Microsoft® Office

Excel 2003

Revised Edition

COMPREHENSIVE

ROBERT T. GRAUER
UNIVERSITY OF MIAMI

MARYANN BARBER
UNIVERSITY OF MIAMI

**Upper Saddle River,
New Jersey 07458**

Library of Congress Cataloging-in-Publication Data

Grauer, Robert T.
  Microsoft Office Excel 2003 : revised comprehensive / Robert T. Grauer, Maryann Barber.
    p. cm.
  Includes index.
  ISBN 0-13-187742-9 (alk. paper)
  1. Microsoft Excel (Computer file) 2. Business--Computer programs. 3. Electronic spreadsheets. I. Barber, Maryann M. II. Title.
  HF5548.4.M523G725 2006
  005.54—dc22
                                                                                                 2005012930

Acquisitions Editor: Melissa Sabella
VP/ Publisher: Natalie E. Anderson
Product Development Manager: Eileen Bien Calabro
Senior Project Manager, Editorial: Eileen Clark
Editorial Assistants: Brian Hoehl, Alana Meyers, and Sandy Bernales
Media Project Manager: Cathleen Profitko
Marketing Manager: Sarah Davis
Marketing Assistant: Lisa Taylor
Managing Editor: Lynda Castillo
Project Manager, Production: Lynne Breitfeller
Production Editor: Greg Hubit
Associate Director, Manufacturing: Vincent Scelta
Manufacturing Buyer: Lynne Breitfeller
Design Manager: Maria Lange
Interior Design: Michael J. Fruhbeis
Cover Design: Michael J. Fruhbeis
Cover Printer: Phoenix Color
Composition and Project Management: Techbooks/GTS
Printer/ Binder: Banta Menasha

Microsoft and the Microsoft Office Specialist logo are trademarks or registered trademarks of Microsoft Corporation in the United States and/or other countries. Prentice Hall is independent from Microsoft Corporation, and not affiliated with Microsoft in any manner. This publication may be used in assisting students to prepare for a Microsoft Office Specialist Exam. Neither Microsoft Corporation, its designated review companies, nor Prentice Hall warrants that use of this publication will ensure passing the relevant Exam.

Use of the Microsoft Office Specialist Approved Courseware Logo on this product signifies that it has been independently reviewed and approved in complying with the following standards:
Acceptable coverage of all content related to the Expert level Microsoft Office Exams entitled "Excel 2003" and sufficient performance-based exercises that relate closely to all required content based on sampling of text.

Copyright © 2006 by Pearson Education, Inc., Upper Saddle River, New Jersey, 07458. All rights reserved. Printed in the United States of America. This publication is protected by Copyright and permission should be obtained from the publisher prior to any prohibited reproduction, storage in a retrieval system, or transmission in any form or by any means, electronic, mechanical, photocopying, recording, or likewise. For information regarding permission(s), write to: Rights and Permissions Department.

                                            10 9 8 7 6 5 4 3 2 1
                                            ISBN 0-13-187742-9

To Marion —
my wife, my lover, and my best friend

Robert Grauer

To Frank and Jessica —
I love you

Maryann Barber

What does this logo mean?

It means this courseware has been approved by the Microsoft® Office Specialist Program to be among the finest available for learning **Microsoft Excel 2003**. It also means that upon completion of this courseware, you may be prepared to take an exam for Microsoft Office Specialist qualification.

What is a Microsoft Office Specialist?

A Microsoft Office Specialist is an individual who has passed exams for certifying his or her skills in one or more of the Microsoft Office desktop applications such as Microsoft Word, Microsoft Excel, Microsoft PowerPoint, Microsoft Outlook, Microsoft Access, or Microsoft Project. The Microsoft Office Specialist Program typically offers certification exams at the "Specialist" and "Expert" skill levels.[*] The Microsoft Office Specialist Program is the only program approved by Microsoft for testing proficiency in Microsoft Office desktop applications and Microsoft Project. This testing program can be a valuable asset in any job search or career advancement.

More Information:

To learn more about becoming a Microsoft Office Specialist, visit www.microsoft.com/officespecialist

To learn about other Microsoft Office Specialist approved courseware from Pearson Education visit www.prenhall.com

---

*The availability of Microsoft Office Specialist certification exams varies by application, application version, and language. Visit www.microsoft.com/officespecialist for exam availability.

Microsoft, the Microsoft Office Logo, PowerPoint, and Outlook are trademarks or registered trademarks of Microsoft Corporation in the United States and/or other countries, and the Microsoft Office Specialist Logo is used under license from owner.

Contents

Preface xiii

MICROSOFT® OFFICE EXCEL 2003

one

Introduction to Excel: What Is a Spreadsheet?   1

Objectives	1
Case Study: Weddings by Molly	1
Introduction to Spreadsheets	2
The Accountant's Ledger	2
The Professor's Grade Book	3
Row and Column Headings	4
Formulas and Constants	5
Introduction to Microsoft Excel	6
Toolbars	7
The File Menu	9
HANDS-ON EXERCISE 1:	
INTRODUCTION TO MICROSOFT EXCEL	11
Modifying a Worksheet	19
The Page Setup Command	21
HANDS-ON EXERCISE 2:	
MODIFYING A WORKSHEET	22
A Better Grade Book	31
Cell Ranges	32
Copy Command	32
Move Operation	34
Learning by Doing	35
HANDS-ON EXERCISE 3:	
CREATING A WORKBOOK	36
Formatting	42
Format Cells Command	43
Alignment	44
Fonts	44
Borders, Patterns, and Shading	46
HANDS-ON EXERCISE 4:	
FORMATTING A WORKSHEET	47
Summary	53
Key Terms	53
Multiple Choice	54
Practice with Excel	56
Mini Cases	65

two

Gaining Proficiency: The Web and Business Applications   67

Objectives	67
Case Study: The Reluctant Entrepreneur	67
Employee Payroll	68
Pointing	70
The Fill Handle	70
Comments	70
HANDS-ON EXERCISE 1:	
PAYROLL	71
Excel and the Internet	78
HANDS-ON EXERCISE 2:	
CREATING A WEB PAGE	80
Web queries	89
The Time Format	91
HANDS-ON EXERCISE 3:	
WEB QUERIES	92
Summary	98
Key Terms	98
Multiple Choice	99
Practice with Excel	101
Mini Cases	113

three

Graphs and Charts: Delivering a Message 115

Objectives	115
Case Study: The Changing Student Population	115
Chart Types	116
Pie Charts	117
Column and Bar Charts	119
Creating a Chart	122
The Chart Wizard	124
Modifying a Chart	126
HANDS-ON EXERCISE 1:	
THE CHART WIZARD	**127**
Multiple Data Series	136
Stacked Column Charts	137
HANDS-ON EXERCISE 2:	
MULTIPLE DATA SERIES	**139**
Object Linking and Embedding	145
HANDS-ON EXERCISE 3:	
OBJECT LINKING AND EMBEDDING	**146**
Summary	153
Key Terms	153
Multiple Choice	154
Practice with Excel	156
Mini Cases	165

four

Using Spreadsheets in Decision Making: What If? 167

Objectives	167
Case Study: Bill's Autos	167
Spreadsheets in Decision Making	168
Analysis of a Car Loan	168
PMT Function	170
FV Function	170
Inserting a Function	171
The Goal Seek Command	172
HANDS-ON EXERCISE 1:	
BASIC FINANCIAL FUNCTIONS	**173**
Home Mortgages	179
Relative versus Absolute References	180
Mixed References	181
HANDS-ON EXERCISE 2:	
ADVANCED FINANCIAL FUNCTIONS	**182**
The Grade Book Revisited	192
Statistical Functions	193
Arithmetic Expressions versus Functions	194
IF Function	195
VLOOKUP Function	196
Working with Large Spreadsheets	197
Freezing Panes	197
Hiding Rows and Columns	197
Printing a Large Worksheet	197
AutoFilter Command	200
HANDS-ON EXERCISE 3:	
THE EXPANDED GRADE BOOK	**201**
Summary	211
Key Terms	211
Multiple Choice	212
Practice with Excel	214
Mini Cases	227

five

Consolidating Data: Worksheet References and File Linking 229

Objectives	229	The Documentation Worksheet	249
Case Study: Tasty Treats	229	**HANDS-ON EXERCISE 3:**	
Consolidating Data	230	THE DOCUMENTATION WORKSHEET	250
The Three-Dimensional Workbook	231	Linking Workbooks	255
Copying Worksheets	232	**HANDS-ON EXERCISE 4:**	
Multiple Workbooks	233	LINKING WORKBOOKS	256
HANDS-ON EXERCISE 1:			
COPYING WORKSHEETS	234	Summary	262
Worksheet References	239	Key Terms	262
3-D Reference	240	Multiple Choice	263
Grouping Worksheets	241	Practice with Excel	265
The AutoFormat Command	241	Mini Cases	273
HANDS-ON EXERCISE 2:			
WORKSHEET REFERENCES	242		

six

Financial Analysis: Forecasting, Rate of Return, and Amortization 275

Objectives	275	**HANDS-ON EXERCISE 3:**	
Case Study: Whispering Woods Golf Club	275	CREATING A TEMPLATE	303
A Financial Forecast	276	The Amortization Schedule	309
Advanced Formatting	278	The Year, Month, and Day Functions	311
Scenario Manager	279	The MATCH and INDEX functions	311
HANDS-ON EXERCISE 1:		**HANDS-ON EXERCISE 4:**	
A FINANCIAL FORECAST	280	CREATING AN AMORTIZATION SCHEDULE	312
Workgroups and Auditing	291		
Data Validation	292	Summary	319
HANDS-ON EXERCISE 2:		Key Terms	319
AUDITING AND WORKGROUPS	294	Multiple Choice	320
The Internal Rate of Return	301	Practice with Excel	322
Creating a Template	301	Mini Cases	334

CONTENTS   vii

seven

List and Data Management: Converting Data to Information   335

Objectives	335
Case Study: Alice Barr Realty	335
List and Data Management	336
Implementation in Excel	337
Data Form Command	338
Sort Command	339
The Text Import Wizard	341
Excel and XML	342
HANDS-ON EXERCISE 1:	
IMPORTING, CREATING,	
AND MAINTAINING A LIST	343
Data versus Information	350
AutoFilter Command	352
Advanced Filter Command	353
Criteria Range	353
Database Functions	355
Insert Name Command	356
Subtotals	357
HANDS-ON EXERCISE 2:	
DATA VERSUS INFORMATION	358
Pivot Tables and Pivot Charts	369
HANDS-ON EXERCISE 3:	
PIVOT TABLES AND PIVOT CHARTS	372
Summary	381
Key Terms	381
Multiple Choice	382
Practice with Excel	384
Mini Cases	396

eight

Data Analysis: A Capstone Chapter   397

Objectives	397
Case Study: The Personal Computer Store	397
Drowning in Data	398
The Admissions Office	399
Implementation in Excel	399
HANDS-ON EXERCISE 1:	
THE ADMISSIONS OFFICE	401
The Graduating Class	408
Implementation in Excel	408
HANDS-ON EXERCISE 2:	
THE GRADUATING CLASS	410
The Men's Store	416
HANDS-ON EXERCISE 3:	
THE MEN'S STORE	418
The Restaurant	425
Implementation in Excel	425
HANDS-ON EXERCISE 4:	
THE RESTAURANT	427
Summary	433
Key Words and Concepts	433
Multiple Choice	434
Practice with Excel	436
Mini Cases	447

nine

Automating Repetitive Tasks: Macros and Visual Basic for Applications   449

Objectives	449
Case Study: Universal Health Services	449
Introduction to Macros	450
HANDS-ON EXERCISE 1:	
INTRODUCTION TO MACROS	**452**
Relative versus Absolute References	461
The Personal Macro Workbook	462
HANDS-ON EXERCISE 2:	
THE PERSONAL MACRO WORKBOOK	**463**
Data Management Macros	470
HANDS-ON EXERCISE 3:	
DATA MANAGEMENT MACROS	**472**
Visual Basic for Applications	480
HANDS-ON EXERCISE 4:	
CREATING ADDITIONAL MACROS	**481**
Loops and Decision Making	492
If Statement	492
Do Statement	493
HANDS-ON EXERCISE 5:	
LOOPS AND DECISION MAKING	**494**
Summary	501
Key Terms	501
Multiple Choice	502
Practice with Excel	504
Mini Cases	514

ten

A Professional Application: An Enhanced Amortization Schedule   515

Objectives	515
Case Study: Retirement Planning	515
Application Development	516
The Enhanced Amortization Schedule	517
Date Functions	520
HANDS-ON EXERCISE 1:	
THE ENHANCED AMORTIZATION	
SCHEDULE WORKBOOK	**521**
Exploring VBA Syntax	528
Three Simple Procedures	528
HANDS-ON EXERCISE 2:	
EXPLORING VBA SYNTAX	**530**
Event Procedures	539
User Forms	541
HANDS-ON EXERCISE 3:	
EVENT PROCEDURES	**542**
More Complex Procedures	551
HANDS-ON EXERCISE 4:	
PERIODIC OPTIONAL PAYMENTS	**553**
Summary	560
Key Terms	560
Multiple Choice	561
Practice with Excel and VBA	563
Mini Cases	574

eleven

Extending VBA: Processing Worksheets and Workbooks 575

Objectives	575
Case Study: Bon Voyage Travel	575
The Expense Summary Application	576
A Quick Review	577
The Dir Function	578
HANDS-ON EXERCISE 1:	
CREATE THE SUMMARY WORKBOOK	**579**
Displaying a Specific Worksheet	585
Error Trapping	585
HANDS-ON EXERCISE 2:	
ERROR TRAPPING	**587**
Processing Worksheets in a Workbook	593
Adding Employees to	
the Summary Worksheet	595
HANDS-ON EXERCISE 3:	
CREATE THE SUMMARY WORKSHEET	**597**
A Better Summary Workbook	605
HANDS-ON EXERCISE 4:	
A BETTER SUMMARY WORKBOOK	**607**
Summary	612
Key Terms	612
Multiple Choice	613
Practice with Excel and VBA	615
Mini Cases	624

Appendix A: Toolbars	625
Appendix B: Solver	635
Appendix C: Using XML	653

GETTING STARTED WITH VBA

Getting Started with VBA: Extending Microsoft® Office 2003   669

Objectives	669
Case Study: On-the-Job Training	669
Introduction to VBA	670
The MsgBox Statement	671
The InputBox Function	672
Declaring Variables	673
The VBA editor	674
HANDS-ON EXERCISE 1:	
INTRODUCTION TO VBA	675
If . . . Then . . . Else Statement	684
Case Statement	686
Custom Toolbars	687
HANDS-ON EXERCISE 2:	
DECISION MAKING	688
For . . . Next Statement	696
Do Loops	697
Debugging	698
HANDS-ON EXERCISE 3:	
LOOPS AND DEBUGGING	700
Putting VBA to Work (Microsoft Excel)	709
HANDS-ON EXERCISE 4:	
EVENT-DRIVEN PROGRAMMING (MICROSOFT EXCEL)	711
Putting VBA to Work (Microsoft Access)	720
HANDS-ON EXERCISE 5:	
EVENT-DRIVEN PROGRAMMING (MICROSOFT ACCESS)	722
Summary	730
Key Terms	730
Multiple Choice	731

MICROSOFT® WINDOWS® XP

Getting Started with Microsoft® Windows® XP   733

Objectives	733
Case Study: Unforeseen Circumstances	733
Welcome to Windows XP	734
The Desktop	735
Moving and Sizing a Window	735
Anatomy of a Window	738
Pull-down Menus	739
Dialog Boxes	740
Help and Support Center	741
HANDS-ON EXERCISE 1:	
WELCOME TO WINDOWS XP	742
Files and Folders	750
The Exploring Office Practice Files	752
Connecting to the Internet	752
HANDS-ON EXERCISE 2:	
DOWNLOAD THE PRACTICE FILES	753
Windows Explorer	761
Personal Folders	761
Moving and Copying a File	763
Deleting a File	763
Backup	763
HANDS-ON EXERCISE 3:	
WINDOWS EXPLORER	764
Increasing Productivity	773
The Control Panel	773
Shortcuts	774
The Search Companion	775
HANDS-ON EXERCISE 4:	
INCREASING PRODUCTIVITY	776
Fun with Windows XP	784
Windows Media Player	784
Digital Photography	785
Windows Messenger	786
HANDS-ON EXERCISE 5:	
FUN WITH WINDOWS XP	787
Summary	796
Key Terms	796
Multiple Choice	797
Practice with Windows XP	799
Mini Cases	804

INDEX	805

Preface

THE EXPLORING OFFICE SERIES FOR 2003

Continuing a tradition of excellence, Prentice Hall is proud to announce the new *Exploring Microsoft Office 2003* series by Robert T. Grauer and Maryann Barber. The hands-on approach and conceptual framework of this comprehensive series helps students master all aspects of the Microsoft Office 2003 software, while providing the background necessary to transfer and use these skills in their personal and professional lives.

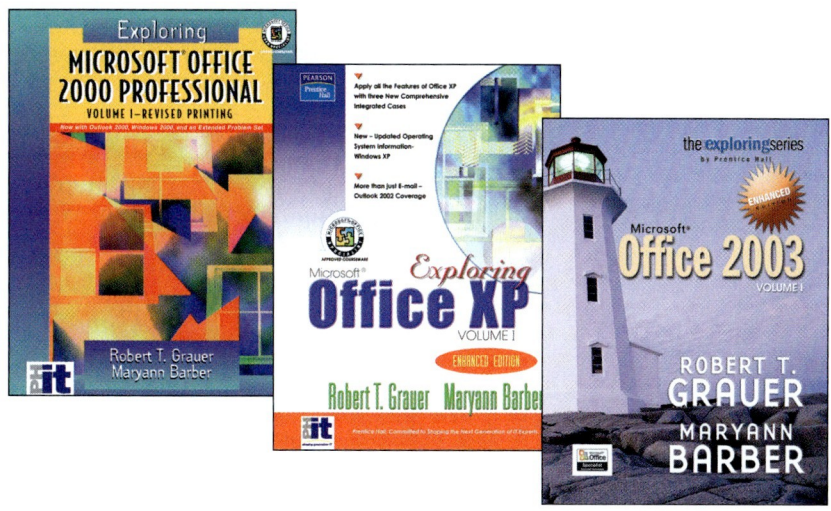

The entire series has been revised to include the new features found in the Office 2003 Suite, which contains Word 2003, Excel 2003, Access 2003, PowerPoint 2003, Publisher 2003, FrontPage 2003, and Outlook 2003.

In addition, this edition includes fully revised end-of-chapter material that provides an extensive review of concepts and techniques discussed in the chapter. Each chapter now begins with an *introductory case study* to provide an effective overview of what the reader will be able to accomplish, with additional *mini cases* at the end of each chapter for practice and review. The conceptual content within each chapter has been modified as appropriate and numerous end-of-chapter exercises have been added.

The new *visual design* introduces the concept of *perfect pages*, whereby every step in every hands-on exercise, as well as every end-of-chapter exercise, begins at the top of its own page and has its own screen shot. This clean design allows for easy navigation throughout the text.

Continuing the success of the website provided for previous editions of this series, Exploring Office 2003 offers expanded resources that include online, interactive study guides, data file downloads, technology updates, additional case studies and exercises, and other helpful information. Start out at **www.prenhall.com/grauer** to explore these resources!

Organization of the Exploring Office 2003 Series

The new Exploring Microsoft Office 2003 series includes five combined Office 2003 texts from which to choose:

- ***Volume I*** is Microsoft Office Specialist certified in each of the core applications in the Office suite (Word, Excel, Access, and PowerPoint). Five additional modules (*Essential Computing Concepts, Getting Started with Windows XP, The Internet and the World Wide Web, Getting Started with Outlook,* and *Integrated Case Studies*) are also included. ***Volume I Enhanced Edition*** adds 18 new chapter-opening case studies, two new integrated case studies, 30 additional end-of-chapter problems, and 20 new mini cases to the existing Volume I.

- ***Volume II*** picks up where Volume I leaves off, covering the advanced topics for the individual applications. A *Getting Started with VBA* module has been added.

- The ***Plus Edition*** extends the coverage of Access and Excel to six and seven chapters, respectively (as opposed to four chapters each in Volume I). It also maintains the same level of coverage for PowerPoint and Word as in Volume I so that both applications are Microsoft Office Specialist certified. The Plus Edition includes a new module on XML but does not contain the Essential Computing Concepts or Internet modules.

- The ***Brief Microsoft Office 2003*** edition provides less coverage of the core applications than Volume I (a total of 10 chapters as opposed to 18). It also includes the *Getting Started with Windows XP* and *Getting Started with Outlook* modules.

- ***Getting Started with Office 2003*** contains the first chapter from each application (Word, Excel, Access, and PowerPoint), plus three additional modules: *Getting Started with Windows XP, The Internet and the World Wide Web,* and *Essential Computing Concepts*.

Individual texts for Word 2003, Excel 2003, Access 2003, and PowerPoint 2003 provide complete coverage of the application and are Microsoft Office Specialist certified. For shorter courses, we have created brief versions of the Exploring texts that give students a four-chapter introduction to each application. Each of these volumes is Microsoft Office Specialist certified at the Specialist level.

This series has been approved by Microsoft to be used in preparation for Microsoft Office Specialist exams.

The Microsoft Office Specialist program is globally recognized as the standard for demonstrating desktop skills with the Microsoft Office suite of business productivity applications (Microsoft Word, Microsoft Excel, Microsoft PowerPoint, Microsoft Access, and Microsoft Outlook). With a Microsoft Office Specialist certification, thousands of people have demonstrated increased productivity and have proved their ability to utilize the advanced functionality of these Microsoft applications.

By encouraging individuals to develop advanced skills with Microsoft's leading business desktop software, the Microsoft Office Specialist program helps fill the demand for qualified, knowledgeable people in the modern workplace. At the same time, Microsoft Office Specialist helps satisfy an organization's need for a qualitative assessment of employee skills.

Instructor and Student Resources

The **Instructor's CD** that accompanies the Exploring Office series contains:

- Student data files
- Solutions to all exercises and problems
- PowerPoint lectures
- Instructor's manuals in Word format that enable the instructor to annotate portions of the instructor manuals for distribution to the class
- Instructors may also use our *test creation software,* TestGen and QuizMaster. TestGen is a test generator program that lets you view and easily edit test-bank questions, create tests, and print in a variety of formats suitable to your teaching situation. Exams can be easily uploaded into WebCT, BlackBoard, and CourseCompass. QuizMaster allows students to take the tests created with TestGen on a local area network.

Prentice Hall's Companion Website at www.prenhall.com/grauer offers expanded IT resources and downloadable supplements. This site also includes an online study guide for students containing true/false and multiple choice questions and practice projects.

WebCT www.prenhall.com/webct

Gold level customer support available exclusively to adopters of Prentice Hall courses is provided free-of-charge upon adoption and provides you with priority assistance, training discounts, and dedicated technical support.

Blackboard www.prenhall.com/blackboard

Prentice Hall's abundant online content, combined with Blackboard's popular tools and interface, result in robust Web-based courses that are easy to implement, manage, and use—taking your courses to new heights in student interaction and learning.

CourseCompass www.coursecompass.com

CourseCompass is a dynamic, interactive online course management tool powered by Blackboard. This exciting product allows you to teach with marketing-leading Pearson Education content in an easy-to-use, customizable format.

Training and Assessment www2.phgenit.com/support

Prentice Hall offers Performance Based Training and Assessment in one product, Train&Assess IT. The Training component offers computer-based training that a student can use to preview, learn, and review Microsoft Office application skills. Web or CD-ROM delivered, Train IT offers interactive multimedia, computer-based training to augment classroom learning. Built-in prescriptive testing suggests a study path based not only on student test results but also on the specific textbook chosen for the course.

The Assessment component offers computer-based testing that shares the same user interface as Train IT and is used to evaluate a student's knowledge about specific topics in Word, Excel, Access, PowerPoint, Windows, Outlook, and the Internet. It does this in a task-oriented, performance-based environment to demonstrate proficiency as well as comprehension on the topics by the students. More extensive than the testing in Train IT, Assess IT offers more administrative features for the instructor and additional questions for the student.

Assess IT also allows professors to test students out of a course, place students in appropriate courses, and evaluate skill sets.

OPENING CASE STUDY

New! Each chapter now begins with an introductory case study to provide an effective overview of what students will accomplish by completing the chapter.

CHAPTER 1
Getting Started with Microsoft® Windows® XP

OBJECTIVES

After reading this chapter you will:

1. Describe the Windows desktop.
2. Use the Help and Support Center to obtain information.
3. Describe the My Computer and My Documents folders.
4. Differentiate between a program file and a data file.
5. Download a file from the Exploring Office Web site.
6. Copy and/or move a file from one folder to another.
7. Delete a file, and then recover it from the Recycle Bin.
8. Create and arrange shortcuts on the desktop.
9. Use the Search Companion.
10. Use the My Pictures and My Music folders.
11. Use Windows Messenger for instant messaging.

hands-on exercises

1. WELCOME TO WINDOWS XP
   Input: None
   Output: None

2. DOWNLOAD PRACTICE FILES
   Input: Data files from the Web
   Output: Welcome to Windows XP (a Word document)

3. WINDOWS EXPLORER
   Input: Data files from exercise 2
   Output: Screen Capture within a Word document

4. INCREASING PRODUCTIVITY
   Input: Data files from exercise 3
   Output: None

5. FUN WITH WINDOWS XP
   Input: None
   Output: None

CASE STUDY
UNFORESEEN CIRCUMSTANCES

Steve and his wife Shelly have poured their life savings into the dream of owning their own business, a "nanny" service agency. They have spent the last two years building their business and have created a sophisticated database with numerous entries for both families and nannies. The database is the key to their operation. Now that it is up and running, Steve and Shelly are finally at a point where they could hire someone to manage the operation on a part-time basis so that they could take some time off together.

Unfortunately, their process for selecting a person they could trust with their business was not as thorough as it should have been. Nancy, their new employee, assured them that all was well, and the couple left for an extended weekend. The place was in shambles on their return. Nancy could not handle the responsibility, and when Steve gave her two weeks' notice, neither he nor his wife thought that the unimaginable would happen. On her last day in the office Nancy "lost" all of the names in the database—the data was completely gone!

Nancy claimed that a "virus" knocked out the database, but after spending nearly $1,500 with a computer consultant, Steve was told that it had been cleverly deleted from the hard drive and could not be recovered. Of course, the consultant asked Steve and Shelly about their backup strategy, which they sheepishly admitted did not exist. They had never experienced any problems in the past, and simply assumed that their data was safe. Fortunately, they do have hard copy of the data in the form of various reports that were printed throughout the time they were in business. They have no choice but to manually reenter the data.

Your assignment is to read the chapter, paying special attention to the information on file management. Think about how Steve and Shelly could have avoided the disaster if a backup strategy had been in place, then summarize your thoughts in a brief note to your instructor. Describe the elements of a basic backup strategy. Give several other examples of unforeseen circumstances that can cause data to be lost.

733

New! A listing of the input and output files for each hands-on exercise within the chapter. Students will stay on track with what is to be accomplished.

Perfect Pages

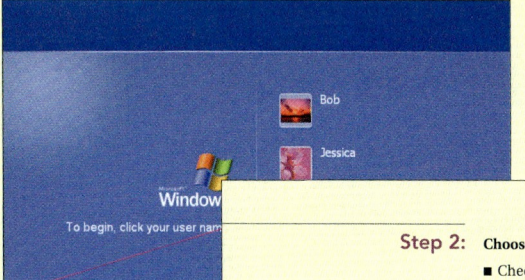

hands-on exercise

1 Welcome to Windows XP

Objective To log on to Windows XP and customize the desktop; to open the My Computer folder; to move and size a window; to format a floppy disk and access the Help and Support Center. Use Figure 7 as a guide.

Step 1: **Log On to Windows XP**

- Turn on the computer and all of the peripheral devices. The floppy drive should be empty prior to starting your machine.
- Windows XP will load automatically, and you should see a login screen similar to Figure 7a. (It does not matter which version of Windows XP you are using.) The number and names of the potential users and their associated icons will be different on your system.
- Click the icon for the user account you want to access. You may be prompted for a password, depending on the security options in effect.

Click icon for user account to be accessed

(a) Log On to Windows XP (step 1)
FIGURE 7 Hands-on Exercise 1

USER ACCOUNTS
The available user names are cr... Windows XP, but you can add or d... click Control Panel, switch to the Ca... the desired task, such as creating ... then supply the necessary informati... user accounts in a school setting.

742 GETTING STARTED WITH MICROSOFT WINDOWS XP

Each step in the hands-on exercises begins at the top of the page to ensure that students can easily navigate through the text.

Step 2: **Choose the Theme and Start Menu**

- Check with your instructor to see if you are able to modify the desktop and other settings at your school or university. If your network administrator has disabled these commands, skip this step and go to step 3.
- Point to a blank area on the desktop, click the **right mouse button** to display a context-sensitive menu, then click the **Properties command** to open the Display Properties dialog box. Click the **Themes tab** and select the **Windows XP theme** if it is not already selected. Click **OK**.
- We prefer to work without any wallpaper (background picture) on the desktop. **Right click** the desktop, click **Properties**, then click the **Desktop tab** in the Display Properties dialog box. Click **None** as shown in Figure 7b, then click **OK**. The background disappears.
- The Start menu is modified independently of the theme. **Right click** a blank area of the taskbar, click the **Properties command** to display the Taskbar and Start Menu Properties dialog box, then click the **Start Menu tab**.
- Click the **Start Menu option button**. Click **OK**.

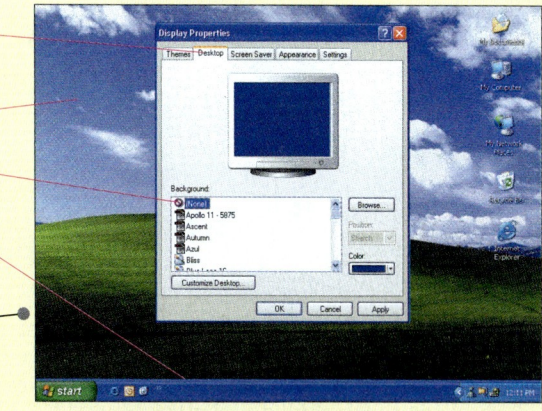

Click Desktop tab
Click right mouse button to display shortcut menu
Click None
Right click blank area on taskbar

(b) Choose the Theme and Start Menu (step 2)
FIGURE 7 Hands-on Exercise 1 (*continued*)

IMPLEMENT A SCREEN SAVER
A screen saver is a delightful way to personalize your computer and a good way to practice with basic commands in Windows XP. Right click a blank area of the desktop, click the Properties command to open the Display Properties dialog box, then click the Screen Saver tab. Click the down arrow in the Screen Saver list box, choose the desired screen saver, then set the option to wait an appropriate amount of time before the screen saver appears. Click OK to accept the settings and close the dialog box.

New! Larger screen shots with clear callouts.

Boxed tips provide students with additional information.

MICROSOFT OFFICE EXCEL 2003 REVISED 743

xvii

MINI CASES AND PRACTICE EXERCISES

New!
We've added mini cases at the end of each chapter for expanded practice and review.

MINI CASES

The Financial Consultant
A friend of yours is in the process of buying a home and has asked you to compare the payments and total interest on a 15- and 30-year loan at varying interest rates. You have decided to analyze the loans in Excel, and then incorporate the results into a memo written in Microsoft Word. As of now, the principal is $150,000, but it is very likely that your friend will change his mind several times, and so you want to use the linking and embedding capability within Windows to dynamically link the worksheet to the word processing document. Your memo should include a letterhead that takes advantage of the formatting capabilities within Word; a graphic logo would be a nice touch.

Fun with the If Statement
Open the *Chapter 4 Mini Case—Fun with the If Statement* workbook in the Exploring Excel folder, then follow the directions in the worksheet to view a hidden message. The message is displayed by various If statements scattered throughout the worksheet, but the worksheet is protected so that you cannot see these formulas. (Use Help to see how to protect a worksheet.) We made it easy for you, however, because you can unprotect the worksheet since a password is not required. Once the worksheet is unprotected, pull down the Format menu, click the Cells command, click the Protection tab, and clear the Hidden check box. Prove to your professor that you have done this successfully, by changing the text of our message. Print the completed worksheet to show both displayed values and cell formulas.

The Lottery
Many states raise money through lotteries that advertise prizes of several million dollars. In reality, however, the actual value of the prize is considerably less than the advertised value, although the winners almost certainly do not care. One state, for example, recently offered a twenty million dollar prize that was to be distributed in twenty annual payments of one million dollars each. How much was the prize actually worth, assuming a long-term interest rate of five percent? Use the PV (Present Value) function to determine the answer. What is the effect on the answer if payments to the recipient are made at the beginning of each year, rather than at the end of each year?

A Penny a Day
What if you had a rich u salary each day for the r prised at how quickly th use the Goal Seek comm (if any) will your uncle p uncle pay you on the 31

The Rule of 72
Delaying your IRA for on when you begin. Tha a calculator, using the "F long it takes money to money earning 8% ann money doubles again in your IRA at age 21, rath initial contribution. Us lose, assuming an 8% ra determine the exact am

New!
Each project in the end-of-chapter material begins at the top of a page—now students can easily see where their assignments begin and end.

PRACTICE WITH EXCEL

1. **Theme Park Admissions:** A partially completed version of the worksheet in Figure 3.13 is available in the Exploring Excel folder as *Chapter 3 Practice 1*. Follow the directions in parts (a) and (b) to compute the totals and format the worksheet, then create each of the charts listed below.
   a. Use the AutoSum command to enter the formulas to compute the total number of admissions for each region and each quarter.
   b. Select the entire worksheet (cells A1 through F8), then use the AutoFormat command to format the worksheet. You do not have to accept the entire design, nor do you have to use the design we selected. You can also modify the design after it has been applied to the worksheet by changing the font size of selected cells and/or changing boldface and italics.
   c. Create a column chart showing the total number of admissions in each quarter as shown in Figure 3.13. Add the graphic shown in the figure for emphasis.
   d. Create a pie chart that shows the percentage of the total number of admissions in each region. Create this chart in its own chart sheet with an appropriate name.
   e. Create a stacked column chart that shows the total number of admissions for each region and the contribution of each quarter within each region. Create this chart in its own chart sheet with an appropriate name.
   f. Create a stacked column chart showing the total number of admissions for each quarter and the contribution of each region within each quarter. Create this chart in its own chart sheet with an appropriate name.
   g. Change the color of each of the worksheet tabs.
   h. Print the entire workbook, consisting of the worksheet in Figure 3.13 plus the three additional sheets that you create. Use portrait orientation for the Sales Data worksheet and landscape orientation for the other worksheets. Create a custom header for each worksheet that includes your name, your course, and your instructor's name. Create a custom footer for each worksheet that includes the name of the worksheet. Submit the completed assignment to your instructor.

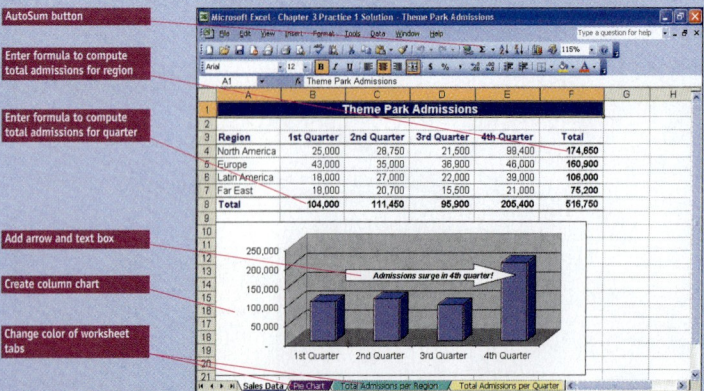

FIGURE 3.13 Theme Park Admissions (exercise 1)

156 CHAPTER 3: GRAPHS AND CHARTS

xviii

NEW! DATA ANALYSIS

New!
This capstone chapter reviews material from previous chapters while simultaneously introducing new features for data analysis.

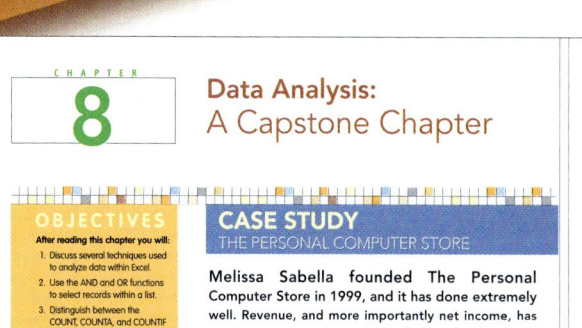

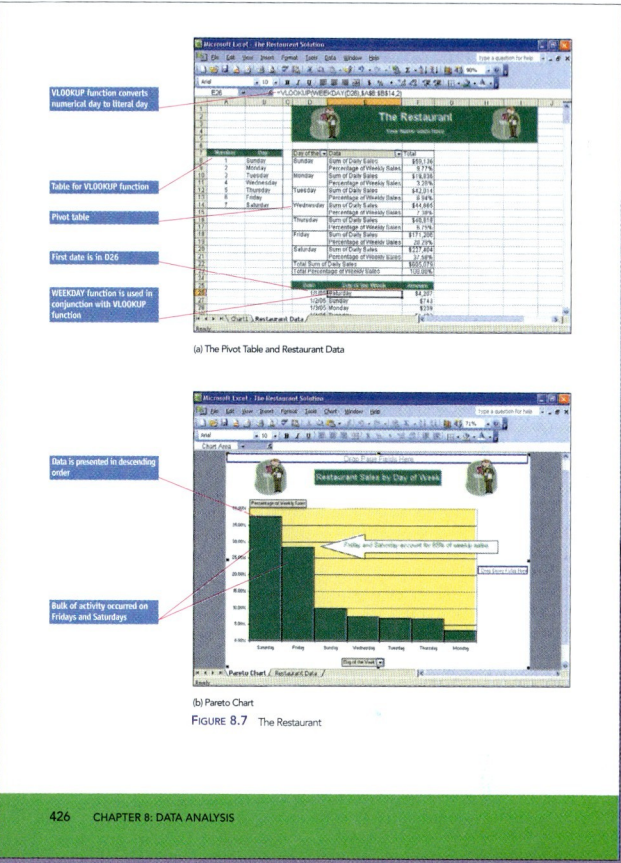

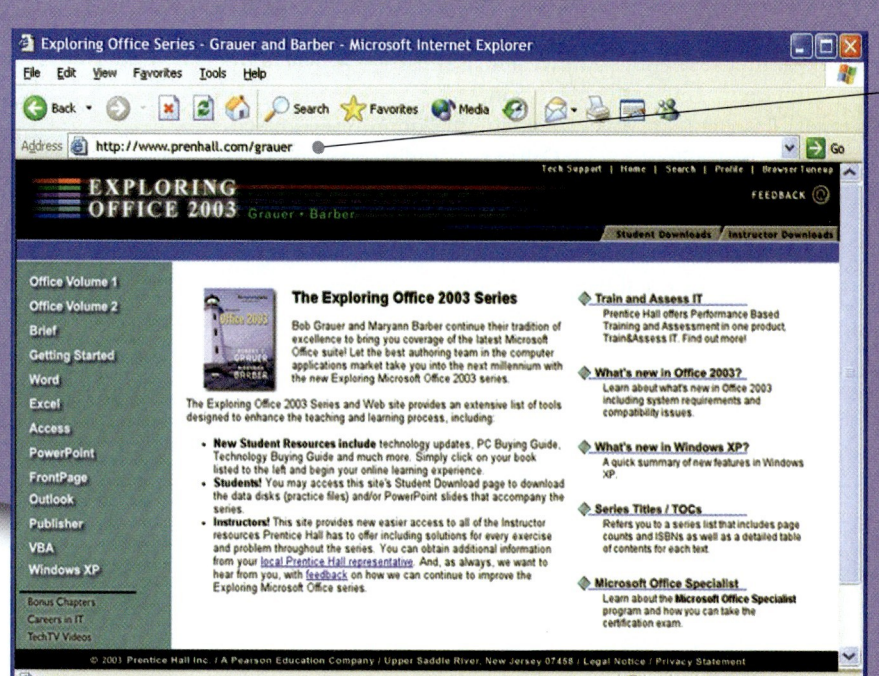

Companion Web site

New!
Updated and enhanced Companion Web site. Find everything you need—student practice files, PowerPoint lectures, online study guides, and instructor support (solutions)!

www.prenhall.com/grauer

Acknowledgments

We want to thank the many individuals who have helped to bring this project to fruition. Melissa Sabella and Jodi McPherson, our editors at Prentice Hall, have provided new leadership in extending the series to Office 2003. Cathi Profitko did an absolutely incredible job on our Web site. Shelly Martin was the creative force behind the chapter-opening case studies. Sarah Davis and Emily Knight coordinated the marketing and continue to inspire us with suggestions for improving the series. Greg Hubit has been masterful as the external production editor for every book in the series from its inception. Eileen Clark coordinated the myriad details of production and the certification process. Lynne Breitfeller was the project manager and manufacturing buyer. Jessica Street created the Instructor Resources CD. Lori Brice was the project manager at Techbooks/GTS and in charge of composition. Chuck Cox did his usual fine work as copyeditor. Cindy Stevens, Tom McKenzie, and Michael Olmstead wrote the instructor manuals. Michael Fruhbeis developed the innovative and attractive design. We also want to acknowledge our reviewers who, through their comments and constructive criticism, greatly improved the series.

Richard Albright, Goldey-Beacom College
Lynne Band, Middlesex Community College
Don Belle, Central Piedmont Community College
Richard Blamer, John Carroll University
Stuart P. Brian, Holy Family College
Carl M. Briggs, Indiana University School of Business
Kimberly Chambers, Scottsdale Community College
Jill Chapnick, Florida International University
Alok Charturvedi, Purdue University
Barbara Cierny, William Rainey Harper College
Jerry Chin, Southwest Missouri State University
Dean Combellick, Scottsdale Community College
Cody Copeland, Johnson County Community College
Larry S. Corman, Fort Lewis College
Janis Cox, Tri-County Technical College
Douglass Cross, Clackamas Community College
Martin Crossland, Southwest Missouri State University
Bill Daley, University of Oregon
Paul E. Daurelle, Western Piedmont Community College
Shawna DePlonty, Sault College of Applied Arts and Technology
Rory J. De Simone, University of Florida
Carolyn DiLeo, Westchester Community College
Judy Dolan, Palomar College
William J. Dorin, Indiana University Northwest
David Douglas, University of Arkansas
Carlotta Eaton, Radford University
Beverly Fite, Amarillo College
Judith M. Fitspatrick, Gulf Coast Community College
James Franck, College of St. Scholastica
Raymond Frost, Central Connecticut State University
Susan Fry, Boise State University

Midge Gerber, Southwestern Oklahoma State University
James Gips, Boston College
Vernon Griffin, Austin Community College
Ranette Halverson, Midwestern State University
Michael Hassett, Fort Hays State University
Barbara Anne Hearn, Community College of Philadelphia
Mike Hearn, Community College of Philadelphia
Wanda D. Heller, Seminole Community College
Fred Hills, McLennan Community College
Bonnie Homan, San Francisco State University
Ernie Ivey, Polk Community College
Dana Johnson, North Dakota State University
Walter Johnson, Community College of Philadelphia
Mike Kelly, Community College of Rhode Island
Jane King, Everett Community College
Rose M. Laird, Northern Virginia Community College
Jackie A. Lamoureux, Albuquerque TVI
David Langley, University of Oregon
John Lesson, University of Central Florida
Maurie Lockley, University of North Carolina at Greensboro
Daniela Marghitu, Auburn University
David B. Meinert, Southwest Missouri State University
Alan Moltz, Naugatuck Valley Technical Community College
Kim Montney, Kellogg Community College
Bill Morse, DeVry Institute of Technology
Kevin Pauli, University of Nebraska
Mary McKenry Percival, University of Miami
Laura McManamon, University of Dayton
Joseph M. Manzo, Lehigh University
Marguerite Nedreberg, Youngstown State University
Joshua L. Mindel, San Francisco State University
James Pepe, Bentley College
Jim Pruitt, Central Washington University
Delores Pusins, Hillsborough Community College
Gale E. Rand, College Misericordia
Judith Rice, Santa Fe Community College
David Rinehard, Lansing Community College
Behrooz Saghafi, Chicago State University
Marilyn Salas, Scottsdale Community College
Herach Safarian, College of the Canyons
John Shepherd, Duquesne University
Barbara Sherman, Buffalo State College
Karl L. Smart, Central Michigan University
Carol Smith, Johnson Community College
Robert Spear, Prince George's Community College
Diane Stark, Phoenix College
Michael Stewardson, San Jacinto College—North
Helen Stoloff, Hudson Valley Community College

... continued

Jessica Street, Broward Community College
Joe Teng, Barry University
Margaret Thomas, Ohio University
Mike Thomas, Indiana University School of Business
Suzanne Tomlinson, Iowa State University
Karen Tracey, Central Connecticut State University
Antonio Vargas, El Paso Community College
Sally Visci, Lorain County Community College
William Wagner, Villanova University
David Weiner, University of San Francisco
Connie Wells, Georgia State University
Wallace John Whistance-Smith, Ryerson Polytechnic University
Karen Wisniewski, County College of Morris
Jack Zeller, Kirkwood Community College

A final word of thanks to the unnamed students at the University of Miami who make it all worthwhile. Most of all, thanks to you, our readers, for choosing this book. Please feel free to contact us with any comments and suggestions.

Robert T. Grauer
rgrauer@miami.edu
www.prenhall.com/grauer

Maryann Barber
mbarber@miami.edu

CHAPTER 1

Introduction to Excel:
What Is a Spreadsheet?

OBJECTIVES

After reading this chapter you will:

1. Describe several potential spreadsheet applications.
2. Distinguish among a constant, a formula, and a function.
3. Distinguish between a workbook and a worksheet.
4. Explain how the rows and columns in a worksheet are labeled.
5. Download the practice files for use in hands-on exercises.
6. Insert or delete rows and columns in a worksheet.
7. Print a worksheet to show displayed values or cell contents.
8. Distinguish between relative and absolute references.
9. Copy and/or move cell formulas within a worksheet.
10. Format a worksheet; use borders and shading; change fonts and alignment.

hands-on exercises

1. **INTRODUCTION TO EXCEL**
   Input: Grade Book
   Output: Grade Book Solution

2. **MODIFYING A WORKSHEET**
   Input: Grade Book Solution (from exercise 1)
   Output: Grade Book Solution (additional modifications)

3. **CREATING A WORKBOOK**
   Input: None
   Output: Better Grade Book Solution

4. **FORMATTING A WORKSHEET**
   Input: Better Grade Book Solution (from exercise 3)
   Output: Better Grade Book Solution (additional modifications)

CASE STUDY
WEDDINGS BY MOLLY

Molly Ketcherside is a wedding consultant who specializes in all aspects of wedding planning. The business is only one year old, but Molly already has a proven history of superbly run events resulting in many happy newlyweds. She offers her clients a complete wedding package that includes the cocktail hour, dinner, and beverage (including alcohol). The client chooses the type of dinner (e.g., chicken, salmon, filet mignon, or some type of combination), which determines the cost per guest and specifies the number of guests. The cost of the reception is obtained by simple multiplication.

Molly provides a detailed budget to all of her clients that divides the cost of a wedding into three major categories—the ceremony, the reception (based on the package selected), and other items such as music and photography. She asks each client for their total budget, and then works closely with the client to allocate that amount over the myriad items that will be necessary. Molly promises to take the stress out of planning and she advertises a turnkey operation, from invitations to thank-you notes. She assures her clients that their needs will be met without the client overextending themselves financially. ■

Your assignment is to read the chapter, focusing on spreadsheet formulas and basic spreadsheet commands. You will then open the partially completed *Chapter 1 Case Study—Weddings by Molly* workbook and enter the appropriate formulas to compute the cost of the wedding. (The worksheet already contains the estimated costs.) If you do the assignment correctly, the total cost of this dream wedding should be $25,000. Molly also wants her clients to see where their money is going, so you are asked to enter formulas to calculate the percentage of the total for each item; for example, the $500 wedding cake represents two percent of the total cost of $25,000. Format the worksheet attractively and add a photograph or clip art showing the happy couple. Copy the completed worksheet, then change the various cost estimates to plan your own affair. Print both worksheets. Each worksheet should be printed twice, once to show the displayed values and once to show the cell formulas.

INTRODUCTION TO SPREADSHEETS

The case study on the previous page illustrates one way in which spreadsheets are used by managers and executives. We suggest that you complete the chapter and then return to the case study to create the actual spreadsheet. Our objective throughout the chapter is to provide a broad-based introduction to spreadsheets in general and to Microsoft Excel in particular. We present the basic concepts behind a spreadsheet and then we describe the specific Excel commands that enable you to modify an existing spreadsheet or to create a new spreadsheet. The additional illustrations within the chapter are set in the context of an accountant's ledger and a professor's grade book, with the latter implemented on the computer. Our philosophy throughout the chapter, and indeed throughout the entire text, is to present the "how and why" and then enable you to apply what you have learned through a series of hands-on exercises at the computer.

The Accountant's Ledger

A **spreadsheet** is the computerized equivalent of an accountant's ledger. As with the ledger, it consists of a grid of rows and columns that enables you to organize data in a readily understandable format. Figures 1.1a and 1.1b show the same information displayed in ledger and spreadsheet format, respectively.

"What is the big deal?" you might ask. The big deal is that after you change an entry (or entries), the spreadsheet will, automatically and almost instantly, recompute all of the formulas. Consider, for example, the profit projection spreadsheet shown in Figure 1.1b. As the spreadsheet is presently constructed, the unit price is $20 and the projected sales are 1,200 units, producing gross sales of $24,000 ($20/unit × 1,200 units). The projected expenses are $19,200, which yields a profit of $4,800 ($24,000 – $19,200). If the unit price is increased to $22 per unit, the spreadsheet recomputes the formulas, adjusting the values of gross sales and net profit. The modified spreadsheet of Figure 1.1c appears automatically.

With a calculator and bottle of correction fluid or a good eraser, the same changes could also be made to the ledger. But imagine a ledger with hundreds of entries and the time that would be required to make the necessary changes to the ledger by hand. The same spreadsheet will be recomputed automatically by the computer. And the computer will not make mistakes. Herein lie the advantages of a spreadsheet—the ability to make changes, and to have the computer carry out the recalculation faster and more accurately than could be accomplished manually.

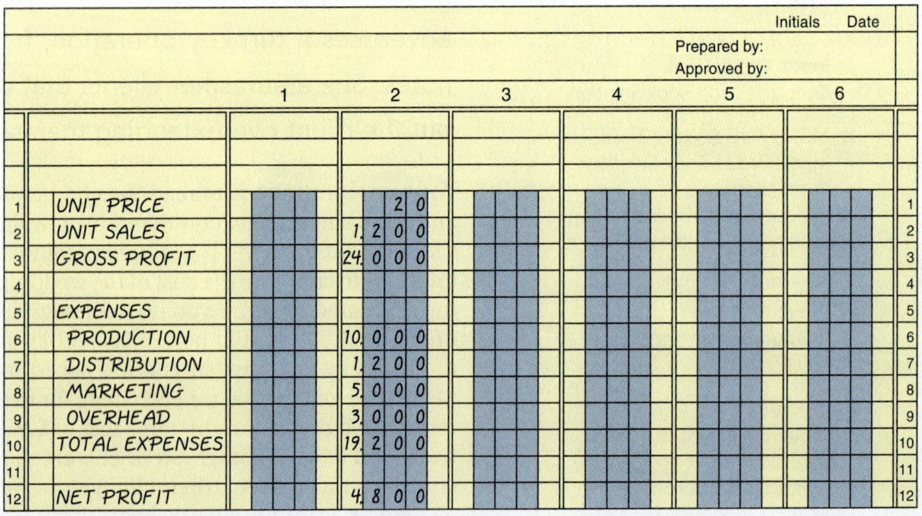

		1	2	3	4	5	6	
1	UNIT PRICE		20					1
2	UNIT SALES		1,200					2
3	GROSS PROFIT		24,000					3
4								4
5	EXPENSES							5
6	PRODUCTION		10,000					6
7	DISTRIBUTION		1,200					7
8	MARKETING		5,000					8
9	OVERHEAD		3,000					9
10	TOTAL EXPENSES		19,200					10
11								11
12	NET PROFIT		4,800					12

(a) The Accountant's Ledger

FIGURE 1.1 The Accountant's Ledger

Unit price is $20

Gross sales calculated automatically

Gross sales are recalculated

Unit price increased to $22

	A	B
1	Profit Projection	
2		
3	Unit Price	$20
4	Unit Sales	1,200
5	Gross Sales	$24,000
6		
7	Expenses	
8	Production	$10,000
9	Distribution	$1,200
10	Marketing	$5,000
11	Overhead	$3,000
12	Total Expenses	$19,200
13		
14	Net Profit	$4,800

Net profit calculated automatically

(b) Original Spreadsheet

	A	B
1	Profit Projection	
2		
3	Unit Price	$22
4	Unit Sales	1,200
5	Gross Sales	$26,400
6		
7	Expenses	
8	Production	$10,000
9	Distribution	$1,200
10	Marketing	$5,000
11	Overhead	$3,000
12	Total Expenses	$19,200
13		
14	Net Profit	$7,200

Net profit is recalculated

(c) Modified Spreadsheet

FIGURE 1.1 The Accountant's Ledger (*continued*)

The Professor's Grade Book

A second example of a spreadsheet, one with which you can easily identify, is that of a professor's grade book. The grades are recorded by hand in a notebook, which is nothing more than a different kind of accountant's ledger. Figure 1.2 contains both manual and spreadsheet versions of a grade book.

Figure 1.2a shows a handwritten grade book as it has been done since the days of the little red schoolhouse. For the sake of simplicity, only five students are shown, each with three grades. The professor has computed class averages for each exam, as well as a semester average for every student. The final counts *twice* as much as either test; for example, Adams's average is equal to (100+90+81+81)/4 = 88. This is the professor's grading scheme, and it is incorporated into the manual grade book and equivalent spreadsheet.

Figure 1.2b shows the grade book as it might appear in a spreadsheet, and is essentially unchanged from Figure 1.2a. Walker's grade on the final exam in Figure 1.2b is 90, giving him a semester average of 85 and producing a class average on the final of 75.2 as well. Now consider Figure 1.2c, in which the grade on Walker's final has been changed to 100, causing Walker's semester average to change from 85 to 90, and the class average on the final to go from 75.2 to 77.2. As with the profit projection, a change to any entry within the grade book automatically recalculates all other dependent formulas as well. Hence, when Walker's final exam was regraded, all dependent formulas (the class average for the final as well as Walker's semester average) were recomputed.

As simple as the idea of a spreadsheet may seem, it provided the first major reason for managers to have a personal computer on their desks. Essentially, anything that can be done with a pencil, a pad of paper, and a calculator can be done faster and far more accurately with a spreadsheet. The spreadsheet, like the personal computer, has become an integral part of every type of business. Indeed, it is hard to imagine that these calculations were ever done by hand. The spreadsheet has become an integral part of corporate culture.

Final counts twice so average is computed as (100+90+81+81)/4

	TEST 1	TEST 2	FINAL	AVERAGE
ADAMS	100	90	81	88
BAKER	90	76	87	85
GLASSMAN	90	78	78	81
MOLDOF	60	60	40	50
WALKER	80	80	90	85
CLASS AVERAGE	84.0	76.8	75.2	
NOTE: FINAL COUNTS DOUBLE				

(a) The Professor's Grade Book

Walker's original grade is 90

	A	B	C	D	E
1	Student	Test 1	Test 2	Final	Average
2					
3	Adams	100	90	81	88.0
4	Baker	90	76	87	85.0
5	Glassman	90	78	78	81.0
6	Moldof	60	60	40	50.0
7	Walker	80	80	90	85.0
8					
9	Class Average	84.0	76.8	75.2	

(b) Original Grades

Grade on Walker's final is changed to 100

Formulas recompute automatically

	A	B	C	D	E
1	Student	Test 1	Test 2	Final	Average
2					
3	Adams	100	90	81	88.0
4	Baker	90	76	87	85.0
5	Glassman	90	78	78	81.0
6	Moldof	60	60	40	50.0
7	Walker	80	80	100	90.0
8					
9	Class Average	84.0	76.8	77.2	

(c) Modified Spreadsheet

FIGURE 1.2 The Professor's Grade Book

Row and Column Headings

A spreadsheet is divided into rows and columns, with each row and column assigned a heading. Rows are given numeric headings ranging from 1 to 65,536 (the maximum number of rows allowed). Columns are assigned alphabetic headings from column A to Z, then continue from AA to AZ and then from BA to BZ and so on, until the last of 256 columns (column IV) is reached.

The intersection of a row and column forms a ***cell***, with the number of cells in a spreadsheet equal to the number of rows times the number of columns. The professor's grade book in Figure 1.2, for example, has 5 columns labeled A through E, 9 rows numbered from 1 to 9, and a total of 45 cells. Each cell has a unique ***cell reference***; for example, the cell at the intersection of column A and row 9 is known as cell A9. *The column heading always precedes the row heading in the cell reference.*

Formulas and Constants

Figure 1.3 is an alternate view of the professor's grade book that shows the cell contents rather than the computed values. Cell E3, for example, does not contain the number 88 (Adams's average for the semester), but rather the formula to compute the average from the exam grades. Indeed, it is the existence of the formula that lets you change the value of any cell containing a grade for Adams (cells B3, C3, or D3), and have the computed average in cell E3 change automatically.

To create a spreadsheet, one goes from cell to cell and enters either a constant or a formula. A ***constant*** is an entry that does not change. It may be a number, such as a student's grade on an exam, or it may be descriptive text (a label), such as a student's name. A ***formula*** is a combination of numeric constants, cell references, arithmetic operators, and/or functions (described below) that displays the result of a calculation. You can ***edit*** (change) the contents of a cell by returning to the cell and reentering the constant or formula.

A formula always begins with an equal sign. Consider, for example, the formula in cell E3, =(B3+C3+2*D3)/4, which computes Adams's semester average. The formula is built in accordance with the professor's rules for computing a student's semester average, which counts the final twice as much as the other tests. Excel uses symbols +, –, *, /, and ^ to indicate addition, subtraction, multiplication, division, and exponentiation, respectively, and follows the normal rules of arithmetic precedence. Any expression in parentheses is evaluated first, then within an expression exponentiation is performed first, followed by multiplication or division in left to right order, then finally addition or subtraction.

The formula in cell E3 takes the grade on the first exam (in cell B3), plus the grade on the second exam (in cell C3), plus two times the grade on the final (in cell D3), and divides the result by four. Thus, should any of the exam grades change, the semester average (a formula whose results depend on the individual exam grades) will also change. This, in essence, is the basic principle behind the spreadsheet and explains why, when one number changes, various other numbers throughout the spreadsheet change as well.

A formula may also include a ***function***, or predefined computational task, such as the AVERAGE function in cells B9, C9, and D9. The function in cell B9, for example, =AVERAGE(B3:B7), is interpreted to mean the average of all cells starting at cell B3 and ending at cell B7 and is equivalent to the formula =(B3+B4+B5+B6+B7)/5. You can appreciate that functions are often easier to use than the corresponding formulas, especially with larger spreadsheets (and classes with many students). Excel contains a wide variety of functions that help you to create very powerful spreadsheets. Financial functions, for example, enable you to calculate the interest payments on a car loan or home mortgage.

Constant (entry that does not change)

Function (predefined computational task)

Formula (mathematical expression)

	A	B	C	D	E
1	Student	Test 1	Test 2	Final	Average
2					
3	Adams	100	90	81	=(B3+C3+2*D3)/4
4	Baker	90	76	87	=(B4+C4+2*D4)/4
5	Glassman	90	78	78	=(B5+C5+2*D5)/4
6	Moldof	60	60	40	=(B6+C6+2*D6)/4
7	Walker	80	80	90	=(B7+C7+2*D7)/4
8					
9	Class Average	=AVERAGE(B3:B7)	=AVERAGE(C3:C7)	=AVERAGE(D3:D7)	

FIGURE 1.3 The Professor's Grade Book (cell formulas)

INTRODUCTION TO MICROSOFT EXCEL

Figure 1.4 displays the professor's grade book as it is implemented in Microsoft Excel. Microsoft Excel is a Windows application, and thus shares the common user interface with which you are familiar. (It's even easier to learn Excel if you already know another Office application such as Microsoft Word.) You should recognize, therefore, that the desktop in Figure 1.4 has two open windows—an application window for Microsoft Excel and a document window for the workbook.

Each window has its own Minimize, Maximize (or Restore), and Close buttons. Both windows have been maximized and thus the title bars have been merged into a single title bar that appears at the top of the application window. The title bar reflects the application (Microsoft Excel) as well as the name of the workbook (Grade Book) on which you are working. A menu bar appears immediately below the title bar. Two toolbars, which are discussed in depth on page 8, appear below the menu bar. Vertical and horizontal scroll bars appear at the right and bottom of the document window.

The *Ask a Question box* appears to the right of the menu bar and provides instant access to the Help facility. The *task pane* at the right of the window provides access to several basic tasks in Excel. Different task panes are displayed at different times, depending on what you want to accomplish. The Getting Started task pane is the one you see when Excel is started initially. It lists the last several workbooks that were opened and also provides access to help. The Help task pane is shown in Figure 1.4.

The terminology is important, and we distinguish among spreadsheet, worksheet, and workbook. Excel refers to a spreadsheet as a **worksheet**. Spreadsheet is a generic term; *workbook* and *worksheet* are unique to Excel. An Excel **workbook** contains one or more worksheets. The professor's grades for this class are contained in the CIS120 worksheet within the Grade Book workbook. This workbook also contains additional worksheets (CIS223 and CIS316) as indicated by the worksheet tabs at the bottom of the window. These worksheets contain the professor's grades for other courses that he or she is teaching this semester.

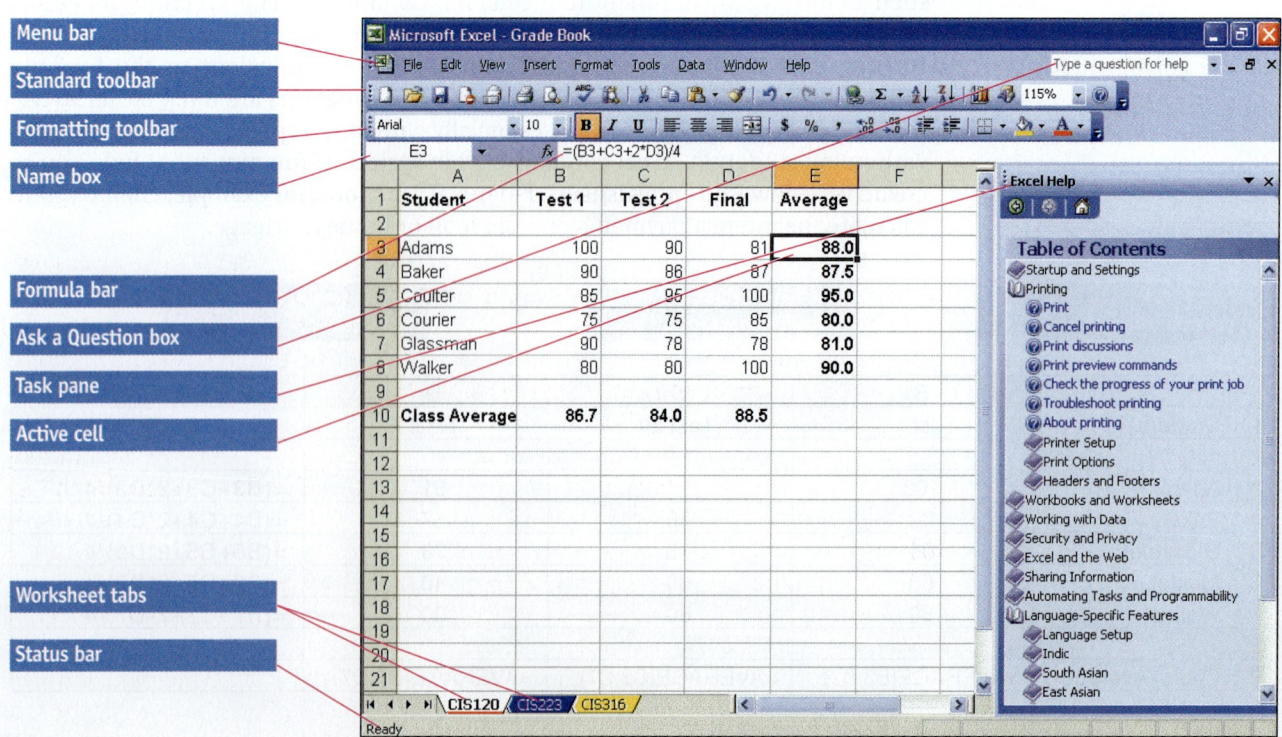

FIGURE 1.4 The Professor's Grade Book

Figure 1.4 resembles the grade book shown earlier, but it includes several other elements that enable you to create and/or edit the worksheet. The heavy border around cell E3 indicates that it (cell E3) is the ***active cell***. (The row and column headings are also highlighted to indicate the active cell.) Any entry made at this time is made into the active cell, and any commands that are executed affect the contents of the active cell. The active cell can be changed by clicking a different cell, or by using the arrow keys to move to a different cell.

The displayed value in cell E3 is 88.0, but as indicated earlier, the cell contains a formula to compute the semester average rather than the number itself. The contents of the active cell, =(B3+C3+2*D3)/4, are displayed in the ***formula bar*** near the top of the worksheet. The cell reference for the active cell, cell E3 in Figure 1.4, appears in the ***Name box*** at the left of the formula bar. The essence of Excel is the automatic recalculation of the formulas in a workbook; i.e., change a value in any cell and the entire workbook is recalculated. Change Adams's grade on the final exam, for example, and the displayed values for his semester average in cell E3, as well as the class average in cell D10, are updated automatically.

The ***status bar*** at the bottom of the worksheet keeps you informed of what is happening as you work within Excel. It displays information about a selected command or an operation in progress.

THE EXCEL WORKBOOK

An Excel workbook is the electronic equivalent of the three-ring binder. A workbook contains one or more worksheets (or chart sheets), each of which is identified by a tab at the bottom of the workbook. The worksheets in a workbook are normally related to one another; for example, each worksheet may contain the sales for a specific division within a company. The advantage of a workbook is that all of its worksheets are stored in a single file, which is accessed as a unit.

Toolbars

Excel provides several different ways to accomplish the same task. Commands may be accessed from a pull-down menu, from a shortcut menu (which is displayed by pointing to an object and clicking the right mouse button), and/or through keyboard equivalents. Commands can also be executed from one of many ***toolbars*** that appear immediately below the menu bar. The Standard and Formatting toolbars are displayed by default. The toolbars appear initially on the same line, but can be separated as described in the hands-on exercise that follows.

The ***Standard toolbar*** contains buttons corresponding to the most basic commands in Excel—for example, opening and closing a workbook, printing a workbook, and so on. The icon on the button is intended to be indicative of its function (e.g., a printer to indicate the Print command). You can also point to the button to display a ***ScreenTip*** showing the name of the button.

The ***Formatting toolbar*** appears under the Standard toolbar and provides access to common formatting operations such as boldface, italics, or underlining. It also enables you to change the alignment of entries within a cell and/or change the font or color. The easiest way to master the toolbars is to view the buttons in groups according to their general function, as shown in Figure 1.5.

The toolbars may appear overwhelming at first, but there is absolutely no need to memorize what the individual buttons do. That will come with time. Indeed, if you use another Office application such as Microsoft Word, you may already recognize many of the buttons on the Standard and Formatting toolbars. Note, too, that many of the commands in the pull-down menus are displayed with an image that corresponds to a button on a toolbar.

Opens a new workbook; opens an existing workbook; saves a workbook; prevents a workbook from being copied or edited; sends a workbook via e-mail

Prints the workbook; previews the workbook prior to printing

Checks the spelling; opens Research in the task pane

Cuts or copies the selecton to the clipboard; pastes the clipboard contents; copies the formatting of the selected cells

Undoes or redoes a previously executed command

Inserts a hyperlink; sums the suggested range; performs an ascending or descending sort

Starts the Chart Wizard; displays the Drawing toolbar

Changes the magnification

Opens Help in the task pane

(a) The Standard Toolbar

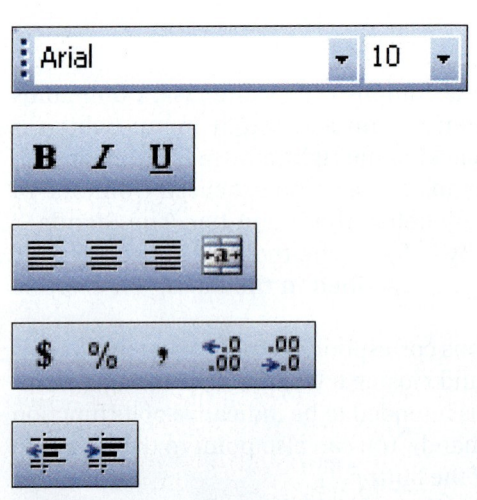

Changes the font or point size

Toggles boldface, italic, and underline on and off

Aligns left, center, right; merges cells and centers

Applies accounting, percentage, or comma formatting; increases or decreases the number of decimals

Decreases or increases the indent

Applies a border; applies a background color; applies a font color

(b) The Formatting Toolbar

FIGURE 1.5   Toolbars

THE FILE MENU

The *File menu* is a critically important menu in virtually every Windows application. It contains the Save and Open commands to save a workbook on disk, then subsequently retrieve (open) that workbook at a later time. The File menu also contains the **Print command** to print a workbook, the **Close command** to close the current workbook but continue working in the application, and the **Exit command** to quit the application altogether.

The **Save command** copies the workbook that you are working on (i.e., the workbook that is currently in memory) to disk. The command functions differently the first time it is executed for a new workbook, in that it displays the Save As dialog box as shown in Figure 1.6a. The dialog box requires you to specify the name of the workbook, the drive (and an optional folder) in which the workbook is to be stored, and its file type. All subsequent executions of the command save the workbook under the assigned name, replacing the previously saved version with the new version.

The *file name* (e.g., My First Spreadsheet) can contain up to 255 characters including spaces, commas, and/or periods. (Periods are discouraged, however, since they are too easily confused with DOS extensions.) The Save In list box is used to select the drive (which is not visible in Figure 1.6a) and the optional folder (e.g., Exploring Excel). The **Places bar** provides shortcuts to any of its folders without having to search through the Save In list box. Click the Desktop icon, for example, and the file is saved on the Windows desktop. You can also use the My Documents folder, which is accessible from every application in Microsoft Office.

The *file type* defaults to an Excel workbook. You can, however, choose a different format to maintain compatibility with earlier versions of Microsoft Excel. You can also save any Excel workbook as a Web page.

The **Save As command** saves a copy of an existing workbook under a different name, and/or a different file type, and is useful when you want to retain a copy of the original workbook. The command results in two copies of the workbook. The original workbook is kept on disk under the original name. A copy of the workbook is saved on disk under the new name and remains in memory. The Save As command also lets you save a workbook in a different file format such as text or CSV (comma-separated values) in order to convert the Excel data to a format required by another application.

The **Open command** is the opposite of the Save command as it brings a copy of an existing workbook into memory, enabling you to work with that workbook. The Open command displays the Open dialog box in which you specify the file name, the drive (and optionally the folder) that contains the file, and the file type. Microsoft Excel will then list all files of that type on the designated drive (and folder), enabling you to open the file you want.

The Save and Open commands work in conjunction with one another. The Save As dialog box in Figure 1.6a, for example, saves the file My First Spreadsheet in the Exploring Excel folder. The Open dialog box in Figure 1.6b loads that file into memory so that you can work with the file, after which you can save the revised file for use at a later time.

The toolbars in the Save As and Open dialog boxes have several buttons in common that facilitate the execution of either command. The Views button lets you display the files in many different views. The Details view shows the file size as well as the date and time a file was last modified. The Preview view shows the beginning of a workbook, without having to open the workbook. The List view displays only the file names, and thus lets you see more files at one time. The Properties view shows information about the workbook, including the date of creation and number of revisions. Other buttons provide limited file management without having to go to My Computer or Windows Explorer. You can, for example, delete a file, create a new folder, or start your Web browser from either dialog box.

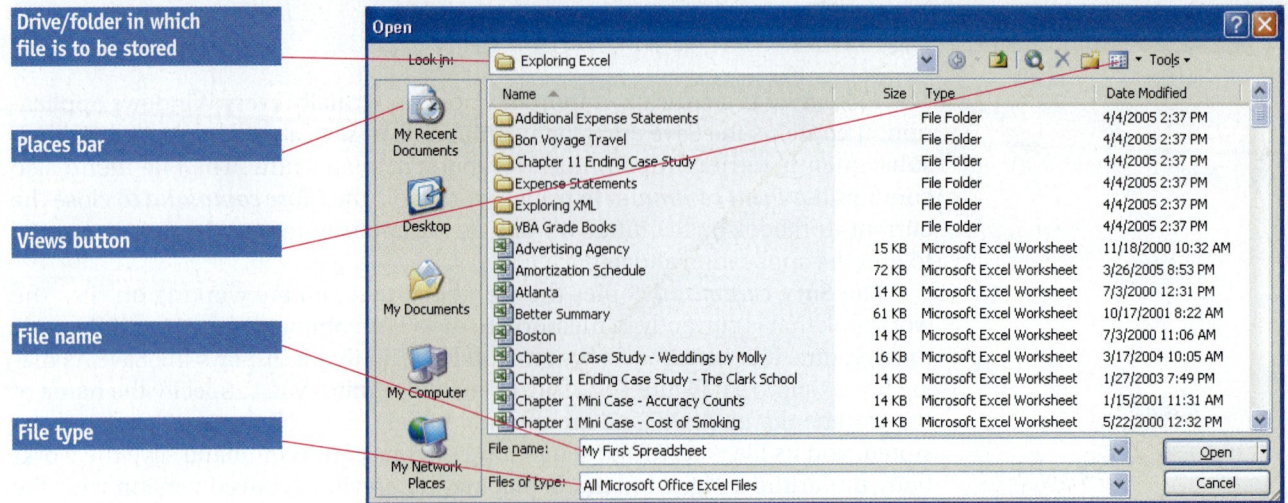

(a) Save As Dialog Box (Details View)

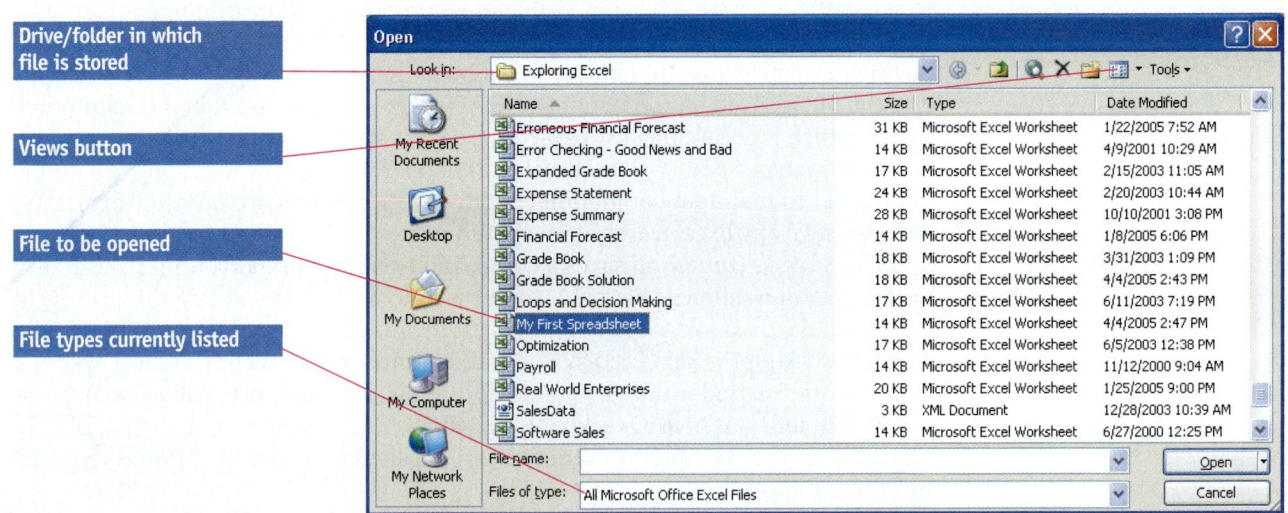

(b) Open Dialog Box (Details View)

FIGURE 1.6   The Save and Open Commands

FILE MANAGEMENT AT YOUR FINGERTIPS

Use the toolbar in the Open and/or Save As dialog box to perform basic file management within any Office application. You can select any existing file or folder, and delete it or rename it. You can also create a new folder, which is very useful when you begin to work with a large number of documents. You can also use the Views button to change the way the files are listed within the dialog box.

hands-on exercise

1 Introduction to Microsoft Excel

Objective To start Microsoft Excel; to open, modify, and print an existing workbook. Use Figure 1.7 as a guide in the exercise.

Step 1: **Log On to Windows XP**

- Turn on the computer and all of its peripherals. The floppy drive should be empty prior to starting your machine.
- Your system will take a minute or so to get started, after which you should see a logon screen similar to Figure 1.7a. Do not be concerned if the appearance of your desktop is different from ours.
- Click the icon for the user account you want to access. You may be prompted for a password, depending on the security options in effect.
- You should be familiar with basic file management and very comfortable moving and copying files from one folder to another. If not, you may want to review the material in the Windows XP section of this text.

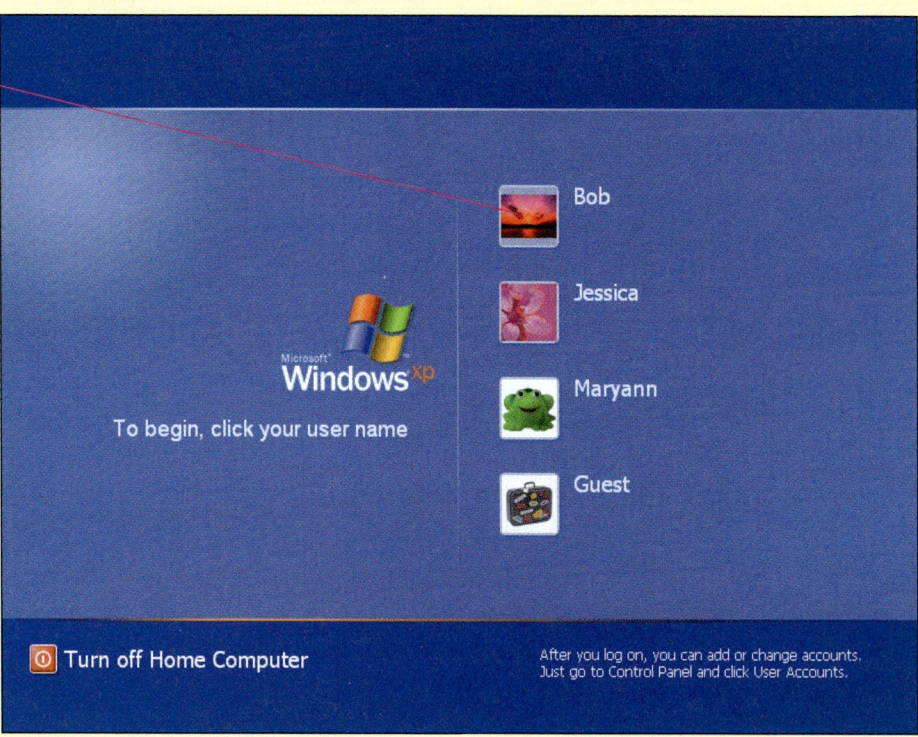

Click icon for your user account

(a) Log On to Windows XP (step 1)

FIGURE 1.7 Hands-on Exercise 1

USER ACCOUNTS

The available user names are created automatically during the installation of Windows XP, but you can add or delete users at any time. Click the Start button, click Control Panel, switch to the Category view, and select User Accounts. Choose the desired task, such as creating a new account or changing an existing account, then supply the necessary information. Do not expect, however, to be able to modify accounts in a school setting.

Step 2: **Download the Practice Files**

- Start Internet Explorer and go to **www.prenhall.com/grauer**. Click the book for **Office 2003**, which takes you to the Office 2003 home page.
- Click the **Student Downloads tab** in the upper-right portion of the window to go to the Student Download page as shown in Figure 1.7b.
- Click the link to download the file for the **Exploring Excel 2003 Revised Edition**. You will see the File Download box asking what you want to do. Click the **Save button**. The Save As dialog box appears.
- Click the **down arrow** in the Save In list box and select the drive and folder where you want to save the file. Click **Save**.
- Start Windows Explorer to select the drive and folder where you saved the file, then double click the file and follow the onscreen instructions. Check with your instructor for additional information.

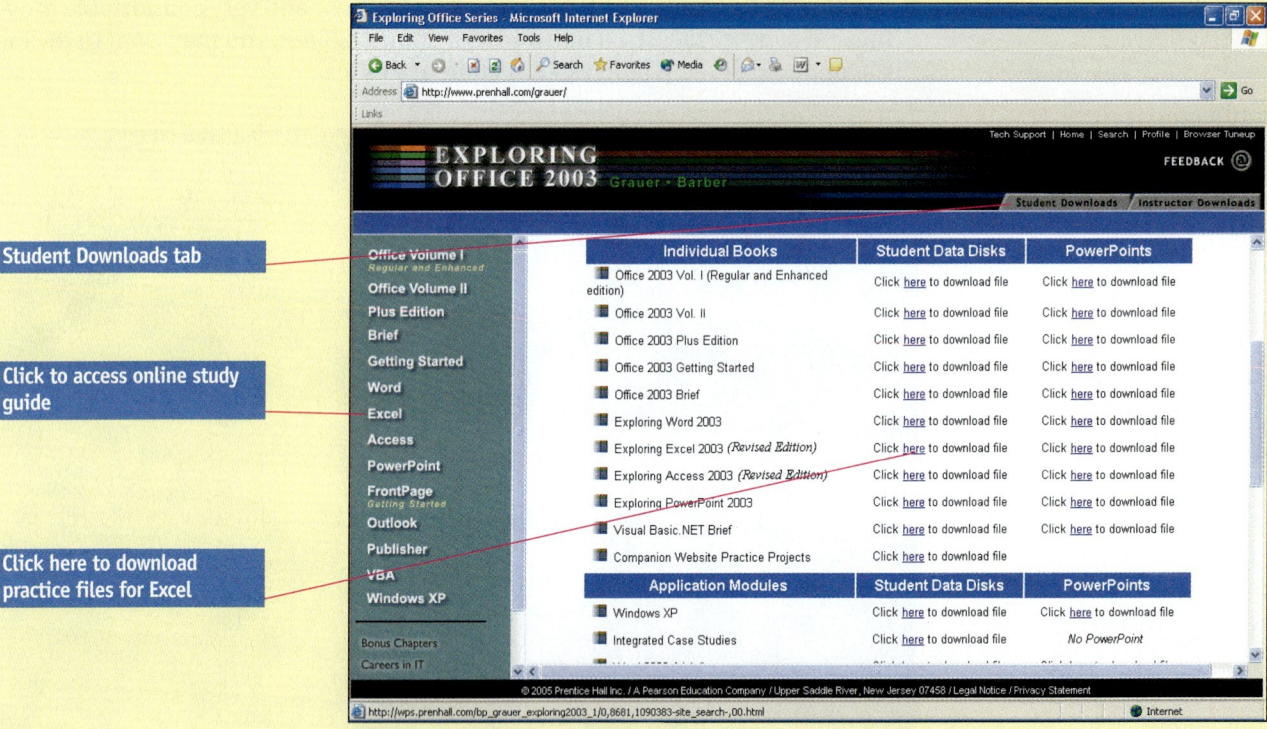

(b) Download the Practice Files (step 2)

FIGURE 1.7 Hands-on Exercise 1 (*continued*)

EXPLORE OUR WEB SITE

The Exploring Office Series Web site offers an online study guide (multiple-choice, true/false, and matching questions) for each individual textbook to help you review the material in each chapter. You can take practice quizzes by yourself and/or e-mail the results to your instructor. These online study guides are available via the tabs in the left navigation bar. You can return to the Student Download page at any time by clicking the tab toward the top of the window and/or you can click the link to Home to return to the home page for the Office 2003 Series. And finally, you can click the Feedback button at the top of the screen to send a message directly to Bob Grauer.

Step 3: **Start Excel**

- Click the **Start button** to display the Start menu. Click (or point to) the **All Programs button**, click **Microsoft Office**, then click **Microsoft Excel 2003** to start the program.

- Right click the Office Assistant if it appears. Click the **Hide command**.

- If necessary, click the **Maximize button** in the application window so that Excel takes the entire desktop as shown in Figure 1.7c. Click the **Maximize button** in the document window (if necessary) so that the document window is as large as possible.

- Pull down the **View menu** and click the **Task Pane command** to display (hide) the task pane. The command functions as a toggle switch; that is, execute the command and the task pane is open. Execute the command a second time and the task pane is closed.

- The Getting Started task pane appears initially. Click the down arrow in the task pane to see what other panes are available. The Help task pane is shown in Figure 1.7c. Close the task pane by clicking its **Close button**.

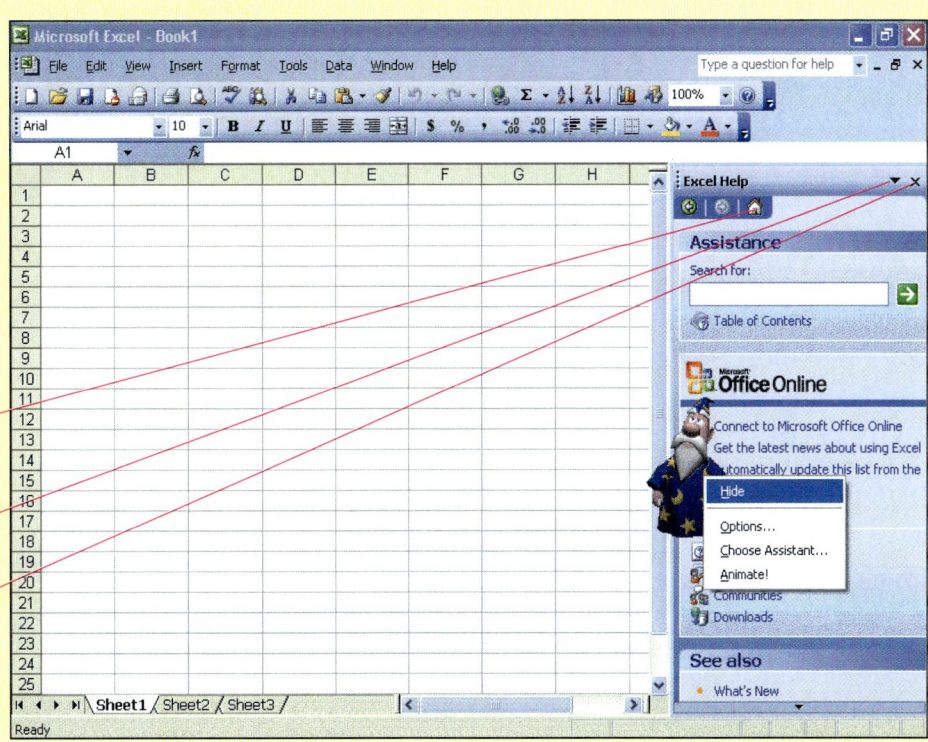

(c) Start Excel (step 3)

FIGURE 1.7 Hands-on Exercise 1 (*continued*)

SEPARATE THE TOOLBARS

You may see the Standard and Formatting toolbars displayed on one row to save space within the application window. If so, we suggest that you separate the toolbars, so that you see all of the buttons on each. Click the down arrow at the end of any visible toolbar to display toolbar options, then click the option to show the buttons on two rows. Click the down arrow a second time to show the buttons on one row if you prefer this configuration.

Step 4: **Open the Workbook**

- Pull down the **File menu** and click **Open** (or click the **Open button** on the Standard toolbar). You should see a dialog box similar to the one in Figure 1.7d.
- Click the **drop-down arrow** on the Views button, then click **Details** to change to the Details view. Click and drag the vertical border between two columns to increase (or decrease) the size of a column.
- Click the **drop-down arrow** on the Look In list box. Click the appropriate drive, drive C or drive A, depending on the location of your data.
- Double click the **Exploring Excel folder** to make it the active folder (the folder from which you will retrieve and into which you will save the workbook).
- Click the **down scroll arrow** if necessary in order to click **Grade Book** to select the professor's grade book. Click the **Open command button** to open the workbook and begin the exercise.

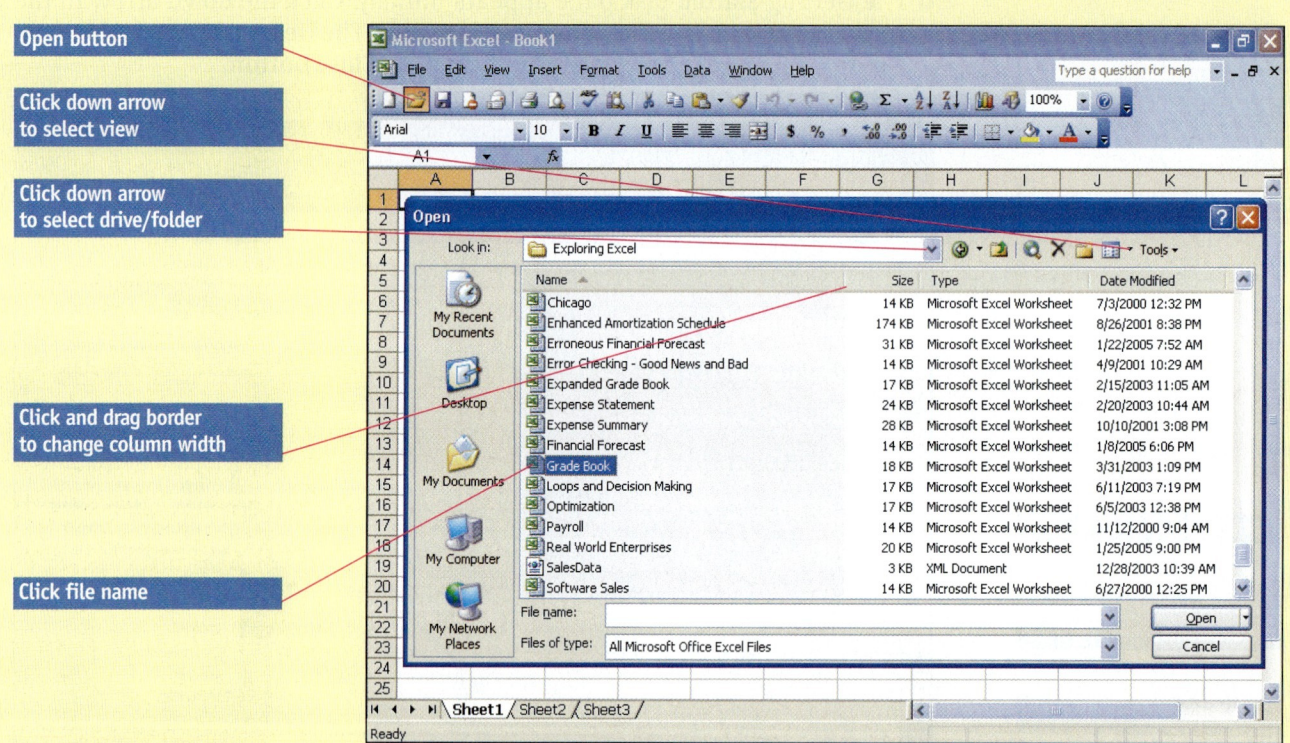

(d) Open the Workbook (step 4)

FIGURE 1.7 Hands-on Exercise 1 (*continued*)

THE MENUS MAY CHANGE

Microsoft Office gives you the option of displaying short menus (ending in a double arrow to show additional commands), as opposed to complete menus with all commands. We prefer the complete menus because that is the way you learn an application, but the settings may be different on your system. Pull down the Tools menu, click the Customize command to display the Customize dialog box, click the Options tab, and check the box to always show full menus.

Step 5: **The Save As Command**

- Pull down the **File menu**. Click **Save As** to display the dialog box shown in Figure 1.7e.

- Enter **Grade Book Solution** as the name of the new workbook. (A file name may contain up to 255 characters. Spaces and commas are allowed in the file name.)

- Click the **Save button**. Press the **Esc key** or click the **Close button** if you see a Properties dialog box.

- There are now two identical copies of the file on disk: "Grade Book" and "Grade Book Solution," which you just created. The title bar shows the latter name, which is the workbook currently in memory.

- You will work with "Grade Book Solution" but can always return to the original "Grade Book" if necessary.

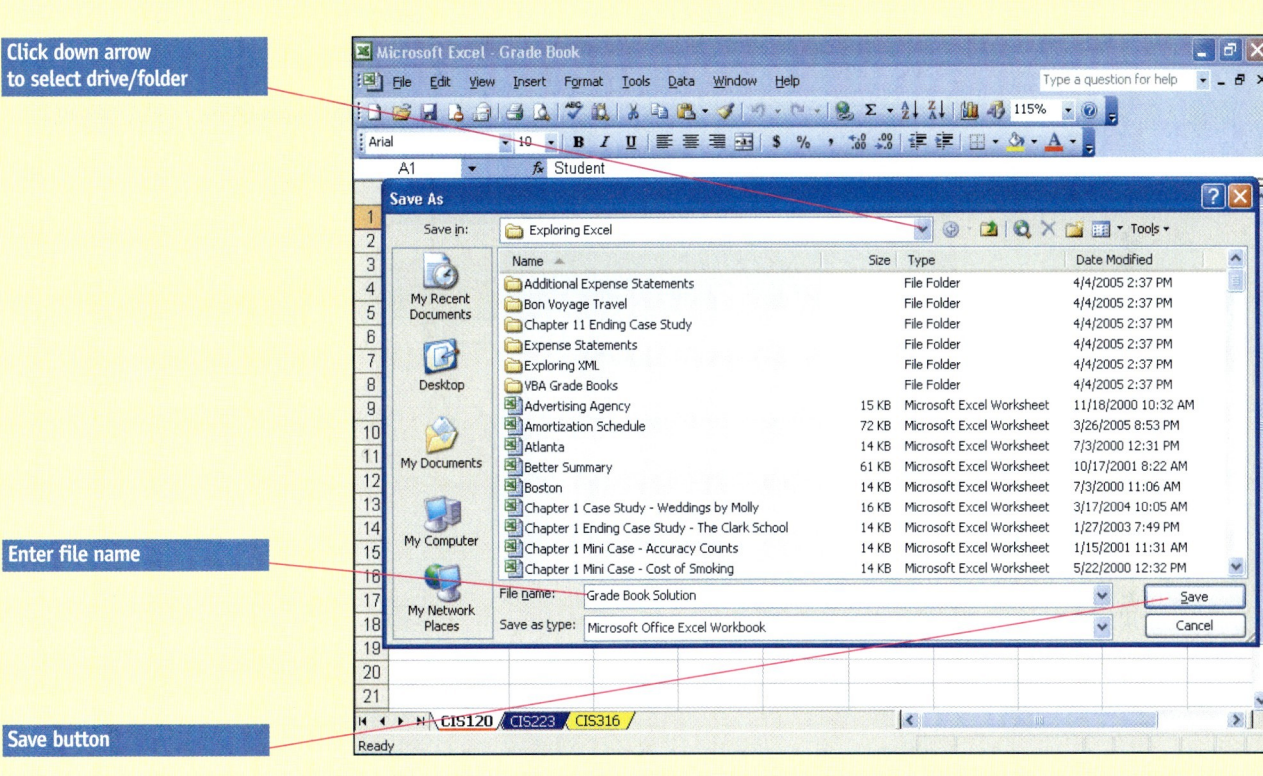

(e) The Save As Command (step 5)

FIGURE 1.7 Hands-on Exercise 1 (*continued*)

QUIT WITHOUT SAVING

There will be times when you do not want to save the changes to a workbook—for example, when you have edited it beyond recognition and wish you had never started. Pull down the File menu and click the Close command, then click No in response to the message asking whether to save the changes. Pull down the File menu, click the file's name at the bottom of the menu to reopen the file, then begin all over.

Step 6: **The Active Cell, Formula Bar, and Worksheet Tabs**

- You should see the workbook in Figure 1.7f. Click in **cell B3**, the cell containing Adams's grade on the first test. Cell B3 is now the active cell and is surrounded by a heavy border. The Name box indicates that cell B3 is the active cell, and its contents are displayed in the formula bar.

- Click in **cell B4** (or press the **down arrow key**) to make it the active cell. The Name box indicates cell B4 while the formula bar indicates a grade of 90.

- Click in **cell E3**, the cell containing the formula to compute Adams's semester average; the worksheet displays the computed average of 88.0, but the formula bar displays the formula, =(B3+C3+2*D3)/4, to compute that average based on the test grades.

- Click the **CIS223 tab** to view a different worksheet within the same workbook. This worksheet contains the grades for a different class.

- Click the **CIS316 tab** to view this worksheet. Click the **CIS120 tab** to return to this worksheet and continue with the exercise.

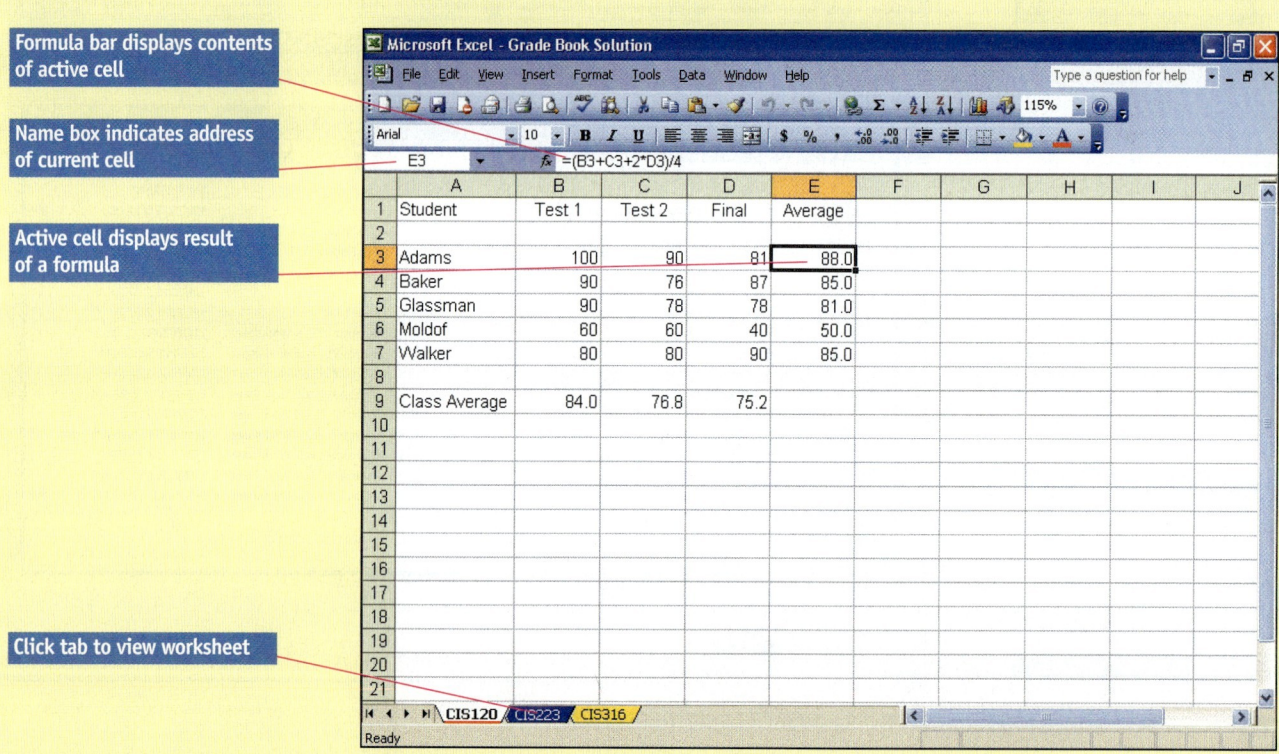

(f) The Active Cell, Formula Bar, and Worksheet Tabs (step 6)

FIGURE 1.7 Hands-on Exercise 1 (*continued*)

ADD COLOR TO THE WORKSHEET TABS

Select (click) the worksheet tab for which you want to change the tab color. (If you don't see the worksheet you want, click the tab scrolling buttons to display the tab, and then click the tab.) Pull down the Format menu, click the Sheet command, then click Tab Color to display a color palette. Click the color you want, and then click OK. You can also right click a worksheet tab to display a context-sensitive menu, and change the color from there.

Step 7: Experiment (What If?)

- Click in **cell C4**, the cell containing Baker's grade on the second test. Enter a corrected value of **86** (instead of the previous entry of 76). Press **Enter** (or click in another cell).

- The effects of this change ripple through the worksheet, automatically changing the computed value for Baker's average in cell E4 to 87.5. The class average on the second test in cell C9 changes to 78.8.

- Change Walker's grade on the final from 90 to **100**. Press **Enter** (or click in another cell). Walker's average in cell E7 changes to 90.0, while the class average in cell D9 changes to 77.2.

- Your worksheet should match Figure 1.7g. Save the workbook.

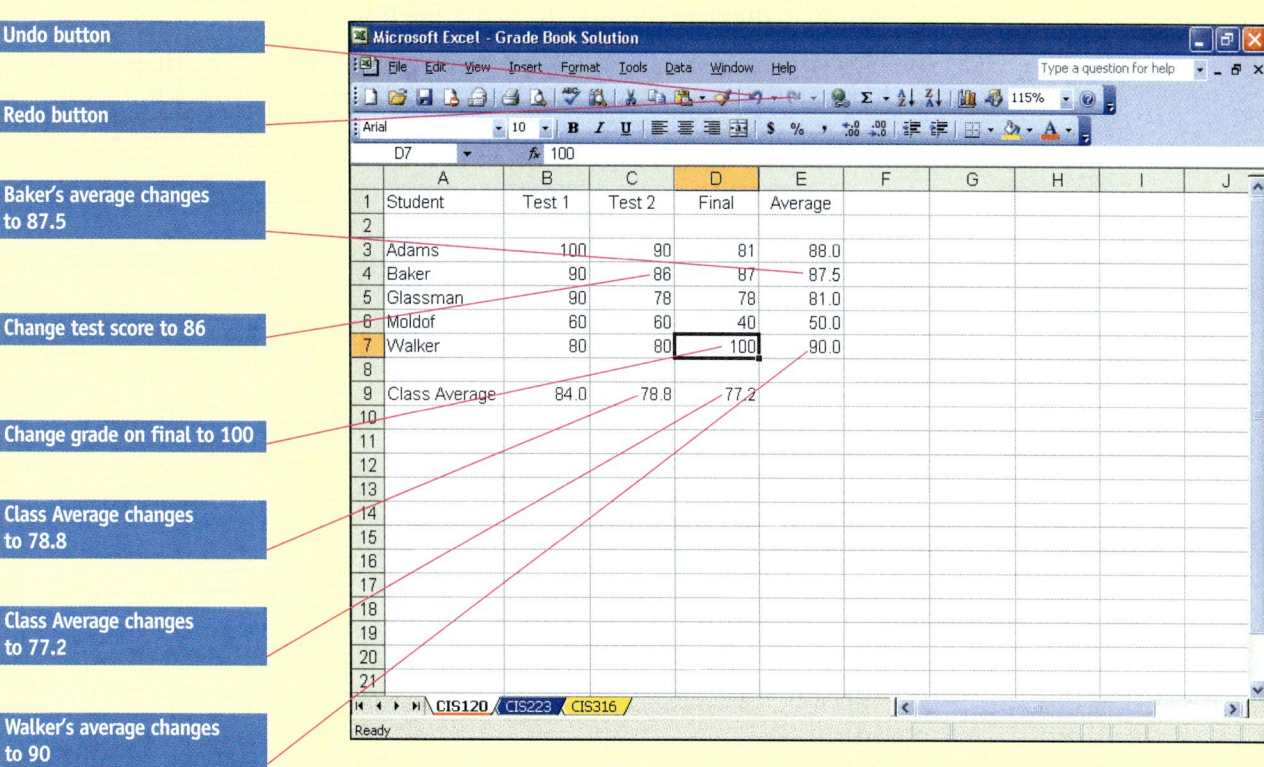

(g) Experiment (What If?) (step 7)

FIGURE 1.7 Hands-on Exercise 1 (*continued*)

THE UNDO AND REDO COMMANDS

The Undo command lets you undo the last several changes to a workbook. Click the down arrow next to the Undo button on the Standard toolbar to display a reverse-order list of your previous commands, then click the command you want to undo, which also cancels all of the preceding commands. Undoing the fifth command in the list, for example, will also undo the preceding four commands. The Redo command redoes (reverses) the last command that was undone. It, too, displays a reverse-order list of commands, so that redoing the fifth command in the list will also redo the preceding four commands.

Step 8: **Help with Excel**

- There are several different ways to request help, but in any event, the best time to obtain help is when you don't need any. Try either of the following:
  - Pull down the **Help menu** and click the command to **Show the Office Assistant**. Click the Assistant, then enter the question, "**How do I undo a command?**" in the Assistant's balloon and click **Search**, or
  - Type the question directly in the **Ask a Question list box** in the upper right of the Excel window and press **Enter**.

- Excel will display a message indicating that it is searching the Office Web site. You should see a task pane with the results as shown in Figure 1.7h.

- Click the link that is most appropriate, for example, **Undo or redo an action**. A new window opens containing the detailed help information. Click the **Print button** in the Help window, then click the **Print command button**.

- Close the Help window. Close the task pane. Pull down the **Help menu** and hide the Office Assistant. Exit Excel if you do not want to continue with the next exercise at this time.

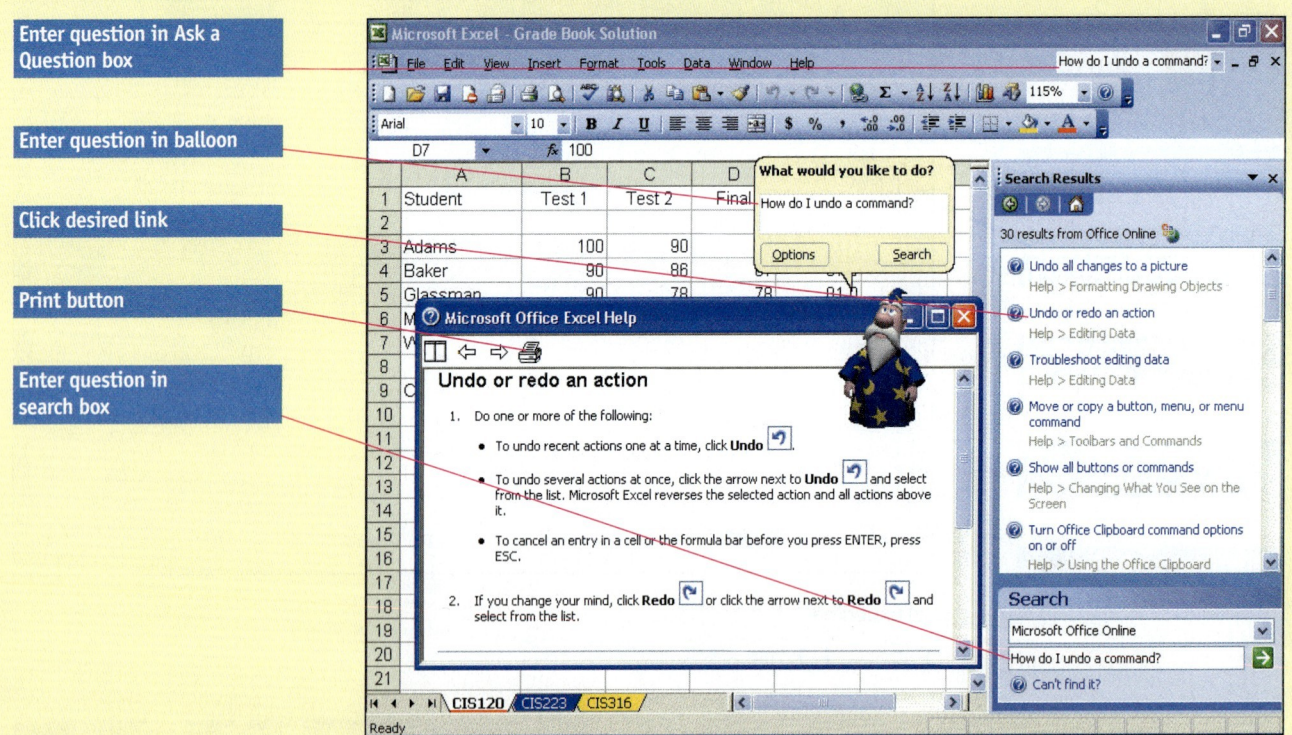

(h) Help with Excel (step 8)

FIGURE 1.7 Hands-on Exercise 1 (*continued*)

ABOUT MICROSOFT EXCEL

Pull down the Help menu and click About Microsoft Excel to display the specific release number as well as other licensing information, including the Product ID. This Help screen also contains two very useful command buttons, System Info and Technical Support. The first button displays information about the hardware installed on your system, including the amount of memory and available space on the hard drive. The Technical Support button provides information on obtaining technical assistance.

MODIFYING A WORKSHEET

We trust that you completed the hands-on exercise without difficulty and that you are more confident in your ability than when you first began. The exercise was not complicated, but it did accomplish several objectives and set the stage for a second exercise, which follows shortly.

Consider now Figure 1.8, which contains a modified version of the professor's grade book. Figure 1.8a shows the grade book at the end of the first hands-on exercise and reflects the changes made to the grades for Baker and Walker. Figure 1.8b shows the worksheet as it will appear at the end of the second exercise. Several changes bear mention:

1. One student has dropped the class and two other students have been added. Moldof appeared in the original worksheet in Figure 1.8a, but has somehow managed to withdraw; Coulter and Courier did not appear in the original grade book but have been added to the worksheet in Figure 1.8b.

2. A new column containing the students' majors has been added.

The implementation of these changes is accomplished through a combination of the *Insert command* (to add individual cells, rows, or columns) and/or the *Delete command* (to remove individual cells, rows, or columns). Execution of either command automatically adjusts the cell references in existing formulas to reflect the insertion or deletion of the various cells. The Insert and Delete commands can also be used to insert or delete a worksheet. The professor could, for example, add a new sheet to a workbook to include grades for another class and/or delete a worksheet for a class that was no longer taught. We focus initially, however, on the insertion and deletion of rows and columns within a worksheet.

	A	B	C	D	E
1	Student	Test 1	Test 2	Final	Average
2					
3	Adams	100	90	81	88.0
4	Baker	90	86	87	87.5
5	Glassman	90	78	78	81.0
6	Moldof	60	60	40	50.0
7	Walker	80	80	100	90.0
8					
9	Class Average	84.0	78.8	77.2	

Moldof will be dropped from class

(a) After Hands-on Exercise 1

	A	B	C	D	E	F
1	Student	Major	Test 1	Test 2	Final	Average
2						
3	Adams	CIS	100	90	81	88.0
4	Baker	MKT	90	86	87	87.5
5	Coulter	ACC	85	95	100	95.0
6	Courier	FIN	75	75	85	80.0
7	Glassman	CIS	90	78	78	81.0
8	Walker	CIS	80	80	100	90.0
9						
10	Class Average		86.7	84.0	88.5	

A new column has been added (Major)

Two new students have been added

Moldof has been deleted

(b) After Hands-on Exercise 2

FIGURE 1.8 The Modified Grade Book

Figure 1.9 displays the cell formulas in the professor's grade book and corresponds to the worksheets in Figure 1.8. The "before" and "after" worksheets reflect the insertion of a new column containing the students' majors, the addition of two new students, Coulter and Courier, and the deletion of an existing student, Moldof.

Let us consider the formula to compute Adams's semester average, which is contained in cell E3 of the original grade book, but in cell F3 in the modified grade book. The formula in Figure 1.9a referenced cells B3, C3, and D3 (the grades on test 1, test 2, and the final). The corresponding formula in Figure 1.9b reflects the fact that a new column has been inserted, and references cells C3, D3, and E3. The change in the formula is made automatically by Excel, without any action on the part of the user other than to insert the new column. The formulas for all other students have been adjusted in similar fashion.

Some students (all students below Baker) have had a further adjustment to reflect the addition of the new students through insertion of new rows in the worksheet. Glassman, for example, appeared in row 5 of the original worksheet, but appears in row 7 of the revised worksheet. Hence the formula to compute Glassman's semester average now references the grades in row 7, rather than in row 5 as in the original worksheet.

Finally, the formulas to compute the class averages have also been adjusted. These formulas appeared in row 9 of Figure 1.9a and averaged the grades in rows 3 through 7. The revised worksheet has a net increase of one student, which automatically moves these formulas to row 10, where the formulas are adjusted to average the grades in rows 3 through 8.

	A	B	C	D	E
1	Student	Test1	Test2	Final	Average
2					
3	Adams	100	90	81	=(B3+C3+2*D3)/4
4	Baker	90	86	87	=(B4+C4+2*D4)/4
5	Glassman	90	78	78	=(B5+C5+2*D5)/4
6	Moldof	60	60	40	=(B6+C6+2*D6)/4
7	Walker	80	80	100	=(B7+C7+2*D7)/4
8					
9	Class Average	=AVERAGE(B3:B7)	=AVERAGE(C3:C7)	=AVERAGE(D3:D7)	

Function references grades in rows 3–7

Formula references grades in B3, C3, and D3

(a) Before

	A	B	C	D	E	F
1	Student	Major	Test1	Test2	Final	Average
2						
3	Adams	CIS	100	90	81	=(C3+D3+2*E3)/4
4	Baker	MKT	90	86	87	=(C4+D4+2*E4)/4
5	Coulter	ACC	85	95	100	=(C5+D5+2*E5)/4
6	Courier	FIN	75	75	85	=(C6+D6+2*E6)/4
7	Glassman	CIS	90	78	78	=(C7+D7+2*E7)/4
8	Walker	CIS	80	80	100	=(C8+D8+2*E8)/4
9						
10	Class Average		=AVERAGE(C3:C8)	=AVERAGE(D3:D8)	=AVERAGE(E3:E8)	

Function changes to reference grades in rows 3–8 (due to addition of 2 new students and deletion of 1)

Formula changes to reference grades in C3, D3, and E3 due to addition of new column

(b) After

FIGURE 1.9 The Insert and Delete Commands

THE PAGE SETUP COMMAND

The **Page Setup command** gives you complete control of the printed worksheet as illustrated in Figure 1.10. Many of the options may not appear important now, but you will appreciate them as you develop larger and more complicated worksheets later in the text.

The Page tab in Figure 1.10 determines the orientation and scaling of the printed page. **Portrait orientation** (8½ × 11) prints vertically down the page. **Landscape orientation** (11 × 8½) prints horizontally across the page and is used when the worksheet is too wide to fit on a portrait page. The option buttons indicate mutually exclusive items, one of which *must* be selected; that is, a worksheet must be printed in either portrait or landscape orientation. Option buttons are also used to choose the scaling factor. You can reduce (enlarge) the output by a designated scaling factor, or you can force the output to fit on a specified number of pages. The latter option is typically used to force a worksheet to fit on a single page.

The Margins tab not only controls the margins, but will also center the worksheet horizontally and/or vertically. The Margins tab also determines the distance of the header and footer from the edge of the page.

The Header/Footer tab lets you create a header (and/or footer) that appears at the top (and/or bottom) of every page. The pull-down list boxes let you choose from several preformatted entries, or alternatively, you can click the appropriate command button to customize either entry.

The Sheet tab offers several additional options. The Gridlines option prints lines to separate the cells within the worksheet. The Row and Column Headings option displays the column letters and row numbers. Both options should be selected for most worksheets. Information about the additional entries can be obtained by clicking the Help button.

The Print Preview command button is available from all four tabs within the Page Setup dialog box. The command shows you how the worksheet will appear when printed and saves you from having to rely on trial and error.

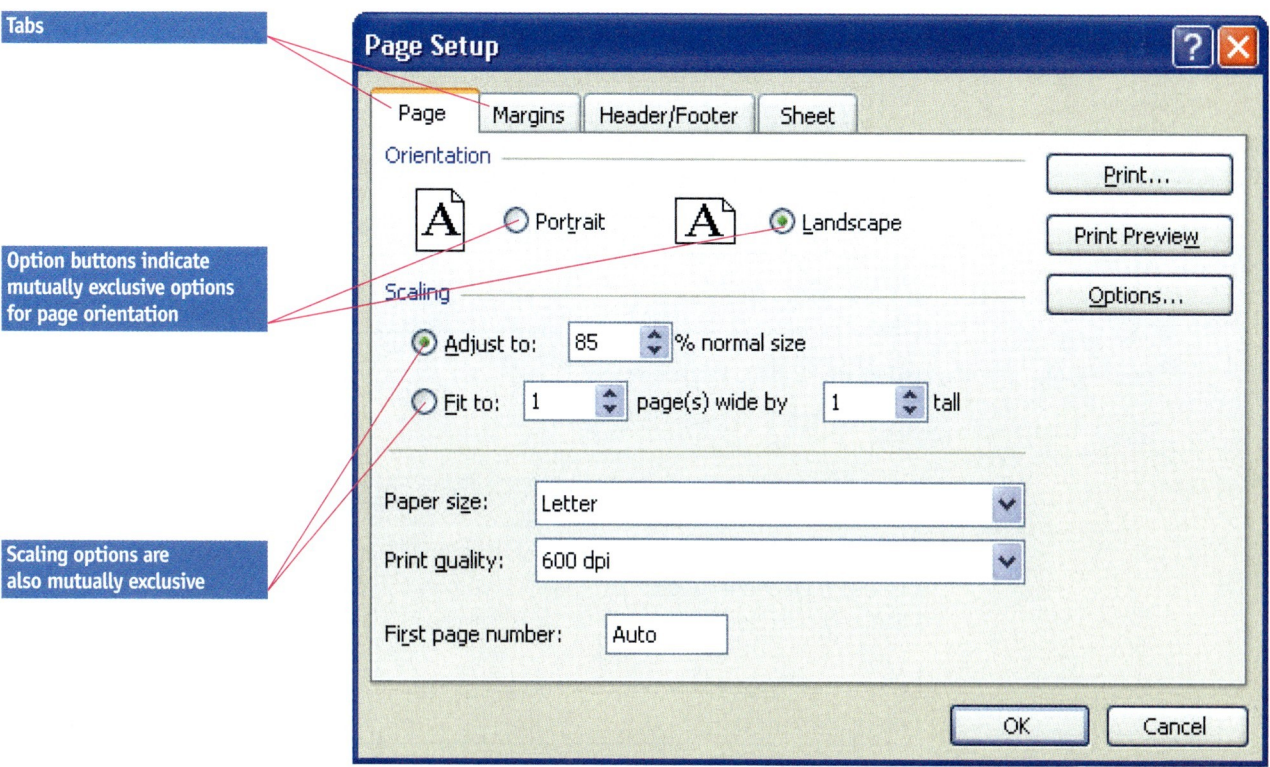

FIGURE 1.10   The Page Setup Command

hands-on exercise

2 Modifying a Worksheet

Objective To open an existing workbook; to insert and delete rows and columns of a worksheet; to print cell formulas and displayed values; to use the Page Setup command. Use Figure 1.11 as a guide.

Step 1: **Open an Existing Workbook**

- Start Excel. Click the **Open button** on the Standard toolbar. You should see a dialog box similar to the one in Figure 1.11a. Click the **drop-down arrow** on the Views button and click **Details** to change to the Details view.

- Click the **drop-down arrow** on the Look In list box and select drive C or drive A, depending on the location of your data. Double click the **Exploring Excel folder** to make it the active folder.

- Scroll until you can open (double click) the **Grade Book Solution** workbook from the previous exercise.

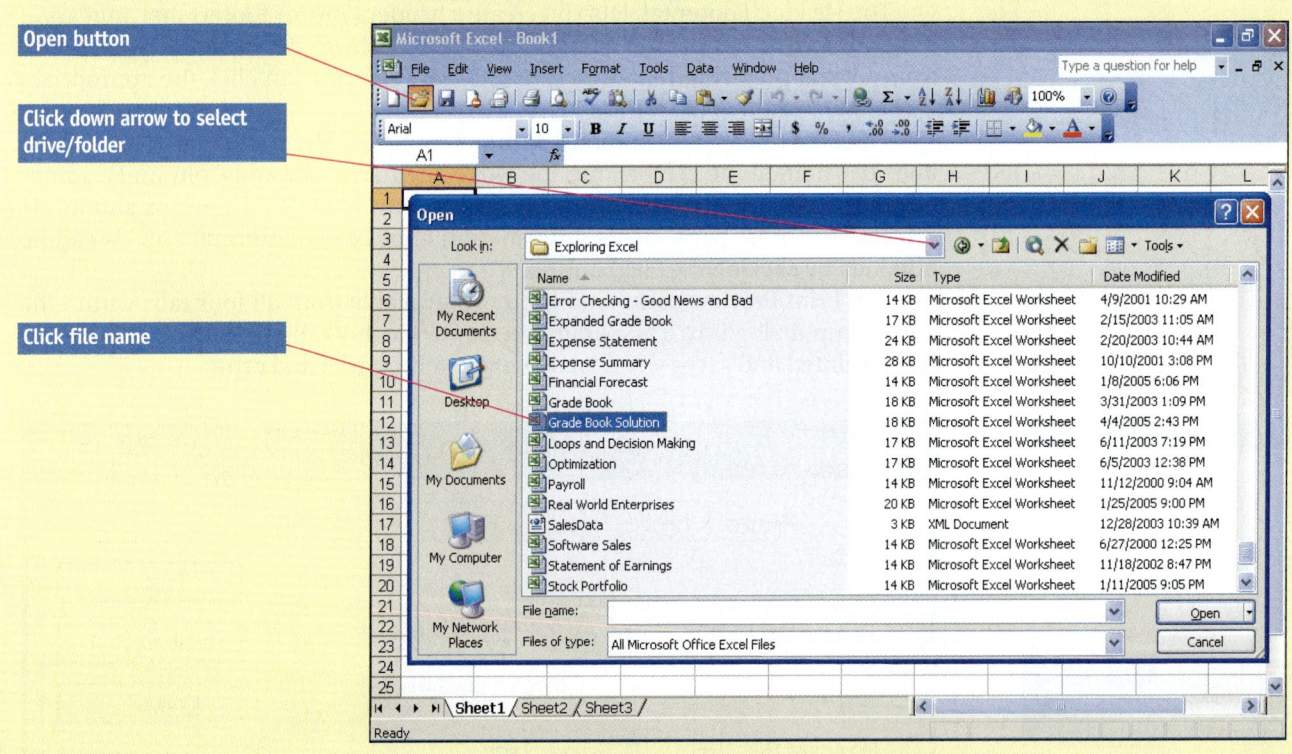

(a) Open an Existing Workbook (step 1)

FIGURE 1.11 Hands-on Exercise 2

THE GETTING STARTED TASK PANE

Pull down the View menu and click the Task Pane command to open the task pane. If necessary, click the down arrow in the task pane to select the Getting Started task pane. Look in the "Open" area of the task pane and you will see links to the last several workbooks that were opened in the application. You can also click the link to the open folder labeled "More . . .", which will display the File Open dialog box.

Step 2: **Delete a Row**

- Click any cell in **row 6** (the row you will delete). Pull down the **Edit menu**. Click **Delete** to display the dialog box in Figure 1.11b. Click **Entire row**. Click **OK** to delete row 6.

- Moldof has disappeared from the grade book, and the class averages (now in row 8) have been updated automatically.

- You can restore the row you just deleted if you made a mistake. Pull down the **Edit menu** and click **Undo Delete** (or click the **Undo button** on the Standard toolbar) to reverse the last command.

- The row for Moldof has been put back into the worksheet.

- Click any cell in **row 6**, and this time delete the entire row for good.

- Save the workbook.

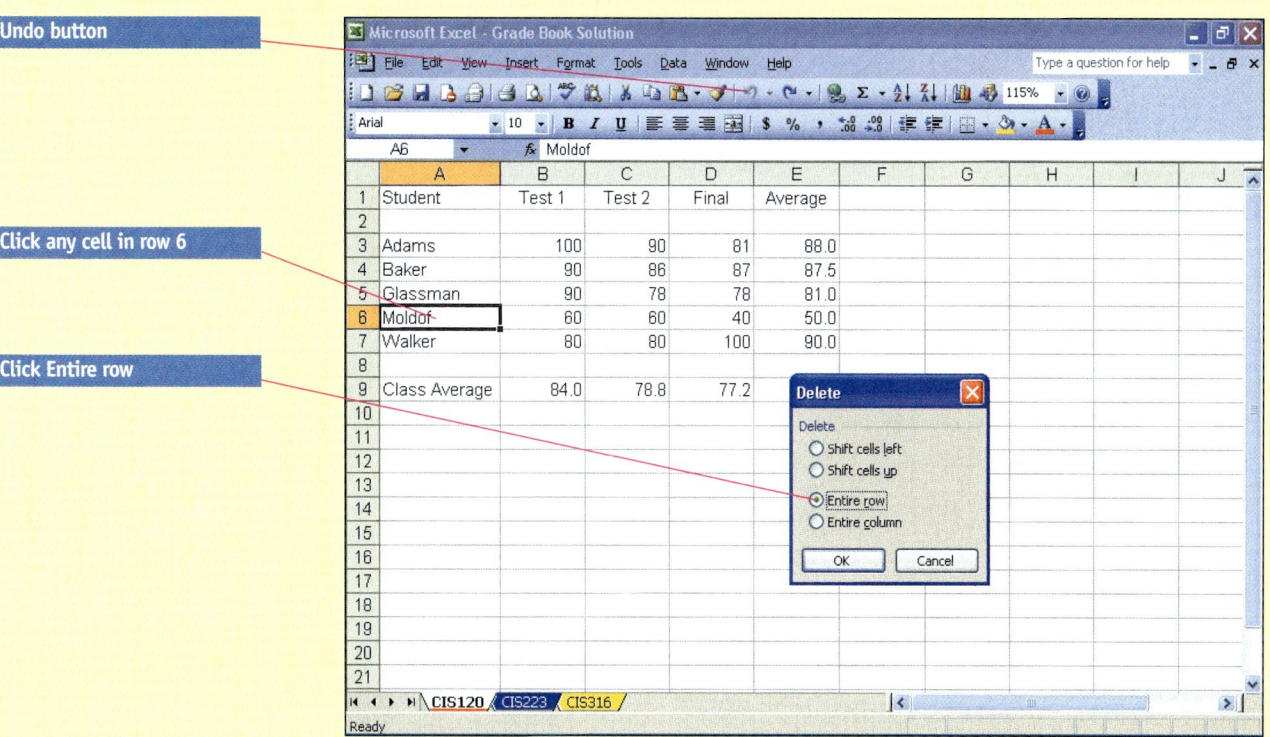

(b) Delete a Row (step 2)

FIGURE 1.11 Hands-on Exercise 2 (*continued*)

INSERT COMMENT COMMAND

You can add a comment, which displays a ScreenTip when you point to the cell, to any cell in a worksheet to explain a formula or other piece of information associated with that cell. Click in the cell that is to hold the comment, pull down the Insert menu, and click Comment to display a box in which you enter the comment. Click outside the box when you have completed the entry. Point to the cell (which should have a tiny red triangle) and you will see the comment you just created.

Step 3: **Insert a Row**

- Click any cell in **row 5** (the row containing Glassman's grades). Pull down the **Insert menu**. Click **Rows** to add a new row above the current row.

- A new row is inserted into the worksheet with the same formatting as in the row above. (Thus you can ignore the Format Painter button, which allows you to change the formatting.) Row 5 is now blank, and Glassman is now in row 6.

- Enter the data for the new student in row 5 as shown in Figure 1.11c. Click in **cell A5**. Type **Coulter**. Press the **right arrow key** or click in **cell B5**. Enter the test grades of 85, 95, 100 in cells B5, C5, and D5, respectively.

- Enter the formula to compute the semester average, **=(B5+C5+2*D5)/4**. Be sure to begin the formula with an equal sign. Press **Enter**.

- Click the **Save button** on the Standard toolbar, or pull down the **File menu** and click **Save** to save the changes made to this point.

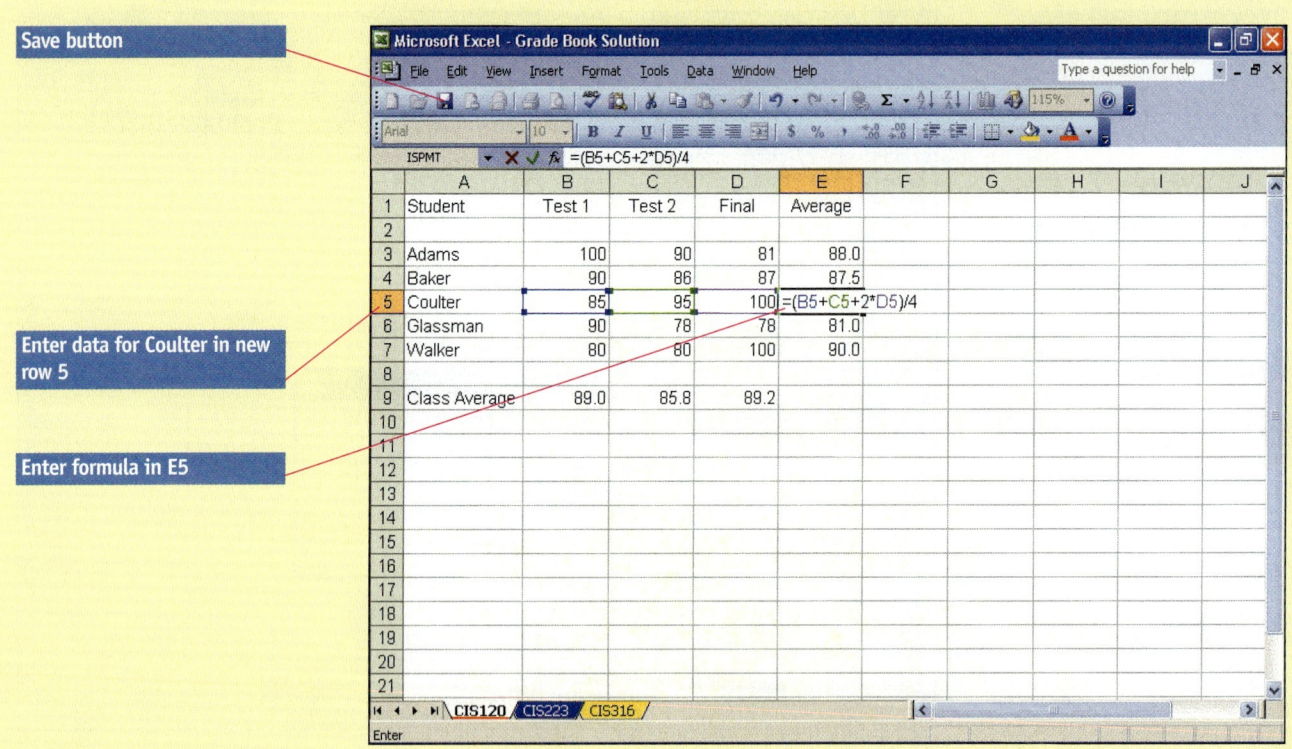

(c) Insert a Row (step 3)

FIGURE 1.11 Hands-on Exercise 2 (*continued*)

CORRECTING MISTAKES

The fastest way to change the contents of an existing cell is to double click in the cell in order to make the changes directly in the cell rather than on the formula bar. Use the mouse or arrow keys to position the insertion point at the point of correction. Press the Ins key to toggle between insert and overtype and/or use the Backspace or Del key to erase a character. Press the Home and End keys to move to the first and last characters in the cell, respectively. (If this feature does not work, pull down the Tools menu, click the Options command, select the Edit tab, and check the box to Edit directly in a cell.)

Step 4: **The AutoComplete Feature**

- Point to the row heading for **row 6** (which now contains Glassman's grades), then click the **right mouse button** to select the row and display a shortcut menu.

- Click **Insert** to insert a new row 6, which moves Glassman to row 7 as shown in Figure 1.11d.

- Click in **cell A6**. Type **C**, the first letter in "Courier," which also happens to be the first letter in "Coulter," a previous entry in column A. If the AutoComplete feature is on (see boxed tip), Coulter's name will be automatically inserted in cell A6 with "oulter" selected.

- Type **ourier** (the remaining letters in "Courier," which replace "oulter."

- Enter Courier's grades in the appropriate cells (75, 75, and 85 in cells B6, C6, and D6, respectively). Click in **cell E6**. Enter the formula to compute the semester average, **=(B6+C6+2*D6)/4**. Press **Enter**.

- Save the workbook.

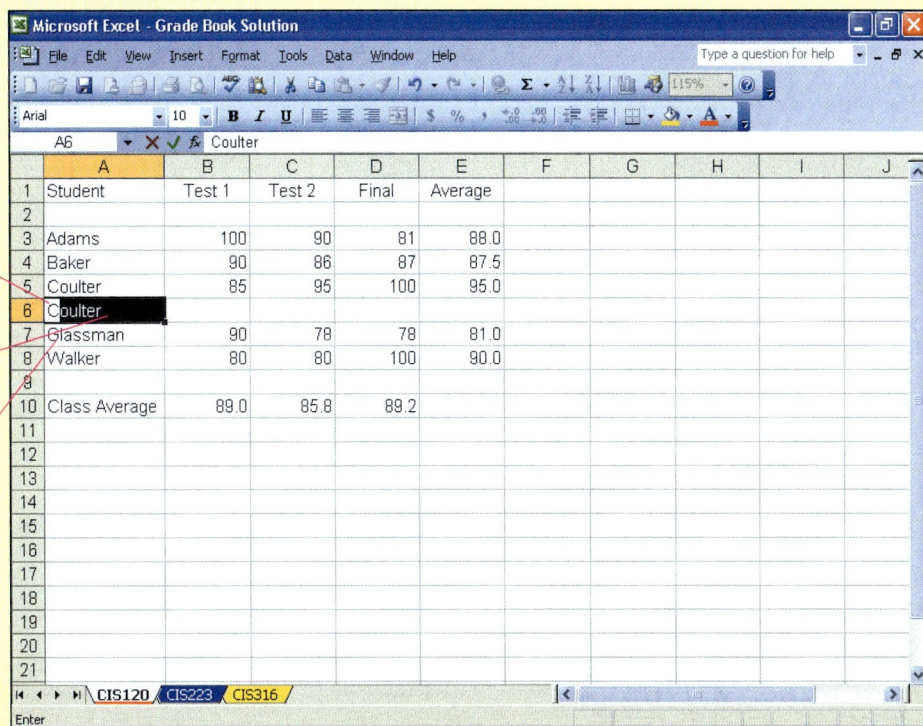

(d) The AutoComplete Feature (step 4)

FIGURE 1.11   Hands-on Exercise 2 (*continued*)

AUTOCOMPLETE

As soon as you begin typing a label into a cell, Excel searches for and (automatically) displays any other label in that column that matches the letters you typed. It's handy if you want to repeat a label, but it can be distracting if you want to enter a different label that just happens to begin with the same letter. To turn the feature on (off), pull down the Tools menu, click Options, then click the Edit tab. Check (clear) the box to enable (disable) the AutoComplete feature.

Step 5: **Insert a Column**

- Point to the column heading for column B, then click the **right mouse button** to display a shortcut menu as shown in Figure 1.11e.

- Click **Insert** to insert a new column, which becomes the new column B. All existing columns have been moved to the right.

- Click in **cell B1**. Type **Major**.

- Click in **cell B3**. Enter **CIS** as Adams's major. Press the **down arrow** to move automatically to the major for the next student.

- Type **MKT** in cell B4. Press the **down arrow**. Type **ACC** in cell B5. Press the **down arrow**. Type **FIN** in cell B6.

- Press the **down arrow** to move to cell B7. Type **C** (AutoComplete will automatically enter "IS" to complete the entry). Press the **down arrow** to move to cell B8. Type **C** (the AutoComplete feature again enters "IS"), then press **Enter** to complete the entry.

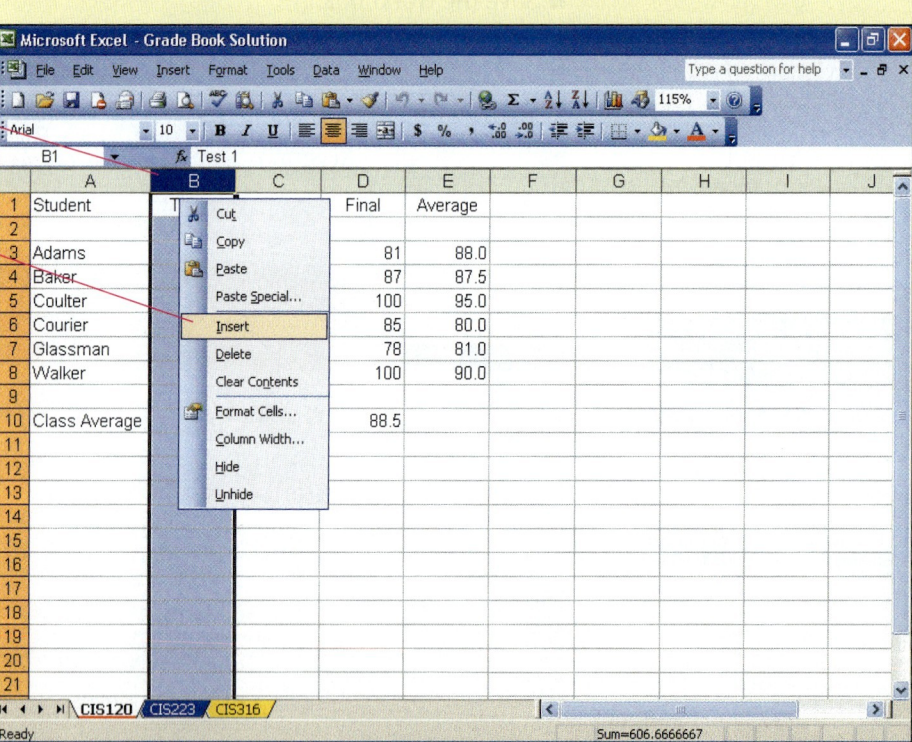

Point to column heading and click right mouse button to display shortcut menu

Click Insert

(e) Insert a Column (step 5)

FIGURE 1.11 Hands-on Exercise 2 (*continued*)

INSERTING AND DELETING INDIVIDUAL CELLS

You can insert and/or delete individual cells, as opposed to an entire row or column. To insert a cell, click in the cell where you want the new cell to go, pull down the Insert menu, then click Cells to display the Insert dialog box. Click the appropriate option button to shift cells right or down and click OK. To delete a cell or cells, select the cell(s), pull down the Edit menu, click the Delete command, then click the option button to shift cells left or up.

Step 6: **Display the Cell Formulas**

- Pull down the **Tools menu**. Click **Options** to display the Options dialog box. Click the **View tab**. Check the box for **Formulas**. Click **OK**. (You can also press **Ctrl+~** to toggle between cell formulas and displayed values.)
- The worksheet should display the cell formulas as shown in Figure 1.11f. The Formula Auditing toolbar is displayed automatically.
- If necessary, click the **right scroll arrow** on the horizontal scroll bar until column F, the column containing the formulas to compute the semester averages, comes into view.
- If necessary (i.e., if the formulas are not completely visible), double click the border between the column headings for columns F and G. This increases the width of column F to accommodate the widest entry in that column.

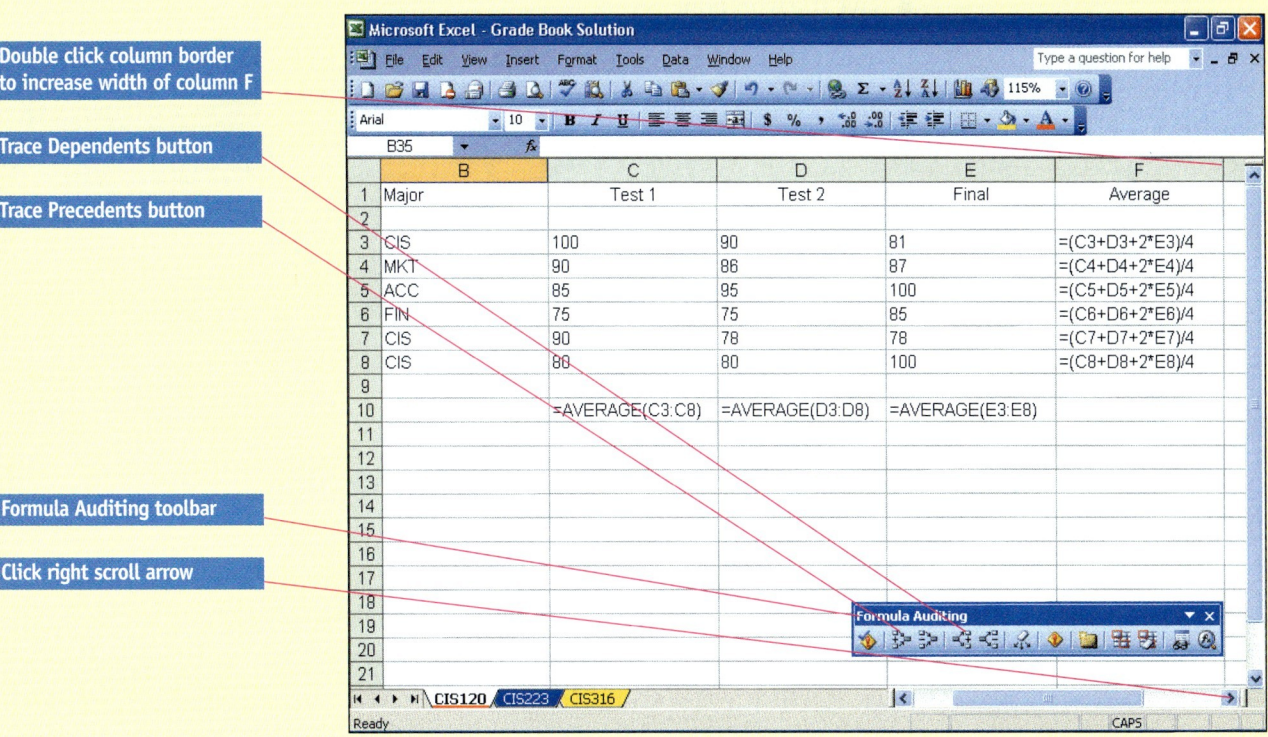

(f) Display the Cell Formulas (step 6)

FIGURE 1.11 Hands-on Exercise 2 (*continued*)

THE FORMULA AUDITING TOOLBAR

The Formula Auditing Toolbar appears automatically any time the display is changed to show cell formulas rather than displayed values. The toolbar is designed to help you detect and correct errors in cell formulas. Click in any cell containing a formula, then click the Trace Precedents button to show the cells that are used in calculating the formula in the selected cell. You can also click in any cell displaying a value and use the Trace Dependents button to show those cells whose formula references the selected cell. Click the Remove All Arrows button to erase the arrows from the display.

Step 7: **The Page Setup Command**

- Pull down the **File menu**. Click the **Page Setup command** to display the Page Setup dialog box as shown in Figure 1.11g.
- Click the **Page tab**. Click the **Landscape option button**. Click the option button to **Fit to 1 page**.
- Click the **Margins tab**. Check the box to center the worksheet horizontally.
- Click the **Sheet tab**. Check the boxes to print Row and Column Headings and Gridlines.
- Click the **Header/Footer tab**. Click the **drop-down arrow** on the Footer list box and select **CIS120**, which corresponds to the worksheet name.
- Click **OK** to exit the Page Setup dialog box.
- Save the workbook.

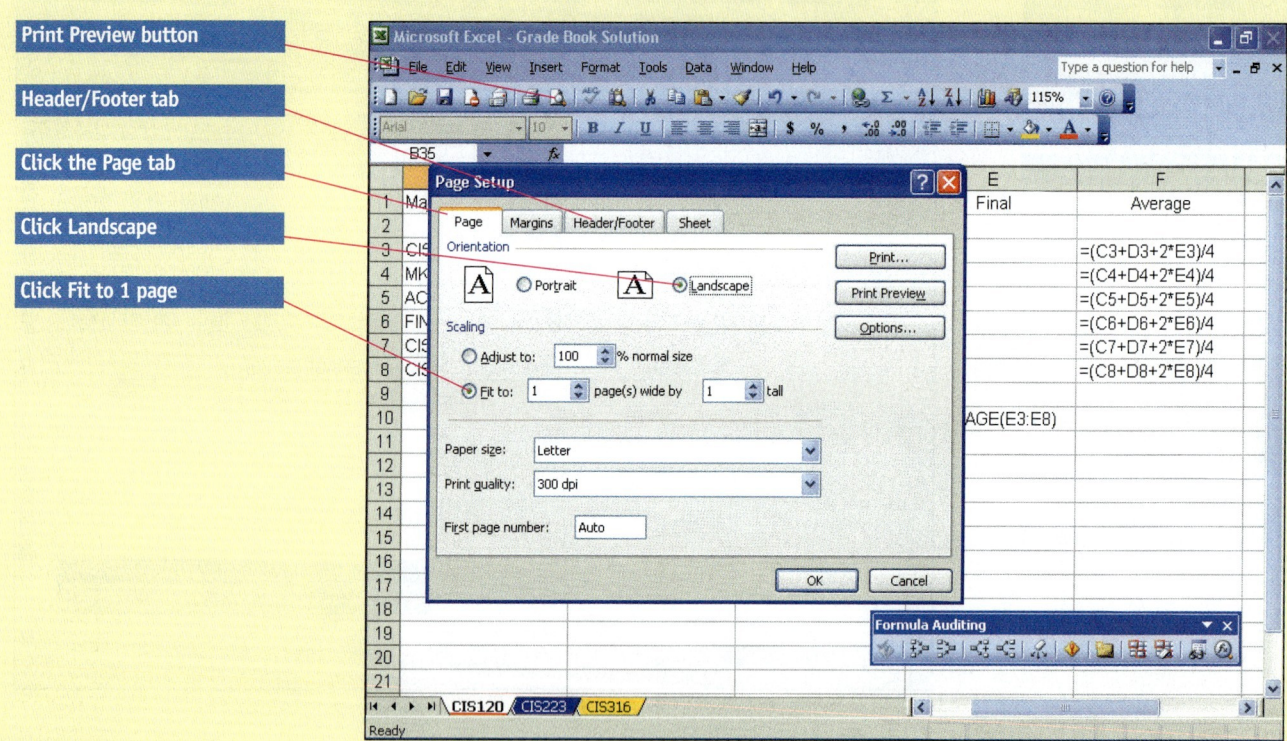

(g) The Page Setup Command (step 7)

FIGURE 1.11   Hands-on Exercise 2 (*continued*)

KEYBOARD SHORTCUTS—THE DIALOG BOX

Press Tab or Shift+Tab to move forward (backward) between fields in a dialog box, or press the Alt key plus the underlined letter to move directly to an option. Use the space bar to toggle check boxes on or off and the up (down) arrow keys to move between options in a list box. Press Enter to activate the highlighted command button and Esc to exit the dialog box without accepting the changes. These are universal shortcuts and apply to any Windows application.

Step 8: **The Print Preview Command**

- Pull down the **File menu** and click **Print Preview** (or click the **Print Preview button** on the Standard toolbar).

- Click the **Margins button** to toggle the margin lines on and off. (You can click and drag any margin line to change the position of the worksheet on the page and/or to change the column widths.)

- Your monitor should match the display in Figure 1.11h. (The Page Setup dialog box is also accessible from this screen.)

- Click the **Print command button** to display the Print dialog box, then click **OK** to print the worksheet.

- Press **Ctrl+~** to switch to displayed values rather than cell formulas. Click the **Print button** on the Standard toolbar to print the worksheet without displaying the Print dialog box.

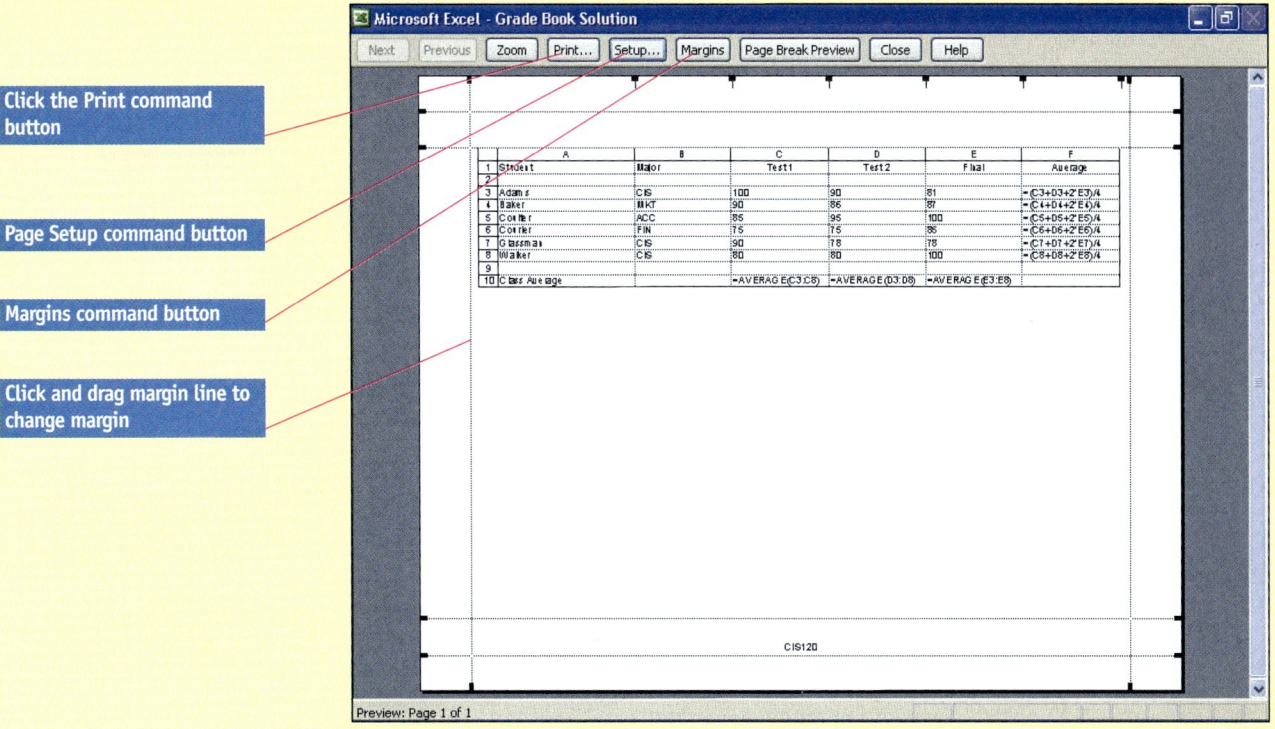

(h) The Print Preview Command (step 8)

FIGURE 1.11 Hands-on Exercise 2 (continued)

IDENTIFY YOUR WORKSHEETS

Use the Page Setup command to create a custom header and/or footer to identify your worksheets. Pull down the File menu, click the Page Setup command, and click the Header/Footer tab, then click the Custom Header or Custom Footer button. You can insert your own text in any desired font, as well as the date and time the worksheet was printed. You can also specify the folder, file name, and/or the worksheet name. All of the buttons are clearly marked with instructions within the dialog box.

Step 9: **Insert and Delete a Worksheet**

- Pull down the **Insert menu** and click the **Worksheet command** to insert a new worksheet. The worksheet is inserted as Sheet1.
- Click in **cell A1**, type **Student**, and press **Enter**. Enter the labels and student data as shown in Figure 1.11i. Enter the formulas to calculate the students' semester averages in column D. (The midterm and final count equally.)
- Enter the formulas in row 7 to compute the class averages on each exam. If necessary, click and drag the column border between the column headings for columns A and B to widen column A.
- Double click the name of the worksheet (Sheet1) to select the name. Type a new name, **CIS101**, to replace the selected text and press **Enter**. If necessary, click and drag the worksheet tab to the beginning of the workbook.
- Click the worksheet tab for **CIS223**. Pull down the **Edit menu** and click the **Delete Sheet command**. Click **Delete** when you are warned that the worksheet will be permanently deleted.
- Save the workbook. Print the new worksheet. Exit Excel if you do not want to continue with the next exercise at this time.

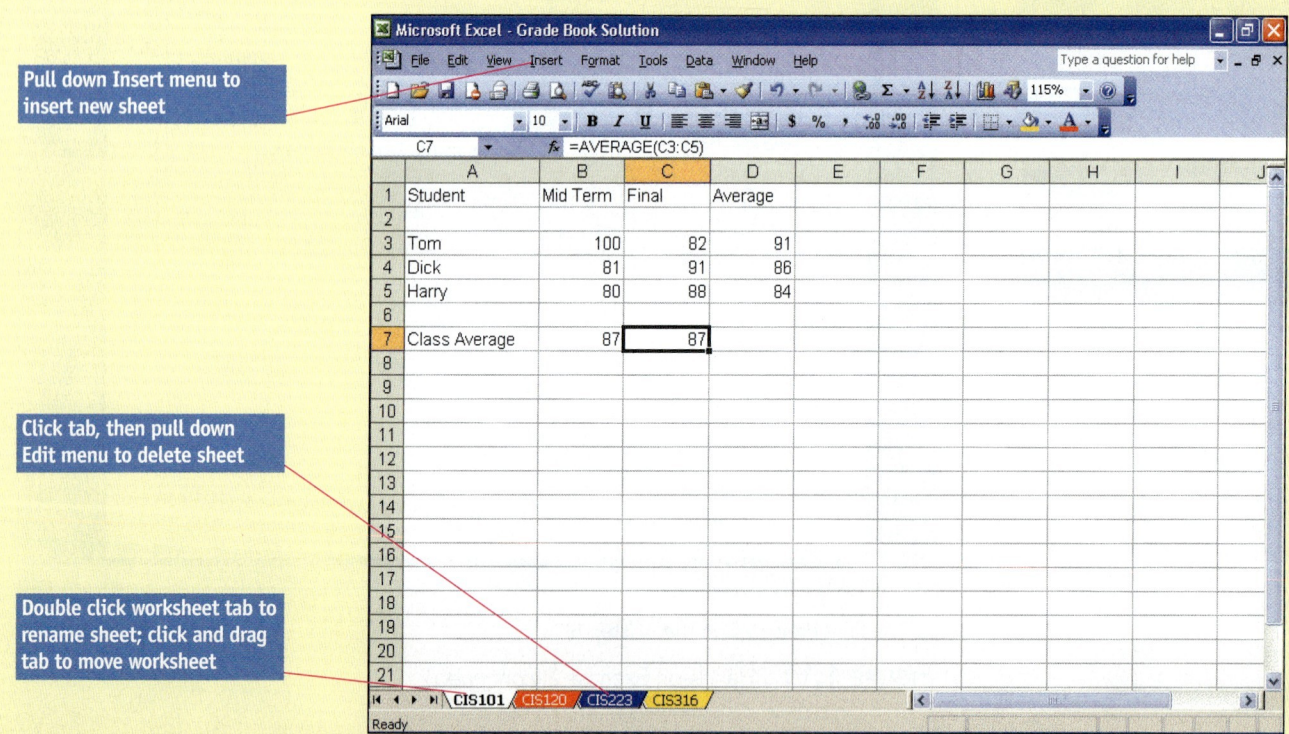

(i) Insert and Delete a Worksheet (step 9)

FIGURE 1.11 Hands-on Exercise 2 (*continued*)

MOVING, COPYING, AND RENAMING WORKSHEETS

The fastest way to move a worksheet is to click and drag the worksheet tab. You can copy a worksheet in similar fashion by pressing and holding the Ctrl key as you drag the worksheet tab. To rename a worksheet, double click its tab to select the current name, type the new name, and press the Enter key.

A BETTER GRADE BOOK

Figure 1.12 contains a much improved version of the professor's grade book. The most *obvious* difference is in the appearance of the worksheet, as a variety of formatting commands have been used to make it more attractive. The exam scores and semester averages are centered under the appropriate headings. The exam weights are formatted with percentages, and all averages are displayed with exactly one decimal point. Boldface and italics are used for emphasis. Shading and borders are used to highlight various areas of the worksheet. The title has been centered over the worksheet and is set in a larger typeface.

The most *significant* differences, however, are that the weight of each exam is indicated within the worksheet, and that the formulas to compute the students' semester averages reference these cells in their calculations. The professor can change the contents of the cells containing the exam weights and see immediately the effect on the student averages.

The isolation of cells whose values are subject to change is one of the most important concepts in the development of a spreadsheet. This technique lets the professor explore alternative grading strategies. He or she may notice, for example, that the class did significantly better on the final than on either of the first two exams. The professor may then decide to give the class a break and increase the weight of the final relative to the other tests. But before the professor says anything to the class, he or she wants to know the effect of increasing the weight of the final to 60%. What if the final should count 70%? The effect of these and other changes can be seen immediately by entering the new exam weights in the appropriate cells at the bottom of the worksheet.

Title is centered in larger font size; it is also in boldface and italics

Formatting includes boldface, shading, and borders

Exam weights are used to calculate the semester average

	A	B	C	D	E
1		*CIS120 - Spring Semester*			
2					
3	**Student**	**Test 1**	**Test 2**	**Final**	**Average**
4	Costa, Frank	70	80	90	82.5
5	Ford, Judd	70	85	80	78.8
6	Grauer, Jessica	90	80	98	91.5
7	Howard, Lauren	80	78	98	88.5
8	Krein, Darren	85	70	95	86.3
9	Moldof, Adam	75	75	80	77.5
10					
11	**Class Averages**	78.3	78.0	90.2	
12					
13	**Exam Weights**	25%	25%	50%	

FIGURE 1.12 A Better Grade Book

ISOLATE ASSUMPTIONS

The formulas in a worksheet should always be based on cell references rather than on specific values—for example, B13 or $B$13 rather than .25. The cells containing these values should be clearly labeled and set apart from the rest of the worksheet. You can then vary the inputs (or assumptions on which the worksheet is based) to see the effect within the worksheet. The chance for error is also minimized because you are changing the contents of a single cell rather than changing the multiple formulas that reference those values.

CELL RANGES

Every command in Excel operates on a rectangular group of cells known as a *range*. A range may be as small as a single cell or as large as the entire worksheet. It may consist of a row or part of a row, a column or part of a column, or multiple rows and/or columns. The cells within a range are specified by indicating the diagonally opposite corners, typically the upper-left and lower-right corners of the rectangle. Many different ranges could be selected in conjunction with the worksheet of Figure 1.12. The exam weights, for example, are found in the range B13:D13. The students' semester averages are found in the range E4:E9. The student data is contained in the range A4:E9.

The easiest way to select a range is to click and drag—click at the beginning of the range, then press and hold the left mouse button as you drag the mouse to the end of the range where you release the mouse. Once selected, the range is highlighted and its cells will be affected by any subsequent command. The range remains selected until another range is defined or until you click another cell anywhere on the worksheet.

COPY COMMAND

The ***Copy command*** duplicates the contents of a cell, or range of cells, and saves you from having to enter the contents of every cell individually. Figure 1.13 illustrates how the command can be used to duplicate the formula to compute the class average on the different tests. The cell that you are copying from, cell B11, is called the ***source range***. The cells that you are copying to, cells C11 and D11, are the ***destination range***. The formula is not copied exactly, but is adjusted as it is copied, to compute the average for the pertinent test.

The formula to compute the average on the first test was entered in cell B11 as =AVERAGE(B4:B9). The range in the formula references the cell seven rows above the cell containing the formula (i.e., cell B4 is seven rows above cell B11) as well as the cell two rows above the formula (i.e., cell B9). When the formula in cell B11 is copied to C11, it is adjusted so that the cells referenced in the new formula are in the same relative position as those in the original formula; that is, seven and two rows above the formula. The formula in cell C11 becomes =AVERAGE(C4:C9). The formula in cell D11 becomes =AVERAGE(D4:D9).

	A	B	C	D	E
1		*CIS120 - Spring Semester*			
2					
3	Student	Test 1	Test 2	Final	Average
4	Costa, Frank	70	80	90	=$B$13*B4+$C$13*C4+$D$13*D4
5	Ford, Judd	70	85	80	=$B$13*B5+$C$13*C5+$D$13*D5
6	Grauer, Jessica	90	80	98	=$B$13*B6+$C$13*C6+$D$13*D6
7	Howard, Lauren	80	78	98	=$B$13*B7+$C$13*C7+$D$13*D7
8	Krein, Darren	85	70	95	=$B$13*B8+$C$13*C8+$D$13*D8
9	Moldof, Adam	75	75	80	=$B$13*B9+$C$13*C9+$D$13*D9
10					
11	Class Averages	=AVERAGE(B4:B9)	=AVERAGE(C4:C9)	=AVERAGE(D4:D9)	
12					
13	Exam Weights	25%	25%	50%	

- Formula was entered in B11
- Relative addresses adjust when formula is copied
- Absolute addresses stay the same when formula is copied
- Relative addresses adjust when formula is copied

FIGURE 1.13 The Copy Command

Figure 1.13 also illustrates how the Copy command is used to copy the formula for a student's semester average, from cell E4 (the source range) to cells E5 through E9 (the destination range). This is slightly more complicated than the previous example because the formula is based on a student's grades, which vary from one student to the next, and on the exam weights, which do not. The cells referring to the student's grades should adjust as the formula is copied, but the addresses referencing the exam weights should not.

The distinction between cell references that remain constant versus cell references that change is made by means of a dollar sign. An **absolute reference** remains constant throughout the copy operation and is specified with a dollar sign in front of the column and row designation, for example, $B$13. A **relative reference**, on the other hand, adjusts during a copy operation and is specified without dollar signs, for example, B4. (A **mixed reference** uses a single dollar sign to make the column absolute and the row relative, for example, $A5. Alternatively, you can make the column relative and the row absolute as in A$5.)

Consider, for example, the formula to compute a student's semester average as it appears in cell E4 of Figure 1.13:

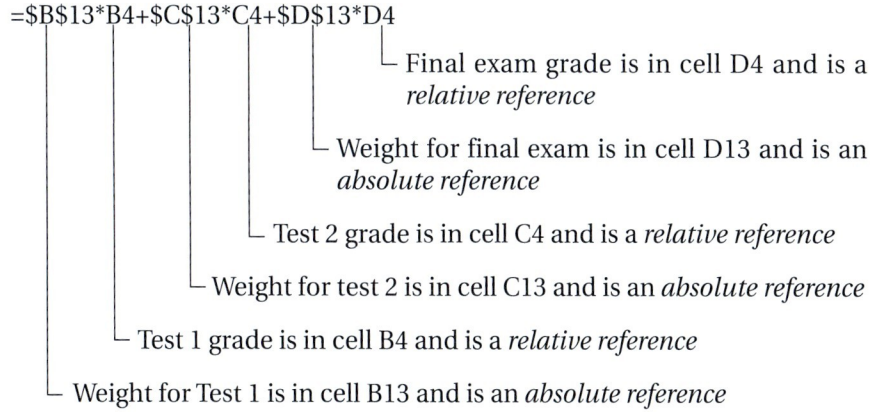

The formula in cell E4 uses a combination of relative and absolute addresses to compute the student's semester average. Relative addresses are used for the exam grades (found in cells B4, C4, and D4) and change automatically when the formula is copied to the other rows. Absolute addresses are used for the exam weights (found in cells B13, C13, and D13) and remain constant.

The copy operation is implemented by using the **clipboard** common to all Windows applications and a combination of the Copy and Paste commands from the Edit menu. (Office 2003 also supports the **Office Clipboard** that can hold 24 separate items. All references to the "clipboard" in this chapter, however, are to the Windows clipboard.) The contents of the source range are copied to the clipboard, from where they are pasted to the destination range. The contents of the clipboard are replaced with each subsequent Copy command but are unaffected by the Paste command. Thus, you can execute the Paste command several times in succession to paste the contents of the clipboard to multiple locations.

MIXED REFERENCES

Most spreadsheets can be developed using only absolute or relative references such as $A1$1 or A1 respectively. Mixed references, where only the row ($A1) or column (A$1) changes, are more subtle, and thus are typically not used by beginners. Mixed references are necessary in more sophisticated worksheets and add significantly to the power of Excel.

MOVE OPERATION

The ***move operation*** is not used in the grade book, but its presentation is essential for the sake of completeness. The move operation transfers the contents of a cell (or range of cells) from one location to another. The concept of relative and absolute references does not apply, as adjustments are made automatically as needed to both types of references. After the move is completed, the cell(s) where the move originated (that is, the source range) is (are) empty. This is in contrast to the Copy command, where the entries remain in the source range and are duplicated in the destination range. Several examples are presented in Figure 1.14.

A simple move operation is depicted in Figure 1.14a, in which the contents of cell A3 are moved to cell C3, with the formula in cell C3 unchanged after the move. In other words, the move operation simply picks up the contents of cell A3 (a formula that adds the values in cells A1 and A2) and puts it down in cell C3. The source range, cell A3, is empty after the move operation has been executed.

Figure 1.14b depicts a situation where the formula itself remains in the same cell, but one of the values it references is moved to a new location; that is, the entry in A1 is moved to C1. The formula in cell A3 is adjusted to follow the moved entry to its new location; that is, the formula is now =C1+A2.

The situation is different in Figure 1.14c as the contents of all three cells—A1, A2, and A3—are moved. After the move has taken place, cells C1 and C2 contain the 5 and the 2, respectively, with the formula in cell C3 adjusted to reflect the movement of the contents of cells A1 and A2. Once again the source range (A1:A3) is empty after the move is completed.

	A	B	C
1	5		
2	2		
3	=A1+A2		

(a) Example 1 (only cell A3 is moved)

	A	B	C
1	5		
2	2		
3			=A1+A2

Source range is empty after move

	A	B	C
1	5		
2	2		
3	=A1+A2		

(b) Example 2 (only cell A1 is moved)

	A	B	C
1			5
2	2		
3	=C1+A2		

Cell reference is adjusted to follow moved entry

	A	B	C
1	5		
2	2		
3	=A1+A2		

(c) Example 3 (all three cells in column A are moved)

FIGURE 1.14 The Move Operation

	A	B	C
1			5
2			2
3			=C1+C2

Both cell references adjust to follow moved entries

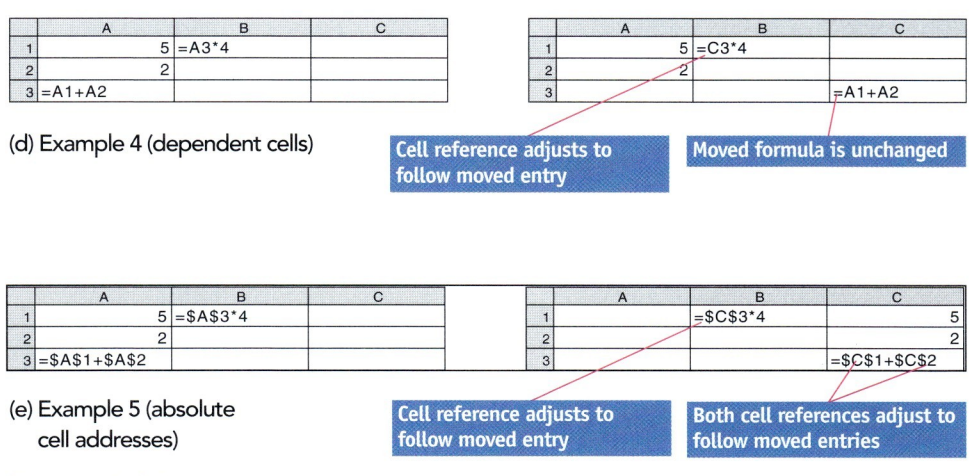

(d) Example 4 (dependent cells)

(e) Example 5 (absolute cell addresses)

FIGURE 1.14 The Move Operation (*continued*)

Figure 1.14d contains an additional formula in cell B1, which is *dependent* on cell A3, which in turn is moved to cell C3. The formula in cell C3 is unchanged after the move because *only* the formula was moved, *not* the values it referenced. The formula in cell B1 changes because cell B1 refers to an entry (cell A3) that was moved to a new location (cell C3).

Figure 1.14e shows that the specification of an absolute reference has no meaning in a move operation, because the cell addresses are adjusted as necessary to reflect the cells that have been moved. Moving a formula that contains an absolute reference does not adjust the formula. Moving a value that is specified as an absolute reference, however, adjusts the formula to follow the cell to its new location. Thus all of the absolute references in Figure 1.14e are changed to reflect the entries that were moved.

The move operation is a convenient way to improve the appearance of a worksheet after it has been developed. It is subtle in its operation, and we suggest you think twice before moving cell entries because of the complexities involved.

The move operation is implemented by clicking and dragging a cell from one location to another or by using the Windows clipboard and a combination of the Cut and Paste commands. The contents of the source range are transferred to the clipboard, from which they are pasted to the destination range. (Executing a Paste command after a Cut command empties the clipboard. This is different from pasting after a Copy command, which does not affect the contents of the clipboard.)

LEARNING BY DOING

As we have already indicated, there are many different ways to accomplish the same task. You can execute commands using a pull-down menu, a shortcut menu, a toolbar, or the keyboard. In the exercise that follows we emphasize pull-down menus (the most basic technique) but suggest various shortcuts as appropriate.

Realize, however, that while the shortcuts are interesting, it is far more important to focus on the underlying concepts in the exercise, rather than specific key strokes or mouse clicks. The professor's grade book was developed to emphasize the difference between relative and absolute cell references. The grade book also illustrates the importance of isolating assumptions so that alternative strategies (e.g., different exam weights) can be considered.

hands-on exercise

3 Creating a Workbook

Objective To create a new workbook; to copy formulas containing relative and absolute references. Use Figure 1.15 as a guide in doing the exercise.

Step 1: **Create a New Workbook**

- Start Excel. A blank workbook should appear automatically in the application window. Close the task pane.
- If necessary, separate the Standard and Formatting toolbars. Pull down the **View menu**, click **Toolbars**, click **Customize**, and click the **Options tab**. Check the box that indicates the Standard and Formatting toolbars should be displayed on two rows. Close the dialog box.
- Click in **cell A1**. Enter the title of the worksheet, **CIS120 - Spring Semester**.
- Enter the column headings in row 3 as in Figure 1.15a. Click in **cell A3** and type **Student**, then press the **right arrow key** to move to **cell B3**. Type **Test 1**.
- Press the **right arrow key** to move to **cell C3**. Type **Test 2**. Enter the words **Final** and **Average** in cells D3 and E3, respectively.

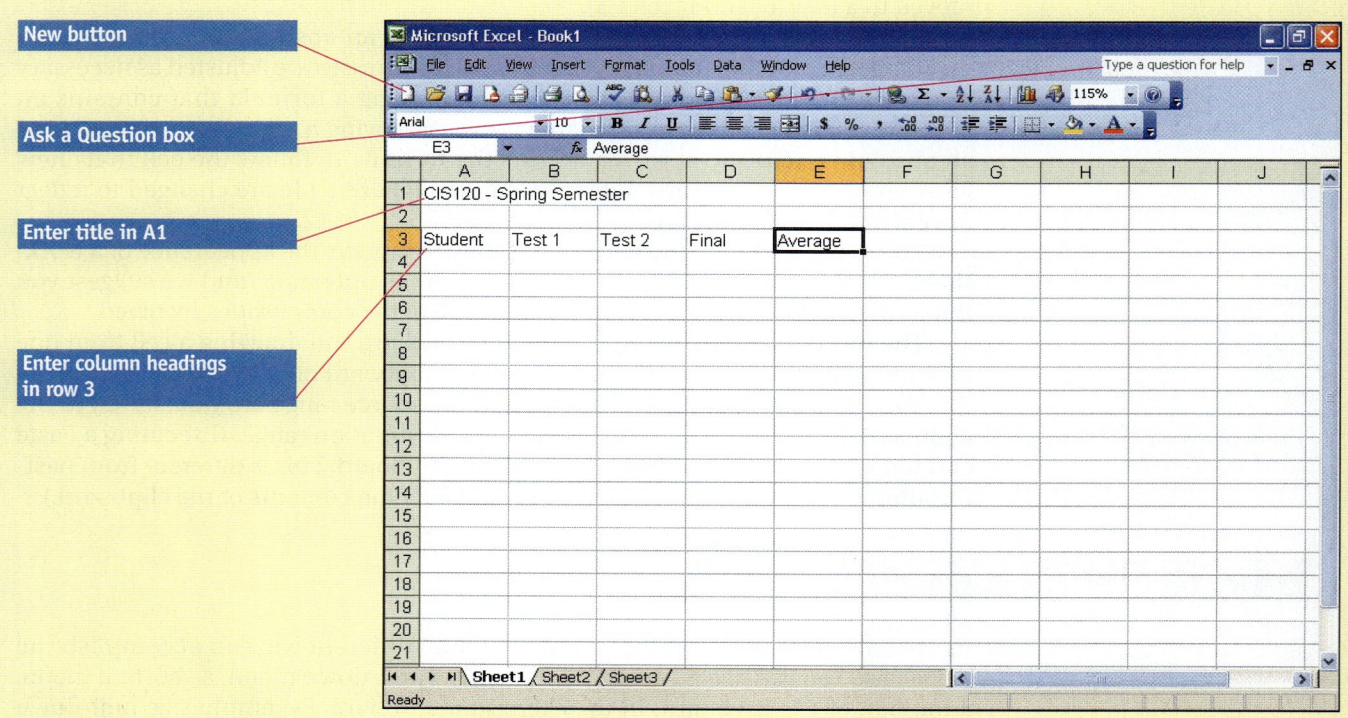

(a) Create a New Workbook (step 1)

FIGURE 1.15 Hands-on Exercise 3

ASK A QUESTION

Click in the "Ask a Question" list box to the right of the menu bar, type a question, press enter, and Excel returns a list of Help topics. Click any topic that appears to open the Help window with detailed information. You can ask multiple questions during an Excel session, then click the down arrow in the list box to return to an earlier question, which will return you to the Help topics.

Step 2: **Save the Workbook**

- Pull down the **File menu** and click **Save** (or click the **Save button** on the Standard toolbar) to display the Save As dialog box as shown in Figure 1.15b. (The Save As dialog box always appears the first time you save a workbook, so that you can give the workbook a name.)

- Click the **drop-down arrow** on the Save In list box. Click the appropriate drive, drive C or drive A, depending on where you are saving your Excel workbooks.

- Double click the **Exploring Excel folder** to make it the active folder (the folder in which you will save the document).

- Click and drag **Book1** (the default entry) in the File name text box to select it, then type **Better Grade Book** as the name of the workbook.

- Click the **Save button** in the Save As dialog box or press the **Enter key**. The title bar changes to reflect the name of the workbook.

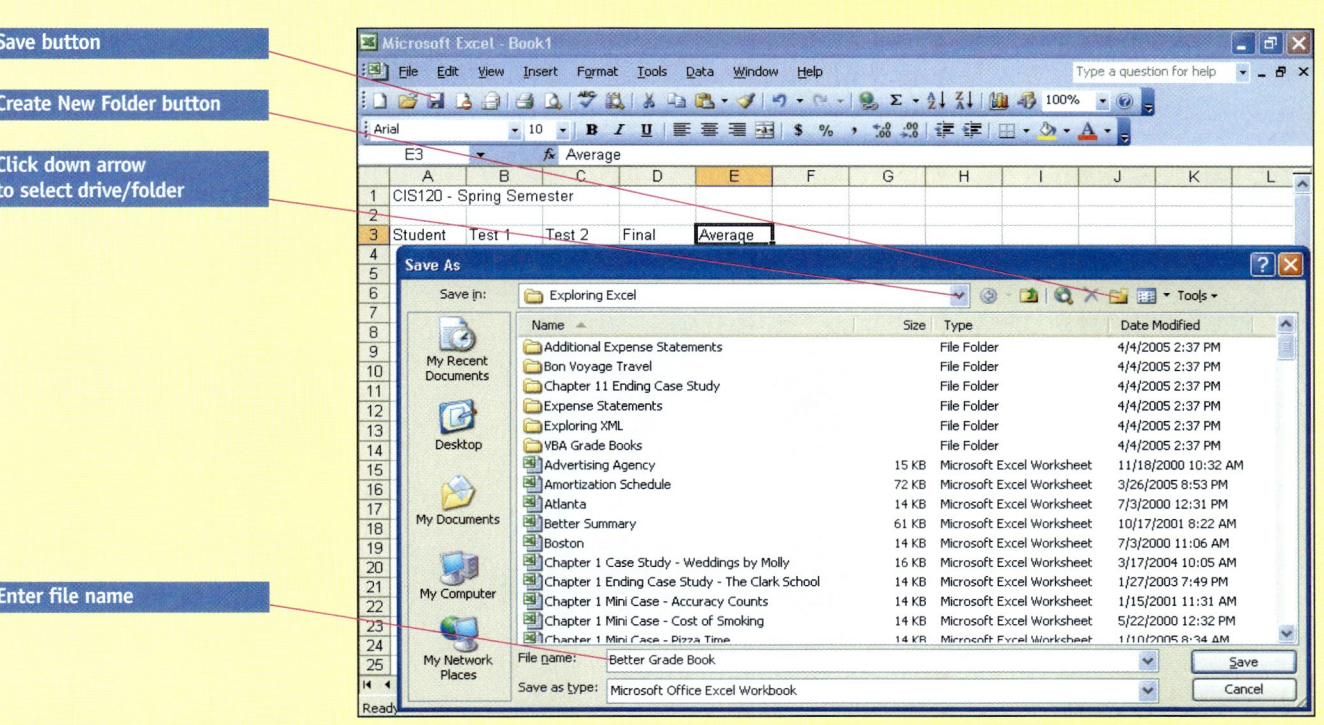

(b) Save the Workbook (step 2)

FIGURE 1.15 Hands-on Exercise 3 (*continued*)

CREATE A NEW FOLDER

Do you work with a large number of different workbooks? If so, it may be useful to store those workbooks in different folders, perhaps one folder for each subject you are taking. Pull down the File menu, click the Save As command to display the Save As dialog box, then click the Create New Folder button to display the associated dialog box. Enter the name of the folder, then click OK. Once the folder has been created, use the Look In box to change to that folder the next time you open that workbook.

Step 3: **Enter Student Data and Literal Information**

- Click in **cell A4** and type **Costa, Frank**, then enter Frank's grades on the two tests and the final as shown in Figure 1.15c. Do *not* enter Frank's semester average in cell E4 as that will be entered as a formula.

- If necessary, click and drag the border between columns A and B so that you can read Frank Costa's complete name. Check that you entered the data for this student correctly. If you made a mistake, return to the cell and retype the entry.

- Enter the names and grades for the other students in rows 5 through 9. Do *not* enter the student averages.

- Complete the entries in column A by typing **Class Averages** and **Exam Weights** in **cells A11** and **A13**, respectively.

- Enter the exam weights in row 13. Click in **cell B13** and enter **.25**, press the **right arrow key** to move to **cell C13** and enter **.25**, then press the **right arrow key** to move to **cell D13** and enter **.5**. Press **Enter**.

- Do *not* be concerned that the exam weights do not appear as percentages as they will be formatted in a later exercise. Save the workbook.

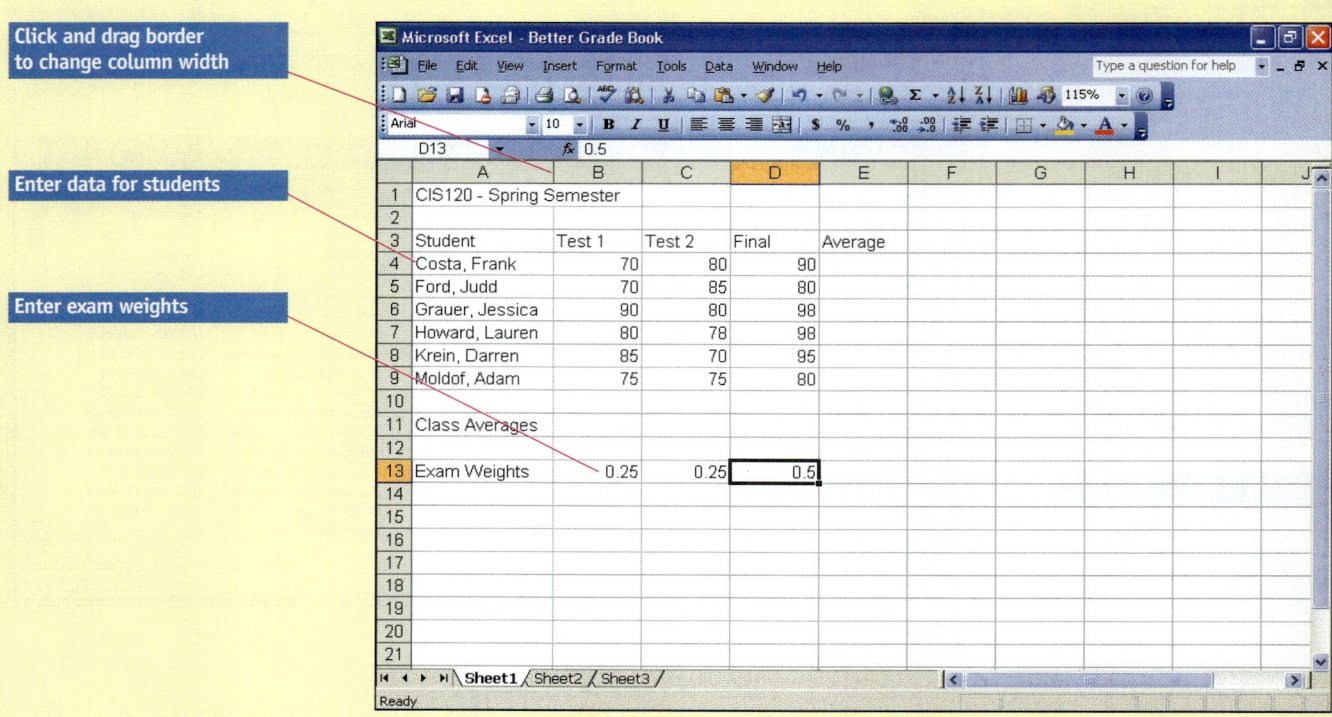

Click and drag border to change column width

Enter data for students

Enter exam weights

(c) Enter Student Data and Literal Information (step 3)

FIGURE 1.15 Hands-on Exercise 3 (*continued*)

COLUMN WIDTHS AND ROW HEIGHTS

Drag the border between column headings to change the column width; for example, to increase (decrease) the width of column A, drag the border between column headings A and B to the right (left). Double click the right boundary of a column heading to change the column width to accommodate the widest entry in that column. Use the same techniques to change the row heights. See practice exercise 2 at the end of the chapter.

Step 4: **Compute the Student Semester Averages**

- Click in **cell E4** and type the formula **=$B$13*B4+$C$13*C4+$D$13*D4** to compute the semester average for the first student. Press **Enter**. Check that the displayed value in cell E4 is 82.5 as shown in Figure 1.15d.

- Click in **cell E4** to make this the active cell, then click the **Copy button** on the Standard toolbar. A moving border will surround cell E4, indicating that its contents have been copied to the clipboard.

- Click and drag to select **cells E5** through **E9** as the destination range. Click the **Paste button** to copy the contents of the clipboard to the destination range. Ignore the Paste Options button that appears automatically any time the Paste command is executed.

- Press **Esc** to remove the moving border around cell E4. The Paste Options button also disappears.

- Click in **cell E5** and look at the formula. The cells that reference the grades have changed to B5, C5, and D5. The cells that reference the exam weights—$B$13, $C$13, and $D$13—are the same as in cell E4.

- Save the workbook.

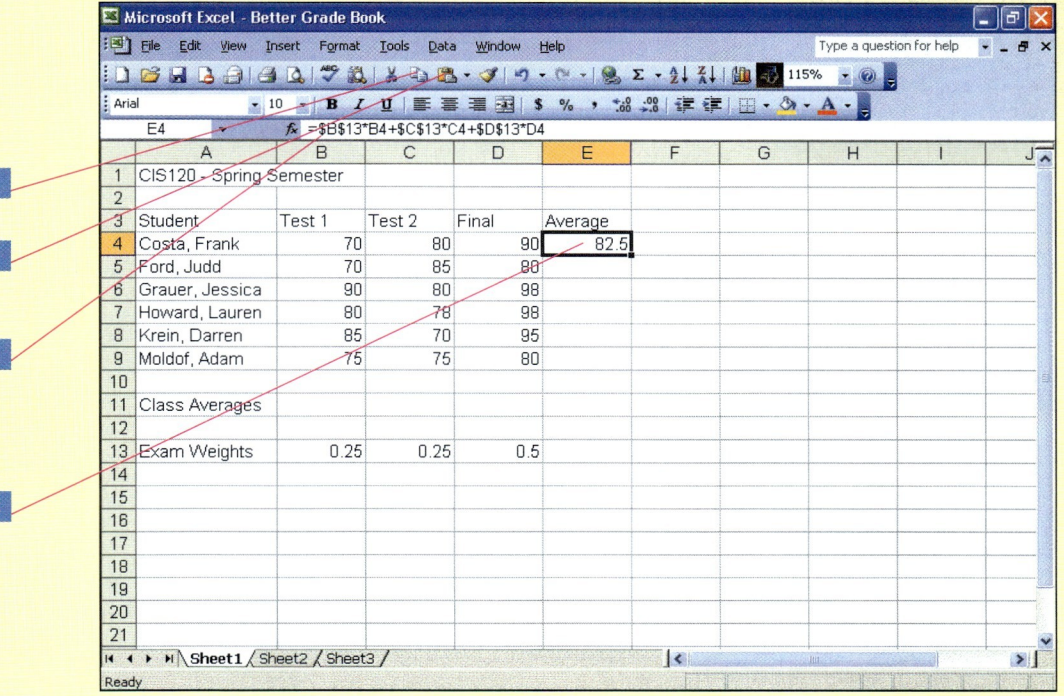

(d) Compute the student Semester Averages (step 4)

FIGURE 1.15 Hands-on Exercise 3 (*continued*)

THE PASTE OPTIONS BUTTON

The Paste Options button (includes options from the Paste Special command) and provides flexibility when you paste the contents of the clipboard into a worksheet. Press Esc to ignore the options and you automatically paste both the cell formulas and associated formatting. Alternatively, you can click the down arrow to display options to copy values rather than formulas with or without formatting, Formatting is discussed in detail later in the chapter.

Step 5: **Compute the Class Averages**

- Click in **cell B11** and type the formula **=AVERAGE(B4:B9)** to compute the class average on the first test. Press the **Enter key** when you have completed the formula.

- Point to cell B11, then click the **right mouse button** to display a context-sensitive menu, then click the **Copy command**. You should see a moving border around cell B11, indicating that the contents of this cell have been copied to the clipboard.

- Click and drag to select **cells C11** and **D11** as shown in Figure 1.15e. Click the **Paste button** on the standard toolbar to copy the contents of the clipboard to the destination range. Press **Esc** to remove the moving border.

- Click anywhere in the worksheet to deselect cells C11 through D11. Cells C11 and D11 should contain 78 and 90.16667, the class averages on Test 2 and the Final, respectively. Do not worry about formatting at this time.

- Save the workbook.

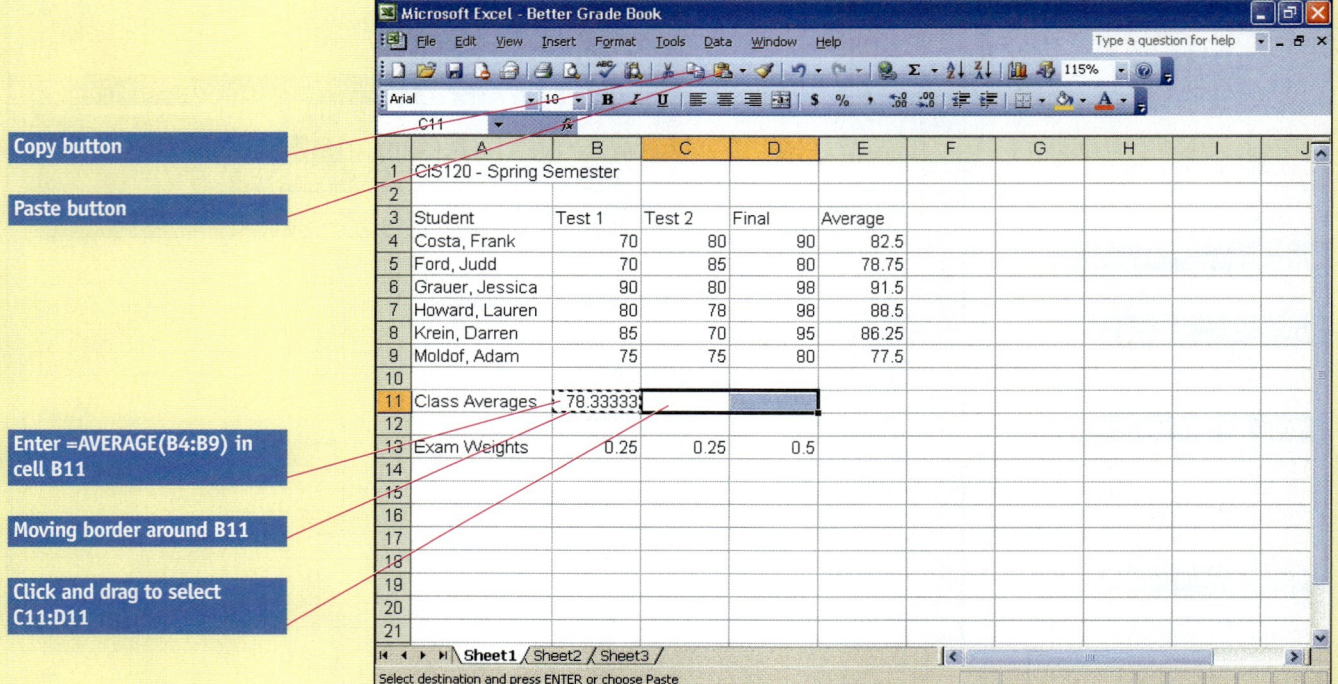

(e) Compute the Class Averages (step 5)

FIGURE 1.15 Hands-on Exercise 3 (*continued*)

TWO DIFFERENT CLIPBOARDS

The Office clipboard holds a total of up to 24 objects from multiple applications, as opposed to the Windows clipboard, which stores only the results of the last Cut or Copy command. Thus, each time you execute a Cut or Copy command, the contents of the Windows clipboard are replaced, whereas the copied object is added to the objects already in the Office clipboard. To display the Office clipboard, open the task pane, click the down arrow, and select clipboard. Leave the clipboard open as you execute multiple cut and copy operations to observe what happens.

Step 6: **Change the Exam Weights**

- Change the entries in **cells B13** and **C13** to **.20** and the entry in **cell D13** to **.60**. The semester average for every student changes automatically; for example, Costa and Moldof change to 84 and 78, respectively, as shown in Figure 1.15f.

- The professor decides this does not make a significant difference and wants to go back to the original weights. Click the **Undo button** three times to reverse the last three actions. You should see .25, .25, and .50 in cells B13, C13, and D13, respectively.

- Click in **cell A15** and type the label **Grading Assistant**. Press **Enter**. Type your name in **cell A16**, so that you will get credit for this assignment.

- Save the workbook. You do not need to print the workbook yet, since we will do that at the end of the next exercise, after we have formatted the workbook.

- Exit Excel if you are not ready to begin the next exercise at this time.

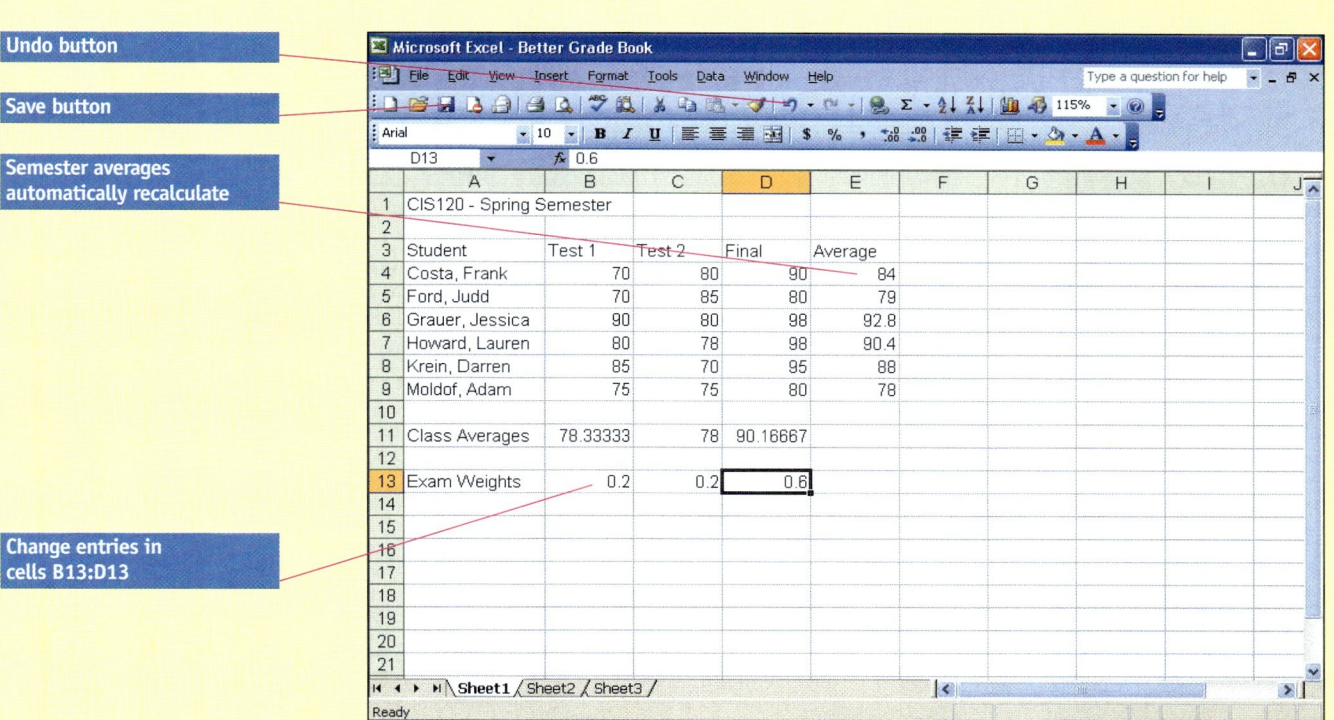

(f) Change the Exam Weights (step 6)

FIGURE 1.15 Hands-on Exercise 3 (*continued*)

CHANGE THE ZOOM PERCENTAGE

You can increase or decrease the size of a worksheet as it appears on the monitor by clicking the down arrow on the zoom box and selecting an appropriate percentage. If you are working with a large spreadsheet and cannot see it at one time on the screen, choose a number less than 100%. Conversely, if you find yourself squinting because the numbers are too small, select a percentage larger than 100%. Changing the magnification on the screen does not affect printing; that is, worksheets are always printed at 100% unless you change the scaling within the Page Setup command.

FORMATTING

Figure 1.16a shows the grade book as it exists at the end of the third hands-on exercise, without concern for its appearance. Figure 1.16b shows the grade book as it will appear at the end of the next exercise after it has been formatted. The differences between the two are due entirely to formatting. Consider:

- The exam weights are formatted as percentages in Figure 1.16b, as opposed to decimals in Figure 1.16a.
- The class and semester averages are displayed with a single decimal place in Figure 1.16b as opposed to a variable number of places in Figure 1.16a.
- Boldface and italic are used for emphasis, as are shading and borders.
- Exam grades and computed averages are centered under their respective headings, as are the exam weights.
- The worksheet title is centered across all five columns.

	A	B	C	D	E
1	CIS120 - Spring Semester				
2					
3	Student	Test 1	Test 2	Final	Average
4	Costa, Frank	70	80	90	82.5
5	Ford, Judd	70	85	80	78.75
6	Grauer, Jessica	90	80	98	91.5
7	Howard, Lauren	80	78	98	88.5
8	Krein, Darren	85	70	95	86.25
9	Moldof, Adam	75	75	80	77.5
10					
11	Class Averages	78.33333333	78	90.16666667	
12					
13	Exam Weights	0.25	0.25	0.5	

- Class Averages are not uniformly formatted
- Percentages are not formatted

(a) At the End of Hands-on Exercise 3

	A	B	C	D	E
1	*CIS120 - Spring Semester*				
2					
3	**Student**	**Test 1**	**Test 2**	**Final**	**Average**
4	Costa, Frank	70	80	90	82.5
5	Ford, Judd	70	85	80	78.8
6	Grauer, Jessica	90	80	98	91.5
7	Howard, Lauren	80	78	98	88.5
8	Krein, Darren	85	70	95	86.3
9	Moldof, Adam	75	75	80	77.5
10					
11	**Class Averages**	78.3	78.0	90.2	
12					
13	**Exam Weights**	25%	25%	50%	

- Title is centered across columns; font is larger and both bold and italic
- Shading, borders, and boldface are used for emphasis
- Test grades are centered in columns
- Uniform number of decimal places
- Percent formatting has been applied

(b) At the End of Hands-on Exercise 4

FIGURE 1.16 Developing the Grade Book

FORMAT CELLS COMMAND

The ***Format Cells command*** controls the formatting for numbers, alignment, fonts, borders, and patterns (color). Execution of the command produces a tabbed dialog box in which you choose the particular formatting category, then enter the desired options. All formatting is done within the context of ***select-then-do***. You select the cells to which the formatting is to apply, then you execute the Format Cells command (or click the appropriate button on the Formatting toolbar).

Once a format has been assigned to a cell, the formatting remains in the cell and is applied to all subsequent values that are entered into that cell. You can, however, change the formatting by executing a new formatting command. You can also remove the formatting by using the Clear command in the Edit menu. Note, too, that changing the format of a number changes the way the number is displayed, but does not change its value. If, for example, you entered 1.2345 into a cell, but displayed the number as 1.23, the actual value (1.2345) would be used in all calculations involving that cell. The numeric formats are shown in Figure 1.17a and described below.

- ***General format*** is the default format for numeric entries and displays a number according to the way it was originally entered. Numbers are shown as integers (e.g., 123), decimal fractions (e.g., 1.23), or in scientific notation (e.g., 1.23E+10) if the number exceeds 11 digits.

- ***Number format***, which displays a number with or without the 1000 separator (e.g., a comma) and with any number of decimal places. Negative numbers can be displayed with parentheses and/or can be shown in red.

- ***Currency format***, which displays a number with the 1000 separator and an optional dollar sign (which is placed immediately to the left of the number). Negative values can be preceded by a minus sign or displayed with parentheses and/or can be shown in red.

- ***Accounting format***, which displays a number with the 1000 separator, an optional dollar sign (at the left border of the cell, vertically aligned within a column), negative values in parentheses, and zero values as hyphens.

- ***Date format***, which displays the date in different ways, such as March 14, 2001, 3/14/01, or 14-Mar-01.

- ***Time format***, which displays the time in different formats, such as 10:50 PM or the equivalent 22:50 (24-hour time).

- ***Percentage format***, whereby the number is multiplied by 100 for display purposes only, a percent sign is included, and any number of decimal places can be specified.

- ***Fraction format***, which displays a number as a fraction, and is appropriate when there is no exact decimal equivalent. A fraction is entered into a cell by preceding the fraction with an equal sign—for example, = 1/3.

- ***Scientific format***, which displays a number as a decimal fraction followed by a whole number exponent of 10; for example, the number 12345 would appear as 1.2345E+04. The exponent, +04 in the example, is the number of places the decimal point is moved to the left (or right if the exponent is negative). Very small numbers have negative exponents.

- ***Text format***, which left aligns the entry and is useful for numerical values that have leading zeros and should be treated as text, such as ZIP codes.

- ***Special format***, which displays a number with editing characters, such as hyphens in a Social Security number.

- ***Custom format***, which allows you to develop your own formats.

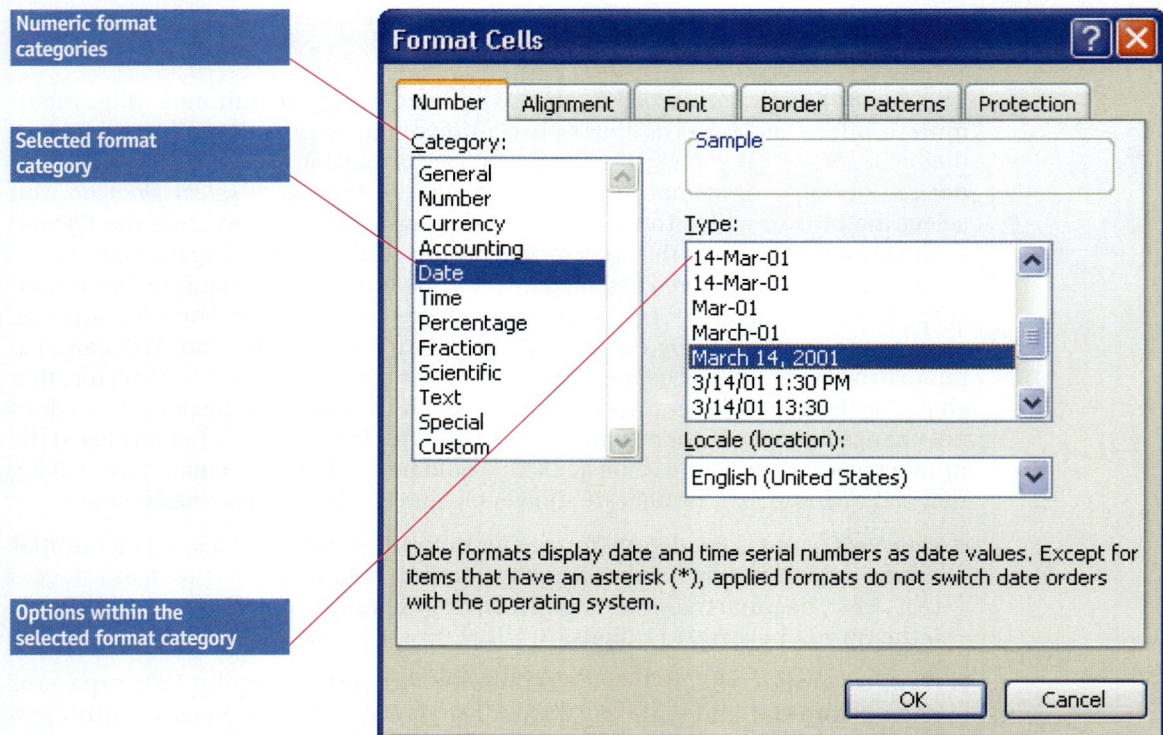

(a) The Number Tab

FIGURE 1.17 The Format Cells Command

Alignment

The contents of a cell (whether text or numeric) may be aligned horizontally and/or vertically as indicated by the dialog box of Figure 1.17b. The default horizontal **alignment** is general, which left-aligns text and right-aligns date and numbers. You can also center an entry across a range of selected cells (or **merge cells**), as in the professor's grade book, which centered the title in cell A1 across columns A through E. Clear the box to merge cells if you want to **split cells** that have been previously merged. The Fill option under Horizontal alignment distributes the characters in the cell across the entire width of that cell.

Vertical alignment is important only if the row height is changed and the characters are smaller than the height of the row. Entries may be vertically aligned at the top, center, or bottom (the default) of a cell.

It is also possible to wrap the text within a cell to emulate the word wrap of a word processor. You select multiple cells and merge them together. And finally, you can achieve some interesting effects by rotating text up to 90° in either direction.

Fonts

You can use the same fonts in Excel as you can in any other Windows application. All fonts are WYSIWYG (What You See Is What You Get), meaning that the worksheet you see on the monitor will match the printed worksheet.

Any entry in a worksheet may be displayed in any font, style, or point size as indicated by the dialog box of Figure 1.17c. The example shows Arial, Bold Italic, and 14 points, and corresponds to the selection for the worksheet title in the improved grade book. Special effects, such as subscripts or superscripts, are also possible. You can even select a different color, but you will need a color printer to see the effect on the printed page.

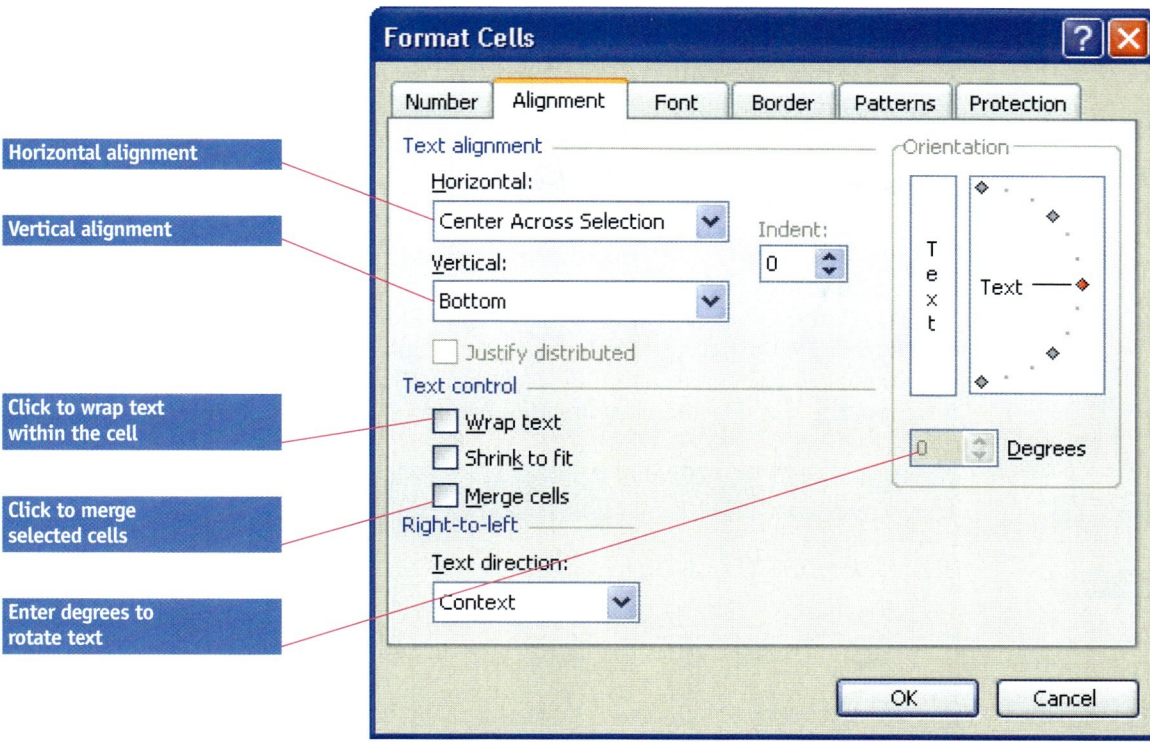

(b) The Alignment Tab

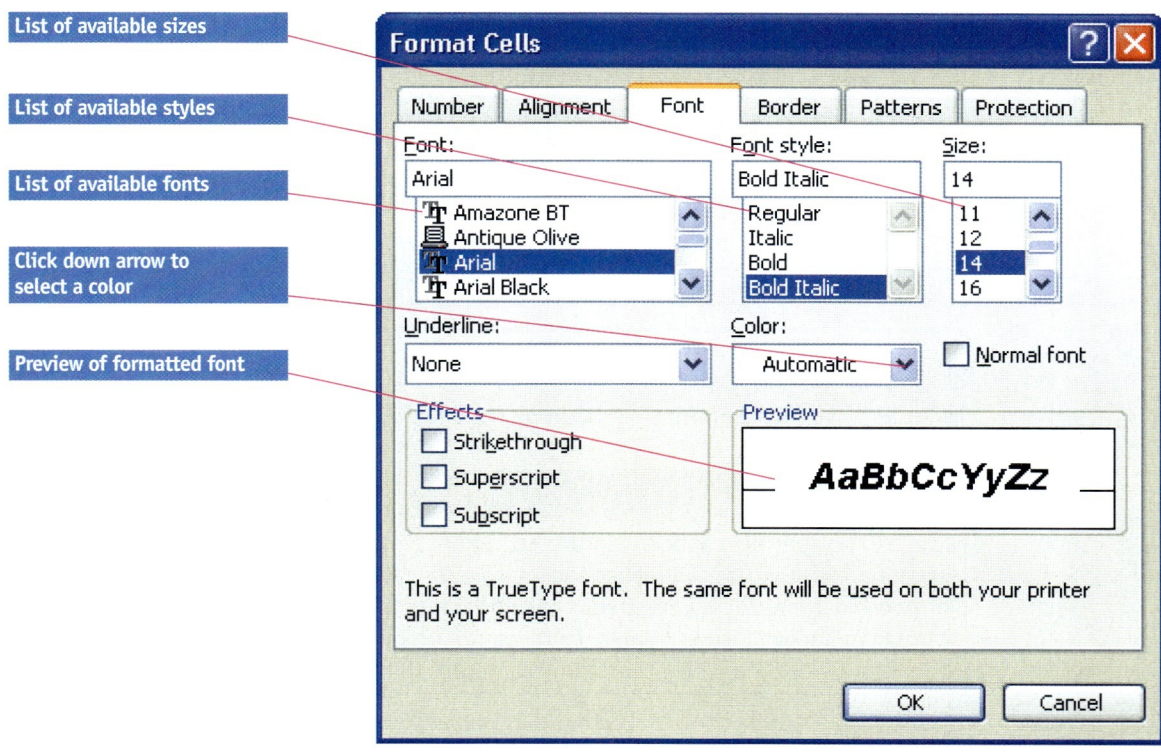

(c) The Font Tab

FIGURE 1.17 The Format Cells Command (*continued*)

Borders, Patterns, and Shading

The **Border tab** in Figure 1.17d enables you to create a border around a cell (or cells) for additional emphasis. You select (click) the line style at the right of the dialog box, then you click the left, right, top, and/or bottom border. You can outline the entire cell or selected cells, or you can choose the specific side or sides; for example, thicker lines on the bottom and right sides produce a drop shadow, which is very effective. You can also specify a different line style and/or a different color for the border, but you will need a color printer to see the effect on the printed output.

The **Patterns tab** (not shown in the figure) lets you choose a different color in which to shade the cell and further emphasize its contents. The Pattern drop-down list box lets you select an alternate pattern, such as dots or slanted lines. Click OK to accept the settings and close the dialog box.

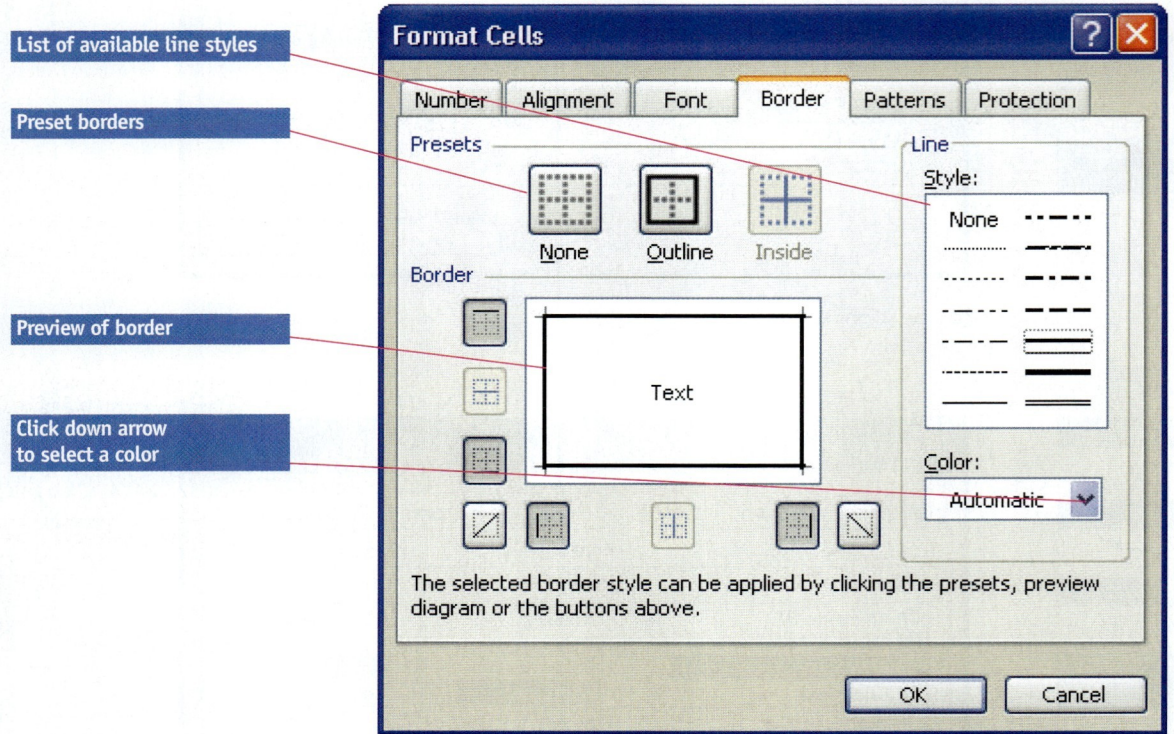

(d) The Border Tab

FIGURE 1.17 The Format Cells Command (*continued*)

USE RESTRAINT

More is not better, especially in the case of too many typefaces and styles, which produce cluttered worksheets that impress no one. Limit yourself to a maximum of two typefaces per worksheet, but choose multiple sizes and/or styles within those typefaces. Use boldface or italics for emphasis, but do so in moderation, because if you emphasize too many elements, the effect is lost.

hands-on exercise
4 Formatting a Worksheet

Objective To format a worksheet using boldface, italic, shading, and borders; to change the font and/or alignment of a selected entry. Use Figure 1.18 as a guide in the exercise.

Step 1: Center the Title

- Open **Better Grade Book** from the previous exercise. Click in **cell A1** to select the cell containing the title of the worksheet. Click the **Bold button** on the Formatting toolbar to boldface the title. Click the **Italic button** to italicize the title.

- Click in **cell A15** and click the **Bold button**. Click the **Bold button** a second time, and the boldface disappears. Click the **Bold button** again, and you are back to boldface. The same is true of the Italic button; that is, the Bold and Italic buttons function as toggle switches.

- Click in **cell A1**. Click the **down arrow** on the Font size list box and change the size to **14** to further accentuate the title.

- Click and drag to select **cells A1** through **E1**, which represents the width of the entire worksheet. Click the **Merge and Center button** on the Formatting toolbar as shown in Figure 1.18a to center the title across the width of your worksheet.

- Save the workbook.

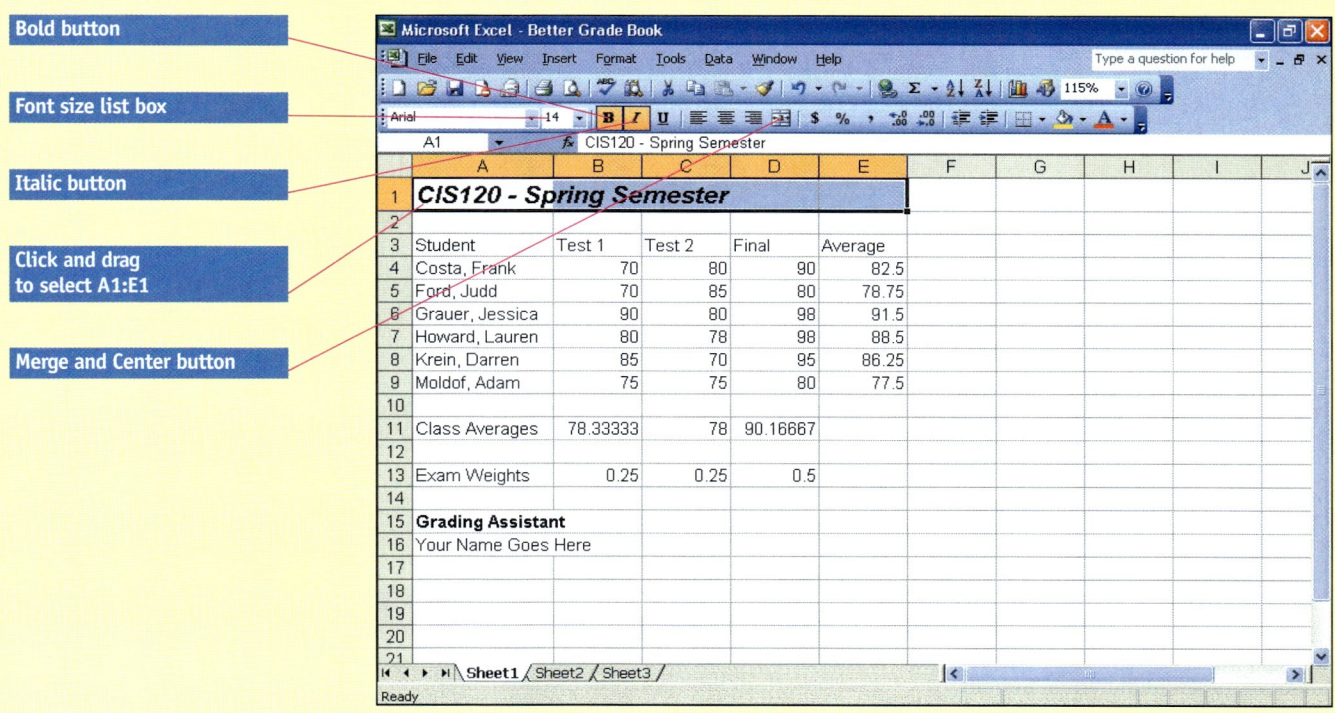

(a) Center the Title (step 1)

FIGURE 1.18 Hands-on Exercise 4

MICROSOFT OFFICE EXCEL 2003 REVISED 47

Step 2: **Format the Exam Weights**

- Click and drag to select **cells B13** through **D13**. Pull down the **Format menu**, then click the **Cells command** to display the dialog box in Figure 1.18b.

- If necessary, click the **Number tab**. Click **Percentage** in the Category list box. Click the **down spin arrow** in the Decimal Places box to select **zero decimals**, then click **OK**. The exam weights are displayed with percent signs and no decimal places.

- You can also use the buttons on the Formatting toolbar to accomplish the same formatting. First remove the formatting by clicking the **Undo button** on the Standard toolbar to cancel the formatting command.

- Check that cells B13 through D13 are still selected. Click the **Percent Style button** on the Formatting toolbar. (You can also pull down the **Format menu**, click the **Style command**, then choose the **Percent Style** from the Style Name list box.) Once again cells B13 through D13 are displayed in percent format.

- Save the workbook.

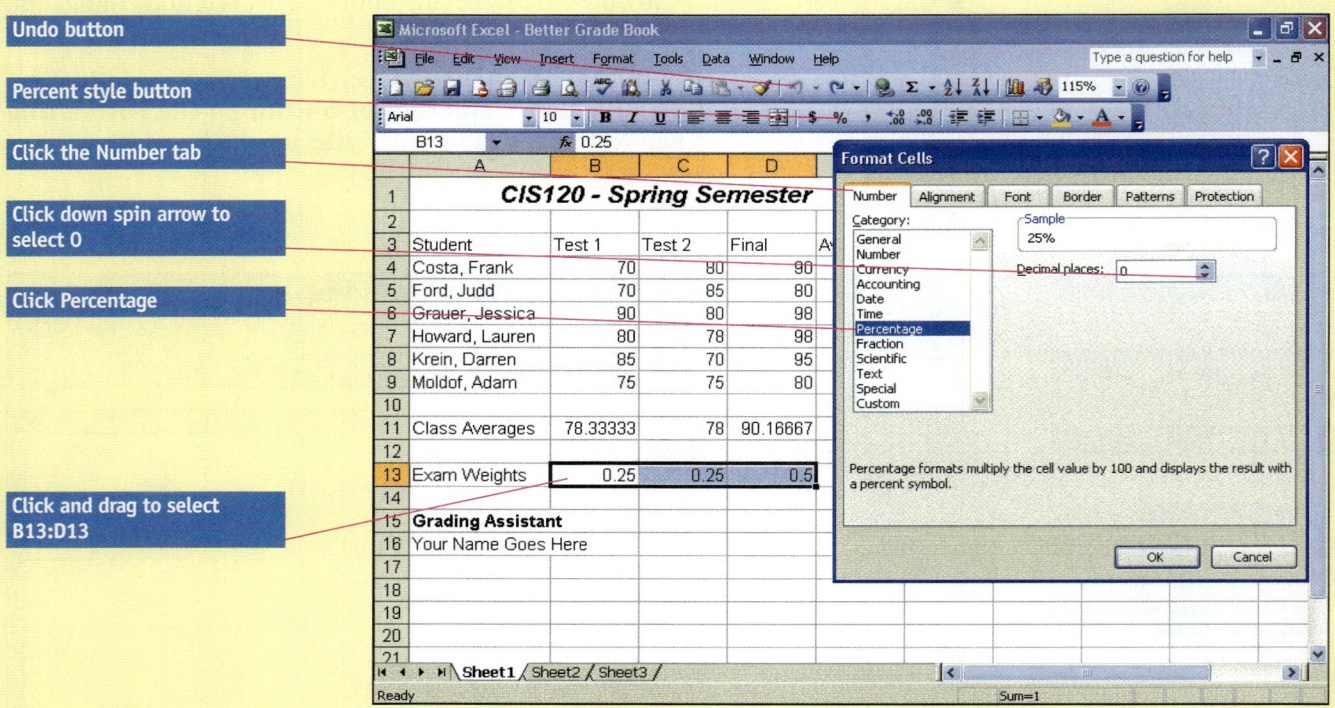

(b) Format the Exam Weights (step 2)

FIGURE 1.18   Hands-on Exercise 4 (*continued*)

THE MENU OR THE TOOLBAR

The Formatting toolbar is often the easiest way to implement a variety of formatting operations. There are buttons for boldface, italic, and underlining (each of which functions as a toggle switch). There are also buttons for alignment (including merge and center), currency, percent, and comma formats, together with buttons to increase or decrease the number of decimal places. You can find various buttons to change the font, point size, color, and borders.

Step 3: **Format the Class Averages**

- Click and drag to select **cells B11** through **D11**. Now press and hold the **Ctrl key** as you click and drag to select **cells E4** through **E9**. Using the Ctrl key in this way allows you to select noncontiguous (nontouching) cells as shown in Figure 1.18c.

- Format the selected cells using the Formatting toolbar or the Format menu:
  - To use the Format menu, pull down the **Format menu**, click **Cells**, click the **Number tab**, then click **Number** in the Category list box. Click the **down spin arrow** in the Decimal Places text box to reduce the decimal places to one. Click **OK**.
  - To use the Formatting toolbar, click the appropriate button repeatedly to increase or decrease the number of decimal places to one.

- Click and drag to select **cells B3** through **E13**. Click the **Center button** to center the numeric data in the worksheet under the respective column headings.

- Save the workbook.

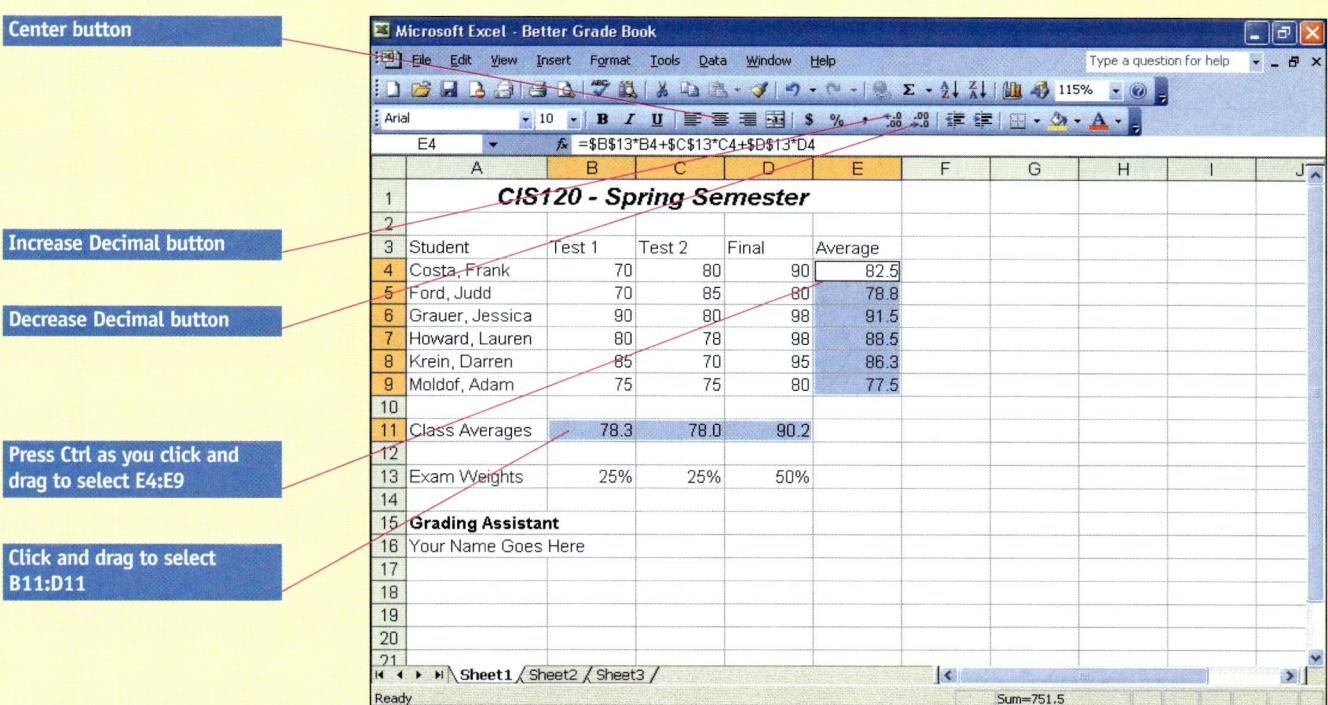

(c) Format the Class Averages (step 3)

FIGURE 1.18 Hands-on Exercise 4 (*continued*)

CLEAR THE FORMATS, BUT KEEP THE CONTENTS

You can clear the formatting in a cell and retain the contents, and/or you can clear contents but retain the formatting. Click and drag over the cell(s) for which the command is to apply, then pull down the Edit menu, click the Clear command, and choose the appropriate option—for example, the option to clear Formats. Click the tiny square immediately below the name box (to the left of the header for column A) to select the entire worksheet, then clear the formats for the worksheet. You can then repeat the steps in this exercise to practice the various formatting commands.

Step 4: Borders and Color

- Click and drag to select **cells A3** through **E3**. Press and hold the **Ctrl key** as you click and drag to select the range **A11:E11**.
- Continue to press the **Ctrl key** as you click and drag to select **cells A13:E13**. All three cell ranges should be selected, which means that any formatting command you execute will apply to all of the selected cells.
- Pull down the **Format menu** and click **Cells** (or point to any of the selected cells and click the **right mouse button** to display a shortcut menu, then click **Format Cells**). Click the **Border tab** to display the dialog box in Figure 1.18d.
- Choose a line width from the Style section. Click the **Top** and **Bottom** boxes in the Border section. Click **OK** to exit the dialog box.
- Check that all three ranges are still selected (A3:E3, A11:E11, *and* A13:E13). Click the **down arrow** on the **Fill Color button** on the Formatting toolbar. Click **yellow** (or whatever color appeals to you).
- Click the **Bold button** on the Formatting toolbar. Click outside the selected cells to see the effects of the formatting change. Save the workbook.

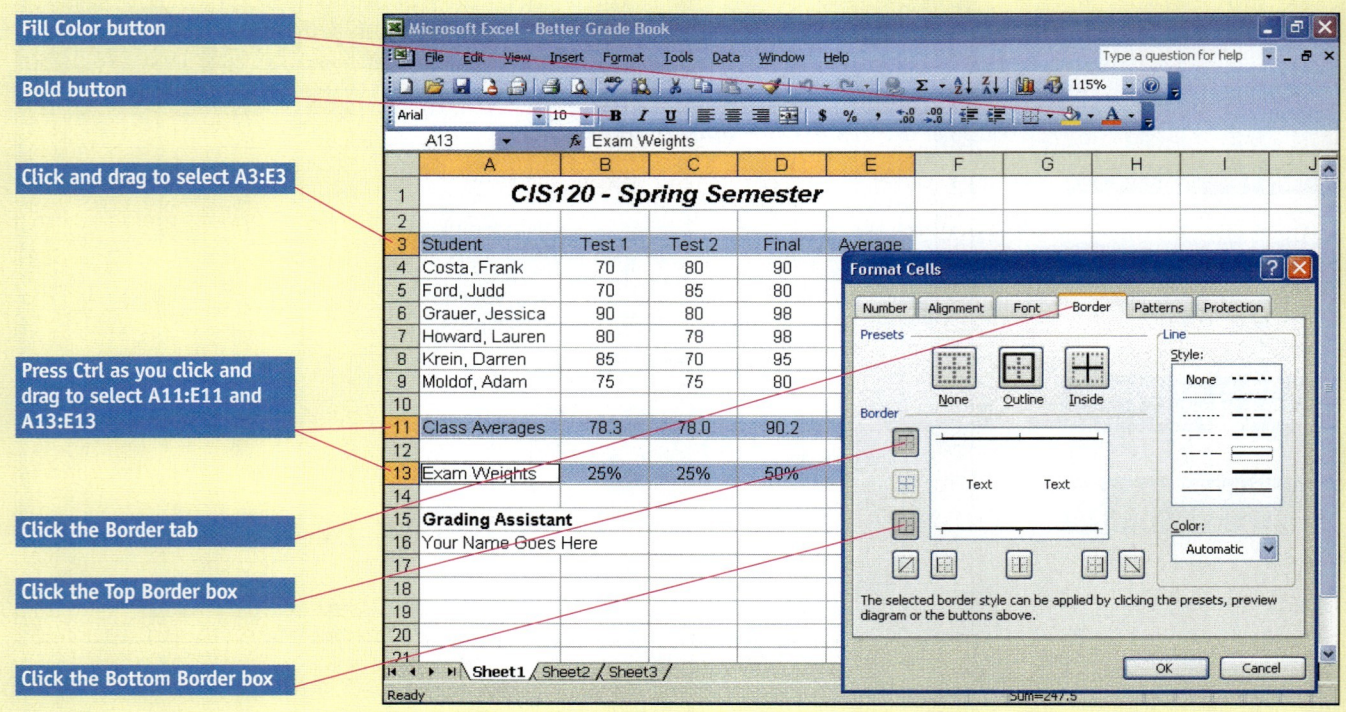

(d) Borders and Color (step 4)

FIGURE 1.18 Hands-on Exercise 4 (*continued*)

USE A PEN TO DRAW THE BORDER

You can draw borders of any thickness or color around the cells in a worksheet using a "pen," as opposed to a menu command. Click the down arrow on the Borders button on the Standard toolbar, then click the Draw Borders command to change the mouse pointer to a pen and simultaneously display the Borders toolbar. Click the Line Color or Line Style buttons to change the appearance of the border, then draw the borders directly in the worksheet. Close the Borders toolbar when you are finished.

Step 5: **The Completed Worksheet**

- Check that your worksheet matches ours as shown in Figure 1.18e. Pull down the **File menu**. Click **Page Setup** to display the Page Setup dialog box.
  - Click the **Margins tab**. Check the box to center the worksheet horizontally.
  - Click the **Sheet tab**. Check the boxes to print **Row and Column Headings** and **Gridlines**.
  - Click the **Header/Footer tab**. If necessary, click the **drop-down arrow** on the Header list box. Scroll to the top of the list and click **(none)** to remove the header. Click the **drop-down arrow** on the Footer list box. Scroll to the top of the list and click **(none)** to remove the footer. Click **OK**.

- Click the **Print Preview button** to preview the worksheet before printing:
  - If you are satisfied with the appearance of the worksheet, click the **Print button** within the Preview window, then click **OK** to print the worksheet.
  - If you are not satisfied with the appearance of the worksheet, click the **Setup button** within the Preview window to make the necessary changes.

- Save the workbook.

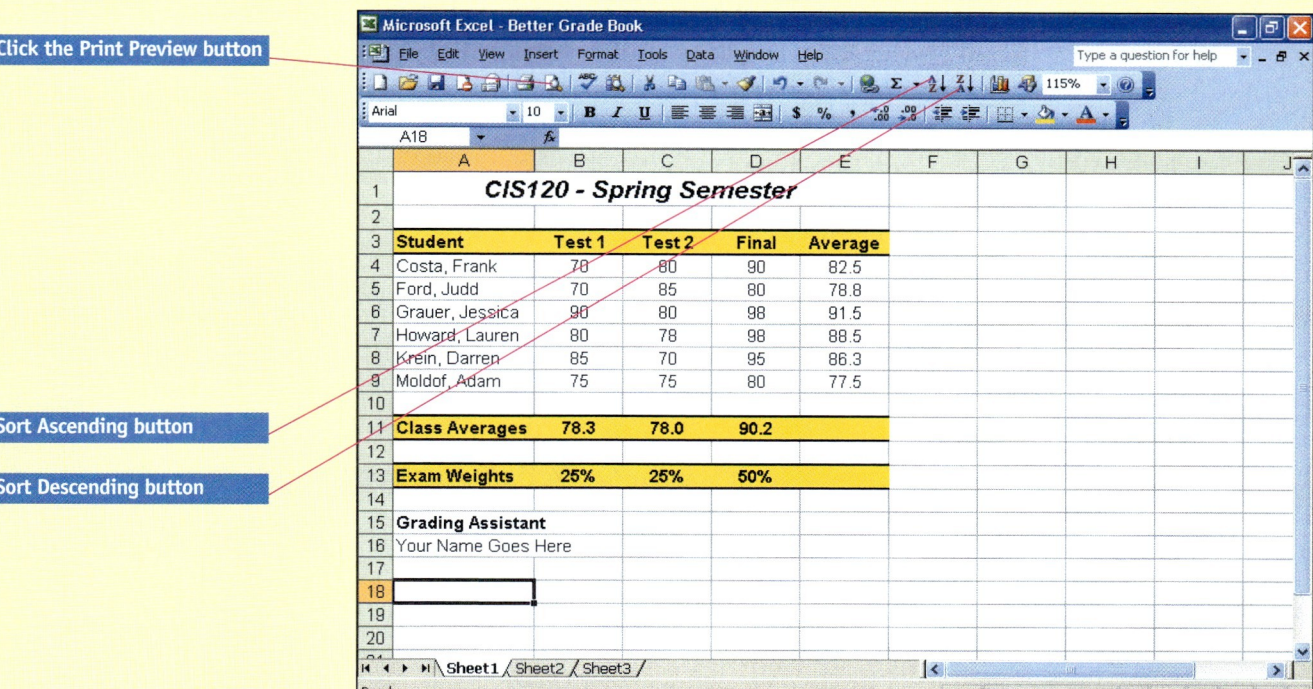

(e) The Completed Worksheet (step 5)

FIGURE 1.18 Hands-on Exercise 4 (*continued*)

SORT THE STUDENTS

The students are listed on the worksheet in alphabetical order, but you can rearrange the list according to any other field, such as the average or the result of a specific exam. Click on a single cell containing the student data in the column on which you want to sort, then click the Sort Ascending or Sort Descending button on the Standard toolbar. Click the Undo button if the result is different from what you intended.

Step 6: **Print the Cell Formulas**

- Pull down the **Tools menu**, click **Options**, click the **View tab**, check the box for **Formulas**, then click **OK**. You should see the cell formulas.

- Pull down the **File menu**. Click **Page Setup** to display the Page Setup dialog box. Click the **Page tab**. Click the **Landscape Orientation button**. Click the option button to **Fit to 1 Page**. Click **OK** to exit the Page Setup dialog box.

- Click the **Print Preview button** to preview the worksheet before printing.
  - Click the **Margins button** to display gridlines within the Print Preview window. Click and drag the column indicators to widen columns as necessary so that the cell formulas are completely visible.
  - Click the **Setup button** to display the Page Setup dialog box. Click the **Header/Footer tab**. Click the button to create a **Custom Header**.
  - Click in the **left section** and enter your name. Click in the **center section** and enter your course and your instructor's name.
  - Click in the **right section**. Click the **Date button**, press the **space bar**, then click the **Time button** to complete the custom header as shown in Figure 1.18f. Click **OK** to close the Header dialog box, then click **OK** to close the Page Setup dialog box. Print the worksheet.

- Pull down the **File menu**. Click **Exit**. Click **No** if prompted to save changes.

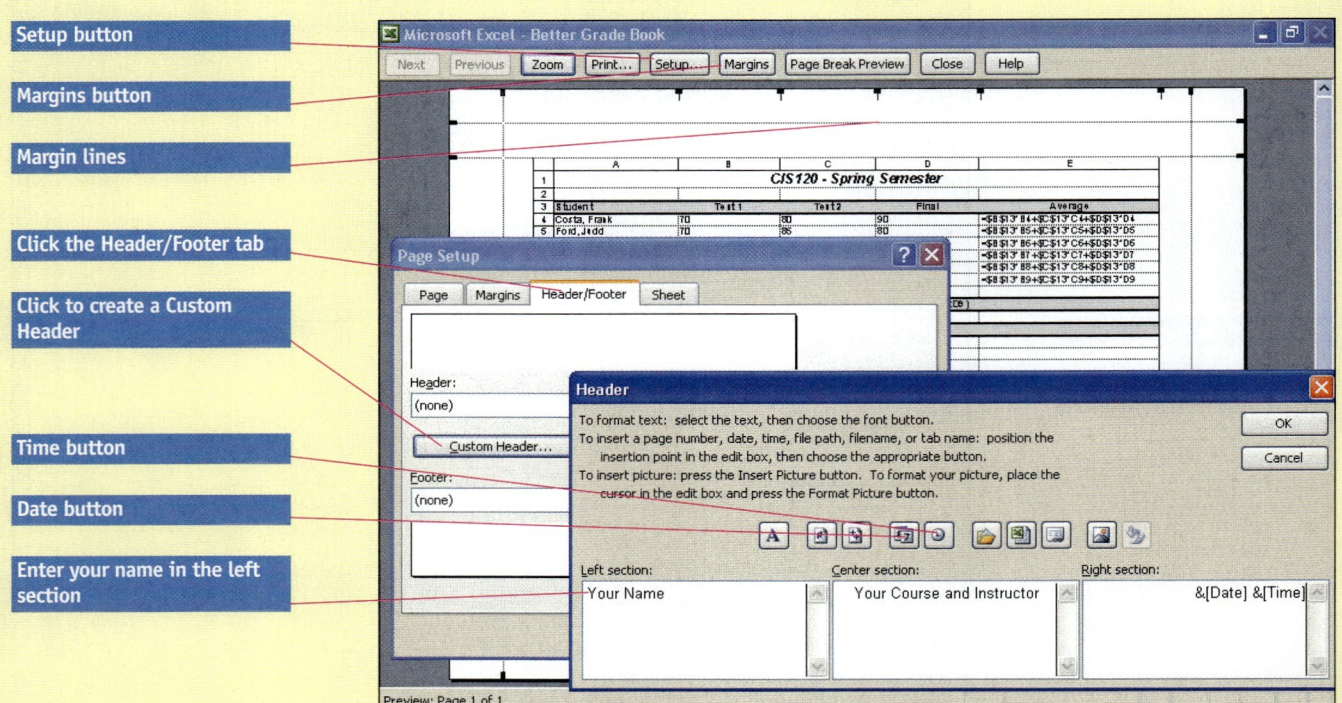

(f) Print the Cell Formulas (step 6)

FIGURE 1.18   Hands-on Exercise 4 (*continued*)

FIND AND REPLACE

Anyone familiar with a word processor takes the Find and Replace command for granted, but many people are surprised to learn that the same commands are also found in Excel. The commands are found in the Edit menu and provide the same options as in Microsoft Word. You can replace text and/or formatting throughout a worksheet. See practice exercise 5 at the end of the chapter.

SUMMARY

A spreadsheet is the computerized equivalent of an accountant's ledger. It is divided into rows and columns, with each row and column assigned a heading. The intersection of a row and column forms a cell. Spreadsheet is a generic term. Workbook and worksheet are Excel specific. An Excel workbook contains one or more worksheets.

Every cell in a worksheet (spreadsheet) contains either a formula or a constant. A formula begins with an equal sign and is a combination of numeric constants, cell references, arithmetic operators, and/or functions. A constant is an entry that does not change and may be numeric or descriptive text.

The Insert and Delete commands add or remove individual cells, rows, or columns of a worksheet. The commands are also used to insert or delete worksheets within a workbook. The Open command brings a workbook from disk into memory. The Save command copies the workbook in memory to disk.

The Page Setup command provides complete control over the printed page, enabling you to print a worksheet with or without gridlines or row and column headings. The Page Setup command also controls margins, headers and footers, centering the worksheet on a page, and orientation. The Print Preview command shows the worksheet as it will print; this command should be used prior to printing.

All worksheet commands operate on a cell or group of cells known as a range. A range is selected by dragging the mouse to highlight the range; the range remains selected until another range is selected or you click another cell in the worksheet. Noncontiguous (nonadjacent) ranges may be selected in conjunction with the Ctrl key.

The formulas in a cell or range of cells may be copied or moved anywhere within a worksheet. An absolute reference remains constant throughout a copy operation, whereas a relative address is adjusted for the new location. Absolute and relative references have no meaning in a move operation.

Formatting is done within the context of select-then-do; that is, select the cell or range of cells, then execute the appropriate command. The Format Cells command controls the formatting for numbers, alignment, font, borders, and patterns (colors). The Formatting toolbar simplifies the formatting process.

KEY TERMS

Term	Page
Absolute reference	33
Accounting format	43
Active cell	7
Alignment	44
Ask a Question box	6
Assumptions	31
Border tab	46
Cell	4
Cell reference	4
Clipboard	33
Close command	9
Constant	5
Copy command	32
Currency format	43
Custom format	43
Date format	43
Delete command	19
Destination range	32
Edit	5
Exit command	9
File menu	9
File name	9
File type	9
Format Cells command	43
Formatting toolbar	7
Formula	5
Formula bar	7
Fraction format	43
Function	5
General format	43
Insert command	19
Landscape orientation	21
Merge cells	44
Mixed reference	33
Move operation	34
Name box	7
Number format	43
Office Assistant	18
Office Clipboard	33
Open command	9
Page Setup command	21
Patterns tab	46
Percentage format	43
Places bar	9
Portrait orientation	21
Print command	9
Range	32
Relative reference	33
Save command	9
Save As command	9
Scientific format	43
ScreenTip	7
Select-then-do	43
Source range	32
Special format	43
Split cells	44
Spreadsheet	2
Standard toolbar	7
Status bar	7
Task pane	6
Text format	43
Time format	43
Toolbars	7
Workbook	6
Worksheet	6

MULTIPLE CHOICE

1. Which of the following is true?
   - (a) A worksheet contains one or more workbooks
   - (b) A workbook contains one or more worksheets
   - (c) A spreadsheet contains one or more worksheets
   - (d) A worksheet contains one or more spreadsheets

2. The cell at the intersection of the second column and third row is cell:
   - (a) B3
   - (b) 3B
   - (c) C2
   - (d) 2C

3. What is the effect of typing F5+F6 into a cell *without* a beginning equal sign?
   - (a) The entry is equivalent to the formula =F5+F6
   - (b) The cell will display the contents of cell F5 plus cell F6
   - (c) The entry will be treated as a text entry and display F5+F6 in the cell
   - (d) The entry will be rejected by Excel, which will signal an error message

4. The Open command:
   - (a) Brings a workbook from disk into memory
   - (b) Brings a workbook from disk into memory, then erases the workbook on disk
   - (c) Stores the workbook in memory on disk
   - (d) Stores the workbook in memory on disk, then erases the workbook from memory

5. The Save command:
   - (a) Brings a workbook from disk into memory
   - (b) Brings a workbook from disk into memory, then erases the workbook on disk
   - (c) Stores the workbook in memory on disk
   - (d) Stores the workbook in memory on disk, then erases the workbook from memory

6. In the absence of parentheses, the order of operation is:
   - (a) Exponentiation, addition or subtraction, multiplication or division
   - (b) Addition or subtraction, multiplication or division, exponentiation
   - (c) Multiplication or division, exponentiation, addition or subtraction
   - (d) Exponentiation, multiplication or division, addition or subtraction

7. Cells A1, A2, and A3 contain the values 10, 20, and 40, respectively. What value will be displayed in a cell containing the cell formula =A1/A2*A3+1?
   - (a) 1.125
   - (b) 21
   - (c) 20.125
   - (d) Impossible to determine

8. The entry =AVERAGE(A4:A6):
   - (a) Is invalid because the cells are not contiguous
   - (b) Computes the average of cells A4 and A6
   - (c) Computes the average of cells A4, A5, and A6
   - (d) None of the above

9. Which of the following was suggested with respect to printing a workbook?
   - (a) Print the displayed values only
   - (b) Print the cell formulas only
   - (c) Print both the displayed values and cell formulas
   - (d) Print neither the displayed values nor the cell formulas

10. Which options are mutually exclusive in the Page Setup menu?
    - (a) Portrait and landscape orientation
    - (b) Cell gridlines and row and column headings
    - (c) Left and right margins
    - (d) All of the above

...continued

multiple choice

11. If cells A1, A2, and A3 contain the values 1, 2, and 5, respectively, what value will be displayed in a cell containing the formula =(A3-A1)/A2^2+A2?

    (a) 1
    (b) 3
    (c) .0625
    (d) .4

12. Which of the following best describes the formula used to compute a student's semester average, when the weights of each exam are isolated at the bottom of a spreadsheet?

    (a) The student's individual grades are entered as absolute references, and the exam weights are entered as relative references
    (b) The student's individual grades are entered as relative references, and the exam weights are entered as absolute references
    (c) All cell references are relative
    (d) All cell references are absolute

13. Cell B11 contains the formula, =SUM (B3:B9). What will the contents of cell C11 be if the formula in cell B11 is copied to cell C11?

    (a) =SUM (C3:C9)
    (b) =SUM (B3:B9)
    (c) =SUM ($B$3:$B$9)
    (d) =SUM ($C$3:$C$9)

14. Given that cell E6 contains the formula, =B6*$B$12+C6*$C$12+D6*$D$12. What will be the formula in cell E7 if the contents of cell E6 are copied to that cell?

    (a) =B7*$B$12+C7*$C$12+D7*$D$12
    (b) =B7*$B$13+C7*$C$13+D7*$D$13
    (c) =B6*$B$13+C6*$C$13+D6*$D$13
    (d) None of the above

15. A formula containing the reference =D$5 is copied to a cell one column over and two rows down. How will the entry appear in its new location?

    (a) =E5
    (b) =E$5
    (c) =E$6
    (d) =$E5

16. The formula =B3+C4 is stored in cell D5. What will the formula be if row two is deleted from the worksheet?

    (a) =B2+C4
    (b) =B3+C3
    (c) =B3+C4
    (d) =B2+C3

17. You are creating a sales forecast, and have entered the sales for 2005 into cell B4. The expected rate of increase is in cell C2. What formula would you enter into cell C4 to compute the sales for 2006, given that you will copy that formula to cells D4:E4 to calculate the forecast for 2007 and 2008?

    (a) =B4+B4*C2
    (b) =$B$4+$B$4*C2
    (c) =B4*(1+$C$2)
    (d) None of the above

18. What is the end result of clicking in a cell, then clicking the Italic button on the Formatting toolbar twice in a row?

    (a) The cell contents are displayed in italic
    (b) The cell contents are displayed in ordinary (nonitalicized) type
    (c) The cell contents are unchanged and appear exactly as they did prior to clicking the Italic button twice in a row
    (d) Impossible to determine

ANSWERS

1. b
2. a
3. c
4. a
5. c
6. d
7. b
8. c
9. c
10. a
11. b
12. b
13. a
14. a
15. b
16. d
17. c
18. c

PRACTICE WITH EXCEL

1. **Isolate Assumptions:** Figure 1.19 displays a new grade book with a different grading scheme. Students take three exams worth 100 points each, submit a term paper and various homework assignments worth 50 points each, then receive a grade for the semester based on their total points. The maximum number of points (the point threshold) is 400. A student's semester average is computed by dividing his or her total points by the point threshold. Open the partially completed workbook in *Chapter 1 Practice 1* in the Exploring Excel folder and proceed as follows:

   a. Click in cell G4 and enter a formula to compute Anderson's total points. Click in cell H4 and enter a formula that will compute Anderson's semester average. Be sure this formula includes an absolute reference to cell B16.

   b. Click and drag to select the formulas in cells G4 and H4, then copy these formulas to cells G5 through H12.

   c. Click in cell B14 and enter a formula that will compute the class average on the first exam. Copy this formula to cells C14 to H14.

   d. Format the worksheet appropriately, but you need not match our formatting exactly. Note, too, that we have wrapped the text in cells B3 through H3 in order to use a narrower column width. (Select the cells, pull down the Format Cells command, click the Alignment tab, then check the box to wrap text.)

   e. Add your name as the grading assistant, then print the worksheet twice, once to show displayed values and once to show the cell formulas. Use landscape printing and be sure that the worksheet fits on one sheet of paper.

   f. The professor is concerned about the grades being too low and wants to introduce a curve. He does this by reducing the point threshold on which the students' semester averages are based. Click in cell B16 and change the threshold to 350, which automatically raises the average of every student.

   g. Print the displayed values that reflect the change in part (e). Can you see the value of isolating the assumptions within a worksheet?

   h. Add a cover page, then submit the complete assignment (four pages in all, counting the cover page) to your instructor as proof that you did this exercise.

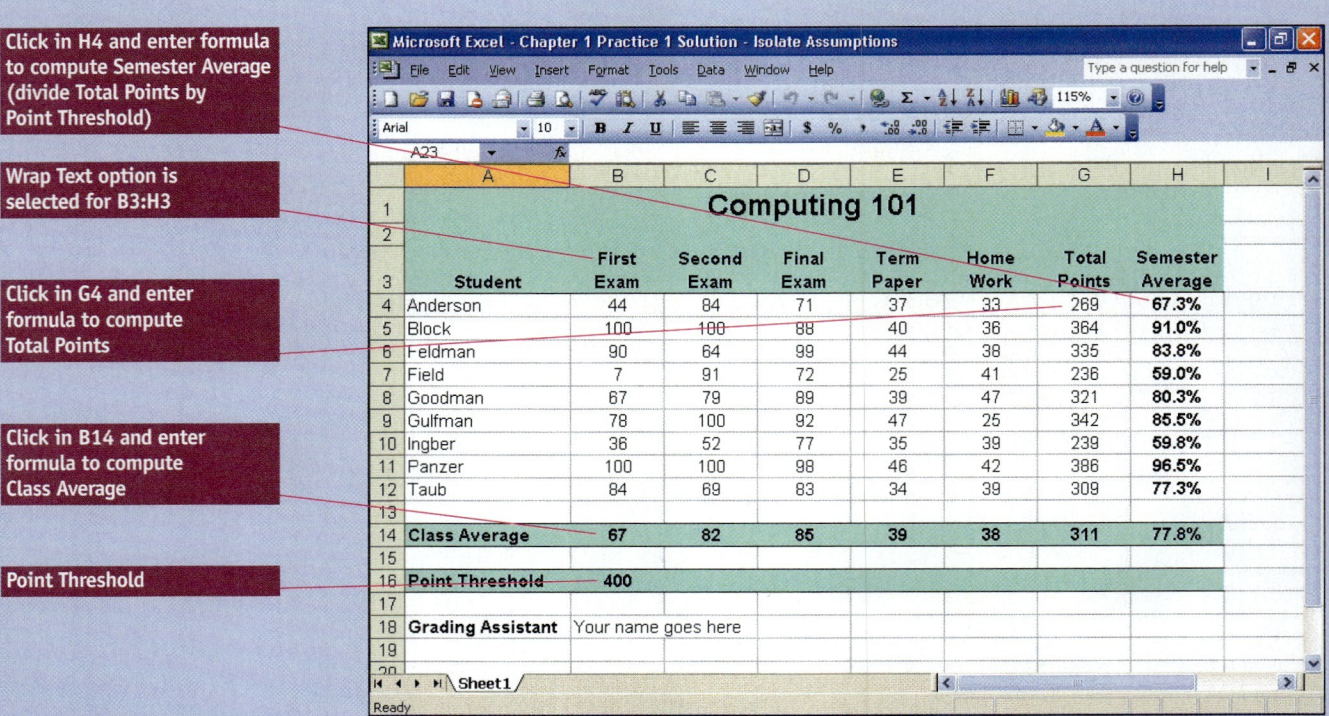

FIGURE 1.19 Isolate Assumptions (exercise 1)

practice exercises

2. **Practice with Formatting:** The workbook in Figure 1.20 provides practice with formatting and basic cell operations. Open the partially completed workbook in *Chapter 1 Practice 2*, and then format the workbook using the instructions in each cell. The formatting is very straightforward, but inserting and deleting cells is a little trickier since it can affect cells that have been merged together. You will find it easier therefore if you start in cell A1 and work your way down the worksheet, one row at a time. Proceed as follows:

   a. Click in cell A1 and enter your name, then change the formatting to 16 point white text on a blue background as shown in the figure.

   b. Move to cell A3 and format the text as indicated. You can use the Format Cells command and/or the various tools on the Formatting toolbar as you see fit. Move to cell B3 and italicize the text in green. Format cells A4 through B7 in similar fashion. Follow the instructions in cell B5 to change the width of column B.

   c. Follow the instructions in cells A8 to A12 to format the contents of cells B8 to B12, respectively. (No additional formatting is required for cells A8 to A12 at this time.)

   d. Click in cell A13, then click the Merge and Center button to split the merged cell into two cells. (The Merge and Center button functions as a toggle switch: Click it once, the selected cells are merged; click it a second time, and the merged cell is split.) Follow the instructions in the cell to change the row height and other formatting. Cell B13 should be blank when you are finished.

   e. Click in cell A14, click the Format Painter tool, and then click and drag cells A8 through A12 to apply the formatting from cell A14.

   f. Right click the row indicator for row 15 and insert a new row, and then move the contents of cell A20 to the newly inserted cell A15.

   g. Change the width of column A to 55, merge cells A16 and B16, then complete the indicated formatting for the merged cell.

   h. Print the completed workbook for your instructor. Use the Page Setup command to display gridlines and row and column headings. Change to landscape printing and center the worksheet horizontally on the page. Create a custom header that contains your name, your school, and your instructor's name. Add a custom footer that contains the name of the workbook, and the date and time you completed the assignment.

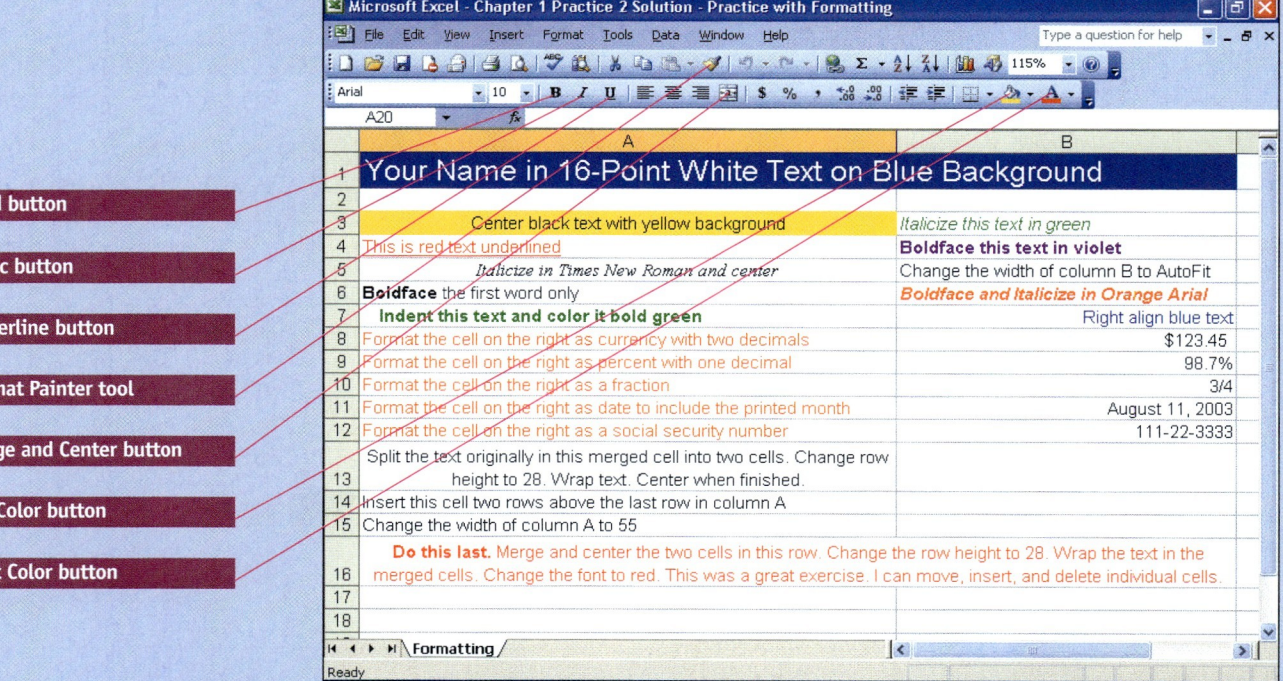

FIGURE 1.20 Practice with Formatting (exercise 2)

practice exercises

3. **The Calendar:** There are many ways to create a calendar within Microsoft Office. The most important step, however, is to design the calendar with the computer off; then once you know the type of calendar (e.g., weekly or monthly) and the desired look, it is relatively easy to create regardless of the application.

   a. Start a new workbook. Click and drag to select cells D1 through F1, click the Merge and Center button, then change the format of the merged cells to text. Enter the month for which you will create the calendar—for example, November 2005 as shown in Figure 1.21. Click and drag to merge cells D2 through F2 in similar fashion, and enter your name. Change the row height, column width, font size, and color as appropriate.

   b. Click in cell B3 and enter "Sunday", the day on which our calendar will begin. Click and drag the fill handle to cells C3 to H3 to automatically enter the remaining days of the week (using the AutoFill capability within Excel).

   c. Click and drag to select cells B3 through H3 and click the Bold button. Pull down the Format menu, click the Cells command, click the Alignment tab, and then choose Center for the Vertical Alignment. Increase the row height to see the vertical alignment. Change the formatting of the text as desired.

   d. Click in the appropriate cell in row four (cell D4 in our figure) and enter 1 for the first day of the month. Enter the remaining days of the month into rows four through eight as appropriate, then increase the row height in rows 4 through 7 so that the calendar fills the page. (We specified a row height of 65.) Change the vertical alignment to the top of each cell and format the text as appropriate—for example, 14 point bold.

   e. Use the Insert Picture command to insert an appropriate piece of clip art. Complete the formatting by changing the fill color in cells B3 through H3, B3 through B8, and H3 through H8.

   f. Insert a second worksheet and create a weekly calendar. The calendar should show the days of the week going across the top, and the times of the day down the side. The rest of the design is up to you.

   g. Use the Page Setup command to change to landscape printing, then print both calendars for your instructor.

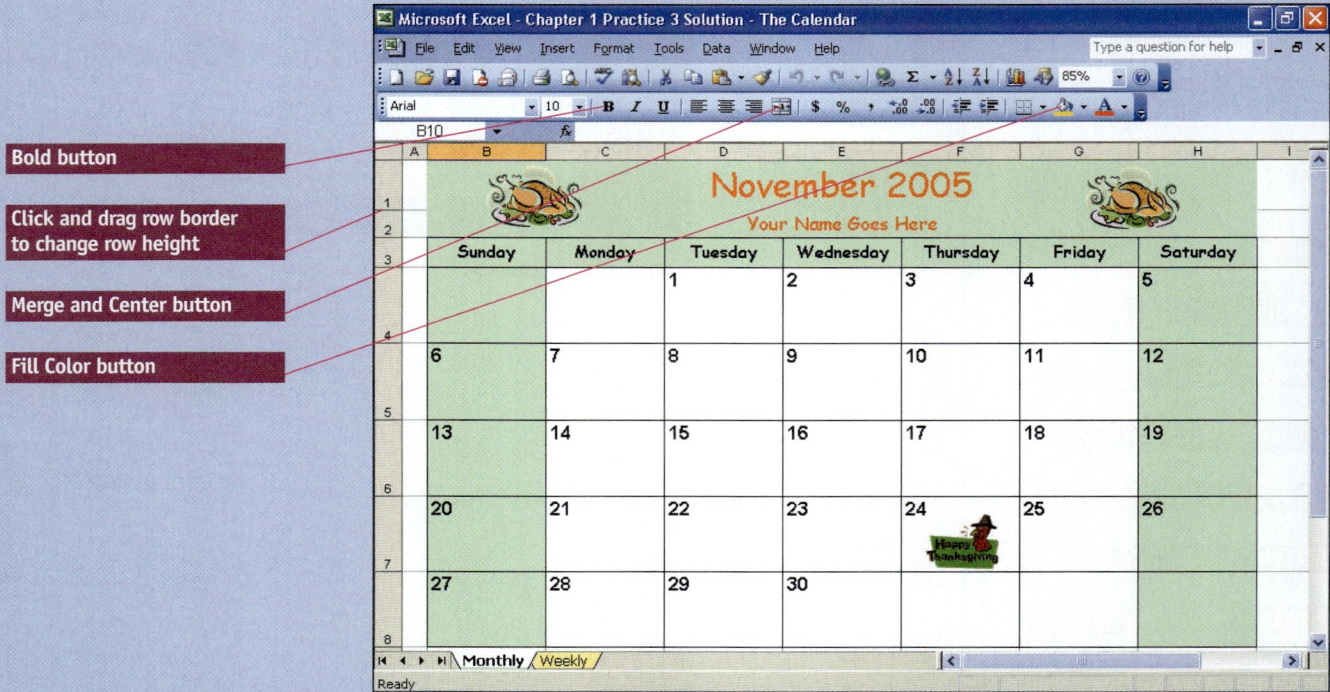

FIGURE 1.21 The Calendar (exercise 3)

practice exercises

4. **The Checkbook:** Figure 1.22 displays a worksheet that can be used to balance your checkbook. Your assignment is to create a similar worksheet using real or hypothetical data. Proceed as follows:

   a. Start Excel. If necessary, click the New button on the Standard toolbar to display a blank workbook. Click in cell A1 and enter the title with your name as shown. Enter the labels for cells A2 through F2. Do not worry about formatting at this time.

   b. Enter the initial balance in cell F3. Enter the data for your first check in row 4. To enter a date, just type the date without an equal sign; e.g., type 6/2 to display June 2 of the current year. Do not worry about the precise formatting at this time.

   c. Click in cell F4 and enter the formula to compute the balance. The formula should be entered in such a way that the balance is computed correctly, regardless of whether the transaction is a check (withdrawal) or deposit.

   d. Enter data for at least 6 additional transactions in cells A through E of the appropriate rows. Copy the formula to compute the balance for these transactions from cell F4.

   e. Skip one row after the last transaction, then enter the formulas to verify that the balance is correct. The formula for cell F18 (in our worksheet) is the initial balance, minus the sum of all checks and withdrawals, plus the sum of all deposits. The displayed value should equal the balance after the last transaction. Pull down the Insert menu and click the Comment command to enter a comment in that cell that explains the formula in cell F18.

   f. Format the completed worksheet as shown in Figure 1.22. You do not have to duplicate our formatting exactly, but you are to use date and currency formatting in the appropriate cells.

   g. Print the completed workbook to show both displayed values and cell formulas. Use the Page Setup command to display gridlines and row and column headings. Center the worksheet horizontally on the page. Create a custom header that contains your name, your school, and your instructor's name. Add a custom footer that contains the name of the workbook, and the date and time you completed the assignment.

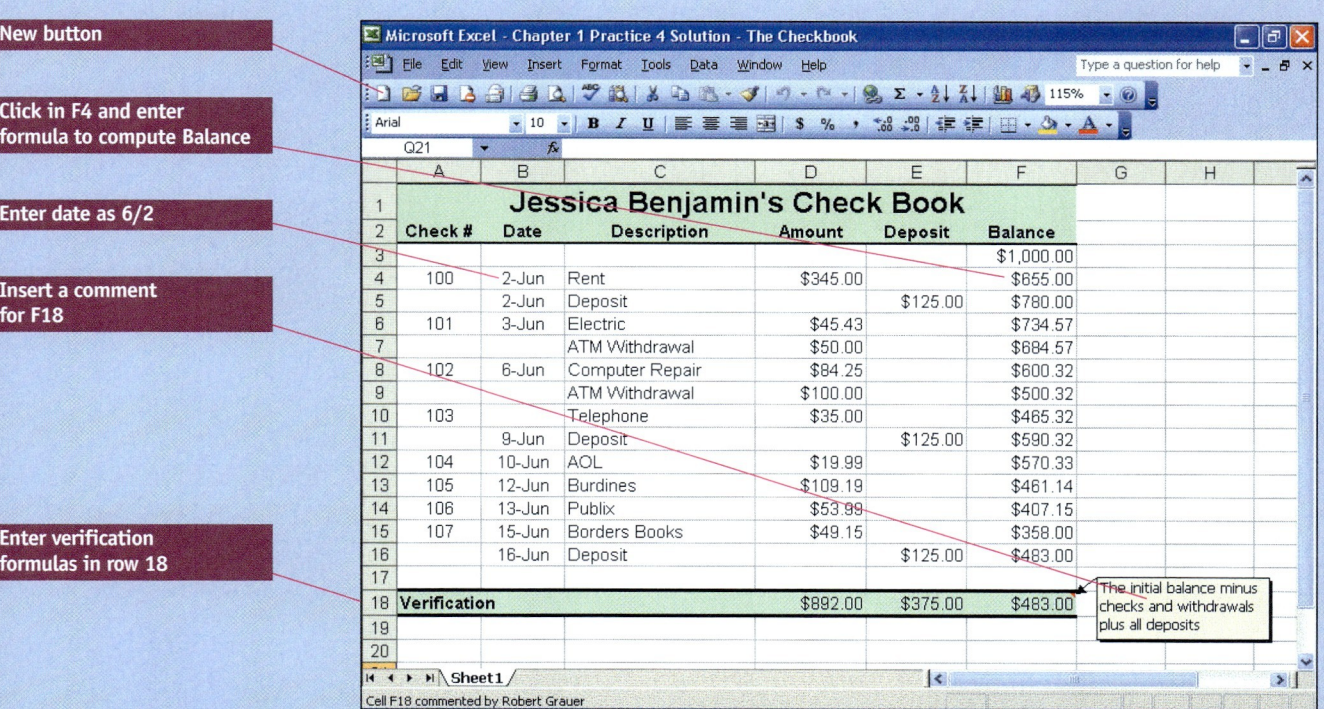

FIGURE 1.22   The Checkbook (exercise 4)

practice exercises

5. **Judson Ford Realty:** The worksheet in Figure 1.23 displays the sales for Judson Ford Realty for the month of October. You can open a partially completed version of this worksheet in *Chapter 1 Practice 5,* but it is up to you to complete the worksheet so that it matches Figure 1.23. The notes in the worksheet and/or the column headings should be self-explanatory with respect to entering the various formulas, but the information is repeated below.

   a. The percentage of the asking price in cell E4 is the sales price divided by the asking price. Format the result as a percent with one decimal place.
   b. The price per square foot in cell F4 is the selling price divided by the number of square feet.
   c. The realtor's commission in cell G4 is a percentage of the selling price and is based on the commission percentage in cell B14.
   d. The net to the homeowner in cell H4 is the selling price minus the commission to the realtor.
   e. Copy the formulas in row 4 to the remaining rows in the worksheet.
   f. Format the worksheet in an appropriate fashion, but you need not match our formatting exactly. Note, too, that we have wrapped the text in row 3 in order to use a narrower column width. (Select cells A3 through H3, pull down the Format Cells command, click the Alignment tab, then check the box to wrap text.)
   g. Compute the agency statistics as shown in row 12. Use the Average, Max, and Min functions in cells H17 through H19 to display these values for the properties that were sold during the month.
   h. Use the Find and Replace command to change the text in the various addresses. Change all occurrences of "Str" to "Street", "Rd" to "Road", and "Ave" to "Avenue". You also need to replace the Courier New font with Arial throughout the worksheet.
   i. Add your name in cell G14, then print the worksheet to show both displayed values and cell formulas. Change to landscape printing and add a custom header and/or a custom footer.
   j. Create a cover sheet, then submit the assignment to your instructor.

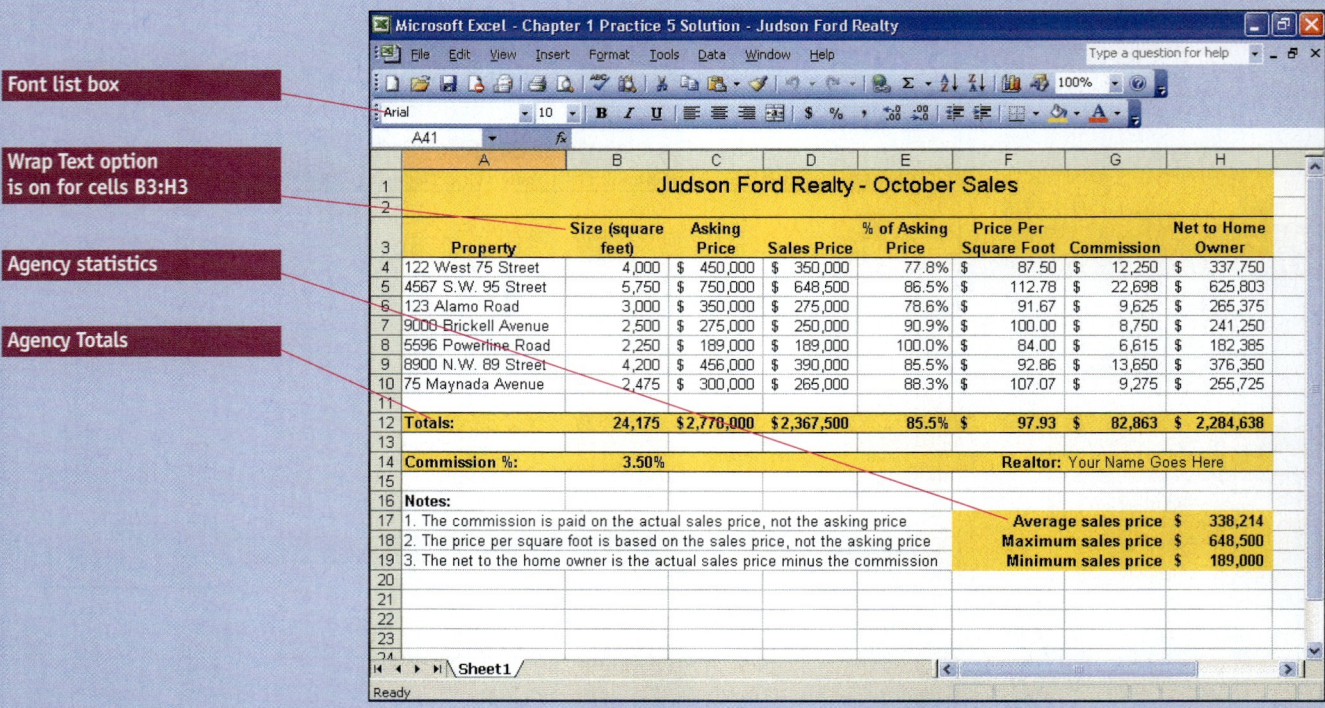

FIGURE 1.23 Judson Ford Realty (exercise 5)

60 CHAPTER 1: INTRODUCTION TO EXCEL

practice exercises

6. **The Solar System:** The potential uses of a spreadsheet are limited only by your imagination as can be seen by Figure 1.24, which displays a spreadsheet with information about our solar system. Open the partially completed version of the workbook in *Chapter 1 Practice 6*, then complete the worksheet by developing the formulas for the first planet, copying those formulas to the remaining rows in the worksheet, then formatting appropriately.

   a. Click in cell C15 and enter your weight on Earth. You can specify your weight in pounds rather than kilograms.

   b. Click in cell C16 and enter the function =Pi() as shown in Figure 1.24. The displayed value for the cell shows the value of Pi to several decimal places. The contents of the cell, however, contain the indicated function as can be seen in the formula bar.

   c. Click in cell D4 and enter the formula to compute the diameter of the first planet (Mercury). The diameter of a planet is equal to twice its radius.

   d. Click in cell E4 and enter the formula to compute the circumference of a planet. The circumference is equal to the diameter times the constant Pi.

   e. Click in cell F4 and enter the formula to compute the surface area, which is equal to four times Pi times the radius squared. (This is the formula to compute the surface area of a sphere, which is different from the formula to compute the area of a circle.)

   f. Click in cell G4 and enter the formula to compute your weight on Mercury, which is your weight on Earth times the relative gravity of Mercury compared to that of Earth.

   g. Copy the formulas in row 4 to the remainder of the worksheet, then format the worksheet appropriately. You need not copy our formatting exactly. Add your name in cell E15 as indicated.

   h. The worksheet contains a hyperlink to a Web site by Bill Arnett, which has additional information about the planets. If you click the hyperlink within Excel, your browser will open automatically, and you will be connected to the site, provided you have an Internet connection.

   i. Print the worksheet two ways, once with displayed values, and once to show the cell contents. Use landscape orientation and appropriate scaling so that the worksheet fits on a single page.

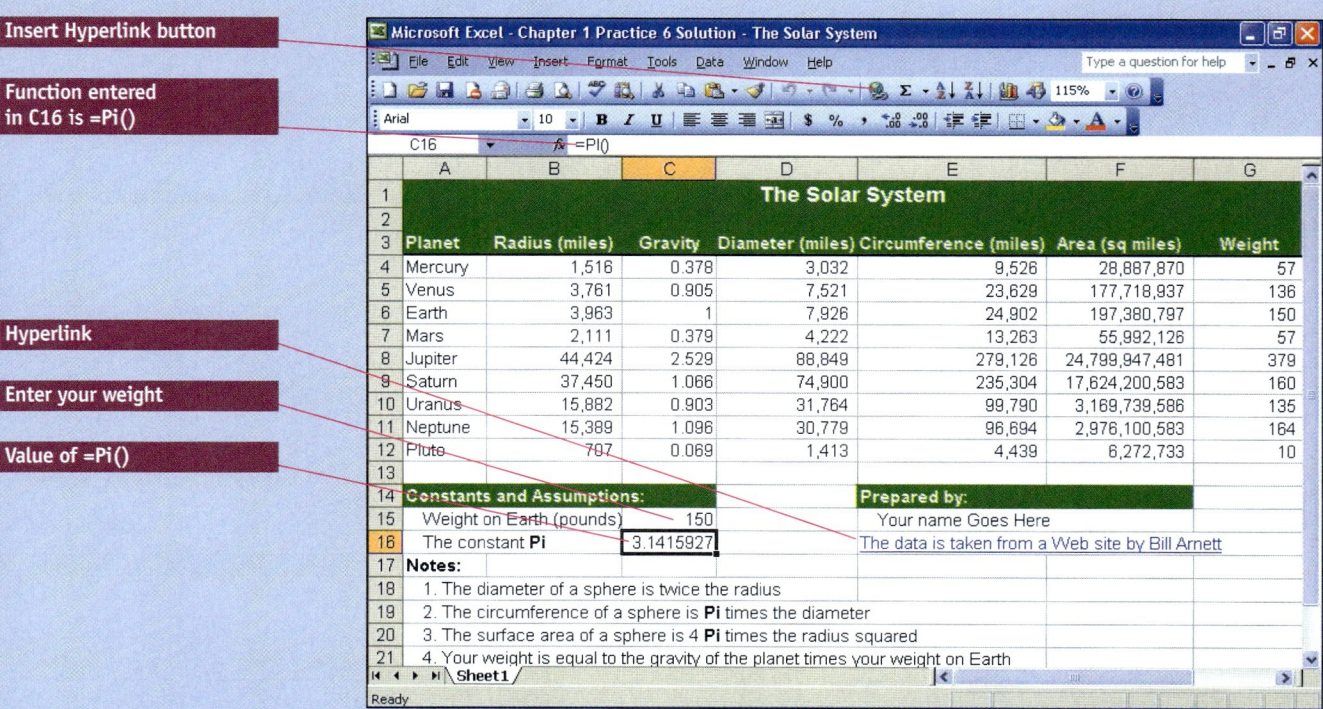

FIGURE 1.24 The Solar System (exercise 6)

practice exercises

7. **Student Budget:** Figure 1.25 displays a hypothetical budget for a nine-month academic year. You can use the partially completed version of this worksheet in the *Chapter 1 Practice 7* workbook, or you can create your own budget. If you use our file, then the totals in your worksheet should correspond exactly to those in Figure 1.25, whereas if you create your own budget, the numbers will differ. The worksheet is straightforward, but we want to call your attention to the following:
   a. Enter the data (the labels for the various income and expense categories as well as the specific amounts) in the body of the worksheet.
   b. Use the Sum function in cell K4 to compute the total for the first income source for the academic year. Copy this formula to the remaining cells in this column.
   c. Use the Sum function in cell B8 to compute the total income for September. Copy this formula to the remaining cells in this row. (The total income for the year can be obtained by summing either cells K4 through K7 or cells B8 through J8.) Use a similar approach to determine the total expenses for each month in row 18.
   d. Compute the deficit or surplus for each month in row 20. If necessary, adjust your numbers to show at least one month where you run a deficit. Negative numbers should be formatted in red and be enclosed in parentheses.
   e. Compute the minimum and maximum monthly expense in cells B22 and B23, respectively.
   f. Merge and center the cells in row 1, and enter your name to identify the worksheet as your own. Format it appropriately. Print the worksheet two ways, to show both displayed values and cell formulas, then submit both pages to your instructor. Be sure to use the Page Setup command to specify landscape printing, and appropriate scaling so that the entire worksheet fits on a single page.
   g. Extend the exercise by exploring potential sources for financial aid. Your school or university may offer scholarships or work study programs of which you are currently unaware. Outside agencies may provide similar help. Summarize your findings and bring them to class for discussion.

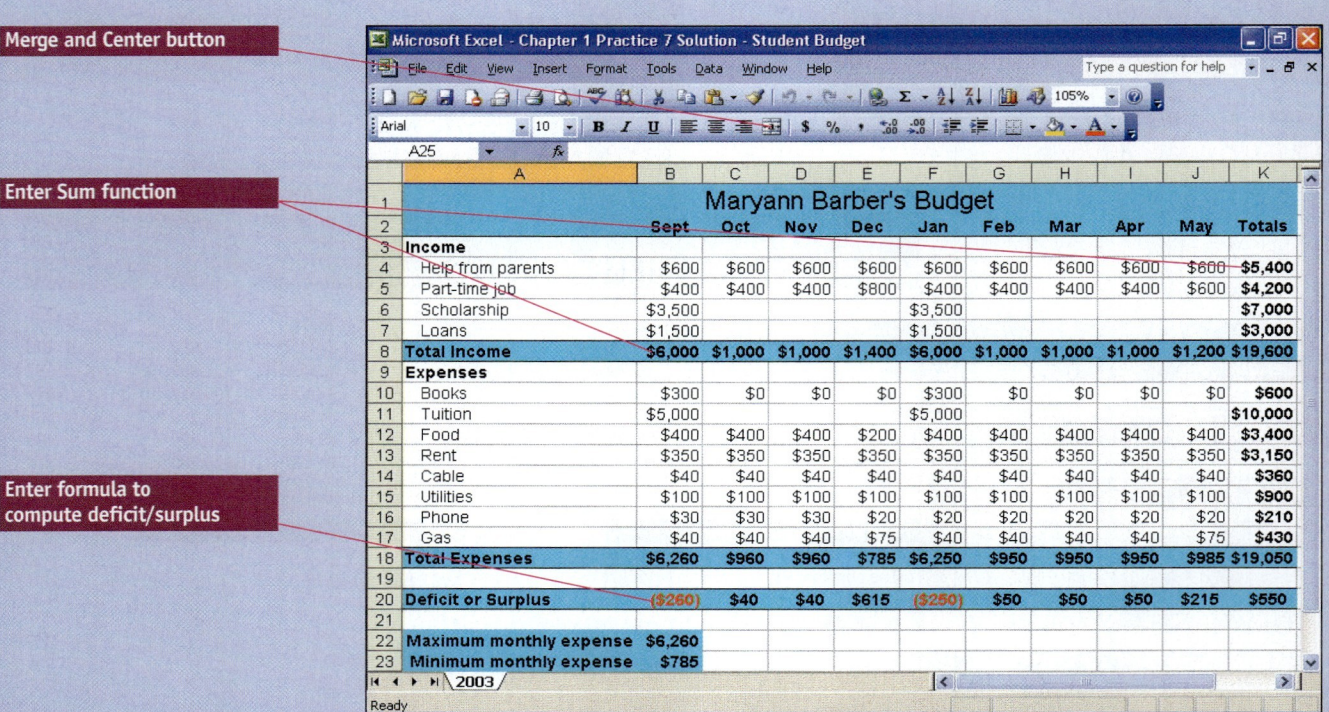

FIGURE 1.25 Student Budget (exercise 7)

practice exercises

8. **Excel Templates:** This chapter introduced you to the basics of Excel and showed you how to create your own spreadsheets. It is often convenient, however, to use a workbook that was created by someone else that is tailored to a specific application. This type of workbook is called a template and it contains text, formulas, and formatting, but no specific data. Proceed as follows:

   a. Start Excel. Pull down the View menu to display the task pane, then click the down arrow in the task pane to display the New Workbook task pane. Look in the Other templates area and click the link to On My Computer to display the Templates dialog box. Click the Spreadsheet Solutions tab.

   b. You should see several templates that were installed locally with the installation of Microsoft Office. Select the *Timecard* template and click OK. (You can open the *Chapter 1 Practice 8* workbook in the Exploring Excel folder if this template is not available on your system.)

   c. Click in cell E10, type your name, and press the Tab key to move to cell I10. Enter your student number (do not be concerned that the worksheet asks for an employee number rather than a student number). Press the Tab key to move to cell M9 where you enter the note in Figure 1.26.

   d. Click in cell D20 and type the name of the first course you are taking. Use the Tab key to move across the row to enter your study hours for the week. You cannot, however, move to column Q because the total is calculated automatically. Click in cell D22 and start to enter the data for your second course. Enter the data for your remaining courses in similar fashion.

   e. The worksheet is currently protected, which means you cannot change the contents of the cells containing labels and formulas. Pull down the Tools menu, click Protection, and then click the Unprotect Sheet command. (A password is not required.) You can now modify the worksheet to fit your specific application, for example, logging study hours instead of an employee worksheet. Click in cell P5 and enter Study Hours. Make additional modifications as you see fit. (We changed the name of the worksheet tab to Study Schedule.) Print the completed worksheet for your instructor. Save the workbook as *Chapter 1 Practice 8 Solution—Study Schedule*.

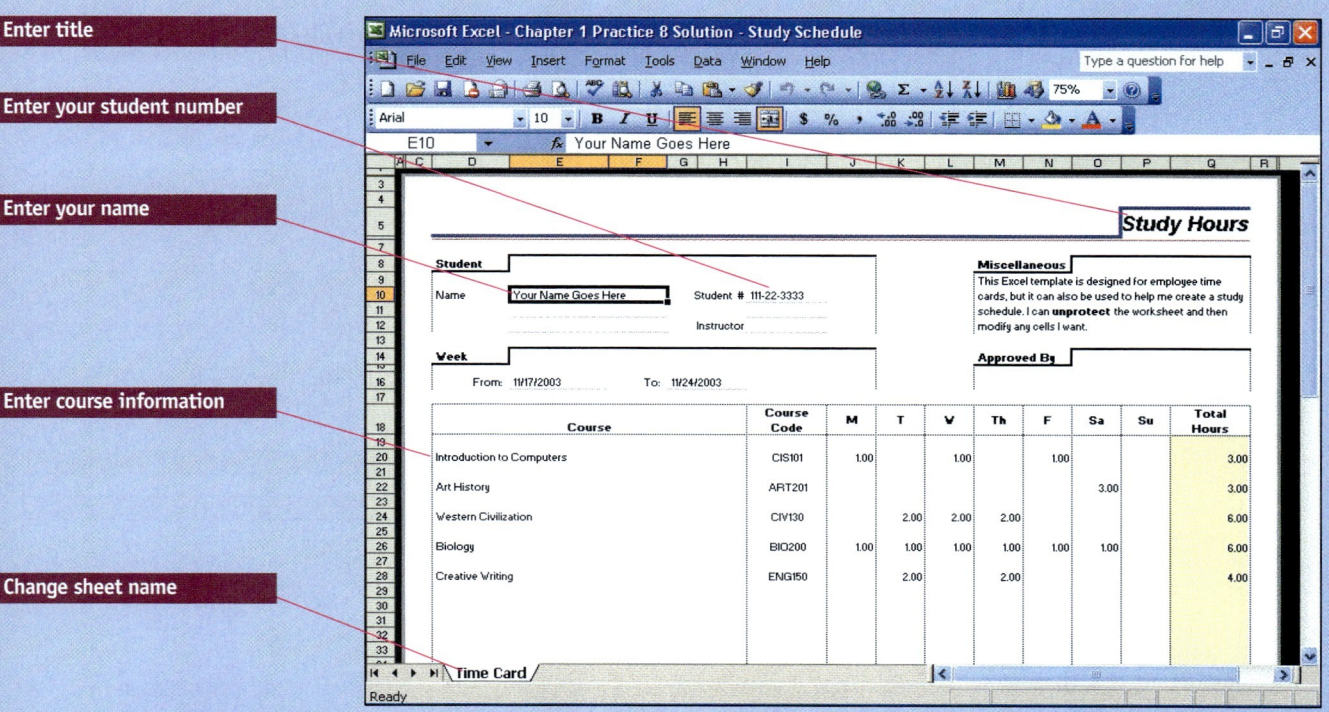

FIGURE 1.26 Excel Templates (exercise 8)

MICROSOFT OFFICE EXCEL 2003 REVISED

practice exercises

9. **Municipal Museums:** Figure 1.27 displays a spreadsheet that is used to compute the daily revenue for the museums in your city. Open the partially completed workbook in *Chapter 1 Practice 9—Municipal Museums*, and then complete the workbook to match Figure 12. You do not have to match our formatting exactly, but the displayed values should be the same.

   a. Click in cell E5 and enter the formula to compute the ticket revenue for the first museum. Be sure to use the appropriate combination of relative and absolute references so that you can copy this formula to the corresponding cells for the other museums.
   b. Click in cell H5 and enter the formula to compute the gift shop revenue (which is the sum of food and merchandise revenue). Enter the formula for total revenue (ticket revenue plus gift shop revenue) in cell I5. Copy the formulas in cell H5 and I5 to the rows for the other museums.
   c. Click in cell B10 and enter the appropriate Sum function to compute the total number of adult tickets that were sold. Copy the formula in cell B10 to the remaining cells in row 10 to compute the other totals.
   d. Format the worksheet. Click in cell E5 and apply the Currency format (with no decimals). Remain in cell E5, double click the Format Painter tool on the Standard toolbar, then copy this format to the appropriate cells in the worksheet.
   e. Click and drag cells B1 to I1, then click the Merge and Center button on the Formatting toolbar. Change the font size as necessary. Complete the formatting by changing alignments and fonts, using a fill color, and applying borders as you see fit.
   f. Pull down the Insert menu, click the Picture command, click Clip Art, then search for an appropriate museum image. Move and size the clip art as shown.
   g. Use the Page Setup command to create a custom footer that contains the date and time the worksheet is printed, the name of the worksheet, and your name. Be sure to specify landscape printing and appropriate scaling so that the entire worksheet fits on a single page.
   h. Print the worksheet twice to show both displayed values and cell formulas. Add a cover sheet to complete the assignment.

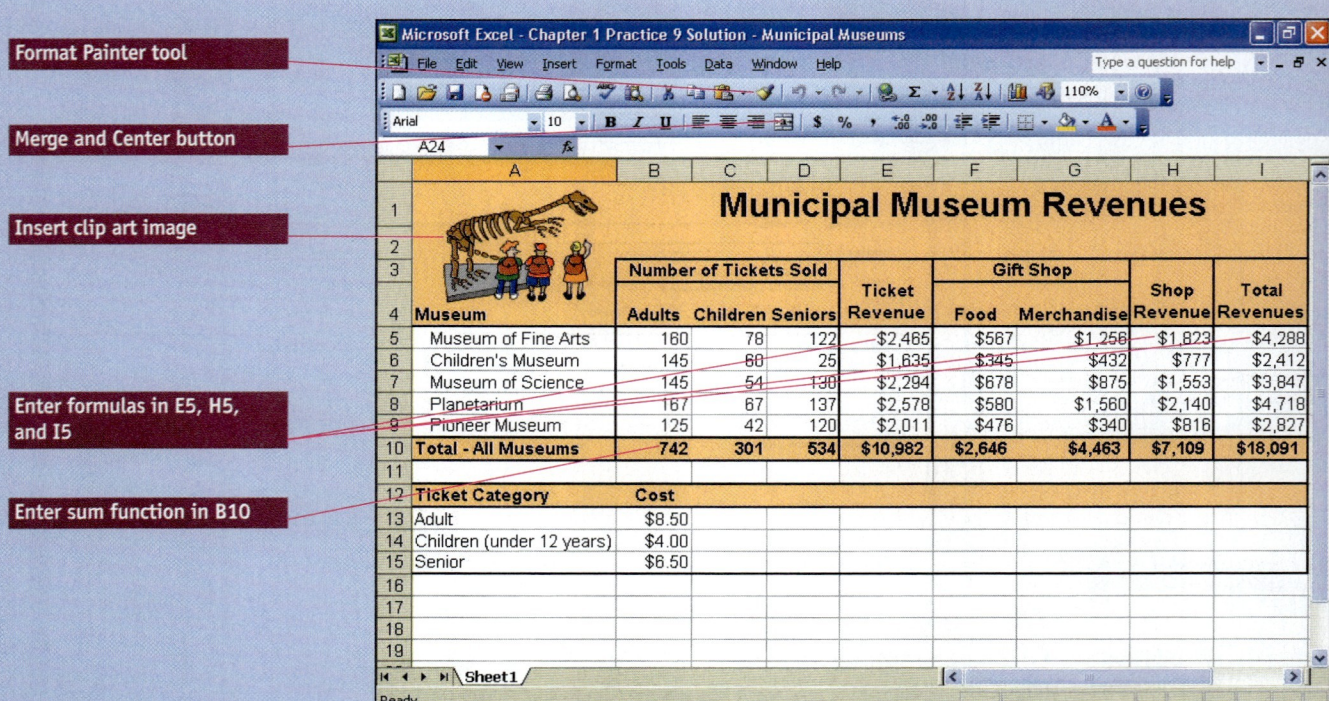

Figure 1.27 Municipal Museums (exercise 9)

MINI CASES

Online Study Guide

Every chapter in the Exploring Office series has an online component that helps you to review the conceptual material in the chapter. Go to www.prenhall.com/grauer after you have completed the chapter and click the icon for the Office 2003 book to go to the home page for this series. Click the appropriate title in the left pane—for example, Excel—then click the down arrow in the list box at the top of the screen to select the appropriate chapter, such as Excel Chapter 1. Click the link to online study guide in the left pane and take the quiz that consists of objective questions (multiple choice, true/false, and matching).

Click the "Submit Answers for Grading" button at the bottom of the quiz so that you can see your results. Scroll to the bottom of the answer screen, and then e-mail the results to yourself in HTML format. Print the e-mail message for your instructor.

The Cost of Smoking

Smoking is hazardous to your health as well as your pocketbook. A one-pack-a-day habit, at $3/pack, will cost you more than $1000 per year. For the same money you could buy 20 concert tickets at $50 each, or more than 500 gallons of gas at $2.00 per gallon. Open the partially completed *Chapter 1 Mini Case—Cost of Smoking* workbook and compute the number of various items that you could buy over the course of a year in lieu of cigarettes. We have entered approximate prices, but you need not use our numbers and/or you can substitute additional items of your own.

Accuracy Counts

The *Chapter 1 Mini Case—Accuracy Counts* workbook in the Exploring Excel folder was the last assignment completed by your predecessor prior to his unfortunate dismissal. The worksheet contains a significant error, which caused your company to underbid a contract and assume a subsequent loss of $100,000. As you look for the error, don't be distracted by the attractive formatting. The shading, lines, and other touches are nice, but accuracy is more important than anything else. Write a memo to your instructor describing the nature of the error. Include suggestions in the memo on how to avoid mistakes of this nature in the future.

Pizza Time

This mini case enables you to combine your knowledge of Excel with your love for pizza to determine the best buy at your local pizza place. Is it the personal pan pizza, an 8-inch pie cut into four slices for $6.99, or is it one of the larger pies at a higher price? Open the *Chapter 1 Mini Case—Pizza Time* workbook in the Exploring Excel folder and complete the indicated calculations to find out. The workbook contains information for the three sizes currently offered: the diameter of the pie, the price, and the number of slices.

Your assignment is to compute the cost per slice, the area of each pie in square inches, and the cost per square inch. Use the Excel function Pi() to compute the area of each pie, then divide the cost of the pie by its area to determine the cost per square inch. Add an appropriate clip art image to the completed worksheet, then format the worksheet in attractive fashion. Use the Page Setup command to add a custom footer with your name and today's date.

Planning for Disaster

This case has nothing to do with spreadsheets per se, but it is perhaps the most important case of all, as it deals with the question of backup. Do you have a backup strategy? Do you even know what a backup strategy is? You had better learn, because eventually you will wish you had one. You will erase a file, be unable to read from a floppy disk, or worse yet suffer a hardware failure in which you are unable to access the hard drive. The problem always seems to occur the night before an assignment is due. Describe in 250 or fewer words the backup strategy you plan to implement in conjunction with your work in this class.

mini cases

Chapter Recap—The Clark School

The Clark School has been severely impacted by a statewide cutback in funding for extracurricular activities. The school needs money badly and has settled on a door-to-door sale of food items by its students as the initial fund-raiser. The goal is to raise $5,000 for the purchase of new instruments for the music program. The plan is for students to present a catalog to their parents and other potential customers, who are asked to indicate their choices and provide immediate payment.

Melissa Edwards, the individual in charge of fund-raising, has settled on cookie dough as the featured product. Melissa has contracted with an organization that offers ten flavors of the dough, each in a two-pound tub that sells for $8.00 to $10.00 per tub. The school keeps a specified percentage of the selling price (50% in this instance) as profit. The students take the orders and collect the money. The organization delivers the cookie dough to the school, and the students deliver the cookie dough to their customers.

The principal has asked for a progress report midway through the fund-raiser. He wants to know whether the $5,000 goal has been met, and if not, how far the school is from meeting its goal.

Your assignment is to review the chapter, paying special attention to Hands-on Exercises 3 and 4, which describe how to create and format a spreadsheet. You will put yourself in Melissa's place and open the workbook, *Chapter 1 Ending Case Study—The Clark School*, which contains the sales data through day 15 of the fund-raiser. Your task is to complete the worksheet by adding the formulas to compute the profit to date, check the profit against the intended goal, and finally, format the spreadsheet in an attractive fashion for presentation to the principal. Print the completed worksheet to show both displayed values and cell formulas.

CHAPTER 2

Gaining Proficiency:
The Web and Business Applications

OBJECTIVES

After reading this chapter you will:

1. Gain proficiency in using relative and absolute references to create a worksheet.
2. Explain the importance of isolating assumptions in a worksheet.
3. Use the fill handle to copy a formula to adjacent cells.
4. Use pointing to enter a formula.
5. Insert a hyperlink into a worksheet.
6. Save a worksheet as a Web page, and then view the page in a Web browser.
7. Import data from a Web query into a workbook; refresh the query to obtain current information.
8. Describe the Today() function and its use in date arithmetic.
9. Describe the Time format; calculate the elapsed time between two values.

hands-on exercises

1. PAYROLL
   Input: Payroll
   Output: Payroll Solution

2. CREATING A WEB PAGE
   Input: Statement of Earnings
   Output: Statement of Earnings Solution (workbook and MHT document)

3. WEB QUERIES
   Input: Stock Portfolio
   Output: Stock Portfolio Solution

CASE STUDY
THE RELUCTANT ENTREPRENEUR

Ken Arnold was living the American dream until globalization and outsourcing disrupted his life. **Ken is happily married, he has a beautiful home, and** until recently he had a high-paying job at the local manufacturing plant. All of this changed one month ago, when Ken was laid off from the company where he had worked for 15 years. Ken's company offered a relocation package, but he does not want to move because his daughter is in high school and because his wife owns a thriving beauty shop. He has decided to make the best of a bad situation and go into business for himself.

Ken has always enjoyed landscaping and outdoor work. His home is a showplace, and through the years Ken has helped friends and family to design and implement tropical gardens. Now he needs to earn a living from his hobby. You are a close friend and have designed a worksheet for Ken that will compute the required hourly wage, based on the hours worked per week and the number of weeks worked per year, to achieve a desired income level. ∎

Your assignment is to read the chapter, paying special attention to the first hands-on exercise, which explains how to use relative and absolute references, and how to create a flexible worksheet by isolating the assumptions on which the worksheet is based. You will then open the partially completed *Chapter 2 Case Study—The Reluctant Entrepreneur* workbook and complete the worksheet.

Your task is to enter the appropriate formulas into the body of the worksheet so that you see the hourly wage necessary to achieve a desired level of income. Start with an initial income of $50,000 and use increments of $5,000 up to an annual income of $250,000. Create the worksheet to accommodate 40, 50, and 60-hour work weeks. (If you do the assignment correctly, you will see that Ken can earn $100,000 a year by charging $50, $40, and $33.33 an hour, respectively, for a 40, 50, and 60-hour work week.) Add a hyperlink at the top of the worksheet that points to a Web site offering tips for a small business. Format the worksheet in an attractive fashion, then print the completed worksheet for your instructor.

EMPLOYEE PAYROLL

This chapter introduces several new capabilities to increase your proficiency in Excel. We begin with pointing, which is a preferred way to enter a cell formula. We present the fill handle to facilitate copying a formula to other rows or columns within a worksheet. We introduce the Today() function and the use of date arithmetic. We also discuss the various Web capabilities that are built into Excel. You will learn how to add a hyperlink to a worksheet and how to save a worksheet as a Web page for viewing in a browser such as Internet Explorer or Netscape Navigator. You will also learn how to create a Web query to download information from the Web directly into an Excel worksheet.

The spreadsheet in Figure 2.1 shows how Excel can be used to compute a simple payroll. Figure 2.1a shows the displayed values and Figure 2.1b contains the underlying formulas. The concepts necessary to develop the spreadsheet were presented in the previous chapter. The intent here is to reinforce the earlier material, with emphasis on the use of **relative** and **absolute references** in the various cell formulas.

The calculation of an individual's gross pay depends on the employment practices of the organization. The formula used in the worksheet is simply an algebraic statement of how employees are paid, in this example, straight time for regular hours, and time-and-a-half for each hour of overtime. The first employee, Adams, earns $400 for 40 regular hours (40 hours at $10/hour) plus $60 for overtime (4 overtime hours $\times$ $10/hour $\times$ 1.5 for overtime). The formula to compute Adams's gross pay is entered into cell E2 as follows:

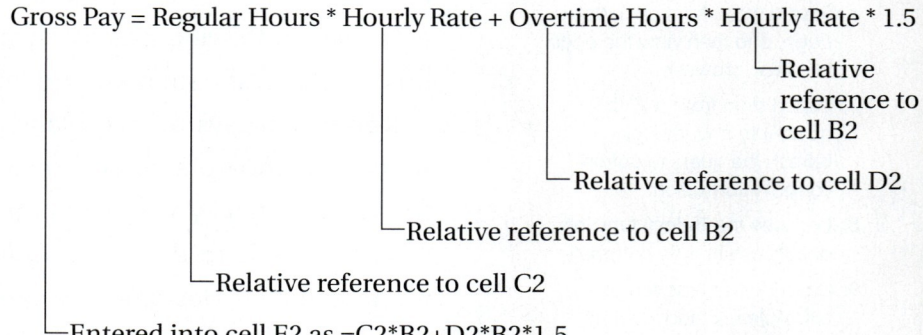

The cell references in the formula are relative references, which means that they will change when copied to another cell. Thus, you can copy the formula in cell E2 to the other rows in column E to compute the gross pay for the other employees. The formula in cell E3, for example, becomes =C3*B3+D3*B3*1.5, as can be seen from the displayed formulas in Figure 2.1b.

The withholding tax is computed by multiplying an individual's gross pay by the withholding tax rate. (This is an approximate calculation because the true withholding tax rate is implemented on a sliding scale; that is, the more an individual earns, the higher the tax rate. We use a uniform rate, however, to simplify the example.) The formula in cell F2 to compute the withholding tax uses a combination of relative and absolute references as follows:

Withholding Tax = Gross Pay * Withholding Rate
                                                                                                           Absolute reference to cell C11
                                                 Relative reference to cell E2
              Entered into cell F2 as =E2*$C$11

CHAPTER 2: GAINING PROFICIENCY

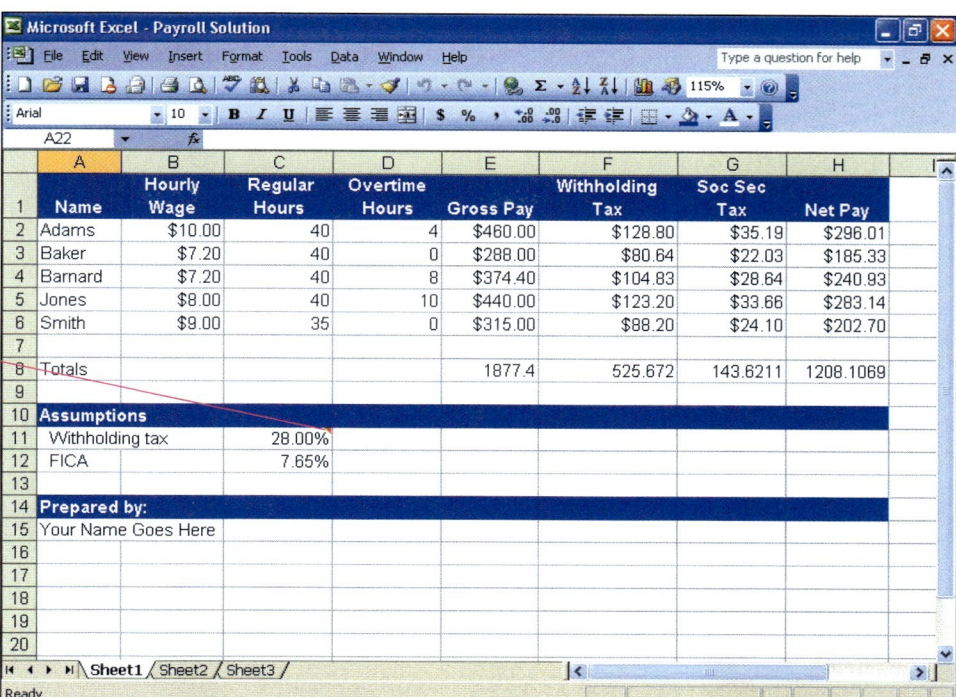

(a) Displayed Values

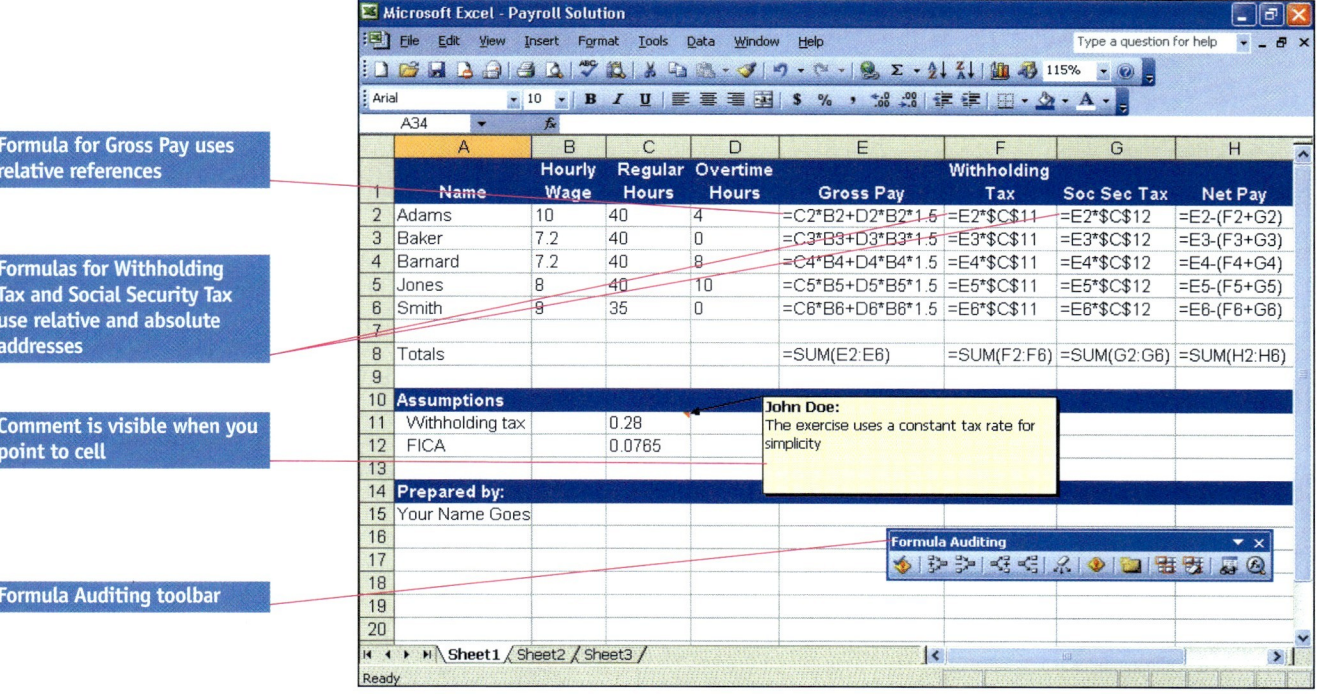

(b) Cell Formulas

FIGURE 2.1   Payroll

It is important to emphasize that the formula to compute the withholding tax contains an absolute reference to the tax rate (cell C11), as opposed to the actual constant (.28 in this example). The distinction may seem trivial, but most assuredly it is not, as two important objectives are achieved. First, the user sees those factors that affect the results of the spreadsheet in a separate assumption area (e.g., the withholding rate). Second, the user can change the value in one place, cell C11, then have the change automatically reflected in the calculations for all of the employees. The calculation of the employee's Social Security tax in cell G2 is performed in similar fashion and includes an absolute reference to cell C12.

The remaining formulas in the worksheet are also straightforward. An employee's net pay is computed by subtracting the deductions (the withholding tax and the Social Security tax) from the gross pay. Thus the net pay for the first employee is entered in cell H2 using the formula =E2–(F2+G2). The cell references are relative, which enables us to copy the formula to the remaining rows in column H, and thus calculate the net pay for the other employees.

The employee totals for gross pay, withholding tax, social security tax, and net pay are computed using the SUM function in the appropriate cells in row 8. The formula to compute the gross pay, =SUM(E2:E6), is entered into cell E8, after which it is copied to the remaining cells in row 8.

Pointing

Any cell reference can be entered into a formula by typing the address explicitly into a cell. Entering addresses in this way is not recommended, however, because it is all too easy to make a mistake, such as typing A40 when you really mean A41. **Pointing** to the cell is a more accurate method, since you use the mouse (or arrow keys) to select the cell directly when you build the formula. In essence you (1) Click in the cell that will contain the formula, (2) Type an equal sign to begin entering the formula, and (3) Click in the cell you want to reference. You then type any arithmetic operator, then continue pointing to additional cells using the steps we just described. And finally, you press the Enter key to complete the formula. It's easier than it sounds, and you get to practice in our next exercise.

The Fill Handle

There are several ways to copy the contents of a cell. You can use the Copy and Paste buttons on the Standard toolbar, the associated keyboard shortcuts, and/or the corresponding commands in the Edit menu. You can also use the ***fill handle,*** a tiny black square that appears in the lower-right corner of a selected cell. All you do is (1) Select the cell or cells to be copied, (2) Point to the fill handle for the selected cell(s), which changes the mouse pointer to a thin crosshair, (3) Click and drag the fill handle over the destination range, and (4) Release the mouse to complete the operation. (The fill handle can be used to copy only to adjacent cells.) Again, it's easier than it sounds, and as you may have guessed, it's time for our next hands-on exercise, in which you build the payroll worksheet in Figure 2.1.

Comments

The **Insert Comment command** creates the equivalent of a ScreenTip that displays information about the worksheet. Cell C11 in Figure 2.1a contains a tiny red triangle to indicate the presence of a comment, which appears as a ScreenTip when you point to the cell, as shown in Figure 2.1b. (An option can be set to display the comment permanently, but most people opt for just the triangle.) Comments may be subsequently edited, or deleted altogether if they are no longer appropriate.

hands-on exercise

1 Payroll

Objective Develop a spreadsheet for a simplified payroll to illustrate relative and absolute references. Use pointing to enter formulas and the fill handle to copy formulas. Use Figure 2.2 as a guide in the exercise.

Step 1: **Compute the Gross Pay**

- Start Excel. Open the **Payroll workbook** in the **Exploring Excel folder** to display the worksheet in Figure 2.2a.

- Save the workbook as **Payroll Solution** so that you may return to the original workbook if necessary.

- Click in **cell E2,** the cell that contains the gross pay for the first employee. Press the **equal sign** on the keyboard to begin pointing, click in **cell C2** (which produces a moving border around the cell), press the **Asterisk key**, then click in **cell B2**. You have entered the first part of the formula to compute an employee's gross pay.

- Press the **plus sign**, click in **cell D2**, press the **Asterisk**, click in **cell B2**, press the **Asterisk**, type **1.5**, then press **Enter**. You should see 460 as the displayed value for cell E2.

- Click in **cell E2**, then check to be sure that the formula you entered matches the formula in the formula bar in Figure 2.2a. If necessary, click in the formula bar and make the appropriate changes so that you have the correct formula in cell E2.

- Enter your name in cell A15. Save the workbook.

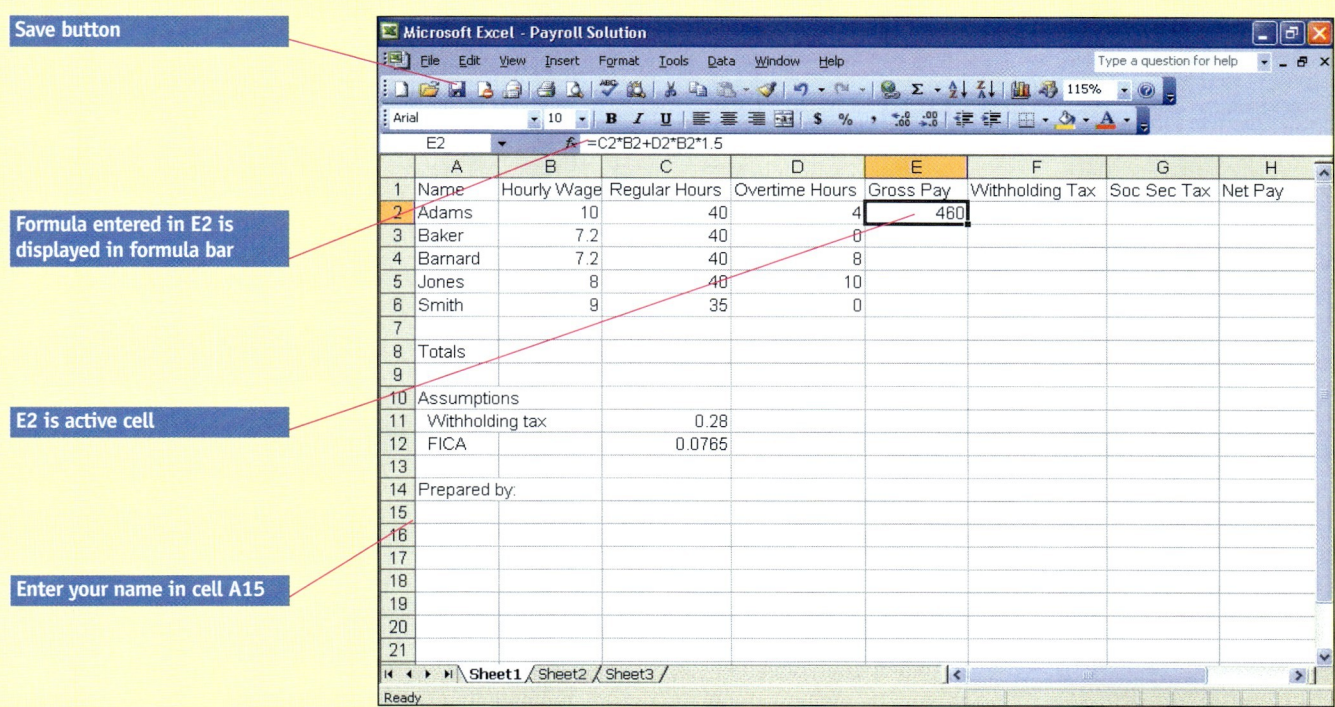

(a) Compute the Gross Pay (step 1)

FIGURE 2.2 Hands-on Exercise 1

Step 2: **Complete the Calculations**

- Click in **cell F2**, the cell that contains the withholding tax for the first employee. Press the **equal sign** on the keyboard to begin pointing, then click in **cell E2**, the cell that contains the employee's gross pay.
- Press the **Asterisk key**, then click in **cell C11**, the cell that contains the withholding tax. Cell F2 should now contain the formula, =E2*C11, but this is not quite correct.
- Check that the insertion point (the flashing vertical line) is within (or immediately behind) the reference to cell C11, then press the **F4 key** to change the cell reference to $C$11 as shown in Figure 2.2b.
- Press **Enter**. The displayed value in cell F2 should be 128.8, corresponding to the withholding tax for this employee.
- Use pointing to enter the remaining formulas for the first employee. Click in **cell G2**, then enter the formula **=E2*$C$12**. The displayed value is 35.19, corresponding to the Social Security Tax.
- Click in **cell H2**, and enter the formula **=E2−(F2+G2)**. The displayed value is 296.01, corresponding to the net pay for this individual.
- Save the workbook.

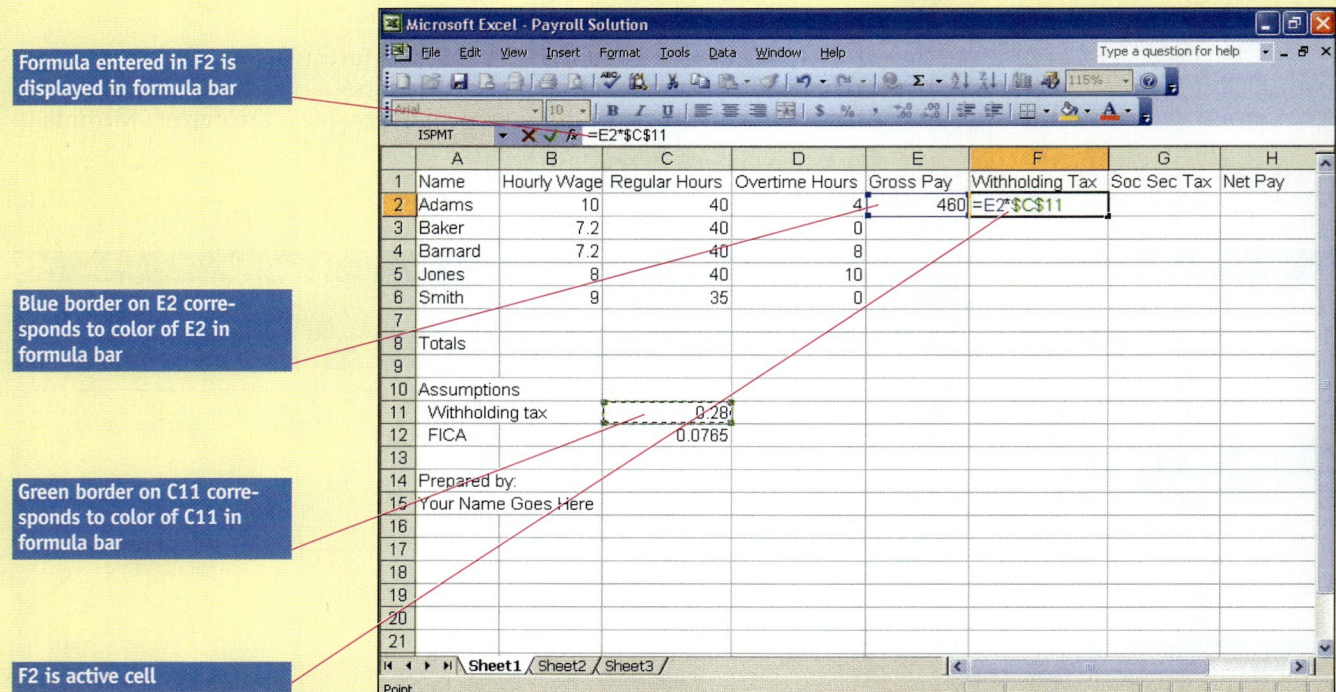

(b) Complete the Calculations (step 2)

FIGURE 2.2 Hands-on Exercise 1 (*continued*)

THE F4 KEY

The F4 key cycles through relative, absolute, and mixed references. Click on any reference within the formula bar; for example, click on A1 in the formula =A1+A2. Press the F4 key once, and it changes to an absolute reference. Press the F4 key a second time, and it becomes a mixed reference, A$1; press it again, and it is a different mixed reference, $A1. Press the F4 key a fourth time, and return to the original relative reference, A1.

Step 3: **Copy the Formulas**

- Click in **cell E2**, then click and drag to select **cells E2:H2**, as shown in Figure 2.2c. Point to the **fill handle** in the lower-right corner of cell H2. The mouse pointer changes to a thin crosshair.

- Drag the **fill handle** to cell H6 (the lower-right cell in the range of employee calculations). A dim border appears as you drag the fill handle as shown in Figure 2.2c.

- Release the mouse to complete the copy operation. The formulas for the first employee have been copied to the corresponding rows for the other employees.

- Click in **cell E3**, the cell containing the gross pay for the second employee. You should see the formula =C3*B3+D3*B3*1.5. Now click in **cell F3**, the cell containing the withholding tax for the second employee.

- You should see the formula =E3*$C$11, which contains a relative reference (cell E3) that is adjusted from one row to the next, and an absolute reference (cell $C$11) that remains constant from one employee to the next.

- Save the workbook.

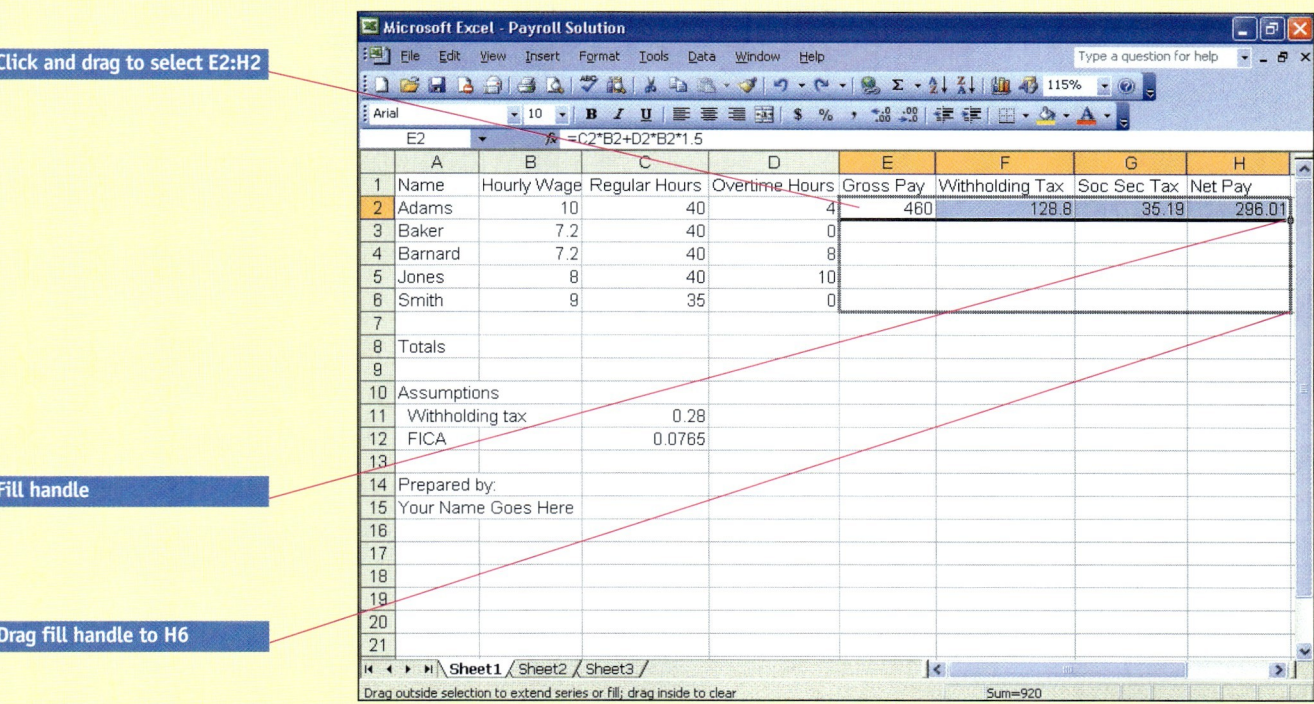

(c) Copy the Formulas (step 3)

FIGURE 2.2 Hands-on Exercise 1 (*continued*)

IT'S ONLY ALGEBRA

There are several ways to enter the formula to compute an employee's gross pay. You could, for example, factor out the hourly rate and enter the formula as =B3*(C3+D3*1.5). It doesn't matter how you enter the formula as long as the results are algebraically correct. What is important is the combination of relative and absolute references, so that the formula is copied correctly from one row to the next.

Step 4: Compute the Totals

- Click in **cell E8**, the cell that is to contain the total gross pay for all employees. Type the **=sign**, type **SUM(**, then click and drag over **cells E2** through **E6**.

- Type a **closing parenthesis**, and then press **Enter** to complete the formula. Cell E8 should display the value 1877.4. Now click in **cell E8** and you should see the function, =SUM(E2:E6).

- Click and drag the **fill handle** in cell E8 to the remaining cells in this row (cells F8 through H8). Release the mouse to complete the copy operation.

- You should see 1208.1069 in cell H8, corresponding to the total net pay for all employees. Click in **cell H8** to view the formula, =SUM(H2:H6), which results from the copy operation.

- Save the workbook.

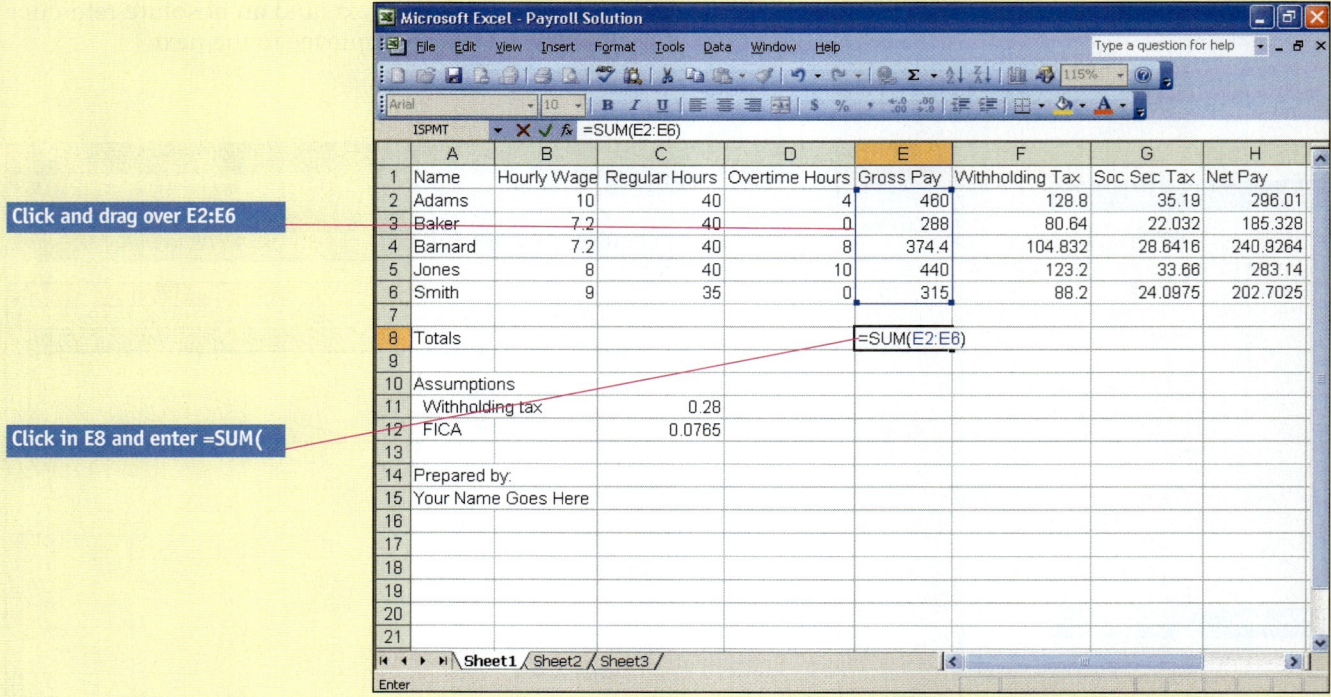

(d) Compute the Totals (step 4)

FIGURE 2.2 Hands-on Exercise 1 (*continued*)

FORMULAS VERSUS FUNCTIONS

There are in essence two ways to compute the total gross pay for all employees, using the SUM function, or the equivalent formula (e.g., =E2+E3+E4+E5+E6). The function is preferable for two reasons. First, it's easier to enter, and therefore less prone to error. Second, the function adjusts automatically to include any additional employees that will be entered within the cell range. Try inserting a new employee between the existing employees in rows 3 and 4, then observe how the values for this employee will be included automatically in the computed totals. The function also adjusts for deleted rows, whereas the formula does not.

Step 5: **Format the Spreadsheet**

- Click in **cell B2**, then click and drag to select **cells B2** through **B6**. Press and hold the **Ctrl key** as you click and drag to select cells **E2** through **H8** (in addition to the previously selected cells).

- Pull down the **Format menu** and click the **Cells command** to display the Format Cells dialog box in Figure 2.2e. Click the **Number tab** and choose **Currency** from the Category list box. Specify **2** as the number of decimal places.

- If necessary, choose the **$ sign** as the currency symbol. (Note, too, that you can select a variety of alternative symbols such as the British Pound or the Euro symbol for the European Community.) Click **OK** to accept the settings and close the dialog box.

- Click and drag to select **cells C11** and **C12**, then click the **Percent Style button** on the Formatting toolbar. Click the **Increase/Decrease Decimals buttons** to format each number to two decimal places.

- Save the workbook.

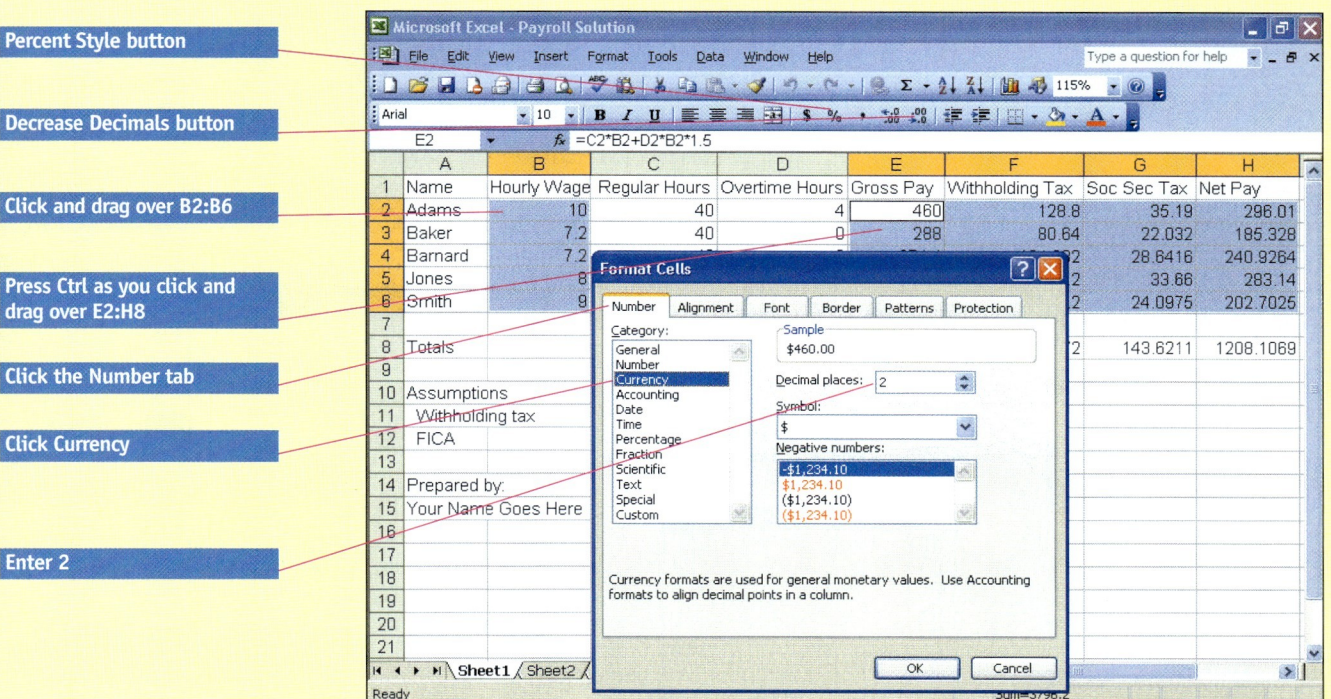

(e) Format the Spreadsheets (step 5)

FIGURE 2.2 Hands-on Exercise 1 (*continued*)

THE FORMAT STYLE COMMAND

A style is a collection of formats such as the font, alignment, and number of decimal places. Common styles, such as percent or currency, are represented by buttons on the Formatting toolbar and are most easily applied by clicking the appropriate tool. You can also apply the style by pulling down the Format menu, clicking the Style command, and selecting the style from the Style Name list box. The latter allows you to modify the definition of existing styles and/or to create a new style.

Step 6: Complete the Formatting

- Click and drag to select **cells A1** through **H1**. Press and hold the **Ctrl key**, then click and drag to select **cells A10** through **H10** in addition to the cells in row 1. Continue to press and hold the **Ctrl key**, then click and drag to select cells **A14** through **H14**.

- Click the **Fill Color arrow** on the Formatting toolbar, then select **blue** as the fill color. Click the **Font Color arrow** on the Formatting toolbar, then select **white** as the color for the text. Click the **Bold button** so that the text stands out from the fill color.

- Click and drag to select **cells A1** through **H1** (which also deselects the cells in rows 10 and 14). Click the **Right mouse button** to display a context-sensitive menu, then click the **Format Cells command** to display the dialog box in Figure 2.2f.

- Click the **Alignment tab,** then check the box to **Wrap text** in a cell. Click **OK** to accept the settings and close the dialog box.

- Click the **Center button** to center the text as well. Reduce the width of columns C and D. Save the workbook.

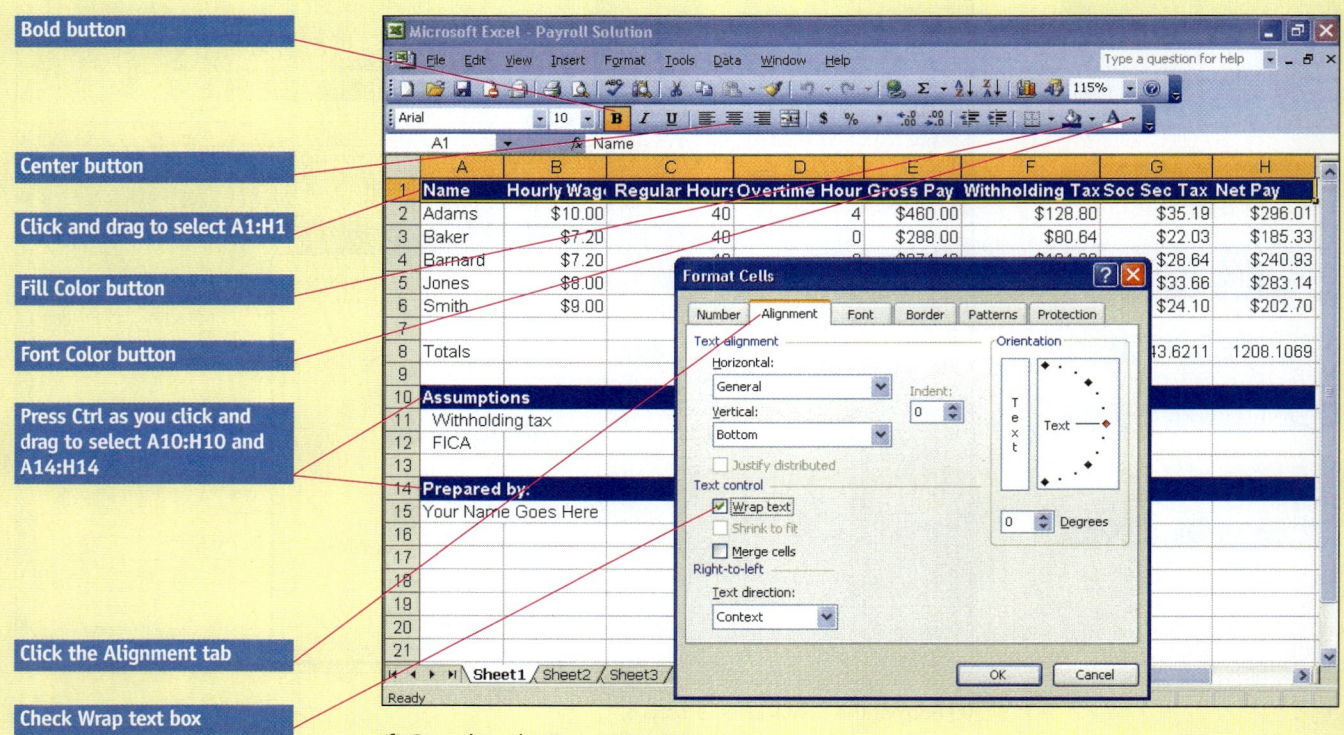

(f) Complete the Formatting (step 6)

FIGURE 2.2 Hands-on Exercise 1 (*continued*)

SORT THE EMPLOYEE LIST

The employees are listed on the worksheet in alphabetical order, but you can rearrange the list according to any other field, such as the net pay. Click a single cell containing employee data in the column on which you want to sort, then click the Sort Ascending or Sort Descending button on the Standard toolbar. Click the Undo button if the result is different from what you intended.

Step 7: **The Completed Workbook**

- Click in **cell C11**. Pull down the **Insert menu** and click **Comment**, then insert the text of the comment as shown in Figure 2.2g. (The name that appears in the comment box will be different on your system.)

- Click in any other cell when you have finished inserting the comment. The text of the comment is no longer visible, but you should still see the tiny triangle. Now point to cell C11 and you see the text of the comment.

- Pull down the **File menu** and click the **Page Setup command** to display the Page Setup dialog box. Click the **Page tab**. Click the **Landscape Option button**. Click the option to **Fit to 1 page**.

- Click the **Margins tab**. Check the box to center the worksheet horizontally. Click the **Sheet tab**. Check the boxes to print **Row and Column Headings** and **Gridlines.** Click **OK**. Print the worksheet.

- Save the workbook. Press **Ctrl+~** to show the cell formulas rather than the displayed values. Adjust the column widths as necessary, then print the worksheet a second time.

- Close the workbook. Exit Excel if you do not want to continue with the next exercise at this time.

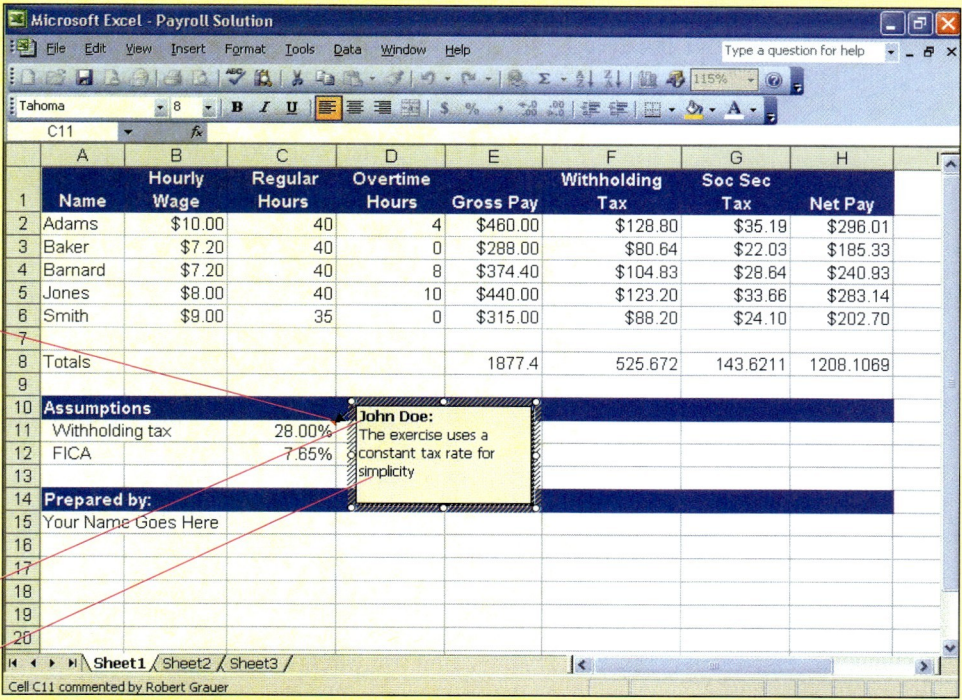

(g) The Completed Workbook (step 7)

FIGURE 2.2 Hands-on Exercise 1 (*continued*)

EDIT AND DELETE COMMENTS

Point to any cell that contains a comment, then click the right mouse button to display a context-sensitive menu with commands to edit or delete a comment. (The menu also contains the option to show or hide the comment.) The name that appears within the comment box corresponds to the user name set during installation. Pull down the Tools menu, click the Option command, click the General tab, then go to the User Name area to modify this information.

MICROSOFT OFFICE EXCEL 2003 REVISED 77

EXCEL AND THE INTERNET

The ***Internet*** is closely tied to Microsoft Excel through three basic capabilities. First, you can insert a ***hyperlink*** (a reference to another document) into any Excel worksheet, then view the associated document by clicking the link without having to start your Web browser manually. Second, you can save any Excel workbook as a ***Web page*** (or ***HTML document***), which in turn can be displayed through a Web browser. And finally, you can download information from a Web server directly into an Excel workbook through a ***Web query*** (a capability that we illustrate later in the chapter).

Consider, for example, Figure 2.3a, which contains an Excel worksheet that displays a consolidated statement of earnings for a hypothetical company. The information in this worksheet is typical of what companies publish in their annual report, a document that summarizes the financial performance of a corporation. Every public corporation is required by law to publish this type of information so that investors may evaluate the strength of the company. The annual report is mailed to the shareholders, and it is typically available online as well.

The worksheet in Figure 2.3a is easy to create, and you do not have to be a business major to understand the information. Indeed, if you have any intention of investing in the stock market, you should be able to analyze the data in the worksheet, which conveys basic information about the financial strength of a company to potential investors. In essence, the worksheet shows the sales for the company in the current year, subtracts the expenses to obtain the earnings before taxes, displays the income taxes that were paid, then arrives at the net earnings after taxes.

The worksheet also contains a calculation that divides the net earnings for the company by the number of shares to determine the earnings per share (a number that is viewed closely by investors). There is also comparable information for the previous year to show the increase or decrease for each item. And finally, the worksheet contains a hyperlink or reference to a specific Web site, such as the home page for the corporation. You can click the link from within Excel, and provided you have an Internet connection, your Web browser will display the associated page. Once you click the link, its color will change, just as it would if you were viewing the page in Netscape Navigator or Internet Explorer.

The Web page in Figure 2.3b is, for all intents and purposes, identical to the worksheet in Figure 2.3a. Look closely, however, and you will see that the Web page in Figure 2.3b is displayed in Internet Explorer, whereas the worksheet in Figure 2.3a is displayed in Microsoft Excel. The ***Save as Web Page command*** converts a worksheet to a Web page. The page can be uploaded to the Internet, but it can also be viewed from a PC or local area network, as was done in Figure 2.3b. Use the ***Web Page Preview command*** in the File menu to view the page, or open the page directly in your browser.

Our next exercise has you create the worksheet in Figure 2.3a, after which you create the Web document in Figure 2.3b. All applications in Microsoft Office incorporate a concept known as ***round trip HTML***, which means that you can subsequently edit the Web page in the application that created it originally. In other words, you start with an Excel worksheet, save it as a Web page, then you can open the Web page and return to Excel to edit the document.

SINGLE FILE WEB PAGES

Web documents are written in HTML or HyperText Markup Language. Microsoft Office 2003 also recognizes the Single File Web Page (MHTML) format, in which all of the elements of a Web page (text and graphics) are saved as a single file. The address bar of a Web browser displays the document name and extension, which may appear as htm (or html) or mht, depending on how the Web page was created initially.

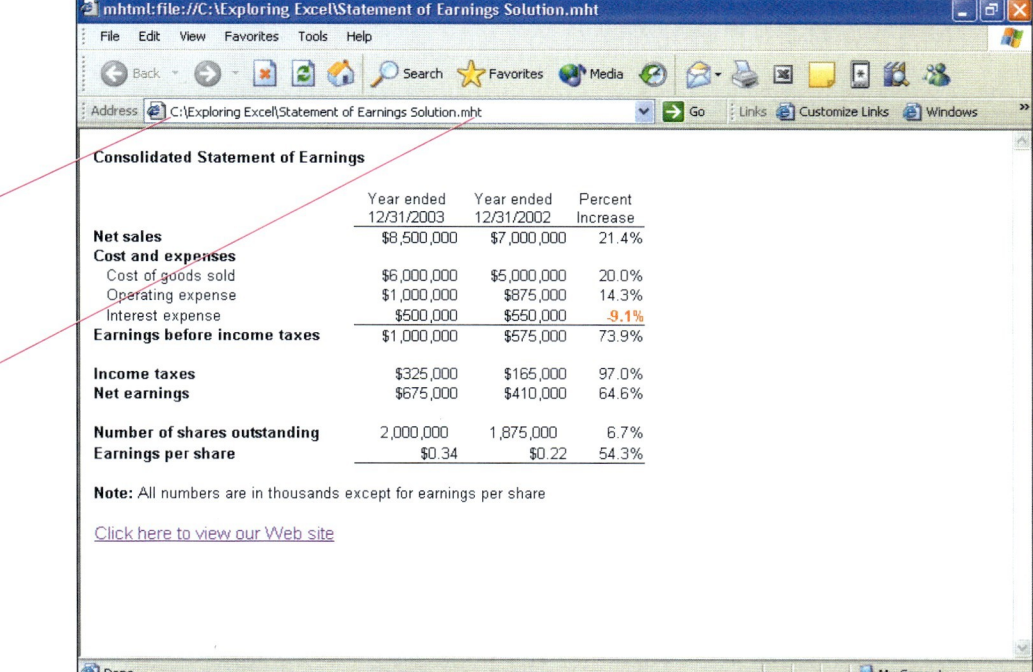

(a) Excel Worksheet

(b) Web Page

FIGURE 2.3 Consolidated Statement of Earnings

hands-on exercise 2

Creating a Web Page

Objective To insert a hyperlink into an Excel workbook; to save a workbook as an HTML document, then subsequently edit the Web page. Use Figure 2.4 as a guide in the exercise.

Step 1: **Compute the Net Earnings**

- Open the **Statement of Earnings workbook** in the **Exploring Excel folder**. Save the workbook as **Statement of Earnings Solution** so that you can always go back to the original workbook if necessary.

- We have entered the labels and data for you, but you have to create the formulas. Click in **cell B9**. Type an **equal sign**, then click in **cell B4** to begin the pointing operation.

- Type a **minus sign**, type **SUM(**, then click and drag to select **cells B6** through **B8** as shown in Figure 2.4a.

- Type a **closing parenthesis**, then press the **Enter key** to complete the formula. You should see 1000000 as the displayed value in cell B9.

- Click in **cell B12**, then use pointing to enter the formula for net earnings, **=B9–B11**.

- Click in **cell B15**, then use pointing to enter the formula for earnings per share, **=B12/B14**.

- Copy the formulas in cells B9, B12, and B15 to the corresponding cells in column C. You have to copy the formulas one at a time.

- Save the workbook.

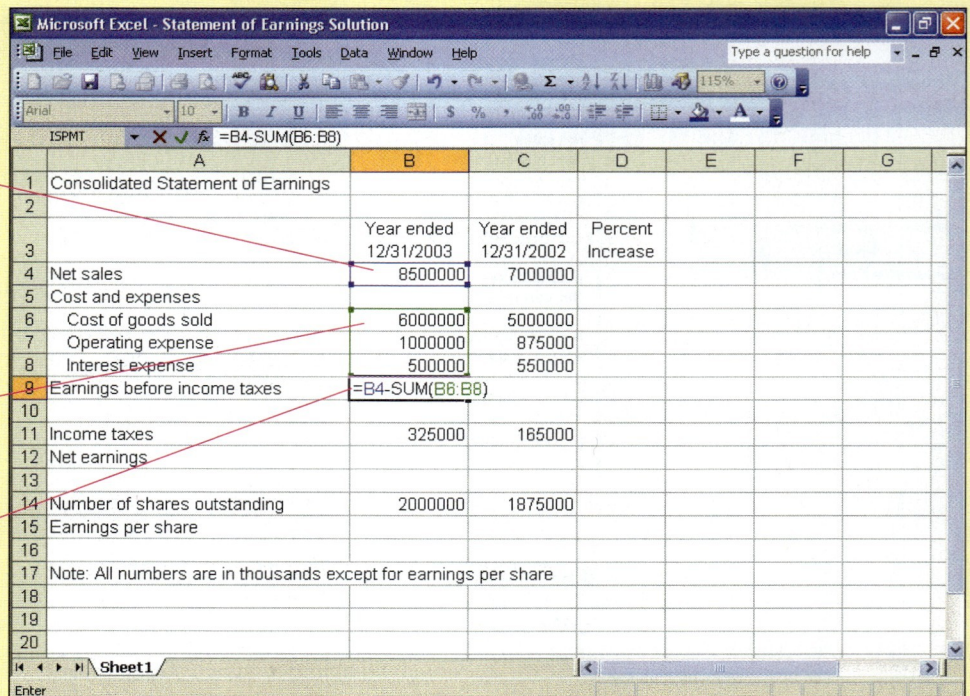

(a) Compute the Net Earnings (step 1)

FIGURE 2.4 Hands-on Exercise 2

Step 2: **Compute the Percent Increase**

- Click in **cell D4**, then enter the formula to compute the percent increase from the previous year. Use pointing to enter the formula, **=(B4-C4)/C4**.

- You should see .214286 as the displayed value in cell D4 as shown in Figure 2.4b. Do not worry about formatting at this time.

- Click in **cell D4**. Click the **Copy button** on the Standard toolbar (or use the **Ctrl+C** keyboard shortcut) to copy the contents of this cell to the clipboard. You should see a moving border around cell D4.

- Press and hold the **Ctrl key** to select **cells D6** through **D9**, **D11**, and **D12**, and **D14** and **D15** as shown in Figure 2.4b. (We have selected a noncontiguous range of cells, because we do not want to copy the formula to cells D10 or D13.)

- Click the **Paste button** on the Standard toolbar (or use the **Ctrl+V** keyboard shortcut) to paste the contents of cell D4 into these cells. Ignore the Paste Options button if it appears.

- Press the **Esc key** to remove the moving border around cell D4.

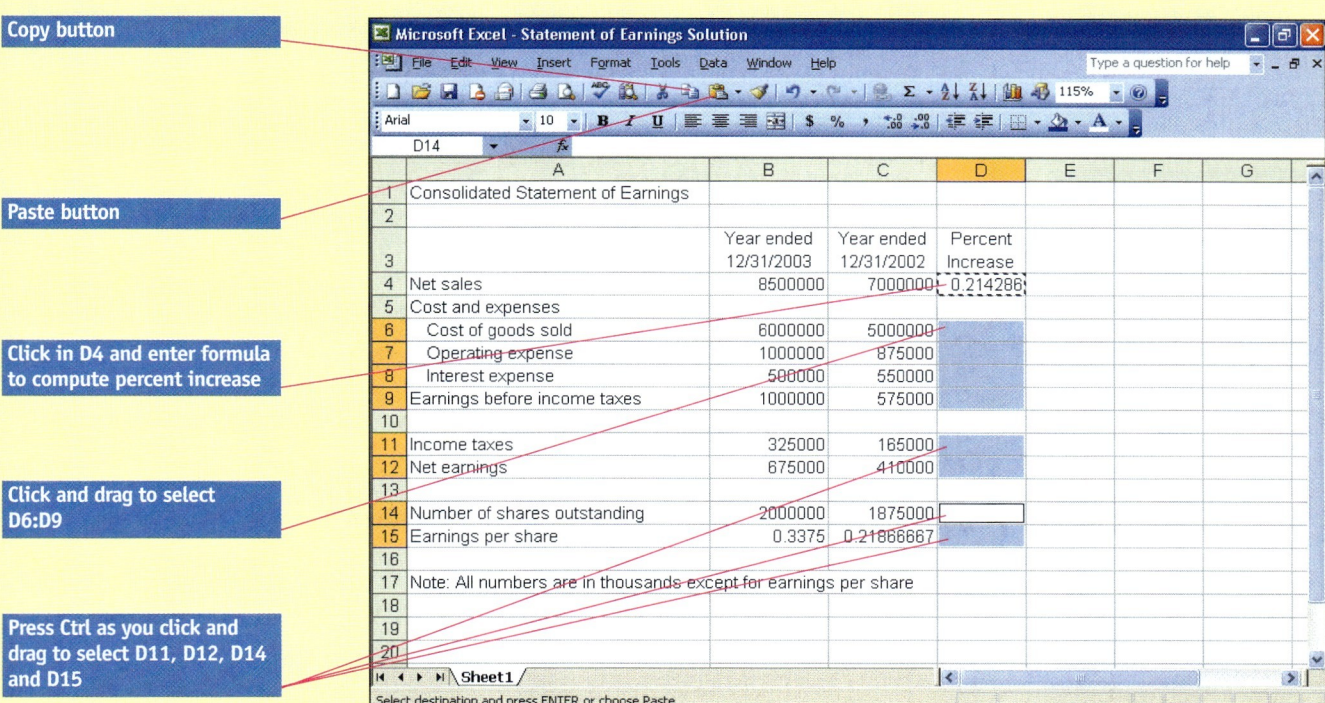

(b) Compute the Percent Increase (step 2)

FIGURE 2.4 Hands-on Exercise 2 (*continued*)

USE POINTING TO ENTER CELL FORMULAS

A cell reference can be typed directly into a formula, or it can be entered more easily through pointing. The latter is also more accurate as you use the mouse or arrow keys to reference cells directly. To use pointing, select (click) the cell to contain the formula, type an equal sign to begin entering the formula, click (or move to) the cell containing the reference, then press the F4 key as necessary to change from relative to absolute references. Type any arithmetic operator to place the cell reference in the formula, then continue pointing to additional cells. Press the Enter key to complete the formula.

Step 3: **Format the Worksheet**

- Format the worksheet as shown in Figure 2.4c. Click in **cell A1**, then press and hold the **Ctrl key** to select **cells A4**, **A5**, **A9**, **A11**, **A12**, **A14**, and **A15**. Click the **Bold button** on the Formatting toolbar (or use the **Ctrl+B** keyboard shortcut).

- Double click in **cell A17**, then click and drag over **Note:** within the cell to select this portion of the label. Press **Ctrl+B** to boldface the selected text.

- Remember that boldfacing the contents of a cell functions as a toggle switch; that is, click the Boldface button and the text is bold. Click the button a second time and the boldface is removed.

- Select **cells B3** through **D3**, **B8** through **D8**, and **B15** through **D15** as shown in Figure 2.4c. Click the **down arrow** on the Borders button on the Formatting toolbar to display the available borders. Click the bottom border icon to implement this formatting in the selected cells.

- Complete the formatting in the remainder of the worksheet by using currency, comma, and percent formats as appropriate. Save the workbook.

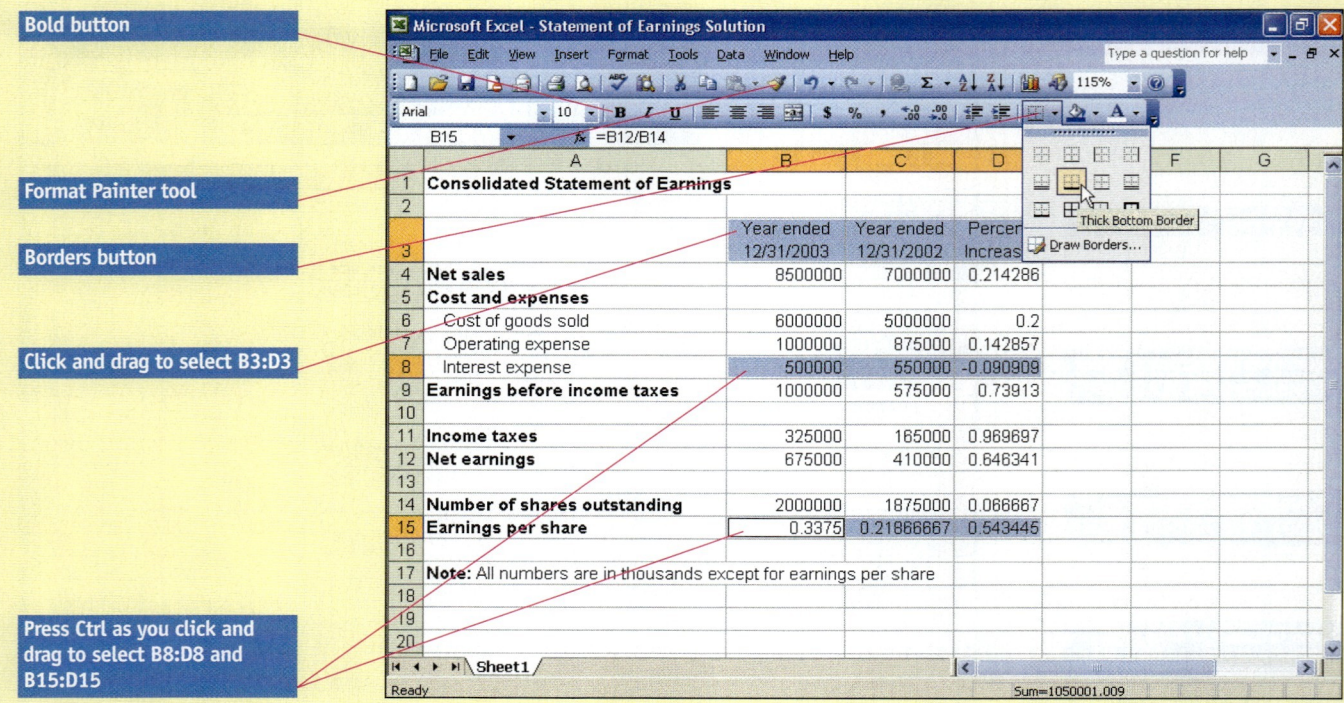

(c) Format the Worksheet (step 3)

FIGURE 2.4 Hands-on Exercise 2 (*continued*)

THE FORMAT PAINTER

The Format Painter copies the formatting of the selected cell to other cells in the worksheet. Click the cell whose formatting you want to copy, then double click the Format Painter button on the Standard toolbar. The mouse pointer changes to a paintbrush to indicate that you can copy the current formatting; just click and drag the paintbrush over the cells that you want to assume the formatting of the original cell. Repeat the painting process as often as necessary, then click the Format Painter button a second time to return to normal editing.

Step 4: **Conditional Formatting**

- Click and drag to select **cells D4** through **D15**, the cells that contain the percentage increase from the previous year.

- Pull down the **Format menu** and click the **Conditional Formatting command** to display the Conditional Formatting dialog box.

- Check that the Condition 1 list box displays Cell Value Is. Click the **down arrow** in the relationship list box and choose **less than**. Press **Tab** to move to the next list box and enter a **zero** as shown in Figure 2.4d.

- Click the **Format button** to display the Format Cells dialog box. Click the **Font tab**, click the **down arrow** on the Color list box and choose **Red**. Choose Bold as the Font style. Click **OK** to close the Format Cells dialog box.

- Click **OK** to close the Conditional Formatting dialog box. The decrease in the interest expense should be displayed in bold red as –9.1%.

- Save the workbook.

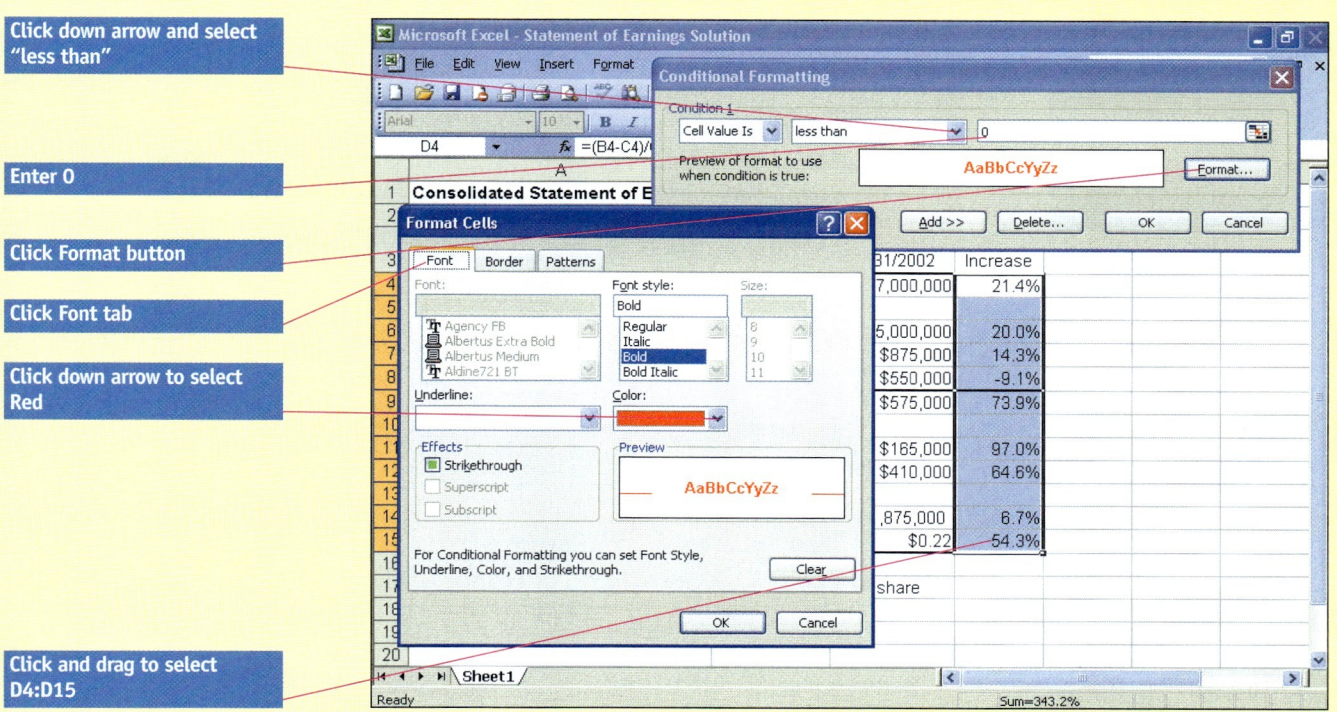

(d) Conditional Formatting (step 4)

FIGURE 2.4 Hands-on Exercise 2 (*continued*)

ADDING MULTIPLE CONDITIONS

Use the Conditional Formatting command to impose additional conditions with alternative formats depending on the value within a cell. You can, for example, display negative values in red (as was done in this example) and positive values (above a certain number) in blue. Pull down the Format menu and click the Conditional Formatting command, then click the Add button within the dialog box to add the additional conditions. Conditional formatting is a lesser-known feature that adds significantly to the appearance of a worksheet.

Step 5: **Insert the Hyperlink**

- Click in **cell A19**. Pull down the **Insert menu** and click the **Hyperlink command** (or click the **Insert Hyperlink button** on the Standard toolbar) to display the Insert Hyperlink dialog box in Figure 2.4e. Click in the **Text to display** text box and enter **Click here to view our Web site**.
- Click **Existing File or Web Page**, then click the button for **Browsed Pages**, then click in the Address text box (toward the bottom of the dialog box) and enter the Web address such as **www.prenhall.com/grauer** (the http:// is assumed). Click **OK** to accept the settings and close the dialog box.
- The hyperlink should appear as an underlined entry in the worksheet. Point to the hyperlink (the Web address should appear as a ScreenTip), then click the link to start your browser and view the Web page. You need an Internet connection to see the actual page.
- You are now running two applications, Excel and the Web browser, each of which has its own button on the Windows taskbar. Click the **Excel button** to continue working (and correct the hyperlink if necessary).
- Save the workbook.

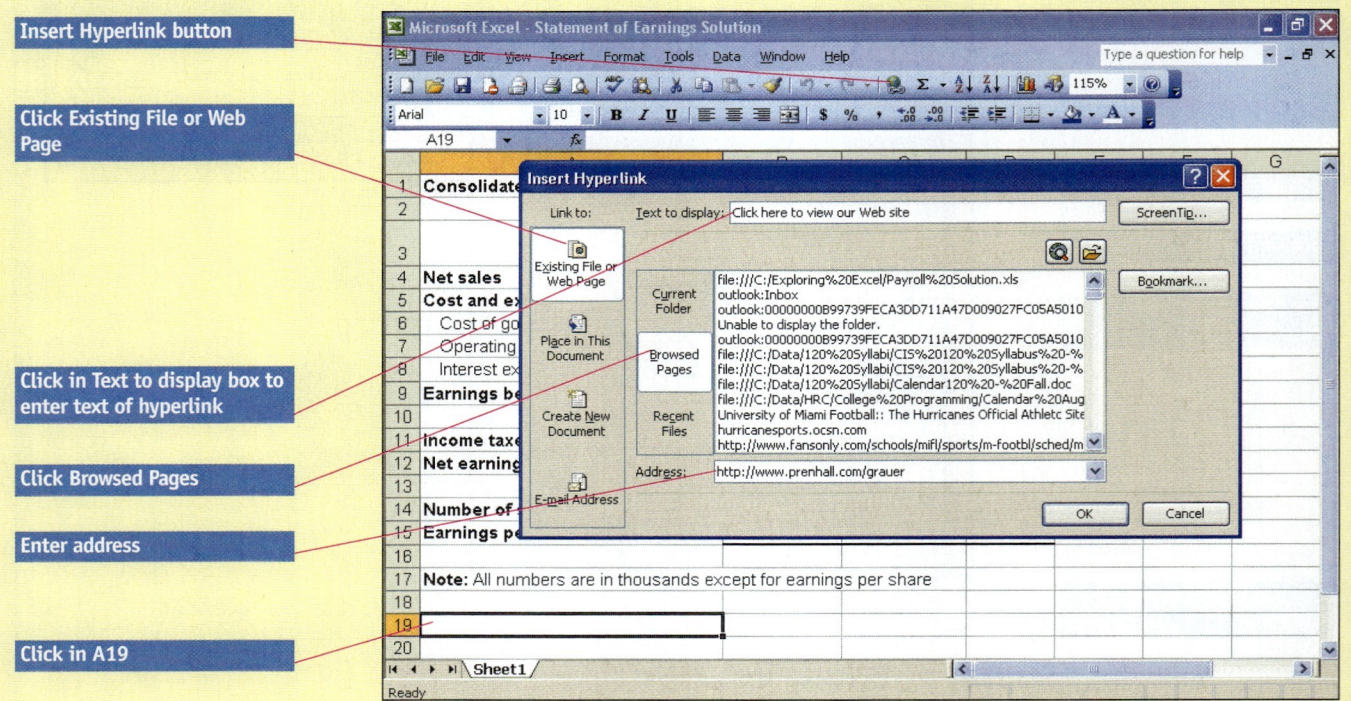

(e) Insert the Hyperlink (step 5)

FIGURE 2.4 Hands-on Exercise 2 (*continued*)

SELECTING (EDITING) A HYPERLINK

In an ideal world you will enter all the information for a hyperlink correctly on the first attempt. But what if you make a mistake and need to edit the information? You cannot select a hyperlink by clicking it, because that displays the associated Web page. You can, however, right click the cell containing the hyperlink to display a context-sensitive menu, then click the Edit Hyperlink command to display the associated dialog box in which to make the necessary changes. (The menu also enables you to remove the hyperlink.)

Step 6: **Save the Web Page**

- Pull down the **File menu** and click the **Save as Web Page command** to display the Save As dialog box in Figure 2.4f. Note the following:
  - The **Exploring Excel folder** is entered automatically as the default folder, since that is the location of the original workbook.
  - **Statement of Earnings Solution** is entered automatically as the name of the Web page, corresponding to the name of the workbook, Statement of Earnings Solution.
  - The default file type is **Single File Web Page**, as opposed to HTML.
  - It does not matter whether you save the entire workbook or a single sheet, since the workbook contains only a single sheet. However, you need to specify a single sheet if and when you want to add interactivity (i.e., Excel functionality) when the page is opened through a Web browser.

- Click the **Save button**. There are now two versions of the workbook on disk, both with the same name (Statement of Earnings Solution), but with different extensions, corresponding to a Web page and Excel workbook.

- Close Microsoft Excel. (We will restart the application later in the exercise.)

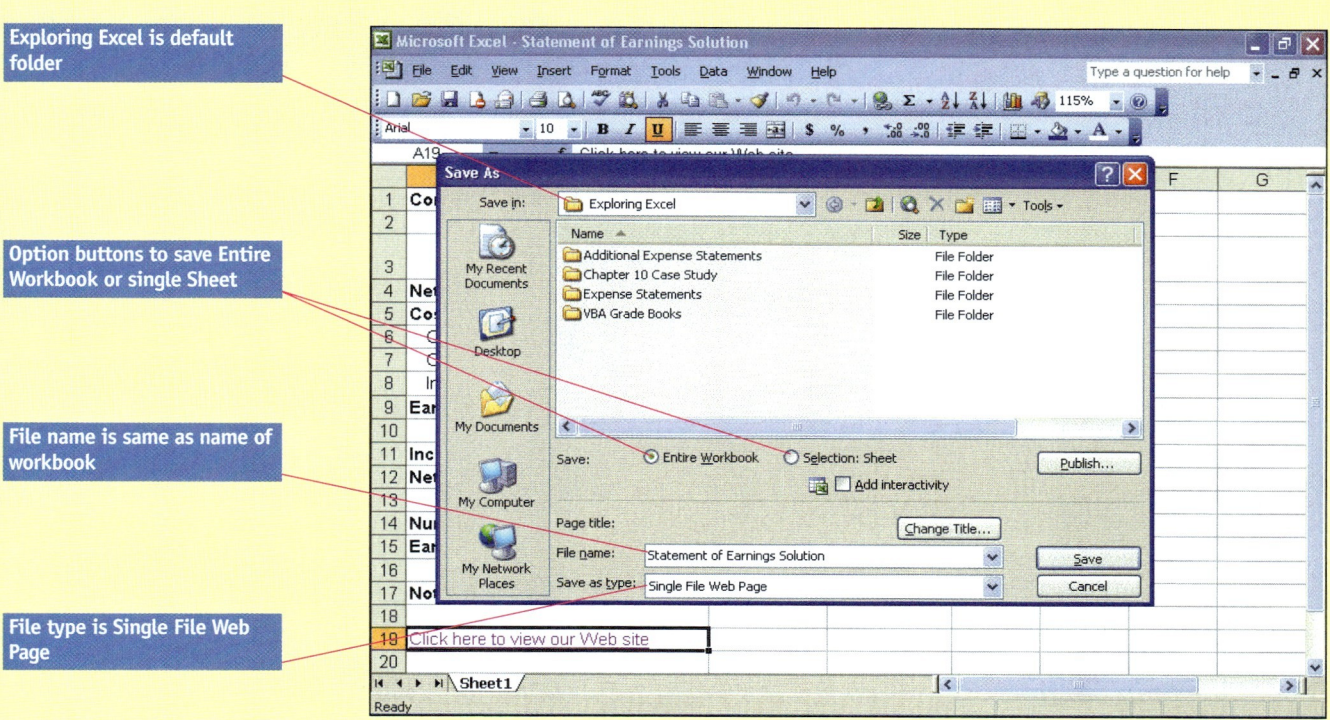

(f) Save the Web Page (step 6)

FIGURE 2.4 Hands-on Exercise 2 (*continued*)

CHANGE THE DEFAULT FILE LOCATION

The default file location is the folder Excel uses to open and save a workbook unless it is otherwise instructed. To change the default location, pull down the Tools menu, click Options, and click the General tab. Enter the name of the new folder (e.g., C:\Exploring Excel) in the Default File Location text box, then click OK. The next time you access the Open or Save command from the File menu, the Look In text box will reflect the change.

Step 7: **Start Windows Explorer**

- Click the **Start button,** start **Windows Explorer**, then change to the Exploring Excel folder. The location of this folder depends on whether you have your own computer.
  - If you are working from a floppy disk, select drive A in the left pane.
  - If you are working on your own computer, expand drive C in the left pane, then scroll until you can select the Exploring Excel folder.
- Either way, you should see the contents of the Exploring Excel folder in the right pane as shown in Figure 2.4g. As indicated, there are two versions of the Statement of Earnings Solution with different icons and file types.
- Right click the file with the Excel icon and file type to display a shortcut menu, then click the **Delete command** to delete this file. You do not need the Excel workbook any longer because you can edit the workbook from the Web page through the concept of round trip HTML.
- Double click the Web page version of the earnings statement to view the document in your default browser.

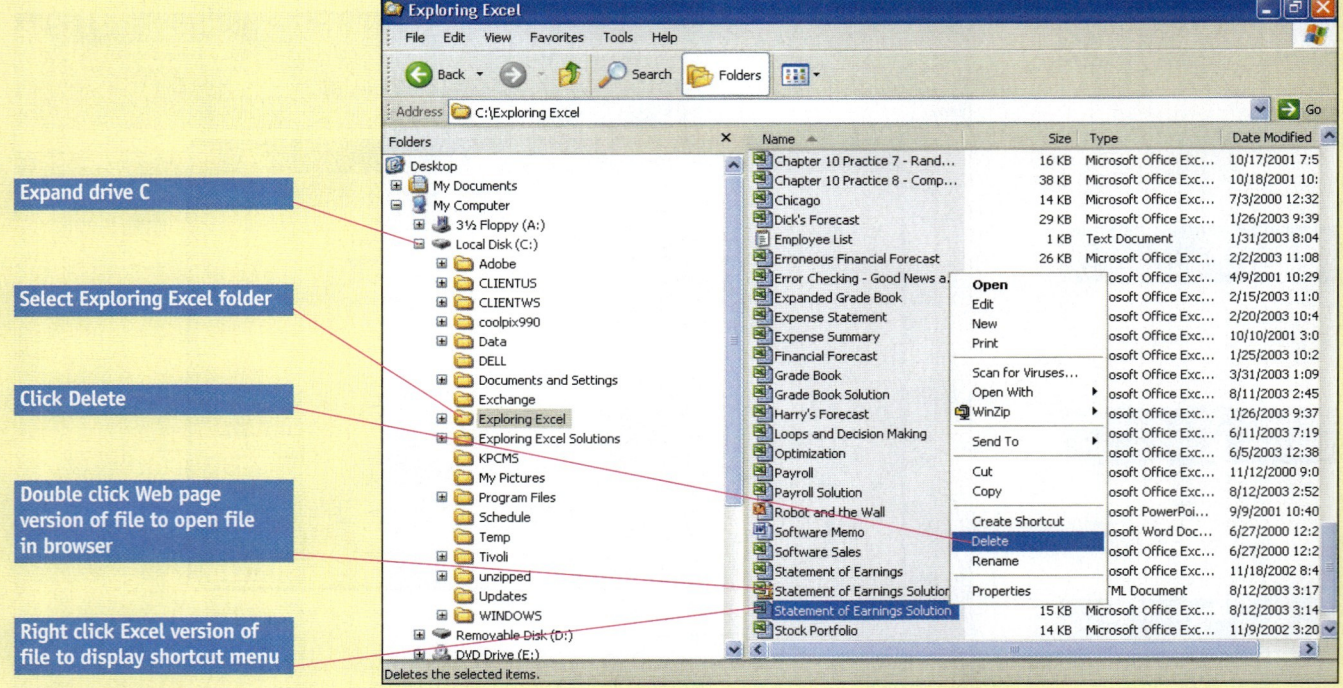

(g) Start Windows Explorer (step 7)

FIGURE 2.4   Hands-on Exercise 2 (*continued*)

ROUND TRIP HTML

Each application in Microsoft Office lets you open an HTML document in both Internet Explorer and the application that created the Web page initially. In other words, you can start with an Excel worksheet and use the Save as Web Page command to convert the document to a Web page, then view that page in a Web browser. You can then reopen the Web page in Excel (the application that created it initially) with full access to all Excel commands in order to edit the document.

Step 8: **View the Web Page**

- You should see the Statement of Earnings Solution displayed within Internet Explorer (or Netscape Navigator) as shown in Figure 2.4h. The Web page looks identical to the worksheet that was displayed earlier in Excel.

- Click the hyperlink that was inserted through the Insert Hyperlink command to view the Web site. You should see our Web site (**www.prenhall.com/grauer**), if that was the address you used earlier.

- Click the **Back button** on the Standard Buttons toolbar to return to the Statement of Earnings Solution Web page. Look carefully at the Address bar and note that unlike other Web documents, this page is displayed from your local system (drive C or drive A), depending on the location of the file.

- Click the **Edit with Microsoft Excel button** on the Standard Buttons toolbar to start Excel in order to modify the Web page.

- Both applications, Internet Explorer and Microsoft Excel, are open as can be seen by the taskbar, which contains buttons for both.

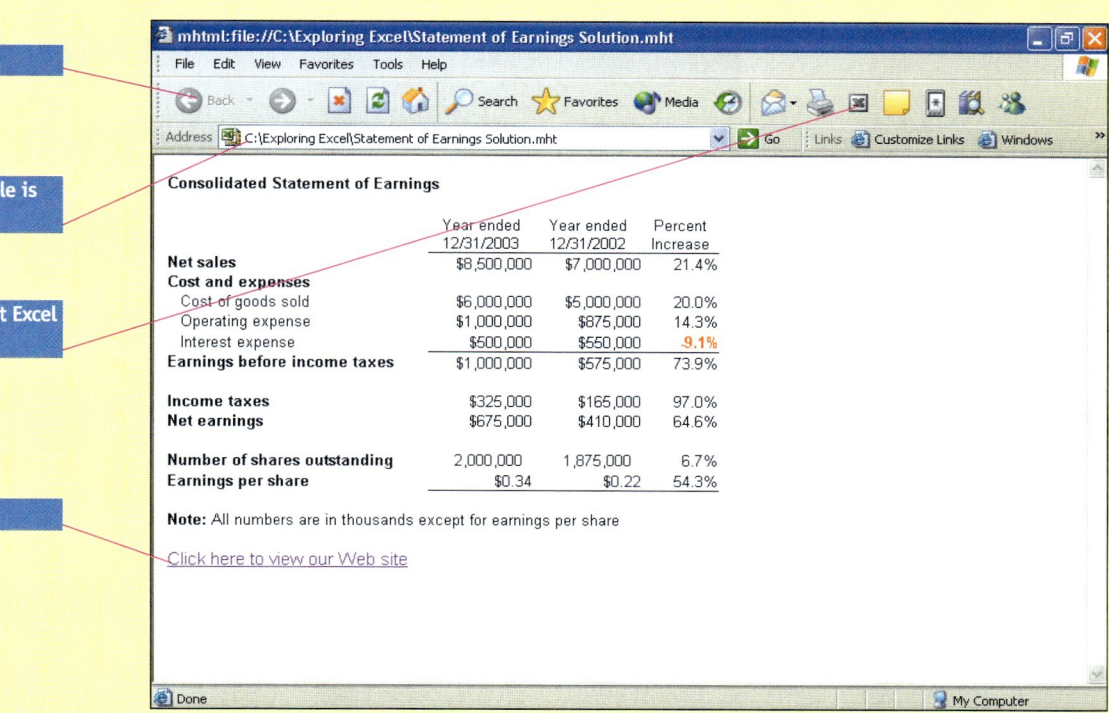

(h) View the Web Page (step 8)

FIGURE 2.4 Hands-on Exercise 2 (*continued*)

MULTITASKING

Multitasking, the ability to run multiple applications at the same time, is one of the primary advantages of the Windows environment. Minimizing an application is different from closing it, and you want to minimize, rather than close, an application to take advantage of multitasking. Closing an application removes it from memory so that you have to restart the application if you want to return to it later in the session. Minimizing, however, leaves the application open in memory, but shrinks its window to a button on the Windows taskbar.

Step 9: **Edit the Web Page**

- You should be back in Microsoft Excel as shown in Figure 2.4i. Click in **cell A21** and enter the label, **Prepared by**, followed by your name.
- Save the worksheet.
- Click the **Internet Explorer button** on the taskbar to return to your browser. The change you made (the addition of your name) is not yet visible because the browser displays the previous version of the page.
- Click the **Refresh button** on the Standard Buttons toolbar to bring in the most current version of the worksheet. Your changes should now be visible. (You may, however, have to close, then reopen Internet Explorer to see the change.)
- Pull down the **File menu** (within Internet Explorer) and click the **Print command,** then click the **Print command button** to print the Web page for your instructor.
- Close Internet Explorer. Exit Excel if you do not wish to continue with the next exercise at this time.

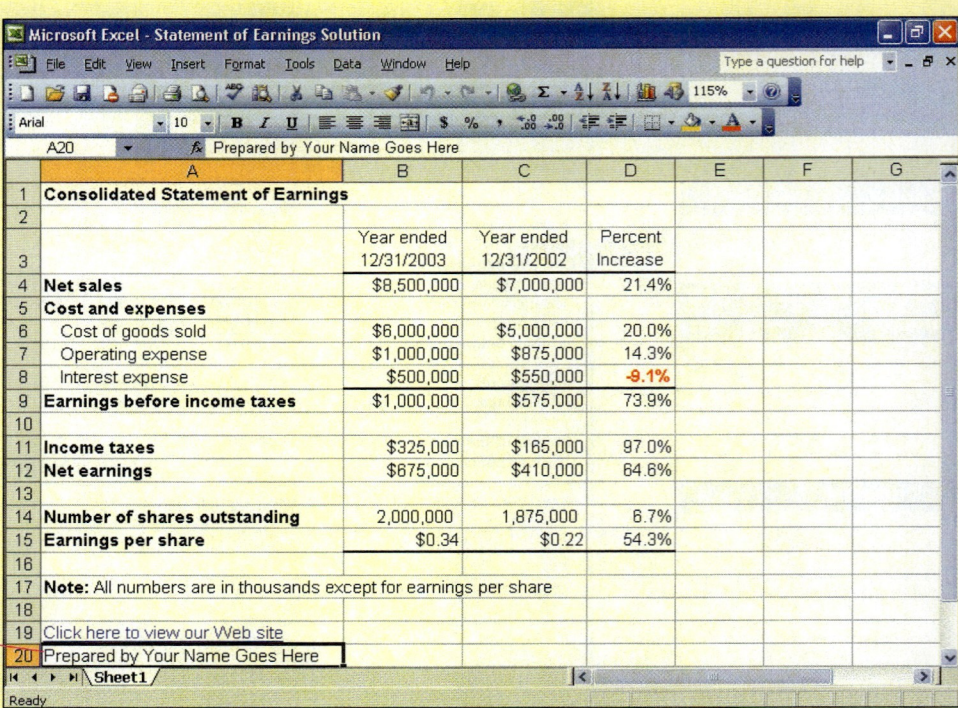

Click in A21 and enter your name

(i) Edit the Web Page (step 9)

FIGURE 2.4 Hands-on Exercise 2 (*continued*)

USE A TEMPLATE

A template is a partially completed workbook that is used to create other workbooks. It typically contains formulas and formatting but no specific data. Thus you open a template and enter the information that is specific to your application, then you save the template as an ordinary workbook. Excel provides several business templates.

WEB QUERIES

Our next example is a worksheet to maintain a stock portfolio and compute the gain or loss associated with investment. The worksheet in Figure 2.5 lists several stocks, each with its recognized symbol, and records the purchase price, number of shares, and date of purchase of each investment. This information is "fixed" for each stock at the time of purchase. The worksheet then uses the current (today's) price to determine the gain or loss. It also uses today's date to compute the length of time the investment was held. The interesting thing about the worksheet is that the current price is obtained via a **Web query**, a capability that enables Excel to go to a specific site on the Web to retrieve the information. The worksheet is time sensitive, and thus the values you see on your computer will be different from those in Figure 2.5.

The top half of the worksheet is typical of the worksheets we have studied thus far. The bottom portion (from row 14 down) represents the result of the Web query, which is entered into the worksheet via the **Import External Data command**. Execution of this command prompts you for the location of the result (e.g., cell A14 in Figure 2.5) and the location of the parameters (or stock symbols), for which you want to determine the price (cells A5 through A10 in this example). Excel does the rest and places the results of the query into the worksheet. The results of the query can be continually updated through the **Refresh command**, which is represented by the Exclamation Point button on the **External Data toolbar**.

The worksheet in Figure 2.5 also illustrates the use of *date arithmetic* to determine the length of time an investment is held. (This is an important consideration for investors who can reduce their tax liability through a capital gains tax break on investments held for more than one year.) Date arithmetic is made possible through a simple concept by which Excel stores all dates as integers (serial numbers) beginning with January 1, 1900. Thus, January 1, 1900 is stored as the number 1, January 2, 1900 as the number 2, and so on.

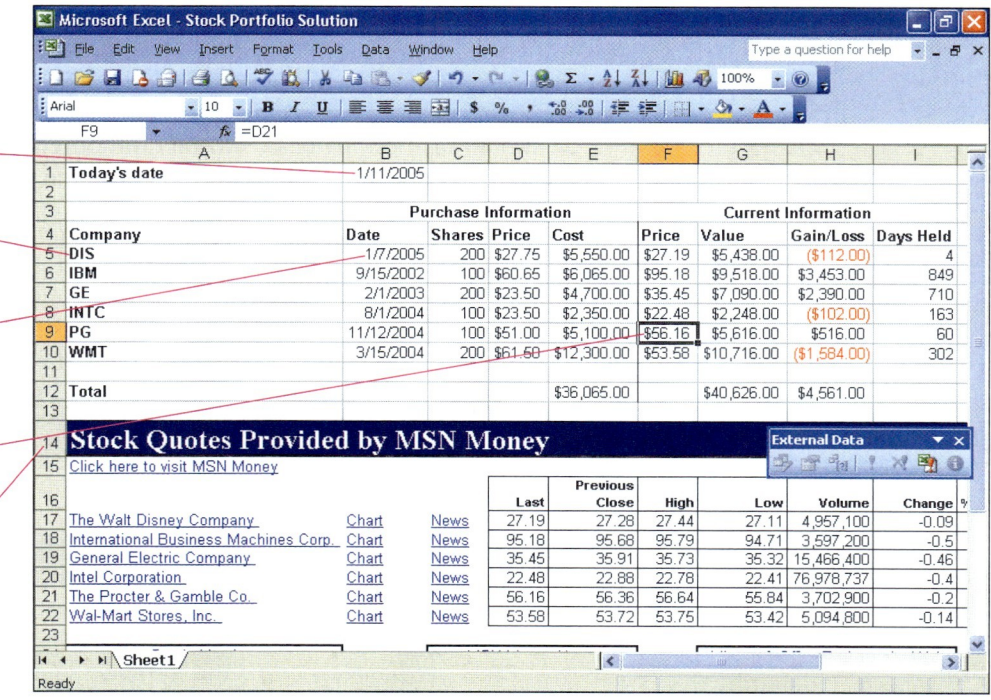

(a) The Excel Worksheet

FIGURE 2.5 Web Queries

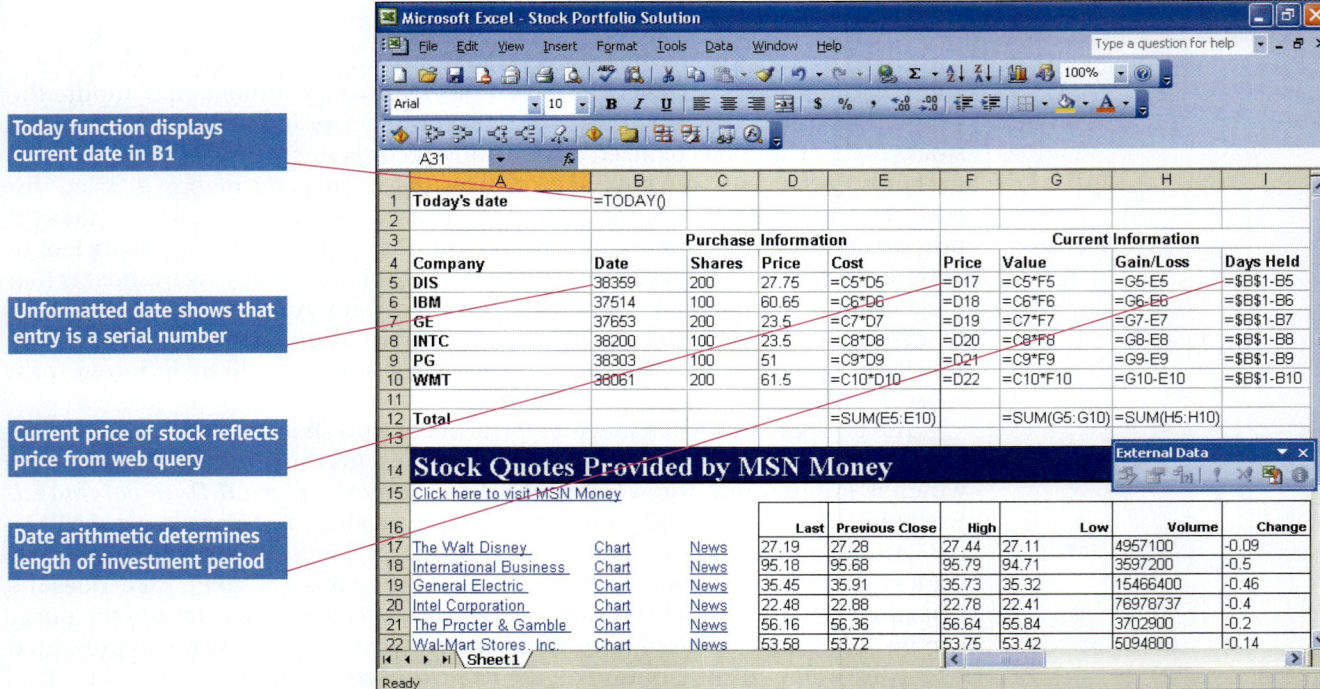

(b) Cell Formulas

FIGURE 2.5   Web Queries (*continued*)

The ***Today( ) function*** returns the current date (i.e., the date on which the spreadsheet is opened). If, for example, you entered the Today( ) function into a spreadsheet that was created on May 14, and you opened the spreadsheet a month later, the value of the function would be automatically updated to June 14. The fact that dates are stored as integers enables you to add or subtract two different dates and/or to use a date in any type of arithmetic computation. A person's age can be computed by subtracting the date of birth from today's date, and dividing the result by 365.

In similar fashion, you can subtract the purchase date of an investment from today's date to determine the number of days the investment was held. Look now at the formula in cell I5 of Figure 2.5b, which subtracts the date of purchase (cell B5) from an absolute reference to today's date (cell B1) to compute the length of the investment. The formula in cell I5 (=$B$1–B5) can then be copied to the remaining rows in column I to determine the length of each investment.

A date is entered in different ways, most easily by typing the date in conventional fashion such as 12/31/99 or 12/31/1999. If you specify a two-digit year, then any year from 00 to 29, is assumed to be in the 21st century; for example, 1/21/00, will be stored as January 21, 2000. (The number 29 is arbitrary, and you will have to ask Microsoft why it was chosen.) To avoid confusion, you should enter all four digits of the year—for example, 10/31/2001 for October 31, 2001.

YOU MUST UNDERSTAND THE PROBLEM

The formulas to compute the cost of an investment, its current value, the associated gain or loss, and the number of days the investment was held have nothing to do with Excel per se. Neither did the formulas to compute the gross pay, net pay, and so on in the payroll example. In other words, Excel is a means to an end, rather than an end unto itself, and you must understand the underlying problem.

The Time Format

Excel enables you to work with time as well as with dates as illustrated in Figure 2.6, which depicts the "billable hours" for an attorney. Each row in the worksheet records the date, the activity, the client, the time started, the time ended, and the hours worked. The figure displays two different views of the workbook, with displayed values in the upper window and cell formulas in the lower window.

Just as dates are internally stored as serial numbers, times are stored internally as decimal fractions, from 0 to .9999. Midnight (12:00 AM) is stored as 0. Noon (12:00 PM) is stored as 0.5 as it represents half a day. In similar fashion, 6:00 AM and 6:00 PM are stored as .25 and .75, respectively. 11:59:59 PM (one second before midnight) is stored as .9999. To enter time into a worksheet, type the time (hours:minutes), type a space, then type either "a" or "p" for AM or PM, respectively. (You can also use military time, for example, 15:00 for 3:00 PM).

To calculate the elapsed time between two values, subtract the starting time from the ending time. The result is the fraction of a day that has elapsed, which is then converted to the elapsed time in hours by multiplying by 24. It's easier than it sounds when you consider a specific example, such as row 7 in Figure 2.6, where we calculate the hours spent on researching a brief. The attorney began at 3:00 PM and finished at 6:00 PM. He (she) spent three hours on this activity. The corresponding cell formulas are in the lower window. We see that 3:00 PM and 6:00 PM are stored as .625 and .75, respectively. (3:00 PM is 15 hours after midnight, which is equivalent to 15/24 or .625. In similar fashion 6:00 PM is equivalent to .75.) The difference between the starting time and ending time is .125 of a day or 3 hours (.125 * 24).

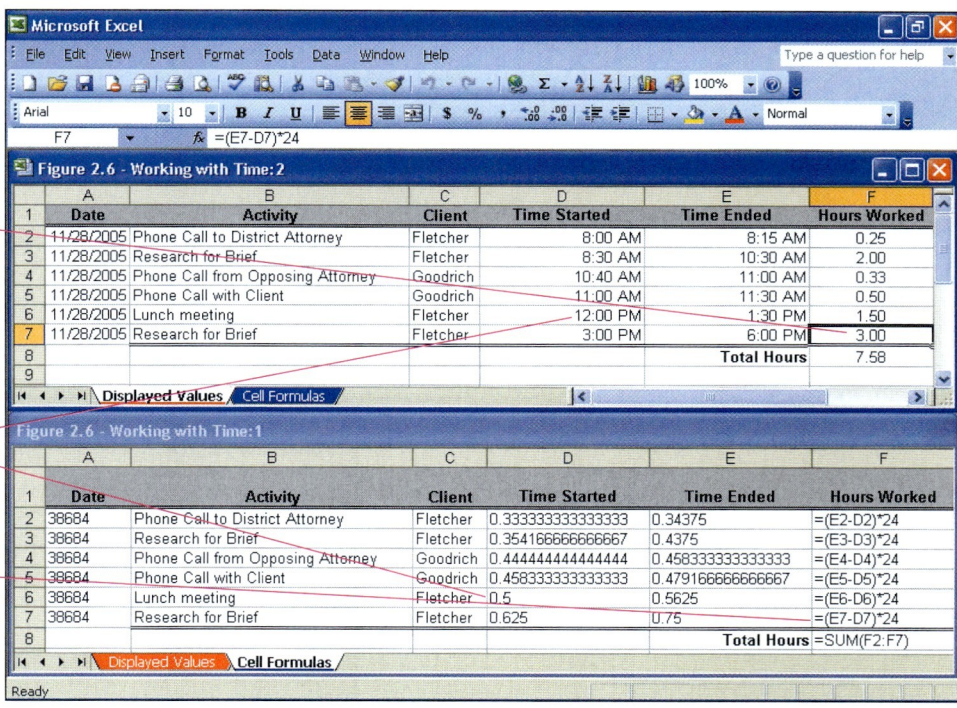

FIGURE 2.6 Working with Time

hands-on exercise

3 Web Queries

Objective Include a Web query into a worksheet to retrieve current stock prices from the Internet. (The exercise requires an Internet connection.) Use the Today() function to illustrate the use of date arithmetic. Use Figure 2.7 as a guide in the exercise.

Step 1: **Open the Stock Portfolio**

- Open the **Stock Portfolio workbook** in the **Exploring Excel folder** to display the worksheet in Figure 2.7a.

- Save the workbook as **Stock Portfolio Solution** so that you can return to the original workbook if necessary.

- Cell B1 displays today's date, 1/11/2005 in our figure, but a different date on your machine. Click in **cell B1**, and note that it contains the function, **=Today()**. Thus, the displayed value in cell B1 will always reflect the current date.

- Click in **cell B5**, the cell containing the date on which the shares in DIS were purchased. The contents of cell B5 are 1/7/2005 (there is no equal sign). This is a "fixed" date, and its value will not change from one day to the next.

- Pull down the **Data menu**, click **the Import External Data command**, then choose **Import Data command** to display the Select Data Source dialog box in Figure 2.7a.

- Choose the **MSN MoneyCentral Investor Stock Quotes** query, then click the **Open button**.

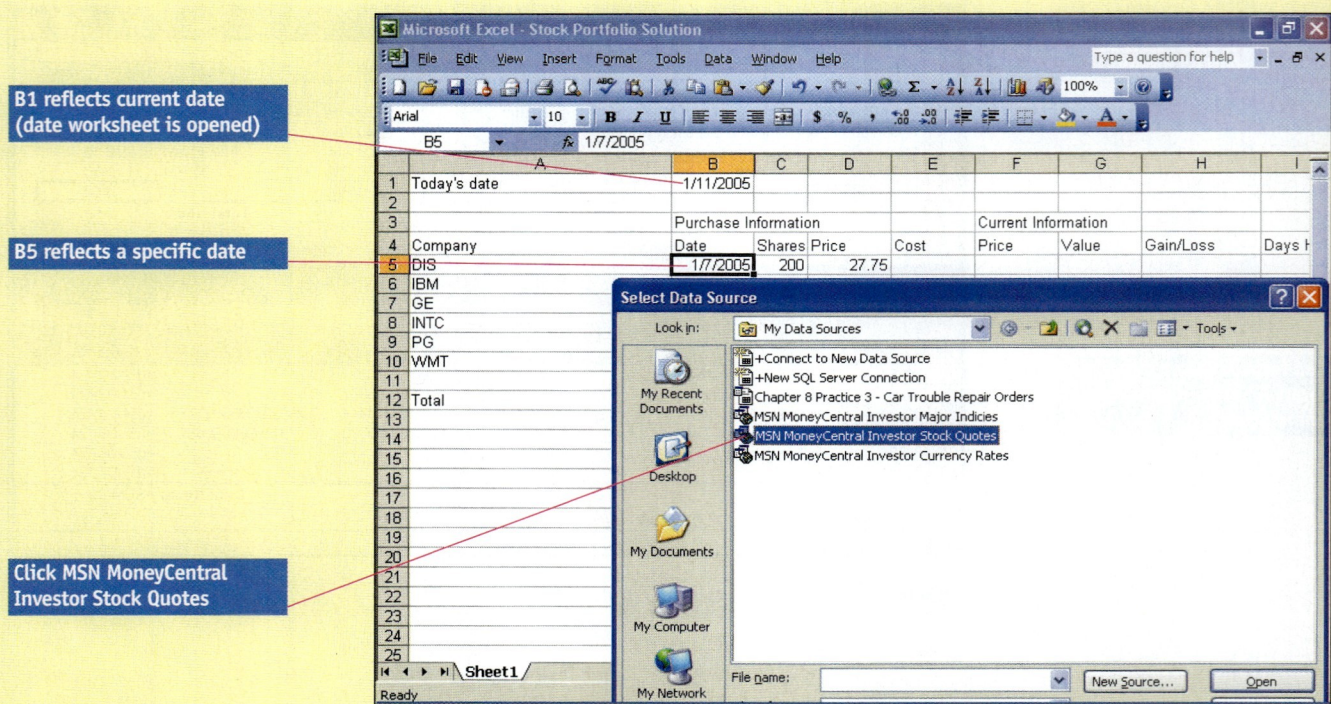

(a) Open the Stock Portfolio (step 1)

FIGURE 2.7 Hands-on Exercise 3

92 CHAPTER 2: GAINING PROFICIENCY

Step 2: **Complete the Web Query**

- The Import Data dialog box opens and prompts you for information about the Web query. Click the option button to put the data into the existing worksheet, then click in **cell A14** to indicate the location within the current worksheet. Click **OK**.

- Click and drag to select **cells A5** through **A10**, as the cells containing the stock symbols as shown in Figure 2.7b. Check the box to use this value reference for future refreshes. Click **OK**.

- Your system will pause as Excel goes to the Web to retrieve the information, provided you have an Internet connection. You should then see the stock quotes provided by MSN Money Central Investor.

- Do not be concerned if the column widths change as a result of the query. (You can widen them later.)

- Save the workbook.

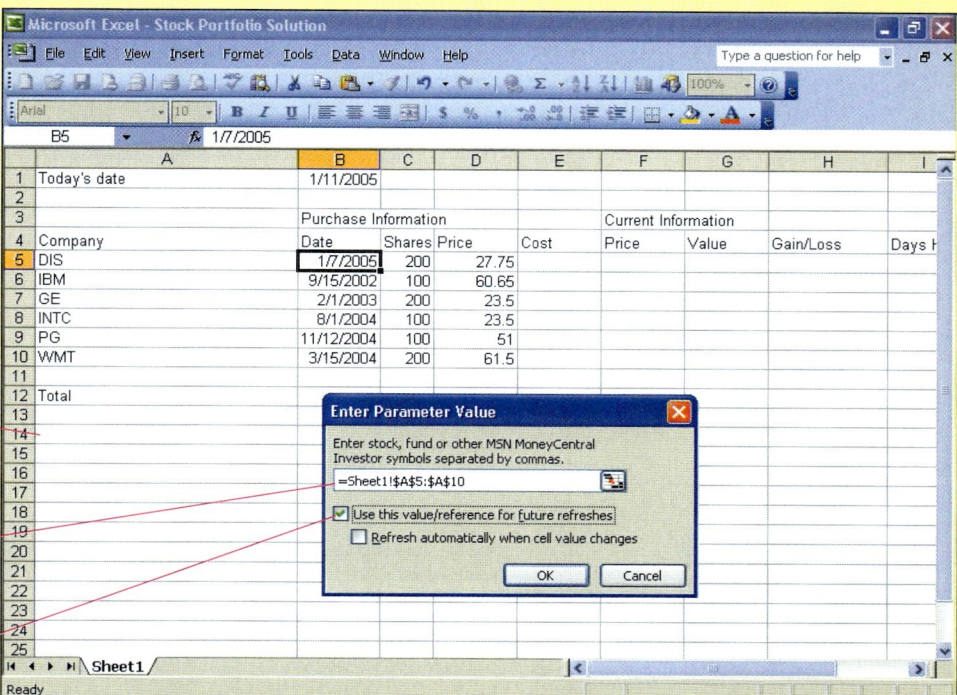

(b) Complete the Web Query (step 2)

FIGURE 2.7 Hands-on Exercise 3 (*continued*)

CREATE A NEW WEB QUERY

Web queries in earlier versions of Microsoft Office were limited in that you had to use existing queries. Office 2003, however, makes it easy to create new queries from virtually any Web page. Pull down the Data menu, click the Import External Data command, then click New Web query to display the associated dialog box. Enter the address of any Web page (try your favorite professional sport) that contains the data you want, then look for the yellow arrows that indicate the data may be imported.

MICROSOFT OFFICE EXCEL 2003 REVISED

Step 3: **Compute the Gain/Loss**

- You should see the information that was obtained via the Web query as shown in Figure 2.7c. Use pointing to enter the cell references to complete the formulas for the first investment.
  - Click in **cell E5** (the cell that contains the cost of the investment) and enter the formula, **=C5*D5**.
  - Click in **cell F5** (the cell that contains today's price), and enter the formula **=D17**, which references the cell that contains the current price of **DIS**.
  - Click in **cell G5** (the cell that contains today's value of the investment) and enter the formula, **=C5*F5**.
  - Click in **cell H5** (the cell that contains the gain or loss) and enter the formula, **=G5−E5**, corresponding to today's value minus the cost.
  - Click in **cell I5** (the cell that contains the days held) and enter the formula, **=$B$1−B5**.

- If necessary, change the format in cell I5 to reflect a number, rather than a date. Click in **cell I5**, pull down the **Format menu**, click the **Cells command**, click the **Number tab**, choose **Number** as the category, and specify **zero decimal places**. Click **OK**.

- Save the workbook.

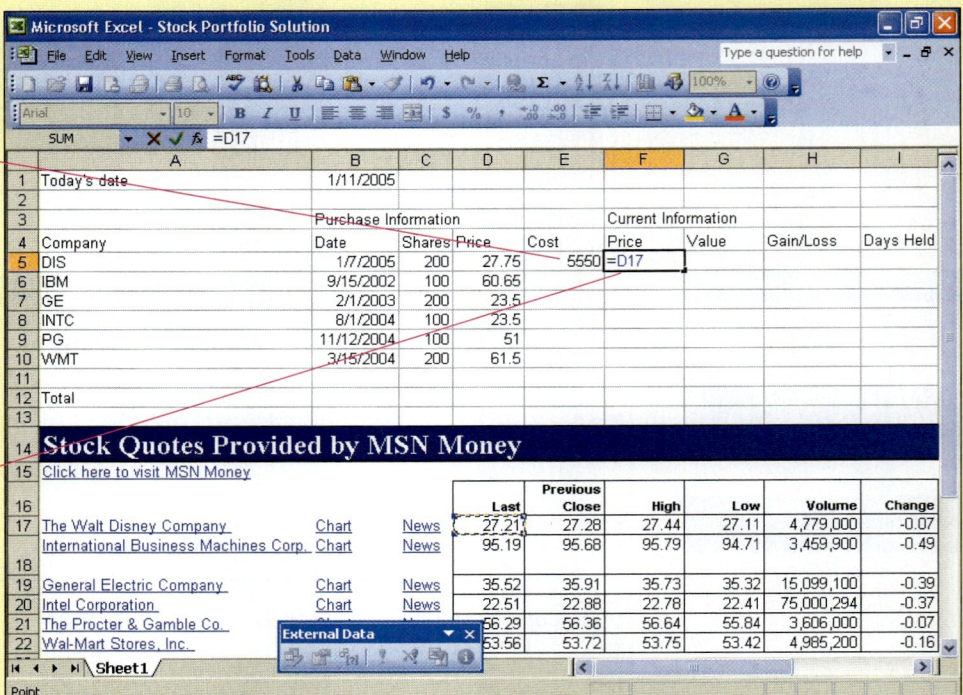

(c) Compute the Gain/Loss (step 3)

FIGURE 2.7 Hands-on Exercise 3 (*continued*)

POUND SIGNS AND COLUMN WIDTH

The appearance of pound signs (########) within a cell indicates that the column is too narrow to display the computed results. Double click the right border of the column heading to change the column width to accommodate the widest entry in that column. For example, to increase the width of column B, double click the border between the column headings for columns B and C.

Step 4: **Copy the Formulas**

- Click and drag to select **cells E5** through **I5**, the cells containing the formulas associated with the first investment, as shown in Figure 2.7d.

- Point to the fill handle in the lower-right corner of cell I5, then click and drag the fill handle to copy the formulas in row 5 to rows 6 through 10. Release the mouse to complete the copy operation.

- Click in **cell E12**, the cell that contains the total cost of your investments. Type =SUM(then click and drag to select **cells E5:E10**.

- Type a **closing parenthesis**, then press the **Enter key**. Cell E12 should contain the formula **=SUM(E5:E10)**.

- Copy the formula in cell E12 to **cells G12** and **H12**. The displayed value in cell E12 should be 36065. The displayed values in cells G12 and H12 depend on the current stock prices. The value of your portfolio will be very different from ours.

- Save the workbook.

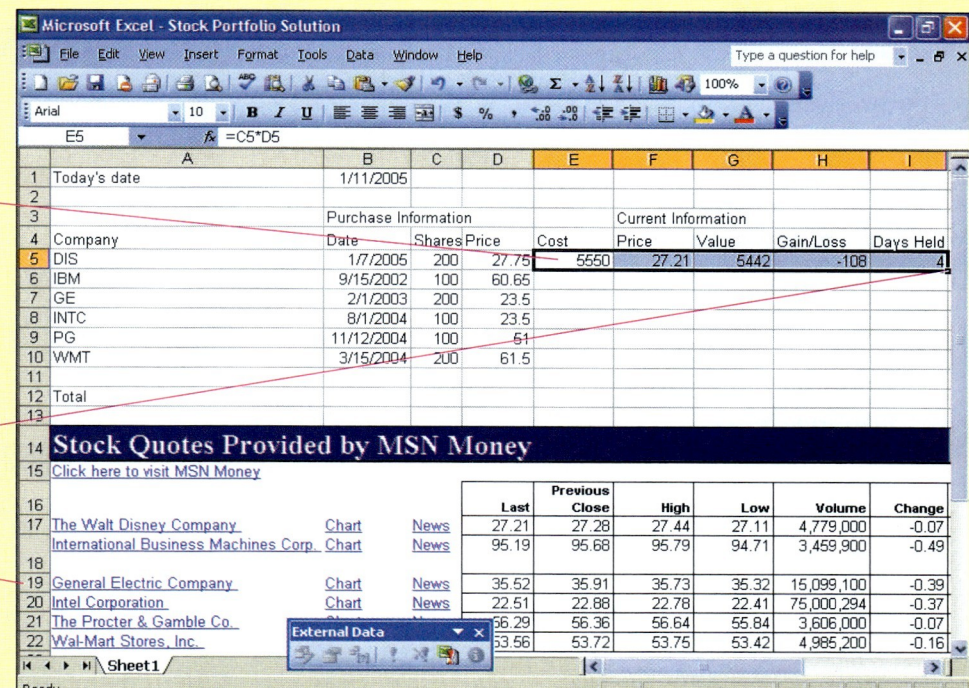

(d) Copy the Formulas (step 4)

FIGURE 2.7 Hands-on Exercise 3 (*continued*)

THE RESEARCH TASK PANE

Microsoft Office Excel 2003 introduces a research pane that connects you directly to various research tools on the Web. Pull down the Tools menu and click the Research command to display the Research task pane. Enter the name of the company for which you want information in the Search for text box, click the down arrow in the Reference Books list box, and then select Gale Company Profiles. Excel retrieves basic corporate information such as the company's address, phone, ticker symbol, and revenue, and displays the results in the task pane. Close the task pane when you are finished reading the information.

Step 5: **Format the Worksheet**

- Click and drag to select **cells D5** through **H12**, the cells that contain dollar amounts. Pull down the **Format menu**, click the **Cells command** to display the Format Cells dialog box, then click the **Number tab**. Format these cells in **Currency format,** with **two decimal places**. Display negative values in **red** and enclosed in **parentheses**. Click **OK**.

- Select all of the cells that contain a label (**cell A1**, **cells A3** through **I4**, **A5** through **A10**, and **cell A12**). Click the **Bold button** to boldface this information.

- Click and drag to select cells **B3** through **E3**, then click the **Merge and Center button**. Merge **cells F3** through **I3** in similar fashion.

- Click and drag to select **cells E4** through **E12**. Click the **down arrow** on the Borders button on the Formatting toolbar, then click the **right border icon** as shown in Figure 2.7e. Click **cell A1** (to deselect these cells). You should see a vertical line separating the purchase information from the current values.

- Adjust the column widths if necessary. Save the workbook.

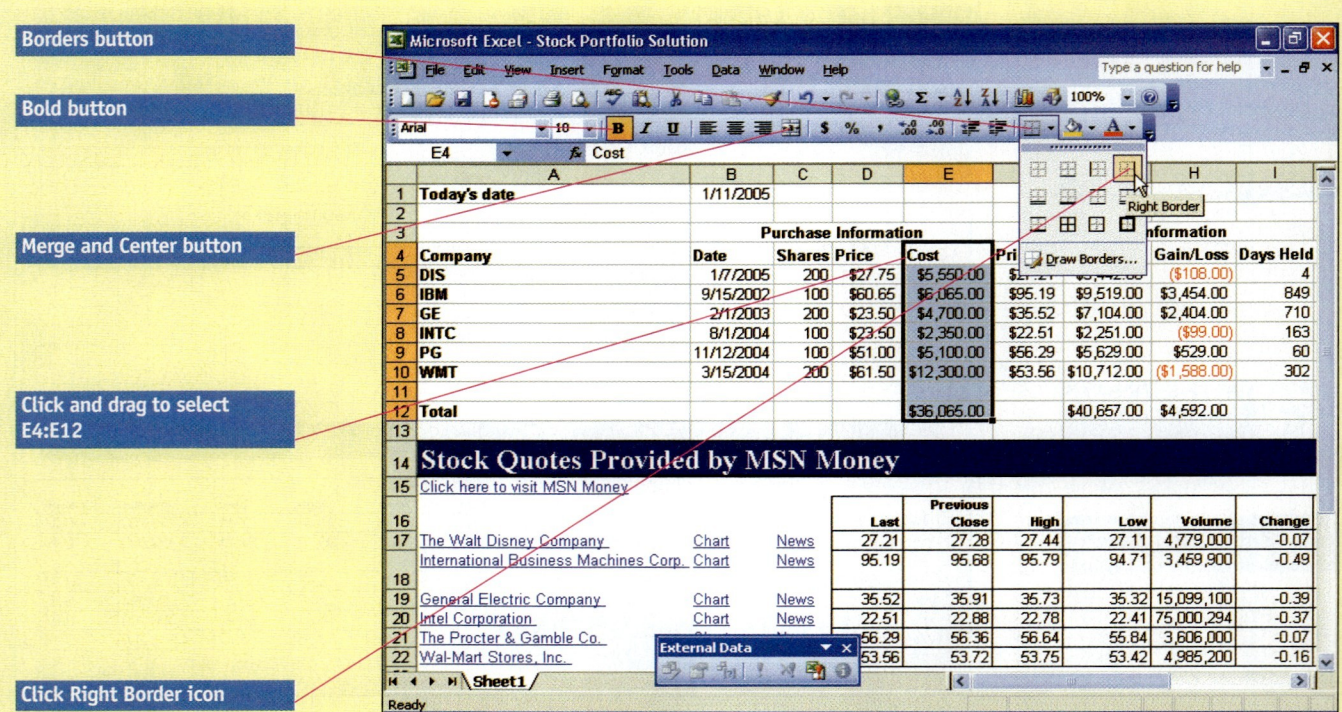

(e) Format the Worksheet (step 5)

FIGURE 2.7 Hands-on Exercise 3 (*continued*)

CAPITAL GAINS AND CONDITIONAL FORMATTING

The Internal Revenue Service offers a significant tax break on stock transactions that are considered a "long-term" capital gain (more than one year under today's tax code). Click and drag to select cells I5 through I10, the cells that show how long a stock has been held. Pull down the Format menu, click the Conditional Formatting command, then enter the condition as cell value is >365. Click the Format button, click the Font tab, then choose a different color (e.g., blue) to highlight those investments that qualify for this consideration.

Step 6: **Refresh the Query**

- Right click anywhere within the Web query (i.e., within cells A14 to I22) to display the context-sensitive menu in Figure 2.7f. Click the **Refresh External Data command** to retrieve the current prices from the Web. Click **OK**.

- The numbers in your worksheet will change, provided you have an Internet connection and the stock market is open. The column widths may also change since the Web query automatically adjusts the width of its columns (see boxed tip).

- Adjust the column widths if necessary. (Remember, the value of your portfolio will be very different from ours.)

- Save the workbook a final time. Print the workbook twice, once to show the displayed values, and once to show the cell contents.

- Now that you have completed this exercise, you can experiment further with the various links within the Web query. Scroll to the bottom of the query, for example, then click the link for Symbol Lookup to find the symbol for your favorite stock or index.

- Good luck with your stock portfolio, and congratulations on a job well done.

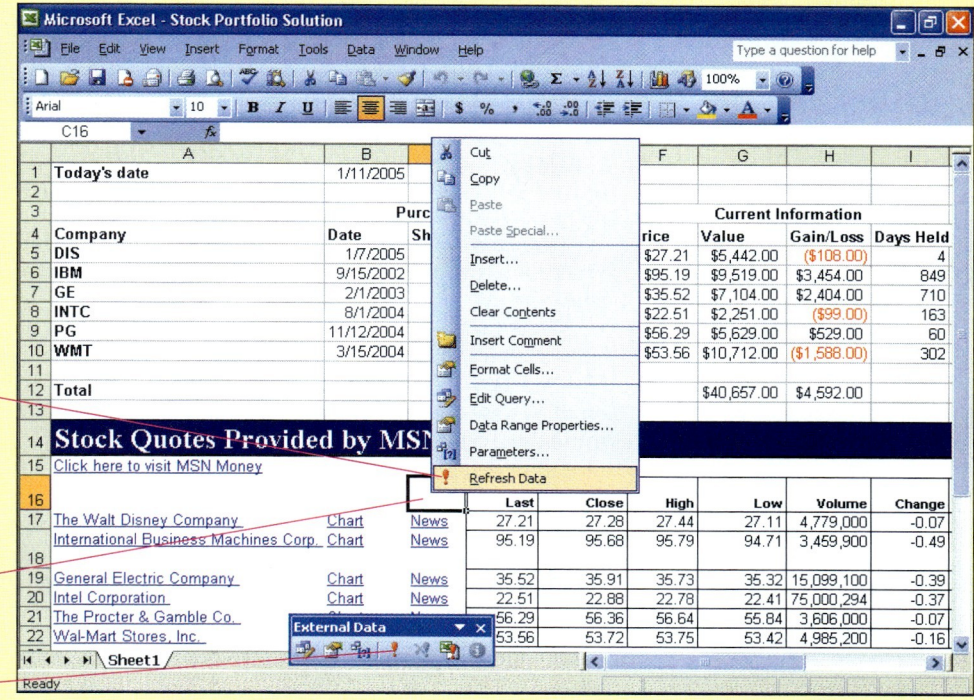

(f) Refresh the Query (step 6)

FIGURE 2.7 Hands-on Exercise 3 (*continued*)

DATA RANGE PROPERTIES

The Web query associated with MSN Stock quotes will, by default, change the column widths in the entire worksheet each time the query is refreshed. You can prevent this from happening by right clicking in the query area, then clicking the Data Range Properties command to display the associated dialog box. Clear the check box to Adjust column width, then click OK to accept the settings and close the dialog box. The next time you refresh the query, the column widths will not change.

SUMMARY

The distinction between relative, absolute, and mixed references, coupled with the importance of isolating the assumptions on which a worksheet is based, are basic concepts in spreadsheet design. A relative reference (such as A1) changes both the row and column, when the cell containing the reference is copied to other cells in the worksheet. An absolute reference (such as $A$1) remains constant throughout the copy operation. A mixed reference, either $A1 or A$1, modifies the row or column, respectively. Most spreadsheets can be built through combinations of relative and absolute addresses. Mixed references are required for more advanced spreadsheets.

The initial conditions and/or assumptions on which a spreadsheet is based should be isolated so that their values can be easily changed. The formulas in the main body of the spreadsheet typically contain absolute references to these assumptions. The placement of the assumptions and initial conditions is not a requirement of Excel per se, but is crucial to the development of accurate and flexible worksheets. The Insert Comment command creates the equivalent of a screen tip.

Pointing and the fill handle are two techniques that facilitate the development of a spreadsheet. Although any cell reference can be entered into a formula by typing the reference directly, it is easier and more accurate to enter the reference through pointing. In essence, you click in the cell that contains the formula, type an equal sign to begin the formula, then use the mouse (or arrow keys) to enter the various cell references.

The fill handle, a tiny black square in the lower-right corner of the selected cell(s), is the easiest way to copy a cell formula to adjacent cells. Just select the cell or cells to be copied, point to the fill handle for the selected cell(s), click and drag the fill handle over the destination range, and release the mouse.

A hyperlink can be inserted into any Excel worksheet, then the associated page viewed by clicking the link, without having to start the Web browser manually. Any worksheet or workbook can be saved as a Web page, which in turn can be stored on a Web server and displayed through a Web browser. Microsoft Office now recognizes the Single File Web Page format, which stores all of the elements on a Web page (text and graphics) as a single file.

Information from the Web can also be downloaded and inserted directly into an Excel workbook through a Web query. Office 2003 enables you to create your own Web queries from virtually any Web page.

Dates are entered into a worksheet by typing the date in conventional fashion such as 11/24/2000 or December 24, 2000. Either way all dates are stored as integers, beginning with January 1, 1900; that is January 1, 1900 is stored as the number 1. This simple concept enables date arithmetic, whereby calculations can be made between two dates to determine the number of days that have elapsed. The Today() function always returns the current date and is used in conjunction with date arithmetic.

Times are stored internally as decimal fractions, from 0 to .9999. Midnight (12:00 AM) is stored as 0. Noon (12:00 PM) is stored as 0.5 as it represents half a day. To calculate the elapsed time between two values, subtract the starting time from the ending time. The result is the fraction of a day that has elapsed, which is then converted to the elapsed time in hours by multiplying by 24.

KEY TERMS

Absolute reference 68	Insert Comment command 70	Save as Web Page command 78
Conditional formatting 83	Insert Hyperlink command 84	Single File Web Page 78
Date arithmetic 89	Internet 78	Template 88
External Data toolbar 89	Now() function 91	Time format .91
Fill handle 70	Pointing 70	Today( ) function 90
HTML document 78	Refresh command 89	Web page 78
Hyperlink 78	Relative reference 68	Web Page Preview command 78
Import External Data command .89	Research task pane 95	Web query 89
	Round trip HTML 78	

MULTIPLE CHOICE

1. The formula to compute the gross pay of an employee in the payroll example that was developed in this chapter uses:
   (a) Absolute references for hourly wage, regular hours, and overtime hours
   (b) Relative references for hourly wage, regular hours, and overtime hours
   (c) Mixed references for hourly wage, regular hours, and overtime hours
   (d) Impossible to determine

2. Which of the following best describes the formula to compute the withholding tax of an employee in the payroll example that was developed in this chapter?
   (a) It contains a relative reference to gross pay and an absolute reference to the withholding rate
   (b) It contains an absolute reference to gross pay and a relative reference to the withholding rate
   (c) It contains absolute references to both the gross pay and withholding tax
   (d) It contains relative references to both the gross pay and withholding tax

3. Cell D12 contains the formula, =SUM (A12:C12). What will the contents of cell D13 be, if the formula in cell D12 is copied to cell D13?
   (a) =SUM (A12:C12)
   (b) =SUM (A13:C13)
   (c) =SUM (A12:C13)
   (d) =SUM (A13:C12)

4. A formula containing the entry =$B$3 is copied to a cell one column over and two rows down. How will the entry appear in its new location?
   (a) =$C$5
   (b) =$B$3
   (c) =B3
   (d) =C5

5. Pointing is used to build formulas, as opposed to typing in the formula because:
   (a) It is easier to vary inputs to the formulas
   (b) It makes it easier to format the formulas
   (c) It is significantly faster than typing in the formulas
   (d) It is more accurate than typing in the cell addresses

6. A Web browser such as Internet Explorer can display a page from:
   (a) A local drive such as drive A or drive C
   (b) A drive on a local area network
   (c) The World Wide Web
   (d) All of the above

7. What is the best way to enter the current price of a stock into an Excel worksheet?
   (a) Copy the price directly from today's copy of *The Wall Street Journal*
   (b) Save the worksheet as a Web page
   (c) Create a Web query, then refresh the query to obtain the current price
   (d) Use Internet Explorer to locate a Web page that contains the current price

8. The estimated sales for the first year of a financial forecast are contained in cell B3. The sales for year two are assumed to be 10% higher than the first year, with the rate of increase (10%) stored in cell C23 at the bottom of the spreadsheet. Which of the following is the best way to enter the sales for year two?
   (a) =B3+B3*.10
   (b) =B3+B3*C23
   (c) =B3+B3*$C$23
   (d) All of the above are equivalent entries

9. Which of the following requires an Internet connection?
   (a) Using Internet Explorer to view a Web page that is stored locally
   (b) Updating the values that are obtained through a Web query
   (c) Clicking a hyperlink that references a document that is stored on drive C
   (d) All of the above

10. Cell F6 contains the formula =AVERAGE(B6:D6). What will be the contents of cell F7 if the entry in cell F6 is *moved* to cell F7?
    (a) =AVERAGE(B6:D6)
    (b) =AVERAGE(B7:D7)
    (c) =AVERAGE($B$6:$D$6)
    (d) =AVERAGE($B$7:$D$7)

...continued

multiple choice

11. What will be stored in a cell if 2/5 is entered in it?
  (a) 2/5
  (b) .4
  (c) The date value February 5 of the current year
  (d) 2/5 or .4, depending on the format in effect

12. You type 11/24/00 into a cell, press the Enter key, and expect to see Nov 24, 2000. Instead you see the value 36854. Which of the following is the most likely explanation?
  (a) Something is radically wrong with the date function
  (b) The cell is formatted to display a numeric value rather than a date
  (c) You should have used an equal sign to enter the date
  (d) None of the above makes any sense at all

13. Which of the following formulas can be used to compute an individual's age, given that the individual's birth date is stored in cell A4?
  (a) =(Today( )–A4)/365
  (b) =(Today–A4)/365
  (c) =(A4–Today)/365
  (d) =(A4–Today( ))/365

14. Microsoft Excel and Internet Explorer are both open and display the "same" worksheet. You make a change in the Excel file that is not reflected in the Web page. What is the most likely explanation?
  (a) The two files are not linked to one another
  (b) The files are stored locally, as opposed to a Web server
  (c) You did not refresh the Web page in Microsoft Excel
  (d) You did not refresh the Web page in Internet Explorer

15. You notice that the values in a specific column are displayed in three different colors, red for values less than zero, blue for values greater than $100,000, and black otherwise. How is this possible?
  (a) The colored formatting is automatically built into every Excel worksheet
  (b) A Web query was used to implement the red and blue formatting
  (c) Conditional formatting was applied to the column
  (d) It is not possible; that is, the question is in error

16. A red triangle in the upper-right corner of a cell indicates that:
  (a) There is an error in the cell formula
  (b) The cell is not formatted
  (c) The contents have been copied from another cell
  (d) The cell contains a comment

17. The formula =B3+C4 is stored in cell D5. What will the formula be if a row is inserted above the second row?
  (a) =B3+C4
  (b) =B4+C5
  (c) =C3+D4
  (d) =B2+C3

18. You want to add the contents of cells C1, C2, C3, and C4 but expect that additional values may be inserted within the column of numbers at a later time. Which formula automatically adjusts to *include* the additional entries?
  (a) =C1+C2+C3+C4
  (b) =SUM(C1:C4)
  (c) Both entries will automatically adjust
  (d) Neither entry will adjust if rows are inserted

ANSWERS

1. b	7. c	13. a
2. a	8. c	14. d
3. b	9. b	15. c
4. b	10. a	16. d
5. d	11. c	17. b
6. d	12. b	18. b

PRACTICE WITH EXCEL

1. **Alternate Payroll:** Figure 2.8 contains an alternate version of the payroll that was created in the first hands-on exercise in the chapter. The new spreadsheet includes the number of dependents for each employee and a fixed deduction per dependent, which combine to reduce an individual's taxable income. An employee with two dependents, for example, would have his or her taxable income reduced by $100 ($50 per dependent). The revised spreadsheet also isolates the overtime rate as an assumption at the bottom of the worksheet, which enables the user to change the overtime rate in a single place should that become necessary.

   a. Open the *Chapter 2 Practice 1* workbook, and then complete the spreadsheet so that the displayed values match ours. Use the appropriate combination of relative and absolute references in row 4, so that you can copy the formulas in this row to the remaining rows in the worksheet.

   b. Click in cell F12 and enter the appropriate Sum function to compute the total gross pay for all employees. Copy this formula to the remaining cells in this row.

   c. Format the worksheet in an attractive fashion. You do not have to match our formatting exactly, but you are to display all dollar amounts with the currency symbol and two decimal places.

   d. Substitute your name for the employee named "Grauer", then sort the worksheet so that the employees appear in alphabetical order. (Click anywhere within column A and click the Sort Ascending button on the Standard toolbar. Note, too, that there must be a blank row above the total row, or else it will be sorted with the other rows.) Shade the row containing your name.

   e. Print the completed worksheet twice, once with displayed values, and once to show the cell formulas. Use the Page Setup command to switch to landscape printing and force the output onto one page. Print gridlines and row and column headings. Change the column widths as appropriate.

   f. Change the overtime rate in cell E14 to 2.00; that is, an employee is paid double time for each overtime hour. Change the withholding rate in cell E16 to 25%. Print the displayed values to reflect these changes.

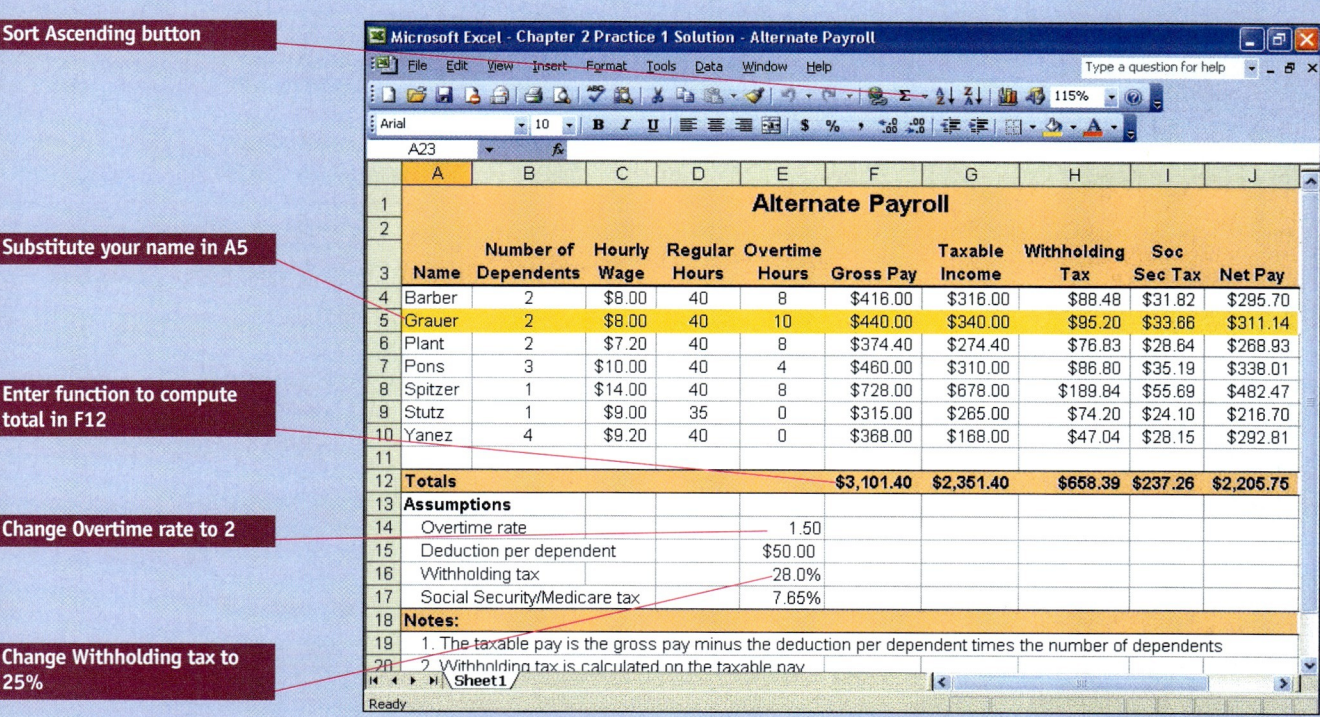

FIGURE 2.8 Alternate Payroll (exercise 1)

practice exercises

2. **The Sports Statistician:** Figure 2.9 illustrates how Excel can be used to tabulate statistics for a hypothetical softball league. Open the partially completed worksheet in *Chapter 2 Practice 2* workbook, and proceed as follows:

   a. An individual batting average is computed by dividing the number of hits by the number of at bats (e.g., 30/80 or .375 for Maryann Barber). The batting average should be formatted to three decimal places. (Create the Custom format .000 to eliminate the 0 before the batting average to display .375, rather than the default numerical format of 0.000.)

   b. Compute the total bases for an individual by multiplying the number of singles by one, the number of doubles by two, the number of triples by three, and the number of home runs by four, then adding the results.

   c. The slugging percentage is computed by dividing the total bases by the number of at bats (e.g., 48/80 or .600 for Maryann Barber). The slugging average should be formatted to three decimal places.

   d. The team totals for all columns except batting average and slugging percentage are determined by summing the appropriate values. The team batting average and slugging percentage are computed by dividing the number of hits and total bases, respectively, by the number of at bats.

   e. Substitute your name for Jessica Grauer (our league is coed), sort the players in alphabetical order, then format the worksheet so that it matches Figure 2.9.

   f. Add an appropriate clip art image somewhere in the worksheet using the same technique as in any Office application. Pull down the Insert menu, click (or point to) Picture, then click Clip Art to open the task pane. Click in the Search text box. Enter "baseball" to search for any clip art image that is described with this keyword and click the Go button.

   g. Print the completed worksheet twice, once with displayed values, and once to show the cell formulas. Use the Page Setup command for the cell formulas to switch to landscape printing and force the output onto one page. Print gridlines and row and column headings. Add a cover sheet, then submit all three pages (cover sheet, displayed values, and cell formulas) to your instructor.

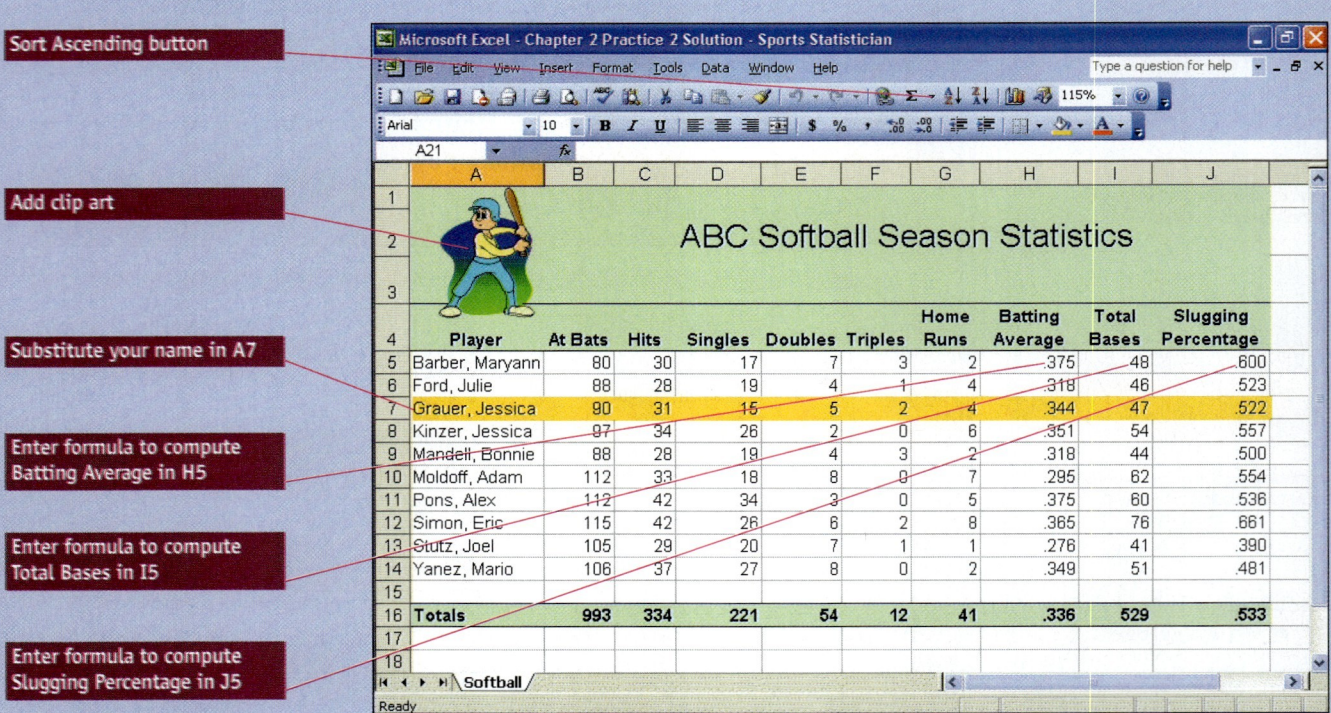

FIGURE 2.9 The Sports Statistician (exercise 2)

practice exercises

3. **Web Pages and Hyperlinks:** The Web page in Figure 2.10 is based on the partially completed *Chapter 2 Practice 3* workbook in the Exploring Excel folder. Your assignment is to complete the workbook in Excel, then save the workbook as a Web page. (You can view the Web page locally as in Figure 2.10, without loading it onto a Web server.) Proceed as follows:

   a. Compute the total points for each player by multiplying the number of free throws, 2-point field goals, and 3-point field goals by 1, 2, and 3, respectively.

   b. Compute the points per game for each player by dividing the total points by the number of games. Display the result to one decimal point. Compute the rebounds per game in similar fashion.

   c. Add clip art as you see fit. We used the same image twice to bracket the title of the worksheet, but feel free to improve on our design. Format your page to match ours.

   d. Add your name as the statistician in the bottom of the worksheet. Instead of merely typing your name, however, add your name as a hyperlink that points to your home page if you have one. If you do not have a home page, use any Web address that is appropriate, such as www.nba.com for the National Basketball Association. In any event, the text should say, "Click here for John Doe's (substitute your name) Home Page".

   e. Print the completed workbook from Excel to show both displayed values and cell formulas. Use the Page Setup command to display gridlines and row and column headings.

   f. Save the workbook as a Web page, then open the workbook in Internet Explorer. How does the printed Web page compare to the printed workbook?

   g. This exercise demonstrates how easy it is to create a Web page from an Excel worksheet and view it locally within Internet Explorer. To place a page on the Web, you will need Internet access, and further, you will need storage space on a Web server. Check with your instructor to see if these resources are available to you, and if so, find out the steps necessary to upload your page to the server. Send a note to your instructor that contains the Web address where he or she may view your Web page.

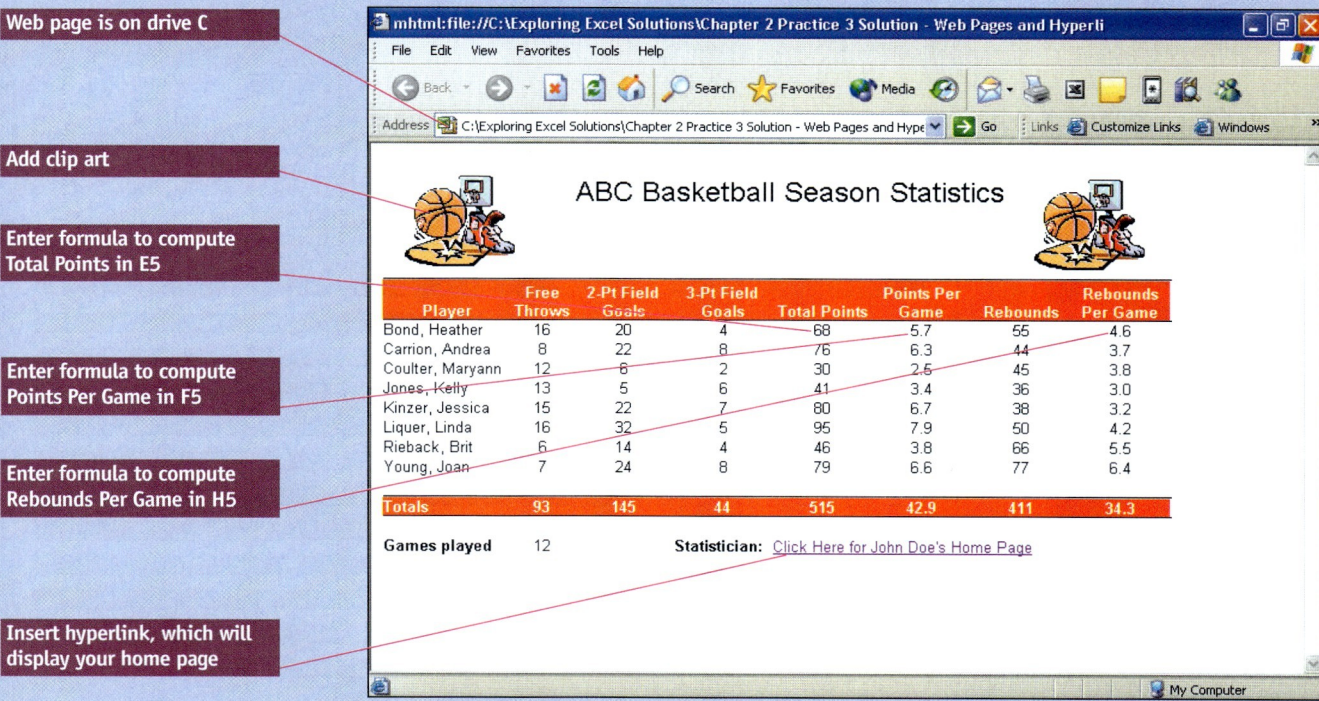

FIGURE 2.10 Web Pages and Hyperlinks (exercise 3)

practice exercises

4. **The Workout Schedule:** The worksheet in Figure 2.11 is essentially an exercise in formatting, but it also tests your ability to copy efficiently within a worksheet. You do not have to duplicate our document exactly, but you are required to have the equivalent functionality. You can create the document entirely on your own, or you can follow our suggested procedure.

   a. Open a new workbook. Click in cell B4 and enter "Day". Click in cell C4 and type "Monday". Click and drag to select cells C4 through E4, click the Merge and Center button to create a single cell, then use the Borders button to place a border around the merged cell. Drag the fill handle of this cell to enter the remaining days of the week into row 4.

   b. Enter "EXERCISE" and "SET" into cells A5 and B5, respectively. Select both cells, change the fill color to black and the text color to white. Center the text. Click the Bold button so that the text stands out.

   c. Enter 1, 2, and 3 into cells C5, D5, and E5, respectively. Click in cell B5, click the Format Painter button, and copy the formatting to cells C5 through E5. Copy these cells to the remaining cells in this row.

   d. Center "Pounds" and "Reps" in cells B6 and B7, respectively. Change the fill color in cell B7. Place a border around cells B6 and B7, then copy the formatting to the remaining cells in rows 6 and 7. (You can use the Format Painter and/or the Paste Special command, after which you choose formats.)

   e. Adjust the width of column A. Add the appropriate border around the merged cell in A6. Copy rows 6 and 7 to the remaining rows in the worksheet.

   f. Merge cells B1 through Q1 to enter the title of the worksheet. Merge cells B2 through Q2 and enter your name. Change the row height in rows 1 to 4 as appropriate, and then insert an appropriate logo in the upper-left portion of the worksheet.

   g. Print the completed worksheet in landscape mode. Be sure the worksheet fits on a single sheet of paper. Use the Page Setup command to add a footer that shows the name of the worksheet (i.e., the week of the workout).

   h. Copy the completed worksheet to two additional worksheets within the workbook. Rename all three worksheets to indicate the week of the workout.

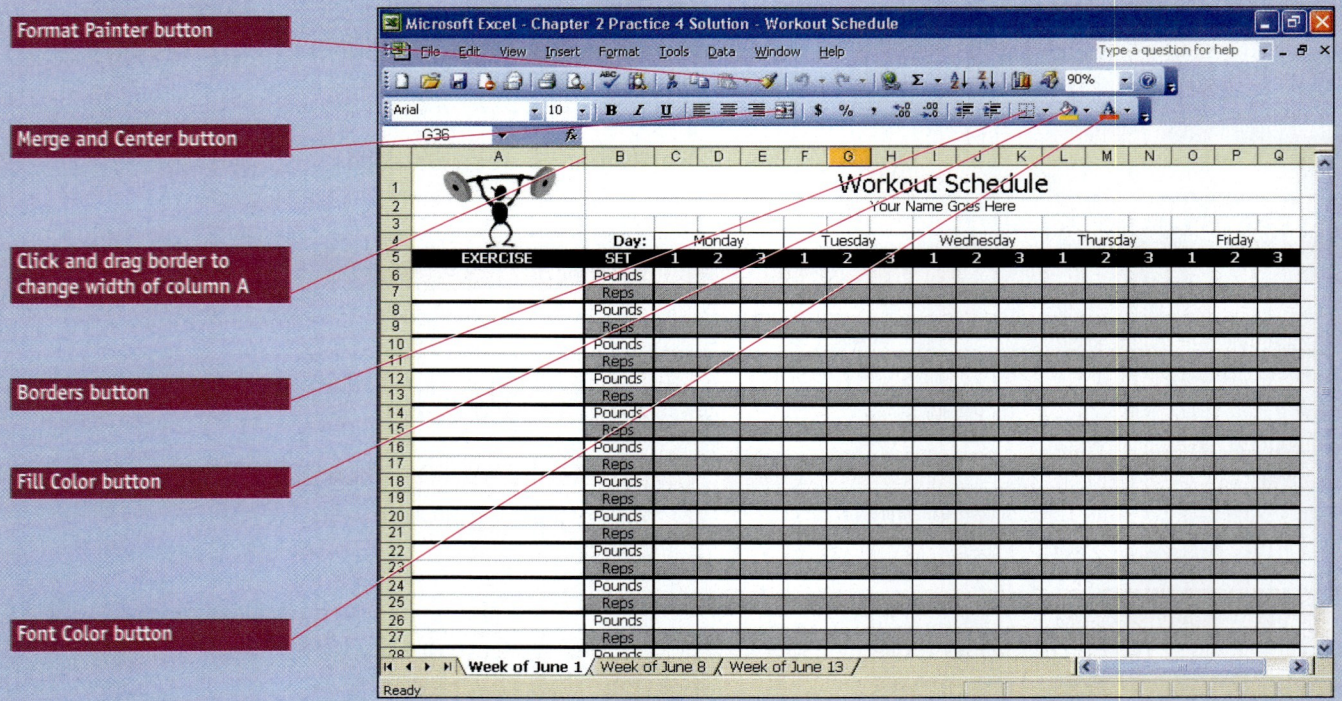

FIGURE 2.11 The Workout Schedule (exercise 4)

practice exercises

5. **An Exercise in Conversion:** The worksheet in Figure 2.12 displays a series of common conversion factors and the associated set of equivalent values. Open the partially completed workbook in *Chapter 2 Practice 5*, and then complete the workbook to match Figure 2.12. You do not have to match our formatting exactly, nor do you have to enter the identical values into column G.

   a. Click in cell E8 and enter the formula, =1/E7. (Cell E7 contains the value to convert inches to centimeters; the reciprocal of that value will convert centimeters to inches.) Enter the appropriate formula into cell E19 to convert kilograms to pounds.

   b. A kilobyte is mistakenly thought of as 1,000 bytes, whereas it is actually 1,024 (2^{10}) bytes. In similar fashion, a megabyte and a gigabyte are 2^{20} and 2^{30} bytes, respectively. Use this information to enter the appropriate formulas to display the conversion factors in cells E21, E22, and E23.

   c. Enter the formulas for the first conversion into row 7. Click in cell H7 and enter =C7. Click in cell J7 and enter =E7*G7. Click in cell K7 and enter =D7. Copy the formulas in row 7 to the remaining rows in the worksheet. (The use of formulas for columns H through K builds flexibility into the worksheet; that is, you can change any of the conversion factors on the left side of the worksheet, and the right side will be updated automatically.)

   d. Enter a set of values in column G for conversion; for example, enter 12 in column G7 to convert 12 inches to centimeters. The result should appear automatically in cell J7. Shade cells G7 through G23.

   e. Convert the entry in cell B3 to a hyperlink for www.onlineconversion.com.

   f. Use the Merge and Center command as necessary throughout the worksheet to approximate the formatting in Figure 2.12. Change the orientation in Column B so that the various labels are displayed as indicated.

   g. Display a border around groups of cells as shown in Figure 2.12. The easiest way to do this is to select the cells, then click the down arrow on the Borders tool on the Formatting toolbar to choose the appropriate border.

   h. Print the displayed values and the cell formulas for your instructor. Be sure to show the row and column headings as well as the gridlines. Use landscape printing to be sure the worksheet fits on a single sheet of paper.

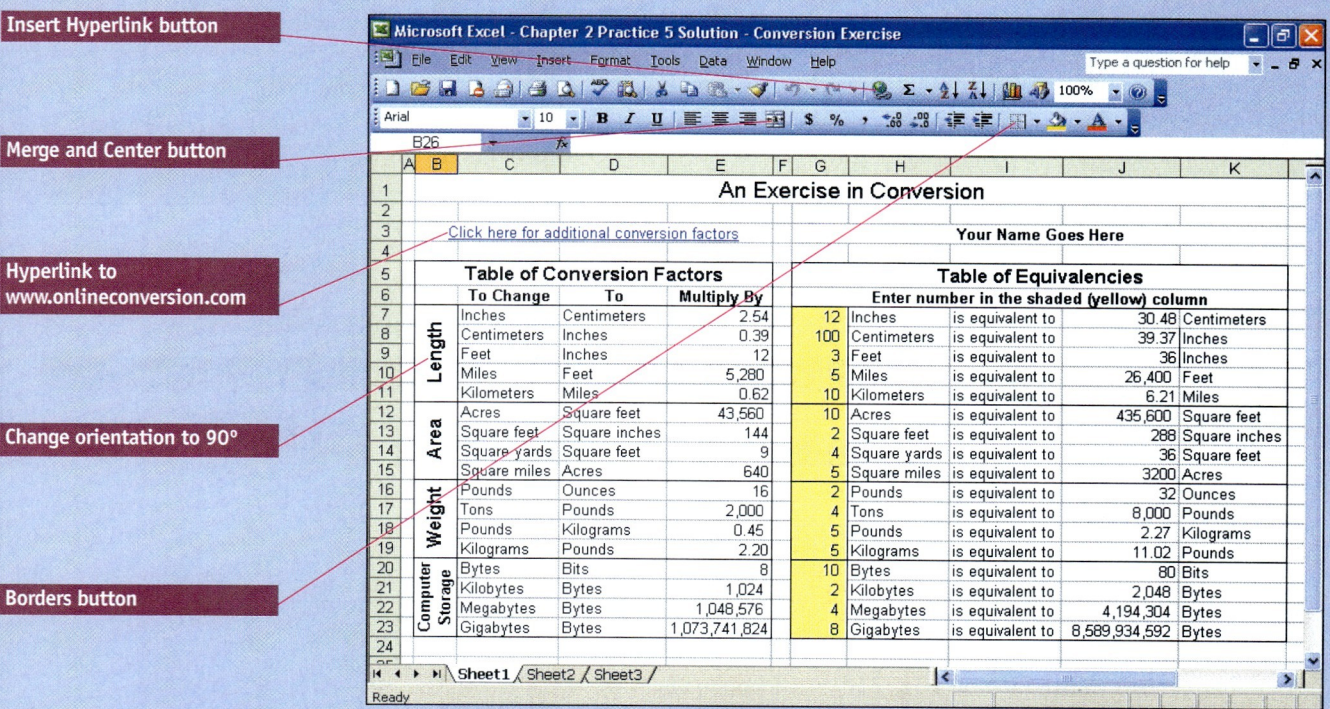

FIGURE 2.12 An Exercise in Conversion (exercise 5)

practice exercises

6. **Web Queries:** Microsoft Office includes a Web query to determine the exchange rates for popular currencies as can be seen in Figure 2.13. The worksheet contains formulas for two parallel sets of conversions, from British pounds to dollars, and from dollars to British pounds. Open the partially completed workbook in *Chapter 2 Practice 6*, then proceed as follows:

   a. Use the Import External Data command to enter the Web query (MS MoneyCentral Investor Currency Rates) into the worksheet, starting in cell A13. Click in cell B11 and enter the appropriate cell reference within the query (cell B23 in our example, which is not visible in Figure 2.13) to obtain the current value of the conversion factor. Use the value in cell B11 to convert the amounts in British pounds to the equivalent dollar amounts. Note that Microsoft is continually changing the content of its queries to include different currencies, so you may have to enter a different cell address.

   b. Click in cell E11 and enter the conversion factor to convert dollars to pounds. (This is the reciprocal of the value in cell B11.) Complete the entries in column E, which convert dollars to the equivalent amount in British pounds.

   c. Format the worksheet to match Figure 2.13. Be sure to use the appropriate currency symbols for dollars and pounds. Add your name and today's date as shown.

   d. Click the tab for the Euro (European Currency) worksheet and enter the formulas for the appropriate conversion from Euros to dollars and vice versa. You do not have to enter the query on this worksheet, because you can reference the values in the existing query. The entry in cell B11 of the Euro worksheet is Pounds!B33 on our worksheet (remember, the query changes continually so you may have to adjust the cell reference). Click in cell B11 of the Euro worksheet, type an equal sign to begin pointing, click the Pounds worksheet, and click in the cell containing the appropriate conversion, then click Enter to finish the formula.

   e. Format the Euro worksheet and include the European Currency Symbol as appropriate. Print both worksheets for your instructor.

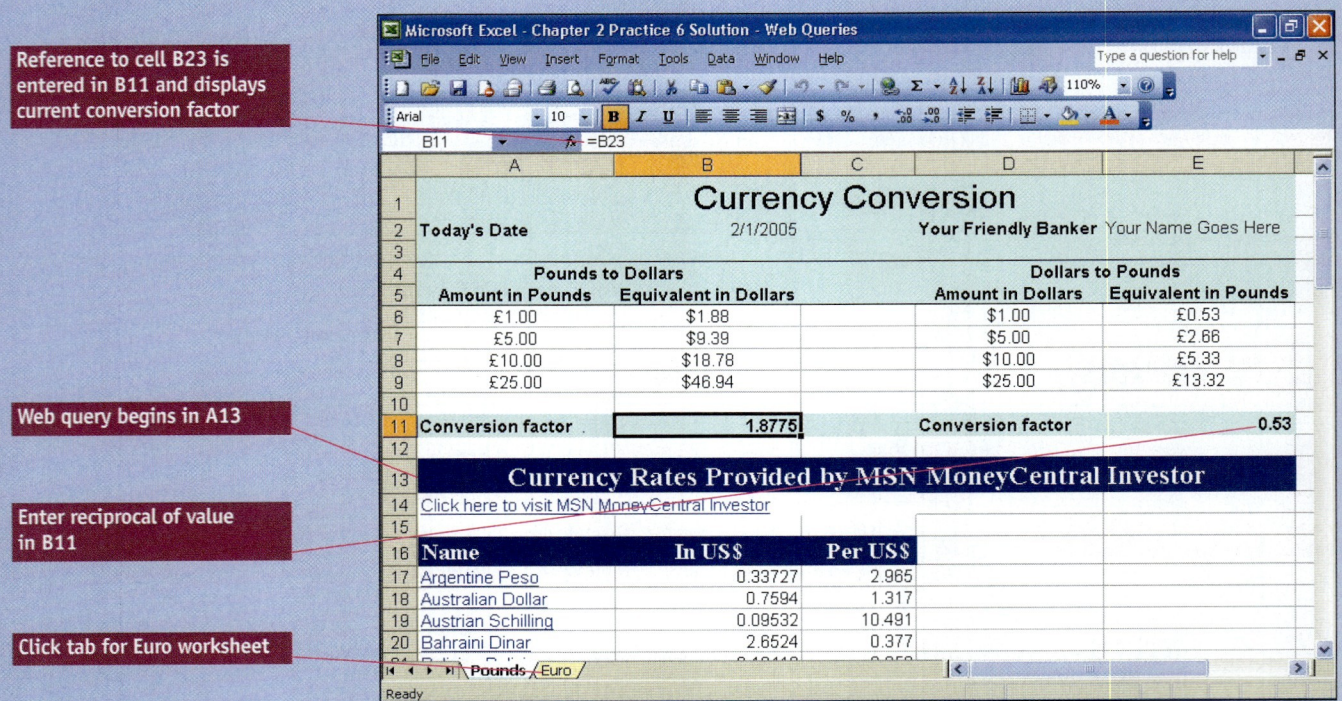

FIGURE 2.13 Web Queries (exercise 6)

practice exercises

7. **Buying a PC:** The worksheet in Figure 2.14 is intended to help you evaluate PC configurations from different vendors. The technical specifications for a PC are continually changing, so the minimum requirements in our worksheet may no longer be appropriate. Still, the partially completed worksheet in *Chapter 2 Practice 7* is a good starting place for your research. Open the workbook and proceed as follows:

   a. Enter the names of three vendors you would consider into cells C3, D3, and E3, respectively. Enter the associated Web sites into cells C4, D4, and E4. Visit the Web site of each vendor to determine an appropriate configuration that the vendor is currently offering. Specifications change all the time, and our minimum specifications in column B may be out of date. Thus, adjust the entries in column B as you see fit. Highlight any cell where you have modified the specification.

   b. Enter the costs associated with each system selected in part (a) in row 6. Your system will include some or all of the specifications at no additional charge. Enter the dollar amount of any item that is not included into the bundled price in the appropriate cell in the body of the worksheet.

   c. Software is probably extra. The vendor may include a basic version of the operating system—for example, Windows XP Home edition—but there will (most likely) be a charge if you want to upgrade. The same is true for Microsoft Office; that is, you have to purchase the version of the Office suite that contains the four major applications.

   d. Enter the appropriate Sum function into cell C25. You also need to enter the shipping, sales tax, and formula for the grand total into the appropriate cells in column C. Copy the formulas for the cells in column C to the corresponding cells in columns D and E.

   e. Enter your name into cell B3 as indicated. Enter a function to determine today's date into cell B4. Insert an appropriate piece of clip art into the upper-left portion of the worksheet.

   f. Format the completed worksheet. You do not have to match our formatting exactly, but you are to display dollar amounts with the currency symbol and no decimal places.

   g. Print the completed worksheet two ways, once with displayed values and once with cell formulas. Be sure the worksheet fits on one page and that you display gridlines and row and column headings.

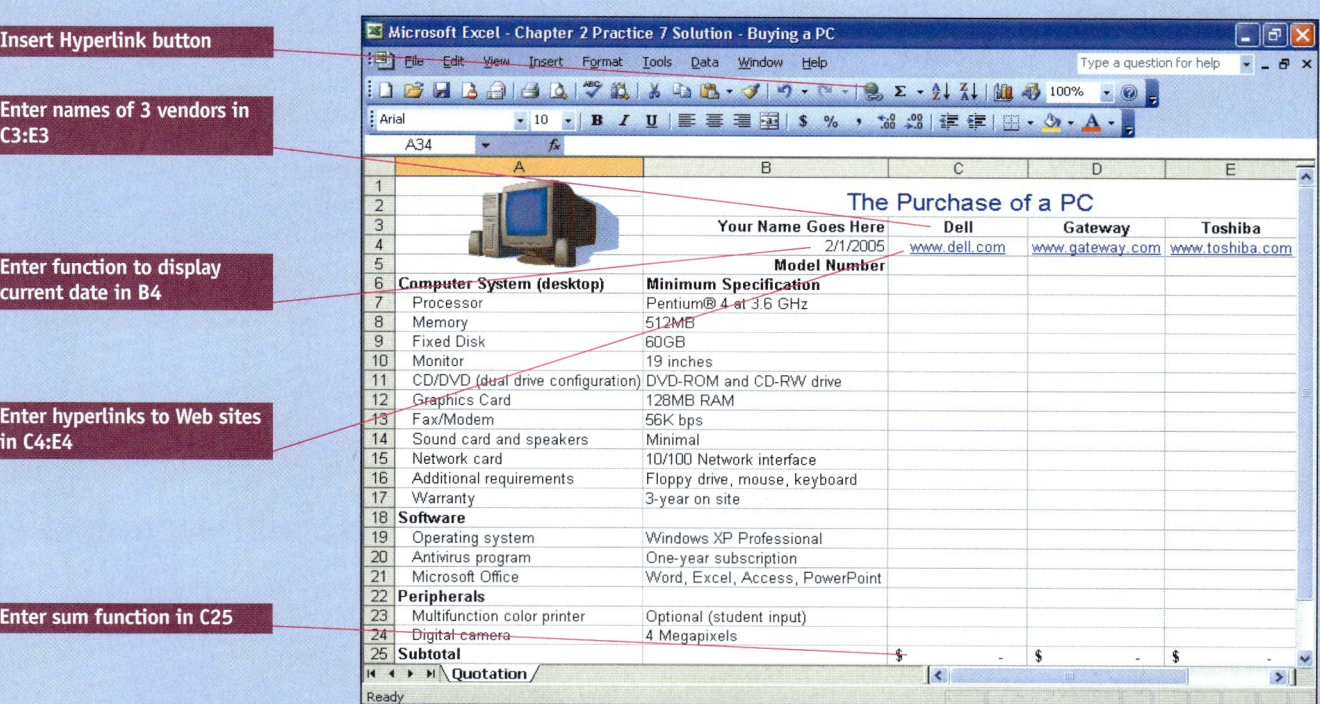

FIGURE 2.14 Buying a PC (exercise 7)

MICROSOFT OFFICE EXCEL 2003 REVISED

practice exercises

8. **Mixed References:** Most spreadsheets can be developed using a combination of relative and absolute references. Occasionally, however, you will need to incorporate mixed references as in a multiplication table. This assignment asks you to create a worksheet similar to the one in Figure 2.15. You can extend the range of the table and/or use different formatting. You are required, however, to use a formula containing mixed references in the first cell of the table (cell B4 in our figure) that can be copied to the remaining entries in this row, after which the entire row can be copied to the remaining rows in the worksheet.

   a. Enter the row and column headings into row 3 and column A, respectively. One way to create these values is through the AutoFill feature. Simply enter 1 and 2 into the first two cells for the row headings, select both of these cells, then drag the fill handle to continue the series in the remaining cells. Repeat the process to enter the column headings.

   b. The interesting part of this problem is the initial formula in the body of the worksheet (we don't want you to enter the results manually); that is, you need mixed references for the formula in cell B4. The formula is easy if you ask yourself the right questions. The product in cell B4 multiplies the value in cell A4 by the value in cell B3. Ask yourself questions about what happens to the formula when it is copied to the remaining rows and columns in the worksheet. Will the first number always come from column A? (Yes.) Will it always come from row 4? (No.) Will the second number always come from column B? (No.) Will it always come from row 3? (Yes.) The answers tell you how to create the mixed references.

   c. Copy the formula in cell B4 to the remaining columns in this row. Now copy row 4 to the remaining rows in the worksheet. Verify that the worksheet is correct by checking the displayed value at the bottom right of the table (144 in our example.)

   d. Add your name to the worksheet and submit it to your instructor. Remember, this worksheet is for a young person, so formatting is important. Print the cell formulas as well so that you can see how the mixed reference changes throughout the worksheet. Submit the complete assignment to your instructor. Using mixed references correctly is challenging, but once you arrive at the correct solution, you will have learned a lot about this very powerful spreadsheet feature.

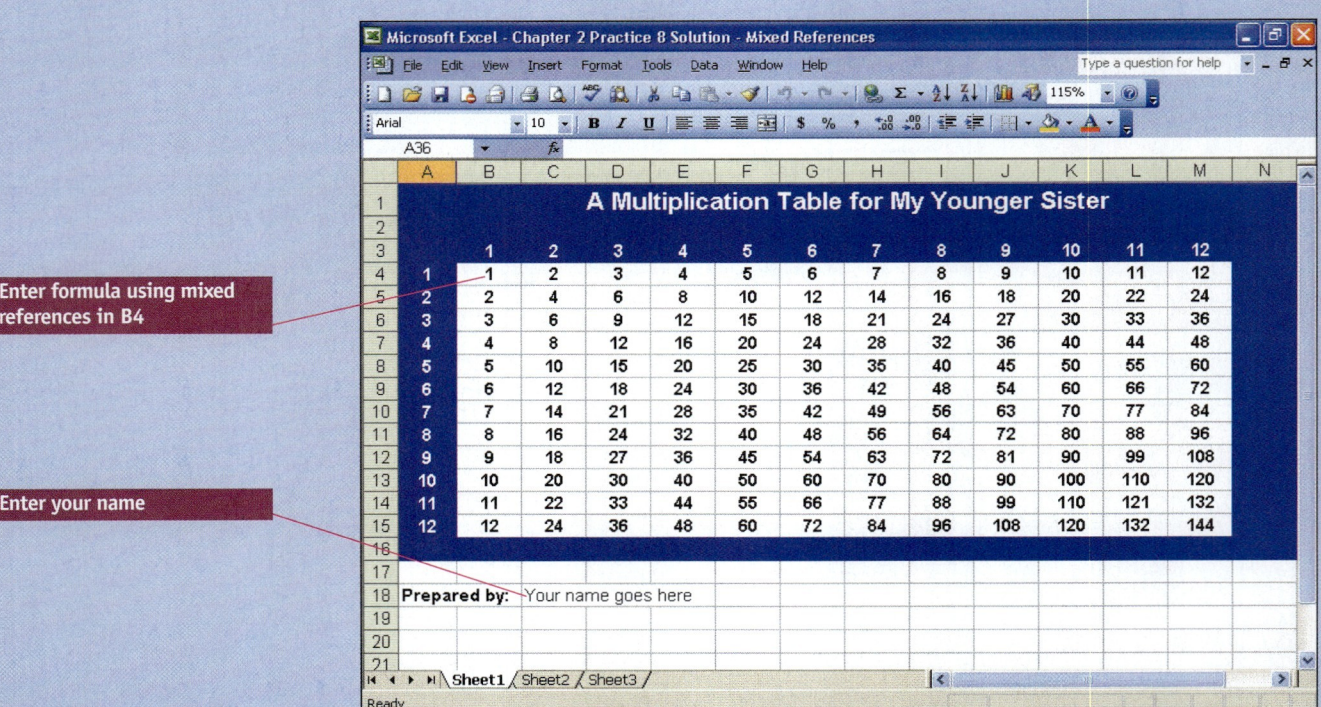

FIGURE 2.15 Mixed References (exercise 8)

practice exercises

9. **The Housing Office:** Open the partially completed workbook in *Chapter 2 Practice 9—The Housing Office*, and then complete the workbook to match Figure 2.16. You do not have to match our formatting or clip art exactly, but the displayed values should be the same.

   a. Click in cell D4 and enter the formula to compute the revenue from room rental. Click in cell E4 and enter the formula to compute the revenue from the meal plan. Be sure that both formulas use a combination of relative and absolute addresses. Note, too, that each double room has two students, each of whom is required to pay for the room as well as the meal plan.

   b. Click in cell F4 and enter the formula to compute the total revenue for the first residence hall. Copy the formulas in cells D4 through F4 into the remaining rows in the worksheet.

   c. Click in cell B10 and enter the appropriate function to compute the total number of double rooms. Copy this formula into the remaining columns in this row. Format the completed worksheet in an attractive fashion.

   d. Use the Insert Picture command to add an appropriate clip art image, then copy the clip art as shown in the figure.

   e. Use the Page Setup command to create a custom footer that contains the date and time the worksheet is printed, the name of the worksheet, and your name. Be sure to specify landscape printing, and appropriate scaling so that the entire worksheet fits on a single page. Print the worksheet twice, to show both displayed values and cell formulas.

   f. Copy the completed worksheet within the current workbook and then rename the new worksheet "Next Year" as shown in the figure. Select the new worksheet, then increase the price of a double room, single room, and meal plan by $100, $200, and $300, respectively. Change the formatting in the new worksheet to a different background color to distinguish the worksheet. Print the new worksheet to show the displayed values. (The cell formulas are the same as the previous worksheet.)

   g. Add a cover sheet and submit all three printouts to your instructor.

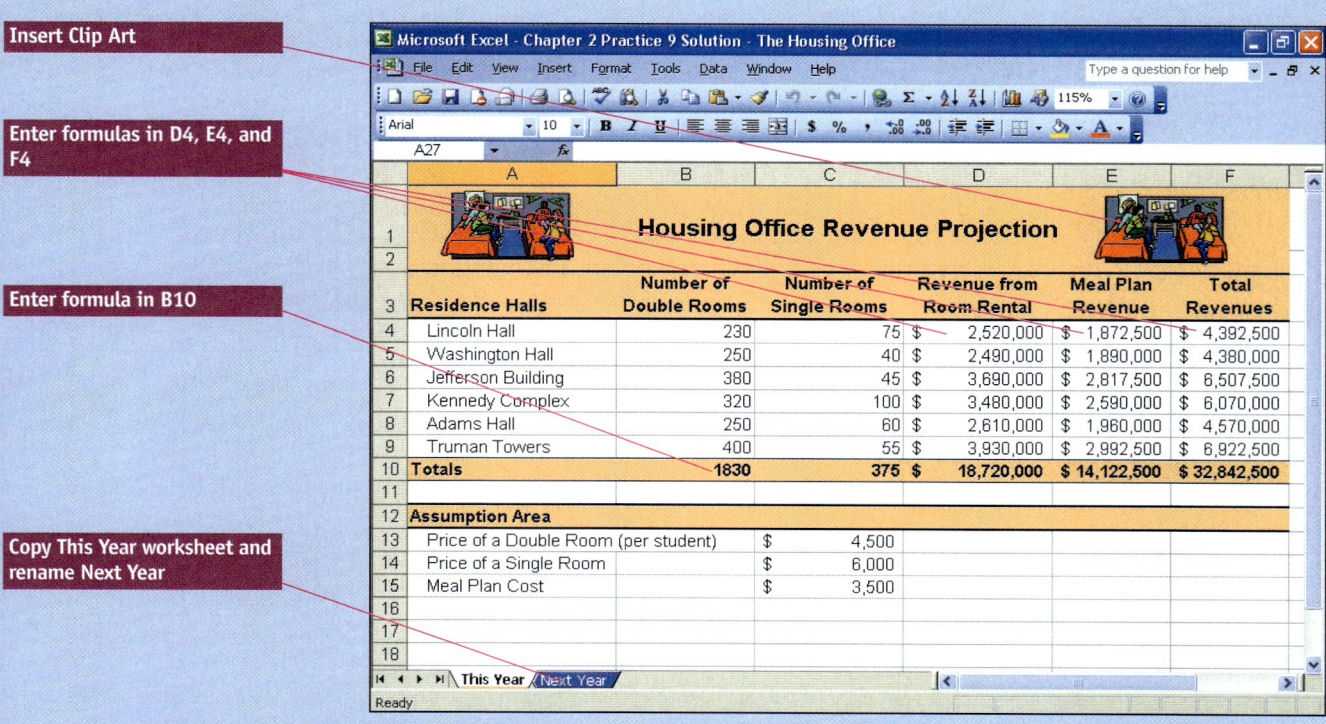

FIGURE 2.16 The Housing Office (exercise 9)

practice exercises

10. **Financial Forecast:** Financial planning and budgeting is one of the most common business applications of spreadsheets. Figure 2.17 depicts one such illustration, in which the income and expenses of Get Rich Quick Enterprises are projected over a six-year period. You don't have to be a business major to do the assignment. You do, however, need to follow a logical approach to develop the worksheet. We have entered the text in column A and the assumptions in the bottom of the partially completed workbook, *Chapter 2 Practice 10*, in the Exploring Excel folder. Open the workbook and proceed as follows.

   a. Develop the formulas for the first year of the forecast based on the initial conditions at the bottom of the spreadsheet. The projected income for the first year of the forecast (cell B7) is $225,000, based on sales of 75,000 units at a price of $3.00 per unit. The overhead (fixed costs) consists of the production facility at $50,000 and administrative expenses of $25,000. The variable costs for the same year are broken down into manufacturing of $75,000 (75,000 units at $1.00 per unit) and sales of $15,000 (75,000 units at $.20 per unit). Subtracting the total expenses from the estimated income yields a net income before taxes of $60,000. The income tax is subtracted from this amount, leaving net earnings of $38,400 in the first year.

   b. Develop the formulas for the second year, based on the values in year 1 and the assumed rates of increase at the bottom of the worksheet. Use an appropriate combination of relative and absolute references so that these formulas can be copied to the remaining columns in the worksheet. We suggest you use pointing to enter the formulas into column C.

   c. Copy the formulas for year 2 (in column C) to the remaining years of the forecast (columns D through G). Check that your worksheet is correct by comparing the displayed values to Figure 2.17.

   d. Format the completed worksheet. You do not have to match our formatting exactly, but you are to display dollar amounts with the currency symbol and appropriate decimal places.

   e. Add your name somewhere in the worksheet. Print the completed worksheet two ways, once with displayed values and once with cell formulas. Use landscape printing and force the worksheet to one page. Display gridlines and row and column headings.

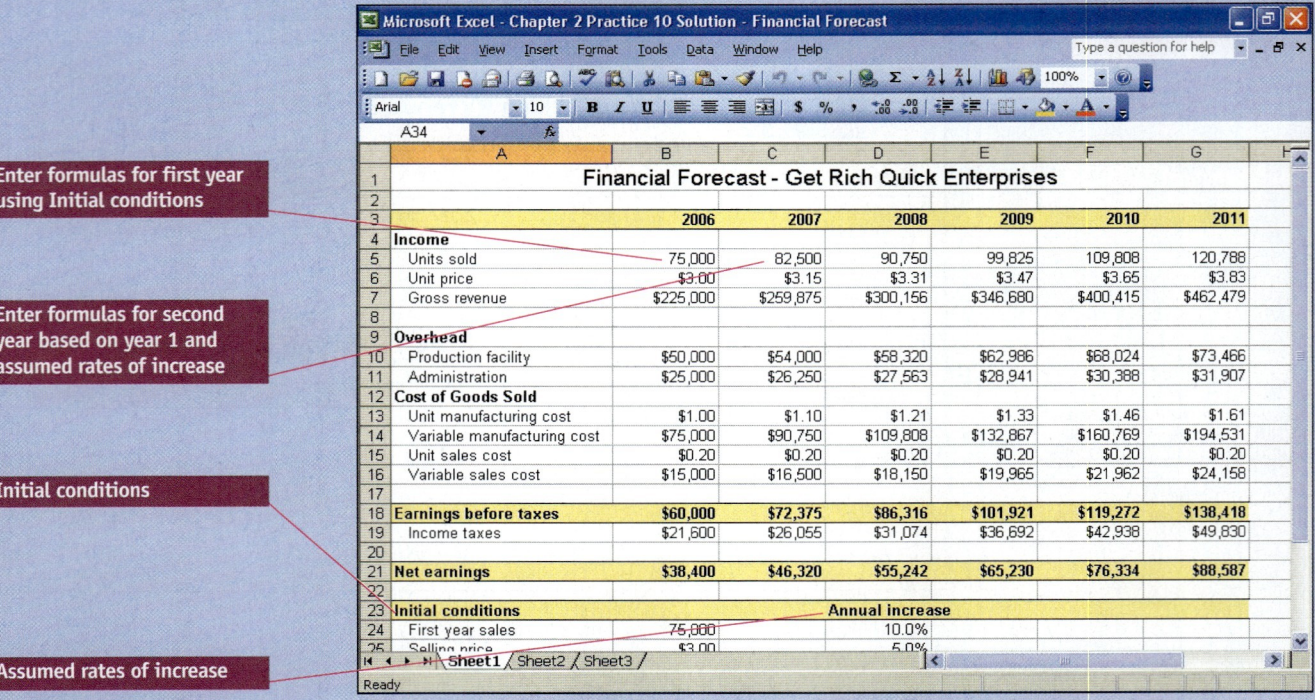

FIGURE 2.17 Financial Forecast (exercise 10)

practice exercises

11. **ABC Theaters:** Figure 2.18 displays a spreadsheet that is used to compute the weekly revenue for a chain of movie theatres. Open the partially completed workbook in *Chapter 2 Practice 11—ABC Theaters*, and then complete the workbook to match Figure 2.18. You do not have to match our formatting exactly, but the displayed values should be the same.

   a. Click in cell D4 and enter a formula, using a combination of relative and absolute references, to compute the ticket revenues for the first theatre.

   b. Enter the appropriate formulas into cells E4 and F4 for the first theatre. Copy the formulas in cells D4, E4, and F4 to the appropriate rows for the other theatres. You can tell that your formulas are correct if you get the same numerical result as in our figure.

   c. Click in cell B9 and enter the function to compute the total number of evening tickets that were sold. Copy this formula to the appropriate cells in row 9 to compute the other totals.

   d. Format the worksheet in attractive fashion. Insert an appropriate clip art image at the upper left, then copy the image as shown in the figure. (Use the Rotate or Flip command in the Draw menu on the Drawing toolbar to flip the figure.) You do not have to match our formatting or clip art.

   e. Use the Page Setup command to create a custom footer that contains the date and time the worksheet is printed, the name of the worksheet, and your name. Be sure to specify landscape printing and appropriate scaling so that the entire worksheet fits on a single page. Print the worksheet twice, to show both displayed values and cell formulas.

   f. Copy the completed worksheet within the current workbook and then rename the new worksheet "Next Year" as shown in the figure. Select the new worksheet, then increase the price of an evening ticket, afternoon ticket, and concession revenue per ticket to $7, $5, and $4, respectively. Change the formatting in the new worksheet to a different background color to distinguish the worksheet. Print the new worksheet to show the displayed values. (The cell formulas are the same as for the previous worksheet.)

   g. Add a cover sheet and submit all three printouts to your instructor.

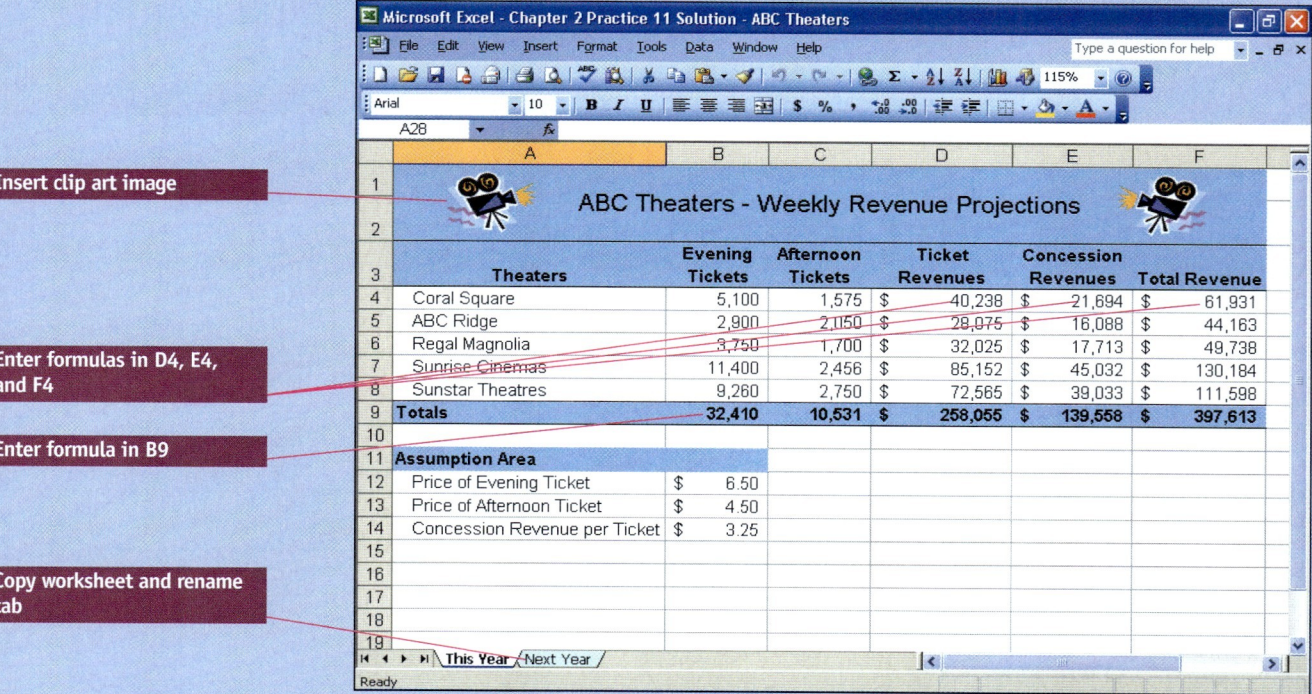

FIGURE 2.18 ABC Theaters (exercise 11)

practice exercises

12. **Second Hand Rose:** The worksheet in Figure 2.19 displays the hours worked and associated wages for three employees of the Second Hand Rose consignment shop. Your assignment is to open the partially completed *Chapter 2 Practice 12—Second Hand Rose* workbook and enter the appropriate formulas to determine the hours worked for each employee. Proceed as follows:

   a. Click in cell B4, the "time in" for Maryann on Monday morning, and change the format in this cell so that it displays a time, as opposed to a decimal fraction. Times are stored internally as decimal fractions, from 0 to .9999. Midnight (12:00 AM) is stored as 0. Noon (12:00 PM) is stored as 0.5 as it represents half a day. Use the Format Painter tool to change the time in and time out for all employees.

   b. Click in cell D4 and enter the formula to compute the hours Maryann worked on Monday, then (if necessary) reformat the result as a number. (To calculate the elapsed time between two values, subtract the starting time from the ending time. The result is the fraction of a day that has elapsed, which is then converted to the elapsed time in hours by multiplying by 24.)

   c. Copy the formula in cell D4 to cells D5 through D9 to compute her hours for the remainder of the week. Now copy the formulas in cells D4 through D9 to G4 through G9 and to J4 through J9. The Copy command works because you have used relative references in your formulas.

   d. Compute the total hours worked for Maryann for the week and the associated weekly earnings. Copy the entries in cells C10 and C12 to G10 and G12, and again to J10 and J12.

   e. Format the worksheet in attractive fashion. We used a variety of techniques, including the time format, merging cells, and borders and shading. Change the name of the worksheet tab to reflect the current week—for example, "Week of March 16".

   f. Insert an appropriate piece of clip art into the upper-left portion of the worksheet.

   g. Print the completed workbook twice to show both the displayed values and cell formulas. Use the Page Setup command to display gridlines, row and column headings, and to ensure the entire worksheet fits on one page. Change to landscape printing and center the worksheet horizontally. Add a custom footer that contains your name, the name of the worksheet, the date, and time.

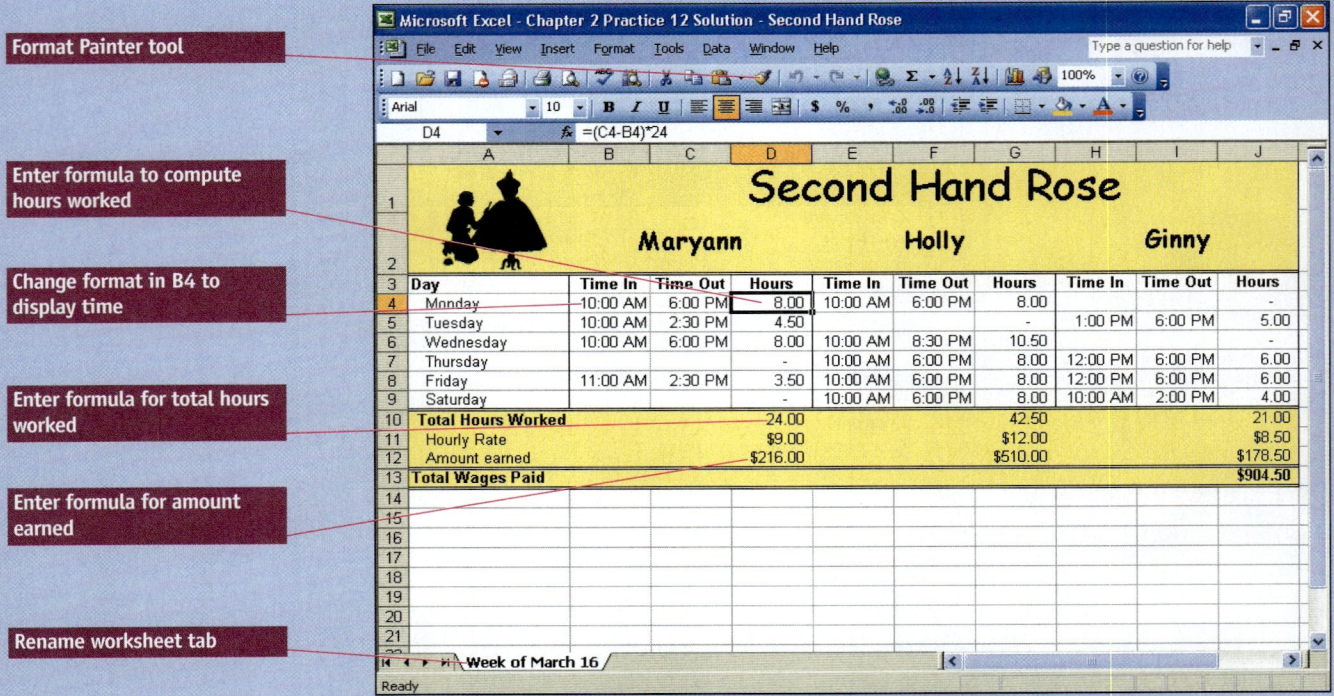

FIGURE 2.19 Second Hand Rose (exercise 12)

MINI CASES

Accounting 101—Straight Line Depreciation

Every asset depreciates (loses value) over time. It's similar to the value of your car, which loses value with every mile you drive. The straight line method of depreciation assumes that an asset depreciates at a uniform rate over its projected life. The amount of value that the asset loses each year is the depreciation expense for that year. To determine the depreciation amount for each year, take the cost of the asset, subtract its residual (salvage) value, and then divide the result by the number of years the asset will be used. Assume, for example, that an asset cost $25,000 new, that it will last for 8 years, at the end of which time it will have a $5,000 salvage value. The annual depreciation expense for this asset is ($25,000 − $5,000)/8 or $2,500.

Your assignment is to open the *Chapter 2 Mini Case—Accounting 101* workbook in the Exploring Excel folder in order to enter the necessary formulas to compute the annual depreciation expense. You also have to determine the accumulated deprecation for each year (the sum of all depreciation taken so far, including the current year) as well as the value of the asset (its cost minus the accumulated depreciation). Add your name to the worksheet, enter today's date and the appropriate formatting, then print the worksheet twice, once with displayed values, and once to show the cell formulas.

Wishful Thinking CD Portfolio

It must be nice to have a portfolio of CDs (Certificates of Deposit) where all you do is collect the interest. Your assignment is to open the *Chapter 2 Mini Case—Wishful Thinking CD Portfolio* workbook to determine the total interest earned by the portfolio. The formulas should be straightforward. The maturity date is computed by adding the term (converted to days) to the purchase date. Determine the days until maturity by subtracting today's date from the maturity date. The annual income is determined by multiplying the amount of the CD times its interest rate. The estimated tax is found by multiplying the annual income by the tax rate. The net income is the annual income minus the estimated tax. If you do the exercise correctly, the net income should be almost $15,000.

Format the completed worksheet in an attractive fashion. Add your name into cell A19. Print the worksheet twice, once with displayed values, and once to show the cell formulas. You might also do a little research on the Web to see what the current interest rates on CDs of varying term are. What is the FDIC? Is the investment in a CD insured to its full value? Add a cover sheet, then submit all three pages, together with the answers to the discussion questions, to your instructor as proof you completed this exercise.

Your Net Worth

Your net worth is the sum of all your assets (such as cash, mutual funds, the value of your home and furniture, and so on) minus the sum of all your liabilities (credit card debt, home mortgages, taxes, etc.) Create a simple worksheet that could be used to calculate your net worth, and then complete the worksheet by adding hypothetical data. *Wishful thinking is encouraged.* Submit the completed worksheet to your instructor.

The Birthday Problem

How much would you bet *against* two people in your class having the same birthday? Don't be too hasty, for the odds of two classmates sharing the same birthday (month and day) are much higher than you would expect: There is a fifty percent chance (.5063) in a class of 23 students that two people will have been born on the same day. The probability jumps to seventy percent (.7053) in a class of thirty, and to ninety percent (.9025) in a class of forty-one.

Open the partially completed *Chapter 2 Mini Case—The Birthday Problem* workbook, which contains the basic formula you will need to determine the probabilities. Your assignment is to complete the workbook by copying the formulas we provide to the remaining rows in the worksheet. Print the completed worksheet for your instructor, and then see whether the probabilities hold in your class.

mini cases

Billable Hours

Attorneys are not shy about billing their clients for all activities associated with a specific legal matter. Open the partially completed *Chapter 2 Mini Case—Billable Hours* workbook and enter the appropriate formula for the first activity to compute the hours worked (or billable hours). Copy this formula to the remaining rows in the worksheet, then total the billable hours for the indicated week. Compute the total amount billed by multiplying the hourly rate by the billable hours. Add your name as indicated, format the worksheet appropriately, then print it two ways, once with displayed values and once to show the cell formulas. Be sure to include the grid lines and row and column headings. Use the Page Setup command to include a custom footer that includes the date and time the worksheet was completed.

Chapter Recap—The Proper Tip

There is no perfect answer to the question, "how much to tip." It helps to realize, however, that the word "tip" is an acronym for the phrase "to insure promptness." One should focus, therefore, on the server's ability to meet your requests: Did he or she hustle and try to please you; was the server professional; did he or she try to rectify a bad situation if there was one? It is truly impolite to omit a tip even if the service was poor, but there is a range of amounts that sends a clear message to your server. This is generally accepted to be between 10% and 20% of the pretax total of the meal.

Lynne Breitfeller has decided to make the calculation easy for herself by creating a simple worksheet that will calculate the appropriate tip, based on the amount of the meal and the level of service. Lynne intends to make the worksheet completely general; she wants to be able to vary the suggested percentages and/or the amount of the bill and see the recommended tip. This is an unusual application, but it is intended to show that Excel can be applied to virtually any numeric calculation.

Your assignment is to review the chapter, paying special attention to Hands-on Exercises 1 and 2, which explain how to use relative and absolute references, and how to save and edit a Web page. You will then put yourself in Lynne's place and create a new workbook that calculates the suggested tip for poor, average, and excellent service on bills ranging from $10 to $200 in increments of $5. Use 10%, 15%, and 20% as the percentages for the different levels of service. Isolate all of the assumptions so that you can change the amount of the bill and/or the suggested percentages. Add a hyperlink to your favorite restaurant or dining etiquette Web site on the worksheet, then save the worksheet as a Web page. Print a copy of the completed worksheet to show both the displayed values and cell formulas. Print a second copy of the worksheet from your Internet browser.

CHAPTER 3

Graphs and Charts:
Delivering a Message

OBJECTIVES

After reading this chapter you will:

1. Describe how a chart can be used to deliver a message.
2. List several types of charts and describe the purpose of each.
3. Distinguish between an embedded chart versus a chart in its own chart sheet.
4. Use the Chart Wizard to create and modify a chart.
5. Use the Drawing toolbar to enhance a chart by adding lines and objects.
6. Distinguish between data series in rows versus columns.
7. Differentiate between a stacked column chart versus a side-by-side column chart.
8. Create a Word document that is linked to a worksheet and an associated chart.

hands-on exercises

1. THE CHART WIZARD
   Input: Software Sales
   Output: Software Sales Solution

2. MULTIPLE DATA SERIES
   Input: Software Sales Solution (from first exercise)
   Output: Software Sales Solution (additional modifications)

3. OBJECT LINKING AND EMBEDDING
   Input: Software Sales Solution (from second exercise)
   Output: Software Sales Solution (additional modifications); Software Memo Solution (Word document)

CASE STUDY
THE CHANGING STUDENT POPULATION

Congratulations. You have just been hired as a student intern in the Admissions Office. Nicole Beaudry, the Dean of Admissions, has asked you to start tomorrow morning to help her prepare for an upcoming presentation with the Board of Trustees in which she will report on enrollment trends over the past four years. Daytime enrollments have been steady, while enrollments in evening and distance (online) learning are increasing significantly. Nicole has asked for a chart(s) to summarize the data. She would also like your thoughts on what impact (if any), the Internet and the trend to lifelong learning have had on the college population. The dean has asked you to present the information in the form of a memo addressed to the Board of Trustees with the data and graph embedded onto that page.

Dean Beaudry will be presenting her findings on "The Changing Student Population" to the university's Board of Trustees in two weeks. She will speak briefly, and will then open the floor for questions and discussion amongst the group. She has invited you to the meeting to answer specific questions pertaining to these trends from a student's perspective. This is an outstanding opportunity for you to participate with a key group of individuals who support the university. Be prepared to present yourself appropriately!

Your assignment is to read the chapter, paying special attention on how to create a Word document that is linked to an Excel worksheet and chart. You will then open up the *Chapter 3 Case Study—The Changing Student Population* workbook and compute the summary totals for each year and each type of enrollment. You are to format the worksheet attractively and create an appropriate chart that shows how each type of enrollment has changed over time. You can then create the Word document, which includes the worksheet and chart to describe your results. Submit the completed document to your instructor.

CHART TYPES

The chapter-opening case study provides one example of how charts are used to facilitate the presentation of quantitative data. Indeed, business has always known that the graphic representation of data is an attractive, easy-to-understand way to convey information. We suggest that you read the chapter, and then return to the case study to complete the associated workbook and apply what you have learned.

The chapter begins by emphasizing the importance of determining the message to be conveyed by a chart. It describes the different types of charts available within Excel and how to choose among them. It explains how to create a chart using the Chart Wizard, how to embed a chart within a worksheet, and how to create a chart in a separate chart sheet. It also describes how to use the Drawing toolbar to enhance a chart by creating lines, objects, and 3-D shapes.

The second half of the chapter explains how one chart can plot multiple sets of data, and how several charts can be based on the same worksheet. It also describes how to create a compound document, in which a chart and its associated worksheet are dynamically linked to a memo created by a word processor. All told, we think you will find this to be one of the most enjoyable chapters in the text.

A *chart* is a graphic representation of data in a worksheet. The chart is based on descriptive entries called *category labels*, and on numeric values called *data points*. The data points are grouped into one or more *data series* that appear in row(s) or column(s) on the worksheet. In every chart there is exactly one data point in each data series for each value of the category label.

The worksheet in Figure 3.1 will be used throughout the chapter as the basis for the charts we will create. Your manager believes that the sales data can be understood more easily from charts than from the strict numerical presentation of a worksheet. You have been given the assignment of analyzing the data in the worksheet and are developing a series of charts to convey that information.

The sales data in the worksheet can be presented several ways—for example, by city, by product, or by a combination of the two. Ask yourself which type of chart is best suited to answer the following questions:

- What percentage of the total revenue comes from each city? What percentage comes from each product?

- What is the dollar revenue produced by each city? What is the revenue produced by each product?

- What is the rank of each city with respect to sales?

- How much revenue does each product contribute in each city?

In every instance, realize that a chart exists only to deliver a message, and that *you cannot create an effective chart unless you are sure of what that message is.* The next several pages discuss various types of business charts, each of which is best suited to a particular type of message. After you understand how charts are used conceptually, we will create various charts in Excel.

	A	B	C	D	E	F
1		Superior Software Sales				
2						
3		Miami	Denver	New York	Boston	Total
4	Word Processing	$50,000	$67,500	$9,500	$141,000	$268,000
5	Spreadsheets	$44,000	$18,000	$11,500	$105,000	$178,500
6	Database	$12,000	$7,500	$6,000	$30,000	$55,500
7	Total	$106,000	$93,000	$27,000	$276,000	$502,000

FIGURE 3.1   Superior Software

Pie Charts

A *pie chart* is the most effective way to display proportional relationships. It is the type of chart to select whenever words like *percentage* or *market share* appear in the message to be delivered. The pie, or complete circle, denotes the total amount. Each slice of the pie corresponds to its respective percentage of the total.

The pie chart in Figure 3.2a divides the pie representing total sales into four slices, one for each city. The size of each slice is proportional to the percentage of total sales in that city. The chart depicts a single data series, which appears in cells B7 through E7 on the associated worksheet. The data series has four data points corresponding to the total sales in each city.

To create the pie chart, Excel computes the total sales ($502,000 in our example), calculates the percentage contributed by each city, and draws each slice of the pie in proportion to its computed percentage. Boston's sales of $276,000 account for 55 percent of the total, and so this slice of the pie is allotted 55 percent of the area of the circle.

An *exploded pie chart*, as shown in Figure 3.2b, separates one or more slices of the pie for emphasis. Another way to achieve emphasis in a chart is to choose a title that reflects the message you are trying to deliver. The title in Figure 3.2a, for example, *Revenue by Geographic Area*, is neutral and leaves the reader to develop his or her own conclusion about the relative contribution of each area. By contrast, the title in Figure 3.2b, *New York Accounts for Only 5% of Revenue,* is more suggestive and emphasizes the problems in this office. Alternatively, the title could be changed to *Boston Exceeds 50% of Total Revenue* if the intent were to emphasize the contribution of Boston.

Three-dimensional pie charts may be created in exploded or nonexploded format as shown in Figures 3.2c and 3.2d, respectively. Excel also enables you to add arrows and text for emphasis.

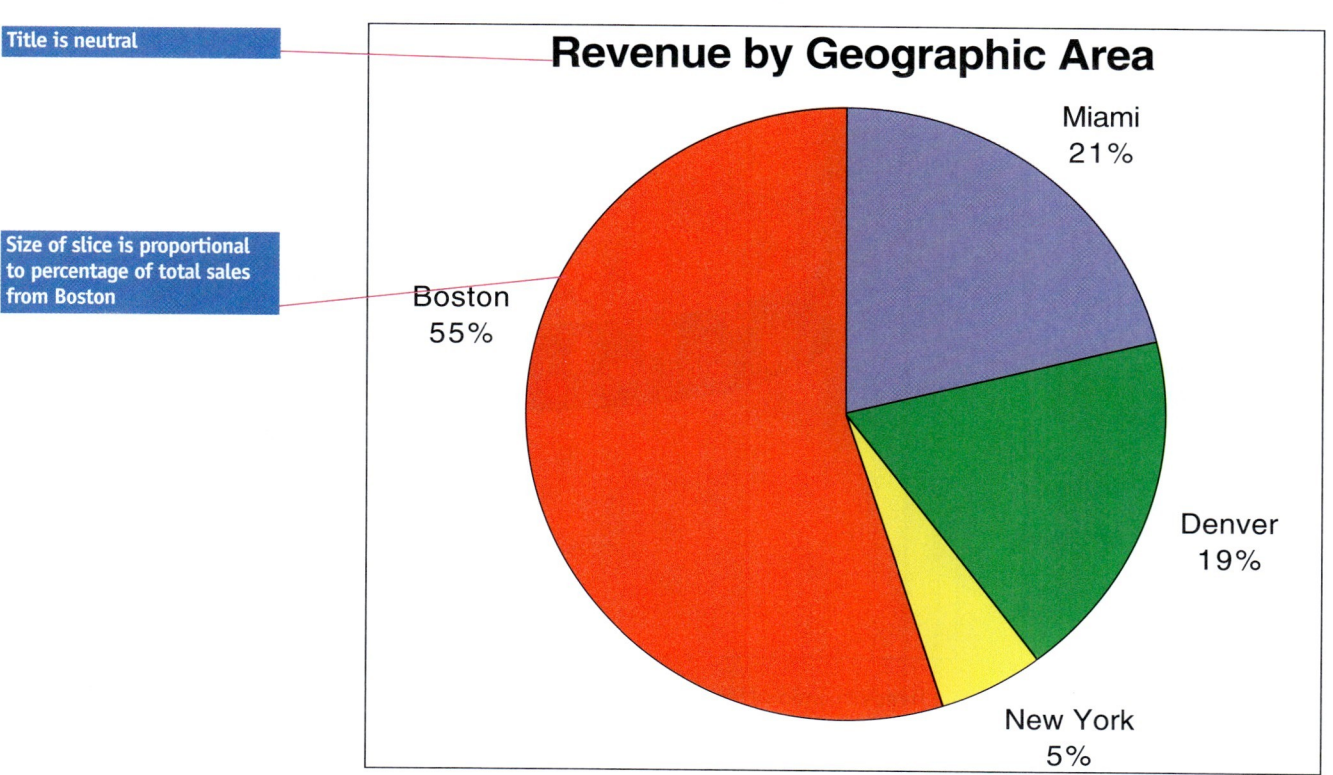

(a) Simple Pie Chart

FIGURE 3.2 Pie Charts

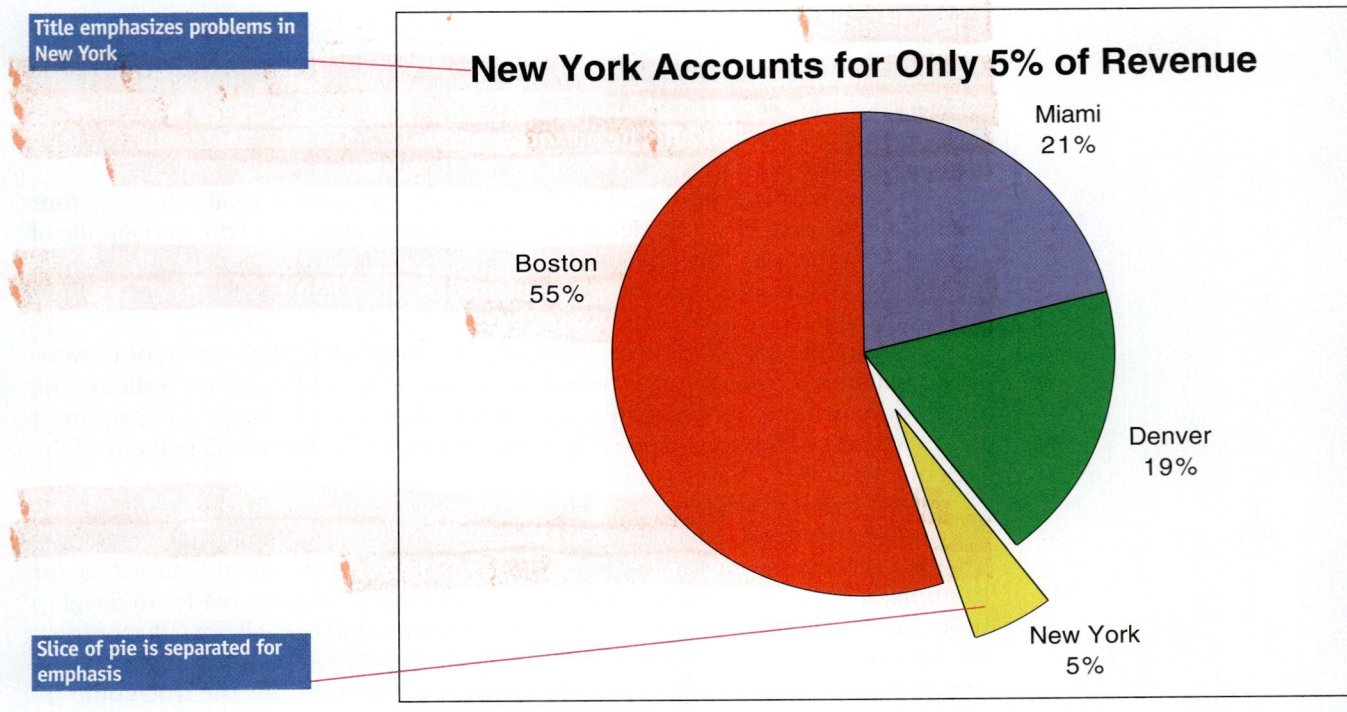

(b) Exploded Pie Chart

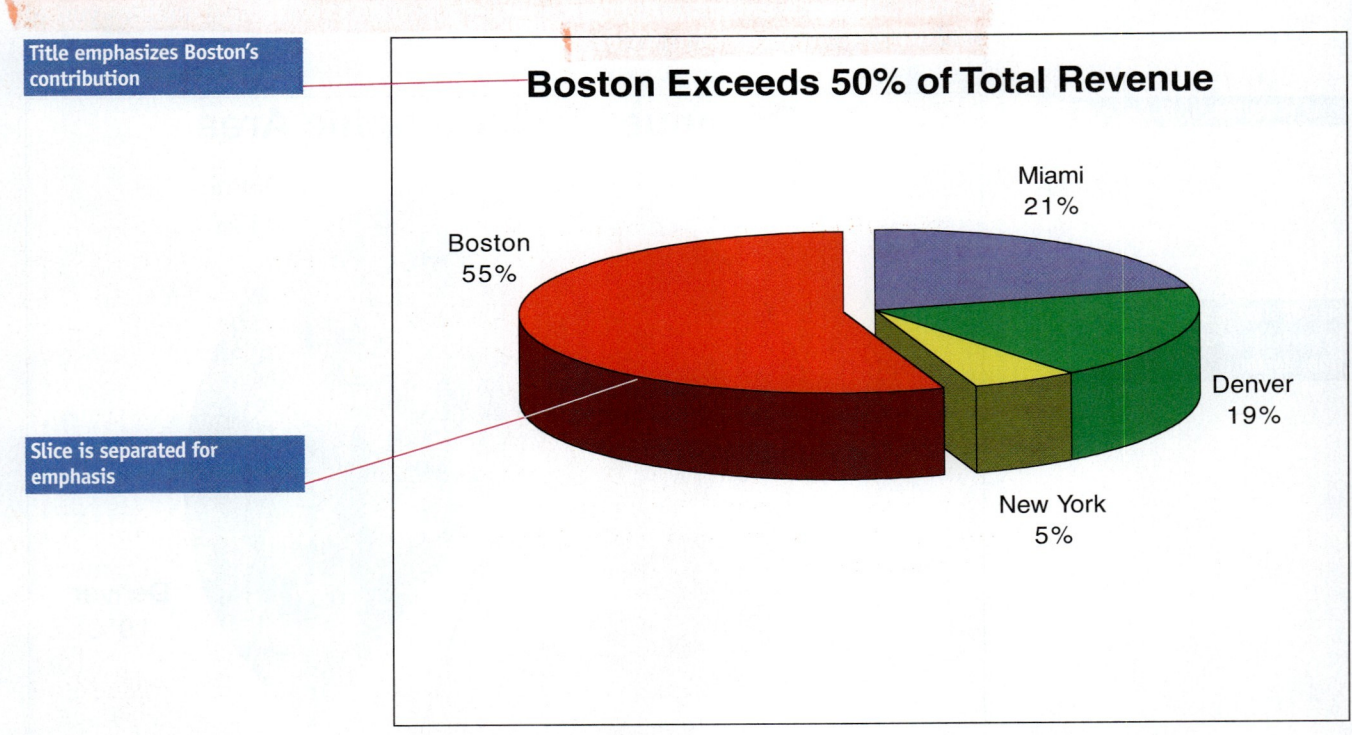

(c) Three-dimensional Pie Chart

FIGURE 3.2 Pie Charts (*continued*)

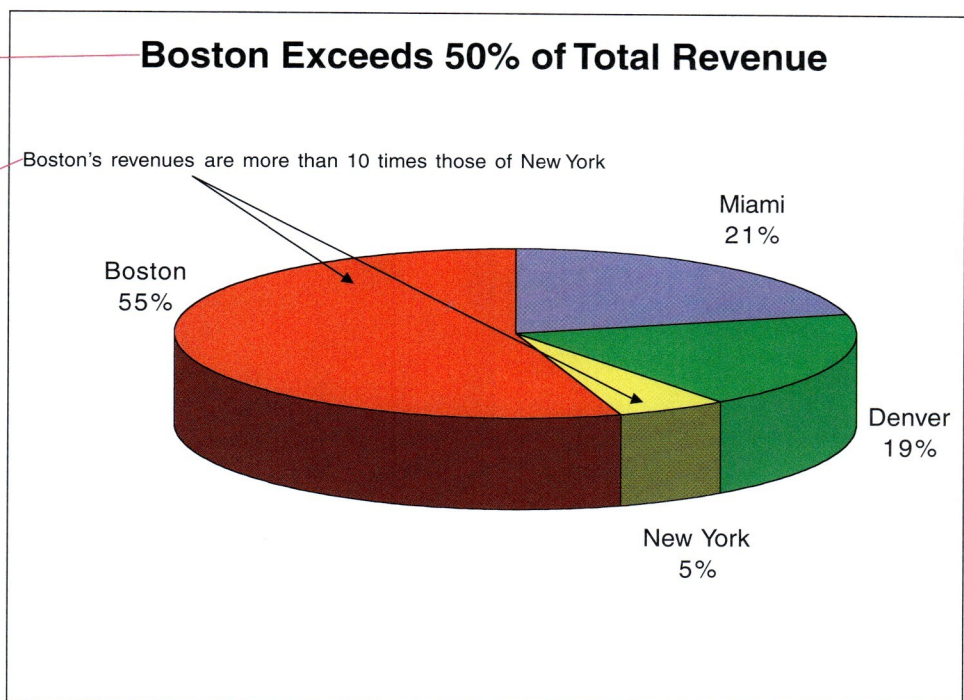

(d) Enhanced Pie Chart

FIGURE 3.2 Pie Charts (continued)

A pie chart is easiest to read when the number of slices is limited (i.e., not more than six or seven), and when small categories (percentages less than five) are grouped into a single category called "Other."

Column and Bar Charts

A *column chart* is used when there is a need to show actual numbers rather than percentages. The column chart in Figure 3.3a plots the same data series as the earlier pie chart, but displays it differently. The category labels (Miami, Denver, New York, and Boston) are shown along the *X* (horizontal) *axis*. The data points (monthly sales) are plotted along the *Y* (vertical) *axis*, with the height of each column reflecting the value of the data point.

A column chart can be given a horizontal orientation and converted to a *bar chart* as in Figure 3.3b. Some individuals prefer the bar chart over the corresponding column chart because the longer horizontal bars accentuate the difference between the items. Bar charts are also preferable when the descriptive labels are long, to eliminate the crowding that can occur along the horizontal axis of a column chart. As with the pie chart, a title can lead the reader and further emphasize the message, as with *Boston Leads All Cities* in Figure 3.3b.

KEEP IT SIMPLE

Keep it simple. This rule applies to both your message and the means of conveying that message. Excel makes it almost too easy to change fonts, styles, the shape of columns, type sizes, and colors, but such changes will often detract from, rather than enhance, a chart. More is not necessarily better, and you do not have to use a feature just because it is there. Remember that a chart must ultimately succeed on the basis of content, and content alone.

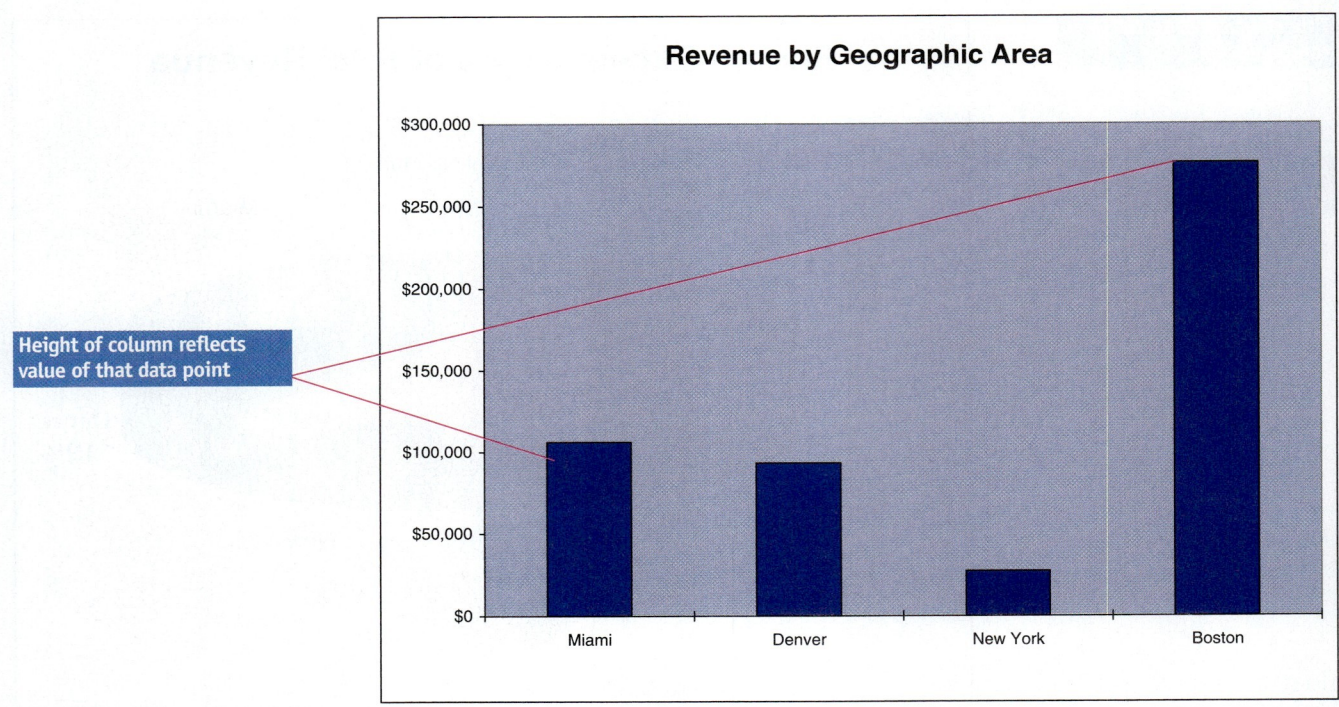

(a) Column Chart

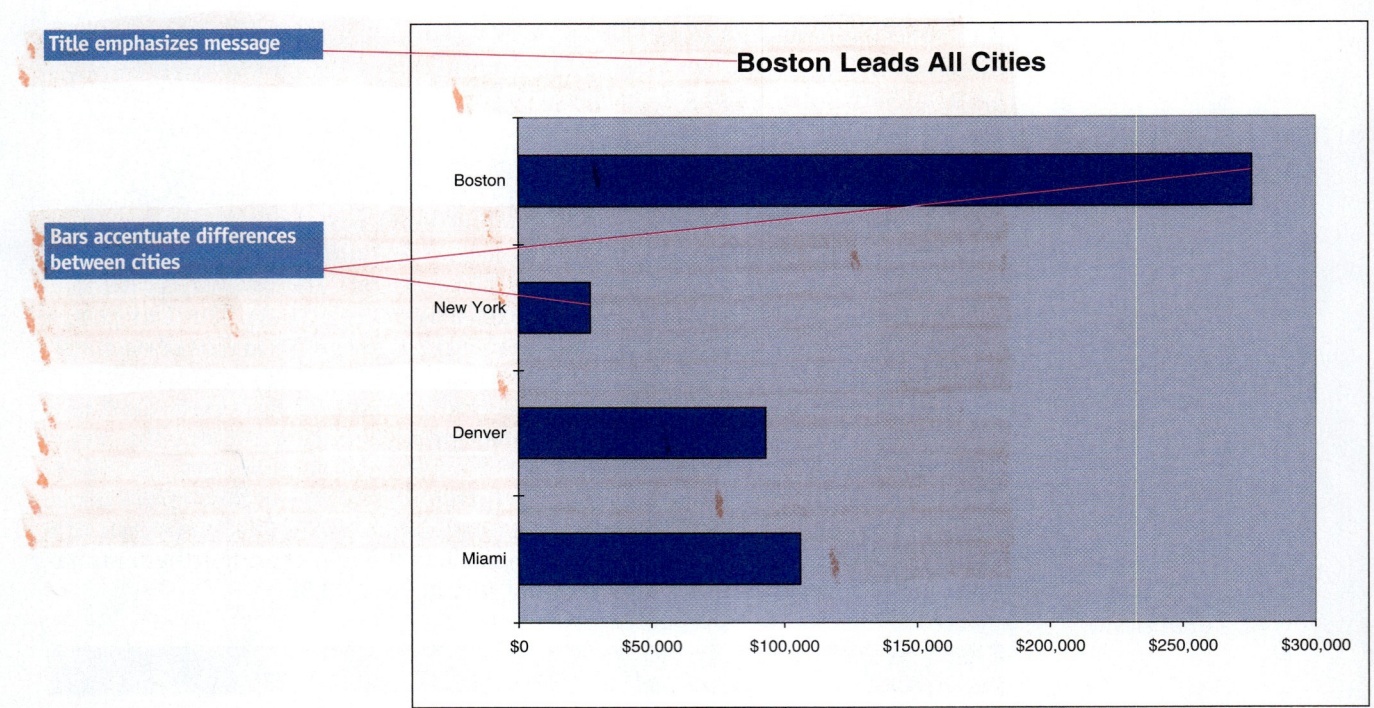

(b) Horizontal Bar Chart

FIGURE 3.3 Column/Bar Charts

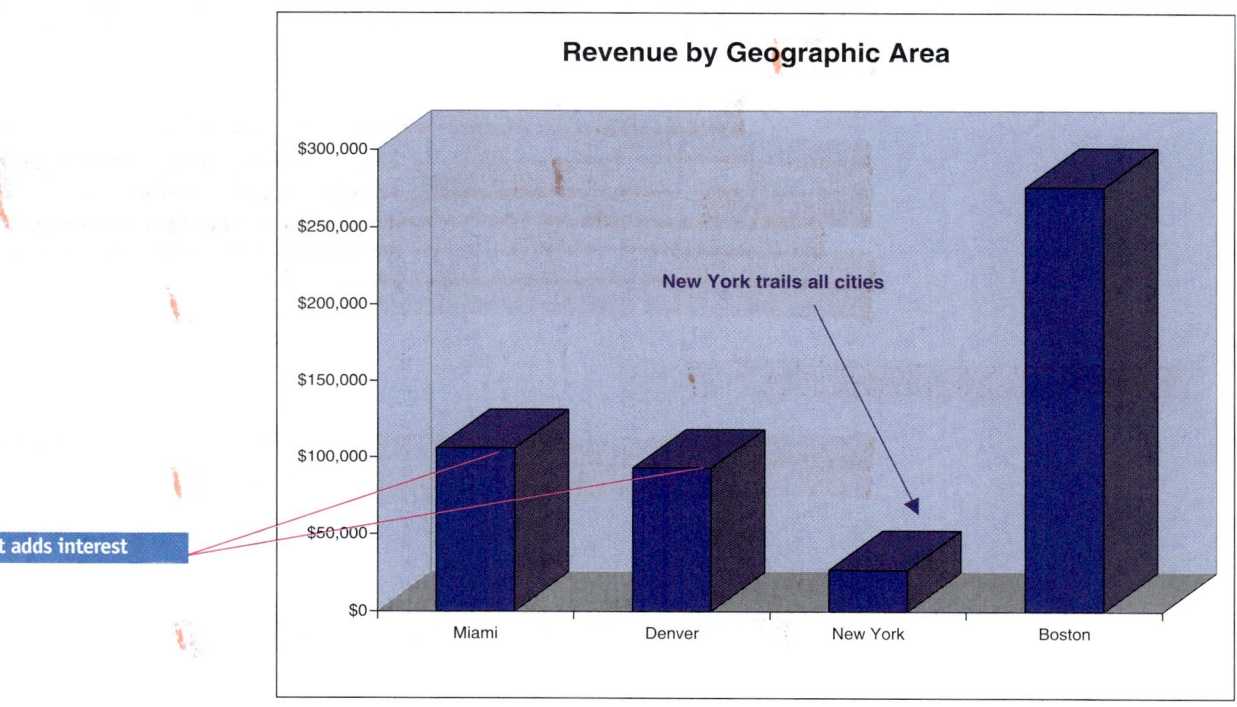

(c) Three-dimensional Column Chart

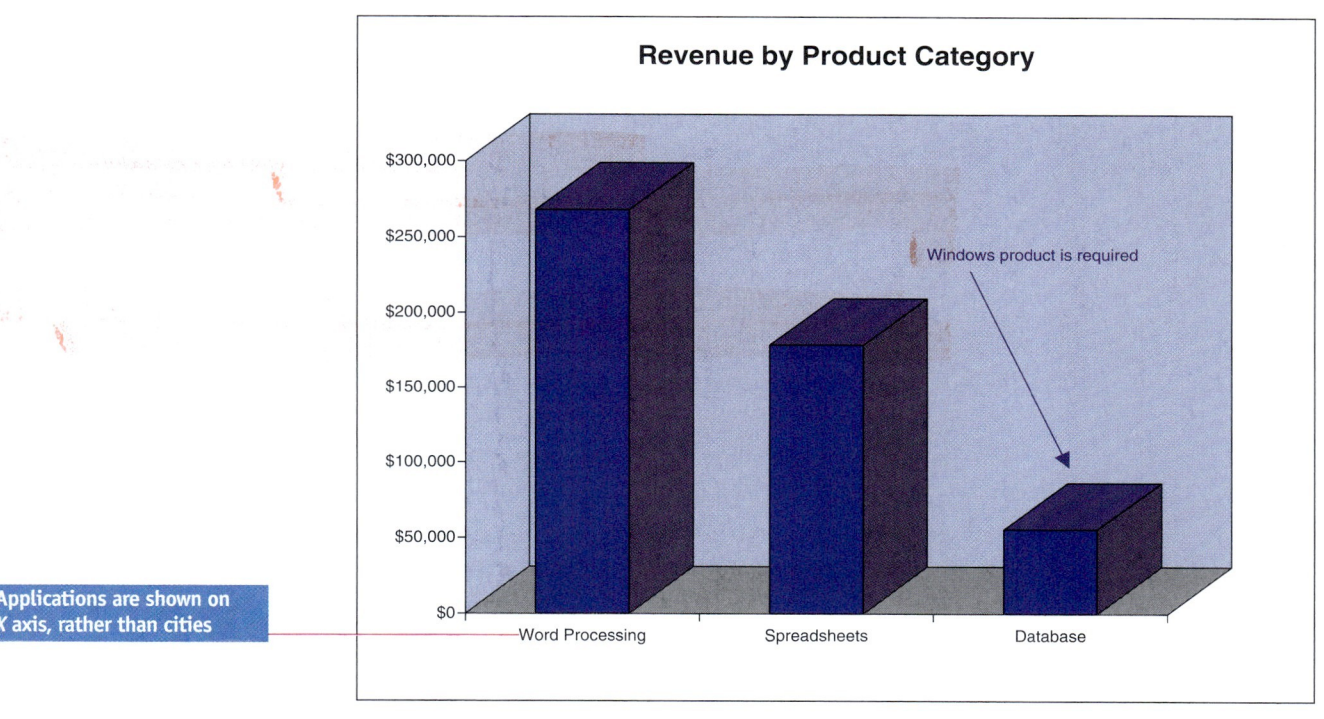

(d) Alternate Column Chart

FIGURE 3.3 Column/Bar Charts (*continued*)

The special effect of a ***three-dimensional column chart*** can produce added interest as shown in Figures 3.3c and 3.3d. Figure 3.3d plots a different set of numbers than we have seen so far (the sales for each product, rather than the sales for each city). The choice between the charts in Figures 3.3c and 3.3d depends on the message you want to convey—whether you want to emphasize the contribution of each city or each product. The title can be used to emphasize the message. Arrows, text, and 3-D shapes can be added to either chart to enhance the message.

As with a pie chart, column and bar charts are easiest to read when the number of categories is relatively small (seven or fewer). Otherwise, the columns (bars) are plotted so close together that labeling becomes impossible.

CREATING A CHART

There are two ways to create a chart in Excel. You can *embed* the chart in a worksheet, or you can create the chart in a separate ***chart sheet***. Figure 3.4a displays an embedded column chart. Figure 3.4b shows a pie chart in its own chart sheet. Both techniques are valid. The choice between the two depends on your personal preference.

Regardless of where it is kept (embedded in a worksheet or in its own chart sheet), a chart is linked to the worksheet on which it is based. The charts in Figure 3.4 plot the same data series (the total sales for each city). Change any of these data points on the worksheet, and both charts will be updated automatically to reflect the new data.

Both charts are part of the same workbook (Software Sales) as indicated in the title bar of each figure. The tabs within the workbook have been renamed to indicate the contents of the associated sheet. Additional charts may be created and embedded in the worksheet and/or placed on their own chart sheets. And, as previously stated, if you change the worksheet, the chart (or charts) based upon it will also change.

Study the column chart in Figure 3.4a to see how it corresponds to the worksheet on which it is based. The descriptive names on the X axis are known as category labels and match the entries in cells B3 through E3. The quantitative values (data points) are plotted on the Y axis and match the total sales in cells B7 through E7. Even the numeric format matches; that is, the currency format used in the worksheet appears automatically on the scale of the Y axis.

The ***sizing handles*** on the ***embedded chart*** indicate it is currently selected and can be sized, moved, or deleted the same way as any other Windows object:

- To size the selected chart, point to a sizing handle (the mouse pointer changes to a double arrow), then drag the handle in the desired direction.

- To move the selected chart, point to the chart (the mouse pointer is a single arrow), then drag the chart to its new location.

- To copy the selected chart, click the Copy button to copy the chart to the clipboard, click in the workbook where you want the copied chart to go, then click the Paste button to paste the chart at that location.

- To delete the selected chart, press the Del key.

The same operations apply to any of the objects within the chart (such as its title), as will be discussed in the next section on enhancing a chart. Note, too, that both figures contain the chart toolbar that enables you to modify a chart after it has been created.

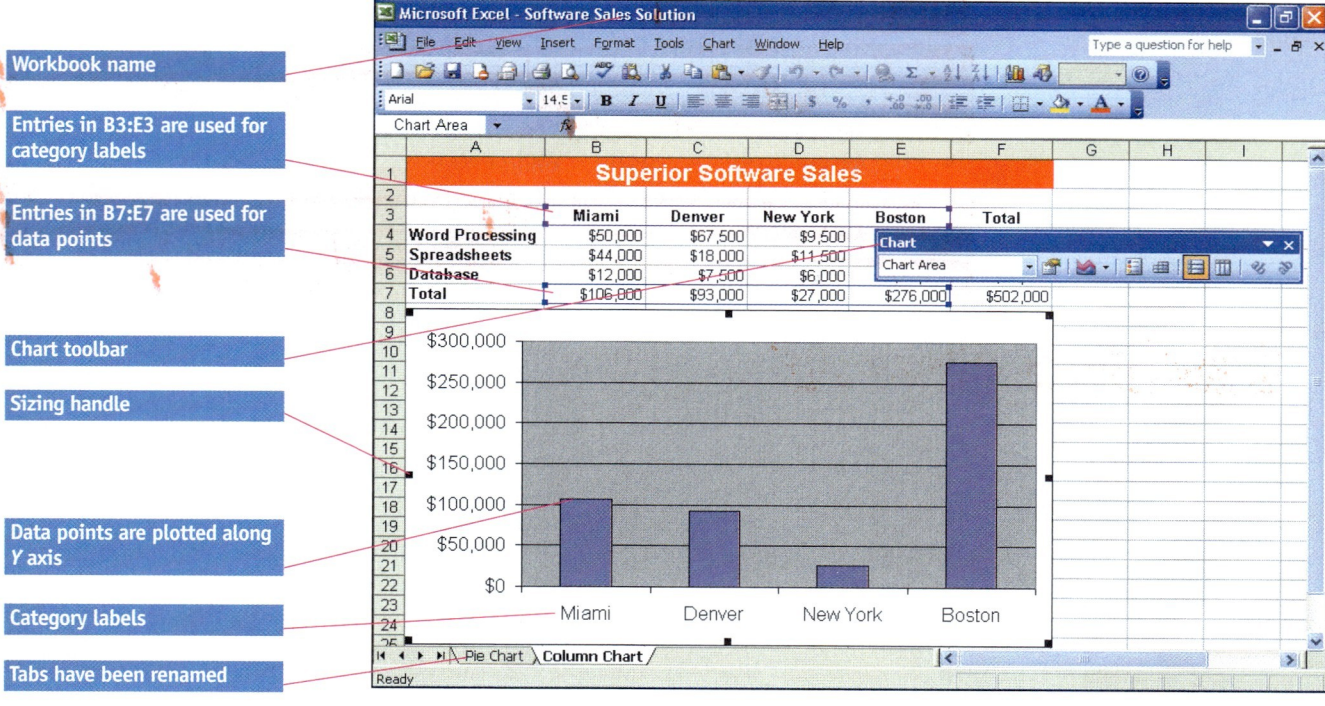

(a) Embedded Chart

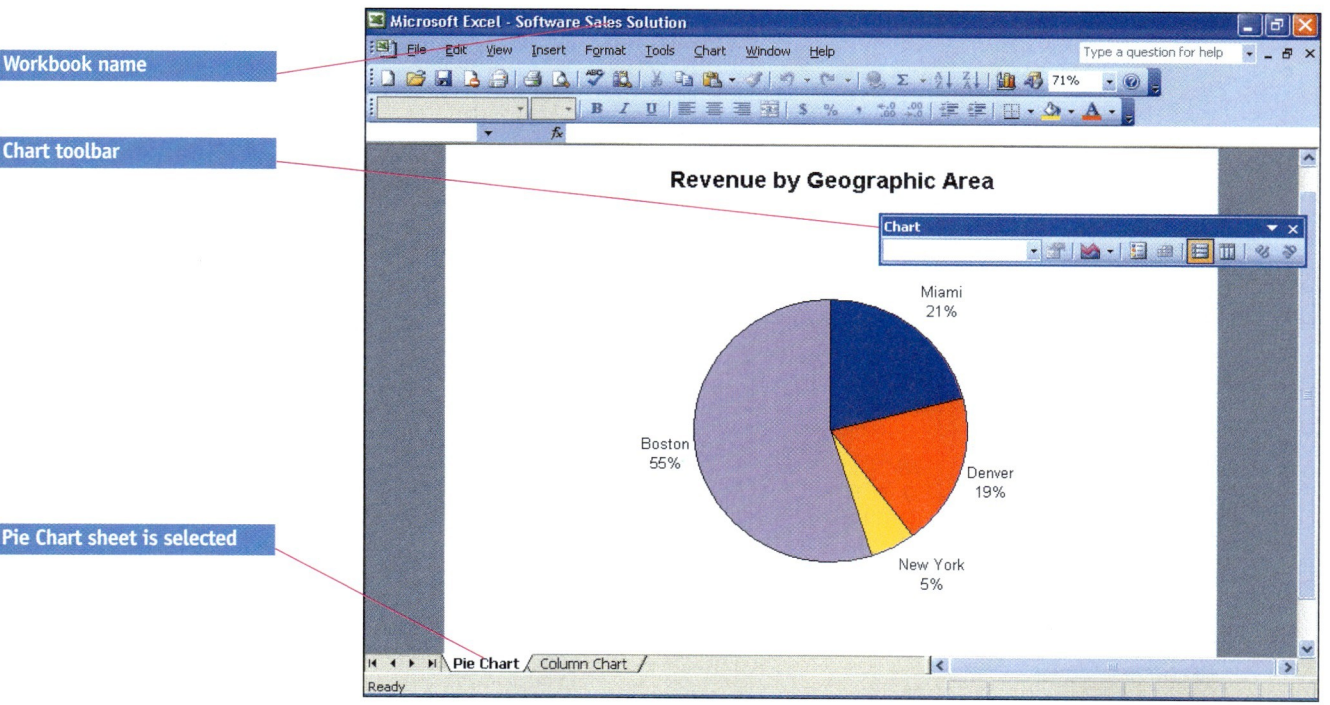

(b) Chart Sheet

FIGURE 3.4 Creating a Chart

The Chart Wizard

The **Chart Wizard** is the easiest way to create a chart. Just select the cells that contain the data as shown in Figure 3.5a, click the Chart Wizard button on the Standard toolbar, and let the wizard do the rest. The process is illustrated in Figure 3.5, which shows how the wizard creates a column chart to plot total sales by geographic area (city).

The steps in Figure 3.5 appear automatically as you click the Next command button to move from one step to the next. You can retrace your steps at any time by pressing the Back command button, access the Office Assistant for help with the Chart Wizard, or abort the process with the Cancel command button.

Step 1 in the Chart Wizard (Figure 3.5b) asks you to choose one of the available *chart types*. Step 2 (Figure 3.5c) shows you a preview of the chart and enables you to confirm (and, if necessary, change) the category names and data series specified earlier. (Only one data series is plotted in this example. Multiple data series are illustrated later in the chapter.) Step 3 (Figure 3.5d) asks you to complete the chart by entering its title and specifying additional options (such as the position of a legend and gridlines). And finally, step 4 (Figure 3.5e) has you choose whether the chart is to be created as an embedded chart (an object) within a specific worksheet, or whether it is to be created in its own chart sheet. The entire process takes but a few minutes.

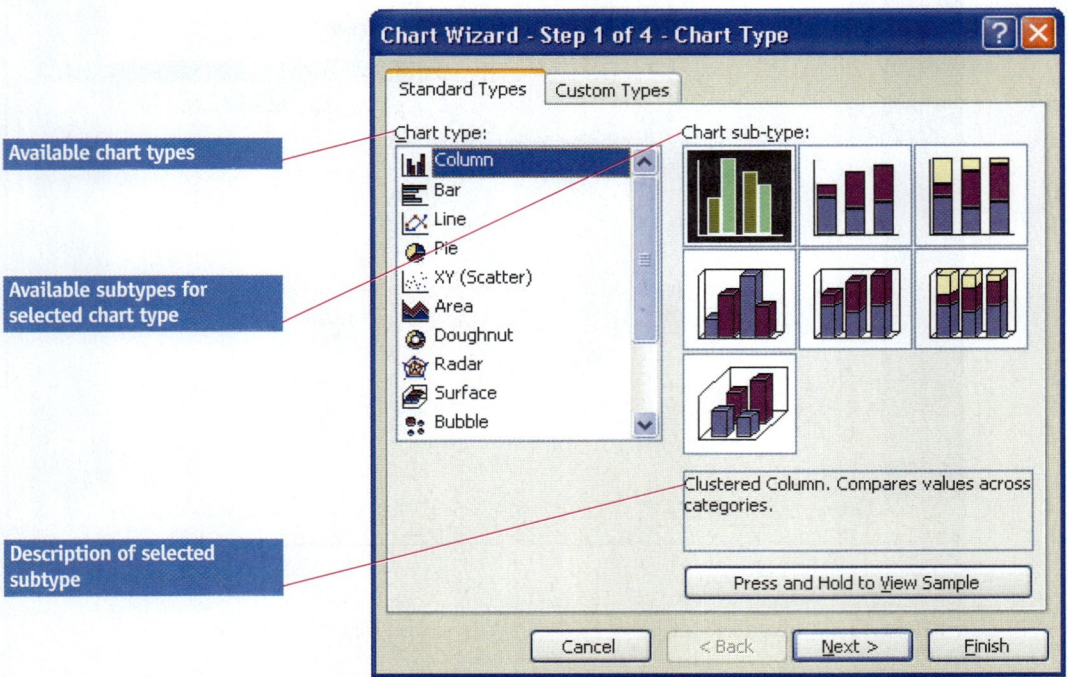

(a) The Worksheet

(b) Select the Chart Type (step 1)

FIGURE 3.5 The Chart Wizard

124 CHAPTER 3: GRAPHS AND CHARTS

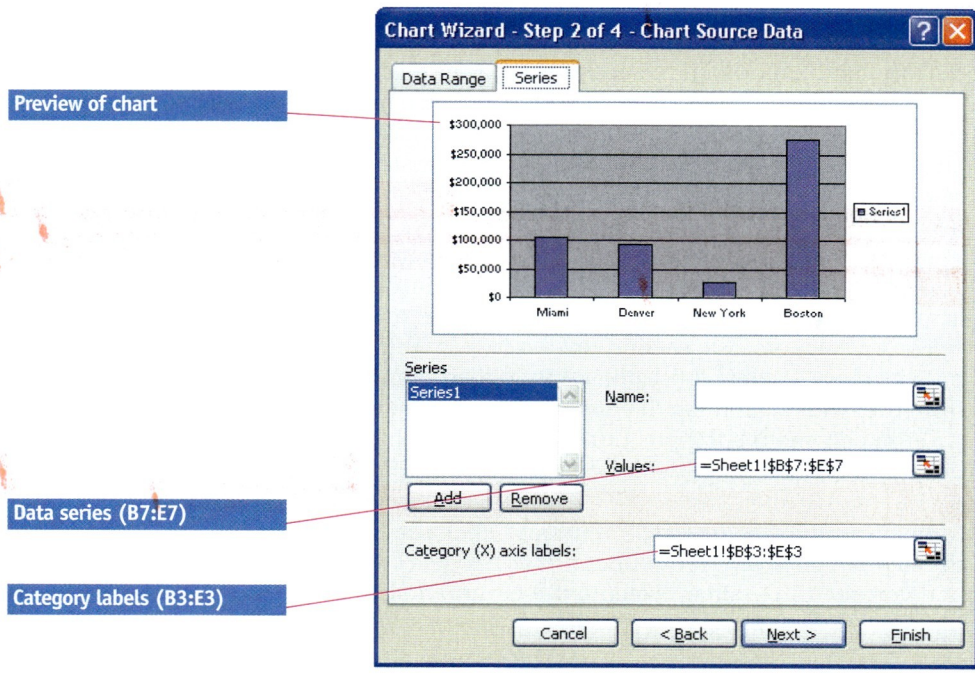

(c) Check the Data Series (step 2)

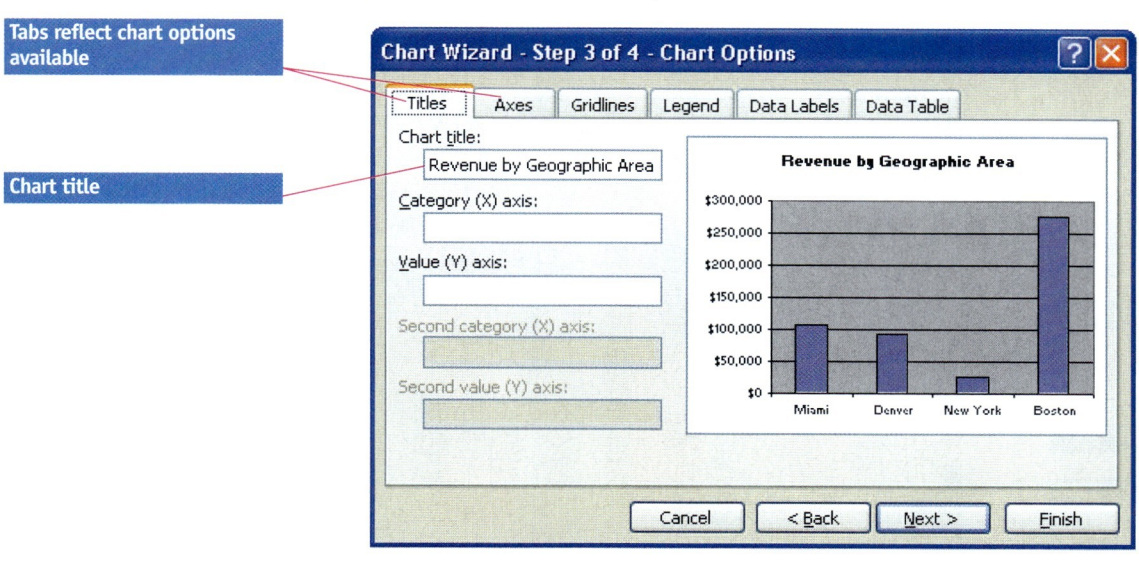

(d) Complete the Chart Options (step 3)

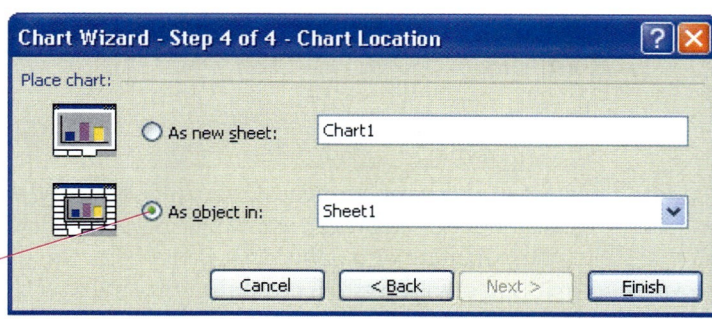

(e) Choose the Location (step 4)

FIGURE 3.5 The Chart Wizard (*continued*)

Modifying a Chart

A chart can be modified in several ways after it has been created. You can change the chart type and/or the color, shape, or pattern of the data series. You can add (or remove) gridlines and/or a legend. You can add labels to the data series. You can also change the font, size, color, and style of existing text anywhere in the chart by selecting the text, then changing its format. All of these features are implemented from the Chart menu or by using the appropriate button on the **Chart toolbar**.

You can also use the **Drawing toolbar** to add text boxes, arrows, and other objects for added emphasis. Figure 3.6, for example, contains a three-dimensional arrow with a text box within the arrow to call attention to the word processing sales. It also contains a second text box with a thin arrow in reference to the database product. Each of these objects is created separately using the appropriate tool from the Drawing toolbar. It's easy, as you will see in our next exercise.

You can change the position of any toolbar by dragging the move handle of a docked toolbar or the title bar of a floating toolbar. (If you drag a floating toolbar to the edge of the program window, it becomes a docked toolbar.) To display a toolbar, pull down the View menu and click the Toolbars command, then check the toolbar. The command functions as a toggle switch; i.e., execute the command and you see the toolbar. Execute the command a second time and the toolbar is hidden.

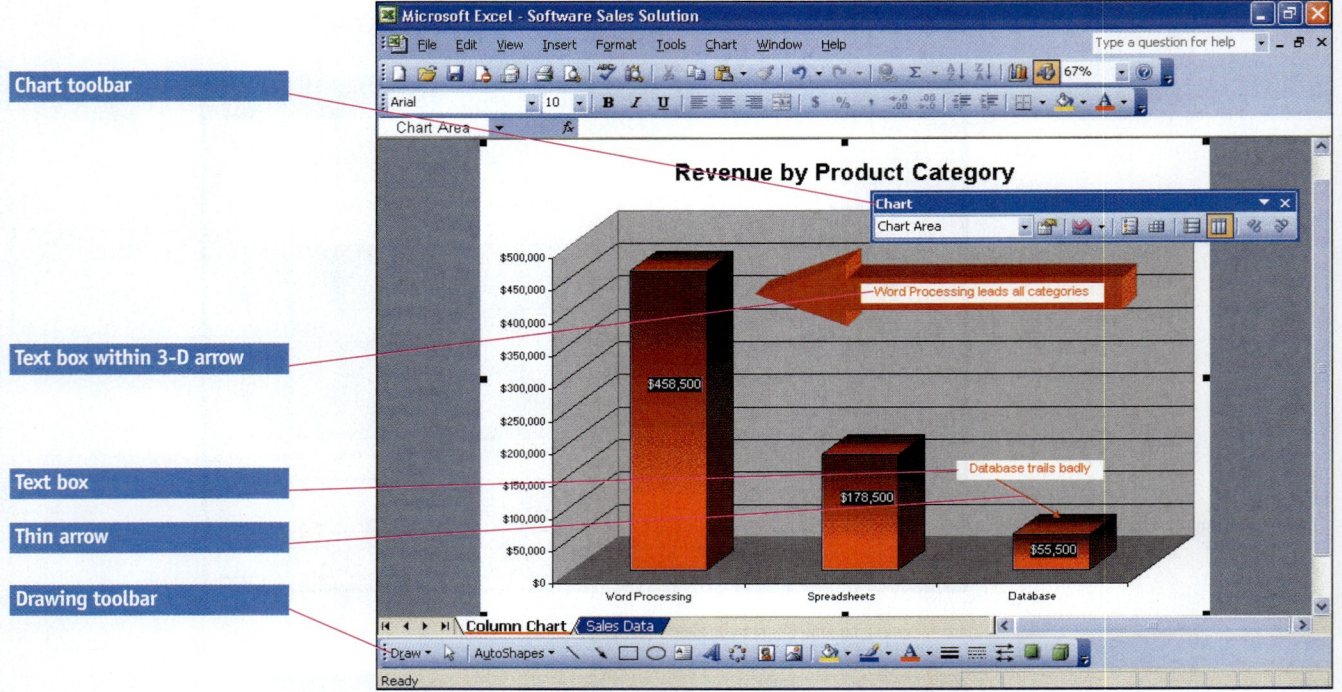

FIGURE 3.6 Enhancing a Chart

SET A TIME LIMIT

Excel enables you to customize virtually every aspect of every object within a chart. That is the good news. It's also the bad news, because you can spend inordinate amounts of time for little or no gain. It's fun to experiment, but set a time limit and stop when you reach the allocated time. The default settings are often adequate to convey your message, and further experimentation might prove counterproductive.

hands-on exercise

1 The Chart Wizard

Objective To create and modify a chart by using the Chart Wizard; to embed a chart within a worksheet; to enhance a chart to include arrows and text. Use Figure 3.7 as a guide in the exercise.

Step 1: **The AutoSum Command**

- Start Excel. Open the **Software Sales workbook** in the **Exploring Excel folder**. Save the workbook as **Software Sales Solution**.

- Click and drag to select **cells B7** through **E7** (the cells that will contain the total sales for each location). Click the **AutoSum button** on the Standard toolbar to compute the total for each city.

- The totals are computed automatically as shown in Figure 3.7a. The formula bar shows that Cell B7 contains the Sum function to total all of the numeric entries immediately above the cell.

- Click and drag to select **cells F4** through **F7**, then click the **AutoSum button**. The Sum function is entered automatically into these cells to total the entries to the left of the selected cells.

- Click and drag to select **cells B4** through **F7** to format these cells with the currency symbol and no decimal places.

- **Boldface** the row and column headings and the totals. Center the entries in **cells B3** through **F3**.

- Save the workbook.

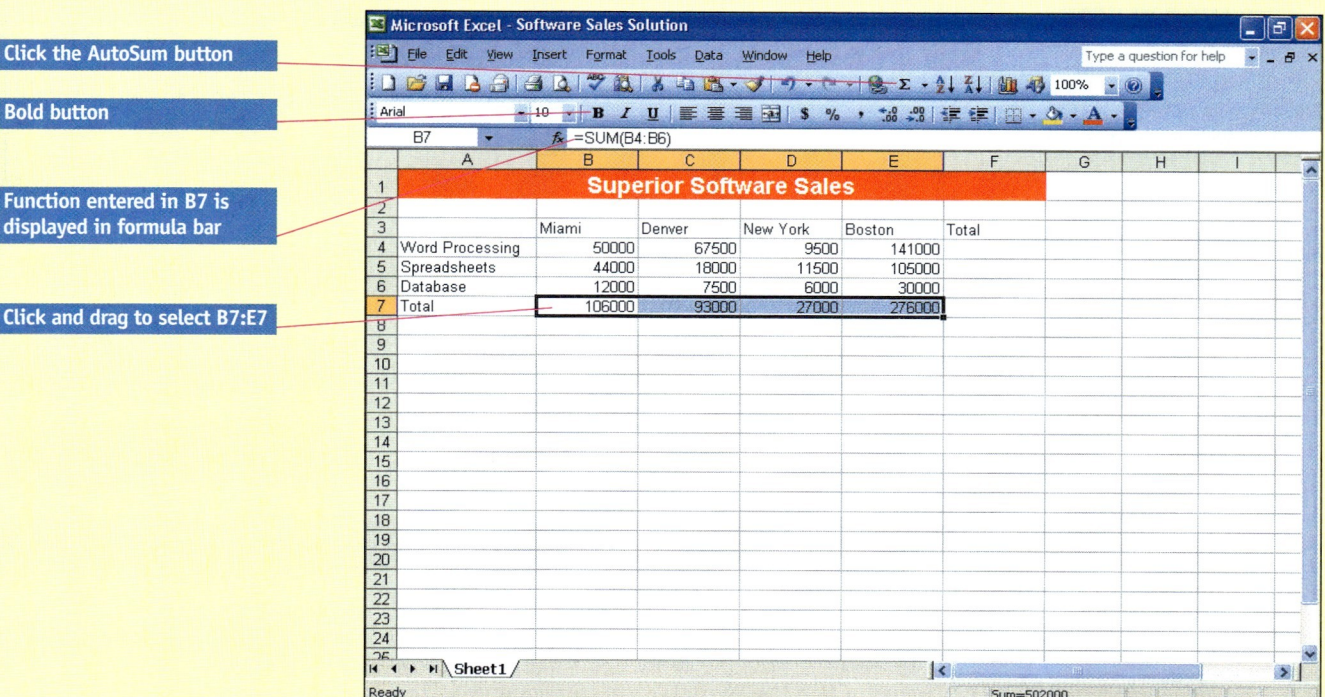

(a) The AutoSum Command (step 1)

FIGURE 3.7 Hands-on Exercise 1

MICROSOFT OFFICE EXCEL 2003 REVISED   127

Step 2: Start the Chart Wizard

- Separate the toolbars if they occupy the same row. Pull down the **Tools menu**, click the **Customize command**, click the **Options tab**, then check the box that displays the toolbars on two rows.

- Drag the mouse over **cells B3** through **E3** to select the category labels (the names of the cities). Press and hold the **Ctrl key** as you drag the mouse over **cells B7** through **E7** to select the data series (the cells containing the total sales for the individual cities).

- Check that cells B3 through E3 and B7 through E7 are selected. Click the **Chart Wizard button** on the Standard toolbar to start the wizard. If you don't see the button, pull down the **Insert menu** and click the **Chart command**.

- You should see the dialog box for step 1 of the Chart Wizard as shown in Figure 3.7b. The **Column** chart type and **Clustered column** subtype are selected.

- Click (and hold) the button to see a sample chart. Click **Next**.

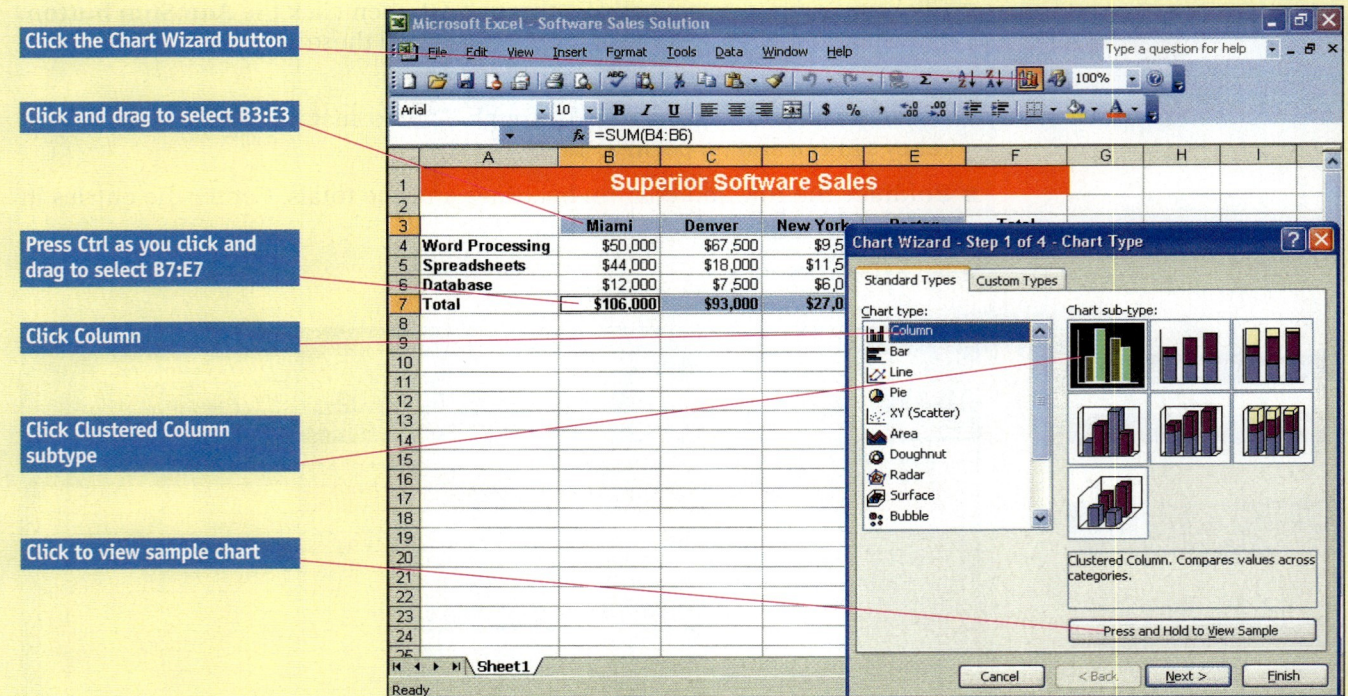

(b) Start the Chart Wizard (step 2)

FIGURE 3.7 Hands-on Exercise 1 (*continued*)

RETRACE YOUR STEPS

The Chart Wizard guides you every step of the way, but what if you make a mistake or change your mind? Click the Back command button at any time to return to a previous screen to enter different information, then continue working with the wizard. Click the Next button to proceed to the next step. Click Finish when the chart is complete.

Step 3: **The Chart Wizard (continued)**

- You should see step 2 of the Chart Wizard. Click the **Series tab** in the dialog box so that your screen matches Figure 3.7c.

- The values (the data being plotted) are in cells B7 through E7. The Category labels for the *X* axis are in cells B3 through E3. Click **Next** to continue.

- You should see step 3 of the Chart Wizard. If necessary, click the **Titles tab**, then click in the text box for the Chart title.

- Type **Revenue by Geographic Area**. Click the **Legend tab** and clear the box to show a legend. Click **Next**.

- You should see step 4 of the Chart Wizard. If necessary, click the option button to place the chart **As object** in Sheet1 (the name of the worksheet in which you are working).

- Click **Finish**.

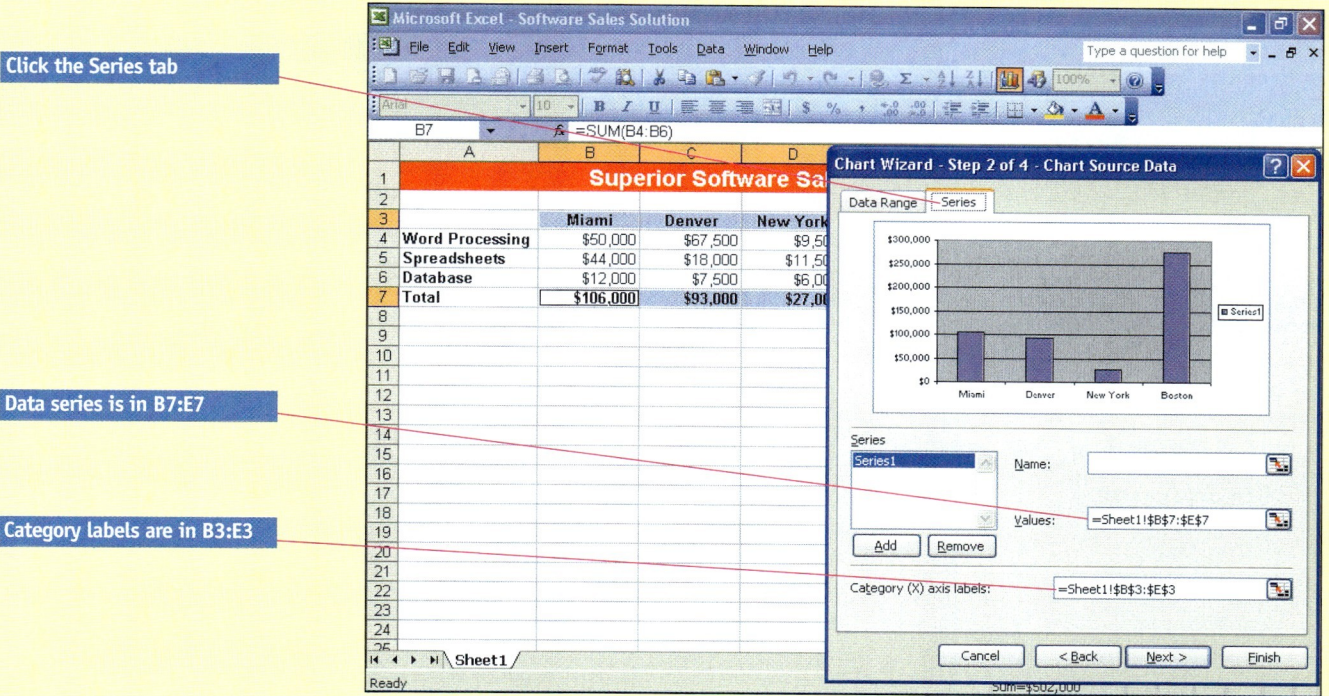

(c) The Chart Wizard (continued) (step 3)

FIGURE 3.7 Hands-on Exercise 1 (*continued*)

THE F11 KEY

The F11 key is the fastest way to create a chart in its own sheet. Select the data, including the legends and category labels, then press the F11 key to create the chart according to the default format built into the Excel column chart. After the chart has been created, you can use the menu bar, Chart toolbar, or shortcut menus to choose a different chart type and/or customize the formatting.

Step 4: **Move and Size the Chart**

- You should see the completed chart as shown in Figure 3.7d. The sizing handles indicate that the chart is selected and will be affected by subsequent commands. The Chart toolbar is displayed automatically whenever a chart is selected.

- Move and/or size the chart just as you would any other Windows object:
  - To move the chart, click the chart (background) area to select the chart (a ScreenTip, "Chart Area," is displayed), then click and drag (the mouse pointer changes to a four-sided arrow) to move the chart.
  - To size the chart, drag a corner handle (the mouse pointer changes to a double arrow) to change the length and width of the chart simultaneously, keeping the chart in proportion as it is resized.

- Click outside the chart to deselect it. The sizing handles disappear and the Chart toolbar is no longer visible.

- Save the workbook.

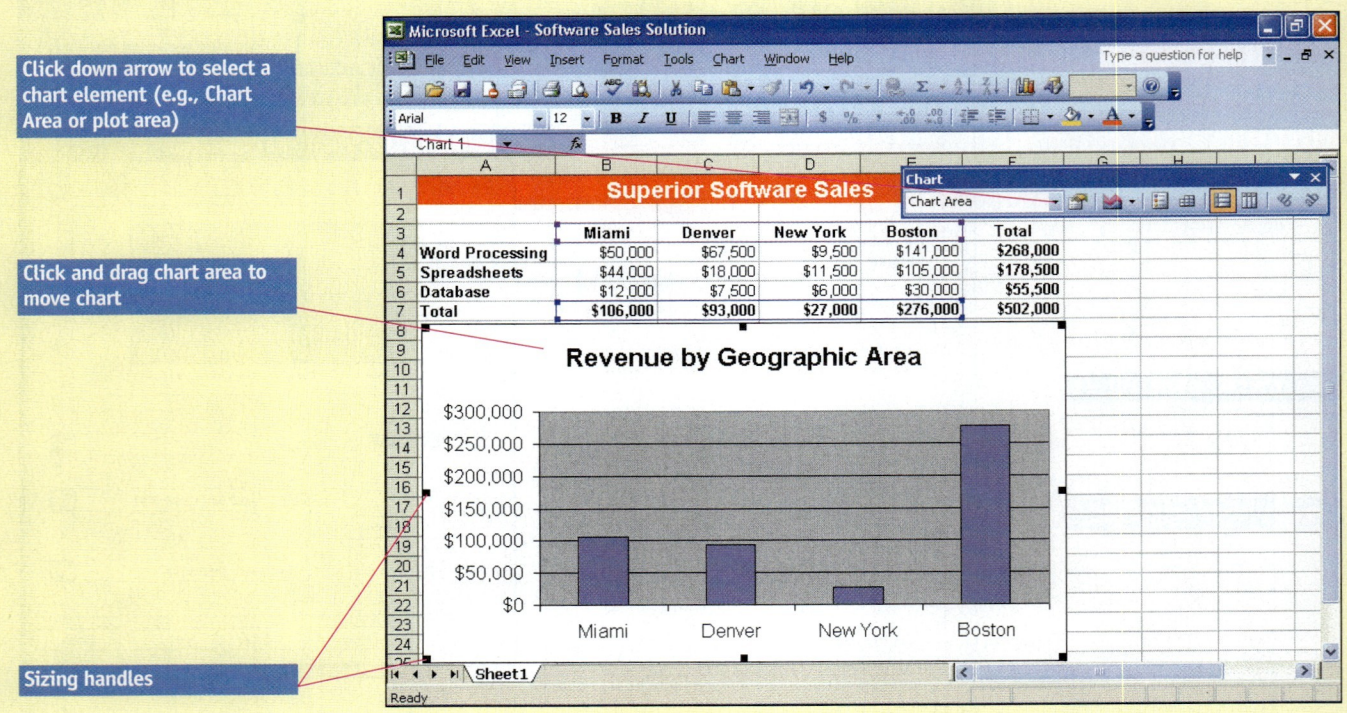

(d) Move and Size the Chart (step 4)

FIGURE 3.7 Hands-on Exercise 1 (*continued*)

EMBEDDED CHARTS

An embedded chart is treated as an object that can be moved, sized, copied, or deleted just as any other Windows object. To move an embedded chart, click the background of the chart to select the chart, then drag it to a new location in the worksheet. To size the chart, select it, then drag any of the eight sizing handles in the desired direction. To delete the chart, select it, then press the Del key. To copy the chart, select it, click the Copy button on the Standard toolbar to copy the chart to the clipboard, click elsewhere in the workbook where you want the copied chart to go, then click the Paste button.

Step 5: Change the Worksheet

- Any changes in a worksheet are automatically reflected in the associated chart. Click in **cell B4**, change the entry to **$400,000**, and press the **Enter key**.

- The total sales for Miami in cell B7 change automatically to reflect the increased sales for word processing, as shown in Figure 3.7e. The column for Miami also changes in the chart and is now larger than the column for Boston.

- Click in **cell B3**. Change the entry to **Chicago**. Press **Enter**. The category label on the *X* axis changes automatically.

- Click the **Undo button** to change the city back to Miami. Click the **Undo button** a second time to return to the initial value of $50,000. The worksheet and chart are restored to their earlier values.

- Save the workbook.

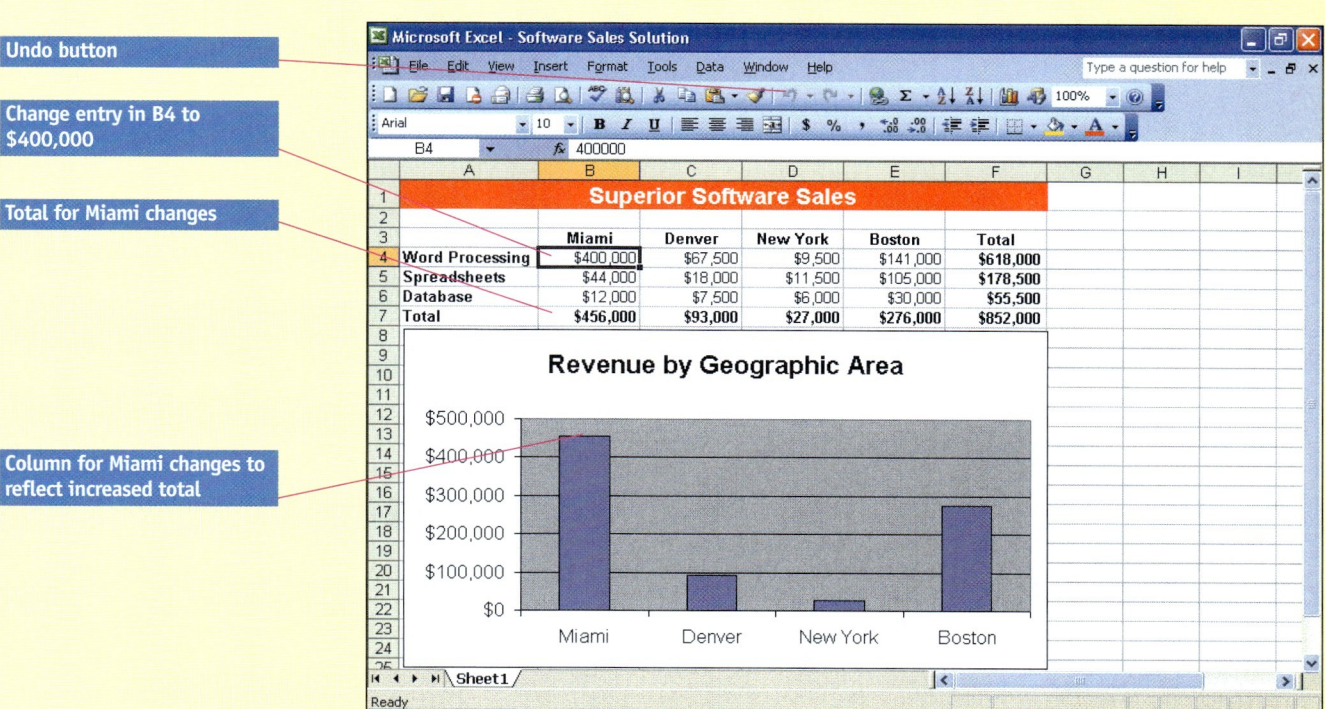

(e) Change the Worksheet (step 5)

FIGURE 3.7 Hands-on Exercise 1 (*continued*)

THE AUTOFORMAT COMMAND

The AutoFormat command does not do anything that could not be done through individual formatting commands, but it does provide inspiration by suggesting several attractive designs. Select the cells you want to format, pull down the Format menu, and click the AutoFormat command to display the AutoFormat dialog box. Select (click) a design, then click the Options button to determine the formats to apply (font, column width, patterns, and so on). Click OK to close the dialog box and apply the formatting. Click the Undo button if you do not like the result. See practice exercise 1 at the end of the chapter.

Step 6: **Change the Chart Type**

- Click the **chart** (background) **area** to select the chart, click the **drop-down arrow** on the Chart type button on the Chart toolbar, then click the **3-D Pie Chart icon**. The chart changes to a three-dimensional pie chart.

- Point to the chart area, click the **right mouse button** to display a shortcut menu, then click the **Chart Options command** to display the Chart Options dialog box shown in Figure 3.7f.

- Click the **Data Labels tab**, then click the check boxes for Category name and Percentage. Click **OK** to accept the settings and close the dialog box.

- The pie chart changes to reflect the options you just specified. Modify each component as necessary:
  - Select (click) the (gray) **Plot area**. Click and drag the sizing handles to increase the size of the plot area within the embedded chart.
  - Point to any of the labels, click the **right mouse button** to display a shortcut menu, and click **Format Data Labels** to display a dialog box. Click the **Font tab**, and select a smaller point size. It may also be necessary to click and drag each label away from the plot area.

- Make other changes as necessary. Save the workbook.

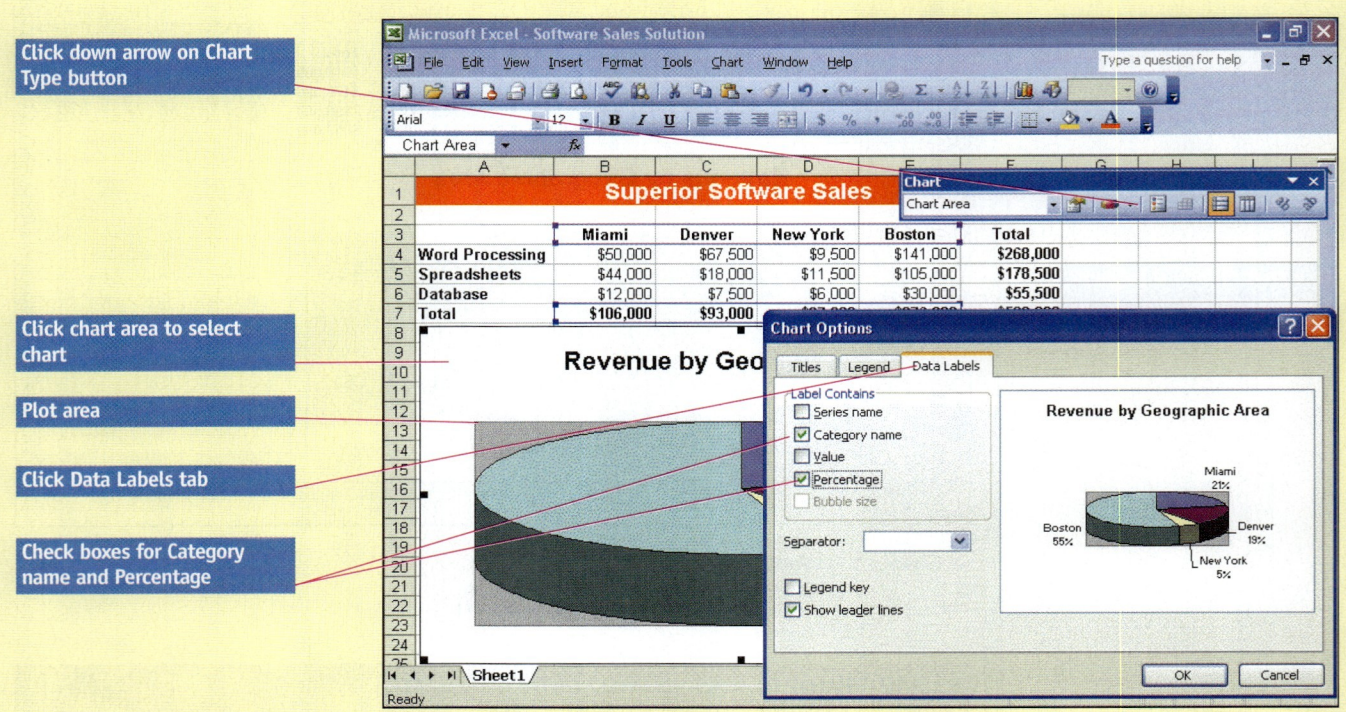

(f) Change the Chart Type (step 6)

FIGURE 3.7 Hands-on Exercise 1 (*continued*)

ADDITIONAL CHART TYPES

Excel offers multiple chart types, each with several formats. Line charts are best to display time-related information such as a five-year trend of sales or profit data. A combination chart uses two or more chart types to display different kinds of data or when different scales are required for multiple data series. See practice exercise 6 at the end of the chapter.

Step 7: **Create a Second Chart**

- Click and drag to select **cells A4** through **A6** in the worksheet. Press and hold the **Ctrl key** as you drag the mouse to select **cells F4** through **F6**.

- Click the **Chart Wizard button** on the Standard toolbar to start the Chart Wizard and display the dialog box for step 1 as shown in Figure 3.7g. The Column Chart type is already selected. Click the **Clustered column with a 3-D visual effect subtype**. Press and hold the indicated button to preview the chart with your data. Click **Next**.

- Click the **Series tab** in the dialog box for step 2 to confirm that you selected the correct data points. The values for Series1 should consist of cells F4 through F6. The Category labels for the *X* axis should be cells A4 through A6. Click **Next**.

- You should see step 3 of the Chart Wizard. Click the **Titles tab**, then click in the text box for the Chart title. Type **Revenue by Product Category**. Click the **Legend tab** and clear the box to show a legend. Click **Next**.

- You should see step 4 of the Chart Wizard. Select the option button to create the chart **As new sheet** (Chart1). Click **Finish**.

- The 3-D column chart has been created in the chart sheet labeled Chart1.

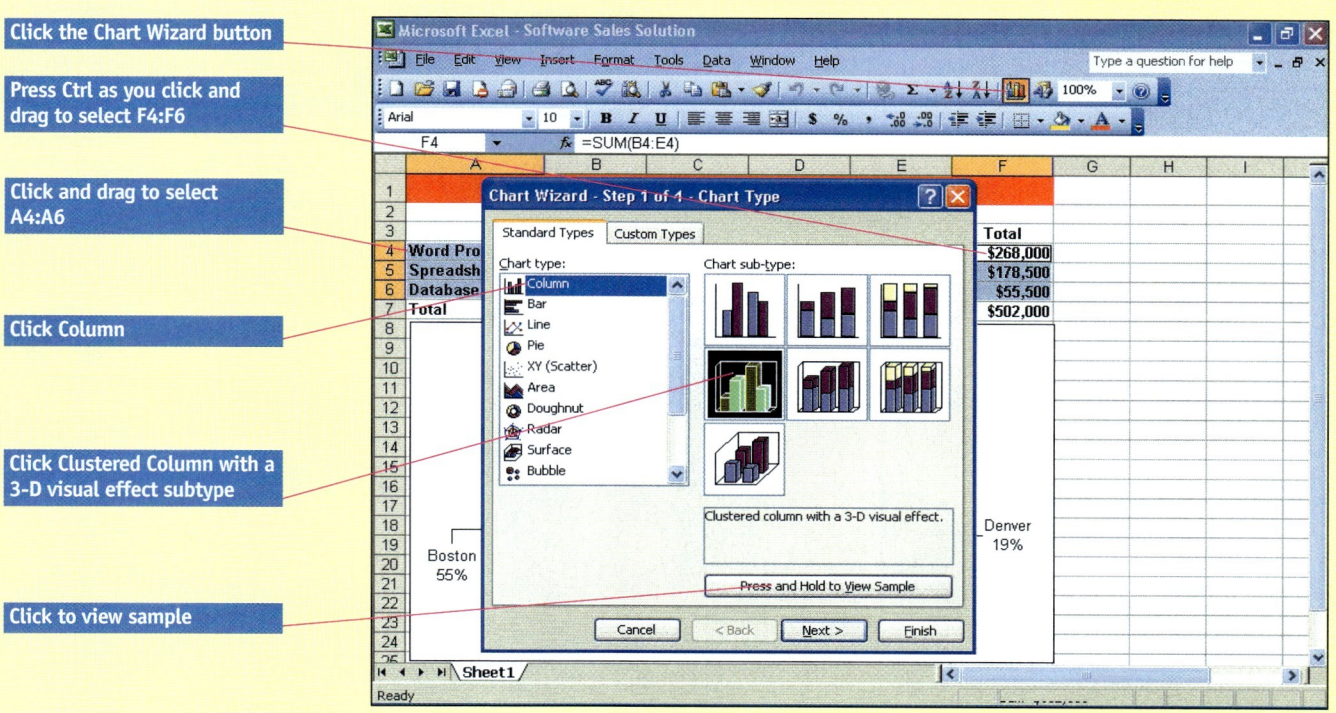

(g) Create a Second Chart (step 7)

FIGURE 3.7 Hands-on Exercise 1 (*continued*)

ANATOMY OF A CHART

A chart is composed of multiple components (objects), each of which can be selected and changed separately. Point to any part of a chart to display a ScreenTip indicating the name of the component, then click the mouse to select that component and display the sizing handles. You can then click and drag the object within the chart and/or click the right mouse button to display a shortcut menu with commands pertaining to the selected object.

Step 8: Add a Text Box

- Point to any visible toolbar, click the **right mouse button** to display a shortcut menu listing the available toolbars, then click **Drawing** to display the Drawing toolbar as shown in Figure 3.7h.

- Click the **Text Box button** on the Drawing toolbar. Click in the chart (the mouse pointer changes to a thin crosshair), then click and drag to create a text box. Release the mouse, then enter the text, **Word Processing leads all categories**.

- Point to the thatched border around the text box, then right click the border to display a context-sensitive menu. Click **Format Text Box** to display the Format Text dialog box. Click the **Font tab** and change the font to **12 point bold**. Choose **Red** as the font color.

- Click the **Colors and Lines tab** and select **white** as the fill color. Click **OK**. You should see red text on a white background. If necessary, size the text box so that the text fits on one line. Do not worry about the position of the text box.

- Click the title of the chart. You will see sizing handles around the title to indicate it has been selected. Click the **drop-down arrow** in the Font Size box on the Formatting toolbar. Click **22** to increase the size of the title. Save the workbook.

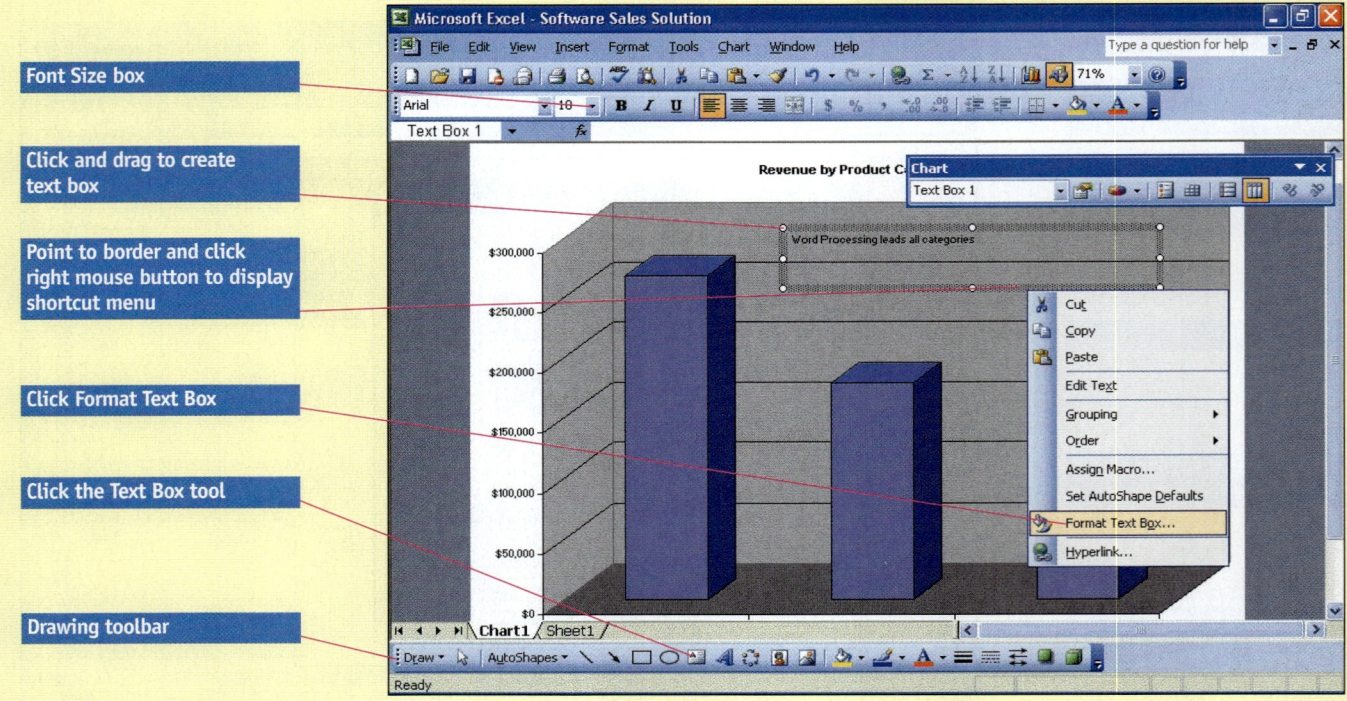

(h) Add a Text Box (step 8)

FIGURE 3.7 Hands-on Exercise 1 (*continued*)

FLOATING TOOLBARS

Any toolbar can be docked along the edge of the application window, or it can be displayed as a floating toolbar within the application window. To move a docked toolbar, drag the move handle. To move a floating toolbar, drag its title bar. To size a floating toolbar, drag any border in the direction you want to go. Double click the title bar of any floating toolbar to dock it. A floating toolbar will dim and disappear if it is not used.

Step 9: **Create a 3-D Shape**

- Click on the **AutoShapes button** and, if necessary, click the down arrow to display additional commands. Click **Block Arrows**. Select an arrow style.

- Click in the chart (the mouse pointer changes to a thin crosshair), then click and drag to create an arrow. Release the mouse.

- Click the **3-D button** on the drawing toolbar and click **3-D Style 1** as shown in Figure 3.7i. Right click the arrow and click the **Format AutoShape command** to display the Format AutoShape dialog box. Click the **Colors and Lines tab**. Choose **Red** as the fill color. Click **OK**, then size the arrow.

- Select (click) the text box you created in the previous step, then click and drag the text box out of the way. Select (click) the **3-D arrow** and position it next to the word processing column.

- Click and drag the text box on top of the arrow. If you do not see the text, right click the arrow, click the **Order command**, and click **Send to Back**.

- Save the workbook, but do not print it at this time. Exit Excel if you do not want to continue with the next exercise at this time.

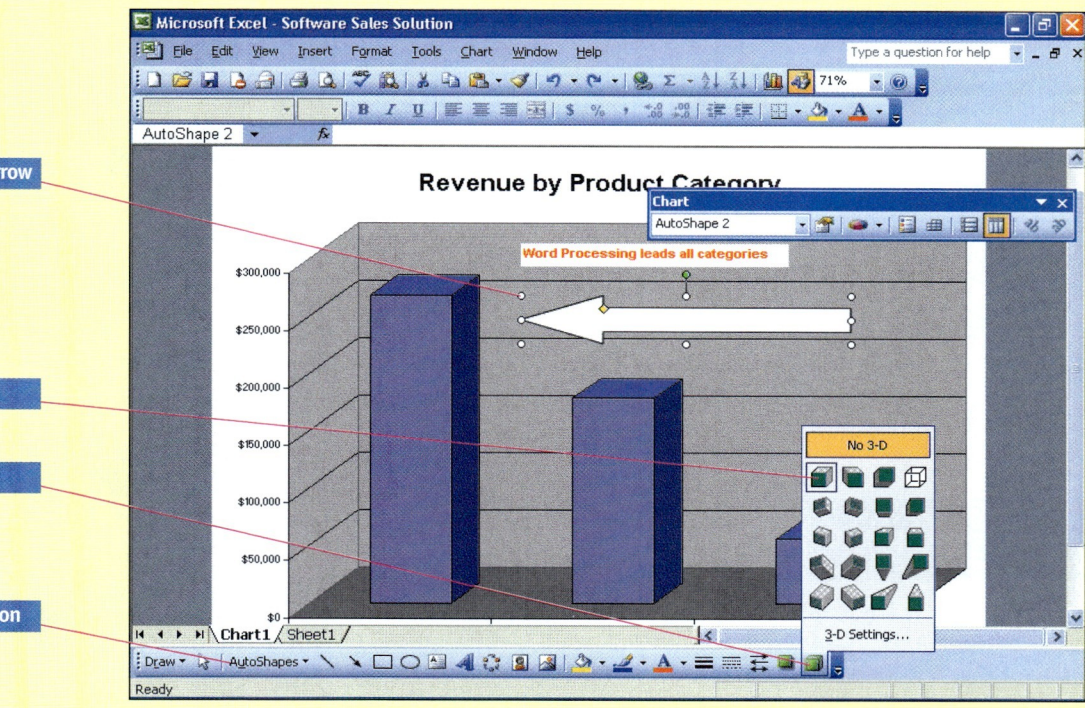

(i) Create a 3-D Shape (step 9)

FIGURE 3.7 Hands-on Exercise 1 (*continued*)

FORMAT THE DATA SERIES

Use the Format Data Series command to change the color, shape, or pattern of the columns within the chart. Right click any column to select the data series (be sure that all three columns are selected), then click Format Data Series to display the Format Data Series dialog box. Experiment with the various options, especially those on the Shape and Patterns tabs within the dialog box. Click OK when you are satisfied with the changes.

MULTIPLE DATA SERIES

The charts presented so far displayed only a single data series such as the total sales by location or the total sales by product category. Although such charts are useful, it is often more informative to view *multiple data series* on the same chart. Figure 3.8a displays the worksheet we have been using throughout the chapter. Figure 3.8b displays a side-by-side column chart that plots multiple data series that exist as rows (B4:E4, B5:E5, and B6:E6) within the worksheet. Figure 3.8c displays a chart based on the same data when the series are in columns (B4:B6, C4:C6, D4:D6, and E4:E6).

Both charts plot a total of twelve data points (three product categories for each of four locations), but they group the data differently. Figure 3.8b displays the data by city in which the sales of three product categories are shown for each of four cities. Figure 3.8c is the reverse and groups the data by product category. This time the sales in the four cities are shown for each of three product categories. The choice between the two charts depends on your message and whether you want to emphasize revenue by city or by product category. It sounds complicated, but it's not; Excel will create either chart for you according to your specifications.

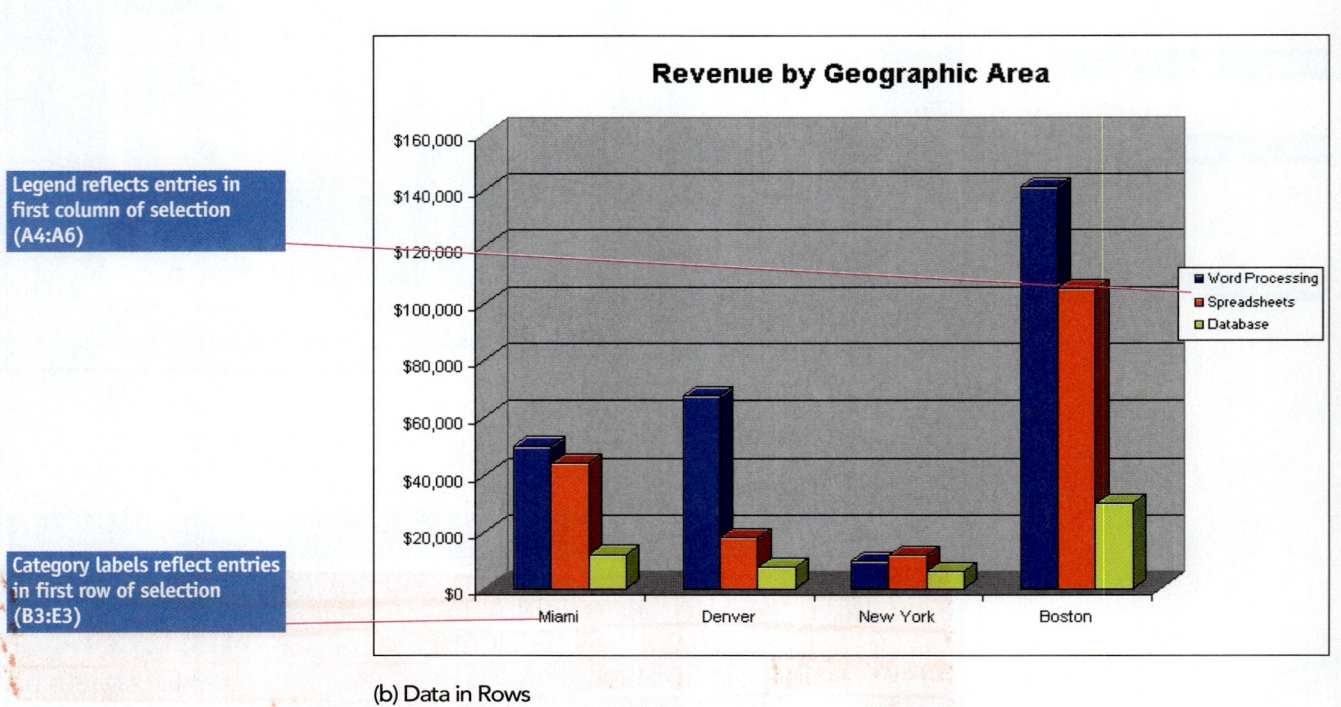

(a) Worksheet Data

(b) Data in Rows

FIGURE 3.8 Side-by-Side Column Charts

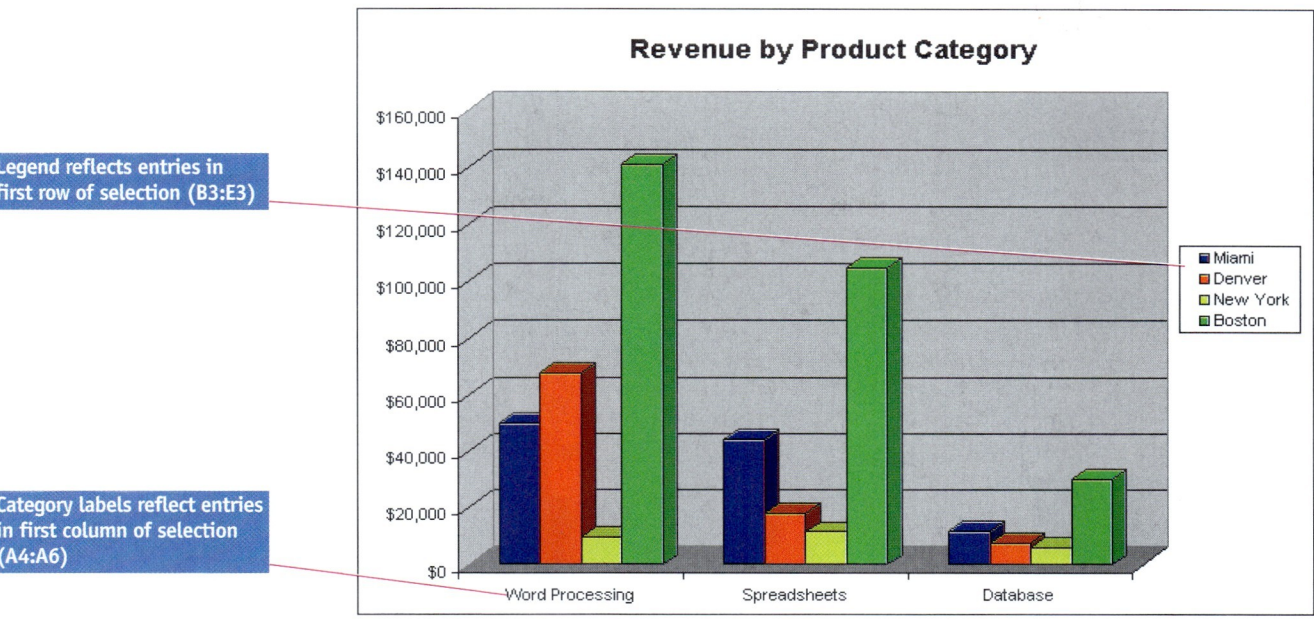

(c) Data in Columns

FIGURE 3.8 Side-by-Side Column Charts (*continued*)

- If you specify that the data series are in rows (Figure 3.8b), the wizard will:
  - ❑ Use the first row (cells B3 through E3) for the category labels
  - ❑ Use the remaining rows (rows four, five, and six) for the data series
  - ❑ Use the first column (cells A4 through A6) for the legend text

- If you specify the data series are in columns (Figure 3.8c), the wizard will:
  - ❑ Use the first column (cells A4 through A6) for the category labels
  - ❑ Use the remaining columns (columns B, C, D, and E) for the data series
  - ❑ Use the first row (cells B3 through E3) for the legend text

Stacked Column Charts

The next decision is the choice between ***side-by-side column charts*** versus ***stacked column charts*** such as those shown in Figure 3.9. Stacked column charts also group data in one of two ways, in rows or in columns. Thus Figure 3.9a is a stacked column chart with the data in rows. Figure 3.9b is also a stacked column chart, but the data is in columns.

The choice of side-by-side versus stacked column charts depends on the intended message. If you want the audience to see the individual sales in each city or product category, then the side-by-side columns in Figure 3.8 are more appropriate. If, on the other hand, you want to emphasize the total sales for each city or product category, the stacked columns are preferable. The advantage of the stacked column is that the totals are clearly shown and can be easily compared. The disadvantage is that the segments within each column do not start at the same point, making it difficult to determine the actual sales for the individual categories.

Note, too, that the scale on the *Y* axis is different for charts with side-by-side columns versus charts with stacked columns. The side-by-side columns in Figure 3.8 show the sales of each product category and so the *Y* axis goes only to $160,000. The stacked columns in Figure 3.9, however, reflect the total sales for all products in each city and thus the scale goes to $300,000. Realize, too, that for a stacked column chart to make sense, its numbers must be additive. You would not, for example, convert a column chart that plots units and dollar sales side by side to a stacked column chart, because units and dollars are not additive.

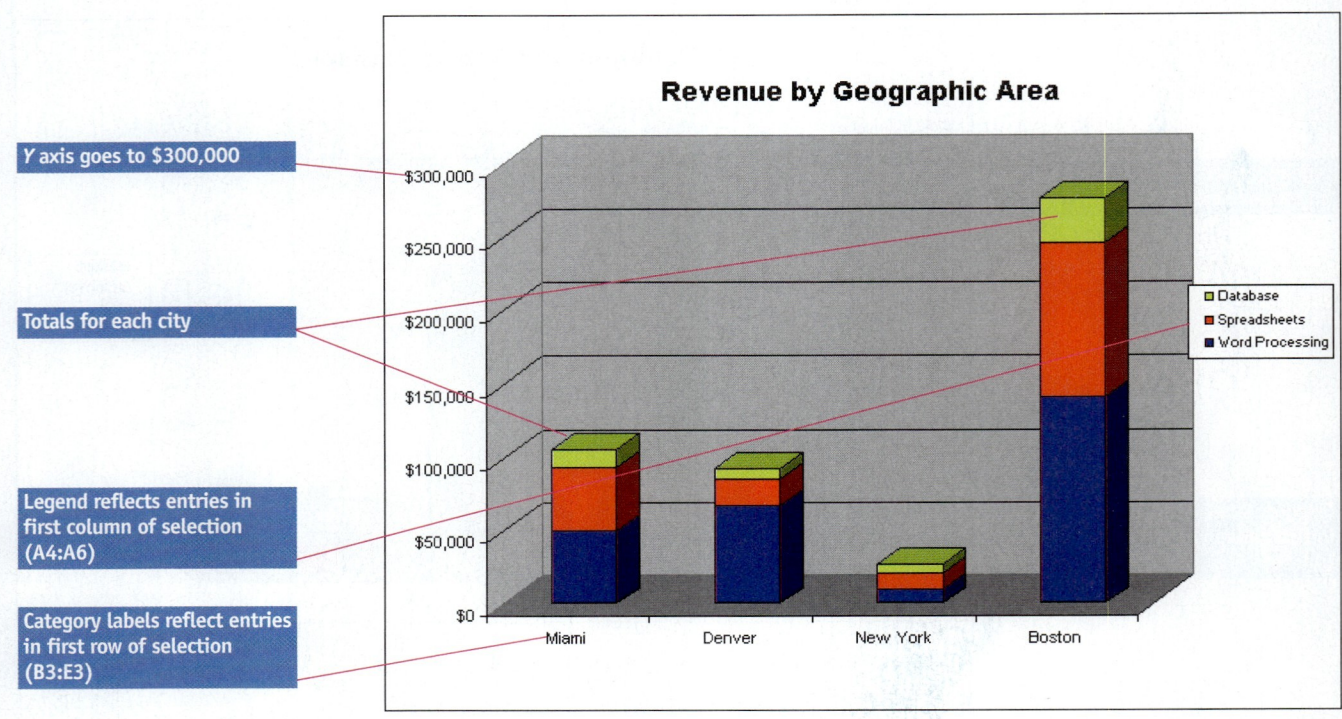

(a) Data in Rows

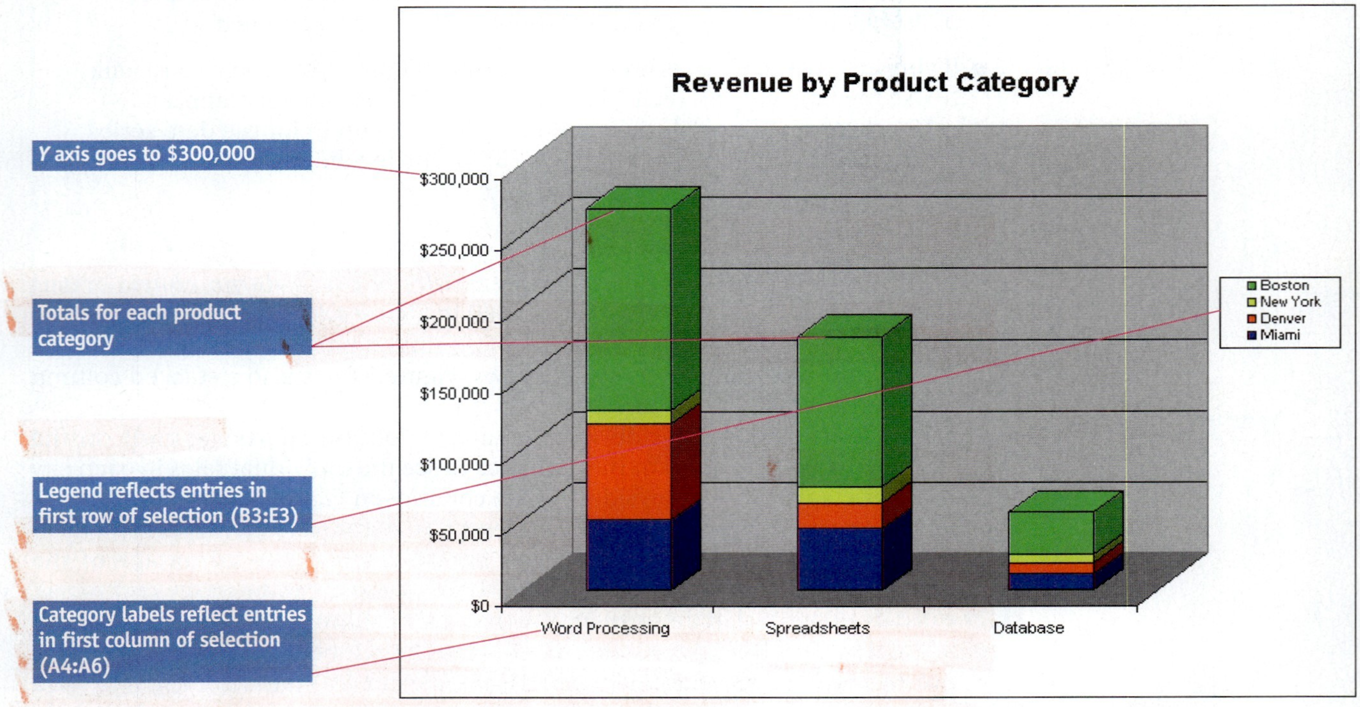

(b) Data in Columns

FIGURE 3.9 Stacked Column Charts

hands-on exercise 2

Multiple Data Series

Objective To plot multiple data series in the same chart; to differentiate between data series in rows and columns. Use Figure 3.10 as a guide.

Step 1: **Rename the Worksheets**

- Open the **Software Sales Solution workbook** from the previous exercise as shown in Figure 3.10a.

- Point to the workbook tab labeled **Sheet1**, click the **right mouse button** to display a shortcut menu, then click the **Rename command**. The name of the worksheet (Sheet1) is selected.

- Type **Sales Data** to change the name of the worksheet to the more descriptive name. Press the **Enter key**. Right click the worksheet tab a second time, click the **Tab Color command**, then change the color to **blue**. Click **OK**.

- Change the name of the Chart1 sheet to **Column Chart**. Change the tab color to **red**. Close the Drawing toolbar. Save the workbook.

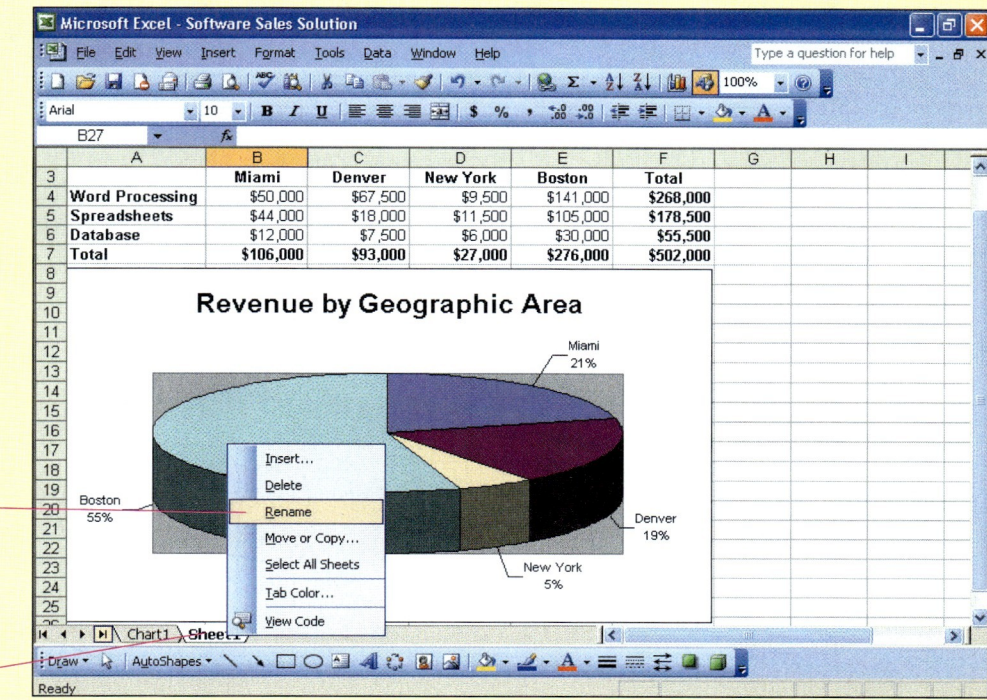

(a) Rename the Worksheets (step 1)

FIGURE 3.10 Hands-on Exercise 2

HIDING AND UNHIDING A WORKSHEET

A chart delivers a message more effectively than the corresponding numeric data, and thus it may be convenient to hide the associated worksheet on which the chart is based. Click the tab of the worksheet you want to hide, pull down the Format menu, click Sheet, and then click the Hide command. (Reverse the process to unhide the worksheet. Pull down the Format menu, click Sheet, click the Unhide command, and then click the name of the worksheet you want to see.)

MICROSOFT OFFICE EXCEL 2003 REVISED

Step 2: **The Chart Wizard**

- Click the **Sales Data tab**, then click and drag to select **cells A3** through **E6**. Click the **Chart Wizard button** on the Standard toolbar to start the wizard.

- Select **Column** as the chart type and **Clustered column with a 3-D visual effect** as the subtype. Click **Next** to continue with the Chart Wizard.

- You should see step 2 of the Chart Wizard as shown in Figure 3.10b. The data range should be specified as **Sales Data!$A$3:$E$6**. The option button for **Series in Rows** should be selected. Click **Next**.

- You should see step 3 of the Chart Wizard. Click the **Titles tab**. Click the text box for Chart title. Type **Revenue by City**. Click **Next**.

- You should see step 4 of the Chart Wizard. Click the option button for **As new sheet**. Type **Revenue by City** in the associated text box. Click **Finish**.

- Excel creates the new chart in its own sheet named Revenue by City. Change the tab color of the chart sheet to **red**. Save the workbook.

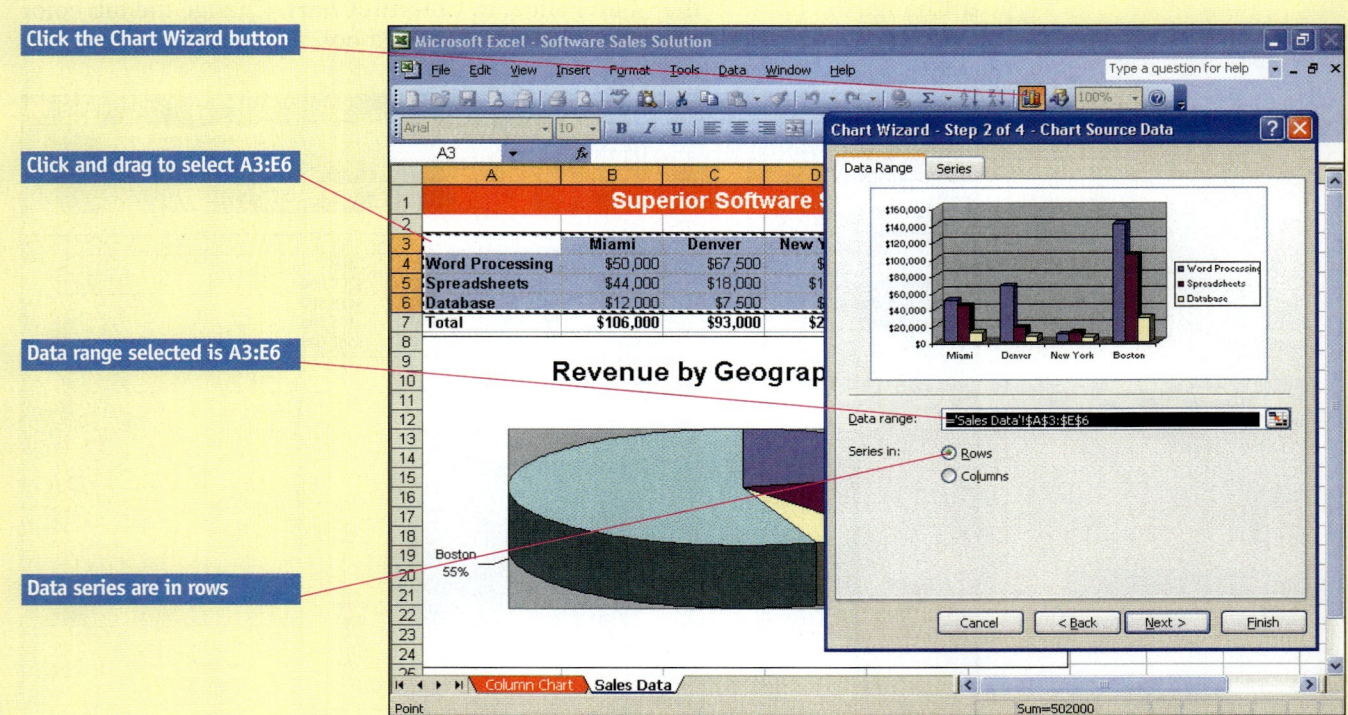

(b) The Chart Wizard (step 2)

FIGURE 3.10 Hands-on Exercise 2 (*continued*)

DATA IN ROWS VERSUS COLUMNS

The choice between data series in rows versus columns depends on the message you want to convey. If the data series are in rows (as in this example), the contribution of each city is emphasized. The first row in the selected range from the worksheet (cells A3 through E6) appears on the *X* axis, and the first column is used as the legend. To view the individual data series, pull down the Chart menu, click the Source Data command to display the associated dialog box, then click the Series tab. You will find three data series (Word processing, Spreadsheets, and Database), each with four data points.

Step 3: **Copy the Chart**

- Click anywhere in the chart title to select the title. Click the **Font Size list box** and change to **18 point** type to enlarge the title.

- Point to the tab named **Revenue by City**. Click the **right mouse button**. Click **Move or Copy** to display the dialog box in Figure 3.10c.

- Click **Sales Data** in the Before Sheet list box. Check the box to **Create a Copy**. Click **OK**.

- A duplicate worksheet called Revenue by City(2) is created and appears before (to the left of) the Sales Data worksheet. (You can also press and hold the Ctrl key as you drag the worksheet tab to create a copy of the worksheet.)

- Double click the newly created worksheet tab to select the name. Enter **Revenue by Product** as the new name.

- Save the workbook.

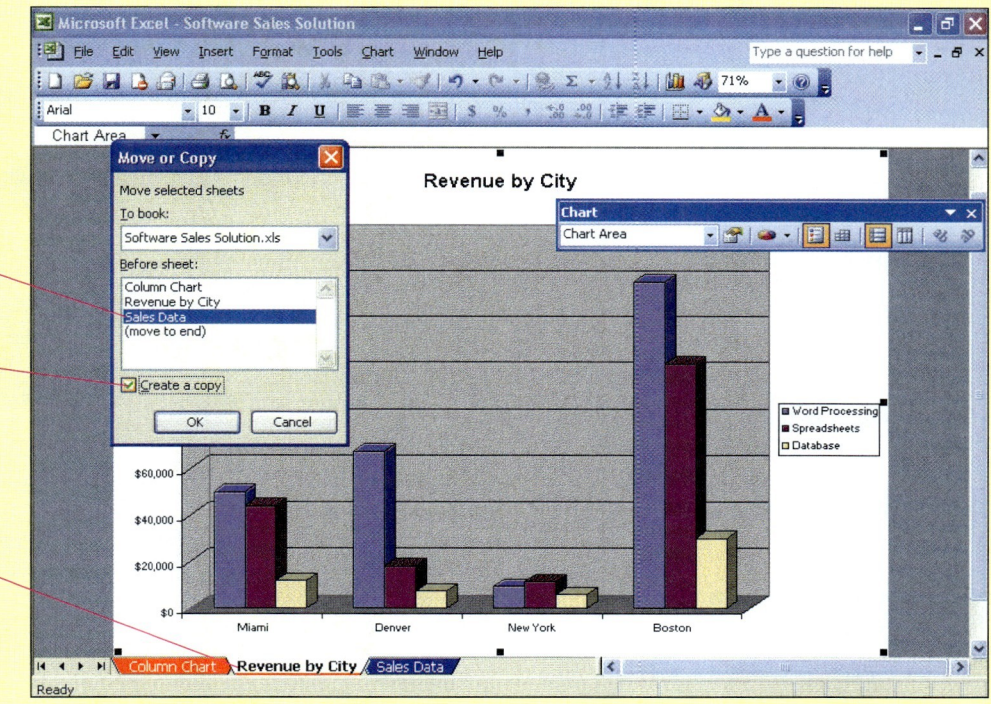

(c) Copy the Chart (step 3)

FIGURE 3.10 Hands-on Exercise 2 (*continued*)

MOVING AND COPYING A WORKSHEET

The fastest way to move or copy a chart sheet is to drag its tab. To move a sheet, point to its tab, then click and drag the tab to its new position. To copy a sheet, press and hold the Ctrl key as you drag the tab to the desired position for the second sheet. Rename the copied sheet (or any sheet for that matter) by double clicking its tab to select the existing name. Enter a new name for the worksheet, then press the Enter key. You can also right click the worksheet tab to change its color. See practice exercise 1 at the end of the chapter.

Step 4: **Change the Source Data**

- Click the **Revenue by Product tab** to make it the active sheet. Click anywhere in the title of the chart, drag the mouse over the word **City** to select the text, then type **Product Category** to replace the selected text. Click outside the title to deselect it.

- Pull down the **Chart menu**. If necessary, click the double arrow to see more commands, click **Source Data** and click the **Data Range tab** (you will see the Sales Data worksheet). Click the **Columns option button** so that your screen matches Figure 3.10d.

- Click the **Series tab** and note the following:
  - The original chart plotted the data in rows. There were three data series (one series for each product).
  - The new chart (shown in the dialog box) plots the data in columns. There are four data series (one for each city as indicated in the Series list box).

- Click **OK** to close the Source Data dialog box.

- Save the workbook.

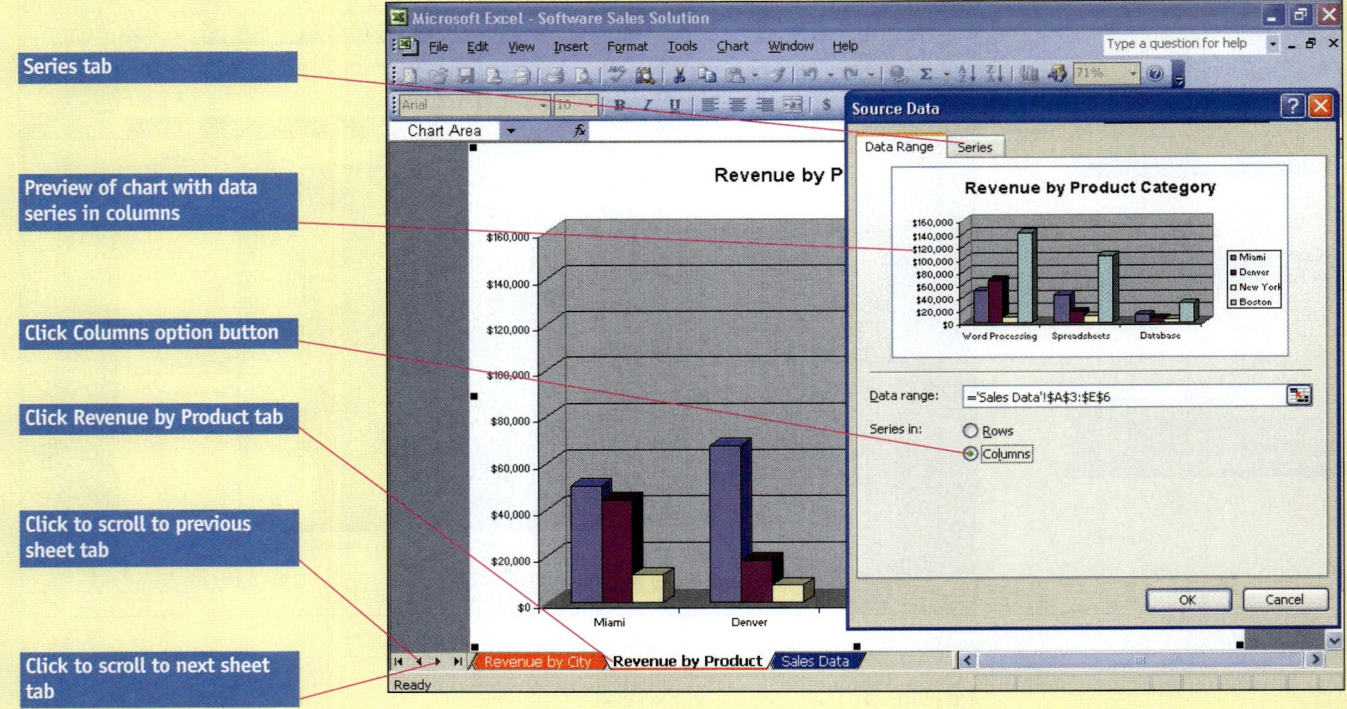

(d) Change the Source Data (step 4)

FIGURE 3.10 Hands-on Exercise 2 (*continued*)

THE HORIZONTAL SCROLL BAR

The horizontal scroll bar contains four scrolling buttons to scroll through the sheet tabs in a workbook. Click ◀ or ▶ to scroll one tab to the left or right. Click ◀◀ or ▶▶ to scroll to the first or last tab in the workbook. Once the desired tab is visible, click the tab to select it. Change the color of any tab by right clicking the tab and selecting Tab Color from the context-sensitive menu. See practice exercise 1 at the end of the chapter.

142 CHAPTER 3: GRAPHS AND CHARTS

Step 5: **Change the Chart Type**

- Pull down the **Chart menu** and click the **Chart Type command** to display the associated dialog box.

- Select the **Stacked Column with a 3-D visual effect** chart (the middle entry in the second row). Click **OK**. The chart changes to a stacked column chart.

- Pull down the **Chart menu** and click the **Chart Options command** to display the associated dialog box. Click the **Legend tab** and check the option button to display the legend at the **bottom** of the chart.

- Click the **Data Labels tab**. Check the box to display the **Value** of each chart component as shown in Figure 3.10e.

- Experiment further with the various options that are available. Click the **Data Table tab**, then check the box to show the data table. We think the table is cluttered in this example, and thus we clear the box to show the table.

- Click **OK** to accept the existing settings and close the Chart Options dialog box. Save the workbook.

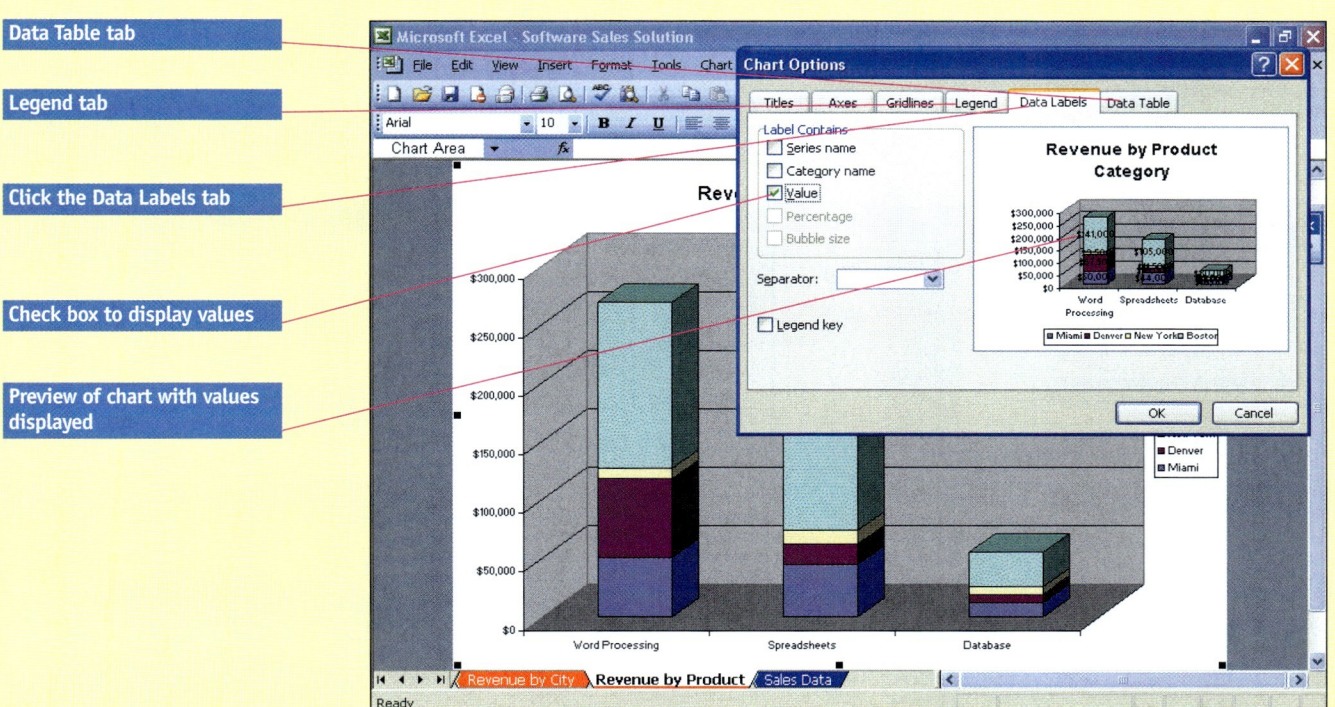

(e) Change the Chart Type (step 5)

FIGURE 3.10 Hands-on Exercise 2 (*continued*)

THE RIGHT MOUSE BUTTON

Point to a cell (or group of selected cells), a chart or worksheet tab, a toolbar, or chart (or a selected object on the chart), then click the right mouse button to display a shortcut menu. All shortcut menus are context-sensitive and display commands appropriate for the selected item. Right clicking a toolbar, for example, enables you to display (hide) additional toolbars. Right clicking a sheet tab enables you to rename, move, copy, or delete the sheet.

Step 6: **Print the Workbook**

- Click the **Print Preview button** on the Standard toolbar to display the Print Preview screen. Click the **Margins button** on the Print Preview toolbar to toggle the (display of the) margins on and off.

- Click the **Setup button** to display the Page Setup dialog box. Click the **Page tab** in the Page Setup dialog box. Click the option button for **landscape**.

- Click the **Header/Footer tab** in the Page Setup dialog box, then click the button to create a **Custom Footer** to display the Footer dialog box as shown in Figure 3.10f.

- Click the text box for the left section and **enter your name**. Click the text box for the center section and **enter your instructor's name**.

- Click the text box for the right section. Click the **Date button**, press the **space bar**, and then click the **Time button**. Click **OK** to accept these settings and close the Footer dialog box. Click **OK** to close the Page Setup dialog box.

- Print the completed chart for your instructor. Use the **Page Setup command** as appropriate prior to printing the other charts in the workbook.

- Save the workbook. Exit Excel if you do not want to continue with the next exercise at this time.

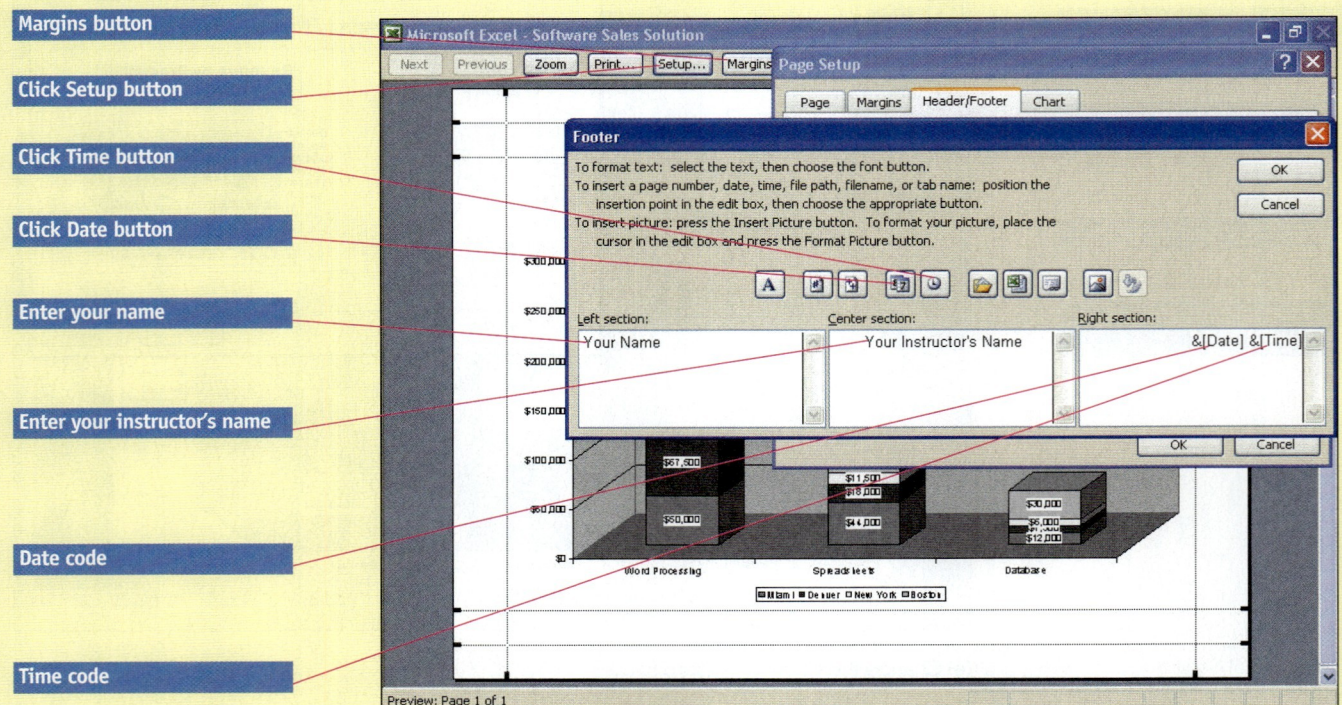

(f) Print the Workbook (step 6)

FIGURE 3.10 Hands-on Exercise 2 (*continued*)

PRINT ONLY WHAT YOU NEED

Why print an entire workbook if you need only a single worksheet? Press and hold the Ctrl key as you click the tab(s) of the worksheet(s) that you want to print. Pull down the File menu, click the Print command, click the option button for Active Sheet(s) in the Print What area, then click OK. (You can also print selected cells within a worksheet by selecting the cells, then clicking the Selection option button.)

144   CHAPTER 3: GRAPHS AND CHARTS

OBJECT LINKING AND EMBEDDING

The applications within Microsoft Office enable you to create a document in one application that contains data (objects) from another application. The memo in Figure 3.11, for example, was created in Microsoft Word, and it contains ***objects*** (a worksheet and a chart) that were developed in Microsoft Excel. The Excel objects are linked to the Word document, so that any changes to the Excel workbook are automatically reflected in the Word document.

The following exercise uses ***Object Linking and Embedding (OLE)*** to create a Word document containing an Excel worksheet and chart. As you do the exercise, both applications (Word and Excel) will be open, and it will be necessary to switch back and forth between them. This in turn demonstrates the ***multitasking*** capability within Windows and the use of the ***taskbar*** to switch between the open applications.

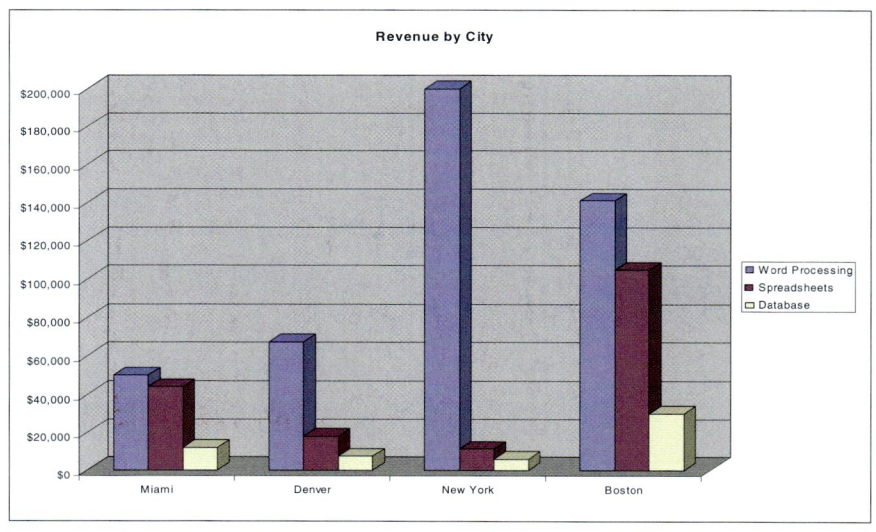

FIGURE 3.11 Object Linking and Embedding

hands-on exercise 3

Object Linking and Embedding

Objective To create a compound document consisting of a memo, worksheet, and chart. Use Figure 3.12 as a guide in the exercise.

Step 1: **Open the Software Sales Document**

- Click the **Start button**, click **All Programs**, click **Microsoft Office**, then click **Microsoft Office Word 2003** to start Word. Hide the Office Assistant if it appears.

- If necessary, click the **Maximize button** in the application window so that Word takes the entire desktop as shown in Figure 3.12a. (The Open dialog box is not yet visible.)

- Pull down the **File menu** and click **Open** (or click the **Open button** on the Standard toolbar).
  - Click the **drop-down arrow** in the Look In list box. Click the appropriate drive, drive C or drive A, depending on the location of your data.
  - Double click the **Exploring Excel folder** (we placed the Word memo in the Exploring Excel folder) to open the folder. Double click the **Software Memo** to open the document.
  - Save the document as **Software Memo Solution**.

- Pull down the **View menu**. Click **Print Layout** to change to the Print Layout view. Pull down the **View menu**. Click **Zoom**. Click **Page Width**. Click **Ok**.

- The software memo is open on your desktop.

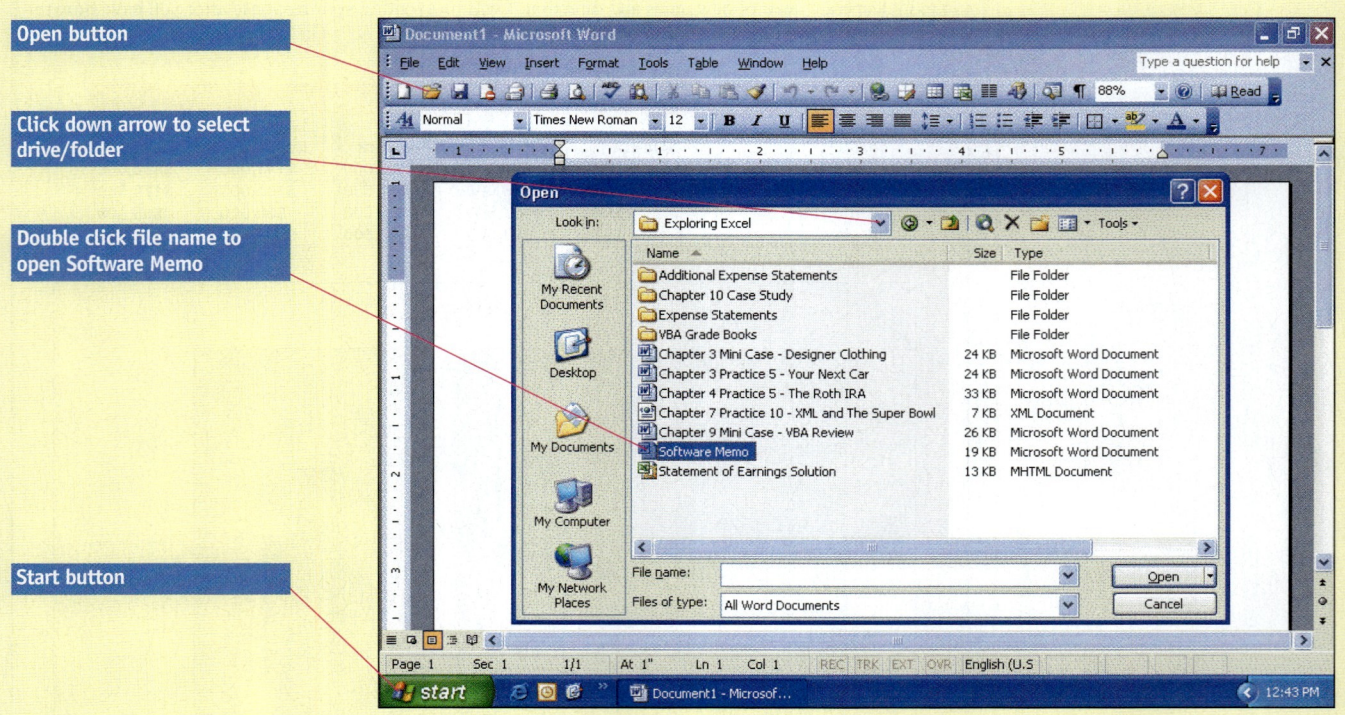

(a) Open the Software Sales Document (step 1)

FIGURE 3.12 Hands-on Exercise 3

Step 2: **Copy the Worksheet**

- Open the **Software Sales Solution workbook** from the previous exercise.
  - If you did not close Microsoft Excel at the end of the previous exercise, you will see its button on the taskbar. Click the **Microsoft Excel button** to return to the Software Sales Solution workbook.
  - If you closed Microsoft Excel, click the **Start button** to start Excel, then open the Software Sales Solution workbook.
- The taskbar should now contain a button for both Microsoft Word and Microsoft Excel. Click either button to move back and forth between the open applications. End by clicking the **Microsoft Excel button**.
- Click the tab for **Sales Data**. Click and drag to select **A1** through **F7** to select the entire worksheet as shown in Figure 3.12b.
- Point to the selected area and click the **right mouse button** to display the shortcut menu. Click **Copy**.
- A moving border appears around the entire worksheet, indicating that it has been copied to the clipboard.

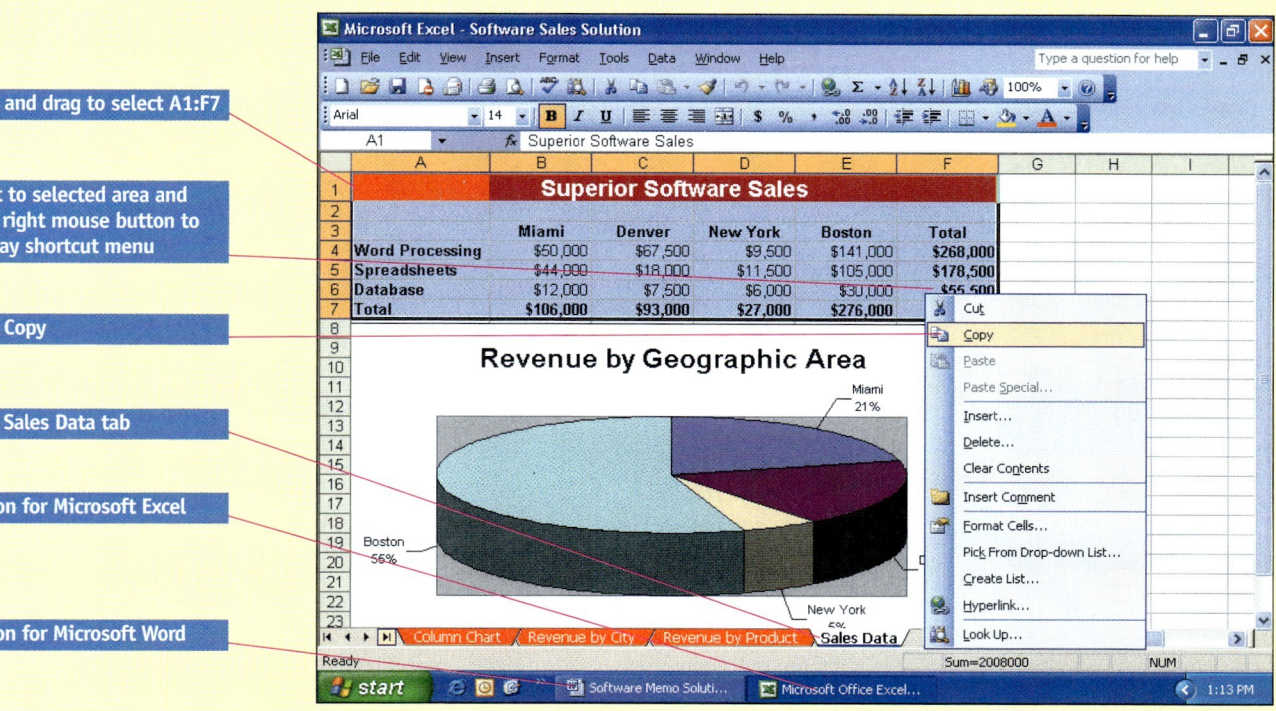

(b) Copy the Worksheet (step 2)

FIGURE 3.12   Hands-on Exercise 3 (*continued*)

THE WINDOWS TASKBAR

Multitasking, the ability to run multiple applications at the same time, is one of the primary advantages of the Windows environment. Each button on the taskbar appears automatically when its application or folder is opened, and disappears upon closing. (The buttons are resized automatically according to the number of open windows.) The taskbar can be moved to the left or right edge of the desktop, or to the top of the desktop, by dragging a blank area of the taskbar to the desired position.

MICROSOFT OFFICE EXCEL 2003 REVISED   147

Step 3: **Create the Link**

- Click the **Microsoft Word button** on the taskbar to return to the memo as shown in Figure 3.12c. Press **Ctrl+End** to move to the end of the memo, which is where you will insert the Excel worksheet.
- Pull down the **Edit menu**. If necessary, click the **double arrow** to see more commands, then click **Paste Special** to display the dialog box in Figure 3.12c.
- Click **Microsoft Excel Worksheet Object** in the As list. Click the **Paste link option button**. Click **OK** to insert the worksheet into the document.
- Right click the worksheet to display a context-sensitive menu, click **Format Object** to display the associated dialog box, and click the **Layout tab**.
- Choose **Square** in the Wrapping Style area, then click the option button to **Center** the object. Click **OK** to accept the settings and close the dialog box.
- Save the memo.

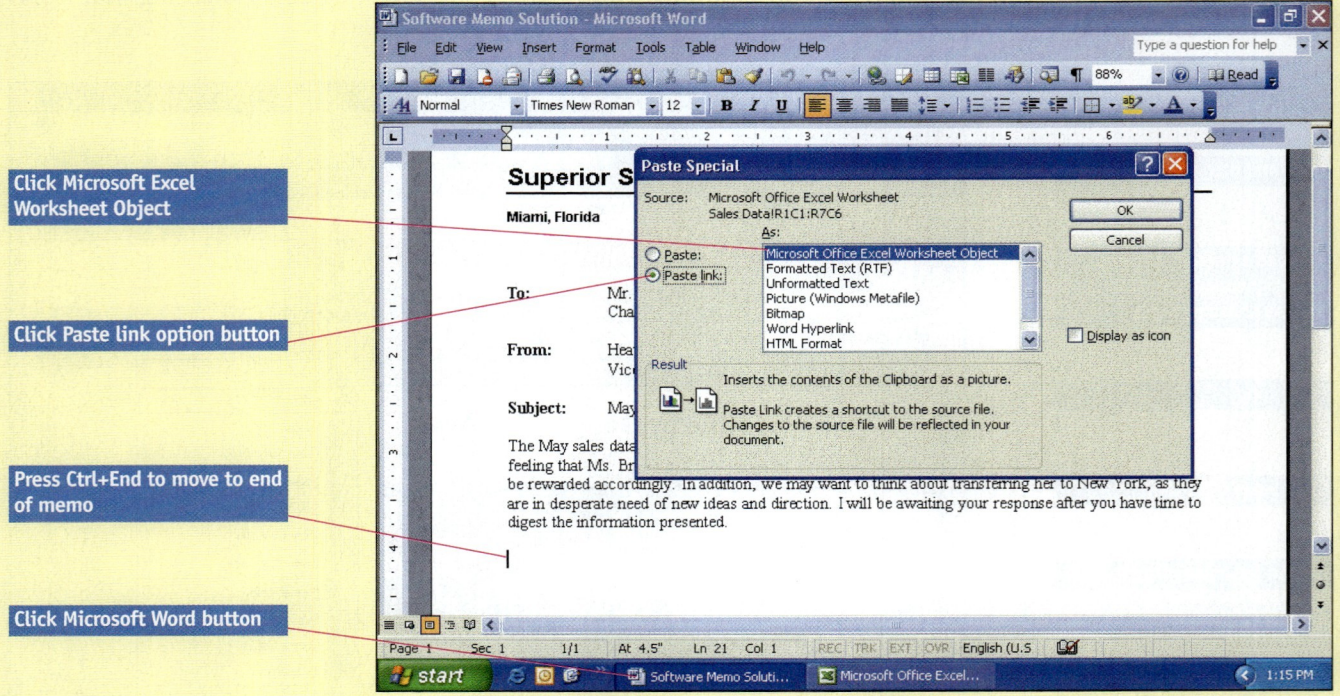

(c) Create the Link (step 3)

FIGURE 3.12 Hands-on Exercise 3 (*continued*)

THE COMMON USER INTERFACE

The common user interface provides a sense of familiarity from one Office application to the next. The applications share a common menu structure with consistent ways to execute commands from those menus. The Standard and Formatting toolbars are present in both applications. Many keyboard shortcuts are also common, such as Ctrl+Home and Ctrl+End to move to the beginning and end of a document, respectively.

Step 4: **Copy the Chart**

- Click the **Microsoft Excel button** on the taskbar to return to the worksheet.
- Click outside the selected area (cells A1 through F7) to deselect the cells. Press **Esc** to remove the moving border.
- Click the **Revenue by City tab** to select the chart sheet. Point to the chart area, then click the left mouse button to select the chart.
- Be sure you have selected the entire chart and that you see the same sizing handles as in Figure 3.12d.
- Pull down the **Edit menu** and click the **Copy command** (or click the **Copy button** on the Standard toolbar).
- A moving border appears around the entire chart, indicating that the chart has been copied to the clipboard. You can now link the chart to the Word document.

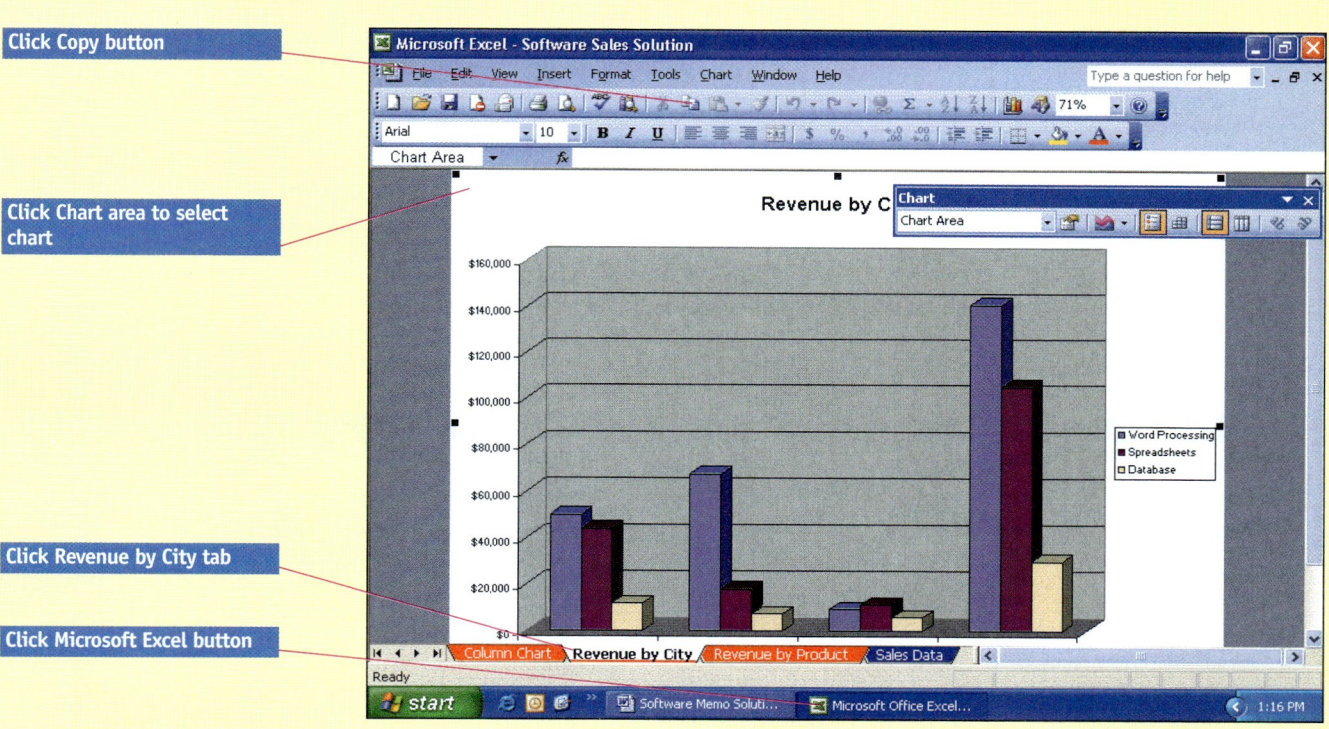

(d) Copy the Chart (step 4)

FIGURE 3.12 Hands-on Exercise 3 (*continued*)

ALT+TAB STILL WORKS

Alt+Tab was a treasured shortcut in the first version of Windows that enabled users to switch back and forth between open applications. The shortcut also works in all subsequent versions of Windows. Press and hold the Alt key while you press and release the Tab key repeatedly to cycle through the open applications, whose icons are displayed in a small rectangular window in the middle of the screen. Release the Alt key when you have selected the icon for the application you want.

MICROSOFT OFFICE EXCEL 2003 REVISED

Step 5: **Add the Chart**

- Click the **Microsoft Word button** on the taskbar to return to the memo. Double click below the worksheet to set the insertion point.

- Pull down the **Edit menu**. Click **Paste Special**. Click the **Paste link option button**. If necessary, click **Microsoft Excel Chart Object**. Click **OK** to insert the chart into the document.

- Right click the chart to display a context-sensitive menu, click **Format Object**, click the **Layout tab**, and choose **Square** in the Wrapping Style area. Click **OK**.

- Zoom to **Whole Page** to facilitate moving and sizing the chart. You need to reduce its size so that it fits on the same page as the memo. Thus scroll to the chart and click the chart to select it. This displays the sizing handles as shown in Figure 3.12e.

- Click and drag a corner sizing handle inward to make the chart smaller. Move the chart to the first page and center it on the page below the spreadsheet.

- Select the chart. Pull down the **Format menu**, and click the **Object command** to display the Format Object dialog box.

- Click the **Colors and Lines tab**. Click the **down arrow** in the Line color area, choose a color, and click **OK** to place a border around the chart.

- Zoom to **Page Width**. Look carefully at the worksheet and chart in the document. The sales for Word Processing in New York are currently $9,500, and the chart reflects this amount. Save the memo.

- Point to the **Microsoft Excel button** on the taskbar and click the **right mouse button** to display a shortcut menu. Click **Close** to close Excel. Click **Yes** if prompted to save the changes to the Software Sales Solution workbook.

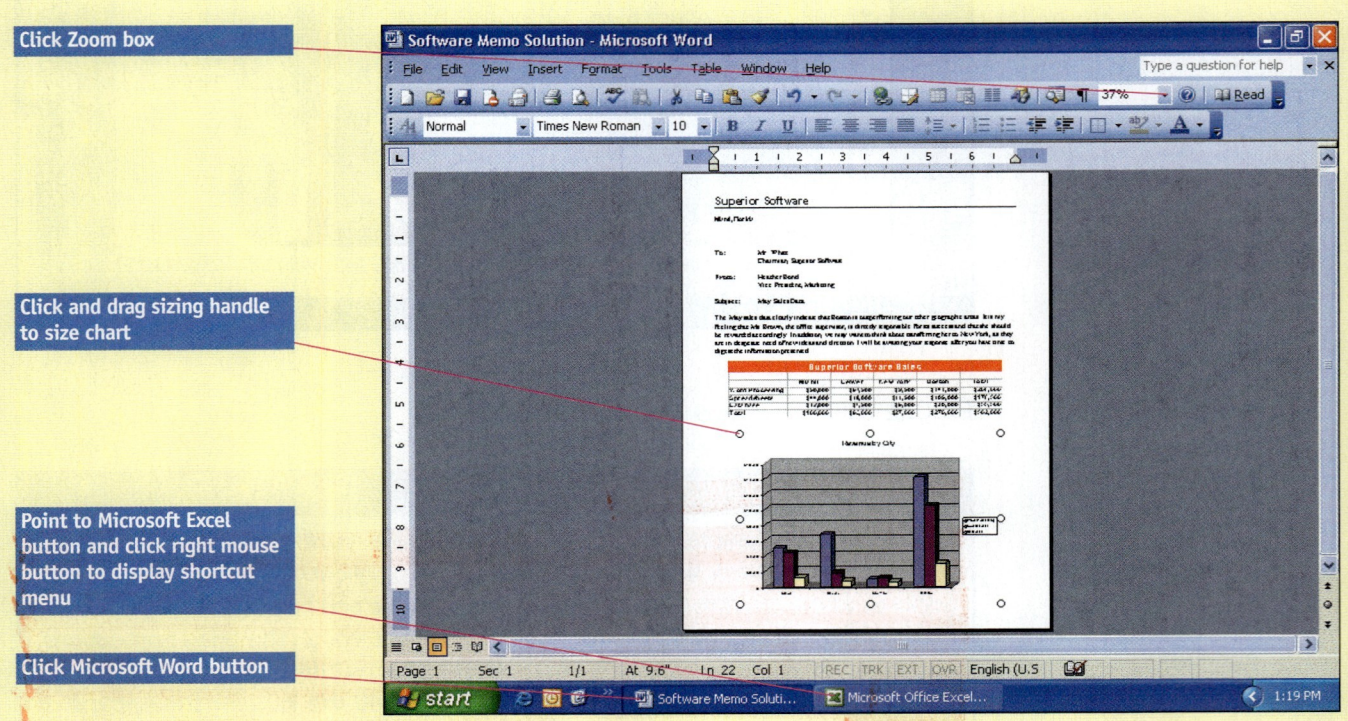

(e) Add the Chart (step 5)

Figure 3.12 Hands-on Exercise 3 (*continued*)

150   CHAPTER 3: GRAPHS AND CHARTS

Step 6: Modify the Worksheet

- Click anywhere in the worksheet to select the worksheet and display the sizing handles as shown in Figure 3.12f.

- The status bar indicates that you can double click to edit the worksheet. Thus, double click anywhere within the worksheet to start Excel, the application that created the chart originally, in order to change the data.

- The system pauses as it loads Excel and reopens the Software Sales Solution workbook. If necessary, click the **Maximize button** to maximize the Excel window. Hide the Office Assistant if it appears.

- If necessary, click the **Sales Data tab** within the workbook. Click in **cell D4**. Type **$200,000**. Press **Enter**.

- Click the **|◄ button** to scroll to the **Revenue by City tab** to select the chart sheet. The chart has been modified automatically and it now reflects the increased sales for New York.

- Save the workbook.

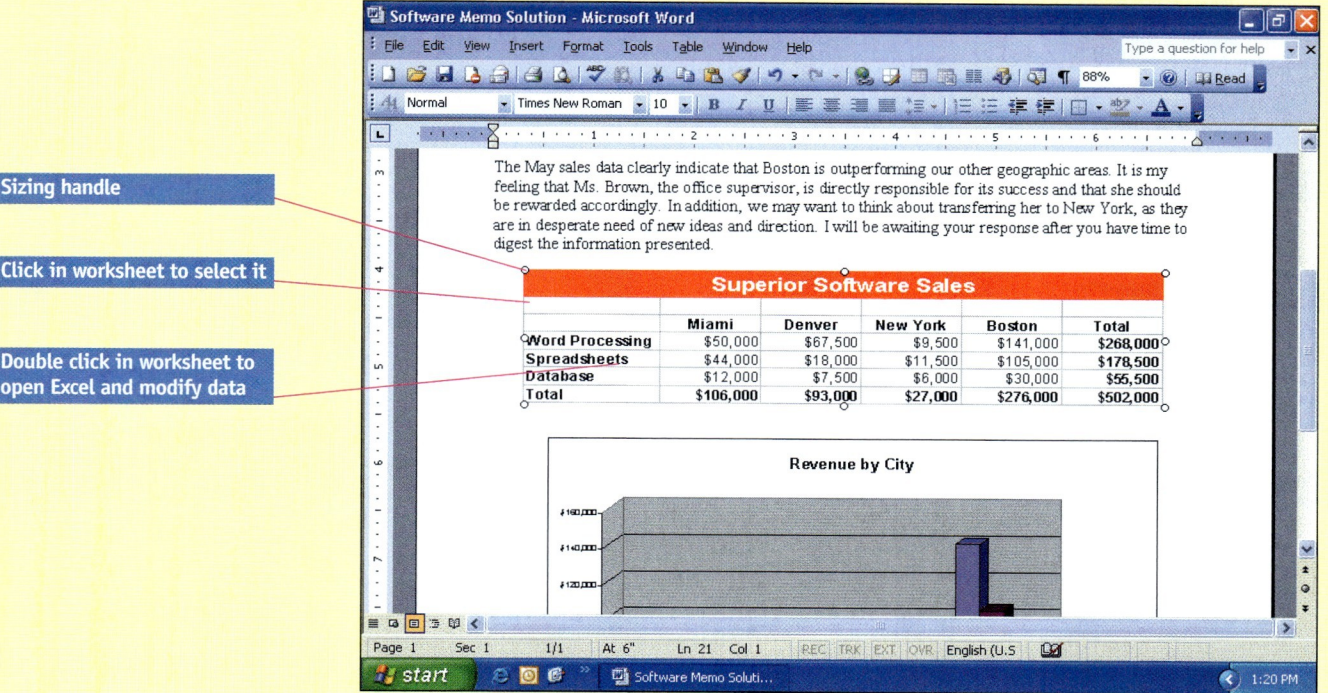

(f) Modify the Worksheet (step 6)

FIGURE 3.12 Hands-on Exercise 3 (*continued*)

LINKING VERSUS EMBEDDING

A linked object maintains its connection to the source file. An embedded object does not. Thus, a linked object can be placed in any number of destination files, each of which maintains a pointer (link) to the same source file. Any change to the object in the source file is reflected automatically in every destination file containing that object.

Step 7: Update the Links

- Click the **Microsoft Word button** on the taskbar to return to the Software Memo. The worksheet and chart should be updated automatically. If not:
  - Pull down the **Edit menu**. Click **Links** to display the Links dialog box in Figure 3.12g.
  - Select the link(s) to update. (You can press and hold the **Ctrl key** to select multiple links simultaneously.)
  - Click the **Update Now button** to update the selected links.
  - Close the Links dialog box.

- The worksheet and chart should both reflect $200,000 for word processing sales in New York.

- Zoom to the **Whole Page** to view the completed document. Click and drag the worksheet and/or the chart within the memo to make any last-minute changes. Save the memo a final time.

- Print the completed memo and submit it to your instructor. Exit Word. Exit Excel. Save the changes to the Software Sales Solution workbook if you are prompted to do so.

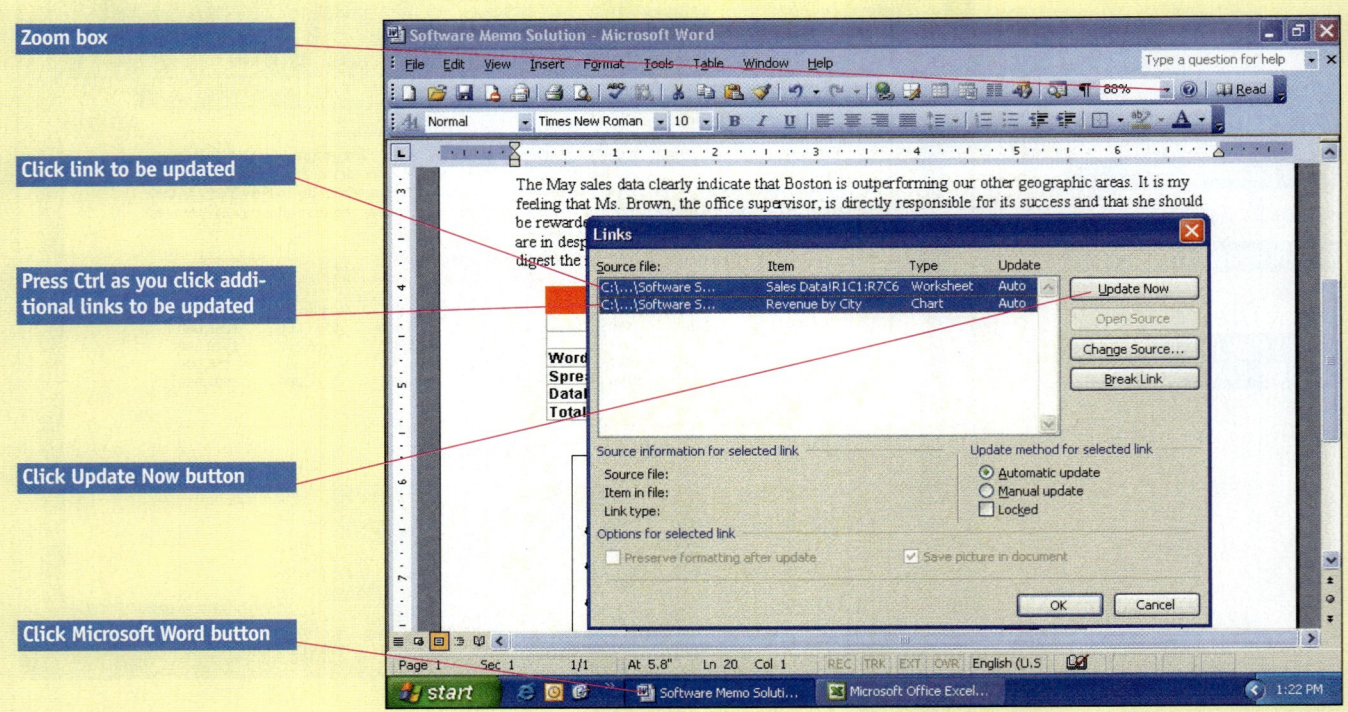

(g) Update the Links (step 7)

FIGURE 3.12 Hands-on Exercise 3 (*continued*)

LINKING WORKSHEETS

A Word document can be linked to an Excel chart and/or worksheet; that is, change the chart in Excel, and the Word document changes automatically. The chart itself is linked to the underlying worksheet; change the worksheet, and the chart changes. Worksheets can also reference one another; for example, a summary worksheet for the corporation as a whole can reflect data from detail worksheets for individual cities. See practice exercises 7 and 8 at the end of the chapter.

SUMMARY

A chart is a graphic representation of data in a worksheet. The type of chart chosen depends on the message to be conveyed. A pie chart is best for proportional relationships. A column or bar chart is used to show actual numbers rather than percentages. A line chart is preferable for time-related data. A combination chart uses two or more chart types when different scales are required for different data series.

The title of a chart can help to convey the message. A neutral title such as *Revenue by City* leaves the reader to draw his or her own conclusion. Using a different title such as *Boston Leads All Cities* or *New York Is Trailing Badly* sends a very different message.

The Chart Wizard is an easy way to create a chart. Once created, a chart can be enhanced with arrows and text boxes found on the Drawing toolbar. These objects can be moved or sized and/or modified with respect to their color and other properties. The chart itself can also be modified using various commands from the Chart menu or tools on the Chart toolbar. A toolbar may be docked along the edge of a window or it may be floating within the window. All toolbars are displayed or hidden using the Toolbar command in the View menu.

A chart may be embedded in a worksheet or created in a separate chart sheet. An embedded chart may be moved within a worksheet by selecting it and dragging it to its new location. An embedded chart may be sized by selecting it and dragging any of the sizing handles in the desired direction.

Multiple data series may be specified in either rows or columns. If the data is in rows, the first row is assumed to contain the category labels, and the first column is assumed to contain the legend. Conversely, if the data is in columns, the first column is assumed to contain the category labels, and the first row the legend. The Chart Wizard makes it easy to switch from rows to columns and vice versa.

The choice between a side-by-side and a stacked-column chart depends on the intended message. A side-by-side chart shows the contribution of each data point, but the total for each series is not as clear as with a stacked-column chart. The stacked-column chart, on the other hand, shows the totals clearly, but the contribution of the individual data points is obscured since the segments do not start at zero. It is important that charts are created accurately and that they do not mislead the reader. Stacked-column charts should not add dissimilar quantities such as units and dollars.

Object Linking and Embedding enables the creation of a compound document containing data (objects) from multiple applications. The essential difference between linking and embedding is whether the object is stored within the compound document (embedding) or in its own file (linking). An embedded object is stored in the compound document, which in turn becomes the only user (client) of that object. A linked object is stored in its own file, and the compound document is one of many potential clients of that object. The same chart can be linked to a Word document and a PowerPoint presentation.

KEY TERMS

Bar chart 119	Docked toolbar 134	Pie chart 117
Category label 116	Drawing toolbar 126	Side-by-side column charts 137
Chart 116	Embedded chart 122	Sizing handles 122
Chart sheet .122	Exploded pie chart 117	Stacked column charts 137
Chart toolbar 126	Floating toolbar 134	Taskbar 145
Chart type 124	Multiple data series 136	Three-dimensional column chart 122
Chart Wizard 124	Multitasking 145	
Column chart 119	Object 145	Three-dimensional pie chart 117
Data point 116	Object Linking and Embedding (OLE) 145	X axis 119
Data series .116		Y axis 119

MULTIPLE CHOICE

1. Which type of chart is best to portray proportion or market share?
   (a) Pie chart
   (b) Line
   (c) Column chart
   (d) Combination chart

2. Which of the following is a true statement about the Chart Wizard?
   (a) It is accessed via a button on the Standard toolbar
   (b) It enables you to choose the type of chart you want as well as specify the location for that chart
   (c) It enables you to retrace your steps via the Back command button
   (d) All of the above

3. Which of the following chart types is *not* suitable to display multiple data series?
   (a) Pie chart
   (b) Horizontal bar chart
   (c) Column chart
   (d) All of the above are equally suitable

4. Which of the following is best to display additive information from multiple data series?
   (a) A column chart with the data series stacked one on top of another
   (b) A column chart with the data series side by side
   (c) Both (a) and (b) are equally appropriate
   (d) Neither (a) nor (b) is appropriate

5. A workbook must contain:
   (a) A separate chart sheet for every worksheet
   (b) A separate worksheet for every chart sheet
   (c) Both (a) and (b)
   (d) Neither (a) nor (b)

6. Which of the following is true regarding an embedded chart?
   (a) It can be moved elsewhere within the worksheet
   (b) It can be made larger or smaller
   (c) Both (a) and (b)
   (d) Neither (a) nor (b)

7. Which of the following will produce a shortcut menu?
   (a) Pointing to a workbook tab and clicking the right mouse button
   (b) Pointing to an embedded chart and clicking the right mouse button
   (c) Pointing to a selected cell range and clicking the right mouse button
   (d) All of the above

8. Which of the following is done *prior* to invoking the Chart Wizard?
   (a) The data series are selected
   (b) The location of the embedded chart within the worksheet is specified
   (c) Both (a) and (b)
   (d) Neither (a) nor (b)

9. Which of the following will display sizing handles when selected?
   (a) An embedded chart
   (b) The title of a chart
   (c) A text box or arrow
   (d) All of the above

10. How do you switch between open applications?
    (a) Click the appropriate button on the taskbar
    (b) Use Alt+Tab to cycle through the applications
    (c) Both (a) and (b)
    (d) Neither (a) nor (b)

... continued

multiple choice

11. A Word document is linked to an Excel worksheet and associated chart. Which of the following best describes the way the documents are stored on disk?
    (a) A single file contains the Word document, the worksheet, and the associated chart
    (b) There are two files—one for the Word document and one for the Excel workbook, which contains both the worksheet and associated chart
    (c) There are three files—one for the Word document, one for the Excel worksheet, and one for the Excel chart
    (d) None of the above

12. To represent multiple data series on the same chart:
    (a) The data series must be in rows and the rows must be adjacent to one another on the worksheet
    (b) The data series must be in columns and the columns must be adjacent to one another on the worksheet
    (c) The data series may be in rows or columns so long as they are adjacent to one another
    (d) The data series may be in rows or columns with no requirement to be next to one another

13. If multiple data series are selected and rows are specified:
    (a) The first row will be used for the category labels
    (b) The first column will be used for the legend
    (c) Both (a) and (b)
    (d) Neither (a) nor (b)

14. If multiple data series are selected and columns are specified:
    (a) The first column will be used for the category (X axis) labels
    (b) The first row will be used for the legend
    (c) Both (a) and (b)
    (d) Neither (a) nor (b)

15. Which of the following is true about the scale on the Y axis in a column chart that plots multiple data series side-by-side versus one that stacks the values one on top of another?
    (a) The scale for the stacked columns chart contains larger values than the side-by-side chart
    (b) The scale for the side-by-side columns contains larger values than the stacked columns
    (c) The values on the scale will be the same for both charts
    (d) The values will be different, but it is not possible to tell which chart has higher values

16. A workbook includes a revenue worksheet with two embedded charts. The workbook also includes one chart in its own worksheet. How many files does it take to store this workbook?
    (a) 1
    (b) 2
    (c) 3
    (d) 4

17. Assume that cells A1 through E5 have been selected, after which the Chart Wizard is used to create a side-by-side column chart. Which of the following is true, given that the data is plotted in rows?
    (a) The category names are in cells B1 through E1
    (b) The legends are in cells A2 through A5
    (c) Both (a) and (b)
    (d) Neither (a) nor (b)

18. Which of the following creates a dynamic link between a workbook and a word processing memo?
    (a) Copy, Paste Special, and Paste Link
    (b) Copy and Paste
    (c) Cut, Paste Special, and Paste Link
    (d) Cut and Paste

ANSWERS

1. a
2. d
3. a
4. a
5. d
6. c
7. d
8. a
9. d
10. c
11. b
12. d
13. c
14. c
15. a
16. a
17. c
18. a

PRACTICE WITH EXCEL

1. **Theme Park Admissions:** A partially completed version of the worksheet in Figure 3.13 is available in the Exploring Excel folder as *Chapter 3 Practice 1*. Follow the directions in parts (a) and (b) to compute the totals and format the worksheet, then create each of the charts listed below.

    a. Use the AutoSum command to enter the formulas to compute the total number of admissions for each region and each quarter.
    b. Select the entire worksheet (cells A1 through F8), then use the AutoFormat command to format the worksheet. You do not have to accept the entire design, nor do you have to use the design we selected. You can also modify the design after it has been applied to the worksheet by changing the font size of selected cells and/or changing boldface and italics.
    c. Create a column chart showing the total number of admissions in each quarter as shown in Figure 3.13. Add the graphic shown in the figure for emphasis.
    d. Create a pie chart that shows the percentage of the total number of admissions in each region. Create this chart in its own chart sheet with an appropriate name.
    e. Create a stacked column chart that shows the total number of admissions for each region and the contribution of each quarter within each region. Create this chart in its own chart sheet with an appropriate name.
    f. Create a stacked column chart showing the total number of admissions for each quarter and the contribution of each region within each quarter. Create this chart in its own chart sheet with an appropriate name.
    g. Change the color of each of the worksheet tabs.
    h. Print the entire workbook, consisting of the worksheet in Figure 3.13 plus the three additional sheets that you create. Use portrait orientation for the Sales Data worksheet and landscape orientation for the other worksheets. Create a custom header for each worksheet that includes your name, your course, and your instructor's name. Create a custom footer for each worksheet that includes the name of the worksheet. Submit the completed assignment to your instructor.

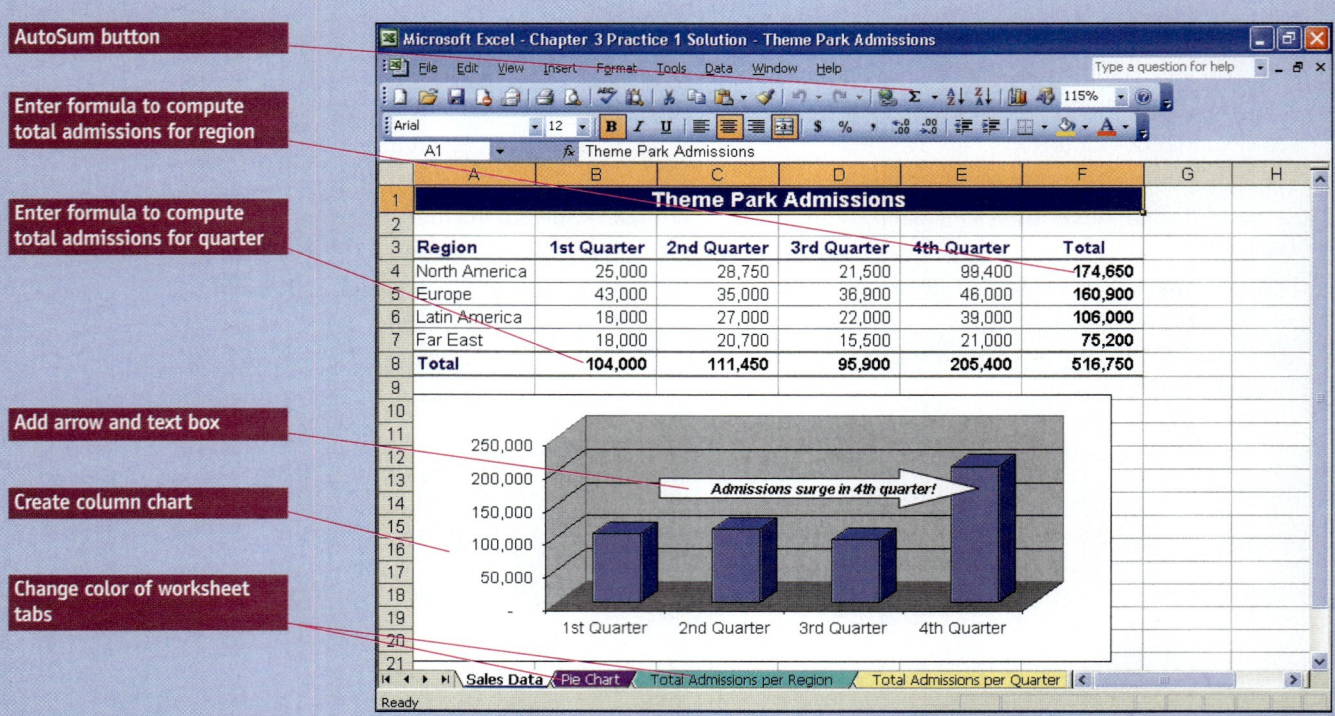

FIGURE 3.13 Theme Park Admissions (exercise 1)

practice exercises

2. **Hotel Bookings:** The workbook in Figure 3.14 was created by the Director of Marketing for a South Florida hotel chain. The workbook contains a worksheet and several charts that show hotel bookings for different counties according to the source of the booking. Your assignment is to open the partially completed version of the workbook, which is available in the Exploring Excel folder as *Chapter 3 Practice 2—Hotel Bookings*, and proceed as follows:

   a. Use the AutoSum command to enter the formulas to compute the total number of bookings for each county and each source.
   b. Select the entire worksheet (cells A1 through F6), then use the AutoFormat command to format the worksheet. You do not have to accept the entire design nor do you have to use the design we selected. You may also modify the design after it has been applied to the worksheet by changing the font size of selected cells and/or changing boldface and italics.
   c. Create a column chart showing the total dollar amount for each county as shown in Figure 3.14. Create the graphic to emphasize Monroe's poor bookings.
   d. Create a pie chart that shows the percentage of the total bookings for each source. Create this chart in its own chart sheet. Rename the sheet as appropriate.
   e. Create a stacked column chart that shows the total dollar amount for each booking source and the relative contribution of each county towards the total. Create this chart in its own chart sheet. Rename the sheet as appropriate.
   f. Create a stacked column chart showing the total dollar amount for each county and the relative contribution of each booking source towards the total. Create this chart in its own chart sheet. Rename the sheet as appropriate.
   g. Change the color of each of the worksheet tabs.
   h. Print the entire workbook, consisting of the worksheet in Figure 3.14 plus the three additional chart sheets that you created. Use portrait orientation for the Sales Data worksheet and landscape orientation for the other sheets. Create a custom footer for each sheet that includes your name, the date and time the sheet is printed, and the name of the sheet. Add a cover sheet, and then submit the completed assignment to your instructor.

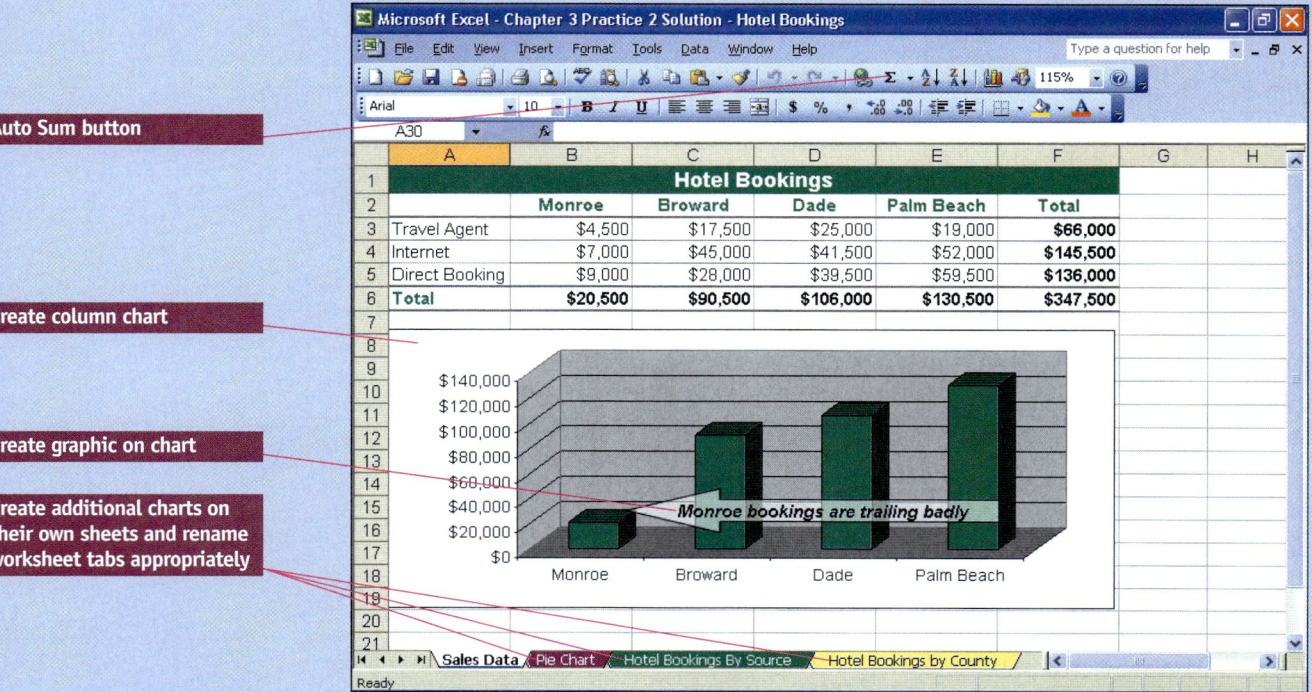

FIGURE 3.14   Hotel Bookings (exercise 2)

practice exercises

3. **Flexibility in Charting:** The worksheet in Figure 3.15 displays the second quarter revenues for each salesperson in TalkAway, Inc., a local cellular company. Open the partially completed workbook in *Chapter 3 Practice 3* to complete the worksheet, then create the chart in Figure 3.15. The intent of this exercise is to show you several formatting options that are available in conjunction with charts. It's fun to experiment, but set a reasonable time limit.

   a. Use the AutoSum command to enter the formulas to compute the total sales for each month and for each salesperson.
   b. Format the worksheet in attractive fashion. You do not have to duplicate our formatting exactly, but you are to highlight the data in row four. In addition, use boldface to emphasize the totals for each salesperson and each month.
   c. Use the Chart wizard to create a column chart that displays the total sales for each salesperson for the second quarter.
   d. Right click any column (data series) within the chart to display a context-sensitive menu, then click the Format Data Series command. Click the Shape tab within the dialog box to change the shape of each column. Click the Data Labels tab to display the dollar value for each salesperson.
   e. Click the second column to select just this column. Click the right mouse button, click the Format Data Point command, click the Pattern tab in the associated dialog box, then change the color of this column.
   f. Click in Cell A4 and enter your name instead of Grauer. The value on the *X* axis changes automatically to reflect the entry in cell A4.
   g. Click the AutoShapes button on the Drawing toolbar to add a callout indicating that this column represents your sales data. Right click the border of the AutoShape, click the Format AutoShape command, click the Colors and Lines tab, and add a fill color.
   h. Right click the border of the chart, click the Format Chart Area command, then change the border to include rounded corners with a shadow effect.
   i. Print the completed worksheet for your instructor.

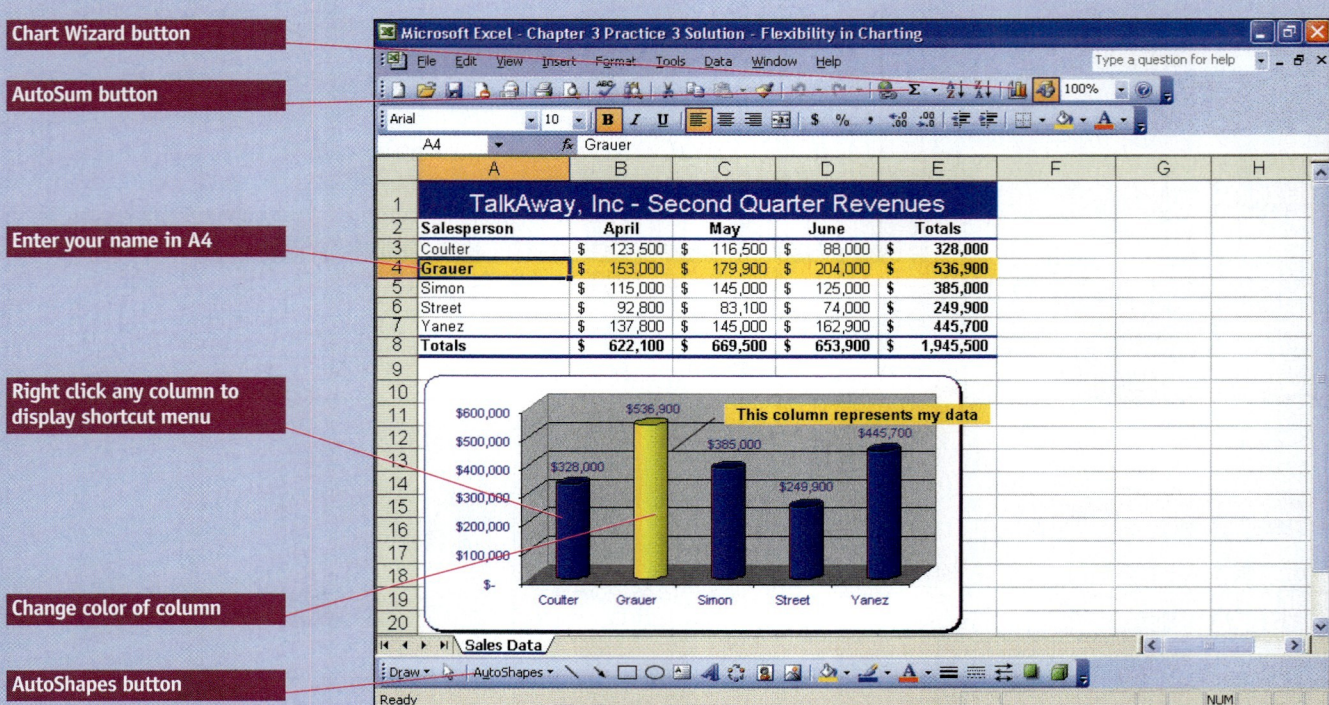

FIGURE 3.15 Flexibility in Charting (exercise 3)

practice exercises

4. **Page Break Preview:** Open the partially completed workbook in *Chapter 3 Practice 4* and create the four charts shown in Figure 3.16. Use the AutoSum and AutoFormat commands to complete the worksheet. Select cells A2 through E6 as the basis for each of the four charts in the figure. The charts should appear as embedded objects on the worksheet, but do not be concerned about the placement of each chart until you have completed all four charts.

   a. The first chart is a side-by-side column chart that emphasizes the sales in each city (the data is in rows).
   b. The second chart is a stacked column version of the chart in part (a).
   c. The third chart (that begins in column H of the worksheet) is a side-by-side column chart that emphasizes the sales in each product line (the data is in columns).
   d. The last chart is a stacked column version of the chart in part (c).
   e. Pull down the View command, then change to the Page Break Preview view as shown in Figure 3.16. You will see one or more dotted lines that show where the page breaks will occur. You will also see the message in Figure 3.16 indicating that you can change the location of the page breaks. Click OK after you have read the message.
   f. Remove any existing page breaks by clicking and dragging the solid blue line that indicates the break. (You can insert horizontal or vertical page breaks by clicking the appropriate cell, pulling down the Insert menu, and selecting Page Break.) Pull down the View menu and click Normal view to return to the normal view.
   g. Add your name to the completed worksheet, then print the worksheet and four embedded charts on one page. If necessary, change to landscape printing for a more attractive layout. Use the Page Setup command to create a custom header with your name, your course, and your instructor's name. Create a custom footer that contains today's date, the name of the workbook, and the current time.
   h. Write a short note to your instructor that describes the differences between the charts. Suggest a different title for one or more charts that helps to convey a specific message.

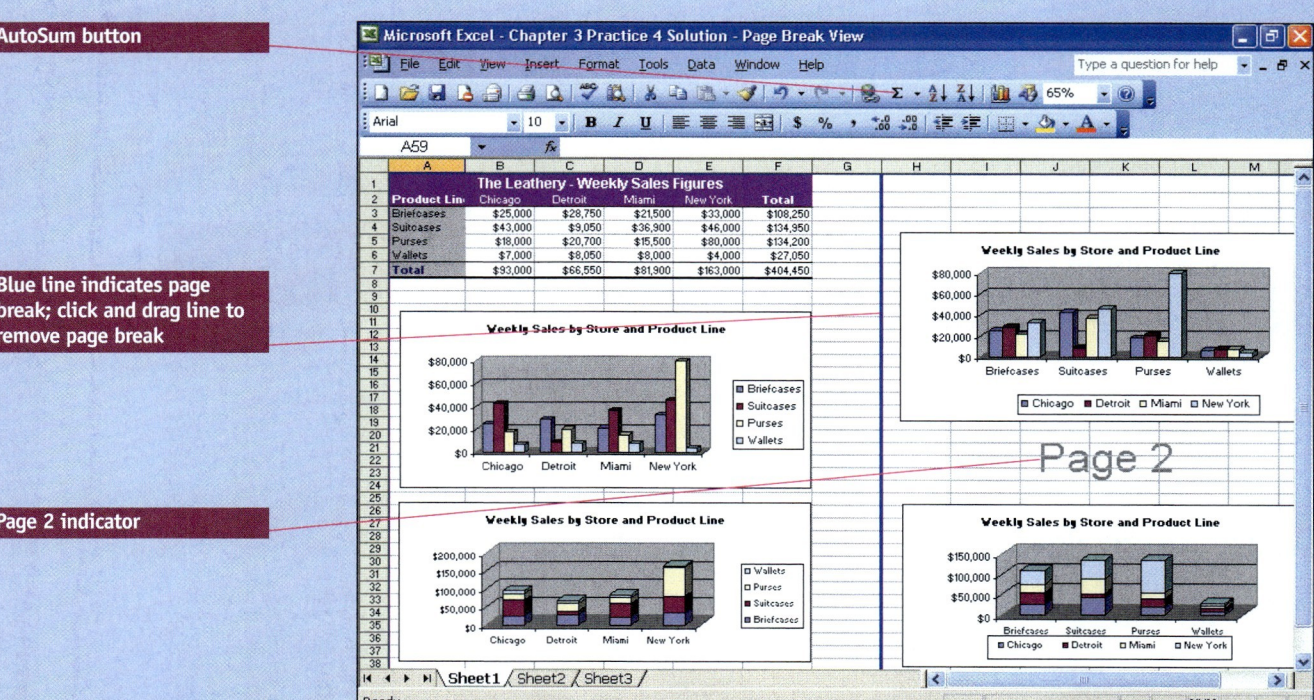

FIGURE 3.16 Page Break Preview (exercise 4)

practice exercises

5. **Your Next Car:** The Word document in Figure 3.17 displays descriptive information about a car you are interested in, a picture of the car, and a hyperlink to the Web site where the information was obtained. In addition, the document is linked to an Excel workbook that computes the car payment for you, based on the loan parameters that you provide. Your assignment is to create a similar document based on any car you choose. Proceed as follows:

   a. Use your favorite search engine to locate a Web site that contains information about the car you are interested in. You can go to the Web site of the manufacturer and/or you can go to a general site such as carpoint.msn.com, which contains information about all makes and models. Select the car you want and obtain the retail price of the car.

   b. Open the *Chapter 3 Practice 5* workbook in the Exploring Excel folder. Enter the price of the car, a hypothetical down payment, the interest rate of the car loan, and the term of the loan in the indicated cells. The monthly payment will be determined automatically by the PMT function that is stored in the workbook. (The PMT function is covered in detail in Chapter 4.) Save the workbook.

   c. Click and drag to select cells A3 through B9 (the cells that contain the information you want to insert into the Word document). Click the Copy button.

   d. Open the partially completed Word document, *Chapter 3 Practice 5,* that is stored in the Exploring Excel folder. Pull down the Edit menu, click the Paste Special command, and then choose the option to link the worksheet data to the Word document. Move and size the inserted worksheet to its approximate position in the document. Save the Word document.

   e. Use the taskbar to return to the Excel workbook. Change the amount of the down payment and/or the interest rate for your loan. Save the workbook. Close Excel. Return to the Word document, which should reflect the updated loan information. (You may have to update the link.)

   f. Return to the Web page that contains the information about your car. Right click the picture of the car that appears within the Web page, and click the Save As command to save the picture of the car to your computer. Use the Insert Picture command to insert the picture that you just obtained.

   g. Complete the Word document by inserting descriptive information about your car.

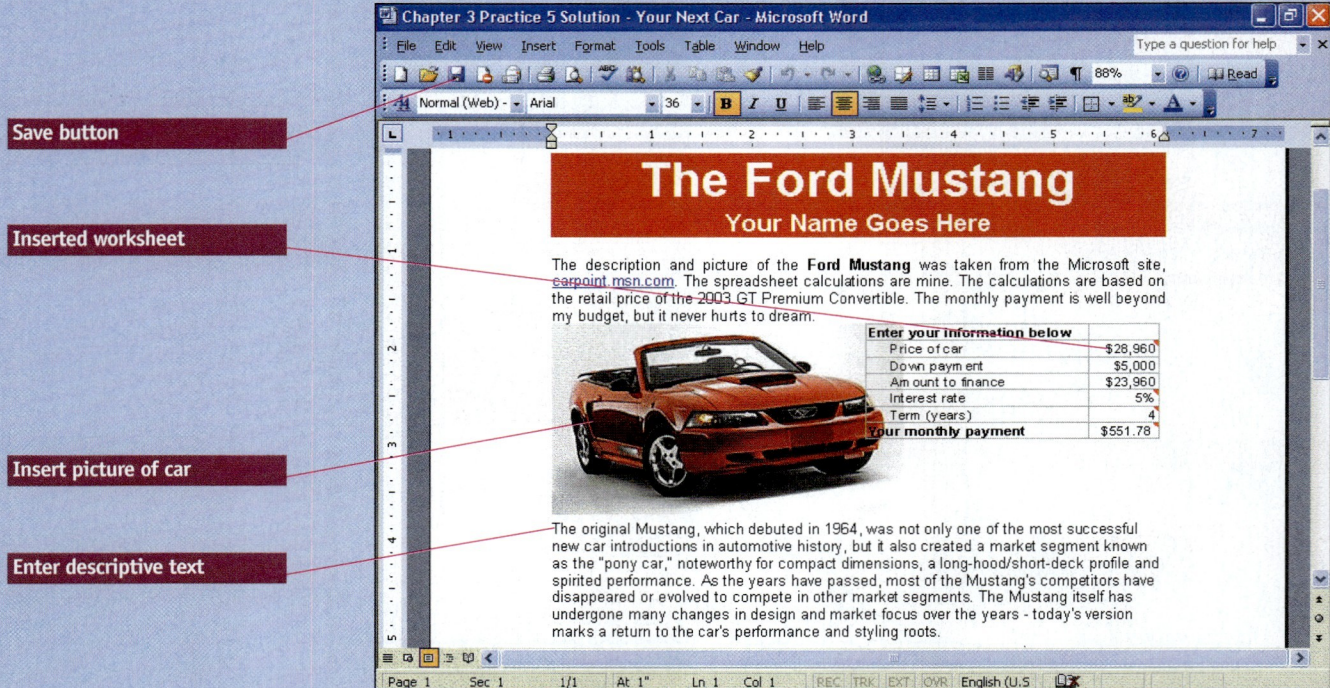

FIGURE 3.17 Your Next Car (exercise 5)

practice exercises

6. **Irrational Exuberance:** Figure 3.18 contains a combination chart to display different kinds of information on different scales for multiple data series. A column chart is specified for the revenue and profits, while a line chart is used for the stock price. Two different scales are necessary because the magnitudes of the numbers differ significantly.

   a. Open the partially completed workbook in *Chapter 3 Practice 6* and format the worksheet appropriately.
   b. Select the entire worksheet (cells A1 through F4), then invoke the Chart Wizard. Click the Custom Types tab in step 1 of the Chart Wizard, choose Line-Column on 2 Axes as the chart type, then in step 2 specify the data in rows. The Chart Wizard will do the rest.
   c. Modify the completed chart so that its appearance is similar to our figure. We made the chart wider and moved the legend to the bottom. (Right click the legend, click the Format Legend command, click the Placement tab, then click the Bottom option button.)
   d. Customize the border around the chart. Right click the completed chart, choose the Format Chart Area command, click the Patterns tab, then choose the style, thickness, and color of the border.
   e. Insert your name somewhere in the worksheet, then print the completed worksheet for your instructor. Use the Page Setup command to change to landscape orientation. Center the worksheet and chart horizontally on the page.
   f. Create a custom header for the worksheet that includes your name, your course, and your instructor's name. Create a custom footer that contains the name of the file in which the worksheet is contained, today's date, and the current time.
   g. What do you think should be the more important factor influencing a company's stock price, its revenue (sales) or its profit (net income)? Could the situation depicted in the worksheet occur in the real world? Summarize your thoughts in a brief note to your instructor.

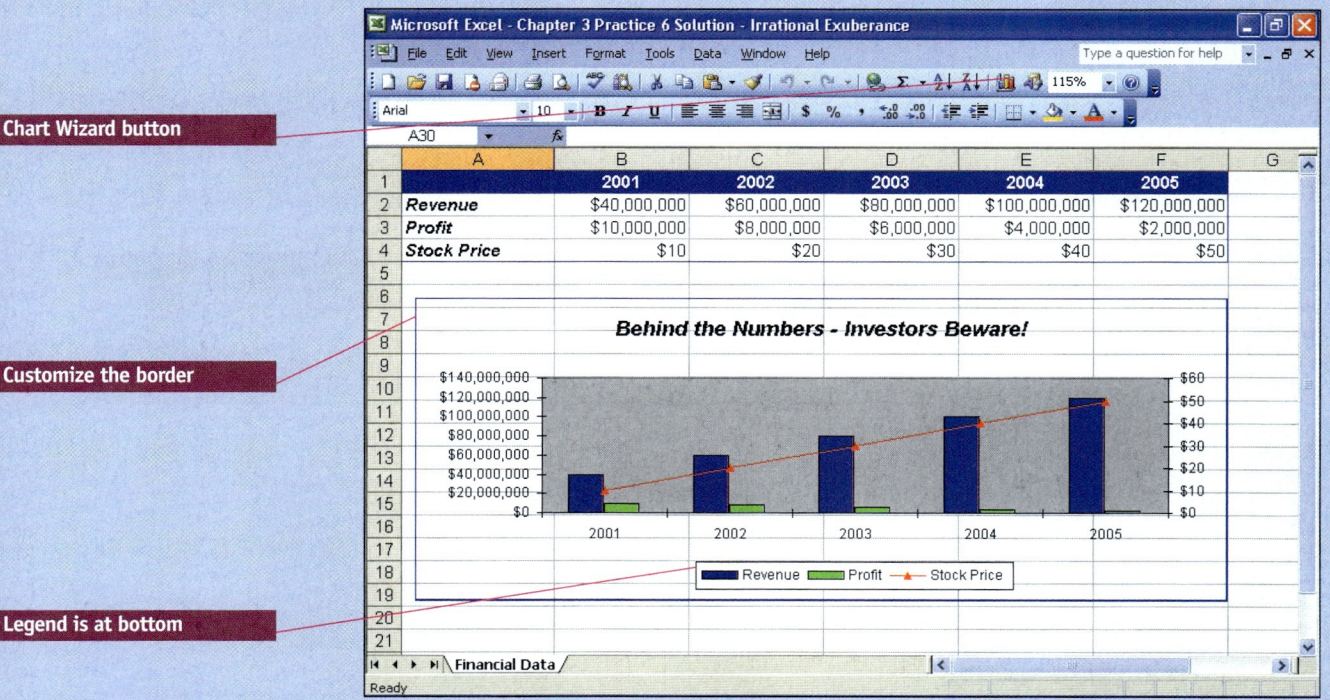

FIGURE 3.18 Irrational Exuberance (exercise 6)

practice exercises

7. **Worksheet References:** The worksheet in Figure 3.19 appears similar to the example that was used throughout the chapter. Look closely, however, and you will see that the workbook contains individual worksheets for each city, in addition to a worksheet for the corporation as a whole. The formulas in the corporate worksheet reference cells in the worksheets of the individual cities. For example, the entry in cell B3 of the Corporate worksheet contains the formula =Phoenix!F2 to indicate that the entry comes from cell F2 in the Phoenix worksheet. Other cells in the table reference other cells in the Phoenix worksheet as well as cells in the other worksheets.

   a. Open the *Chapter 3 Practice 7* workbook in the Exploring Excel folder. Select the Corporate worksheet by clicking the Worksheet tab. (The color of the tab for this worksheet is different from the tabs for the individual cities.) You can enter the formulas in this worksheet explicitly, but it is easier to use pointing, especially when referencing cells in other worksheets.

   b. Click (select) cell B3 in the Corporate worksheet. Type an = sign, click the Phoenix worksheet tab, click in cell F2 of this worksheet, and press the Enter key. Click in cell C3, type an = sign, click the Minneapolis tab, click in cell F2 of that worksheet, and press Enter. Repeat the process to enter the sales for San Francisco and Los Angeles.

   c. Select cells B3 through E3, then drag the fill handle to row 5 to copy the formulas for the other product lines. The copy operation works because the worksheet references are absolute, but the cell references are relative.

   d. Use the AutoSum button to compute the totals for the corporation as a whole in column F.

   e. Use the AutoFormat command to format the worksheet in an attractive fashion. (You do not have to duplicate our formatting exactly.)

   f. Use the completed worksheet as the basis for a stacked column chart with the data plotted in rows.

   g. Use the Page Setup command to display gridlines and row and column headings for each worksheet. Create a custom footer that contains your name, the name of the worksheet, and today's date. Print the entire workbook and submit the completed assignment to your instructor.

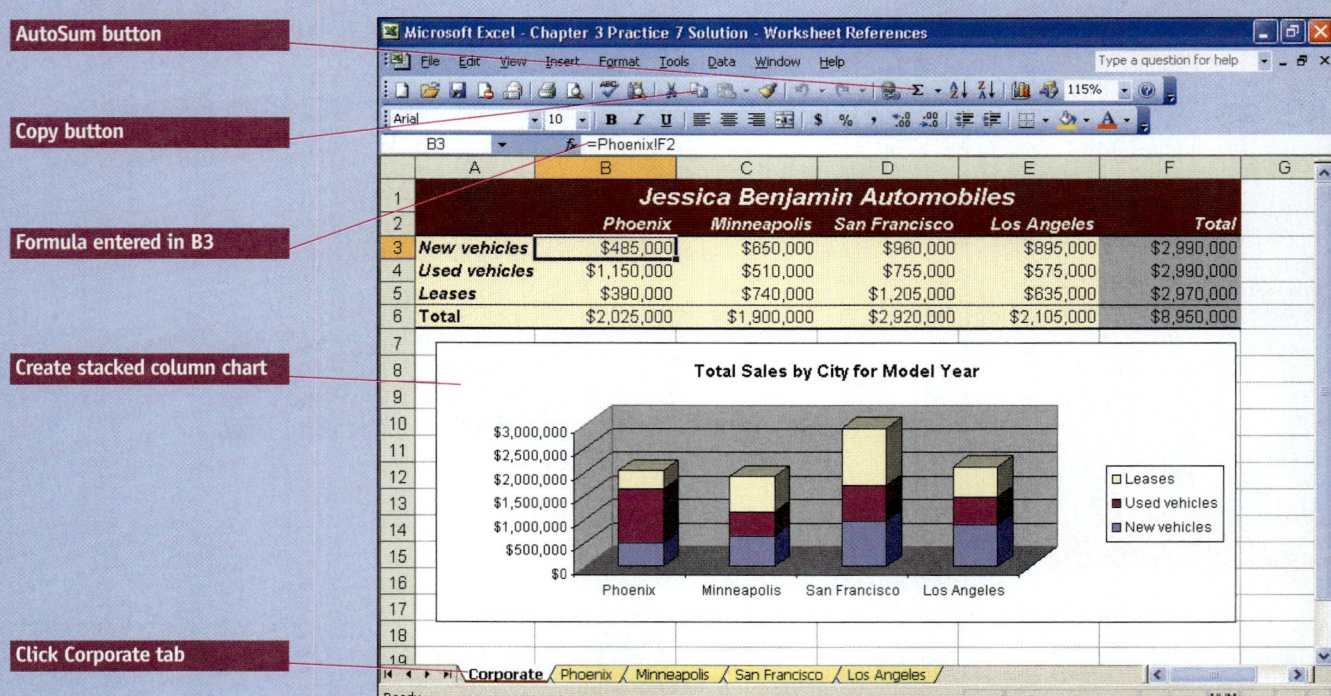

FIGURE 3.19 Worksheet References (exercise 7)

practice exercises

8. **Additional Practice:** The worksheet in Figure 3.20 contains a year-to-year comparison of sales data in both graphical and tabular form. Open the partially completed workbook in *Chapter 3 Practice 8* and proceed as follows:

   a. Select the Year to Year Comparison worksheet. Click in cell B3 of this worksheet, type an equal sign, click the worksheet tab labeled Previous Year, click in cell B8 of this worksheet, and press Enter. The formula for cell B3 should appear in the formula bar as ='Previous Year'!B8, indicating that the value for this cell is obtained from another worksheet in the same workbook. Copy the formula in cell B3 to cells C3 through E3.

   b. Click in cell B4 and use the same technique as in part (a) to obtain the sales for the first quarter for the current year. Copy this formula to cells C4 through E4.

   c. Use the AutoSum command to compute the total sales for the previous year (cell F3 in this worksheet). Compute the total sales for the current year in cell F4.

   d. Enter the formulas to compute the dollar increase for the first quarter in cell B5. Copy the formula in cell B5 to cells D5 through F5.

   e. Format the worksheet as shown in Figure 3.20. Try to duplicate our formatting. Use the Chart Wizard to create a side-by-side column chart that compares the sales in the current year to those in the previous year for each quarter. Display a legend at the bottom of the chart.

   f. Right click each data series individually within the chart, select the Format Data Series command, and then change the colors of the current and previous years to green and white, respectively.

   g. Use the AutoShapes button on the Drawing toolbar to create the arrow in the figure. Enter the indicated text as shown.

   h. Add your name to the title of the worksheet in cell A1. Print the completed worksheet for your instructor. Be sure to show gridlines and row and column headings.

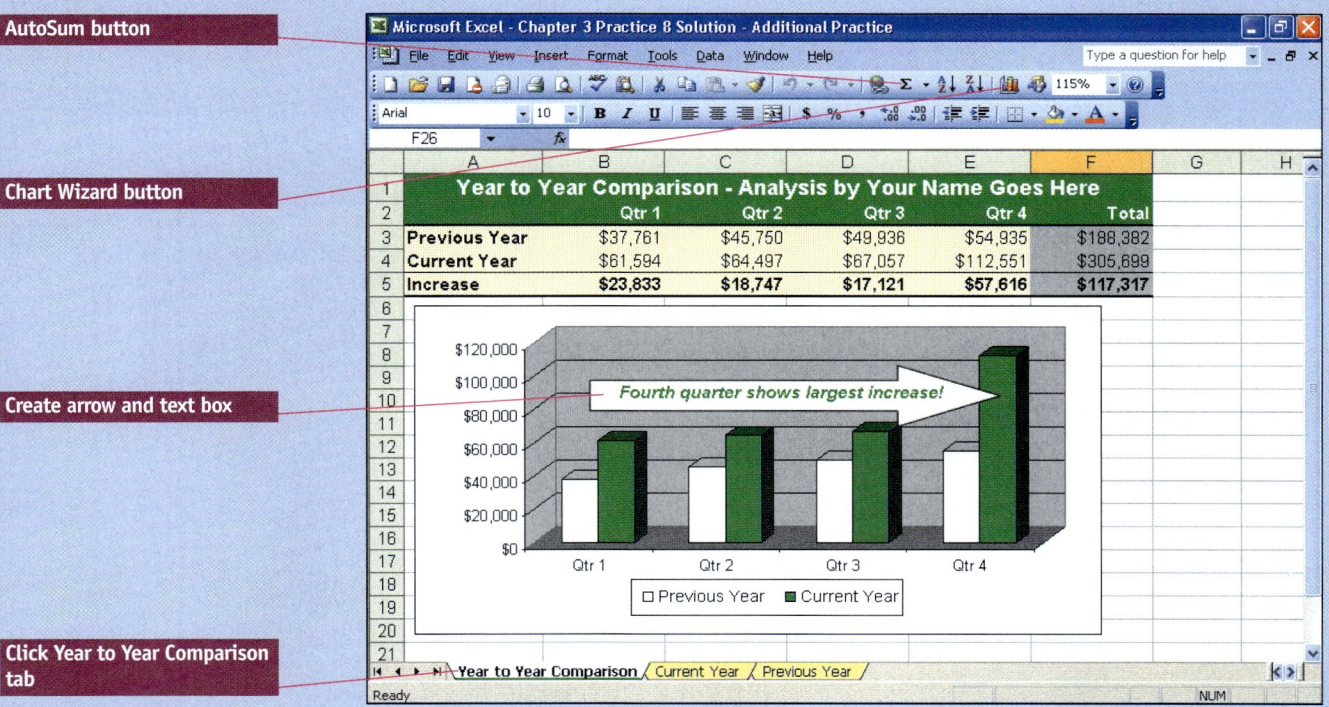

FIGURE 3.20 Additional Practice (exercise 8)

practice exercises

9. **A Combination Chart:** The workbook in Figure 3.21 is used by a regional airline to compare this year's revenue to that of last year for three classes of aircraft. Your assignment is to open the partially completed *Chapter 3 Practice 9—Combination Chart* workbook, calculate the dollar and percent increases as shown in the Year to Year Comparison worksheet, then create the corresponding combination chart.

   a. Click the worksheet tab labeled Year to Year Comparison, then click in cell B3 of this worksheet as shown in Figure 3.21. Type an equal sign, click the worksheet tab labeled Last Year, click in cell F3 of this worksheet, and press Enter. The formula for this cell appears in the formula bar as ='Last Year'!F3, indicating that the value for this cell is obtained from another worksheet in the same workbook. Enter a similar formula in cell C3 to display the total revenues for this year.

   b. Click in cell D3 and compute the dollar increase from last year to this year. (This formula does not require reference to the other worksheets.) Click in cell E3 and enter the formula to compute the corresponding percent increase from last year to this year.

   c. Copy the formulas from cells B3:E3 to B4:E5. Add the appropriate formulas in B6:D6 to compute the totals. Copy the formula in cell E5 to cell E6 to determine the percent increase.

   d. Format the completed worksheet so that it approximates Figure 3.21.

   e. Create a combination chart that plots both the dollar amount of the increase and the percent of the increase for each plane as well as for the company as a whole as shown in Figure 3.21. Press and hold the Ctrl key as you select cells A2 through A6, D2 through D6, and E2 through E6. Start the Chart Wizard, click the Custom Types tab in step 1 of the Wizard, then choose the Line-Column on 2 Axes chart. Specify that the data is in columns and that the legend is to appear at the bottom of the worksheet.

   f. Print the completed workbook to show the displayed values for all three worksheets. Display the cell formulas on the Year to Year Comparison worksheet, then select cells A1 through E6 to show cell values.

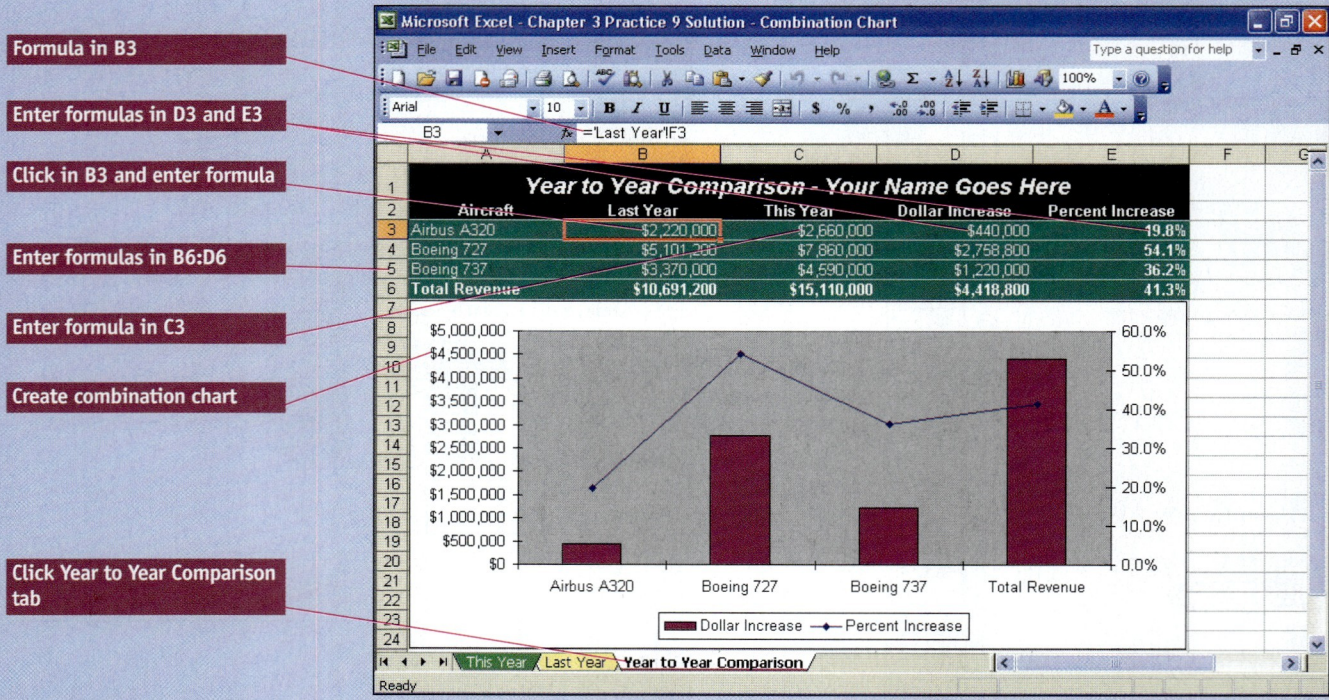

FIGURE 3.21 A Combination Chart (exercise 9)

MINI CASES

The Convention Planner

Your first task as a convention planner is to evaluate the hotel capacity for the host city in order to make recommendations as to which hotels should host the convention. The data can be found in the *Chapter 3 Mini Case—Convention Planner* workbook, which contains a single worksheet showing the number of rooms in each hotel, divided into standard and deluxe categories, together with the associated room rates. Complete the worksheet by computing the total number of rooms in each category. Format the worksheet in an attractive way. Create a stacked column chart that shows the total capacity for each hotel. Create a second chart that shows the percentage of total capacity for each hotel. Store each chart in its own worksheet, and then print the entire workbook for your instructor.

Designer Clothing

This assignment asks you to complete a worksheet and associated chart for a Designer Clothing boutique, and then link these Excel objects to an appropriate memo. Open the partially completed *Chapter 3 Mini Case—Designer Clothing* workbook; compute the sales totals for each individual salesperson as well as the totals for each quarter, then format the resulting worksheet in an attractive fashion. Include your name in the title of the worksheet (cell A1). We have started the memo for you and have saved the text in the *Chapter 3 Mini Case—Designer Clothing* Word document. Open the Word document, and then link the Excel worksheet to the Word document. Repeat the process to link the Excel chart to the Word document. Print the completed document for your instructor.

PowerPoint Presentations

The chapter described how to link an Excel chart and/or worksheet to a Word document, but you can use the same technique to link these objects to a PowerPoint presentation. Open the *Chapter 3 Mini Case—Theme Park Admissions* PowerPoint presentation that is found in the Exploring Excel folder. Now open your solution to the *Chapter 3 Practice 1—Theme Park Admissions* exercise, and link the worksheet and charts in the completed workbook to the appropriate slides in the presentation. Print the completed presentation (six slides per page) for your instructor.

Exploded Pie Charts

The *Chapter 3 Mini Case—Exploded Pie Chart* workbook contains a worksheet with summary data for the Tom Laquer Men's Wear Boutique. There are four stores and three categories of sales. Your assignment is to complete the worksheet to show the summary data, using the AutoSum and AutoFormat commands as appropriate. Once this is accomplished, you can create the two required charts. The first chart is an exploded pie chart that shows the percentage of total sales that is attributed to each city. The second chart is also a pie chart that shows the percentage of sales attributed to each product line. Replace "Tom Laquer" with your name, and then print the completed workbook for your instructor.

The Petting Zoo

The Children's Petting Zoo is a popular local attraction that opened last year. There are four classes of exhibits: dogs, cats, birds, and reptiles. The administration wants to analyze the visitation data from the first year of operation to determine the most popular exhibit to guide its plans for expansion. A summary of the data, showing the number of visits to each exhibit in each quarter, has been entered into the *Chapter 3 Mini Case—Petting Zoo* workbook. Your task is to create two charts from the numerical data. The first chart is an exploded pie chart that shows the percentage of total visits from each exhibit class. The second chart is a stacked column chart that shows the total number of visits for each exhibit (and the amount of that total in each quarter). Each chart is to appear in its own chart sheet. Print the completed workbook for your instructor.

mini cases

Chapter Recap—Tax Cuts and Dinner

What if people split a dinner check using the principles of the progressive income tax that is central to our tax code? Five lifelong friends of various means meet once a week for dinner and split the $100 check according to their ability to pay. Tom, Dick, and Harry are of relatively modest means and pay $1, $4, and $9, respectively. Ben and Ken are far more prosperous and pay $18 and $68, respectively.

The friends were quite satisfied with the arrangement until the owner offered a rebate. "You are excellent customers, and I will reduce the cost of your meal by $15." The question became how to divide the $15 windfall in order to give everyone his fair share? The proprietor suggested that they allocate the savings according to the amount each contributed to the original check. He made a quick calculation, and then rounded each person's share to an integer; e.g., Tom's new bill should have been 85 cents, but it was decided he would eat for free. In similar fashion, Dick now owes $3, Harry $7, Ben $15, and Ken $60. (Ken, the most prosperous individual, made up the difference with respect to the cents that were dropped.) The new total is $85 and everyone saves money.

Once outside the restaurant the friends began to compare their savings. Tom and Dick each complained that they saved only $1. Harry grumbled that he saved only $2. Ben thought it unfair that Ken saved more than the other four friends combined. Everyone continued to pick on Ken. The next week Ken felt so uncomfortable that he did not show up, so his former friends ate without him. But when the bill came they were $60 short.

Your assignment is to review the chapter and then create a simple worksheet and associated set of charts that show the amounts the friends pay before and after the rebate. The numbers in the case are not contrived; that is, they represent the proportion of income taxes that are paid by five different income groups. The 20% of families that represent the lowest income group pays approximately 1% of the total tax bill. The second 20% pays 4%, the third 20% pays 9%, the fourth 20% pays 18%, and the uppermost 20% pays 68%. This example was inspired by an anonymous e-mail message.

CHAPTER 4

Using Spreadsheets in Decision Making: What If?

OBJECTIVES

After reading this chapter you will:

1. Use the PMT function to calculate the payment of a car loan or mortgage.
2. Use the FV function to determine the future value of a retirement account.
3. Explain how the Goal Seek command facilitates the decision-making process.
4. Use mixed references to vary two parameters in a table.
5. Use the AVERAGE, MAX, MIN, and COUNT functions.
6. Use the IF and VLOOKUP functions to implement decision making.
7. Freeze, unfreeze, hide, and unhide rows and columns in a worksheet.
8. Use the AutoFilter command to display selected records in a list.
9. Describe the options in the Page Setup command used with large worksheets.

hands-on exercises

1. BASIC FINANCIAL FUNCTIONS
   Input: None
   Output: Basic Financial Functions
2. ADVANCED FINANCIAL FUNCTIONS
   Input: None
   Output: Advanced Financial Functions
3. THE EXPANDED GRADE BOOK
   Input: Expanded Grade Book
   Output: Expanded Grade Book Solution

CASE STUDY
BILL'S AUTOS

Bill Jennings is looking for salespeople to work weekends and a few holidays. You love cars, you need a part-time job, and you can really use the extra money. Bill has a broad inventory of used cars that is popular with college students on a tight budget. Most of his vehicles range in price from ten to fifteen thousand dollars, and Bill has worked out an arrangement with the local credit union to offer special student financing, based on a 3–5-year time span. For the majority of these auto loans, the interest rates have recently been running between 4% and 9%, depending upon credit history and current income.

Bill has offered you a job, provided you can create an easy-to-read, one-page car payment calculator for prospective customers. Bill admits to being a micromanager, and he has very definite ideas on what he wants it to look like. Therefore he has provided you with a worksheet to help get you started. Knowing the value of making a strong first impression, this is your chance to get started on the right foot, provided the finished product looks great, is flexible, and most importantly, is accurate!

Your assignment is to read the chapter, paying special attention to the discussion on financial functions and mixed references. You will then open the *Chapter 4 Case Study—Bill's Autos* worksheet to use as the starting point in creating a flexible car payment calculator. The user should be able to vary the amount of the loan, interest rate, and/or the term (years) to see the results of varying monthly car payments. It will be important to use the correct financial function and cell references when calculating the payments.

In addition, you need to add appropriate formatting to the worksheet to make it attractive enough for handing out to prospective customers. Be sure to pay attention to how it will look when printed—use various commands within Page Setup to modify the printed document. Upon completion, submit two copies of the worksheet to your instructor, one displaying cell formulas and one displaying the values.

SPREADSHEETS IN DECISION MAKING

Excel is a truly fascinating program, but it is only a means to an end. A spreadsheet is first and foremost a tool for decision making, and the objective of this chapter is to show you just how valuable that tool can be. Decisions typically involve money, and so we begin by introducing two financial functions, PMT and FV, either of which is entered directly into a worksheet.

The PMT (Payment) function calculates the periodic payment on a loan, such as one you might incur with the purchase of an automobile. The FV (Future Value) function determines the future value of a series of periodic payments, such as annual contributions to a retirement account. Either function can be used in conjunction with the Goal Seek command that lets you enter the desired end result (such as the monthly payment on a car loan) and from that, determines the input (e.g., the price of the car) to produce that result.

The second half of the chapter presents an expanded version of the professor's grade book that uses several commands associated with large spreadsheets. We describe scrolling and explain how its effects are modified by freezing and/or hiding rows and columns in a worksheet. We describe various statistical functions such as MAX, MIN, COUNT, and COUNTA as well as the IF and VLOOKUP functions that provide decision making within a worksheet. We also review the important concepts of relative and absolute cell references, as well as the need to isolate the assumptions and initial conditions in a worksheet.

Analysis of a Car Loan

Figure 4.1 shows how a worksheet might be applied to the purchase of a car. In essence you need to know the monthly payment, which depends on the price of the car, the down payment, and the terms of the loan. In other words:

- Can you afford the monthly payment on the car of your choice?
- What if you settle for a less expensive car and receive a manufacturer's rebate?
- What if you work next summer to earn money for a down payment?
- What if you extend the life of the loan and receive a better interest rate?
- Have you accounted for additional items such as insurance, gas, and maintenance?

The answers to these and other questions determine whether you can afford a car, and if so, which car, and how you will pay for it. The decision is made easier by developing the worksheet in Figure 4.1, and then by changing the various parameters as indicated.

Figure 4.1a contains the ***template***, or "empty" worksheet, in which the text entries and formulas have already been entered, the formatting has already been applied, but no specific data has been input. The template requires that you enter the price of the car, the manufacturer's rebate, the down payment, the interest rate, and the length of the loan. The worksheet uses these parameters to compute the monthly payment. (Implicit in this discussion is the existence of a PMT function within the worksheet program, which is explained in the next section.)

The availability of the worksheet lets you consider several alternatives, and therein lies its true value. You quickly realize that the purchase of a $14,999 car as shown in Figure 4.1b is prohibitive because the monthly payment is almost $500. Settling for a less expensive car, coming up with a substantial down payment, and obtaining a manufacturer's rebate in Figure 4.1c help considerably, but the $317 monthly payment is still too steep. Extending the loan to a fourth year at a lower interest rate in Figure 4.1d reduces the monthly payment to (a more affordable) $244.

No specific data has been input

	A	B
1	Price of car	
2	Manufacturer's rebate	
3	Down payment	
4	Amount to finance	=B1-(B2+B3)
5	Interest rate	
6	Term (in years)	
7	Monthly payment	=PMT(B5/12,B6*12,-B4)

(a) The Template

Data entered

	A	B
1	Price of car	$14,999
2	Manufacturer's rebate	
3	Down payment	
4	Amount to finance	$14,999
5	Interest rate	9%
6	Term (in years)	3
7	Monthly payment	$476.96

(b) Initial Parameters

Less expensive car

Rebate

Down payment made

	A	B
1	Price of car	$13,999
2	Manufacturer's rebate	$1,000
3	Down payment	$3,000
4	Amount to finance	$9,999
5	Interest rate	9%
6	Term (in years)	3
7	Monthly payment	$317.97

(c) Less Expensive Car with Down Payment and Rebate

Lower interest rate

Longer term

	A	B
1	Price of car	$13,999
2	Manufacturer's rebate	$1,000
3	Down payment	$3,000
4	Amount to finance	$9,999
5	Interest rate	8%
6	Term (in years)	4
7	Monthly payment	$244.10

(d) Longer Term and Better Interest Rate

FIGURE 4.1 Spreadsheets in Decision Making

PMT Function

A *function* is a predefined formula that accepts one or more *arguments* as input, performs the indicated calculation, then returns another value as output. Excel has more than 100 different functions in various categories. Financial functions, such as the PMT function we are about to study, are especially important in business.

The *PMT function* requires three arguments (the interest rate per period, the number of periods, and the amount of the loan), from which it computes the associated payment on a loan. The arguments are placed in parentheses and are separated by commas. Consider the PMT function as it might apply to Figure 4.1b:

=PMT(.09/12,36,−14999)
- Amount of loan (as a *negative* amount)
- Number of periods (3 years × 12 months/year)
- Interest rate per period (annual rate divided by 12)

Instead of using specific values, however, the arguments in the PMT function are supplied as cell references, so that the computed payment can be based on values supplied by the user elsewhere in the worksheet. Thus, the PMT function is entered as =PMT(B5/12,B6*12,−B4) to reflect the terms of a specific loan whose arguments are in cells B4, B5, and B6. (The principal is entered as a negative amount so that the worksheet will display a positive value.)

FV Function

The *FV function* returns the future value of an investment based on constant periodic payments and a constant interest rate. It can be used to determine the future value of a retirement plan such as an IRA (Individual Retirement Account) or 401K, two plans that are very popular in today's workplace. Under either plan, an individual saves for his or her retirement by making a fixed contribution each year. The money is allowed to accumulate tax-free until retirement, and it is an excellent way to save for the future.

Assume, for example, that you plan to contribute $3,000 a year to an IRA, that you expect to earn 7% annually, and that you will be contributing for 40 years (i.e., you began contributing at age 25 and will continue to contribute until age 65). The future value of that investment—the amount you will have at age 65—would be $598,905! All told, you would have contributed $120,000 ($3,000 a year for 40 years). The difference, more than $470,000, results from compound interest over the life of your investment.

The FV function is entered into a worksheet in similar fashion to the PMT function. There are three arguments—the interest rate (also called the rate of return), the number of periods, and the periodic investment. The FV function corresponding to our earlier example would be:

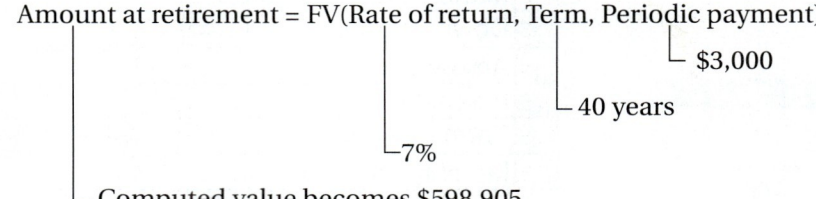

Amount at retirement = FV(Rate of return, Term, Periodic payment)
- $3,000
- 40 years
- 7%
- Computed value becomes $598,905

It's more practical, however, to enter the values into a worksheet, then use cell references within the FV function. If, for example, cells A1, A2, and A3 contained the rate of return, term, and annual contribution, respectively, the resulting FV function would be =FV(A1, A2, −A3). The periodic payment is preceded by a minus sign, just as the principal in the PMT function.

Inserting a Function

The ***Insert Function command*** places a function into a worksheet. You can select a function from a category as was done in Figure 4.2a, or you can enter a brief description of the function you are searching for. The Function Arguments dialog box in Figure 4.2b appears after you choose the function and is where you enter the various arguments. (Only the first three arguments are required for the Future Value function.) Excel displays the calculated value of each argument as well as the value of the function within the dialog box.

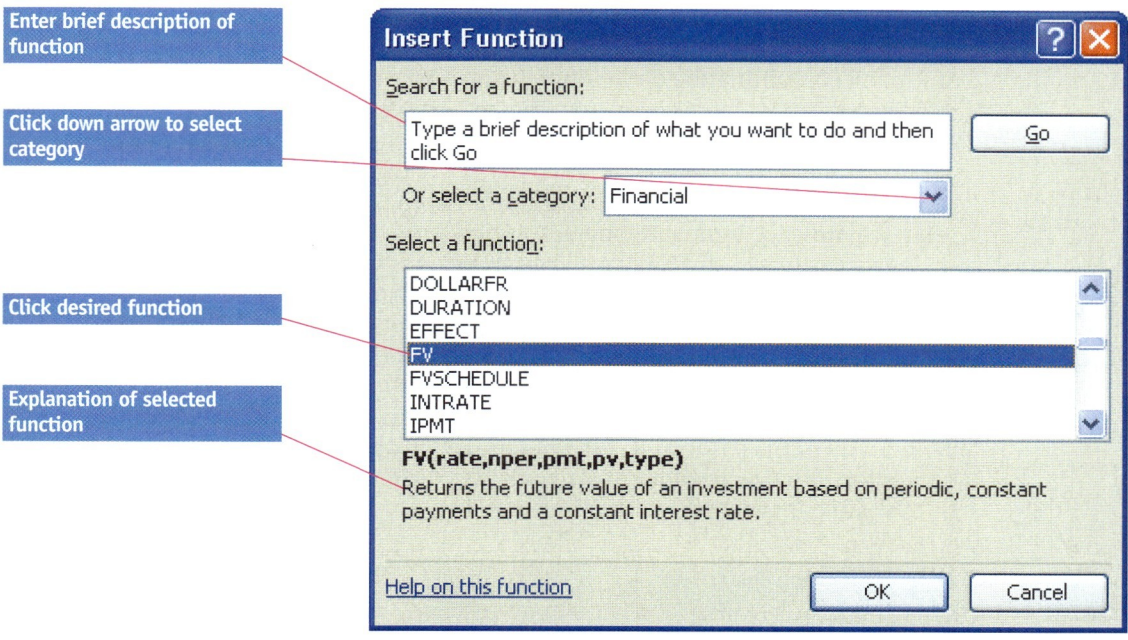

(a) Select the Function

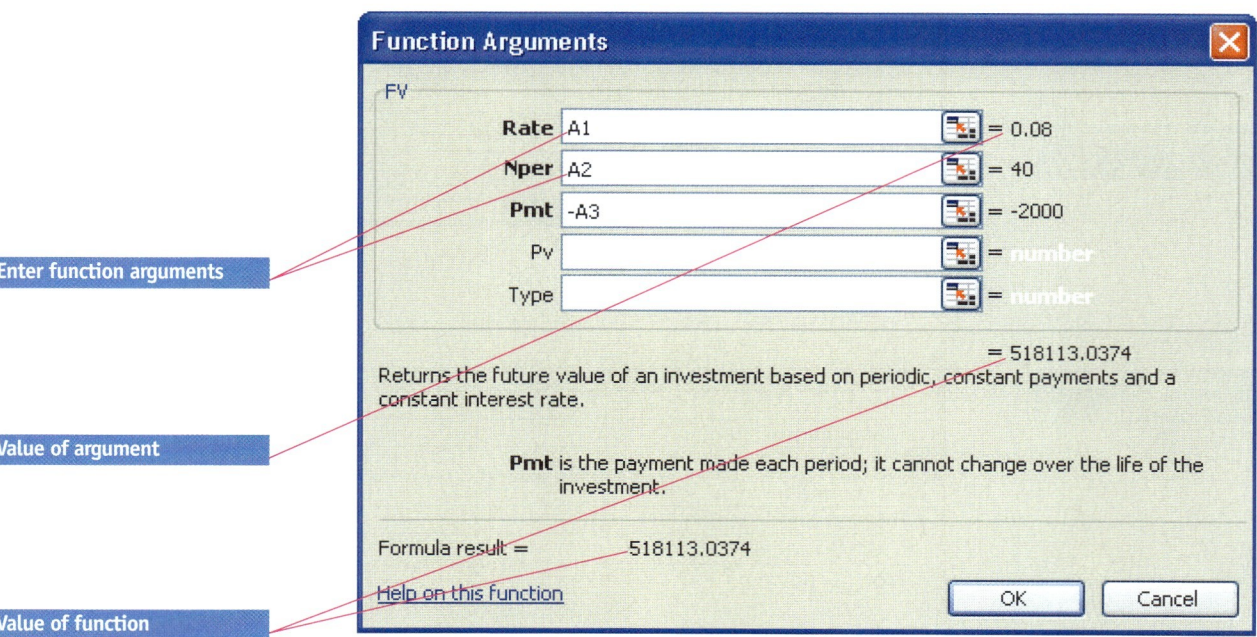

(b) Enter the Argument

FIGURE 4.2 Inserting a Function

The Goal Seek Command

The analysis in Figure 4.1 enabled us to reduce the projected monthly payment from $476 to a more affordable $244. What if, however, you can afford a payment of only $200, and you want to know the maximum you can borrow in order to keep the payment to the specified amount? The ***Goal Seek command*** is designed to solve this type of problem, as it enables you to set an end result (such as the monthly payment) in order to determine the input (the price of the car) to produce that result. Only one input (the price of the car, the interest rate, or the term) can be varied at a time.

Figure 4.3 extends our earlier analysis to illustrate the Goal Seek command. You create the spreadsheet as usual, then you pull down the Tools menu, and select the Goal Seek command to display the dialog box in Figure 4.3a. Enter the address of the cell containing the dependent formula (the monthly payment in cell B7) and the desired value of this cell ($200). Indicate the cell whose contents should be varied (the price of the car in cell B1), then click OK to execute the command. The Goal Seek command then varies the price of the car until the monthly payment returns the desired value of $200. (Not every problem has a solution, in which case Excel returns a message indicating that a solution cannot be found.)

In this example, the Goal Seek command is able to find a solution and returns a purchase price of $12,192 as shown in Figure 4.3b. You now have all the information you need. Find a car that sells for $12,192 (or less), hold the other parameters to the values shown in the figure, and your monthly payment will be (at most) $200.

The analysis in Figure 4.3 illustrates how a worksheet is used in the decision-making process. An individual defines a problem, then develops a worksheet that includes all of the associated parameters. He or she can then plug in specific numbers, changing one or more of the variables until a decision can be reached. Excel is invaluable in arriving at the solution.

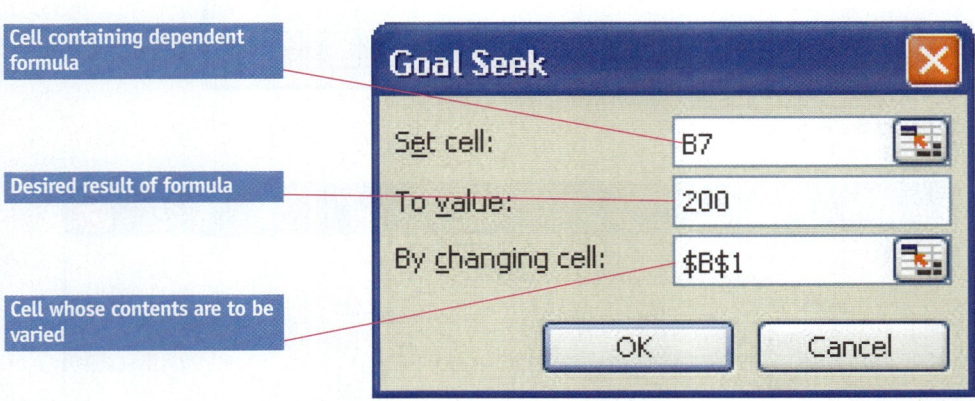

(a) Set the Maximum Payment

	A	B
1	Price of car	$12,192
2	Manufacturer's rebate	$1,000
3	Down payment	$3,000
4	Amount to finance	$8,192
5	Interest rate	8%
6	Term (in years)	4
7	Monthly payment	$200.00

(b) Solution

FIGURE 4.3   The Goal Seek Command

hands-on exercise 1

Basic Financial Functions

Objective To illustrate the PMT and FV functions; to illustrate the Goal Seek command. Use Figure 4.4 as a guide in the exercise.

Step 1: **Enter the Descriptive Labels**

- Start Excel. If necessary, click the **New button** on the Standard toolbar to open a new workbook as shown in Figure 4.4a.

- Click in **cell A1**, type the label **Basic Financial Functions**, then press the **Enter key** to complete the entry. Enter the remaining labels for column A.

- Click and drag the column border between columns A and B to increase the column width of column A to accommodate the widest entry in column A (other than cell A3).

- Click in **cell B4** and type **$14,999** corresponding to the price of the automobile you hope to purchase. Be sure to include the dollar sign as you enter the data to format the cell automatically.

- Enter **$1,000** and **$3,000** in **cells B5** and **B6**, respectively, corresponding to the manufacturer's rebate and down payment, respectively.

- Click in **cell B7**. Use pointing to enter the formula **=B4−(B5+B6)**, which calculates the amount to finance (i.e., the principal of the loan).

- Enter **9%** and **3** in **cells B8** and **B9**. (If necessary, click in **cell B9**, pull down the **Edit menu**, select the **Clear command**, and choose the **Format command** to remove the dollar sign.)

- All of the loan parameters have been entered.

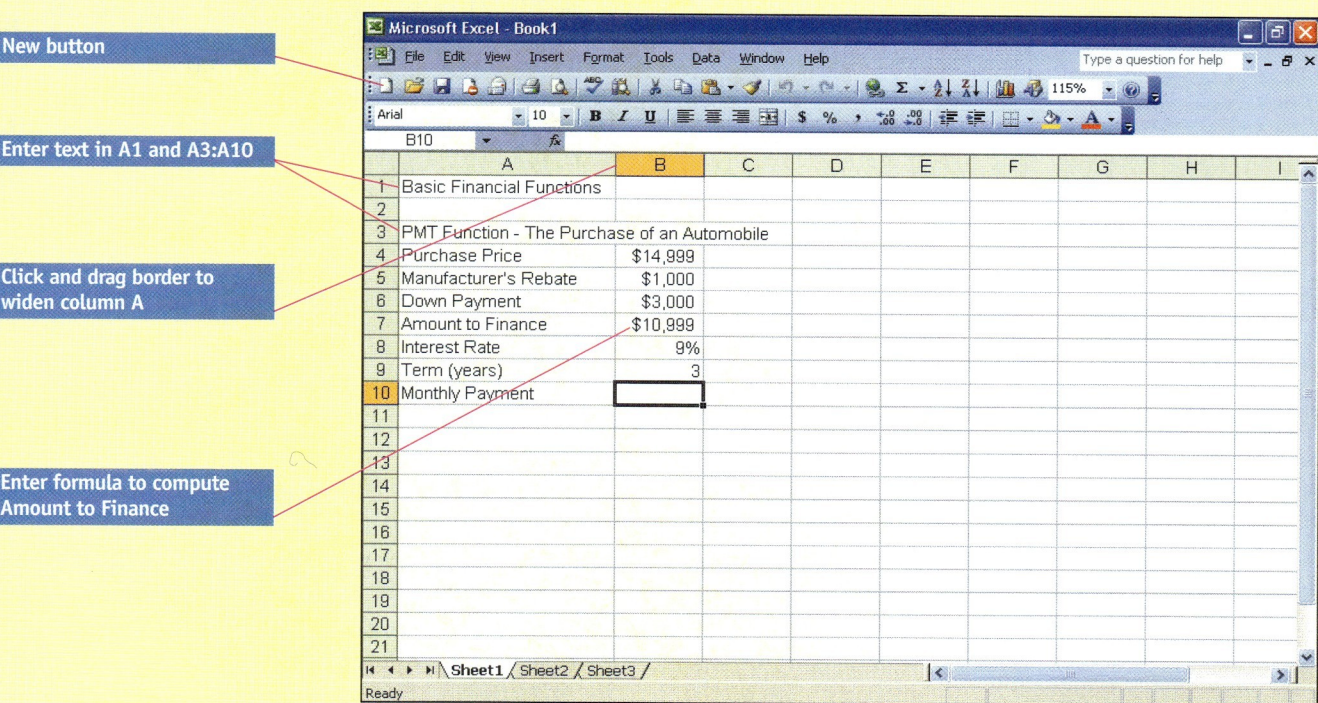

(a) Enter the Descriptive Labels (step 1)

FIGURE 4.4 Hands-on Exercise 1

Step 2: **Insert a Function**

- Click in **cell B10**. Pull down the **Insert menu** and click the **Function command** (or click the **Insert Function button** on the formula bar) to display the Insert Function dialog box.

- Click the **down arrow** in the Select a Category list box and select **Financial**, select the **PMT function** and click **OK** to display the Function Arguments dialog box in Figure 4.4b.

- Click the **Rate text box** and use pointing to enter the rate. Click in **cell B8** of the worksheet, then type **/12**, so that the text box contains the entry B8/12.

- Click the **Nper text box** and use pointing to enter the number of periods. Click in **cell B9**, then type ***12**, so that the formula bar contains the entry B9*12.

- Click the **Pv text box**. Type a – sign, then click in **cell B7**. You should see 349.7652595 as the value for the PMT function. Click **OK** to close the Function Arguments dialog box.

- Pull down the **File menu** and click the **Save command** (or click the **Save button** on the Standard toolbar) to display the Save As dialog box, then save the workbook as **Basic Financial Functions** in the **Exploring Excel** folder.

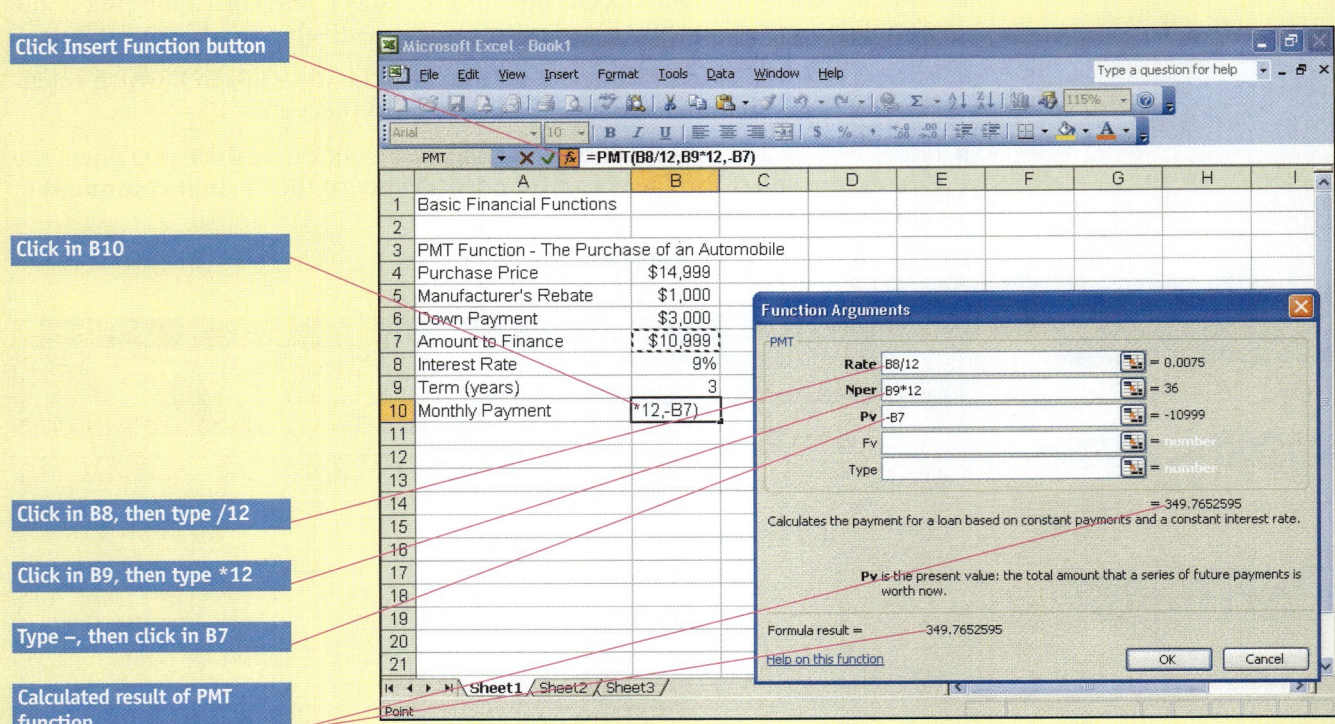

(b) Insert a Function (step 2)

FIGURE 4.4 Hands-on Exercise 1 (*continued*)

SEARCH FOR THE FUNCTION

It's easy to select a function if you know its name, but what if you are unsure of the name or don't know the category in which the function is found? Click the Insert Function button on the formula bar to display the Insert Function dialog box, type a keyword such as "payment" in the Search text box, then click the Go button. Excel returns nine functions in this example, one of which is the PMT function that you are looking for.

Step 3: **The Goal Seek Command**

- You can reduce the monthly payment in various ways. Click in **cell B4** and change the price of the car to **$13,999**. The monthly payment drops to $317.97.
- Change the interest rate to **8%** and the term of the loan to **4** years. The payment drops to $244.10.
- You can reduce the payment still further by using the Goal Seek command to fix the payment at a specified level. Click in **cell B10**, the cell containing the formula for the monthly payment.
- Pull down the **Tools menu**. Click **Goal Seek** to display the dialog box in Figure 4.4c. Click in the **To value** text box. Type **200** (the desired payment).
- Click in the **By changing cell** text box. Type **B4**, the cell containing the price of the car. This is the cell whose value will be determined. Click **OK**.
- The Goal Seek command returns a successful solution consisting of $12,192 and $200 in cells B4 and B10, respectively. Click **OK** to accept the solution and close the Goal Seek dialog box.
- Save the workbook.

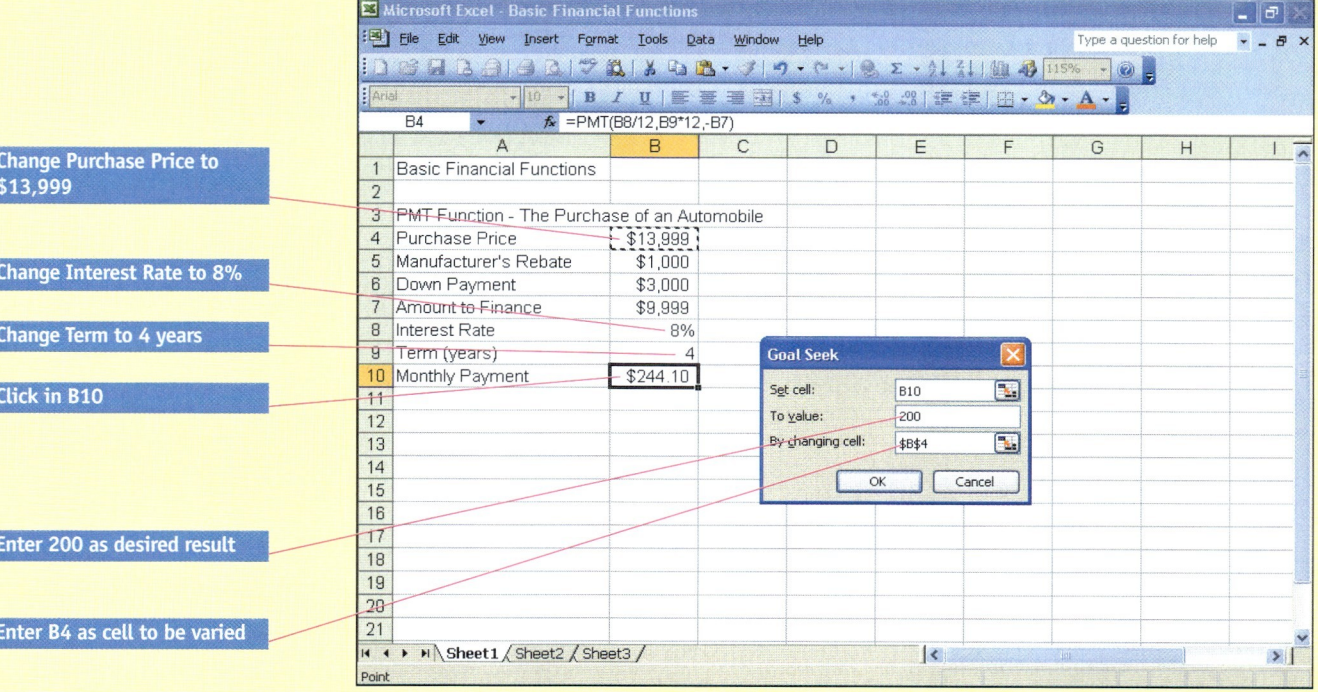

(c) The Goal Seek command (step 3)

FIGURE 4.4   Hands-on Exercise 1 (*continued*)

THE FORMATTING IS IN THE CELL

Once a number format has been assigned to a cell, either by including the format as you entered a number, or through execution of a formatting command, the formatting remains in the cell. Thus, to change the contents in a formatted cell, all you need to do is enter the new number without the formatting. Entering 5000, for example, into a cell that was previously formatted as currency will display the number as $5,000. To remove the formatting, pull down the Edit menu, select the Clear command, then choose Format.

Step 4: **The Future Value (FV) Function**

- Check your work carefully to be sure that your worksheet matches the top half of Figure 4.4d. Make corrections as necessary.
- Enter the labels in **cells A13** through **A17** as shown in the figure. Click in **cell B14** and type **$3,000** corresponding to the annual contribution. Be sure to include the dollar sign.
- Enter **7%** (type the percent sign) and **40** in **cells B15** and **B16**, respectively.
- Click in **cell B17**, type **=FV(** . You will see a ScreenTip that shows the arguments in the FV function. There are five arguments, but only the first three (rate, nper, and pv) are required. (The last two arguments are enclosed in square brackets to indicate they are optional.)
- Use pointing to complete the function, which is **=FV(B15,B16,–B14)**. Press **Enter** when you have finished.
- You should see $598,905.34 in cell B17. This is the amount you will have at retirement, given that you save $3,000 a year for 40 years and earn 7% interest over the life of your investment.
- Save the workbook.

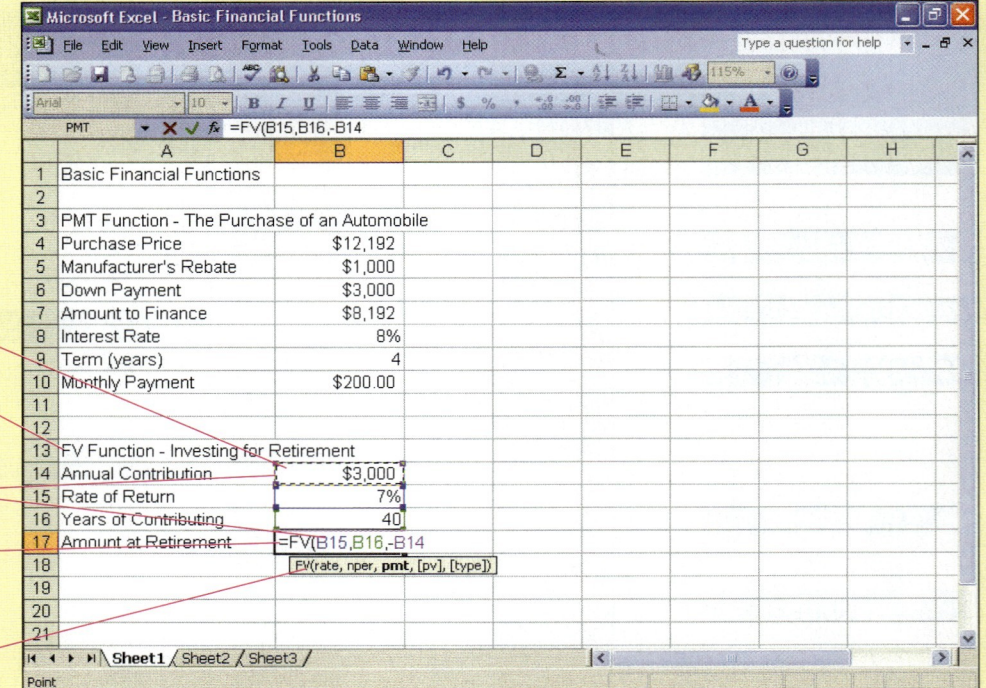

(d) The Future Value (FV) Function (step 4)

FIGURE 4.4 Hands-on Exercise 1 (*continued*)

IT'S COLOR CODED

Double click in the cell that contains the FV function, then look closely at the arguments within the function to see that each argument is a different color. Each color corresponds to the border color of the referenced cell. You can change any reference in the function (e.g., from B15 to C15) by dragging the color-coded border surrounding cell B15 (the reference you want to change) to cell C15 (the new reference).

Step 5: **Format the Worksheet**

- Your workbook should match Figure 4.4e except for the formatting. Click and drag **cells A1** and **B1**, then click the **Merge and Center button**.
- Click the **down arrow** on the Font Size list box to change the font size to **12**. Click the **Bold button** to boldface the title.
- Click **cell A3**. Press and hold the **Ctrl key** as you click cells **A10:B10, A13**, and **A17:B17** to select all of these cells. Click the **Bold button** to boldface the contents of these cells.
- Click and drag to select **cells A4** through **A9**. Press and hold the **Ctrl key** as you click and drag to select **cells A14** through **A16** (in addition to cells A4 through A9).
- Click the **Increase Indent button** on the Formatting toolbar to indent the labels as shown in Figure 4.4e.
- Click in **cell A19** and enter your name, then click the **Bold button** to boldface the type.
- Save the workbook.

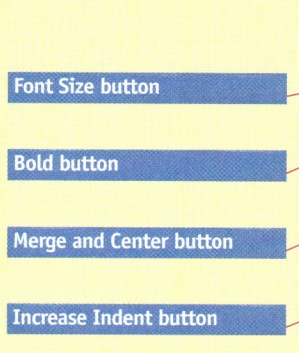
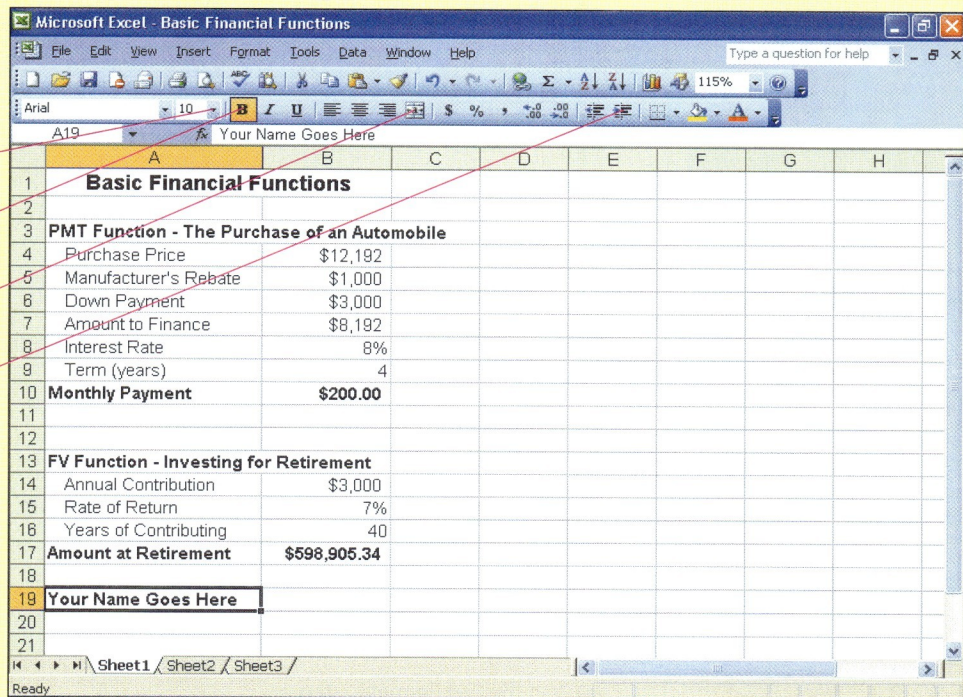

(e) Format the Worksheet (step 5)

FIGURE 4.4 Hands-on Exercise 1 (*continued*)

SELECTING NONCONTIGUOUS RANGES

You can apply the same formatting to noncontiguous (nonadjacent) cells within a worksheet by using the Ctrl key to select the cells. Click and drag to select the first cell range, then press and hold the Ctrl key as you select a second range. Continue to press the Ctrl key to select additional ranges, then format all of the selected cells with a single command. Click anywhere in the worksheet to deselect the cells.

Step 6: **Print the Cell Formulas**

- Pull down the **File menu** and click the **Page Setup command** to display the Page Setup dialog box. Click the **Sheet tab**, then check the boxes to print gridlines and row and column headings.

- Click the **Margins tab** and check the box to center the worksheet horizontally. Click **OK** to accept the settings and close the dialog box.

- Save the workbook. Click the **Print Preview button** on the Standard toolbar to be sure you are satisfied with the appearance of the workbook. Click the **Print button**, then click **OK** to print the worksheet.

- Press **Ctrl+`** to display the cell contents, as opposed to the displayed values. Preview the worksheet in this format, then print it when you are satisfied with its appearance. Press **Ctrl+`** to return the worksheet to displayed values.

- Submit printouts—the displayed values and the cell formulas—to your instructor as proof that you did this exercise.

- Exit Excel if you do not want to continue with the next exercise at this time.

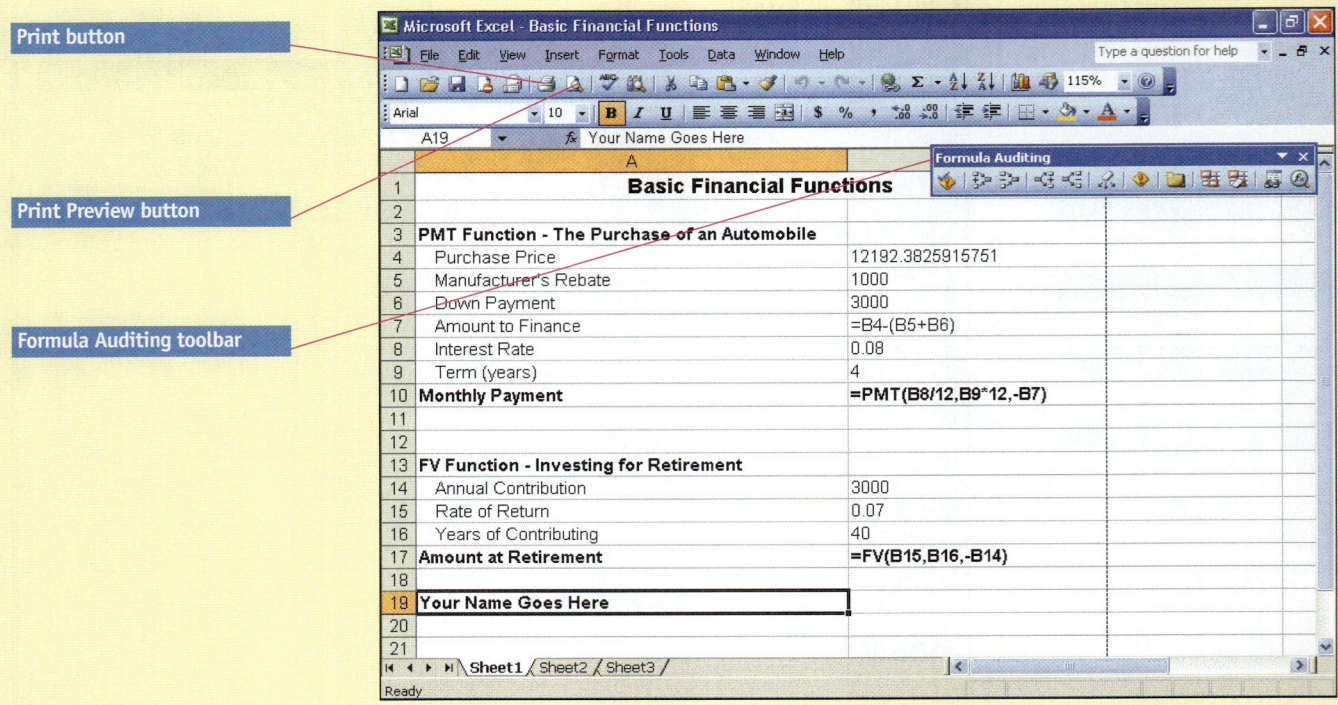

(f) Print the Cell Formulas (step 6)

FIGURE 4.4 Hands-on Exercise 1 (*continued*)

ARE THE PAYMENTS MONTHLY OR ANNUAL?

The FV function in this example computes the future value of a series of annual payments, with the term and interest rate specified as annual values, and thus there is no need to multiply or divide these values by 12. The car payment in the previous example, however, was on a monthly basis. Thus the annual interest rate was divided by 12 (to obtain the monthly rate), while the term of the loan was multiplied by 12, in order to put the numbers on a monthly basis.

HOME MORTGAGES

The PMT function is used in our next example in conjunction with the purchase of a home. The example also reviews the concept of relative and absolute addresses from Chapter 2. In addition, it introduces several other techniques to make you more proficient in Excel.

The spreadsheets in Figure 4.5 illustrate a variable rate mortgage, which will be developed over the next several pages. The user enters the amount he or she wishes to borrow and a starting interest rate, and the spreadsheet displays the associated monthly payment. The spreadsheet in Figure 4.5a enables the user to see the monthly payment at varying interest rates, and to contrast the amount of the payment for a 15-year and a 30-year mortgage.

Most first-time buyers opt for the longer term, but they would do well to consider a 15-year mortgage. Note, for example, that the difference in monthly payments for a $100,000 mortgage at 7.5% is only $227.80 (the difference between $927.01 for a 15-year mortgage versus $699.21 for the 30-year mortgage). This is a significant amount of money, but when viewed as a percentage of the total cost of a home (property taxes and maintenance), it becomes less important, especially when you consider the substantial saving in interest over the life of the mortgage.

Figure 4.5b expands the spreadsheet to show the total interest over the life of the loan for both the 15-year and the 30-year mortgage. The total interest on a $100,000 loan at 7.5% is $151,717 for a 30-year mortgage, but only $66,862 for a 15-year mortgage. In other words, you will pay back the $100,000 in principal plus another $151,717 in interest if you select the longer term.

Difference in monthly payment between a 30-year and a 15-year mortgage at 7.5%

	A	B	C	D
1	Amount Borrowed		$100,000	
2	Starting Interest		7.50%	
3				
4		Monthly Payment		
5	Interest	30 Years	15 Years	Difference
6	7.50%	$699.21	$927.01	$227.80
7	8.50%	$768.91	$984.74	$215.83
8	9.50%	$840.85	$1,044.22	$203.37
9	10.50%	$914.74	$1,105.40	$190.66
10	11.50%	$990.29	$1,168.19	$177.90
11	12.50%	$1,067.26	$1,232.52	$165.26

(a) Difference in Monthly Payment

Less interest is paid on a 15-year loan ($66,862 vs $151,717 on a 30-year loan)

	A	B	C	D	E
1	Amount Borrowed			$100,000	
2	Starting Interest			7.50%	
3					
4		30 Years		15 Years	
5	Interest	Monthly Payment	Total Interest	Monthly Payment	Total Interest
6	7.50%	$699.21	$151,717	$927.01	$66,862
7	8.50%	$768.91	$176,809	$984.74	$77,253
8	9.50%	$840.85	$202,708	$1,044.22	$87,960
9	10.50%	$914.74	$229,306	$1,105.40	$98,972
10	11.50%	$990.29	$256,505	$1,168.19	$110,274
11	12.50%	$1,067.26	$284,213	$1,232.52	$121,854

(b) Total Interest

FIGURE 4.5 15-Year versus 30-Year Mortgage

Relative versus Absolute References

Figure 4.6 displays the cell formulas for the mortgage analysis. All of the formulas are based on the amount borrowed and the starting interest, in cells C1 and C2, respectively. You can vary either or both of these parameters, and the worksheet will automatically recalculate the monthly payments.

The similarity in the formulas from one row to the next implies that the copy operation will be essential to the development of the worksheet. You must, however, remember the distinction between a ***relative*** and an ***absolute reference***—that is, a cell reference that changes during a copy operation (relative) versus one that does not (absolute). Consider the PMT function as it appears in cell B6:

=PMT(A6/12,30*12,–$C$1)

└ The amount of the loan, –$C$1, is an absolute reference that remains constant

└ Number of periods (30 years*12 months/year)

└ The interest rate, A6/12, is a relative reference that changes

The entry A6/12 (which is the first argument in the formula in cell B6) is interpreted to mean "divide the contents of the cell one column to the left by 12." Thus, when the PMT function in cell B6 is copied to cell B7, it (the copied formula) is adjusted to maintain this relationship and will contain the entry A7/12. The Copy command does not duplicate a relative address exactly, but adjusts it from row to row (or column to column) to maintain the relative relationship. The cell reference for the amount of the loan should not change when the formula is copied, and hence it is specified as an absolute address. Absolute references use a dollar sign before the row and column reference—for example, $C$1.

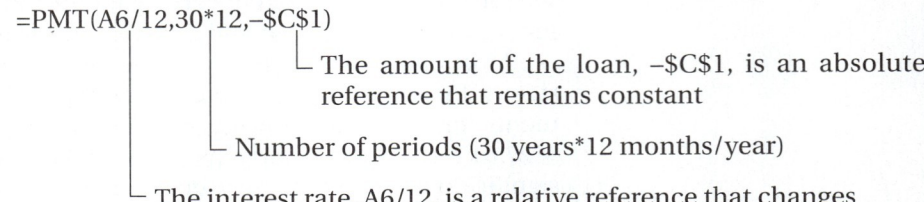

FIGURE 4.6 Cell Formulas

ISOLATE ASSUMPTIONS

The formulas in a worksheet should be based on cell references rather than specific values—for example, C1 or $C$1 rather than $100,000. The cells containing these values should be clearly labeled and set apart from the rest of the worksheet. You can then vary the inputs (assumptions) to the worksheet and immediately see the effect. The chance for error is also minimized because you are changing the contents of a single cell, rather than changing multiple formulas.

Mixed References

Figure 4.7 displays a new worksheet that uses the FV function to calculate the value of an *IRA (Individual Retirement Account)* under various combinations of interest rates and years for investing. The annual contribution is $3,000 in all instances (the maximum that is allowed under current law). The interest rates appear in row 5, while the years for investing are shown in column B. The intersection of a row and column contains the future value of a series of $3,000 investments for the specific interest rate and year combination. Cell E21, for example, shows that $3,000 a year, invested over 40 years at 7%, will compound to $598,905.

The key to the worksheet is to realize that the Future Value function requires *mixed references* for both the interest rate and number of years. The interest rate will always come from row 5, but the column will vary. In similar fashion, the number of years will always come from column B, but the row will vary. Using this information we can enter the appropriate formula into cell C6, then copy that formula to the remaining cells in row 6, and finally copy row 6 to the remaining rows in the worksheet. The key to the worksheet is the formula in cell C6. Consider:

Future Value = FV(C$5, $B6, –$D$3)

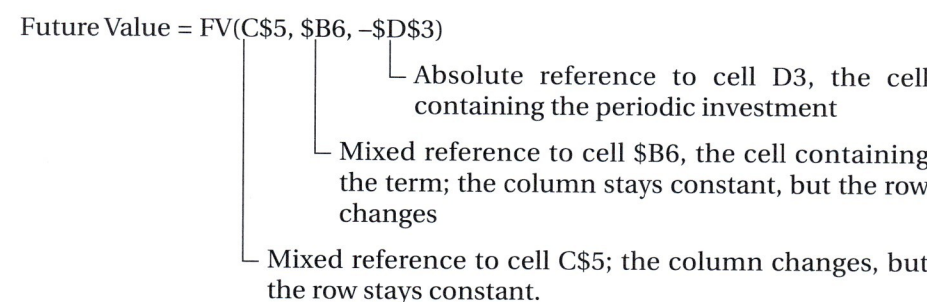

- Absolute reference to cell D3, the cell containing the periodic investment
- Mixed reference to cell $B6, the cell containing the term; the column stays constant, but the row changes
- Mixed reference to cell C$5; the column changes, but the row stays constant.

The majority of spreadsheets can be developed using a combination of relative and absolute references. Occasionally, however, you will need to incorporate mixed references as you will see in our next exercise.

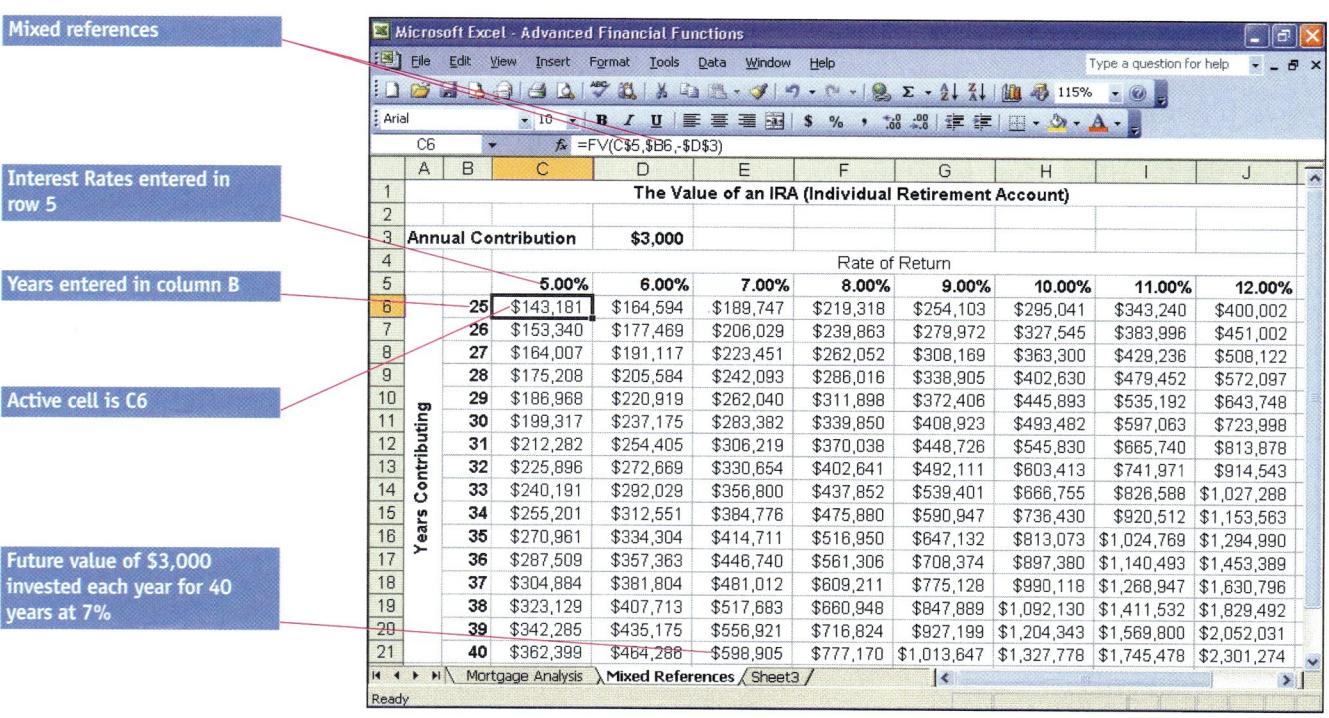

FIGURE 4.7 Mixed References

hands-on exercise 2

Advanced Financial Functions

Objective To use relative, absolute, and mixed references in conjunction with the PMT and FV functions; to practice various formatting commands. Use Figure 4.8 as a guide in the exercise.

Step 1: **The Spell Check**

- Start Excel and begin a new workbook. Click in **cell A1**. Type **Amount Borrowed**. Do not be concerned that the text is longer than the cell width, as cell B1 is empty and thus the text will be displayed in its entirety. Press the **Enter key** or **down arrow** to complete the entry.

- Type **Starting Interest** in **cell A2**. Click in **cell A4**. Type **Monthly Payment**. Enter the remaining labels in **cells A5** through **D5**, as shown in Figure 4.8a without concern for the column width.

- We suggest that you deliberately misspell one or more words in order to try the spell check. Click in **cell A1** to begin the spell check at the beginning of the worksheet.

- Click the **Spelling button** on the Standard toolbar to initiate the spell check as shown in Figure 4.8a. Make corrections, as necessary, just as you would in Microsoft Word.

- Click in **cell C1**. Type **$100,000** (include the dollar sign). Press the **Enter key** or **down arrow** to complete the entry and move to **cell C2**. Type **7.5%** (include the percent sign). Press **Enter**.

- Save the workbook as **Advanced Financial Functions** in the **Exploring Excel folder** on the appropriate drive.

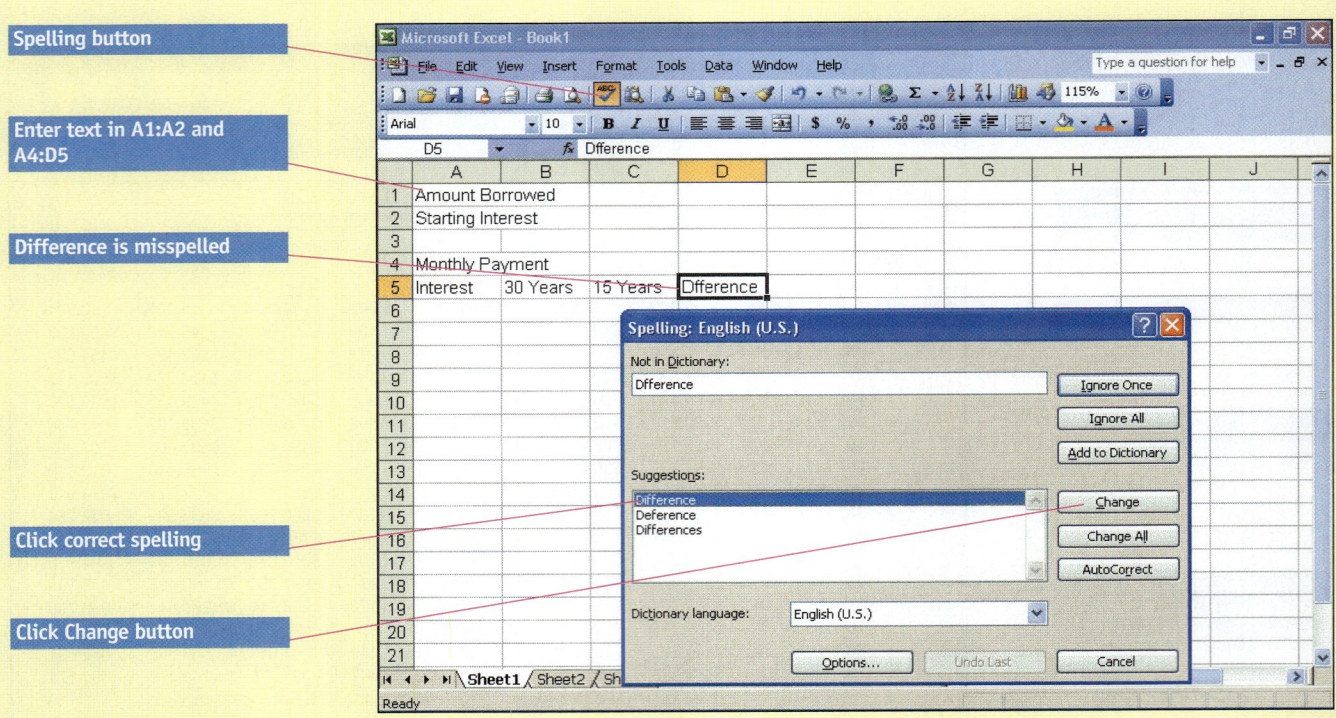

(a) The Spell Check (step 1)

FIGURE 4.8 Hands-on Exercise 2

CHAPTER 4: USING SPREADSHEETS IN DECISION MAKING

Step 2: **The Fill Handle**

- Click in **cell A6**. Use pointing to enter the formula **=C2** to reference the starting interest rate in cell C2.

- Click in **cell A7**. Use pointing to enter the formula **=A6+.01** to compute the interest rate in this cell, which is one percent more than the interest rate in row 6. Press **Enter**.

- Click in **cell A7**. Point to the **fill handle** in the lower-right corner of cell A7. The mouse pointer changes to a thin crosshair.

- Drag the **fill handle** over **cells A8** through **A11**. A border appears to indicate the destination range as in Figure 4.8b. Release the mouse to complete the copy operation. The formula and associated percentage format in cell A7 have been copied to cells A8 through A11.

- Click in **cell C2**. Type **5%**. The entries in cells A6 through A11 change automatically. Click the **Undo button** on the Standard toolbar to return to the 7.5% interest rate.

- Save the workbook.

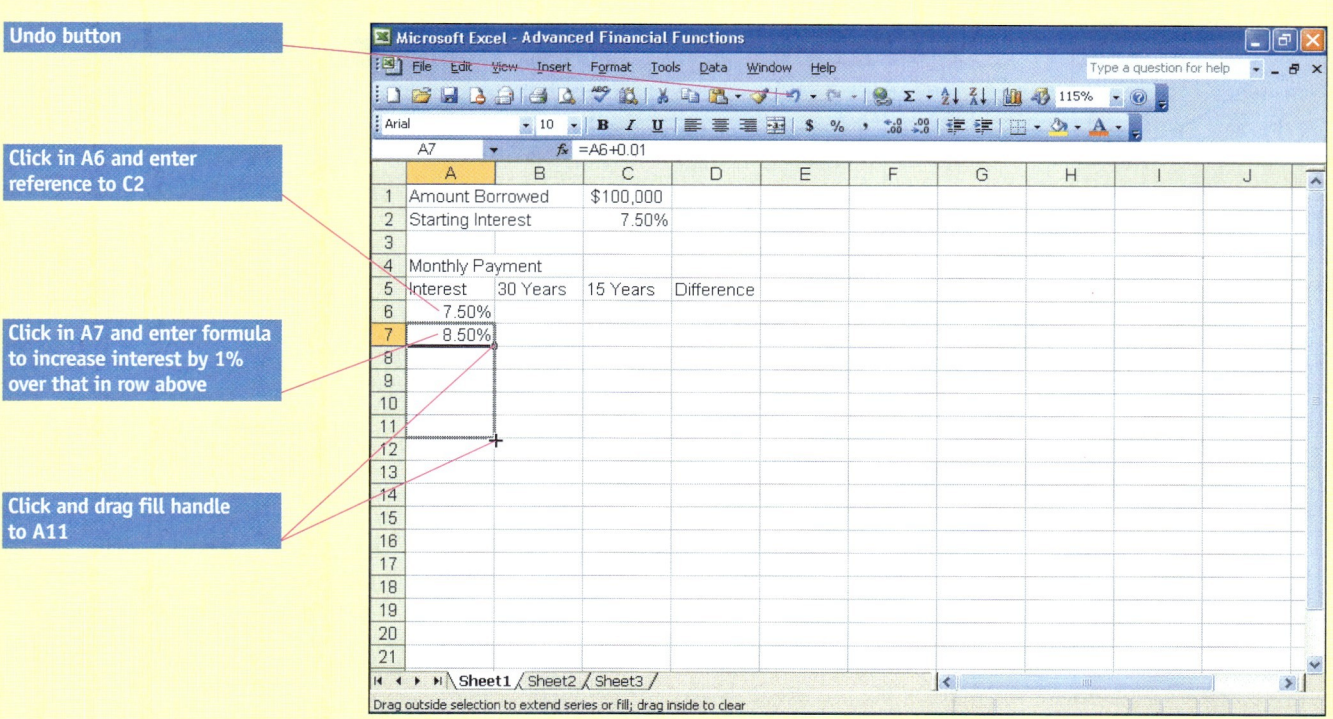

(b) The Fill Handle (step 2)

FIGURE 4.8 Hands-on Exercise 2 (*continued*)

FIND AND REPLACE

Anyone familiar with a word processor takes the Find and Replace commands for granted, but did you know the same capabilities exist in Excel? Pull down the Edit menu and choose either command. You have the same options as in the parallel command in Word, such as a case-sensitive (or insensitive) search. Use the command in the current worksheet to change "Interest" to "Interest Rate".

Step 3: **Determine the 30-year Payments**

- Click in **cell B6** and enter the formula **=PMT(A6/12,30*12,–$C$1)** as shown in Figure 4.8c. Note the ScreenTip that appears as you enter the function to indicate the order of the arguments. Note, too, that you can enter the references directly or you can use pointing (click the **F4 key** as necessary to change from relative to absolute addresses).

- Click in **cell B6**, which should display the value $699.21, as shown in Figure 4.8c. Click and drag the **fill handle** in the bottom-right corner of cell B6 over cells B7 through B11. Release the mouse to complete the copy operation.

- The PMT function in cell B6 has been copied to cells B7 through B11. The payment amounts are visible in cells B7 through B10, but cell B11 may display a series of number signs, meaning that the cell (column) is too narrow to display the computed results in the selected format.

- Check that cells B6:B11 are still selected. Pull down the **Format menu**, click **Column**, then click **AutoFit Selection** from the cascaded menu. Cell B11 should display $1,067.26.

- Save the workbook.

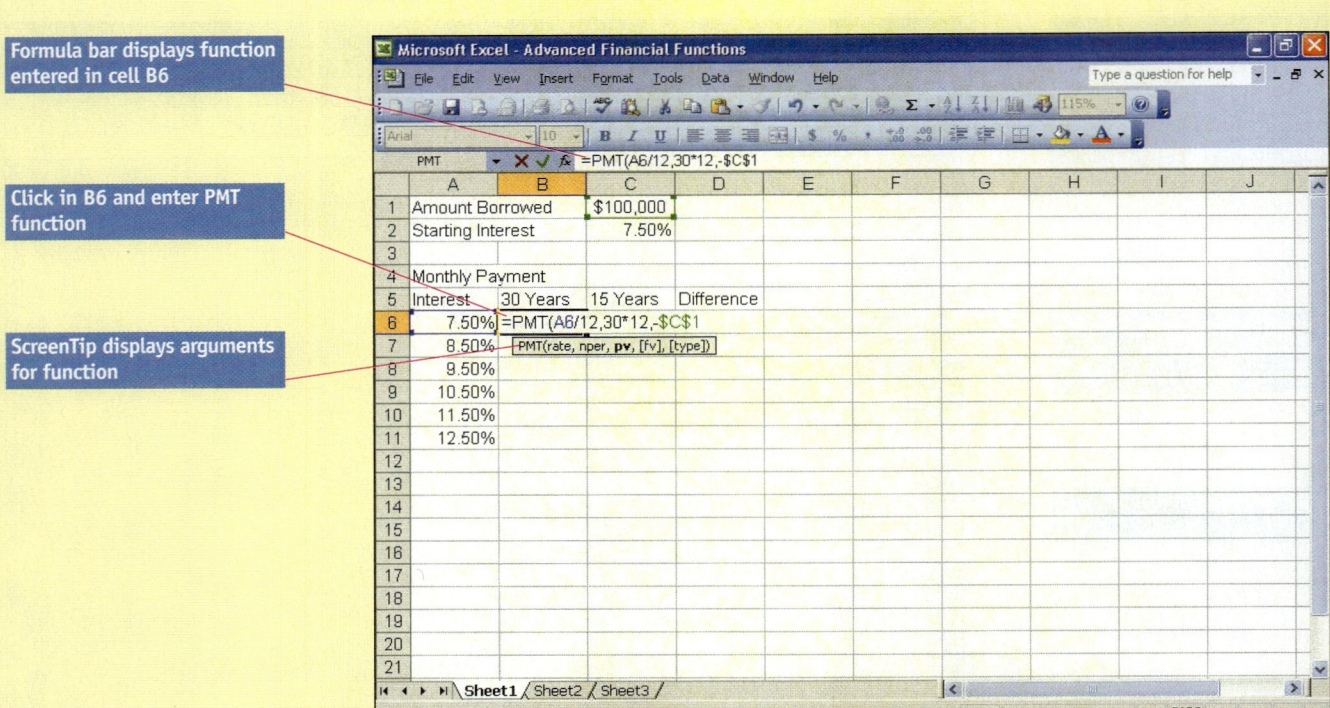

(c) Determine the 30-year Payments (step 3)

FIGURE 4.8 Hands-on Exercise 2 (*continued*)

POUND SIGNS AND COLUMN WIDTH

The appearance of pound signs within a cell indicates that the cell width (column width) is insufficient to display the computed results in the selected format. Double click the right border of the column heading to change the column width to accommodate the widest entry in that column. For example, to increase the width of column B, double click the border between the column headings for columns B and C.

Step 4: **Determine the 15-year Payments**

- Click in **cell C6** and enter the formula **=PMT(A6/12,15*12,–$C$1)** as shown in Figure 4.8d. Note the ScreenTip that appears as you enter the function to indicate the order of the arguments. You can enter the references directly, or you can use pointing (click the **F4 key** as necessary to change from relative to absolute addresses).
- Press **Enter** to complete the formula. Check that cell C6 displays the value $927.01. Make corrections as necessary.
- Use the **fill handle** to copy the contents of **cell C6** to **cells C7** through **C11**.
- If necessary, increase the width of column C. Cell C11 should display $1,232.52 if you have done this step correctly.
- Click in **cell D6** and enter the formula **=C6–B6**, then copy this formula to the remaining cells in this column. Cell D11 should display $165.26.
- Save the workbook.

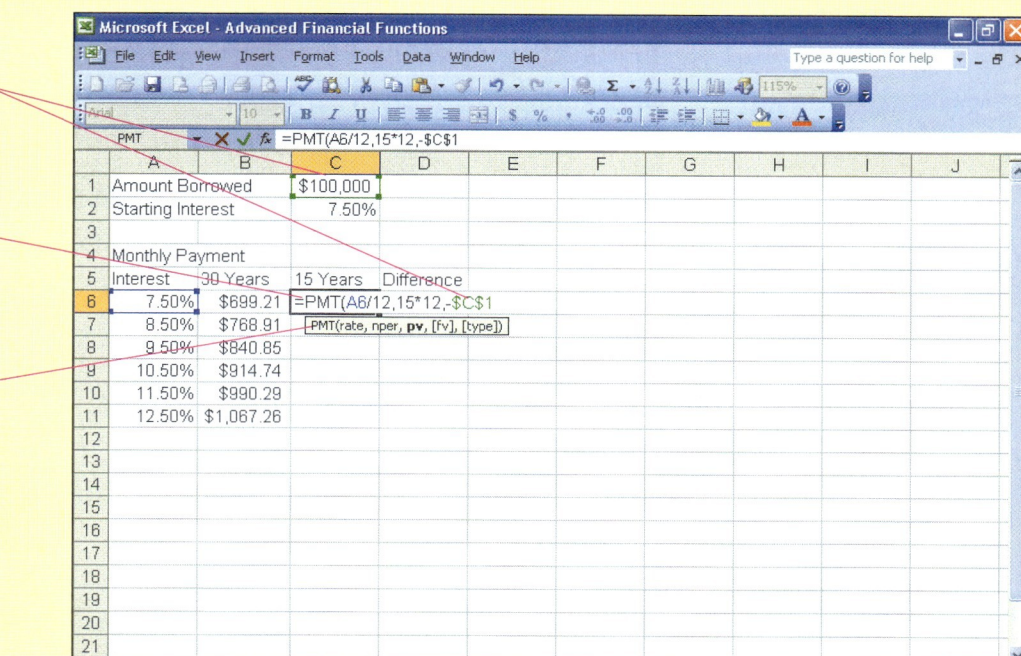

(d) Determine the 15-year Payments (step 4)

FIGURE 4.8 Hands-on Exercise 2 (*continued*)

KEYBOARD SHORTCUTS—CUT, COPY, AND PASTE

Ctrl+X (the X is supposed to remind you of a pair of scissors), Ctrl+C, and Ctrl+V are keyboard shortcuts to cut, copy, and paste, respectively, and apply to Excel as well as to Windows applications in general. The keystrokes are easier to remember when you realize that the operative letters X, C, and V are next to each other at the bottom left side of the keyboard. There is no need to memorize the keyboard shortcuts, but as you gain proficiency, they will become second nature.

Step 5: Format the Worksheet

- Click in cell **A13** and enter the label **Financial Consultant**. Enter **your name** in **cell A14**. Add formatting as necessary using Figure 4.8e as a guide.

- Click **cell A4**. Drag the mouse over cells **A4** through **D4**. Click the **Merge and Center button** on the Formatting toolbar to center the entry.

- Center the column headings in row 5. Add boldface and/or italics to the text and/or numbers as you see fit. Widen columns as necessary.

- Pull down the **File menu** and click the **Page Setup command** to display the Page Setup dialog box.

- Click the **Margins tab**. Check the box to center the worksheet horizontally. Click the **Sheet tab**. Check the boxes to include row and column headings and gridlines. Click **OK** to exit the Page Setup dialog box.

- Save the workbook. Pull down the **File menu**, click the **Print command** to display the Print dialog box, then click **OK** to print the worksheet. Press **Ctrl+~** to display the cell formulas. Widen the columns as necessary, then print.

- Press **Ctrl+~** to return to displayed values.

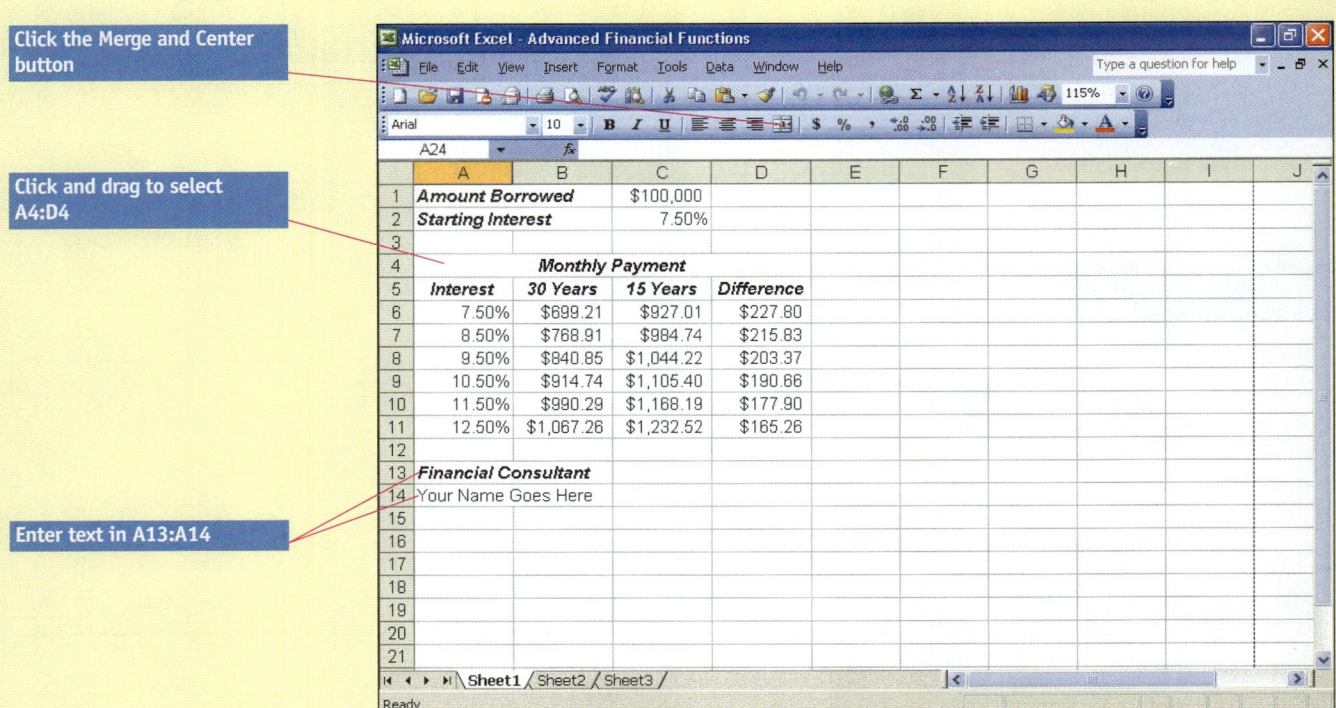

(e) Format the Worksheet (step 5)

FIGURE 4.8 Hands-on Exercise 2 (*continued*)

THE PPMT AND IPMT FUNCTIONS

The PMT function determines the periodic payment for a loan, which in turn is composed of two components, interest and principal. The amount of the payment that goes toward interest decreases each period, and conversely, the amount for the principle increases. These values can be computed through the IPMT and PPMT functions, respectively, which are used to compute the amortization (payoff) schedule for the loan.

Step 6: **Merge and Center Text**

- Click the **Sheet2 tab** to change to this worksheet. Click in **cell A1** and enter the title of the worksheet, **The Value of an IRA (Individual Retirement Account)**.

- Enter the indicated labels in **cells A3** and **C4** as shown in Figure 4.8f. Click in **cell A6** and type the label **Years Contributing**.

- Click and drag to select **cells A6** through **A21**, then click the **Merge and Center button** on the Standard toolbar to merge the cells. Right click within the merged cell, then click the **Format Cells command** to display the Format cells dialog box. Click the **Alignment tab**.

- Enter **90** in the Degrees list box to change to 90 degrees. Click the **down arrow** on the Vertical list box and choose **Center**. Click **OK**. Click the **Undo button** if the results are different from what you intended.

- Click and drag to select **cells A1** through **J1**, then click the **Merge and Center button** to center the title. Merge and center cells **C4** through **J4** in similar fashion.

- Click and drag the border between columns A and B to make the column narrower, as appropriate. Save the workbook.

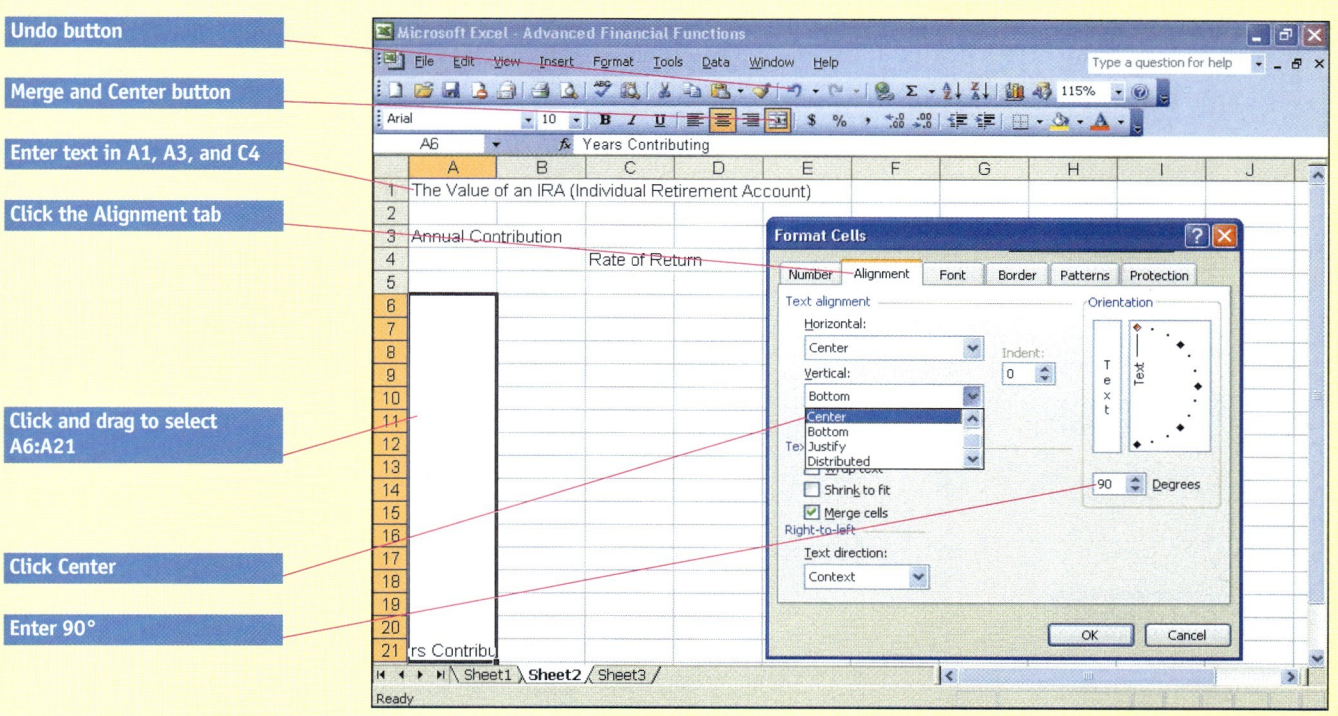

(f) Merge and Center Text (step 6)

FIGURE 4.8 Hands-on Exercise 2 (*continued*)

THE MERGE AND CENTER COMMAND

The Merge and Center command combines multiple cells into a single cell and is best used in conjunction with the headings in a worksheet. Cells can be merged horizontally or vertically, then the text in the merged cells can be aligned in a variety of styles. Text can also be rotated to provide interest in the worksheet. If necessary, you can restore the individual cells and remove the associated formatting using the Edit Clear command. Click in the merged cell, pull down the Edit menu, and click the Clear command. Click Formats to restore the individual cells to the default format.

Step 7: **Enter the Row and Column Headings**

- Check that the labels in your worksheet match those in Figure 4.8g. Click in **cell D3** and enter **$3,000**. Click in **cell C5** and type **5.00%**. Be sure to include the decimal point, zeros, and percent sign.

- Click in **cell D5** and enter the formula **=C5+.01**, then click and drag the **fill handle** to copy this formula to cells **E5** through **J5**.

- Click in **cell B6** and type the number **25**. Click in **cell B7** and enter the formula **=B6+1**, then click and drag the **fill handle** to copy this formula to **cells B8** through **B21**.

- Double click the **Sheet2 tab** to select the worksheet name, then type **Mixed References** as the name of this worksheet. Double click the **Sheet1 tab** to select the worksheet name, then type **Mortgage Analysis** as the name of this worksheet.

- Click the newly named **Mixed References worksheet tab** to return to this worksheet and continue working.

- Save the workbook.

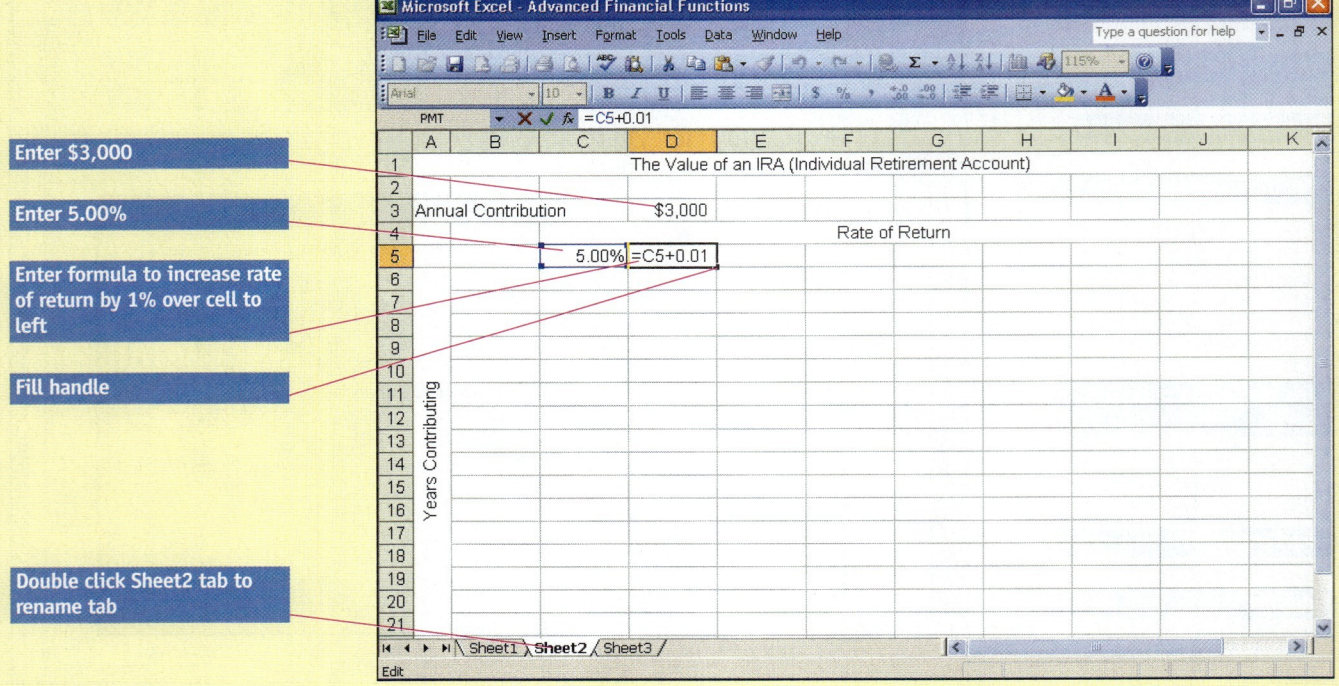

(g) Enter the Row and Column Headings (step 7)

FIGURE 4.8 Hands-on Exercise 2 (*continued*)

AUTOMATIC FORMATTING

Excel converts any number entered with a beginning dollar sign to currency format, and any number entered with an ending percent sign to percentage format. The automatic formatting enables you to save a step by typing $100,000 or 7.5% directly into a cell, rather than entering 100000 or .075 and having to format the number. The formatting is applied to the cell and affects any subsequent numbers in that cell. (Use the Clear command in the Edit menu to remove the formatting.)

Step 8: **Create the Mixed References**

- Click in **cell C6**. Pull down the **Insert menu** and click **Function** (or click the **Insert Function button** on the formula bar) to display the Insert Function dialog box.
- Click the **drop-down arrow**, then click **Financial** in the Select a Category list box. Click **FV** in the Select a Function list box. Click **OK**.
- Click and drag the Function Arguments dialog box so that you can see the underlying cells as shown in Figure 4.8h.
- Click the text box for rate, click in **cell C5**, then press the **F4 key** until you see **C$5** within the dialog box.
- Press **Tab** to move to (or click in) the **Nper text box**, click in **cell B6**, then press the **F4 key** until you see $B6 within the dialog box.
- Press **Tab** to move to (or click in) the **Pmt text box**, type a **minus sign**, click in **cell D3**, then press the **F4 key** until you see **−$D$3** in the dialog box.
- Check that the entries on your screen match those in Figure 4.8h, then click **OK**. Cell C6 should display the value $143,181.
- Save the workbook.

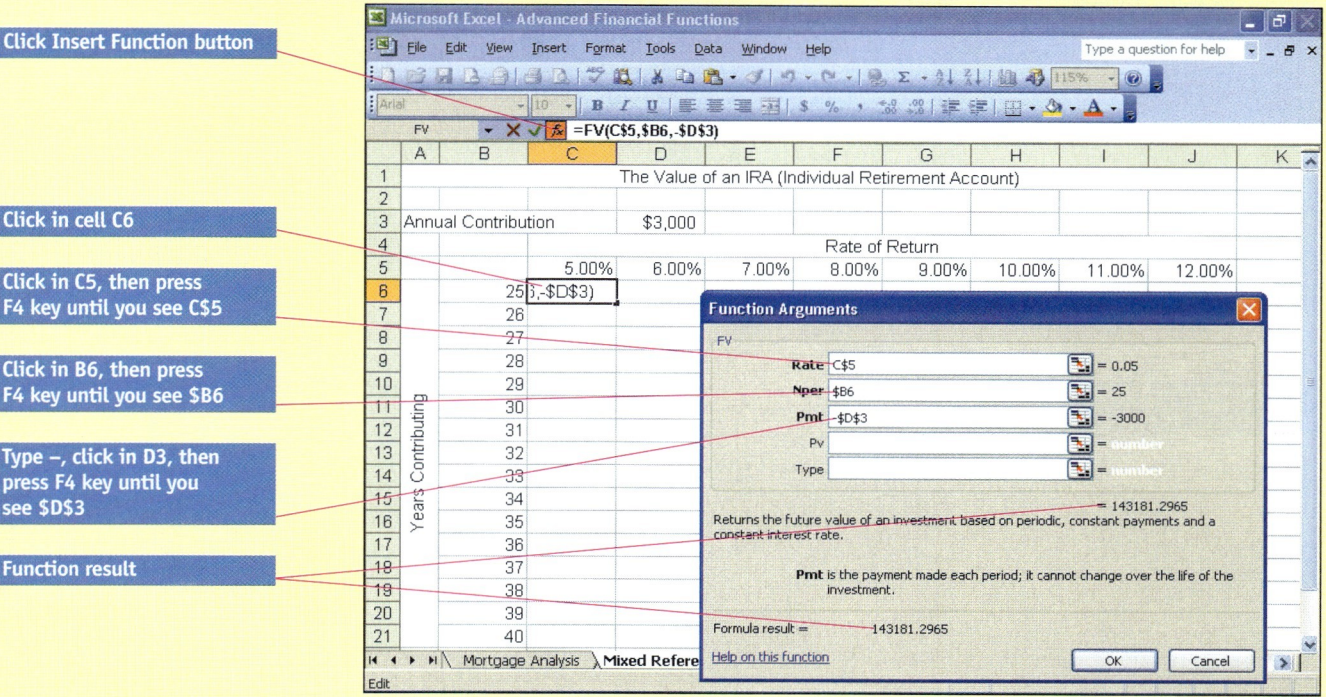

(h) Create the Mixed References (step 8)

FIGURE 4.8 Hands-on Exercise 2 (*continued*)

MIXED REFERENCES ARE NOT DIFFICULT

Mixed references are not difficult, provided you think clearly about what is required. In our example the interest rate should always come from row 5, but the column should change. Hence you enter C$5 for this parameter within the FV function. In similar fashion, the term of the investment should always come from column B, but the row should change. Thus you enter $B6 for this parameter. It's easy and it's powerful.

MICROSOFT OFFICE EXCEL 2003 REVISED 189

Step 9: **Copy the Formula**

- If necessary, click in **cell C6**, the cell that contains the formula you just created. Click and drag the **fill handle** in **cell C6** to **cells D6** through **J6**.

- Change the formatting to **zero decimal places**, then change column widths as necessary. Cell J6 should display the value $400,002.

- If necessary, select **cells C6** through **J6** as shown in Figure 4.8i. Click and drag the fill handle in **cell J6** to **cell J21** to copy the entire row to the remaining rows in the worksheet.

- Release the mouse. Cell J21 should display the value $2,301,274, corresponding to the future value of a $3,000 investment for 40 years at 12 percent. Change column widths as necessary.

- Click in **cell C6**, then press the **right arrow** to move from one cell to the next in this row to see how the cell formulas change to reflect the mixed references. Return to cell C6, then press the **down arrow** to view the cell formulas for the other cells in this column.

- Save the workbook.

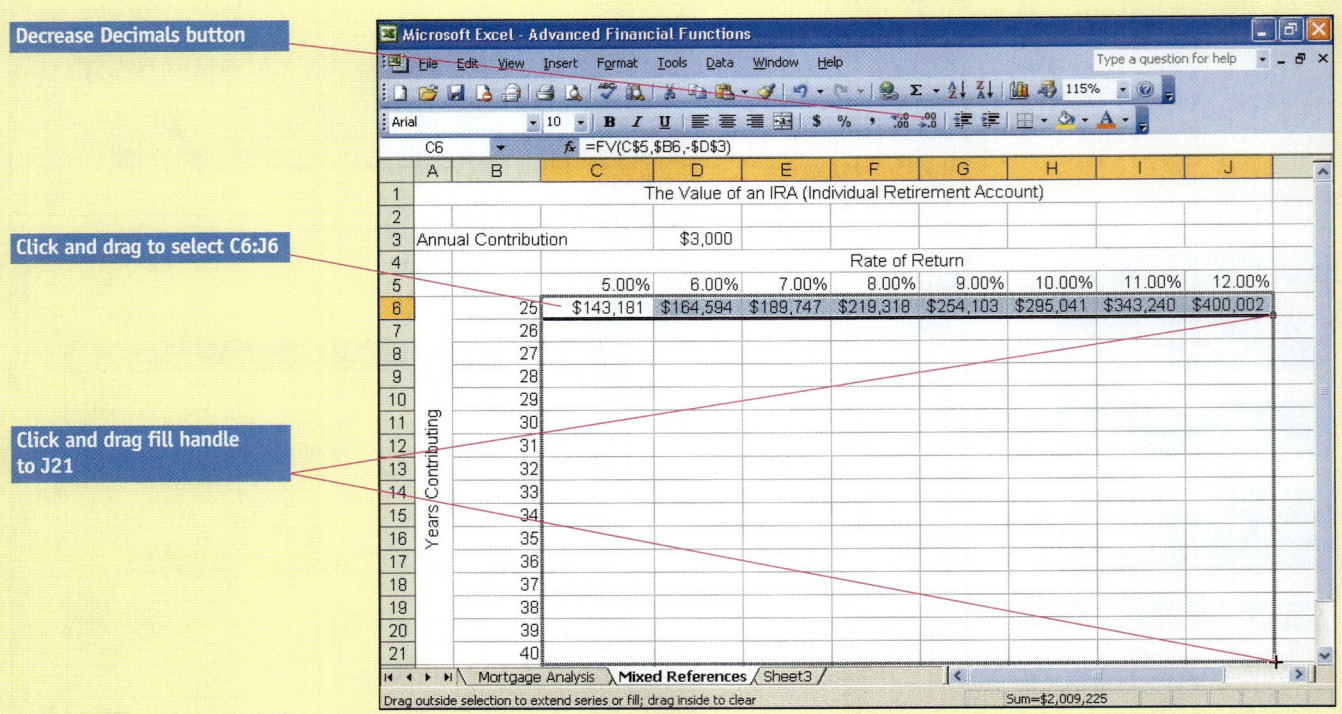

(i) Copy the Formula (step 9)

FIGURE 4.8   Hands-on Exercise 2 (*continued*)

> ### THE ARRANGE WINDOWS COMMAND
>
> It can be advantageous to view multiple worksheets within a workbook at the same time, with each worksheet in its own window. Pull down the Window menu and click the New Window command to open another window. Pull down the Window menu a second time, click the Arrange command, then click the option button that indicates how you want to display the windows; e.g., horizontal to display the windows one on top of another. Each window provides a different view of the workbook. Click in either window, then click the worksheet tab you want to display.

Step 10: **The Finishing Touches**

- Check that the numbers in your worksheet match those in Figure 4.8j. Make corrections as necessary.

- Use the **Page Setup command** to include gridlines and row and column headings. Use landscape formatting if necessary.

- Print the worksheet two ways, once with the displayed values and once with the cell contents.

- Add a cover sheet, then submit all five pages (the cover sheet, the displayed values and cell formulas for the mortgage analysis from step 5, and the displayed values and cell formulas from this step) to your instructor as proof that you completed this exercise.

- Exit Excel if you do not want to continue with the next exercise at this time.

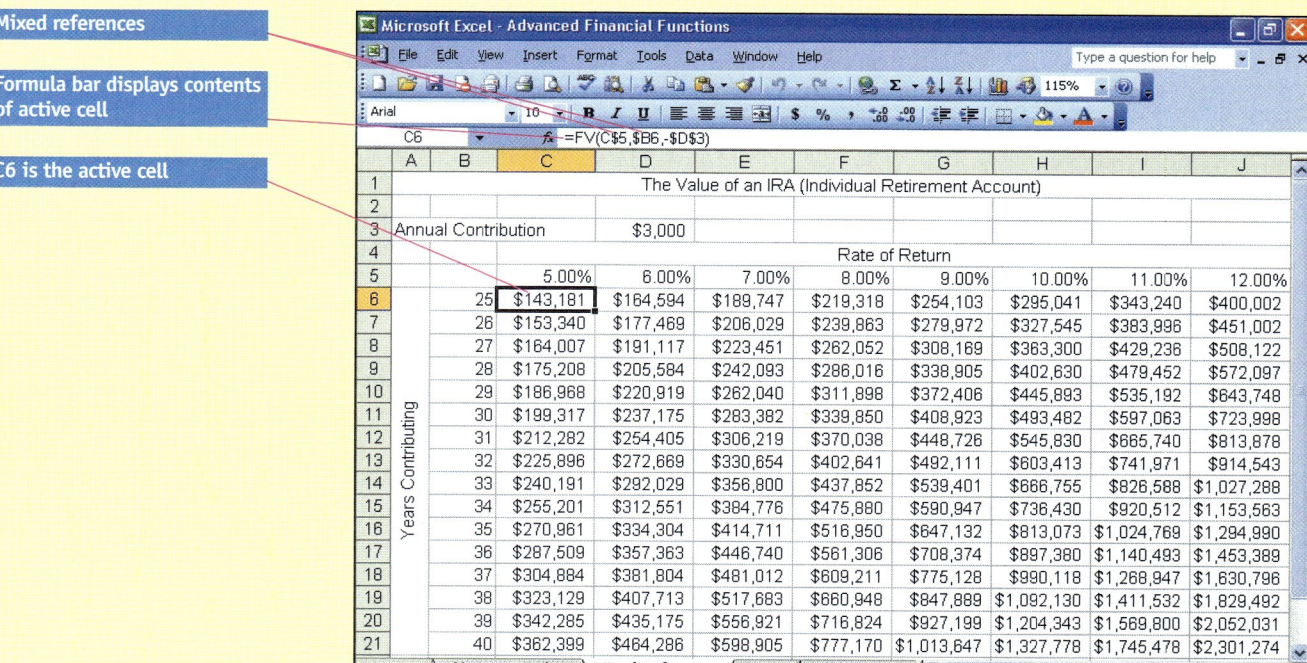

(j) The Finishing Touches (step 10)

FIGURE 4.8 Hands-on Exercise 2 (*continued*)

START SAVING EARLY

The longer you invest, the more time that compound interest has to work its magic. Investing $3,000 for 40 years at 7%, for example, yields a future value of $598,905. Delay for five years—that is, invest for 35 years rather than 40—and the amount goes down to $414,711. Put another way—Start your IRA at age 25, and 40 years later you will have accumulated more than half a million dollars. Wait until age 30, and you wind up with significantly less. The out-of-pocket difference is only $15,000 ($3,000 a year for five years), but the end result at retirement is more than $180,000. Too many people try to time the stock market, which is impossible. It is the time *in* the market that matters.

THE GRADE BOOK REVISITED

Financial functions are only one of several categories of functions that are included in Excel. Our next example presents an expanded version of the professor's grade book. It introduces several new functions and shows how those functions can aid in the professor's determination of a student's grade. The expanded grade book is shown in Figure 4.9. Consider:

Statistical functions: The AVERAGE, MAX, and MIN functions are used to compute the statistics on each test for the class as a whole. The range on each test is computed by subtracting the minimum value from the maximum value.

IF function: The IF function conditionally adds a homework bonus of three points to the semester average, prior to determining the letter grade. The bonus is awarded to those students whose homework is "OK." Students whose homework is not "OK" do not receive the bonus.

VLOOKUP function: The expanded grade book converts a student's semester average to a letter grade, in accordance with the table shown in the lower-right portion of the worksheet. A student with an average of 60 to 69 will receive a D, 70 to 79 a C, 80 to 89 a B, and 90 or higher an A. Any student with an average less than 60 receives an F.

The Sort command: The rows within a spreadsheet can be displayed in any sequence by clicking on the appropriate column within the list of students, then clicking the Ascending or Descending sort button on the Standard toolbar. The students in Figure 4.9 are listed alphabetically, but could just as easily have been listed by Social Security number.

	A	B	C	D	E	F	G	H	I	J
1	Professor's Grade Book - Final Semester Averages									
2										
3	Name	Soc Sec Num	Test 1	Test 2	Test 3	Test 4	Test Average	Homework	Semester Average	Grade
4	Adams, John	111-22-3333	80	71	70	84	77.8	Poor	77.8	C
5	Barber, Maryann	444-55-6666	96	98	97	90	94.2	OK	97.2	A
6	Boone, Dan	777-88-9999	78	81	70	78	77.0	OK	80.0	B
7	Borow, Jeff	123-45-6789	65	65	65	60	63.0	OK	66.0	D
8	Brown, James	999-99-9999	92	95	79	80	85.2	OK	88.2	B
9	Carson, Kit	888-88-8888	90	90	90	70	82.0	OK	85.0	B
10	Coulter, Sara	100-00-0000	60	50	40	79	61.6	OK	64.6	D
11	Fegin, Richard	222-22-2222	75	70	65	95	80.0	OK	83.0	B
12	Ford, Judd	200-00-0000	90	90	80	90	88.0	Poor	88.0	B
13	Glassman, Kris	444-44-4444	82	78	62	77	75.2	OK	78.2	C
14	Goodman, Neil	555-55-5555	92	88	65	78	80.2	OK	83.2	B
15	Milgrom, Marion	666-66-6666	94	92	86	84	88.0	OK	91.0	A
16	Moldof, Adam	300-00-0000	92	78	65	82	79.8	Poor	79.8	C
17	Smith, Adam	777-77-7777	60	50	65	80	67.0	Poor	67.0	D
18										
19	Average		81.9	78.3	71.4	80.5	HW Bonus	3	Grading Criteria	
20	Highest Grade		96.0	98.0	97.0	95.0			0	F
21	Lowest Grade		60.0	50.0	40.0	60.0			60	D
22	Range		36.0	48.0	57.0	35.0			70	C
23									80	B
24	Exam Weights		20%	20%	20%	40%			90	A

Statistical functions determine average, highest, and lowest grades on tests

IF function determines Semester Average

VLOOKUP Function determines Grade

FIGURE 4.9 The Expanded Grade Book

Statistical Functions

The *MAX*, *MIN*, and *AVERAGE functions* return the highest, lowest, and average values, respectively, from an argument list. The list may include individual cell references, ranges, numeric values, functions, or mathematical expressions (formulas). The *statistical functions* are illustrated in the worksheet of Figure 4.10.

The first example, =AVERAGE(A1:A3), computes the average for cells A1 through A3 by adding the values in the indicated range (70, 80, and 90), then dividing the result by three, to obtain an average of 80. Additional arguments in the form of values and/or cell addresses can be specified within the parentheses; for example, the function =AVERAGE(A1:A3,200), computes the average of cells A1, A2, and A3, and the number 200.

Cells that are empty or cells that contain text values are *not* included in the computation. Thus since cell A4 is empty, the function =AVERAGE(A1:A4) will also return an average value of 80 (240/3). In similar fashion, the function =AVERAGE(A1:A3,A5) includes only three values in its computation (cells A1, A2, and A3) because the text entry in cell A5 is excluded. The results of the MIN and MAX functions are obtained in a comparable way, as indicated in Figure 4.10. Empty cells and text entries are not included in the computation.

The COUNT and COUNTA functions each tally the number of entries in the argument list and are subtly different. The *COUNT function* returns the number of cells containing a numeric entry, including formulas that evaluate to numeric results. The *COUNTA function* includes cells with text as well as numeric values. The functions =COUNT(A1:A3) and =COUNTA(A1:A3) both return a value of 3 as do the two functions =COUNT(A1:A4) and =COUNTA(A1:A4). (Cell A4 is empty and is excluded from the latter computations.) The function =COUNT(A1:A3,A5) also returns a value of 3 because it does not include the text entry in cell A5. However, the function =COUNTA(A1:A3,A5) returns a value of 4 because it includes the text entry in cell A5.

Function	Value
=AVERAGE(A1:A3)	80
=AVERAGE(A1:A3,200)	110
=AVERAGE(A1:A4)	80
=AVERAGE(A1:A3,A5)	80
=MAX(A1:A3)	90
=MAX(A1:A3,200)	200
=MAX(A1:A4)	90
=MAX(A1:A3,A5)	90
=MIN(A1:A3)	70
=MIN(A1:A3,200)	70
=MIN(A1:A4)	70
=MIN(A1:A3,A5)	70
=COUNT(A1:A3)	3
=COUNT(A1:A3,200)	4
=COUNT(A1:A4)	3
=COUNT(A1:A3,A5)	3
=COUNTA(A1:A3)	3
=COUNTA(A1:A3,200)	4
=COUNTA(A1:A4)	3
=COUNTA(A1:A3,A5)	4

(a) Illustrative Functions

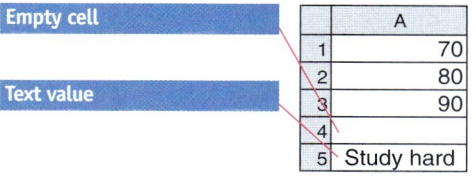

(b) The Spreadsheet

FIGURE 4.10 Statistical Functions with a Text Entry

Arithmetic Expressions versus Functions

Many worksheet calculations, such as an average or a sum, can be performed in two ways. You can enter a formula such as =(A1+A2+A3)/3, or you can use the equivalent function =AVERAGE(A1:A3). *The use of functions is generally preferable* as shown in Figure 4.11.

The two worksheets in Figure 4.11a may appear equivalent, but the **SUM function** is superior to the arithmetic expression. This is true despite the fact that the entries in cell A5 of both worksheets return a value of 100.

Consider what happens if a new row is inserted between existing rows 2 and 3, with the entry in the new cell equal to 25 as shown in Figure 4.11b. The SUM function adjusts automatically to include the new value (returning a sum of 125) because the SUM function was defined originally for the cell range *A1 through A4*. The new row is inserted within these cells, moving the entry in cell A4 to cell A5, and changing the range to include cell A5.

No such accommodation is made in the arithmetic expression, which was defined to include four *specific* cells rather than a range of cells. The addition of the new row modifies the cell references (since the values in cells A3 and A4 have been moved to cells A4 and A5), and does not include the new row in the adjusted expression.

Similar reasoning holds for deleting a row. Figure 4.11c deletes row 2 from the *original* worksheets, which moves the entry in cell A4 to cell A3. The SUM function adjusts automatically to =SUM(A1:A3) and returns the value 80. The formula, however, returns an error (to indicate an illegal cell reference) because it is still attempting to add the entries in four cells, one of which no longer exists. In summary, a function expands and contracts to adjust for insertions or deletions, and should be used wherever possible.

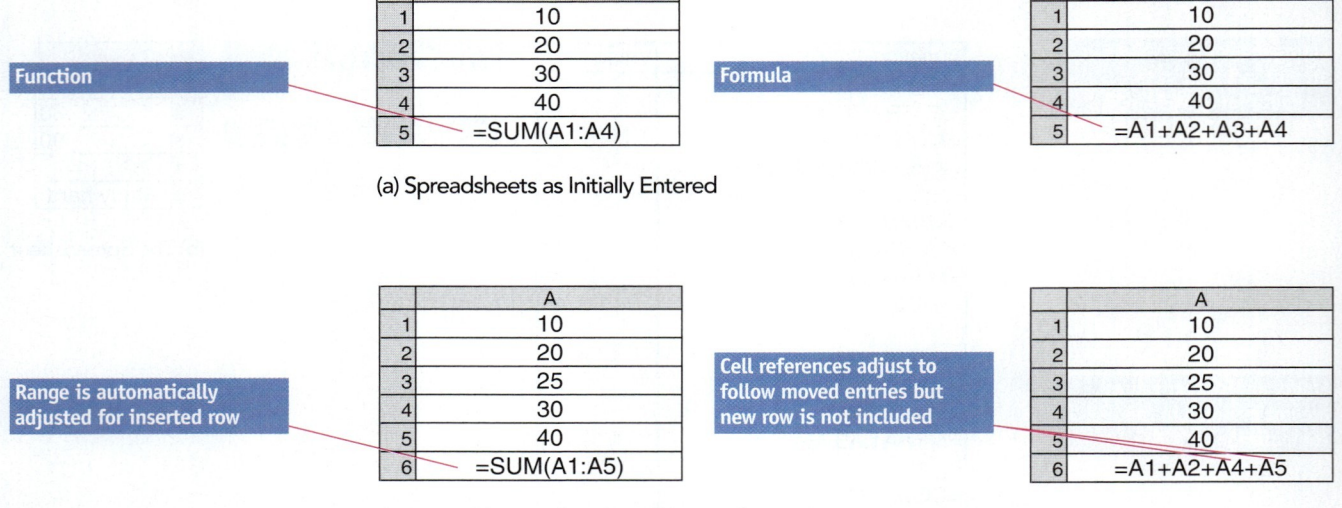

FIGURE 4.11 Arithmetic Expressions versus Functions

IF Function

The **IF function** enables decision making to be implemented within a worksheet. It has three arguments: a condition that is either true or false, the value if the condition is true, and the value if the condition is false. Consider:

=IF(condition,value-if-true,value-if-false)

- Condition is either true or false
- Value returned for a true condition
- Value returned for a false condition

The IF function returns either the second or third argument, depending on the result of the condition; that is, if the condition is true, the function returns the second argument. If the condition is false, the function returns the third argument.

The condition includes one of the six **relational operators** in Figure 4.12a. The IF function is illustrated in the worksheet in Figure 4.12b, which is used to create the examples in Figure 4.12c. The arguments may be numeric (1000 or 2000), a cell reference to display the contents of the specific cell (B1 or B2), a formula (=B1+10 or =B1−10), a function (MAX(B1:B2) or MIN(B1:B2)), or a text entry enclosed in quotation marks ("Go" or "Hold").

Operator	Description
=	Equal to
<>	Not equal to
<	Less than
>	Greater than
<=	Less than or equal to
>=	Greater than or equal to

	A	B	C
1	10	15	April
2	10	30	May

(a) Relational Operators

(b) The Spreadsheet

IF Function	Evaluation	Result
=IF(A1=A2,1000,2000)	10 is equal to 10: TRUE	1000
=IF(A1<>A2,1000,2000)	10 is not equal to 10: FALSE	2000
=IF(A1<>A2,B1,B2)	10 is not equal to 10:FALSE	30
=IF(A1<B2,MAX(B1:B2),MIN(B1:B2))	10 is less than 30: TRUE	30
=IF(A1<A2,B1+10,B1-10)	10 is less than 10:FALSE	5
=IF(A1=A2,C1,C2)	10 is equal to 10: TRUE	April
=IF(SUM(A1:A2)>20,"Go","Hold")	10+10 is greater than 20:FALSE	Hold

(c) Examples

FIGURE 4.12 The IF Function

The IF function is used in the grade book of Figure 4.9 to award a bonus for homework. Students whose homework is "OK" receive the bonus, whereas other students do not. The IF function to implement this logic for the first student is:

=IF(H4="OK",G4+$H$19,G4)

- Condition determines if homework is "OK"
- Average is incremented by the bonus in cell H19 if homework is "OK"
- Average is unchanged if homework *not* "OK"

The IF function compares the value in cell H4 (the homework grade) to the literal "OK." If the condition is true (the homework is "OK"), the bonus in cell H19 is added to the student's test average in cell G4. If, however, the condition is false (the homework is not "OK"), the average is unchanged.

VLOOKUP Function

Consider, for a moment, how the professor assigns letter grades to students at the end of the semester. He or she computes a test average for each student and conditionally awards the bonus for homework. The professor then determines a letter grade according to a predetermined scale; for example, 90 or above is an A, 80 to 89 is a B, and so on.

The **VLOOKUP** (vertical lookup) *function* duplicates this process within a worksheet by assigning an entry to a cell based on a numeric value contained in another cell. The **HLOOKUP** (horizontal lookup) *function* is similar in concept except that the table is arranged horizontally. In other words, just as the professor knows where on the grading scale a student's numerical average will fall, the VLOOKUP function determines where within a specified table (the grading criteria) a numeric value (a student's average) is found, and retrieves the corresponding entry (the letter grade).

The VLOOKUP function requires three arguments: the value to look up, the range of cells containing the table in which the value is to be looked up, and the column number within the table that contains the result. These concepts are illustrated in Figure 4.13, which was taken from the expanded grade book in Figure 4.9. The table in Figure 4.13 extends over two columns (I and J), and five rows (20 through 24); that is, the table is located in the range I20:J24. The **breakpoints** or matching values (the lowest numeric value for each grade) are contained in column **I** (the first column in the table) and are in ascending order. The corresponding letter grades are found in column **J**.

The VLOOKUP function in cell J4 determines the letter grade (for John Adams) based on the computed average in cell I4. Consider:

=VLOOKUP(I4,$I$20:$J$24,2)

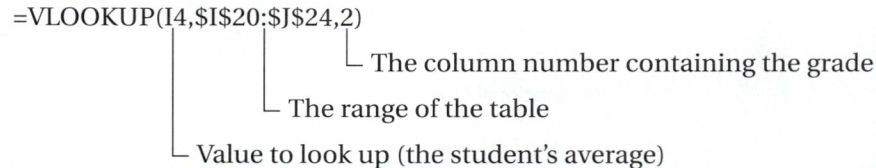

The first argument is the value to look up, which in this example is Adams's computed average, found in cell I4. A relative reference is used so that the address will adjust when the formula is copied to the other rows in the worksheet.

	A	. . .	G	H	I	J
1		Professor's Grade Book - Final Semester Averages				
2						
3	Name		Test Average	Homework	Semester Average	Grade
4	Adams, John		77.8	Poor		
.	.	.	.	.	.	.
.	.	.	.	.	.	.
.	.	.	.	.	.	.
19	Average		HW Bonus	3	Grading Criteria	
20	Highest Grade				0	F
21	Lowest Grade				60	D
22	Range				70	C
23					80	B
24	Exam Weights				90	A

FIGURE 4.13 The VLOOKUP Function

WORKING WITH LARGE SPREADSHEETS

A large worksheet, such as the extended grade book, can seldom be seen on the monitor in its entirety. It's necessary, therefore, to learn how to view the distant parts of a worksheet, to keep certain parts of the worksheet in constant view, and/or to hide selected rows and columns. These concepts are illustrated in Figure 4.14. Figure 4.14a displays the initial worksheet, with cell A1 selected as the active cell, so that you see the upper-left portion of the worksheet, rows 1 through 20 inclusive, and columns A through I inclusive. You cannot see the semester grades in column J, nor can you see the class averages and other statistics that begin in row 21.

Clicking the right arrow on the horizontal scroll bar (or pressing the right arrow key when the active cell is already in the rightmost column of the screen) causes the entire screen to move one column to the right. In similar fashion, clicking the down arrow in the vertical scroll bar (or pressing the down arrow key when the active cell is in the bottom row of the screen) causes the entire screen to move down one row. This is known as *scrolling* and it comes about automatically as the active cell is changed as you work with the worksheet.

Freezing Panes

Scrolling brings the distant portions of a worksheet into view, but it also moves the headings for existing rows and/or columns off the screen. You can, however, retain the headings by freezing panes as shown in Figure 4.14b. The letter grades and the grading criteria are visible as in the previous figure, but so too are the names at the left of the worksheet and the column headings at the top of the worksheet.

Look closely at Figure 4.14b and you will see column B (containing the Social Security numbers) is missing, as are rows 4 through 7 (the first four students). You will also notice a horizontal line under row 3 and a vertical line after column A, to indicate that these rows and columns have been frozen. This is accomplished through the **Freeze Panes command** that always displays the desired row or column headings (column A and rows 1, 2, and 3 in this example) regardless of the scrolling in effect. The rows and/or columns that are frozen are the ones above and to the left of the active cell when the command is issued. The **Unfreeze Panes command** returns to normal scrolling.

Hiding Rows and Columns

Figure 4.14c illustrates the ability to hide rows and/or columns in a worksheet. We have hidden columns C through F (inclusive) that contain the results of the individual tests, and rows 19 through 24 that contain the summary statistics. The "missing" rows and columns remain in the workbook but are hidden from view. The cells are not visible in the monitor, nor do they appear when the worksheet is printed. To hide a row or column, click the row or column heading to select the entire row or column, then execute the Hide command from within the Format menu. **Unhiding cells** is trickier because you need to select the adjacent rows or columns prior to executing the Unhide command.

Printing a Large Worksheet

The **Page Break Preview command** (in the View menu) lets you see and/or modify the page breaks that will occur when the worksheet is printed as shown in Figure 4.14d. The dashed blue line between columns H and I indicates that the worksheet will print on two pages, with columns A to H on page 1 and columns I and J on page 2. The dialog box shows that you adjust (eliminate) the page break by dragging the dashed line to the right.

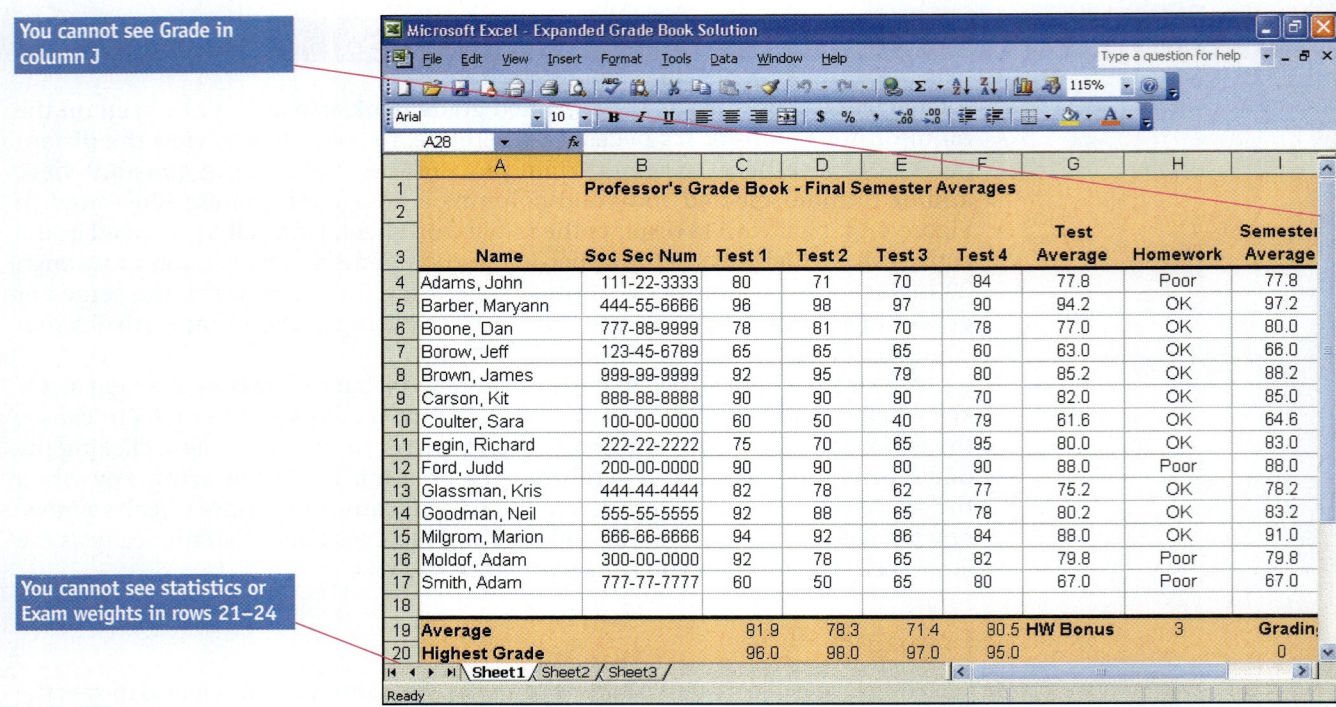

(a) The Grade Book

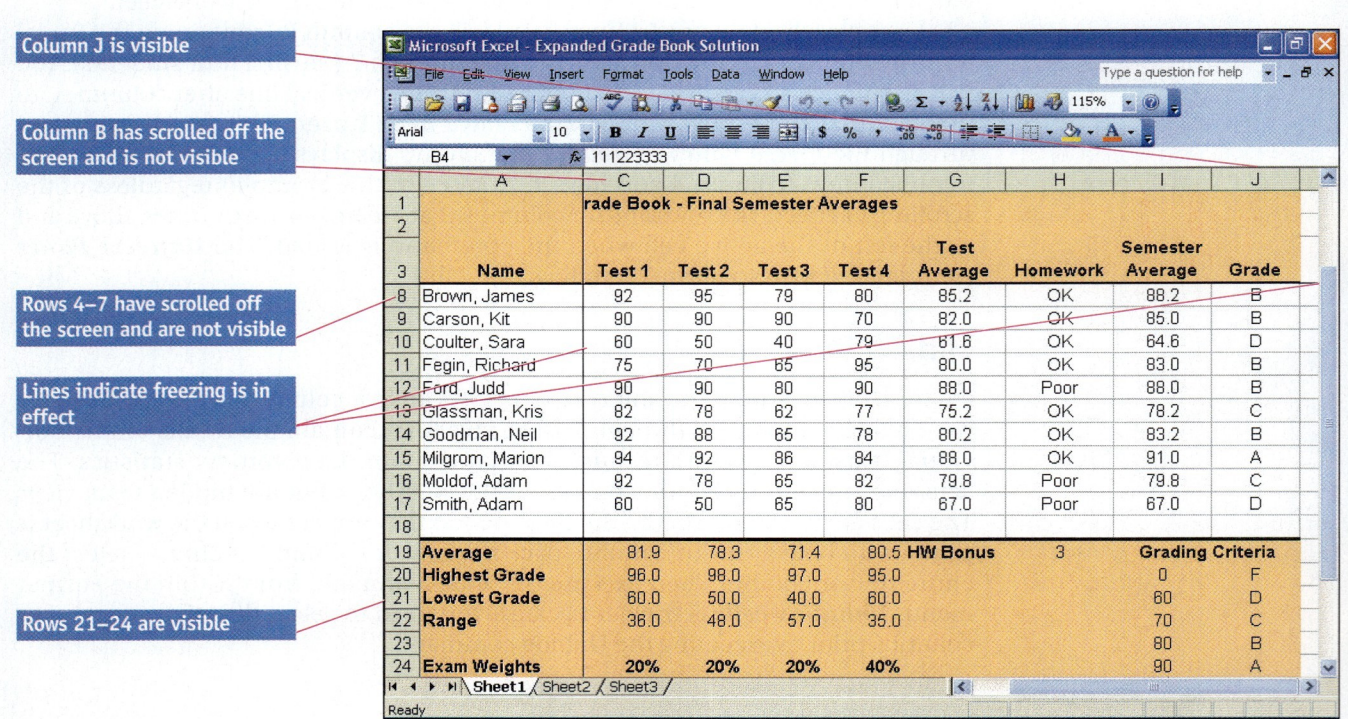

(b) Freezing Panes

FIGURE 4.14 Working with Large Spreadsheets

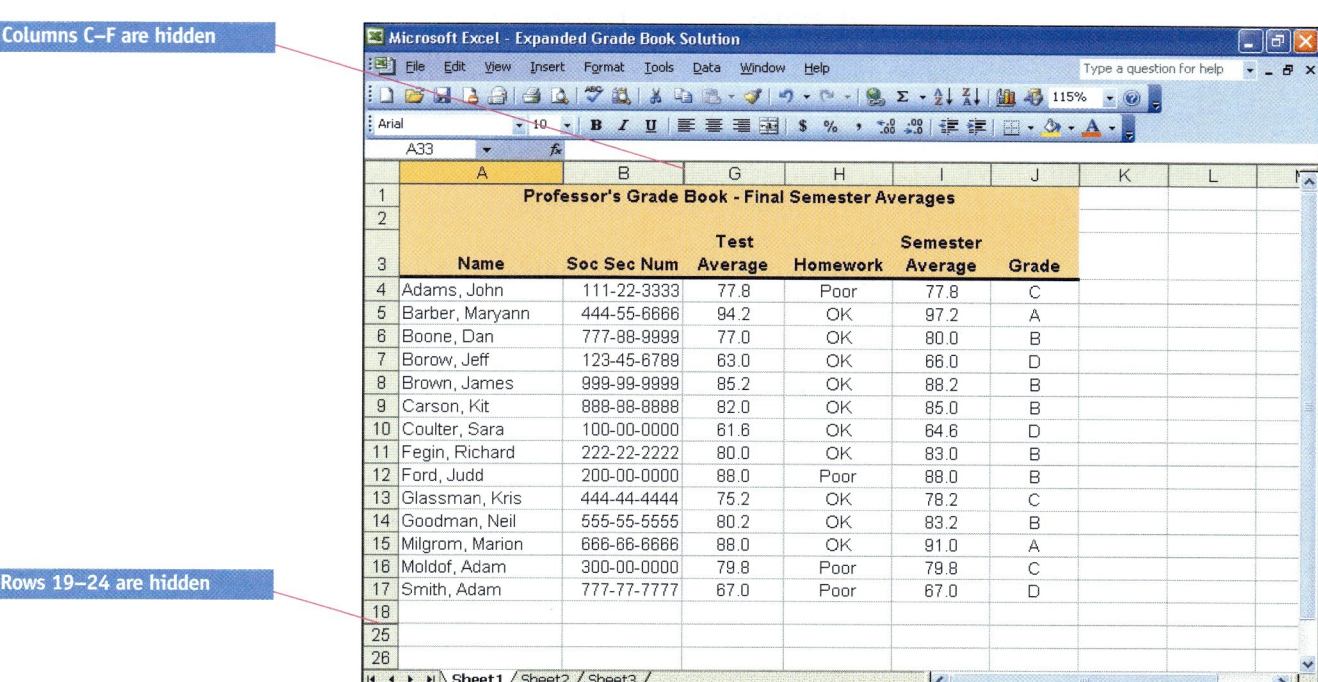

(c) Hiding Rows and Columns

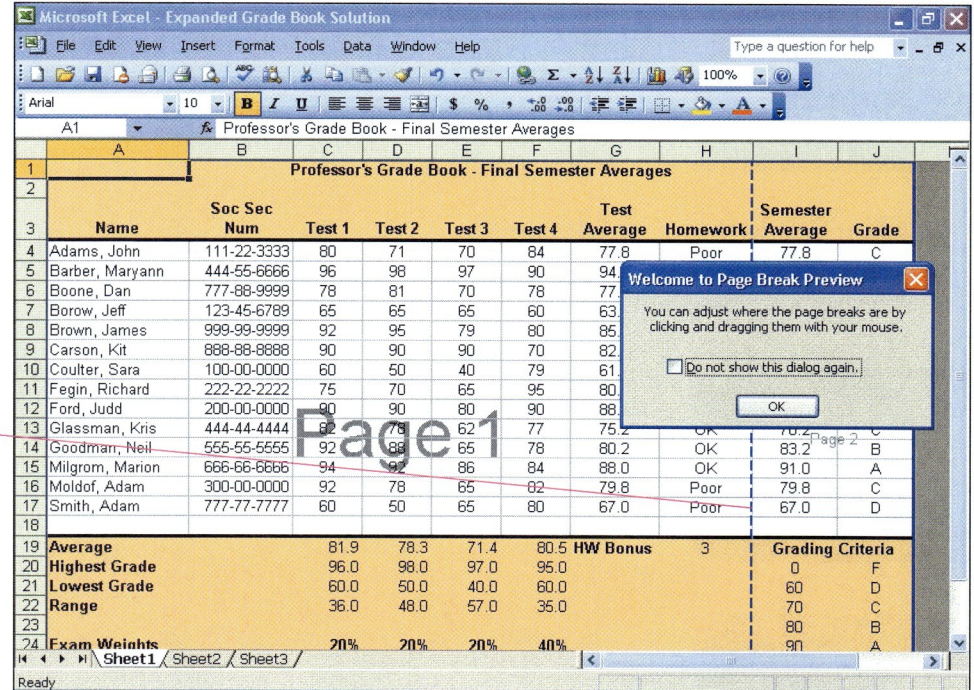

(d) Page Break Preview

FIGURE 4.14 Working with Large Spreadsheets (*continued*)

AutoFilter Command

The ***AutoFilter command*** lets you display a selected set of students (rows) within a worksheet as shown in Figure 4.15. The hidden rows are *not* deleted, but are simply not displayed. We begin with Figure 4.15a, which shows the list of all students (with selected columns hidden from view). Look closely at the column headings in row three and note the presence of drop-down arrows that appear in response to the AutoFilter command.

Clicking a drop-down arrow produces a list of the unique values for that column, enabling you to establish the criteria-selected records. To display the students with poor homework, for example, click the drop-down arrow for Homework, then click Poor from the resulting list. Figure 4.15b shows three students in rows 4, 12, and 17 that satisfy the filter. The remaining students are still in the worksheet but are not shown because of the selection criterion.

A filter condition can be imposed on multiple columns as shown in Figure 4.15c. As indicated, the worksheet in Figure 4.15b displays only the students with poor homework. Clicking the arrow next to Grade, then clicking "B", will filter the list further to display the students who received a "B" *and* who have poor homework. Only one student meets both conditions, as shown in Figure 4.15c. The drop-down arrows next to Homework and Grade are displayed in blue to indicate that a filter is in effect for these columns.

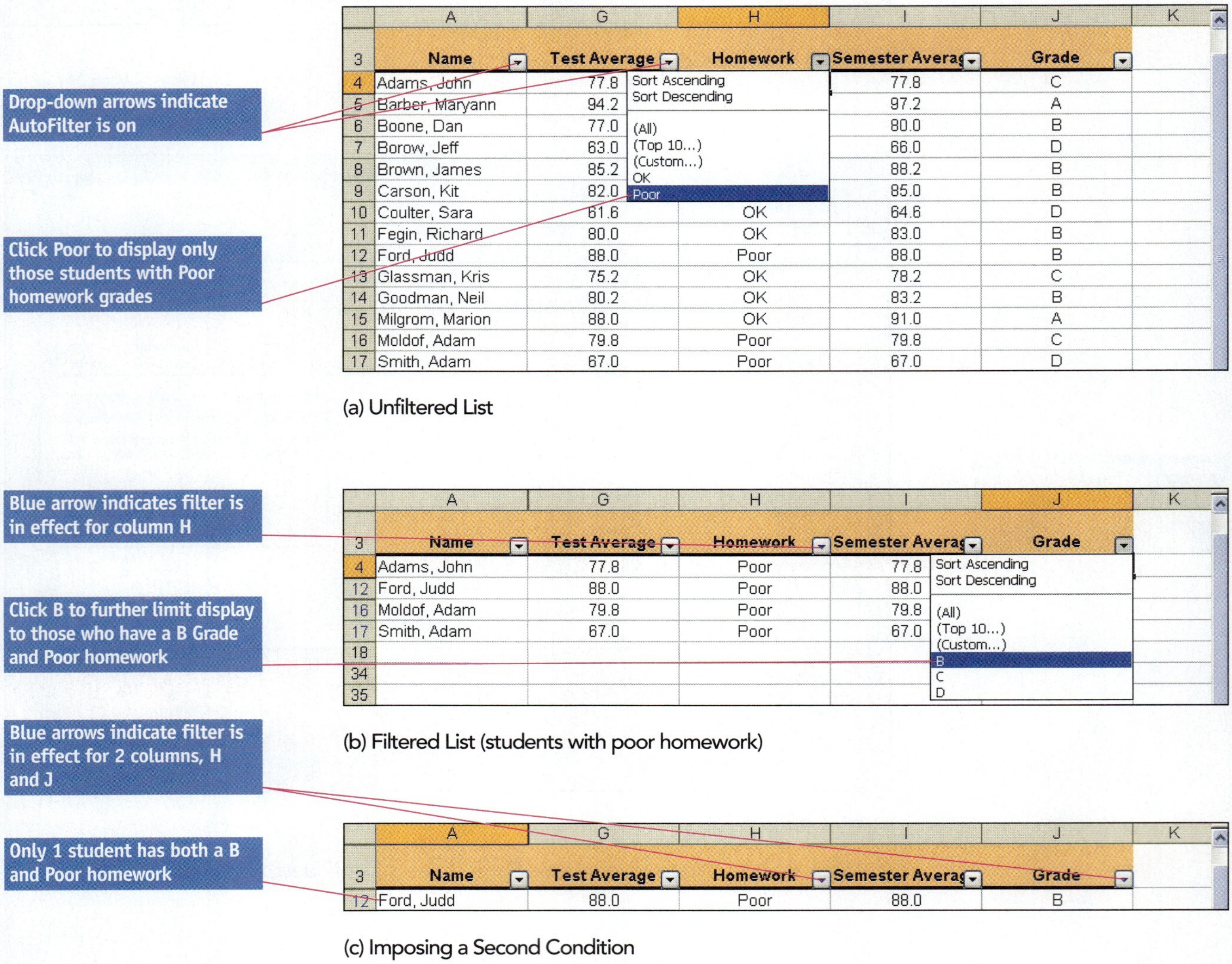

Drop-down arrows indicate AutoFilter is on

Click Poor to display only those students with Poor homework grades

(a) Unfiltered List

Blue arrow indicates filter is in effect for column H

Click B to further limit display to those who have a B Grade and Poor homework

(b) Filtered List (students with poor homework)

Blue arrows indicate filter is in effect for 2 columns, H and J

Only 1 student has both a B and Poor homework

(c) Imposing a Second Condition

FIGURE 4.15 The AutoFilter Command

hands-on exercise

3 The Expanded Grade Book

Objective To develop the expanded grade book; to use statistical (AVERAGE, MAX, and MIN) and logical (IF and VLOOKUP) functions; to demonstrate scrolling and the Freeze Panes command. Use Figure 4.16 as a guide.

Step 1: **The Fill Handle**

- Open the **Expanded Grade Book** in the **Exploring Excel folder**. Click in **cell C3**, the cell containing the label Test 1 as shown in Figure 4.16a.

- Click and drag the **fill handle** over **cells D3**, **E3**, and **F3** (a ScreenTip shows the projected result in cell F3), then release the mouse. Cells D3, E3, and F3 contain the labels Test 2, Test 3, and Test 4, respectively.

- Save the workbook as **Expanded Grade Book Solution** so that you can always return to the original workbook if necessary.

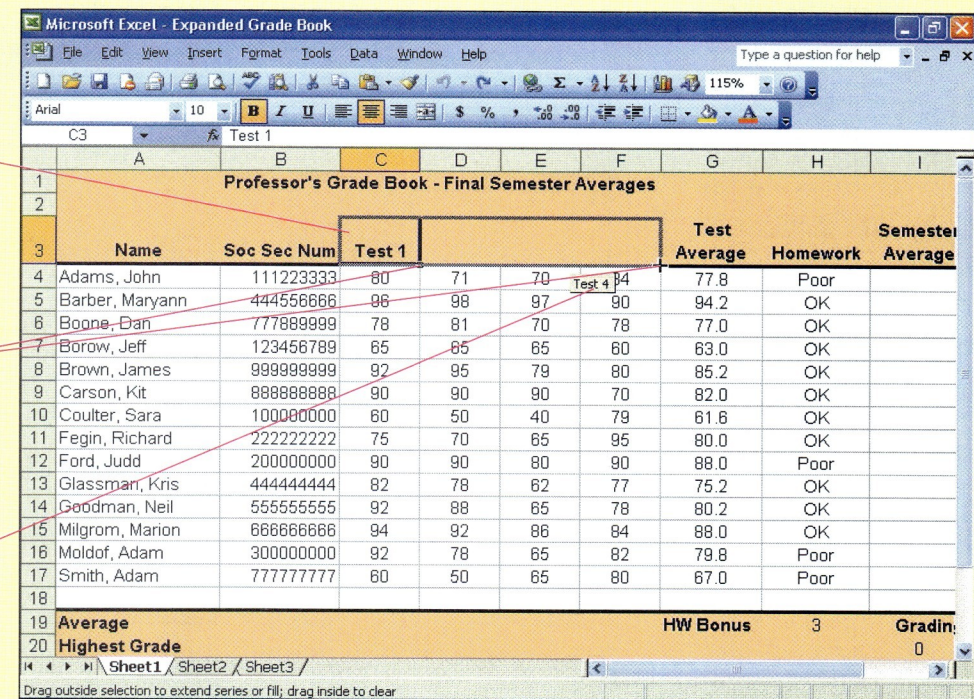

(a) The Fill Handle (step 1)

FIGURE 4.16 Hands-on Exercise 3

THE AUTOFILL CAPABILITY

The AutoFill capability is the fastest way to enter certain series into contiguous cells. Enter the starting value(s) in a series, then drag the fill handle to the adjacent cells. Excel completes the series based on the initial value. Type January (or Jan) or Monday (or Mon) then drag the fill handle in the direction you want to fill. Excel will enter the appropriate months or days of the week, respectively. You can also type text followed by a number, such as Product 1 or Quarter 1, then use the fill handle to extend the series.

Step 2: **Format the Social Security Numbers**

- Click and drag to select **cells B4** through **B17**, the cells containing the unformatted Social Security numbers.
- Point to the selected cells and click the **right mouse button** to display a shortcut (context-sensitive) menu.
- Click the **Format Cells command**, click the **Number tab**, then click **Special** in the Category list box as shown in Figure 4.16b.
- Click **Social Security Number** in the Type box, then click **OK** to accept the formatting and close the Format Cells dialog box. These *hypothetical* Social Security numbers are displayed with hyphens. Do *not* give your Social Security number to anyone without a good reason.
- Save the workbook.

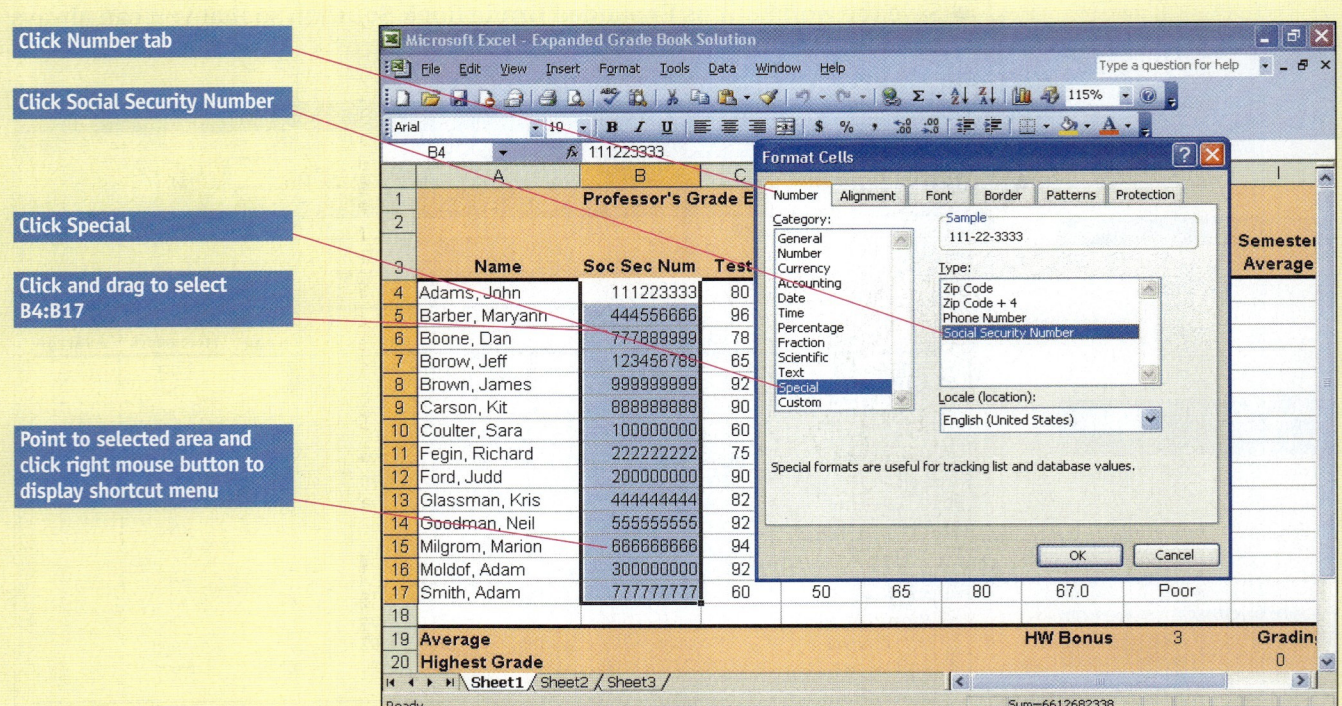

(b) Format the Social Security Numbers (step 2)

FIGURE 4.16 Hands-on Exercise 3 (*continued*)

THE LEFT AND RIGHT FUNCTIONS

A professor may want to post grades, but cannot do so by student name or Social Security number. One can, however, create an "ID number" consisting of the left- or rightmost digits in the Social Security number. Insert a new column into the worksheet, then go to the cell for the first student in this column (e.g., cell C4 if you insert a new column C). Enter the function =LEFT(B4,4) to display the first four digits from cell B4, corresponding to the first four (leftmost) digits in Adams's Social Security Number. You could also enter the function =RIGHT(B4,4) to display the last four (rightmost) digits. Hide the columns containing the names and Social Security numbers, then post the grades. See practice exercise 9 at the end of the chapter.

Step 3: **The Freeze Panes Command**

- Press **Ctrl+Home** to move to **cell A1**. Click the **right arrow** on the horizontal scroll bar until column A scrolls off the screen. Cell A1 is still the active cell, because scrolling with the mouse does not change the active cell.

- Press **Ctrl+Home**. Press the **right arrow key** until column A scrolls off the screen. The active cell changes as you scroll with the keyboard.

- Press **Ctrl+Home** again, then click in **cell B4**. Pull down the **Window menu**. Click **Freeze Panes** as shown in Figure 4.16c. You will see a line to the right of column A and below row 3.

- Click the **right arrow** on the horizontal scroll bar (or press the **right arrow key**) repeatedly until column J is visible. Note that column A is visible (frozen), but that one or more columns are not shown.

- Click the **down arrow** on the vertical scroll bar (or press the **down arrow key**) repeatedly until row 25 is visible. Note that rows 1 through 3 are visible (frozen), but that one or more rows are not shown.

- Press **Ctrl+Home** to go to **B4**.

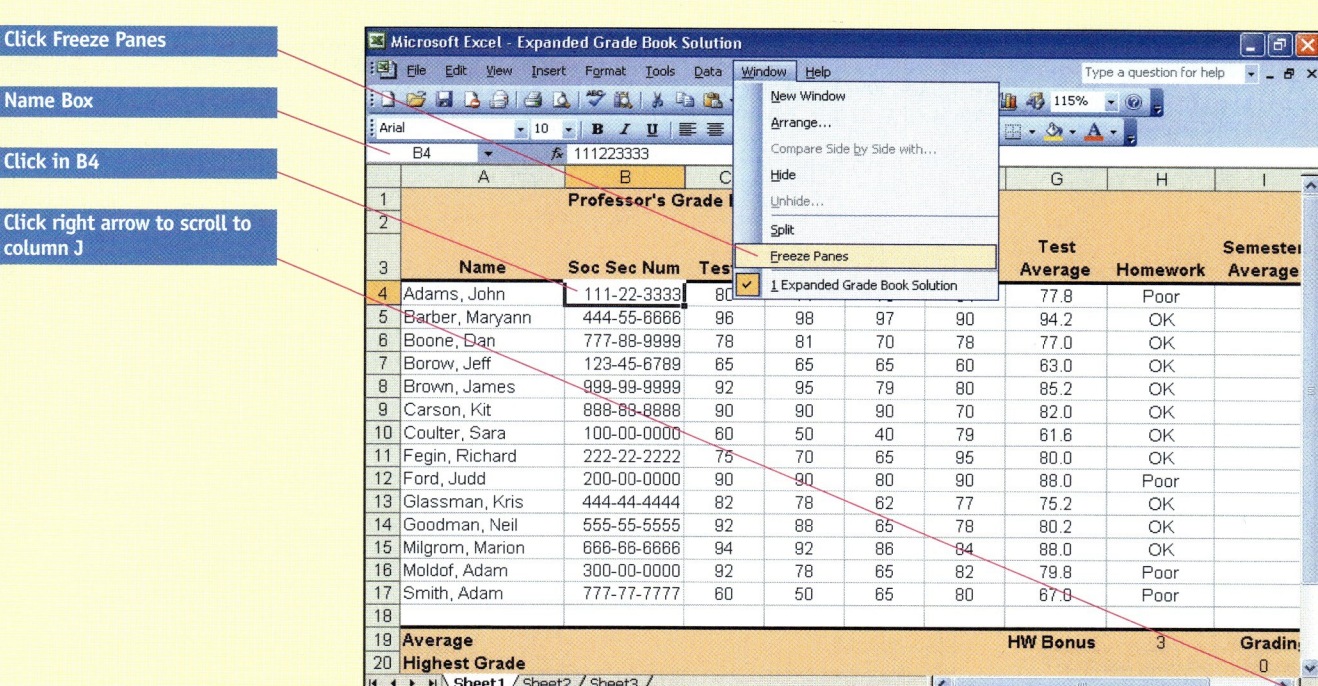

(c) The Freeze Panes Command (step 3)

FIGURE 4.16   Hands-on Exercise 3 (*continued*)

GO TO A SPECIFIC CELL

Ctrl+Home and Ctrl+End will take you to the upper-left and bottom-right cells within a worksheet, but how do you get to a specific cell? One way is to click in the Name box (to the left of the formula bar), enter the cell reference (e.g., K250), and press the Enter key. You can also pull down the Edit menu and click the Go To command (or press the F5 key) to display the Go To dialog box, enter the address of the cell in the Reference text box, then press Enter to go directly to the cell.

Step 4: **The IF Function**

- Scroll until Column I is visible on the screen. Click in **cell I4**.
- Click the **Insert Function button** on the formula bar. Click the **down arrow** on the Select a Category list box and click **Logical**. Click **IF** in the Select a Function list box, then click **OK** to display the Function Arguments dialog box in Figure 4.16d.
- You can enter the arguments directly, or you can use pointing as follows:
    - Click the **Logical_test** text box. Click **cell H4** in the worksheet. (You may need to click and drag the top border of the dialog box to move it out of the way.) Type **="OK"** to complete the logical test.
    - Click the **Value_if_true** text box. Click **cell G4** in the worksheet, type a **plus sign**, click **cell H19** in the worksheet (scrolling if necessary), and finally press the **F4 key** (see boxed tip) to convert the reference to cell H19 to an absolute reference ($H$19).
    - Click the **Value_if_false** text box. Click **cell G4** in the worksheet.
- Check that the dialog box on your worksheet matches the one in Figure 4.16d. Click **OK** to insert the function into your worksheet.
- Save the workbook.

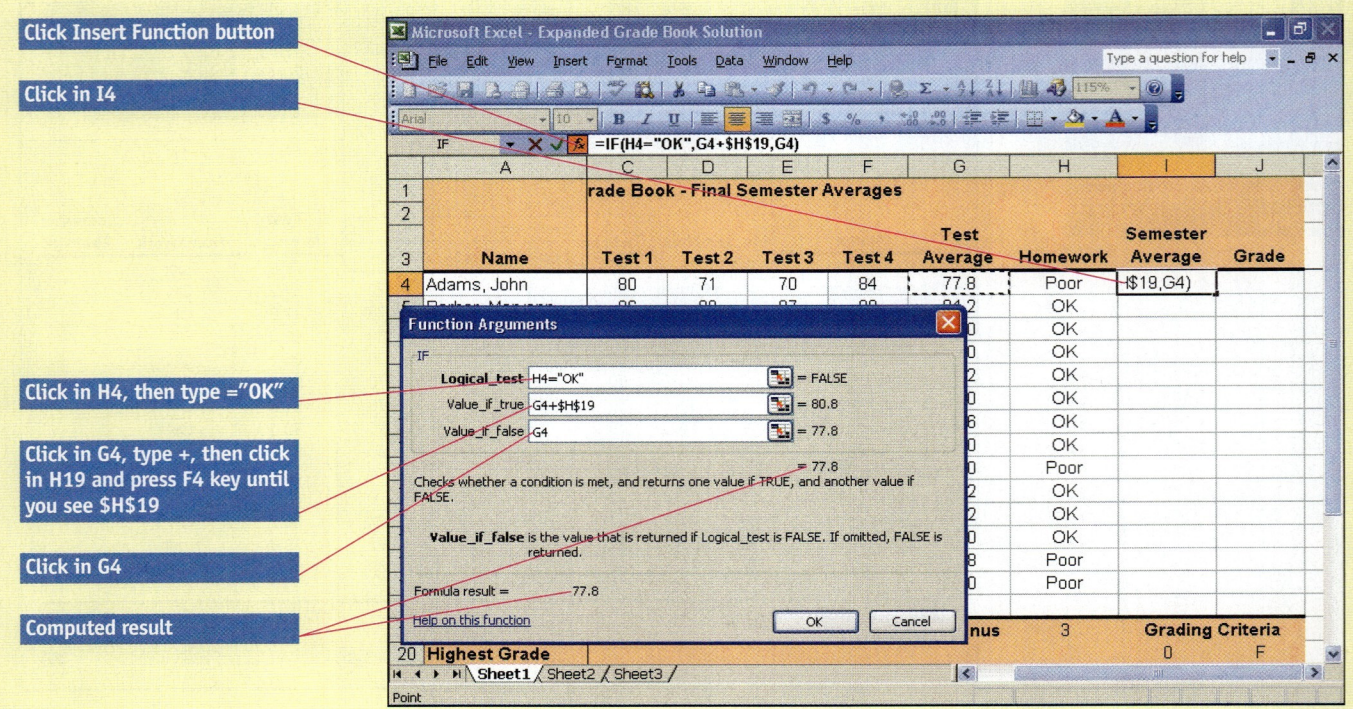

(d) The IF Function (step 4)

FIGURE 4.16 Hands-on Exercise 3 (*continued*)

THE F4 KEY

The F4 key cycles through relative, absolute, and mixed addresses. Click on any reference within the formula bar; for example, click on A1 in the formula =A1+A2. Press the F4 key once, and it changes to an absolute reference. Press the F4 key a second time, and it becomes a mixed reference, A$1; press it again, and it is a different mixed reference, $A1. Press the F4 key a fourth time, and return to the original relative address, A1.

Step 5: **The VLOOKUP Function**

- Click in **cell J4**. Click the **Insert Function button** on the formula bar. Click **Lookup & Reference** from the Select a Category list box. Scroll in the Function Name list box until you can select **VLOOKUP**. Click **OK** to display the Function Arguments dialog box in Figure 4.16e.

- Enter the arguments for the VLOOKUP function as shown in the figure. You can enter the arguments directly, or you can use pointing as follows:
  ❑ Click the **Lookup_value** text box. Click **cell I4** in the worksheet.
  ❑ Click the **Table_array** text box. Click **cell I20** and drag to **cell J24** (scrolling if necessary). Press the **F4 key** to convert to an absolute reference.
  ❑ Click the **Col_index_num** text box. Type **2**.

- Check that the dialog box on your worksheet matches the one in Figure 4.16e. Make corrections as necessary.

- Click **OK** to insert the completed function into your worksheet.

- Save the workbook.

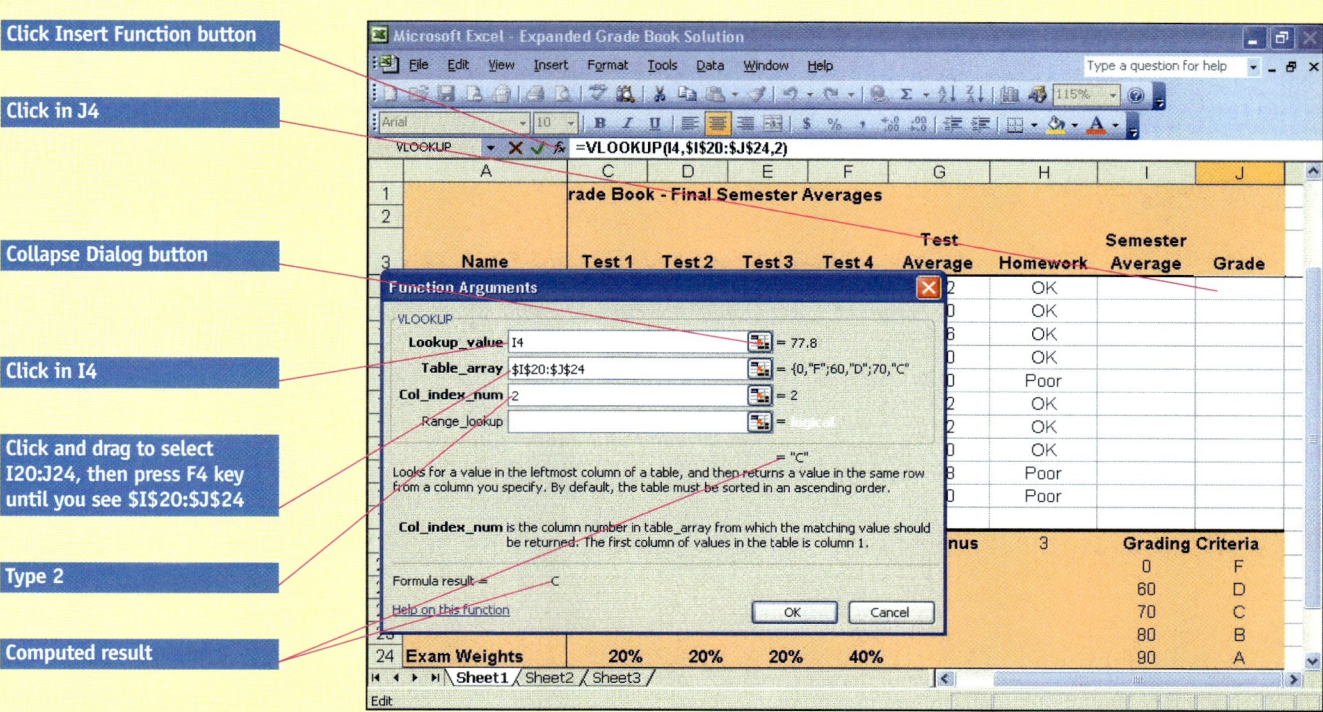

(e) The VLOOKUP Function (step 5)

FIGURE 4.16 Hands-on Exercise 3 (*continued*)

THE COLLAPSE DIALOG BUTTON

You can enter a cell reference in one of two ways: You can type it directly in the Function Arguments dialog box, or click the cell in the worksheet. The Function Arguments dialog box typically hides the necessary cell, however, in which case you can click the Collapse Dialog button (which appears to the right of any parameter within the dialog box). This collapses (hides) the Function Arguments dialog box so that you can click the underlying cell, which is now visible. Click the Collapse Dialog button a second time to display the entire dialog box.

Step 6: **Copy the IF and VLOOKUP Functions**

- If necessary, scroll to the top of the worksheet. Select **cells I4** and **J4** as in Figure 4.16f.

- Point to the **fill handle** in the lower-right corner of the selected range. The mouse pointer changes to a thin crosshair.

- Drag the **fill handle** over **cells I5** through **J17**. A border appears, indicating the destination range as shown in Figure 4.16f. Release the mouse to complete the copy operation.

- If you have done everything correctly, Adam Smith should have a grade of D based on a semester average of 67.

- Check that the semester averages in column I are formatted to one decimal place.

- Save the workbook.

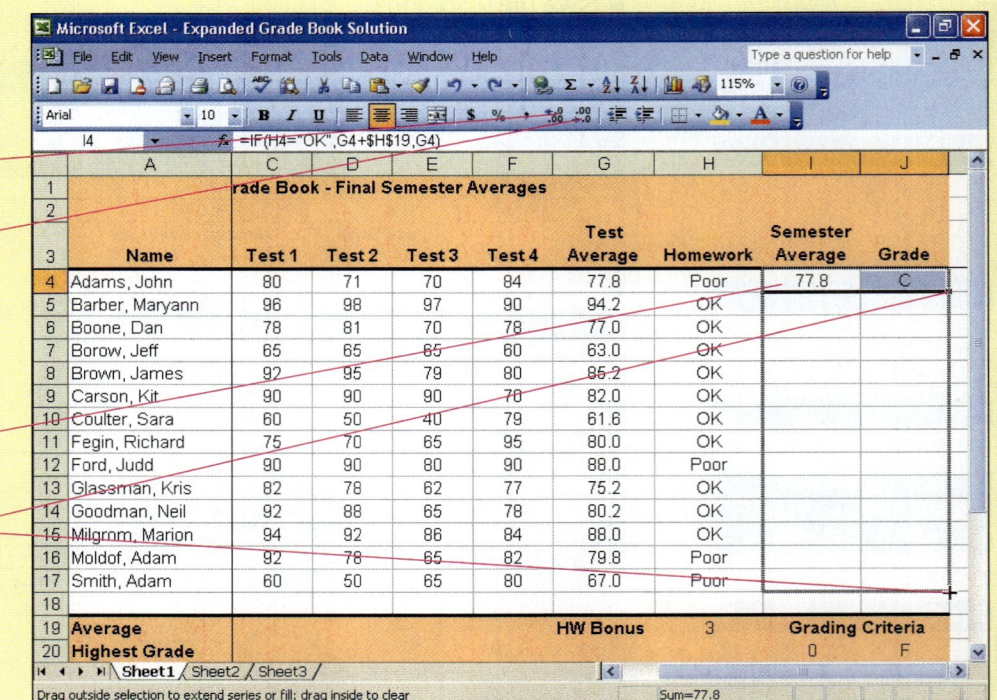

(f) Copy the IF and VLOOKUP Functions (step 6)

FIGURE 4.16 Hands-on Exercise 3 (*continued*)

THE ROUND FUNCTION

Adam Moldof has a semester average of 79.8, which returns a grade of C according to the strict interpretation of the VLOOKUP function. Your instructor might give Adam a break and round his average to 80, but the computer will not. Changing the format to display zero decimal places is not the answer, since formatting affects the display of a number, but not how the number is stored internally. The solution is to use the ROUND function in conjunction with the formula to compute the semester average. See exercise 9 at the end of the chapter.

Step 7: **Create the Summary Statistics**

- Scroll until you can click in **cell C19**. Type **=AVERAGE(C4:C17)**. Press **Enter**. Cell C19 should display 81.9 as shown in Figure 4.16g.

- Click in **cell C20** and enter the formula **=MAX(C4:C17)**. Click in **cell C21** and enter the formula **=MIN(C4:C17)**.

- Click in **cell C22** and enter the formula **=C20–C21**. Check that the displayed values match those in Figure 4.16g.

- Click and drag to select **cells C19** through **C22**, then click and drag the **fill handle** to **cell F22**. Release the mouse.

- Click outside the selection to deselect the cells. You will see the summary statistics for the other tests.

- Save the workbook.

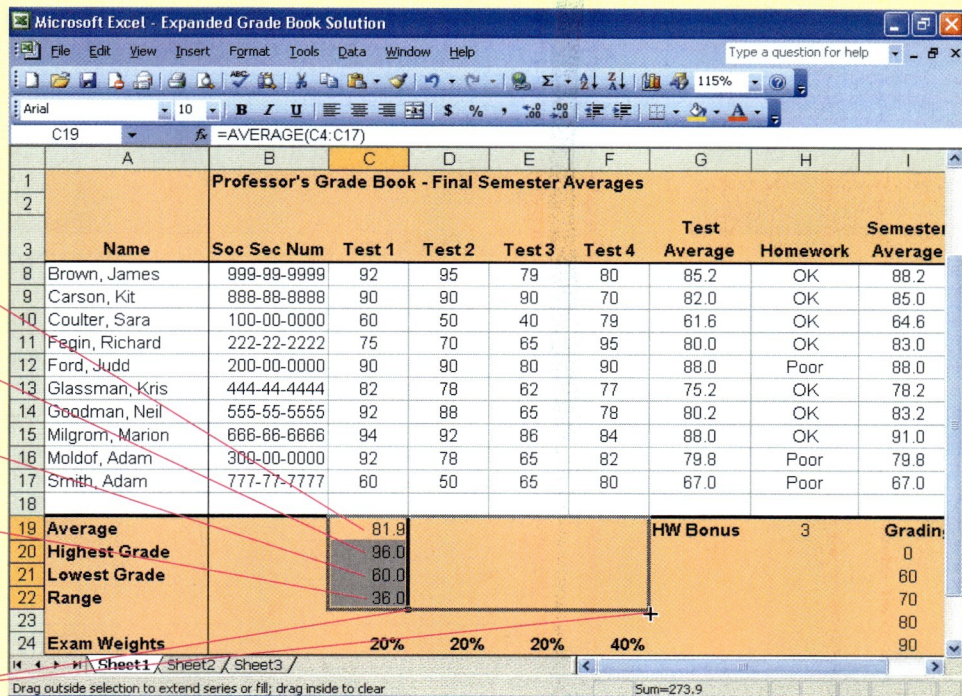

(g) Create the Summary Statistics (step 7)

FIGURE 4.16   Hands-on Exercise 3 (*continued*)

RANK IN CLASS

Use the Rank function to determine a student's rank in class. (Excel also has functions for quartiles and percentiles.) Add a new column to the worksheet, column K in this example, then click in the cell for the first student in the list (cell K4). Enter the function =RANK(I4,$I$4:$I$17), where I4 contains the value you want to look up (the individual student's semester average) and $I$4:$I$17 references the set of numbers on which to base the rank. The latter is entered as an absolute reference so that the cell formula may be copied to the remaining cells in column K. See practice exercise 9 at the end of the chapter.

Step 8: **The Page Break Preview Command**

- Pull down the **View menu** and click the **Page Break Preview command** to see the potential page breaks as shown in Figure 4.16h. Click **OK** if you see the welcome message.
- Click and drag the dashed blue line to the right to eliminate the page break. (You can also drag the solid blue line that appears on the right border to the left to create a page break.)
- Pull down the **View menu** and click **Normal** to return to the Normal view.
- Pull down the **File menu**. Click **Page Setup** to display the Page Setup dialog box. Click the **Margins tab**. Check the box to center the worksheet horizontally.
- Click the **Sheet tab**. Check the boxes to display the **Row and Column Headings** and the **Gridlines**.
- Click the **Print Preview button** to display the completed spreadsheet. Click the **Print button** and click **OK** to print the workbook.
- Print the worksheet with the cell formulas.

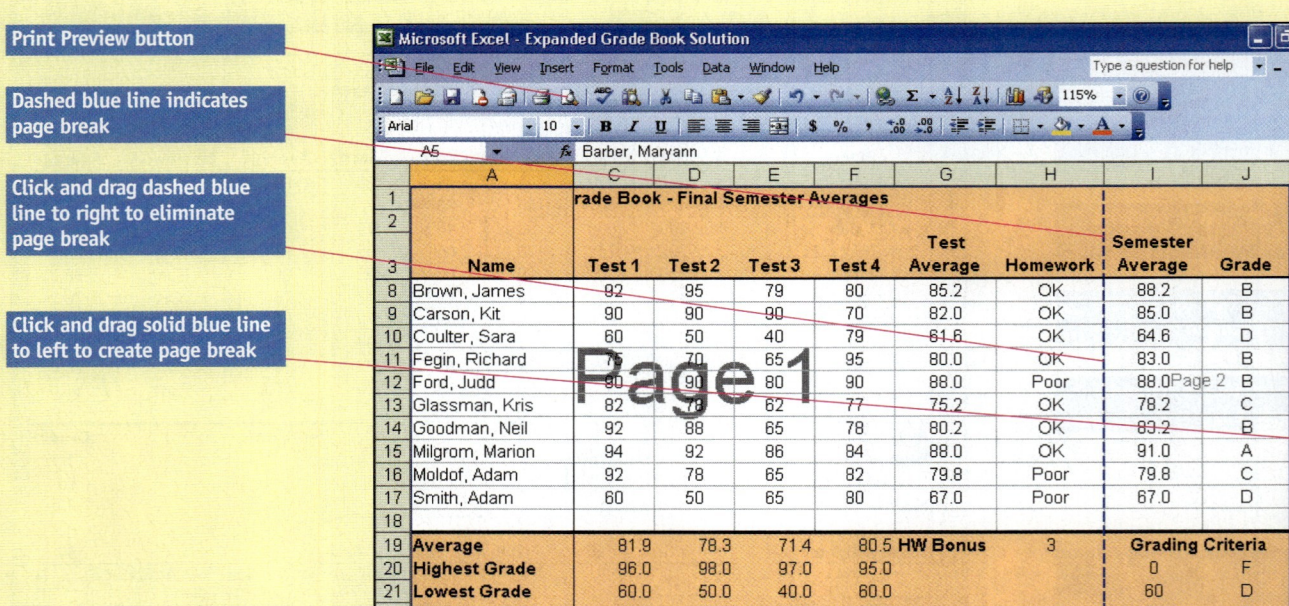

(h) The Page Break Preview Command (step 8)

FIGURE 4.16 Hands-on Exercise 3 (*continued*)

USE NESTED IFS FOR MORE COMPLEX DECISION MAKING

A "nested IF" (or "IF within an IF") is a common logic structure in every programming language. It could be used in the expanded grade book to implement more complicated logic such as a variable homework bonus (of –2, 3, and 5), depending on the grade (for poor, OK, and good, respectively). The IF function in Excel has three arguments—a condition, a value if the condition is true, and a value if the condition is false. A nested IF simply replaces the true and/or false value with another IF statement. See practice exercise 9 at the end of the chapter.

Step 9: **Hide the Rows and Columns**

- Click and drag the column headings for **columns C** through **F** to select these columns, point to the selected columns, then click the **right mouse button** to display the context-sensitive menu in Figure 4.16i. Click **Hide** to hide these columns.

- Click and drag the row headings for **rows 19** through **24** to select these rows, point to the selected rows, click the **right mouse button**, and click the **Hide command**. Print the worksheet.

- Now reverse the process and unhide the rows, but leave the columns hidden. Click and drag to select the row headings for **rows 18** and **25** (which are contiguous), right click to display a context-sensitive menu, then click the **Unhide command**.

- You should see all of the rows in the entire worksheet (within the limitations of scrolling). Save the workbook.

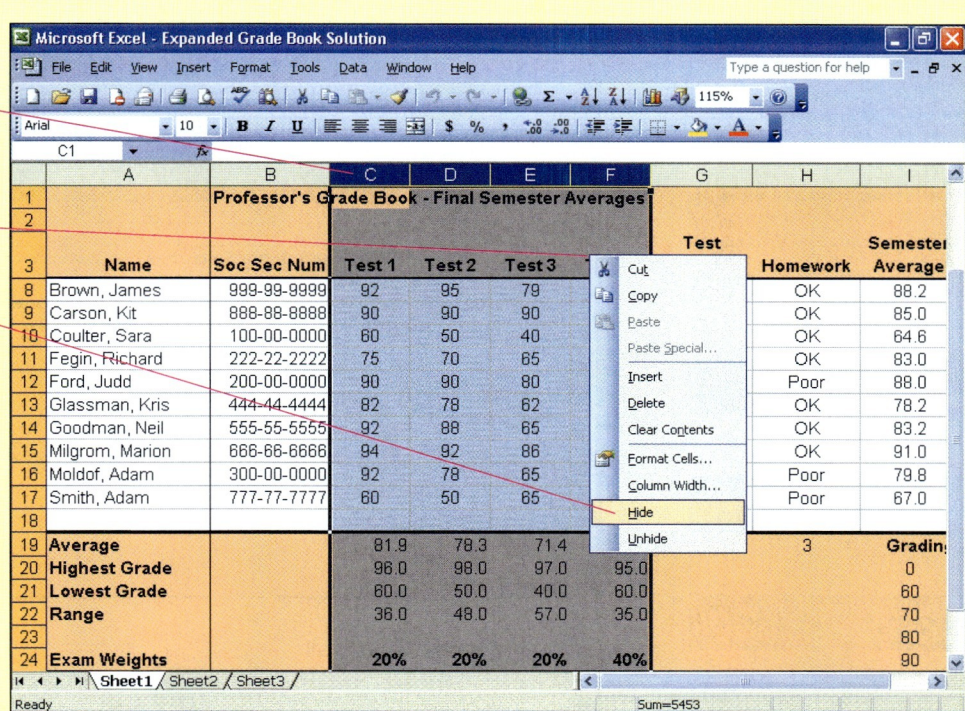

(i) Hide the Rows and Columns (step 9)

FIGURE 4.16 Hands-on Exercise 3 (*continued*)

UNHIDING ROWS AND COLUMNS

Hiding a row or column is easy: You just select the row or column(s) you want to hide, click the right mouse button, then select the Hide command from the shortcut menu. Unhiding a row or column is trickier because you cannot see the target cells. To unhide a column, for example, you need to select the columns on either side; for example, select columns A and C if you are trying to unhide column B. To unhide column A, however, click in the Name box and enter A1. Pull down the Format menu, click Column, then click the Unhide command.

MICROSOFT OFFICE EXCEL 2003 REVISED 209

Step 10: **The AutoFilter Command**

- Click anywhere within the list of students. Pull down the **Data menu**, click the **Filter command**, then click **AutoFilter**. The worksheet is essentially unchanged except that each column heading is followed by a drop-down arrow.

- Click the **drop-down arrow** in cell H3 (the column containing the students' homework grades). Click **Poor**. The list of students changes to show only those students who received this grade on their homework as shown in Figure 4.16j.

- Click the **drop-down arrow** in cell J3, then select **B** from the drop-down list of grade values. The list changes to show the one student who managed to receive a "B" despite having poor homework.

- Add your name and title (**Grading Assistant**) in cells G26 and G27. Save the workbook, then print it for your instructor.

- Pull down the **Data menu**, click **Filter**, and click the **AutoFilter command** to remove the filter and display all of the students.

- Exit Excel. Congratulations on a job well done.

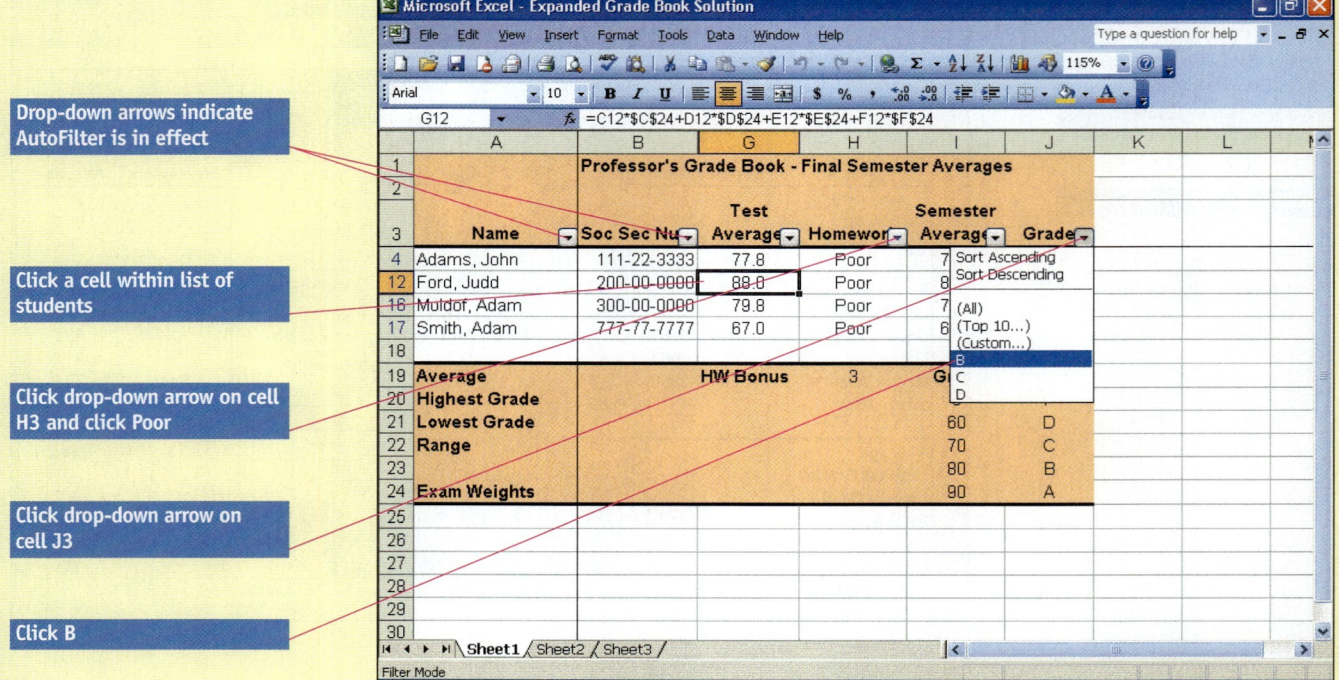

(j) The AutoFilter Command (step 10)

FIGURE 4.16 Hands-on Exercise 3 (*continued*)

SET PRINT AREAS

Press and hold the Ctrl key as you click and drag to select one or more areas in the worksheet, then pull down the File menu, select the Print Area command, and click Set Print Area. The print area is enclosed in dashed lines. The next time you execute the Print command, you will print just the print area(s), with each print area appearing on a separate page. Use the Print Area command in the File menu to clear the print area.

SUMMARY

Excel contains several categories of built-in functions. The PMT function computes the periodic payment for a loan based on three arguments (the interest rate per period, the number of periods, and the amount of the loan). The PMT function was used in worksheets to compute a car payment and a home mortgage. The IPMT and PPMT functions determine the amount of each payment that goes toward interest and principal, respectively.

The FV function returns the future value of an investment based on constant periodic payments and a constant interest rate. The function is associated with Individual Retirement Accounts and 401K retirement plans. A spreadsheet was developed using mixed references to create a two-level table showing the future value of a retirement account at different interest rates and time periods.

Statistical functions were also discussed. The AVERAGE, MAX, and MIN functions return the average, highest, and lowest values in the argument list. The COUNT function returns the number of cells with numeric entries. The COUNTA function displays the number of cells with numeric and/or text entries.

The IF, VLOOKUP, and HLOOKUP functions implement decision making within a worksheet. The IF function has three arguments: a condition, which is evaluated as true or false; a value if the test is true; and a value if the test is false. The VLOOKUP and HLOOKUP functions also have three arguments: the value to look up, the range of cells containing the table, and the column or row number within the table that contains the result.

Several options were presented for working with large spreadsheets. Scrolling enables you to view any portion of a large worksheet but moves the labels for existing rows and/or columns off the screen. The Freeze Panes command keeps the row and/or column headings on the screen while scrolling within a large worksheet. The Page Break Preview command lets you see and/or modify the page breaks that will occur when a worksheet is printed. The AutoFilter command displays a selected set of rows within a worksheet according to a specified set of criteria. The hidden rows are not deleted but are simply not displayed.

A spreadsheet is first and foremost a tool for decision making, and thus Excel includes several commands to aid in that process. The Goal Seek command lets you enter the desired end result of a spreadsheet model (such as the monthly payment on a car loan) and determines the input (the price of the car) necessary to produce that result. The assumptions and initial conditions in a spreadsheet should be clearly labeled and set apart from the rest of the worksheet. This facilitates change and reduces the chance for error.

The hands-on exercises introduced several techniques to make you more proficient. The fill handle is used to copy a cell or group of cells to a range of adjacent cells. Pointing is a more accurate way to enter a cell reference into a formula as it uses the mouse or arrow keys to select the cell as you build the formula. The AutoFill capability creates a series based on the initial value(s) you supply.

KEY TERMS

Absolute reference 180
Arguments 170
Assumptions 180
AutoFill capability 201
AutoFilter command 200
AVERAGE function 193
Breakpoint 196
COUNT function...............193
COUNTA function 193
Freeze Panes command 197
Function 170
FV function 170
Goal Seek command 172
HLOOKUP function 196
IF function 195
Insert Function command 171
IRA (Individual Retirement
    Account) 181
MAX function 193
MIN function 193
Mixed reference 181
Nested IF 208
Page Break Preview command ...197
PMT function.................170
Relational operator 195
Relative reference 180
Scrolling 197
Sort command 192
Statistical functions 193
SUM function 194
Template 168
Unfreeze Panes command 197
Unhiding cells 197
VLOOKUP function 196

MULTIPLE CHOICE

1. Which of the following options may be used to print a large worksheet?
   (a) Landscape orientation
   (b) Scaling
   (c) Reduced margins
   (d) All of the above

2. If the results of a formula contain more characters than can be displayed according to the present format and cell width,
   (a) The extra characters will be truncated under all circumstances
   (b) All of the characters will be displayed if the cell to the right is empty
   (c) A series of asterisks will be displayed
   (d) A series of pound signs will be displayed

3. Which cell—A1, A2, or A3—will contain the amount of the loan, given the function =PMT(A1,A2,A3)?
   (a) A1
   (b) A2
   (c) A3
   (d) Impossible to determine

4. Which of the following will compute the average of the values in cells D2, D3, and D4?
   (a) The function =AVERAGE(D2:D4)
   (b) The function =AVERAGE(D2,D4)
   (c) Both (a) and (b)
   (d) Neither (a) nor (b)

5. The function =IF(A1>A2,A1+A2,A1*A2) returns
   (a) The product of cells A1 and A2 if cell A1 is greater than A2
   (b) The sum of cells A1 and A2 if cell A1 is less than A2
   (c) Both (a) and (b)
   (d) Neither (a) nor (b)

6. Which of the following is the preferred way to sum the values contained in cells A1 to A4?
   (a) =SUM(A1:A4)
   (b) =A1+A2+A3+A4
   (c) Either (a) or (b) is equally good
   (d) Neither (a) nor (b) is correct

7. Which of the following will return the highest and lowest arguments from a list of arguments?
   (a) HIGH/LOW
   (b) LARGEST/SMALLEST
   (c) MAX/MIN
   (d) All of the above

8. Which of the following is a *required* technique to develop the worksheet for the mortgage analysis?
   (a) Pointing
   (b) Copying with the fill handle
   (c) Both (a) and (b)
   (d) Neither (a) nor (b)

9. Given that cells B6, C6, and D6 contain the numbers 10, 20, and 30, respectively, what value will be returned by the function =IF(B6>10,C6*2,D6*3)?
   (a) 10
   (b) 40
   (c) 60
   (d) 90

10. Which of the following is not an input parameter to the Goal Seek command?
    (a) The cell containing the end result
    (b) The desired value of the end result
    (c) The cell whose value will change to reach the end result
    (d) The value of the input cell that is required to reach the end result

... continued

multiple choice

11. What is the correct order of the arguments for the FV function?
    (a) Interest Rate, Term, Principal
    (b) Term, Interest Rate, Principal
    (c) Interest Rate, Term, Annual Amount
    (d) Term, Interest Rate, Annual Amount

12. Which function will return the number of nonempty cells in the range A2 through A6, including in the result cells that contain text as well as numeric entries?
    (a) =COUNT(A2:A6)
    (b) =COUNTA(A2:A6)
    (c) =COUNT(A2,A6)
    (d) =COUNTA(A2,A6)

13. The annual interest rate, term in years, and principal of a loan are stored in cells A1, A2, and A3, respectively. Which of the following is the correct PMT function, given monthly payments?
    (a) =PMT(A1,A2,–A3)
    (b) =PMT(A1/12,A2*12,–A3)
    (c) =PMT(A1*12, A2/12,–A3)
    (d) =PMT(A1,A2,A3)

14. The worksheet displayed in the monitor shows columns A and B, skips columns C, D, E, and F, then displays columns G, H, I, J, and K. What is the most likely explanation for the missing columns?
    (a) The columns were previously deleted
    (b) The columns are empty and thus are automatically hidden from view
    (c) Either (a) or (b) is a satisfactory explanation
    (d) Neither (a) nor (b) is a likely reason

15. Given the function =VLOOKUP(C6,D12:F18,3)
    (a) The entries in cells D12 through D18 are in ascending order
    (b) The entries in cells D12 through D18 are in descending order
    (c) The entries in cells F12 through F18 are in ascending order
    (d) The entries in cells F12 through F18 are in descending order

16. A formula containing the entry =$B3 is copied to a cell one column over and two rows down. How will the entry appear in its new location?
    (a) =$B3
    (b) =B3
    (c) =$C5
    (d) =$B5

17. You expect to contribute $2,000 a year for 10 years to a retirement plan and expect an annual return of 7%. Which of the following functions can you use to determine the expected future value?
    (a) =FV(.07/12,10*12,–2000)
    (b) =FV(.07,10,–2000)
    (c) =FV(.07/12,10*12, 2000)
    (d) =FV(.07,10, 2000)

18. Which of the following computes the monthly payment for a car loan of $10,000 that is amortized over 3 years at 5%?
    (a) =PMT(.05/12,36,–10000)
    (b) =PMT(.05,36,–10000)
    (c) =PMT(.05,3,–10000)
    (d) =PMT(.05,3,10000)

ANSWERS

1. d	7. c	13. b
2. d	8. d	14. d
3. c	9. d	15. a
4. a	10. d	16. d
5. d	11. c	17. b
6. a	12. b	18. a

PRACTICE WITH EXCEL

1. **Calculating Your Retirement:** Retirement is years away, but it is never too soon to start planning. The Future Value function enables you to calculate the amount of money you will have at retirement, based on a series of uniform contributions, made by you and/or your employer, during your working years. Once you reach retirement, however, you do not withdraw all of the money immediately, but withdraw it periodically as a monthly pension. Your assignment is to create a new worksheet similar to the one in Figure 4.17. Note the following:

   a. The accrual phase uses the FV function to determine the amount of money you will accumulate. The total contribution in cell B7 is a formula based on a percentage of your annual salary, plus a matching contribution from your employer. The 6.2% in our figure corresponds to the percentages that are currently in effect for Social Security. (In actuality, the government currently deducts 7.65% from your paycheck, and allocates 6.2% for Social Security and the remaining 1.45% for Medicare.)

   b. The future value of your contributions (i.e., the amount of your "nest egg") depends on the assumptions in the left side of the worksheet. The 6% interest rate is conservative and can be achieved by investing in bonds, as opposed to equities. The 45 years of contributions corresponds to an individual entering the work force at age 22 and retiring at 67 (the age at which today's worker will begin to collect Social Security).

   c. The pension phase uses the PMT function to determine the payments you will receive in retirement. The formula in cell E4 is a simple reference to the amount accumulated in cell B10. The formula in cell E7 uses the PMT function to compute your monthly pension based on your nest egg, the interest rate, and the years in retirement. Note that accrual phase uses an *annual* contribution in its calculations, whereas the pension phase determines a *monthly* pension.

   d. Add a hyperlink to the page that goes to the Social Security Administration (www.ssa.gov), and then compare your calculation to the benefits provided by the government. Is Social Security providing a good return on your investment?

   e. Add your name to the worksheet, print the worksheet both ways to show displayed values and cell formulas, add a cover sheet, and then submit the assignment to your instructor.

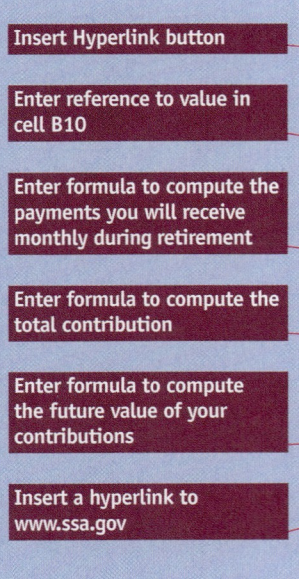

FIGURE 4.17 Calculating Your Retirement (exercise 1)

practice exercises

2. **Alternate Grade Book:** Figure 4.18 displays an alternate version of the grade book that was used in the third hands-on exercise. The student names have changed as has the professor's grading scheme. Open the partially completed version of this worksheet in the *Chapter 4 Practice 2* workbook in the Exploring Excel folder, then complete the workbook as follows:

   a. The test average is computed by dropping the student's lowest grade, then giving equal weight to the three remaining tests. Steve Weinstein's test average, for example, is computed by dropping the 70 on test 1, then taking the average of 80, 90, and 100, his grades for tests 2, 3, and 4. You will need to use the SUM, MIN, and COUNT functions to implement this requirement.

   b. Students are required to complete a designated number of homework assignments (12 in Figure 4.18), then receive a bonus or penalty for every additional or missing homework assignment. Andrea Carrion completed 9 homework assignments, rather than 12, and thus has a 6-point penalty (2 points per each missing assignment). Steve Weinstein, however, receives a 3-point bonus (1 point for each extra assignment). The bonus or penalty is added to the test average to determine the semester average.

   c. The grade for the course is based on the semester average and table of grading criteria according to an HLOOKUP function within the worksheet.

   d. Format the worksheet in an attractive manner. You do not have to duplicate our formatting exactly, but you are to use conditional formatting to display all failing grades and homework penalties in red.

   e. Add your name to the worksheet. Print the worksheet twice, once with displayed values and once with cell formulas. Use the Page Setup command to display grid lines and row and column headings. Add a custom header with your name, the course you are taking and your instructor's name. Create a custom footer with today's date and the current time.

   f. Print the worksheet a second time to reflect Maryann's comment. Add a cover sheet, and then submit both copies of the worksheet together with the cell formulas to your instructor.

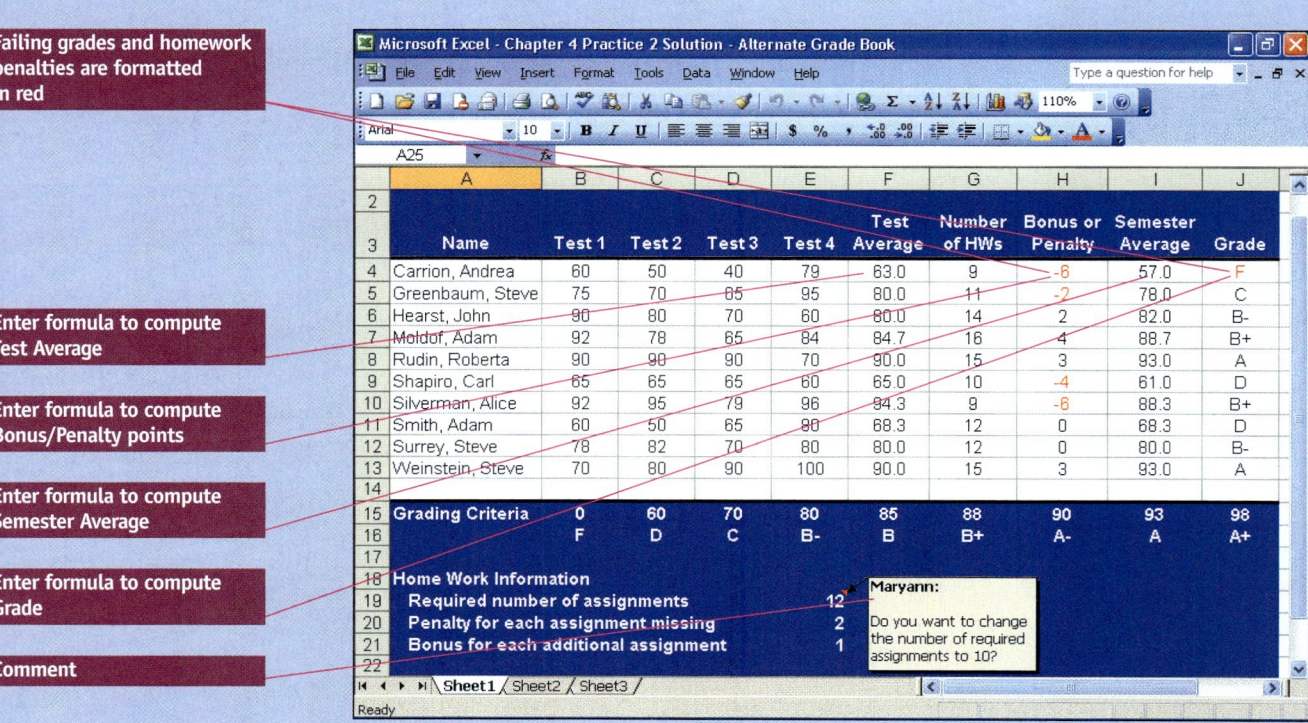

FIGURE 4.18 Alternate Grade Book (exercise 2)

practice exercises

3. **Expanded Payroll:** Figure 4.19 displays an expanded version of the payroll example that was used earlier in the text. The assumptions used to determine an individual's net pay are listed in the worksheet and repeated below. Open the partially completed *Chapter 4 Practice 3* workbook in the Exploring Excel folder. Be sure to use the appropriate combination of relative and absolute addresses so that the formulas in row 2 may be copied to the remaining rows in the worksheet and, further, so that you can easily modify any of the underlying assumptions.

   a. Click in cell E2 to compute the employee's regular pay (regular hours worked times the hourly wage). The number of regular hours worked does not appear explicitly in the worksheet, but is calculated from the total hours worked and the overtime threshold (which is entered in the assumption area). Barber, for example, works a total of 48 hours, 40 regular, and 8 (every hour over the threshold) of overtime.
   b. Click in cell F2 and compute the overtime pay, which is the pay for all hours above the overtime threshold (40 hours in Figure 4.19). The employee receives the overtime rate (1.5 in this worksheet) times the hourly wage for every hour over the threshold.
   c. The gross pay in cell G2 is the sum of the regular pay and the overtime pay. The taxable pay in cell H2 is computed by subtracting the deduction per dependent times the number of dependents.
   d. The withholding tax in cell I2 is based on the taxable pay and the tax table. Use a VLOOKUP function to determine the tax rate, then multiply by the taxable pay.
   e. The Social Security/Medicare tax in cell J2 is a fixed percentage of gross pay.
   f. The Net Pay in cell K2 is equal to the gross pay minus the withholding and Social Security tax.
   g. Copy the formulas in row 2 to the remaining rows in the worksheet.
   h. Add your name to the worksheet, then print the worksheet to show both displayed values and cell formulas.
   i. Change the overtime threshold in cell D13 to 35 and the overtime rate in cell D14 to 2. Print the worksheet a second time to show the resulting displayed values.
   j. Add a cover sheet and submit all of the printouts to your instructor.

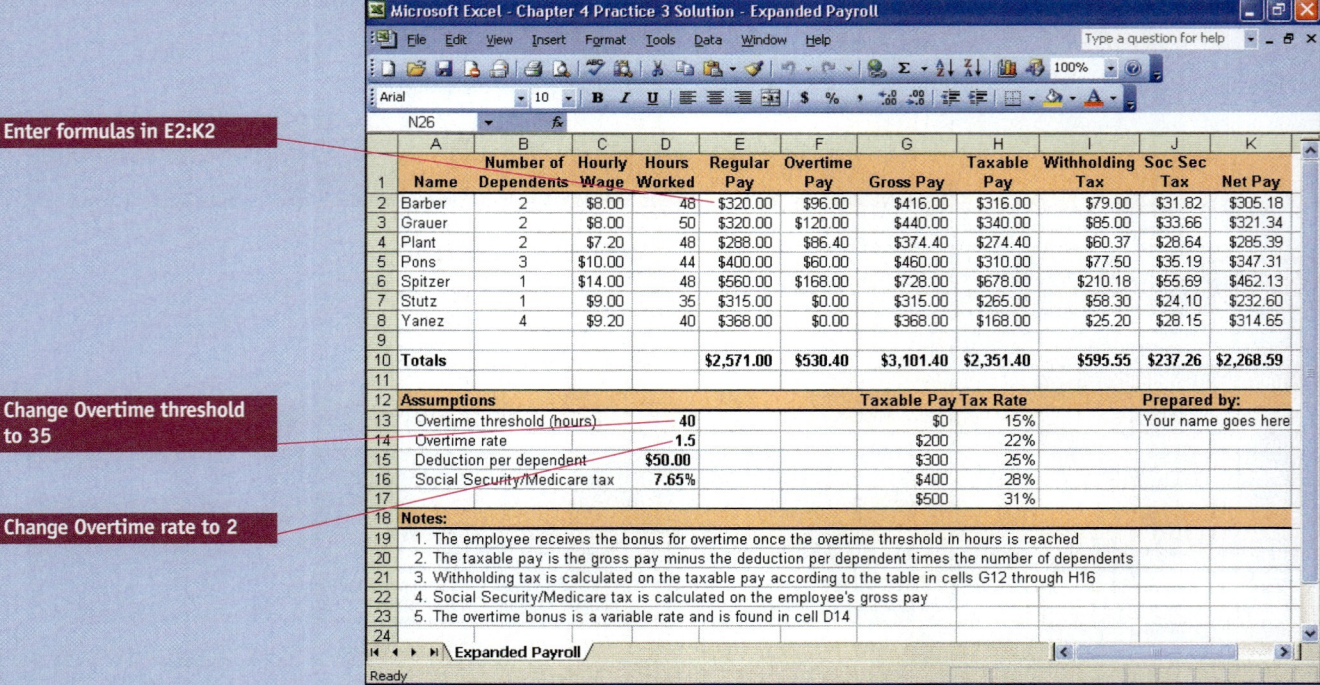

FIGURE 4.19 Expanded Payroll (exercise 3)

practice exercises

4. **Fuel Estimates:** Figure 4.20 displays a worksheet an airline uses to calculate the fuel requirements and associated cost for available flights. Open the partially completed worksheet in the *Chapter 4 Practice 4* workbook, and then complete the workbook to match our figure. Note the following:

   a. The fuel required for each flight is dependent on the type of aircraft and the number of flying hours. Use a VLOOKUP function in the formula to determine gallons per hour based on the type of plane, then multiply the result by the number of flying hours to compute the amount of fuel for each flight. (The table for the VLOOKUP function extends over three columns.)

   b. Use the fuel required from part (a) to compute the additional requirements for reserve fuel and holding fuel, which must then be added to the initial fuel requirements to get the total fuel needed for a trip. These parameters are shown at the bottom of the worksheet and are susceptible to change. Use the appropriate combination of relative and absolute references so that the formulas for the first flight can be copied to the remaining rows in the worksheet.

   c. The estimated fuel cost for each flight is the number of gallons times the price per gallon. There is a price break, however, if the fuel required reaches or exceeds a threshold number of gallons. The Boeing-727 flight from Miami to Los Angeles, for example, requires 6,050 gallons, which exceeds the threshold, and therefore qualifies for the reduced price of fuel.

   d. Your worksheet should be completely flexible and amenable to change; that is, the hourly fuel requirements, price per gallon, price threshold, and holding and reserve percentages are all subject to change.

   e. Print the worksheet to show both displayed values and cell formulas. Use the Page Setup command to create a custom header and a custom footer that includes your name, your instructor's name, the name of your course, today's date, and the current time.

   f. Change the threshold for the price break to 3,500 gallons. Change the price per gallon to $1.50 and $1.75 if the threshold is met or not met, respectively. Print the spreadsheet to reflect these new values. Add a cover sheet and submit all of your printouts to your instructor.

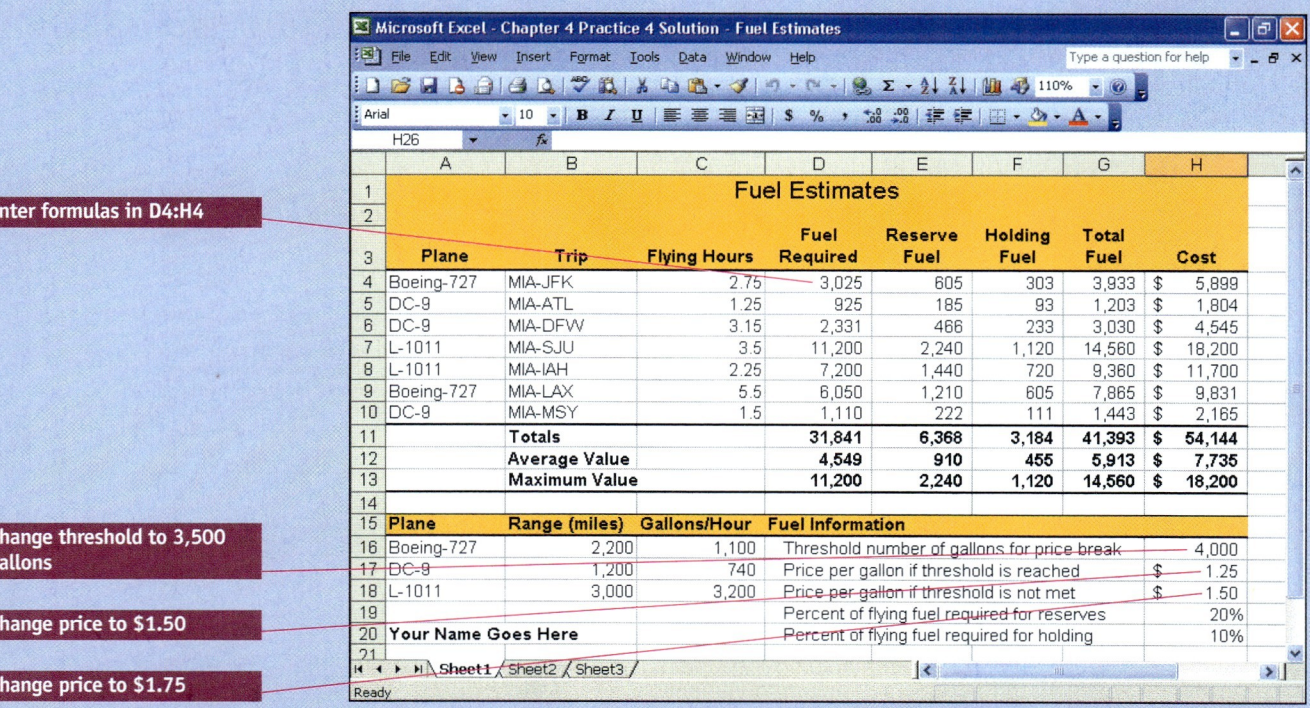

FIGURE 4.20 Fuel Estimates (exercise 4)

practice exercises

5. **The Roth IRA:** Figure 4.21 displays a Word document with an Excel worksheet and associated chart that displays the value of an IRA for various combinations of interest rates and years invested. (The chart is not visible in Figure 4.21.) A partially completed version of that worksheet is found in the Exploring Excel folder, as is the associated Word document. Your assignment is to complete the worksheet, create the associated line chart, and then link the Excel objects to the Word document.

   a. Open the partially completed *Chapter 4 Practice 5* workbook. Click in cell C5 and enter the appropriate FV function using mixed references. Mixed references are not difficult if you ask yourself the right questions. The interest rate for the calculation in cell C5 will come from cell B5. Will the interest rate for other cells always come from column B? (Yes, so the reference to the column is absolute.) Will the interest rate always come from row 5? (No, so the reference to the column is relative.) Use similar reasoning to determine that the reference to the number of years in cell C4 should be expressed as C$4. Copy the formula in cell C5 to the remaining rows and columns in the worksheet. You should see the same dollar amounts as in Figure 4.21.

   b. The worksheet is designed so that the user can change the starting interest rate and associated increment, 4.50% and .5%, respectively in the figure, then have those values reflected in the body of the spreadsheet. The user can also change the number of years for the investment and the associated increment, as well as the annual contribution. Change the values in the assumption area of the worksheet to see how the worksheet changes.

   c. Create a line chart in its own chart sheet that shows the value of a Roth IRA at different interest rates for different time periods.

   d. Open the associated *Chapter 4 Practice 5* Word document in the Exploring Excel folder and link the portion of the worksheet shown in Figure 4.21 to the Word document. Return to Excel and link the line chart to a second page in the Word document. Save the workbook. Exit Excel.

   e. Add your name to the memo after the salutation, "To the New Graduate", then print the completed memo and submit it to your instructor. Compound interest has been called the eighth wonder of the world. Use it to your advantage!

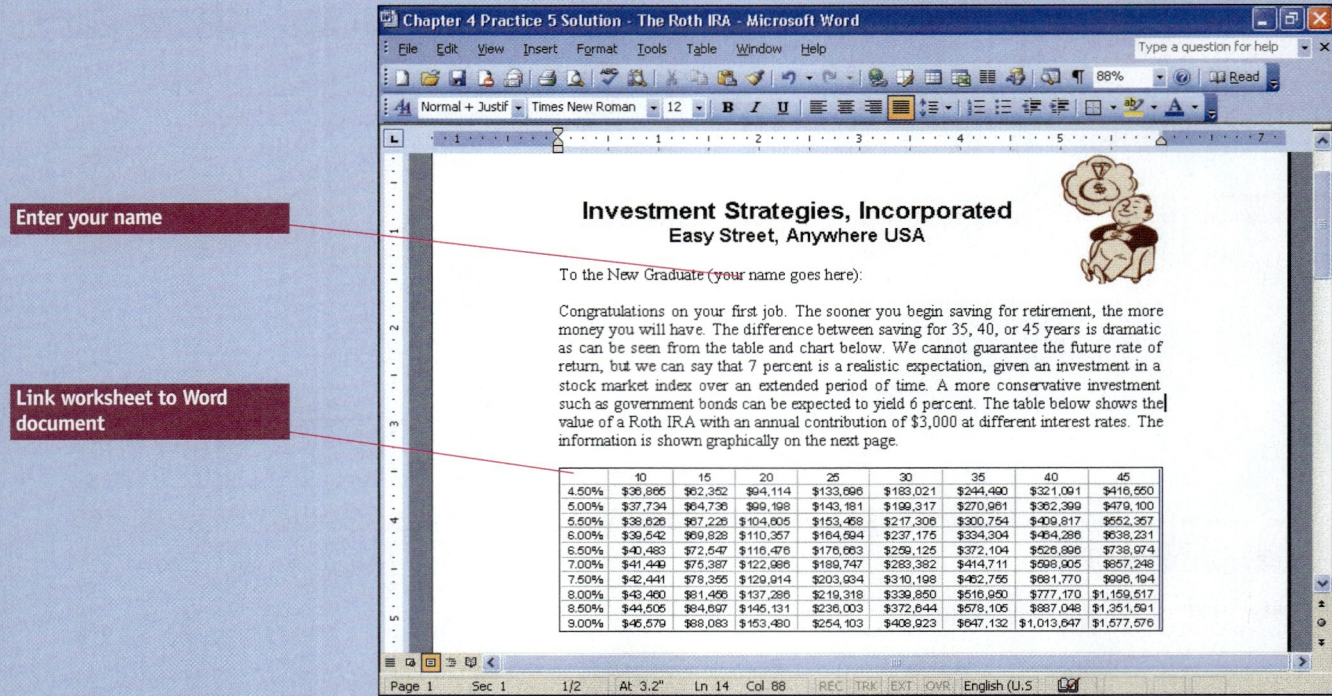

FIGURE 4.21 The Roth IRA (exercise 5)

practice exercises

6. **Celebrity Birthdays:** The spreadsheet in Figure 4.22 compares the age of its developer to that of several celebrities. It is a sophisticated spreadsheet that uses a nested IF function, the absolute value function, and conditional formatting. Open the partially completed version of this spreadsheet in *Chapter 4 Practice 6* and proceed as follows:
   a. Enter your name and birth date in cells B4 and B5, respectively. Enter the function to display today's date in cell E4. Enter the formula to compute your age in cell E5.
   b. Click in cell C8 and enter a nested IF function to indicate whether you are older, younger, or the same age as the celebrity in this row. Start the IF function as follows: =IF($B$5<B8,"older by",IF($B$5>B8, ...)). The absolute reference is to your birth date in cell B5; that is, if your birth date is less than the celebrity's birth date, you are older. If this condition is not true, the second IF function should tell whether you are younger or you are the same age.
   c. Apply conditional formatting to the formula in cell C8 to display the result in red, blue, or green, depending on whether you are older, younger, or the same age.
   d. Click in cell D8 and enter the formula to compute the difference in age, which is to appear as a positive number, regardless of whether you are older or younger than the celebrity. The easiest way to ensure positive numbers is to use the ABS (absolute value) function. (A zero age difference should not appear in the worksheet, however. Pull down the Tools menu, click the Options command, click the View tab, and then clear the box to display zero values.)
   e. Click in cell E8 and enter the appropriate IF function to display the word "years" if you are either older or younger than the celebrity. The cell should be blank if you are the same age. Center the entry.
   f. Copy the formulas in row 8 to the remaining rows of the worksheet. Be sure to test the worksheet completely; that is, change your birth date temporarily to match the birthday of a celebrity to see if you display the same age in column D.
   g. Click the link to find celebrity birthdays and add a person who is not in the original workbook. (We added Ashton Kutcher.) Boldface and highlight the row you added.
   h. Print the spreadsheet to show the displayed values in alphabetical order by the celebrities' last name. Print the cell formulas.

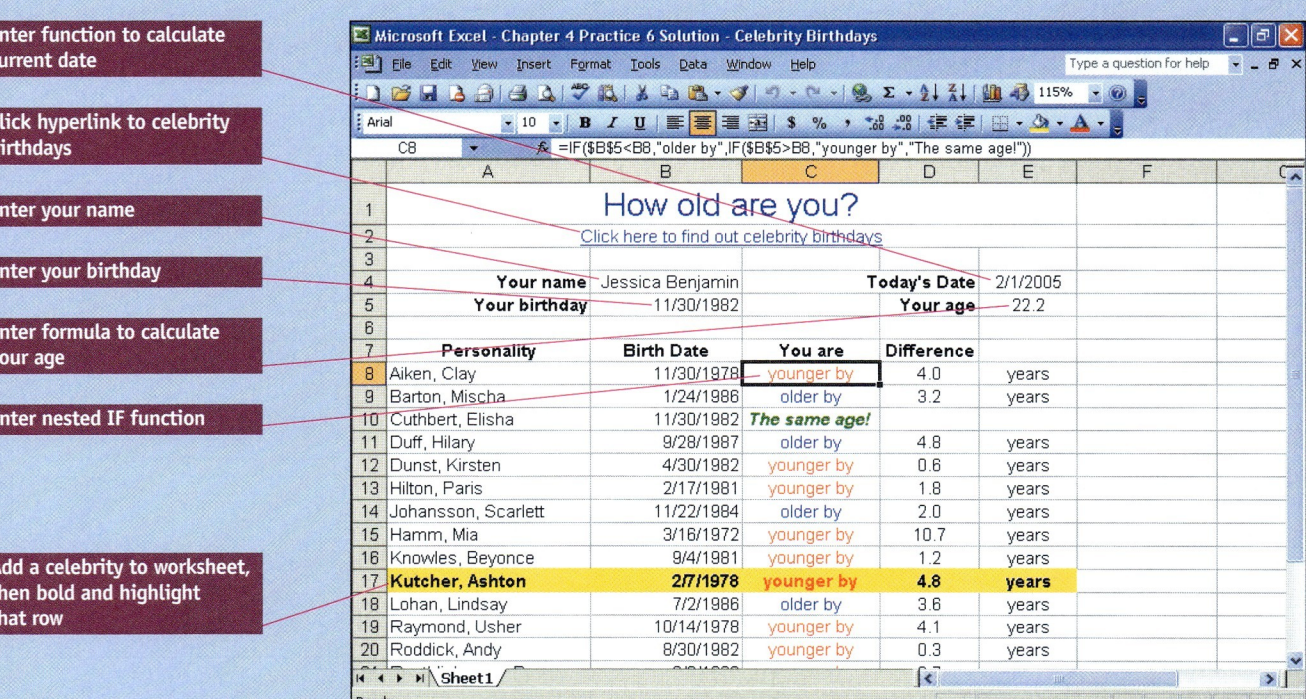

FIGURE 4.22 Celebrity Birthdays (exercise 6)

MICROSOFT OFFICE EXCEL 2003 REVISED   219

practice exercises

7. **The Health Club:** The worksheet in Figure 4.23 displays a list of new members in the Totally Fit Gym. Your assignment is to open the partially completed workbook in *Chapter 4 Practice 7*, in order to complete the workbook so that it matches our figure. You do not have to match our formatting exactly, but you are required to duplicate the functionality. Proceed as follows:

   a. Click in Cell C4 and enter the appropriate VLOOKUP function to determine the cost of the individual's membership. Your formula should contain an absolute reference to the table of membership costs that is contained in cells A17 through C19.

   b. Click in cell E4 and use an IF function to determine the annual total, which consists of the cost of membership plus an optional locker fee. Now click in cell G4 to compute the total amount due, which is the annual total times the number of years the individual has chosen.

   c. The down payment in cell H4 depends on the type of membership and is not dependent on the number of years. Thus Allen, George, and Grauer all have a required down payment of $250 for the deluxe membership, even though they selected a different number of years.

   d. Compute the balance (which is the total due minus the down payment) in cell I4. Use the PMT function to determine the monthly payment in cell J4.

   e. Copy the formulas in row 4 to the remaining rows in the worksheet.

   f. Enter your last name in cell A8 in place of "Grauer". Sort the client list in alphabetical order, then select the row containing your name and shade it.

   g. Enter the appropriate statistical functions in column H to determine summary statistics. Your values should match ours.

   h. Format the completed worksheet as you see fit. Insert clip art somewhere in the worksheet to serve as a logo.

   i. Print the displayed values and cell formulas for your instructor. Use landscape printing so that the worksheet fits on one page. Be sure that the grid lines and the row and column headings appear.

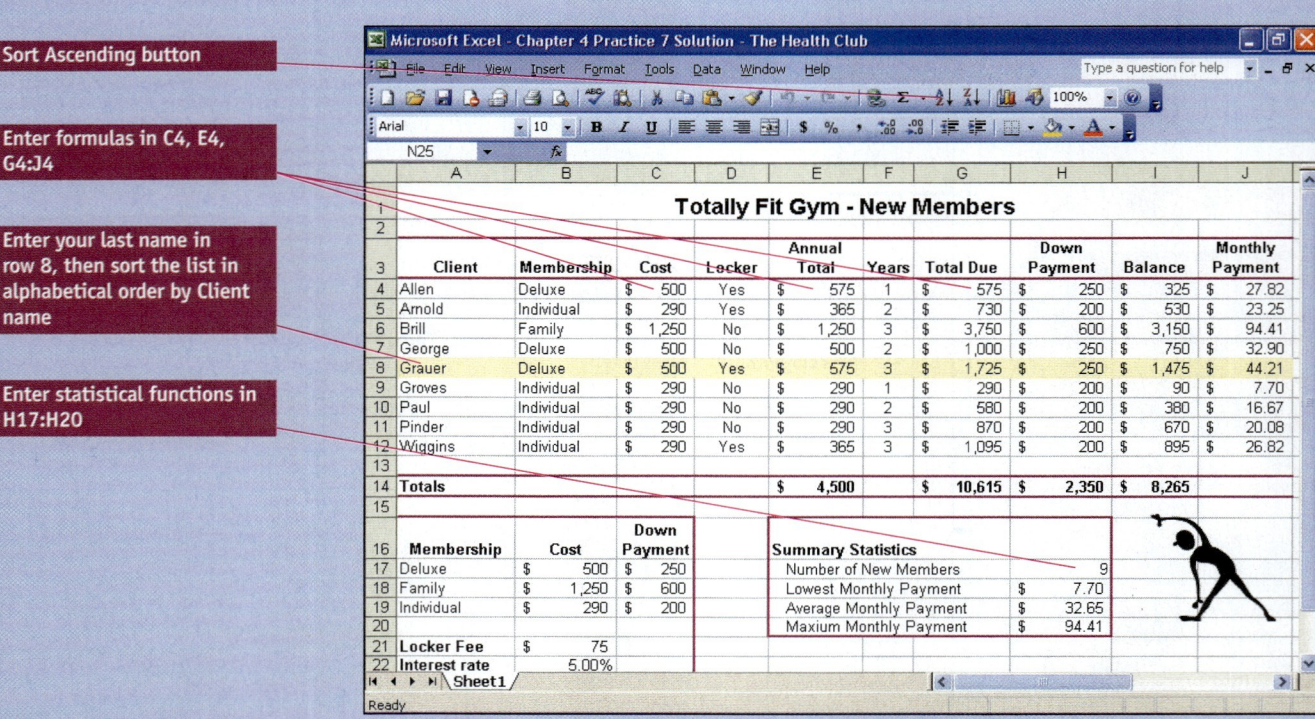

FIGURE 4.23 The Health Club (exercise 7)

practice exercises

8. **Big Bopper Bank:** The workbook in Figure 4.24 reviews multiple Excel functions that were discussed in the chapter. The selling price and term of each loan are entered into columns B and C. All of the other entries (the interest rate, down payment, amount to be financed, and monthly payment) are determined from these parameters and the table at the bottom of the worksheet. Open the partially completed workbook in *Chapter 4 Practice 8—Big Bopper Bank* and proceed as follows:

   a. Click in cell D4 and enter the appropriate formula to determine the interest rate, which depends on the term of the loan. (You will need to use the VLOOKUP function in your formula to reference the table in cells A15 through C17.) You should see 6.25% since Allen has selected a 30-year loan.

   b. Click in cell C4 and enter 15 years instead of 30 years as the term of the loan. The interest rate should change to 5.75% if your VLOOKUP function is correct. Change the loan back to 30 years.

   c. Click in cell E4 and enter the formula to compute the required down payment, which is found by multiplying the percentage rate for the down payment times the selling price of the home. The percentage rate for the down payment depends on the term of the loan, so you will need to use the VLOOKUP function to determine the correct percentage.

   d. Complete the formulas in row four. The amount to be financed is the selling price minus the down payment. The monthly payment is computed using the PMT function. Copy the formulas to the rows for the other customers.

   e. Enter the appropriate functions to compute the summary statistics at the bottom of the worksheet in cells C19 through C22.

   f. Enter your name in cell A6 in place of Barber, and then highlight the row containing your data. Sort the customers so that they appear in alphabetical order. Be sure you sort the worksheet correctly.

   g. Format the completed worksheet. (You do not have to duplicate our formatting exactly.) Use the Insert Picture command to insert an appropriate graphic.

   h. Print the completed worksheet. Be sure that you print both the displayed values and cell formulas and that the worksheet fits on one page. Include gridlines and row and column headings.

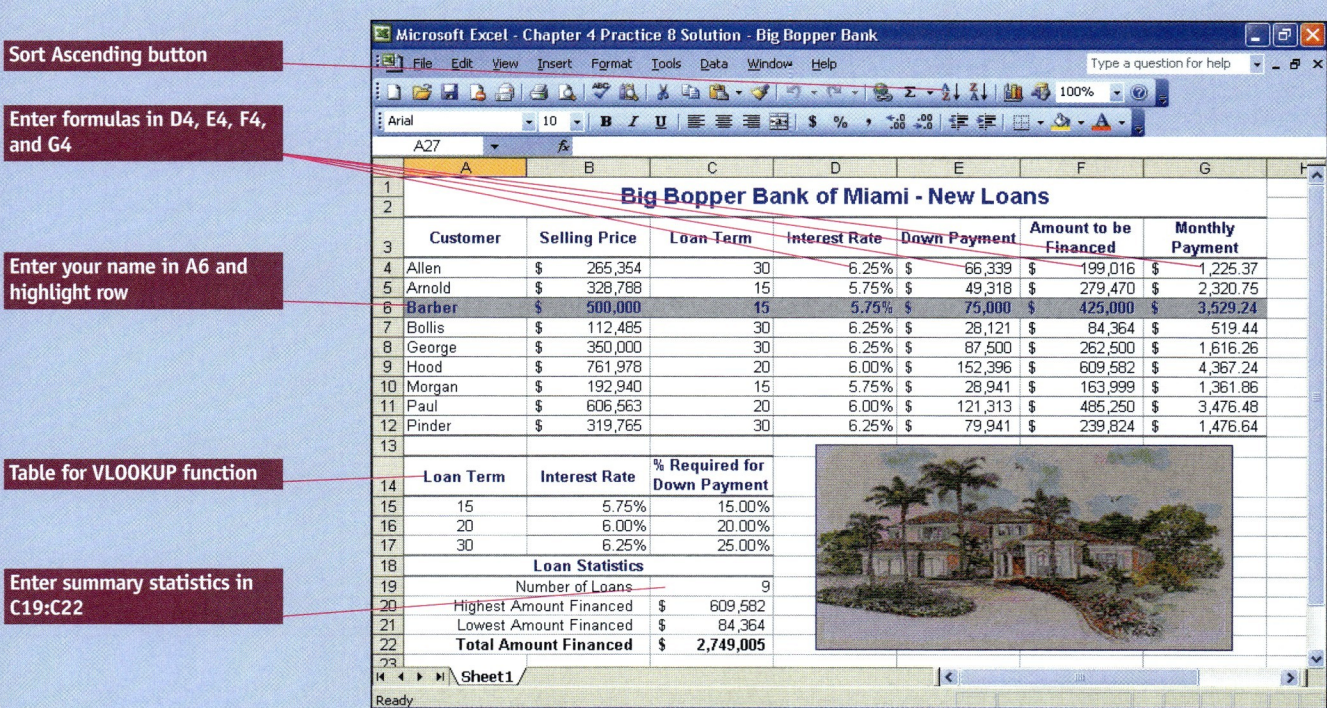

FIGURE 4.24 Big Bopper Bank (exercise 8)

MICROSOFT OFFICE EXCEL 2003 REVISED

practice exercises

9. **Nested IFs and Other Functions:** Figure 4.25 displays a modified version of the expanded grade book that illustrates a variety of Excel functions that are used individually and in conjunction with one another. This is a challenging exercise that introduces additional functions that were not covered in the chapter. Open the partially completed workbook in *Chapter 4 Practice 9*, then proceed as follows:

   a. Click in cell A4 (not shown in Figure 4.25), pull down the Window menu, and click the Freeze Panes command so that the first three rows are always visible.

   b. The professor has decided to give students a break and drop the lowest test grade if the student has taken all five exams. Click in cell G4 and enter the formula to compute the student's test average and drop the lowest grade if the student has taken all five exams.

   c. The professor gives his students a second break by rounding the computed average. (Alex Pons, for example, would get a C rather than a B if his average were not rounded.) Click in Cell H4 and enter the function =ROUND(G4,0). (The zero indicates the number of decimal places in the rounded number.)

   d. Students are allowed to take the course for credit only and thus the formula to compute the semester grade must determine whether the student elected this option, and if so, whether the student has passed. Click in cell J4 and enter the formula =IF(I4="Yes", IF(H4>=$H$27, "Pass", "F"), VLOOKUP(H4,$G$22:$H$26,2)).

   e. Use the Rank function to determine each student's rank in class according to the computed value of his or her semester average. (Use Help to learn how to enter the Rank function.)

   f. Copy the formulas in row four to the remaining rows in the worksheet.

   g. Compute the summary statistics for each exam as shown in rows 21 through 25.

   h. Use the COUNTIF function to determine the grade distribution. The entry in cell K22, for example, is COUNTIF($J$4:$J$19,"=F"). (Use Help if you need more information.)

   i. Format the worksheet in attractive fashion. You do not have to duplicate our formatting exactly, but you are required to use conditional formatting to display grades of A and F in blue and red, respectively.

   j. Print the completed worksheet to show both displayed values and cell formulas.

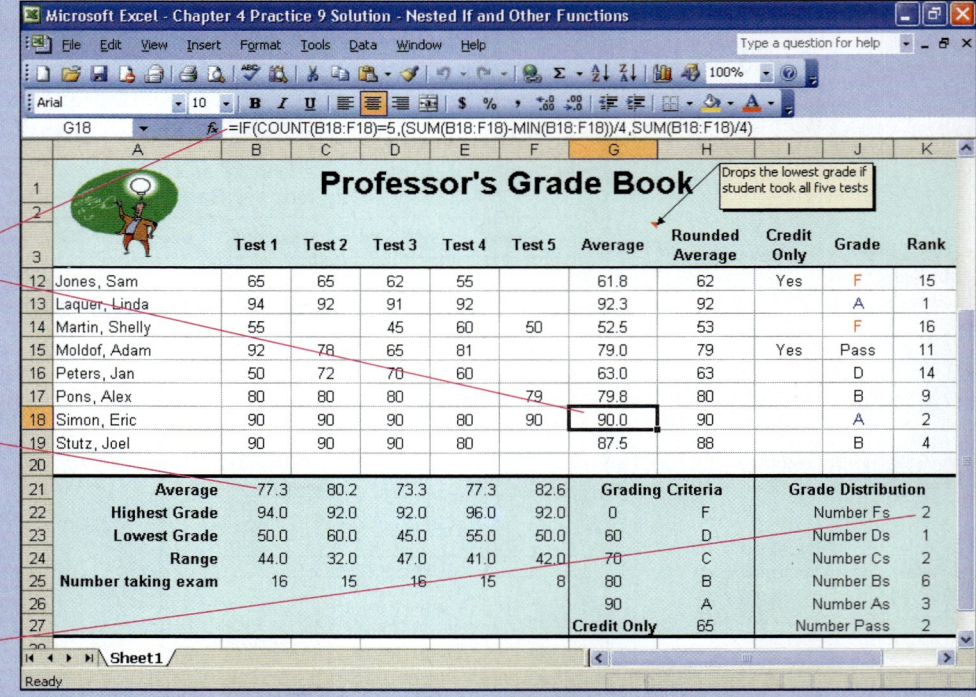

FIGURE 4.25 Nested IFs and Other Functions (exercise 9)

222 CHAPTER 4: USING SPREADSHEETS IN DECISION MAKING

practice exercises

10. **Election 2004:** The election has come and gone, but it is interesting to analyze the results of both the popular and electoral votes as shown in Figure 4.26. You will find a partially completed version of this figure in the file, *Chapter 4 Practice 10—Election 2004*. Open the workbook and proceed as follows:

    a. Enter an appropriate IF function in cells D9 and F9 to determine the number of electoral votes for each candidate. The electoral votes are awarded on an all-or-nothing basis; that is, the candidate with the larger popular vote wins all of that state's electoral votes. The other candidate gets zero votes. (Pull down the Tools menu, click the Options command, click the View tab, and then clear the box to display zero values.)

    b. Copy the entries in cells D9 and F9 to the remaining rows in the respective columns. Format these columns to display red and blue values, for Mr. Bush and Mr. Kerry, respectively.

    c. Enter a formula into cell G9 to determine the difference in the popular vote between the two candidates. The result should always appear as a positive number. You can do this in one of two ways: by using either an absolute value function or an appropriate IF function. Copy this formula to the remaining rows in the column.

    d. Click in cell H9 and determine the percentage differential in the popular vote. This is the difference in the number of votes, divided by the total number of votes.

    e. Enter the appropriate SUM functions in cells B4, B5, C4, and C5 to determine the electoral and popular vote totals for each candidate.

    f. Use the Insert Picture command to add an appropriate clip art image.

    g. Add your name as indicated. Use the Page Setup command to reduce the top and bottom margins to three quarters of an inch and to ensure that the worksheet fits on one page. Adjust the column widths as necessary. Create a custom footer that shows the date and time the worksheet was printed. Print the displayed values, then print the worksheet a second time to show the cell formulas.

    h. Use the Sort command to display the states in a different sequence, such as the smallest (or largest) vote differential. Print the worksheet in this sequence. Add a title page and submit the completed assignment to your instructor.

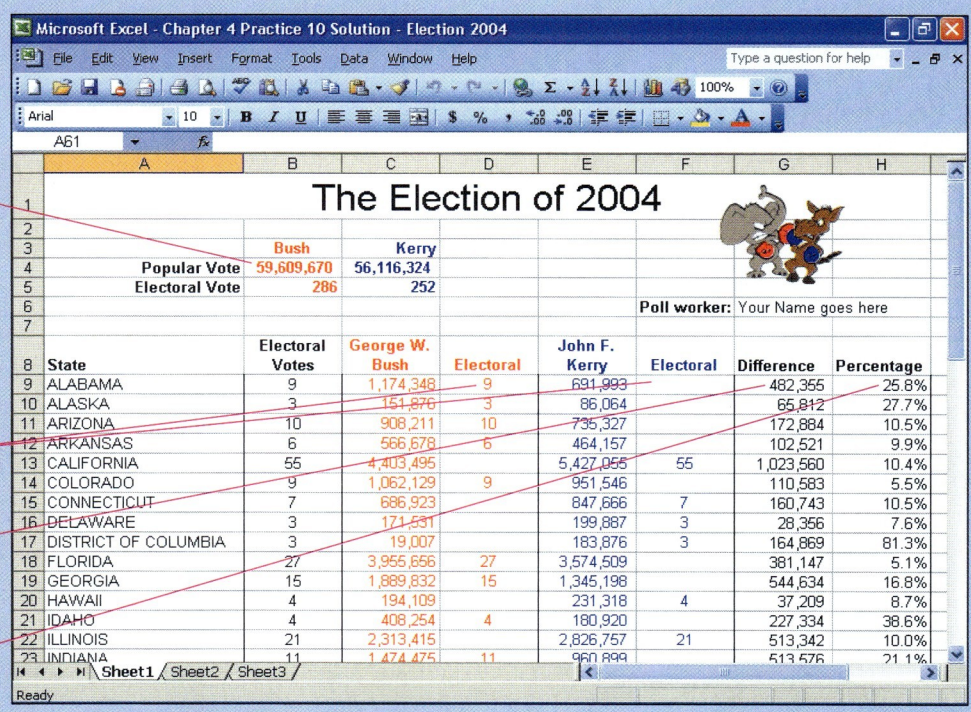

FIGURE 4.26 Election 2004 (exercise 10)

MICROSOFT OFFICE EXCEL 2003 REVISED

practice exercises

11. **The Shopping Mall:** The worksheet in Figure 4.27 displays leasing information for stores in a shopping mall. The data for each store includes the occupancy date, the duration of the lease, and the number of square feet in the store. The assumption area at the bottom of the worksheet contains a table that determines the annual price per square foot (the longer the lease, the cheaper the cost). There are additional adjustments for large stores (a $1.50 reduction in the price per square foot) and small stores (a $1 increase in the price per square foot). Open the partially completed *Chapter 4 Practice 11—The Shopping Mall* workbook and proceed as follows:

   a. Select cells B3 through B13, pull down the Format menu, click the Cells command to display the Format Cells dialog box, click the Number tab, then choose the appropriate Date format as shown in Figure 4.27.

   b. Click in cell D3 and enter the appropriate formula (as shown in Figure 4.27) to compute the expiration date. The formula may seem complicated, but it adjusts for leap year and it terminates the lease on the exact date; for example, the expiration date for the five-year lease that began on January 1, 2002 is December 31, 2006.

   c. Click in cell F3 and enter the appropriate VLOOKUP function to determine the annual price per square foot, which is based on the length of the lease.

   d. Enter a nested IF function in cell G3 to compute the adjusted price per square foot, given that those stores larger than 2000 square feet pay a reduced rate, while stores smaller than 1200 square feet pay a premium.

   e. Enter the formulas to compute the annual rent (price per square foot times the square footage) and monthly rent in cells H3 and I3, respectively.

   f. Copy the formulas in row three to the remaining rows of the worksheet. Enter the appropriate SUM or AVERAGE functions in row 14.

   g. Format the completed worksheet. You do not have to match our formatting exactly. Insert a clip art image in the upper left of the worksheet.

   h. Print the completed worksheet to show displayed values and cell formulas. Use the Page Setup command to ensure that the worksheet fits on a single page.

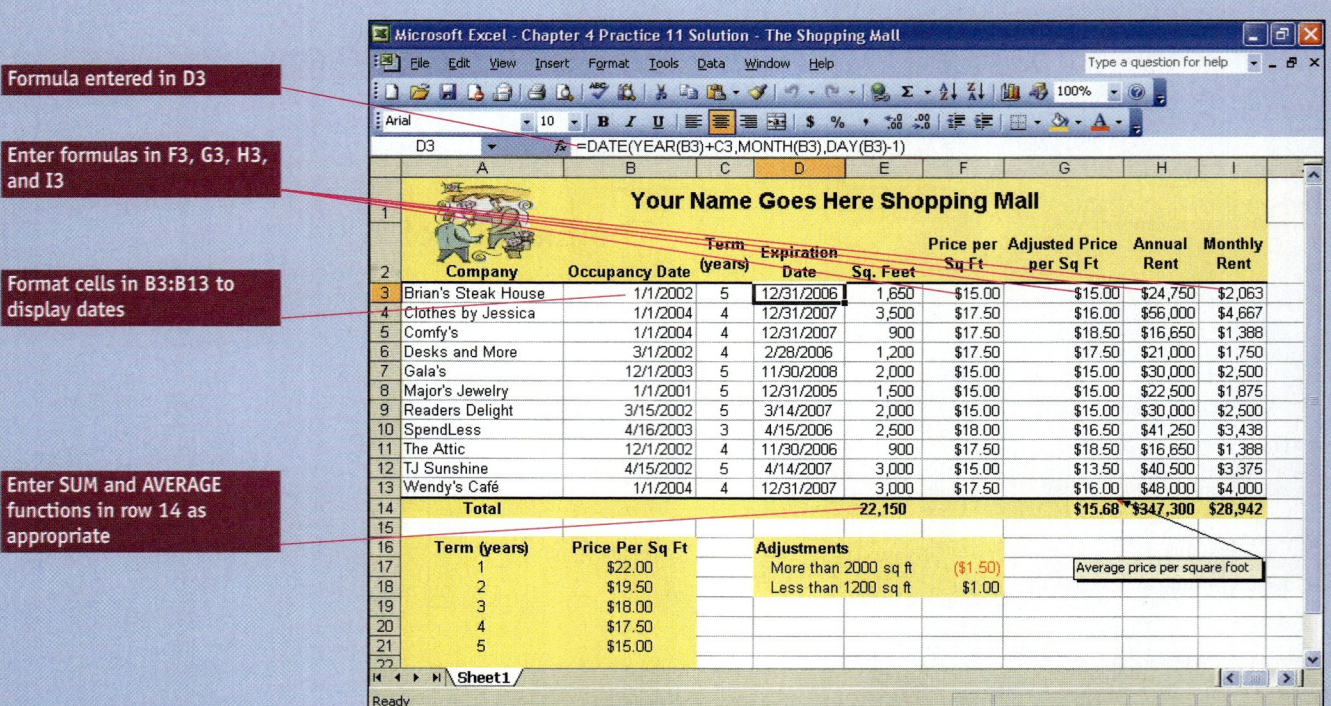

FIGURE 4.27 The Shopping Mall (exercise 11)

practice exercises

12. **Barber Academy:** The worksheet in Figure 4.28 computes the tuition, lunch, insurance, and other fees associated with newly admitted students at an exclusive prep school. The heading information appears at the top of the worksheet, the individual students appear in the middle of the worksheet, and the assumptions and summary calculations appear at the bottom. (This is a large worksheet and hence not all of the students are visible at one time.) Open the partially completed workbook in *Chapter 4 Practice 12—Barber Academy* and proceed as follows:

   a. Click in cell A4 (not shown in Figure 4.28), pull down the Window menu, and click the Freeze Panes command so that the first three rows are always visible.

   b. Click in cell C4 and enter the appropriate VLOOKUP function to compute the tuition. Click in cell D4 and enter a second VLOOKUP function to compute the associated cost for lunch. Use a third VLOOKUP function in cell E4 to compute the insurance premium, which is applied to just the tuition. The tuition, lunch fee, and insurance all depend on the level of school in which the student is enrolling, as shown by the table in the assumption area.

   c. Click in cell H4 and enter the formula to determine the cost for bus transportation. The formula requires both an IF function and a VLOOKUP function; that is, you have to determine whether the student requests bus service and then you have to calculate the cost of the service based on the distance from school.

   d. Click in cell I4 and compute the total bill for the first student, which includes the tuition, lunch, insurance, and optional bus transportation. Copy the formulas in row four to the remaining rows of the worksheet. Enter the appropriate SUM functions into row 27 to compute the totals for the academy.

   e. Enter the appropriate functions to compute the summary statistics for the academy as a whole in the lower-right portion of the worksheet.

   f. Format the completed worksheet. (You do not have to match our formatting.) Insert a clip art image as you see fit.

   g. Print the completed worksheet to show both displayed values and cell formulas. Be sure the worksheet fits on a single page.

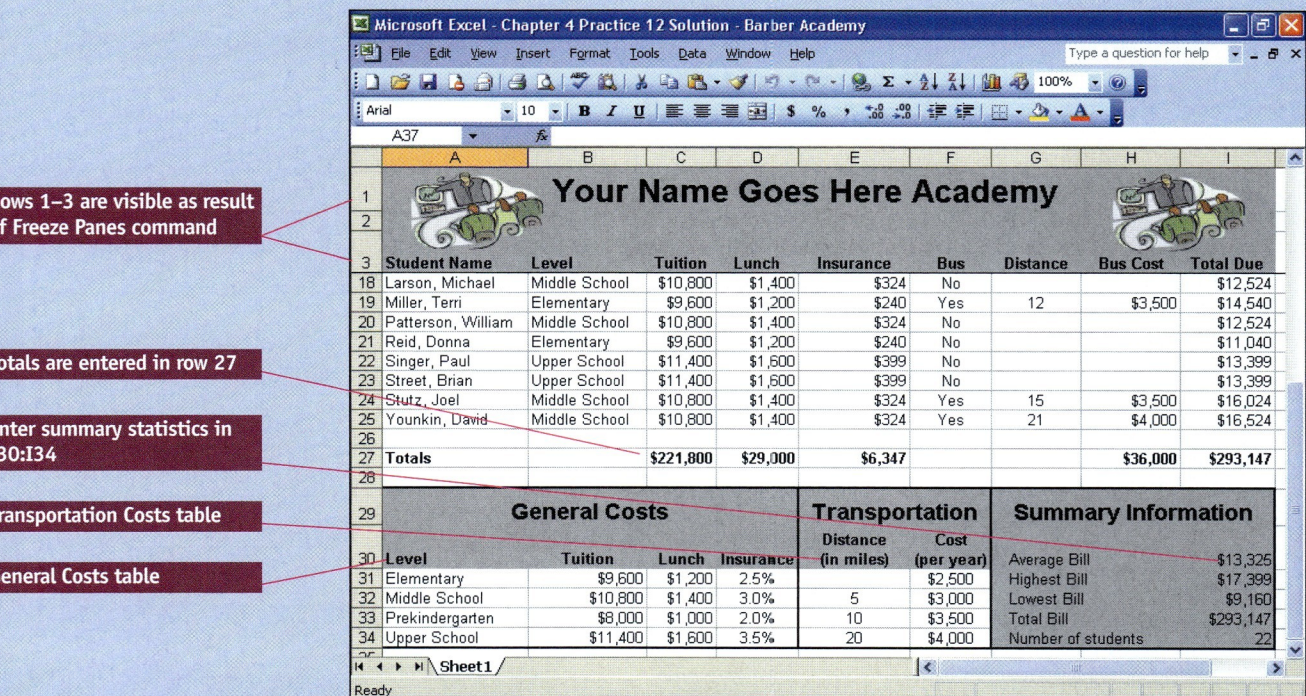

FIGURE 4.28 Barber Academy (exercise 12)

practice exercises

13. **Excel Jeopardy:** How well do you know Microsoft Excel? The presentation in Figure 4.29 contains a Jeopardy game with 25 answers and questions that review material from Chapters 1 through 4. All you have to do is open the presentation and play the game. Thus, open the *Chapter 4 Practice 13—Excel Jeopardy* presentation and proceed as follows:

    a. Pull down the Slide Show menu and click the View Show command (or click the F5 key) to view the slide show, which begins with the title slide. Click the mouse to move to slide 2 (the board). The names of the categories will appear one after another, after which you can select any question in any category. Each dollar amount is a hyperlink to another slide in the presentation.

    b. Select (click) a question, such as the $400 question in the Excel 101 category, to display the clue, "Used at the beginning of every formula". Click the mouse to display the answer "What is an equal sign?" (that appears in the form of a question), then click the answer to return to slide 2 (the board). Before you click, be sure you see the tiny hand indicating that you are clicking the hyperlink, as opposed to clicking the background of the slide.

    c. You should be back on slide 2, the Jeopardy board. Look closely and you will see that the color of the text (i.e., the 400) has changed, indicating that the hyperlink has been followed. Select a different question, view the answer, and return to the game board so that you can be sure of the navigation.

    d. Select a classmate and play the game. There is no buzzer, so you have to determine an equitable way to gain control of the board and keep score. We leave the details to you.

    e. Print the presentation in a variety of ways. Select the first two slides, pull down the File menu, click the Print command, choose the option button for Selection, and select Slides in the Print What list box. Click OK to print. Pull down the Print menu a second time and print the entire presentation in Outline view. Study the outline and be sure that you can answer all of the questions.

    f. You will find additional games for the other Office applications (Word, PowerPoint, and Access) in the appropriate folders after downloading the practice files from our Web site. The Word game, for example, is found in the Exploring Word folder and reviews material from Chapters 1 through 4 in the Word section.

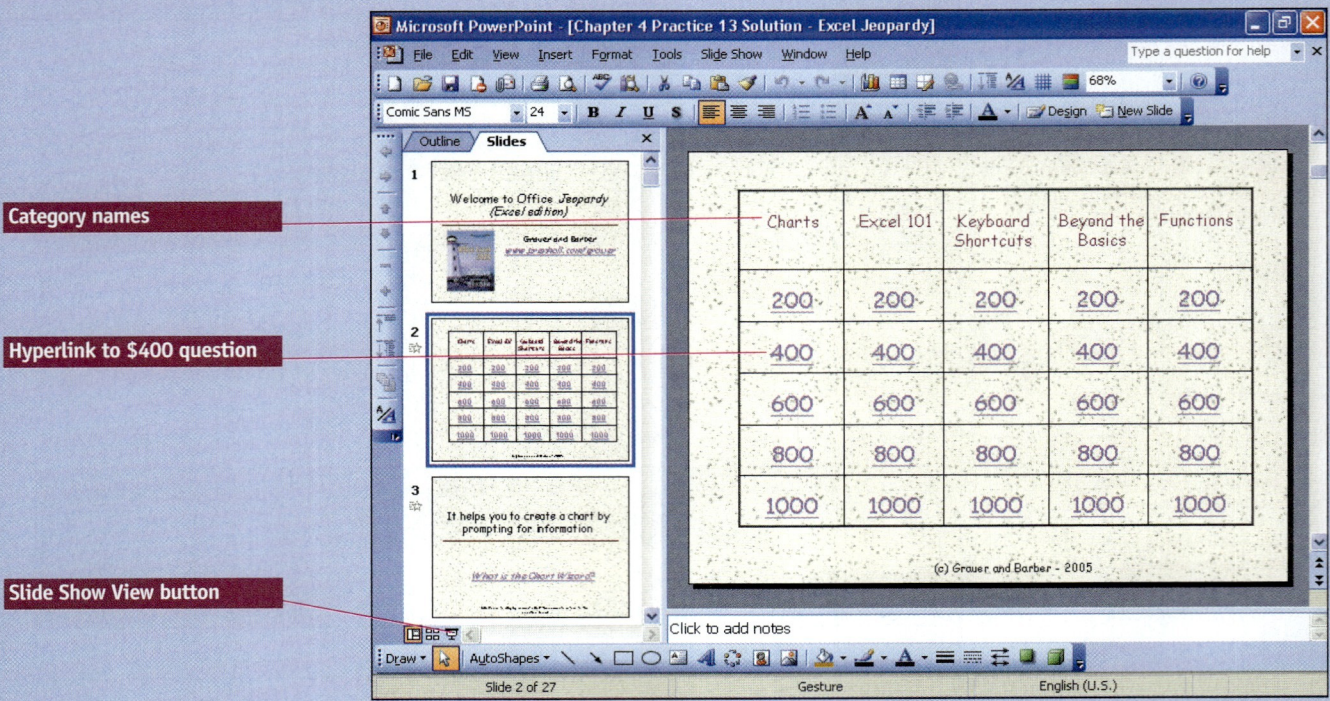

FIGURE 4.29 Excel Jeopardy (exercise 13)

MINI CASES

The Financial Consultant

A friend of yours is in the process of buying a home and has asked you to compare the payments and total interest on a 15- and 30-year loan at varying interest rates. You have decided to analyze the loans in Excel, and then incorporate the results into a memo written in Microsoft Word. As of now, the principal is $150,000, but it is very likely that your friend will change his mind several times, and so you want to use the linking and embedding capability within Windows to dynamically link the worksheet to the word processing document. Your memo should include a letterhead that takes advantage of the formatting capabilities within Word; a graphic logo would be a nice touch.

Fun with the If Statement

Open the *Chapter 4 Mini Case—Fun with the If Statement* workbook in the Exploring Excel folder, then follow the directions in the worksheet to view a hidden message. The message is displayed by various If statements scattered throughout the worksheet, but the worksheet is protected so that you cannot see these formulas. (Use Help to see how to protect a worksheet.) We made it easy for you, however, because you can unprotect the worksheet since a password is not required. Once the worksheet is unprotected, pull down the Format menu, click the Cells command, click the Protection tab, and clear the Hidden check box. Prove to your professor that you have done this successfully, by changing the text of our message. Print the completed worksheet to show both displayed values and cell formulas.

The Lottery

Many states raise money through lotteries that advertise prizes of several million dollars. In reality, however, the actual value of the prize is considerably less than the advertised value, although the winners almost certainly do not care. One state, for example, recently offered a twenty million dollar prize that was to be distributed in twenty annual payments of one million dollars each. How much was the prize actually worth, assuming a long-term interest rate of five percent? Use the PV (Present Value) function to determine the answer. What is the effect on the answer if payments to the recipient are made at the beginning of each year, rather than at the end of each year?

A Penny a Day

What if you had a rich uncle who offered to pay you "a penny a day," and then double your salary each day for the next month? It does not sound very generous, but you will be surprised at how quickly the amount grows. Create a simple worksheet that enables you to use the Goal Seek command to answer the following questions. On what day of the month (if any) will your uncle pay you more than one million dollars? How much money will your uncle pay you on the 31st day?

The Rule of 72

Delaying your IRA for one year can cost you as much as $64,000 at retirement, depending on when you begin. That may be hard to believe, but you can check the numbers without a calculator, using the "Rule of 72." This financial rule of thumb states that to find out how long it takes money to double, divide the number 72 by the interest rate; for example, money earning 8% annually will double in approximately 9 years (72 divided by 8). The money doubles again in 18 years, again in 27 years, and so on. Now assume that you start your IRA at age 21, rather than 20, effectively losing 45 years of compound interest for the initial contribution. Use the rule of 72 to determine approximately how much you will lose, assuming an 8% rate of return. Check your calculation by creating a worksheet to determine the exact amount.

mini cases

Study Break—Excel Crossword Puzzle

We enjoy a good puzzle and with that in mind, we have created a unique crossword puzzle that reviews the material from Chapters 1 to 4. Many of the clues are taken from the end-of-chapter list of key terms and concepts, but additional clues come from elsewhere in the chapter. Open the *Chapter 4 Mini Case—Excel Crossword Puzzle* Word document in the Exploring Excel folder, give yourself one hour, and do your best to complete the puzzle. Add your name at the top of the page, and submit the puzzle to your instructor. Our students find this exercise to be an excellent review for an exam.

Signs of the Zodiac

Many people look forward to reading their daily horoscope, which is based on the sign under which they were born. Your assignment is to open the partially completed *Chapter 4 Mini Case—Signs of the Zodiac* workbook, enter your name and birthday into cells C3 and C4, then enter the appropriate formulas into cell C5 and C6 to compute your age and astrological sign. The latter requires a VLOOKUP function that uses your birth date as an argument to search a table that contains the signs of the Zodiac and the appropriate dates. We have done the 'hard part' for you by creating the table; all you have to do is develop the appropriate VLOOKUP function. Print the completed spreadsheet two ways, once to show displayed values, and once to show the cell formulas. Try to explain how the VLOOKUP function works and how the various breakpoints are entered as specific dates, which in turn requires knowledge of the DATE and YEAR functions within Excel. Complete the spreadsheet by adding a hyperlink to a Web site for your horoscope.

Chapter Recap—Vacation Time

Emily Knight is the office manager for a regional office of a large, multinational corporation. As office manager, she handles some extremely confidential employee information, including Social Security number, salary, and bonus information. It is also her responsibility to monitor the amount of vacation time each employee has accrued, and how much of that they have used thus far this year.

The Human Resources department has asked Emily to prepare a worksheet for a selected set of employees that will show the weeks of vacation granted to each employee, the number of days already used, and the number of days remaining. The amount of vacation is based on the employee's years of service, which changes continually; that is, the worksheet must reference today's date when computing the amount of vacation time. The worksheet should also contain summary statistics for the group of employees that shows the average number of days used, as well as the maximum and minimum number of days remaining. Your predecessor began the worksheet but left unexpectedly. Emily has asked you to step in and complete the worksheet as quickly as possible.

Your assignment is to review the chapter, paying special attention to Hands-on Exercise 3, which describes the use of statistical and logical functions. You will then open the *Chapter 4 Ending Case Study—Vacation Time* workbook, which contains the employee data for the regional sales office, and complete the worksheet. Use the VLOOKUP function to determine the vacation time for each employee by referencing the table at the bottom of the worksheet. You will also need the IF function to display the number of days remaining. And finally, you will have to enter the formulas for the summary statistics table at the bottom of the worksheet. Print the completed worksheet for your instructor. Print the worksheet twice to show both displayed values and cell formulas. Use the Page Setup command to create a custom footer that contains your name.

CHAPTER 5

Consolidating Data:
Worksheet References and File Linking

OBJECTIVES

After reading this chapter you will:

1. Describe two ways to consolidate data from multiple workbooks.
2. Distinguish between a cell reference and a worksheet reference.
3. Select multiple worksheets to enter common formulas and formatting.
4. Use the AutoFormat command.
5. Explain the advantage of using a function rather than a formula to consolidate data.
6. Create a documentation worksheet.
7. Use a workbook reference to link one workbook to another.

hands-on exercises

1. COPYING WORKSHEETS
   Input: Atlanta, Boston, and Chicago (three workbooks)
   Output: Corporate Sales

2. WORKSHEET REFERENCES
   Input: Corporate Sales workbook (from exercise 1)
   Output: Corporate Sales (with additional modifications)

3. THE DOCUMENTATION WORKSHEET
   Input: Corporate Sales workbook (from exercise 2)
   Output: Corporate Sales (with additional modifications)

4. LINKING WORKBOOKS
   Input: Atlanta, Boston, and Chicago (three workbooks)
   Output: Corporate Links

CASE STUDY
TASTY TREATS

The Tasty Treats Ice Cream Shoppe offers old-fashioned, homemade ice cream in a comfortable setting that has a strong appeal to young families. The first store was opened three years ago in Coral Springs, Florida. Everyone loves ice cream, and the store was an instant hit. Two other stores in other South Florida communities quickly followed, both with similar success.

Joe Pascale, the owner of Tasty Treats, has received an unsolicited offer to sell the three stores. Joe has bigger plans, however, and wants to expand further before selling out at what he hopes will be a much better price. He knows that he needs to evaluate the overall performance of the chain before opening additional stores, and thus he is especially interested in the comparative results of the various ice cream products he sells.

Joe knows you are studying Excel at the local college and he has asked for your help in return for a small stipend and all the ice cream you can eat. Each store manager has entered the sales data for last year in a separate workbook. Your task is to consolidate the data into a single workbook that shows the total sales for each quarter and each ice cream category. The information should be shown in spreadsheet as well as graphical form.

Your assignment is to read the chapter, paying special attention to the two different ways in which to consolidate data. You can use either technique for the solution; that is, you can create a summary workbook with multiple worksheets, or you can create a summary workbook that links to the individual workbooks. In any event, start with the partially completed *Chapter 5 Case Study—Tasty Treats Summary* workbook in the Exploring Excel folder. Data for the individual stores (Coral Springs, Bay Heights, and Key West) is found in three additional workbooks in the same folder. Print the completed summary workbook for your instructor to show both displayed values and cell formulas. Print the associated chart as well.

CONSOLIDATING DATA

Assume that you are the marketing manager for a national corporation with offices in several cities. Each branch manager reports to you on a quarterly basis, providing information about each product sold in his or her office. Your job is to consolidate the data into a single report. The situation is depicted graphically in Figure 5.1. Figures 5.1a, 5.1b, and 5.1c show reports for the Atlanta, Boston, and Chicago offices, respectively. Figure 5.1d shows the summary report for the corporation.

Atlanta Office

	Qtr 1	Qtr 2	Qtr 3	Qtr 4
Product 1	$10	$20	$30	$40
Product 2	$1,100	$1,200	$1,300	$1,400
Product 3	$200	$200	$300	$400

(a) Atlanta Data

Boston Office

	Qtr 1	Qtr 2	Qtr 3	Qtr 4
Product 1	$55	$25	$35	$45
Product 2	$150	$250	$350	$450
Product 3	$1,150	$1,250	$1,350	$1,400

(b) Boston Data

Chicago Office

	Qtr 1	Qtr 2	Qtr 3	Qtr 4
Product 1	$850	$950	$1,050	$1,150
Product 2	$100	$0	$300	$400
Product 3	$75	$150	$100	$200

(c) Chicago Data

Corporate Totals

	Qtr 1	Qtr 2	Qtr 3	Qtr 4
Product 1	$915	$995	$1,115	$1,235
Product 2	$1,350	$1,450	$1,950	$2,250
Product 3	$1,425	$1,600	$1,750	$2,000

(d) Corporate Summary

FIGURE 5.1 Consolidating Data

You should be able to reconcile the corporate totals for each product in each quarter with the detail amounts in the individual offices. Consider, for example, the sales of Product 1 in the first quarter. The Atlanta office has sold $10, the Boston office $55, and the Chicago office $850; thus, the corporation as a whole has sold $915 ($10+$55+$850). In similar fashion, the Atlanta, Boston, and Chicago offices have sold $1,100, $150, and $100, respectively, of Product 2 in the first quarter, for a corporate total of $1,350.

The chapter presents two approaches to computing the corporate totals in Figure 5.1. One approach is to use the three-dimensional capability within Excel, in which one workbook contains multiple worksheets. The workbook contains a separate worksheet for each of the three branch offices, and a fourth worksheet to hold the corporate data. An alternate technique is to keep the data for each branch office in its own workbook, then create a summary workbook that uses file linking to reference cells in the other workbooks.

There are advantages and disadvantages to each technique, as will be discussed in the chapter. As always, the hands-on exercises are essential to mastering the conceptual material.

THE THREE-DIMENSIONAL WORKBOOK

An Excel workbook is the electronic equivalent of the three-ring loose-leaf binder. It contains one or more worksheets, each of which is identified by a worksheet tab at the bottom of the document window. The workbook in Figure 5.2, for example, contains four worksheets. The title bar displays the name of the workbook (Corporate Sales). The tabs at the bottom of the workbook window display the names of the individual worksheets (Summary, Atlanta, Boston, and Chicago). The highlighted tab indicates the name of the active worksheet (Summary). To display a different worksheet, click on a different tab; for example, click the Atlanta tab to display the Atlanta worksheet.

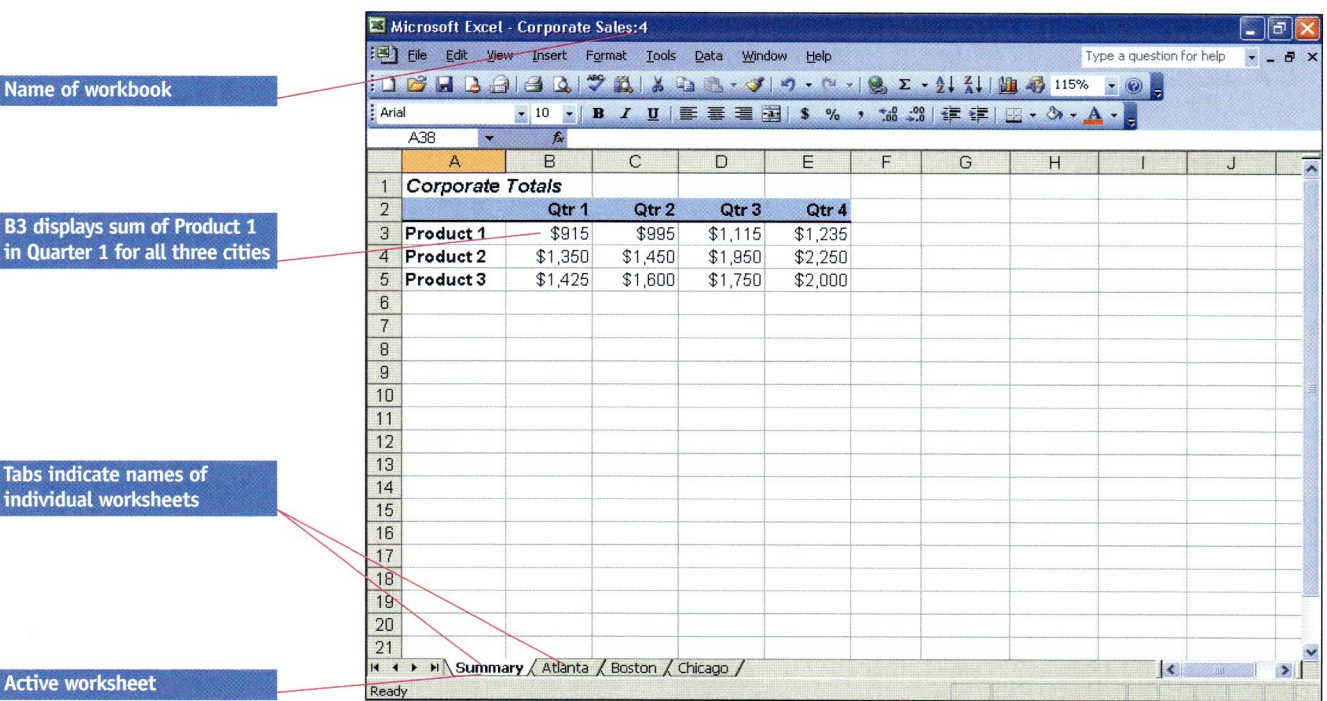

FIGURE 5.2   A Three-dimensional Workbook

The Summary worksheet shows the total amount for each product in each quarter. The data in the worksheet reflects the amounts shown earlier in Figure 5.1; that is, each entry in the Summary worksheet represents the sum of the corresponding entries in the worksheets for the individual cities. The amounts in the individual cities, however, are not visible in Figure 5.2. It is convenient, therefore, to open multiple windows to view the individual city worksheets at the same time you view the summary sheet.

Figure 5.3 displays the four worksheets in the Corporate Sales workbook, with a different sheet displayed in each window. The individual windows are smaller than the single view in Figure 5.2, but you can see at a glance how the Summary worksheet consolidates the data from the individual worksheets. The **New Window command** (in the Window menu) is used to open each additional window. Once the windows have been opened, the **Arrange command** (in the Window menu) is used to tile or cascade the open windows.

Only one window can be active at a time, and all commands apply to just the active window. In Figure 5.3, for example, the window in the upper left is active, as can be seen by the highlighted title bar. (To activate a different window, just click in that window.)

Copying Worksheets

The workbook in Figure 5.3 summarizes the data in the individual worksheets, but how was the data placed into the workbook? You could, of course, manually type in the entries, but there is an easier way, given that each branch manager sends you a workbook with the data for his or her office. All you have to do is copy the data from the individual workbooks into the appropriate worksheets in a new corporate workbook. (The specifics for how this is done are explained in detail in a hands-on exercise.)

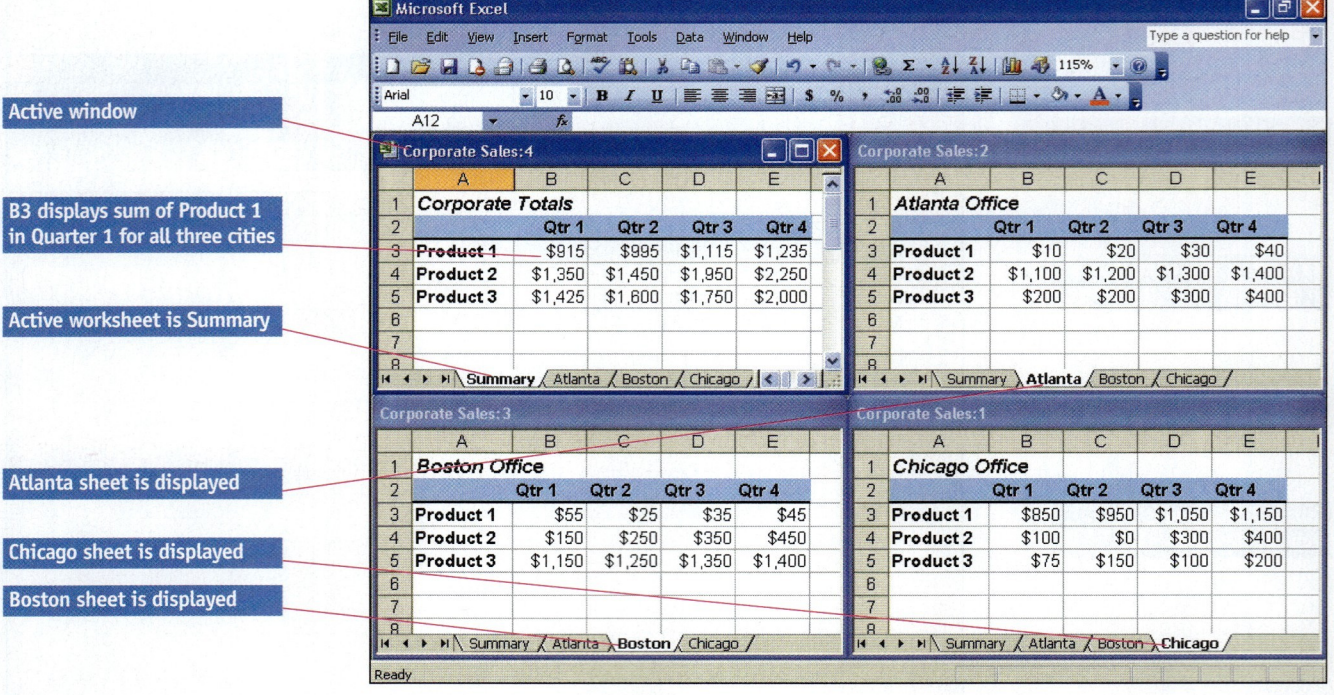

FIGURE 5.3   Multiple Worksheets

Multiple Workbooks

Consider now Figure 5.4, which at first glance appears to be almost identical to Figure 5.3. The two figures are very different, however. Figure 5.3 displayed four different worksheets from the same workbook. Figure 5.4, on the other hand, displays four different workbooks. There is one workbook for each city (Atlanta, Boston, and Chicago) and each of these workbooks contains only a single worksheet. The fourth workbook, Corporate Sales, contains four worksheets (Atlanta, Boston, Chicago, and Summary) and is the workbook displayed in Figure 5.3.

There are advantages and disadvantages to each technique. The single workbook in Figure 5.3 is easier for the manager in that he or she has all of the data in one file. The disadvantage is that the worksheets have to be maintained by multiple people (the manager in each city), and this can lead to confusion in that several individuals require access to the same workbook. The multiple workbooks of Figure 5.4 facilitate the maintenance of the data, but four separate files are required to produce the summary information. Both approaches are explored in detail within the chapter. The choice is up to you.

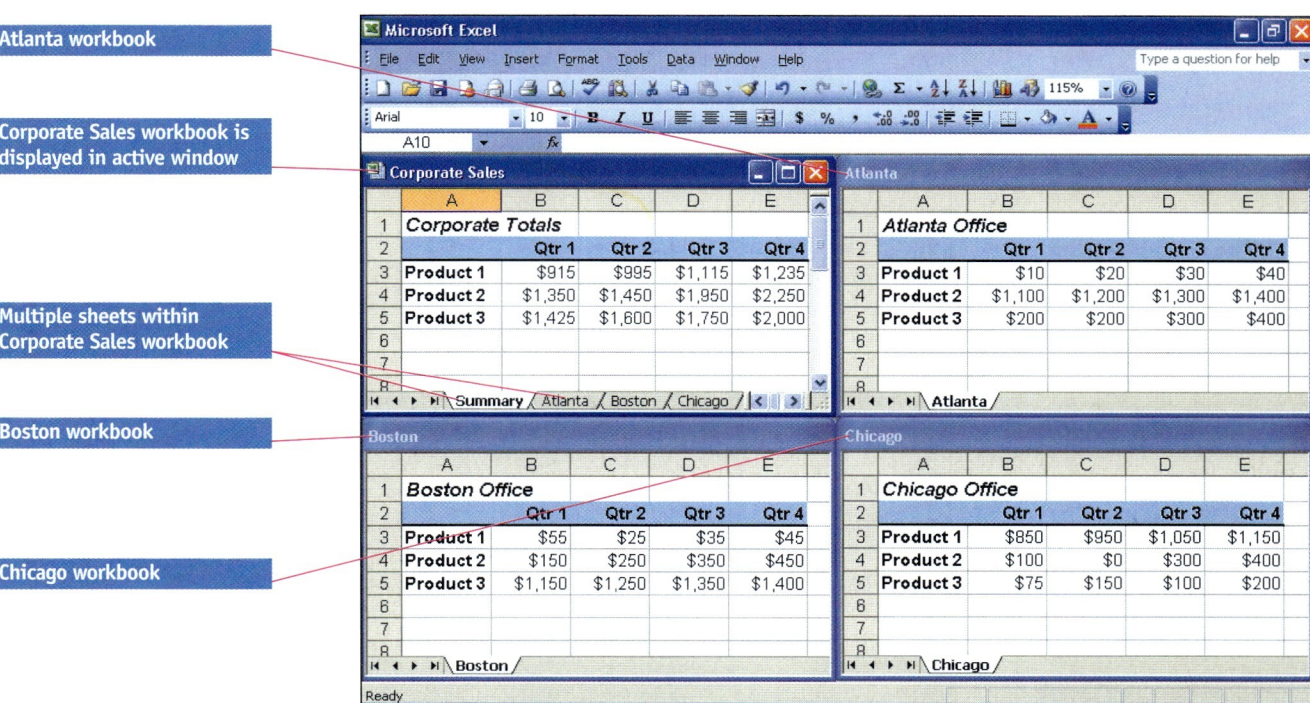

FIGURE 5.4   Multiple Workbooks

THE HORIZONTAL SCROLL BAR

The horizontal scroll bar contains four scrolling buttons to scroll through the worksheet tabs in a workbook. (The default workbook has three worksheets.) Click ◀ or ▶ to scroll one tab to the left or right. Click ◀◀ or ▶▶ to scroll to the first or last tab in the workbook. Once the desired tab is visible, click the tab to select it. The number of tabs that are visible simultaneously depends on the setting of the horizontal scroll bar; that is, you can drag the tab split bar to change the number of tabs that can be seen at one time.

hands-on exercise

1 Copying Worksheets

Objective To open multiple workbooks; to use the Windows Arrange command to tile the open workbooks; to copy a worksheet from one workbook to another. Use Figure 5.5 as a guide in the exercise.

Step 1: **Open a New Workbook**

- Start Excel. Close the task pane if it is open. If necessary, click the **New button** on the Standard toolbar to open a new workbook as shown in Figure 5.5a.

- Delete all worksheets except for Sheet1:
  - Click the tab for **Sheet2**. Press the **Shift key** as you click the tab for **Sheet3**.
  - Point to the tab for **Sheet3** and click the **right mouse button** to display a shortcut menu. Click **Delete**.

- The workbook should contain only Sheet1 as shown in Figure 5.5a. Save the workbook as **Corporate Sales** in the **Exploring Excel folder**.

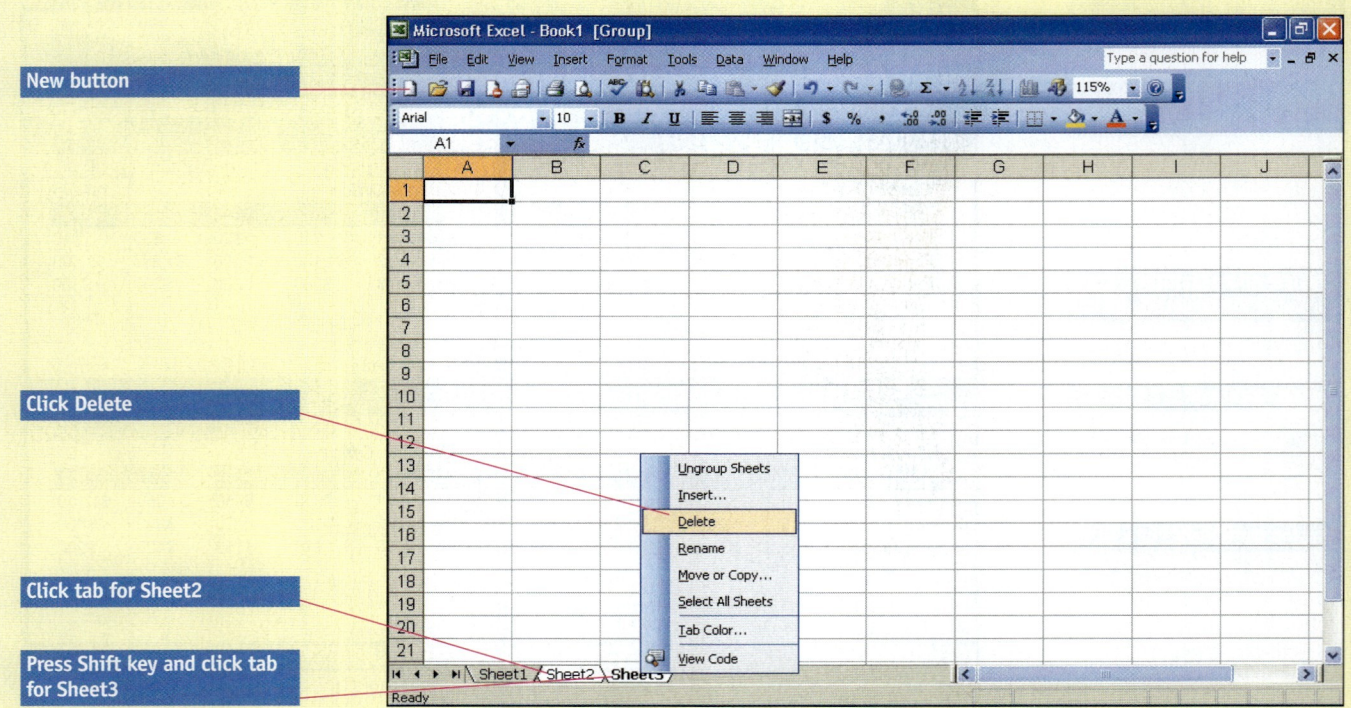

(a) Open a New Workbook (step 1)

FIGURE 5.5 Hands-on Exercise 1

THE RIGHT MOUSE BUTTON

Point to any object, then click the right mouse button to display a context-sensitive menu with commands appropriate to the item you are pointing to. Right clicking a cell, for example, displays a menu with selected commands from the Edit, Insert, and Format menus. Right clicking a toolbar displays a menu that lets you display (hide) additional toolbars. Right clicking a worksheet tab enables you to rename, move, copy, or delete a worksheet.

Step 2: **Open the Individual Workbooks**

- Pull down the **File menu**. Click **Open** to display the Open dialog box. (If necessary, open the Exploring Excel folder.)

- Click the **Atlanta workbook**, then press and hold the **Ctrl key** as you click the **Boston** and **Chicago workbooks** to select all three workbooks at the same time.

- Click **Open** to open the selected workbooks. The workbooks will be opened one after another with a brief message appearing on the status bar as each workbook is opened.

- Pull down the **Window menu**, which should indicate the four open workbooks at the bottom of the menu. Only one of the workbooks is visible at this time.

- Click **Arrange** to display the Arrange Windows dialog box. If necessary, select the **Tiled option**, then click **OK**. You should see four open workbooks as shown in Figure 5.5b. (Do not be concerned if your workbooks are arranged differently from ours.)

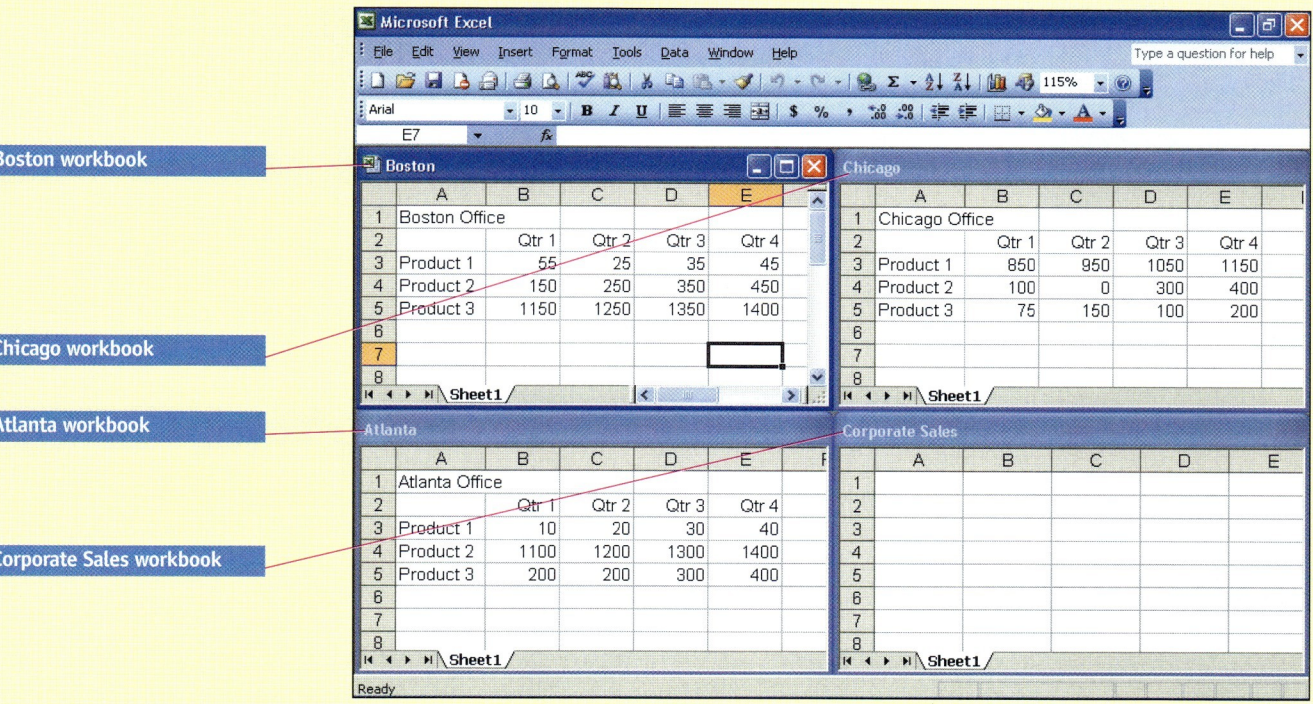

(b) Open the Individual Workbooks (step 2)

FIGURE 5.5   Hands-on Exercise 1 (*continued*)

DOWNLOAD THE PRACTICE FILES (DATA DISK)

The hands-on exercises in the text reference a series of practice files that are downloaded from our Web site. Go to www.prenhall.com/grauer, click the book icon for the series you want, and click the Student Download tab near the top of the window. Select the file you need according to the book you are using. Save the file to your desktop, then double click and follow the onscreen instructions. The installation procedure creates an Exploring Excel folder, which contains the files you need—for example, the Atlanta, Boston, and Chicago workbooks that are required for this exercise.

Step 3: **Copy the Atlanta Data**

- Click in the **Atlanta workbook** to make it the active workbook. Reduce the column widths (if necessary) so that you can see the entire worksheet.
- Click and drag to select **cells A1 through E5** as shown in Figure 5.5c. Pull down the **Edit menu** and click **Copy** (or click the **Copy button**).
- Click in **cell A1** of the **Corporate Sales workbook**.
- Click the **Paste button** on the Standard toolbar to copy the Atlanta data into this workbook. Press **Esc** to remove the moving border from the copy range.
- Point to the **Sheet1 tab** at the bottom of the Corporate Sales worksheet window, then click the **right mouse button** to produce a shortcut menu. Click **Rename**, which selects the worksheet name.
- Type **Atlanta** to replace the existing name and press **Enter**. The worksheet tab has been changed from Sheet1 to Atlanta. Reduce column widths as necessary.
- Click the **Save button** to save the active workbook (Corporate Sales).

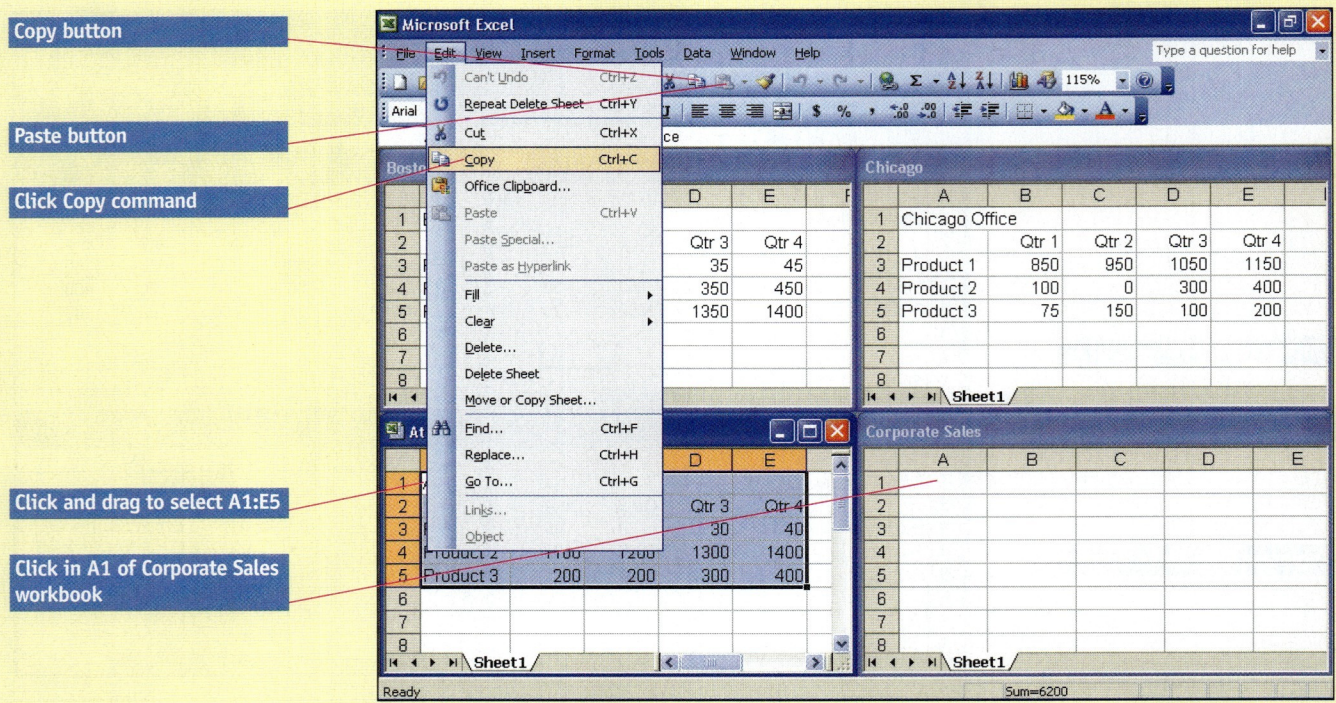

(c) Copy the Atlanta Data (step 3)

FIGURE 5.5 Hands-on Exercise 1 (*continued*)

CHANGE THE ZOOM SETTING

You can increase or decrease the size of a worksheet as it appears on the monitor by clicking the down arrow on the Zoom box and selecting an appropriate percentage. If you are working with a large spreadsheet and cannot see it at one time on the screen, choose a number less than 100%. Conversely, if you find yourself squinting because the numbers are too small, select a percentage larger than 100%. Changing the magnification on the screen does not affect printing; that is, worksheets are printed at 100% unless you change the scaling within the Page Setup command.

Step 4: **Copy the Boston and Chicago Data**

- Click in the **Boston workbook** to make it the active workbook as shown in Figure 5.5d.

- Click the **Sheet1 tab**, then press and hold the **Ctrl key** as you drag the tab to the right of the Atlanta tab in the Corporate Sales workbook. You will see a tiny spreadsheet with a plus sign as you drag the tab. The plus sign indicates that the worksheet is being copied; the ▼ symbol indicates where the worksheet will be placed.

- Release the mouse, then release the Ctrl key. The worksheet from the Boston workbook should have been copied to the Corporate Sales workbook and appears as Sheet1 in that workbook.

- The Boston workbook should still be open; if it isn't, it means that you did not press the Ctrl key as you were dragging the tab to copy the worksheet. If this is the case, pull down the **File menu**, reopen the Boston workbook, and if necessary, tile the open windows.

- Double click the **Sheet1 tab** in the Corporate Sales workbook to rename the tab. Type **Boston** as the new name, then press the **Enter key**.

- The Boston worksheet should appear to the right of the Atlanta worksheet; if the worksheet appears to the left of Atlanta, click and drag the tab to its desired position. (The ▼ symbol indicates where the worksheet will be placed.)

- Repeat the previous steps to copy the Chicago data to the Corporate Sales workbook, placing the new sheet to the right of the Boston sheet. Rename the copied worksheet **Chicago**.

- Save the Corporate Sales workbook. (The Summary worksheet will be built in the next exercise.)

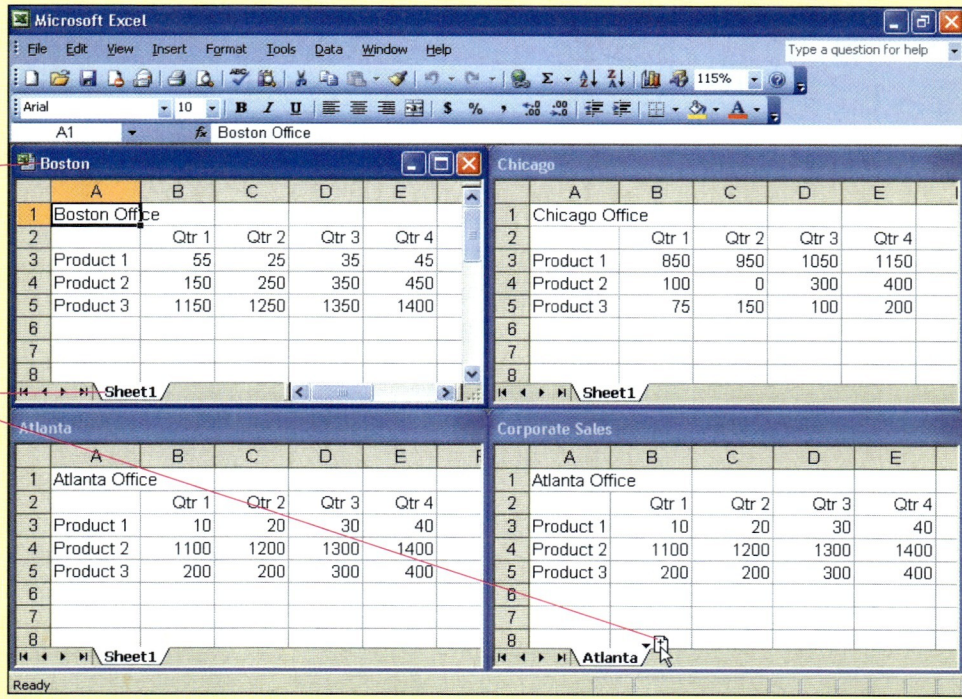

(d) Copy the Boston and Chicago Data (step 4)

FIGURE 5.5 Hands-on Exercise 1 (*continued*)

Step 5: **The Corporate Sales Workbook**

- Check that the Corporate Sales workbook is the active workbook. Click the **Maximize button** so that this workbook takes the entire screen.
- The Corporate Sales workbook contains three worksheets, one for each city, as can be seen in Figure 5.5e.
- Click the **Atlanta tab** to display the worksheet for Atlanta.
- Click the **Boston tab** to display the worksheet for Boston.
- Click the **Chicago tab** to display the worksheet for Chicago.
- Close all of the open workbooks, saving changes if requested to do so.
- Exit Excel if you do not want to continue with the next hands-on exercise at this time.

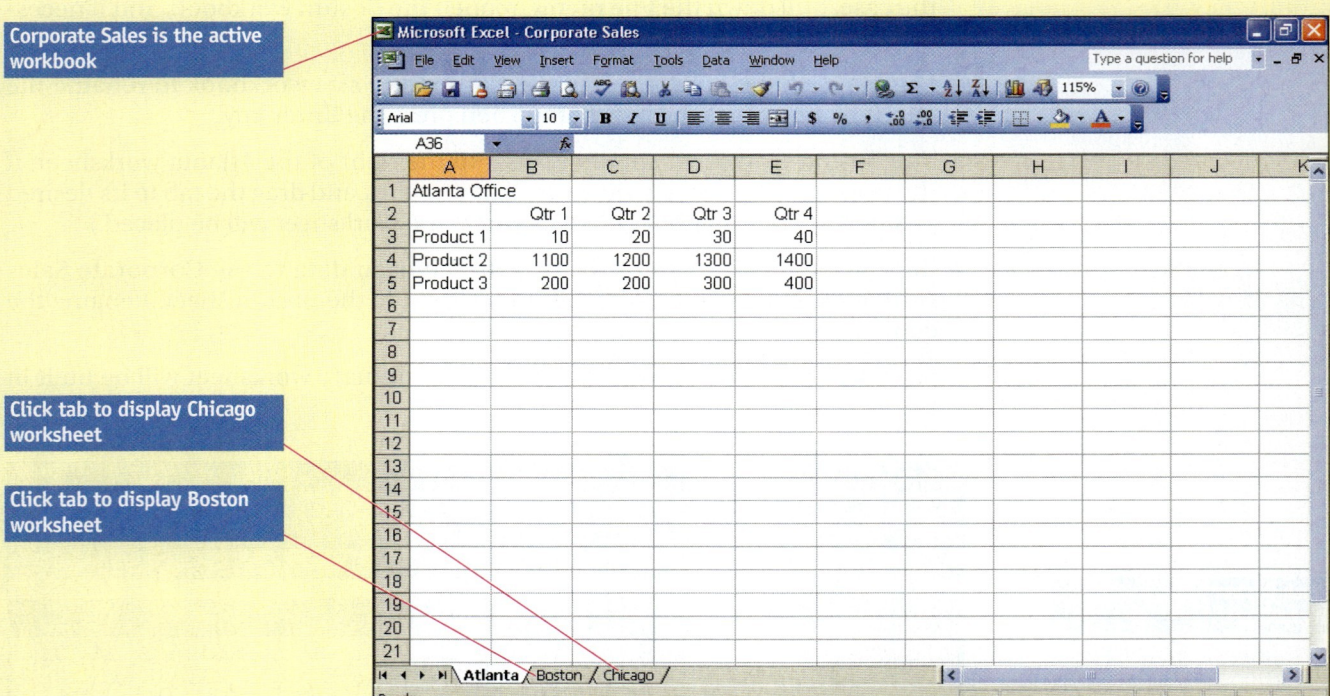

(e) The Corporate Sales Workbook (step 5)

FIGURE 5.5 Hands-on Exercise 1 (*continued*)

MOVING AND COPYING WORKSHEETS

You can move or copy a worksheet within a workbook by dragging its tab. To move a worksheet, click its tab, then drag the tab to the new location (a black triangle shows where the new sheet will go). To copy a worksheet, click its tab, then press and hold the Ctrl key as you drag the tab to its new location. The copied worksheet will have the same name as the original worksheet, followed by a number in parentheses indicating the copy number. Add color to your workbook by changing the color of a worksheet tab. Right click the worksheet tab, click the Tab Color command, select a new color, and click OK.

WORKSHEET REFERENCES

The presence of multiple worksheets in a workbook creates an additional requirement for cell references. You continue to use the same row and column convention when you reference a cell on the current worksheet; that is, cell A1 is still A1. What if, however, you want to reference a cell on another worksheet within the same workbook? It is no longer sufficient to refer to cell A1 because every worksheet has its own cell A1.

To reference a cell (or cell range) in a worksheet other than the current (active) worksheet, you need to preface the cell address with a ***worksheet reference***; for example, Atlanta!A1 references cell A1 in the Atlanta worksheet. A worksheet reference may also be used in conjunction with a cell range—for example, Summary!B2:E5 to reference cells B2 through E5 on the Summary worksheet. Omission of the worksheet reference in either example defaults to the cell reference in the active worksheet.

An exclamation point separates the worksheet reference from the cell reference. The worksheet reference is always an absolute reference. The cell reference can be either relative (e.g., Atlanta!A1 or Summary!B2:E5) or absolute (e.g., Atlanta!$A$1 or Summary!$B$2:$E$5).

Consider how worksheet references are used in the Summary worksheet in Figure 5.6. Each entry in the Summary worksheet computes the sum of the corresponding cells in the Atlanta, Boston, and Chicago worksheets. The cell formula in cell B3, for example, would be entered as follows:

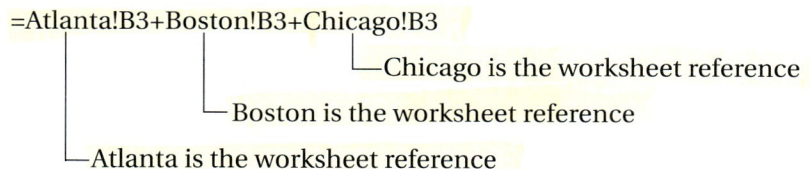

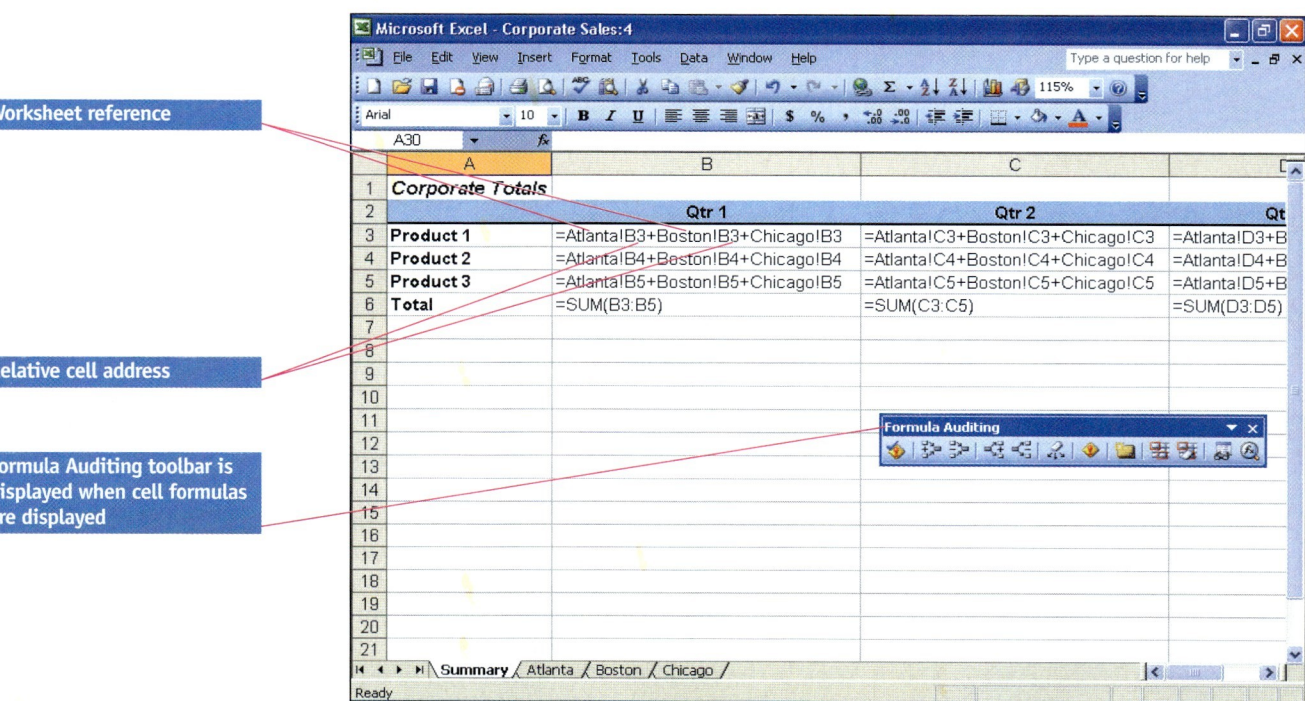

FIGURE 5.6 Worksheet References

The combination of relative cell references and constant worksheet references enables you to enter the formula once (into cell B3), then copy it to the remaining cells in the worksheet. In other words, you enter the formula into cell B3 to compute the total sales for Product 1 in Quarter 1, then you copy that formula to the other cells in row 3 (C3 through E3) to obtain the totals for Product 1 in Quarters 2, 3, and 4. You then copy the entire row (B3 through E3) to rows 4 and 5 (cells B4 through E5) to obtain the totals for Products 2 and 3 in all four quarters.

The proper use of relative and absolute references in the original formula in cell B3 is what makes it possible to copy the cell formulas. Consider, for example, the formula in cell C3 (which was copied from cell B3):

=Atlanta!C3+Boston!C3+Chicago!C3

- Chicago is the worksheet reference
- Boston is the worksheet reference
- Atlanta is the worksheet reference

The worksheet references remain absolute (e.g., Atlanta!) while the cell references adjust for the new location of the formula (cell C3). Similar adjustments are made in all of the other copied formulas.

3-D Reference

A **3-D reference** is a range that spans two or more worksheets in a workbook—for example, =SUM(Atlanta:Chicago!B3) to sum cell B3 in the Atlanta, Boston, and Chicago worksheets. The sheet range is specified with a colon between the beginning and ending sheets. An exclamation point follows the ending sheet, followed by the cell reference. The worksheet references are constant and will not change if the formula is copied. The cell reference may be relative or absolute.

Three-dimensional references can be used in the Summary worksheet as an alternative way to compute the corporate total for each product–quarter combination. To compute the corporate sales for Product 1 in Quarter 1 (which appears in cell B3 of the Summary worksheet), you would use the following function:

=SUM(Atlanta:Chicago!B3)

- Cell reference
- Ending worksheet
- Beginning worksheet

The 3-D reference includes all worksheets between the Atlanta and Chicago worksheets. (Only one additional worksheet, Boston, is present in the example, but the reference would automatically include any additional worksheets that were inserted between Atlanta and Chicago. In similar fashion, it would also adjust for the deletion of worksheets between Atlanta and Chicago.) Note, too, that the cell reference is relative and thus the formula can be copied from cell B3 in the Summary worksheet to the remaining cells in row 3 (C3 through E3). Those formulas can then be copied to the appropriate cells in rows 4 and 5.

A 3-D reference can be typed directly into a cell formula, but it is easier to enter the reference by pointing. Click in the cell that is to contain the 3-D reference, then enter an equal sign to begin the formula. To reference a cell in another worksheet, click the tab for the worksheet you want to reference, then click the cell or cell range you want to include in the formula. To reference a range from multiple worksheets, click in the cell in the first worksheet, press the Shift key as you click the tab for the last worksheet in the range, then click in the cell in the last worksheet.

Grouping Worksheets

The worksheets in a workbook are often similar to one another in terms of content and/or formatting. In Figure 5.3, for example, the formatting is identical in all four worksheets of the workbook. You can format the worksheets individually or more easily through grouping.

Excel provides the capability for *grouping worksheets* to enter or format data in multiple worksheets at the same time. Once the worksheets are grouped, anything you do in one of the worksheets is automatically done to the other sheets in the group. You could, for example, group all of the worksheets together when you enter row and column labels, when you format data, or when you enter formulas to compute row and column totals. You must, however, ungroup the worksheets when you enter data into a specific worksheet. Grouping and ungrouping is illustrated in the following hands-on exercise.

The AutoFormat Command

The formatting commands within Excel can be applied individually (as you have done throughout the text), or automatically and collectively by choosing a predefined set of formatting specifications. Excel provides several such designs as shown in Figure 5.7. You can apply any of these designs to your worksheet by selecting the range to be formatted, then executing the *AutoFormat command* from within the Format menu.

The AutoFormat command does not do anything that could not be done through the individual commands, but it does provide inspiration by suggesting several attractive designs. You can enter additional formatting commands after the AutoFormat command has been executed, as you will see in our next exercise.

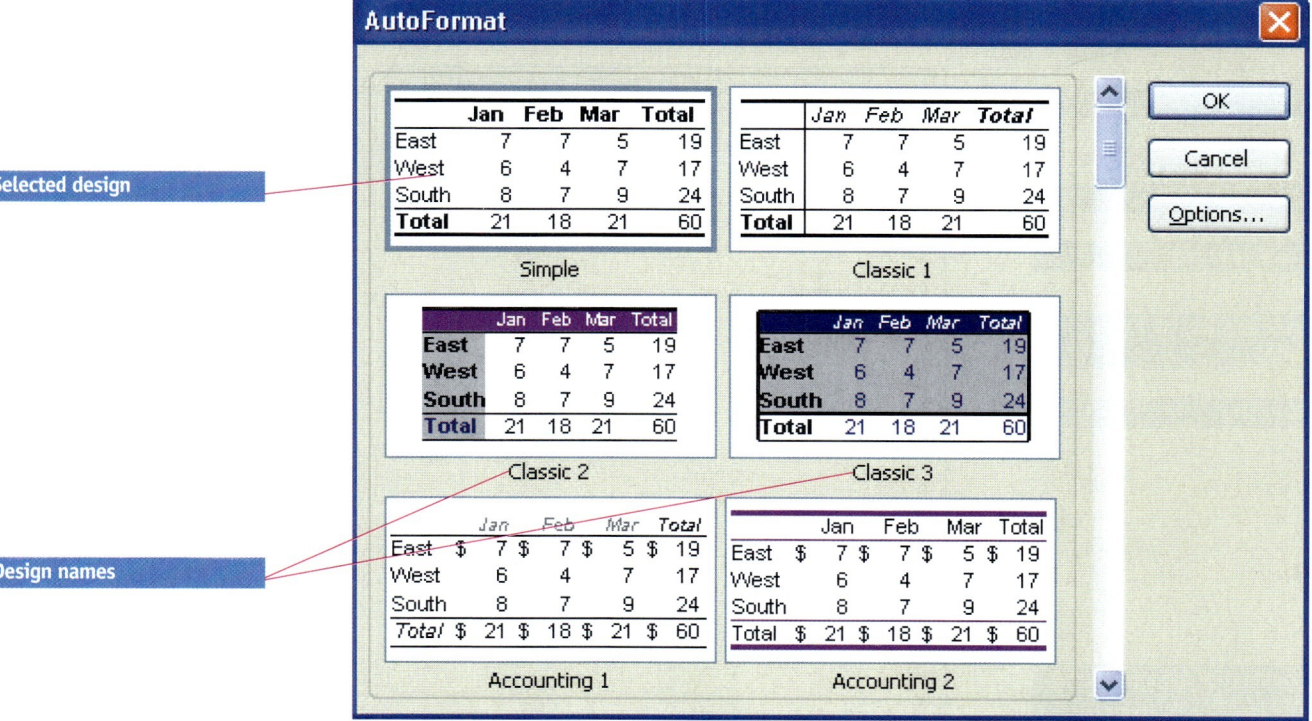

FIGURE 5.7 The AutoFormat Command

hands-on exercise
2 Worksheet References

Objective To use 3-D references to summarize data from multiple worksheets within a workbook; to group worksheets to enter common formatting and formulas; to open multiple windows to view several worksheets at the same time. Use Figure 5.8 as a guide in the exercise.

Step 1: Insert a Worksheet

- Start Excel. Open the **Corporate Sales workbook** created in the previous exercise. The workbook contains three worksheets.

- If necessary, click the ◄ to display all three tabs. Click the **Atlanta tab** to select this worksheet. Pull down the **Insert menu**, and click the **Worksheet command**. You should see a new worksheet, Sheet1.

- Double click the **tab** of the newly inserted worksheet to select the name. Type **Summary** and press **Enter**. The name of the new worksheet has been changed.

- Click in **cell A1** of the Summary worksheet. Type **Corporate Totals** as shown in Figure 5.8a.

- Click in **cell B2**. Enter **Qtr 1**. Click in **cell B2**, then point to the fill handle in cell B2. The mouse pointer changes to a thin crosshair.

- Click and drag the fill handle over **cells C2**, **D2**, and **E2**. A border appears to indicate the destination range. Release the mouse. Cells C2 through E2 contain the labels Qtr 2, Qtr 3, and Qtr 4, respectively. Right align the column labels.

- Click in **cell A3**. Enter **Product 1**. Use the AutoFill capability to enter the labels **Product 2** and **Product 3** in cells A4 and A5.

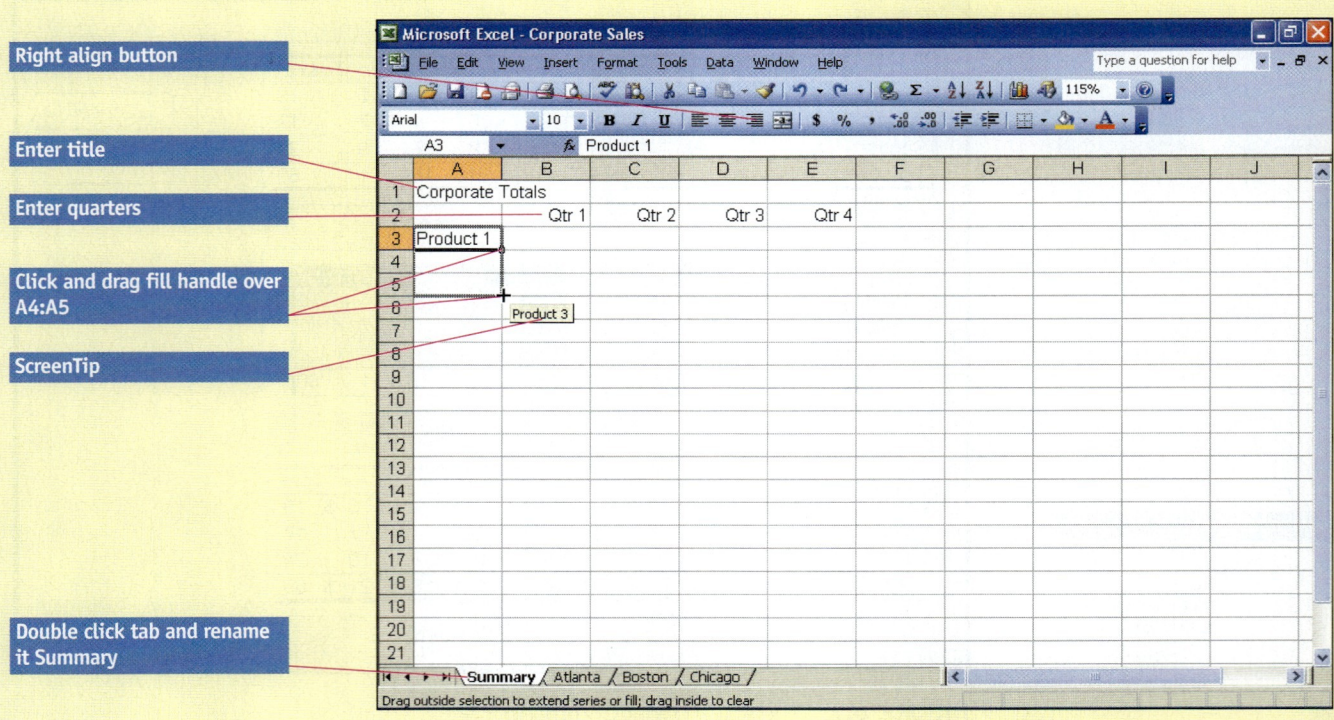

(a) Insert a Worksheet (step 1)

FIGURE 5.8 Hands-on Exercise 2

Step 2: **Sum the Worksheets**

- Click in **cell B3** of the Summary worksheet as shown in Figure 5.8b. Enter **=SUM(Atlanta:Chicago!B3)**, then press the **Enter key**. You should see 915 as the sum of the sales for Product 1 in Quarter 1 for the three cities (Atlanta, Boston, and Chicago).

- Click the **Undo button** on the Standard toolbar to erase the function so that you can reenter the function by using pointing.

- Check that you are in cell B3 of the Summary worksheet. Enter **=SUM(**.
    - Click the **Atlanta tab** to begin the pointing operation.
    - Press and hold the **Shift key**, click the **Chicago tab** (scrolling if necessary), then release the Shift key and click **cell B3**. The formula bar should now contain =SUM(Atlanta:Chicago!B3.
    - Press the **Enter key** to complete the function (which automatically enters the closing right parenthesis) and return to the Summary worksheet.

- You should see once again the displayed value of 915 in cell B3 of the Summary worksheet.

- If necessary, click in **cell B3**, then drag the fill handle over **cells C3 through E3** to copy this formula and obtain the total sales for Product 1 in all four quarters.

- Be sure that cells B3 through E3 are still selected, then drag the fill handle to **cell E5**. You should see the total sales for all products in all quarters.

- Click **cell E5** to examine the formula in this cell and note that the worksheet references are constant (i.e., they remained the same), whereas the cell references are relative (they were adjusted). Click in other cells to review their formulas in similar fashion.

- Save the workbook.

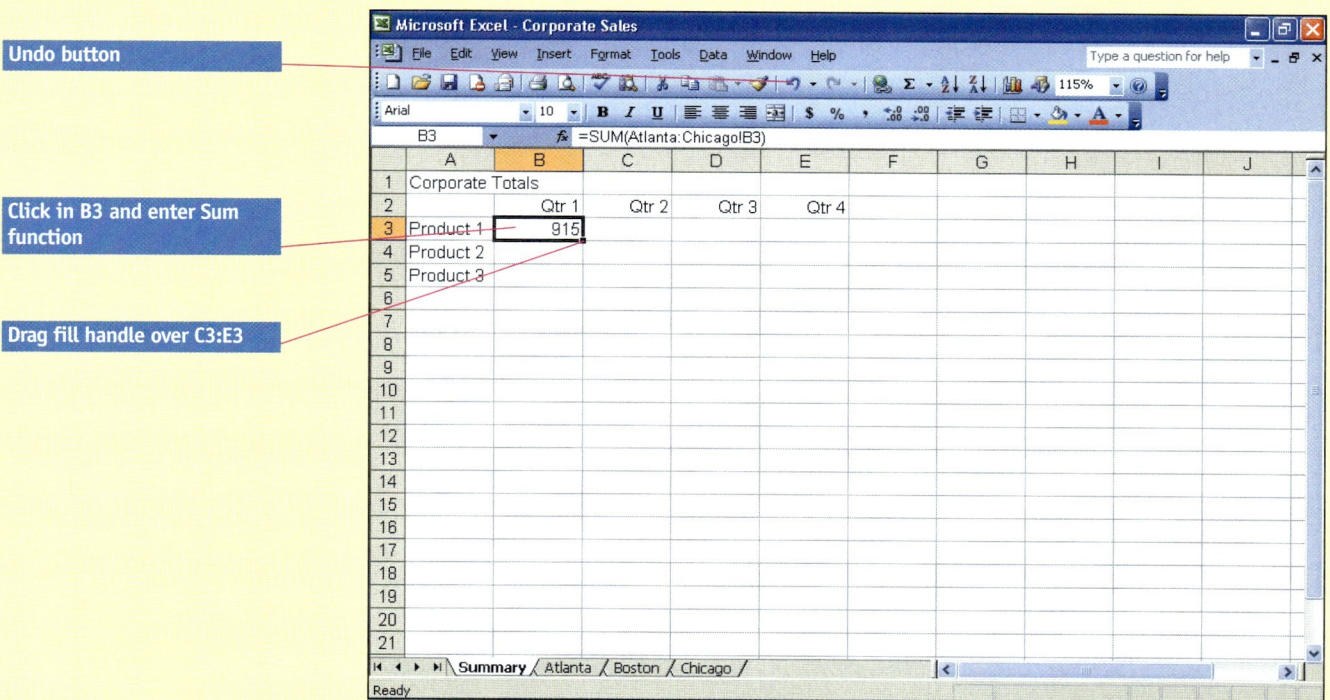

(b) Sum the Worksheets (step 2)

FIGURE 5.8 Hands-on Exercise 2 (*continued*)

Step 3: **The Arrange Windows Command**

- Pull down the **Window menu**, which displays the names of the open windows.
- The Corporate Sales workbook should be the only open workbook. Close any other open workbooks, including Book1.
- Pull down the **Window menu** a second time. Click **New Window** to open a second window. Note, however, that your display will not change at this time.
- Pull down the **Window menu** a third time. Click **New Window** to open a third window. Open a fourth window in similar fashion.
- Pull down the **Window menu** once again. You should see the names of the four open windows as shown in Figure 5.8c.
- Click **Arrange** to display the Arrange Windows dialog box. If necessary, select the **Tiled option**, then click **OK**. You should see four tiled windows.

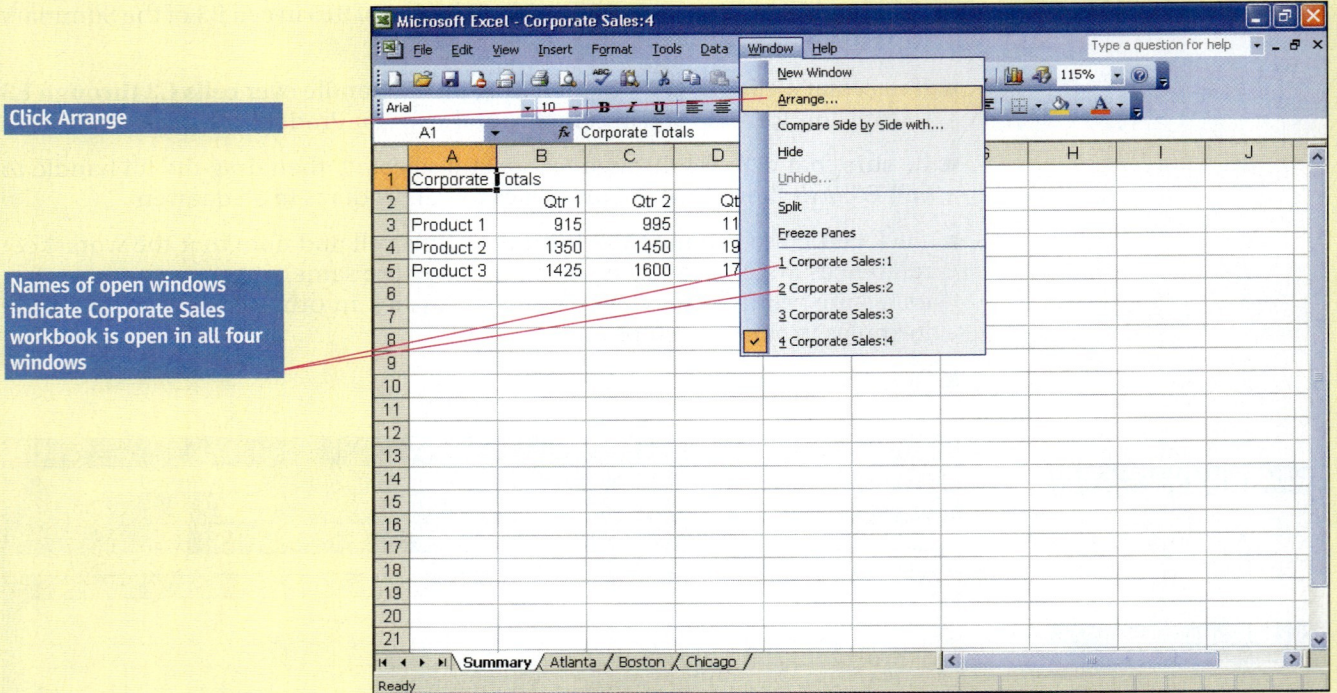

(c) The Arrange Windows Command (step 3)

FIGURE 5.8 Hands-on Exercise 2 (*continued*)

POINTING TO CELLS IN OTHER WORKSHEETS

A worksheet reference can be typed directly into a cell formula, but it is easier to enter the reference by pointing. Click in the cell that is to contain the reference, then enter an equal sign to begin the formula. To reference a cell in another worksheet, click the tab for the worksheet you want to reference, then click the cell or cell range you want to include in the formula. Complete the formula as usual, continuing to first click the tab whenever you want to reference a cell in another worksheet.

Step 4: **Changing Data**

- Click in the **upper-right window** in Figure 5.8d. Click the **Atlanta tab** to display the Atlanta worksheet in this window.

- Click the **lower-left window**. Click the **Boston tab** to display the Boston worksheet in this window.

- Click in the **lower-right window**. Click the **Tab scrolling button** until you can see the Chicago tab, then click the **Chicago tab**.

- Note that cell B3 in the Summary worksheet displays the value 915, which reflects the total sales for Product 1 in Quarter 1 for Atlanta, Boston, and Chicago (10, 55, and 850, respectively).

- Click in **cell B3** of the Chicago worksheet. Enter **250**. Press **Enter**. The value of cell B3 in the Summary worksheet changes to 315 to reflect the decreased sales in Chicago.

- Click the **Undo button** on the Standard toolbar. The sales for Chicago revert to 850 and the Corporate total is again 915.

- Save the workbook.

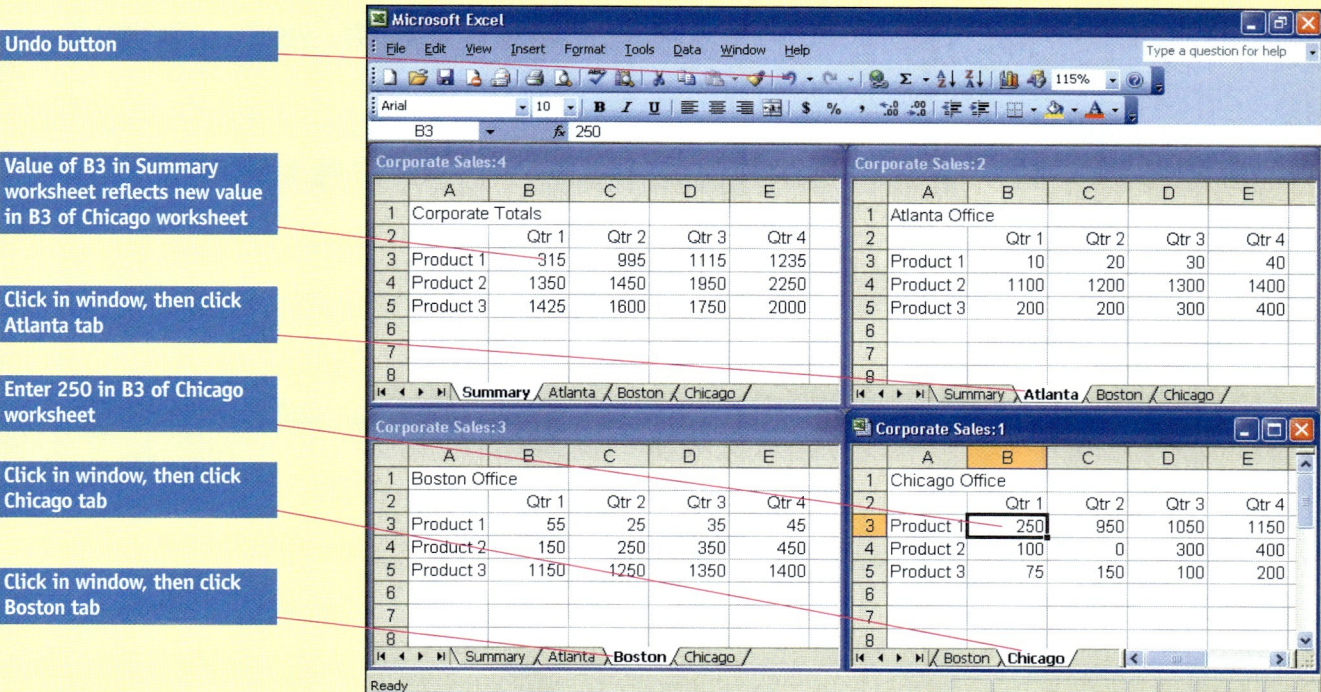

(d) Changing Data (step 4)

FIGURE 5.8   Hands-on Exercise 2 (*continued*)

CONTEXT-SENSITIVE MENUS

A context-sensitive menu provides an alternate (and generally faster) way to execute common commands. Point to a tab, then click the right mouse button to display a menu with commands to insert, delete, rename, move, copy, change color, or select all worksheets. Point to the desired command, then click the left mouse button to execute the command from the shortcut menu. Press the Esc key or click outside the menu to close the menu.

Step 5: **Group Editing**

- Click in the window where the Summary worksheet is active. Point to the split box separating the tab scrolling buttons from the horizontal scroll bar. (The pointer becomes a two-headed arrow.) Click and drag to the right until you can see all four tabs at the same time.

- If necessary, click the **Summary tab**. Press and hold the **Shift key** as you click the tab for the **Chicago worksheet**. All four tabs should be selected (and thus displayed in white) as shown in Figure 5.8e. You should also see [Group] in the title bar.

- Enter **Total** in **cell A6**. The text is centered in cell A6 of all four worksheets.

- Click in cell **B6** and enter the function **=SUM(B3:B5)**. Note that the formula is entered in all four sheets simultaneously because of group editing. Copy this formula to **cells C6 through E6**.

- Stay in the Summary worksheet and scroll until you can see column F. Enter **Total** in **cell F2**. Click in **cell F3** and enter the function **=SUM(B3:E3)**. Copy this formula to **cells F4 through F6**.

- Save the workbook.

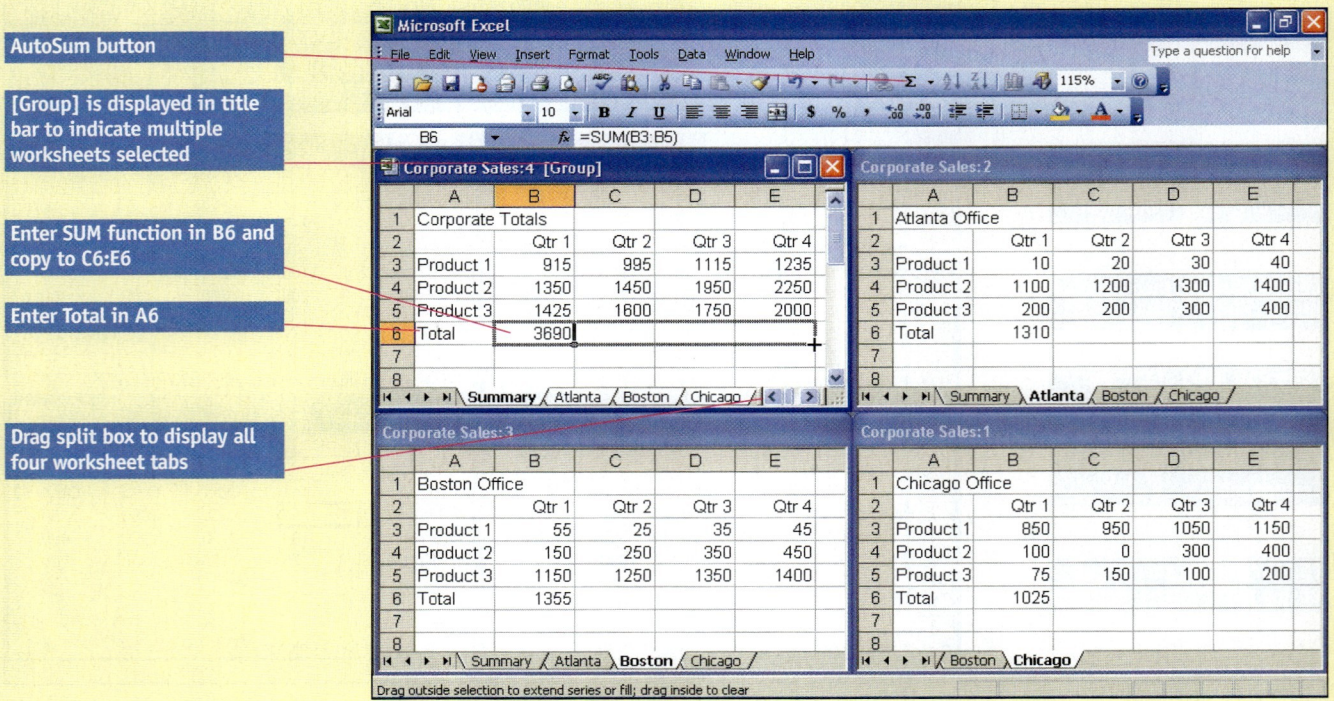

(e) Group Editing (step 5)

FIGURE 5.8 Hands-on Exercise 2 (*continued*)

THE AUTOSUM BUTTON

The AutoSum button on the Standard toolbar invokes the Sum function over a range of cells. To sum a single row or column, click in the blank cell at the end of the row or column, click the AutoSum button to see the suggested function, then click the button a second time to enter the function into the worksheet. To enter a sum function for multiple rows or columns, select the cell range prior to clicking the AutoSum button.

Step 6: **The AutoFormat Command**

- Be sure that all four tabs are still selected so that group editing is still in effect. Click and drag to select **cells A1 through F6** as shown in Figure 5.8f. (You may need to scroll in the worksheet to select all of the cells.)

- Pull down the **Format menu** and click the **AutoFormat command** to display the AutoFormat dialog box. Choose a format that appeals to you, then click the **Options button** to determine which parts of the format you want to apply.

- Experiment freely by selecting different designs and/or checking and unchecking the various check boxes within a design. Set a time limit, then make a decision. We chose the **Colorful 2** format and left all of the boxes checked. Click **OK**.

- The format is applied to all four selected sheets. You cannot see the effects in the summary worksheet, however, until you click elsewhere in the worksheet to deselect the cells.

- Save the workbook.

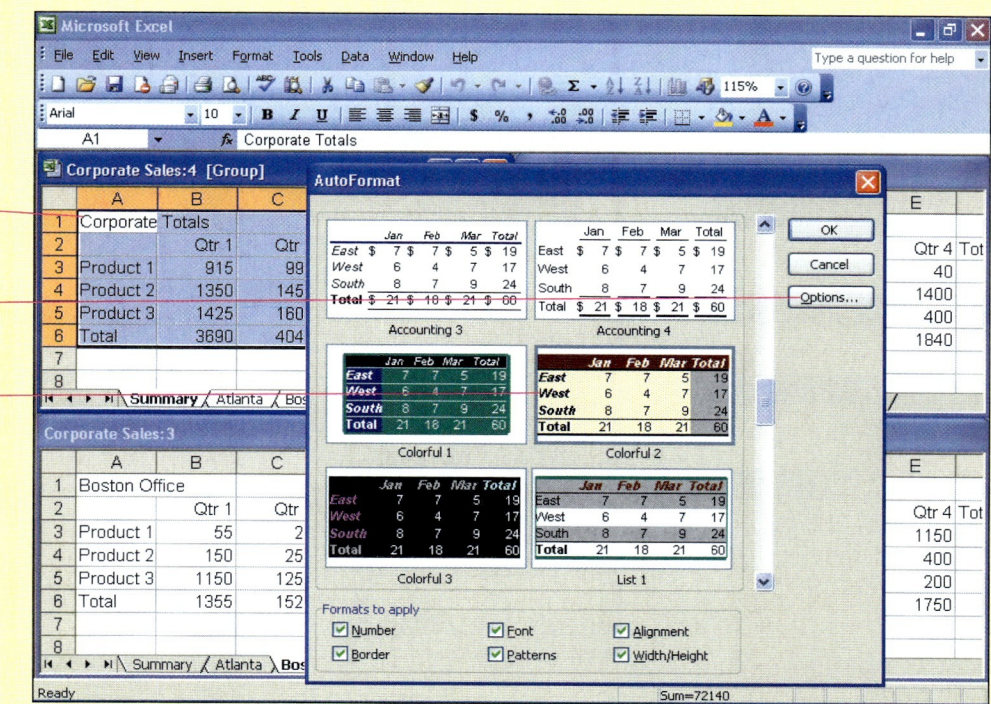

(f) The AutoFormat Command (step 6)

FIGURE 5.8 Hands-on Exercise 2 (*continued*)

SELECT MULTIPLE WORKSHEETS

You can group multiple worksheets simultaneously, then perform the same operation on the selected sheets at one time. To select adjacent worksheets, click the first sheet in the group, then press and hold the Shift key as you click the last sheet in the group. If the worksheets are not adjacent to one another, click the first tab, then press and hold the Ctrl key as you click the tab of each additional sheet. Excel indicates that grouping is in effect by appending [Group] to the workbook name in the title bar. Click any tab (other than the active sheet) to deselect the group.

MICROSOFT OFFICE EXCEL 2003 REVISED

Step 7: **The Finishing Touches**

- Click and drag to select **cells B3 through F6**, then pull down the **Format menu** and click the **Cells command** to display the Format Cells dialog box in Figure 5.8g. (You can also right click the selected cells, then select the **Format Cells command** from the context-sensitive menu.)

- Click the **Number tab**, click **Currency**, and set the number of decimal places to **zero**. Click **OK**.

- Change the width of columns B through F as necessary to accommodate the additional formatting. It's easiest to select all of the columns at the same time, then click and drag the border between any two of the selected columns to change the width of all selected columns.

- Click the **Atlanta tab** to ungroup the worksheets. Save the workbook. Close all four windows. Exit Excel if you do not want to continue with the next exercise at this time.

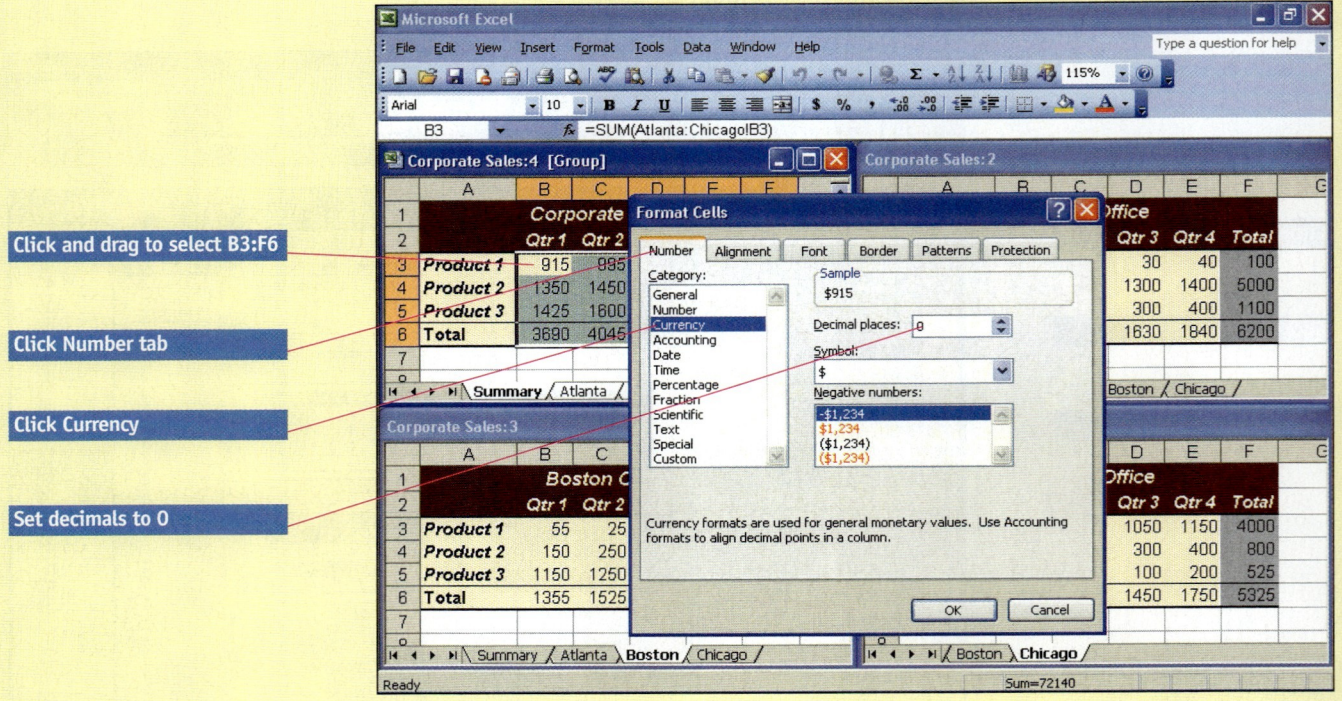

(g) The Finishing Touches (step 7)

FIGURE 5.8 Hands-on Exercise 2 (*continued*)

THE OPTIMAL (AUTOFIT) COLUMN WIDTH

The appearance of pound signs within a cell indicates that the cell width (column width) is insufficient to display the computed results in the selected format. Double click the right border of the column heading to change the column width to accommodate the widest entry in that column. For example, to increase the width of column B, double click the border between the column headings for columns B and C.

THE DOCUMENTATION WORKSHEET

Throughout the text we have emphasized the importance of properly designing a worksheet and of isolating the assumptions and initial conditions on which the worksheet is based. A workbook can contain up to 255 worksheets, and it, too, should be well designed so that the purpose of every worksheet is evident. Documenting a workbook, and the various worksheets within it, is important because spreadsheets are frequently used by individuals other than the author. You are familiar with every aspect of your workbook because you created it. Your colleague down the hall (or across the country) is not, however, and that person needs to know at a glance the purpose of the workbook and its underlying structure. Even if you don't share your worksheet with others, you will appreciate the documentation six months from now, when you have forgotten some of the nuances you once knew so well.

One way of documenting a workbook is through the creation of a ***documentation worksheet*** that describes the contents of each worksheet within the workbook as shown in Figure 5.9. The worksheet in Figure 5.9 has been added to the Corporate Sales workbook that was created in the first two exercises. (The Insert menu contains the command to add a worksheet.)

The documentation worksheet shows the author and date the spreadsheet was last modified. It contains a description of the overall workbook, a list of all the sheets within the workbook, and the contents of each. The information in the documentation worksheet may seem obvious to you, but it will be greatly appreciated by someone seeing the workbook for the first time.

The documentation worksheet is attractively formatted and takes advantage of the ability to wrap text within a cell. The description in cell B6, for example, wraps over several lines (just as in a word processor). The worksheet also takes advantage of color and larger fonts to call attention to the title of the worksheet. The grid lines have been suppressed through the View tab in the Options command of the Tools menu. The documentation worksheet is an important addition to any workbook.

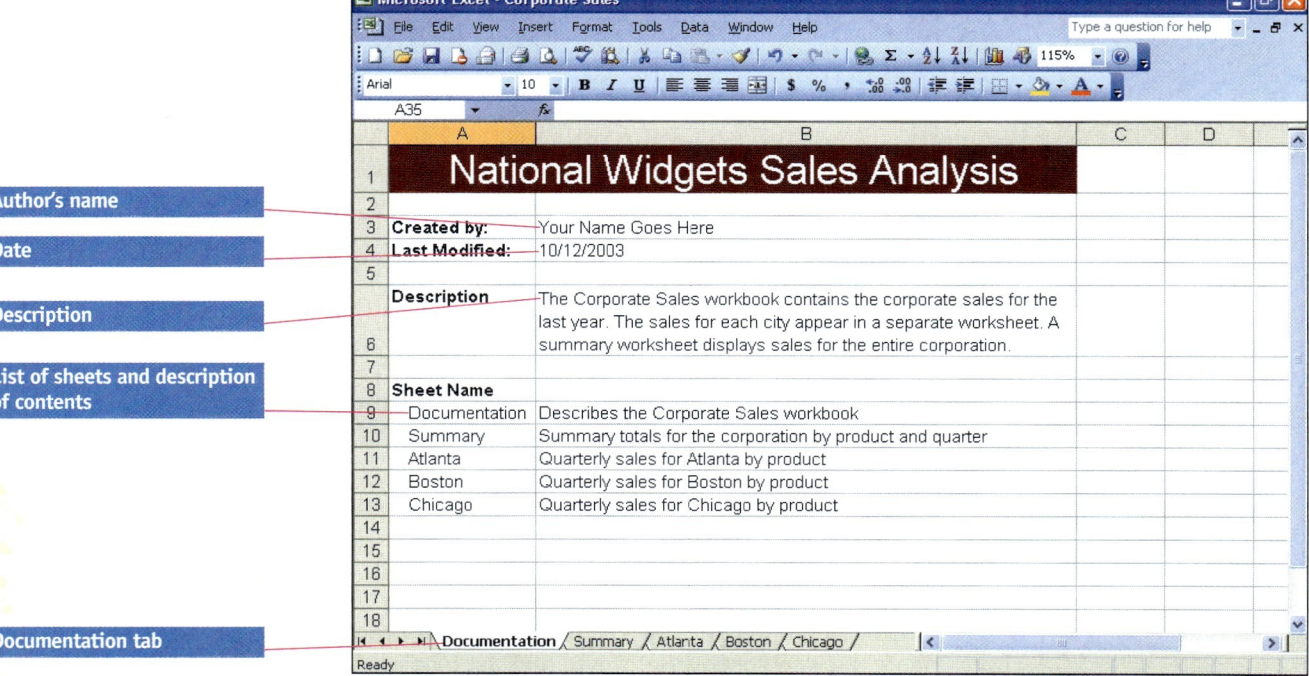

FIGURE 5.9 The Documentation Worksheet

hands-on exercise 3

The Documentation Worksheet

Objective To improve the design of a workbook through the inclusion of a documentation worksheet; to illustrate sophisticated formatting.

Step 1: **Add the Documentation Worksheet**

- Open the **Corporate Sales workbook** that was created in the previous exercise. Maximize the window. If necessary, click the **Atlanta tab** to turn off the group-editing feature. Click the **Summary tab** to select this worksheet.

- Pull down the **Insert menu** and click the **Worksheet command** to insert a new worksheet to the left of the Summary worksheet. Double click the **tab** of the new worksheet. Enter **Documentation** as the new name and press **Enter**.

- Enter the descriptive entries in column A as shown in Figure 5.10a. Enter your name in **cell B3**. Enter **=Today( )** in cell B4. Press **Enter**. Click the **Left Align button** to align the date as shown in the figure. Save the workbook.

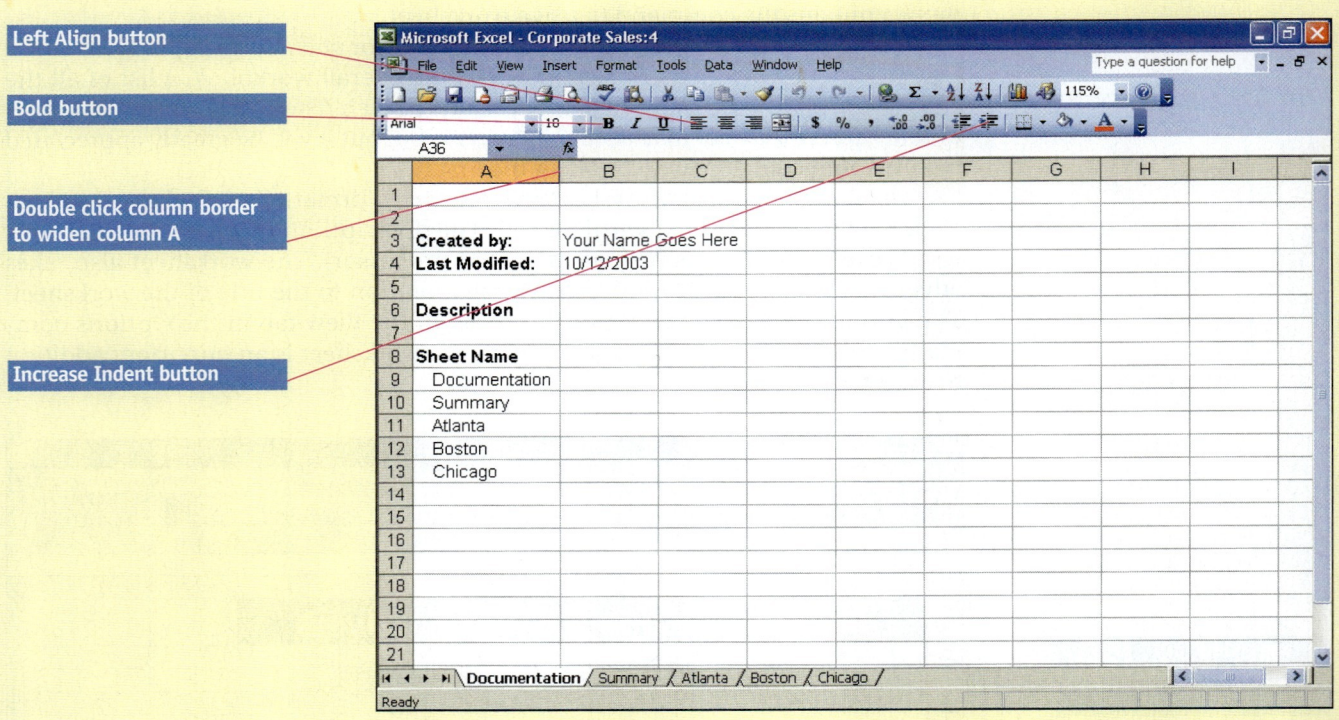

(a) Add the Documentation Worksheet (step 1)

FIGURE 5.10 Hands-on Exercise 3

WORKBOOK PROPERTIES

A documentation worksheet is one way to describe the author and other properties of a workbook. Excel also documents various properties automatically, but gives you the opportunity to modify that information. Pull down the File menu and click the Properties command to display the associated dialog box and explore the various tabs within the dialog box. Some properties are entered for you, such as the author in the Summary tab, the worksheet names in the Contents tab, and the date the worksheet was created and last modified in the Statistics tab. Other properties can be modified as necessary, especially in the Custom tab.

Step 2: **The Wrap Text Command**

- Increase the width of column B as shown in Figure 5.10b, then click in **cell B6** and enter the descriptive entry shown in the formula bar.

- Do not press the Enter key until you have completed the entire entry. Do not be concerned if the text in cell B6 appears to spill into the other cells in row six. Press the **Enter key** when you have completed the entry.

- Click in **cell B6**, then pull down the **Format menu** and click **Cells** (or right click **cell B6** and click the **Format Cells command**) to display the dialog box in Figure 5.10b.

- Click the **Alignment tab**, click the box to **Wrap Text** as shown in the figure, then click **OK**. The text in cell B6 wraps to the width of column B.

- Point to **cell A6**, then click the **right mouse button** to display a shortcut menu. Click **Format Cells** to display the Format Cells dialog box. If necessary, click the **Alignment tab**, click the **drop-down arrow** in the Vertical list box, and select **Top**. Click **OK**. Save the workbook.

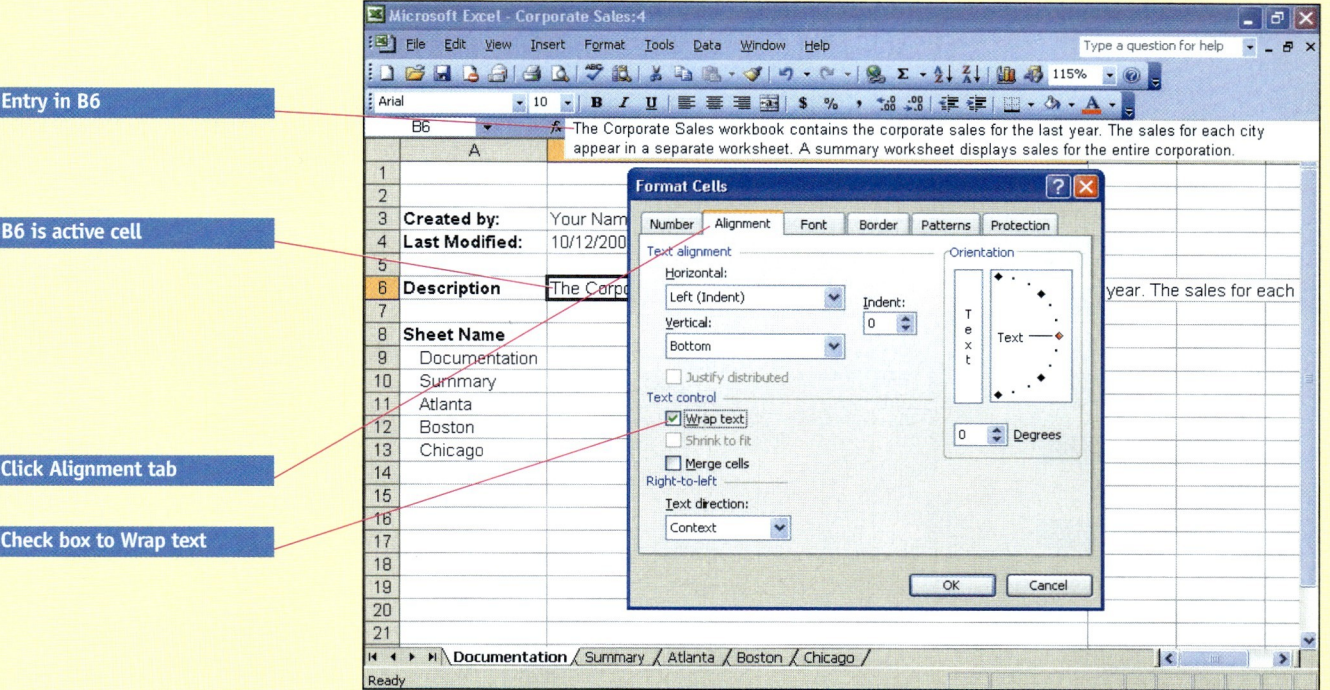

(b) The Wrap Text Command (step 2)

FIGURE 5.10   Hands-on Exercise 3 (*continued*)

EDIT WITHIN A CELL

Double click in the cell whose contents you want to change, then make the changes directly in the cell itself rather than on the formula bar. Use the mouse or arrow keys to position the insertion point at the point of correction. Press the Ins key to toggle between the insertion and overtype modes and/or use the Del key to delete a character. Press the Home and End keys to move to the first and last characters, respectively. If this feature does not work, pull down the Tools menu, click the Options command, click the Edit tab, then check the box to edit directly in a cell.

Step 3: **Add the Worksheet Title**

- Click in **cell A1**. Enter **National Widgets Sales Analysis**. Change the font size to **22**.

- Click and drag to select **cells A1 and B1**. Click the **Merge and Center button** to center the title across cells A1 and B1.

- Check that cells A1 and B1 are still selected. Pull down the **Format menu**. Click **Cells** to display the Format Cells dialog box as shown in Figure 5.10c.
  - Click the **Patterns tab**. Click the **Dark Red** color (to match the color used in the Colorful 2 AutoFormat that was applied in the previous exercise).
  - Click the **Font tab**. Click the drop-down arrow in the **Color list box**. Click the **White** color.
  - Click **OK** to accept the settings and close the Format Cells dialog box.

- Click outside the selected cells to see the effects of the formatting change. You should see white letters on a dark red background.

- Complete the text entries in **cells B9 through B13**. (Refer to Figure 5.9.) Add any additional documentation and formatting that you think is appropriate.

- Click in **cell A1**. Click the **Spelling button** to check the worksheet for spelling. Make corrections as necessary. Save the workbook.

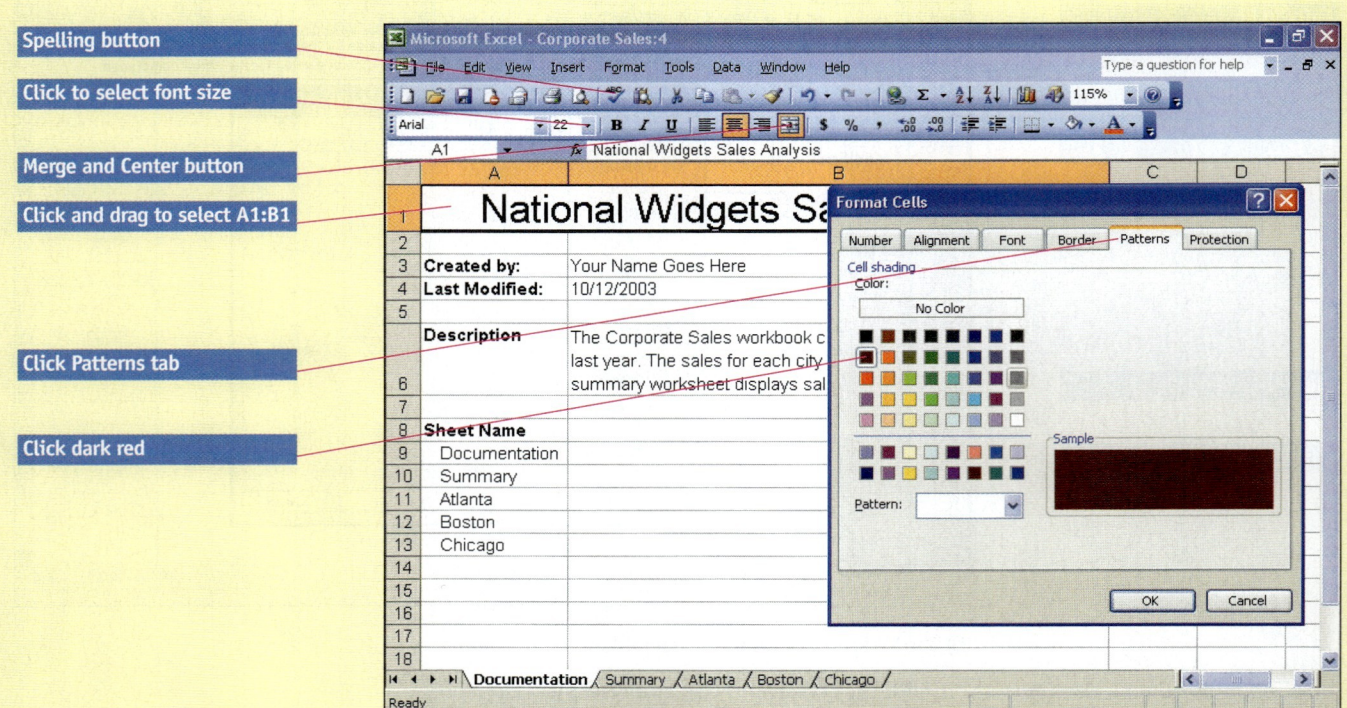

(c) Add the Worksheet Title (step 3)

FIGURE 5.10 Hands-on Exercise 3 (*continued*)

THE SPELL CHECK

Anyone familiar with a word processor takes the spell check for granted, but did you know the same capability exists within Excel? Click the Spelling button on the Standard toolbar to initiate the spell check, then implement corrections just as you do in Microsoft Word.

Step 4: **The Page Setup Command**

- If necessary, click the **Documentation tab** at the bottom of the window, then press and hold the **Shift key** as you click the tab for the **Chicago worksheet**. All five worksheet tabs should be selected, as shown in Figure 5.10d.

- Pull down the **File menu** and click the **Page Setup command** to display the Page Setup dialog box.
  - Click the **Header/Footer tab**. Click the **down arrow** on the Header list box and choose **Documentation** (the name of the worksheet). Click the **down arrow** on the Footer list box and choose **Corporate Sales** (the name of the workbook).
  - Click the **Margins tab**, then click the check box to center the worksheet horizontally. Change the top margin to **2 inches**.
  - Click the **Sheet tab**. Check the boxes to include row and column headings and gridlines. Click **OK** to exit the Page Setup dialog box.

- Save the workbook. Pull down the **File menu**. Click **Print** to display the Print dialog box. Click the option button to print the **Entire Workbook**. (Use the Preview command as necessary to ensure that the individual worksheets fit on a single page.) Click **OK**.

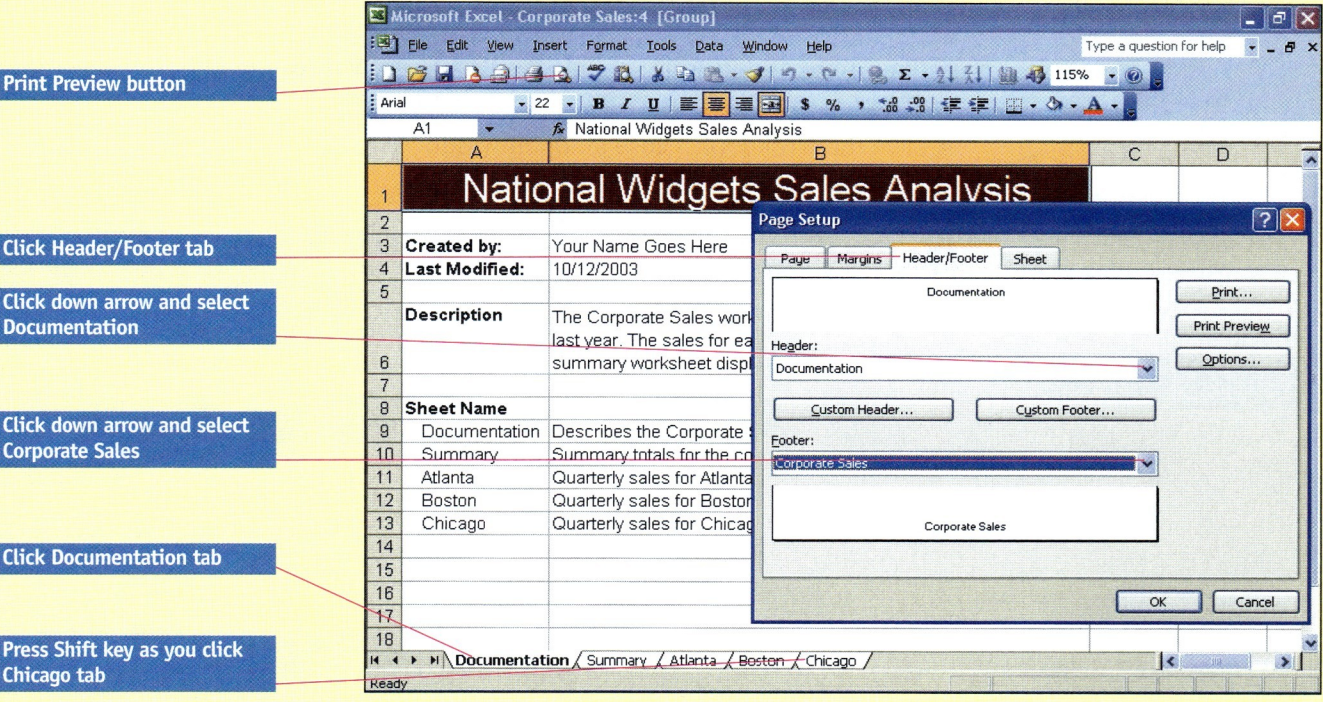

(d) The Page Setup Command (step 4)

FIGURE 5.10   Hands-on Exercise 3 (*continued*)

THE PRINT PREVIEW COMMAND

Use the Print Preview command to check the appearance of a worksheet to save time as well as paper. (Legend has it that the command was created by an unknown Microsoft programmer who tired of walking down the hall to pick up the printout.) You can execute the command by clicking the Print Preview button on the Standard toolbar or from the Print Preview command button within the Page Setup dialog box.

Step 5: **Print the Cell Formulas**

- Right click the **Summary tab** to display a context-sensitive menu, then click the **Ungroup Sheets command** to remove the group editing.

- Pull down the **View menu**, click **Custom Views** to display the Custom Views dialog box. Click the **Add button** to display the Add View dialog box.

- Enter **Displayed Values** as the name of the view (this is different from Figure 5.10e). Be sure that the Print Settings box is checked, and click **OK**.

- Press **Ctrl+~** to display the cell formulas. Double click the column borders between adjacent columns to increase the width of each column so that the cell formulas are completely visible.

- Pull down the **File menu** and click the **Page Setup command**. Click the **Page tab** and change to **Landscape orientation**. Click the option button to **Fit to 1 page**. Click **OK** to accept these settings and close the Page Setup dialog box. Click the **Print button** to print the summary worksheet.

- Pull down the **View menu**, click **Custom Views** to display the Custom View dialog box, then click the **Add button** to display the Add View dialog box. Enter **Cell Formulas** as shown in Figure 5.10f, verify that the Print Settings box is checked, and click **OK**.

- Pull down the **View menu**, click **Custom Views** to display the Custom View dialog box, then double click the **Displayed Values** view that was created earlier. You can switch back and forth at any time.

- Save the workbook. Close all open windows. Exit Excel if you do not want to continue with the next exercise at this time.

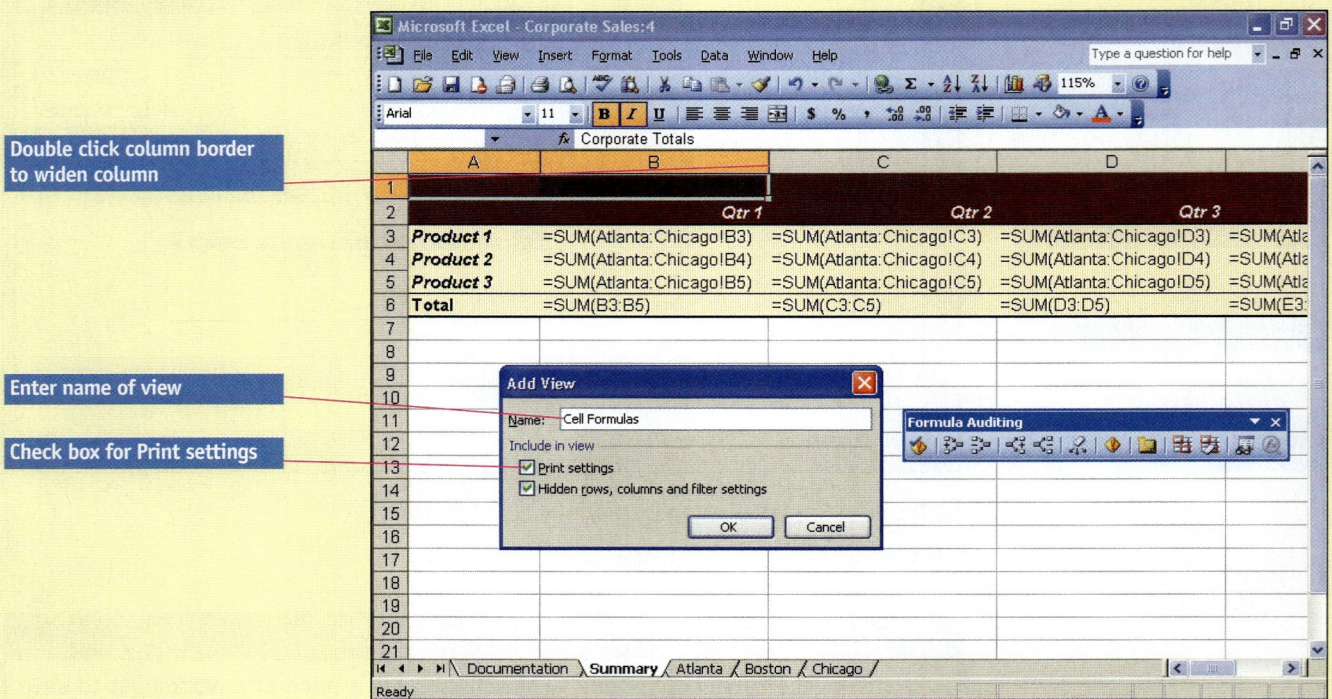

(e) Print the Cell Formulas (step 5)

FIGURE 5.10 Hands-on Exercise 3 (*continued*)

LINKING WORKBOOKS

There are two approaches to combining data from multiple sources. You can store all of the data on separate sheets in a single workbook, then create a summary worksheet within that workbook that references values in the other worksheets. Alternatively, you can retain the source data in separate workbooks, and create a summary workbook that references (links to) those workbooks.

Linking is established through the creation of ***external references*** that specify a cell (or range of cells) in another workbook. The ***dependent workbook*** (the Corporate Links workbook in our next example) contains the external references and thus reflects (is dependent on) data in the source workbook(s). The ***source workbooks*** (the Atlanta, Boston, and Chicago workbooks in our example) contain the data referenced by the dependent workbook.

Figure 5.11 illustrates the use of linking within the context of the example we have been using. Four different workbooks are open, each with one worksheet. The Corporate Links workbook is the dependent workbook and contains external references to obtain the summary totals. The Atlanta, Boston, and Chicago workbooks are the source workbooks.

Cell B3 is the active cell, and its contents are displayed in the formula bar. The corporate sales for Product 1 in the first quarter are calculated by summing the corresponding values in the source workbooks. Note how the workbook names are enclosed in square brackets to indicate the external references to the Atlanta, Boston, and Chicago workbooks.

The formulas to compute the corporate totals for Product 1 in the second, third, and fourth quarters contain external references similar to those shown in the formula bar. The ***workbook references*** and sheet references are absolute, whereas the cell reference may be relative (as in this example) or absolute. Once the formula has been entered into cell B3, it may be copied to the remaining cells in this row to compute the totals for Product 1 in the remaining quarters.

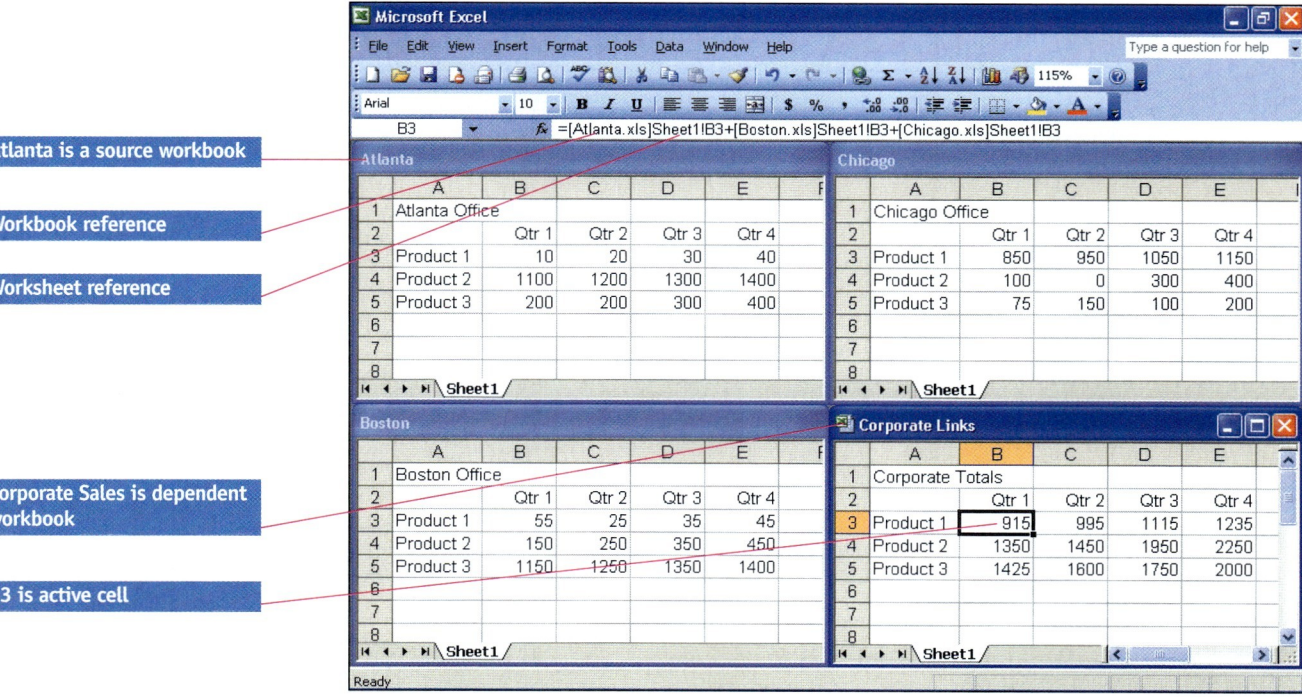

FIGURE 5.11   File Linking

hands-on exercise 4

Linking Workbooks

Objective To create a dependent workbook with external references to multiple source workbooks; to use pointing to create the external reference rather than entering the formula explicitly. Use Figure 5.12 as a guide in doing the exercise.

Step 1: Open the Workbooks

- Start Excel. If necessary, click the **New Workbook button** on the Standard toolbar to open a new workbook.

- Delete all worksheets except for Sheet1. Save the workbook as **Corporate Links** in the **Exploring Excel folder**.

- Pull down the **File menu**. Click **Open** to display the Open dialog box. Click the **Atlanta workbook**. Press and hold the **Ctrl key** as you click the **Boston** and **Chicago workbooks** to select all three workbooks at the same time as shown in Figure 5.12a.

- Click **Open** to open the selected workbooks. The workbooks will be opened one after another, with a brief message appearing on the status bar as each workbook is opened.

- Pull down the **Window menu**, which should indicate four open workbooks at the bottom of the menu. Click **Arrange** to display the Arrange Windows dialog box. If necessary, select the **Tiled option**, then click **OK**.

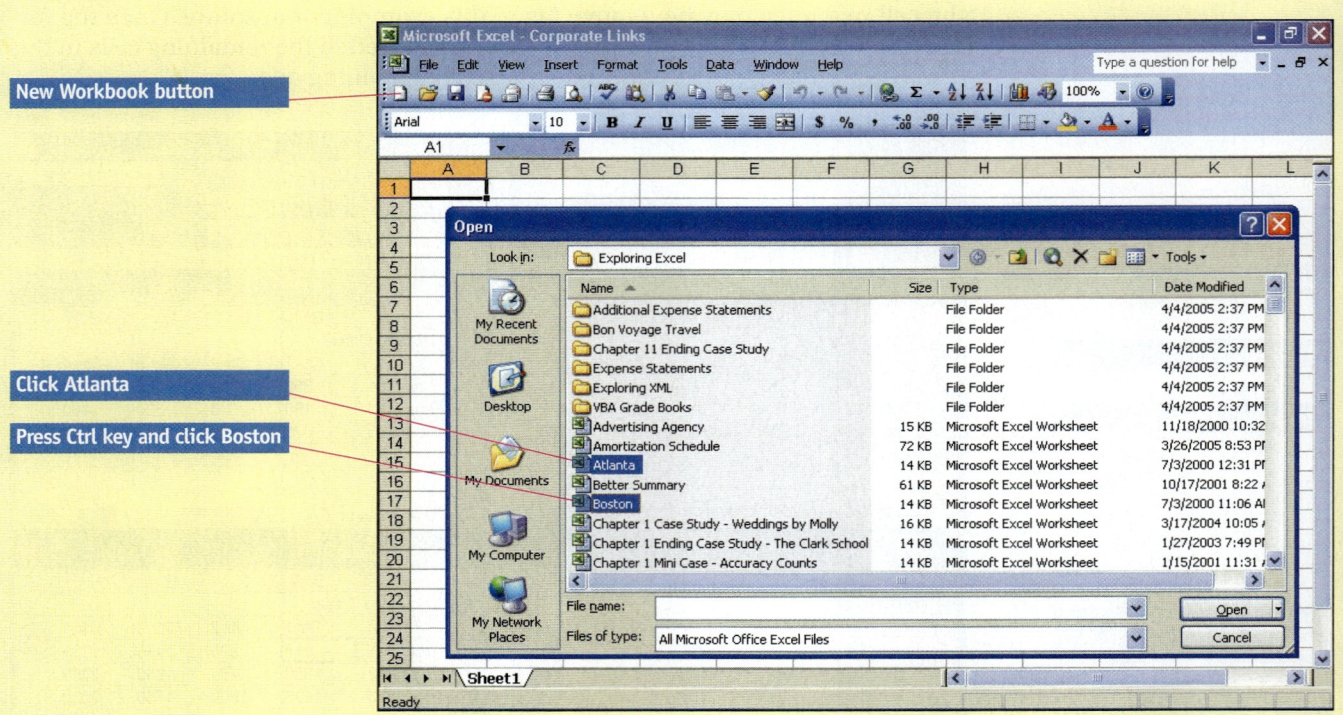

(a) Open the Workbooks (step 1)

FIGURE 5.12 Hands-on Exercise 4

256 CHAPTER 5: CONSOLIDATING DATA

Step 2: **The AutoFill Command**

- You should see four open workbooks as shown in Figure 5.12b, although the row and column labels have not yet been entered in the Corporate Links workbook. (Do not be concerned if your workbooks are arranged differently.)

- Click in **cell A1** in the **Corporate Links workbook** to make this the active cell in the active workbook. Enter **Corporate Totals**.

- Click **cell B2**. Enter **Qtr 1**. Click in **cell B2**, then point to the fill handle in the lower-right corner. The mouse pointer changes to a thin crosshair.

- Drag the fill handle over **cells C2**, **D2**, **and E2**. A border appears, to indicate the destination range. Release the mouse. Cells C2 through E2 contain the labels Qtr 2, Qtr 3, and Qtr 4, respectively.

- Right-align the entries in **cells B2 through E2**, then reduce the column widths so that you can see the entire worksheet in the window.

- Click **cell A3**. Enter **Product 1**. Use the AutoFill capability to enter the labels **Product 2** and **Product 3** in cells A4 and A5.

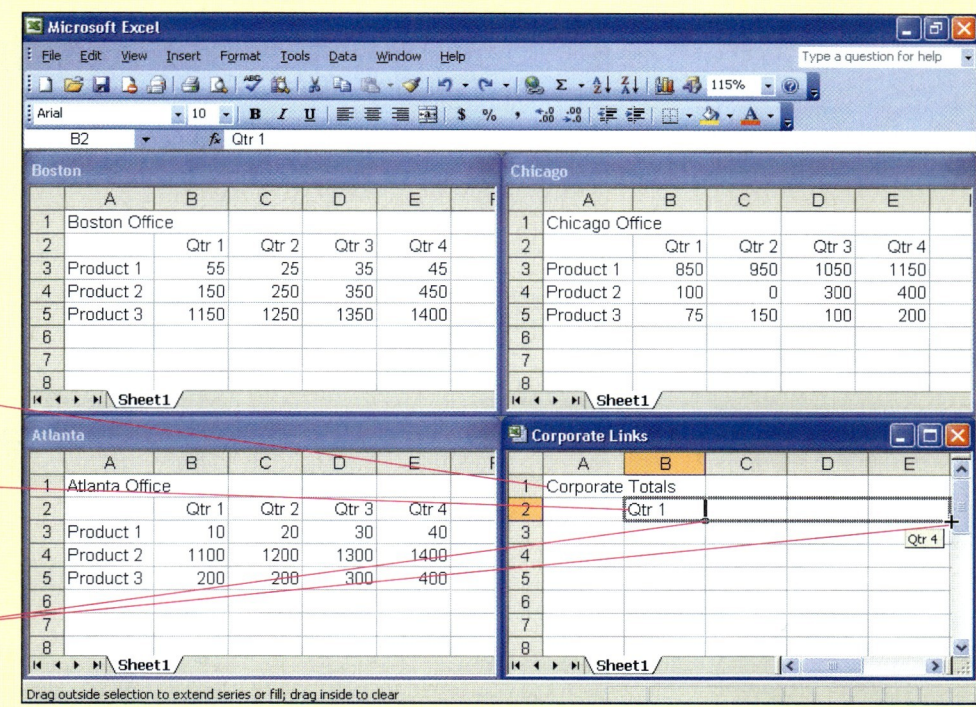

(b) The AutoFill Command (step 2)

FIGURE 5.12 Hands-on Exercise 4 (*continued*)

CREATE A CUSTOM SERIES

The AutoFill command is the fastest way to enter a series into adjacent cells. Type the first entry in the series (such as January, Monday, or Quarter 1), then click and drag the fill handle to adjacent cells to complete the series. You can also create your own series. Pull down the Tools menu, click Options, click the Custom Lists tab, and select New List. Enter the items in your series separated by commas (e.g., Tom, Dick, and Harry), click Add, and click OK. The next time you type Tom, Dick, or Harry in a cell you can use the fill handle to complete the series.

Step 3: **File Linking**

- Click **cell B3** of the **Corporate Links workbook**. Enter an **equal sign** so that you can create the formula by pointing.

- Click in the window for the **Atlanta workbook**. Click **cell B3**. The formula bar should display =[ATLANTA.XLS]Sheet1!$B$3. Press the **F4 key** continually until the cell reference changes to B3.

- Enter a **plus sign**. Click in the window for the **Boston workbook**. Click **cell B3**. The formula expands to include +[BOSTON.XLS]Sheet1!$B$3. Press the **F4 key** continually until the cell reference changes to B3.

- Enter a **plus sign**. Click in the window for the **Chicago workbook**. Click **cell B3**. The formula expands to include +[CHICAGO.XLS]Sheet1!$B$3. Press the **F4 key** continually until the cell reference changes to B3.

- Press **Enter**. The formula is complete, and you should see 915 in cell B3 of the Corporate Links workbook. Click in **cell B3**. The entry on the formula bar should match the entry in Figure 5.12c.

- Save the workbook.

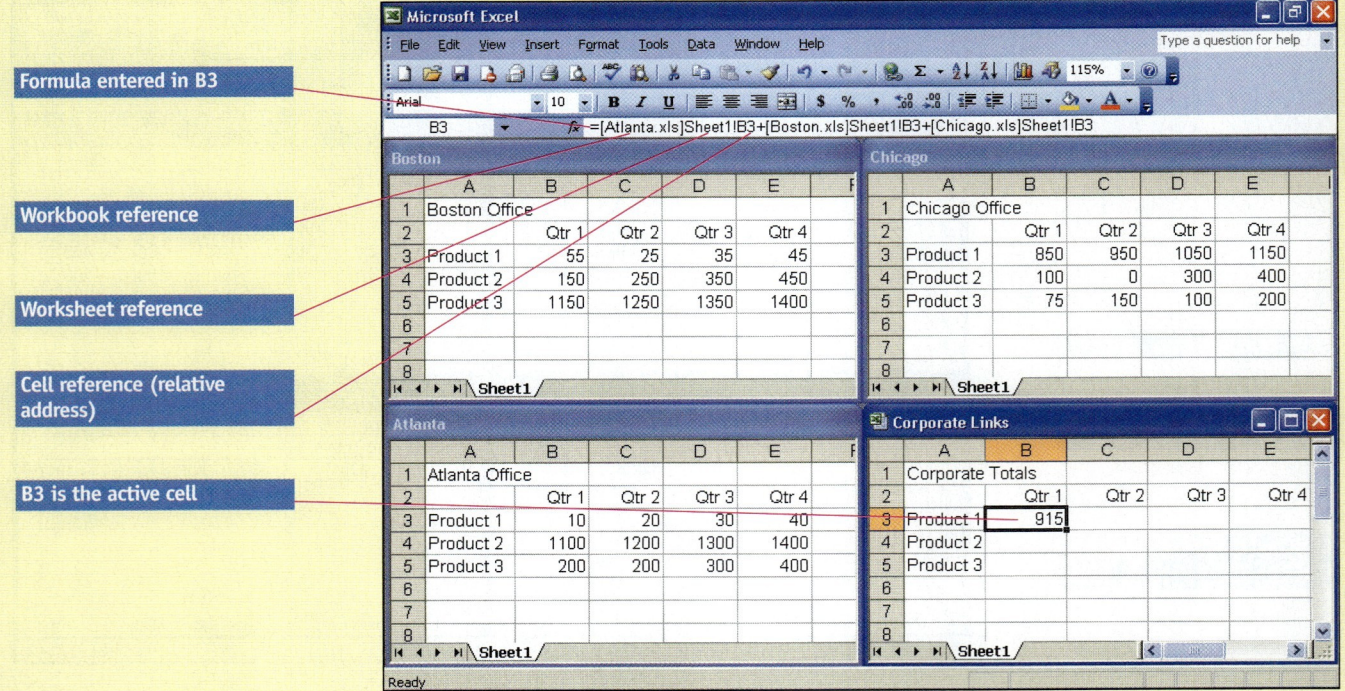

(c) File Linking (step 3)

FIGURE 5.12 Hands-on Exercise 4 (*continued*)

THE F4 KEY

The F4 key cycles through relative, absolute, and mixed addresses. Click on any reference within the formula bar; for example, click on A1 in the formula =A1+A2. Press the F4 key once, and it changes to an absolute reference, $A$1. Press the F4 key a second time, and it becomes a mixed reference, A$1; press it again, and it is a different mixed reference, $A1. Press the F4 key a fourth time, and it returns to the original relative address, A1.

Step 4: **Copy the Cell Formulas**

- If necessary, click **cell B3** in the **Corporate Links workbook**, then drag the fill handle over **cells C3 through E3** to copy this formula to the remaining cells in row 3.

- Be sure that cells B3 through E3 are still selected, then drag the fill handle to **cell E5**. You should see the total sales for all products in all quarters as shown in Figure 5.12d.

- Click **cell E5** to view the copied formula as shown in the figure. Note that the workbook and sheet references are the same but that the cell references have adjusted.

- Save the workbook.

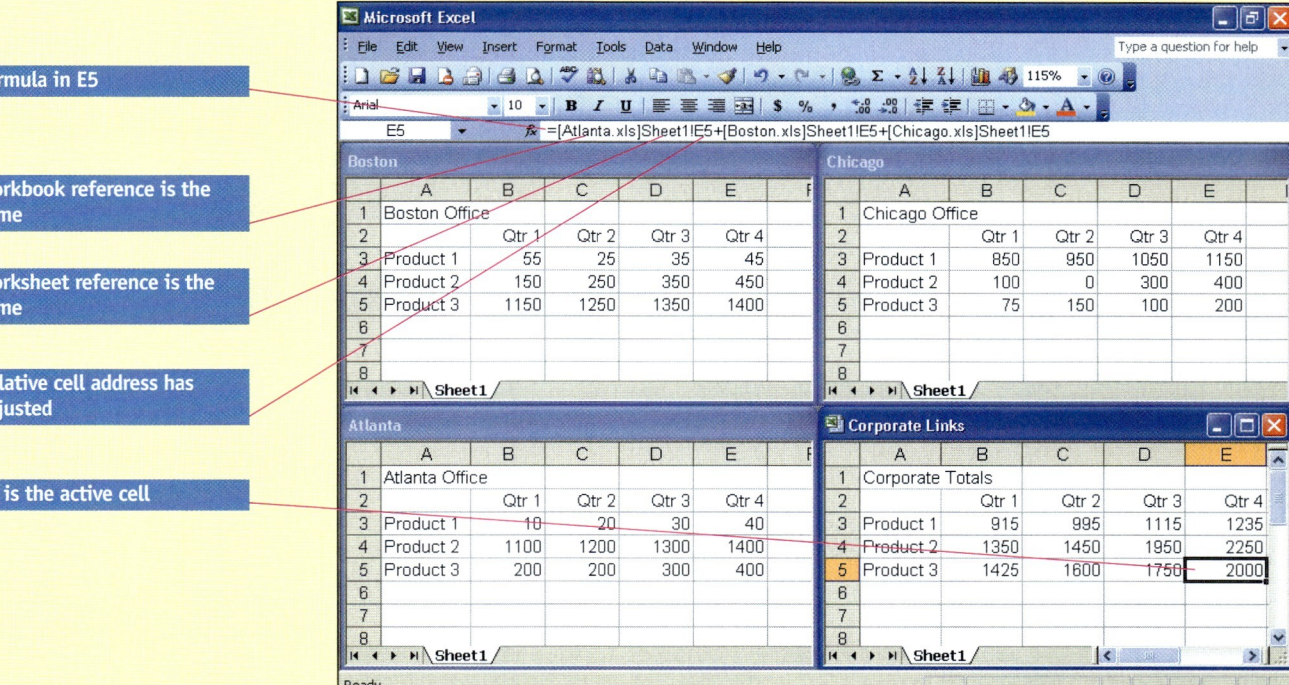

(d) Copy the Cell Formulas (step 4)

FIGURE 5.12 Hands-on Exercise 4 (*continued*)

DRIVE AND FOLDER REFERENCE

An external reference is updated regardless of whether or not the source workbook is open. The reference is displayed differently, depending on whether or not the source workbook is open. The references include the path (the drive and folder) if the source workbook is closed; the path is not shown if the source workbook is open. The external workbooks must be available to update the summary workbook. If the location of the workbooks changes (as may happen if you copy the workbooks to a different folder), pull down the Edit menu and click the Links command, then change the source of the external data.

Step 5: **Create a Workspace**

- Pull down the **File menu** and click the **Save Workspace command** to display the Save Workspace dialog box in Figure 5.12e.

- If necessary, click the **down arrow** in the Save in list box to select the **Exploring Excel folder**. Enter **Linked Workbooks** as the file name. Click the **Save button** in the dialog box to save the workspace. Click **Yes** if asked whether to save the changes to the Corporate Links workbook.

- The workspace is saved and you can continue to work as usual. The advantage of the workspace is that you can open all four workbooks with a single command.

- Click the **Close button** in each window to close all four workbooks. Pull down the **File menu**, click the **Open command**, then open the **Linked Workbooks** workspace that you just created.

- Click **Update** when asked whether you want to update the links within the Corporate Links workbook. All four workbooks are open as before.

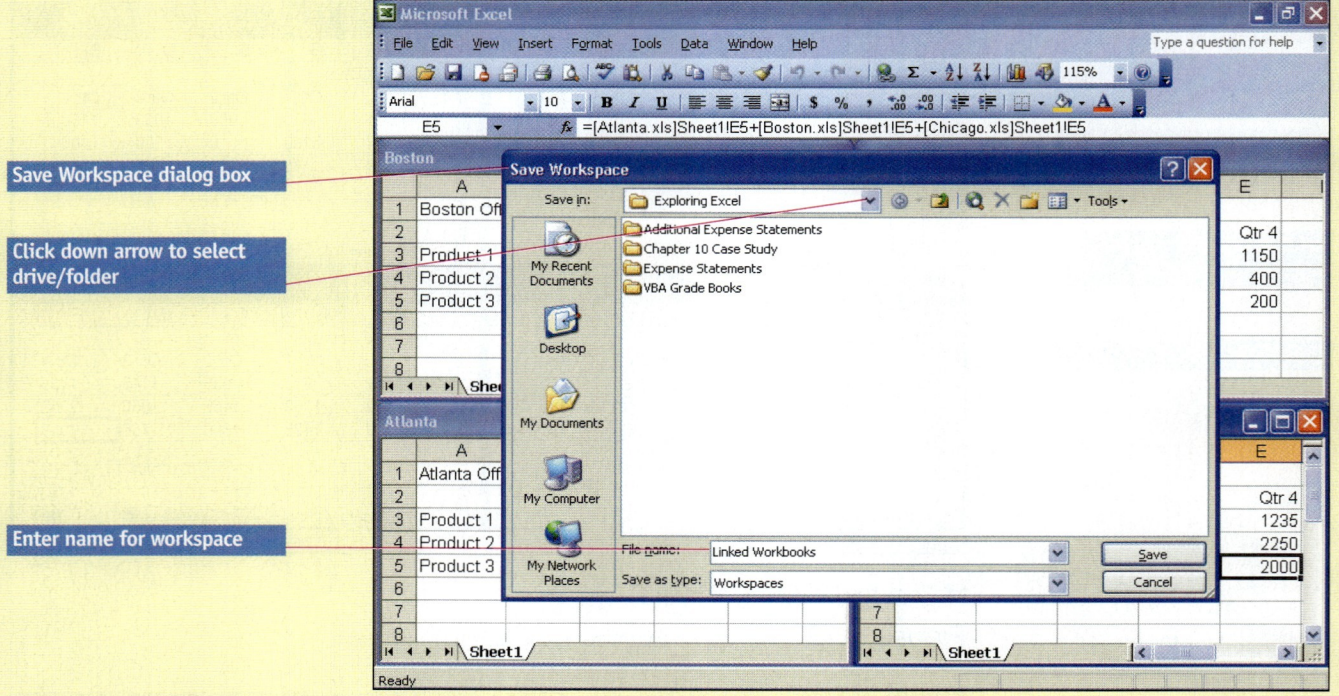

(e) Create a Workspace (step 5)

FIGURE 5.12 Hands-on Exercise 4 (*continued*)

THE WORKSPACE

A workspace enables you to open multiple workbooks in a single step, and further, will retain the arrangement of those workbooks within the Excel window. The workspace file does not contain the workbooks themselves, however, and thus you must continue to save changes you make to the individual workbooks.

Step 6: **Change the Data**

- Click **cell B3** in the **Corporate Links workbook** to make it the active cell. Note that the value displayed in the cell is 915.

- Pull down the **File menu**. Click **Close**. Answer **Yes** if asked whether to save the changes.

- Click in the window containing the **Chicago workbook**, click **cell B3**, enter **250**, and press **Enter**. Pull down the **File menu**. Click **Close**. Answer **Yes** if asked whether to save the changes. Only two workbooks, Atlanta and Boston, are now open.

- Pull down the **File menu** and open the **Corporate Links workbook**. You should see the dialog box in Figure 5.12f, asking whether to update the links. (Note that cell B3 still displays 915). Click **Update** to update the links.

- The value in cell B3 of the Corporate Links workbook changes to 315 to reflect the change in the Chicago workbook, even though the latter is closed.

- If necessary, click in **cell B3**. The formula bar displays the contents of this cell, which include the drive and folder reference for the Chicago workbook, because the workbook is closed.

- Close the Atlanta and Boston workbooks. Close the Corporate Links workbook. Click **Yes** if asked whether to save the changes.

- Saving the source workbook(s) before the dependent workbook ensures that the formulas in the source workbooks are calculated, and that all external references in the dependent workbook reflect current values.

- Exit Excel. Congratulations on a job well done.

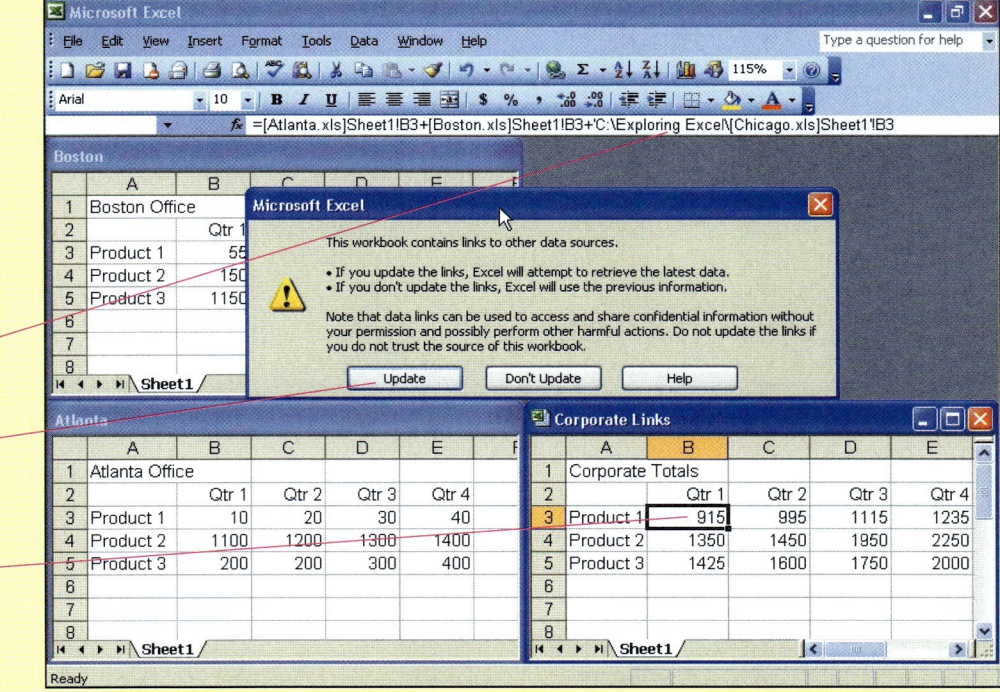

(f) Change the Data (step 6)

FIGURE 5.12 Hands-on Exercise 4 (*continued*)

SUMMARY

The chapter showed how to combine data from different sources into a summary report. The example is quite common and applicable to any business scenario requiring both detail and summary reports. One approach is to store all of the data in separate sheets of a single workbook, then summarize the data in a summary worksheet within that workbook. Alternatively, the source data can be kept in separate workbooks and consolidated through linking to a summary workbook. Both approaches are equally valid, and the choice depends on where you want to keep the source data.

An Excel workbook may contain up to 255 worksheets, each of which is identified by a tab at the bottom of the window. Worksheets may be added, deleted, moved, copied, or renamed through a shortcut menu. The color of the worksheet tab may also be changed. The highlighted tab indicates the active worksheet.

A worksheet reference is required to indicate a cell in another worksheet of the same workbook. An exclamation point separates the worksheet reference from the cell reference; e.g., =Atlanta!C3 references cell C3 in the Atlanta worksheet. The worksheet reference is absolute and remains the same when the formula is copied. The cell reference may be relative or absolute. A 3-D reference refers to a cell or range in another worksheet.

The best way to enter a reference to a cell in a different worksheet (or in a different workbook) is by pointing. Click in the cell that is to contain the formula, type an equal sign, click the worksheet tab that contains the external reference, then click in the appropriate cell. Use the F4 key as you select the cell to switch between relative, absolute, and mixed cell references.

Multiple worksheets may be selected (grouped) to execute the same commands on all of the selected worksheets simultaneously. You can, for example, insert formulas to sum a row or column and/or format the selected worksheets. The AutoFormat command provides access to a predefined set of formats that includes font size, color, boldface, alignment, and other attributes that can be applied automatically to a selected range.

A workbook should be clearly organized so that the purpose of every worksheet is evident. One way of documenting a workbook is through the creation of a documentation worksheet that describes the purpose of each worksheet within the workbook. Multiple worksheets (workbooks) can be displayed at one time, with each worksheet contained in its own window within the Excel application window. The Arrange command in the Window menu is used to tile or cascade the individual worksheets (workbooks).

A workbook may also be linked to cells in other workbooks through an external reference that specifies a cell (or range of cells) in a source workbook. The dependent workbook contains the external references and uses (is dependent on) the data in the source workbook(s). The external workbooks must be available to update the summary workbook. If the location of the workbooks changes (as may happen if you copy the workbooks to a different folder), pull down the Edit menu and click the Links command, then change the source of the external data.

KEY TERMS

3-D reference 240	Dependent workbook 255	New Window command 232
Arrange command 232	Documentation worksheet 249	Source workbook 255
AutoFormat command 241	External reference 255	Workbook properties 250
AutoSum 246	Grouping worksheets 241	Workbook reference 255
Custom view 254	Linking 255	Worksheet reference 239

MULTIPLE CHOICE

1. Which of the following is true regarding workbooks and worksheets?
   (a) A workbook contains one or more worksheets
   (b) Only one worksheet can be selected at a time within a workbook
   (c) Every workbook contains the same number of worksheets
   (d) All of the above

2. Assume that a workbook contains three worksheets. How many cells are included in the function =SUM(Sheet1:Sheet3!A1)?
   (a) Three
   (b) Four
   (c) Twelve
   (d) Twenty-four

3. Assume that a workbook contains three worksheets. How many cells are included in the function =SUM(Sheet1:Sheet3!A1:B4)?
   (a) Three
   (b) Four
   (c) Twelve
   (d) Twenty-four

4. Which of the following is the preferred way to sum the value of cell A1 from three different worksheets?
   (a) =Sheet1!A1+Sheet2!A1+Sheet3!A1
   (b) =SUM(Sheet1:Sheet3!A1)
   (c) Both (a) and (b) are equally good
   (d) Neither (a) nor (b)

5. The reference CIS120!$A$2:
   (a) Is an absolute reference to cell A2 in the CIS120 workbook
   (b) Is a relative reference to cell A2 in the CIS120 workbook
   (c) Is an absolute reference to cell A2 in the CIS120 worksheet
   (d) Is a relative reference to cell A2 in the CIS120 worksheet

6. What does City! refer to in the reference City!A1:F9?
   (a) A cell range
   (b) An error in a formula
   (c) A workbook
   (d) A worksheet

7. Which of the following is true about the reference Sheet1:Sheet3!A1:B2?
   (a) The worksheet reference is relative, the cell reference is absolute
   (b) The worksheet reference is absolute, the cell reference is relative
   (c) The worksheet and cell references are absolute
   (d) The worksheet and cell references are relative

8. You are in the Ready mode and are positioned in cell B2 of Sheet1. You enter an equal sign, click the worksheet tab for Sheet2, click cell B1, and press Enter.
   (a) The content of cell B2 in Sheet1 is =Sheet2!B1
   (b) The content of cell B1 in Sheet2 is =Sheet1!B2
   (c) Both (a) and (b)
   (d) Neither (a) nor (b)

9. You are positioned in cell A10 of Sheet1. You enter an equal sign, click the worksheet tab for the worksheet called This Year, and click cell C10. You then enter a minus sign, click the worksheet tab for the worksheet called LastYear, click cell C10, and press Enter. What are the contents of cell A10?
   (a) =ThisYear:LastYear!C10
   (b) =(ThisYear–LastYear)!C10
   (c) =ThisYear!C10-LastYear!C10
   (d) =ThisYear:C10-LastYear:C10

10. Which of the following can be accessed from a shortcut menu?
    (a) Inserting or deleting a worksheet
    (b) Moving or copying a worksheet
    (c) Renaming a worksheet
    (d) All of the above

... continued

multiple choice

11. You are positioned in cell A1 of Sheet1 of Book1. You enter an equal sign, click in the open window for Book2, click the tab for Sheet1, click cell A1, then press the F4 key continually until you have a relative cell reference. What reference appears in the formula bar?
    (a) =[BOOK1.XLS]Sheet1!$A$1
    (b) =[BOOK1.XLS]Sheet1!A1
    (c) =[BOOK2.XLS]Sheet1!$A$1
    (d) =[BOOK2.XLS]Sheet1!A1

12. The Arrange Windows command can display:
    (a) Multiple worksheets from one workbook
    (b) One worksheet from multiple workbooks
    (c) Both (a) and (b)
    (d) Neither (a) nor (b)

13. Pointing can be used to reference a cell in:
    (a) A different worksheet
    (b) A different workbook
    (c) Both (a) and (b)
    (d) Neither (a) nor (b)

14. The appearance of [Group] within the title bar indicates that:
    (a) Multiple workbooks are open and are all active
    (b) Multiple worksheets are selected within the same workbook
    (c) Both (a) and (b)
    (d) Neither (a) nor (b)

15. Which of the following is true regarding the example on file linking that was developed in the chapter?
    (a) The Atlanta, Boston, and Chicago workbooks were dependent workbooks
    (b) The linked workbook was a source workbook
    (c) Both (a) and (b)
    (d) Neither (a) nor (b)

16. The formula =Office1!A3+Office2!A3+Office3!A3
    (a) References the same cell in three different workbooks
    (b) References the same cell on three different worksheets in the same workbook
    (c) References the same cell on three different worksheets in three different workbooks
    (d) Impossible to determine

17. The formula =City1!$B$1+City2!$B$1+City3!$B$1 specifies that:
    (a) The worksheet references are absolute and the cell references are relative
    (b) The worksheet references are relative and the cell references are absolute
    (c) Both the worksheet and the cell references are absolute
    (d) Both the worksheet and cell references are relative

18. Which of the following is a valid reference to an external workbook?
    (a) =Boston!B3
    (b) =Boston!Sheet2!B3
    (c) Both (a) and (b)
    (d) Neither (a) nor (b)

ANSWERS

1. a
2. a
3. d
4. b
5. c
6. d
7. b
8. a
9. c
10. d
11. d
12. c
13. c
14. b
15. d
16. b
17. c
18. d

PRACTICE WITH EXCEL

1. **Linking Worksheets:** The workbook in Figure 5.13 features a summary worksheet that displays exam results for multiple sections of an introductory computer course. It also contains an individual worksheet for each section of the course. Your assignment is to open the partially completed *Chapter 5 Practice 1* workbook in the Exploring Excel folder, compute the test averages for each section, and then create the summary worksheet.

   a. Select the worksheet for Section N. Press and hold the Shift key as you click the worksheet tab for Section S to group all of the worksheets. Click in cell B10 and enter the formula, =AVERAGE(B3:B8) to compute the average on the first test for the students in Section N. Copy this formula to cells C10 and D10. (The sections have different numbers of students, but the last student in every section appears in row 8 or before. The Average function ignores empty cells within the designated range and thus you can use the same function for all four worksheets.)

   b. Check that the worksheets are still grouped, and then apply the same formatting to each worksheet. You do not have to duplicate our formatting exactly, but you are to merge and center the name of the section in the first row, and use bold text and a colored background. Change the color of the worksheet tab to match the formatting in the worksheet. You will not see the color change until you ungroup the worksheets.

   c. Ungroup the worksheets, then insert a blank worksheet for the summary as shown in Figure 5.13. Enter the title and column headings as shown in rows 1 and 2. Click in cell A3 of the summary worksheet. Type an equal sign, click the Worksheet tab for Section N, click in cell A1 of this worksheet, then press Enter to display the section name in the summary worksheet. Enter the names of the other sections.

   d. Click in cell B3 of the summary worksheet. Type an equal sign, click the Worksheet tab for Section N, click in cell B10, then press Enter to obtain the class average for section N on test 1. Copy the formula in cell B3 to cells C3 and D3 of the summary worksheet. Enter the test grades for the other sections in similar fashion.

   e. Format the summary worksheet in a similar style to the detailed worksheets.

   f. Use the Page Setup command to create a custom footer for all worksheets that includes your name, the name on the worksheet tab, and today's date. Print the worksheet for section N and the summary worksheet for your instructor. Print both worksheets a second time to show the cell formulas rather than the displayed values.

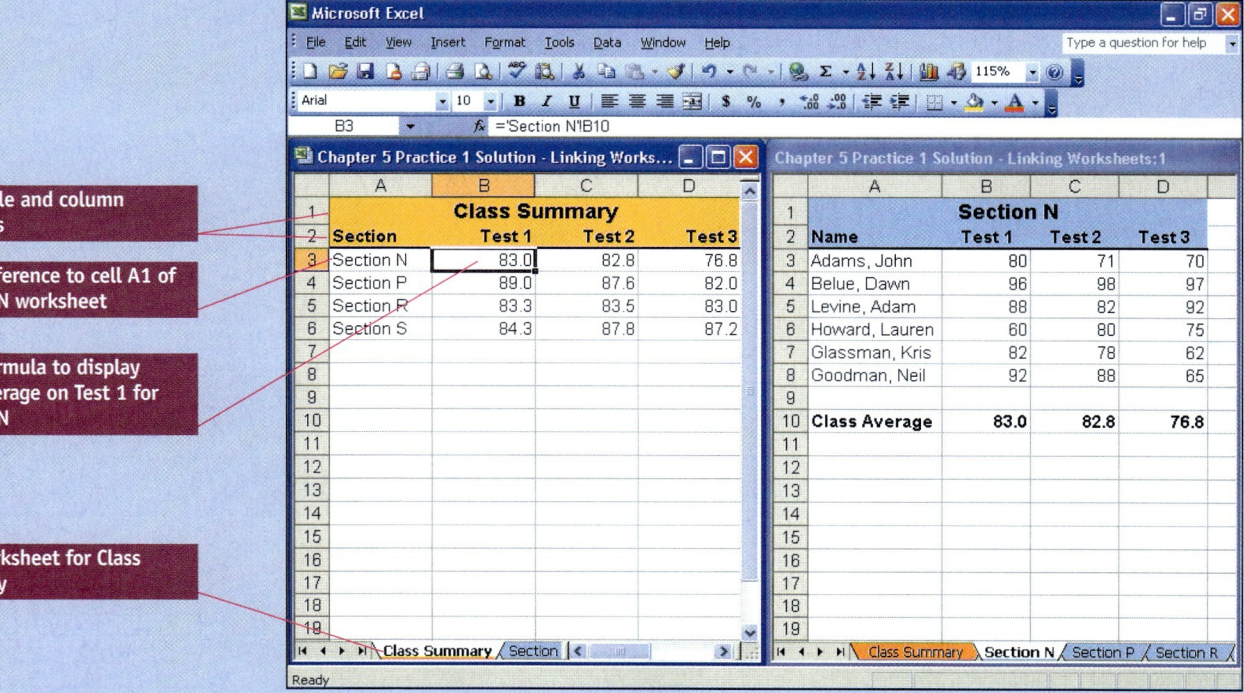

FIGURE 5.13 Linking Worksheets (exercise 1)

practice exercises

2. **Group Editing:** The workbook in Figure 5.14 contains a separate worksheet for each month of the year as well a summary worksheet for the entire year. Each monthly worksheet tallies the expenses for five divisions in each of four categories to compute a monthly total for each division. The summary worksheet is to display the total expense for each division. Thus far, however, only the months of January, February, and March are complete. Your assignment is to open the partially completed *Chapter 5 Practice 2* workbook in the Exploring Excel folder and proceed as follows:

   a. Insert a new worksheet for April to the right of the March worksheet and then enter the appropriate row and column headings. Assume that Division 1 spends $100 in each category, Division 2 spends $200 in each category, Division 3 spends $300 in each category, and so on. Change the worksheet tab to reflect April.

   b. Select the worksheet for January and then press and hold the Shift key as you click the worksheet tab for April. The title bar should reflect group editing. Click in cell F3 to compute the monthly total for Division 1, and then copy this formula to the remaining rows in this column. Compute the totals for each expense category in row eight.

   c. Format the worksheet in an attractive fashion. You do not have to match our formatting exactly, but you should include bold text, borders, and shaded cells as appropriate. Change the color of the worksheet tab. Right click any worksheet tab, click the Ungroup Worksheets command, then view the various monthly worksheets to verify that the formulas and formatting appear in each worksheet.

   d. Click the worksheet tab for the Summary worksheet. Insert a column for April to the right of the column for March. Click in cell B3, type an equal sign, click in the January worksheet, click in cell F3 (the cell that contains the January total for Division 1), and press Enter. Enter the formulas for the remaining months for Division 1 in similar fashion. Click in cell F3 and compute the year-to-date expenses for Division 1, then copy the formulas in cells B3 through F3 to the remaining rows in the Summary worksheet. Format the summary worksheet.

   e. Use the Page Setup command to create a custom footer for all worksheets that includes your name, the name on the worksheet tab, and today's date. Print the worksheet for April and the summary worksheet for your instructor. Print both worksheets a second time to show the cell formulas rather than the displayed values.

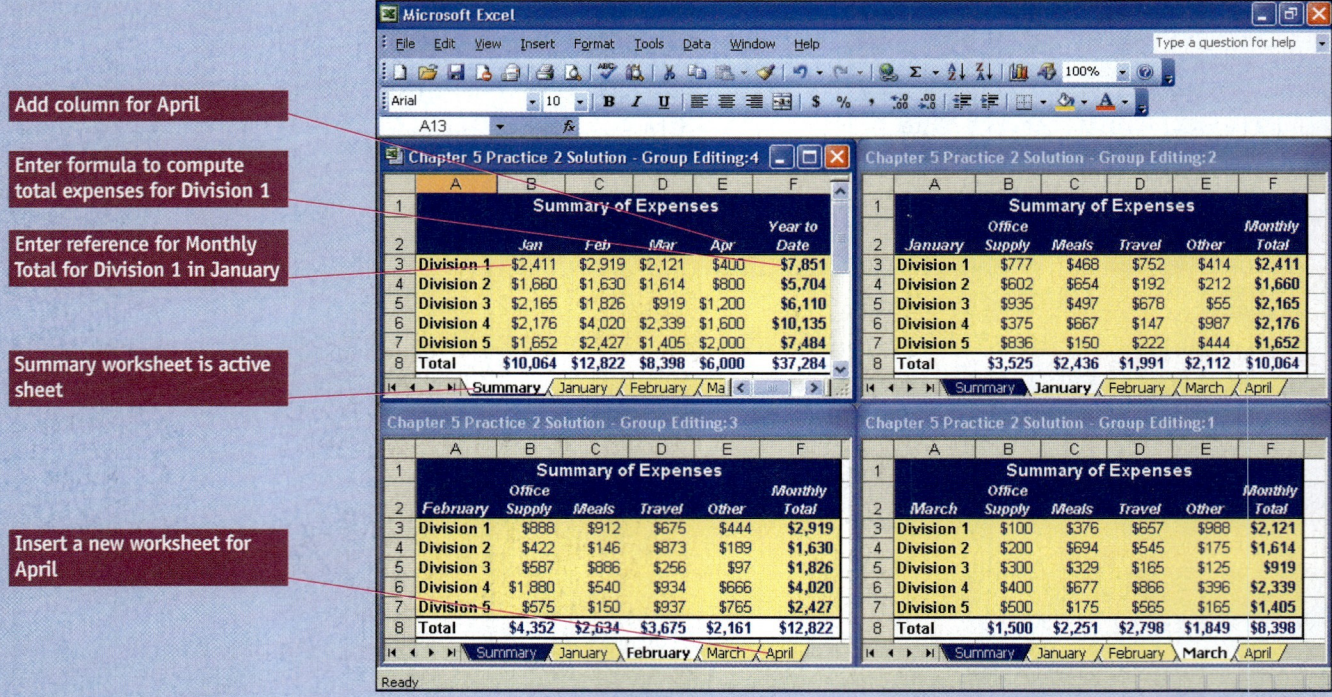

FIGURE 5.14 Group Editing (exercise 2)

practice exercises

3. **Object Linking and Embedding:** This exercise builds on the hands-on exercises within the chapter by creating a Word document that contains an Excel worksheet and associated chart. The chart is to be created in its own chart sheet within the Corporate Sales workbook and then incorporated into the memo. Proceed as follows:

   a. Start Word. Create a simple document that describes the corporate performance as shown in Figure 5.15. You do not have to match our document exactly, but you are required to create a letterhead and include your instructor's name and your name as indicated.

   b. Open the *Corporate Sales* workbook from the third hands-on exercise. Click the worksheet tab that contains the summary data, click and drag to select the completed worksheet, and then click the Copy button. Return to the Word document and click below the first paragraph. Pull down the Edit menu and click the Paste Special command to display the Paste Special dialog box. Select Microsoft Excel Worksheet Object in the displayed list, click the Paste Link button, and then click OK to insert the worksheet. Do not worry about the size or position at this time. Move the cursor so that it is below the worksheet. Add two or three blank lines.

   c. Return to the Excel workbook. Create a side-by-side column chart (in its own chart sheet) that plots the data in rows; that is, the X axis should display the four quarters, and the legend should display the product names. Use the same technique as in part (b) to link the side-by-side column chart to the Word document. Move and size the chart within the memo as necessary. You may find it convenient to change the zoom specification to "Whole Page" so that you can position the chart more easily.

   d. Save the completed document. Print the completed document for your instructor.

   e. Prove to yourself that Object Linking and Embedding really works by returning to the Atlanta worksheet *after* you have created the document in Figure 5.15. Change the sales for product 1 in Quarter 4 to $3,000. Switch back to the Word memo, and the chart should reflect the increase in the sales for product 1. Add a postscript to the memo indicating that the corrected chart reflects the last-minute sale of product 1 in Atlanta, and that you no longer want to discontinue the product. Print the revised memo and submit it to your instructor with the earlier version.

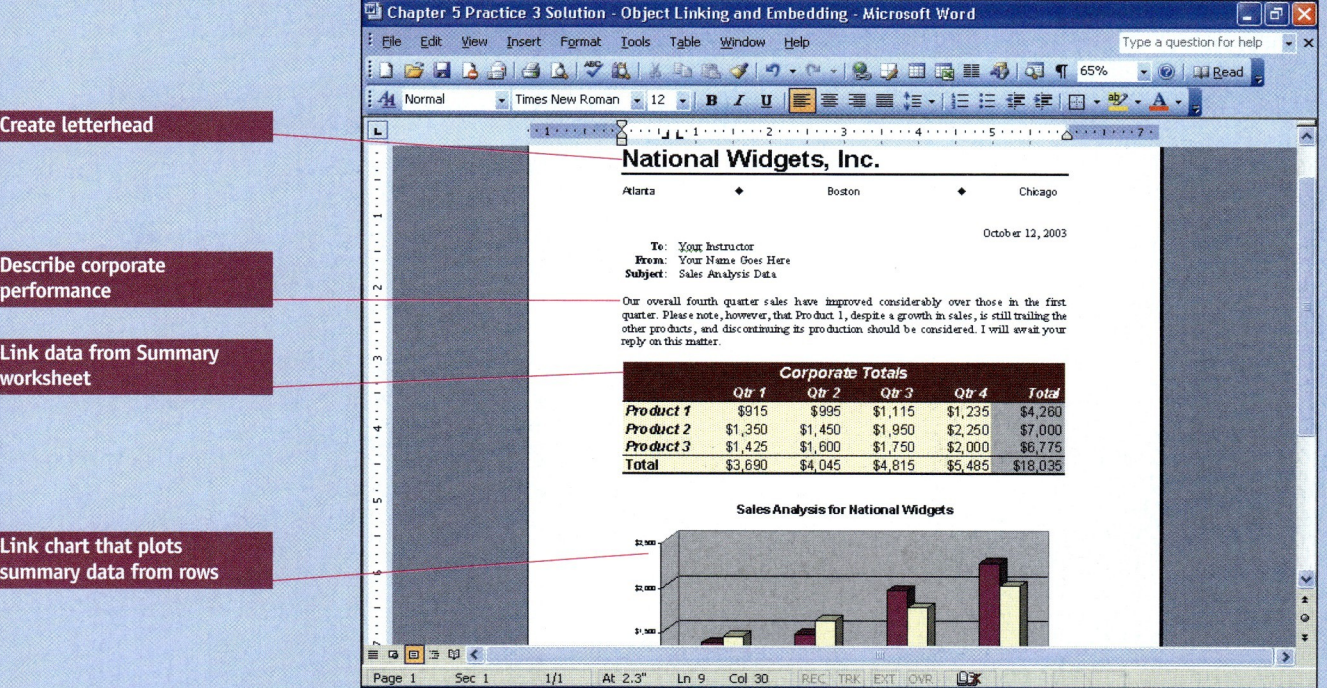

FIGURE 5.15 Object Linking and Embedding (exercise 3)

practice exercises

4. **National Computers:** You will find a partially completed version of the workbook in Figure 5.16 in the *Chapter 5 Practice 4* workbook in the Exploring Excel folder. That workbook has four partially completed worksheets, one for each city. Your assignment is to complete the workbook so that it parallels the Corporate Sales workbook that was used in the first three hands-on exercises in this chapter. Proceed as follows:

   a. Complete the individual worksheets by adding the appropriate formulas to compute the necessary row and column totals, then format these worksheets in attractive fashion. You can apply your own formatting, or you can use the AutoFormat command. You will find it easier, however, to use the group editing feature as you add the totals and apply the formatting, since all of the worksheets contain parallel data. Be sure to ungroup the worksheets after you have applied the formatting.

   b. Add a summary worksheet that provides corporate totals by product line. Apply the formatting from the individual worksheets to the summary worksheet.

   c. Create two side-by-side column charts, each in its own chart sheet, which display the summary information in graphical fashion. One chart should compare the sales revenue for each city by product, the other should compare the revenue for each product by city.

   d. Add a documentation worksheet similar to the worksheet in Figure 5.16. Change the color of the worksheet tabs as appropriate.

   e. Select the first worksheet, then press and hold the Shift key as you click the last worksheet tab to turn on the group editing feature. Use the Page Setup command to create a custom footer that includes your name, the name on the worksheet tab and today's date. Ungroup the worksheets, then change the orientation for the chart sheets to landscape.

   f. Print the entire workbook for your instructor. Print the Corporate (summary) worksheet a second time to show the cell formulas. (Change to landscape printing if necessary.)

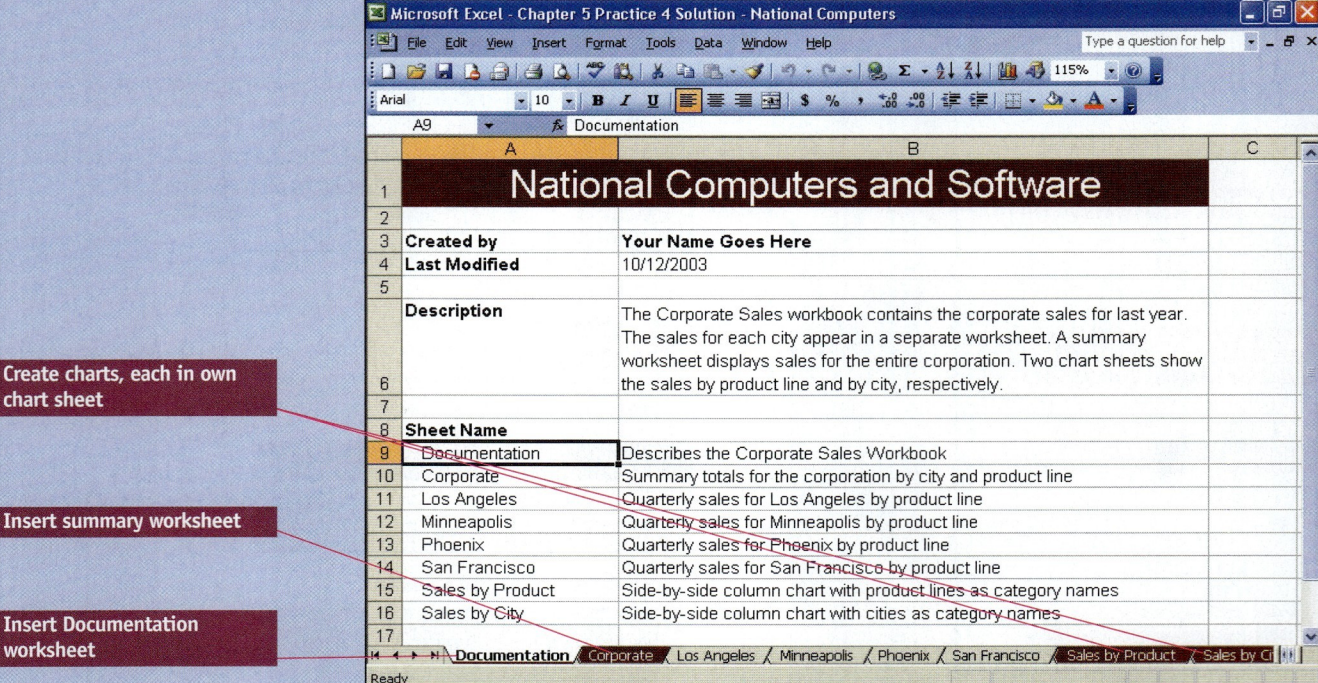

FIGURE 5.16 National Computers (exercise 4)

practice exercises

5. **Weekly Sales:** The workbook in Figure 5.17 contains seven worksheets that provide detailed information on last week's sales for the Definitely Needlepoint boutique. The daily worksheets contain sales data for the indicated day of the week and are identical to one another except for the specific data. The summary worksheet displays the information for each day and computes the weekly total of all receipts in cell H13. In similar fashion, the total sales (across all categories of merchandise) are computed in cell H21, and the value should equal the value in cell H13. Open the *Chapter 5 Practice 5* workbook and complete the summary worksheet.

   a. Select the Monday worksheet. Press and hold the Shift key as you click the worksheet tab for Saturday, so that all six worksheets are selected and the Group editing formula is turned on. Enter the appropriate formulas and/or functions in the Monday worksheet to compute the totals in cells B6, B12, B13, and B21.

   b. Click the Weekly Summary worksheet tab (which also turns off the Group editing feature). Click in cell B4. Type an equal sign, click the worksheet tab for Monday, click in cell B4 of this worksheet, then press the Enter key. Enter the appropriate worksheet references for the remaining days of the week in similar fashion. Click in cell H4, then click the Sum button on the Standard toolbar to obtain the weekly total.

   c. Click and drag to select cells B4 through H4. Click the Copy button. Click and drag to select cells B5 through H21. Pull down the Edit menu, click the Paste Special command, then click the option button to paste the formulas. Delete the entries in cells B14 through H15 because these cells should not contain any formulas.

   d. Enter an IF function in cell A22 that compares the total payments in cell H13 to the total in cell H21. The numbers should be equal; if not, there is a potential accounting error somewhere in the worksheet. Use conditional formatting to display the text in blue or red, depending on whether the numbers check or are in error. (A similar IF function has been entered for you on the daily worksheets in cell A22.)

   e. Use the Page Setup command to create a custom footer for all worksheets that includes your name, the name on the worksheet tab, and today's date. Print the summary worksheet. (Use landscape orientation.) Print the summary worksheet a second time to show the cell formulas.

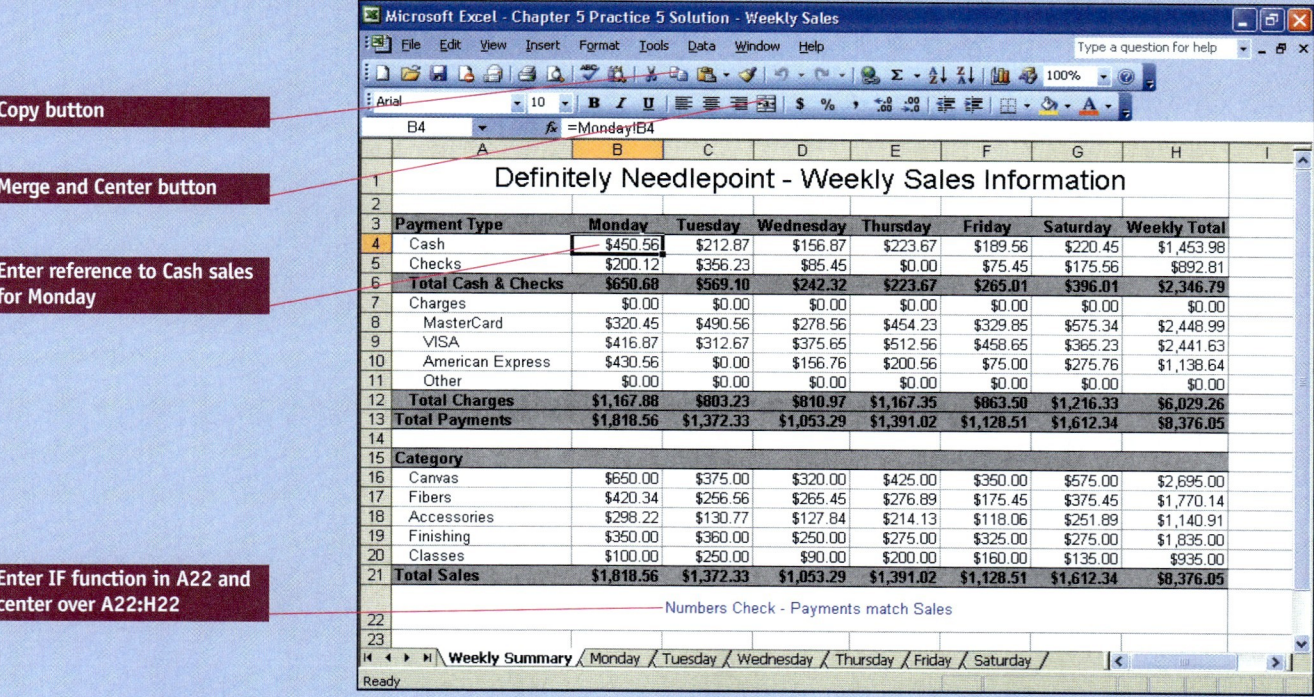

FIGURE 5.17 Weekly Sales (exercise 5)

MICROSOFT OFFICE EXCEL 2003 REVISED

practice exercises

6. **Natural Foods (Workbook References):** The Natural Foods Company began operation last year in New York City by opening three stores in different areas of Manhattan. The manager of each store has prepared a workbook that summarizes the results for last year. Your task is to combine the results from the three individual workbooks into a corporate summary as shown in Figure 5.18.

   a. Open the *Chapter 5 Practice 6—Natural Foods Corporate* workbook, which consists of a single worksheet that will be used to hold the summary data. Open the three workbooks for the individual stores. These are *Chapter 5 Practice 6—Natural Foods Uptown, Chapter 5 Practice 6—Natural Foods Midtown,* and *Chapter 5 Practice 6—Natural Foods Downtown.* Pull down the Window menu and tile the open windows.

   b. Click in the window containing the corporate workbook, then click in cell B3 to make it the active cell. The formula looks complicated, but you can enter it through pointing. Type an = sign, click in the window containing the Downtown workbook, click in cell B3, use the F4 key to change to a relative reference (B3 instead of $B$3), then type a plus sign. Click in the window containing the Midtown workbook, click in cell B3, change to a relative reference, and type a plus sign. Finally, click in the window containing the Uptown workbook, click in cell B3, change to a relative reference, and press Enter to complete the formula. Close the workbooks for the three individual stores.

   c. Use the fill handle to copy the formula in cell B3 to cells B3:E3, then copy the formulas in row 3 to rows 4–8. Enter the appropriate Sum functions in cells F3:F8 and cells B9:F9. Cell F9 should display the value $1,501,937.

   d. Use the AutoFormat command to format the completed worksheet. You do not have to match our formatting exactly.

   e. Create a stacked column chart in its own sheet with the data series in columns as shown. Change the name of the worksheet tab as shown.

   f. Use the Page Setup command to create a custom footer for both sheets containing today's date, the name of the worksheet tab, and your name. Use landscape printing for both worksheets. Print the completed workbook.

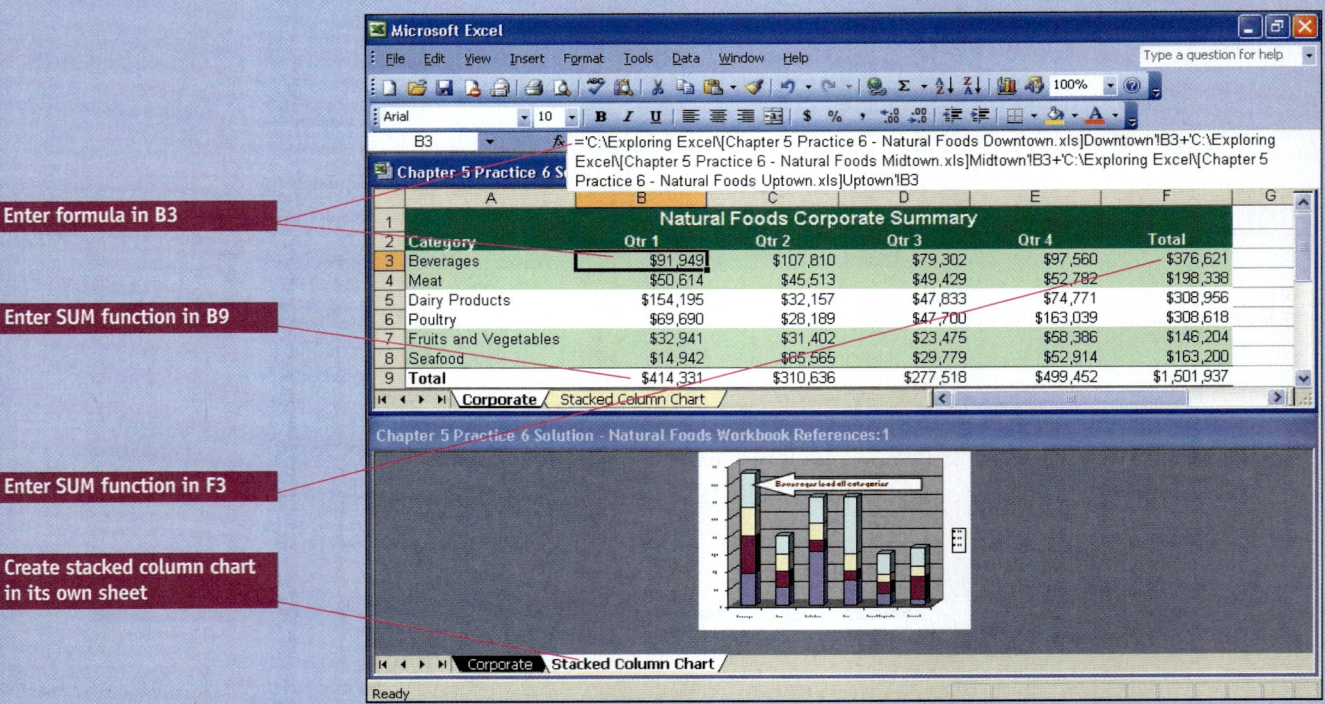

FIGURE 5.18 Natural Foods (Workbook References) (exercise 6)

practice exercises

7. **Natural Foods (Worksheet References):** Figure 5.19 displays an alternative way to create the Corporate workbook for the Natural Foods Company that was introduced in the previous exercise. This time we use a single workbook that contains worksheets for the individual stores, as opposed to referencing external workbooks as in the previous exercise. Proceed as follows:

   a. Open the *Chapter 5 Practice 7—Natural Foods Corporate* workbook, which contains a single worksheet that will hold the summary data. Open the three workbooks for the individual stores (Downtown, Midtown, and Uptown) from the previous exercise, then pull down the Window menu and tile the open windows.

   b. Click the window containing the Downtown workbook, then click and drag the worksheet tab to the Corporate workbook. The Downtown workbook closes automatically. Click and drag the worksheet tabs for the Midtown and Uptown worksheets in similar fashion. The Corporate workbook now contains four worksheets. Pull down the Window menu and open a new window. Open two additional windows, then tile the windows. Activate a different sheet in each window.

   c. Click in the window containing the Corporate worksheet, then click in cell B3 to make it the active cell. Type an = sign, click in the window containing the Downtown worksheet, click in cell B3, then type a plus sign. Click in the window containing the Midtown worksheet, click in cell B3, then type a plus sign. Finally, click in the window containing the Uptown worksheet, click in cell B3, and then press Enter to complete the formula. Use the fill handle to copy the formula in cell B3 to cells B3:E3, then copy the formulas in row 3 to rows 4–8.

   d. Group the four worksheets. Enter the appropriate Sum functions in cells F3:F8 and cells B9:F9. Cell F9 of the Corporate worksheet should display the value $1,501,937. Use the AutoFormat command to format the completed worksheets. Ungroup the worksheets.

   e. Create a stacked column chart in its own sheet with the data series in rows. Change the name of the worksheet tab as shown.

   f. Use the Page Setup command to create a custom footer for every worksheet containing today's date, the name of the worksheet tab, and your name. Print the completed workbook.

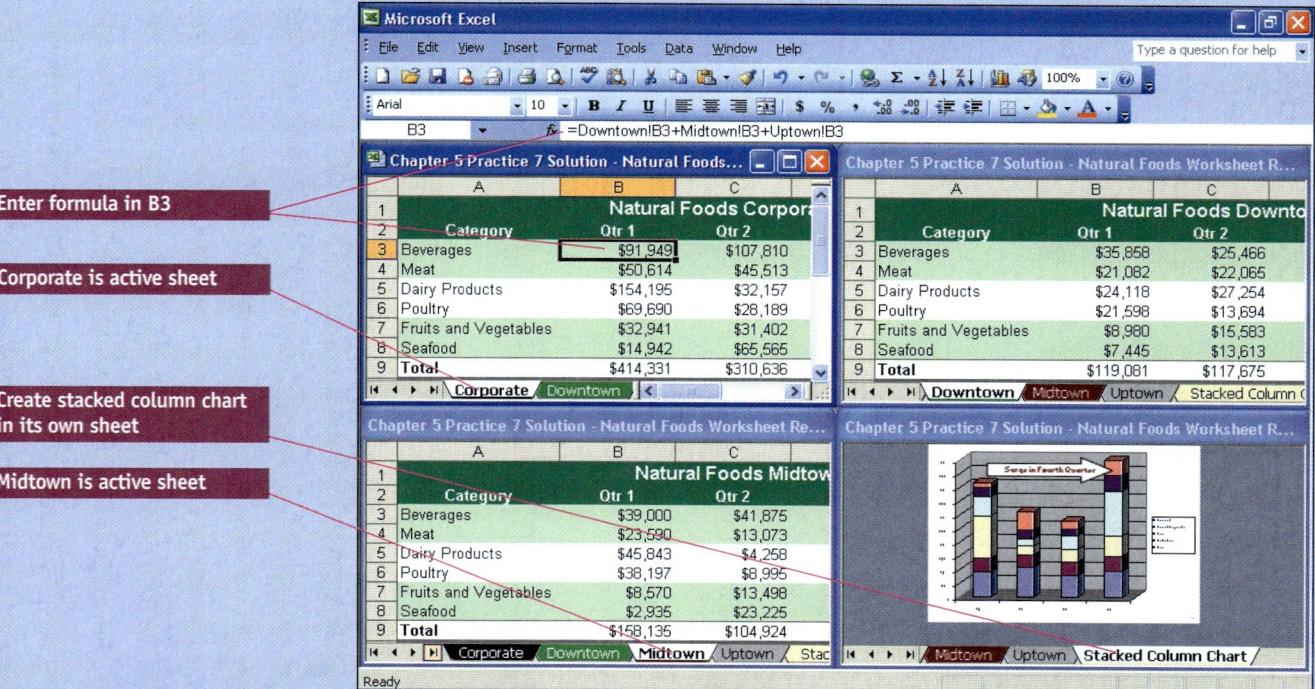

FIGURE 5.19 Natural Foods Worksheet References (exercise 7)

practice exercises

8. **A Look Ahead to Pivot Tables:** A pivot table is an extremely flexible tool that enables you to manipulate the data in multiple worksheets to produce new reports as shown in Figure 5.20. (Pivot tables are covered in more detail in Chapter 8.) Complete the first three hands-on exercises, then follow the instructions below:

   a. Open the Corporate Sales workbook that was completed at the end of the third hands-on exercise. Pull down the Data menu and click the Pivot Table and PivotChart Report command. Click the option buttons to select Multiple Consolidation Ranges and to specify Pivot Table. Click Next.

   b. Click the option button that says I will create the page fields. Click Next.

   c. Specify the range in step 2b of the PivotTable Wizard through pointing. Click the Sheet tab for Atlanta, select cells A2 through E5, then click the Add command button. You should see Atlanta!A$2:$E$5 in the All Ranges list box. Repeat this step for the other two cities.

   d. Remain in step 2b of the PivotTable Wizard. Click the option button for 1 page field. Select (click) the Atlanta range within the All Ranges list box, then click in the Field One list box and type Atlanta. Do not press the Enter key. Select (click) the Boston range within the All ranges list box, then click in the Field One list box and type Boston. Repeat this step for Chicago.

   e. Click Next. Click the option button to create the pivot table on a New Worksheet. Click Finish.

   f. You have a pivot table, but it does not match our figure. Click in cell B3 (the entry in the cell is Column), then click the formula bar and type Quarter, replacing the previous entry. Change the entry in cell A4 from Row to Product. Change the entry in cell A1 from Page1 to City.

   g. Pivot the table to match the figure. Drag Quarter to the row position (cell A4), Product to the column position (cell C3), and City to the row position below Quarter (cell A5). Release the mouse, and the Quarter and City labels will move to the positions shown in the figure.

   h. Format the pivot table so that it matches Figure 5.20. Modify the description on the Documentation worksheet to include the pivot table, then print the pivot table (or the entire workbook if you haven't done so previously).

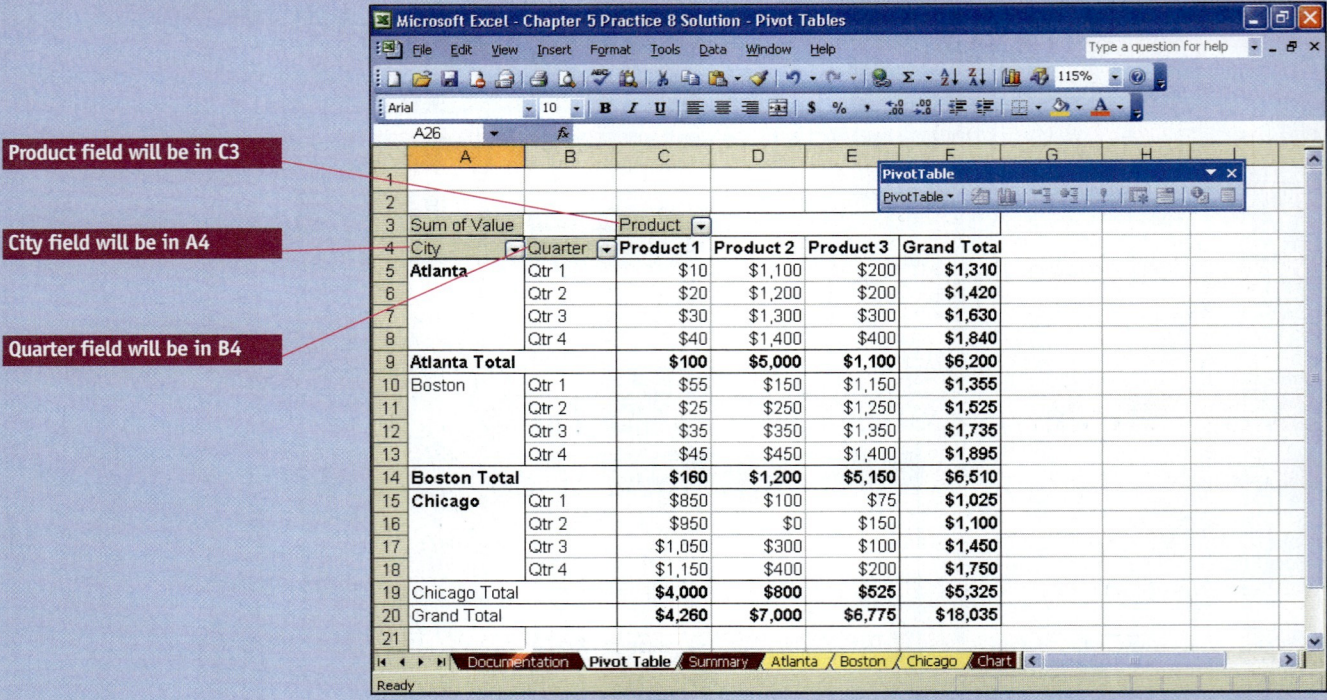

FIGURE 5.20 Pivot Tables (exercise 8)

MINI CASES

Babyland

The Babyland Toy Store has three branches, each of which operates independently. Your job is to consolidate the data in the *Chapter 5 Mini Case—Maplewood*, *Oakwood*, and *Ramblewood* workbooks, each of which is found in the Exploring Excel folder. You are to create a new workbook that contains a worksheet for each store, a summary worksheet that shows the corporate totals for each product in each quarter, and an appropriate chart reflecting the summary data. You are also asked to create a documentation worksheet with your name, date, and a list of all worksheets in the workbook. Print the completed workbook, along with the cell formulas from the summary worksheet, then submit the printout to your instructor as proof you did this exercise. Use the Page Setup command to display your name, today's date, and the name of the worksheet on the output.

Designs by Jessica

The *Chapter 5 Mini Case—Designs by Jessica* workbook in the Exploring Excel folder is only partially complete as it contains worksheets for individual stores, but does not as yet have a summary worksheet. Your job is to retrieve the workbook and create a summary worksheet that shows the corporate totals for each product in each quarter, and then use the summary worksheet as the basis of a three-dimensional column chart reflecting the sales for the past year. Add a documentation worksheet containing your name as financial analyst, then print the entire workbook and submit it to your instructor. Use the Page Setup command to display your name, today's date, and the name of the worksheet on the output.

External References

Each branch manager of Technology Associates creates an identically formatted workbook with the sales information for his or her branch office. Your job as marketing manager is to consolidate the information into a single workbook, and then graph the results appropriately. The branch data is to remain in the individual workbooks; that is, the formulas in your workbook are to contain external references to the *Chapter 5 Mini Case—Eastern*, *Western*, and *Foreign* workbooks in the Exploring Excel folder. Begin by opening the individual workbooks and entering the appropriate formulas to total the data for each product and each quarter. You can then create a summary workbook that reflects the quarterly totals for each branch through external references to the individual workbooks; that is, any change in the individual workbooks should be automatically reflected in the consolidated workbook.

Sophisticates Clothing Time Sheet

The owner of Sophisticates Clothing uses an Excel workbook to compute the weekly wages for its part-time employees. The data for each employee is entered on a separate worksheet, which contains the employee's name, the employee's hourly rate, as well as the time the employee signed in and out each day. Your assignment is to open the partially completed *Chapter 5 Mini Case—Sophisticates Clothing Time Sheet* workbook, compute the number of hours worked for each employee, then use worksheet references to create a summary worksheet with the payroll for that week. It's a simple workbook, and we have entered most of the formatting for you.

The only subtlety pertains to the computation of the hours worked for each employee. It helps to know, therefore, that the time of day is stored internally as a decimal fraction, from 0 to .9999. Midnight (12:00 AM) is stored as 0. Noon (12:00 PM) is stored as 0.5 as it represents half a day. In similar fashion, 6:00 AM and 6:00 PM are stored as .25 and .75, respectively. You can compute the elapsed time between two values, by subtracting the starting time from the ending time. The result is the fraction of a day that has elapsed, which is then converted to the elapsed time in hours by multiplying by 24. (Be sure to multiply by 24 to convert to hours.) Print the completed workbook for your instructor. In addition, print the cell formulas for the Summary worksheet and for one of the employees.

mini cases

Chapter Recap—Bandit's Pizza

Bandit's Pizza offers a tasty pizza at a "steal" of a price, with a strong appeal to the college and family crowds. Their pizzas are generously proportioned, made with a homemade spicy pizza sauce to create a unique zesty flavor, and their list of toppings includes some of the most off-the-wall selections around. This tried and true proven product offering, combined with great customer service, keep their pizzas flying out the door! Bandit's Pizza has expanded from its initial restaurant downtown to two additional sites elsewhere in the city.

The owner, Andreas Marquis, wants to evaluate the overall performance of the chain before expanding further. He is especially interested in the comparative results of three dining categories: dine-in, pick-up, and delivery. Andreas knows you are studying Excel at the local college and asked for your help in return for a small stipend and all the pizza you can eat. You have already prepared a template and distributed it to each restaurant manager, who has entered the sales data for last year. Your next task is to consolidate the data into a single workbook that shows the total sales for each quarter and each dining category. The information should be shown in tabular as well as graphical form.

Your assignment is to review the chapter, paying special attention to the two different ways in which to consolidate data. You can use either technique for the solution; that is, you can create a summary workbook with multiple worksheets, or you can create a summary workbook that links to the individual workbooks. In any event, start with the partially completed *Chapter 5 Ending Case Study—Bandit's Summary* workbook in the Exploring Excel folder. Data for the individual stores (Eastside, Westside, and Downtown) is found in three additional workbooks in the same folder. Print the completed summary workbook for your instructor to show both displayed values and cell formulas. Print the associated chart as well.

CHAPTER

6

Financial Analysis:
Forecasting, Rate of Return, and Amortization

OBJECTIVES

After reading this chapter you will:

1. Develop a spreadsheet model for a financial forecast.
2. Use the Scenario Manager to facilitate decision making.
3. Differentiate between precedent and dependent cells.
4. Use the Formula Auditing toolbar.
5. Track the editing changes that are made to a spreadsheet.
6. Resolve editing conflicts among different users.
7. Use conditional formatting.
8. Create a template.
9. Use the IRR (Internal Rate of Return) function to compute the return on an investment.
10. Define amortization; create an amortization schedule.
11. Use the YEAR, MONTH, DAY, and DATE functions.
12. Use the INDEX and MATCH functions to extract information.

hands-on exercises

1. **A FINANCIAL FORECAST**
   Input: Financial Forecast
   Output: Financial Forecast Solution

2. **AUDITING AND WORKGROUPS**
   Input: Erroneous Financial Forecast
   Output: Erroneous Financial Forecast Solution

3. **CREATING A TEMPLATE**
   Input: Real World Enterprises
   Output: Real World Enterprises Solution

4. **CREATING AN AMORTIZATION SCHEDULE**
   Input: Amortization Schedule
   Output: Amortization Schedule Solution

CASE STUDY
WHISPERING WOODS GOLF CLUB

Gary June was lucky. He made his money with the Internet boom, and then sold out early in 2000 before the market crash. Since then, Gary has played innumerable rounds of golf and dropped his handicap to 5. He can play only so much golf, however, and he is ready for a new challenge, which came upon him quite unexpectedly when he learned the Whispering Woods golf course was for sale.

Gary is thinking of making an offer to buy the club and is using Excel to create a six-year financial forecast. He plans to offer $2.5 million for the club and intends to spend another $1 million immediately for such capital improvements as redoing the greens and enhancing the driving range. The spreadsheet he developed is typical of other financial forecasts, but it does include a limitation on membership. There are currently 130 members and he expects to add another 25 members a year, capping membership at 250. Gary does not plan to charge an initiation fee, but he has set the annual dues rather steeply at $15,000. Capping the membership will ensure that members will always be able to get a tee time, and Gary hopes that this will justify the cost.

Gary's worksheet will be seen by other potential investors who are, at best, casual Excel users. It is important, therefore, to protect the worksheet so that these individuals have access to just the assumptions; they should not be able to modify the formulas. ∎

Your assignment is to read the chapter, paying special attention to the financial forecast that is developed within the chapter. You will then open the partially completed, *Chapter 6 Case Study—Whispering Woods* workbook and develop the appropriate formulas in the body of the worksheet. You are also to compute the rate of return at the end of years two through six of the forecast. Format the completed worksheet, then print the worksheet in landscape orientation with the gridlines and row and column headings. Your name should appear in a custom footer when the worksheet is printed.

A FINANCIAL FORECAST

The chapter-opening case study describes the need for a financial forecast, one of the most common applications of a spreadsheet. We thought it appropriate, however, to focus initially on a less sophisticated example, which we develop throughout the chapter, at the end of which you can complete the case study. We begin therefore with a basic financial forecast and emphasize the importance of isolating the assumptions on which the spreadsheet is based. We introduce the Scenario Manager, which enables you to specify multiple sets of assumptions and input conditions (scenarios), then see the results at a glance. We also introduce the Formula Auditing toolbar and explain how its tools can help ensure the accuracy of a worksheet.

Figure 6.1 displays a financial forecast for Get Rich Quick Enterprises, which contains the projected income and expenses for the company over a five-year period. The spreadsheet enables management to vary any of the *assumptions* at the bottom of the spreadsheet to see the effects on the projected earnings. You don't have to be a business major to follow our forecast. All you have to realize is that the profit for any given year is determined by subtracting expenses from income.

The income is equal to the number of units sold times the unit price. The projected revenue in 2006, for example, is $300,000, based on selling 100,000 units at a price of $3.00 per unit. The variable costs for the same year are estimated at $150,000 (100,000 units times $1.50 per unit). The production facility costs $50,000, and administrative expenses add another $25,000. Subtracting the total expenses from the estimated income yields a net income before taxes of $75,000.

The income and expenses for each succeeding year are based on estimated percentage increases over the previous year, as shown at the bottom of the worksheet. It is absolutely critical to isolate the initial values and assumed rates of increase in this manner, and further, that all entries in the body of the spreadsheet are developed as formulas that reference these cells. The entry in cell C4, for example, is *not* the constant 100,000, but rather a reference to cell C18, which contains the value 100,000.

The distinction may seem trivial, but most assuredly it is not, as two important objectives are achieved. The user sees at a glance which factors affect the results of the spreadsheet (i.e., the cost and earnings projections) and, further, the user can easily change any of those values to see their effect on the overall forecast. Assume, for example, that the first-year forecast changes to 80,000 units sold and that this number will increase at 8% a year (rather than 10%). The only changes in the worksheet are to the entries in cells C18 and E18, because the projected gross revenue is calculated using the values in these cells.

Once you appreciate the necessity of isolating the assumptions and *initial conditions*, you can design the actual spreadsheet. Ask yourself why you are building the spreadsheet in the first place and what you hope to accomplish. (The financial forecast in this example is intended to answer questions regarding projected rates of growth, and more importantly, how changes in the assumptions and initial conditions will affect the income, expenses, and earnings in later years.) This facilitates the creation of the spreadsheet, which is done in five general stages:

1. Enter the row and column headings, and the values for the initial conditions and the assumed rates of change.

2. Develop the formulas for the first year of the forecast based on the initial conditions at the bottom of the spreadsheet.

3. Develop the formulas for the second year based on the values in year one and the assumed rates of change.

4. Copy the formulas for year two to the remaining years of the forecast.

5. Format the spreadsheet, then print the completed forecast.

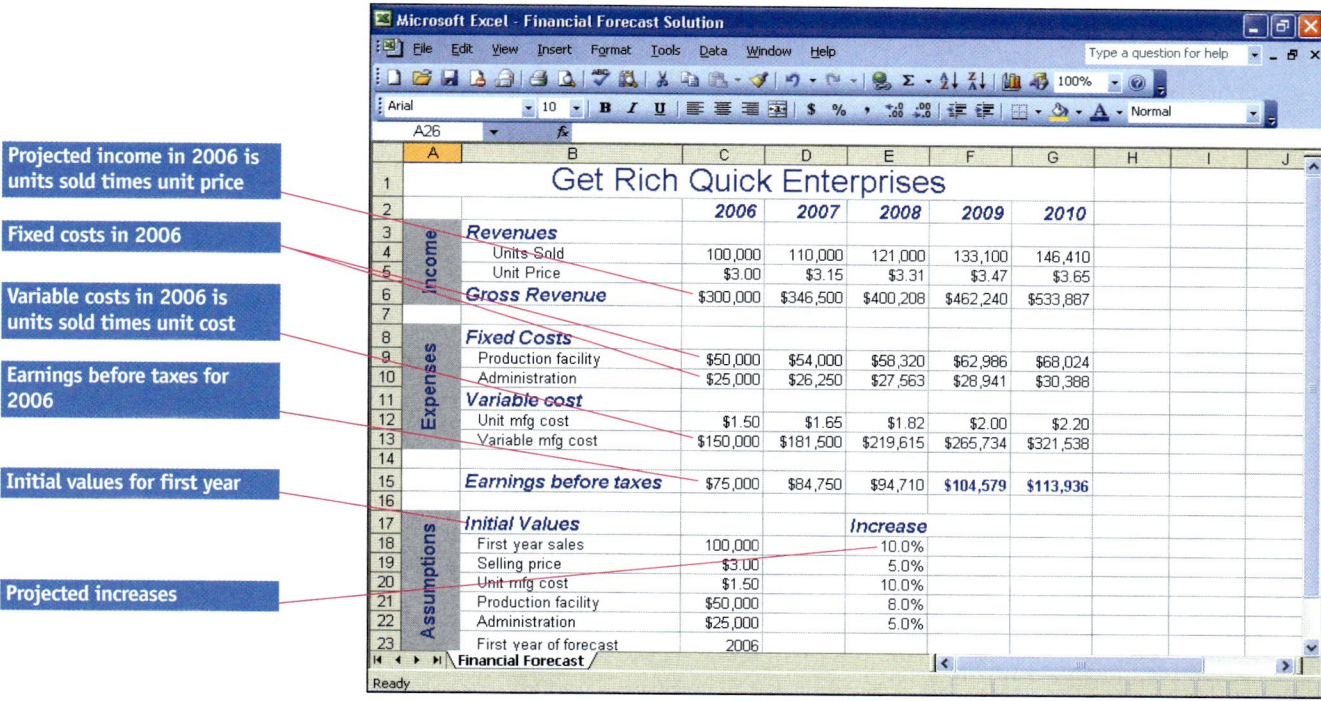

(a) Displayed Values

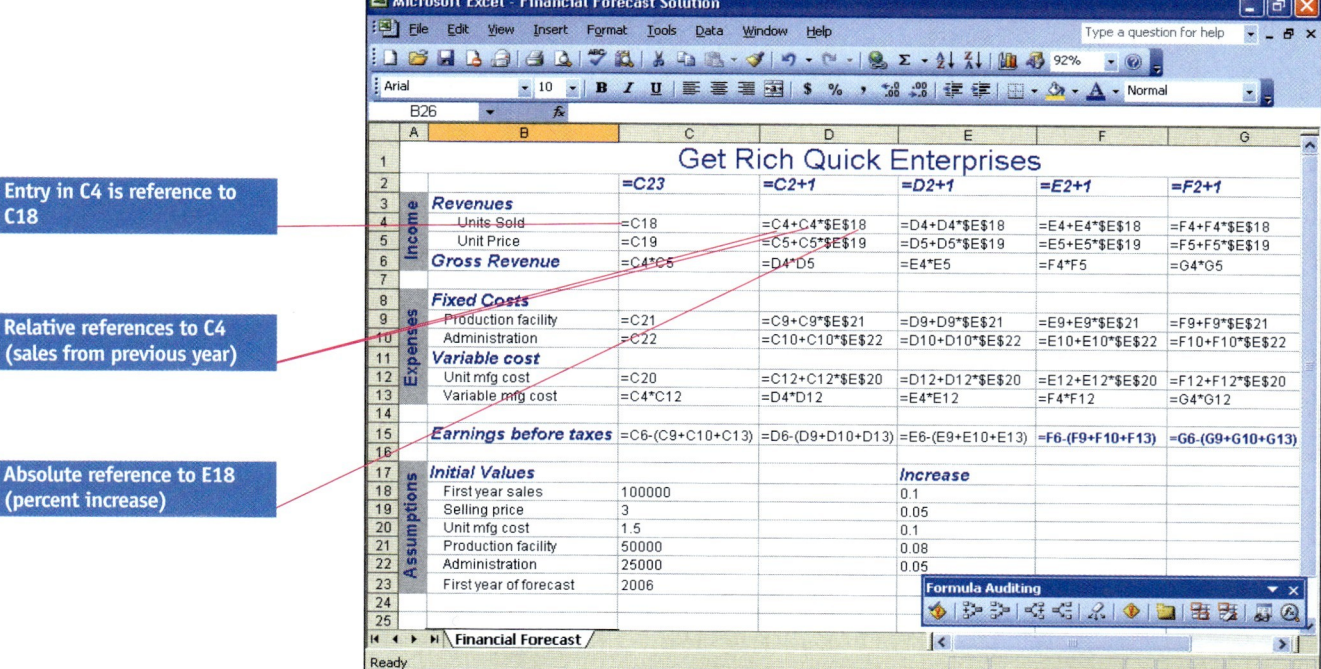

(b) Cell Formulas

FIGURE 6.1 Financial Forecast

Perhaps the most critical step is the development of the formulas for the second year (2007 in Figure 6.1), which are based on the results for 2006 and the assumption about how these results will change for the next year. The units sold in 2007, for example, are equal to the sales in 2006 (cell C4) plus the estimated increase in unit sales (C4*$E$18); that is,

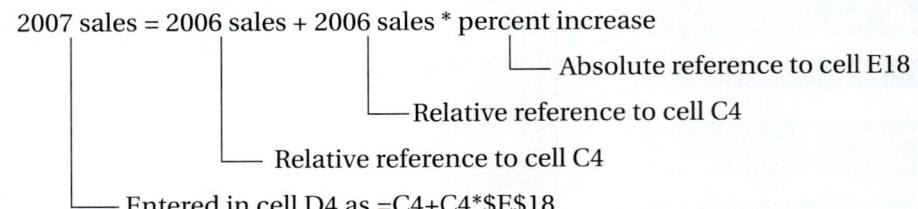

The formula to compute the sales for the year 2007 uses both absolute and relative references, which ensures that it will be copied properly to the other columns for the remaining years in the forecast. An absolute reference ($E$18) is necessary for the cell containing the percent increase in unit sales, because this reference should remain the same when the formula is copied. A relative reference (C4) is used for the sales from the previous year, because this reference should change when the formula is copied. Many of the other formulas in column D are also based on percentage increases from column C, and are developed in similar fashion, as shown in Figure 6.1b.

After the formulas for year two are completed in column D, the entire column is copied to columns E, F, and G to develop the remainder of the forecast. The worksheet is formatted and then printed to complete the exercise. It is now a simple matter to vary any of the assumptions or initial conditions at the bottom of the worksheet and see the result of those changes in the completed forecast.

Advanced Formatting

The spreadsheet in Figure 6.1 incorporates many of the formatting commands that have been used throughout the text. The spreadsheet also illustrates additional capabilities that will be implemented in the hands-on exercise that follows shortly. Some of these features are obvious, such as the ability to ***rotate text*** as seen in column A or the ability to ***indent text*** as was done in column B.

Other capabilities, such as ***conditional formatting***, are more subtle. Look at the projected earnings, for example, and note that amounts over $100,000 are displayed in blue, whereas values under $100,000 are not. One could simply select the two cells and change the font color to blue, but as the earnings change, the cells would have to be reformatted. Accordingly, we implemented the color by selecting the entire row of projected earnings and specifying a conditional format to display the value in blue if it exceeds $100,000, display it in red if it is negative, and default to black otherwise. The use of conditional formatting lets you vary any of the assumptions or initial conditions, which in turn change the projected earnings, yet automatically display the projected earnings in the appropriate color.

The last formatting feature in Figure 6.1 is the imposition of a user-defined style (Main Heading) for various cells in the spreadsheet. A ***style*** (or ***custom format***) is a set of formatting characteristics that is stored under a specific name. You've already used styles throughout the text that were predefined by Excel. Clicking the Comma, Currency, or Percent button on the Formatting toolbar, for example, automatically applies these styles to the selected cells. You can also define your own styles (e.g., Main Heading), as will be done in the hands-on exercise. The advantage of storing the formatting characteristics within a style, as opposed to applying the commands individually, is that you can change the definition of the style, which automatically changes the appearance of all cells defined by that style.

SCENARIO MANAGER

The **Scenario Manager** enables you to specify multiple sets of assumptions (*scenarios*), then see at a glance the results of any given scenario. Each scenario represents a different set of what-if conditions that you want to consider in assessing the outcome of a spreadsheet model. You could, for example, look at optimistic, pessimistic, and most likely (consensus) assumptions, as shown in Figure 6.2. The scenarios are saved with the workbook and are available whenever the workbook is opened.

Figure 6.2a displays the Scenario Manager dialog box that contains the various scenarios that have been created. Each scenario is stored under its own name and is composed of a set of cells whose values vary from scenario to scenario. Figure 6.2b, for example, shows the value of the *changing cells* for the consensus scenario. Figure 6.2c shows the values for the optimistic scenario. (The cells in the dialog box are identified by name, rather than cell reference through the **Define Name command** as will be shown in the next hands-on exercise. First_Year_Sales, for example, refers to cell C18 in the financial forecast. The use of a mnemonic name, as opposed to a cell reference, makes it much easier to understand precisely which values change from one scenario to the next.)

The *scenario summary* in Figure 6.2d compares the effects of the different scenarios to one another by showing the value of one or more *result cells*. We see, for example, that the consensus scenario yields earnings of $113,936 in the fifth year (the same value shown earlier), compared to significantly higher or lower values for the other two scenarios.

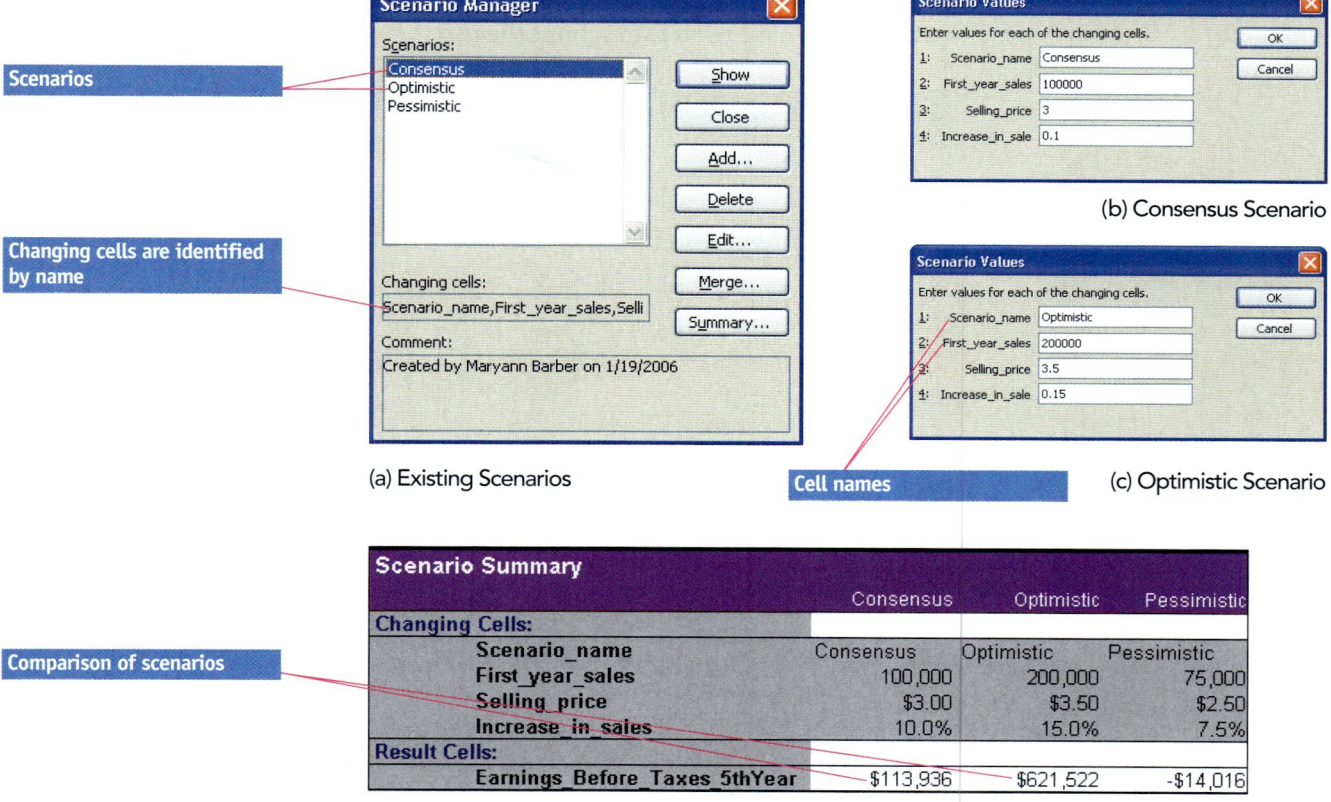

FIGURE 6.2 Scenario Manager

hands-on exercise
1 A Financial Forecast

Objective To develop a spreadsheet for a financial forecast that isolates the assumptions and initial values; to use conditional formatting, styles, indentation, and rotated text to format the spreadsheet. Use Figure 6.3 as a guide in the exercise.

Step 1: **Enter the Formulas for Year One**

- Start Excel. Open the **Financial Forecast workbook** in the **Exploring Excel folder** to display the worksheet in Figure 6.3a. (Cells C4 through C15 are currently empty.)

- Click in **cell C2**. Type **=C23** and press **Enter**. Note that you are not entering the year explicitly, but rather a reference to the cell that contains the year, which is located in the assumptions area of the worksheet.

- Enter the remaining formulas for year one of the forecast:
    - Click in **cell C4**. Type **=C18**. Click in **cell C5**. Type **=C19**.
    - Click in **cell C6**. Type **=C4*C5**. Click in **cell C9**. Type **=C21**.
    - Click in **cell C10**. Type **=C22**. Click in **cell C12**. Type **=C20**.
    - Click in **cell C13**. Type **=C4*C12**.
    - Click in **cell C15**. Type **=C6-(C9+C10+C13)**.

- The cell contents for year one (2006 in this example) are complete. The displayed values in this column should match the numbers shown in Figure 6.3a.

- Save the workbook as **Financial Forecast Solution** in the **Exploring Excel Folder** you have used throughout the text.

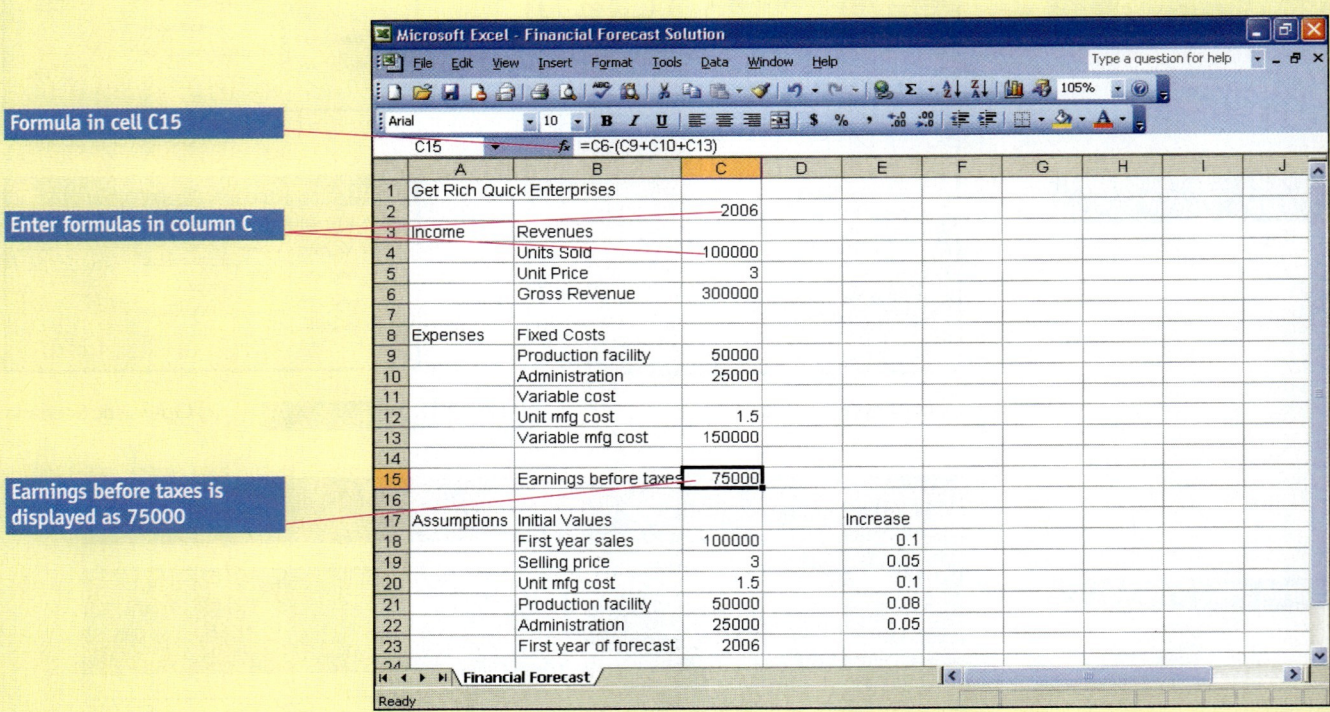

(a) Enter the Formulas for Year One (step 1)

FIGURE 6.3 Hands-on Exercise 1

Step 2: **Enter the Formulas for Year Two**

- Click in **cell D2**. Type **=C2+1** to determine the second year of the forecast.

- Click in **cell D4**. Type **=C4+C4*$E$18**. This formula computes the sales for year two as a function of the sales in year one and the rate of increase.

- Enter the remaining formulas for year two:
  - Click in **cell D5**. Type **=C5+C5*$E$19**. Copy the formula in cell C6 to D6.
  - Click in **cell D9**. Type **=C9+C9*$E$21**.
  - Click in **cell D10**. Type **=C10+C10*$E$22**.
  - Click in **cell D12**. Type **=C12+C12*$E$20**.
  - Copy the formulas in cells C13 and C15 to cells D13 and D15.

- The cell contents for the second year (2007) are complete. The displayed values should match the numbers shown in Figure 6.3b.

- Save the workbook.

Formula in cell D15

Enter formulas in column D

Earnings before taxes is displayed as 84750

(b) Enter the Formulas for Year Two (step 2)

FIGURE 6.3 Hands-on Exercise 1 (*continued*)

USE POINTING TO ENTER CELL FORMULAS

A cell reference can be typed directly into a formula, or it can be entered more easily through pointing. The latter is also more accurate as you use the mouse or arrow keys to reference cells directly. To use pointing, select (click) the cell to contain the formula, type an equal sign to begin entering the formula, click (or move to) the cell containing the reference, then press the F4 key as necessary to change from relative to absolute references. Type any arithmetic operator to place the cell reference into the formula, then continue pointing to additional cells. Press the Enter key to complete the formula.

Step 3: **Copy the Formulas to the Remaining Years**

- Click and drag to select **cells D2 through D15** (the cells containing the formulas for year two). Click the **Copy button** on the Standard toolbar (or use the **Ctrl+C** keyboard shortcut).

- A moving border will surround these cells to indicate that their contents have been copied to the clipboard.

- Click and drag to select **cells E2 through G15** (the cells that will contain the formulas for years three to five). Point to the selection and click the **right mouse button** to display the context-sensitive menu in Figure 6.3c.

- Click **Paste** to paste the contents of the clipboard into the selected cells. The displayed values for the last three years of the forecast should be visible in the worksheet.

- You should see earnings before taxes of 113936 for the last year in the forecast. Press **Esc** to remove the moving border.

- Save the workbook.

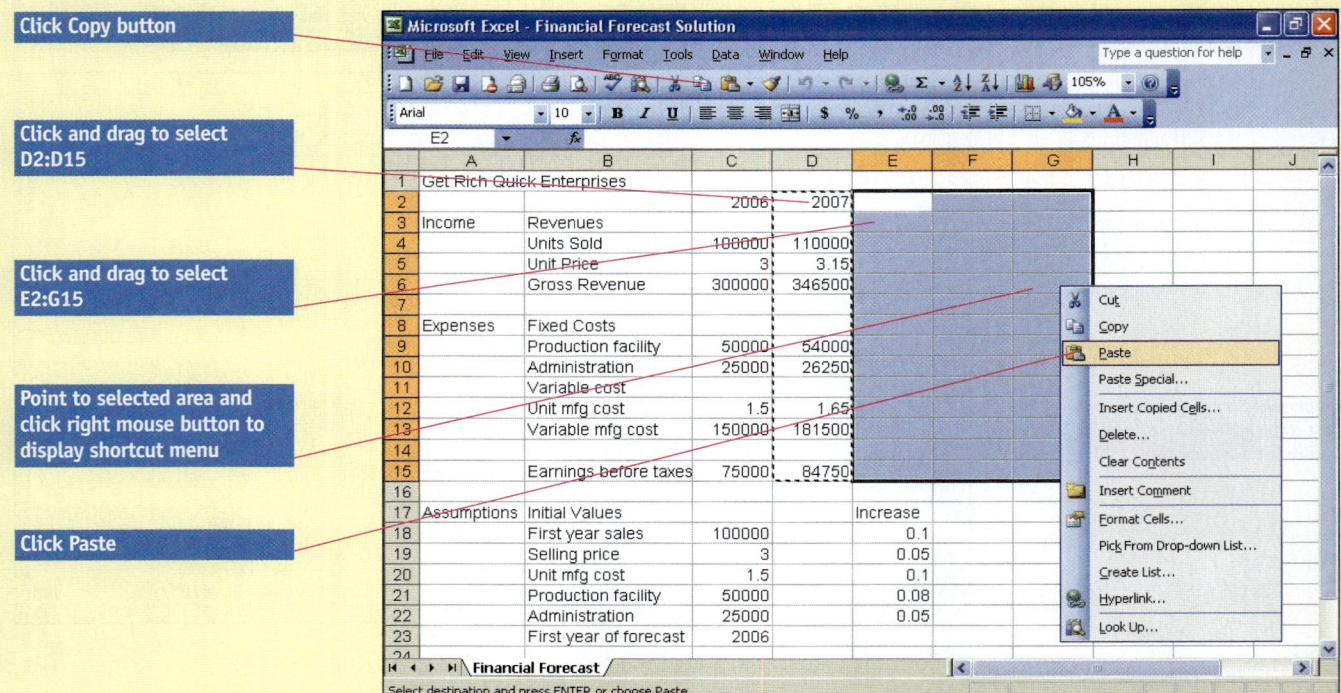

(c) Copy the Formulas to the Remaining Years (step 3)

FIGURE 6.3 Hands-on Exercise 1 (*continued*)

THE FILL HANDLE

There are several ways to copy a formula to cells in adjacent rows or columns. The easiest is the fill handle (the tiny black square) that appears in the lower-right corner of the selected cells. Select the cell (cells) to be copied, then click and drag the fill handle over the destination range. Release the mouse to complete the operation.

Step 4: **Create a Style**

- Point to any toolbar, click the **right mouse button** to display a context-sensitive menu, then click the **Customize command** to display the Customize dialog box. Click the **Commands tab**, then select (click) the **Format category**.

- Click and drag the **Style List box** from within the command section to the right of the font color button on the Formatting toolbar. (You must drag the tool inside the toolbar and will see a large I-beam as you do so.)

- Release the mouse when you position the tool where you want. Click **Close** to close the Custom dialog box.

- The Style list box now appears on the Formatting toolbar as shown in Figure 6.3d. (The Style dialog box is not yet visible.) Click in **cell C2** and note that the Style list box indicates the Normal style (the default style for all cells in a worksheet).

- Change the font in cell C2 to **12 point Arial bold italic**. Click the **down arrow** on the Font Color tool and click **blue**. Pull down the **Format menu** and click the **Style command** to display the Style dialog box.

- The Normal style is already selected. Type **Main Heading** to define a new style according to the characteristics of the selected cell. Click **OK** to create the style and close the dialog box.

- Click and drag to select **cells D2 through G2**. Click the down arrow on the Style list box and select the **Main Heading style** you just created to apply this style to the selected cells.

- Select **cell B3**. Press and hold the **Ctrl key** as you select **cells B6, B8, B11, B15, B17, and E17**, then apply the **Main Heading style** to these cells as well.

- Increase the width of column B so that you can see the text in cell B15. Save the workbook.

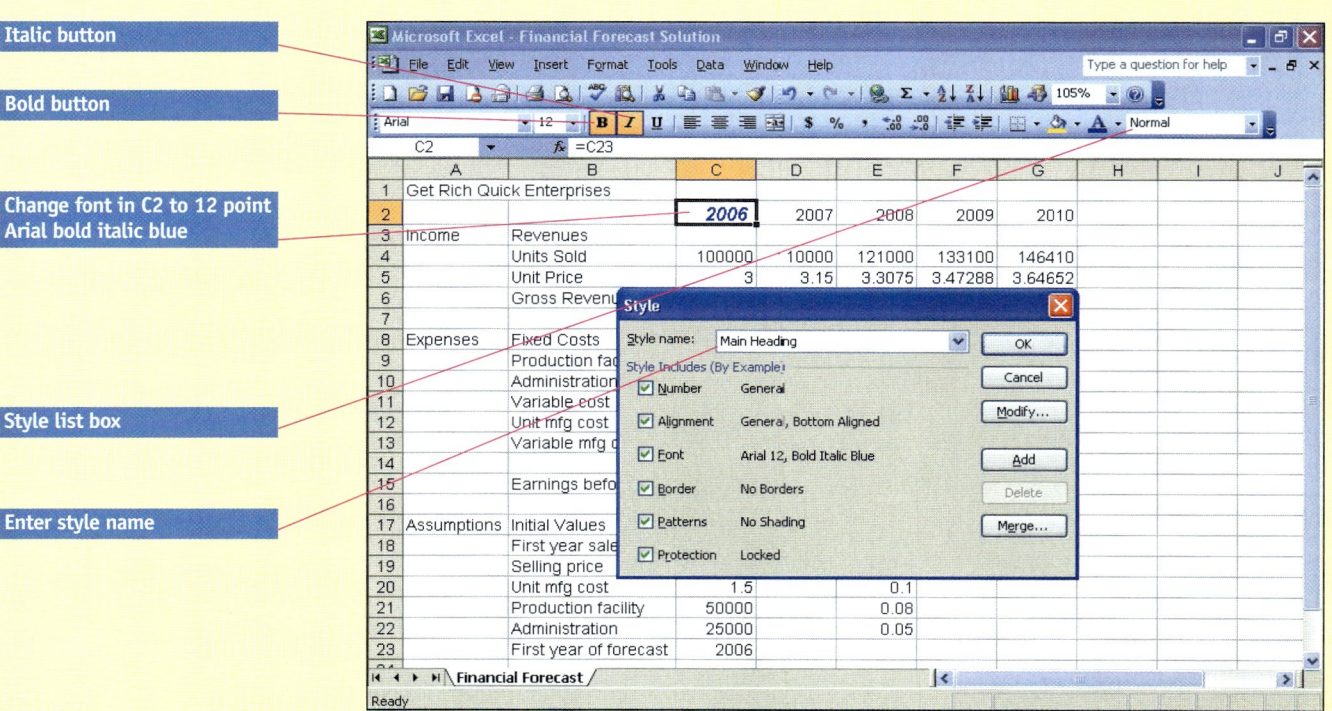

(d) Create a Style (step 4)

FIGURE 6.3 Hands-on Exercise 1 (*continued*)

Step 5: **Rotate and Indent Text**

- Click and drag to select **cell ranges A3:A6, A8:A13, and A17:A23** as shown in Figure 6.3e. Pull down the **Format menu** and click the **Cells command** to display the Format Cells dialog box shown in the figure.

- Click the **Alignment tab** and specify **center alignment** in both the horizontal and vertical list boxes. Check the box to **Merge cells**. Click in the **Degrees text box** and enter **90**.

- Click the **Font tab**, then change the font to **12 point Arial bold**. Change the font color to **blue**.

- Click the **Patterns tab** and choose **gray shading**.

- Click **OK** to accept these changes and close the Format Cells dialog box.

- Click and drag to select the labels in **cells B4 and B5**. Click the **Increase Indent button** on the Formatting toolbar to indent these labels.

- Press and hold the **Ctrl key** as you select **cells B9 and B10, B12 and B13**, and **B18 through B23**. Click the **Increase Indent button** to indent the labels that appear in these cells.

- Save the workbook.

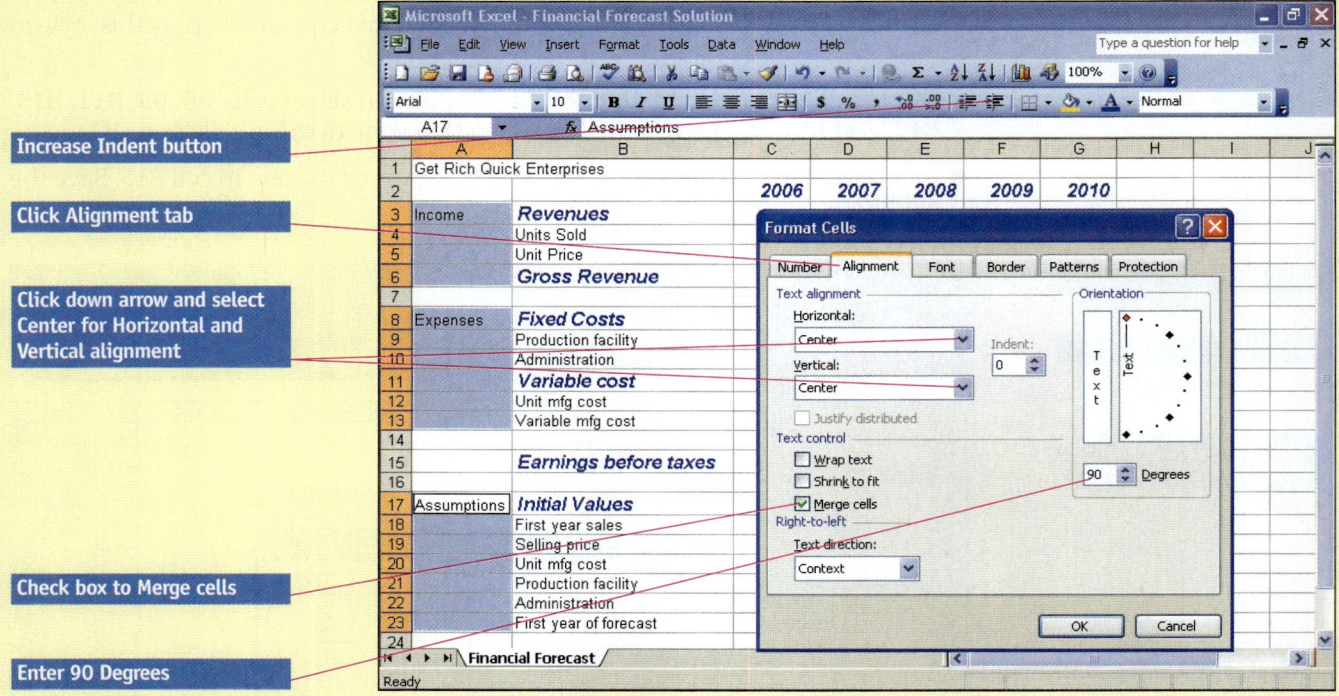

(e) Rotate and Indent Text (step 5)

FIGURE 6.3 Hands-on Exercise 1 (*continued*)

TOGGLE MERGE CELLS ON AND OFF

Click and drag to select multiple cells, then click the Merge and Center button on the Formatting toolbar to merge the cells into a single cell. Click in the merged cell, then click the Merge and Center button a second time and the cell is split. (This is different from Office 2000, where the only way to split cells was to clear the Merge cells check box within the Format Cells dialog box.)

Step 6: **Conditional Formatting**

- Click and drag to select **cells C15 through G15**. Pull down the **Format menu** and click the **Conditional Formatting command** to display the Conditional Formatting dialog box in Figure 6.3f.

- Set the relationships for condition 1 as shown in Figure 6.3f. Click the **Format button** to display the Format Cells dialog box and click the **Font tab**. Change the font style to **bold** and the font color to **blue**. Click **OK**.

- Click the **Add button** and enter the parameters for condition 2 as shown in Figure 6.3f. Click the **Format button**. Change the Font style to **bold** and the color to **red**. Click **OK**.

- Click **OK** to close the Conditional Formatting dialog box. Click any cell to deselect cells C15 to G15. The earnings before taxes for the last two years of the forecast are displayed in bold and in blue, since they exceed $100,000.

- Click in **cell C19**, change the selling price to **2.00**, and press the **Enter key**. The earnings before taxes are displayed in red since they are negative for every year. Click the **Undo button** to return the initial sales price to 3.00.

- Save the workbook.

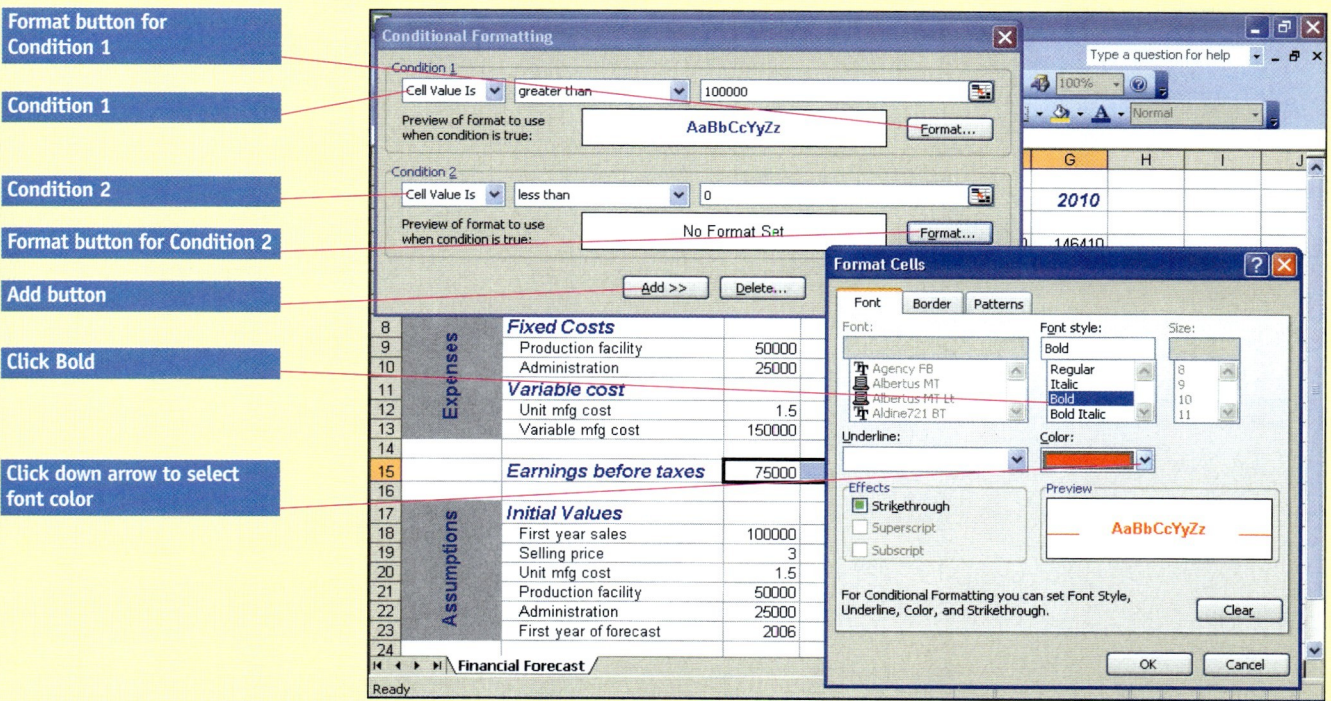

(f) Conditional Formatting (step 6)

FIGURE 6.3 Hands-on Exercise 1 (*continued*)

THE RIGHT MOUSE BUTTON

Point to a cell (or cell range), a worksheet tab, or a toolbar, then click the right mouse button to display a context-sensitive menu. Right clicking a cell, for example, displays a menu with selected commands from the Edit, Insert, and Format menus. Right clicking a toolbar displays a menu that lets you display or hide additional toolbars. Right clicking a worksheet tab enables you to rename, move, copy, or delete the worksheet.

Step 7: **Complete the Formatting**

- Click in **cell A1**. Change the font color to **blue**, and the font size to **22 points**. Click and drag to select **cells A1 through G1**, then click the **Merge and Center button** to center the entry.

- Use Figure 6.3g as a guide to implement the appropriate formatting for the remaining entries in the worksheet. Remember to press and hold the **Ctrl key** if you want to select noncontiguous cells prior to executing a command.

- Add your name into **cell A2**. Save the workbook.

- Print the spreadsheet twice, once to show the displayed values and once to show the cell formulas. Press **Ctrl+~** to toggle between cell formulas and displayed values.

- Submit both printouts to your instructor.

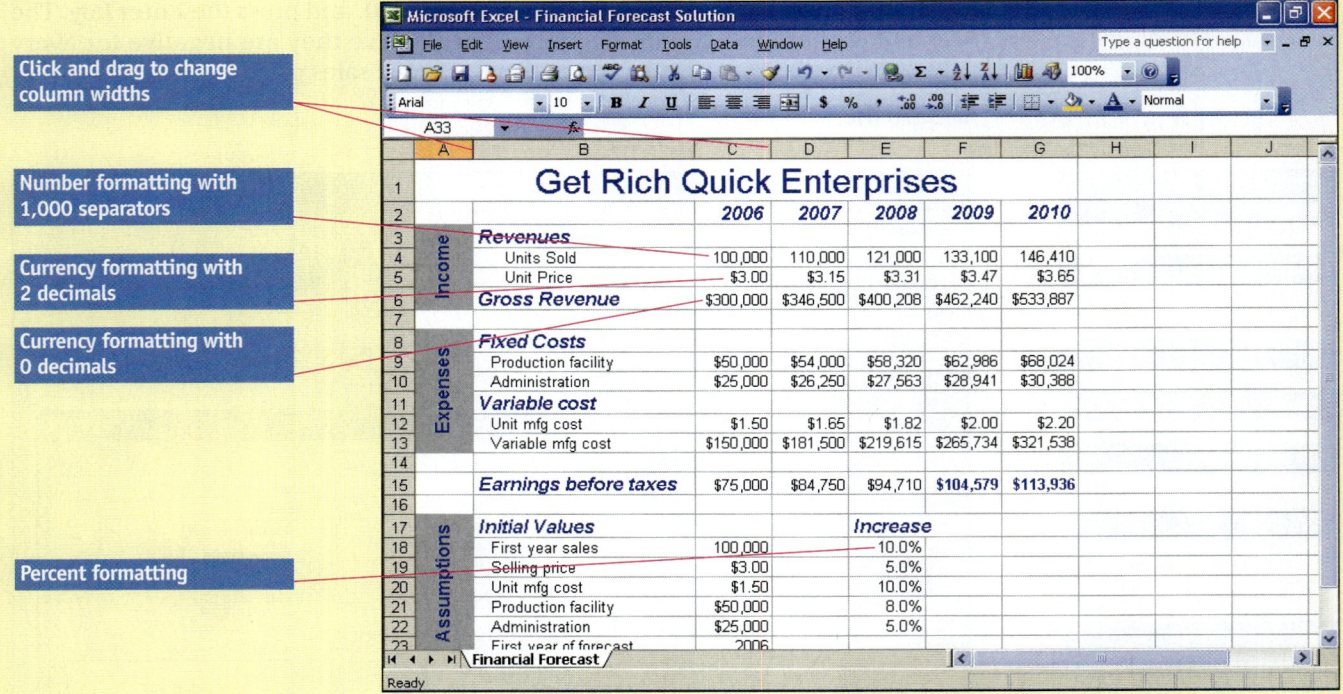

(g) Complete the Formatting (step 7)

FIGURE 6.3 Hands-on Exercise 1 (*continued*)

CREATE A CUSTOM VIEW

Format the spreadsheet to print the displayed values, then pull down the View menu and click Custom Views to display the Custom Views dialog box. Click the button to Add a view, enter the name (e.g., Displayed Values), and click OK. Press Ctrl+~ to display the cell formulas, adjust the column widths as necessary, then pull down the View menu a second time to create a second custom view (e.g., Cell Formulas). You can switch to either view at any time by selecting the Custom Views command and selecting the appropriate view.

Step 8: **The Insert Name Command**

- Click in **cell C18**, pull down the **Insert menu**, select the **Name command**, then click **Define** to display the Define Name dialog box in Figure 6.3h.

- **First_year_sales** is already entered as the default name (because this text appears as a label in the cell immediately to the left of the active cell. Underscores were added between the words, however, because blanks are not permitted in a cell name.) Click **OK** to accept this name.

- Name the other cells that will be used in the various scenarios. Use **Selling_price** as the name for **cell C19**. Enter names of **Increase_in_sales** for **cell E18**, and **Scenario_name** for **cell E23**. (Do not be concerned that cell E23 is currently empty.)

- Save the workbook.

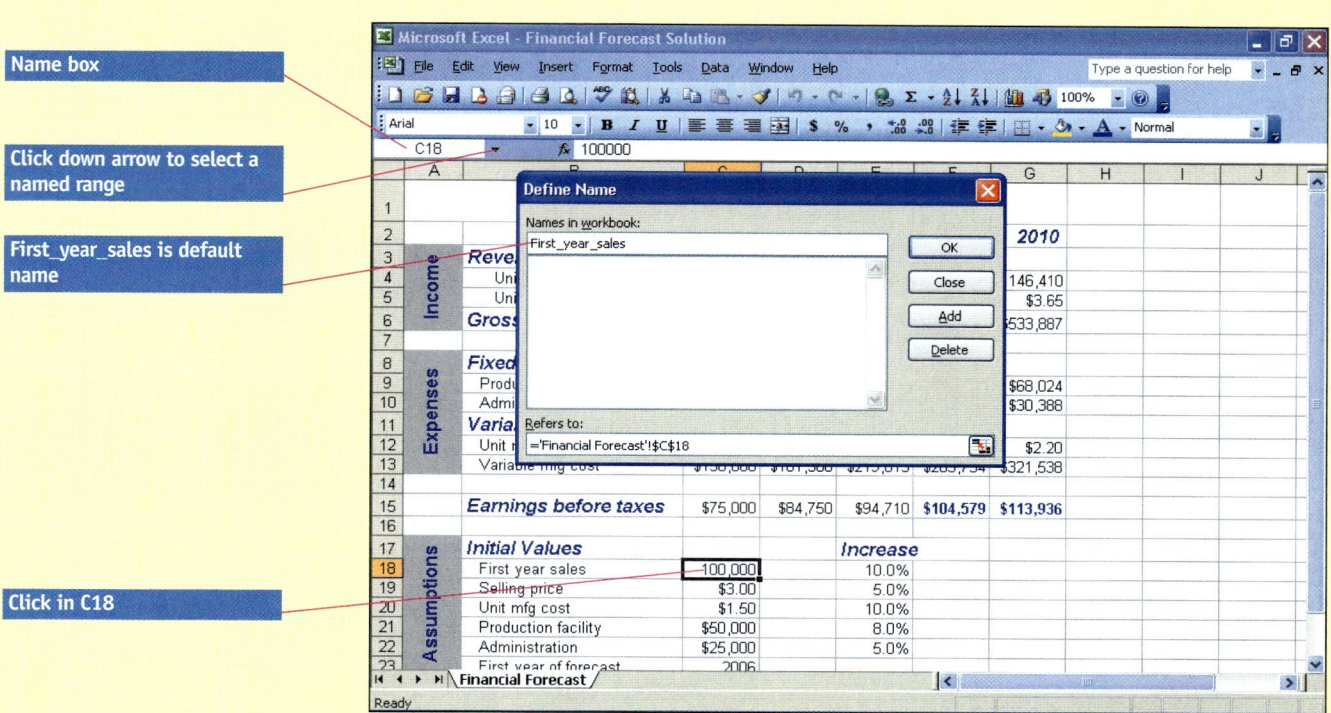

(h) The Insert Name Command (step 8)

FIGURE 6.3 Hands-on Exercise 1 (*continued*)

THE NAME BOX

Use the Name box on the formula bar to define a named range, by first selecting the cell in the worksheet to which the name is to apply, clicking in the Name box to enter the range name, and then pressing the Enter key. Once the name has been defined, you can use the Name box to select a named range by clicking in the box and then typing the appropriate cell reference or name or simply by clicking the drop-down arrow next to the Name box to select the name from a drop-down list. Named ranges make a scenario easier to read since we see mnemonic names, as opposed to cell references such as C18.

Step 9: **Create the Scenarios**

- Click in **cell E23** and type the word **Consensus**. Click in **cell E17**, click the **Format Painter button** on the Formatting toolbar, then click in **cell E23** to copy the format from cell E17.

- Pull down the **Tools menu**. Click **Scenarios** to display the Scenario Manager dialog box. Click the **Add command button** to display the Add Scenario dialog box in Figure 6.3i. Type **Consensus** in the Scenario Name text box.

- Click in the **Changing Cells text box**. Cell E23 (the active cell) is already entered as the first cell in the scenario. Type a comma, then enter **C18, C19, and E18** as the remaining cells in the scenario. Click **OK**.

- You should see the Scenario Values dialog box with the values of this scenario already entered from the corresponding cells in the worksheet.

- Click the **Add command button** to add a second scenario called **Optimistic**. The changing cells are already entered and match the Consensus scenario. Click **OK**. Enter **Optimistic, 200000, 3.5**, and **.15**, as the values for the changing cells. Click **Add**.

- Enter a Pessimistic scenario in similar fashion, using **Pessimistic, 75000, 2.5**, and **.075**, for the changing cells. Click **OK**.

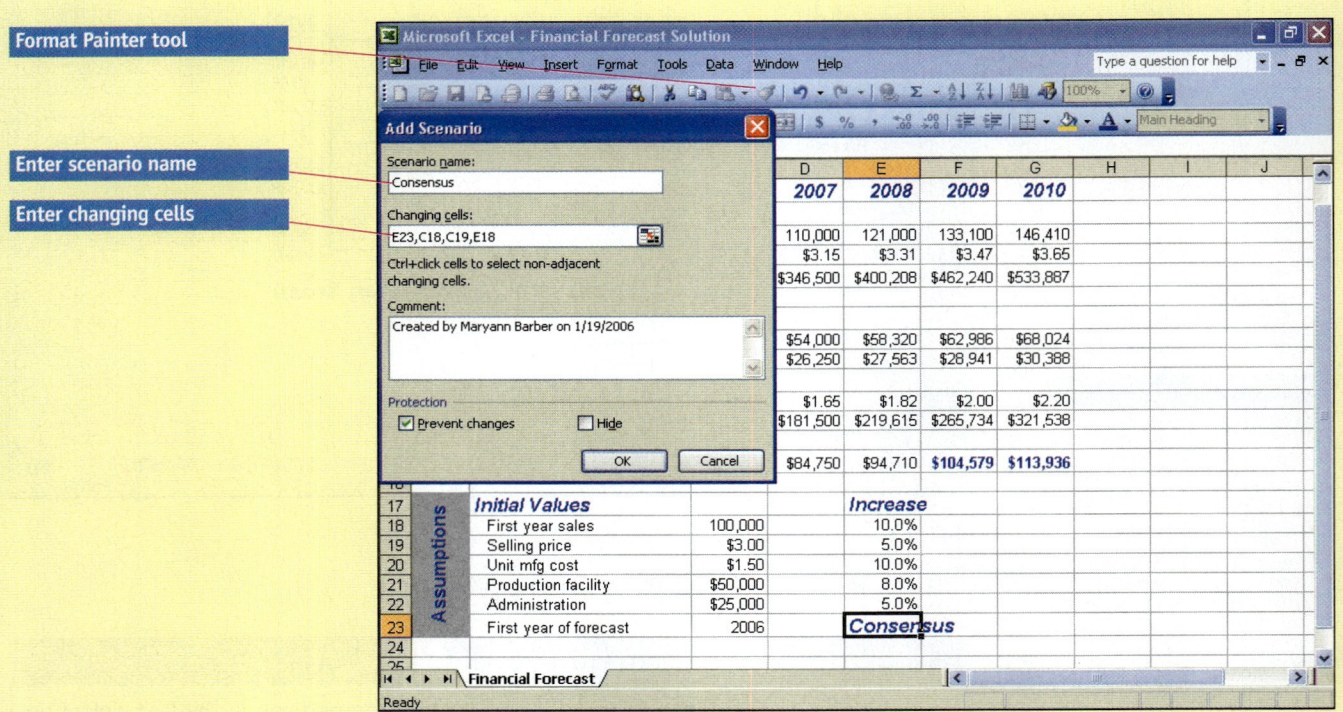

(i) Create the Scenarios (step 9)

FIGURE 6.3 Hands-on Exercise 1 (*continued*)

ISOLATE THE ASSUMPTIONS

The formulas in a worksheet should always be based on cell references that are clearly labeled, set apart from the rest of the worksheet. You can then vary the inputs (or assumptions) on which the worksheet is based to see the effect within the worksheet. You can change the values manually, or store sets of values within a specific scenario.

Step 10: **View the Scenarios**

- The Scenario Manager dialog box should still be open as shown in Figure 6.3j. If necessary, pull down the **Tools menu** and click the **Scenarios command** to reopen the Scenario Manager.

- There should be three scenarios listed—Consensus, Optimistic, and Pessimistic—corresponding to the scenarios that were just created.

- Select the **Optimistic scenario**, then click the **Show button** (or simply double click the scenario name) to display the financial forecast under the assumptions of this scenario.

- Double click the **Pessimistic scenario**, which changes the worksheet to show the forecast under these assumptions.

- Double click the **Consensus scenario** to return to this scenario. Do you see how easy it is to change multiple assumptions at one time by storing the values in a scenario?

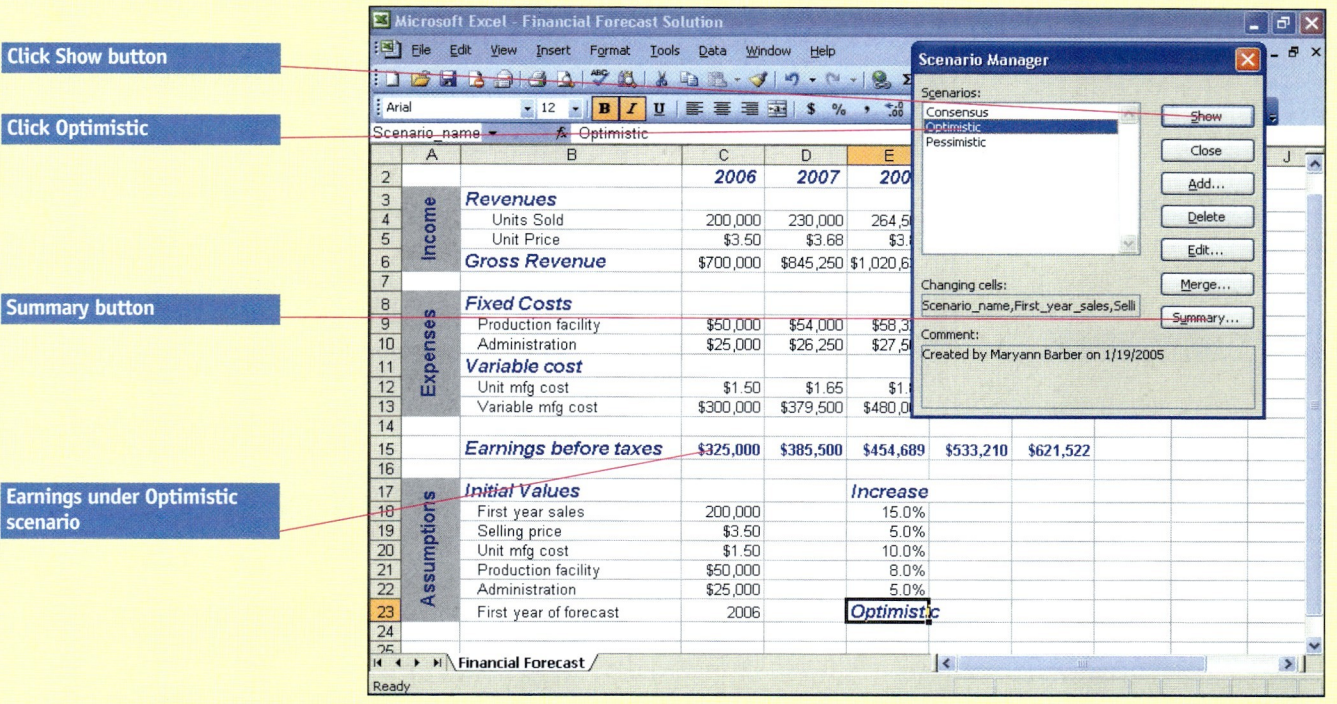

(j) View the Scenarios (step 10)

FIGURE 6.3 Hands-on Exercise 1 (*continued*)

THE SCENARIO LIST BOX

The Scenario Manager list box lets you select a scenario directly from a toolbar. Point to any toolbar, click the right mouse button to display a shortcut menu, then click Customize to display the Customize dialog box. Click the Commands tab, select Tools in the Categories list box, then click and drag the Scenario list box to an empty space on the toolbar. Click Close to close the dialog box and return to the workbook. Click the down arrow on the Scenario list box, which now appears on the toolbar, to choose from the scenarios that have been defined within the current workbook.

Step 11: **The Scenario Summary**

- The Scenario Manager dialog box should still be open. Click the **Summary button** to display the Scenario Summary dialog box.

- If necessary, click the **Scenario Summary option button**. Click in the **Result Cells text box**, then click in **cell G15** (the cell that contains the earnings before taxes in the fifth year of the forecast). Click **OK**.

- You should see a Scenario Summary worksheet as shown in Figure 6.3k. Each scenario has its own column in the worksheet. The changing cells, identified by name rather than cell reference, are listed in column C.

- The Scenario Summary worksheet is an ordinary worksheet to the extent that it can be modified like any other worksheet. Click the header for **row 6**, then press and hold the **Ctrl key** as you click and drag **rows 12 to 14**. Right click the selected cells, then click the **Delete command** from the context-sensitive menu.

- Delete Column D in similar fashion. Add your name to the worksheet. Save the workbook, then print the summary worksheet for your instructor. Close the workbook.

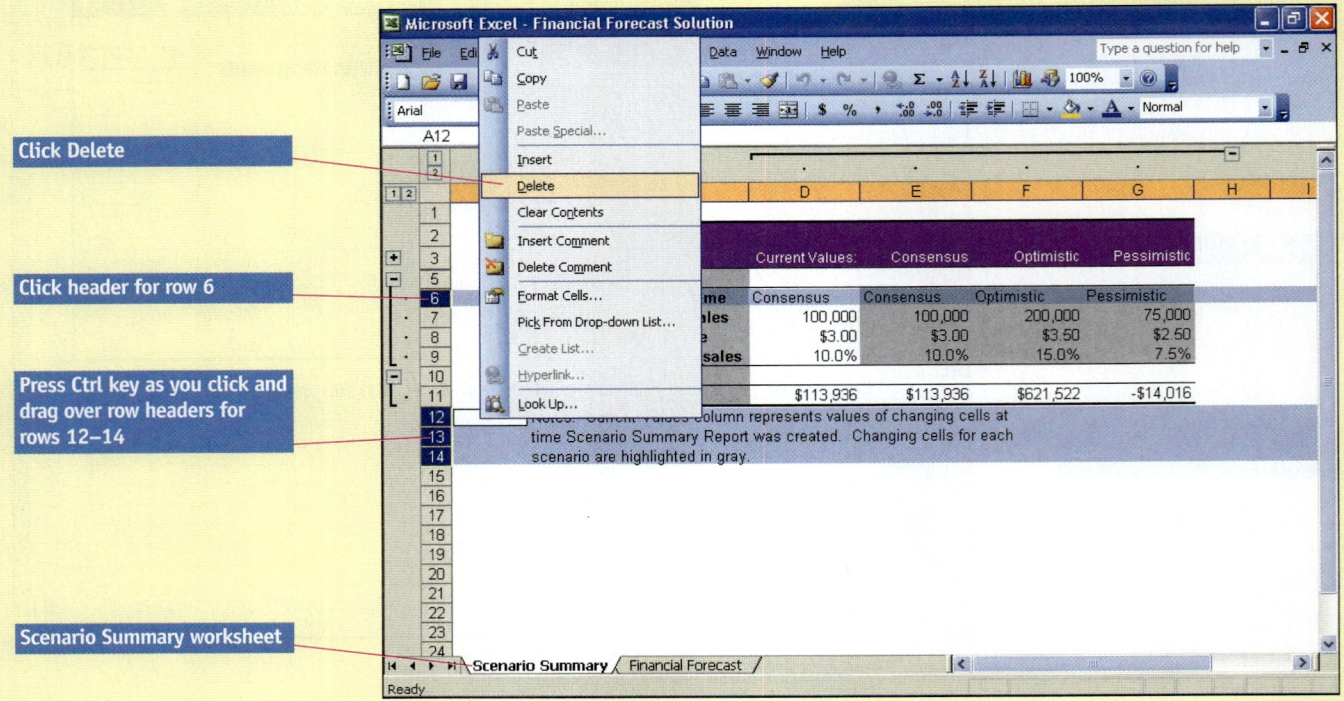

(k) The Scenario Summary (step 11)

FIGURE 6.3 Hands-on Exercise 1 (*continued*)

THE SCENARIO SUMMARY WORKSHEET

You can return to the Scenario Manager to add or modify an individual scenario, after which you can create a new scenario summary. You must, however, execute the command when the original worksheet is displayed on the screen. Note, too, that each time you click the Summary button within the Scenario Manager, you will create another summary worksheet called Scenario Summary 2, Scenario Summary 3, and so on. You can delete the extraneous worksheets by right clicking the worksheet tab, then clicking the Delete command.

WORKGROUPS AND AUDITING

The spreadsheet containing the financial forecast is a tool that will be used by management as the basis for decision making. Executives in the company will vary the assumptions on which the spreadsheet is based to see the effects on profitability, then implement changes in policy based on the results of the spreadsheet. But what if the spreadsheet is in error? Think, for a moment, how business has become totally dependent on the spreadsheet, and what the consequences might be of basing corporate policy on an erroneous spreadsheet.

It's one thing if the assumptions about the expected increases turn out to be wrong because the very nature of a forecast requires us to deal with uncertainty. It's inexcusable, however, if the formulas that use those assumptions are invalid. Thus, it's common for several people to collaborate on the same spreadsheet to minimize the chance for error. One person creates the initial version, then distributes copies to the **workgroup** (the persons working on a project). Each person enters his or her comments and/or proposed changes, then the various workbooks can be merged into a single workbook. It's also possible to create a **shared workbook** and place it on a network drive to give all reviewers access to a common file.

Consider, for example, Figure 6.4, which displays an *erroneous* version of the financial forecast. One of the first things you notice about Figure 6.4 is the comments by different people, Marion, Jodi, and Ben, who have reviewed the spreadsheet and suggested changes. Anyone with access to the shared workbook can change it using the tools on the **Reviewing toolbar** or through the **Track Changes command**. The changes made by different people to cell formulas are even displayed in different colors. You, as the developer, can then review the collective changes and resolve any conflicts that might occur.

How can you, or any of the reviewers, know when a spreadsheet displays invalid results? One way is to "eyeball" the spreadsheet and try to approximate its results. Look for any calculations that are obviously incorrect. Look at the financial forecast, for example, and see whether all the values are growing at the projected rates

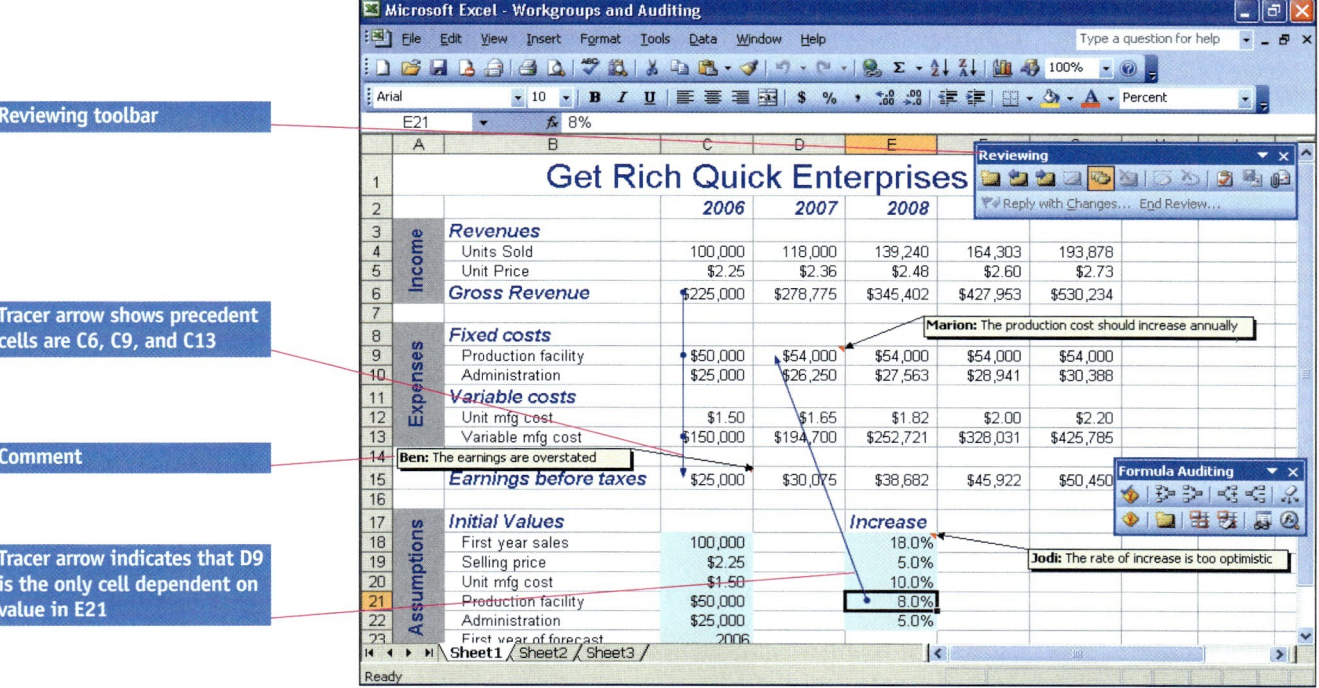

FIGURE 6.4 Workgroups and Auditing

of change. The number of units sold and the unit price increase every year as expected, but the cost of the production facility remains constant after 2007 (Marion's comment). This is an obvious error, because the production facility is supposed to increase at 8% annually, according to the assumptions at the bottom of the spreadsheet. The consequence of this error is that the production costs are too low and hence the projected earnings are too high. The error was easy to find, even without the use of a calculator.

A more subtle error occurs in the computation of the earnings before taxes. Look at the numbers for 2006. The gross revenue is $225,000. The total cost is also $225,000 ($50,000 for the production facility, $25,000 for administration, and $150,000 for the manufacturing cost). The projected earnings should be zero, but are shown incorrectly as $25,000 (Ben's comment), because the administration cost was not subtracted from the gross revenue in determining the profit.

You may be good enough to spot either of these errors just by looking at the spreadsheet. You can also use the **Formula Auditing toolbar** to display the relationships between the various cells in a worksheet. It enables you to trace the **precedents** for a formula and identify the cells in the worksheet that are referenced by that formula. It also enables you to trace the **dependents** of a cell and identify the formulas in the worksheet that reference that cell.

The identification of precedent and/or dependent cells is done graphically by displaying **tracers** on the worksheet. You simply click in the cell for which you want the information, then you click the appropriate button on the Formula Auditing toolbar. The blue lines (tracers) appear on the worksheet, and will remain on the worksheet until you click the appropriate removal button. The tracers always point forward, from the precedent cells to the dependent formula.

Look again at Figure 6.4 to see how the tracers are used. Cell C15 contains the formula to compute the earnings for the first year. There is a tracer (blue line) pointing to this cell, and it indicates the precedents for the cell. In other words, we can see that cells C6, C9, and C13 are used to compute the value of cell C15. Cell C10 is not a precedent, however, and therein lies the error.

The analysis of the cost of the production facility is equally telling. There is a single tracer pointing away from cell E21, indicating that there is only one other cell (cell D9) in the worksheet that depends on the value of cell E21. In actuality, however, cells E9, F9, and G9 should also depend on the value of cell E21. Hence the cost of the production facility does not increase as it is supposed to. Jodi's comment about the unrealistic rate of the sales increase is best addressed through the Data Validation command.

Data Validation

The results of the financial forecast depend on the accuracy of the spreadsheet as well as the underlying assumptions. One way to stop such errors from occurring is through the **Data Validation command**, which enables the developer to restrict the values that can be entered into a cell. If the cell is to contain a text entry, you can limit the values to those that appear in a list such as Atlanta, Boston, or Chicago. In similar fashion, you can specify a quantitative relationship for numeric values such as > 0 or < 100.

Figure 6.5a displays the Settings tab in the Data Validation dialog box in which the developer prevents the value in cell E18 (the annual sales increase) from exceeding 15%. Figure 6.5b shows the type of error alert (a Warning) and the associated message that is to appear if the user does not enter a valid value. Figure 6.5c displays the dialog box the user sees if the criteria are violated, together with the indicated choice of actions. "Yes" accepts the invalid data into the cell despite the warning, "No" returns the user to the cell for further editing, and "Cancel" restores the previous value to the cell. The Formula Auditing toolbar contains a tool to **circle invalid data** if the warning is disregarded.

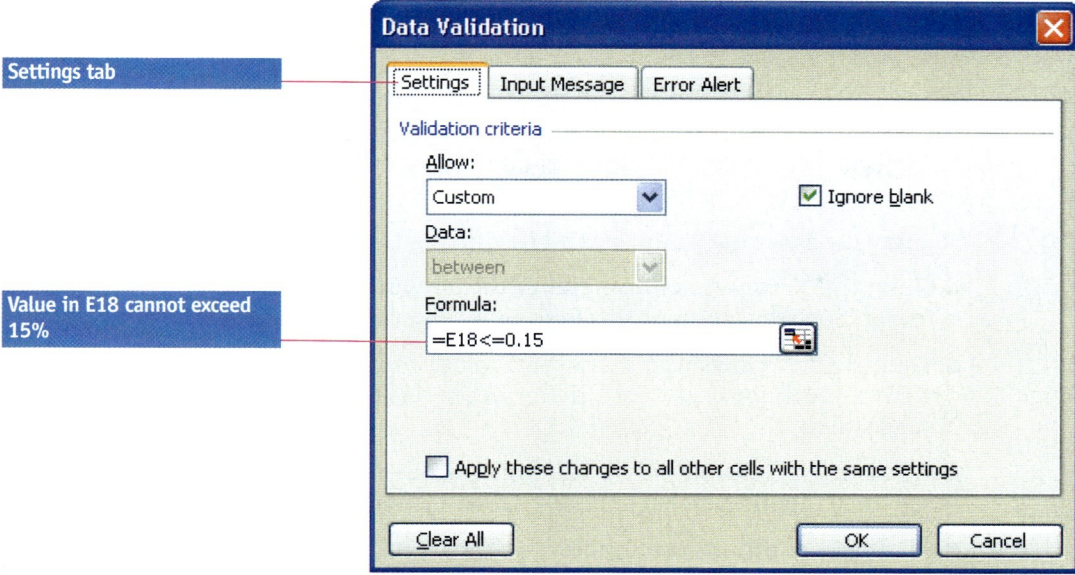

(a) Settings Tab

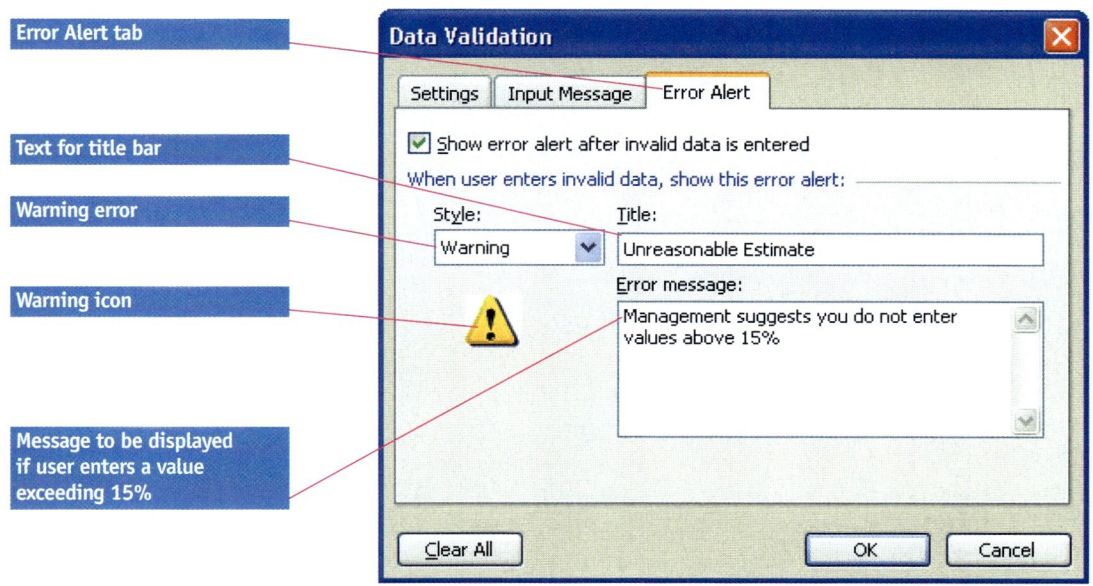

(b) Error Alert Tab

(c) Displayed Error Message

FIGURE 6.5   The Data Validation Command

hands-on exercise 2

Auditing and Workgroups

Objective To illustrate the tools on the Formula Auditing toolbar; to trace errors in spreadsheet formulas; to insert and delete comments; to track changes in a workbook. Use Figure 6.6 as a guide in the exercise.

Step 1: **Display the Formula Auditing and Reviewing Toolbars**

- Open the **Erroneous Financial Forecast workbook** in the **Exploring Excel folder**. Save the workbook as **Erroneous Financial Forecast Solution**.

- The title bar shows that this workbook has been previously established as a shared workbook. It has already been reviewed and changes have been suggested.

- Point to any toolbar, click the **right mouse button** to display a context-sensitive menu, then click **Customize** to display the Customize dialog box.

- Click the **Toolbars tab**, check the boxes for the **Reviewing** and **Formula Auditing toolbars**, then close the dialog box to display the toolbars as in Figure 6.6a.

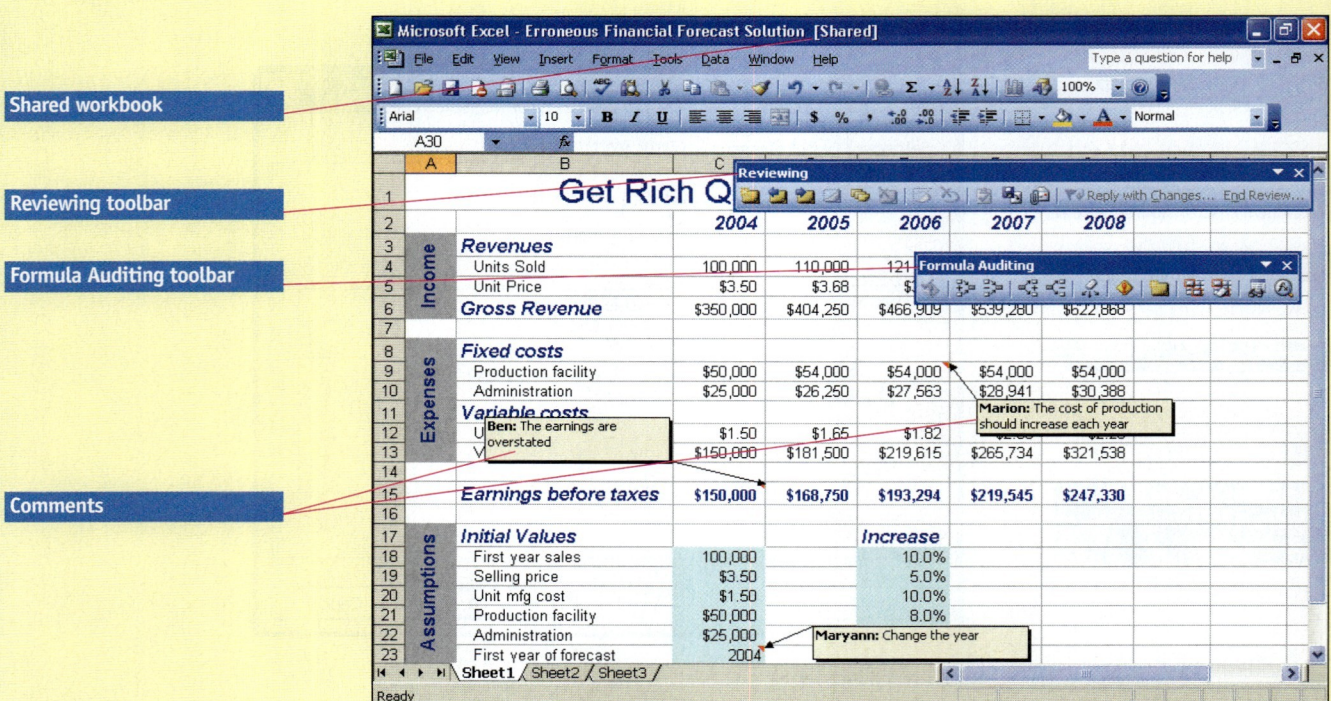

(a) Display the Formula Auditing and Reviewing Toolbars (step 1)

FIGURE 6.6 Hands-on Exercise 2

COMMENTS VERSUS CHANGES

A reviewer can suggest comments through the Insert Comment command and/or enter changes directly through the Track Changes command. Comments are visible immediately when you point to the cell, whereas changes are not visible until Track Changes is turned on. Comments display only the reviewer's name. Changes show the name, date, and time of the change.

Step 2: **Highlight Changes**

- Pull down the **Tools menu**, click (or point to) the **Track Changes command**, then click **Highlight Changes** to display the Highlight Changes dialog box. Set the various options to match our selections in Figure 6.6b. Click **OK**.

- You should see a border around cell C19 to indicate that a change has been made to the contents of that cell. Point to the cell and you will see a ScreenTip indicating that Robert Grauer changed the contents from $2.25 to $3.50.

- Click in **cell C23**. Type **2006** to modify the year (as suggested by Maryann) and press **Enter**. The years change automatically at the top of the forecast.

- Maryann's comment is now obsolete. Thus, right click in **cell C23** to display the context-sensitive menu, then click the **Delete Comment command**.

- The comment is removed from the cell and the red triangle disappears. The cell is still enclosed in a blue border and has a blue triangle to indicate that its value has changed. Point to **cell C23** to see the modification.

- Click the **Hide All Comments button** on the Reviewing toolbar. The comments are still in the worksheet, but are no longer visible.

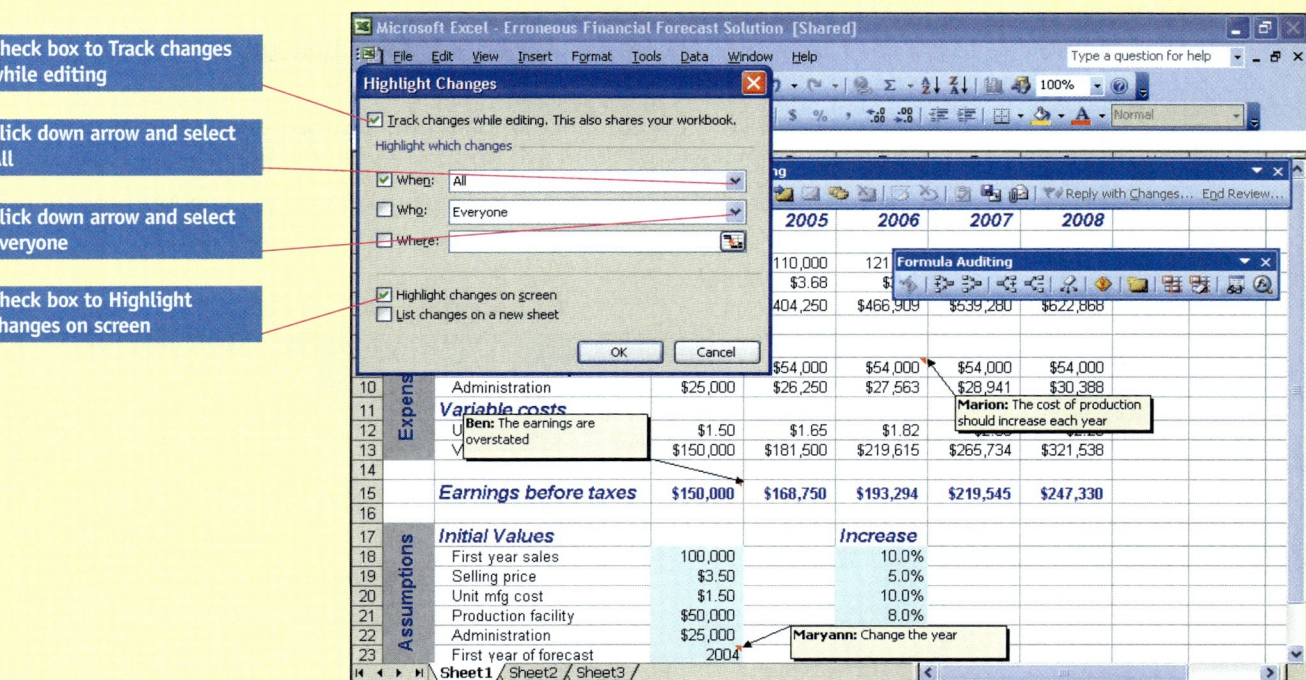

(b) Highlight Changes (step 2)

FIGURE 6.6 Hands-on Exercise 2 (*continued*)

CHANGE THE YEAR

A well-designed spreadsheet facilitates change by isolating the assumptions and initial conditions. 2004 has come and gone, but all you have to do to update the forecast is to click in cell C23, and enter 2006 as the initial year. The entries in cells C2 through G2 (containing years of the forecast) are changed automatically as they contain formulas (rather than specific values) that reference the value in cell C23.

Step 3: **Trace Dependents**

- Point to **cell E9** to display the comment, which indicates that the production costs do not increase after the second year. Click in **cell E21** (the cell containing the projected increase in the cost of the production facility).

- Click the **Trace Dependents button** on the Formula Auditing toolbar to display the dependent cells as shown in Figure 6.6c. Only one dependent cell (cell D9) is shown. This is clearly an error because cells E9 through G9 should also depend on cell E21.

- Click in **cell D9** to examine its formula. The production costs for the second year are based on the first-year costs (cell C9) and the rate of increase (cell E21). The latter, however, was entered as a relative rather than an absolute address.

- Change the formula in **cell D9** to include an absolute reference to cell E21 (i.e., the correct formula is =C9+C9*$E$21). The tracer arrow disappears due to the correction.

- Drag the fill handle in **cell D9** to copy the corrected formula to cells E9, F9, and G9. The displayed value for cell G9 should be $68,024. Delete Marion's comment in cell E9, which is no longer applicable.

- Cells D9 through G9 have a blue border and a blue triangle to indicate that changes were made to these cells.

- Click in **cell E21**. Click the **Trace Dependents button**, and this time it points to the production costs for years two through five in the forecast.

- Click the **Remove Dependent Arrows button** on the Formula Auditing toolbar to remove the arrows.

- Save the workbook.

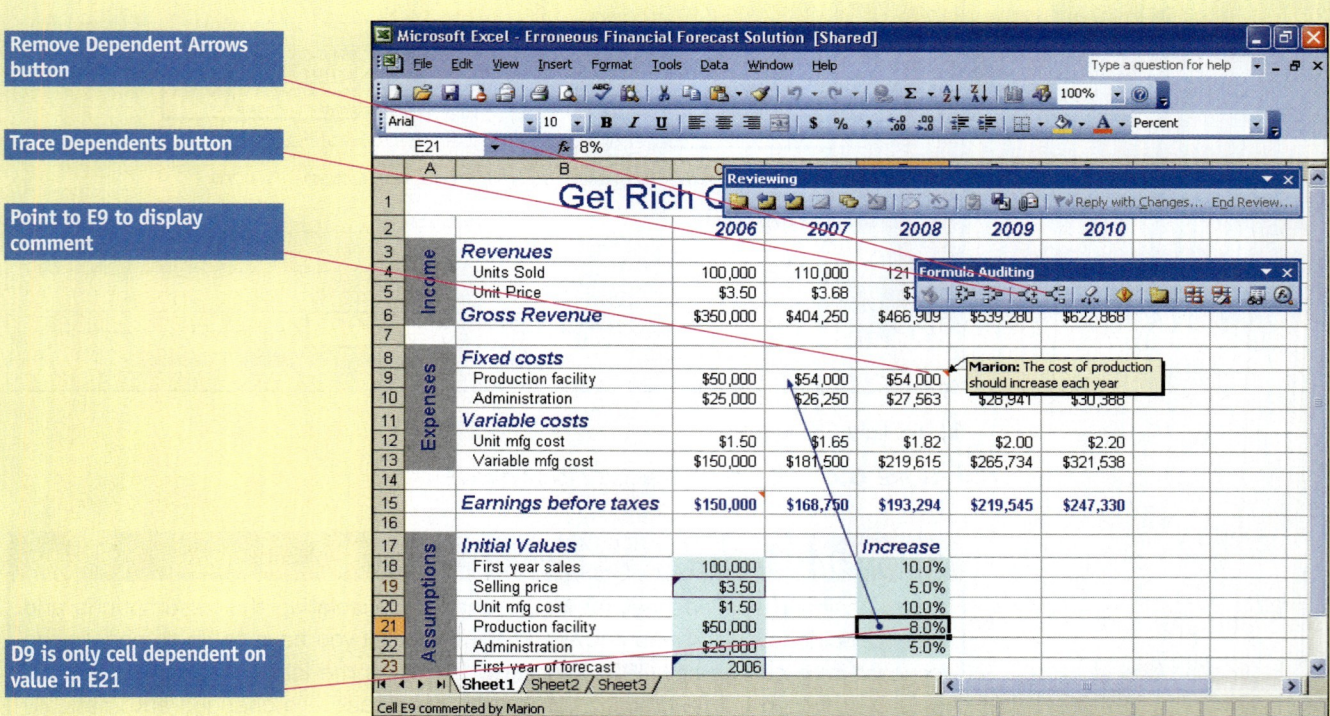

(c) Trace Dependents (step 3)

FIGURE 6.6 Hands-on Exercise 2 (*continued*)

Step 4: **Trace Precedents**

- Point to **cell C15** to display Ben's comment that questions the earnings before taxes. Now click in **cell C15** and click the **Trace Precedents button** to display the precedent cells as shown in Figure 6.6d.

- There is an error in the formula because the earnings do not account for the administration expense (cell C10).

- Change the formula in cell C15 to **=C6-(C9+C10+C13)**. The earnings change to $125,000 after the correction.

- Drag the fill handle in **cell C15** to copy the corrected formula to cells D15 through G15. (The latter displays a value of $202,918 after the correction.)

- Point to **cell C15**. You see both the change and the comment. Now right click in **cell C15** and delete the comment, which is no longer applicable. Only the comment is deleted, not the ScreenTip associated with the change.

- Save the workbook.

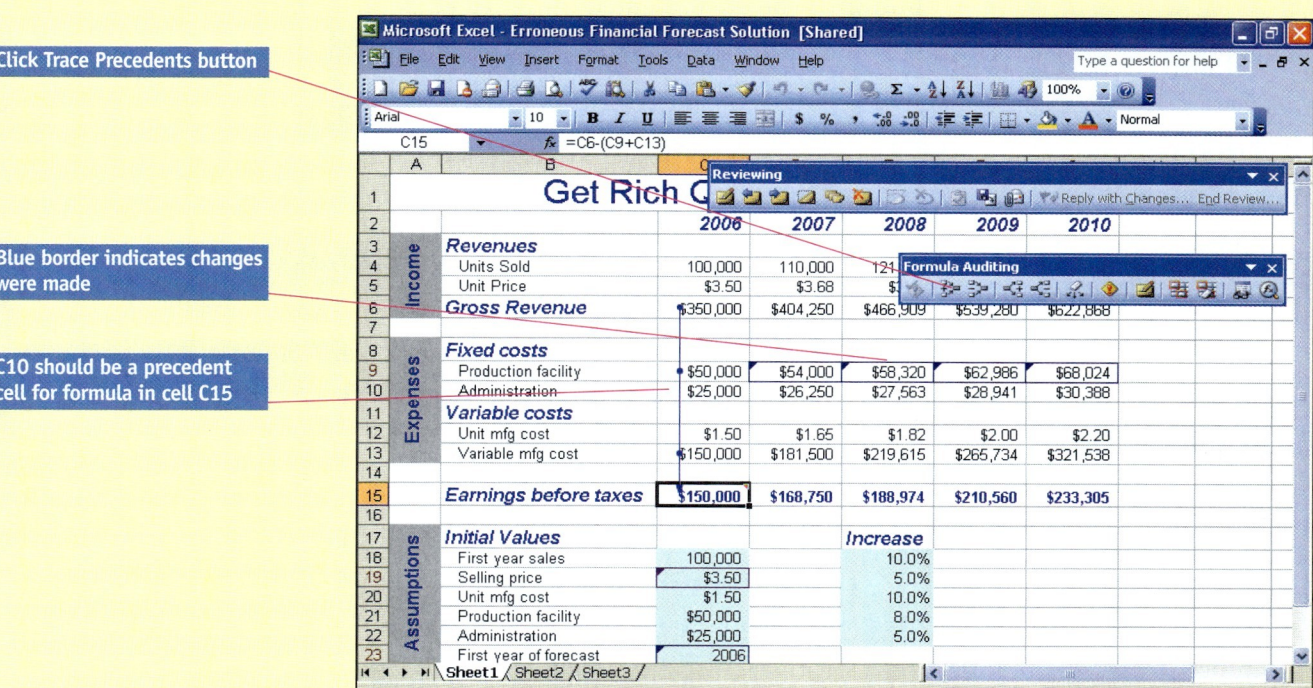

(d) Trace Precedents (step 4)

FIGURE 6.6 Hands-on Exercise 2 (*continued*)

THE FORMULAS ARE COLOR-CODED

The fastest way to change the contents of a cell is to double click in the cell, then make the changes directly in the cell rather than to change the entries on the formula bar. Note, too, that if the cell contains a formula (as opposed to a literal entry), Excel will display each cell reference in the formula in a different color, which corresponds to the border color of the referenced cells elsewhere in the worksheet. This makes it easy to see which cell or cell range is referenced by the formula. You can also click and drag the colored border to a different cell to change the cell formula.

Step 5: **Accept or Reject Changes (resolve conflicts)**

- Pull down the **Tools menu**, click the **Share Workbook command** to display the Share Workbook dialog box, then click the **Advanced tab**.

- Look for the Conflicting Changes Between Users section (toward the bottom of the dialog box), then if necessary, click the option button that says "Ask me which changes win". Click **OK**.

- Pull down the **Tools menu**, click (or point to) the **Track Changes command**, then click **Accept or Reject Changes**. You can accept the default selections in the Selection Changes dialog box. Click **OK**.

- You should see the Accept or Reject Changes dialog box in Figure 6.6e. You see Robert Grauer's change from $2.25 to $3.50. Click the **Reject button**. (The contents of cell C19 change in the worksheet to $2.25, which in turn affects several other values throughout the spreadsheet.)

- Click **Accept** (or press **Ctrl+A**) to accept the next change, which was the change you made earlier in the first year of the forecast. Press the **Accept button** as you are presented with each additional change.

- Save the workbook.

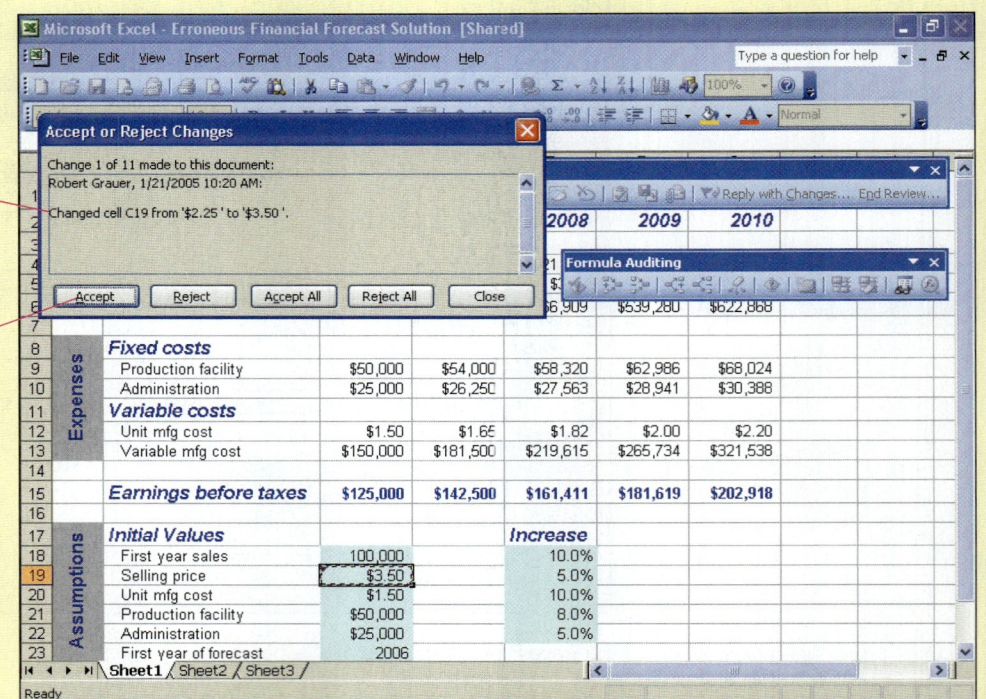

(e) Accept or Reject Changes (step 5)

FIGURE 6.6 Hands-on Exercise 2 (*continued*)

CIRCULAR REFERENCES

A circular reference occurs when a cell formula references itself, either directly or indirectly. Excel indicates the problem automatically and displays a circular reference toolbar which shows the interdependencies of the affected cells. Excel also gives you the option to remove the reference and/or to override the error and calculate the spreadsheet manually using multiple iterations to arrive at a steady state value. See practice exercise 10 at the end of the chapter.

Step 6: **Insert a Comment**

- Click in **cell C19** (the cell containing the selling price for the first year). Pull down the **Insert menu** and click the **Comment command** (or click the **New Comment button** on the Reviewing toolbar).

- A comment box opens, as shown in Figure 6.6f. Enter the text of your comment as shown in the figure, then click outside the comment when you are finished.

- The comment box closes, but a tiny red triangle appears in the upper-right corner of cell C19. (If you do not see the triangle, pull down the **Tools menu**, click **Options**, click the **View tab**, then click the option button in the Comments area to show **Comment Indicator only**.)

- Point to **cell C19** and the text of your comment appears. Point to a different cell and the comment disappears.

- Save the workbook.

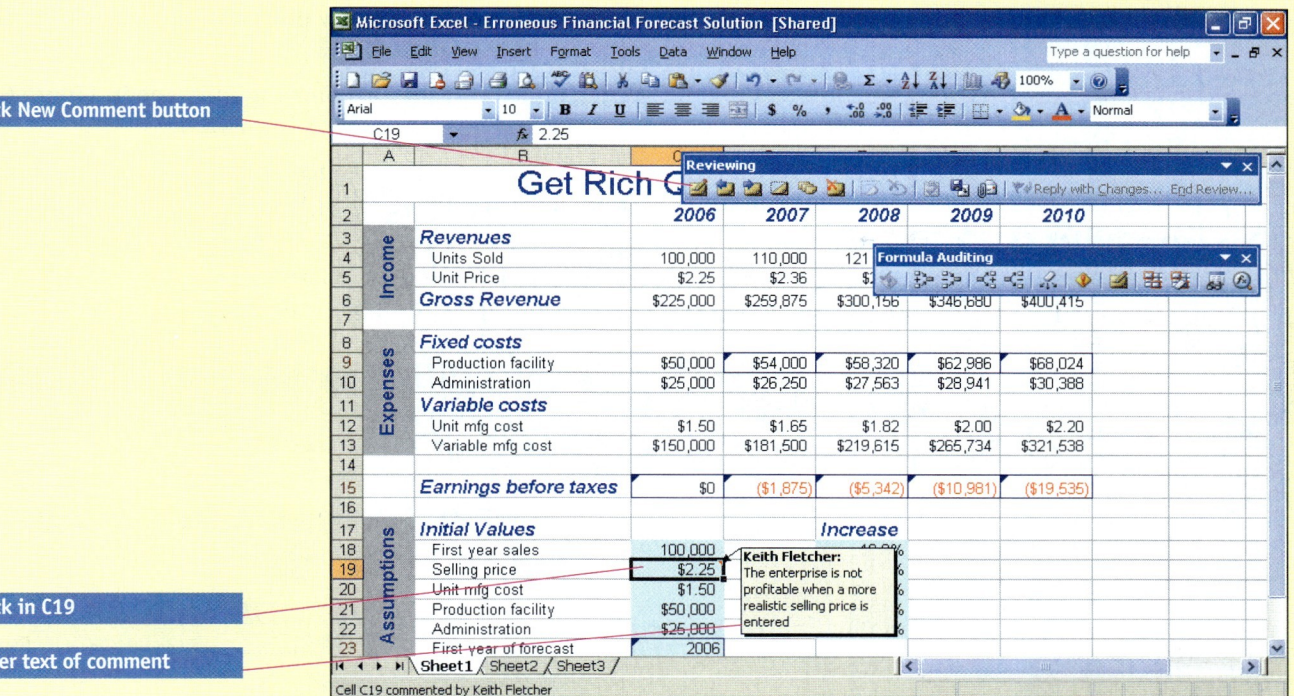

(f) Insert a Comment (step 6)

FIGURE 6.6 Hands-on Exercise 2 (*continued*)

EDITING OR DELETING COMMENTS

The easiest way to edit or delete an existing comment is to point to the cell containing the comment, then click the right mouse button to display a context-sensitive menu, in which you select the appropriate command. You can use the right mouse button to insert a comment by right clicking in the cell, then choosing the Insert Comment command. You can also insert or delete a comment by using the appropriate tool on the Reviewing toolbar.

Step 7: **Data Validation**

- Click in **cell E18**. Type **.18**. Excel displays the error message "Management will not accept a value above 15%." Press **Esc** to cancel. You are not be able to enter a value above .15 into cell E18 because the error type we previously defined was specified as "Stop" rather than a warning.

- Pull down the **Data menu**. The Validation command is dim and not currently accessible because the workbook is currently a shared workbook.

- Pull down the **Tools menu**, click (or point to) the **Track Changes command**, then click **Highlight Changes** to display the Highlight Changes dialog box. Clear the box to track changes while editing. Click **OK**.

- Click in **cell E18**. Pull down the **Data menu**. Click the **Validation command** (which is now accessible) to display the Data Validation dialog box, and if necessary, click the **Error Alert tab**.

- Click the **drop-down arrow** on the Style list box and click **Warning**. Change the text of the message to **Management frowns on values above 15%**. Click **OK** to accept the new settings and close the dialog box.

- Reenter **.18** in **cell E18**. This time you see the Warning message in Figure 6.6g rather than a Stop message. Click **Yes** to accept the new value.

- Add your name somewhere into the workbook. Save the workbook, then print the completed workbook for your professor as proof that you completed the exercise.

- Close the Reviewing and Formula Auditing toolbars. Close the workbook. Exit Excel if you do not want to continue with the next exercise at this time.

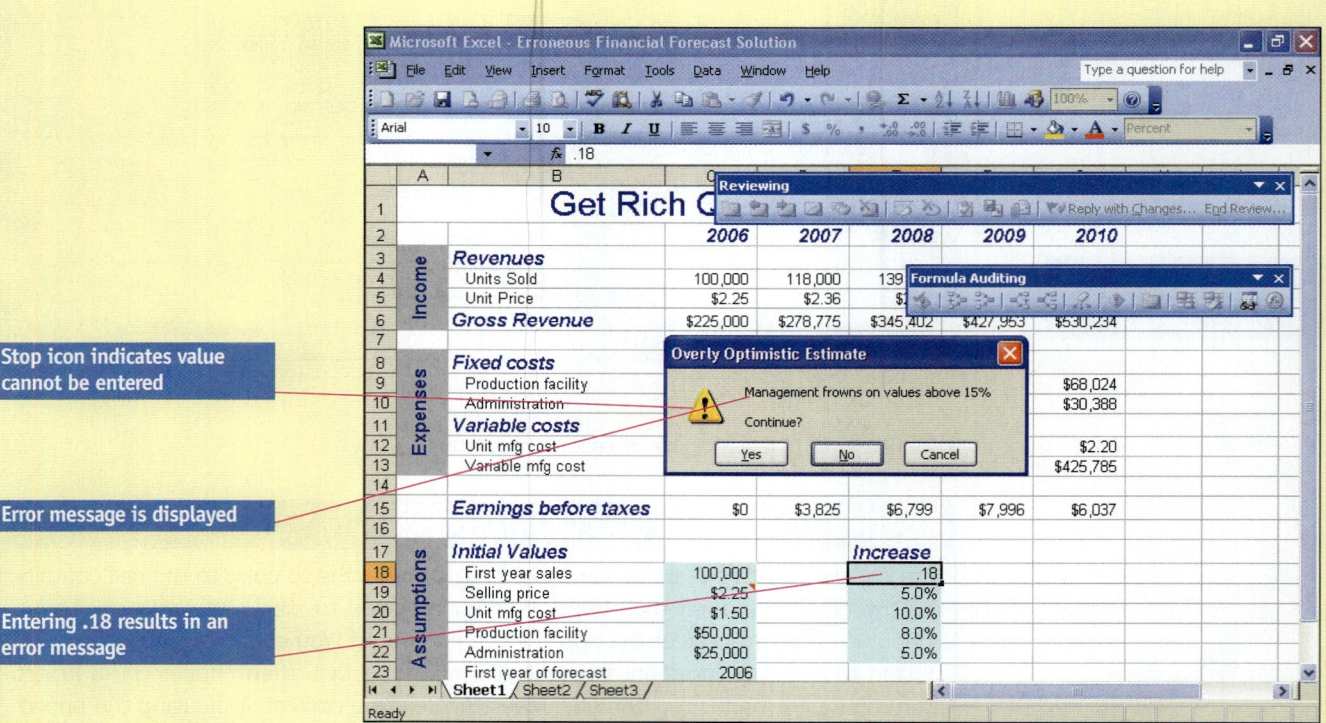

(g) Data Validation (step 7)

FIGURE 6.6 Hands-on Exercise 2 (*continued*)

THE INTERNAL RATE OF RETURN

The worksheet in Figure 6.7 is similar to the original Get Rich Quick worksheet in Figure 6.1 except that it includes additional calculations to make it more realistic. The top portion of the worksheet (through row 16) is identical in both worksheets. We have, however, introduced a tax rate of 20%, to compute the tax and net income for each year. In 2010, for example, the corporation is expected to pay $22,787 in tax (20% of $113,936) to yield a net income of $91,149 ($113,936 − $22,787).

The worksheet in Figure 6.7 also indicates an initial investment of $150,000, which the company is required to invest in order to go into business. Is this a wise decision? In other words, does it make sense to spend $150,000 today, in order to get back $60,000 next year, $67,800 the year after, $75,768 the year after that, and so on until we receive $91,149 in the last year? The investment decision is aided by computing the **Internal Rate of Return (IRR)**, a commonly accepted financial measure that takes into account the time value of money. The Excel **IRR function** requires a single argument, the range of cells that contain the expenses and income at the end of each year. The cell range must contain at least one negative (expense) and one positive (income) value. A second argument, a "guess" at the IRR, is required when the internal rate of return is negative.

Look again at the values in rows 18 and 19 in Figure 6.7. We invest $150,000 initially and receive $60,000 at the end of year one, $67,800 at the end of year two, and so on. The rate of return at the end of year one is −60%; that is, we "lost" $90,000 on our investment of $150,000, and hence the negative return. The IRR improves, however, for each successive year until we achieve a return of 37.7% at the end of the last year. This is the interest rate on the initial investment over five years, which is very favorable, to say the least. (The formula in cell H19 is =IRR(C18:H18). Similar formulas appear in the other cells in this row.)

Creating a Template

The worksheet in Figure 6.7a was created from the **template** in Figure 6.7b. A template is a special type of workbook (it has its own file format) that is used as the basis for other workbooks. It contains text, formatting, formulas, (and/or macros), but it does not contain data; that is, the assumption area at the bottom of the template has been cleared of all values. Look closely, however, and you can see that the formulas are still present in the body of the template; for example, cell D16 is the active cell and its contents are visible in the Formula bar. (The results of the calculations within the body of the spreadsheet are uniformly zero, but the zeros are suppressed through an option in the Tools menu.)

Most templates are based on **protected worksheets** that enable the user to change only a limited number of cells in the worksheet. This prevents the accidental modification of formulas and existing text in the worksheet, while still permitting the user to change the value in any unprotected cell. The financial forecast, for example, enables the user to modify the contents of any cell in the shaded assumption area, but it precludes changes elsewhere in the worksheet. Any attempt to do so produces a protected-cell message on the screen. Protecting a worksheet is a two-step process. First, you **unlock** the cells that are subject to change (all cells in a worksheet are locked initially) and then you **protect** the worksheet. (Locking or unlocking cells has no effect until the worksheet has been protected.)

Protecting a worksheet is generally the last step in creating a template, which is then saved under its own name, but as a template rather than an ordinary workbook. This is very convenient because when the template is subsequently opened, a new workbook is automatically created with a number appended to the name of the template; for example, Real World Enterprises1 as shown in Figure 6.7a. The template should be saved in the **Templates folder** within the Microsoft Office folder so that it can be accessed automatically through the File New command.

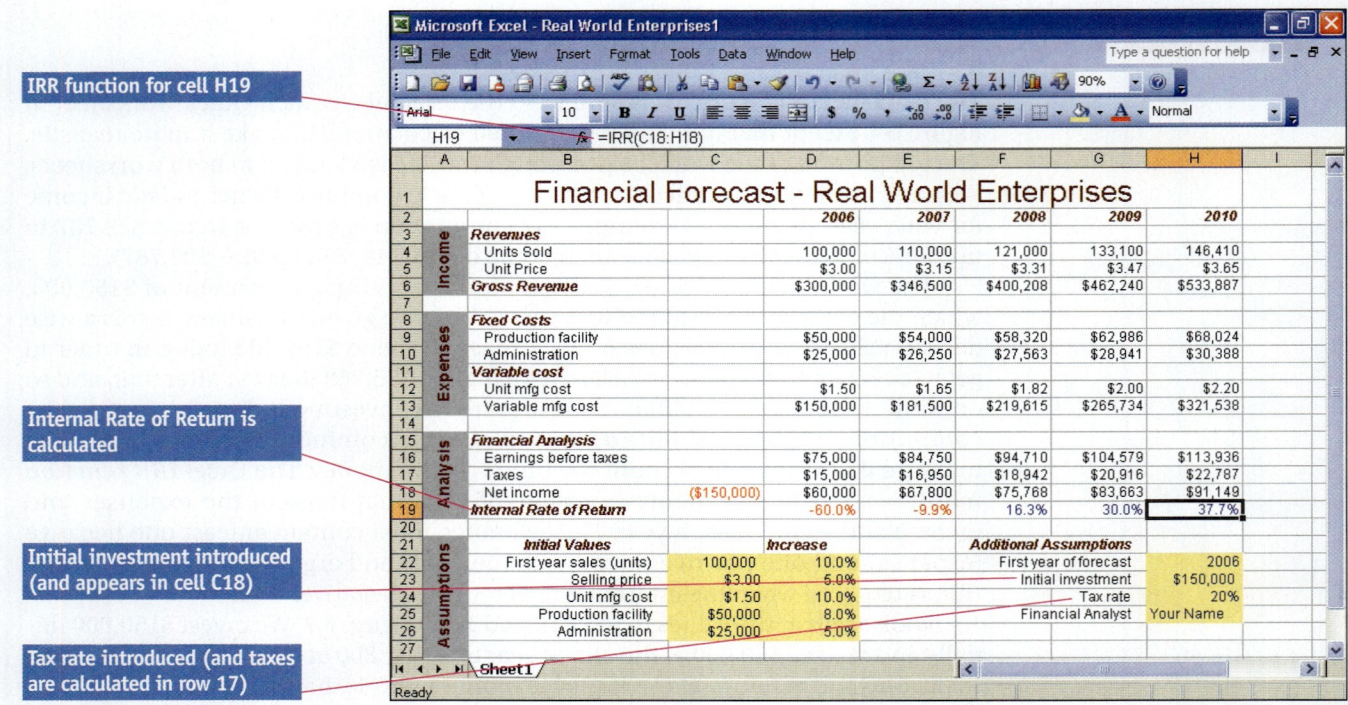

(a) The Internal Rate of Return

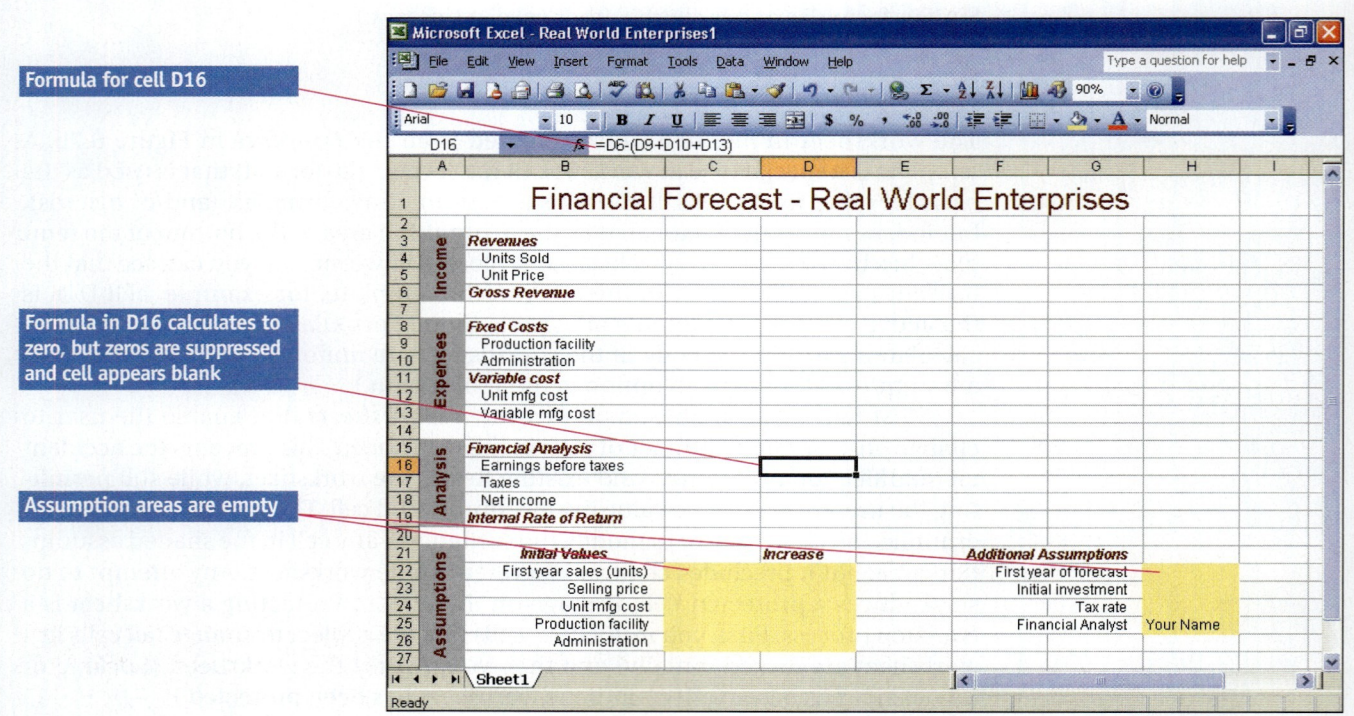

(b) The Template

FIGURE 6.7 Real World Enterprises

hands-on exercise 3

Creating a Template

Objective To use the IRR (Internal Rate of Return) function; to unlock cells in a worksheet, then protect the worksheet; to create a template.

Step 1: **Compute the After Tax Income**

- Open the **Real World Enterprises workbook** in the **Exploring Excel folder**. Save the workbook as **Real World Enterprises Solution**.

- Click in **cell D17**. Type an equal sign, then use pointing to enter the formula to compute the income tax for the first year, **=D16*$H$24**.

- Click in **cell D18**. Type an equal sign, then use pointing to enter the formula to compute the net income for the first year, **=D16-D17**.

- Click and drag to select **cells D17 and D18**, then drag the fill handle to **cells H17:H18**. Format cells **D17:H18** to **Currency format** with zero decimal places. Cell H18 should display $91,149 as shown in Figure 6.8a.

Enter formula into D17

Enter formula into D18

Result in H18 is $91,149 after copy operation and formatting

(a) Compute the After Tax Income (step 1)

FIGURE 6.8 Hands-on Exercise 3

CHANGE THE STYLE

The Real World Enterprises workbook contains two styles that were created by the user, Category and Main Heading. Each style has been applied to multiple cells, for example, cells A3 and B3, respectively. You can change the definition of either style, which in turn will change the appearance of the cells defined by that style. Click in cell B3, for example, pull down the Format menu, and click Style to display the Style dialog box. Click the Modify button to display the Format Cells dialog box, click the Font tab, then change the color. Click OK, and notice how the color changes in multiple cells throughout the workbook.

Step 2: **Compute the Internal Rate of Return**

- Click in **cell C18** and enter **= −H23** to enter the initial investment in this cell. The minus sign indicates this is a cash outlay, as opposed to incoming cash.

- Click in **cell D19** and enter **=IRR(C18:D18)**. You will see the #NUM! error instead of a numerical result because Excel is unable to compute an answer.

- Edit the formula in **cell D18** to **=IRR(C18:D18, −.35)**; the additional parameter is an initial "guess" at the internal rate of return. This time Excel is successful and displays −60%. The "guess" is often needed to calculate negative returns.

- Click in **cell E18** and enter **=IRR(C18:E18, −.35)**. This formula differs from the one in the previous cell in that it also references the income for the second year.)

- Enter the formulas to compute the rate of return for the remaining years of the forecast. You have to enter each formula individually (a "guess" is not required.)

- Change the formatting in **cells D19:H19** to percent with one decimal. The value of cell H19 should change to 37.7% as shown in Figure 6.8b.

- Use conditional formatting (see boxed tip) to display negative and positive returns in red and blue, respectively. Save the workbook.

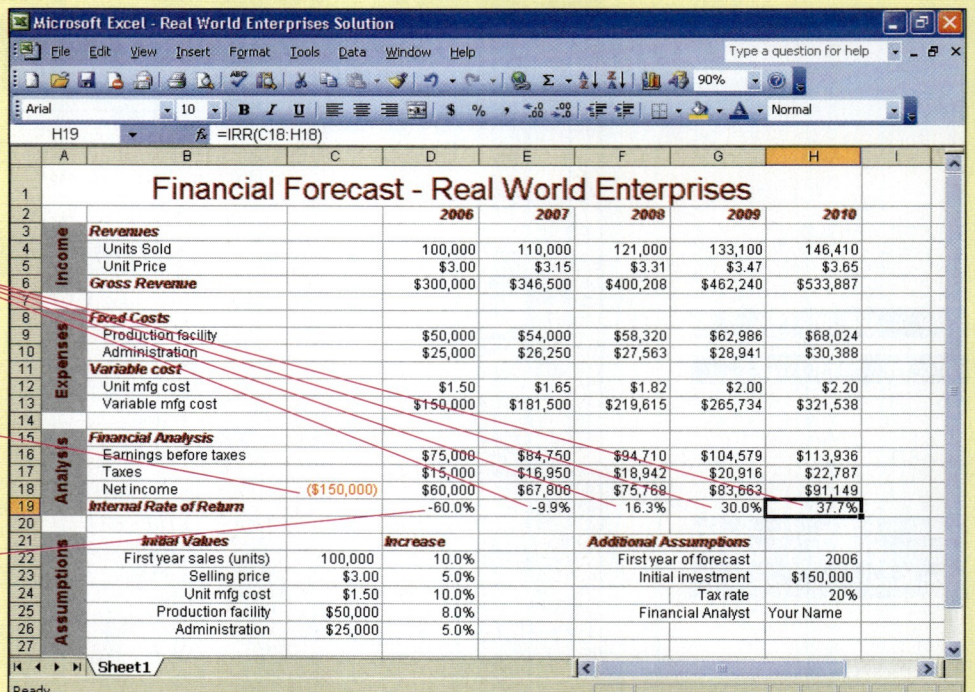

(b) Compute the Internal Rate of Return (step 2)

FIGURE 6.8 Hands-on Exercise 3 (*continued*)

CONDITIONAL FORMATTING

You can change the formatting within a cell according to the displayed value of that cell; for example, you can display negative returns in red and positive returns in blue. Click and drag to select cells D19:H19, pull down the Format menu, and click the Conditional Formatting command. Enter Cell value is less than zero as the first condition, click the Format button, and choose Red as the font color. Click the Add button to enter the second condition, then click OK to accept the conditions and close the Conditional Formatting dialog box.

Step 3: **Protect the Worksheet**

- Click and drag to select **cells C22:D26**. Press and hold the **Ctrl key** as you select cells **H22:H25**. Pull down the **Format menu** and click the **Cells command** to display the Format Cells dialog box.
  - Click the **Protection tab**, and then clear the Locked check box.
  - Click the **Patterns tab**, choose **light yellow**, and click **OK**.

- Pull down the **Tools menu**, click **Protection**, then click the **Protect Sheet command** to display the Protect Sheet dialog box in Figure 6.8c.

- Check that your settings match those in the figure, then click **OK**. (A password is optional. If you do enter a password, be sure you remember it, or else you will not be able to modify the workbook.)

- Check that cell protection works. Try to change the formula in any of the protected cells in the upper part of the spreadsheet. You should see a message indicating that the cell is protected and "read only". Click **OK**.

- Save the workbook. Print the spreadsheet to show the displayed values. Print the spreadsheet a second time to show the cell formulas.

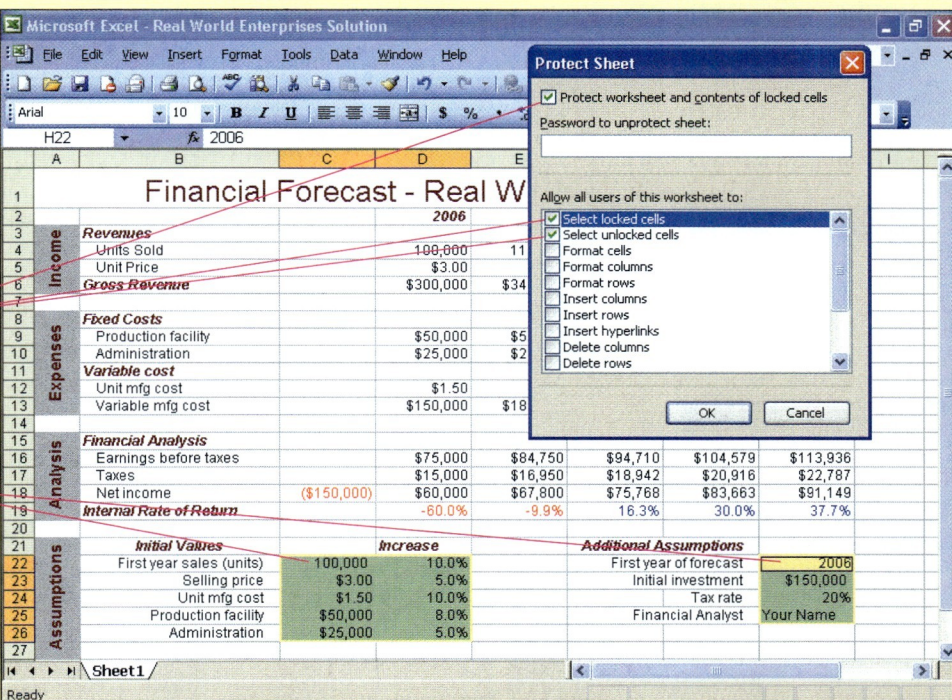

(c) Protect the Worksheet (step 3)

FIGURE 6.8 Hands-on Exercise 3 (*continued*)

PROTECT THE FORMULAS

The formulas in a well-designed worksheet should be based on a set of assumptions and initial conditions that are grouped together for ease of change. The user can change any of the initial values and see the effect ripple throughout the spreadsheet. The user need not, however, have access to the formulas, and thus the formulas should be protected. Remember, protection is a two-step process. First, you unlock the cells that you want to be able to change after the worksheet has been protected, and then you protect the worksheet.

Step 4: **Create the Template**

- A template contains text, formatting, and formulas, but it does not contain specific values. Accordingly, we need to clear the assumption area in order to create the template.

- Click and drag to select **cells C22:D26**, then press the **Del key** to delete the contents of these cells. Click and drag to select **cells H22:H24**, and press the **Del key**. The spreadsheet looks rather awkward with zero values and #NUM errors as shown in Figure 6.8d.

- Pull down the **Tools menu**, click the **Options command**, click the **View tab**, and clear the box to show zero values. Click **OK**. The zeros disappear.

- The #NUM occurs because the IRR function is unable to find a result based on the inputs that were supplied; that is, the body of the spreadsheet contains only zero values and hence the rate of return cannot be calculated.

- The #NUM error will disappear automatically when the spreadsheet is complete, but you can suppress it in the template by using the ISERROR function as described in the boxed tip. This is tricky; try it, but you can skip this step if you cannot make the function work.

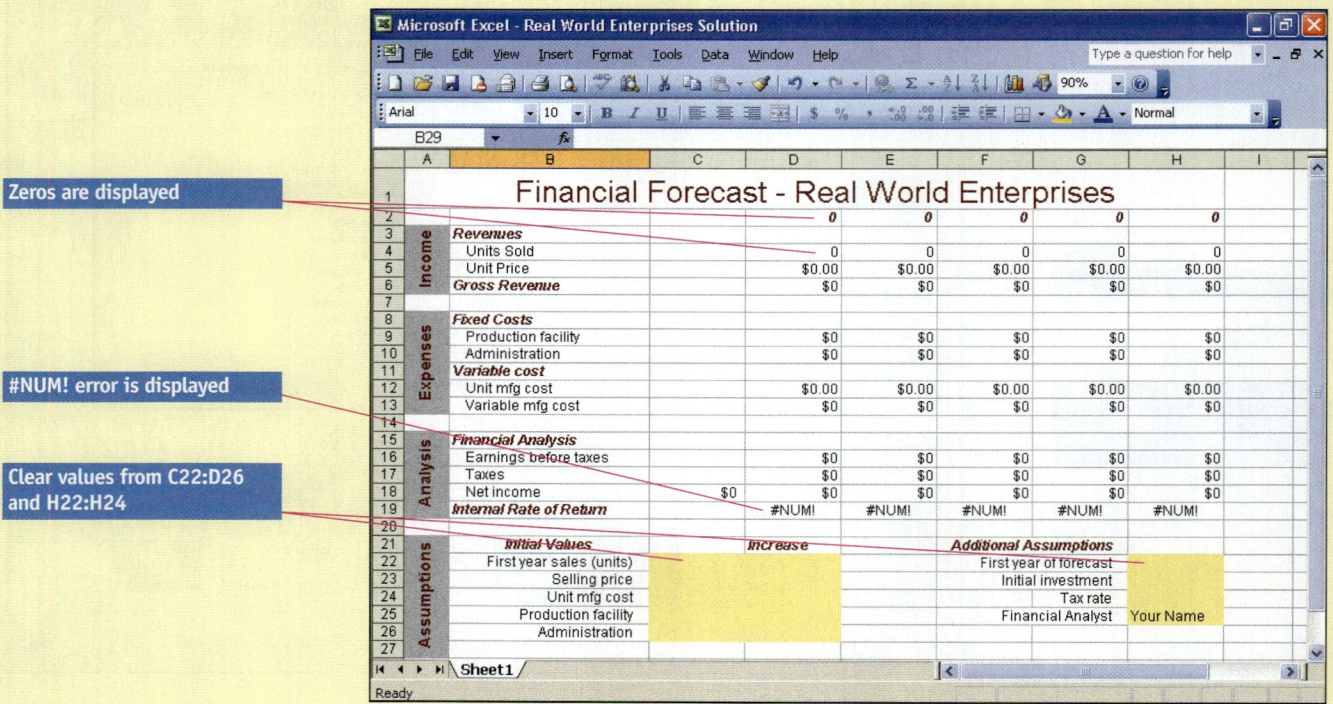

(d) Create the Template (step 4)

FIGURE 6.8 Hands-on Exercise 3 (*continued*)

THE ISERROR FUNCTION

The ISERROR function returns a value of true or false, depending on whether the indicated cell contains an error; you can use the function to test for and then suppress the error by putting in an IF function, =IF(ISERROR(*Formula*),"",*Formula*). Click in cell D19. Type =IF(ISERROR(IRR(C18:D18,−0.35)),"",IRR(C18:D18,−0.35)). The "" will print nothing in the cell if an error exists, that is, if the error condition is true. Enter similar formulas for the other cells in row 19.

Step 5: **Save the Template**

- Pull down the **File menu**; click the **Save As command** to display the Save As dialog box in Figure 6.8e. Enter **Real World Enterprises** as the name of the template.

- Click the **down arrow** in the Save as Type list box and choose **Template**. The folder where you will save the template depends on whether you have your own machine.
  - ❏ If you are working on your own computer and have access to all of its folders, save the template in the **Templates folder** (the default folder that is displayed automatically).
  - ❏ If you are working at school or otherwise sharing a computer, you should change the default folder. Click the **down arrow** in the Save in list box and save the template in the **Exploring Excel folder** that you have used throughout the text.

- Click the **Save button** to save the template.

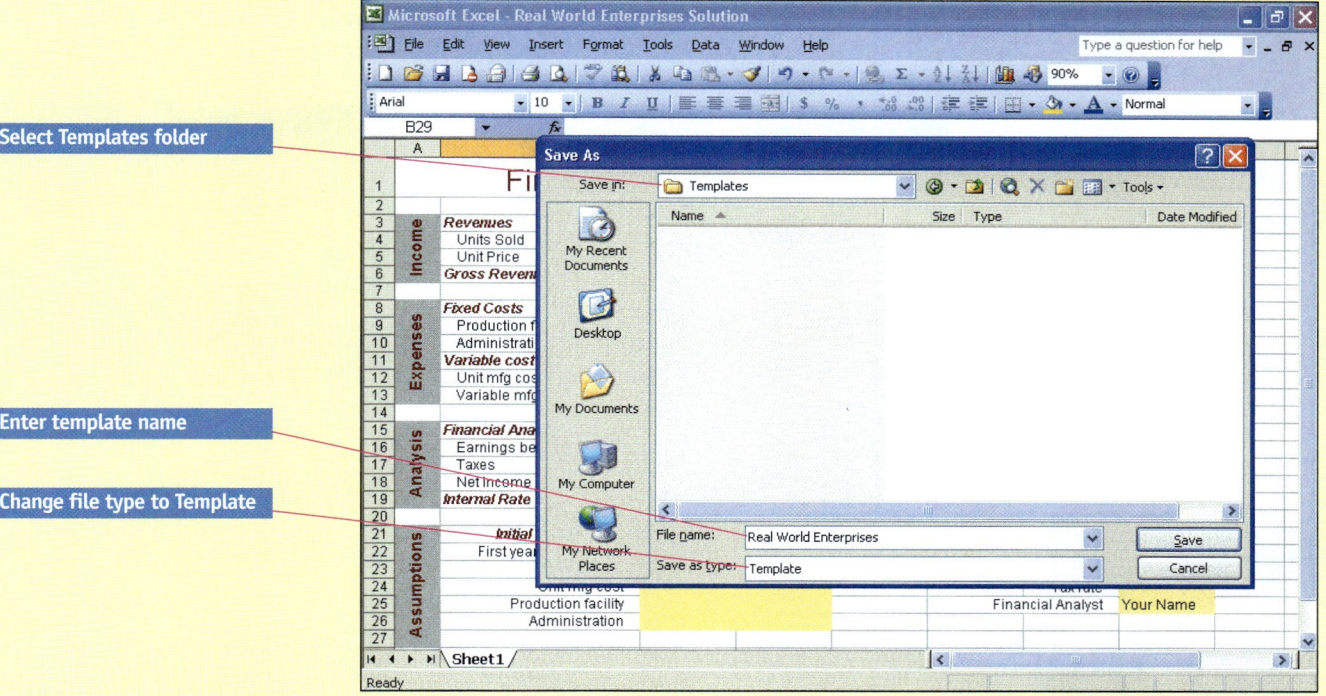

(e) Save the Template (step 5)

FIGURE 6.8 Hands-on Exercise 3 (*continued*)

PROTECT THE WORKBOOK

A template or workbook is not truly protected unless it is saved with a password, because a knowledgeable user can always copy a protected worksheet to a new workbook, and gain full access to that worksheet. You can, however, use password protection to prevent this from happening. Pull down the File menu, click the Save As command to the Save As dialog box, click the Tools button, then click General Options to display the Save Options dialog box. You can enter one or two passwords, one to open the file, and one to modify it. Be careful! Once you save a workbook or template with a password, you cannot open it if you forget the password.

Step 6: **Open the Template**

- Close Excel, and then restart the program. The location of the template depends on where you saved it in the previous step.
  - If you are working on your own computer, open the task pane, click the **down arrow** at the top of the task pane, and select **New Workbook**. Click **On my computer** in the Templates section.
  - If you are working at school or otherwise sharing a computer, start Windows Explorer and change to the **Exploring Excel folder.**

- Double click the **Real World Enterprises template** from either location to create a blank workbook, named **Real World Enterprises1**. (Excel automatically saves a copy of the template as a workbook and assigns it a name consisting of the template's name followed by a number.)

- Enter the initial values and assumptions into the shaded assumption area. Note that as you enter each successive value, additional calculations are displayed in the body of the worksheet as shown in Figure 6.8f. (The template may fail to display an IRR if the initial guess is too far away from the actual result.)

- Print the completed workbook two ways, once with displayed values and once to show the cell formulas. Exit Excel. Congratulations on a job well done.

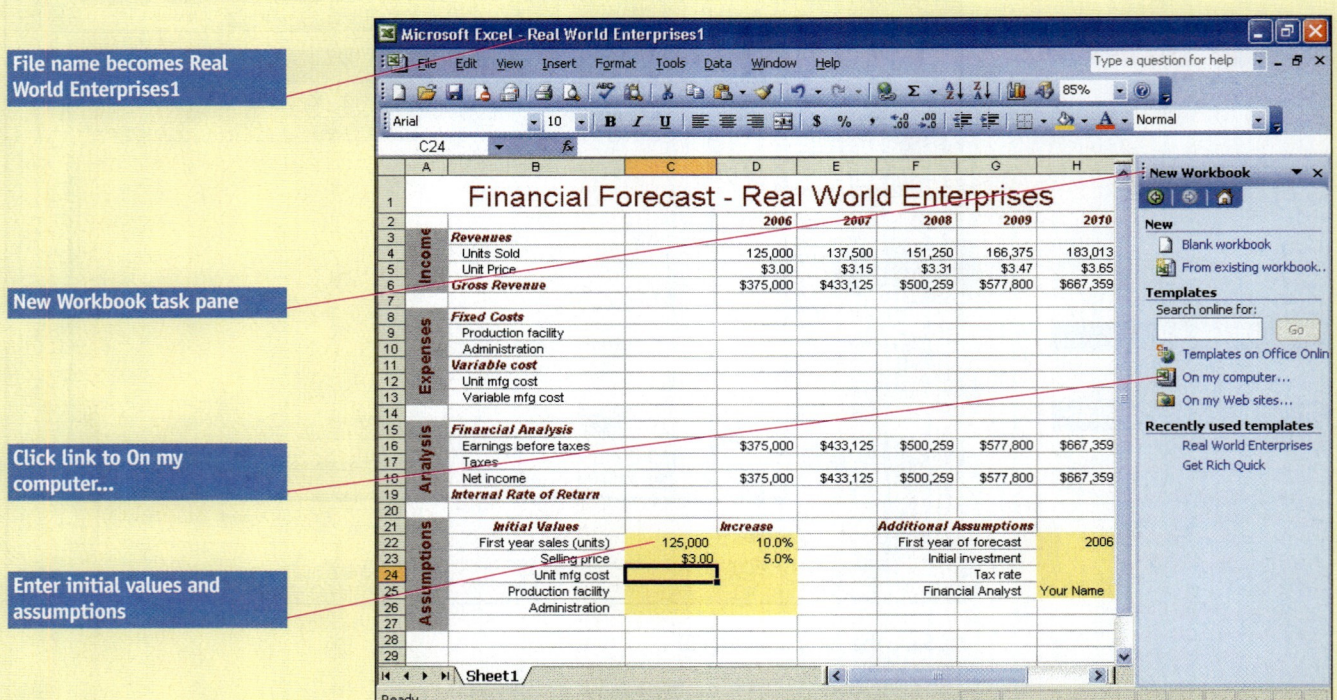

(f) Open the Template (step 6)

FIGURE 6.8 Hands-on Exercise 3 (*continued*)

EVALUATE THE FORMULA

Pull down the View menu, click the Toolbars command, then display the Formula Auditing toolbar. Click in any cell containing a formula, then click the Evaluate button on the Formula Auditing toolbar. You should see the complete formula for the active cell. Click the Evaluate button a second time, and you will see the numeric value for the first cell reference. Continue to click the Evaluate button to see the numeric value of each cell reference until the computed value is shown.

THE AMORTIZATION SCHEDULE

It's easy to borrow money, but with any loan comes the obligation for repayment. That, in turn, takes the form of an ***amortization*** (payment) ***schedule,*** which displays the date of each payment, the amount of each payment that goes toward interest and principal, and the remaining balance, which eventually reaches zero. Figure 6.9 displays the amortization schedules for two hypothetical loans, for an automobile and new home, respectively. The worksheets were created from the same workbook, which is applicable to any type of loan. The parameters for the specific loan are entered into the upper-left portion of the respective worksheets (cells C4 through C10). All of the other values are calculated automatically.

The car loan in Figure 6.9a is for $15,000 at 8% for four years, which results in a monthly payment of $366.19. The payments begin on February 15, 2005 and continue for 48 months until the loan is repaid on January 15, 2009. The total paid by the borrower is $17,577.30 (48 payments of $366.19 each), which is equal to the principal ($15,000) plus the interest over the life of the loan ($2,577.30).

Each payment is divided into two parts, interest and principal, as shown in the body of the worksheet. The details for the first payment appear in row 13. The balance at the beginning of the first period is $15,000. The annual interest rate is 8%. The interest for the entire first year would be $1,200 (8% of $15,000) if no payments were made during the year. Payments are made monthly, however, so the interest is computed monthly as well, and thus the interest for the first month is $100 ($1200/12). The payment of $336.19 is divided in two; $100 goes for interest, and the remainder ($266.19) goes toward principal. The initial balance of $15,000 is then reduced by this amount so that the balance at the end of the first month is $14,733.81; this value is also the beginning balance for the second payment.

The interest for the second period is less than for the previous period because the starting balance is less ($14733.81, as opposed to $15,000). The payment is the same, however, and thus a little less of the payment goes toward interest ($98.23, as opposed to $100), and a little more goes toward principal ($267.97 versus $266.19). The process continues in this fashion until the loan is eventually paid off.

Figure 6.9b displays the amortization worksheet for a different loan: $100,000 at 6.5% for 30 years. This loan also includes an additional parameter: an optional extra payment of $100 each month, which pays off the loan in 250 payments, as opposed to the original 360. The extra payment is a sound strategy if you can afford it; many individuals elect a 30-year mortgage to keep the monthly payments low, but then decide to make an optional payment each month.

The result is a substantial saving in interest; the summary area shows that total interest is $82,506.10, as opposed to $127,544 (which is not shown in the worksheet), which would be the total interest if the user did not make the extra payments. The borrower has paid $25,000 (250 payments of $100 each) in early payments, but this is not truly "additional" money. It is principal that would have been paid eventually during the original 30-year schedule. The borrower has elected to make the payments earlier than necessary to reduce the total interest.

One very significant feature of both worksheets is what you do *not* see, as payments do not appear in the body of the worksheet until all four loan parameters have been entered. This is accomplished by the logical AND function =AND(C4>0,C5>0,C6>0,C7>0), which has been entered into cell D6, but which is hidden from view by the clip art. The ***AND function*** returns one of two values, True or False. It is considered True only if every argument is True, and False otherwise. The AND function checks the values in cells C4 through C7 and returns a value of True after every parameter has been entered, when every entry is greater than zero.

The formula in cell A13 of Figure 6.9a checks the value of cell D6 (which has been assigned the name DataEntered) to determine if all of the required parameters have been supplied, and if so, the payment number is displayed. The other formulas in the row check to see if the value in cell A13 is greater than zero, and if so,

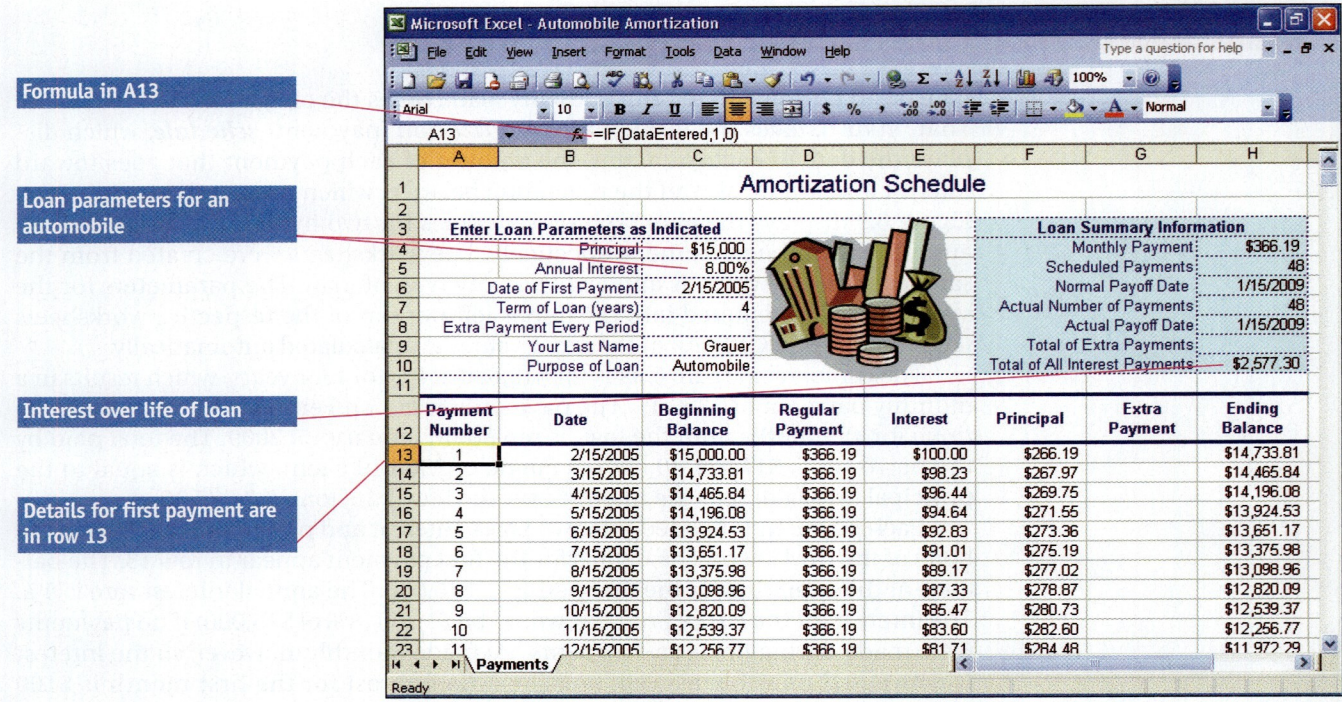

(a) Automobile

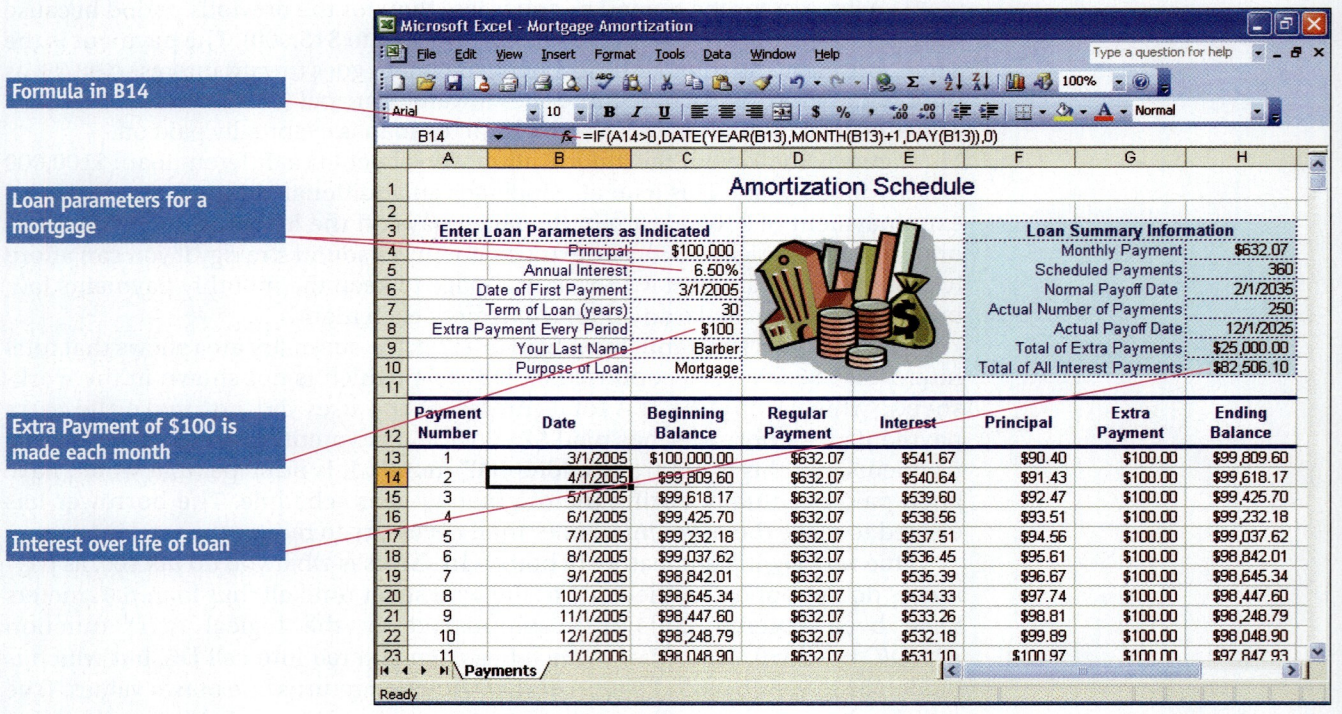

(b) 30-Year Mortgage with Optional Extra Payments

FIGURE 6.9 The Amortization Schedule Workbook

display the result of the respective formulas. If not, a zero is displayed in each cell, which in turn is suppressed through an option in the Tools menu. Note, too, that the body of the worksheet may contain up to 360 potential payments (for a 30-year loan), but only the payments that are actually made appear in the worksheet. The worksheet in Figure 6.9a, for example, contains only 48 payments; the other payments are zeroed out and suppressed via an option in the Tools menu.

The Year, Month, and Day Functions

The calculation of the payment dates in both worksheets is more complicated than you might have expected initially. Recall that Excel stores a date as an integer (serial number) equivalent to the elapsed number of days since January 1, 1900; that is, January 1, 1900, is stored as the number 1; January 2, 1900, as the number 2; and so on. It's easy enough to determine tomorrow's date or yesterday's date because all you have to do is add or subtract one to the integer value of today's date. What if, however, you want to display the same date in every month, such as March 15, April 15, and so on? Do you add 30 or 31? And what if today's date is February 15? Do you add 28 or 29 to display March 15? Excel includes additional date functions that accomplish these tasks very easily.

The ***DAY***, ***MONTH***, and ***YEAR functions*** return the numeric day, month, and year, respectively. The function, =MONTH(B13), for example, returns the numeric month of the date in cell B13. In similar fashion, =MONTH(B13)+1 adds one to the numeric month in cell B13. Excel is smart enough to know that if today's date is sometime in December, next month will occur in January.

The ***DATE function*** has three arguments; year, month, and day. It is combined with the other functions to compute the next month's payment date; for example, the formula in cell B14 is =DATE(YEAR(B13),MONTH(B13)+1,DAY(B13)). The year and the day are taken directly from cell B13. The month, however, is one greater than the value in cell B13. The DATE function then returns a date that is exactly one month from today. (The IF function in Figure 6.9b displays the date only if the payment number is greater than zero.)

The MATCH and INDEX functions

The summary area in Figure 6.9 displays information about the loan as a whole. The calculations for the monthly payment, number of scheduled payments, and normal payoff date are straightforward, as you will see in the next hands-on exercise. So, too, is the calculation of the total amount in extra payments as well as the total paid in interest. (A simple SUM function is used for both.) The determination of the actual number of payments (when extra payments are made) requires the ***MATCH function***. The actual payoff date uses the ***INDEX function***.

The MATCH function has three arguments: the value you are looking up (a zero ending balance), the associated cell range (the cells containing the balance at the end of each period), and the type of match (e.g., whether or not it is an exact match). The type of match is 1, 0, or −1; the −1 in our example specifies the smallest value that is greater than or equal to the lookup value. The function returns the *position* in the list where the match occurs, which corresponds to the actual payment number where the zero balance is reached.

The INDEX function uses the result of the MATCH function to determine the payoff date. The function has three arguments: a cell range in the form of a table (cells A13:H372, which contain all 360 potential payments), a row number within the table (the value returned by the MATCH function), and a column number within the table (column 2, which contains the date of the payment). The INDEX function returns the value in the specified cell, which in our case is the payment date corresponding to the number of payments that were made.

hands-on exercise

4 Creating an Amortization Schedule

Objective To create a flexible amortization schedule that permits optional extra payments of principal. Use Figure 6.10 as a guide in the exercise.

Step 1: **Enter the Loan Parameters**

- Open the **Amortization Schedule workbook** in the **Exploring Excel folder**. Save the workbook as **Amortization Schedule Solution**.

- Click in **cell C4**. Enter **$15,000** as the principal (the amount you are going to borrow). Enter **8%, 2/15/05,** and **4** into **cells C5 through C7,** respectively.

- Click in **cell H4**. Enter the formula **=PMT(C5/12,C7*12,−C4)** to compute the periodic payment. You should see $366.19 as shown in Figure 6.10a.

- Click in **cell H5**. Enter the formula **=C7*12** to compute the number of scheduled payments. You should see 48; that is, there will be 48 monthly payments.

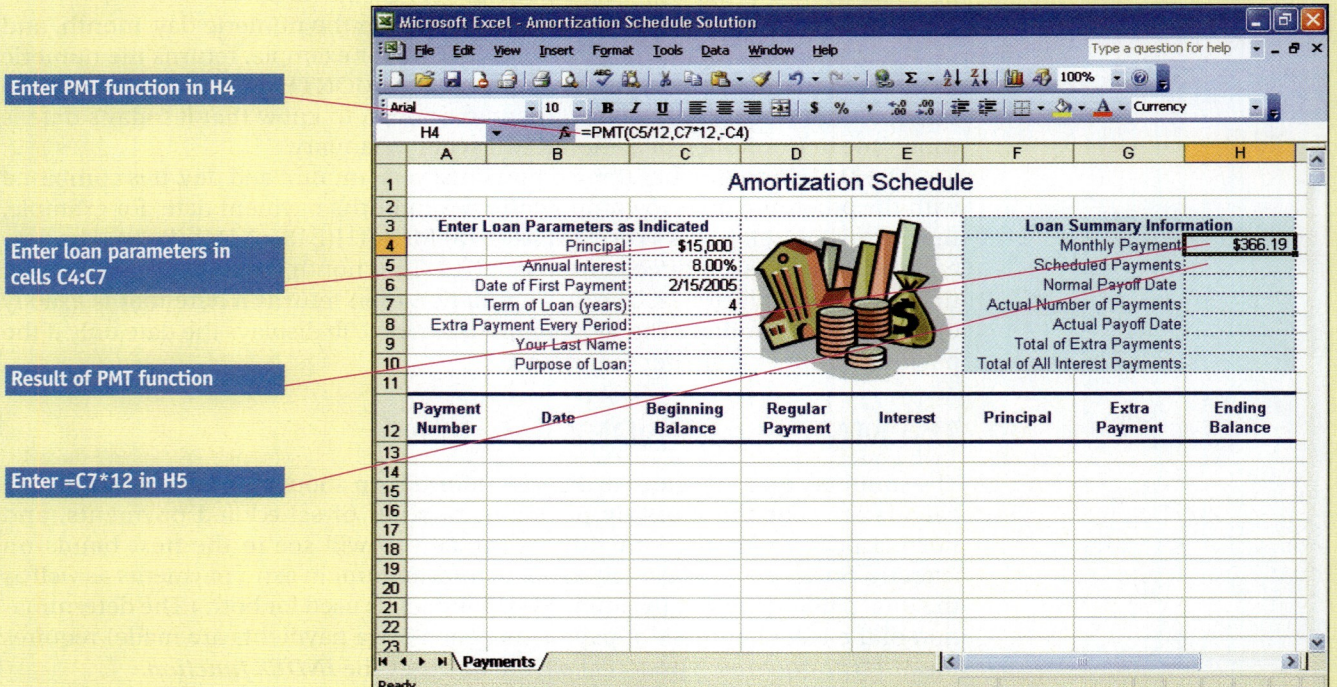

(a) Enter the Loan Parameters (step 1)

FIGURE 6.10 Hands-on Exercise 4

THE PMT FUNCTION

The PMT (payment) function has three required arguments; the interest rate per period, the number of periods, and the principal (amount that you are borrowing). The interest rate is typically entered on an annual basis, whereas the payments are made monthly; thus the interest rate is divided by 12 within the PMT function. In similar fashion, the number of periods is multiplied by 12 to convert the number of years to the equivalent number of months. The principal is equal to the present value of the future sum of periodic payments; it is normally entered with a minus sign so that the calculated payment appears as a positive number within the worksheet.

Step 2: **Enter Formulas for the First Payment**

- Click in **cell A13** and enter the number **1**, which represents the payment number. Click in **cell B13** and enter the formula **=C6** to copy the date of the first payment from the input area.

- Click in **cell C13** and enter **=C4** to obtain the beginning balance. Click in **cell D13** and enter **=$H$4** to get the regular payment. This entry must be absolute because the entries in the remaining rows should always reflect this amount.

- The regular payment is divided into two parts, one for the interest and the remainder for principal.
  - The interest is charged on the unpaid balance at the beginning of the period (cell C13). The interest rate is the annual rate (cell C5) divided by 12. Thus, click in **cell E13** and enter the formula **=($C$5/12)*C13**.
  - The amount of the payment that goes toward principal is the amount left after paying the interest. Click in cell **F13** and enter the formula **=D13-E13**.

- Click in cell **G13** and enter **=$C$8** to reflect the extra payment (if any).

- Finally, click in **cell H13** and enter the formula **=C13-F13-G13** to compute the remaining balance. You should see $14,733.81 as shown in Figure 6.10b.

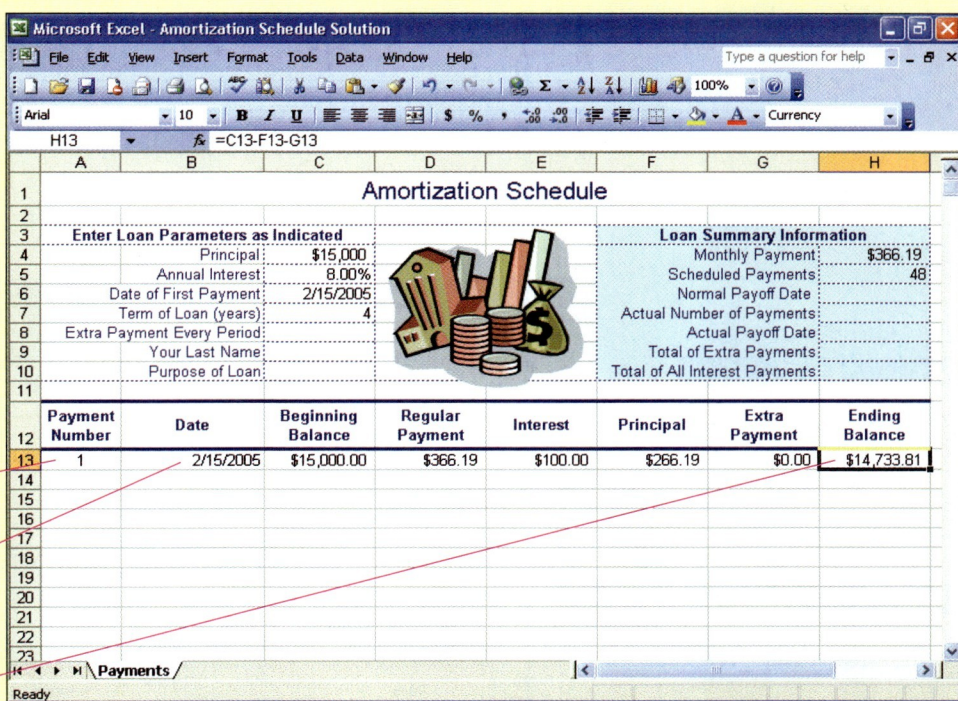

(b) Enter Formulas for the First Payment (step 2)

FIGURE 6.10 Hands-on Exercise 4 (*continued*)

DATA VALIDATION

A good developer anticipates errors that a user may make, and then incorporates the appropriate data validation in the input area of the worksheet. Click in cell C7, for example, (the cell containing the term of the loan) and try to enter a noninteger value and/or a value greater than 30. Either way you will see an error message indicating an invalid entry. To find out which cells have data validation, pull down the Edit menu and click the Go To command (or press the F5 key), click the Special command button, click the option button for Data Validation, then click OK.

Step 3: **Add the If Statements**

- Click and drag the clip art image in order to see the contents of cell D6. The value is currently TRUE because all of the loan parameters have been entered. Click in **cell C7** and press the **Del key**.

- The value in cell D6 is now FALSE because a loan parameter is missing. In addition, the worksheet now contains several "Division by zero" error messages because the PMT function is unable to compute a value when the term of the loan is missing.

- The errors can be hidden by including an IF function to ensure that all of the loan parameters have been entered. Click in **cell A13** and change the formula to **=IF(DataEntered,1,0)**; that is, the value of the cell is one if cell D6 is true, and zero otherwise. (The name DataEntered has been assigned to cell D6.)

- Click in **cell B13** and change its formula to **=IF(A13>0,C6,0)**; that is, there will be a nonzero payment date only if there is a payment. (You will see 1/0/1900, which is the number zero formatted as a date.)

- Click in **cell C13** and change its formula to include a similar If statement: **=IF(A13>0,C4,0)**. Modify the remaining formulas in row 13 to test the value in cell A13 as well.

- Click in **cell H4.** Enter **=IF(DataEntered,PMT(C5/12,C7*12,−C4),0)**. And finally, click in **cell H5** and enter the formula **=IF(DataEntered,C7*12,0)**. The error messages are gone.

- Click in **cell C7** and enter **4**. The values for the first payment reappear. Drag the clip art back to its original position.

- Save the workbook.

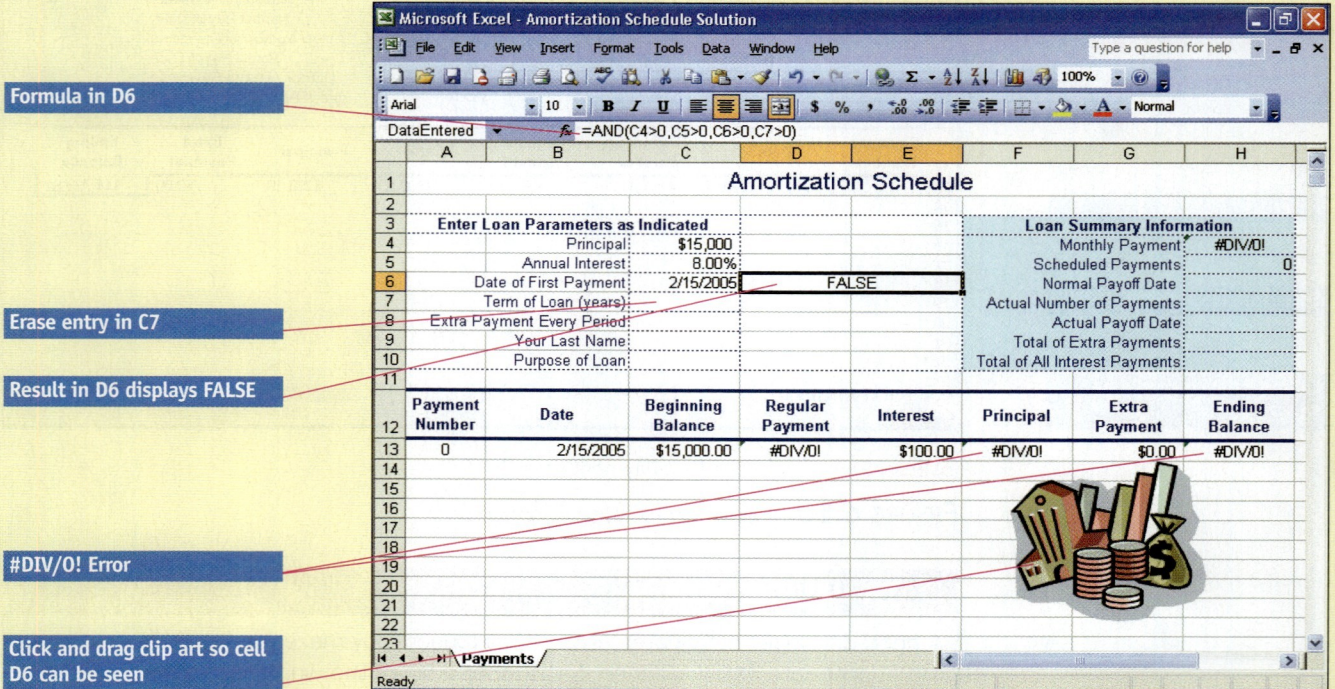

(c) Add the If Statements (step 3)

FIGURE 6.10 Hands-on Exercise 4 (*continued*)

Step 4: **Enter the Formulas for the Second Payment**

- Click in **cell A14** and type the formula **=IF(H13>0, A13+1,0)**; that is, a second payment is necessary only if there is a balance after the first payment.

- The remaining entries in row 14 should appear only if the value in cell A14 is greater than zero. Click in **cell B14** and enter **=IF(A14>0,DATE(YEAR(B13), MONTH(B13)+1,DAY(B13)),0)** as shown in Figure 6.10d. The date should appear as 3/15/2005.

- Click in **cell C14** and enter the formula **=IF(A14>0,H13,0)**; that is, the beginning balance for the second period is equal to the ending balance from the first period.

- The formulas in cells D14 through H14 are the same as those in row 13 but are adjusted through the relative references in these cells. Click and drag to select **cells D13:H13**, then drag the fill handle to create the formulas in row 14. You should see $14,465.84 in cell H14.

- Delete the entry in cell C7 to test the IF functions. You should see zeros throughout rows 13 and 14. Click the **Undo button** on the Standard toolbar to restore the value in cell C7. Save the workbook.

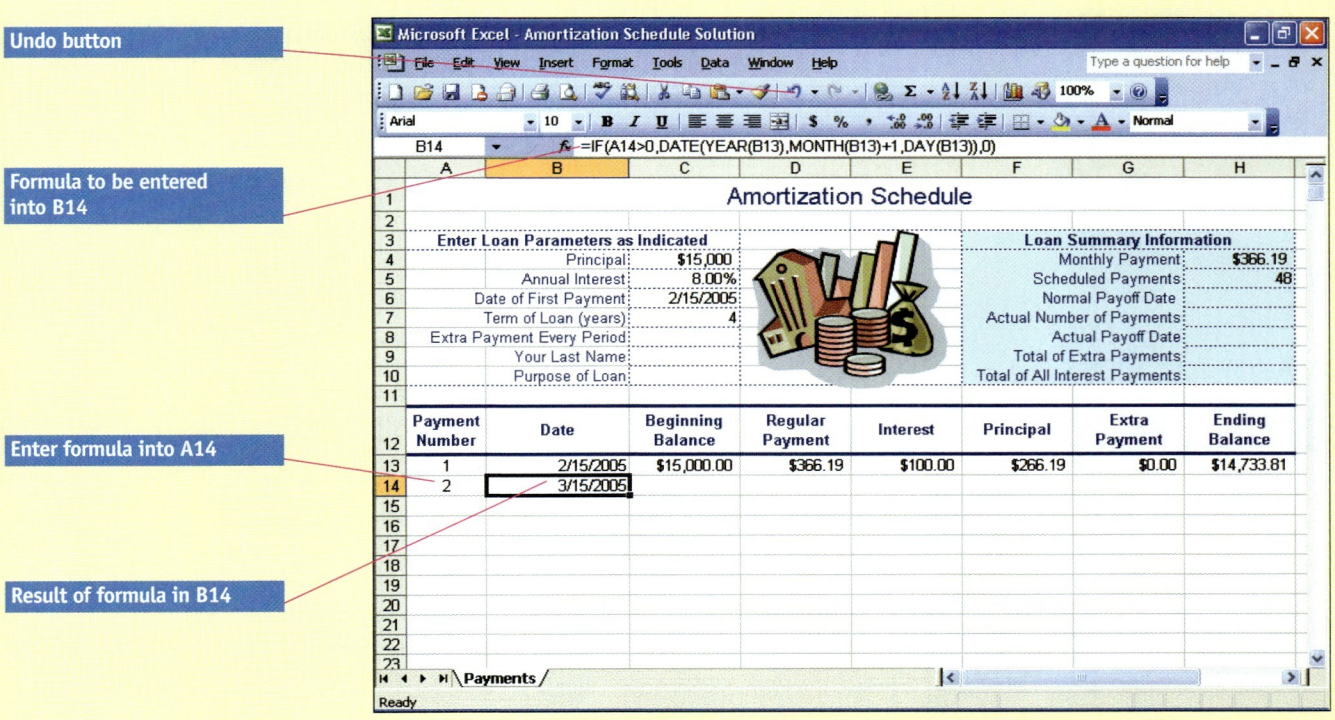

(d) Enter the Formulas for the Second Payment (step 4)

FIGURE 6.10 Hands-on Exercise 4 (*continued*)

THE IPMT AND PPMT FUNCTIONS

The IPMT and PPMT functions compute the portion of a monthly payment that goes toward interest and principal, respectively. These functions refer to the original principal and cannot accommodate extra payments toward principal, and hence are not used in this worksheet. They could, however, be used with simpler amortization tables and/or to verify the calculations of this worksheet in the absence of extra payments. See Help for additional information.

Step 5: **Complete the Payment Schedule**

- The completed spreadsheet is to be as general as possible and capable of creating amortization tables that run to 30 years (to use for conventional mortgages). Click in **cell C7** and temporarily change the term to **30**. The monthly payment is reduced to $110.06.

- Click and drag to select **cells A14:H14**, then drag the fill handle to **row 372**. This takes you to the 360th payment, at which point the balance goes to zero.

- Click in **cell C7** and reset the term of the loan to **4 years**, which in turn restores the monthly payment to $366.19. Scroll down column H until you come to an ending balance of zero, which occurs after four years with the 48th payment.

- Your spreadsheet contains many rows of superfluous zeros. Pull down the **Tools menu**, click the **Options command**, click the **View tab**, and clear the box to show Zero values. Click **OK**. The zeros are no longer visible, but the formulas are still there.

- Save the workbook.

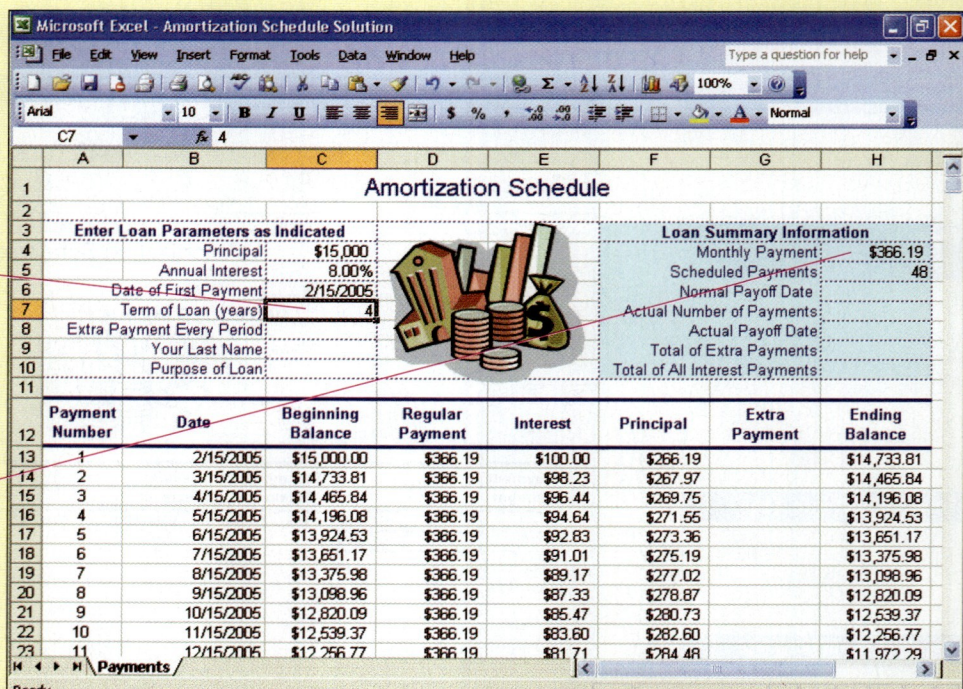

(e) Complete the Payment Schedule (step 5)

FIGURE 6.10 Hands-on Exercise 4 (*continued*)

THE OPTIONS COMMAND

Pull down the Tools menu and click the Options command to display the Options dialog box, from where you can customize virtually every aspect of Excel. The General tab is especially useful as it enables you to change the default file location, the number of worksheets in a new workbook, the default font in a workbook, and/or the number of recently opened files that appear on the file menu. There is no need to memorize anything, just spend a few minutes exploring the options on the various tabs, then think of the Options command the next time you want to change an Excel feature.

Step 6: **Complete the Summary Area**

- Click in **cell C8** and enter **$100** as the optional extra payment that will be made each period. The displayed values change as shown in Figure 6.10f. The formulas in the summary area use predefined range names for simplification.

- Click in **cell H6**. Enter the formula in Figure 6.10f to determine the normal payoff date for the loan. You should see 1/15/2009.

- Click in **cell H7**. Enter **=IF(DataEntered,MATCH(0,EndingBalance,−1)+1,0)** to search the range name EndingBalance (cells H13:H372) for the smallest value that is greater than or equal to zero. In actuality, the balance never goes exactly to zero because of rounding error; thus the row below the match corresponds to the number of actual payments.

- Click in **cell H8**. Enter **=IF(DataEntered,INDEX(AmortizationTable,H7,2),0)**. This returns the entry in column two of the row within the table that was returned by the MATCH function.

- Click in **cell H9**. Enter **=SUM(ExtraPayment)** to determine the total of the extra payments. Click in **cell H10**. Enter **=SUM(Interest)** to determine the total amount paid in interest. You should see the values in Figure 6.10f.

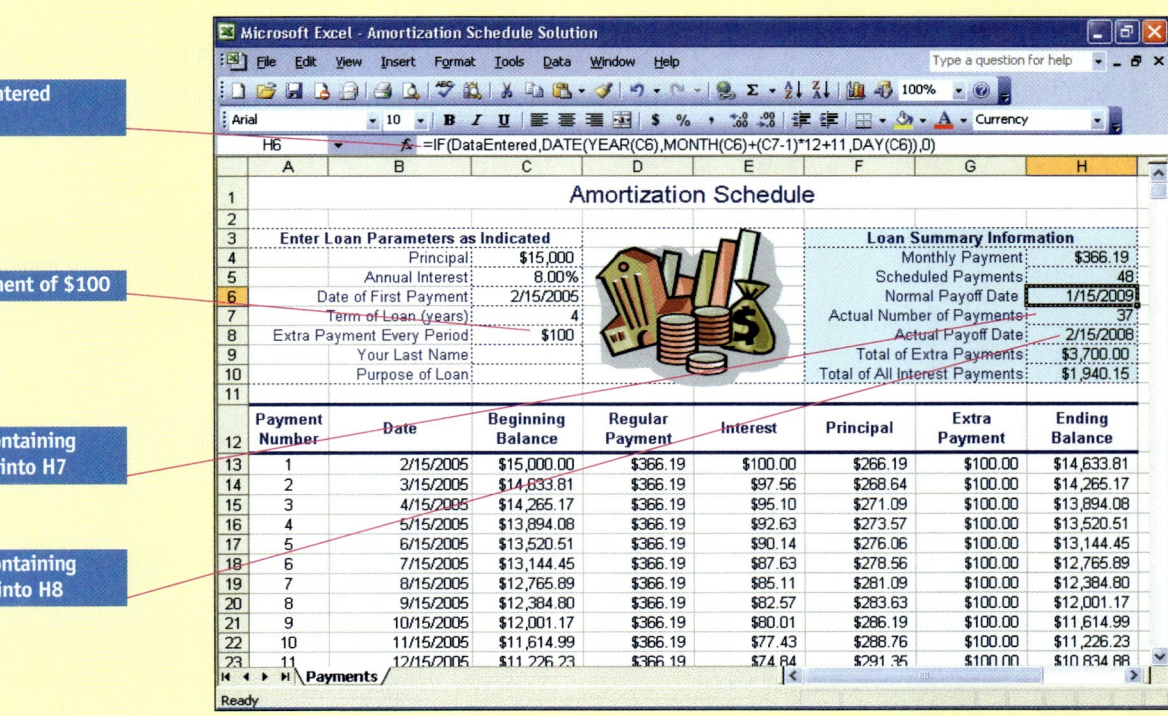

(f) Complete the Summary Area (step 6)

FIGURE 6.10   Hands-on Exercise 4 (*continued*)

PAY OFF YOUR CREDIT CARD

A certain amount of debt is unavoidable; for example, a car loan, a home mortgage, and/or a school loan are obligations that almost everyone incurs at one time or another. The availability of this type of credit increases our standard of living, because without it, we would be unable to purchase these "big ticket" items. Credit card debt is another issue, and while most of us have it, it is expensive, to say the least (the interest rate on a credit card is much higher than for a car loan or mortgage). See exercises 7 and 8 at the end of the chapter.

Step 7: **The Finishing Touches**

- Click the **down arrow** on the Name box and click **AmortizationTable**. Pull down **Format menu** and click the **Conditional Formatting command** to display the associated dialog box.

- Enter **Cell value is greater than zero** as the first condition, click the **Format button**, click the **Patterns tab**, and choose **light blue** as the color. Click **OK** to close the Format Cells dialog box. Click **OK** a second time to close the Conditional Formatting dialog box. The various loan payments should be shaded as shown in Figure 6.10g.

- Click and drag to select **cells C4:C10**, the cells that contain the user inputs. Pull down the **Format menu** and click the **Cells command** to display the Format Cells dialog box. Click the **Protection tab**, and then clear the Locked check box. Click **OK**.

- Pull down the **Tools menu**, click **Protection**, then click the **Protect Sheet command** to display the Protect Sheet dialog box. Click **OK**. (A password is optional. If you do enter a password, be sure you remember it.)

- Enter the parameters for the new loan as shown in Figure 6.10g. The worksheet should accept all of the new parameters since the cells were previously unlocked. Now click in any cell containing a formula and try to change its value. Click **OK** when you see the message indicating a protected cell.

- Print the first page of the completed worksheet for your instructor. Save the workbook. Change to **landscape orientation**, then print the **cell formulas** for the first page.

- Exit Excel. Congratulations on a job well done!

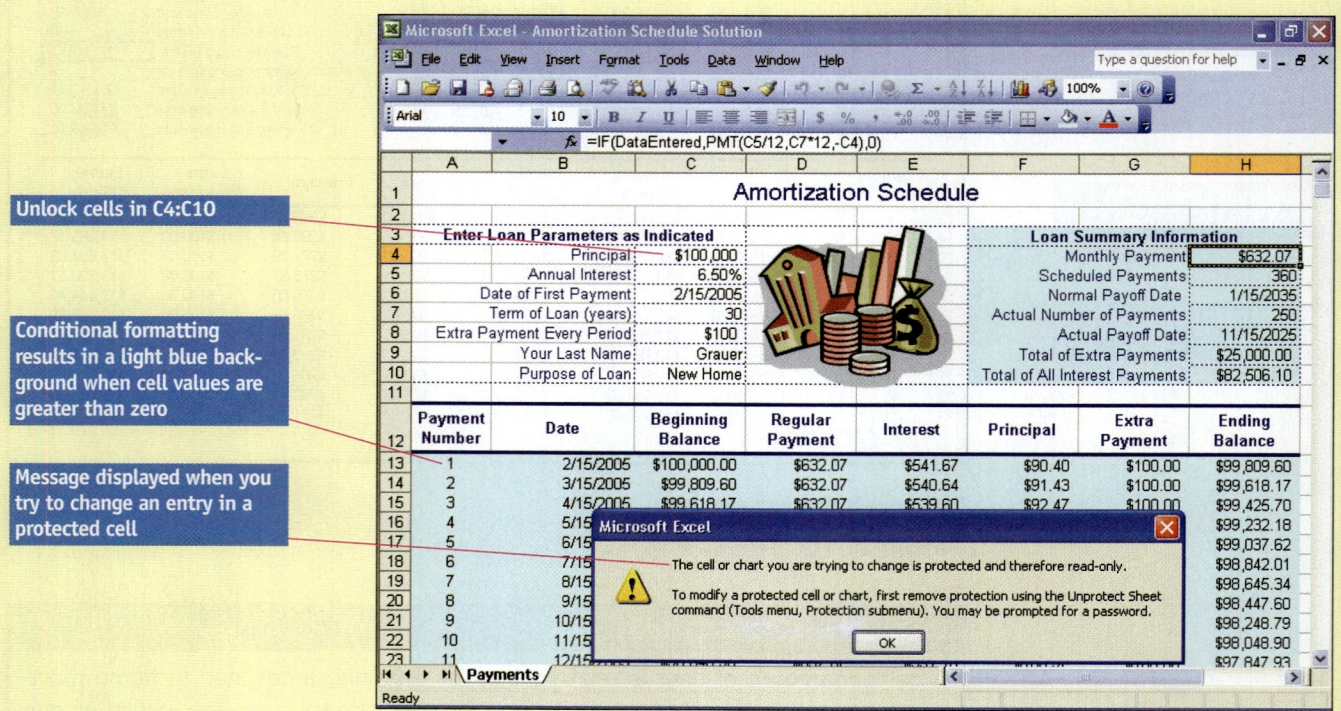

(g) The Finishing Touches (step 7)

FIGURE 6.10 Hands-on Exercise 4 (*continued*)

SUMMARY

A spreadsheet is used frequently as a tool in decision making, and as such, is the subject of continual what-if speculation. Thus, the initial conditions and assumptions on which the spreadsheet is based should be clearly visible so that they can be easily varied. In addition, the formulas in the body of the spreadsheet should be dependent on these cells.

The Scenario Manager lets you specify multiple sets of assumptions (scenarios), then see the results at a glance within the associated worksheet. The scenario summary compares the effects of the different scenarios to one another by showing the value of one or more result cells in a summary table.

Conditional formatting may be implemented to change the appearance of a cell, based on its calculated value. The text in a cell may be rotated vertically to give the cell greater emphasis.

The Formula Auditing toolbar provides a graphical display for the relationships among the various cells in a worksheet. It enables you to trace the precedents for a formula and identify the cells in the worksheet that are referenced by that formula. It also enables you to trace the dependents of a cell and identify the formulas in the worksheet that reference that cell.

A shared workbook may be viewed and/or edited by multiple individuals simultaneously. The changes made by each user can be stored within the workbook, then subsequently reviewed by the developer, who has the ultimate authority to resolve any conflicts that might occur.

The Data Validation command enables you to restrict the values that will be accepted into a cell. You can limit the values to a list for cells containing text entries (e.g., Atlanta, Boston, or Chicago), or you can specify a quantitative relationship for cells that hold numeric values.

A template is a workbook that is used to create other workbooks. It contains text, formatting, formulas, and/or macros, but no specific data. A template that has been saved to the Templates or Spreadsheet Solutions folder is accessed automatically from the link to General Templates in the task pane.

A worksheet may be protected so that its contents cannot be altered or deleted. A protected worksheet may also contain various cells that are unlocked, enabling a user to vary the contents of these cells.

The Excel IRR function requires a single argument, the range of cells that contain the expenses and income at the end of each year. The cell range must contain at least one negative (expense) and one positive (income) value. A second argument, a "guess" at the IRR, is required when the internal rate of return is negative.

The PMT function is used to calculate the periodic payment of a loan based on constant payments and a constant interest rate. An amortization schedule shows the amount of each payment that goes toward interest and toward principal.

KEY TERMS

Amortization schedule 309	Indent text 278	Rotate text 278
AND function 309	INDEX function 311	Scenario 279
Assumptions 276	Initial conditions 276	Scenario Manager 279
Changing cells 279	Insert Comment command 299	Scenario summary 279
Circle invalid data 292	Insert Name command 287	Shared workbook 291
Circular reference 298	Internal rate of return 301	Style 278
Conditional formatting 278	IRR function 301	Template 301
Custom format 278	ISERROR function 306	Templates folder 301
Custom view 286	MATCH function 311	Tracers 292
Data Validation command 292	MONTH function 311	Track Changes command 291
DATE function 311	PMT function 312	Unlock cells 301
DAY function 311	Precedent cells 292	Workgroup 291
Define Name command 279	Protected worksheet 301	YEAR function 311
Dependent cells 292	Result cells 279	
Formula Auditing toolbar 292	Reviewing toolbar 291	

MULTIPLE CHOICE

1. Which of the following best describes the formula to compute the sales in the second year of the financial forecast?
   (a) It contains a relative reference to the assumed rate of increase and an absolute reference to the sales from the previous year
   (b) It contains an absolute reference to the assumed rate of increase and a relative reference to the sales from the previous year
   (c) It contains absolute references to both the assumed rate of increase and the sales from the previous year
   (d) It contains relative references to both the assumed rate of increase and the sales from the previous year

2. The estimated sales for the first year of a financial forecast are contained in cell B3. The sales for year two are assumed to be 10% higher than for the first year, with the rate of increase (10%) stored in cell C23 at the bottom of the spreadsheet. Which of the following is the best way to enter the projected sales for year two, assuming that this formula is to be copied to the remaining years of the forecast?
   (a) =B3+B3*.10
   (b) =B3+B3*C23
   (c) =B3+B3*$C$23
   (d) All of the above are equivalent entries

3. Which of the following describes the placement of assumptions in a worksheet as required by Microsoft Excel?
   (a) The assumptions must appear in contiguous cells but can be placed anywhere within the worksheet
   (b) The assumptions must appear in contiguous cells and, further, must be placed below the main body of the worksheet
   (c) The assumptions are not required to appear in contiguous cells and, further, can be placed anywhere within the worksheet
   (d) None of the above

4. Given that cell D4 contains the formula =D1+D2:
   (a) Cells D1 and D2 are precedent cells for cell D4
   (b) Cell D4 is a dependent cell of cells D1 and D2
   (c) Both (a) and (b)
   (d) Neither (a) nor (b)

5. Which of the following is true, given that cell C23 is displayed with three blue tracers that point to cells E4, F4, and G4, respectively?
   (a) Cells E4, F4, and G4 are dependent cells for cell C23
   (b) Cell C23 is a precedent cell for cells E4, F4, and G4
   (c) Both (a) and (b)
   (d) Neither (a) nor (b)

6. How can you enter a comment into a cell?
   (a) Click the New Comment command on the Formula Auditing toolbar
   (b) Click the New Comment command on the Reviewing toolbar
   (c) Right click in the cell, then select the Insert Comment command
   (d) All of the above

7. Which of the following best describes how to protect a worksheet, but still enable the user to change the value of various cells within the worksheet?
   (a) Protect the entire worksheet, then unlock the cells that are to change
   (b) Protect the entire worksheet, then unprotect the cells that are to change
   (c) Lock the cells that are to change, then protect the entire worksheet
   (d) Unlock the cells that are to change, then protect the entire worksheet

8. Which of the following describes the protection associated with the financial forecast that was developed in the chapter?
   (a) The worksheet is protected and all cells are locked
   (b) The worksheet is protected and all cells are unlocked
   (c) The worksheet is protected and the assumption area is locked
   (d) The worksheet is protected and the assumption area is unlocked

9. Which of the following may be stored within a style?
   (a) The font, point size, and color
   (b) Borders and shading
   (c) Alignment and protection
   (d) All of the above

... continued

multiple choice

10. What is the easiest way to change the formatting of five cells that are scattered throughout a worksheet, each of which has the same style?
    (a) Select the cells individually, then click the appropriate buttons on the Formatting toolbar
    (b) Select the cells at the same time, then click the appropriate buttons on the Formatting toolbar
    (c) Change the format of the existing style
    (d) Reenter the data in each cell according to the new specifications

11. Each scenario in the Scenario Manager:
    (a) Is stored in a separate worksheet
    (b) Contains the value of a single assumption or input condition
    (c) Both (a) and (b)
    (d) Neither (a) nor (b)

12. The Formula Auditing and Reviewing toolbars are floating toolbars by default. Which of the following is (are) true about fixed (docked) and floating toolbars?
    (a) Floating toolbars can be changed to fixed toolbars, but the reverse is not true
    (b) Fixed toolbars can be changed into floating toolbars, but the reverse is not true
    (c) Fixed toolbars can be changed into floating toolbars and vice versa
    (d) Fixed toolbars can be displayed only at the top of the screen

13. You open a template called Expense Account but see Expense Account1 displayed on the title bar. What is the most likely explanation?
    (a) You are the first person to use this template
    (b) Some type of error must have occurred
    (c) All is in order since Excel has appended the number to differentiate the workbook from the template on which it is based
    (d) The situation is impossible

14. Two adjacent cells are enclosed in hairline borders of different colors. Each of these cells also contains a tiny shaded triangle in the upper-left part of the cell. Which of the following is the most likely explanation?
    (a) Conditional formatting is in effect
    (b) Data validation is in effect for the cells in question
    (c) A comment has been entered into each of the cells
    (d) The cells have been changed by different people

15. The value in cell A7 is to be displayed in blue if its value exceeds $100,000. To which cell(s) would you apply conditional formatting? (Cell A7 contains the formula =A5*A6.)
    (a) A5
    (b) A6
    (c) A7
    (d) A5, A6, and A7

16. Which command would you use to restrict the value that can be entered into a specific cell?
    (a) Protect Worksheet command
    (b) Lock Worksheet command
    (c) Data Validation command
    (d) Conditional Formatting command

17. What is the most common reason to protect selected cells in a worksheet?
    (a) To prevent the initial conditions and assumptions from ever being changed
    (b) To prevent formulas in the worksheet from being changed
    (c) To prevent additional scenarios from being added
    (d) To prevent the worksheet from review by outsiders

18. The IRR function has how many *required* arguments?
    (a) One
    (b) Two
    (c) Three
    (d) Four

ANSWERS

1. b	7. d	13. c
2. c	8. d	14. d
3. c	9. d	15. c
4. c	10. c	16. c
5. c	11. d	17. b
6. d	12. c	18. a

PRACTICE WITH EXCEL

1. **Erroneous Payroll:** The worksheet in Figure 6.11 displays an *erroneous* version of a worksheet that computes the payroll for a fictitious company. The worksheet is nicely formatted, but several calculations are in error. Your assignment is to open the *Chapter 6 Practice 1* workbook in the Exploring Excel folder, find the errors, and correct the worksheet. Print the workbook as it exists initially, and then print the corrected workbook at the end of the exercise.

   You can "eyeball" the worksheet to find the mistakes, and/or you can use the Formula Auditing toolbar as shown in Figure 6.11. Note, too, that when you identify an error, such as the incorrect formula for gross pay in cell F4, you must first correct the error, then copy the corrected formula to the remaining cells in that column. The correct specifications are given below:

   a. The gross pay is the regular pay (hourly wage times regular hours) plus the overtime pay (hourly wage times the overtime hours times the overtime rate). The overtime rate is entered as an assumption within the worksheet, making it possible to change the overtime rate in a single place should that become necessary.

   b. The net pay is the gross pay minus the deductions (the withholding tax and the Social Security tax).

   c. The taxable income is the gross pay minus the deduction per dependent multiplied by the number of dependents.

   d. The withholding tax is based on the individual's taxable income. The Social Security tax is based on the individual's gross pay.

   e. Use the Page Setup command to include a custom footer with your name and today's date. Print the corrected worksheet with both displayed values and cell formulas. Add a cover sheet and submit the assignment to your instructor. Do you see the importance of checking a worksheet for accuracy?

   f. Describe the purpose of each tool on the Formula Auditing toolbar. Which tools were used in conjunction with the workbook displayed in Figure 6.11? Was the information useful in finding the errors within the worksheet?

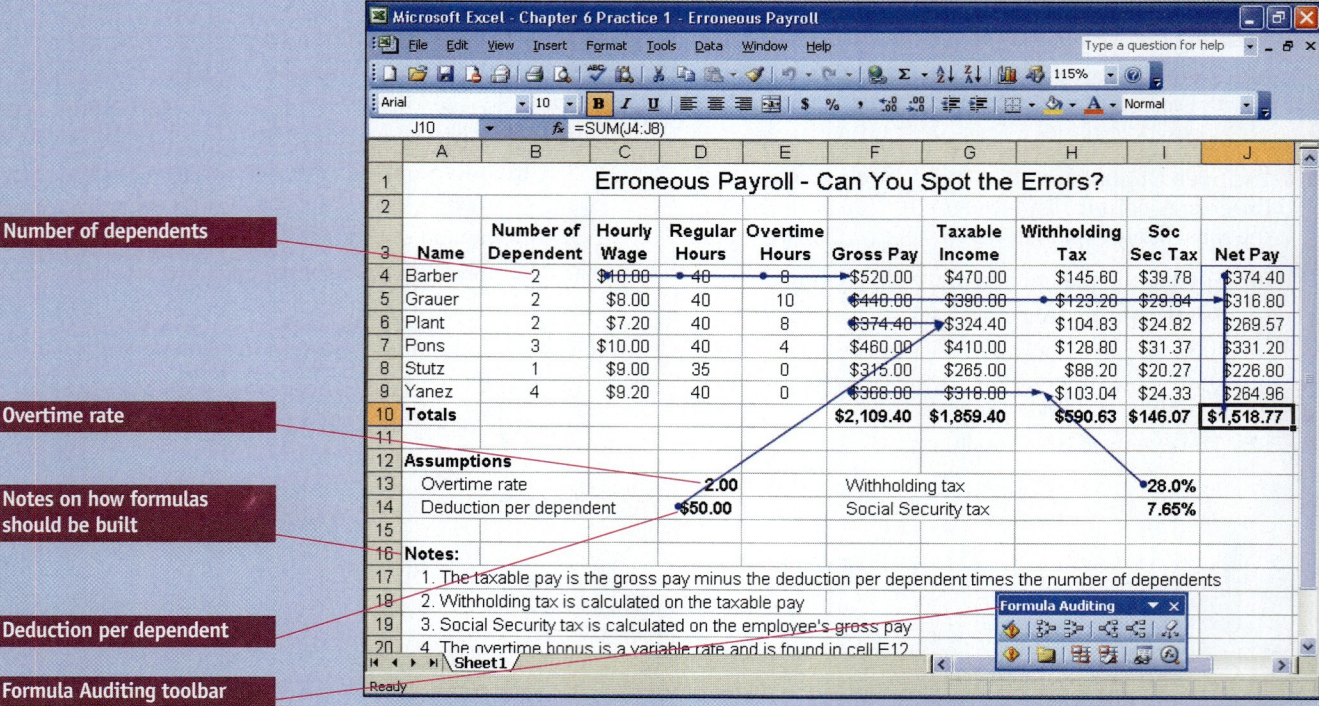

FIGURE 6.11 Erroneous Payroll (exercise 1)

practice exercises

2. **Protection and Validation:** The worksheet in Figure 6.12 will calculate the value of your retirement, based on a set of uniform annual contributions to a retirement account. In essence, you contribute a fixed amount of money each year ($3,000 in Figure 6.12), and the money accumulates at an estimated rate of return (7% in Figure 6.12). You indicate the age when you start to contribute, your projected retirement age, the number of years in retirement, and the rate of return you expect to earn on your money when you retire.

   a. The worksheet determines the total amount you will have contributed, the amount of money you will have accumulated, and the value of your monthly pension. The numbers are impressive, and the sooner you begin to save, the better. The calculations use the Future Value (FV) and Payment (Pmt) functions, respectively.

   b. You will find the completed worksheet in the *Chapter 6 Practice 2* workbook in the Exploring Excel folder. Your assignment is to implement data validation and password protection to ensure that the user does not enter unrealistic numbers nor alter the formulas within the worksheet.

   c. Three validity checks are required as indicated in the assumption area of the worksheet. The retirement age must be 59.5 or greater (as required by current law), the rate of return during the period you are investing money cannot exceed 8%, and the rate of return during retirement cannot exceed 7%. You are to display a warning message if the user violates any of these conditions. The warning will allow the user to override the assumptions.

   d. Enter the parameters that are displayed in Figure 6.12, including the *invalid* entry of .08 in cell B8 by overriding the warning message. Display the Formula Auditing toolbar, then click the button to circle invalid data to display the red circle.

   e. Unlock cells B2 through B8, where the user enters his or her name and assumptions. Protect the remainder of the worksheet. Use "password" as the password.

   f. Enter your name and your assumptions in the completed worksheet, then print the worksheet twice to show both displayed values and cell formulas for your instructor.

   g. A Roth IRA (Individual Retirement Account) is one of the best ways to save for retirement. The money that you contribute is taxed at the time you make your contribution, but the future withdrawals are tax free! In this example, the individual contributed a total of $135,000, which grew to more than $850,000.

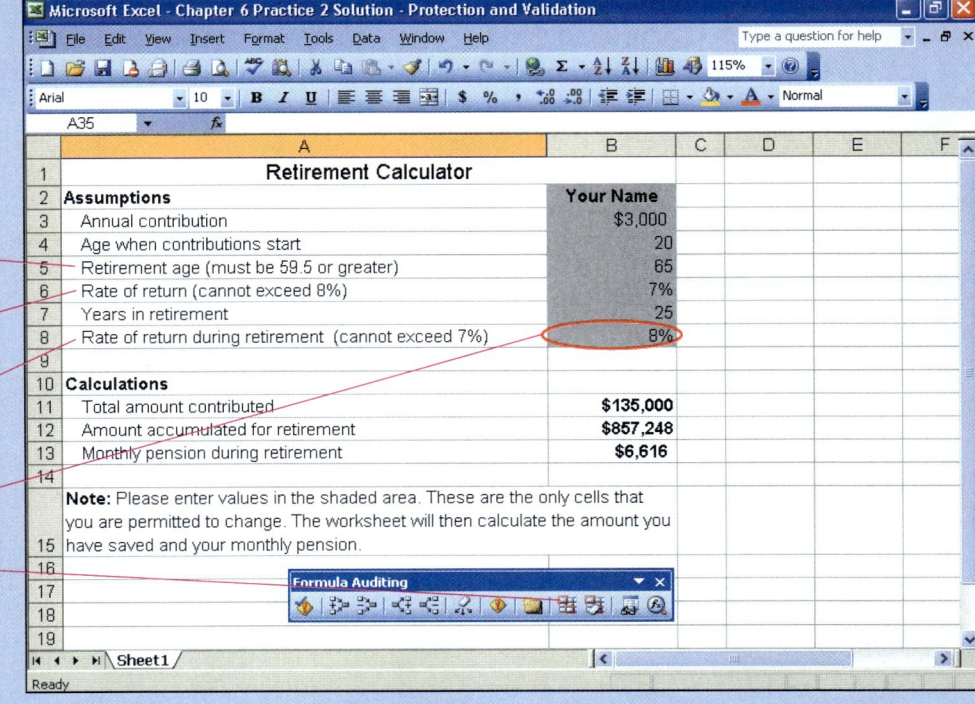

FIGURE 6.12 Protection and Validation (exercise 2)

practice exercises

3. **The Coal Mine:** Figure 6.13 displays a five-year financial forecast for a hypothetical coal mine. The initial investment is substantial ($20,000,000), but so, too, is the return on the investment. Open the partially completed *Chapter 6 Practice 3—The Coal Mine* workbook. Proceed as follows:

   a. Develop the formulas for the first year of the forecast (column D) based on the assumptions and initial conditions at the bottom of the spreadsheet. The projected revenue for the first year is the number of tons of coal that are sold times the price per ton. There are two variable costs, for manufacturing and transportation, which depend on the number of tons that are sold. There is also a fixed cost for sales and administration that is independent of the quantity of coal that is produced. The earnings before taxes are computed by subtracting the total expenses from the anticipated revenue. The after-tax earnings are computed by subtracting the taxes from the earnings before taxes. Note, too, that even the first year of the forecast (cell D2) should be entered as a formula so that the forecast can be easily changed if necessary.

   b. Develop the formulas for the second year based on the values in year one and, where appropriate, the assumed rates of increase at the bottom of the worksheet. Use an appropriate combination of relative and absolute references so that these formulas can be copied to the remaining columns in the worksheet.

   c. Copy the formulas for year two (in column E) to the remaining years of the forecast (columns F through H). Check that your worksheet is correct by comparing the displayed values to those in Figure 6.13.

   d. Enter the formula to display the initial investment in cell C19, then click in cell D20 and enter the function to calculate the internal rate of return at the end of year one. Compute the rate of return for the remaining years.

   e. Format the completed worksheet. You do not have to match our formatting exactly, but you are to display dollar amounts with the currency symbol. Use conditional formatting to display negative returns in red and positive returns in blue.

   f. Enter your name as the financial analyst. Print the completed worksheet two ways, once with displayed values and once with cell formulas. Use landscape printing and force the worksheet to one page. Create a custom footer that includes the date. Display gridlines and row and column headings.

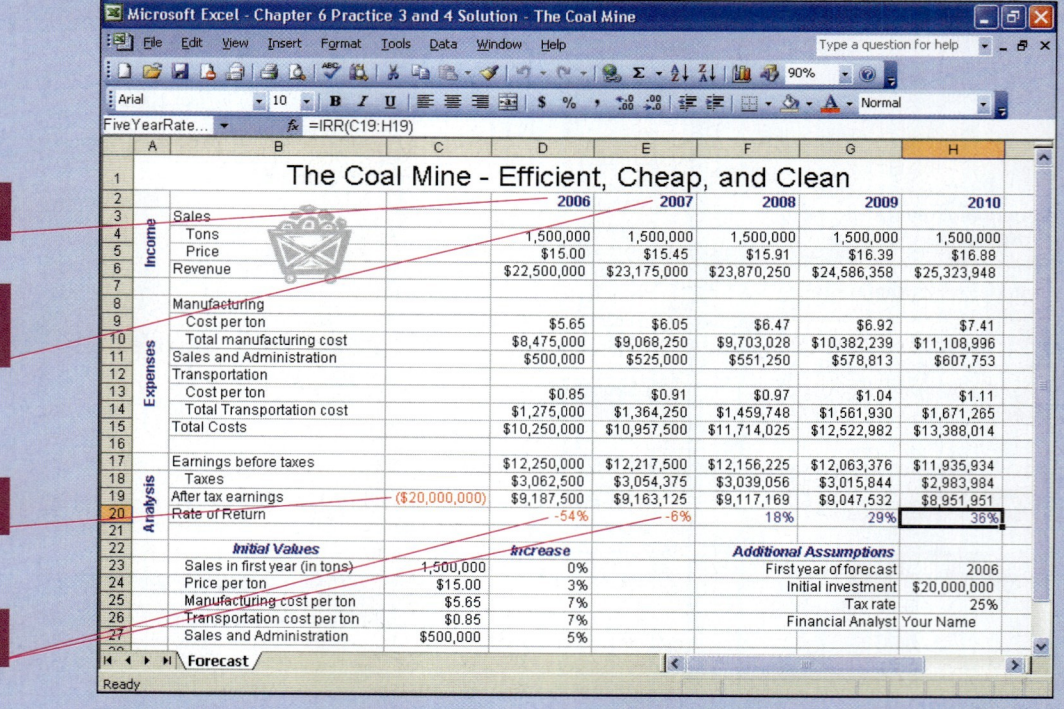

FIGURE 6.13 The Coal Mine (exercise 3)

practice exercises

4. **The Coal Mine—Protection and Scenario Summary:** Figure 6.14 expands the financial forecast for the coal mine to include protected cells and a scenario summary. Open the workbook from the previous exercise. Proceed as follows:

   a. Select the cells that contain the variable inputs for the initial values and additional assumptions (cells C23:D27 and H23:H26). Pull down the Format menu, click the Cells command, click the Patterns tab, and select light gray to shade these cells. Click the Protection tab and clear the Locked box so that the user will be able to change these values. (The worksheet will be protected at the end of the exercise.) Click OK.

   b. We will create three scenarios, each with five input variables in cells C23:C27. The descriptive labels for these cells are found in the adjacent cells B23:B27. Thus we can create all five cell names at once. Select cells B23:C27, pull down the Insert menu, click Name, then click Create to display the Create Names dialog box, and note that the Left column box is checked automatically. Click OK to name the cells.

   c. Click in cell H20. Pull down the Insert menu, click Name, then click Define since you are naming a single cell. Enter FiveYearRateOfReturn. Click OK.

   d. Pull down the Tools menu, click Scenarios, then click the Add command button to display the Add Scenario dialog box. Type Consensus in the Scenario Name text box. Click in the Changing Cells text box, delete H20, then click and drag to select cells C23:C27. Click OK. You should see the Scenario Values dialog box with the values for this scenario already entered. Click the Add button to enter a Pessimistic scenario and take the values from the summary in Figure 6.14. Add the Optimistic Scenario in similar fashion.

   e. The Scenario Manager dialog box should still be open with three scenarios listed. Click the Summary button, click in the Result Cells text box, click cell H20, then click OK to create the Scenario Summary worksheet.

   f. Click the worksheet tab to return to the financial forecast, then pull down the Tools menu and protect the worksheet. Pull down the Window menu, open a second window, then arrange the windows as shown in Figure 6.14. Click in any protected cell (e.g., cell C19) and attempt to change its value. You should see the dialog box in Figure 6.14. Use the Print Screen key to capture the screen in Figure 6.14 in a Word document for your instructor.

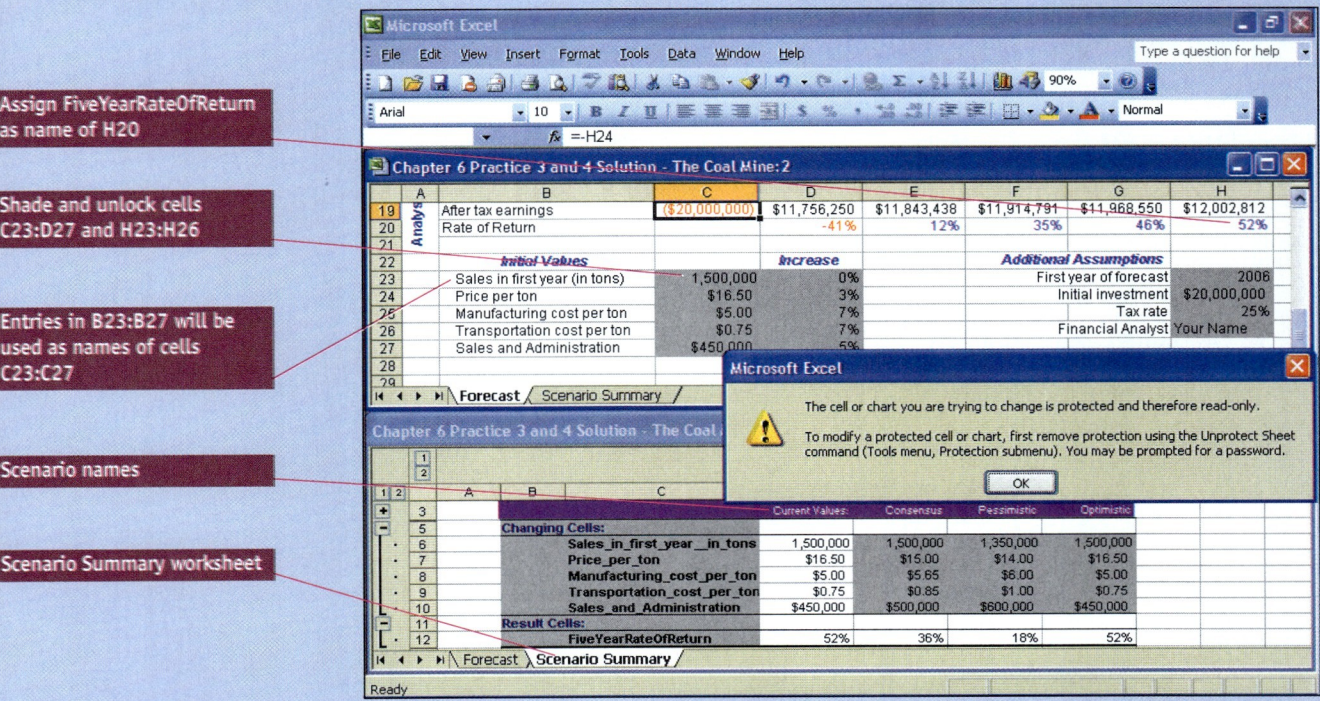

FIGURE 6.14 The Coal Mine (exercise 4)

MICROSOFT OFFICE EXCEL 2003 REVISED

practice exercises

5. **The Gym:** Figure 6.15 displays a six-year financial forecast for a hypothetical gym. The gym begins each year with a number of existing members from the previous year (e.g., 650 in 2006); it also adds a number of new members for that year (e.g., 100 in 2006). There is a limitation, however, on the maximum number of memberships (1,000) and thus there is a subtlety in calculating the number of new members. Open the partially completed *Chapter 6 Practice 5—the Gym* workbook and proceed as follows:

   a. Develop the formulas for the first year of the forecast (column C) based on the assumptions and initial conditions at the bottom of the spreadsheet. Look closely at the formula bar in Figure 6.15 to see how the MIN function is used to limit the number of new members. Note, too, that even the first year of the forecast (cell C2) should be entered as a formula so that the forecast can be easily changed if necessary.
   b. Develop the formulas for the second year based on the values in year one and the assumed rates of increase at the bottom of the worksheet. Use an appropriate combination of relative and absolute references so that these formulas can be copied to the remaining columns in the worksheet. Note, however, that there is a cap on the annual dues and thus the MIN function should be used in conjunction with this formula.
   c. Copy the formulas for year two (in column D) to the remaining years of the forecast (columns E through H). Check that your worksheet is correct by comparing the displayed values to those in Figure 6.15.
   d. Enter the formula to display the initial investment in cell B17, then click in cell C19 and enter the function to calculate the internal rate of return at the end of year one. Compute the rate of return for the remaining years.
   e. Format the completed worksheet. You do not have to match our formatting exactly, but you are to display dollar amounts with the currency symbol. Use conditional formatting to display negative returns in red and positive returns in blue.
   f. Enter your name as the financial analyst. Print the completed worksheet two ways, once with displayed values and once with cell formulas. Use landscape printing and force the worksheet to one page. Create a custom footer that includes the date. Display gridlines and row and column headings.

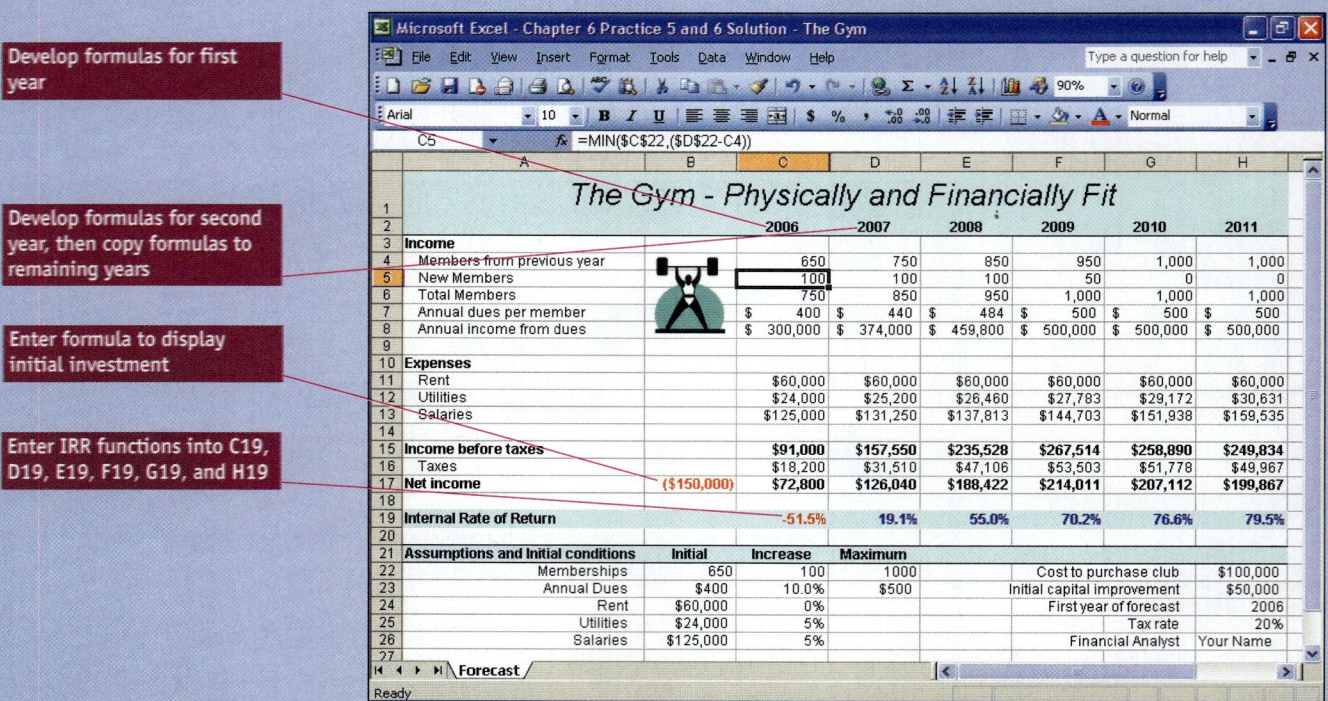

FIGURE 6.15 The Gym (exercise 5)

practice exercises

6. **The Gym—Protection and Scenario Summary:** Figure 6.16 expands the financial forecast for the gym to include protected cells and a scenario summary. Open the workbook from the previous exercise. Proceed as follows:

   a. Select the cells that contain the variable inputs for the initial values and additional assumptions (cells B22:C26, D22:D23, and H22:H26). Pull down the Format menu, click the Cells command, click the Patterns tab, and select light yellow to shade these cells. Click the Protection tab and clear the Locked box so that the user will be able to change these values. (The worksheet will be protected at the end of the exercise.)

   b. We will create three scenarios, each with four input variables in cells B23, C22, D22, and D23. Select cell B23, and then use the Insert Name command to give it a descriptive name. Assign descriptive names to cells C22, D22, and D23 in similar fashion (our names appear in the Scenario Summary worksheet in Figure 6.16). The scenario summary also has two result cells, E19 and H19, which should be named ReturnAfterThreeYears and ReturnAfterSixYears, respectively.

   c. Pull down the Tools menu, click Scenarios, then click the Add command button to display the Add Scenario dialog box. Type Consensus in the Scenario Name text box. Click in the Changing Cells text box, then press and hold the Ctrl key to select cells B23, C22, D22, and D23. Click OK. You should see the Scenario Values dialog box with the values for this scenario already entered. Click the Add button to enter an Optimistic scenario and take the values from the summary in Figure 6.16. Add the Pessimistic scenario in similar fashion.

   d. The Scenario Manager dialog box should still be open with three scenarios listed. Click the Summary button, click in the Result Cells text box, then press and hold the Ctrl key as you select cells E19 and H19. Click OK to create the Scenario Summary worksheet.

   e. Click the worksheet tab to return to the financial forecast, then pull down the Tools menu and protect the worksheet. Pull down the Window menu, open a second window, then arrange the windows as shown in Figure 6.16. Click in any protected cell (e.g., cell B17) and attempt to change its value. You should see the dialog box in Figure 6.16. Use the Print Screen key to capture the screen in Figure 6.16 in a Word document for your instructor.

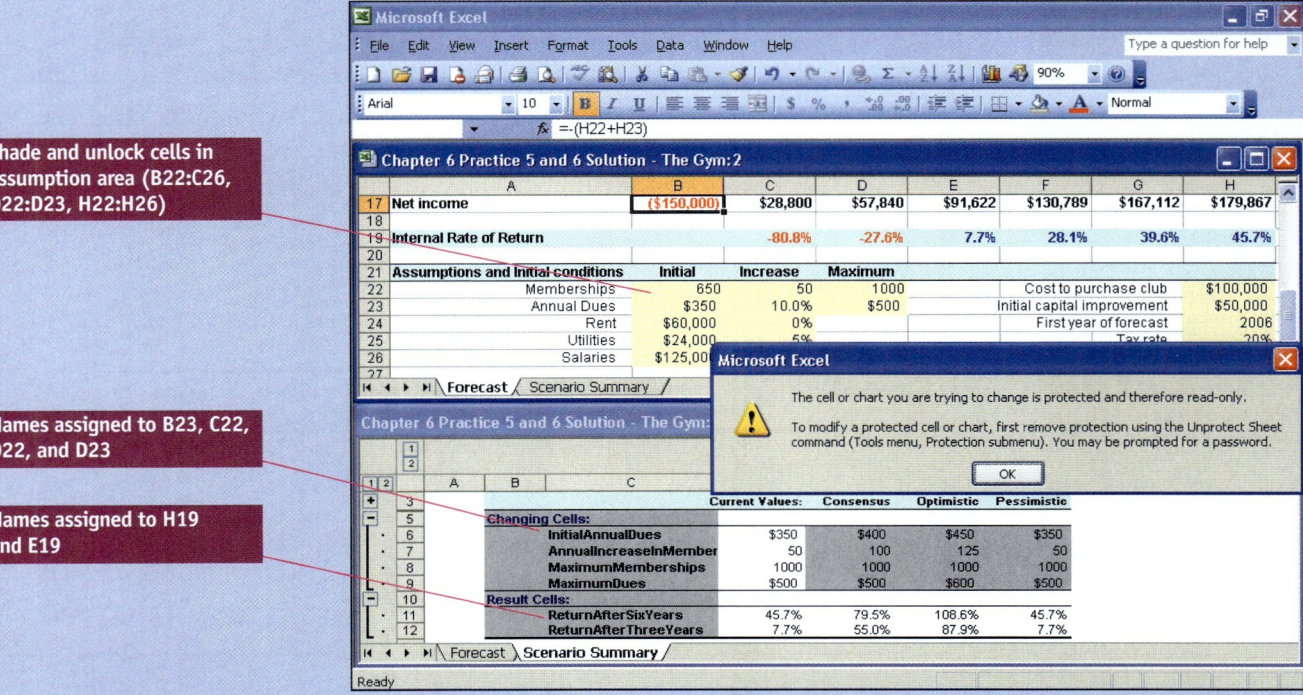

FIGURE 6.16 The Gym— Protection and Scenario Summary (exercise 6)

practice exercises

7. **Pay Off Your Credit Card:** The worksheet in Figure 6.17 resembles the amortization schedule in the chapter, with two significant differences. The interest rate is much higher, but more importantly the individual is still in debt after 180 payments.

   a. Open the *Chapter 6 Practice 7—Pay Off Your Credit Card* workbook. Drag the clip art out of the way. Enter the AND function into cell D7.
   b. Enter the parameters shown into cells C4 through C7. The AND function changes to true after the last value is entered. Return the clip art to its original position.
   c. Create the formulas for the first payment in row 14:
      i. Click in cell A14; enter =IF(DataEntered,1,0). Click in cell B14; enter =IF(A14>0,C6,0). Click in cell C14; enter =IF(A14>0,C4,0).
      ii. Click in cell D14; enter =IF(A14>0,($C$5/12)*C14,0). The interest is charged on the unpaid balance at the beginning of the period.
      iii. Click in cell E14; enter =IF(A14>0,$C$8,0).
      iv. Click in cell F14; enter =IF(A14>0,D14+$C$7*(C14+E14),0). The minimum payment is the interest due, plus the minimum percent required by the credit card company (which is computed on the initial balance plus the new charges.)
      v. Click in cell G14; enter =IF(A14>0,$C$9,0).
      vi. Click in cell H14; enter =IF(A14>0,C14+D14+E14-F14-G14,0).
   d. Create the formulas for the second payment:
      i. Click in cell A15; enter =IF(H14>0,A14+1,0). There is a payment in this period only if there was an ending balance in the previous period.
      ii. Enter =IF(A15>0,DATE(YEAR(B14),MONTH(B14)+1,DAY(B14)),0) into cell B15 to compute the date of the next payment.
      iii. Click in cell C15; enter =IF(A15>0,H14,0).
      iv. Copy the formulas from D14:H14 to cells D15:H15.
   e. Copy cells A15:H15 to the remaining payments (through row 193, where you see payment 180). Suppress the zero values, then format the worksheet. Print this worksheet. The summary statistics will be calculated in the next exercise.

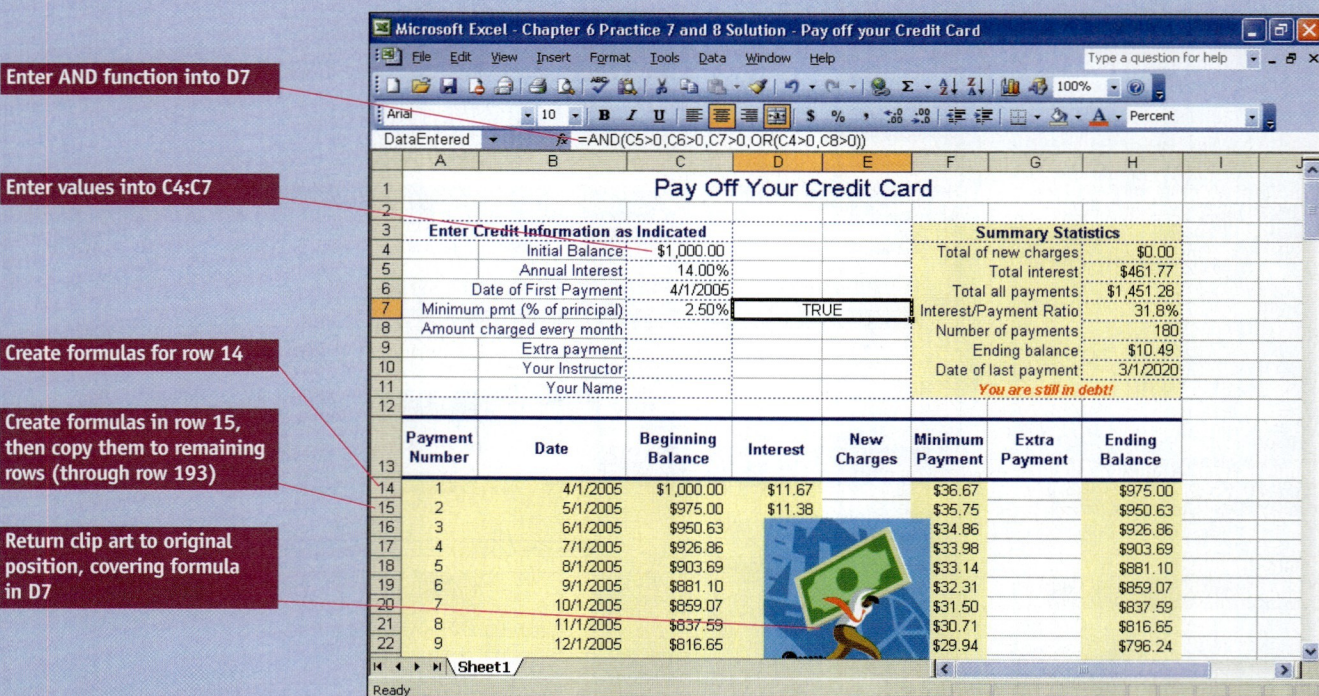

FIGURE 6.17 Pay Off Your Credit Card (exercise 7)

328 CHAPTER 6: FINANCIAL ANALYSIS

practice exercises

8. **Pay Off Your Credit Card (continued):** This exercise continues the development of the credit card worksheet by computing the summary information. It also uses the Goal Seek command to determine the extra payment required to pay off the debt in a specified amount of time. Open the completed workbook from the previous exercise and proceed as follows:

   a. Click in cell H4; enter =SUM(New_Charges). The range name has already been defined in the workbook. An If statement is not required in the formula because zero values are suppressed.
   b. Click in cell H5; enter =SUM(Interest). Click in cell H6 and enter the formula =SUM(Minimum_Payment,Extra_Payment).
   c. Click in cell H7; enter =IF(H6>0,H5/H6,0).
   d. Click in cell H8 and enter the formula in Figure 6.18 to compute the number of payments. (The nested IF calculates the number of payments only if all of the data has been entered.) The range name EndingBalance refers to the balance after the 180th payment when the table ends; that is, if a zero balance is not reached at this point, there are 180 payments.
   e. Click in cell H9; enter =IF(H8>0,INDEX(PaymentTable,H8,8),0).
   f. Click in cell H10; enter =IF(H8>0,INDEX(PaymentTable,H8,2),"").
   g. And finally, click in cell H11 and enter a formula to determine if you are still in debt, or are debt free: =IF(DataEntered,IF(H9<=0, "Congratulations, you are debt free!", "You are still in debt!"),"").
   h. You should see the values in Figure 6.17 *from the previous exercise*.
   i. You made a resolution to get out of debt in two years. Click in cell H8, pull down the Tools menu, and click the Goal Seek command. H8 is already entered in the Set cell text box. Enter 24 and $C$9 into the To value and By Changing Cell text boxes, respectively. Click OK.
   j. Excel indicates a solution. Click OK to close the Goal Seek Status dialog box and display the worksheet in Figure 6.18, which indicates an extra payment of $31.05 each period for 24 periods. At that point you will be out of debt with a credit of $20.97 after the last payment. Print this worksheet.

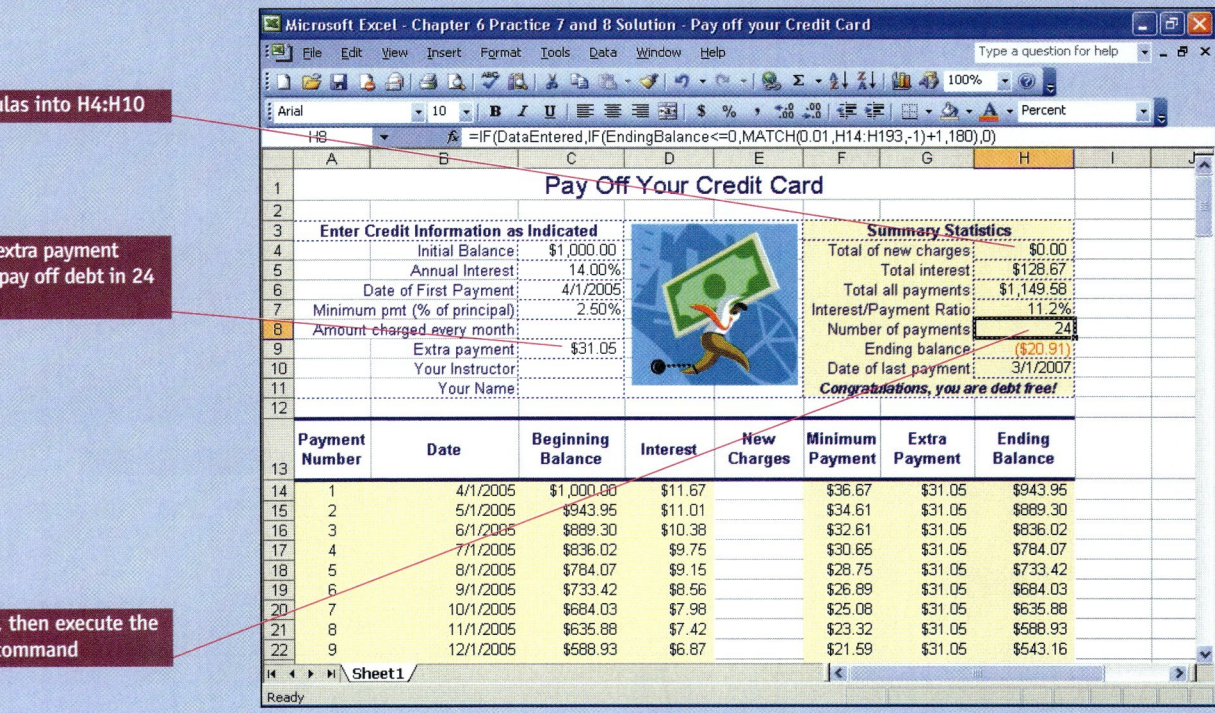

FIGURE 6.18   Pay Off Your Credit Card (continued) (exercise 8)

MICROSOFT OFFICE EXCEL 2003 REVISED   329

practice exercises

9. **Compare and Merge Workbooks:** The consensus workbook in Figure 6.19 is the result of merging three individual workbooks, provided by Tom, Dick, and Harry, each of whom added his comments to a shared workbook. Proceed as follows:

   a. Open the *Chapter 6 Practice 9* workbook that contains the original workbook sent out to each of the three reviewers.

   b. Pull down the Tools menu, click the Compare and Merge Workbooks command to display the associated dialog box, select the individual workbooks for Tom's Forecast, Dick's Forecast, and Harry's Forecast, then click OK. The workbooks will be opened individually, and any changes will be automatically merged into the consensus workbook. If there are conflicting changes (e.g., two individuals make different changes to the same cell), the changes are entered in the order that the workbooks are opened.

   c. Pull down the Tools menu, click Track Changes, and click the Highlight Changes command to display the Highlight Changes dialog box. Clear the Who, When, and Where check boxes so that you will see all of the changes made to the workbook. Check the box to list the changes on a new sheet. Click OK.

   d. A History worksheet is created automatically that shows all of the changes made to the shared workbook. Pull down the Windows menu, click New window, then pull down the Windows menu a second time, click Arrange, and tile the worksheets horizontally to match Figure 6.19. Click the Sales Data tab in one window and the History tab in the other.

   e. Look closely at the History worksheet and note that Harry and Tom changed the value of cell E4 to $90,000 and $125,000, respectively. The value that is shown in the consensus workbook ($125,000 in our figure) depends on the order in which the workbooks were merged. Tom was last in our example, so his change dominates. You can, however, use the Accept or Reject Changes command to go through all of the changes individually and accept (reject) the changes individually. If necessary, use this command to accept Tom's change ($125,000) rather than Harry's.

   f. Print the completed workbook, with both worksheets, for your instructor. Use the Page Setup command to include an appropriate footer that contains today's date and the name of the worksheet.

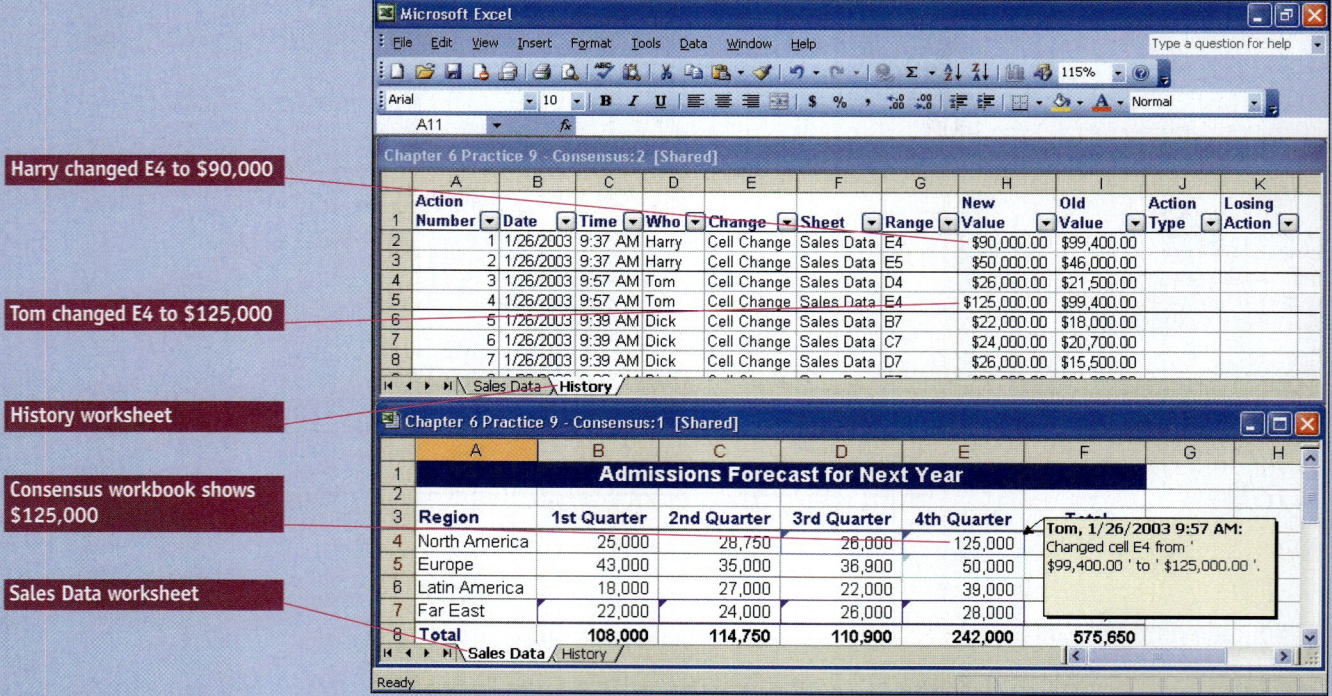

FIGURE 6.19 Compare and Merge Workbooks (exercise 9)

330   CHAPTER 6: FINANCIAL ANALYSIS

practice exercises

10. **Circular References:** A circular reference usually indicates a logic error, but there are instances when it can be valid. Figure 6.20 displays a hypothetical worksheet for an employee profit sharing plan, in which the company contributes 25% of its net income, *after profit sharing is taken into account*, to profit sharing. The net income is determined by subtracting expenses from revenue, but one of those expenses is profit sharing, which in turn creates the circular reference. In other words, the formula in cell B7 depends on the formula in cell B6, which depends on the formula in cell B7. Open the partially completed spreadsheet in *Chapter 6 Practice 10* and proceed as follows:

    a. Click in cell B7 and enter the formula to compute the net income after profit sharing, =B4-B5-B6. Excel indicates that there is a circular reference. Click OK. Close the Help screen if it appears.

    b. The Circular Reference toolbar is displayed automatically, and the status bar shows a circular reference in cell B6. Pull down the View menu, click Toolbars, then click the Formula Auditing toolbar to display this toolbar as well. Click the Show Watch Window button and add cells B6 and B7.

    c. You can now recalculate the spreadsheet manually to see the effects of the circular reference. Pull down the Tools menu, click the Options command, then click the Calculation tab. Check the Iteration box and change the maximum number of iterations to one. Click the Manual option button in the Calculation area. Click OK to accept these settings and close the dialog box.

    d. Press the F9 (recalculate) key continually to see the spreadsheet go through multiple iterations, eventually settling on steady state values of $400,000 and $1,600,000 for the profit sharing and net income, respectively. Note that the profit sharing value of $400,000 is indeed 25% of the net income value of $1,600,000.

    e. Add your name to the worksheet, then print the completed worksheet for your professor. Close the Formula Auditing toolbar and Watch Window. Close the workbook.

    f. Open a blank workbook. Pull down the Tools menu, click the Options command, then click Calculation tab to restore the default settings. Click the option button for Automatic calculation and reset the maximum iterations to 100. Clear the iteration check box.

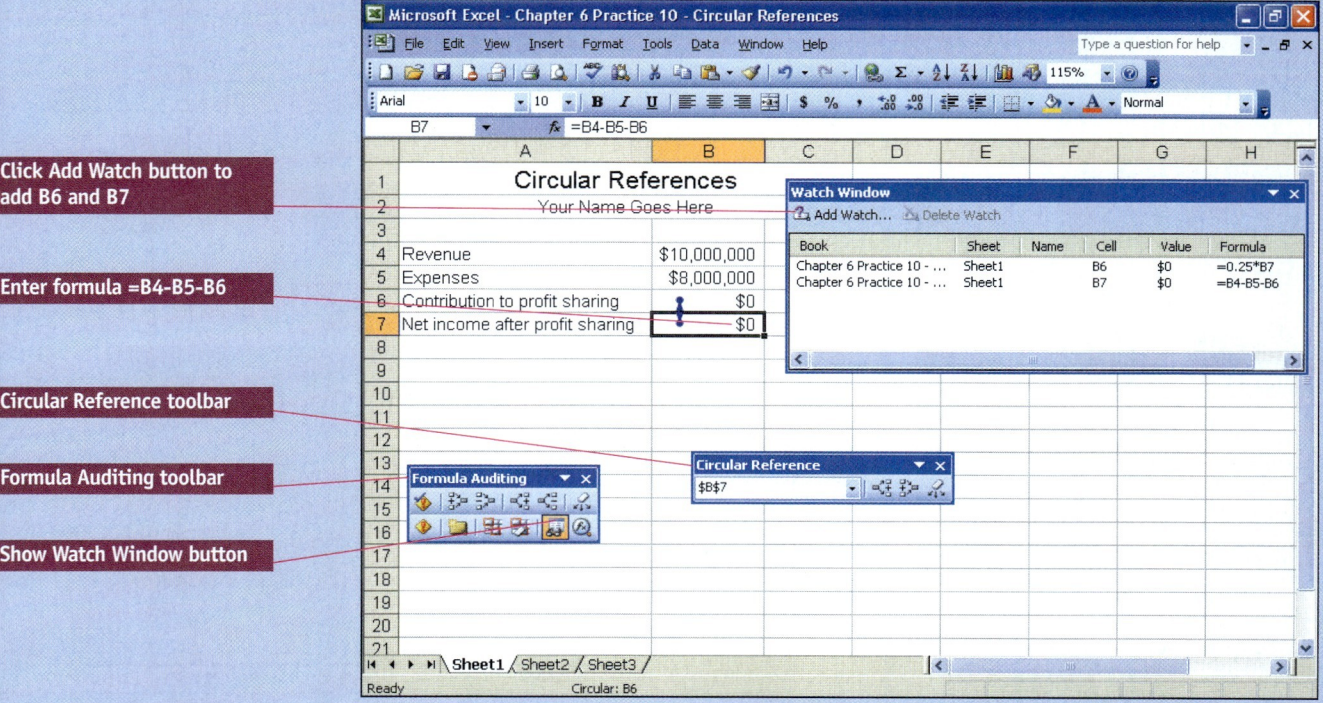

FIGURE 6.20 Circular References (exercise 10)

practice exercises

11. **The Mortgage Calculator:** The worksheet in Figure 6.21 is completely flexible in that it accepts the user's input in the shaded cells and then it computes the associated monthly payments in the body of the worksheet. It also introduces the Evaluate Formula tool on the Formula Auditing toolbar that lets you step through the calculation of any formula within a worksheet. Your assignment is to create the worksheet as shown in Figure 6.21. (You may want to review material on the PMT function and mixed references from Chapter 4.) Open the partially completed *Chapter 6 Practice 11* workbook, then proceed as follows:

   a. Click in cell B8 and enter the formula =E4; that is, the initial interest rate in the body of the spreadsheet is taken from the user's input in cell E4. Click in cell C8 and enter the formula, =B8+$E$5, then copy this formula to the remaining cells in this row. Enter parallel formulas in cells A9 to A19 to compute the various values for the principal amounts that will appear in the table. Check that your formulas are correct by changing the input parameters in rows 4 and 5. Any changes to the input parameters should be reflected in row 8 and/or column A.

   b. The "trick" to this assignment (if any) is to develop the PMT function with the correct mixed references in cell B9. The correct formula is =PMT(B$8/12,$B$6*12,-$A9) as can be seen by looking at the title bar in Figure 6.21. Enter this formula into cell B9 and copy it to the remaining rows and columns in the worksheet.

   c. Display the Formula Auditing toolbar. Click in Cell B9, then click the Evaluate Formula button to display the associated dialog box. You should see the complete formula for cell B9. Now click the Evaluate button, and the numeric value (.045) is substituted for the first argument, B$8. Continue to click the Evaluate button to see the numeric value of each cell reference until the computed value is shown. Do you see how this tool can help you to understand how a formula works?

   d. Enter your name into cell A1 and format the completed worksheet. You do not have to match our formatting exactly, but you are to shade the input parameters.

   e. Unlock cells B4 through B6 and cells E4 and E5, then protect the completed worksheet. Use "password" in lowercase letters as the password.

   f. Print the worksheet two ways, once with displayed values, and once with the cell formulas. Use landscape orientation.

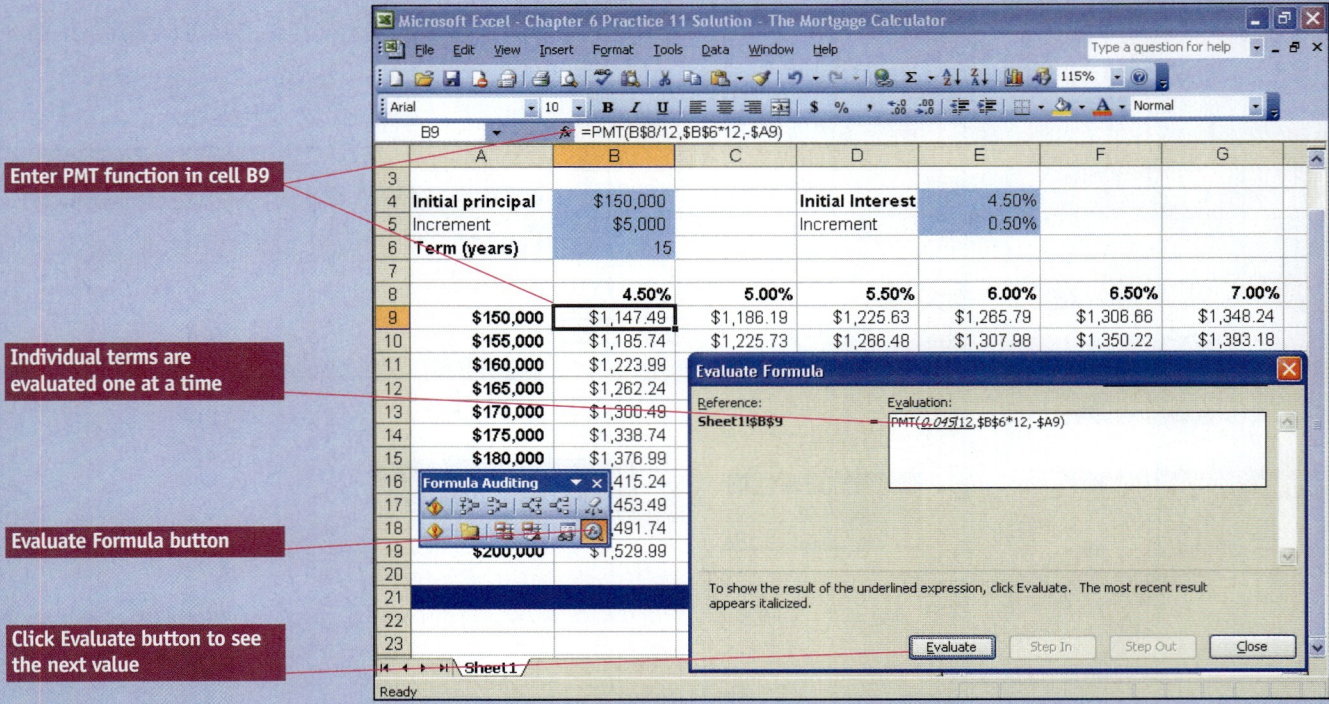

FIGURE 6.21 The Mortgage Calculator (exercise 11)

practice exercises

12. **Data Tables:** A data table is a range of cells (i.e., a table) that shows the results of substituting different values in a formula. The same result can be achieved using mixed references (as was done in the previous exercise), and we invite you to compare the two techniques. Both worksheets in Figure 6.22 function identically; i.e., the user enters values in the shaded cells in rows 4 through 6 and the remaining numbers are calculated automatically. Proceed as follows:

   a. Open the completed workbook from the previous exercise. Double click the worksheet tab and rename the existing worksheet Mixed References. Right click the worksheet, click the Move or Copy command, check the box to Create a copy, click OK, and then rename the copied worksheet Data Tables.

   b. Erase C9:H19. Insert a new column as column A. Click in cell A9 and enter =C4 to take the initial principal from cell C4. Enter =C6 and =F4 in cells A10 and A11, respectively. This seems awkward (it is) but the data table cannot reference the cells at the top of the worksheet because those cells are also referenced in the row and column headings; hence you need the additional column to match the functionality of the mixed references.

   c. Click in cell B8 and enter =PMT(A11/4,A20*12,−A9).

   d. Click and drag to select cells B8 through H19, which constitute the body of the table. Pull down the Data menu and click Table to display the Data table dialog box. Enter A11 and A9 as the row and column input cells, respectively, and click OK. You should see the numbers in Figure 6.22.

   e. Click in cell C9 and view its contents {=TABLE(A11,A9)}. The same formula appears in every cell of the data table.

   f. You can improve the appearance of the data table by hiding the formula in cell B8. Right click the cell, click the Format command, click Cells, click the Number tab, and choose the Custom category. Enter "Principal" in the Type list box to hide the formula. You can further improve the appearance of the worksheet by hiding column A.

   g. Compare the results in the two worksheets. Which technique do you prefer, mixed references or data tables? Would you ever consider a one-variable data table when the same results could be achieved with relative references?

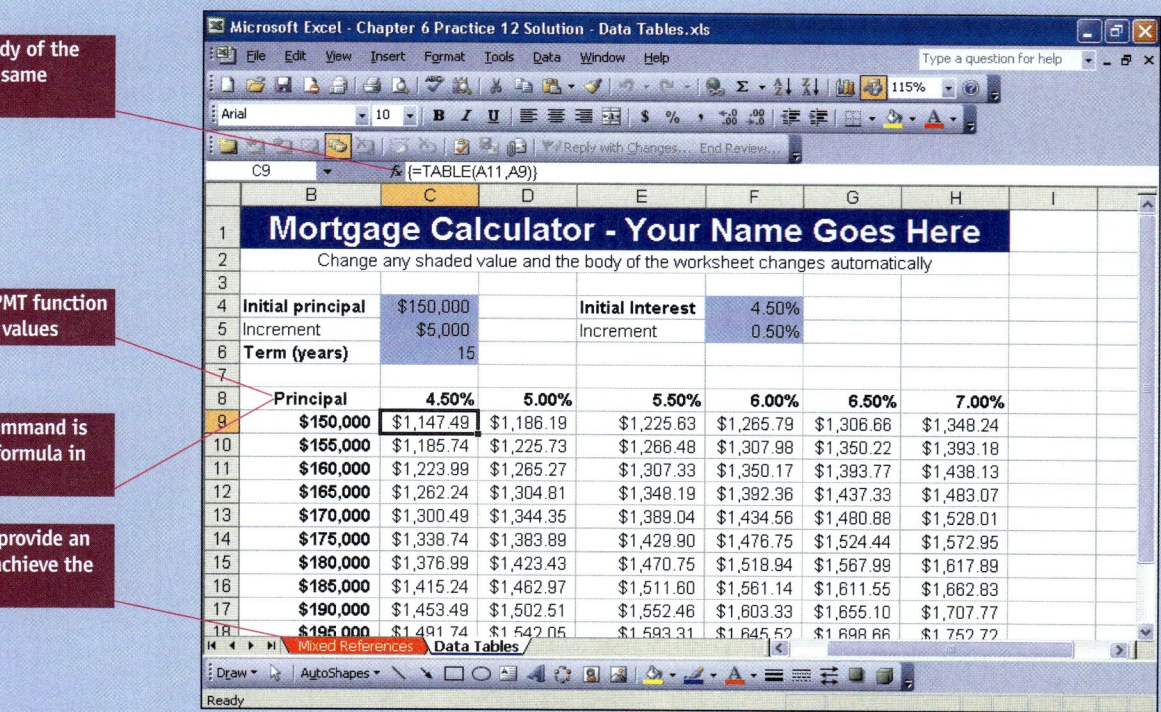

FIGURE 6.22 Data Tables (exercise 12)

MINI CASES

Retirement Planning

Compound interest has been called the eighth wonder of the world. It can work against you, as in the case of credit card and other debt. It works in your favor, however, if you are able to save periodically toward retirement, especially when you begin saving at an early age. The best time to start is when you begin your first job, because the longer your money is invested, the more time it has to grow.

Assume, for example, that you begin saving $25 a week at age 22 and that you continue to save for 45 years until you reach age 67 (the retirement age under Social Security). Let's further assume that you earn an annual return of 8%, which is the historical rate of return for a broad-based investment in the stock market. When you retire, you will have contributed a total of $58,500, but your money will have grown to more than $540,000. The compound interest you earned on your money accounts for almost 90% of your nest egg. Let's say that you delay for 10 years and that all other parameters are the same. Your total contribution is $45,500 ($13,000 less), but your nest egg will be only $241,000, less than half of what you would have had if you had contributed the additional ten years.

Your assignment is to open the *Chapter 6 Mini Case—Retirement Planning* workbook in the Exploring Excel folder. The workbook is complete; that is, all of the formulas have already been entered. All you have to do is enter the parameters in the shaded input area (cells C4 through C8) to see your retirement projection. Print a completed worksheet for your instructor. Print the worksheet a second time to show the cell formulas for the first 24 payments as well as the summary area.

Chapter Recap—Timely Signs

Gary and Tonya Smith are the sole proprietors of Timely Signs, a business that specializes in creating custom signs. The business lost $5,000 last year, and the Smiths are concerned about the future. They currently produce two types of signs—ink-jet signs and vinyl signs—and believe they need to continue to offer both types going forward. Greg Hubit, a family friend and successful entrepreneur, suggested that they create a simple spreadsheet to analyze income and expenses for the year just ended, and then project these numbers for a three- or four-year period.

The Smiths realize that they need to increase sales and/or to reduce costs if their business is to survive. Gary is in favor of focusing on the ink-jet signs. He wants to increase the marketing budget by 20% a year and reduce the selling price of the ink-jet signs by 10% a year. He believes that the aggressive advertising and reduced price will increase demand by 25% a year, and further that the higher volume will reduce the manufacturing cost for the ink-jet signs by 5% a year.

Tonya is in favor of moving their business to a smaller plant where the rent and utilities will decrease 20% a year for the next three years. She proposes to use the savings to increase the marketing budget by 20% a year, and projects a 5% increase in the number of units for each sign. Greg suggests that they focus on reducing costs and urges that they reduce the manufacturing unit cost of both types of signs by 10% a year. Greg would use the savings to increase the marketing budget by 15% a year, which in turn will boost the number of signs in each category by 10% a year.

Your assignment is to review the chapter, open the partially completed *Chapter 6 Ending Case Study—Timely Signs* workbook, and complete the forecast by supplying the missing formulas. If you do the work correctly, you will see that the business should earn just under $3,000 in the fourth year according to the Status Quo scenario that exists within the worksheet. You will then create three new scenarios, one each for Gary (ink-jet focus), Tonya (move location), and Greg (control costs), then combine the results in a scenario summary which you will print for your instructor. Print the completed workbook showing the values for the best scenario.

CHAPTER 7

List and Data Management: Converting Data to Information

OBJECTIVES

After reading this chapter you will:

1. Add, edit, and/or delete records in a list within an Excel worksheet;
2. Use the Text Import Wizard to import data in character format.
3. Define XML; import XML data into an Excel workbook.
4. Describe the Today() function and its use in date arithmetic.
5. Use the Sort command; distinguish between an ascending and a descending sort
6. Use DSUM, DAVERAGE, DMAX, DMIN, and DCOUNT functions.
7. Use the AutoFilter and Advanced Filter commands.
8. Use the Subtotals command.
9. Create a pivot table and corresponding pivot chart.
10. Save a pivot table as a Web page.

hands-on exercises

1. IMPORTING, CREATING, AND MAINTAINING A LIST
   Input: Employee List (text file)
   Output: Employee List Solution

2. DATA VERSUS INFORMATION
   Input: Employee List Solution (from exercise 1)
   Output: Employee List Solution (additional changes)

3. PIVOT TABLES AND PIVOT CHARTS
   Input: Advertising Agency
   Output: Advertising Agency Solution (Excel workbook and Web Page)

CASE STUDY
ALICE BARR REALTY

There are two items that matter most to individuals who sell their home; they want to receive a good price that is at or close to their asking price, and they want to sell their home quickly. Alice Barr Realty claims to meet both objectives, with its slogan, "We get your price and we sell it quickly." This local, highly successful agency was started two years ago when Alice returned to the workforce after raising two children. Her drive, winning personality, and business acumen, coupled with a red-hot real estate market, has enabled Alice to attract outstanding sales agents to her growing business.

A friend of yours is considering an offer from Alice to join her firm, but first he wants to evaluate the accuracy of her claim; that is, do clients realize a quick sale at or near the original asking price? Alice has made her records available in the form of an Excel workbook that lists every property sold during the last quarter, the asking price and selling price for each property, as well as the listing date and sales date. There is an assumption area toward the top of the worksheet that defines the desired percentage of the asking price (95%) and the definition of a quick sale (30 days or fewer).

Your assignment is to read the chapter, paying special attention to the establishment of a list within an Excel workbook and the creation of the associated pivot table. You will then open the partially completed *Chapter 7 Case Study—Alice Barr* workbook in order to evaluate the claim. Your first task is to enter the appropriate IF functions for each property that will display "Yes" or "No" depending on whether the minimum percentage was reached and whether a quick sale was realized. You will then create a pivot table that totals the number of "Yes" and "No" responses to each question. Is Alice's claim justified? Does your answer change if you relax the parameters to 90% of the asking price and 45 days or fewer?

LIST AND DATA MANAGEMENT

All businesses maintain data in the form of lists. Companies have lists of their employees. Magazines and newspapers keep lists of their subscribers. Political candidates monitor voter lists, and so on. This chapter presents the fundamentals of list management as it is implemented in Excel. It begins with the definition of basic terms, such as field and record, then covers the commands to create a list, to add a new record, and to modify or delete an existing record.

The second half of the chapter distinguishes between data and information and describes how one is converted to the other. We introduce the AutoFilter and Advanced Filter commands that display selected records in a list. We use the Sort command to rearrange the list. We discuss database functions and the associated criteria range. We also review date functions and date arithmetic. The chapter ends with a discussion of subtotals, pivot tables, and pivot charts—three powerful capabilities associated with lists.

Imagine that you are the personnel director of a medium-sized company with offices in several cities, and that you manually maintain employee data for the company. Accordingly, you have recorded the specifics of every individual's employment (name, salary, location, title, and so on) in a manila folder, and you have stored the entire set of folders in a file cabinet. You have written the name of each employee on the label of his or her folder and have arranged the folders alphabetically in the filing cabinet.

The manual system just described illustrates the basics of data management terminology. The set of manila folders corresponds to a ***file***. Each individual folder is known as a ***record***. Each data item (fact) within a folder is called a ***field***. The folders are arranged alphabetically in the file cabinet (according to the employee name on the label) to simplify the retrieval of any given folder. Likewise, the records in a computer-based system are also in sequence according to a specific field known as a ***key***.

Excel maintains data in the form of a list. A ***list*** is an area in the worksheet that contains rows of similar data. A list can be used as a simple ***database***, where the rows in a worksheet correspond to records and the columns correspond to fields. The first row contains the column labels or ***field names***, which identify the data that will be entered in that column (field). Each additional row in the list contains a record. Each column represents a field. Each cell in the list area (other than the field names) contains a value for a specific field in a specific record. Every record (row) contains the same fields (columns) in the same order as every other record.

Figure 7.1 contains an employee list with 13 records. There are four fields in every record—name, location, title, and salary. The field names should be meaningful and must be unique. (A field name may contain up to 255 characters, but you should keep them as short as possible so that a column does not become too wide and thus difficult to work with.) The arrangement of the fields within a record is consistent from record to record. The employee name was chosen as the key, and thus the records are in alphabetical order.

Normal business operations require that you make repeated trips to the filing cabinet to maintain the accuracy of the data. You will have to add a folder whenever a new employee is hired. In similar fashion, you will have to remove the folder of any employee who leaves the company, or modify the data in the folder of any employee who receives a raise, changes location, and so on.

Changes of this nature (additions, deletions, and modifications) are known as file maintenance and constitute a critical activity within any system. Indeed, without adequate file maintenance, the data in a system quickly becomes obsolete and the information useless. Imagine the consequences of producing a payroll based on data that is six months old.

	A	B	C	D
1	**Name**	**Location**	**Title**	**Salary**
2	Adams	Atlanta	Trainee	$29,500
3	Adamson	Chicago	Manager	$52,000
4	Brown	Atlanta	Trainee	$28,500
5	Charles	Boston	Account Rep	$40,000
6	Coulter	Atlanta	Manager	$100,000
7	Frank	Miami	Manager	$75,000
8	James	Chicago	Account Rep	$42,500
9	Johnson	Chicag	Account Rep	$47,500
10	Manin	Boston	Accout Rep	$49,500
11	Marder	Chicago	Account Rep	$38,500
12	Milgrom	Boston	Manager	$57,500
13	Rubin	Boston	Account Rep	$45,000
14	Smith	Atlanta	Account Rep	$65,000

- Row 1 contains the field names
- Each row represents a record
- Chicago is misspelled (row 9)
- Account Rep is misspelled (row 10)

FIGURE 7.1 The Employee List

Nor is it sufficient simply to add (edit or delete) a record without adequate checks on the validity of the data. Look carefully at the entries in Figure 7.1 and ask yourself whether a computer-generated report that is intended to show the employees in the Chicago office will include Johnson. Will a report listing account reps include Manin? The answer to both questions is *no* because the data for these employees was entered incorrectly.

Chicago is misspelled in Johnson's record (the "o" was omitted). Account rep is misspelled in Manin's title. *You* know that Johnson works in Chicago, but the computer does not, because it searches for the correct spelling. It also will omit Manin from a listing of account reps because of the misspelled title. Remember, a computer does what you tell it to do, not necessarily what you want it to do. There is a significant difference.

GARBAGE IN, GARBAGE OUT (GIGO)

The information produced by a system is only as good as the data on which it is based. It is absolutely critical, therefore, that you validate the data that goes into a system, or else the associated information will not be correct. No system, no matter how sophisticated, can produce valid output from invalid input. In other words, garbage in—garbage out.

IMPLEMENTATION IN EXCEL

Creating a list is easy because there is little to do other than enter the data. You choose the area in the worksheet that will contain the list, then you enter the field names in the first row of the designated area. Each field name should be a unique text entry. The data for the individual records should be entered in the rows immediately below the row of field names.

Once a list has been created, you can edit any field, in any record, just as you would change the entries in an ordinary worksheet. The ***Insert Rows command*** lets you add new rows (records) to the list. The ***Insert Columns command*** lets you add additional columns (fields). The ***Delete command*** in the Edit menu enables you to delete a row or column. You can also use shortcut menus to execute commands more quickly. And finally, you can also format the entries within a list, just as you format the entries in any other worksheet.

Data Form Command

A ***data form*** provides an easy way to add, edit, and delete records in a list. The ***Form command*** in the Data menu displays a dialog box based on the fields in the list and contains the command buttons shown in Figure 7.2. Every record in the list contains the same fields in the same order (e.g., Name, Location, Title, and Salary in Figure 7.2), and the fields are displayed in this order within the dialog box. You do not have to enter a value for every field; that is, you may leave a field blank if the data is unknown.

Next to each field name is a text box into which data can be entered for a new record, or edited for an existing record. The scroll bar to the right of the data is used to scroll through the records in the list. As indicated, the Data Form command provides an easy way to add, edit, and delete records in a list. It is not required, however, and you can use the Insert and Delete commands within the Edit menu as an alternate means of data entry.

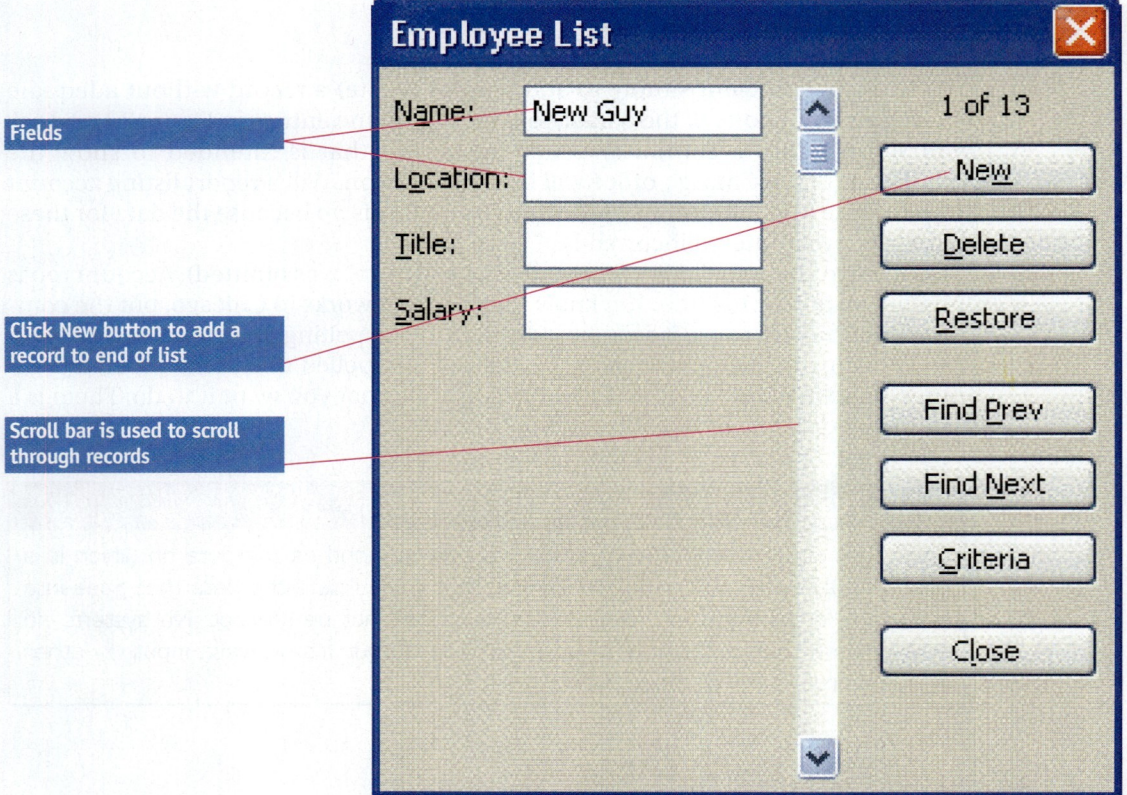

FIGURE 7.2 The Data Form Command

LIST SIZE AND LOCATION

A list can appear anywhere within a worksheet and can theoretically be as large as an entire worksheet (65,536 rows by 256 columns). Practically, the list will be much smaller, giving rise to the following guideline for its placement: Leave at least one blank column and one blank row between the list and the other entries in the worksheet. Excel will then be able to find the boundaries of the list automatically whenever a cell within the list is selected. It simply searches for the first blank row above and below the selected cell, and for the first blank column to the left and right of the selected cell.

The functions of the various command buttons are explained briefly:

- New—Adds a record to the end of a list, then lets you enter data into that record. The formulas for computed fields, if any, are automatically copied to the new record.
- Delete—Permanently removes the currently displayed record. The remaining records move up one row.
- Restore—Cancels any changes made to the current record. (You must press the Restore button before pressing the Enter key or scrolling to a new record.)
- Find Prev—Displays the previous record (or the previous record that matches the existing criteria when criteria are defined).
- Find Next—Displays the next record (or the next record that matches the existing criteria when criteria are defined).
- Criteria—Displays a dialog box in which you specify the criteria for the Find Prev and/or Find Next command buttons to limit the displayed records to those that match the criteria.
- Close—Closes the data form and returns to the worksheet.

Sort Command

Data is easier to understand if it is displayed in a meaningful sequence. The **Sort command** arranges the records in a list according to the value of one or more fields within that list. You can sort the list in **ascending** (low-to-high) or **descending** (high-to-low) **sequence**. (Putting a list in alphabetical order is considered an ascending sort.) You can also sort on more than one field at a time—for example, by location and then alphabetically by last name within each location. The field(s) on which you sort the list is (are) known as the key(s).

Each worksheet in Figure 7.3 displays the same set of employee records, but in a different order. The records in Figure 7.3a are listed alphabetically (in ascending sequence) according to the employees' last names. Adams comes before Adamson, who comes before Brown, and so on. Figure 7.3b displays the identical records but in descending sequence by employee salary. The employee with the highest salary is listed first, and the employee with the lowest salary is last.

Figure 7.3c sorts the employees on two keys—by location, and by descending salary within location. Location is the more important, or primary key. Salary is the less important, or secondary key. The Sort command groups employees according to like values of the primary key (location) in ascending (alphabetical) sequence, then within the like values of the primary key arranges them in descending sequence (ascending could have been chosen just as easily) according to the secondary key (salary). Excel provides a maximum of three keys—primary, secondary, and tertiary.

CHOOSE A CUSTOM SORT SEQUENCE

Alphabetic fields are normally arranged in strict alphabetical order. You can, however, choose a custom sort sequence such as the days of the week or the months of the year. Pull down the Data menu, click Sort, click the Options command button, then click the arrow on the drop-down list box to choose a sequence other than the alphabetic. You can also create your own sequence. Pull down the Tools menu, click Options, click the Custom Lists tab, select NewList, then enter the items in desired sequence in the List Entries Box. Click Add to create the sequence, then close the dialog box.

(a) Ascending Sequence (by name)

Records are in ascending sequence by employee name

	A	B	C	D
1	**Name**	**Location**	**Title**	**Salary**
2	Adams	Atlanta	Trainee	$29,500
3	Adamson	Chicago	Manager	$52,000
4	Brown	Atlanta	Trainee	$28,500
5	Charles	Boston	Account Rep	$40,000
6	Coulter	Atlanta	Manager	$100,000
7	Frank	Miami	Manager	$75,000
8	James	Chicago	Account Rep	$42,500
9	Johnson	Chicago	Account Rep	$47,500
10	Manin	Boston	Account Rep	$49,500
11	Marder	Chicago	Account Rep	$38,500
12	Milgrom	Boston	Manager	$57,500
13	Rubin	Boston	Account Rep	$45,000
14	Smith	Atlanta	Account Rep	$65,000

(b) Descending Sequence (by salary)

Records are in descending sequence by salary

	A	B	C	D
1	**Name**	**Location**	**Title**	**Salary**
2	Coulter	Atlanta	Manager	$100,000
3	Frank	Miami	Manager	$75,000
4	Smith	Atlanta	Account Rep	$65,000
5	Milgrom	Boston	Manager	$57,500
6	Adamson	Chicago	Manager	$52,000
7	Manin	Boston	Account Rep	$49,500
8	Johnson	Chicago	Account Rep	$47,500
9	Rubin	Boston	Account Rep	$45,000
10	James	Chicago	Account Rep	$42,500
11	Charles	Boston	Account Rep	$40,000
12	Marder	Chicago	Account Rep	$38,500
13	Adams	Atlanta	Trainee	$29,500
14	Brown	Atlanta	Trainee	$28,500

(c) Multiple Keys

Location is the primary key (in ascending sequence)

Salary is the secondary key (in descending sequence)

	A	B	C	D
1	**Name**	**Location**	**Title**	**Salary**
2	Coulter	Atlanta	Manager	$100,000
3	Smith	Atlanta	Account Rep	$65,000
4	Adams	Atlanta	Trainee	$29,500
5	Brown	Atlanta	Trainee	$28,500
6	Milgrom	Boston	Manager	$57,500
7	Manin	Boston	Account Rep	$49,500
8	Rubin	Boston	Account Rep	$45,000
9	Charles	Boston	Account Rep	$40,000
10	Adamson	Chicago	Manager	$52,000
11	Johnson	Chicago	Account Rep	$47,500
12	James	Chicago	Account Rep	$42,500
13	Marder	Chicago	Account Rep	$38,500
14	Frank	Miami	Manager	$75,000

FIGURE 7.3 The Sort Command

THE TEXT IMPORT WIZARD

It's easy to create a list in Excel and/or to modify data in that list. What if, however, the data already exists, but it is not in the form of a workbook? This is very common, especially in organizations that collect data on a mainframe, but analyze it on a PC. It can also occur when data is collected by one application, then analyzed in another. Excel provides a convenient solution in the form of the **Text Import Wizard** that converts a text (ASCII) file to an Excel workbook as shown in Figure 7.4. (Conversely, you can export an Excel workbook to another application by using the Save As command and specifying a text file.)

Figures 7.4a and 7.4b each contain the 13 records from the employee list shown, but in different formats. Both figures contain text files. The data in Figure 7.4a is in *fixed width format*, where each field requires the same number of positions in an input record. The data in Figure 7.4b is in *delimited format*, where the fields are separated from one another by a specific character.

You can access either file via the Open command in Excel, which in turn displays step 1 of the Text Import Wizard in Figure 7.4c. The Wizard prompts you for information about the external data, then it converts that data into an Excel workbook as shown in Figure 7.4d.

```
Name        Location    Title           Salary
Adams       Atlanta     Trainee         29500
Adamson     Chicago     Manager         52000
Brown       Atlanta     Trainee         28500
Charles     Boston      Account Rep     40000
Coulter     Atlanta     Manager         100000
Frank       Miami       Manager         75000
James       Chicago     Account Rep     42500
Johnson     Chicago     Account Rep     47500
Manin       Boston      Account Rep     49500
Marder      Chicago     Account Rep     38500
Milgrom     Boston      Manager         57500
Rubin       Boston      Account Rep     45000
Smith       Atlanta     Account Rep     65000
```

(a) Fixed Width

```
Name,Location,Title,Salary
Adams,Atlanta,Trainee,29500
Adamson,Chicago,Manager,52000
Brown,Atlanta,Trainee,28500
Charles,Boston,Account Rep,40000
Coulter,Atlanta,Manager,100000
Frank,Miami,Manager,75000
James,Chicago,Account Rep,42500
Johnson,Chicago,Account Rep,47500
Manin,Boston,Account Rep,49500
Marder,Chicago,Account Rep,38500
Milgrom,Boston,Manager,57500
Rubin,Boston,Account Rep,45000
Smith,Atlanta,Account Rep,65000
```

(b) Delimited

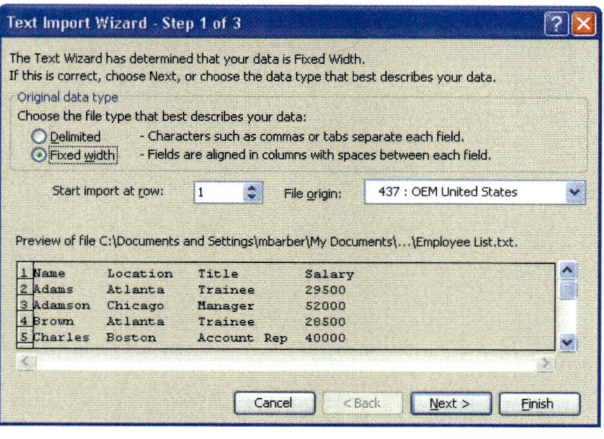

(c) Text Import Wizard

	A	B	C	D
1	Name	Location	Title	Salary
2	Adams	Atlanta	Trainee	$29,500
3	Adamson	Chicago	Manager	$52,000
4	Brown	Atlanta	Trainee	$28,500
5	Charles	Boston	Account Rep	$40,000
6	Coulter	Atlanta	Manager	$100,000
7	Frank	Miami	Manager	$75,000
8	James	Chicago	Account Rep	$42,500
9	Johnson	Chicag	Account Rep	$47,500
10	Manin	Boston	Account Rep	$49,500
11	Marder	Chicago	Accout Rep	$38,500
12	Milgrom	Boston	Manager	$57,500
13	Rubin	Boston	Account Rep	$45,000
14	Smith	Atlanta	Account Rep	$65,000

(d) Workbook

FIGURE 7.4 Importing Data from Other Applications

Excel and XML

A text file is a universal file format, in that it can be read by virtually any application. **XML (Extensible Markup Language)** goes one step further by enabling a developer to create customized tags to define and interpret the data within the file. (XML is an industry standard for structuring data and not a Microsoft product.) XML is not to be confused with **HTML (Hypertext Markup Language)**, nor is it intended as a replacement for HTML.

HTML is intended to display data and it has only a finite set of tags; e.g., <B> or <UL>, for bold and underlining, respectively. XML, however, describes the data and it has an infinite number of tags. XML tags are not defined in any XML standard, however, but are created by the author of the XML document. Consider:

HTML:	XML:
<B>John Doe</B>	<name>
	<first>John</first>
	<last>Doe</last>
	</name>

The HTML code tells us that "John Doe" will appear in boldface, but it does not tell us anything more. We don't know that "John" is the first name or that "Doe" is the last name. XML, on the other hand, is "data about data". You can see at a glance that it is conveying information about a name, and that there is a first name and a last name, within the name. The real advantage of XML, however, is that it is easily expanded (extensible) to include additional information about a person's name such as a prefix or middle initial. We just extend the definition of the elements within the name to include the additional data, and then we mark up the data accordingly by including additional tags.

Microsoft Excel 2003 provides full XML support that enables you to exchange information between an XML source document and an Excel workbook. You attach the XML definition or *schema* to the workbook and then you map the XML elements in the schema to the cells in your workbook. Once this is accomplished you can import and/or export XML data into or out of the individual cells. Figure 7.5a displays the first three employee records in an XML document, Figure 7.5b shows the XML source task pane in which the mapping takes place, and Figure 7.5c displays the associated list within a worksheet.

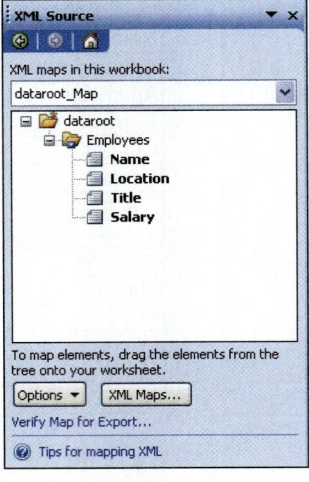

(a) XML Document   (b) XML Source Task Pane   (c) Excel Spreadsheet

FIGURE 7.5 Excel and XML

hands-on exercise 1

Importing, Creating, and Maintaining a List

Objective To use the Text Import Wizard; to add, edit, and delete records in an employee list. Use Figure 7.6 as a guide in the exercise.

Step 1: **The Text Import Wizard**

- Start Excel. Pull down the **File menu** and click the **Open command** (or click the **Open button** on the Standard toolbar) to display the Open dialog box.

- Open the **Exploring Excel folder** that you have used throughout the text. Click the **drop-down arrow** on the Files of Type list box and specify **All Files**, then double click the **Employee List** text document.

- The Text Import Wizard opens automatically as shown in Figure 7.6a. The Wizard recognizes that the file is in Delimited format. Click **Next**.

- Clear the **Tab Delimiter** check box. Check the **Comma Delimiter** check box. Each field is now shown in a separate column. Click **Next**.

- There is no need to change the default format (general) of any of the fields. Click **Finish**. You see the Employee List within an Excel workbook.

- Click and drag to select **cells A1 through D1**, then click the **Bold** and **Center buttons** to distinguish the field names from the data records. Click the **down arrow** for the **Fill Color button** and select **Light Yellow**. Adjust the column widths. Format the Salary field as Currency with zero decimals.

- Save the workbook as **Employee List Solution.** Click the **down arrow** in the Save as type list box and select **Microsoft Excel workbook**. Click **Save**.

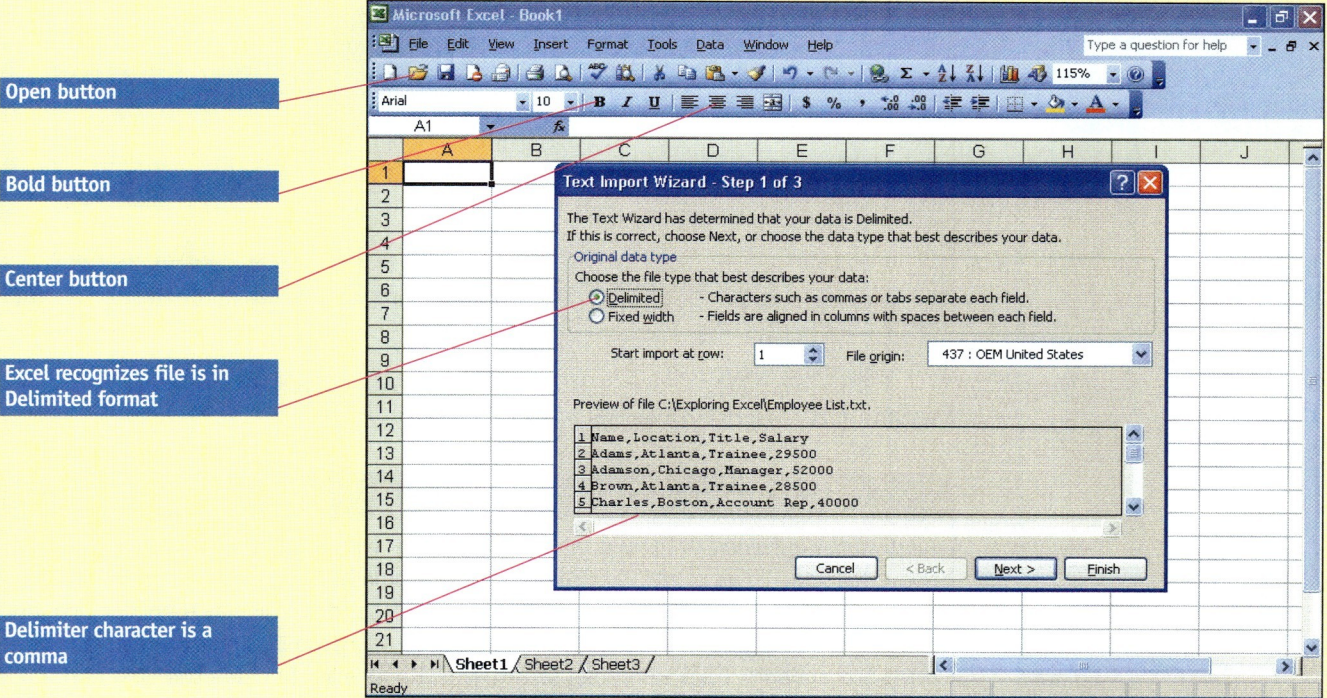

(a) The Text Import Wizard (step 1)

FIGURE 7.6 Hands-on Exercise 1

Step 2: **Add New Records**

- Click a single cell anywhere within the employee list (**cells A1 through D14**). Pull down the **Data menu**. Click **Form** to display a dialog box with data for the first record in the list (Adams).
- Click the **New command button** at the right of the dialog box to clear the text boxes and begin entering a new record.
- Enter the data for **Elofson** as shown in Figure 7.6b, using the **Tab key** to move from field to field within the data form.
- Click the **Close command button** after entering the salary. Elofson has been added to the list and appears in row 15.
- Add a second record for **Gillenson**, who works in **Miami** as an **Account Rep** with a salary of **$55,000**.
- Save the workbook.

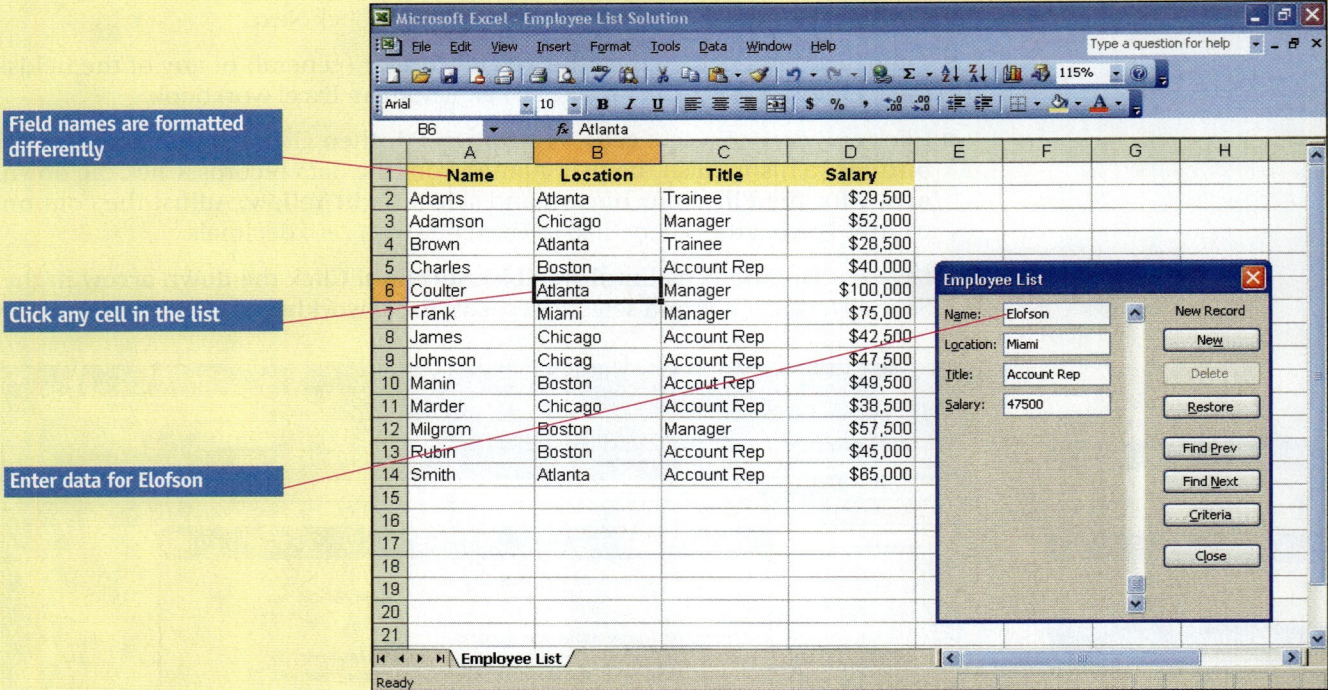

(b) Add New Records (step 2)

FIGURE 7.6 Hands-on Exercise 1 (*continued*)

THE CREATE LIST COMMAND

All previous versions of Excel enabled you to work with a list or area in a worksheet that contained rows of similar data. The user would highlight the field names in the first row, turn the AutoFilter command on and off, and/or display a border around the entire list. Microsoft Excel 2003 introduces a Create List command that does this automatically. Click and drag to select the entire list (include the field names), pull down the Data menu, click the List command, and then click the Create List command. Click anywhere in the list and you will see an asterisk in the last row; enter data in this row and the new record is added to the list automatically.

Step 3: **The Spell Check**

- Select **cells B2:C16** as in Figure 7.6c. Pull down the **Tools menu** and click **Spelling** (or click the **Spelling button** on the Standard toolbar).

- Chicago is misspelled in cell B9 and flagged accordingly. Click the **Change command button** to accept the suggested correction and continue checking the document.

- Account is misspelled in cell C10 and flagged accordingly. Click **Account** in the Suggestions list box, then click the **Change command button** to correct the misspelling.

- Excel will indicate that it has finished checking the selected cells. Click **OK** to return to the worksheet.

- Save the workbook.

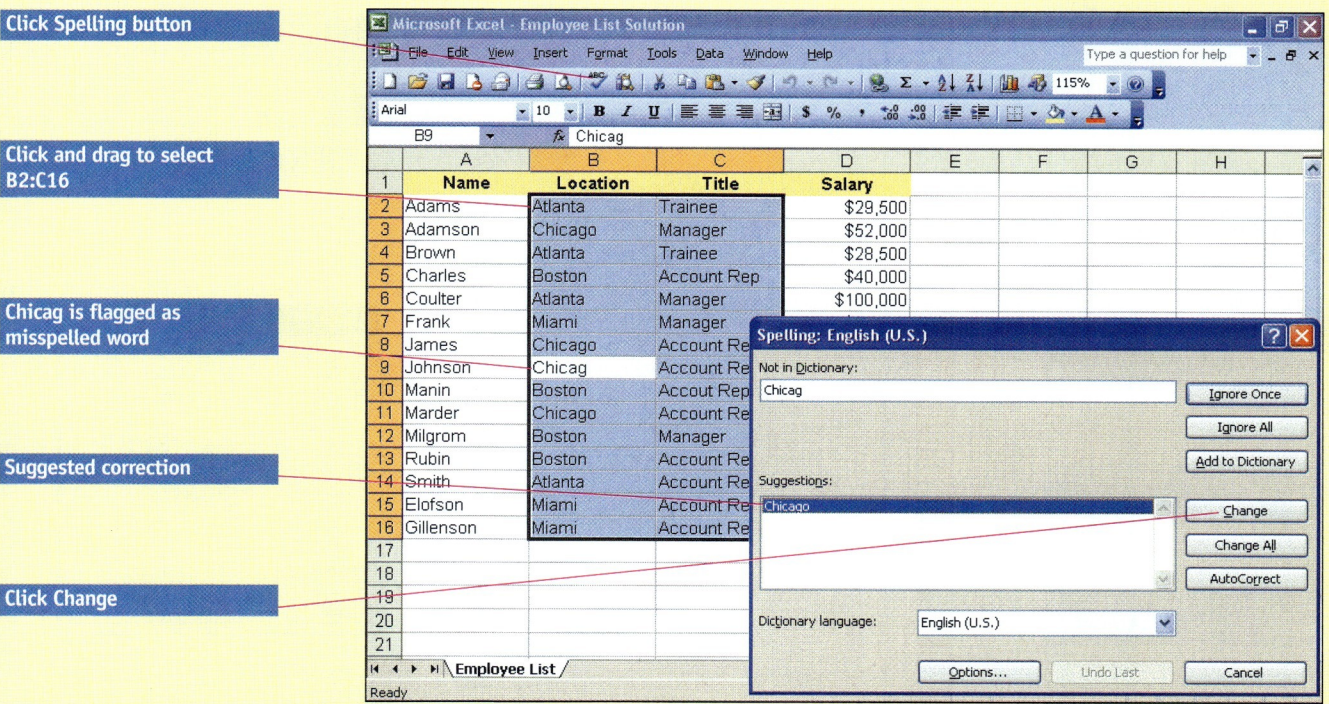

(c) The Spell Check (step 3)

FIGURE 7.6   Hands-on Exercise 1 (*continued*)

CREATE YOUR OWN SHORTHAND

Use the AutoCorrect capability within Microsoft Office to create your own shorthand by having it expand abbreviations such as *cis* for *Computer Information Systems.* Pull down the Tools menu, click AutoCorrect Options to display the associated dialog box, then click the AutoCorrect tab. Type the abbreviation in the Replace text box and the expanded entry in the With text box. Click the Add command button, then click OK to exit the dialog box. The next time you type *cis* in a spreadsheet, it will automatically be expanded to *Computer Information Systems*.

Step 4: **Sort the Employee List**

- Click a single cell anywhere in the employee list (**cells A1 through D16**). Pull down the **Data menu.** Click **Sort** to display the dialog box in Figure 7.6d.
- Click the **drop-down arrow** in the Sort By list box. Select **Location**.
- Click the **drop-down arrow** in the first Then By list box. Select **Name**.
- Be sure the **Header Row option button** is selected (so that the field names are not sorted with the records in the list).
- Check that the **Ascending option button** is selected for both the primary and secondary keys. Click **OK**.
- The employees are listed by location and alphabetically within location.
- Save the workbook.

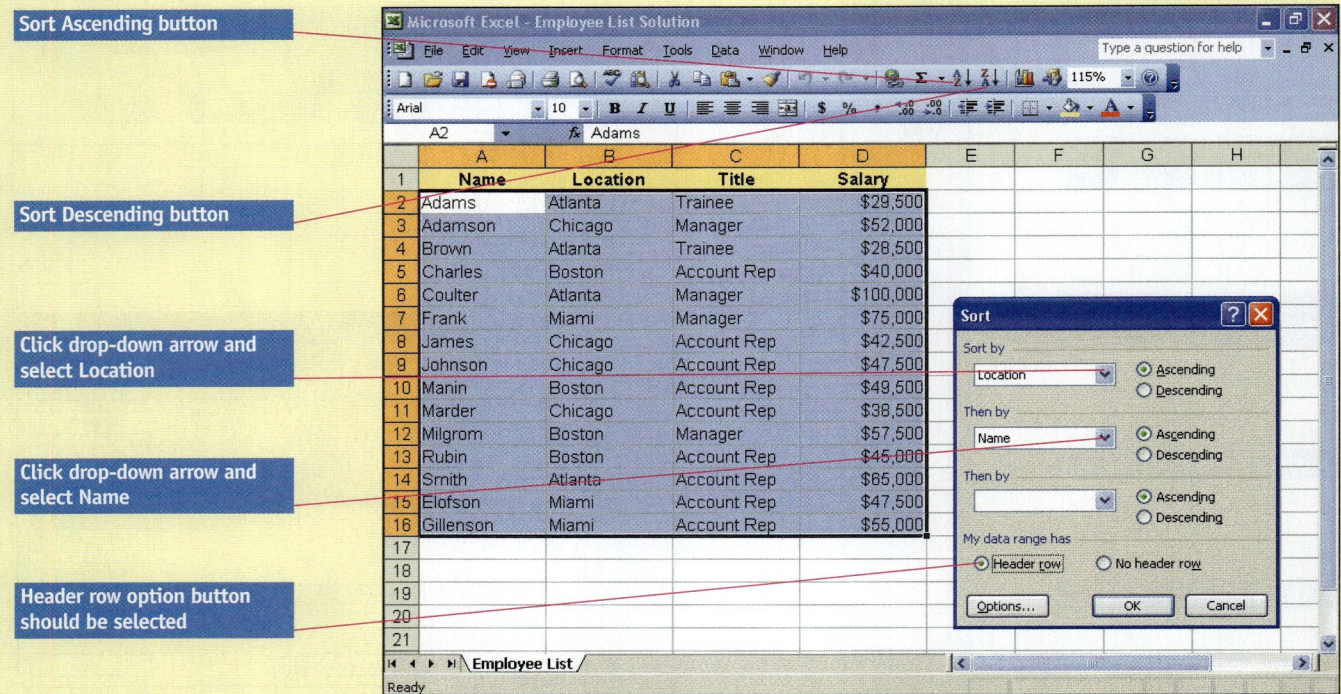

(d) Sort the Employee List (step 4)

FIGURE 7.6 Hands-on Exercise 1 (*continued*)

USE THE SORT BUTTONS

Use the Sort Ascending or Sort Descending button on the Standard toolbar to sort on one or more keys. To sort on a single key, click any cell in the column containing the key, then click the appropriate button, depending on whether you want an ascending or a descending sort. You can also sort on multiple keys, by clicking either button multiple times, but the trick is to do it in the right sequence. Sort on the least significant field first, then work your way up to the most significant. For example, to sort a list by location, and name within location, sort by name first (the secondary key), then sort by location (the primary key).

Step 5: **Delete a Record**

- A record may be deleted by using the Edit Delete command or the Data Form command. To delete a record by using the Edit Delete command:
  - Click the **row heading** in **row 15** (containing the record for Frank, which is slated for deletion).
  - Pull down the **Edit menu**. Click **Delete**. Frank has been deleted.

- Click the **Undo button** on the Standard toolbar. The record for Frank has been restored.

- To delete a record by using the Data Form command:
  - Click a single cell within the employee list. Pull down the **Data menu**. Click **Form** to display the data form. Click the **Criteria button**. Enter **Frank** in the Name text box, then click the **Find Next button** to locate Frank's record.
  - Click the **Delete command button**. Click **OK** in response to the warning message shown in Figure 7.6e. (The record cannot be undeleted as it could with the Edit Delete command.) Click **Close** to close the Data Form.

- Save the workbook.

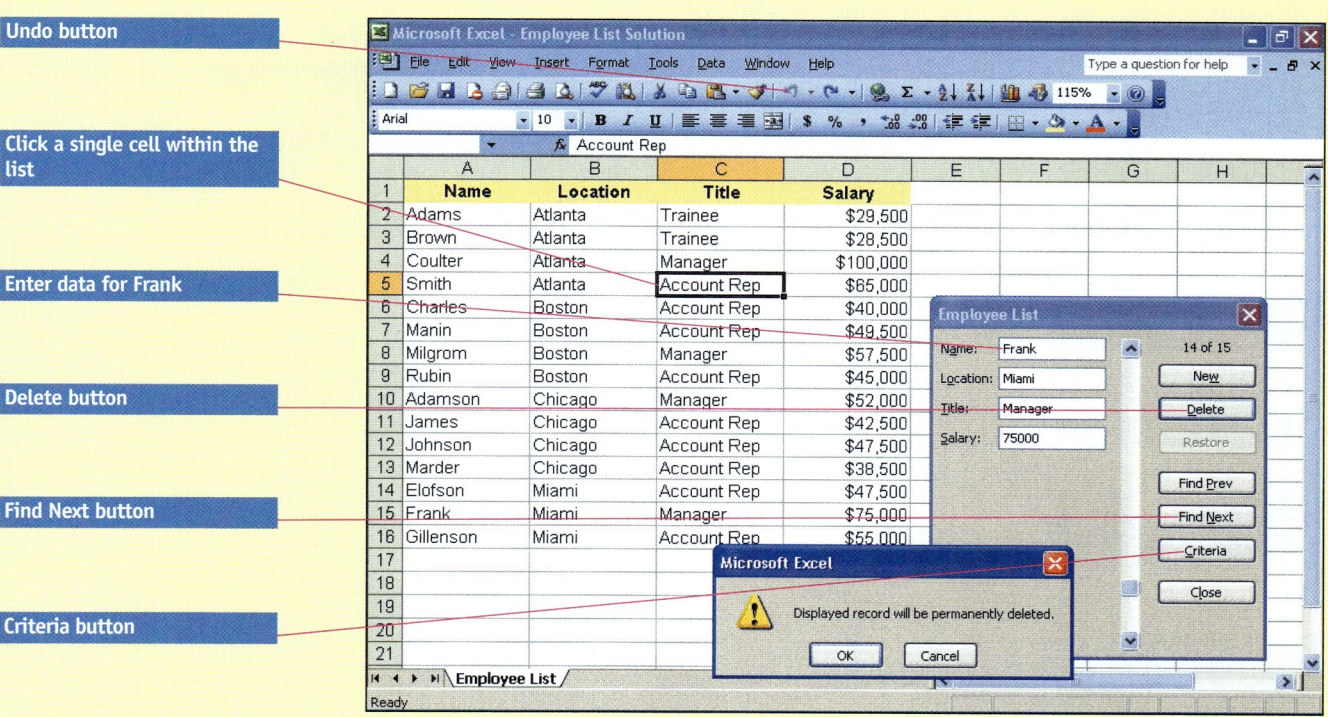

(e) Delete a Record (step 5)

FIGURE 7.6 Hands-on Exercise 1 (*continued*)

EDIT CLEAR VERSUS EDIT DELETE

The Edit Delete command deletes the selected cell, row, or column from the worksheet, and thus its execution will adjust cell references throughout the worksheet. It is very different from the Edit Clear command, which erases the contents (and/or formatting) of the selected cells, but does not delete the cells from the worksheet and hence has no effect on the cell references in formulas that reference those cells. Pressing the Del key erases the contents of a cell and thus corresponds to the Edit Clear command.

Step 6: Enter the Hire Date

- Click the **column heading** in column D. Point to the selection, then click the **right mouse button** to display a shortcut menu. Click **Insert**. The employee salaries have been moved to column E, as shown in Figure 7.6f.

- Click **cell D1**. Type **Hire Date** and press **Enter**. Adjust the column width if necessary. Dates may be entered in several different formats.
  - Type **11/24/98** in cell D2. Press the **down arrow key**.
  - Type **11/24/1998** in cell D3. Press the **down arrow key**.
  - Type **Nov 24, 1998** in cell D4. Type a **comma** after the day but do not type a period after the month. Press the **down arrow key** to move to cell D5.
  - Type **11-24-98** in cell D5. Press **Enter**.

- For ease of data entry, assume that the next several employees were hired on the same day, 3/16/99. Click in **cell D6**. Type **3/16/99**. Press **enter**. Click in **cell D6**. Click the **Copy button** on the Standard toolbar.

- Drag the mouse over cells **D7 through D10**. Click the **Paste button**. Press **Esc** to remove the moving border around cell D6.

- Save the workbook.

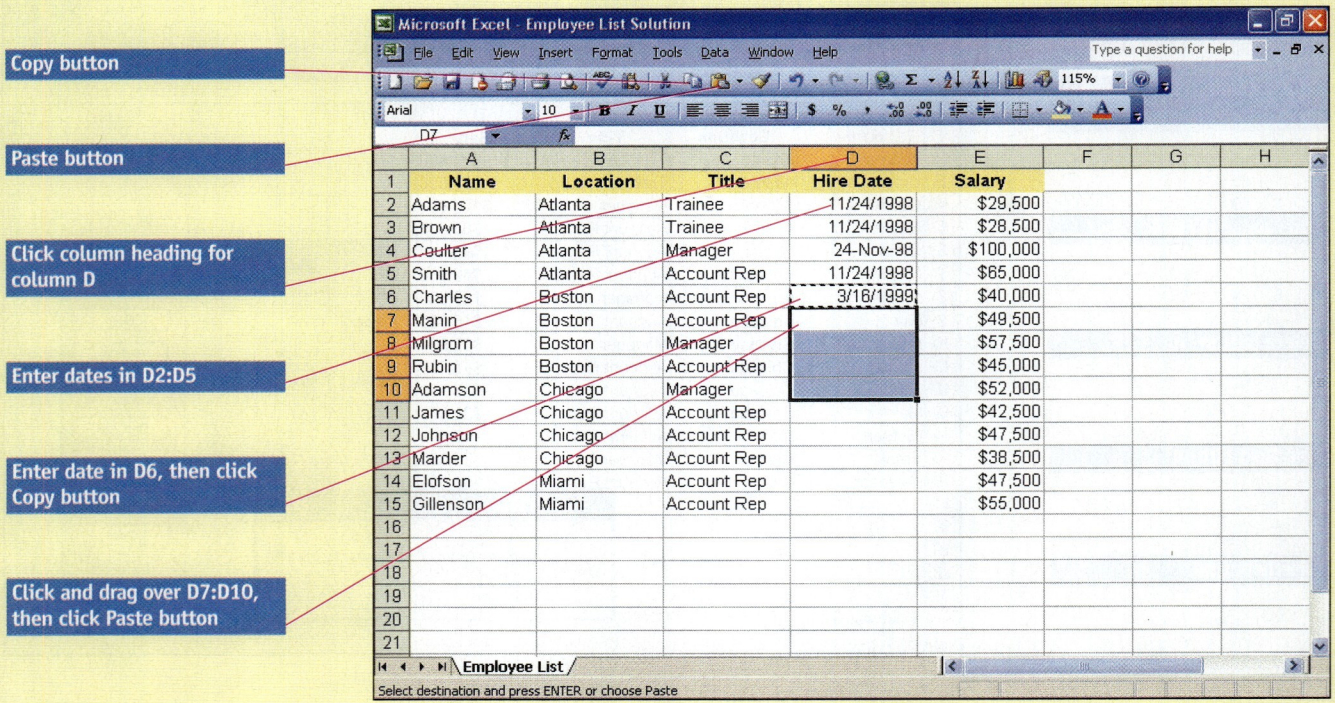

(f) Enter the Hire Date (step 6)

FIGURE 7.6 Hands-on Exercise 1 (*continued*)

TWO-DIGIT DATES AND THE YEAR 2000

Excel assumes that any two-digit year up to and including 29 is in the 21st century; that is, 12/31/29 will be stored as December 31, 2029. (The year 2029 is arbitrary.) Any year after 29, however, is assumed to be in the 20th century; for example, 1/1/30 will be stored as January 1, 1930. When in doubt, however, enter a four-digit year to be sure.

Step 7: **Format the Hire Dates**

- The next five employees were hired one year apart beginning October 31, 1998.
  - Click in cell **D11** and type **10/31/98**. Click in cell **D12** and type **10/31/99**.
  - Select cells **D11 and D12**.
  - Drag the **fill handle** at the bottom of cell D12 over cells **D13**, **D14**, and **D15**. Release the mouse to complete the AutoFill operation.

- Click in the column heading for **column D** to select the column of dates.

- Point to the selected cells and click the **right mouse button** to display a shortcut menu. Click **Format Cells**.

- Click the **Number tab** in the Format Cells dialog box. Click **Date** in the Category list box. Select (click) the date format shown in Figure 7.6g. Click **OK**.

- Click elsewhere in the workbook to deselect the dates. Reduce the width of column D as appropriate. Save the workbook.

- Exit Excel if you do not want to complete the next exercise at this time.

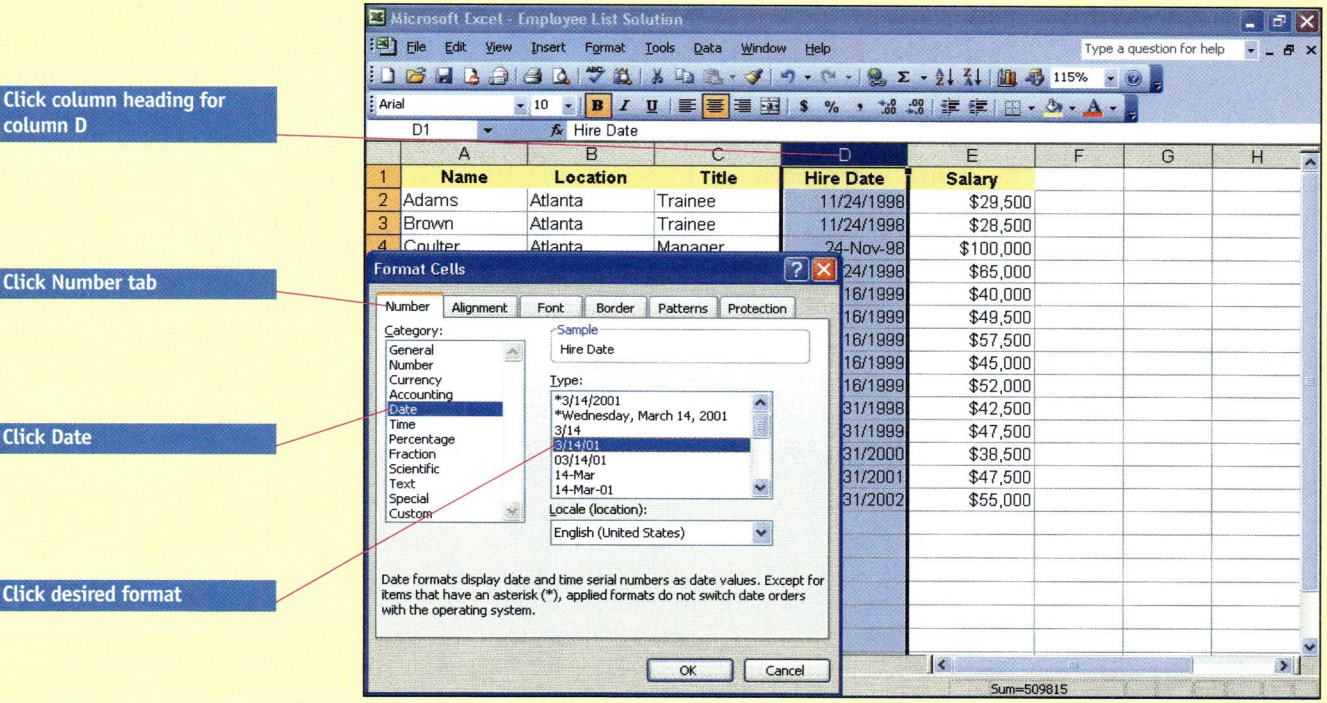

(g) Format the Hire Dates (step 7)

FIGURE 7.6 Hands-on Exercise 1 (*continued*)

EXPORTING DATA FROM EXCEL

We began the exercise by importing data from a text file into an Excel workbook. You can also go in the opposite direction; i.e., you can export the data in an Excel worksheet into a CSV (comma-separated value) or text file, an XML document, or an Access database. Pull down the File menu, click the Save As command, then specify the file type; e.g., a text file. Exporting an Excel worksheet to an Access table is done differently, however, in that you have to import the Excel table from within Access. See the Excel and Access mini case at the end of the chapter.

DATA VERSUS INFORMATION

Data and information are not synonymous. **Data** refers to a fact or facts about a specific record, such as an employee's name, title, or salary. **Information**, on the other hand, is data that has been rearranged into a form perceived as useful by the recipient. A list of employees earning more than $35,000 or a total of all employee salaries are examples of information produced from data about individual employees. Put another way, data is the raw material, and information is the finished product.

Decisions in an organization are based on information rather than raw data; for example, in assessing the effects of a proposed across-the-board salary increase, management needs to know the total payroll rather than individual salary amounts. In similar fashion, decisions about next year's hiring will be influenced, at least in part, by knowing how many individuals are currently employed in each job category.

Organizations maintain data to produce information. Data maintenance entails three basic operations—adding new records, modifying (editing or updating) existing records, and deleting existing records. The exercise just completed showed you how to maintain the data. This section focuses on using that data to create information.

Data is converted to information through a combination of database commands and functions whose capabilities are illustrated by the reports in Figure 7.7. The reports are based on the employee list as it existed at the end of the first hands-on exercise. Each report presents the data in a different way, according to the information requirements of the end-user. As you view each report, ask yourself how it was produced; that is, what was done to the data to produce the information?

Figure 7.7a contains a master list of all employees, listing employees by location, and alphabetically by last name within location. The report was created by sorting the list on two keys, location and name. Location is the more important field and is known as the primary key. Name is the less important field and is called the secondary key. The sorted report groups employees according to like values of the primary key (location), then within the primary key groups the records according to the secondary key (name).

The report in Figure 7.7b displays a subset of the records in the list, which includes only those employees who meet specific criteria. The criteria can be based on any field or combination of fields—in this case, employees whose salaries are between $40,000 and $60,000 (inclusive). The employees are shown in descending order of salary so that the employee with the highest salary is listed first.

The report in Figure 7.7c displays summary statistics for the selected employees—in this example, the salaries for the account reps within the company. Reports of this nature omit the salaries of individual employees (known as detail lines), to present an aggregate view of the organization. Remember, too, that the information produced by any system is only as good as the data on which it is based. Thus, it is very important that organizations take steps to ensure the validity of the data as it is entered into a system.

BIRTH DATE VERSUS AGE

An individual's age and birth date provide equivalent information, as one is calculated from the other. It might seem easier, therefore, to enter the age directly into the list and avoid the calculation, but this would be a mistake. A person's age changes continually, whereas the birth date remains constant. Thus, the date, not the age, should be stored, so that the data in the list remains current. Similar reasoning applies to an employee's hire date and length of service.

Location Report

Name	Location	Title	Service	Hire Date	Salary
Adams	Atlanta	Trainee	4.6	11/24/98	$29,500
Brown	Atlanta	Trainee	4.6	11/24/98	$28,500
Coulter	Atlanta	Manager	4.6	11/24/98	$100,000
Smith	Atlanta	Account Rep	4.6	11/24/98	$65,000
Charles	Boston	Account Rep	4.3	3/16/99	$40,000
Manin	Boston	Account Rep	4.3	3/16/99	$49,500
Milgrom	Boston	Manager	4.3	3/16/99	$57,500
Rubin	Boston	Account Rep	4.3	3/16/99	$45,000
Adamson	Chicago	Manager	4.3	3/16/99	$52,000
James	Chicago	Account Rep	4.7	10/31/98	$42,500
Johnson	Chicago	Account Rep	3.7	10/31/99	$47,500
Marder	Chicago	Account Rep	2.7	10/31/00	$38,500
Elofson	Miami	Account Rep	1.7	10/31/01	$47,500
Gillenson	Miami	Account Rep	0.7	10/31/02	$55,000

(a) Employees by Location and Name within Location

Earnings Between $40,000 and $60,000

Name	Location	Title	Service	Hire Date	Salary
Milgrom	Boston	Manager	4.3	3/16/99	$57,500
Gillenson	Miami	Account Rep	0.7	10/31/02	$55,000
Adamson	Chicago	Manager	4.3	3/16/99	$52,000
Manin	Boston	Account Rep	4.3	3/16/99	$49,500
Johnson	Chicago	Account Rep	3.7	10/31/99	$47,500
Elofson	Miami	Account Rep	1.7	10/31/01	$47,500
Rubin	Boston	Account Rep	4.3	3/16/99	$45,000
James	Chicago	Account Rep	4.7	10/31/98	$42,500
Charles	Boston	Account Rep	4.3	3/16/99	$40,000

(b) Employees Earning Between $40,000 and $60,000, Inclusive

Summary Statistics

Total Salary for Account Reps	$430,500
Average Salary for Account Reps	$47,833
Maximum Salary for Account Reps	$65,000
Minimum Salary for Account Reps	$38,500
Number of Account Reps	9

(c) Account Rep Summary Data

FIGURE 7.7 Data versus Information

AutoFilter Command

A ***filtered list*** displays a subset of records that meet a specific criterion or set of criteria. It is created by the **AutoFilter command** (or the Advanced Filter command discussed in the next section). Both commands temporarily hide those records (rows) that do not meet the criteria. The hidden records are *not* deleted; they are simply not displayed.

Figure 7.8a displays the employee list in alphabetical order. Figure 7.8b displays a filtered version of the list in which only the Atlanta employees (in rows 2, 4, 6, and 15) are visible. The remaining employees are still in the worksheet but are not shown as their rows are hidden.

AutoFilter command places drop-down arrow next to field name

Click to display Atlanta employees only

	A	B	C	D	E
1	Name	Location	Title	Hire Date	Salary
2	Adams	*Sort Ascending* / *Sort Descending* / (All) / (Top 10...) / (Custom...) / **Atlanta** / Boston / Chicago / Miami	Trainee	11/24/98	$29,500
3	Adamson		Manager	3/16/99	$52,000
4	Brown		Trainee	11/24/98	$28,500
5	Charles		Account Rep	3/16/99	$40,000
6	Coulter		Manager	11/24/98	$100,000
7	Elofson		Account Rep	10/31/01	$47,500
8	Gillenson		Account Rep	10/31/02	$55,000
9	James	Chicago	Account Rep	10/31/98	$42,500
10	Johnson	Chicago	Account Rep	10/31/99	$47,500
11	Manin	Boston	Account Rep	3/16/99	$49,500
12	Marder	Chicago	Account Rep	10/31/00	$38,500
13	Milgrom	Boston	Manager	3/16/99	$57,500
14	Rubin	Boston	Account Rep	3/16/99	$45,000
15	Smith	Atlanta	Account Rep	11/24/98	$65,000

(a) Unfiltered List

Only rows 2, 4, 6, and 15 are visible

Only Atlanta employees are displayed

	A	B	C	D	E
1	Name	Location	Title	Hire Date	Salary
2	Adams	Atlanta	Trainee	11/24/98	$29,500
4	Brown	Atlanta	Trainee	11/24/98	$28,500
6	Coulter	Atlanta	Manager	11/24/98	$100,000
15	Smith	Atlanta	Account Rep	11/24/98	$65,000

(b) Filtered List (Atlanta employees)

Click drop-down arrow to further filter list by Title

	A	B	C	D	E
1	Name	Location	Title	Hire Date	Salary
2	Adams	Atlanta	*Sort Ascending* / *Sort Descending* / (All) / (Top 10...) / (Custom...) / Account Rep / **Manager** / Trainee	11/24/98	$29,500
4	Brown	Atlanta		11/24/98	$28,500
6	Coulter	Atlanta		11/24/98	$100,000
15	Smith	Atlanta		11/24/98	$65,000
16					
17					
18					

(c) Imposing a Second Condition

Blue drop-down arrows indicate filter condition is in effect for those fields

	A	B	C	D	E
1	Name	Location	Title	Hire Date	Salary
6	Coulter	Atlanta	Manager	11/24/98	$100,000

(d) Filtered List (Atlanta managers)

FIGURE 7.8 Filter Command

Execution of the AutoFilter command places drop-down arrows next to each column label (field name). Clicking a drop-down arrow produces a list of the unique values for that field, enabling you to establish the criteria for the filtered list. Thus, to display the Atlanta employees, click the drop-down arrow for Location, then click Atlanta.

A filter condition can be imposed on multiple columns as shown in Figure 7.8c. The filtered list in Figure 7.8c contains just the Atlanta employees. Clicking the arrow next to Title, then clicking Manager, will filter the list further to display the employees who both work in Atlanta *and* have Manager as a title. Only one employee meets both conditions, as shown in Figure 7.8d. The drop-down arrows next to Location and Title are displayed in blue to indicate that a filter is in effect for these columns.

The AutoFilter command has additional options as can be seen from the drop-down list box in Figure 7.8c. (All) removes existing criteria in that column. (Custom . . .) enables you to use the relational operators (=, >, <, >=, <=, or <>) within a criterion. (Top 10 . . .) displays the records with the top (or bottom) values in the field, and makes most sense if you sort the list to see the entries in sequence.

Advanced Filter Command

The ***Advanced Filter command*** extends the capabilities of the AutoFilter command in two important ways. It enables you to develop more complex criteria than are possible with the AutoFilter Command. It also enables you to filter the list in place and/or to copy (extract) the selected records to a separate area in the worksheet. The Advanced Filter command is illustrated in detail in the hands-on exercise that follows shortly.

Criteria Range

A ***criteria range*** is used with both the Advanced Filter command and the database functions that are discussed in the next section. It is defined independently of the list on which it operates and exists as a separate area in the worksheet. A criteria range must be at least two rows deep and one column wide as illustrated in Figure 7.9.

The simplest criteria range consists of two rows and as many columns as there are fields in the list. The first row contains the field names as they appear in the list. The second row holds the value(s) you are looking for. The criteria range in Figure 7.9a selects the employees who work in Atlanta; that is, it selects those records where the value of the Location Field is equal to Atlanta.

Multiple values in the same row are connected by an AND and require that the selected records meet *all* of the specified criteria. The criteria range in Figure 7.9b identifies the account reps in Atlanta; that is, it selects any record in which the Location field is Atlanta *and* the Title field is Account Rep. (Both fields must be spelled exactly; e.g., specifying Account Rep*s* instead of Account Rep will not return any employees.)

Values entered in multiple rows are connected by an OR in which the selected records satisfy *any* of the indicated criteria. The criteria range in Figure 7.9c will identify employees who work in Atlanta *or* whose title is Account Rep.

Relational operators may be used with date or numeric fields to return records within a designated range. The criteria range in Figure 7.9d selects the employees hired before January 1, 1993. The criteria range in Figure 7.9e returns employees whose salary is more than $40,000.

An upper and lower boundary may be established for the same field by repeating the field within the criteria range. This was done in Figure 7.9f, which returns all records in which the salary is more than $40,000 but less than $60,000.

First row contains field names

Second row contains filter condition

Name	Location	Title	Hire Date	Salary
	Atlanta			

(a) Employees Who Work in Atlanta

Multiple criteria in same row indicate both must be met

Name	Location	Title	Hire Date	Salary
	Atlanta	Account Rep		

(b) Account Reps Who Work in Atlanta (AND condition)

Multiple criteria in different rows indicate either may be met

Name	Location	Title	Hire Date	Salary
	Atlanta			
		Account Rep		

(c) Employees Who Work in Atlanta or Who Are Account Reps (OR condition)

Name	Location	Title	Hire Date	Salary
			<1/1/93	

(d) Employees Hired before January 1, 1993

Relational operators may be used with dates and numerical data

Name	Location	Title	Hire Date	Salary
				>$40,000

(e) Employees Who Earn More Than $40,000

Lower boundary

Upper boundary

Name	Location	Title	Hire Date	Salary	Salary
				>$40,000	<$60,000

(f) Employees Who Earn More Than $40,000 But Less Than $60,000

Selects records with no entry in Location field

Name	Location	Title	Hire Date	Salary
	=			

(g) Employees without a Location

Empty criteria row returns every record

Name	Location	Title	Hire Date	Salary

(h) All Employees (blank row)

FIGURE 7.9 The Criteria Range

The equal and unequal signs select records with empty and nonempty fields, respectively. An equal sign with nothing after it will return all records without an entry in the designated field; for example, the criteria range in Figure 7.9g selects any record that is missing a value for the Location field. An unequal sign (<>) with nothing after it will select all records with an entry in the field.

An empty row in the criteria range returns *every* record in the list, as shown in Figure 7.9h. All criteria are *case-insensitive* and return records with any combination of upper- and lowercase letters that match the entry. Remember, too, that all text entries must be spelled correctly in order to return the intended records.

THE IMPLIED WILD CARD

Any text entry within a criteria range is treated as though it were followed by the asterisk wild card; that is, *New* is the same as *New**. Both entries will return New York and New Jersey. To match a text entry exactly, begin with an equal sign, enter a quotation mark followed by another equal sign, the entry you are looking for, and the closing quotation mark—for example, = " =New" to return only the entries that say New.

Database Functions

The ***database functions*** DSUM, DAVERAGE, DMAX, DMIN, and DCOUNT operate on *selected* records in a list. These functions parallel the statistical functions (SUM, AVERAGE, MAX, MIN, and COUNT) except that they affect only records that satisfy the established criteria.

The summary statistics in Figure 7.10 are based on the salaries of the managers in the list, rather than the salaries of all employees. Each database function includes the criteria range in cells A17:E18 as one of its arguments, and thus limits the employees that are included to managers. The ***DAVERAGE function*** returns the average salary for just the managers. The ***DMAX*** and ***DMIN functions*** display the maximum and minimum salaries for the managers. The ***DSUM function*** computes the total salary for all the managers. The ***DCOUNT function*** indicates the number of managers.

Each database function has three arguments: the range for the list on which it is to operate, the field to be processed, and the criteria range. Consider, for example, the DAVERAGE function as shown below:

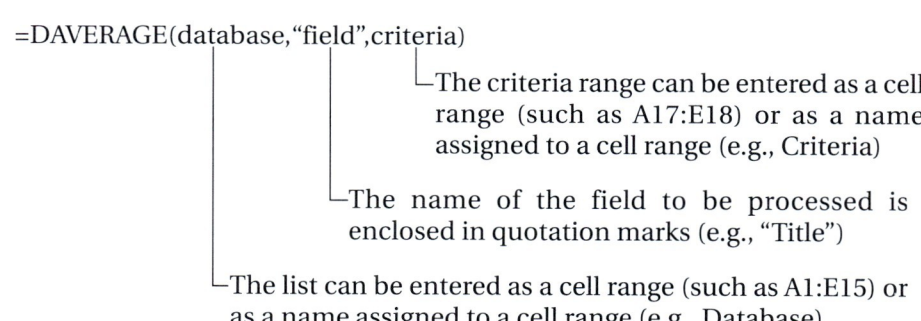

The entries in the criteria range may be changed at any time, in which case the values of the database functions are automatically recalculated. The other database functions have arguments identical to those used in the DAVERAGE function. The functions will adjust automatically if rows or columns are inserted or deleted within the specified range.

	A	B	C	D	E
1	Name	Location	Title	Hire Date	Salary
2	Adams	Atlanta	Trainee	11/24/98	$29,500
3	Adamson	Chicago	Manager	3/16/99	$52,000
4	Brown	Atlanta	Trainee	11/24/98	$28,500
5	Charles	Boston	Account Rep	3/16/99	$40,000
6	Coulter	Atlanta	Manager	11/24/98	$100,000
7	Elofson	Miami	Account Rep	10/31/01	$47,500
8	Gillenson	Miami	Account Rep	10/31/02	$55,000
9	James	Chicago	Account Rep	10/31/98	$42,500
10	Johnson	Chicago	Account Rep	10/31/99	$47,500
11	Manin	Boston	Account Rep	3/16/99	$49,500
12	Marder	Chicago	Account Rep	10/31/00	$38,500
13	Milgrom	Boston	Manager	3/16/99	$57,500
14	Rubin	Boston	Account Rep	3/16/99	$45,000
15	Smith	Atlanta	Account Rep	11/24/98	$65,000
16					
17	Name	Location	Title	Hire Date	Salary
18			Manager		
19					
20					
21			Summary Statistics		
22	Average Salary				$69,833
23	Maximum Salary				$100,000
24	Minimum Salary				$52,000
25	Total Salary				$209,500
26	Number of Employees				3

- Criteria range is A17:E18
- Criteria is Manager
- Summary statistics for Managers

FIGURE 7.10 Database Functions

Insert Name Command

The **Name command** in the Insert menu equates a mnemonic name such as *EmployeeList* to a cell or cell range such as *A1:E15*, then enables you to use that name to reference the cell(s) in all subsequent commands. A name can be up to 255 characters in length, but must begin with a letter or an underscore. It can include upper- or lowercase letters, numbers, periods, and underscore characters but no blank spaces.

Once defined, range names will adjust automatically for insertions and/or deletions within the range. If, in the previous example, you were to delete row 4, the definition of *EmployeeList* would change to A1:E14. And, in similar fashion, if you were to insert a new column between columns B and C, the range would change to A1:F14.

A name can be used in any formula or function instead of a cell address; for example, =SALES–EXPENSES instead of =C1–C10, where Sales and Expenses have been defined as the names for cells C1 and C10, respectively. A name can also be entered into any dialog box where a cell range is required.

THE GO TO COMMAND

Names are frequently used in conjunction with the Go To command. Pull down the Edit menu and click Go To (or click the F5 key) to display a dialog box containing the names that have been defined within the workbook. Double click a name to move directly to the first cell in the associated range and simultaneously select the entire range.

SUBTOTALS

The ***Subtotals command*** uses a summary function (such as SUM, AVERAGE, or COUNT) to compute subtotals for groups of records within a list. The records are grouped according to the value in a specific field, such as location, as shown in Figure 7.11. The Subtotals command inserts a subtotal row into the list whenever the value of the designated field (location in this example) changes from one record to the next.

The subtotal for the Atlanta employees is inserted into the list as we go from the last employee in Atlanta to the first employee in Boston. In similar fashion, the subtotal for Boston is inserted into the list as we go from the last employee in Boston to the first employee in Chicago. A grand total is displayed after the last record. The list must be in sequence, according to the field on which the subtotals will be grouped, prior to executing the Subtotals command.

The summary information can be displayed with different levels of detail. Figure 7.11a displays the salary data for each employee (known as the detail lines), the subtotals for each location, and the grand total. Figure 7.11b suppresses the detail lines but shows both the subtotals and grand total. Figure 7.11c shows only the grand total. The worksheet in all three figures is said to be in outline format, as seen by the ***outline symbols*** at the extreme left of the application window.

The records within the list are grouped to compute the summary information. A plus sign indicates that the group has been collapsed, and that the detail information is suppressed. A minus sign indicates the opposite, namely that the group has been expanded and that the detail information is visible. You can click any plus or minus sign to expand or collapse that portion of the outline. You can also click the symbols (1, 2, or 3) above the plus or minus signs to collapse or expand the rows within the worksheet. Level one shows the least amount of detail and displays only the grand total. Level two includes the subtotals as well as the grand total. Level three includes the detail records, the subtotals, and the grand total.

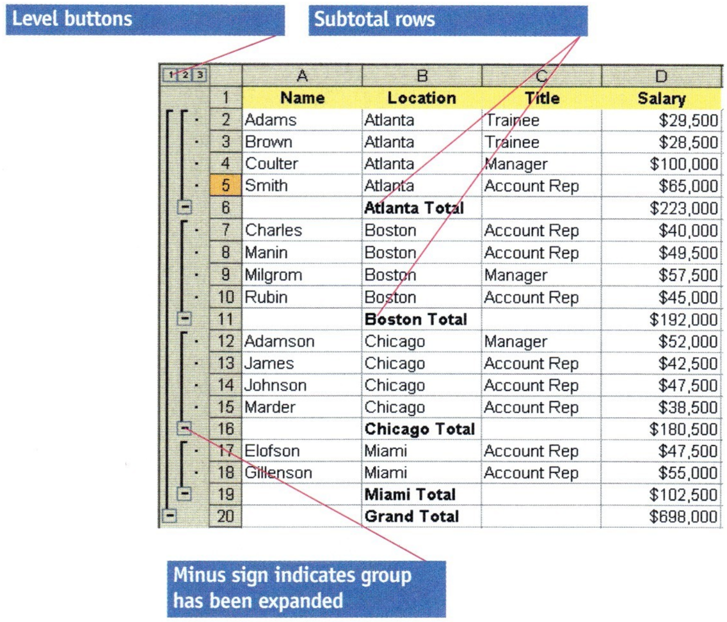

	A	B	C	D
1	Name	Location	Title	Salary
2	Adams	Atlanta	Trainee	$29,500
3	Brown	Atlanta	Trainee	$28,500
4	Coulter	Atlanta	Manager	$100,000
5	Smith	Atlanta	Account Rep	$65,000
6		**Atlanta Total**		**$223,000**
7	Charles	Boston	Account Rep	$40,000
8	Manin	Boston	Account Rep	$49,500
9	Milgrom	Boston	Manager	$57,500
10	Rubin	Boston	Account Rep	$45,000
11		**Boston Total**		**$192,000**
12	Adamson	Chicago	Manager	$52,000
13	James	Chicago	Account Rep	$42,500
14	Johnson	Chicago	Account Rep	$47,500
15	Marder	Chicago	Account Rep	$38,500
16		**Chicago Total**		**$180,500**
17	Elofson	Miami	Account Rep	$47,500
18	Gillenson	Miami	Account Rep	$55,000
19		**Miami Total**		**$102,500**
20		**Grand Total**		**$698,000**

(a) Detail Lines (level 3)

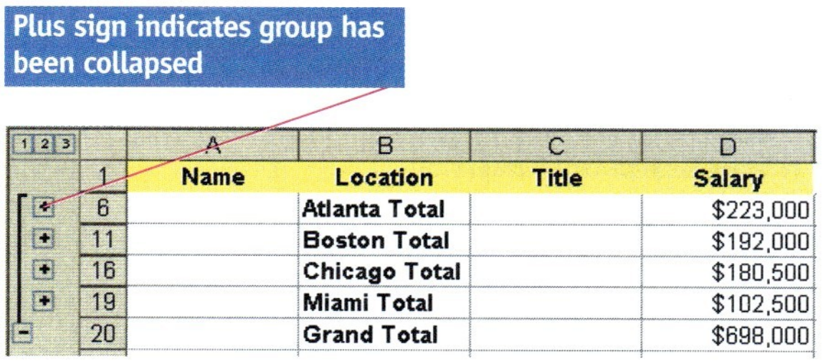

	A	B	C	D
1	Name	Location	Title	Salary
6		**Atlanta Total**		**$223,000**
11		**Boston Total**		**$192,000**
16		**Chicago Total**		**$180,500**
19		**Miami Total**		**$102,500**
20		**Grand Total**		**$698,000**

(b) Location Totals (level 2)

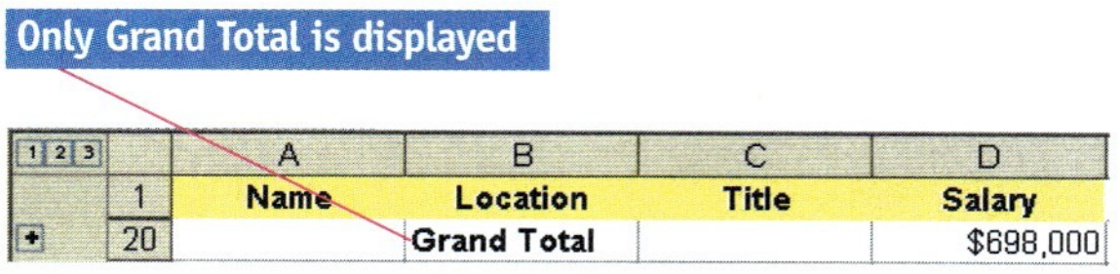

	A	B	C	D
1	Name	Location	Title	Salary
20		**Grand Total**		**$698,000**

(c) Grand Total (level 1)

FIGURE 7.11 Subtotals and Outlining

hands-on exercise 2

Data versus Information

Objective To sort a list on multiple keys; to use the AutoFilter and Advanced Filter commands; to define a named range; to use date arithmetic; to use the DSUM, DAVERAGE, DMAX, DMIN, and DCOUNT functions.

Step 1: **Calculate the Years of Service**

- Open the **Employee List Solution workbook** created in the previous exercise.

- Right click the **column heading** in **column D** to display a shortcut menu. Click **Insert.** The column of hire dates has been moved to column E. Click in **cell D1**. Type **Service** and press **Enter**.

- Click in **cell D2** and enter **=(Today()-E2)/365** as shown in Figure 7.12a. Press **Enter**; the years of service for the first employee are displayed in cell D2.

- Click in **cell D2**, then click the **Decrease Decimal button** on the Formatting toolbar several times to display the length of service with only one decimal.

- Drag the **fill handle** in cell D2 to the remaining cells in that column **(cells D3 through D15)** to compute the length of service for the remaining employees.

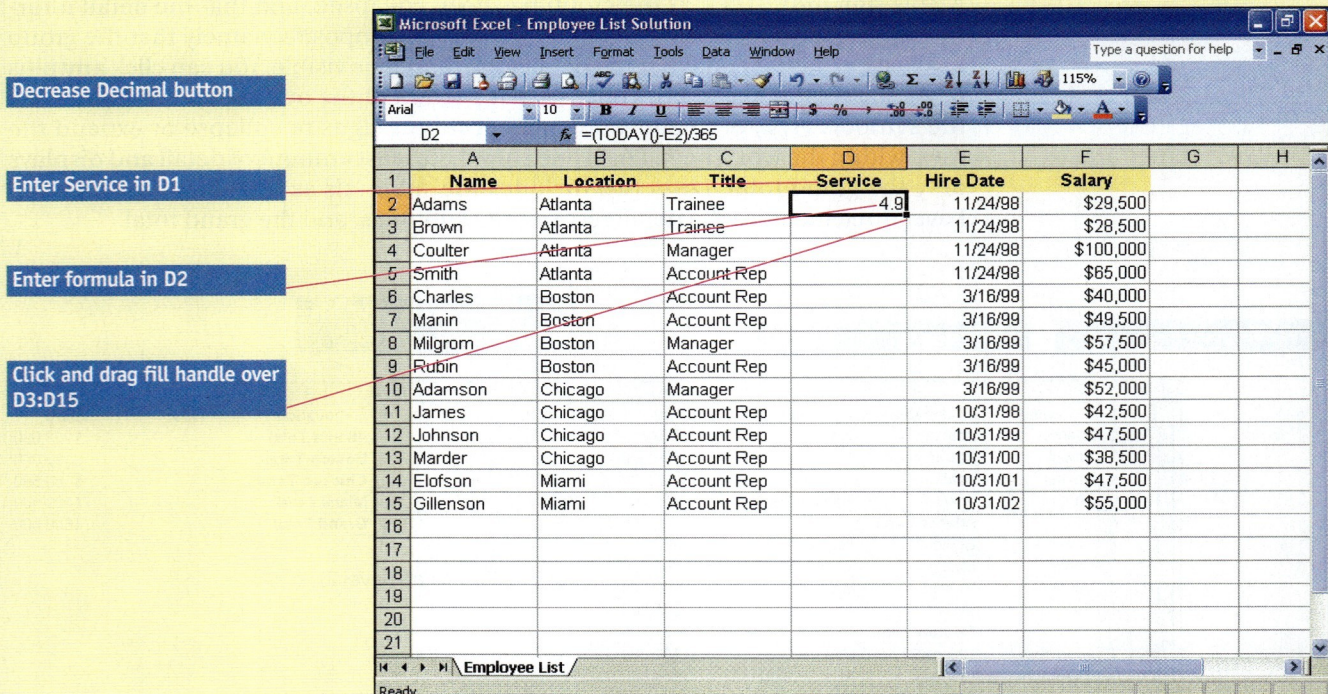

(a) Calculate the Years of Service (step 1)

FIGURE 7.12 Hands-on Exercise 2

DATE ARITHMETIC

Microsoft Excel stores a date as an integer (serial number) starting with January 1, 1900; that is, January 1, 1900 is stored as the number 1, January 2, 1900 as the number 2, and so on. This enables you to use dates in an arithmetic computation. An employee's service, for example, is computed by subtracting the hire date from the Today() function and dividing the result by 365.

Step 2: **The AutoFilter Command**

- Click a single cell anywhere within the list. Pull down the **Data menu**. Click the **Filter command**.
- Click **AutoFilter** from the resulting cascade menu to display the drop-down arrows to the right of each field name.
- Click the **drop-down arrow** next to **Title** to display the list of titles in Figure 7.12b. Click **Account Rep**.
- The display changes to show only those employees who meet the filter. The row numbers for the visible records are blue. The drop-down arrow for Title is also blue, indicating that it is part of the filter condition.
- Click the **drop-down arrow** next to **Location**. Click **Boston** to display only the employees in this city. The combination of the two filter conditions shows only the account reps in Boston.
- Click the **drop-down arrow** next to **Location** a second time. Click **(All)** to remove the filter condition on location. Only the account reps are displayed since the filter on Title is still in effect.
- Save the workbook.

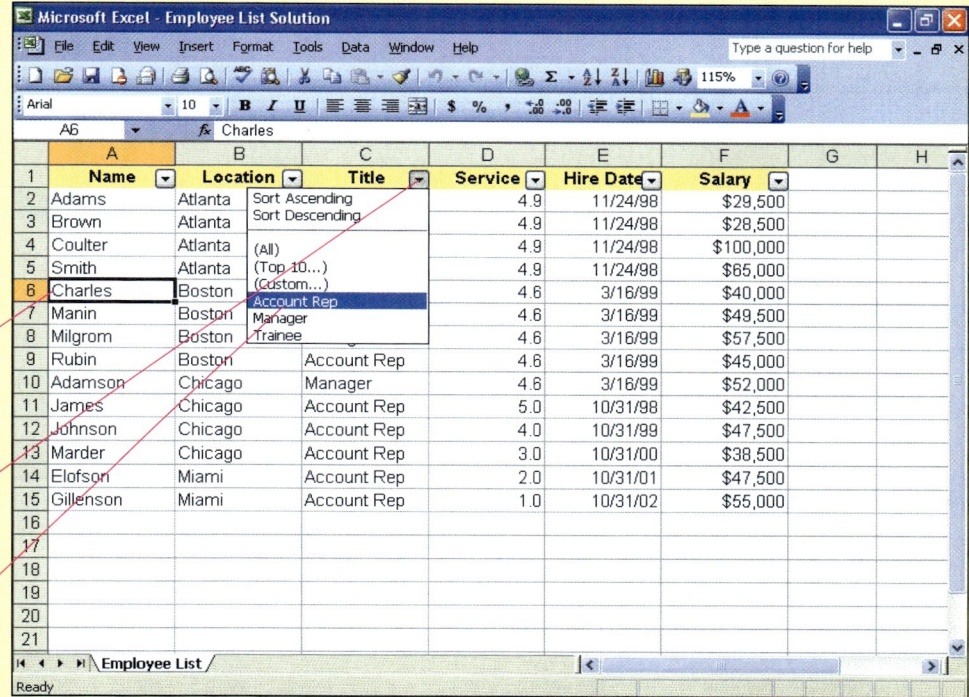

(b) The AutoFilter Command (step 2)

FIGURE 7.12 Hands-on Exercise 2 (*continued*)

THE TOP 10 AUTOFILTER

Use the Top 10 AutoFilter option to see the top (or bottom) 10, or for that matter any number of records in a list. Just turn the AutoFilter condition on, click the down arrow in the designated field, then click Top 10 to display the associated dialog box, where you specify the records you want to view. You can also specify a percentage, as opposed to a number—for example, the top 10% of the records in a list. See exercise 1 at the end of the chapter.

Step 3: **The Custom AutoFilter Command**

- Click the **drop-down arrow** next to **Salary** to display the list of salaries. Click **Custom** to display the dialog box in Figure 7.12c.
- Click the **arrow** in the leftmost drop-down list box for **Salary**, then click the **is greater than** as the relational operator.
- Click in the text box for the salary amount. Type **45000**. Click **OK**.
- The list changes to display only those employees whose title is account rep *and* who earn more than $45,000.
- Pull down the **Data menu**. Click **Filter**. Click **AutoFilter** to toggle the AutoFilter command off, which removes the arrows next to the field names and cancels all filter conditions. All of the records in the list are visible.
- Save the workbook.

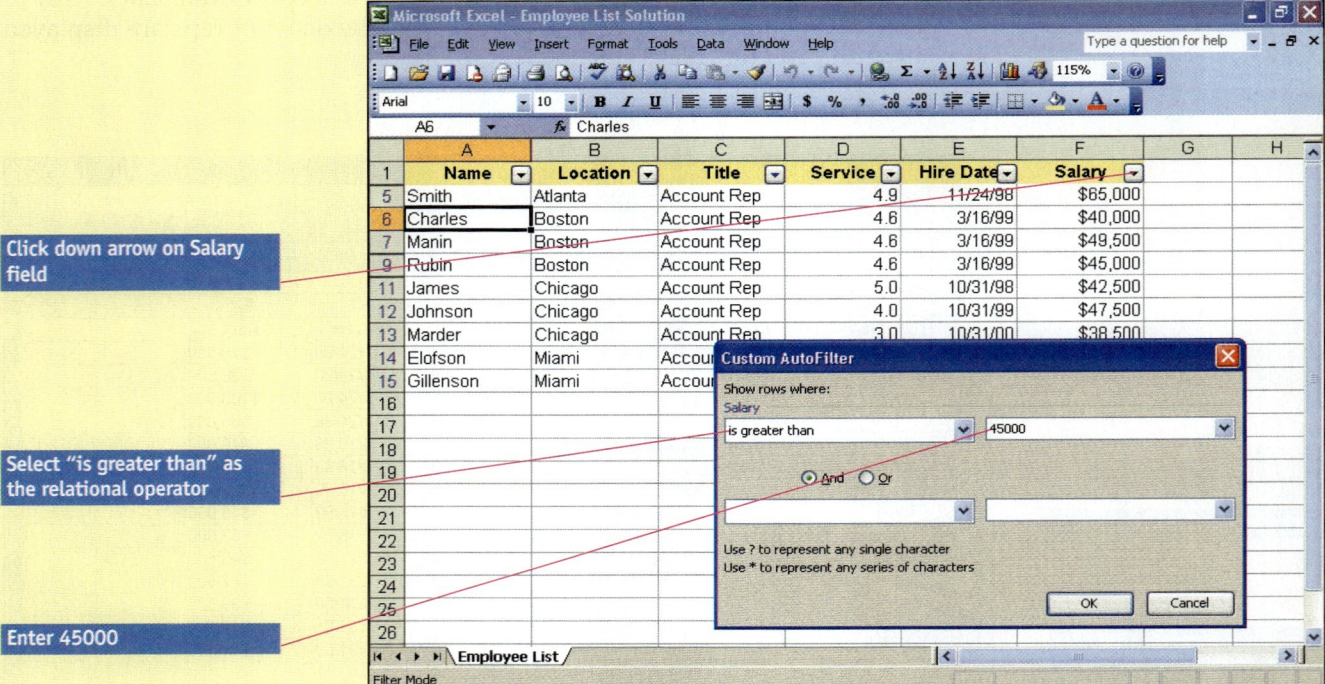

(c) The Custom AutoFilter Command (step 3)

FIGURE 7.12 Hands-on Exercise 2 (*continued*)

THE ANALYSIS TOOLPAK

Do you need to perform a statistical analysis on data within a worksheet? If so, you will want to use the Analysis ToolPak, one of several supplemental programs (or add-ins) that is included with Microsoft Excel. Pull down the Tools menu, click the Add-Ins command to display the associated dialog box, check the box for the Analysis ToolPak, then click OK to load the program. Pull down the Tools menu a second time, and then click the newly added Data Analysis command to access the tool pack, which provides access to a set of statistical functions to provide sophisticated analyses. See practice exercise 9 at the end of the chapter.

Step 4: **The Advanced Filter Command**

- The field names in the criteria range must be spelled exactly the same way as in the associated list. The best way to ensure that the names are identical is to copy the entries from the list to the criteria range.

- Click and drag to select **cells A1 through F1**. Click the **Copy button** on the Standard toolbar. A moving border appears around the selected cells. Click in **cell A17**. Click the **Paste button** on the Standard toolbar to complete the copy operation. Press **Esc** to cancel the moving border.

- Click in **cell C18**. Enter **Manager**. (Be sure you spell it correctly.)

- Click a single cell anywhere within the employee list. Pull down the **Data menu**. Click **Filter**. Click **Advanced Filter** from the resulting cascade menu to display the dialog box in Figure 7.12d. (The list range is already entered because you had selected a cell in the list prior to executing the command.)

- Click in the **Criteria Range** text box. Click in **cell A17** in the worksheet and drag the mouse to cell F18. Release the mouse. A moving border appears around these cells in the worksheet, and the corresponding cell reference is entered in the dialog box.

- Check that the **option button** to Filter the list, in-place is selected. Click **OK**. The display changes to show just the managers; that is, only rows 4, 8, and 10 are visible.

- Click in **cell B18**. Type **Atlanta**. Press **Enter**.

- Pull down the **Data menu**. Click **Filter**. Click **Advanced Filter**. The Advanced Filter dialog box already has the cell references for the list and criteria ranges.

- Click **OK**. The display changes to show just the manager in Atlanta; that is, only row 4 is visible.

- Pull down the **Data menu**. Click **Filter**. Click **Show All** to remove the filter condition. The entire list is visible.

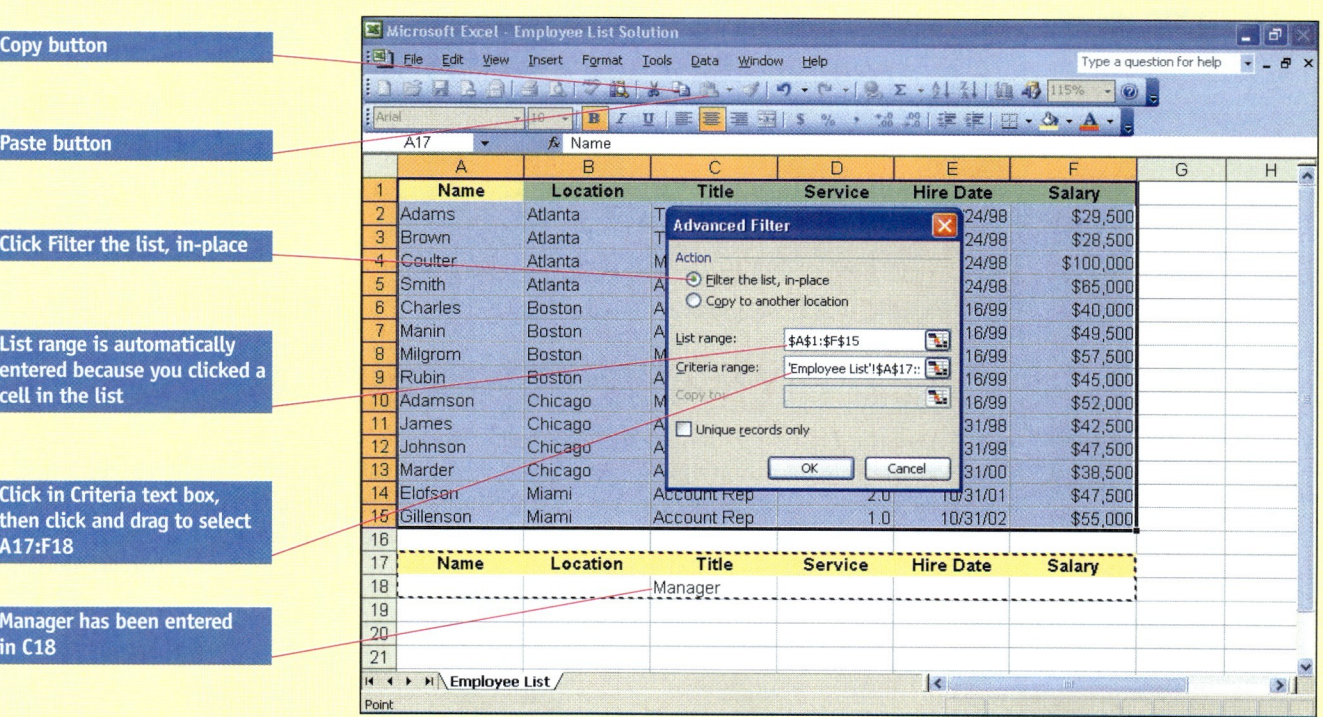

(d) The Advanced Filter Command (step 4)

FIGURE 7.12 Hands-on Exercise 2 (*continued*)

Step 5: **The Insert Name Command**

- Click and drag to select **cells A1 through F15** as shown in Figure 7.12e.

- Pull down the **Insert menu**. Click **Name**. Click **Define**. Type **Database** in the Names in workbook text box. Click **OK**.

- Pull down the **Edit menu** and click **Go To** (or press the **F5 key**) to display the Go To dialog box. There are two names in the box: **Database**, which you just defined, and **Criteria**, which was defined automatically when you specified the criteria range in step 4.

- Double click **Criteria** to select the criteria range **(cells A17 through F18)**. Click elsewhere in the worksheet to deselect the cells.

- Save the workbook.

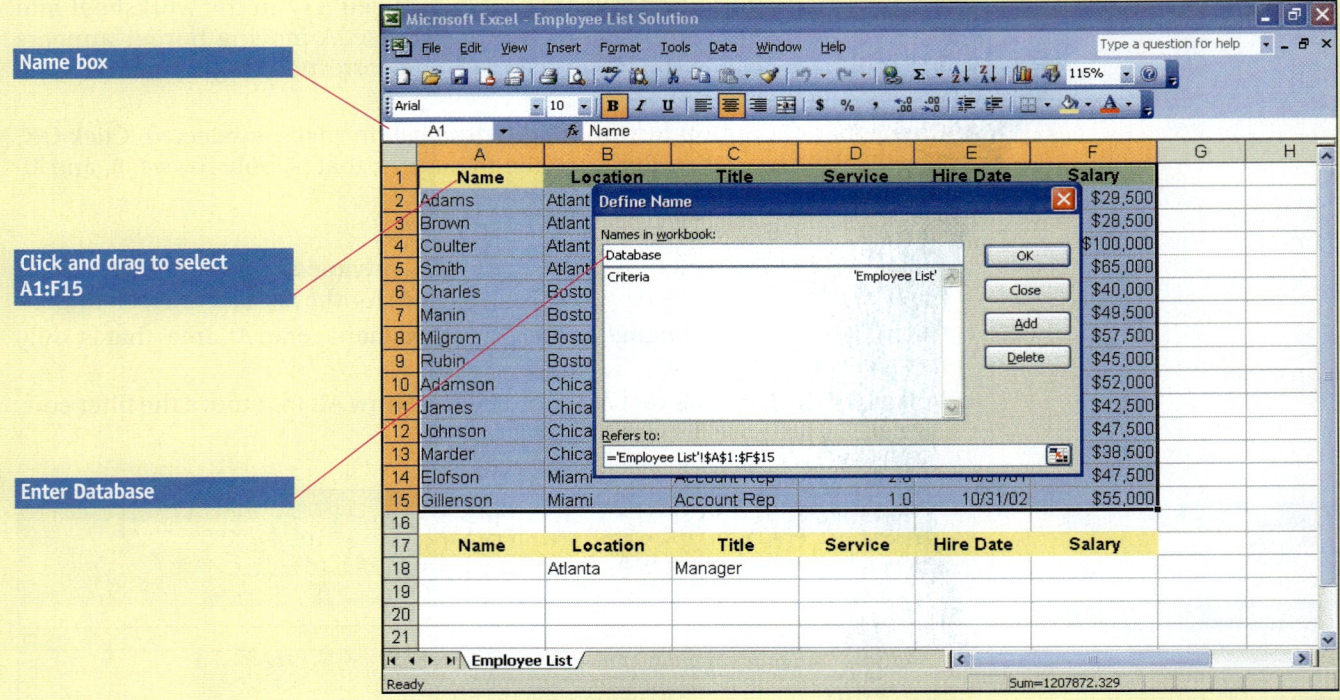

(e) The Insert Name Command (step 5)

FIGURE 7.12 Hands-on Exercise 2 (*continued*)

THE NAME BOX

Use the Name box on the formula bar to select a cell or named range by clicking in the box and then typing the appropriate cell reference or name. You can also click the drop-down arrow next to the Name box to select a named range from a drop-down list. And, finally, you can use the Name box to define a named range, by first selecting the cell(s) in the worksheet to which the name is to apply, clicking in the Name box to enter the range name, and then pressing the Enter key.

Step 6: **Database Functions**

- Click in **cell A21**, type **Summary Statistics**, press the **Enter key**, then click and drag to select cells **A21 through F21**.

- Pull down the **Format menu**, click **Cells**, click the **Alignment tab**, then select **Center Across Selection** as the horizontal alignment. Click **OK**. Change the fill color for this range to **light yellow**.

- Enter the labels for **cells A22 through A26** as shown in Figure 7.12f.

- Click in **cell B18**. Press the **Del key**. The criteria range is now set to select only managers.

- Click in **cell F22**. Click the **Insert Function button** on the formula bar to display the dialog box in Figure 7.12f.

- Select **Database** from the Category list box, select **DAVERAGE** as the function name, then click **OK**.

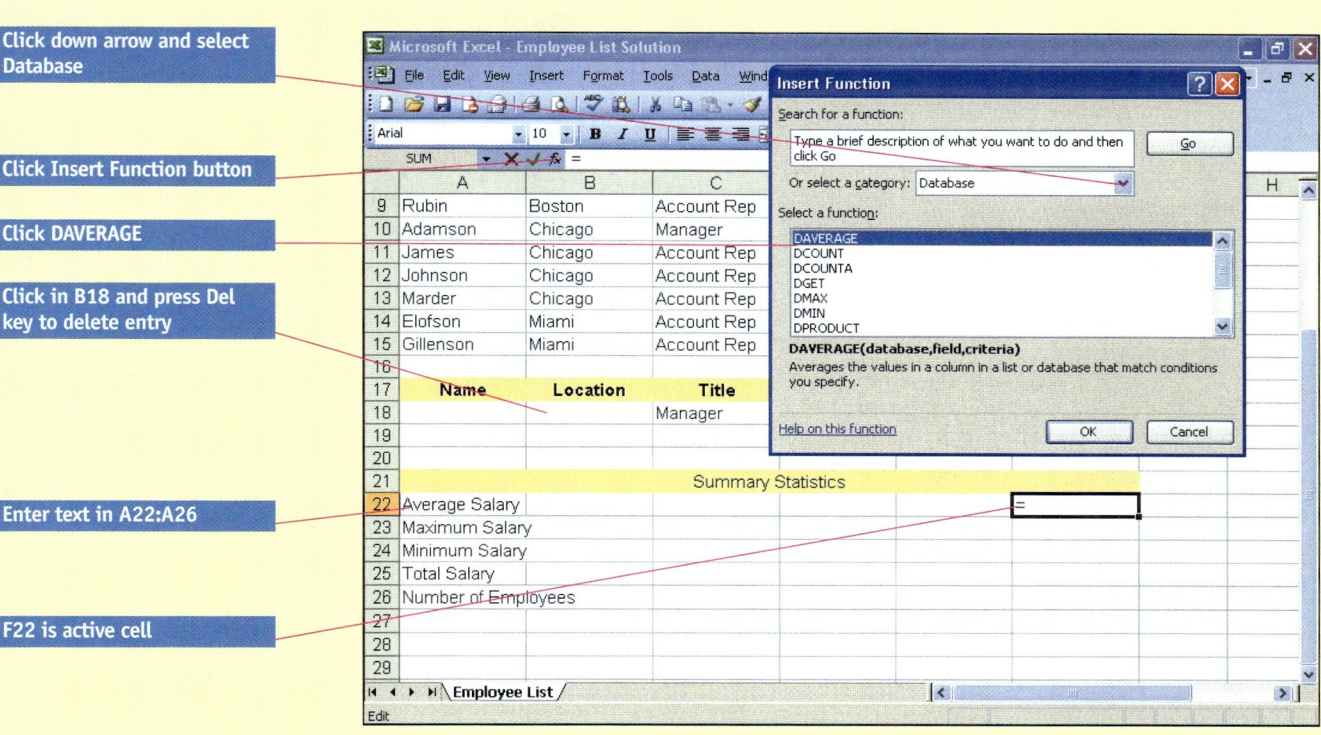

(f) Database Functions (step 6)

FIGURE 7.12 Hands-on Exercise 2 (*continued*)

HIDE A COLUMN

An individual's hire date and length of service convey essentially the same information, and thus there is no need to display both columns. Point to the column heading of the field you wish to hide, then click the right mouse button to select the column and display a shortcut menu. Click the Hide command, and the column is no longer visible (although it remains in the worksheet). To display (unhide) a column, click and drag the adjacent column headings on both sides, click the right mouse button to display a shortcut menu, then click the Unhide command.

Step 7: **The DAVERAGE Function**

- Click the **Database** text box in the dialog box as shown in Figure 7.12g. Type **Database** (the range name defined in step 5), which references the employee list.

- Click the **Field** text box. Type **"Salary"** (you must include the quotation marks), which is the name of the field (column name) within the list that you want to average.

- Click the **Criteria** text box. Type **Criteria** (the range name automatically assigned to the criteria range during the Advanced Filter operation). The dialog box displays the computed value of 69833.33333.

- Click **OK** to enter the DAVERAGE function into the worksheet.

- Save the workbook.

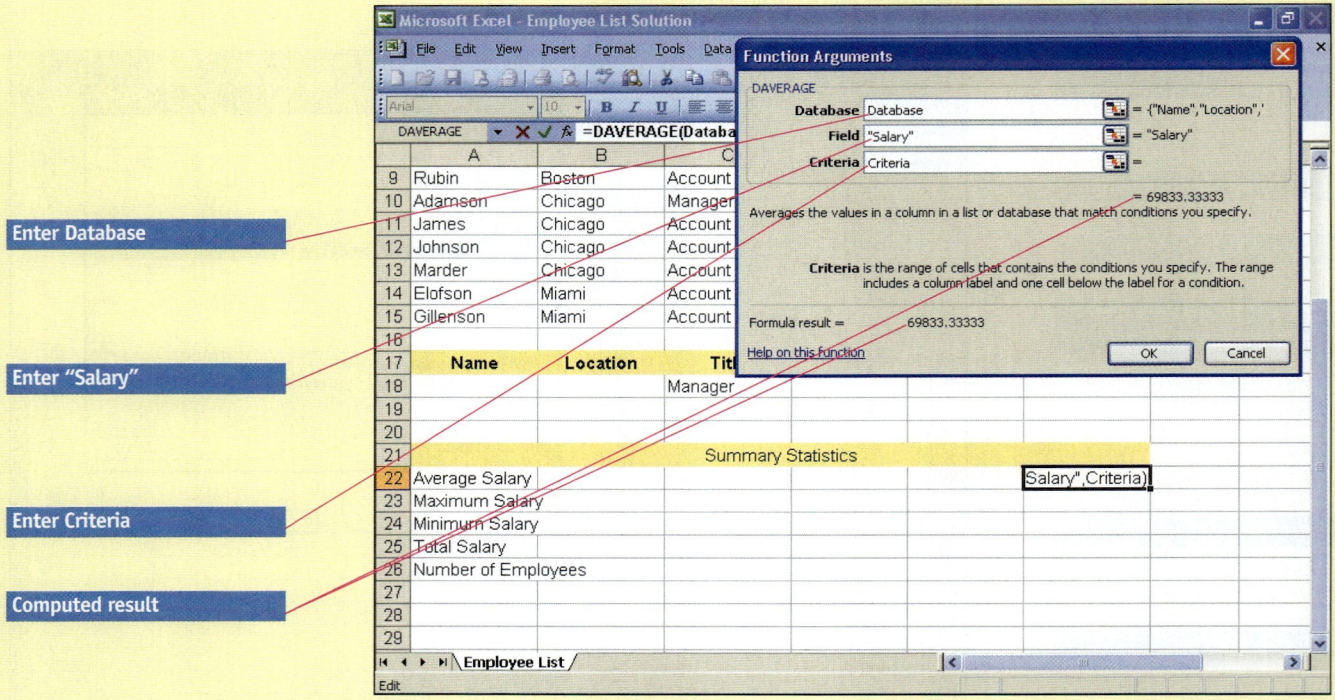

(g) The DAVERAGE Function (step 7)

FIGURE 7.12 Hands-on Exercise 2 (*continued*)

DIVISION BY ZERO—#DIV/0—AND HOW TO AVOID IT

The DAVERAGE function displays a division by zero error message if there are no records that meet the specified criteria. You can hide the error message, however, by using conditional formatting to display the message in white, which renders it invisible. Click in the cell containing the DAVERAGE function, pull down the Format menu, click Conditional formatting, and then click the drop-down arrow in the left list box to select Formula Is. Click in the box to the right and type = ISERROR(F22), where F22 is the cell containing the DAVERAGE function. Click the Format button, click Font, and change the color to white. The message is in the cell but you cannot see it.

Step 8: **The DMAX, DMIN, DSUM, and DCOUNT Functions**

- Enter the DMAX, DMIN, DSUM, and DCOUNT functions in cells F23 through F26, respectively. You can use the **Insert Function button** to enter each function individually, *or* you can copy the DAVERAGE function and edit appropriately:
  - Click in **cell F22**. Drag the **fill handle** to **cells F23 through F26** to copy the DAVERAGE function to these cells.
  - Double click in **cell F23** to edit the contents of this cell, then click within the displayed formula to substitute **DMAX** for DAVERAGE. Press **Enter**.
  - Double click in the remaining cells and edit them appropriately.

- The computed values (except for the DCOUNT function, which has a computed value of 3) are shown in Figure 7.12h.

- Format **cells F22 through F25**, to currency with no decimals.

- Click and drag the border between columns F and G to widen column F as necessary. Save the workbook.

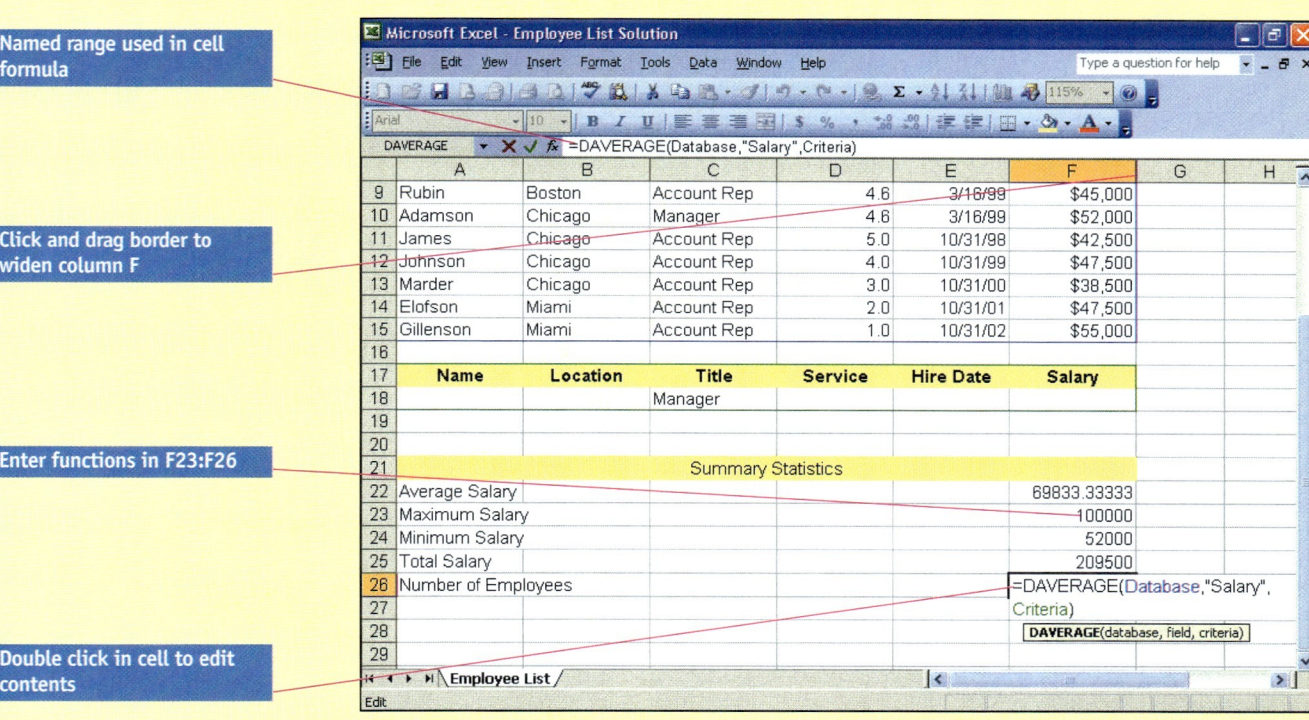

(h) The DMAX, DMIN, DSUM, DCOUNT Functions (step 8)

FIGURE 7.12 Hands-on Exercise 2 (*continued*)

IMPORT DATA FROM ACCESS

The data in a worksheet can be imported from an Access database. Pull down the Data menu, click the Import External Data command, then click Import Data to display the Select Data Source dialog box. Use the Look In list box to locate the folder containing the database and choose Access Databases as the file type. Select the database, then click the Open command to bring the Access table(s) into an Excel workbook.

Step 9: **Change the Criteria**

- Click in the **Name box**. Type **B18** and press **Enter** to make cell B18 the active cell. Type **Chicago** to change the criteria to Chicago managers. Press **Enter**.
- The values displayed by the DAVERAGE, DMIN, DMAX, and DSUM functions change to $52,000, reflecting the one employee (Adamson) who meets the current criteria (a manager in Chicago). The value displayed by the DCOUNT function changes to 1 to indicate one employee as shown in Figure 7.12i.
- Click in **cell C18**. Press the **Del key**.
- The average salary changes to $45,125, reflecting all employees in Chicago.
- Click in **cell B18**. Press the **Del key**.
- The criteria range is now empty. The DAVERAGE function displays $49,857, which is the average salary of all employees in the database.
- Click in **cell C18**. Type **Manager** and press the **Enter key**. The average salary is $69,833, the average salary for all managers.
- Save the workbook.

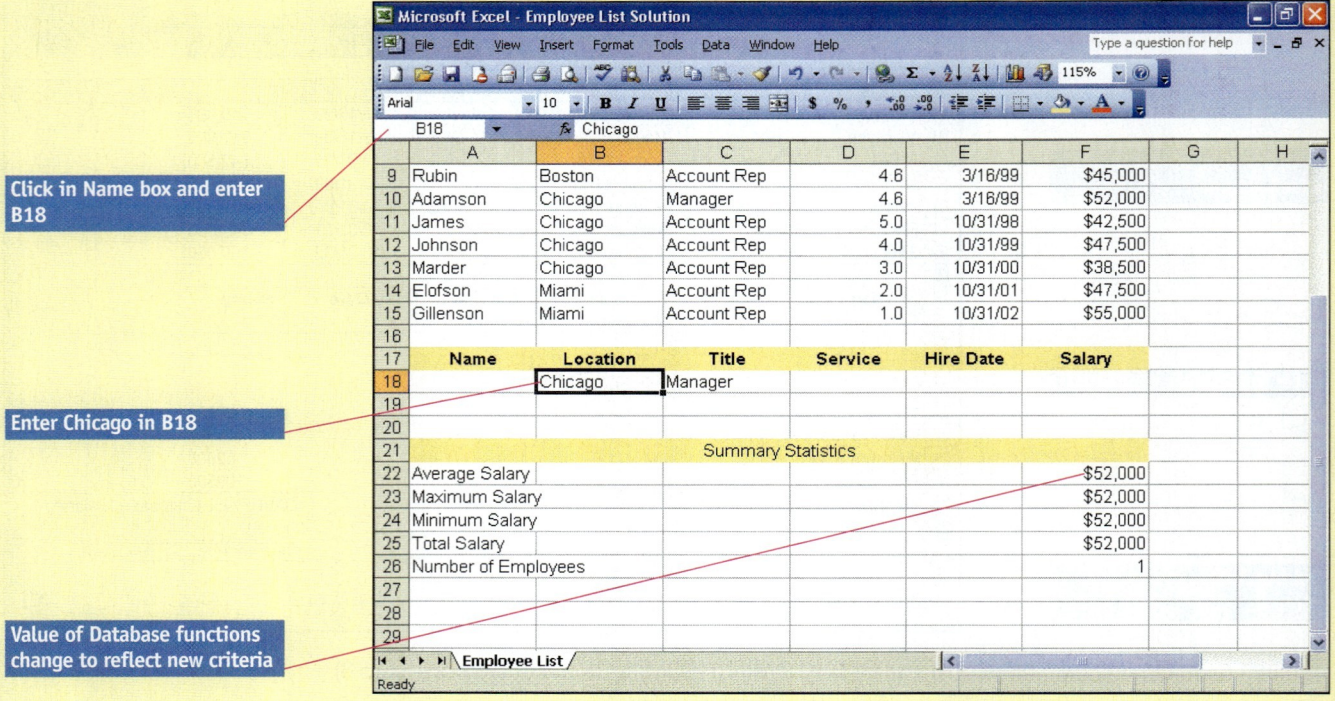

(i) Change the Criteria (step 9)

FIGURE 7.12 Hands-on Exercise 2 (*continued*)

FILTER THE LIST IN PLACE

Use the Advanced Filter command to filter the list in place and display the records that meet the current criteria. Click anywhere in the list, pull down the Data menu, click the Filter command, then choose Advanced Filter to display the Advanced Filter dialog box. Click the option button to filter the list in place, then click OK to display the selected records. You have to execute this command each time the criteria change.

Step 10: **Create the Subtotals**

- A list must be in sequence prior to computing the subtotals. Click any cell in the list in **column C**, the column containing the employee titles, then click the **Sort Ascending button** on the Standard toolbar. The employees should be sequenced according to title as shown in Figure 7.12j.

- Click in any cell in **column F**, the column containing the field for which you want subtotals. Pull down the **Data menu** and click the **Subtotals command**. Click the **drop-down arrow** in the **At each change in** list box. Click **Title** to create a subtotal whenever there is a change in title. Set the other options to match the dialog box in Figure 7.12j. Click **OK** to create the subtotals.

- You should see the three subtotals, one for each title, followed by the grand total for the company. The total for the Account Reps should appear first, and it is equal to $430,500.

- The total for managers is $209,500, but the DSUM command displays $419,000 (see boxed tip). Click in **cell C22**, type ="=Manager" and press **Enter**. The DSUM function returns the correct value.

- Save the workbook.

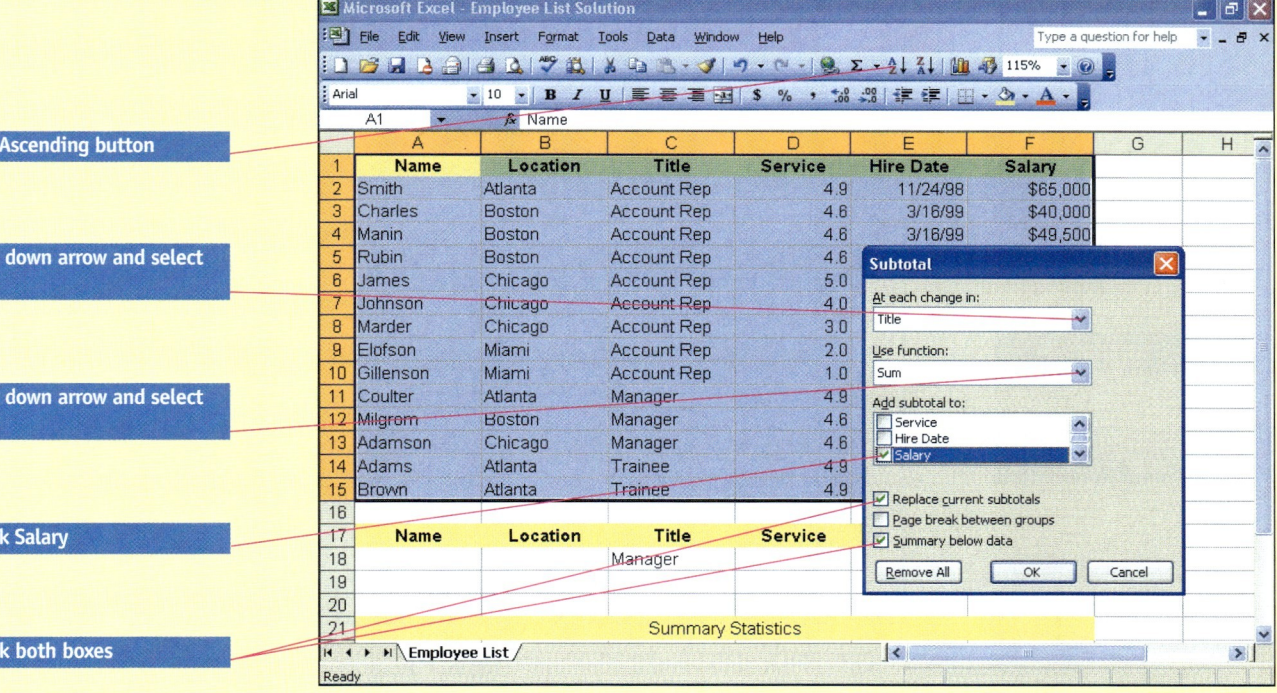

(j) Create the Subtotals (step 10)

FIGURE 7.12   Hands-on Exercise 2 (*continued*)

INCOMPATIBLE FUNCTIONS AND SUBTOTALS

Excel treats any text entry in a criteria row as though it were followed by the asterisk wild card and thus "Manager" returns both "Manager" and "Manager Total". This creates a problem with the Subtotals command, which interprets the total row as another manager record; that is, it returns $419,000 as the total salary for all managers when it should be $209,500. The solution is to modify the criteria entry to include an equal sign: ="=Manager" in place of "Manager".

Step 11: **Collapse and Expand the Subtotals**

- The vertical lines at the left of the worksheet indicate how the data is aggregated within the list. Click the **minus sign** corresponding to the total for the Account Reps.

- The minus sign changes to a plus sign, and the detail lines (the names of the Account Reps) disappear from the worksheet as shown in Figure 7.12k. Click the **plus sign** next to the Account Rep total, and you see the detailed information for each Account Rep.

- Click the **Level 2 button** (under the Name box) to suppress the detail lines for all employees. The list collapses to display the subtotals and grand total.

- Click the **Level 1 button** to suppress the subtotals. The list collapses further to display only the grand total. Click the **Level 3 button** to restore the detail lines and subtotals.

- Click the **Print button** to print the list with the subtotals. Close the workbook. Exit Excel if you do not want to continue with the next exercise at this time.

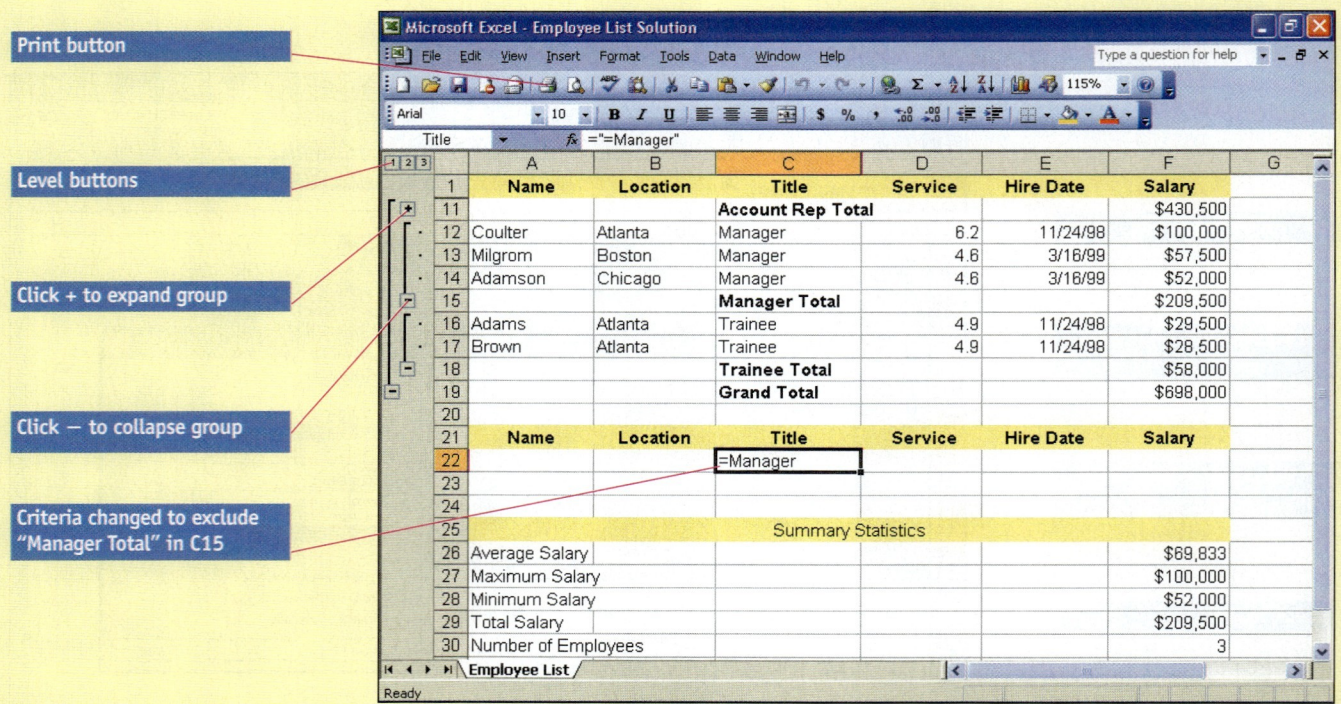

(k) Collapse and Expand the Subtotals (step 11)

FIGURE 7.12 Hands-on Exercise 2 (*continued*)

TWO SETS OF SUBTOTALS

You can obtain multiple sets of subtotals in the same list, provided you do the operations in the correct sequence. First, sort the list according to the sequence you want, for example, by title within location. Click in the list, and compute the subtotals based on the primary key (location in this example). Click on the list a second time and compute the subtotals based on the secondary key (title in this example), but clear the check box to replace the current subtotals. You will see the subtotal for each title in the first location, followed by the subtotal for that location, and so on.

PIVOT TABLES AND PIVOT CHARTS

A ***pivot table*** provides the ultimate flexibility in data analysis. It divides the records in a list into categories, then computes summary statistics for those categories. Pivot tables are illustrated in conjunction with the data in Figure 7.13 that displays sales information for a hypothetical advertising agency. Each record in the list in Figure 7.13a displays the name of the sales representative, the quarter in which the sale was recorded, the type of media, and the amount of the sale.

The pivot table in Figure 7.13b shows the total sales for each Media–Sales Rep combination. Look closely and you will see four shaded buttons, each of which corresponds to a different area in the table. The Media and Sales Rep buttons are in the row and column areas, respectively. Thus, each row in the pivot table displays the data for a different media type (magazine, radio, or TV), whereas each column displays data for a different sales representative. The Quarter button in the page area provides a third dimension. The value in the drop-down list box indicates that all of the records in the underlying worksheet are used to compute the totals in the body of the table. You can, however, display different pages corresponding to the totals in the first, second, third, or fourth quarters. You can also click the arrows next to the other buttons to suppress selected values for the media type or sales representative.

The best feature about a pivot table is its flexibility because you can change the orientation to provide a different analysis of the associated data. Figure 7.13c, for example, displays an alternate version of the pivot table in which the fields have been rearranged to show the total for each combination of quarter and sales representative. You go from one pivot table to another simply by clicking and dragging the buttons corresponding to the field names to different positions.

You can also change the means of computation within the data area. Both of the pivot tables in Figure 7.13 use the Sum function, but you can choose other functions such as Average, Minimum, Maximum, or Count. You can also change the formatting of any element in the table. More importantly, pivot tables are dynamic in that they reflect changes to the underlying worksheet. Thus, you can add, edit, or delete records in the associated list and see the results in the pivot table, provided you execute the ***Refresh command*** to update the pivot table.

The ***Pivot Table Wizard*** is used to create the initial pivot table in conjunction with an optional pivot chart. The ***pivot chart*** in Figure 7.14, for example, corresponds to the pivot table in Figure 7.13b, and at first glance, it resembles any other Excel chart. Look closely, however, and you will see shaded buttons similar to those in the pivot table, enabling you to change the chart by dragging the buttons to different areas. Reverse the position of the Media and Sales Rep buttons, for example, and you have a completely different chart. Any changes to the chart are reflected in the underlying pivot table and vice versa.

Drop-down arrows next to each button on the pivot chart let you display selected values. Click either arrow to display a drop-down list in which you select the values you want to appear in the chart. You could, for example, click the drop-down arrow next to the Sales Rep field and clear the name of any sales rep to remove his/her data from the chart.

Pivot tables may also be saved as Web pages with full interactivity as shown in Figure 7.15. The Address bar indicates that you are viewing a Web document (note the mht extension), as opposed to an Excel workbook. As with an ordinary pivot table, you can pivot the table within the Web page by repositioning the buttons for the row, column, and page fields. The plus and minus next to the various categories enable you to show or hide the detailed information. (The interactivity extends to Netscape as well as Internet Explorer, provided that you install the Office Web components.)

Pivot tables are one of the best-kept secrets in Excel, even though they have been available in the last several releases of Excel. (Pivot charts were introduced in Excel 2000.) Be sure to share this capability with your friends and colleagues.

	A	B	C	D
1	**Sales Rep**	**Quarter**	**Media**	**Amount**
2	Alice	1st quarter	TV	$15,000
3	Alice	1st quarter	Radio	$4,000
4	Alice	2nd quarter	Magazine	$2,000
5	Alice	2nd quarter	Radio	$4,000
6	Alice	3rd quarter	Radio	$2,000
7	Alice	4th quarter	Radio	$4,000
8	Alice	4th quarter	Radio	$1,000
9	Bob	1st quarter	Magazine	$2,000
10	Bob	1st quarter	Radio	$1,000
11	Bob	2nd quarter	Radio	$4,000
12	Bob	3rd quarter	TV	$10,000
13	Bob	4th quarter	Magazine	$10,000
14	Bob	4th quarter	Magazine	$12,000
15	Bob	4th quarter	Radio	$1,000
16	Bob	4th quarter	Magazine	$7,000
17	Carol	1st quarter	Radio	$4,000
18	Carol	2nd quarter	Magazine	$2,000
19	Carol	2nd quarter	Magazine	$7,000
20	Carol	2nd quarter	TV	$10,000
21	Carol	3rd quarter	TV	$8,000
22	Carol	3rd quarter	TV	$18,000
23	Carol	4th quarter	TV	$13,000
24	Ted	1st quarter	Radio	$2,000
25	Ted	2nd quarter	TV	$6,000
26	Ted	2nd quarter	TV	$6,000
27	Ted	3rd quarter	TV	$20,000
28	Ted	3rd quarter	Magazine	$15,000
29	Ted	3rd quarter	Magazine	$2,000
30	Ted	4th quarter	TV	$13,000
31	Ted	4th quarter	TV	$15,000

(a) Sales Data (Excel list)

Quarter is in page area
Computation is Sum of Amount
Media is in row area
Click down arrow to show data for all quarters or to select a specific quarter
Sales Rep is in column area

	A	B	C	D	E	F
1						
2	Quarter	(All)				
3						
4	Sum of Amount	Sales Rep				
5	Media	Alice	Bob	Carol	Ted	Grand Total
6	Magazine	$2,000	$31,000	$9,000	$17,000	$59,000
7	Radio	$15,000	$6,000	$4,000	$2,000	$27,000
8	TV	$15,000	$10,000	$49,000	$60,000	$134,000
9	Grand Total	$32,000	$47,000	$62,000	$79,000	$220,000

(b) Analysis by Media Type and Sales Representative

Media is in page area
Sales Rep is in row area
Quarter is in column area

	A	B	C	D	E	F
1						
2	Media	(All)				
3						
4	Sum of Amount	Quarter				
5	Sales Rep	1st quarter	2nd quarter	3rd quarter	4th quarter	Grand Total
6	Alice	$19,000	$6,000	$2,000	$5,000	$32,000
7	Bob	$3,000	$4,000	$10,000	$30,000	$47,000
8	Carol	$4,000	$19,000	$26,000	$13,000	$62,000
9	Ted	$2,000	$12,000	$37,000	$28,000	$79,000
10	Grand Total	$28,000	$41,000	$75,000	$76,000	$220,000

(c) Analysis by Sales Representative and Quarter

FIGURE 7.13 Pivot Tables

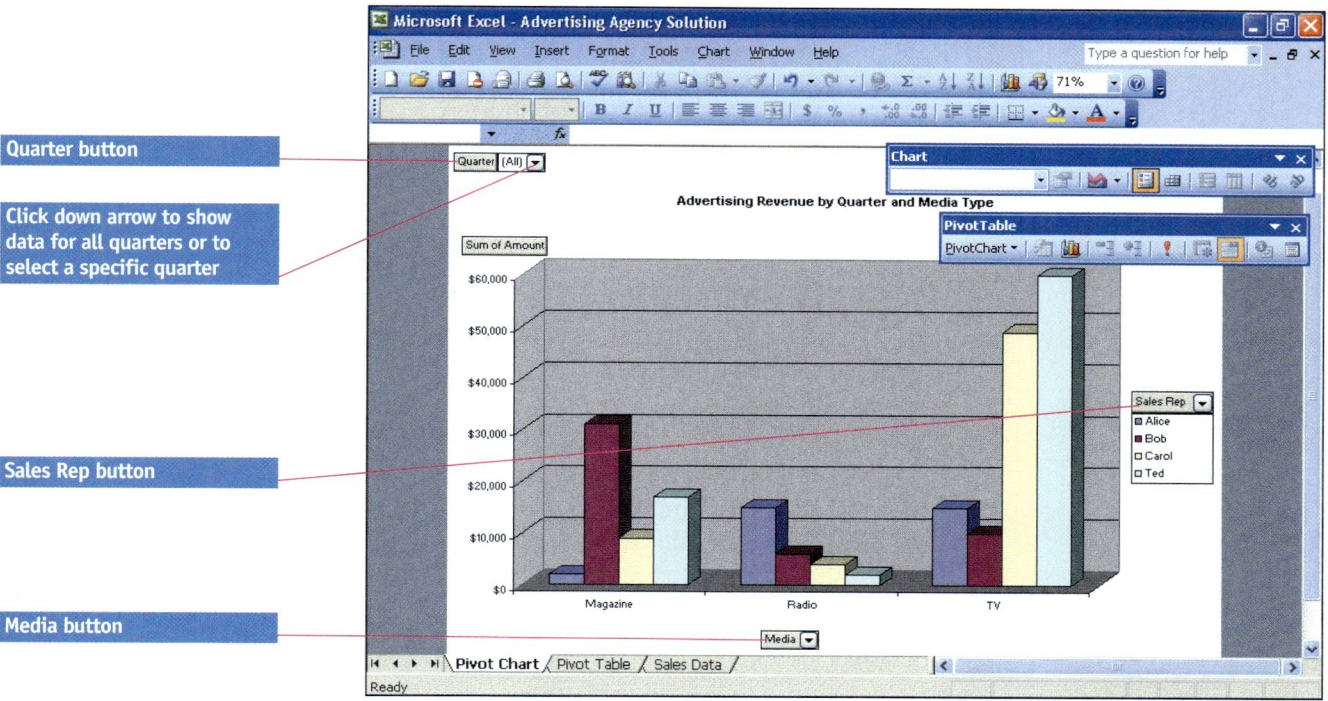

FIGURE 7.14 A Pivot Chart

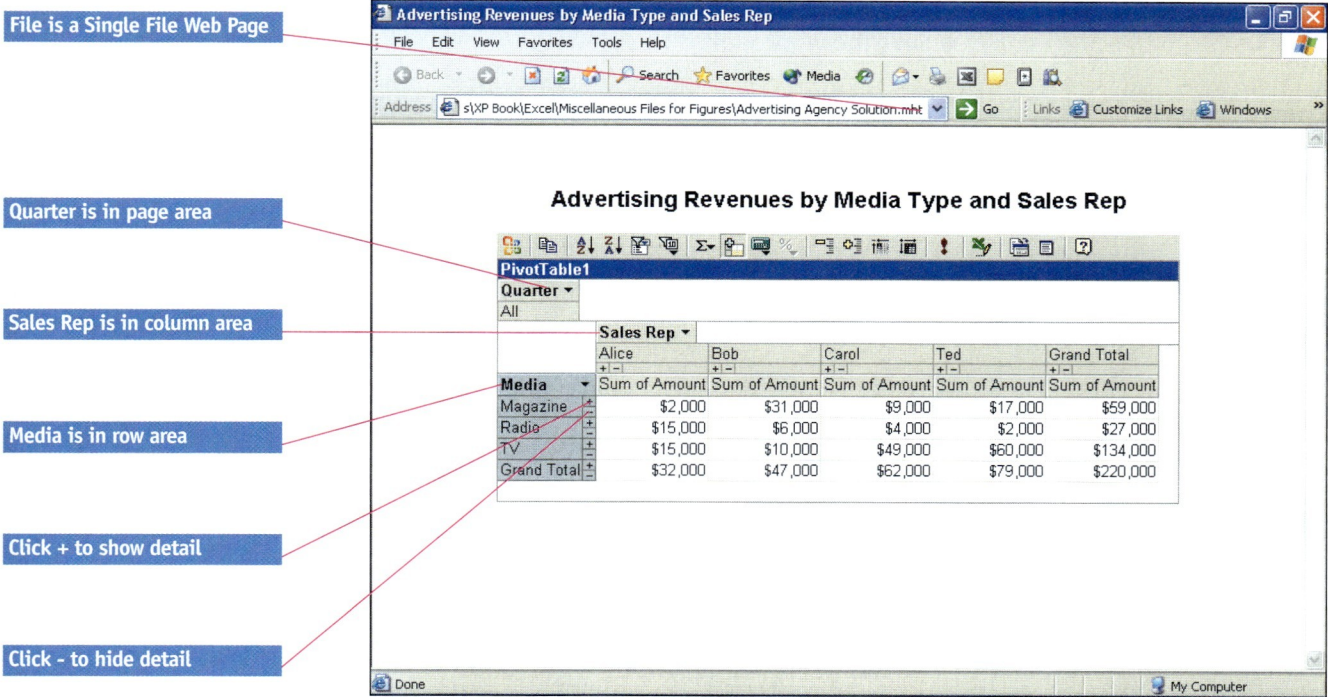

FIGURE 7.15 Pivot Tables on the Web

MICROSOFT OFFICE EXCEL 2003 REVISED   371

hands-on exercise 3
Pivot Tables and Pivot Charts

Objective To create a pivot table and pivot chart; to create a Web page based on the pivot table. Use Figure 7.16 as a guide in the exercise.

Step 1: **Start the Pivot Table Wizard**

- Start Excel. Open the **Advertising Agency workbook** in the **Exploring Excel folder**. Save the workbook as **Advertising Agency Solution** so that you will be able to return to the original workbook.

- The workbook contains a list of sales records for the advertising agency. Each record displays the name of the sales representative, the quarter in which the sale was recorded, the media type, and the amount of the sale.

- Click anywhere in the list of sales data. Pull down the **Data menu**. Click **PivotTable and PivotChart Report** to start the Pivot Table Wizard as shown in Figure 7.16a. Close the Office Assistant if necessary.

- Select the same options as in our figure. The pivot table will be created from data in a Microsoft Excel List or Database. In addition, you want to create a Pivot Chart report (that includes the Pivot Table). Click **Next**.

- Cells A1 through D31 have been selected automatically as the basis of the pivot table. Click **Next**.

- The option button to put the pivot table into a new worksheet is already selected. Click **Finish**. Two additional sheets have been added to the workbook, but the pivot table and chart area are not yet complete.

- Save the workbook.

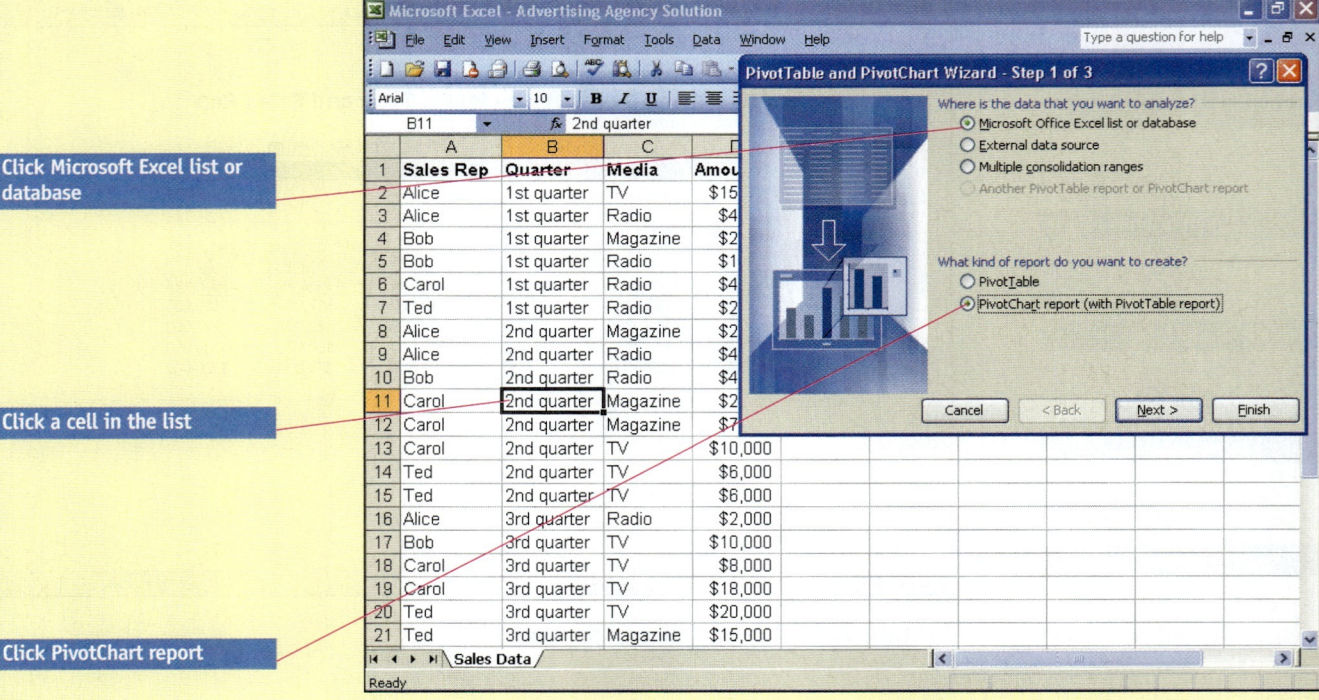

(a) Start the Pivot Table Wizard (step 1)

FIGURE 7.16 Hands-on Exercise 3

Step 2: Complete the Pivot Table

- Click the tab that takes you to the new worksheet (Sheet1 in our workbook). Your screen should be similar to Figure 7.16b. Complete the pivot table as follows:
  - Click the **Media field button** and drag it to the row area.
  - Click the **Sales Rep button** and drag it to the column area.
  - Click the **Quarter field button** and drag it to the page area.
  - Click the **Amount field button** and drag it to the data area.

- You should see the total sales for each sales representative for each type of media within a pivot table.

- Rename the worksheets so that they are more descriptive of their contents. Double click the **Sheet1 tab** (the worksheet that contains the pivot table) to select the name of the sheet. Type **Pivot Table** as the new name, and press **enter**.

- Double click the tab for the **Chart1** worksheet and change its name to **Pivot Chart** in similar fashion.

- Save the workbook.

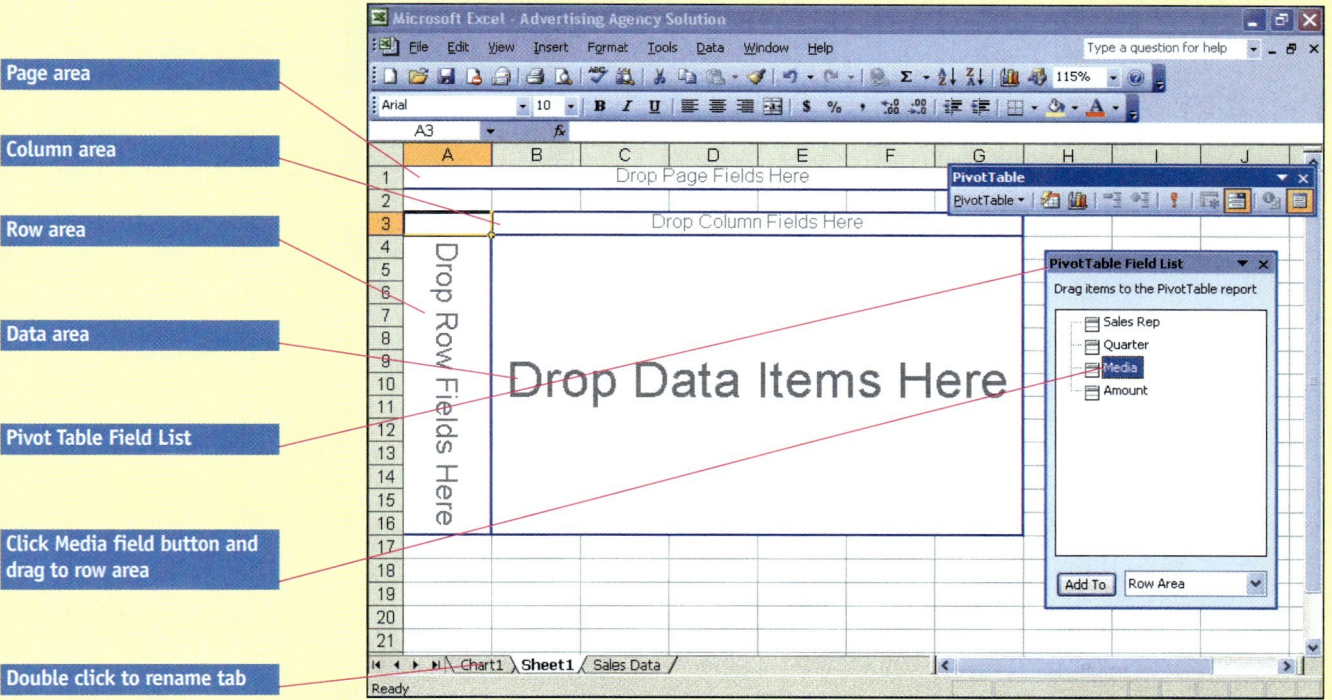

(b) Complete the Pivot Table (step 2)

FIGURE 7.16   Hands-on Exercise 3 (*continued*)

THE PAGE FIELD

A page field adds a third dimension to a pivot table. Unlike items in the row and column fields, however, the items in a page field are displayed one at a time. Creating a page field on Quarter, for example, lets you view the data for each quarter separately, by clicking the drop-down arrow on the page field list box, then clicking the appropriate quarter.

Step 3: **Modify the Sales Data**

- You will replace Bob's name within the list of transactions with your own name. Click the **Sales Data tab** to return to the underlying worksheet. Pull down the **Edit menu** and click the **Replace command** to display the Find and Replace dialog box.

- Enter **Bob** in the Find What dialog box, type **Your Name** (first and last) in the Replace With dialog box, then click the **Replace All button**. Click **OK** after the replacements have been made. Close the Find and Replace dialog box.

- Click the **Pivot Table tab** to return to the pivot table as shown in Figure 7.16c. The name change is not yet reflected in the pivot table because the table must be manually refreshed whenever the underlying data changes.

- Click anywhere in the pivot table, then click the **Refresh Data button** on the Pivot Table toolbar to update the pivot table. (You must click the Refresh button to update the pivot table whenever the underlying data changes.) You should see your name as one of the sales representatives.

- Save the workbook.

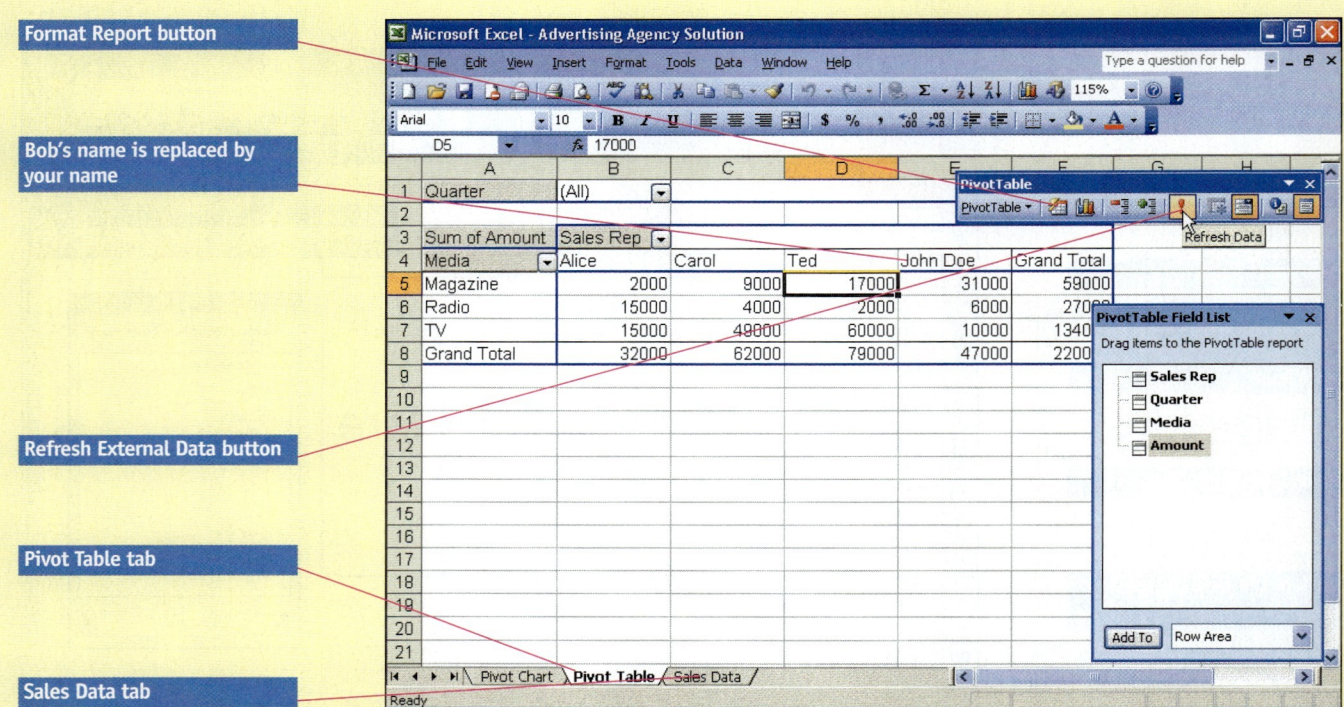

(c) Modify the Sales Data (step 3)

FIGURE 7.16 Hands-on Exercise 3 (*continued*)

THE FORMAT REPORT BUTTON

Why settle for a traditional report in black and white or shades of gray when you can choose from preformatted reports in a variety of styles and colors? Click the Format Report button on the Pivot Table toolbar to display the AutoFormat dialog box, where you select the style of your report. (To return to the default formatting, scroll to the end of the AutoFormat dialog box and select PivotTable Classic.) Use the Undo command if the result is not what you intended.

Step 4: **Pivot the Table**

- You can change the arrangement of a pivot table simply by dragging fields from one area to another. Click and drag the **Quarter field** to the row area. The page field is now empty, and you can see the breakdown of sales by quarter and media type.

- Click and drag the **Media field** to the column area, then drag the **Sales Rep field** to the page area. Your pivot table should match the one in Figure 7.16d.

- Click anywhere in the pivot table, then click the **Field Settings button** on the Pivot Table toolbar to display the PivotTable Field dialog box.

- Click the **Number button**, choose **Currency format** (with zero decimals). Click **OK** to close the Format Cells dialog box. Click **OK** a second time to close the Pivot Table Field dialog box.

- Save the workbook.

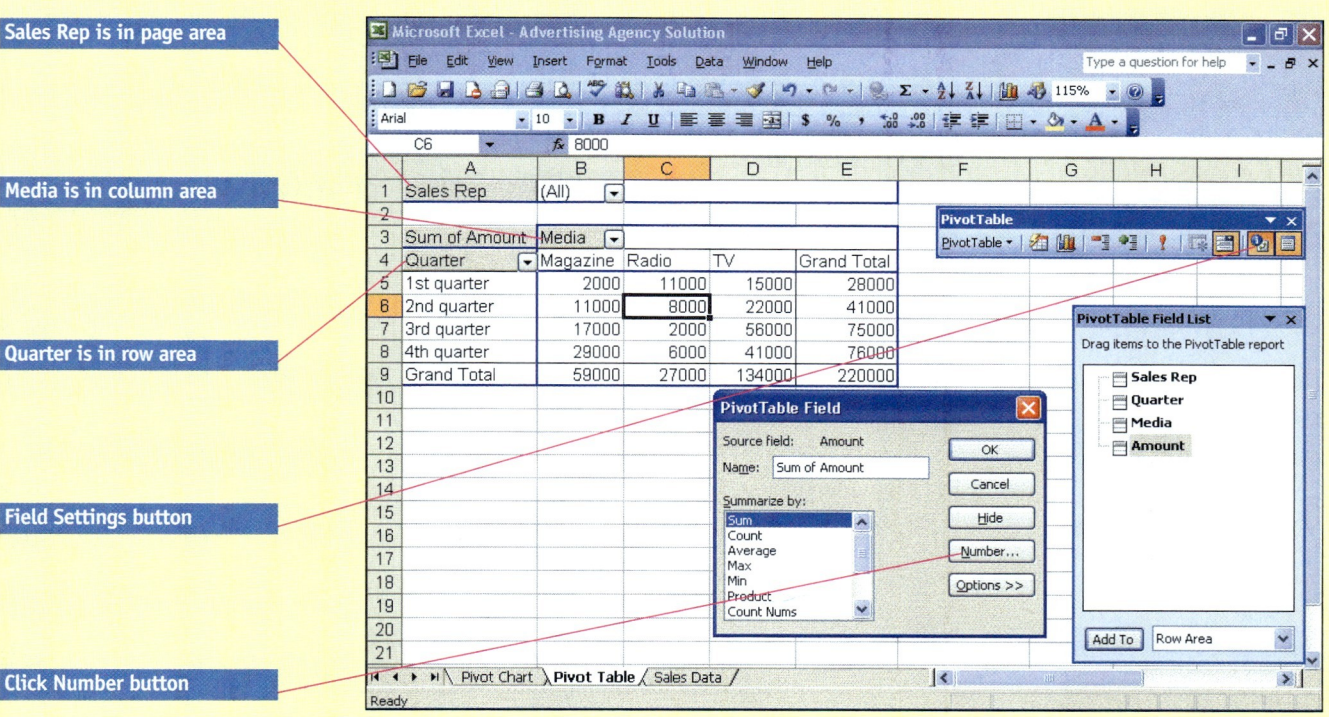

(d) Pivot the Table (step 4)

FIGURE 7.16 Hands-on Exercise 3 (*continued*)

CUSTOMIZE THE PIVOT TABLE

Right click anywhere within a pivot table to display a context-sensitive menu, then click the Table Options command to display the PivotTable Options dialog box. The default settings work well for most tables, but you can customize the table in a variety of ways. You can, for example, suppress the row or column totals or display a specific value in a blank cell. You can also change the formatting for any field within the table by right clicking the field and selecting the Format Cells button from the resulting menu.

Step 5: **Change the Chart Type**

- Click the **Pivot Chart tab** to view the default pivot chart as shown in Figure 7.16e. If necessary, close the field list to give yourself more room in which to work.

- Pull down the **Chart menu** and click the **Chart Type command** to display the dialog box in Figure 7.16e.

- Select the **Clustered column with a 3-D visual effect**. (Take a minute to appreciate the different types of charts that are available.)

- Check the box for **Default formatting**. This is a very important option, because without it, the chart is rotated in an awkward fashion. Click **OK**.

- The chart changes to display a three-dimensional column for each of the media in each quarter.

- Save the workbook.

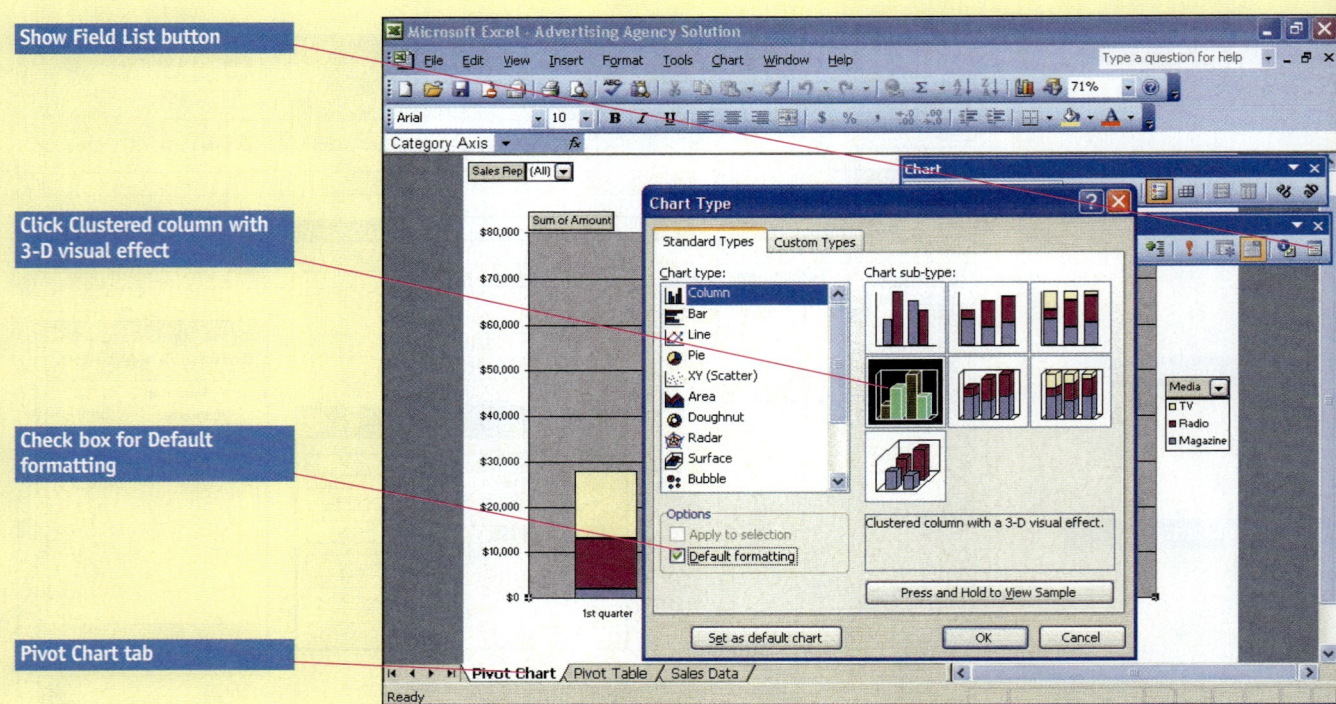

(e) Change the Chart Type (step 5)

FIGURE 7.16 Hands-on Exercise 3 (*continued*)

IT'S A PIVOT CHART

The shaded buttons for Sales Rep, Quarter, and Media that appear on the chart are similar in appearance and function to their counterparts in the underlying pivot table. Thus you can click and drag any of the buttons to a different position on the chart to change the underlying structure. You can also click and drag a field button from the PivotTable Field List to a new position on the chart. (Click the Show Field List button on the Pivot Table toolbar to show or hide the field list.) Any changes to the pivot chart affect the pivot table and vice versa.

Step 6: **Complete the Chart**

- Pull down the **Chart menu**, click **Chart Options** to display the Chart Options dialog box, then click the **Titles tab**. Enter **Advertising Revenue by Quarter and Media Type** as the chart title. Click **OK** to complete the chart as shown in Figure 7.16f.

- Click the **Sales Data tab** to select this worksheet. Press and hold the **Ctrl key** as you select the **Pivot Table tab** to select the worksheet containing the pivot table. Both worksheets are selected and hence both will be affected by the next command.

- Pull down the **File menu**, click the **Page Setup command**, and click the **Sheet tab**. Check the boxes to print **Gridlines** and **Row and Column headings**.

- Click the **Margins tab** and check the box to center the worksheet **horizontally**. Click **OK**.

- Pull down the **File menu** and click the **Print command** to display the Print dialog box. Click the option button to print the entire workbook. Click **OK**.

- Save the workbook.

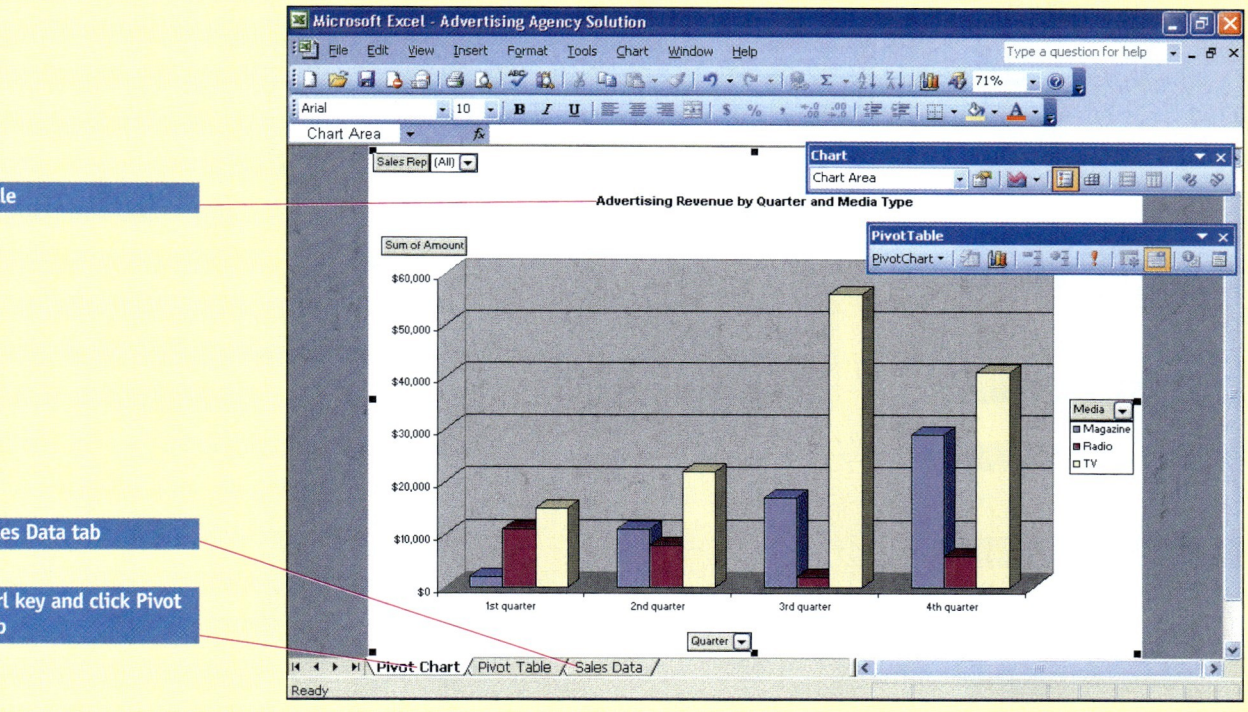

(f) Complete the Chart (step 6)

FIGURE 7.16 Hands-on Exercise 3 (*continued*)

FORMAT THE DATA SERIES

Why settle for a traditional bar chart when you can change the color, pattern, or shape of its components? Right click any column to select a data series to display a shortcut menu, then choose the Format Data Series command to display a dialog box in which you can customize the appearance of the vertical columns. We warn you that it is addictive, and that you can spend much more time than you intended initially. Set a time limit, and stop when you reach it.

Step 7: **Save the Pivot Table as a Web Page**

- Click the **Pivot Chart tab** to deselect the two tabs, then click the **Pivot Table tab**. Click and drag to select the entire pivot table. (If you have difficulty selecting the table, click and drag from the bottom-right cell to the top-left cell.)
- Pull down the **File menu**, click the **Save As Web Page command** to display the Save As dialog box, then click the **Publish button** (within the Save As dialog box) to display the Publish as Web Page dialog box in Figure 7.16g. Click **No** if the Office Assistant offers help.
- Change the name of the web page to **Advertising Agency Solution**. Save it in the **Exploring Excel folder**.
- Check the box to **Add interactivity** and select **Pivot Table functionality**. Check the boxes to **AutoRepublish every time this workbook is saved** and to **Open published web page in browser**.
- Click the **Change button** and enter an appropriate title that includes your name. Click **OK** to close the Set Title dialog box.
- Check that your settings match those in Figure 7.16g. Click the **Publish button** to publish the pivot table.

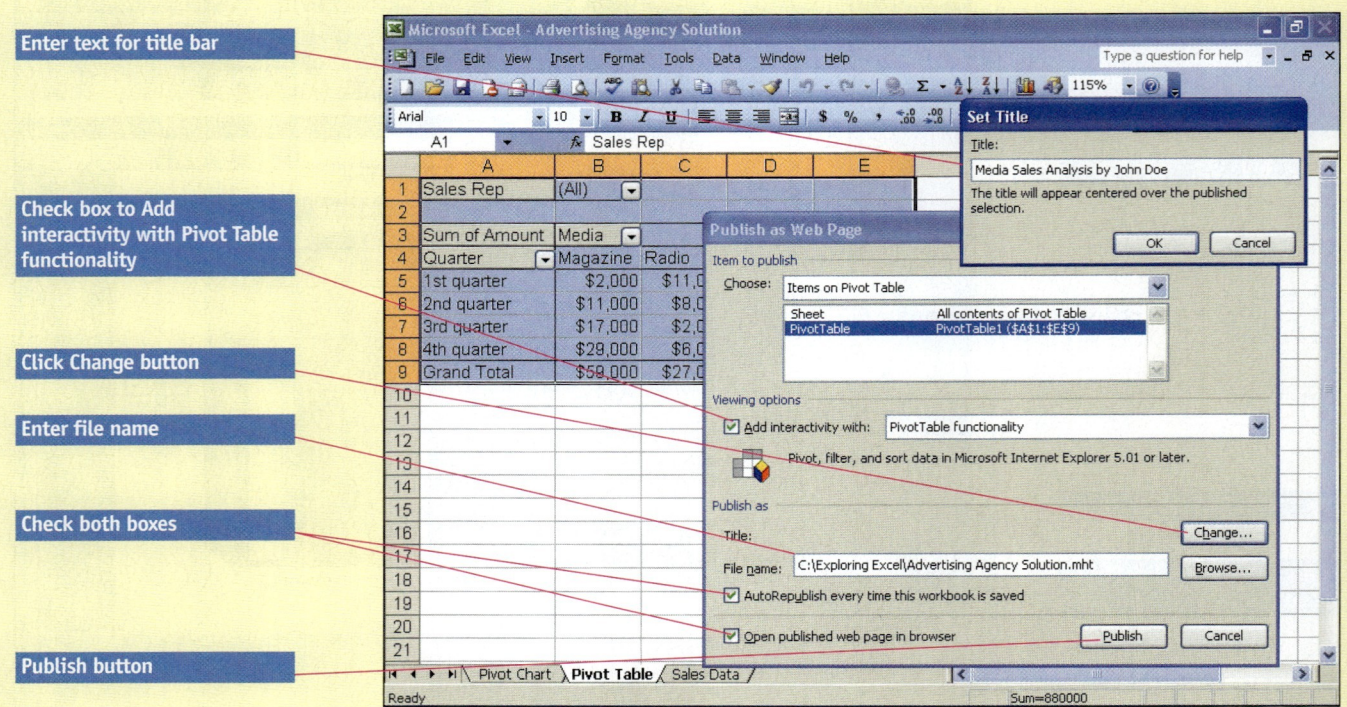

(g) Save the Pivot Table as a Web Page (step 7)

FIGURE 7.16   Hands-on Exercise 3 (*continued*)

SINGLE FILE WEB PAGE

Microsoft Office 2003 introduces the Single File Web Page (MHTML) format that saves all of the elements of a Web page, including text and graphics, in a single file. (A supporting folder to hold the extra elements was created previously.) The new format enables you to upload a single file to a Web server, as opposed to sending multiple files and folders. It also lets you send the entire page as a single e-mail attachment. The new file format is supported by Internet Explorer 4.0 and higher.

Step 8: **Pivot the Web Page**

- The pivot table will open automatically in your browser because of the option you selected in the previous step. If Internet Explorer is your default browser, you will see the pivot table in Figure 7.16h.

- If Netscape Navigator is your default browser, you will be prompted to install the Microsoft Web components, after which you should see the pivot table.

- Pivot the table so that its appearance matches Figure 7.16h. Thus, you need to drag the **Sales Rep button** to the column area and the **Media button** to the row area to the right of the Quarter field. (You can click the **Fields List button** on the Pivot Table toolbar to display/hide the fields in the table, should you lose a field button.)

- Click the **Plus sign** next to each quarter to display the detailed information. Click the **Print button** on the Internet Explorer toolbar to print the pivot table for your instructor.

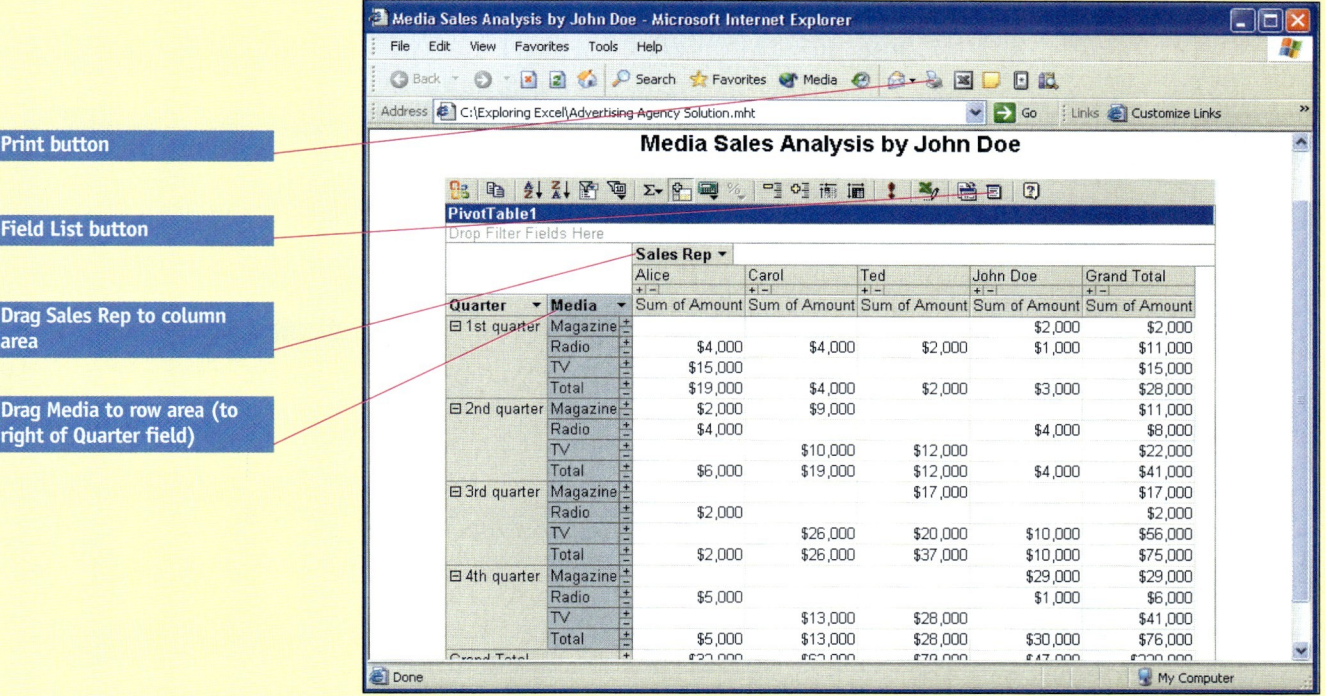

(h) Pivot the Web Page (step 8)

FIGURE 7.16 Hands-on Exercise 3 (*continued*)

XML IS NOT HTML

Extensible Markup Language, or XML for short, is an industry standard for structuring data. It is very different from HTML and it is not intended as a replacement. HTML describes how a document should look; e.g., <B>John Doe</B> indicates that John Doe should appear in boldface, but it does not tell us anything more. You don't know that "John" is the first name or that "Doe" is the last name. XML, on the other hand, is data about data, and it lets you define your own tags; e.g., <name><first>John</first><last>Doe</last></name>. The XML codes can be read by any XML-compliant application and processed accordingly. Formatting can also be implemented in XML through style sheets.

Step 9: Change the Underlying Data

- Click the **Excel button** on the Windows taskbar to return to Excel. Click the **Sales Data worksheet** and change the data for John Doe's (your name) magazine sales in the first quarter from $2000 to $22000.

- Click the **Worksheet tab** for the pivot table. Click anywhere in the pivot table and click the **Refresh External Data button** on the Pivot Table toolbar. The magazine sales in the 1st quarter increase to $22,000 and the grand total changes to $240,000.

- Click the **Save button** to save the changes to the worksheet. You will see the dialog box in Figure 7.16i. Click the option button to **Enable the Autopublish feature**. Click **OK**.

- Return to Internet Explorer. Click the **Refresh button** on the Pivot Table toolbar to update the Web page. The numbers within the Web pivot table change to reflect the change in magazine sales. If the numbers do not refresh, close Internet Explorer, reopen it, and then reopen the Web page from the Exploring Excel folder.

- Close Internet Explorer. Close Excel. Click **Yes** if prompted to save the changes.

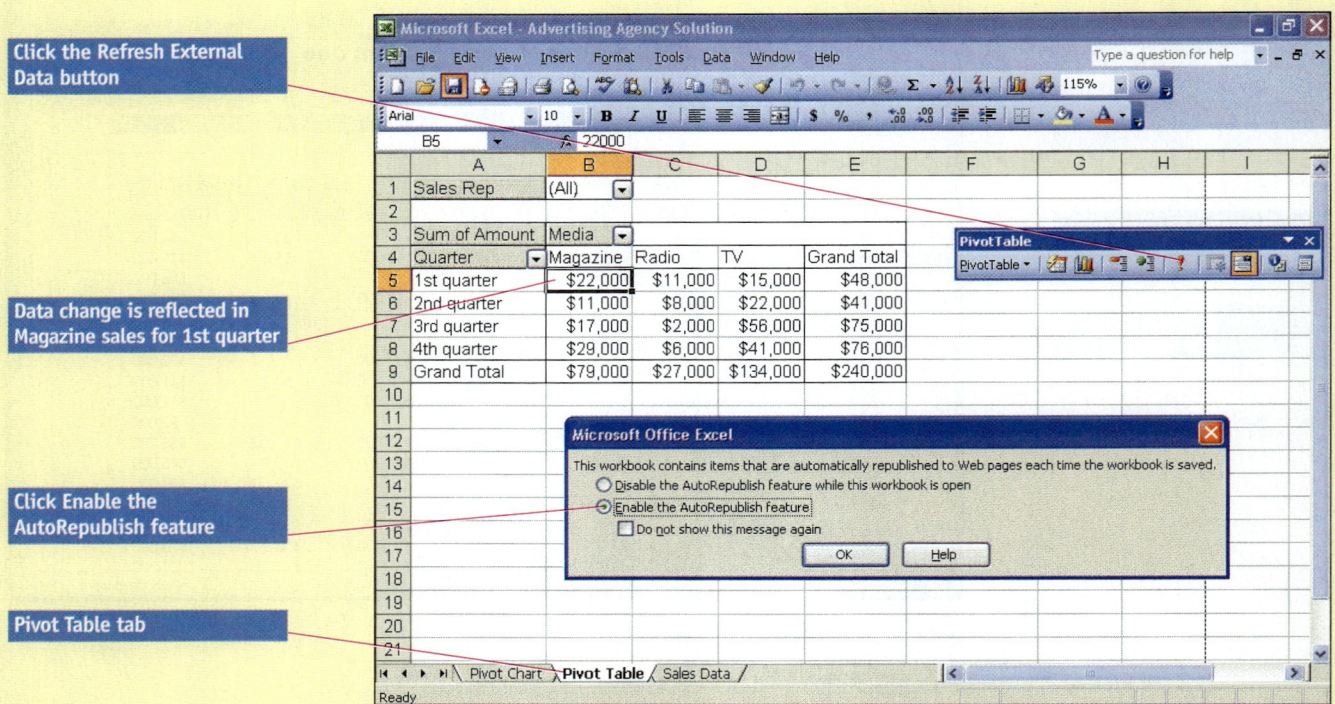

(i) Change the Underlying Data (step 9)

FIGURE 7.16 Hands-on Exercise 3 (*continued*)

THE NEED TO REFRESH

A pivot table and/or a Web page based on a pivot table do not automatically reflect changes in the underlying data. You must first refresh the pivot table as it exists within the workbook, by clicking in the pivot table, then clicking the refresh button on the Pivot Table toolbar. Next, you must save the workbook and enable the AutoPublish feature. And finally, the Single File Web page format requires you to close Internet Explorer, reopen it, and then reopen the Web page.

SUMMARY

A list is an area in a worksheet that contains rows of similar data. The first row in the list contains the column labels (field names). Each additional row contains data for a specific record. A data form provides an easy way to add, edit, and delete records in a list.

The Text Import Wizard converts data in either fixed width or delimited format to an Excel workbook. The wizard is displayed automatically if you attempt to open a text file. Data can also be imported into an Excel workbook from other applications such as Microsoft Access.

XML (Extensible Markup Language) enables a developer to create customized tags to define data within a file. It is an industry standard for structuring data and not a Microsoft product. XML is not to be confused with HTML (Hypertext Markup Language), nor is it intended as a replacement for HTML. Microsoft Excel 2003 provides full XML support to exchange information between an XML source document and an Excel workbook. You attach the XML definition or schema to the workbook and then you map the XML elements in the schema to the cells in your workbook.

A date is stored internally as an integer number corresponding to the number of days since 1900. (January 1, 1900 is stored as the number 1.) The number of elapsed days between two dates can be determined by simple subtraction. The TODAY function always returns the current date (the date on which a worksheet is created or retrieved).

A filtered list displays only those records that meet specific criteria. Filtering is implemented through AutoFilter or the Advanced Filter command. The latter enables you to specify a criteria range and to copy the selected records elsewhere in the worksheet.

The Sort command arranges a list according to the value of one or more keys (known as the primary, secondary, and tertiary keys). Each key may be in ascending or descending sequence.

The database functions (DSUM, DAVERAGE, DMAX, DMIN, and DCOUNT) have three arguments: the associated list, the field name, and the criteria range. The simplest criteria range consists of two rows and as many fields as there are in the list.

The Subtotals command uses a summary function (such as SUM, AVERAGE, or COUNT) to compute subtotals for data groups within a list. The data is displayed in outline view, where outline symbols can be used to suppress or expand the detail records.

A pivot table extends the capability of individual database functions by presenting the data in summary form. It divides the records in a list into categories, then computes summary statistics for those categories. Pivot tables provide the utmost flexibility in that you can vary the row or column categories and/or the way that the statistics are computed. A pivot chart extends the capability of a pivot table to a chart.

KEY TERMS

Advanced Filter command 353	DMAX function 355	Insert Rows command 337
Analysis ToolPak 360	DMIN function 355	ISERROR function 364
Ascending sequence 339	DSUM function 355	Key 336
AutoFilter command 352	Extensible Markup	List 336
Criteria range 353	Language (XML) 342	Outline symbols 357
Data 350	Field 336	Pivot chart 369
Data form 338	Field name 336	Pivot table 369
Database 336	File 336	Pivot Table Wizard 369
Database functions 355	Filtered list 352	Record 336
Date arithmetic 358	Fixed width format 341	Refresh command 369
DAVERAGE function 355	Form command 338	Schema 342
DCOUNT function 355	Hypertext Markup	Single File Web Page 378
Delete command 337	Language (HTML) 342	Sort command 339
Delimited format 341	Information 350	Subtotals command 357
Descending sequence 339	Insert Columns command 337	Text Import Wizard 341
Division by zero 364	Insert Name command 356	TODAY() function 358

MULTIPLE CHOICE

1. Which of the following best describes data management in Excel?
   (a) The rows in a list correspond to records in a file
   (b) The columns in a list correspond to fields in a record
   (c) Both (a) and (b)
   (d) Neither (a) nor (b)

2. How should a list be placed within a worksheet?
   (a) There should be at least one blank row between the list and the other entries in the worksheet
   (b) There should be at least one blank column between the list and the other entries in the worksheet
   (c) Both (a) and (b)
   (d) Neither (a) nor (b)

3. Which of the following is suggested for the placement of database functions within a worksheet?
   (a) Above or below the list with at least one blank row separating the database functions from the list to which they refer
   (b) To the left or right of the list with at least one blank column separating the database functions from the list to which they refer
   (c) Both (a) and (b)
   (d) Neither (a) nor (b)

4. Cells A21:B22 have been defined as the criteria range, cells A21 and B21 contain the field names City and Title, respectively, and cells A22 and B22 contain New York and Manager. The selected records will consist of:
   (a) All employees in New York, regardless of title
   (b) All managers, regardless of the city
   (c) Only the managers in New York
   (d) All employees in New York (regardless of title) or all managers

5. Cells A21:B23 have been defined as the criteria range, cells A21 and B21 contain the field names City and Title, respectively, and cells A22 and B23 contain New York and Manager, respectively. The selected records will consist of:
   (a) All employees in New York regardless of title
   (b) All managers regardless of the city
   (c) Only the managers in New York
   (d) All employees in New York and all managers

6. If employees are to be listed so that all employees in the same city appear together in alphabetical order by the employee's last name:
   (a) City and last name are both considered to be the primary key
   (b) City and last name are both considered to be the secondary key
   (c) City is the primary key and last name is the secondary key
   (d) Last name is the primary key and city is the secondary key

7. Which of the following can be used to delete a record from a database?
   (a) The Edit Delete command
   (b) The Data Form command
   (c) Both (a) and (b)
   (d) Neither (a) nor (b)

8. Which of the following is true about the DAVERAGE function?
   (a) It has a single argument
   (b) It can be entered into a worksheet using the Function Wizard
   (c) Both (a) and (b)
   (d) Neither (a) nor (b)

9. Which of the following can be converted to an Excel workbook?
   (a) A text file in delimited format
   (b) A text file in fixed width format
   (c) Both (a) and (b)
   (d) Neither (a) nor (b)

10. Which of the following is recommended to distinguish the first row in a list (the field names) from the remaining entries (the data)?
    (a) Insert a blank row between the first row and the remaining rows
    (b) Insert a row of dashes between the first row and the remaining rows
    (c) Either (a) or (b)
    (d) Neither (a) nor (b)

...continued

multiple choice

11. The AutoFilter command:
    (a) Permanently deletes records from the associated list
    (b) Requires the specification of a criteria range elsewhere in the worksheet
    (c) Either (a) or (b)
    (d) Neither (a) nor (b)

12. Which of the following is true of the Sort command?
    (a) The primary key must be in ascending sequence
    (b) The secondary key must be in descending sequence
    (c) Both (a) and (b)
    (d) Neither (a) nor (b)

13. What is the best way to enter January 21, 2004 into a worksheet, given that you create the worksheet on that date, and further, that you always want to display that specific date?
    (a) =TODAY()
    (b) 1/21/2004
    (c) Both (a) and (b) are equally acceptable
    (d) Neither (a) nor (b)

14. Which of the following best describes the relationship between the Sort and Subtotals commands?
    (a) The Sort command should be executed before the Subtotals command
    (b) The Subtotals command should be executed before the Sort command
    (c) The commands can be executed in either sequence
    (d) There is no relationship because the commands have nothing to do with one another

15. Which of the following may be implemented in an existing pivot table?
    (a) A row field may be added or deleted
    (b) A column field may be added or deleted
    (c) Both (a) and (b)
    (d) Neither (a) nor (b)

16. How many rows (including the header row) are necessary in a criteria range that selects employees in the New York Office who earn more than $100,000 annually?
    (a) 1
    (b) 2
    (c) 3
    (d) 4

17. You have applied the Advanced Filter command to filter a customer list in place, expecting to see a subset of the entire customer list. All of the customers were displayed, however. What is the most likely reason?
    (a) There is a blank row in the criteria range
    (b) There is a blank row in the list (database)
    (c) Both (a) and (b)
    (d) Neither (a) nor (b)

18. You want to use the Subtotals command to show total salaries for each location with the locations appearing in alphabetical order. What should you do before executing the Subtotals command?
    (a) Sort the list by salary in ascending order
    (b) Sort the list by salary in descending order
    (c) Sort the list by location in ascending order
    (d) Sort the list by location in descending order

ANSWERS

1. c	7. c	13. b
2. c	8. b	14. a
3. a	9. c	15. c
4. c	10. d	16. b
5. d	11. d	17. a
6. c	12. d	18. c

PRACTICE WITH EXCEL

1. **The Top Ten Filter:** Figure 7.17 displays a workbook containing three worksheets, each with a different view of the same data about the United States. Open the *Chapter 7 Practice 1* workbook in the Exploring Excel folder, which contains just the original data worksheet. Proceed as follows:

   a. Click in cell F5 and enter the formula to compute the population density for the first state in the list. Format the cell to display the value to zero decimal places. Copy the formula to the remaining rows in the list.

   b. Format the worksheet appropriately. You do not have to match our formatting exactly.

   c. Right click the worksheet tab, select the command to Move or Copy the worksheet, check the box to create a copy, click OK, and then rename the copied worksheet to Population Density. Copy the worksheet a second time, renaming this worksheet to 13 Original States as shown in our figure. You will now apply the AutoFilter command to each of the new worksheets.

   d. Click the tab for the Population Density worksheet. Turn on the AutoFilter command. Click the down arrow next to the Population Density field, click Top 10 to display the Top 10 AutoFilter dialog box. Be sure that you have the appropriate entries in each of the three list boxes—that is, Top rather than Bottom, 10 for the number of entries, and items rather than percentages. Click OK to display the filtered list, which displays the filtered records in the same order as in the original list. Click in column F, then click the Sort Descending button on the Standard toolbar to display the population densities in descending sequence. Add the appropriate subtitle to this worksheet.

   e. Click the tab for the 13 Original States worksheet and create a filtered list to display the first 13 states admitted to the Union. Sort the list in ascending sequence by year admitted.

   f. Press and hold the Ctrl key as you select all three worksheets to enter the group mode for editing. Create a custom footer that contains your name, the worksheet tab, and today's date. Check the boxes to show gridlines and row and column headings. Force each worksheet to fit on one page.

   g. Print the entire workbook for your instructor. Add a cover sheet to complete the assignment.

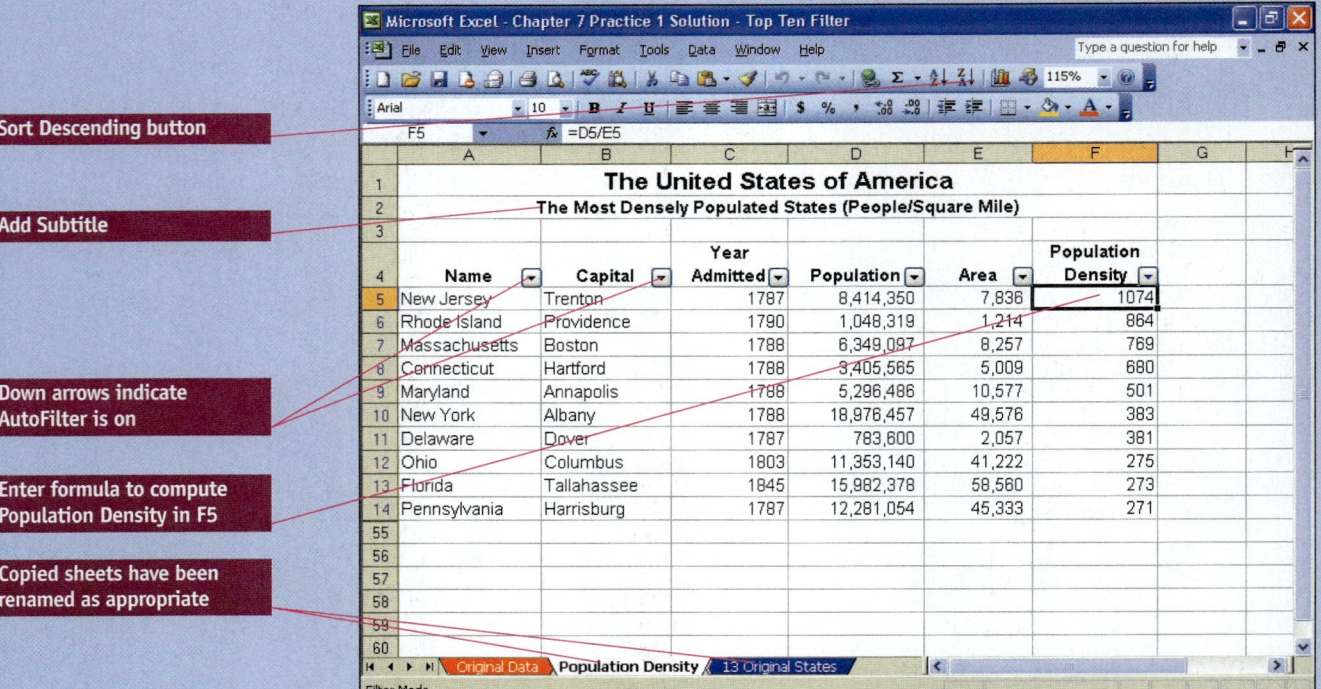

FIGURE 7.17 The Top Ten Filter (exercise 1)

384 CHAPTER 7: LIST AND DATA MANAGEMENT

practice exercises

2. **The Dean's List:** The *Chapter 7 Practice 2* workbook contains a partially completed version of the workbook in Figure 7.18. Your assignment is to open the workbook, then implement the following changes:

   a. Add a transfer student, Jeff Borow, majoring in Engineering. Jeff has completed 14 credits and has 45 quality points. (Jeff's record can be seen in Figure 7.18, but it is not in the workbook that you will retrieve from the Exploring Excel folder.) Do not, however, enter Jeff's GPA or year in school, as both will be computed from formulas in the next two steps.

   b. Enter the appropriate formula in F4 to compute the GPA for the first student (the quality points divided by the number of credits). Copy the formula to the other cells in this column.

   c. Enter the appropriate formula in cell G4 to determine the year in school for the first student. (Use the HLOOKUP function based on the table in cells B24 through E25. The entries in cells A24 and A25 contain labels and are not part of the table per se.) Copy the formula to the other cells in this column.

   d. Format the worksheet attractively. You can use our formatting or develop your own. Sort the list so that the students are listed alphabetically.

   e. Use the Advanced Filter command to filter the list in place so that the only visible students are those on the Dean's List (with a GPA greater than 3.2) as shown in Figure 7.18.

   f. Add your name as the academic advisor in cell A28. Print the worksheet two ways, with displayed values and cell formulas. Use the Page Setup command to specify landscape printing and display gridlines and row and column headings. Be sure that each printout fits on a single sheet of paper.

   g. Remove the filter condition, then print the worksheet in a different sequence—for example, by ascending or descending GPA.

   h. Add a cover sheet, then submit the complete assignment to your instructor.

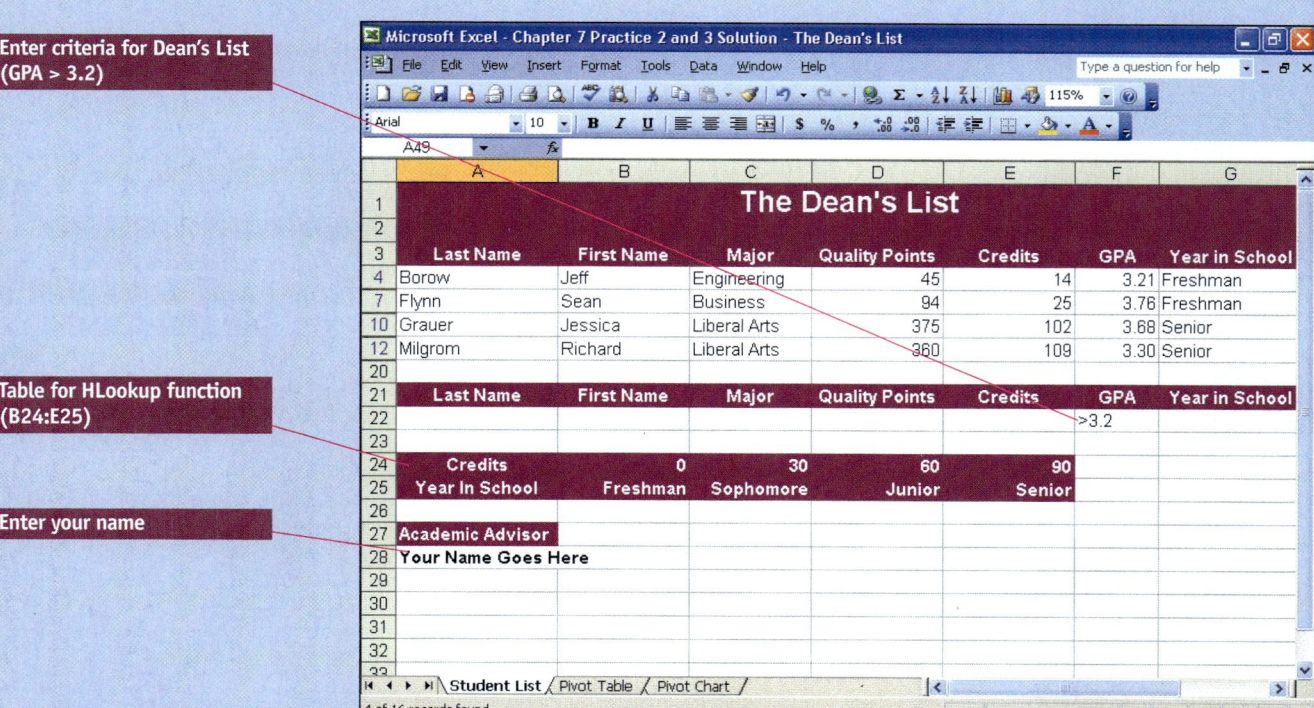

FIGURE 7.18 The Dean's List (exercise 2)

practice exercises

3. **The Pivot Chart:** Complete the previous exercise, then add a pivot table and pivot chart as shown in Figure 7.19. Start the Pivot Table Wizard. In step 1, select the option to create a PivotChart report (with PivotTable report). Specify the range of the pivot table in step 2, then in step 3 select the option to put the pivot table on a new worksheet. Rename the resulting worksheets, Sheet1 and Chart1, to Pivot Table and Pivot Chart as shown in Figure 7.19.

   a. Modify the pivot table so that major and year in school are the row and column fields, respectively. Use GPA as the data field, but be sure to specify the average GPA rather than the sum. Format the GPA to two decimal places.

   b. Change the format of the pivot chart to a 3-D clustered column chart with default formatting. Right click any column within the chart, select the Format Data Series command, then select the Series Order tab. Change the order of the columns to Freshman, Sophomore, Junior, and Senior, as opposed to the default alphabetical order.

   c. Pull down the Chart menu, click the Chart Options command to display the associated dialog box, then select the Data Table tab. Check the box to display the data table. Save the workbook.

   d. Use the Page Setup command to create a custom footer containing your name, the name of the worksheet, and today's date. Check the boxes to include gridlines and row and column headings.

   e. Print the pivot chart as shown in Figure 7.19. You do not need to print the pivot table since the equivalent information is shown in the data table that appears below the pivot chart.

   f. Pivot tables are one of the best-kept secrets in Excel, even though they have been available in the last several releases of Excel. (Pivot charts, however, were first introduced in Excel 2000.) Write a short note to a fellow student that describes how this feature facilitates data analysis.

   g. Add a cover sheet, then submit the complete assignment to your instructor.

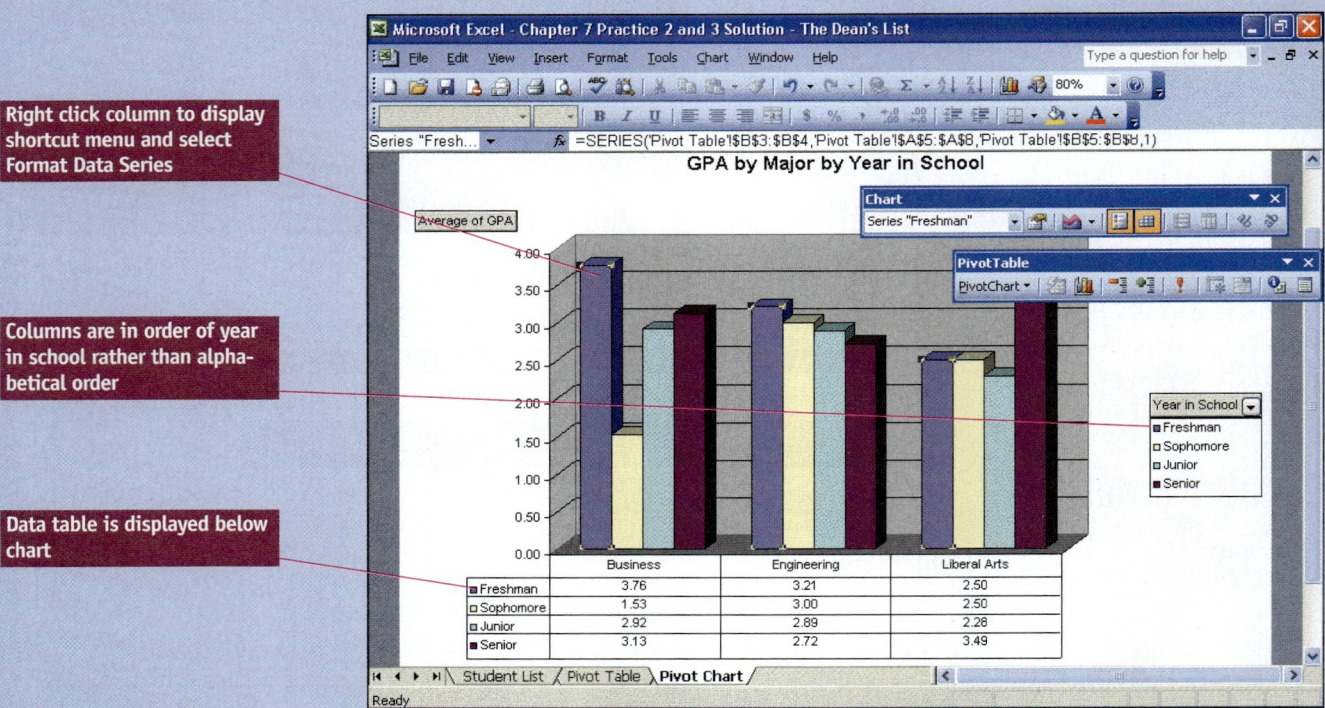

FIGURE 7.19   The Pivot Chart (exercise 3)

practice exercises

4. **Compensation Analysis:** The workbook in Figure 7.20 is used to analyze employee compensation with respect to the dollar amount and percentage of their latest salary increase. Your assignment is to open the partially completed workbook in *Chapter 7 Practice 4* and complete the workbook to match our figure.

   a. Open the workbook, then enter the formula to compute the dollar increase for the first employee in cell G4. Note, however, that not every employee has a previous salary, and thus the formula requires an IF function. Copy this formula to the remaining rows in column G.

   b. Enter the formula to compute the percentage increase for the first employee in cell H4. The percentage increase is found by dividing the amount of the increase by the previous salary. Again, not every employee has a previous salary, and hence the formula requires an IF function to avoid dividing by zero when there is no previous salary. Copy this formula to the remaining rows in column H.

   c. Enter the indicated database functions in rows 21 and 22 to reflect only those employees who have received a raise. Thus, be sure to include the greater than zero entry under Previous Salary in the criteria row.

   d. Format the worksheet in attractive fashion. You can copy our formatting or use your own design. Note, too, that you should suppress the display of zero values. (If necessary, pull down the Tools menu, click the Options command, then click the View tab and clear the box to display zero values.)

   e. Add your name as a financial analyst, then print the worksheet with both displayed values and cell formulas. Use landscape printing as necessary to be sure that the worksheet fits on a single sheet of paper.

   f. Print the worksheet in at least one other sequence—for example, by the smallest (or largest) percentage increase.

   g. Add a cover sheet, then submit the complete assignment to your instructor.

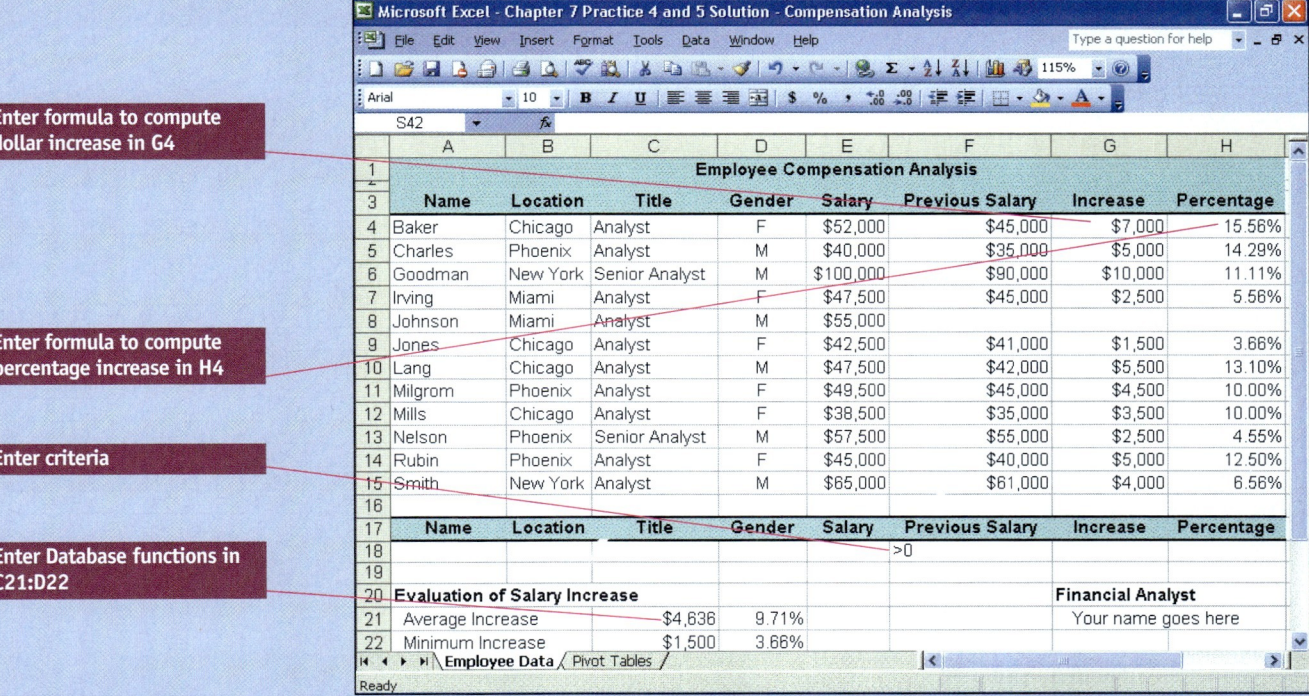

FIGURE 7.20 Compensation Analysis (exercise 4)

practice exercises

5. **Pivot Tables:** The pivot table in Figure 7.21 is based on the compensation analysis in the worksheet from the previous exercise. Open the completed *Chapter 7 Practice 4* workbook (or complete the exercise at this time), then create the associated pivot table. Proceed as follows:

   a. Click anywhere within the Employee table, pull down the Data menu, and create the pivot table in Figure 7.21. You will need to specify two data fields (the salary increase and the percent of salary increase), and choose the average function for each.

   b. Format the pivot table in an attractive fashion. You do not have to duplicate our formatting exactly, but you are to use the currency and percent symbols as appropriate, as well as a reasonable number of decimal places.

   c. Use the same style of formatting for the text (e.g., 10 point Arial) in your pivot table as in the previous exercise, so that your workbook has a uniform look. Use the Options command as described in the previous exercise to suppress the display of zero values.

   d. Use the Page Setup command to create a custom footer containing your name, the name of the worksheet, and today's date. Check the boxes to print the gridlines and row and column headings.

   e. Print the completed workbook for your instructor to show the displayed values for each worksheet. Print the Employee Data worksheet a second time to show the cell formulas.

   f. Save the worksheet, then experiment with pivoting the table by changing the row, column, and/or page fields and/or the function associated with the data fields. Pivot tables are one of the best-kept secrets in Excel even though they have been available in the last several releases of Excel. Write a short note to your instructor that describes how this feature facilitates data analysis.

   g. Add a cover sheet, then submit the complete assignment to your instructor.

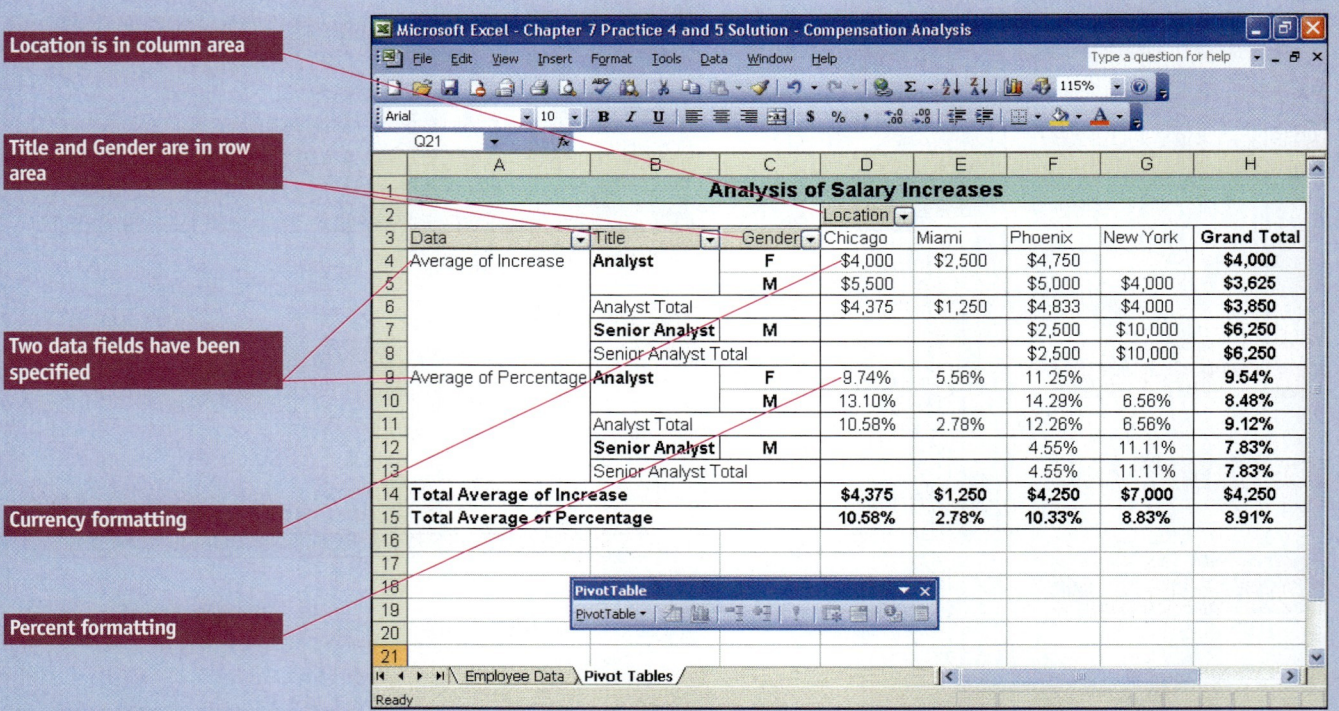

FIGURE 7.21 Pivot Tables (exercise 5)

practice exercises

6. **Compensation Report:** The document in Figure 7.22 consists of a memo created in Microsoft Word that is linked to a pivot table from exercise 5. The document was created in such a way that any change in the pivot table within the Excel workbook will be automatically reflected in the memo.

   a. Complete practice exercises 4 and 5 in this chapter to create the pivot table that will be used in the memo.

   b. Start Word, create a simple letterhead (we used the Drop Cap command in the Format menu to create our letterhead), then enter the text of the memo in Figure 7.22. You can use our text, or modify the wording as you see fit. Be sure to include your name in the signature area.

   c. Use the Windows taskbar to switch to Excel, copy either pivot table to the clipboard, then use the Paste Link command within Word to bring the pivot table into the Word document as a worksheet object.

   d. Move and/or size the table as necessary. Note, too, that you may have to insert or delete hard returns within the memo to space it properly. *Print this version of the memo for your instructor.*

   e. Prove to yourself that the linking really works by returning to Excel to modify the pivot table to show the total (as opposed to average) salary increase. Change the title of the pivot table as well.

   f. Use the Windows taskbar to return to the Word memo, which should show an updated copy of the pivot table. If you did the exercise correctly, you should see $51,000 as the total amount for all salary increases. Modify the text of the memo to say "revised" salary analysis, as opposed to "preliminary," then print this version of the memo for your instructor.

   g. Add a cover sheet, then submit the complete assignment, consisting of both versions of the memo, to your instructor.

   h. Save the Word document. Exit Word. Save the workbook. Exit Excel.

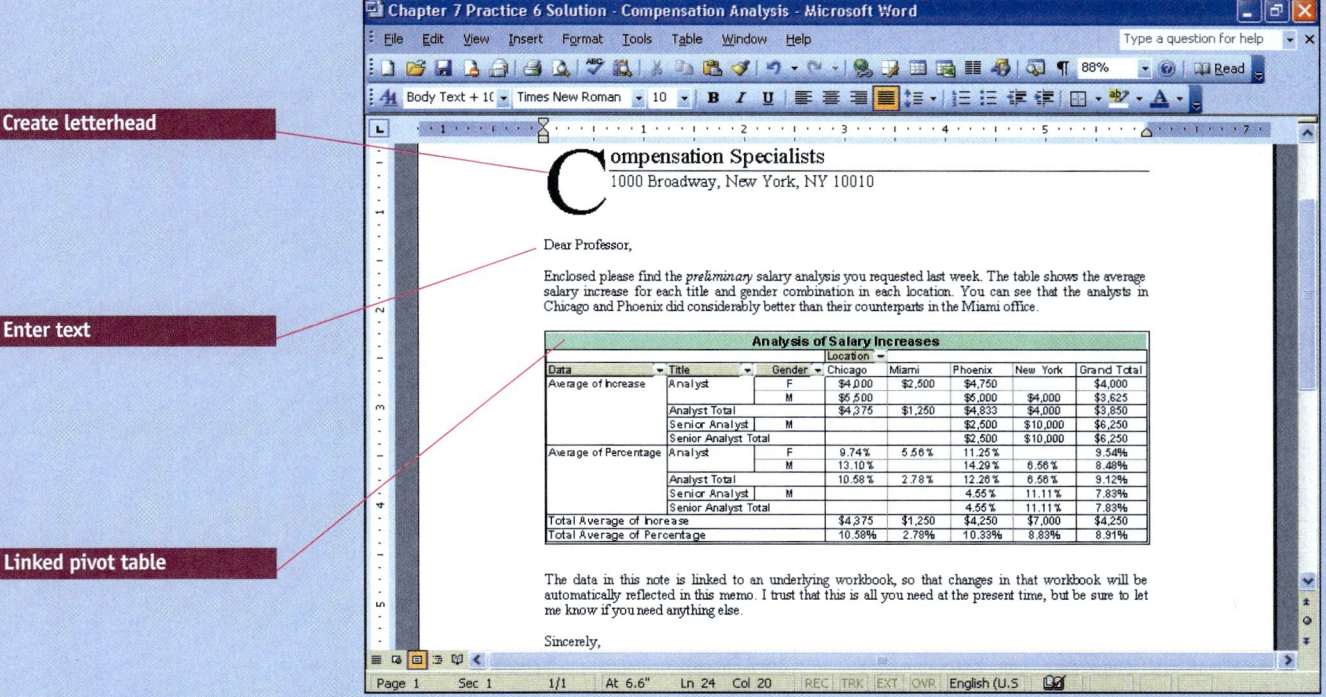

FIGURE 7.22 Compensation Report (exercise 6)

practice exercises

7. **The Wedding:** The workbook in Figure 7.23 uses the Subtotals command to group the guests at a wedding according to table number. The workbook also uses concatenation to string together the various components in each guest's name (prefix, last name, and suffix). Columns A, B, C, and D are hidden, but you can see the appropriate formula in Figure 7.23. Open the partially completed *Chapter 7 Practice 7—The Wedding* workbook and proceed as follows:

   a. Click in cell A3. Pull down the Windows menu and click the Freeze Panes command so that rows 1 and 2 are always visible. Go to cell A80, which is the first blank cell at the bottom of the list of guests. Add your name and that of your guest in the appropriate columns, then enter two as the number attending. You will be sitting at Table 01. Click in cell A81 and enter your instructor's name and guest. Your instructor will be sitting at Table 02.
   b. Click in cell E3 and enter the formula shown in Figure 7.23 to concatenate the fields within each guest's name. Copy this formula to the remaining rows in the worksheet.
   c. Click and drag to select the column headings for columns A, B, C, and D so that all four columns are selected. Pull down the Format menu, click the Column command, then click the Hide command.
   d. Go to cell F3. Click the Sort Ascending button to sequence the guests by table number. Pull down the Data menu and click the Subtotals command to display the associated dialog box. The totals should be calculated at each change in Table; that is, use the Sum function to add the total to the Number field. Check the boxes to replace current subtotals and to place the summary below data.
   e. Highlight the rows that contain your name and your instructor's name. Click and drag to select cells E1:G1, then click the Merge and Center button. Increase the font size in the worksheet title, and then click the Align Right button. Add a clip art image as appropriate.
   f. Print the completed worksheet for your instructor. The worksheet looks better if it is centered and printed on two pages. Pull down the View menu, click the Page Break command, then adjust the break so that the guests at Table 08 start the second page. Use the Page Setup command to repeat rows 1 and 2 on both pages.

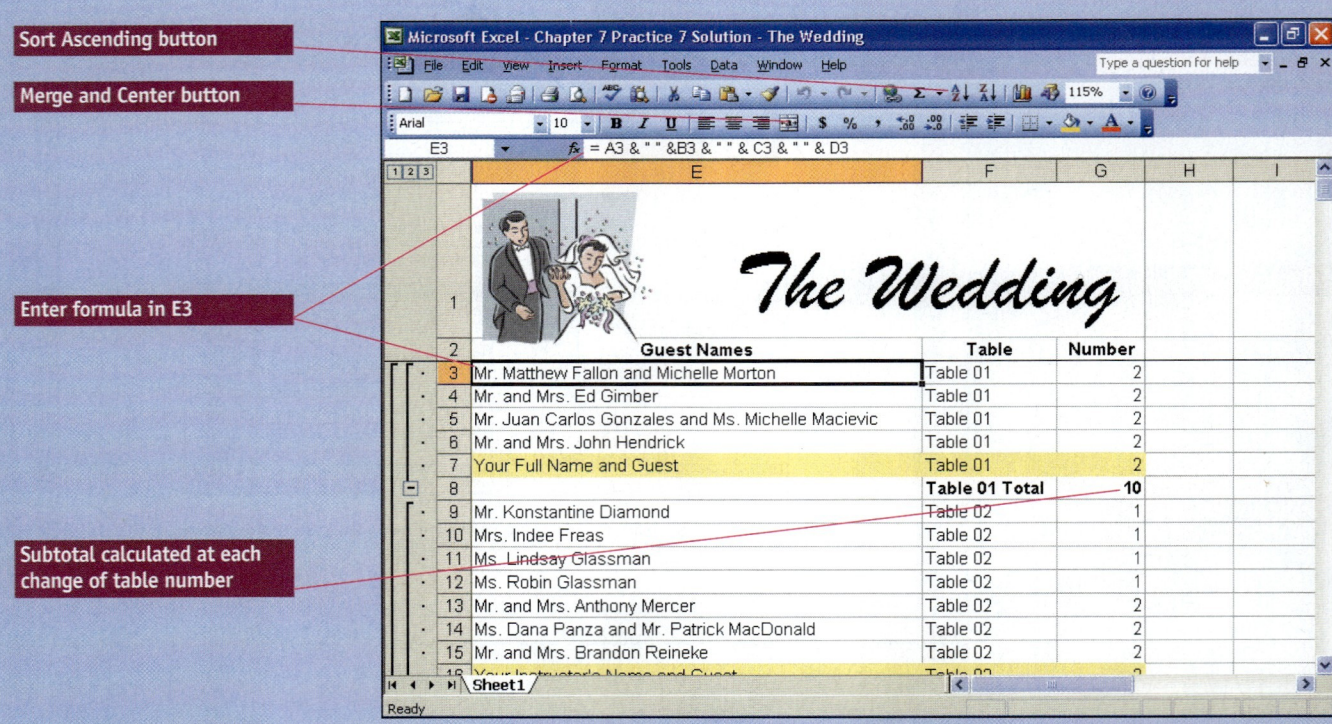

FIGURE 7.23 The Wedding (exercise 7)

practice exercises

8. **Consumer Loans:** The worksheet in Figure 7.24 displays selected loans (those with a loan type of "A") from a comprehensive set of loan records. Your assignment is to open the partially completed *Chapter 7 Practice 8* workbook in the Exploring Excel folder to create the worksheet in our figure.

   a. Open the workbook, then go to cell H4, the cell containing the ending date for the first loan. Enter the formula to compute the ending date, based on the starting date and the term of the loan. For the sake of simplicity, you do not have to account for leap year. Thus, to compute the ending date, multiply the term of the loan by 365 and add that result to the starting date. Be sure to format the starting and ending dates to show a date format.

   b. Go to cell I4 and enter the PMT function to compute the monthly payment for the first loan. Copy the formulas in cells H4 and I4 to the remaining rows in the worksheet.

   c. Enter the indicated criteria in cell D29, then enter the indicated database functions toward the bottom of the worksheet.

   d. Use the Advanced Filter command to filter the list in place to display only those loans that satisfy the indicated criteria as shown in Figure 7.24.

   e. Format the list in attractive fashion. Add your name as the loan officer.

   f. Look closely at the bottom of Figure 7.24 and note the presence of a Pivot Table worksheet. You are to create a pivot table that has the loan type and branch location in the row and column fields, respectively. Your pivot table is to contain two data fields, the total amount of the loans, and the average interest rate.

   g. Print the entire workbook for your instructor. Print both the displayed values and cell formulas for the loans worksheet, but only the displayed values for the pivot table. Use the Page Setup command to create a custom footer containing your name, the name of the worksheet, and today's date. Be sure to print the gridlines and row and column headings.

   h. Add a cover sheet, then submit the complete assignment to your instructor.

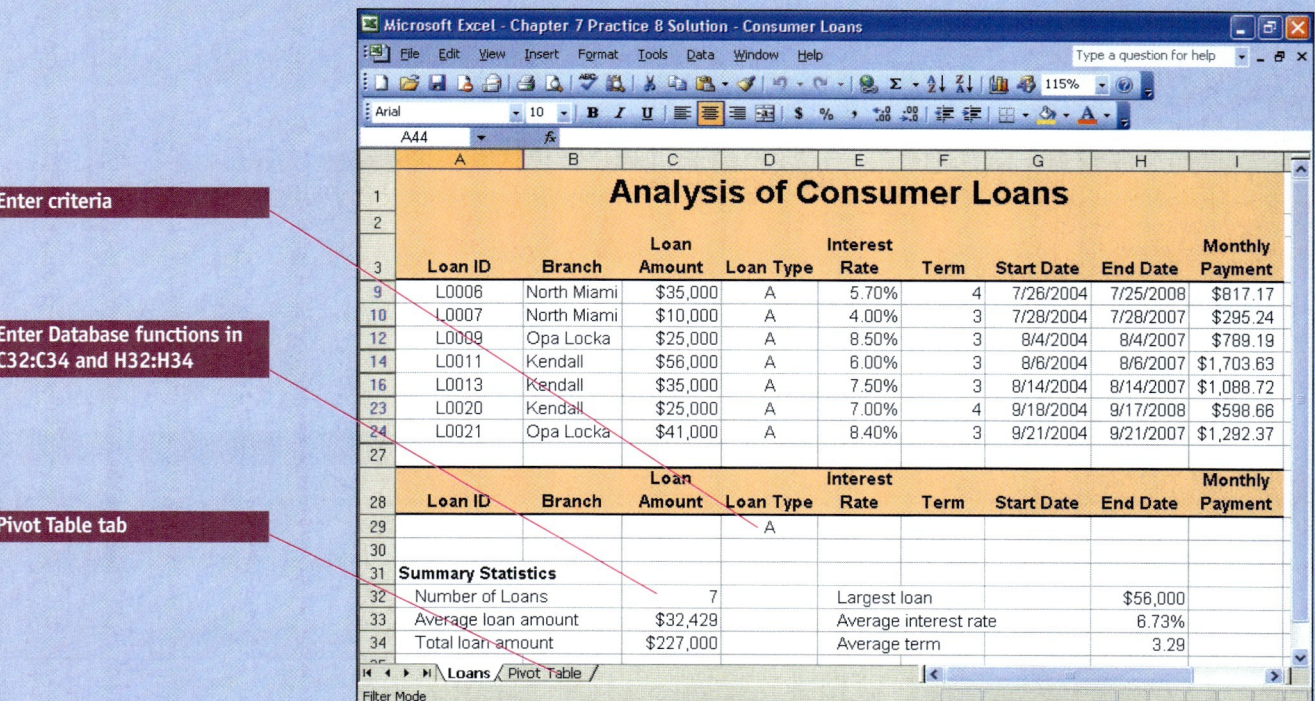

FIGURE 7.24 Consumer Loans (exercise 8)

practice exercises

9. **The Analysis ToolPak:** The degree to which you will benefit from the analysis tools in Excel depends in part on your proficiency in statistics. Even if you are not a statistician, however, you can use a few basic techniques as shown in Figure 7.25. This worksheet uses three tools to perform some basic analysis. Start Excel, open a new workbook, and proceed as follows:

   a. Pull down the Tools menu and click the Add-Ins command to display the associated dialog box. Check the box for the Analysis TookPak. Click OK.

   b. Pull down the Tools menu a second time and click the Data Analysis command that has been added to the Tools menu. Scroll down the list of analysis tools until you can select random number generation. Click OK to display the Random Number Generation dialog box where you specify the type of random numbers that you want to generate.

   c. Enter 1 as the number of variables and 200 as the number of random numbers. Choose Normal as the distribution and enter 0 and 1 as the mean and standard deviation, respectively. Specify cell A2 as the output range and click OK. You should see 200 random numbers in cells A2 through A201. (Your values will be different from ours.) Click in cell A1 and enter Random Number as the column heading.

   d. Pull down the Tools menu, click the Data Analysis command, and then scroll down the list of analysis tools until you can select Descriptive Statistics. Enter A1:A201 as the input range, check the box that indicates there are labels in the first row, specify C1 as the output range, and check the box for summary statistics. Click OK. The descriptive statistics for the 200 random numbers will appear in columns C and D. The mean and standard deviation will differ from the theoretical values of 0 and 1, but they should be close.

   e. Enter the lower bounds for the histogram you are about to create in cells F1 through F13 as shown in Figure 7.25. Execute the Data Analysis command one final time and specify Histogram as the analysis tool. Enter A2:A201 as the input range and F2:F12 as the Bin range. Specify C17 as the output range. Click OK to create the histogram. Note how the values are clustered around the middle, which is what you'd expect from a normal distribution.

   f. Format the worksheet as appropriate and then print the completed worksheet for your instructor. Are you less intimated by statistics than previously?

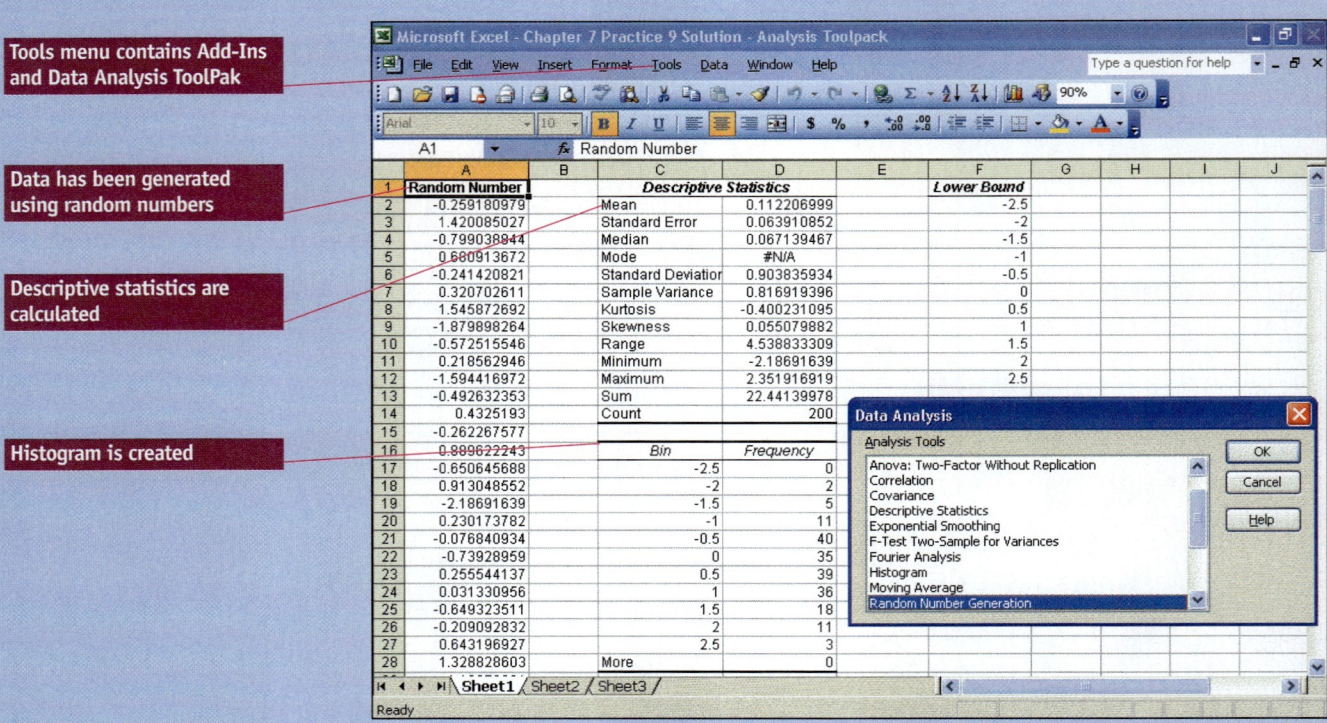

FIGURE 7.25 The Analysis ToolPak (exercise 9)

practice exercises

10. **XML and the Super Bowl:** The workbook in Figure 7.26 was created by importing data from an XML document into an Excel workbook, adding two new fields within the data (Winner and Victory Margin), and inserting two database functions to determine the number of times that each conference has won the big game. Proceed as follows:

   a. Start Excel. Pull down the Data menu, click the Import External Data command, and then click Import Data to display the Select Data Source dialog box. Change to the Exploring Excel folder and specify the file type as XML files. Select the *Chapter 7 Practice 10* XML document and click the Open button. Click OK when you see the message indicating that Excel will create a schema based on the XML source data.

   b. You should see the Import Data dialog box. The option button to put the data as an XML list in an existing worksheet is already selected, with cell A1 specified by default. Change the location of the list to cell A5. Click OK. The XML data is imported into the workbook.

   c. Pull down the View menu and open the XML Source task pane as shown in Figure 7.26. Click the Options button within the task pane to see the available options for an XML list. Press Esc to suppress the option list. Click the XML Maps button to explore a dialog box that allows you to add, delete, or rename an XML map. Close the XML Maps dialog box.

   d. Click in cell F5, type Winner, press the right arrow key to move to cell G5, type Victory Margin, and press Enter. These fields have been added to the list (they appear within the blue border), but they do not appear within the XML map in the task pane.

   e. Click in cell F6 and enter an IF function to determine the winner for that year. Click in cell G6. Enter the appropriate formula to display the victory margin. (Use the absolute value function to display the result as a positive number.) Copy both formulas to remaining rows in the worksheet.

   f. Complete the worksheet by developing the appropriate database functions to determine the number of times each conference has won the Super Bowl. You will need to create two criteria ranges elsewhere in the worksheet.

   g. Format the worksheet in an attractive fashion. Print the complete workbook for your instructor to show both displayed values and cell formulas.

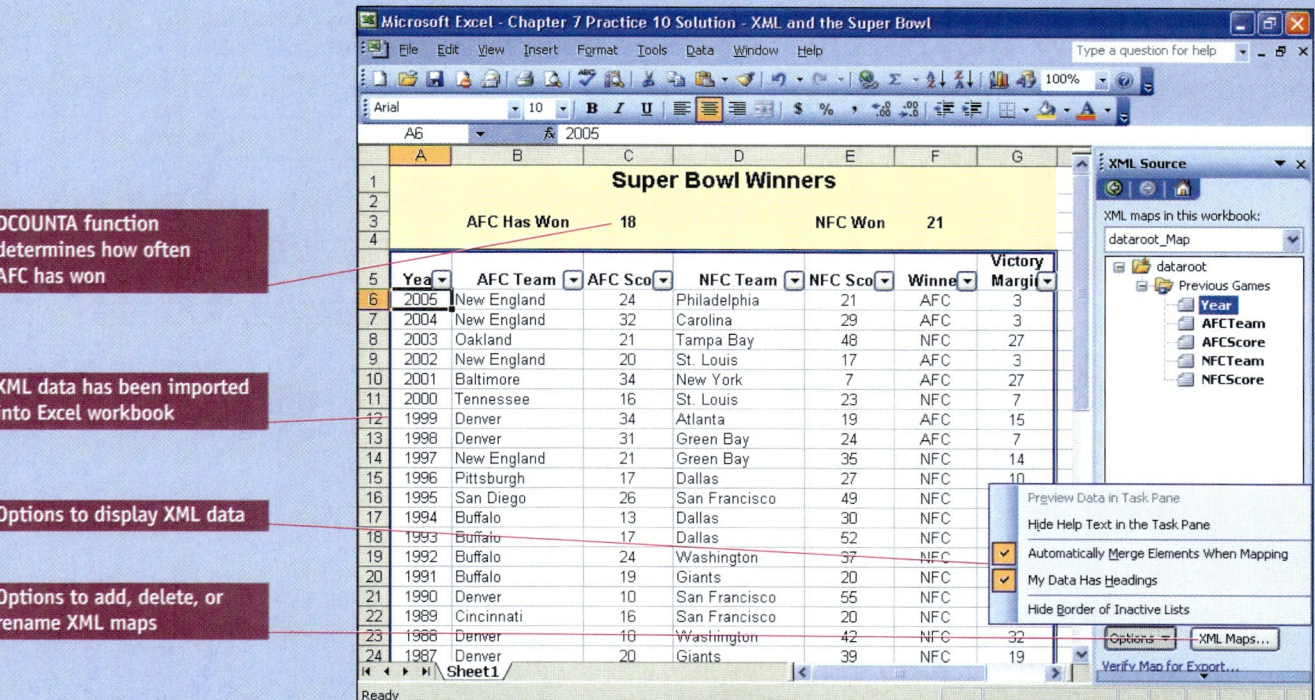

FIGURE 7.26 XML and the Super Bowl (exercise 10)

practice exercises

11. **The Job Search:** The worksheet in Figure 7.27 is used by a personnel officer to search through a long list of applicants to identify qualified individuals to invite to a follow-up interview. This particular example displays the results of a search for account reps requesting less than $45,000 in base salary, who were judged to be experienced in the field, but who do not require relocation. Thirteen individuals were found to satisfy these criteria as can be seen by the DCOUNTA function in cell E5. Open the partially completed *Chapter 7 Practice 11—The Job Search* workbook and proceed as follows:

   a. Use the Insert Name command to define the range names Criteria (cells A8:H9) and Database (A11:H185).

   b. Click in cell E5 and enter the DCOUNTA function in Figure 7.27. You should see 174 qualified applicants since no criteria values have been specified, and thus the function returns every record in the list. Fill in the criteria values and note that as you enter each value, the number of qualified employees is reduced until you see 13 as the final answer.

   c. Click in cell A11. Pull down the Data menu, click the Filter command, then click the Advanced Filter command. Click the option button to filter the list in place, enter Database and Criteria as the list range and criteria range, respectively, then click OK. You should see the filtered list of 13 applicants as shown in Figure 7.27.

   d. Format the worksheet in attractive fashion (you do not have to match our formatting exactly), then print the worksheet for your instructor. Use the Page Setup command to create a custom footer with your name, the date, and the name of the class you are taking. Display gridlines and row and column headings. Be sure the worksheet fits on one page.

   e. Clear the criteria range in cells A9:E9 in order to initiate a second search for bilingual employees who are applying for the position of "Director". (There are no other parameters in your search.) Click in cell A11, and then use the Advanced Filter command to display the names of qualified individuals. Print this worksheet for your instructor. Add a cover sheet, and then submit all three pages to your instructor.

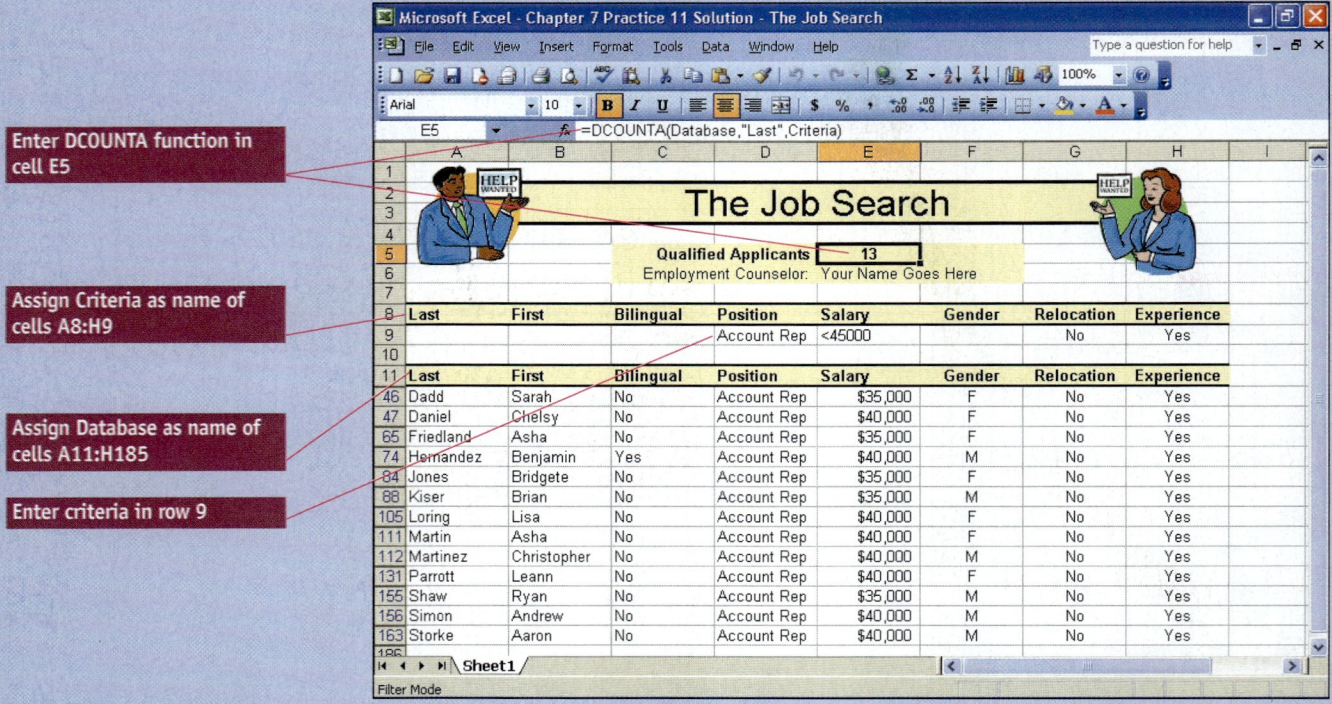

FIGURE 7.27 The Job Search (exercise 11)

practice exercises

12. **The Golf Trader:** The pivot chart in Figure 7.28 is based on the associated pivot table, which in turn is derived from the Source Data worksheet. Pivot tables can help analyze the data and discern trends that are not otherwise visible. Open the *Chapter 7 Practice 12—The Golf Trader* workbook and proceed as follows:

   a. Pull down the Edit menu, click the Replace command, enter "Moldof" as the Find What string, and your last name as the Replace with string. Click the Replace All button, and then click OK when you see the dialog box indicating 111 replacements. Close the Find and Replace Dialog box.

   b. Click in cell A2 (or anywhere within the list). Pull down the Data menu, click the PivotTable and PivotChart Report command, and then click the option button to create a Pivot Chart report with a Pivot Table. Create the pivot table in its own worksheet. The pivot table should have two fields, Category and Salesperson, which serve as the row and column fields, respectively. The Order Amount goes in the data area.

   c. Click on the worksheet tab for Sheet1, which contains the newly created pivot table. Right click any numeric entry within the body of the pivot table, click Field Settings to display the PivotTable Field dialog box, then click the Number command button to display the Format Cells dialog box. Change the formatting to Currency with no decimals. Click OK. Click OK a second time to close the PivotTable dialog box.

   d. Click anywhere in the Grand Total column, then click the Sort Descending button, so that the category with the highest sales total appears first.

   e. Click the worksheet tab for the pivot chart. Pull down the Chart menu, click the Chart Type command, and choose the Stacked Column with 3-D visual effect as the chart type. Check the box for default formatting. Click OK. Use the Chart Options command to display a data table below the chart.

   f. Change the names of the worksheet tabs to match those in Figure 7.28, then print the completed pivot chart for your instructor. Use the Page Setup command to create an appropriate custom footer, which includes the name of each worksheet. Do *not* print the Source Data worksheet, since it runs many pages due to the large quantity of data.

   g. Pivot tables and pivot charts are discussed further in the next chapter.

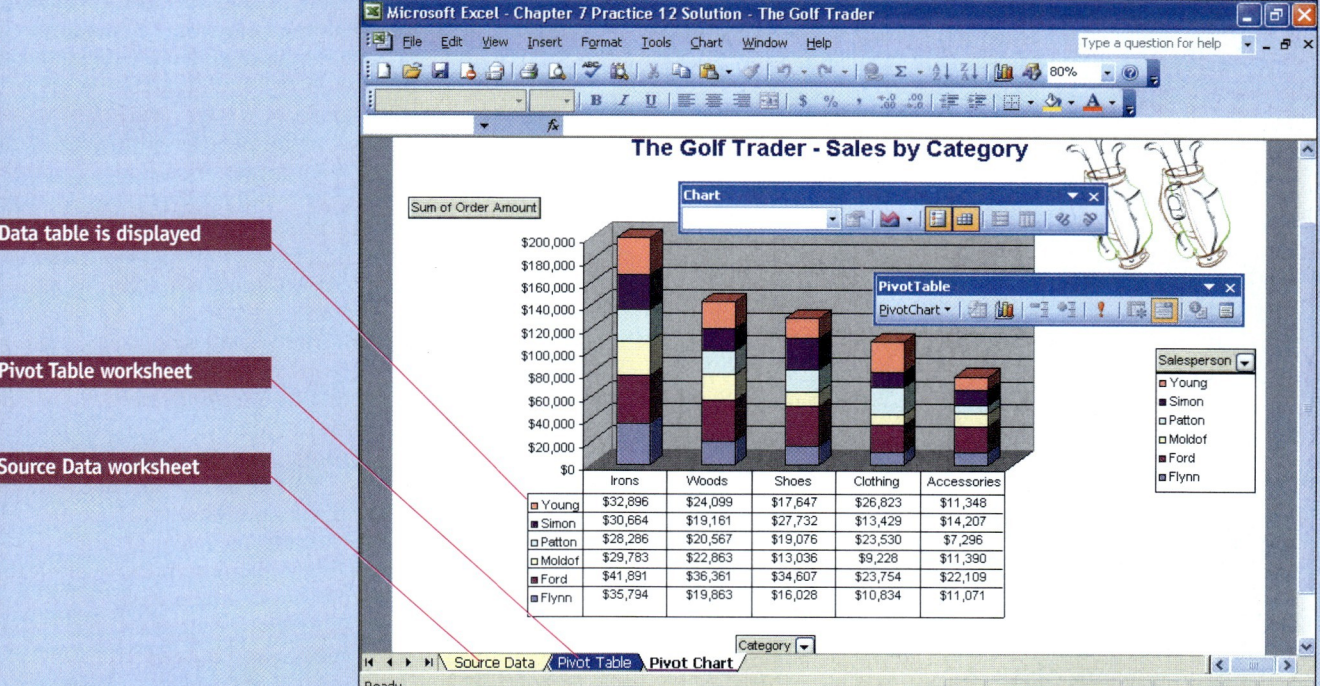

FIGURE 7.28 The Golf Trader (exercise 12)

MICROSOFT OFFICE EXCEL 2003 REVISED

MINI CASES

Asset Allocation

It's several years in the future and you find yourself happily married and financially prosperous. You and your spouse have accumulated substantial assets in a variety of accounts. Some of the money is in a regular account for use today, whereas other funds are in retirement accounts for later use. Much of the money, both regular and retirement, is invested in equities (i.e., the stock market), but a portion of your funds is also in nonequity funds such as money-market checking accounts and bank certificates of deposit. Your accounts are also in different places such as banks and brokerage houses. A summary of your accounts can be found in the *Chapter 7 Mini Case—Asset Allocation* workbook. Your assignment is to open the workbook and develop a pivot table that will enable you and your spouse to keep track of your investments.

Fly by Night Airways

Fly by Night Airways is an independent airline offering charters and special tours. The airline has several independent agents, each of whom books trips for the airline. The data for all trips is maintained in the *Chapter 7 Mini Case—Fly by Night Airlines* Access database that is stored in the Exploring Excel folder. Your assignment is to start a new Excel workbook and import the data from the Access database into the Excel workbook to create a pivot table for data analysis. (Pull down the File menu, click the Open command, specify an Access database in the File Type list box, select the database in the Exploring Excel folder, and then click the Open button.)

Your pivot table should show the amount of contracts by marketing representative and contract status (whether the trip is still in the proposal stage or whether it has already been signed). The table should also have the flexibility to show all trips or trips that do or do not require passage through customs. Use the Page Setup command to create a custom footer that contains your name and the name of the worksheet. Print the completed workbook for your instructor.

Chapter Recap—The Spa Experts

Dan and Tim like to relax. The two fraternity brothers went into business shortly after graduation selling spas and hot tubs. Business has been good, and their expansive showroom and wide selection appeal to a variety of customers. The partners maintain a large inventory to attract the impulse buyer and currently have agreements with three manufacturers: Serenity Spas, The Original Hot Tub, and Port-a-Spa. Each manufacturer offers spas and hot tubs that appeal to different segments of the market with prices ranging from affordable to exorbitant.

The business has grown rapidly, and there is a need to analyze the sales data in order to increase future profits—for example, which vendor generates the most sales? Who is the leading salesperson? Do most customers purchase their spa or finance it? Are sales promotions necessary to promote business, or will customers pay the full price? Dan has created a simple workbook that has sales data for the current month. Each transaction appears on a separate row and contains the name of the salesperson, the manufacturer, and the amount of the sale. There is also an indication of whether the spa was purchased or financed, and whether a promotion was in effect.

Your assignment is to review the chapter, open the *Chapter 7 Ending Case Study—The Spa Experts* workbook, and complete the workbook. A criteria range has been established at the top of the worksheet that displays the sales performance for any combination of salesperson, manufacturer, and/or other fields within the sales list. The summary statistics appear immediately below the criteria range, but you will have to enter the appropriate data management functions to compute the indicated statistics.

Use the Edit command to substitute your name for Jessica Benjamin throughout the worksheet. You can then enter your name in cell B5 (within the criteria range) to view your sales statistics for the month. Create a pivot table and associated pivot chart (each in its own worksheet) that displays summary information by vendor and salesperson.

CHAPTER 8

Data Analysis: A Capstone Chapter

OBJECTIVES

After reading this chapter you will:

1. Discuss several techniques used to analyze data within Excel.
2. Use the AND and OR functions to select records within a list.
3. Distinguish between the COUNT, COUNTA, and COUNTIF functions.
4. Use the CONCATENATE and TRIM functions.
5. Use the Goal Seek command.
6. Use the RANK and QUARTILE functions to order the records in a list.
7. Use the MOD and ROW functions with conditional formatting to shade alternate rows in a spreadsheet.
8. Define a Pareto chart; explain the meaning of the 80/20 rule.
9. Explore the advanced features in pivot tables and pivot charts.
10. Customize a chart by formatting the data series and chart background.

hands-on exercises

1. **THE ADMISSIONS OFFICE**
   Input: The Admissions Office
   Output: The Admissions Office Solution

2. **THE GRADUATING CLASS**
   Input: The Graduating Class
   Output: The Graduating Class Solution

3. **THE MEN'S STORE**
   Input: The MEN'S STORE
   Output: The MEN'S STORE Solution

4. **THE RESTAURANT**
   Input: The Restaurant
   Output: The Restaurant Solution

CASE STUDY
THE PERSONAL COMPUTER STORE

Melissa Sabella founded The Personal Computer Store in 1999, and it has done extremely well. Revenue, and more importantly net income, has grown at a compound rate of 25%. The fact that the store is across the street from a 30,000-student campus has helped, but Melissa's business acumen and personal touch are the real reasons for the success. Indeed, Melissa has made her store "the place" for students to buy their computers, software, and associated accessories. One way she has accomplished this is by building strong relationships with faculty and administrators. Melissa has also created a vibrant student intern program, which provides an unending source of advertising and good will.

You have been working at the store as an intern since the beginning of this semester. One of your primary tasks is to staff the "Service Desk" where you greet customers as they arrive, and more importantly, identify and hopefully solve their problems. If not, you provide the customer with a "loaner computer" while his or her machine is being serviced. You have been on the job for only two months and have already logged almost 200 repair orders. Needless to say, Melissa is very concerned and she has asked you to study the list of repair orders to see if you can discern a pattern, such as which hardware component is failing with the greatest frequency. ■

Your assignment is to read the chapter and study the various ways to analyze data in Microsoft Excel. Look closely at the third example that describes the Pareto Principle or 80/20 rule, which states that 80% (the majority) of the activity is generated from 20% (a minority) of the transactions. You will then open the *Chapter 8 Case Study—The Personal Computer Store* workbook in order to analyze the approximately two hundred repair orders. Create a pivot table that counts the number of problems of each type, and then display this information in a Pareto chart. How closely did the data follow the 80/20 rule?

DROWNING IN DATA

The opening case study describes a problem in which the owner of a small business needs to analyze the available data in order to take corrective action. The problem is not that she is lacking data (there is more than enough), but that she does not know what to do with the data that are available. This problem is more widespread than you might think. It is important, therefore, that every organization establish a coherent policy for ***data analysis***, which in turn requires answers to the following questions:

1. What data is currently available? Is it sufficient? If not, what additional data is required? How often is the data collected?
2. How do we analyze the data we have? How can we present the analysis so that it is clear to management and others in the organization?
3. What future decisions will be made by the business or organization based on the data analysis?

Data analysis is a complex topic, and entire books have been written on the subject. Our premise is that you need not look beyond Excel in many cases, and that you should use what you already know, as opposed to reinventing the wheel. Our objective, therefore, is to show you what you can do within Excel. To that end we have created four different examples in this chapter.

Each example uses a combination of techniques to analyze several hundred records and then present the results in meaningful fashion. Some of the commands have been presented in earlier chapters, but the review is beneficial. Indeed, this is a "capstone chapter" that reviews and extends everything that has come before. Our techniques include the following:

1. ***Sorting*** enables you to find individual records quickly. It can be used to identify groups of records, and/or to show you the top or bottom performers. It is performed in either an ascending or descending sequence and can pertain to a single field or to multiple fields simultaneously.
2. ***Calculating*** can be applied to data within an individual record; for example, you can compute a student's GPA by dividing the quality points by the number of credits or evaluate an employee's performance by comparing actual sales to a stated goal. Calculation can also be applied to the list as a whole by determining overall record counts, averages, totals, and so on.
3. ***Summarizing*** combines the techniques of sorting and calculating. It displays records within groups (e.g., employees by location), and then performs calculations for each group (e.g., the total or average salary for employees in each location). ***Pivot tables*** are the most effective way to summarize data in Excel.
4. ***Filtering*** or selection displays (or performs calculations on) a subset of records that satisfy specific criteria, such as employees in a specific location or customer invoices above a designated amount. Filtering can be implemented using multiple criteria through a combination of the logical "And" and "Or" operations.
5. ***Formatting*** may not seem like an analysis technique, but if you have ever used a highlighting pen, you understand its value. Basic formatting includes changes in color, font, and style (boldface and italics). ***Conditional formatting*** enables you to change the formatting in a cell according to its value; for instance, negative values can be shown in red.
6. ***Charting*** (the graphic representation of data) is an attractive and effective way to convey the results of data analysis. The Chart Wizard is the easiest way to access the many types of charts available with Excel.

THE ADMISSIONS OFFICE

Our first example of data analysis occurs within the Admissions Office of a small liberal arts college as shown in Figure 8.1a. This worksheet displays the complete list of applicants in alphabetical order by last name together with their admissions data (the SAT score and GPA from their high school). The Admissions Office has to analyze the data to determine which students it will admit to next year's freshmen class; that is, it has to answer the following questions:

1. Which students are exceptionally qualified and thus should be granted early admission? Which students are so poorly qualified that they should be denied admission immediately?
2. How should the SAT and GPA scores be weighted to create an admissions score that will objectively evaluate the applicants?
3. What threshold should be established for the admission scores in order to admit a specified number of students?
4. What percentage of the applicants are accepted?

The admissions criteria are subjective, but once established they yield an objective decision. At that point the "human element" comes into play, and the university may look at other factors such as extracurricular activities in reconsidering students who may have been rejected initially. (That decision process is beyond the scope of this discussion.) The university has set the following criteria:

1. Early admission: Students with an SAT score greater than or equal to 1400 *and* a GPA greater than or equal to 3.80 will be admitted immediately
2. Early rejection: Students with an SAT score less than 800 *or* a GPA less than or equal to 1.80 will be rejected immediately
3. Regular admission: the SAT and GPA are weighted equally; thus, the GPA is multiplied by 400 so that the maximum GPA component becomes 1600 (equal to that of the SAT). The threshold for admission is 2700.

Implementation in Excel

The Admissions Office worksheet uses a variety of functions to implement the admission criteria and tabulate the results. The ***AND*** and ***OR functions*** are used to determine the early admission (where both criteria must be satisfied) and early rejection (where either criterion is sufficient), respectively. The ***COUNTIF function*** is used to tally the number of applicants in each admissions category.

The worksheet also illustrates other techniques such as conditional formatting to highlight the admission decisions. The Admissions Officer may also use the worksheet to explore variations in the admissions criteria; for example, he or she can use the ***Goal Seek command*** to set the number of total admissions (cell I9) to a specified number, which in turn will determine the threshold score (in cell D11). In addition, the Admissions Officer can display selected groups of students through the ***AutoFilter command***, such as a list of students who were rejected, in order to review those decisions individually. Figure 8.1b illustrates a ***custom filter***, which displays only the students who were admitted (early admissions and regular decisions).

One last point before we begin, namely that "data is data" regardless of where it originates, and that it is essential to go back and forth between different file formats. The data in the Admissions Office case study originate in an Excel workbook but could just as easily come from a text or ***CSV (Comma Separated Values) file***, an ***XML document***, a ***Web query***, and/or an ***Access database***.

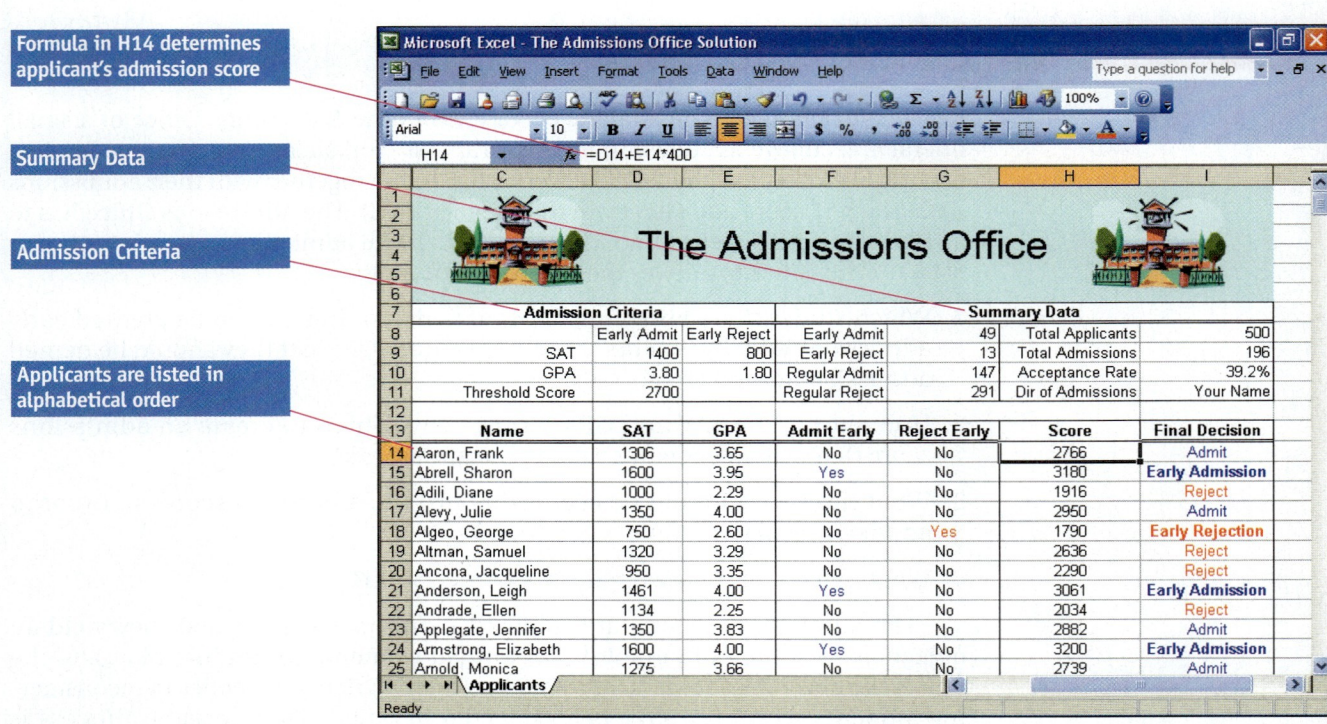

(a) Applicants in Alphabetical Order

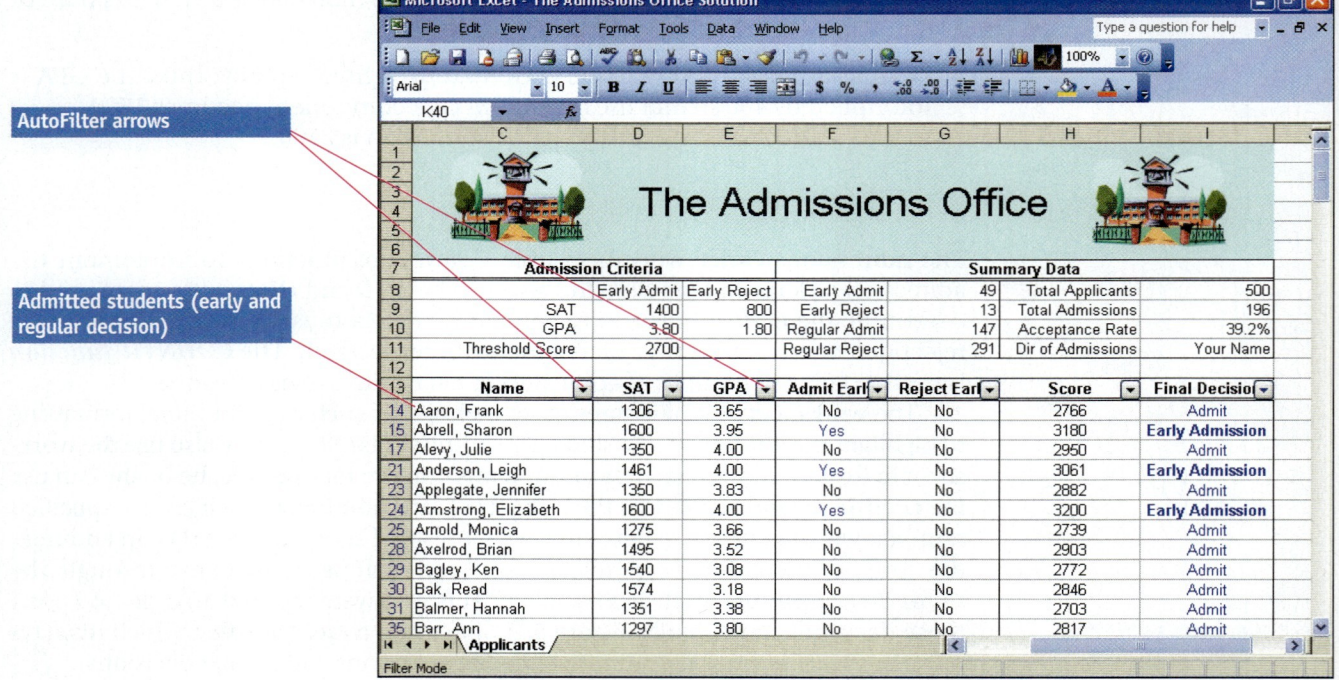

(b) Applicants Who Were Admitted

FIGURE 8.1 The Admissions Office

hands-on exercise

1 The Admissions Office

Objective To examine a list of applicants and determine the acceptances and rejections; to illustrate the AND and OR functions; to use conditional formatting and the AutoFilter command. Use Figure 8.2 as a guide.

Step 1: **Concatenate the Student's Name**

- Open **The Admissions Office workbook** in the **Exploring Excel folder** as shown in Figure 8.2a. Save the workbook as **The Admissions Office Solution** so that you can always return to the original workbook if necessary.

- Click in **cell C14**. Enter the formula =A14 & ", " & B14 to concatenate (join together) the last name, a comma and a space, followed by the first name, to create a single field. Copy this formula to the remaining rows in the worksheet.

- Click and drag the column headings for columns A and B to select these columns. Pull down the **Format menu**, click the **Column command**, then click the **Hide command** to hide these columns.

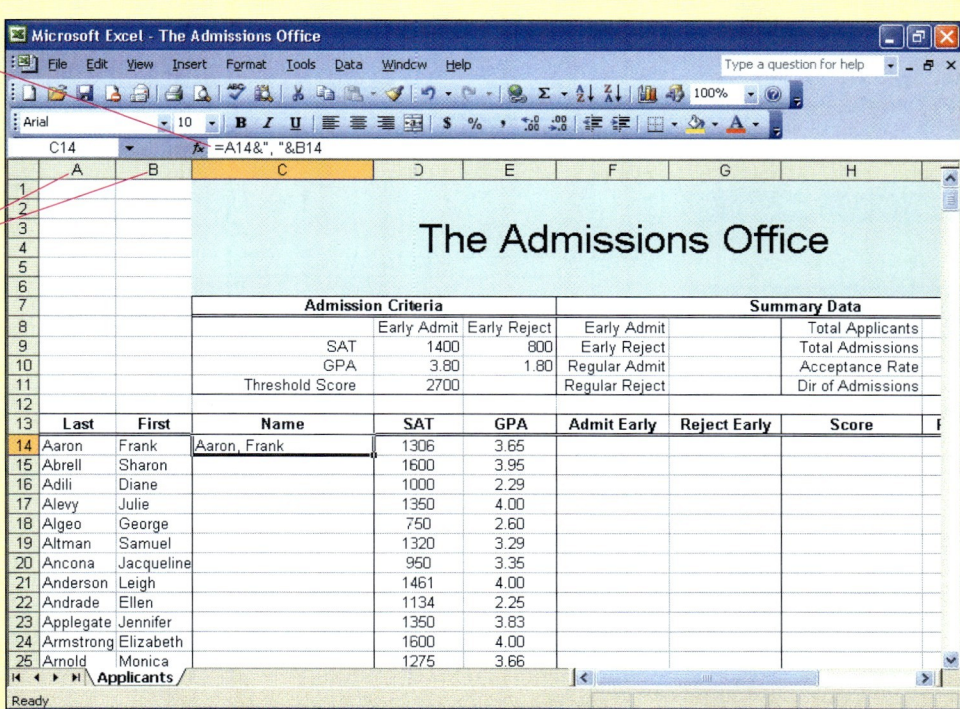

(a) Concatenate the Student's Name (step 1)

FIGURE 8.2 Hands-on Exercise 1

UNHIDING ROWS AND COLUMNS

Hiding a row or column is easy: You just select the row(s) or column(s) you want to hide, click the right mouse button, then select the Hide command from the shortcut menu. Unhiding a row or column is trickier because you cannot see the target cells. To unhide a column, you first need to select the columns on either side; for example, select columns A and C if you are trying to unhide column B. To unhide column A, however, click in the Name box and enter A1. Pull down the Format menu, click Column, then click the Unhide command.

MICROSOFT OFFICE EXCEL 2003 REVISED 401

Step 2: **Enter formulas for Early Admission/Early Rejection**

- Click in **cell F14** and enter the formula **=AND(D14>=$D$9,E14>=$D$10)**. You should see "FALSE" displayed in the cell as this student does not meet the early admissions criteria.

- Modify the formula in cell F14 so that it contains an IF statement, that is, **=IF(AND(D14>=$D$9,E14>=$D$10),"Yes","No")** as shown in Figure 8.2b. This time you see "No" displayed in the cell, which is a more descriptive entry.

- Enter the formula **=IF(OR(D14<$E$9,E14<$E$10),"Yes","No")** into cell G14. You should see "No" displayed in this cell as well since the student does not meet the criteria for early rejection either.

- Select **cells F14:G14**, then drag the fill handle down four or five rows to be sure that it is working correctly. Sharon Abrell should be admitted early, while George Algeo should be rejected early.

- Copy the formulas in cells F14:G14 to the remaining rows in the worksheet. Center the entries. Save the workbook.

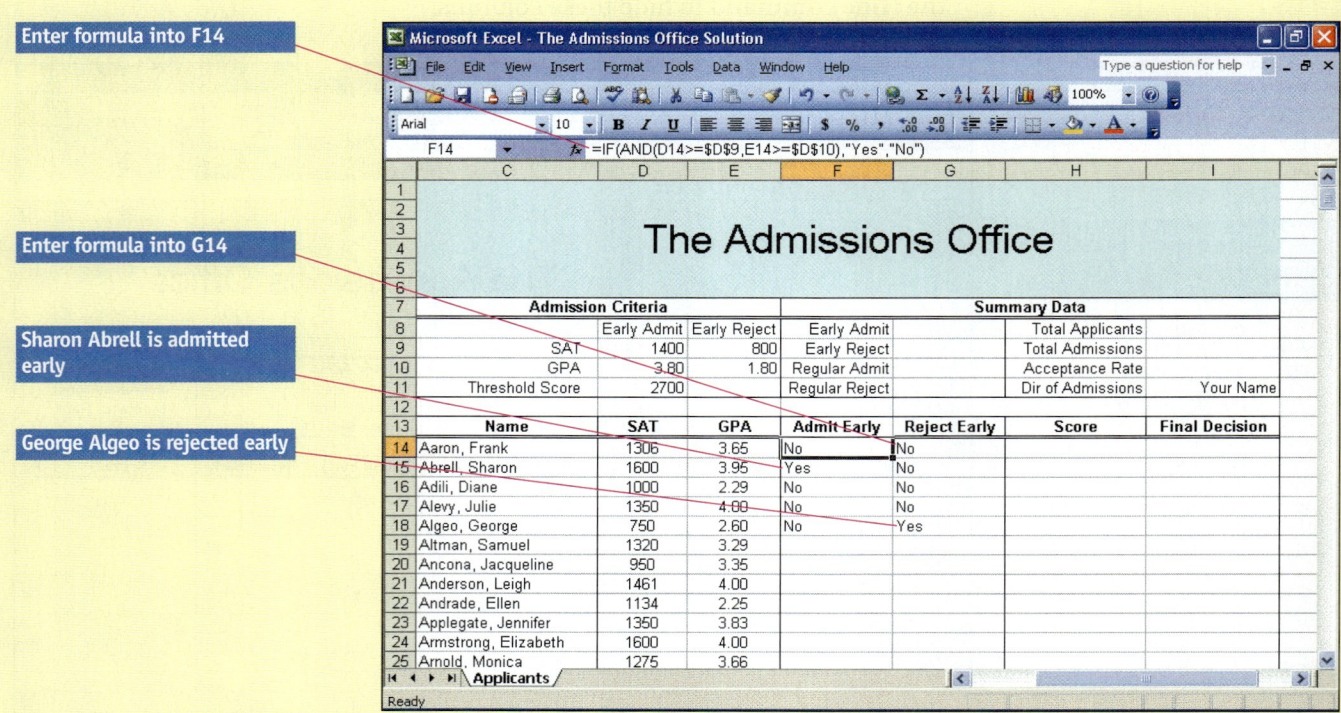

(b) Enter Formulas for Early Admission and Early Rejection (step 2)

FIGURE 8.2 Hands-on Exercise 1 (*continued*)

USE POINTING TO ENTER FORMULAS

A cell reference can be typed directly into a formula, or it can be entered more easily through pointing. Pointing is more accurate because you use the mouse or arrow keys to reference cells directly. To use pointing, select (click in) the cell to contain the formula, type an equal sign to begin the formula, click (or move to) the cell containing the reference, then press the F4 key as necessary to change from relative to absolute or mixed references. Type any arithmetic operator to place the cell reference into the formula, and then continue pointing to additional cells. Press the Enter key to complete the formula.

Step 3: **Enter Formulas for the Admissions Decision**

- Click in **cell H14**. Enter the formula **=D14+E14*400** to compute the applicant's admissions score. You should see 2766 as the numerical result.

- Click in **cell I14** and build the nested If statement shown in the formula bar of Figure 8.2c. You should see "Admit" in cell I14. Copy the formulas in **cells H14:I14** to the remaining rows in the worksheet. Center the entries.

- Click in **cell I14**. Press and hold the **Shift key**, press the **End key**, then press **down arrow key** to select **cells I14:I513**. Pull down the **Insert menu**, click **Name**, then click **Define**. Type **Final_Decision** in the Names in workbook area, then click **OK**.

- Click in **cell G8** and enter the formula **=COUNTIF(Final_Decision,"Early Admission")**. Now click in **cell G9** and enter the formula **=COUNTIF(Final_Decision,"Early Rejection")**. You should see 49 and 13, respectively.

- Click in **cell G10** and enter the formula **=COUNTIF(Final_Decision,"Admit")** to count the number of admissions. Click in **cell G11** and enter the formula **=COUNTIF(Final_Decision,"Reject")** to count the number of rejections. You should see 147 and 291, respectively. Save the workbook.

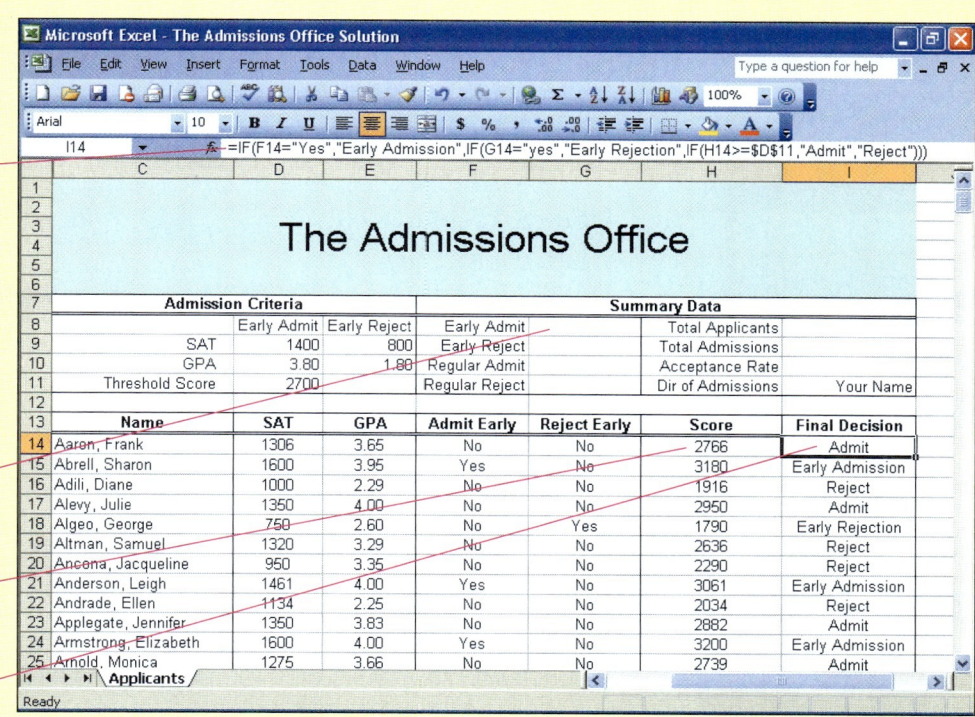

(c) Enter Formulas for the Admissions Decision (step 3)

FIGURE 8.2 Hands-on Exercise 1 (*continued*)

USE A NESTED IF FOR COMPLEX DECISIONS

A nested If statement (an "If" within an "If") is used to build the admissions decision. Thus, If the early admissions statement is "Yes", display "Early Admission"; Else If the early rejection decision is "Yes", display "Early Rejection"; Else If the score is greater than or equal to the threshold, display "Admit"; Else display "Reject". The statement in cell I14 is not difficult to write, but you must balance the number of left and right parentheses.

Step 4: **Implement Conditional Formatting**

- The entries in column I will be displayed in four different color/style combinations according to the admissions decision. Click in **cell I14**, pull down the **Format menu**, and click the **Conditional Formatting command** to display the dialog box in Figure 8.2d.

- Click the **down arrow** in the second list box to select **equal to,** then enter **Early Admission** (do not use quotation marks) in the text box. Click the **Format button**, chose **Bold** as the Font Style and Blue as the color. Click **OK**.

- Click the **Add button** to add a second condition to display **Admit** in **Blue** using **Regular** as the font style. Add the third and last condition to display **Early Rejection** in **Red** with **Bold** as the font style. Click **OK**.

- Click the **down arrow** on the **Font Color button**. Select **Red** as the default color for this cell, which will display all "rejects" in red. (This is necessary because the Conditional Formatting dialog box is limited to three conditions.)

- Double click the **Format Painter tool** on the Standard toolbar, then paint the next several cells in column I to be sure that the conditional formatting is working correctly. Copy the format to the remaining cells in the column. Click the Format Painter tool to turn it off.

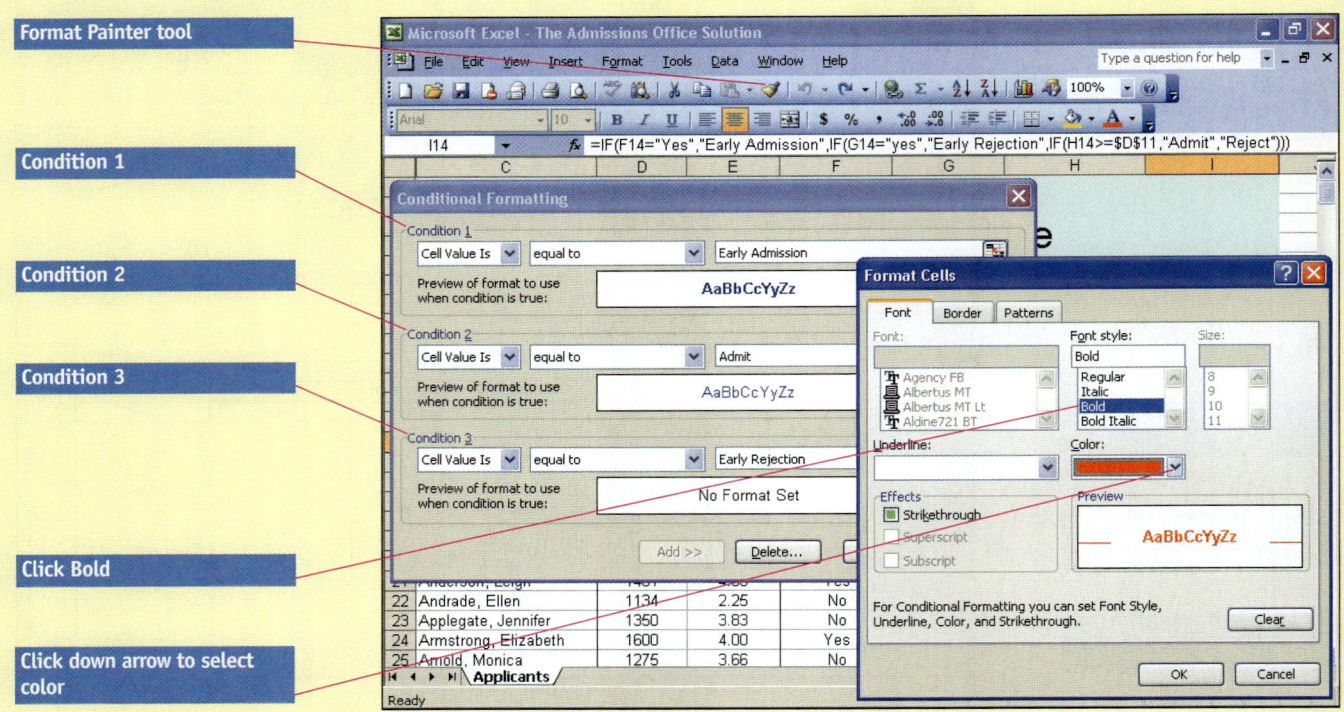

(d) Implement Conditional Formatting (step 4)

FIGURE 8.2   Hands-on Exercise 1 (*continued*)

WHICH CELLS HAVE CONDITIONAL FORMATTING?

It may be helpful to know which cells have conditional formatting if the worksheet does not look the way you expect it to. Pull down the Edit menu and click the Go To command (or press the F5 key), click the Special command button, click the option button for Conditional formats, then click OK to select the cells with conditional formatting. (Click anywhere outside the range to deselect the cells.)

Step 5: **The Finishing Touches**

- Click in **cell I8**. Enter the formula **=COUNTA(Final_Decision)** to count the number of applicants. The COUNTA function is used instead of COUNT because we are counting text entries (the final decisions) instead of numerical values.

- Click in **cell I9**. Enter the formula **=G8+G10** to compute the total number of admissions (early admissions plus regular admissions).

- Click in **cell I10**. Enter the formula **=I9/I8**, then format the result as a percent with one decimal.

- Pull down the **Insert menu**, click the **Picture command**, then click **Clip Art** to display the Clip Art task pane as shown in Figure 8.2e. Enter **university** in the Search for text box, and then click the **Go button**. Scroll until you find an appropriate selection, then click the picture to insert it into the workbook.

- Close the task pane. Size the clip art, then move it to the left of the worksheet title. Select the clip art, press **Ctrl+C** to copy it, then **Ctrl+V** to create a second image. Drag the second image to the right of the title.

- Apply any "last minute" formatting to complete the worksheet; for example, we applied conditional formatting to display the "Yes" for early admission or rejection, in blue and red, respectively. Save the workbook.

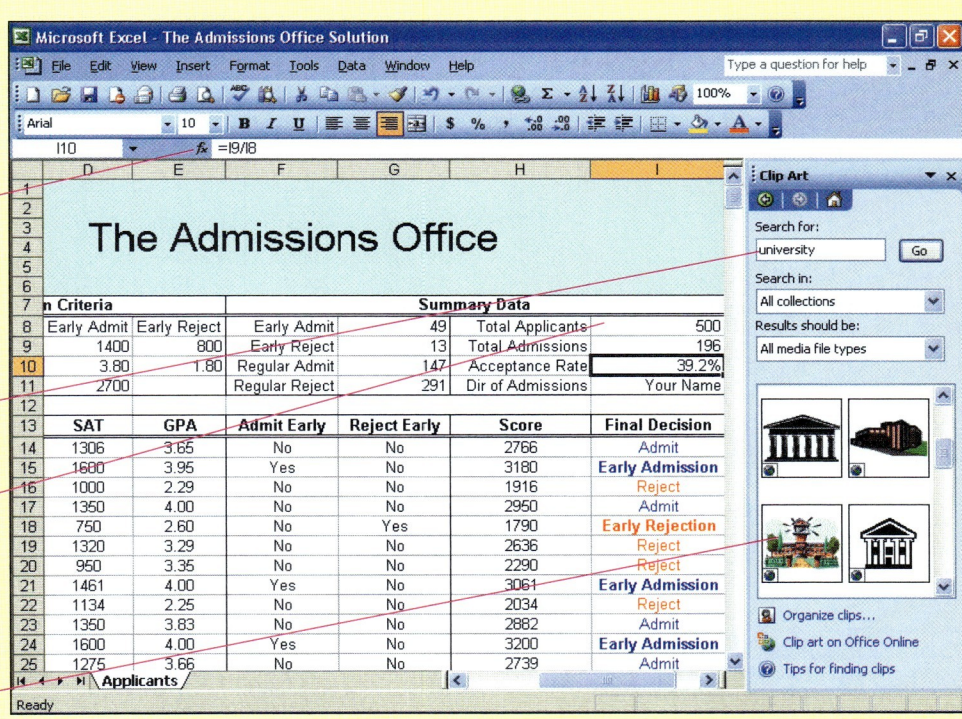

(e) The Finishing Touches (step 5)

FIGURE 8.2 Hands-on Exercise 1 (*continued*)

COUNT, COUNTA, AND COUNTIF

Excel provides multiple COUNT functions, each with a different purpose. The COUNT function includes only the numeric entries within a list, whereas the COUNTA function includes both numeric and nonnumeric entries. The COUNTIF function adds decision making and tallies the number of cells within a range that satisfy a specified condition.

Step 6: **Set the Printing Parameters**

- Pull down the **File menu** and click the **Page Setup command**.
  - Click the **Page tab**. Click the **Scaling option button** to fit to one page wide (leave a blank where it asks for the number of pages "tall").
  - Click the **Margins tab**. Change the **top margin** to **.5** inch. Center the worksheet horizontally.
  - Click the **Header/Footer tab**. Create a custom footer with the date in the left portion, your name in the middle, and an entry to print the page number and total number of pages (such as "Page 1 of 10") in the right.
  - Click the **Sheet tab**. Enter **13:13** in the **Rows to repeat at top** list box.
- Click the **Print Preview button** to preview the printed worksheet as shown in Figure 8.2f. Note the page footer that appears at the bottom of the first page.
- Click the **Next button** to move to the second page, where you see additional applicants. The first line of that page should contain the header row with the student's name, GPA, SAT, and so on.
- Click the **Print button**, then click the **Page(s) button** within the print range, and print pages **1 and 2**.

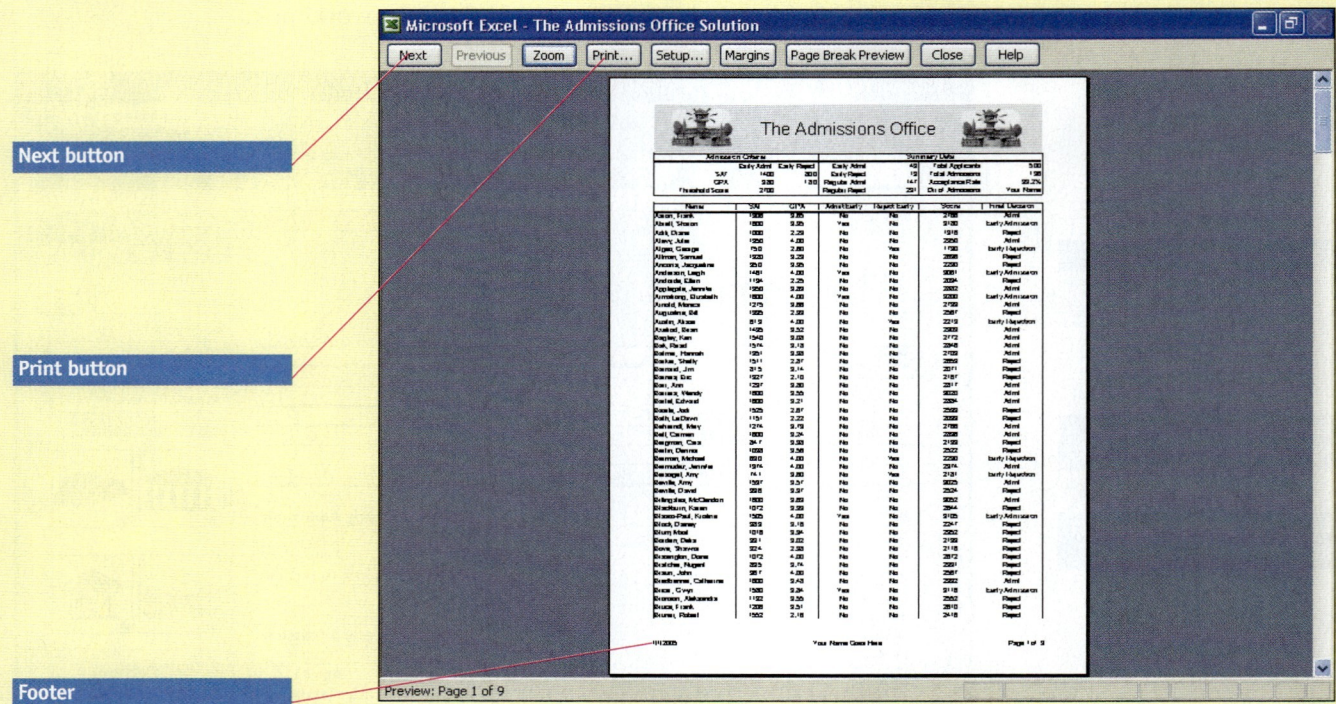

(f) Set the Printing Parameters (step 6)

FIGURE 8.2 Hands-on Exercise 1 (*continued*)

PRINT PREVIEW VERSUS PAGE BREAK PREVIEW

The Print Preview command displays a worksheet as it will be printed including the header and/or the footer. The Page Break Preview command, however, lets you see and/or modify the page breaks by dragging the breaks (indicated by a solid or dashed blue line) to allow more or less on any given page. Pull down the View menu and click the Page Break Preview command to see the worksheet with the intended page breaks. Pull down the View menu a second time and click Normal to return to the familiar view of a spreadsheet.

Step 7: **The AutoFilter Command**

- Click anywhere within the list of applicants. Pull down the **Data menu**, click the **Filter command**, then click **AutoFilter**. Click the **drop down arrow** in the Final Decision column, then click **Reject** to filter the list to see the rejected applicants (does not include the early rejections).

- Click in cell **H16**, then click the **Sort Descending button** to list the selected records in descending sequence by admission score. Jane McElroy just missed with a score of 2697. Two other students were also rejected by a narrow margin.

- The Admissions Officer could change each decision manually, but decides to change the threshold instead. Click in **cell D11** and enter **2690**. The three students are admitted as shown in Figure 8.2g.

- Click the **drop down arrow** in the Final Decision column and click **(Custom...)** to display the associated dialog box. Enter **equals** and **Admit** in the list boxes for the first condition, click the **Or option button**, then enter **equals** and **Early Admission** for the second condition. Click **OK**.

- You should see every student who was admitted. Click in **cell C14**, then click the **Sort Ascending button** to display the students alphabetically. Print the first page of the admitted applicants for your instructor. Save the workbook.

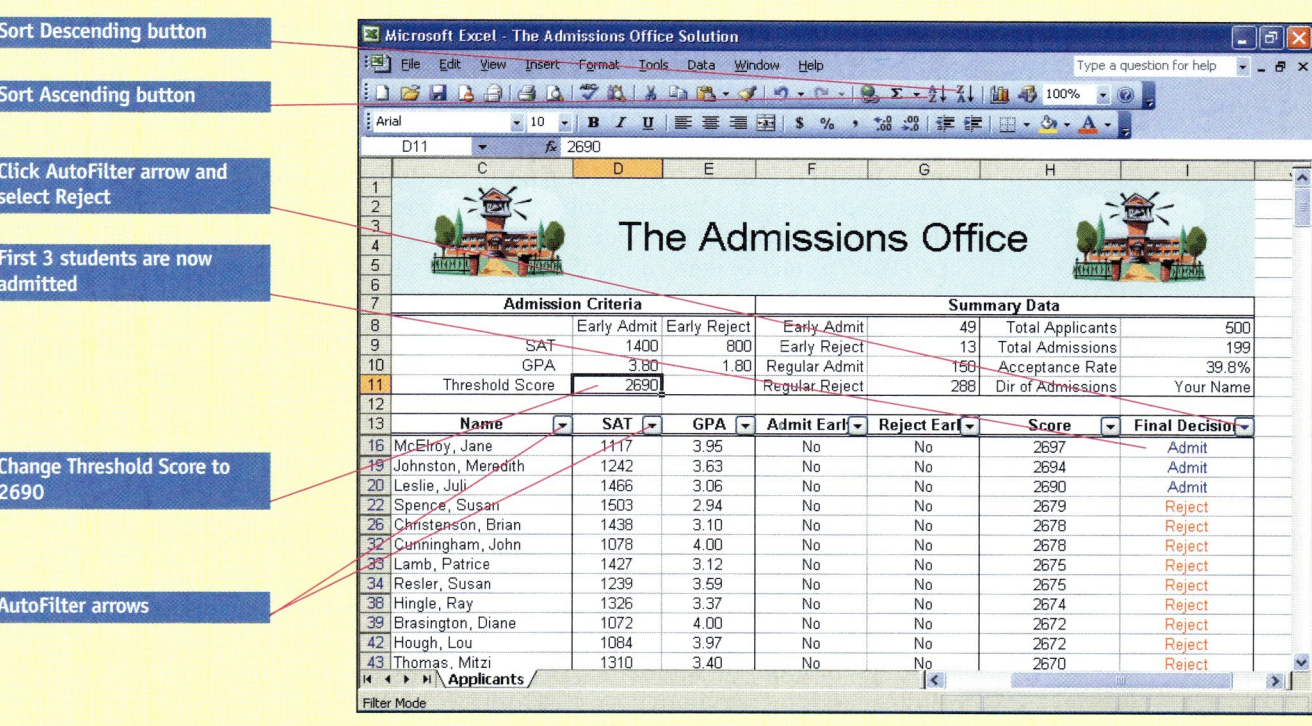

(g) The AutoFilter Command (step 7)

FIGURE 8.2 Hands-on Exercise 1 (*continued*)

THE GOAL SEEK COMMAND

What should the admission score be in order to admit just 25% of applicants? You can find the answer by trial and error, but there is an easier way. Pull down the Tools menu and click the Goal Seek command. Enter I10 in the Set cell text box, .25 in the To value text box, D11 in the By Changing Cell text box, then click OK. Excel returns a threshold value of 2866, which in turn admits 125 students.

THE GRADUATING CLASS

Our second example occurs in the registrar's office immediately prior to graduation. The registrar is presented with the list of graduating seniors, which includes the student's name, major, and GPA and is required to compile individual statistics for each student as well as for the class as a whole. In particular:

1. In which quartile did every student graduate? What is the corresponding rank in class for that student?
2. What are the requirements to graduate with honors? Which students achieved this distinction?
3. What is the average GPA for the graduating class as a whole? What is the GPA for each major?
4. How many students are there in each major?
5. How many students in each major graduated with honors?

Implementation in Excel

The worksheet in Figure 8.3a computes the rank, quartile, and honors distinction (if any) for each graduate. The **RANK function** is straightforward and returns the rank of a number in a list. The **QUARTILE function** has two arguments, the range and the quartile; for example, QUARTILE(Range, 1) and QUARTILE(Range, 2) return the maximum value in the first and second quartile, respectively, corresponding to the 25th and 50th percentile. You can also specify QUARTILE(Range, 0) and QUARTILE(Range, 4) to return the minimum and maximum values in the range. The recognition of an honors distinction for each student is accomplished through a **VLOOKUP function**, which uses the table in cells F4 through G7. The **COUNTIF function** determines the number of students for each honors designation.

Figure 8.3b uses a combination of the **SORT** and **SUBTOTALS commands** to display summary statistics for each major as well as the class as a whole. Our favorite feature, however, is shading the alternate rows in the body of the worksheet in Figure 8.3a. The easiest way to do this is through one of two predefined AutoFormats; for example, the List1 format shades every other row in gray. The technique is simple, but there is a drawback, namely, you may not like the color. More importantly, however, if you update or sort the list, you will have to reapply the formatting.

A better way uses conditional formatting in conjunction with the ROW() function and modulo arithmetic. It may seem complicated at first, but we prefer to think of the technique as powerful and elegant. And once you use it, you will love it. **Modulo arithmetic** deals with the remainder after a division; for example, seven modulo (or mod) two equals one. We take seven and divide it by two. The quotient is three and the remainder is one. Throw away the quotient and keep the remainder. The format of the Excel function is MOD(number, divisor), as in =MOD(7, 2). The result is one as explained earlier. Try another example: =MOD(10,2). The result is zero; that is, ten divided by two is five and the remainder is zero. Throw away the five and keep the zero.

The **ROW function** returns the row number; for example, if you are in any cell in row 15 and you enter the formula =ROW(), the result is 15. That sounds trivial, but you can combine the ROW and **MOD functions** in the expression =MOD(ROW(),2). This returns a result of zero or one, for even and odd rows, respectively. You then use conditional formatting to apply shading whenever the result is zero (one) to shade the even (odd) rows.

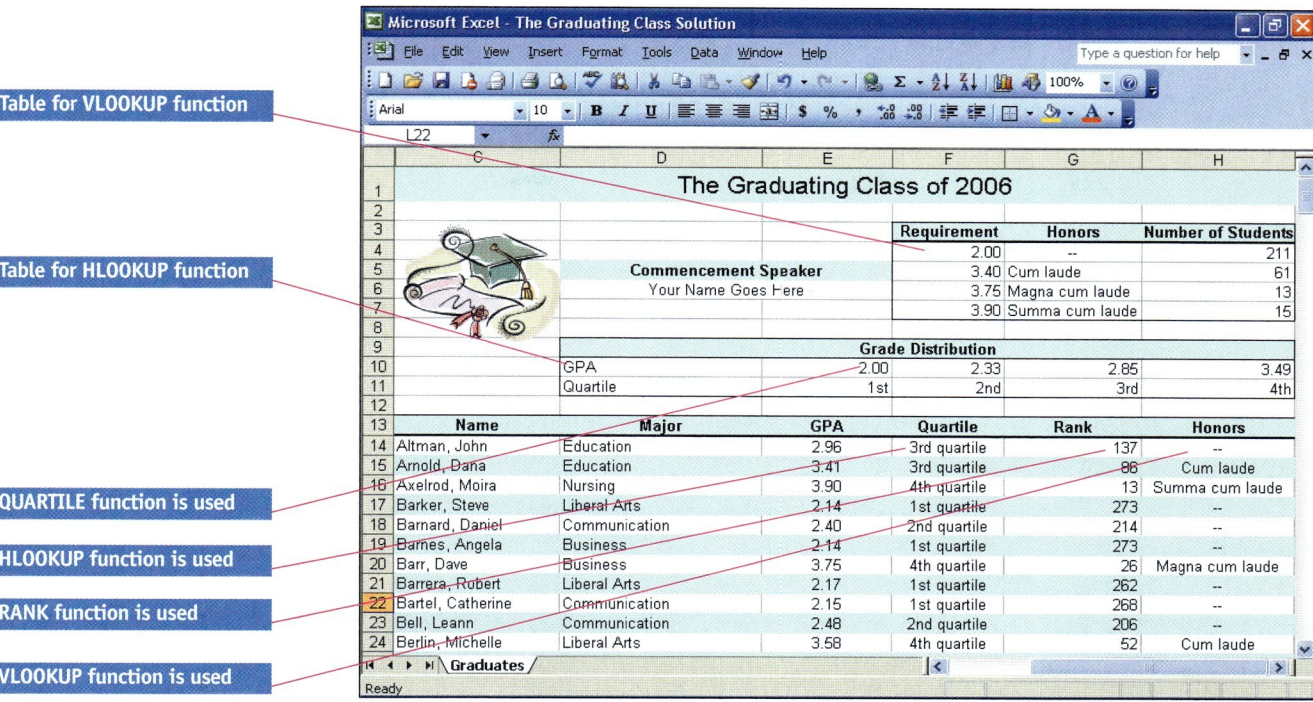

(a) The Graduating Class

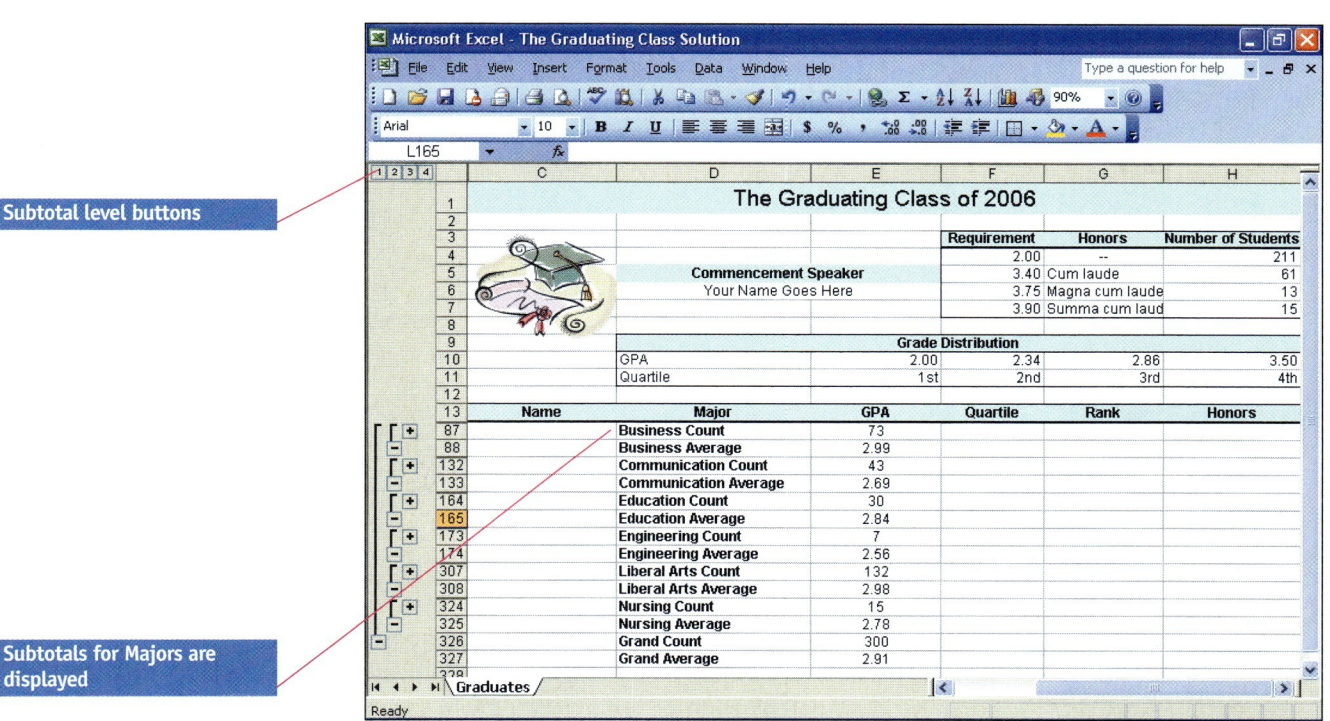

(b) Average GPA by Major

FIGURE 8.3 The Graduating Class

hands-on exercise 2

The Graduating Class

Objective Use the QUARTILE, RANK, and SUBTOTALS functions; shade alternate rows within a worksheet. Use Figure 8.4 as a guide.

Step 1: The CONCATENATE and TRIM Functions

- Open **The Graduating Class workbook** in the **Exploring Excel folder**.

- Click in **cell C14**. Enter the formula **=CONCATENATE(A14,", ",B14)** to concatenate the last name, a comma and a space, followed by the first name.

- You see "Altman   , John". The problem is not with the CONCATENATE function per se, but rather the trailing blanks after the student's last name. Edit the formula to include the TRIM function, **=CONCATENATE(TRIM(A14),", ",B14)** as shown in Figure 8.4a. The trailing blanks are eliminated. Copy the formula in **cell C14** to the remaining rows in the worksheet.

- Hide columns A and B. Save the workbook as **The Graduating Class Solution**.

Formula to be entered into C14

Click and drag to select column headings for columns A and B, then hide columns

Click in C14

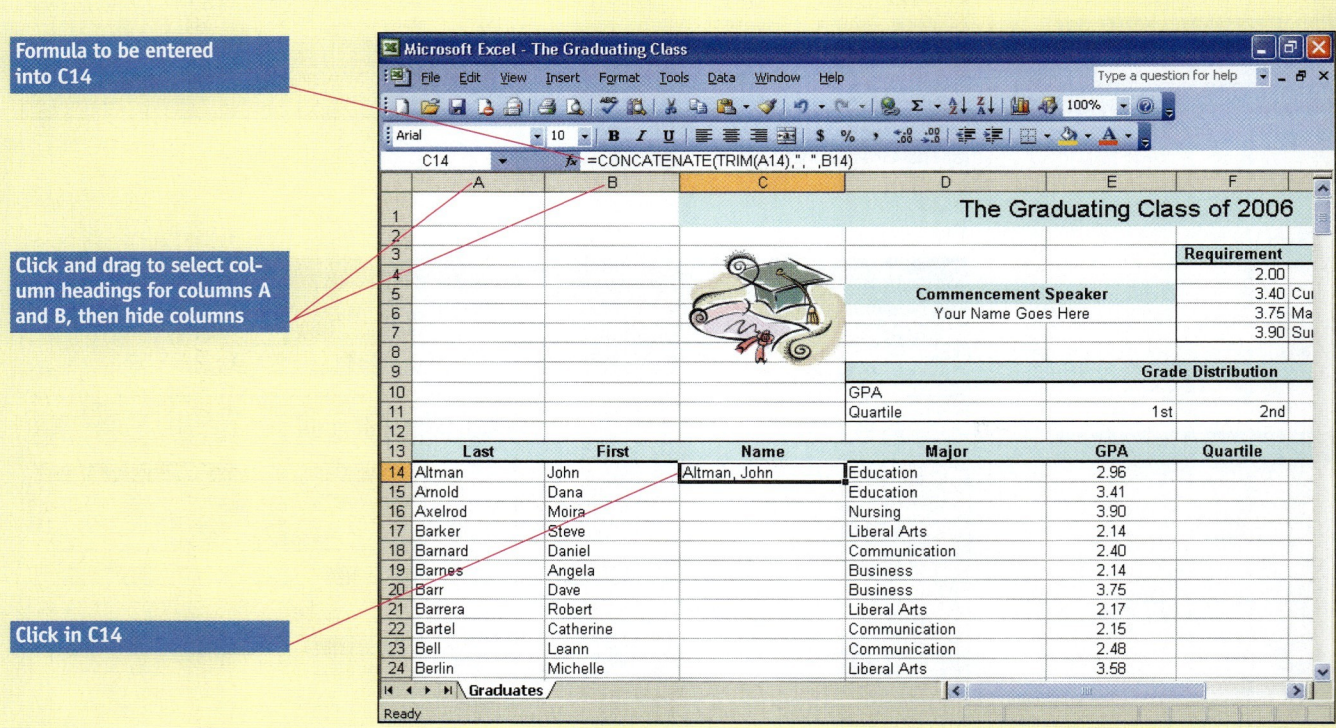

(a) The CONCATENATE and TRIM Functions (step 1)

FIGURE 8.4 Hands-on Exercise 2

CHANGE "ADAMS" TO "Adams"

The right combination of text functions will accomplish wonders if the imported data is not in the desired format. UPPER and LOWER convert an entry to upper and lowercase, respectively, whereas LEFT and RIGHT return the left and right portions of a character string; for example, =LEFT("ADAMS",1) returns the leftmost character or "A". The LEN function returns the number of characters; for example, =LEN("ADAMS") returns five. Now put it all together. Enter "ADAMS" in cell A1, then enter =UPPER(LEFT(A1,1)) & LOWER(RIGHT(A1,(LEN(A1)-1))) in an adjacent cell to convert the name to "Adams". See practice exercise 8.

Step 2: **Determine the Quartile and Rank in Class**

- Click in **cell E14**. Press and hold the **Shift key**, press the **End key**, then press the **down arrow key** to select cells **E14:E313**. Pull down the **Insert menu**, click **Name**, click **Define**, then enter **GPA_LIST** to define the range name. Click **OK**.

- Click in **cell E10**. Enter the formula **=QUARTILE(GPA_LIST,0)** to determine the minimum GPA in the entire list.

- Click and drag the fill handle to copy the formula in cell E10 to **cells F10, G10, and H10**. Change the last argument in cells F10, G10, and H10 to **1, 2,** and **3**, respectively. You should see the values in Figure 8.4b.

- Click in **cell F14**. Enter the formula **=HLOOKUP(E14,$E$10:$H$11,2)**. You should see 3rd as the displayed result; that is, the GPA of 2.96 falls within the 3rd quartile (between 2.85 and 3.49).

- Modify the formula in cell F14 to include the concatenation operator to display 3rd quartile as shown in Figure 8.4b. Center the entry in the cell.

- Click in **cell G14**. Enter the formula **=RANK(E14,GPA_LIST)** to determine the student's rank. Copy the formulas in **cells F14:G14** to the remainder of the list.

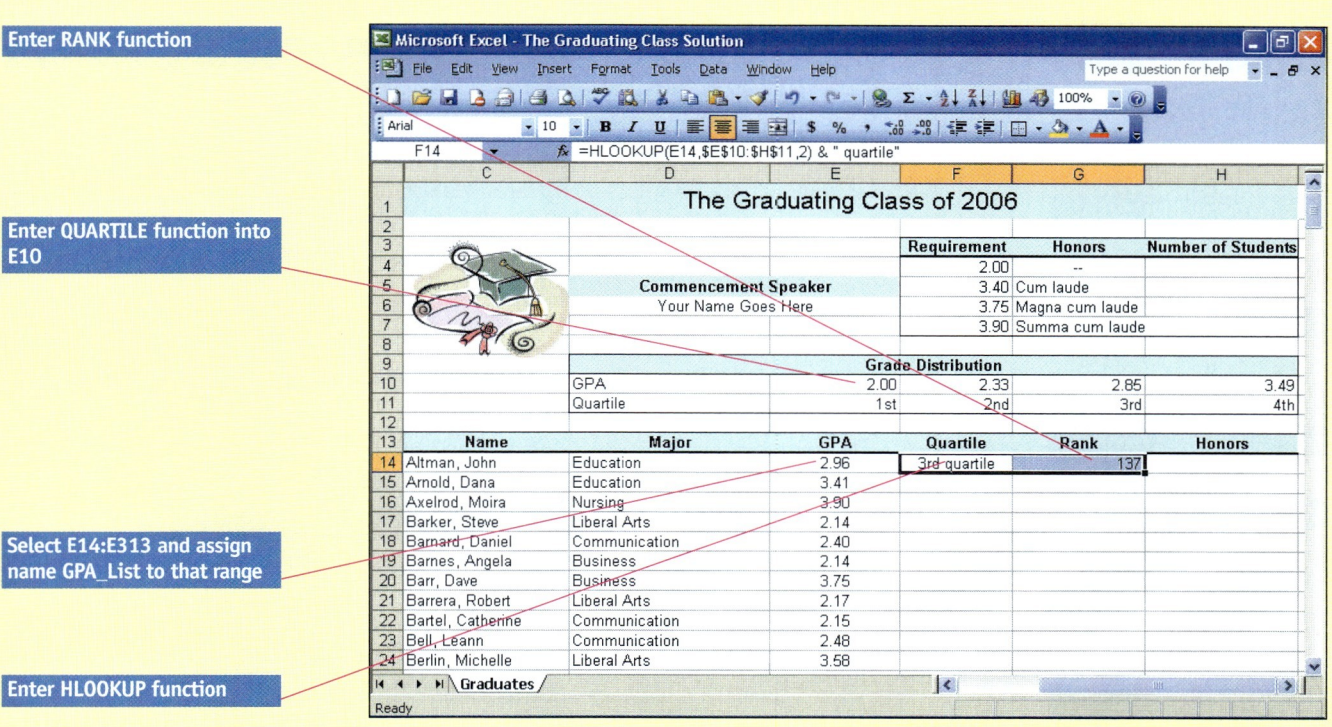

(b) Determine the Quartile and Rank in Class (step 2)

FIGURE 8.4 Hands-on Exercise 2 (*continued*)

THE QUARTILE—MORE WORK THAN YOU EXPECT

The QUARTILE and HLOOKUP functions are used together to display the individual's class standing. The four QUARTILE functions at the top of the spreadsheet compute the starting value for each quartile (2.00, 2.33, 2.85, and 3.49, corresponding to the 1st, 2nd, 3rd, and 4th quartiles). The HLOOKUP function within the body of the worksheet determines where an individual's GPA falls within these values, and returns 1st, 2nd, 3rd, or 4th. Finally the concatenate operator (an ampersand) appends the word "quartile" to the result of the HLOOKUP function.

Step 3: **Shade the Alternate Rows**

- Click and drag to select **cells C14:H14**. Pull down the **Format menu** and click the **Conditional Formatting command** to display the associated dialog box.

- Click the **down arrow** in the Condition 1 list box and choose **Formula is**. Click in the text box and enter the formula **=MOD(ROW(),2)=1**.

- Click the **Format button** to display the Format Cells dialog box. Click the **Patterns tab**, click the desired fill color, then click **OK**. You should see the fill color applied to the Preview box as shown in Figure 8.4c. Click **OK** to close the Conditional Formatting dialog box and return to the spreadsheet.

- Double click the **Format Painter button** on the Standard toolbar, then paint the next few rows in the worksheet. The odd rows are shaded, the even rows are not. Continue to paint the remaining rows in the worksheet (through row 313), then click the **Format Painter button** when you are finished.

- The key to the technique is the expression =MOD(ROW(),2) which returns a result of zero or one for even and odd rows, respectively. The expression is compared to one and hence it is false for the even rows (no conditional formatting) and true for the odd rows (conditional formatting is applied).

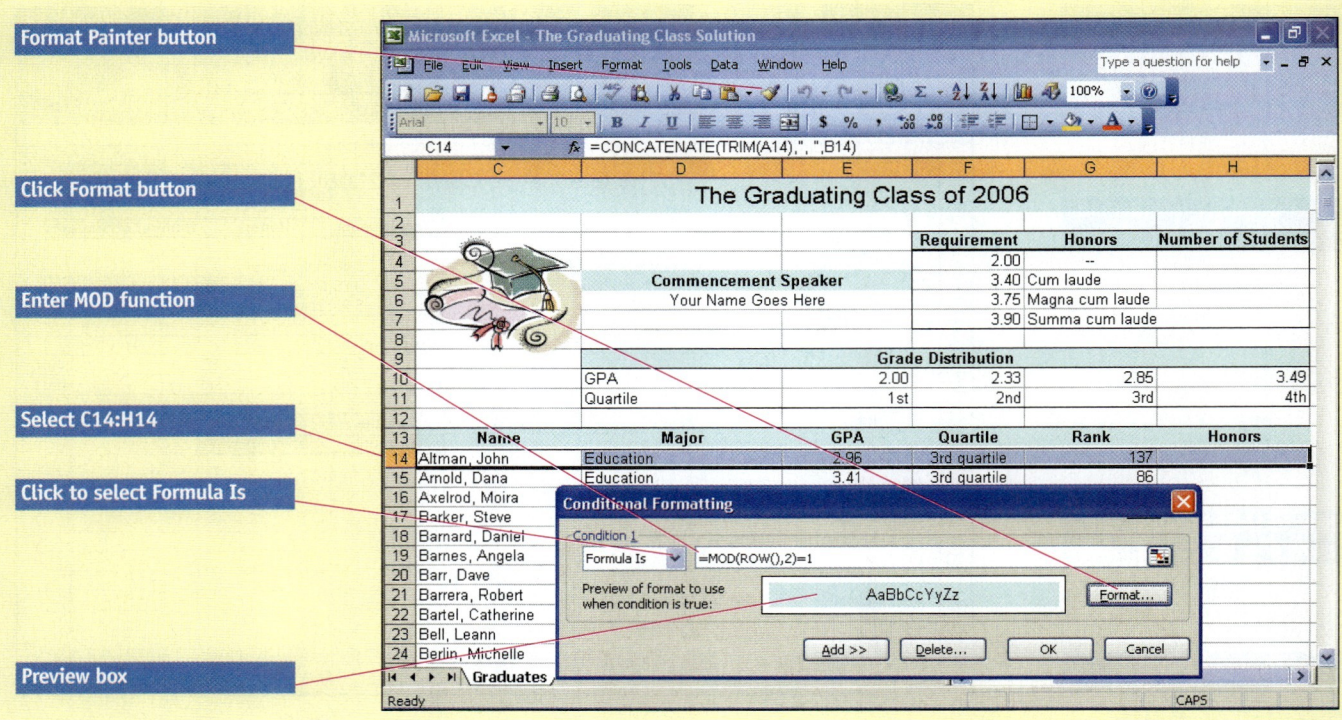

(c) Shade the Alternate Rows (step 3)

FIGURE 8.4 Hands-on Exercise 2 (*continued*)

YOU ALREADY KNOW MODULO ARITHMETIC

Let's assume that today is Monday and that you have an appointment 15 days from today. You don't need a calendar to realize that the appointment falls on Tuesday and indeed, you obtained the result intuitively using modulo arithmetic. In other words, you divided 15 (the number of days to your appointment), by 7 (the number of days in a week), discarded the quotient (two) and then added the remainder (one) to the current day (Monday) to arrive at Tuesday.

Step 4: **Determine the Honors Distinction**

- Click in **cell H14** and enter the formula **=VLOOKUP(E14,$F$4:$G$7,2)**. You should see two dashes in the cell as shown in Figure 8.4d. Center the entry.

- Click and drag the fill handle to the next several cells to be sure that the formula is working correctly.
  - Dana Arnold will graduate Cum laude as her GPA exceeds 3.40.
  - Moira Axelrod will graduate Summa cum laude; note that Moira's GPA of 3.90 is exactly equal to the requirement for this distinction.
  - Dave Barr will graduate Magna cum laude.

- Copy the VLOOKUP formula to the remaining cells in column H.

- Click in **cell H14**. Press and hold the **Shift key**, press the **End key**, then press the **down arrow key** to select the entire column (cells H14:H313). Pull down the **Insert menu**, click **Name**, then click **Define** to display the associated dialog box. Type **HONORS_LIST** as the range name. Click **OK**.

- Click in **cell H4** and enter the formula **=COUNTIF(HONORS_LIST,"--")**. You should see 211 as the displayed value.

- Enter similar formulas into cells H5, H6, and H7 to compute the number of Cum laude, Magna cum laude, and Summa cum laude graduates. You should see 61, 13, and 15, respectively. Save the workbook.

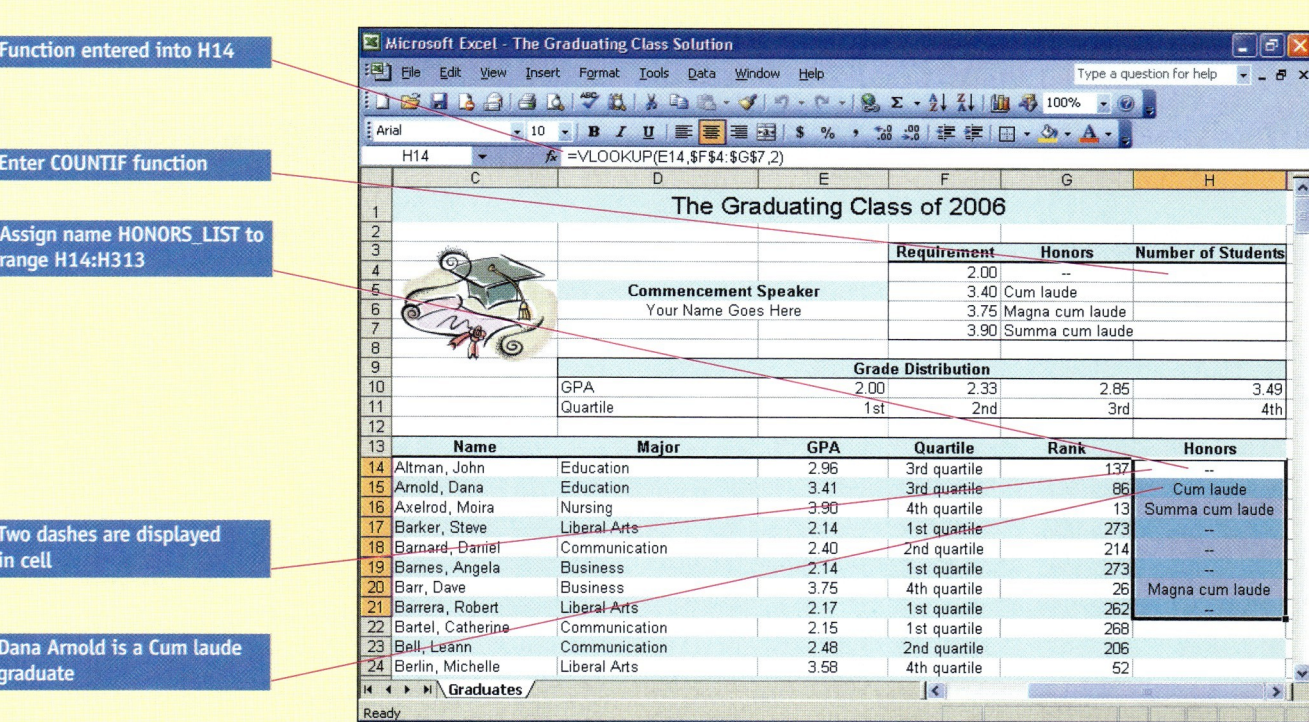

(d) Determine the Honors Distinction (step 4)

FIGURE 8.4 Hands-on Exercise 2 (*continued*)

THE NAME BOX

You can use the Name box to define a named range, by first selecting the cell(s) in the worksheet to which the name is to apply, clicking in the Name box to enter the name (spaces are not allowed), and then pressing the Enter key. (The only way to delete a range name, however, is through the Insert/Name/Define command.)

Step 5: **Print the Honors Students**

- Click in **cell E14**, which contains the GPA for the first student, then click the **Sort Descending** button to display the graduates in descending order of GPA; that is, the highest GPA is listed first.

- Pull down the **Data menu**, click **Filter**, then click the **AutoFilter command**. Click the **drop down arrow** next to the GPA, then click **(Custom…)** to display the associated dialog box.

- Enter **is greater than or equal to** as the condition, then enter **3.40** as the value (the minimum GPA to graduate with honors). Click **OK**.

- Pull down the **File menu**. Click the **Page Setup command** to display the associated dialog box.
    - Click the **Page tab**. Click the **Scaling option button** to fit to one page wide by seven pages tall.
    - Click the **Margins tab**. Change the **top margin** to **.75** inch. Center the worksheet horizontally.
    - Click the **Header/Footer tab**. Create a custom footer with the date in the left portion, your name in the middle, and an entry to print the page number and total number of pages, such as "page 1 of 7".
    - Click the **Sheet tab**. Click in the **Rows to repeat at top** list box and enter **1:13**.

- Print this worksheet for your instructor. Pull down the **Data menu**, click **Filter**, then click **AutoFilter** to toggle the filter off.

- Save the workbook.

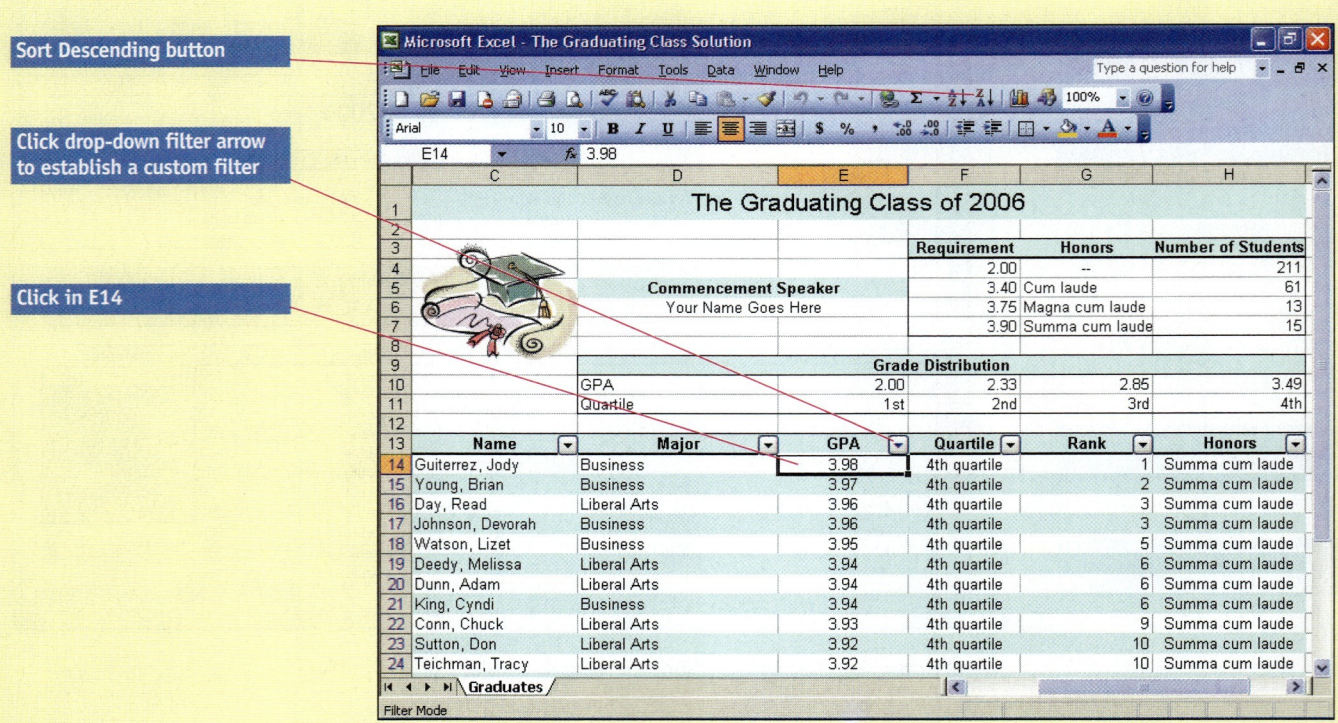

(e) Print the Honors Students (step 5)

FIGURE 8.4 Hands-on Exercise 2 (*continued*)

Step 6: **Compute the Subtotals**

- Click anywhere within the list. Pull down the **Data menu** and click the **Sort command** to display the associated dialog box. Enter **Major** and **Name** in the Sort by and Then by list boxes, respectively.

- Be sure the **Ascending option button** is selected for both fields. The option button for the **Header row** should also be selected. Click **OK**. The students are sorted by major and alphabetically within major.

- Pull down the **Data menu** and click the **Subtotals command** to display the Subtotal dialog box, and then enter the parameters as shown in Figure 8.4f. Be sure that **GPA** is the only field checked within the Add subtotal to list box.

- Click **OK** to compute the subtotals. The subtotals have been computed, but are not yet visible. Click the **Level 2 button** (under the Name box) to show the subtotals and suppress the detail lines within the list. Print this worksheet.

- Pull down the **Data menu**, click the **Subtotals command** to display the Subtotal dialog box, then click the **Remove All button** to clear the subtotals. Save the workbook.

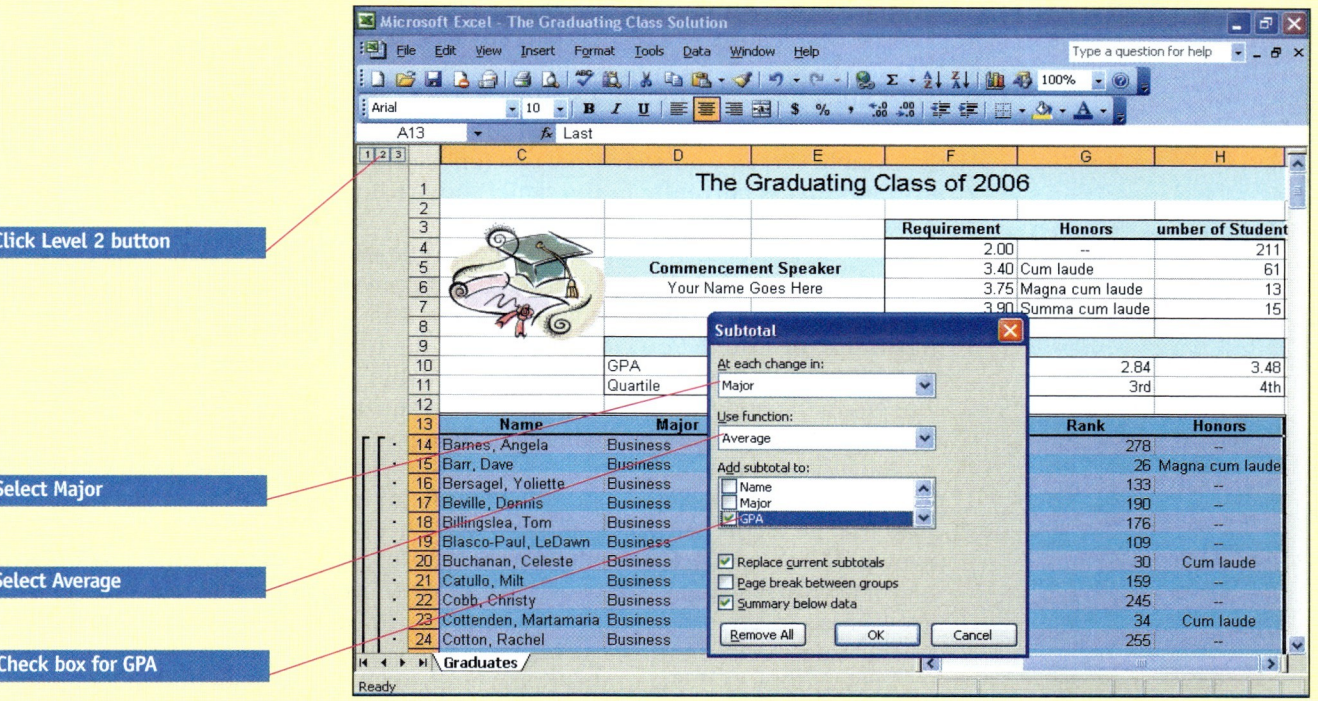

(f) Compute the Subtotals (step 6)

FIGURE 8.4 Hands-on Exercise 2 (*continued*)

TWO SETS OF SUBTOTALS

You can obtain multiple sets of subtotals using different functions, provided you do the operations in the correct sequence. First, sort the list according to the sequence you want; for example, by major. Click in the list, and compute the subtotals using the first function, AVG GPA at each change in major. Click OK. Click in the list a second time, and compute the subtotals using a different function; COUNT GPA, again at each change in major, but *clear* the box to replace the current subtotals. You will see the number of students in each major followed by the average GPA for that major.

MICROSOFT OFFICE EXCEL 2003 REVISED 415

THE MEN'S STORE

Our next example is set in the context of a men's clothing store and extends the discussion of pivot tables from Chapter 7. A pivot table divides the records in a list into categories, and then computes summary statistics for those categories. A *pivot chart* is the graphical equivalent of a pivot table, which at first glance resembles any other chart. A pivot chart, however, contains the same shaded buttons as the corresponding pivot table, enabling you to change the chart by dragging the buttons to different areas. Any changes to the pivot table are automatically reflected in the associated pivot chart and vice versa.

Figure 8.5a displays a pivot table with two **row fields** (Order Date and Category), one **column field** (Salesperson), and one **page field** (Sale Item), which provides a third dimension. The pivot table is based on the underlying Sales Data worksheet, which contains more than 700 records, each with five fields: the order date, the salesperson responsible for the order, the amount of the order, the category or type of merchandise, and an indication of whether the item was on sale or not. The really interesting thing about the pivot table is that the underlying data includes the *order date*, rather than the specific quarter in which a sale was recorded. The **Group and Show Detail command** was used to convert the individual dates to the appropriate quarter for subsequent analysis.

The best feature of a pivot table is its flexibility in that you can change the orientation to provide an entirely different analysis. You can, for example, "pivot the table" and reverse the row and column fields to show the salespersons in rows and the sales categories in the columns. You could also bring the page field to the body of the table to create an additional row (or column) field, and/or you could remove any field that is currently in the table. You are limited only by your imagination and/or information requirements.

You can also change the means of computation within the data area. The pivot table currently uses the Sum function to compute the total sales for each salesperson in each category in each quarter, but you can also choose Average, Minimum, Maximum, or Count. You can also change the formatting of any element in the table. The only limitation is that a pivot table does *not* automatically reflect changes in the underlying data; you must execute the **Refresh command** to update the table whenever the underlying data changes.

Each field in the pivot table has a drop-down list box that enables you to display (or suppress) selected values for that field; for example, the page field indicates that all records in the Sales Data worksheet are reflected in the body of the pivot table. You can, however, change the table to see the data for only the items on sale, or conversely items that were not on sale. In similar fashion, you can click the arrows next to the other buttons to suppress (or display) various values for the quarter, salesperson, and/or sales category.

Look closely at the worksheet tabs in Figure 8.5a and note that in addition to the Sales Data worksheet there is also a worksheet for Grauer, which contains all Grauer transactions throughout the year. The latter worksheet was created with a single click (actually a double click) of the mouse; that is, select the cell in the summary pivot table that contains Grauer's sales for the year, and then double click. The resulting worksheet for Grauer is created automatically.

The pivot chart in Figure 8.5b was created from a modified version of the pivot table (the category field was removed from the row area). A 3-D stacked column was chosen as the chart type, and a data table is displayed under the chart. It is important to realize that a pivot chart is also an ordinary chart in the sense that you can apply any commands or options from the chart menu. Note, too, how the title of the chart helps to convey a message, in this case that the company's sales leveled off after the first quarter. This is a powerful message (as well as a sobering thought) and certainly was not discernible from the more than 700 transactions in the original Sales Data worksheet.

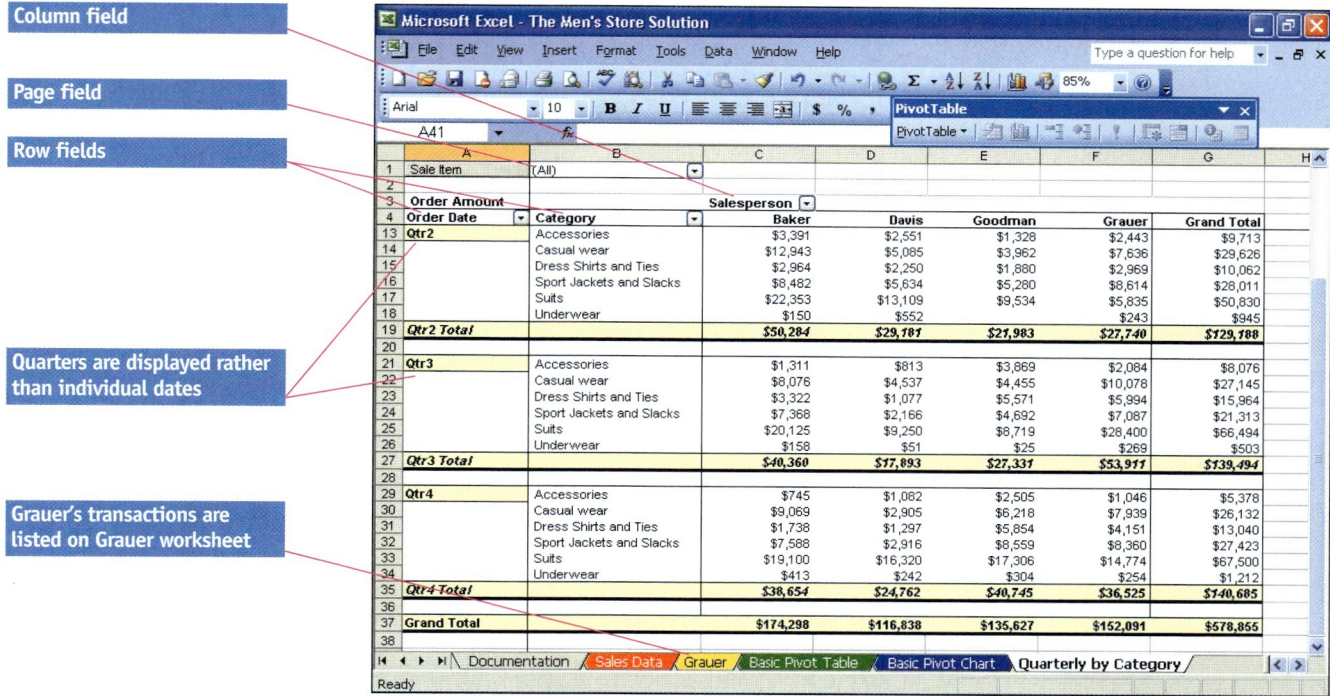

(a) Pivot Table (Quarterly by Category)

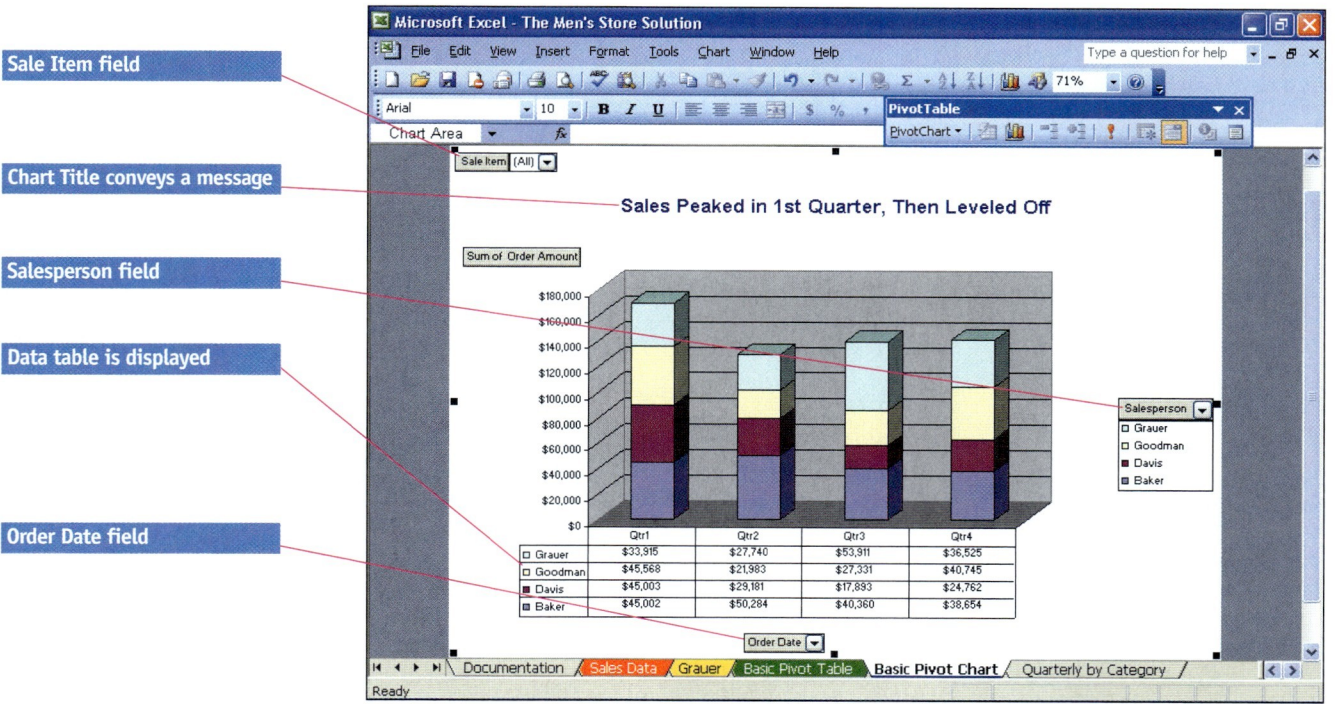

(b) Pivot Chart (Quarterly Sales by Salesperson)

FIGURE 8.5   The Men's Store

hands-on exercise 3: The Men's Store

Objective To import data from a text file into an Excel workbook; to create a pivot table and associated pivot chart; to use the Group and Show Detail command.

Step 1: Import the Data

- Start Excel and close any open workbooks. Pull down the **File menu** and click the **Open command** to display the Open dialog box. Open the **Exploring Excel folder**, click the **down arrow** on the Files of Type list box, and specify **All files**, then double click **The Men's Store** text document.

- The Text Import Wizard opens as shown in Figure 8.6a. The wizard recognizes the file is in Delimited format. Click **Next**. Clear the **Tab Delimiter** check box. Check the **Comma Delimiter** check box. Click **Next**. Click **Finish**.

- Click and drag to select **cells A1:E1**. Click the **Bold button** on the Formatting toolbar. Click the **Center button** as well. Change column widths as necessary.

- Pull down the **File menu** and click the **Save As command**. Click the **down arrow** in the Save as type list box and select **Microsoft Office Excel workbook**. Change the file name to **The Men's Store Solution**. Click the **Save button**.

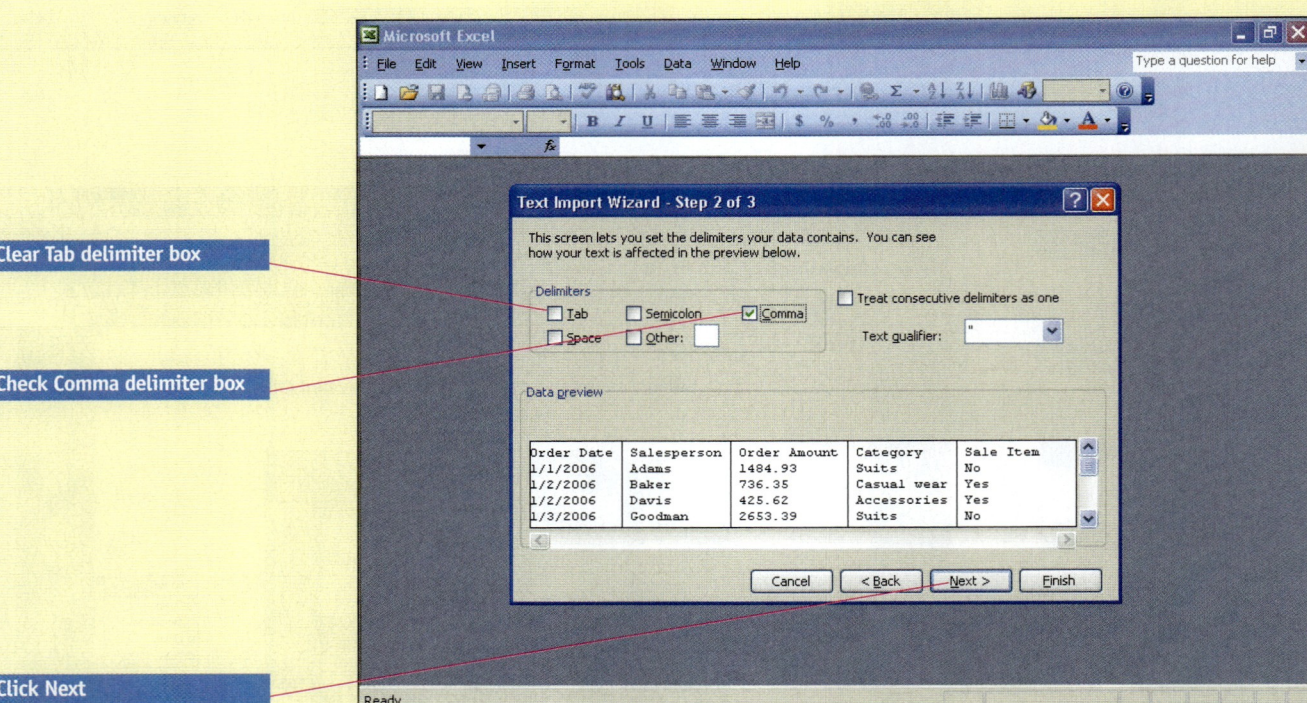

(a) Import the Data (step 1)

FIGURE 8.6 Hands-on Exercise 3

IMPORT DATA FROM ACCESS

The data in a worksheet can be imported from an Access database. Pull down the Data menu, click the Import External Data command, then click Import Data to display the Select Data Source dialog box. Use the Look in list box to locate the folder containing the database and choose Access Databases as the file type. Select the database, and then click the Open command to bring the Access table(s) into an Excel workbook. See practice exercise 3 at the end of the chapter.

418 CHAPTER 8: DATA ANALYSIS

Step 2: **Create the Basic Pivot Table**

- Click anywhere within the list of sales data. Pull down the **Data menu**. Click **PivotTable and PivotChart Report** to start the Pivot Table Wizard.

- The option for **Microsoft Office Excel list or database** is selected. Click the option button for **PivotChart report (with PivotTable report)**. Click **Next**.

- The entire list of sales data is automatically selected. Click **Next**. The option button to place the pivot table in a **New worksheet** is selected. Click **Finish**.

- Click the worksheet tab for **Sheet1**. The Pivot Table toolbar and field list should be open as shown in Figure 8.6b. If not, display the toolbar, and then click the button to **Show Field List**.

- Click and drag the **Sale Item**, **Category**, and **Salesperson fields** from the Pivot Table list to the Page, Row, and Column fields, respectively, as shown in Figure 8.6b. Drag the **Order Amount** to the Data Items field. Close the field list.

- Click anywhere in the **Grand Total column**, then click the **Sort Descending button** to list the sales amounts in descending sequence. Click the **Field Settings button** on the Pivot Table toolbar, click the **Number... button**, then change the format to **Currency** with **no decimals**. Click **OK** twice to accept the settings and close the dialog boxes. Save the workbook.

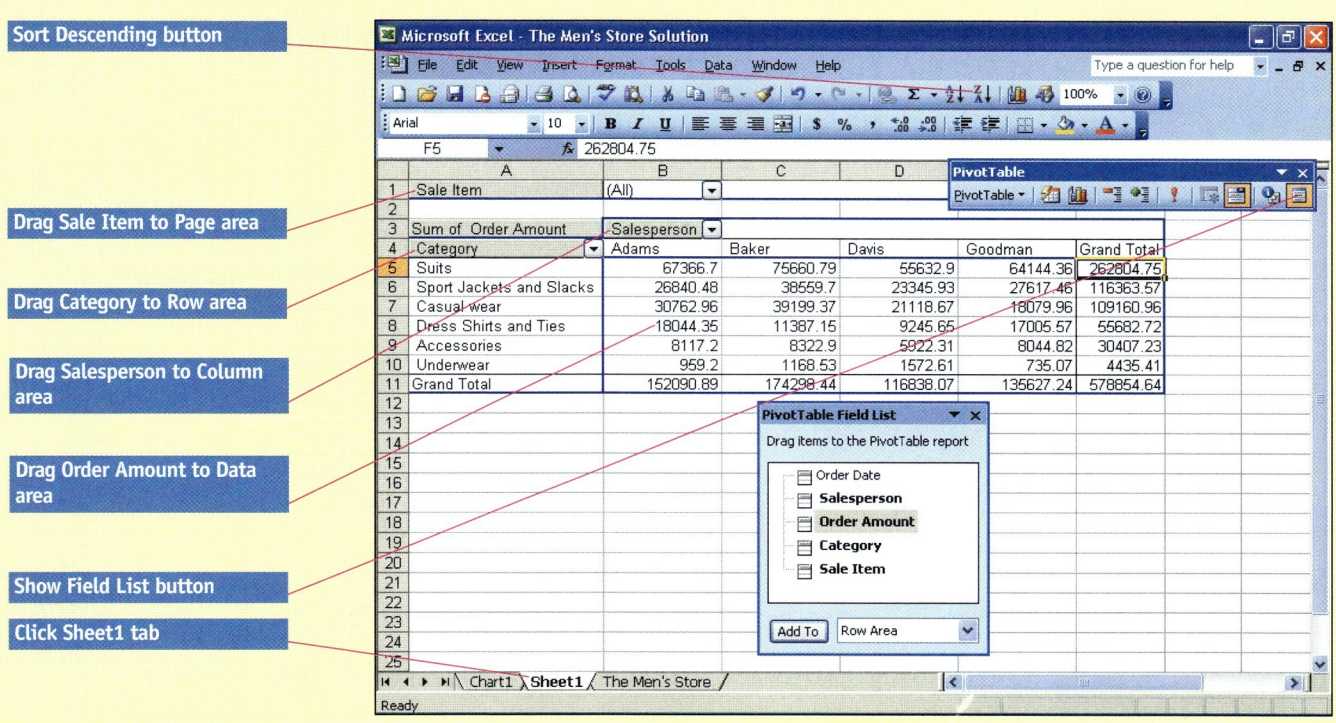

(b) Create the Pivot Table (step 2)

FIGURE 8.6 Hands-on Exercise 3

MULTIPLE CONSOLIDATION RANGES

What if you have several branch managers, each of whom sent you a summary workbook that displays the sales for each product in each quarter for that branch? Your task is to consolidate the information into a single pivot table that allows you to see the sales for each product for the organization as a whole. The solution is to specify multiple consolidation ranges. See practice exercise 7.

Step 3: Modify the Pivot Chart

- Click the **Chart1 tab** to view the initial pivot chart. You should see a stacked column chart as shown in Figure 8.6c, although your chart will be very different.

- Pull down the **Chart menu** and click the **Chart Type command**. Click **Stacked Column with a 3-D visual effect**. Check the box to use **Default formatting**, then click **OK**.

- Pull down the **Chart menu** and click the **Chart Options** command to display the Chart Options dialog box.

- Click the **Legend tab**, then clear the box to Show Legend. Click the **Data Table tab**, then check the box to show the Data Table. Click **OK**.

- Enter the title in Figure 8.6c in **18 point Arial**. Choose **Indigo** as the font color.

- Change to **landscape printing**. Print this chart for your instructor.

- Click **The Men's Store tab** to select the worksheet. Double click the worksheet tab, type **Sales Data**, and then press **Enter** to rename the tab. Rename the **Sheet1** and **Chart1** worksheets to **Basic Pivot Table** and **Basic Pivot Chart**.

- Change the color of one or more worksheet tabs as you see fit; **right click** the worksheet tab, click the **Tab Color command**, select a new color, and click **OK**.

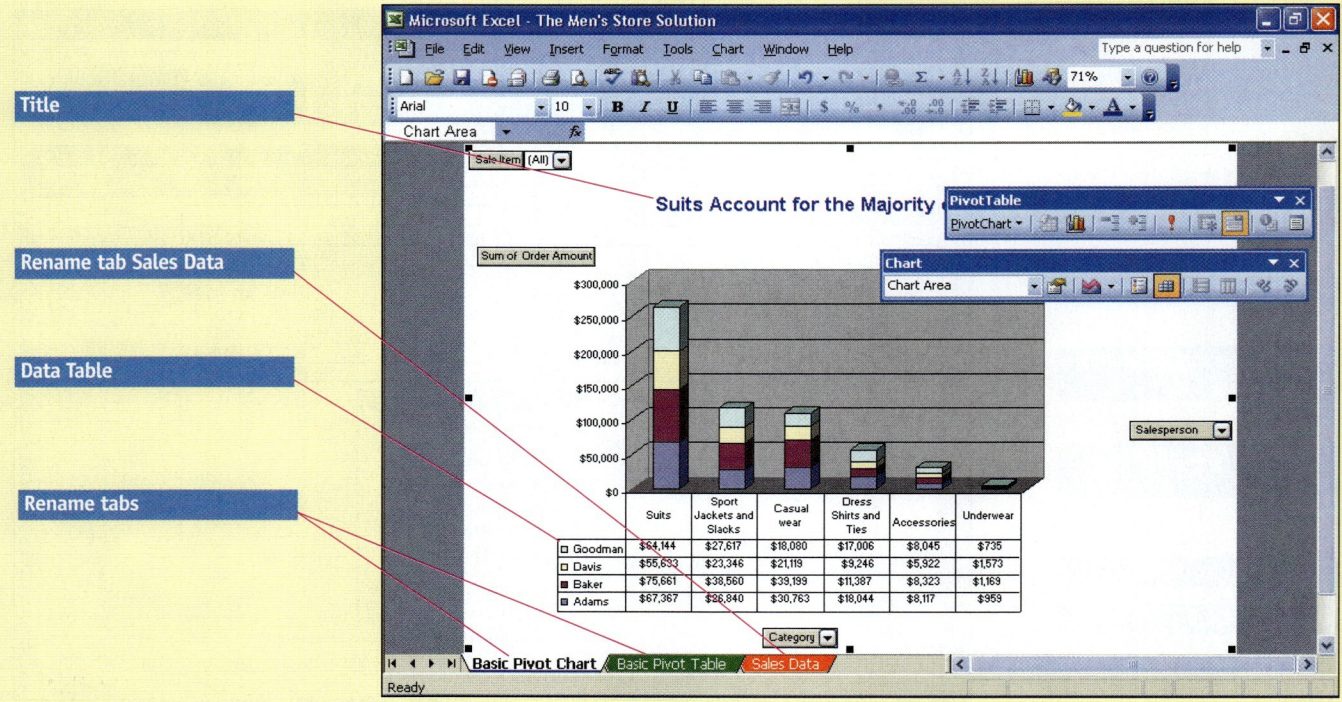

(c) Modify the Pivot Chart (step 3)

FIGURE 8.6 Hands-on Exercise 3 (*continued*)

HIDING AND UNHIDING A WORKSHEET

You can hide a worksheet just as you can hide a row(s) or column(s) within the worksheet. Click the tab of the worksheet you want to hide, pull down the Format menu, click Sheet, and then click the Hide command. Reverse the process to unhide a worksheet; pull down the Format menu, click Sheet, click the Unhide command, and then click the name of the worksheet you want to see.

Step 4: **Pivot the Chart**

- Click the **Basic Pivot Chart tab**. Pull down the **Chart menu**, click the **Chart Type command**, click the **Standard Types tab**, and choose **Clustered Column with 3-D visual effect**.

- Check the box to keep the **Default formatting**. Click **OK**. The chart changes to a side-by-side column chart, but does not yet resemble Figure 8.6d.

- Click and drag the various buttons on the pivot chart until you wind up with the same basic layout as in the figure. Do not worry about how the chart looks in the intermediate stages. If you have trouble, click the **Undo command** and start over.

- Add the chart title as shown in Figure 8.6d. Remove the legend and display the data table.

- Click the **Basic Pivot Table tab** to return to the associated pivot table, which looks very different from when you created it initially. Click in any cell in the body of the table.

- Click the **Field Settings button** on the Pivot Table toolbar to display the PivotTable Field dialog box.

- Click the **Options button** and click the **down arrow** in the Show Data as list box. Scroll to the bottom until you can select **% of Total**. Click **OK**. The pivot table changes to display percentages, as opposed to dollar amounts.

- Click the **Basic Pivot Chart tab** to return to the pivot chart, which should now match Figure 8.6d. Print the chart sheet for your instructor.

- Save the workbook.

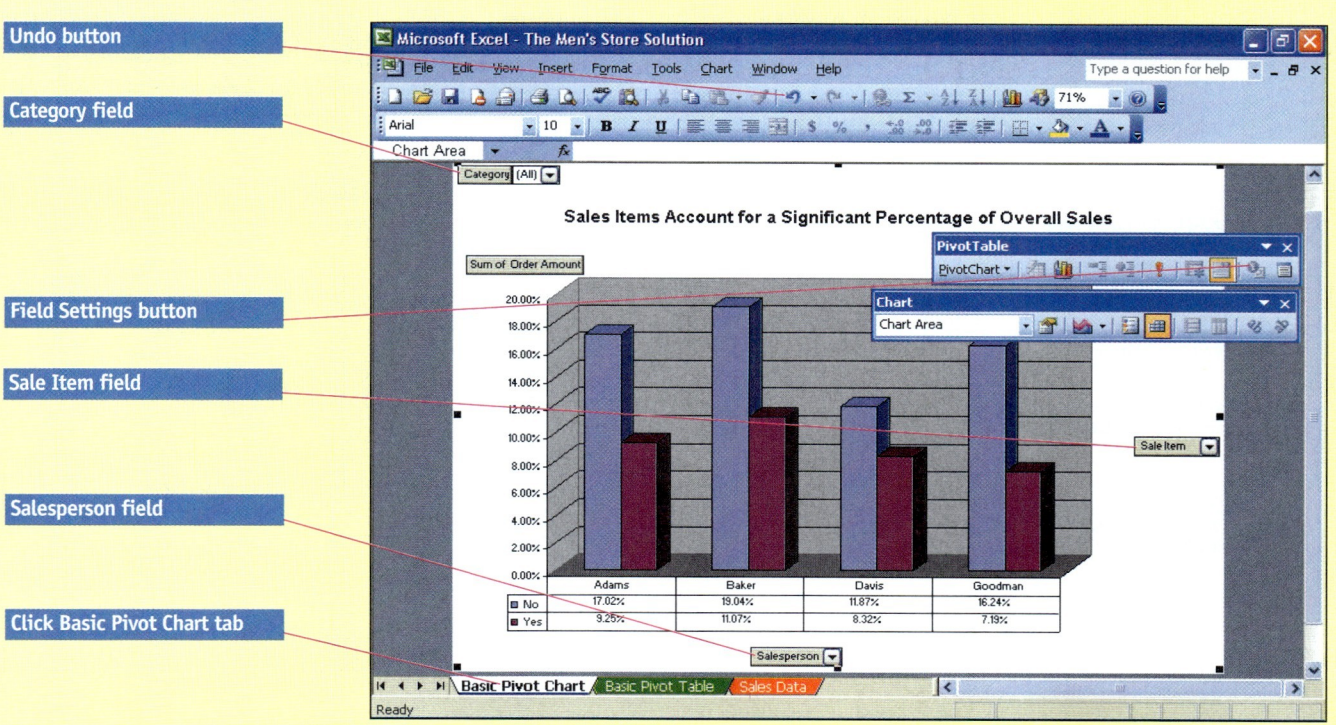

(d) Pivot the Chart (step 4)

FIGURE 8.6 Hands-on Exercise 3 (*continued*)

Step 5: **Group the Data**

- Return to the **Sales Data worksheet**, click anywhere within the list of sales data, pull down the **Data menu**, and click **PivotTable and PivotChart Report** to start the Pivot Table Wizard.

- The option button for **Microsoft Office Excel list or database** is already selected. The **Pivot Table option button** is selected. Click **Next**. The table of sales data is selected. Click **Next**.

- Click **Yes** when asked if you want the new report to be based on the same data as the existing report. The next screen selects the pivot table you just created as the source of the data. Click **Next**.

- The option button for a **New worksheet** is already selected. Click **Finish**. The pivot table is created on Sheet1.

- Click and drag the **Order Date field** to the row area, and then drag the **Order Amount field** to the data area. **Right click** any date, click the **Group and Show Detail command**, and then click **Group** to display the Grouping dialog box.

- Click **Months** in the By area (to toggle this group off), click **Quarters**, then click **OK**. The row field should display four values: Qtr1, Qtr2, Qtr3, and Qtr4.

- Complete the pivot table by dragging **Sale Item** to the page area, **Salesperson** to the column area, and **Category** to the row area (to the right of the order date).

- The completed pivot table is shown in the next step in Figure 8.6f. Rename the worksheet containing the pivot table **Quarterly by Category**. Close the field list.

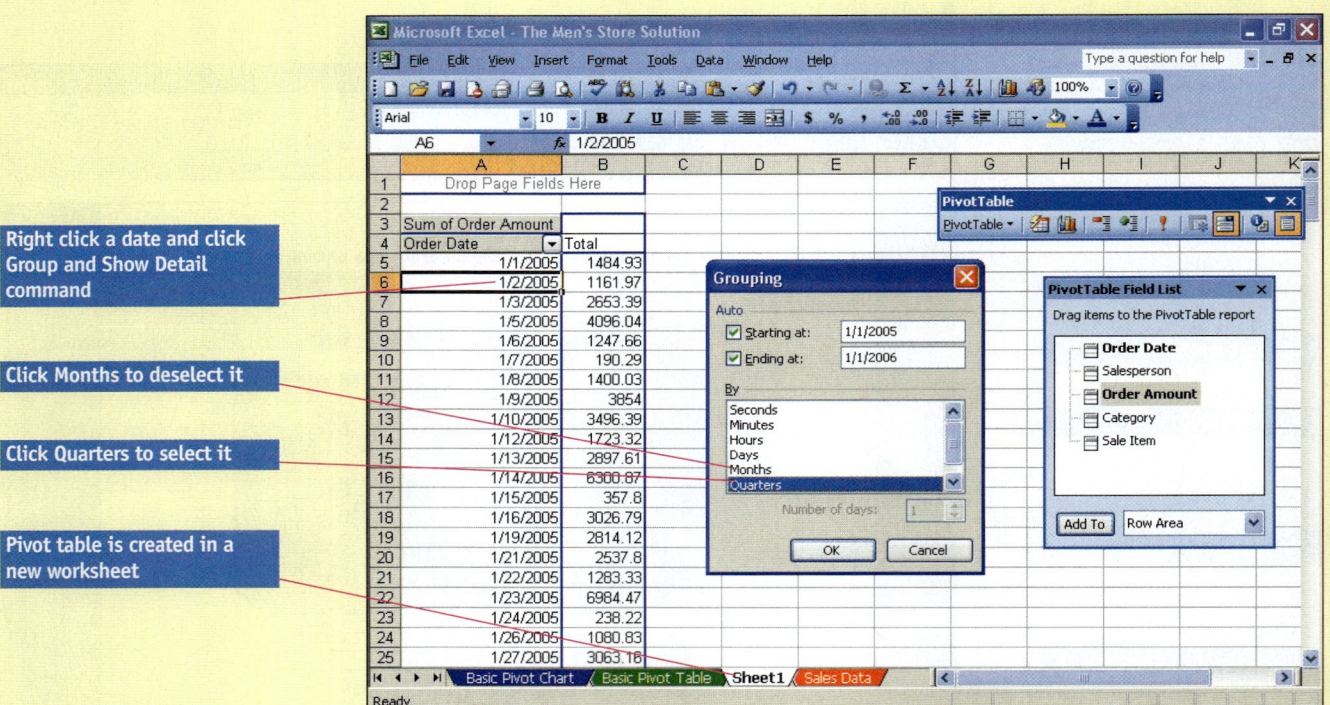

(e) Group the Data (step 5)

FIGURE 8.6 Hands-on Exercise 3 (*continued*)

Step 6: **Refresh the Data**

- Click the tab for the **Sales Data worksheet**, then press **Ctrl+Home to** move cell A1. Pull down the **Edit menu** and click the **Replace command**. Enter **Adams** and **Your Name** (Grauer is used in our worksheet) as the Find What and Replace With string, respectively.

- Click the **Replace All button**. Excel indicates 179 replacements; that is, there were 179 transactions for Adams in the original sales data. Click **OK**. Your name should now appear in the worksheet instead of Adams, starting with the very first transaction on 1/1/2006. Close the Find and Replace dialog box.

- Click the **Quarterly by Category worksheet tab** to view the pivot table and note that Adams appears, as opposed to your name.

- Click anywhere in the pivot table, then click the **Refresh Data button** (the exclamation point) on the Pivot table toolbar. You should see your name (Grauer in our example) instead of Adams in the column headings.

- Click anywhere in the pivot table, click the **Format Report button** on the Pivot Table toolbar, scroll through the list of available formats, then click **OK** when you see the format you like. (We chose the Table 4 format.)

- Click the **Field Settings button** on the PivotTable toolbar. Change the **Number format** to **currency** with **zero decimals**.

- Scroll down in the pivot table until you come to the grand total row, which contains the totals for each salesperson. **Double click** in the cell containing your total ($152,091).

- Excel creates a new worksheet (e.g., Sheet5) that contains the 179 sales transactions associated with your name. Double click the **worksheet tab**, type your name (Grauer in our example), and press **Enter** to rename the worksheet.

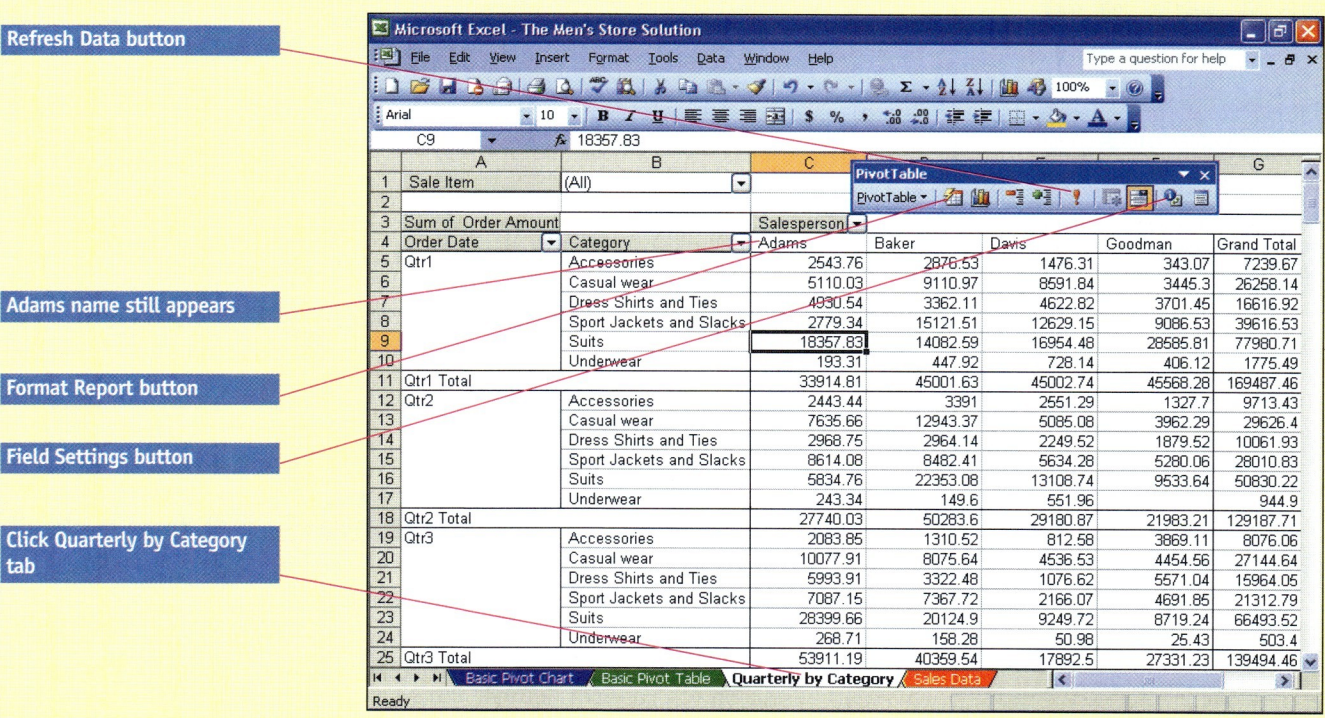

(f) Refresh the Data (step 6)

FIGURE 8.6 Hands-on Exercise 3 (*continued*)

Step 7: The Documentation Worksheet

- Pull down the **Insert menu** and click the **Worksheet command** to insert a new worksheet. Double click the worksheet tab, type **Documentation** as the new name, then press **Enter**.

- Your workbook should contain all of the worksheet tabs in Figure 8.6g, although the order may be different. Click and drag the various worksheet tabs to match our sequence, then change the color of the tabs as you see fit.

- Select the worksheet containing your sales data. Click anywhere in the **Order Date column**, then click the **Sort Ascending button** on the Standard toolbar. The data is sequenced by order date. The first transaction occurred on January 1, 2005. Print the first page of transactions for your instructor.

- Enter the text for the Documentation worksheet as shown in Figure 8.6g. Insert clip art as appropriate, format the Documentation worksheet as you see fit, then print this worksheet for your instructor. Save the workbook.

- Exit Excel if you do not want to continue with the next exercise at this time.

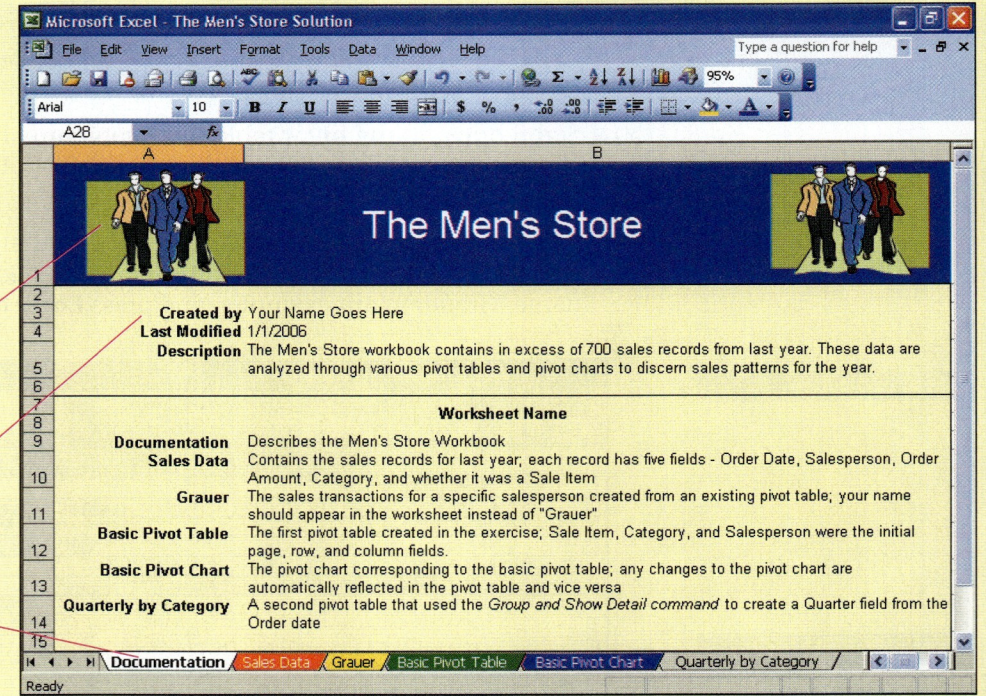

(g) The Documentation Worksheet (step 7)

FIGURE 8.6 Hands-on Exercise 3 (*continued*)

GENERATING TEST DATA

This exercise, like the three that preceded it, depended on the availability of several hundred records for analysis. The data in all four exercises was purely hypothetical and a figment of our imagination. How then did we obtain the data, and further, how did we "force" the data to display reasonable trends in each example? We relied heavily on the random number function in Excel; for example, =RAND() generates a random number that is uniformly distributed from zero to one. Once you know the existence of this function, you can use various formulas to create data that conforms to desired values; =100+500*RAND() generates a random number between 100 and 600. See practice exercise 9 at the end of the chapter.

THE RESTAURANT

Our last example analyzes the weekly sales data of a neighborhood restaurant. No one works harder than the proprietor of an independent restaurant who does not have the benefit of a large chain with the attendant purchasing power and advertising potential. The owner must depend on his or her individual resources to sustain a business in a very competitive environment. The workload is endless as the owner feels compelled to remain open every day of the week, but is this decision justified in terms of the actual receipts? The worksheet in Figure 8.7 is intended to answer this and other questions about the restaurant. Consider:

1. What was the restaurant's revenue for last year? On which day(s) of the week did the restaurant do the best? Should additional staff be hired for those days?

2. On which day(s) of the week did the restaurant do the poorest? Should the restaurant remain open on those days?

3. How closely does the daily revenue follow the Pareto Principle or 80/20 rule?

4. Display this information in graphical form.

Implementation in Excel

The pivot table in Figure 8.7a is based on the 365 data points that appear in the body of the worksheet. Each data point represents the sales for one day. We are given the date (starting in cell D26) and the sales for that day (cell F26). The day of the week is computed using a combination of the WEEKDAY and VLOOKUP functions. The **WEEKDAY function** returns a numerical value from 1 to 7, corresponding to the days of the week, from Sunday to Saturday, respectively. The VLOOKUP function in cell E26 takes the numerical result and applies it to the table of weekday names to display the day of the week.

The pivot table analyzes the data by the day of the week, computing the total receipts and corresponding percentage for each day over the course of the year, such as $227,404 and 37.58% for Saturday. The pivot chart in Figure 8.7b is an example of a ***Pareto chart***, named for Vilfredo Pareto, a 19th century economist who is credited with establishing the ***Pareto Principle*** or ***80/20 rule***. Pareto found that 80% of the activity in a system is attributable to 20% of the transactions. For example, 80% of the questions in your class may arise from 20% of the students. Pareto established the principal when he examined land holdings in Italy and observed that 80% of the land was owned by 20% of the population.

The percentages may not hold exactly, but the principle is valid; that is, the bulk of activity in any system stems from a relatively small percentage of the transactions. The analysis of the restaurant data, for example, shows that 65% of the weekly revenue is attributable to Friday and Saturday (two days or 28% of the week). To create the Pareto chart, the rows (days of the week) in the pivot table are displayed in descending sequence according to the sales receipts for each day. This sequence is reflected automatically in the associated pivot chart, which is an essential characteristic of a Pareto chart; that is, the data is displayed in descending magnitude to emphasize the relative importance of the different data series.

CREATE A PIVOT CHART AFTER THE FACT

A pivot chart is created automatically with the associated pivot table, provided you select the appropriate option button, PivotChart report (*with PivotTable report*). What if, however, you go through all the trouble to modify the pivot table, and then realize you forgot to create the pivot chart? You don't have to start over. Just click anywhere in the pivot table, then click the Chart Wizard button on the Standard toolbar to create the pivot chart.

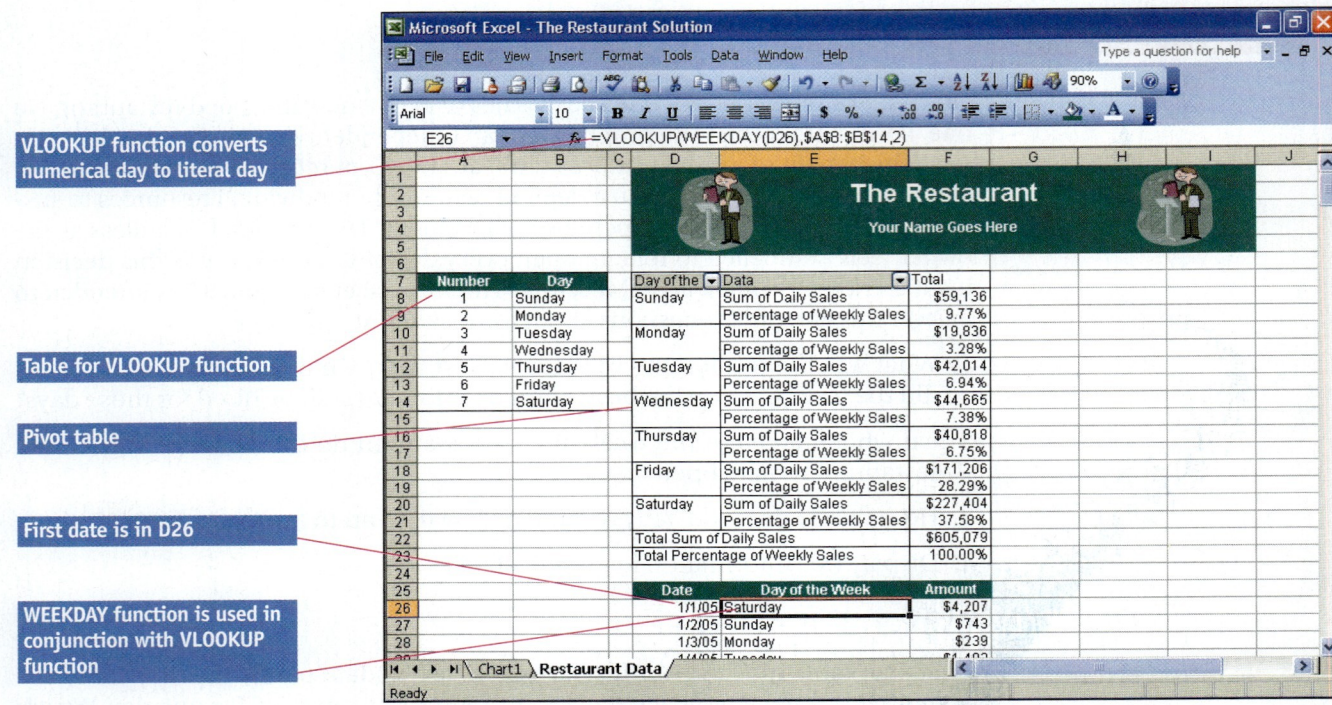

(a) The Pivot Table and Restaurant Data

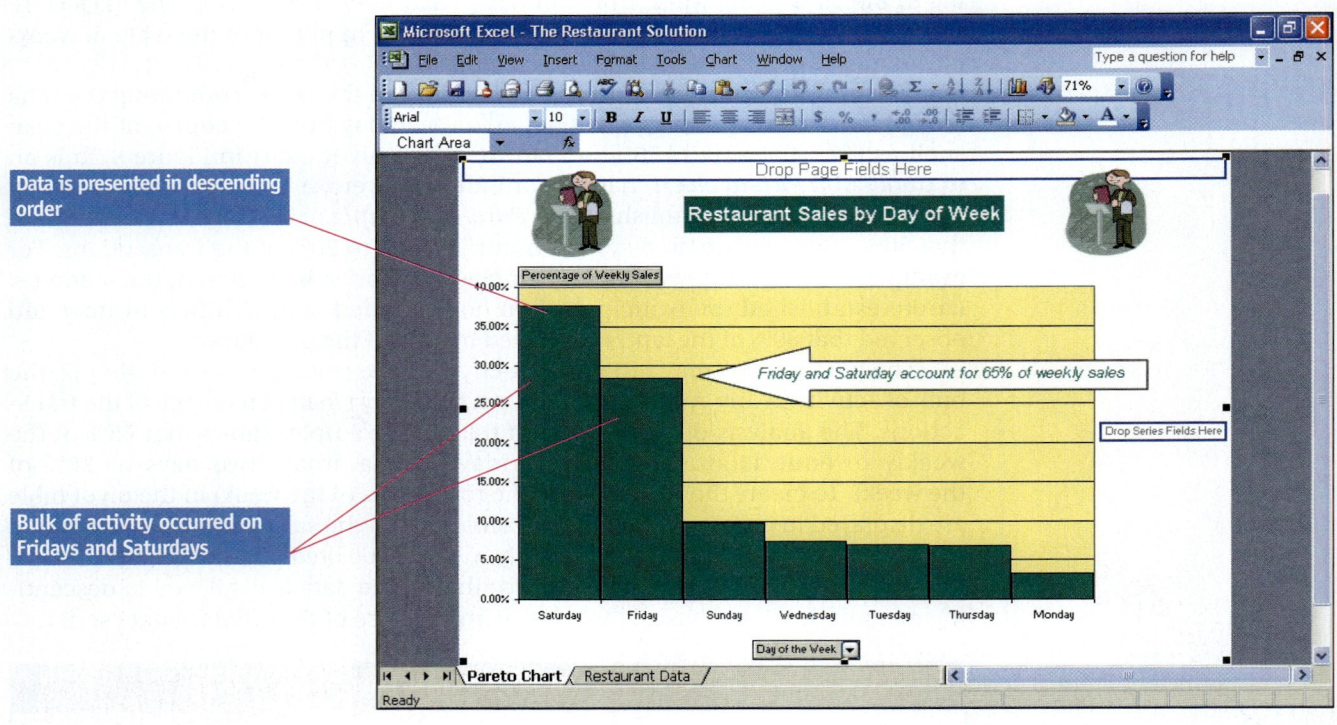

(b) Pareto Chart

FIGURE 8.7 The Restaurant

426 CHAPTER 8: DATA ANALYSIS

hands-on exercise
4 The Restaurant

Objective To display the day of the week given a calendar date; to create a pivot table and corresponding pivot chart; to determine percentage values within a pivot table; to convert the pivot chart to a Pareto chart. Use Figure 8.8.

Step 1: **Determine the Day of the Week**

- Open **The Restaurant workbook** in the **Exploring Excel folder**. Click in **cell E26**, type **=WEEKDAY(D26)**, and press **Enter**. You should see the number 7, which corresponds to the number for Saturday.

- Click in **cell E26**, press the **F2 key** to edit the existing formula, then modify the formula as shown in Figure 8.8a. Press **Enter**. This time you see Saturday.

- Copy the formula in **cell E26** to the remaining rows in the column. Click and drag to select the column headings for columns A, B, and C. Right click, then click the **Hide command** since we no longer need to reference the table.

- Save the workbook as **The Restaurant Solution**.

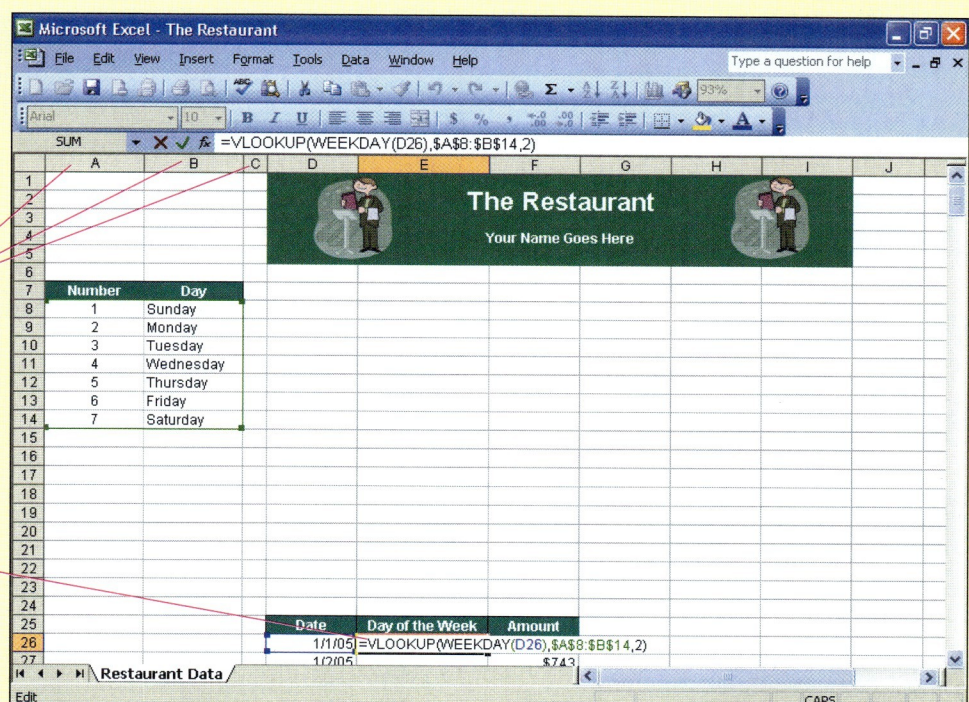

(a) Determine the Day of the Week (step 1)

FIGURE 8.8 Hands-on Exercise 4

DATE FORMATS AND DATE ARITHMETIC

A date is entered into a worksheet by typing the date directly into a cell; for example, 1/21/2005 to enter January 1, 2005. Once entered, a date can be displayed in a variety of formats such as January 21, 2005; 21-Jan-05; 1/21/2005; or 1/1/05. Regardless of the format, however, a date is stored internally as a serial number, starting with January 1, 1900, which is stored as the number 1. This enables date arithmetic; thus, to calculate the number of days between two dates, simply subtract one date from the other, then display the result as a number.

Step 2: **Create the Pivot Table**

- Click anywhere within the list of sales data. Pull down the **Data menu**. Click **PivotTable and PivotChart Report** to start the Pivot Table Wizard.

- The option button for **Microsoft Office Excel list or database** is already selected. Click the option button for **PivotChart report (with PivotTable report)**. Click **Next**.

- The entire list of sales data is automatically selected. Click **Next**. Click the option button to place the PivotTable report in an **Existing worksheet**. Click in the associated text box and then click in **cell D7**.

- Click the **Layout . . . button** to display the dialog box in Figure 8.8b. Click the **Day of the week button** at the right of the dialog box and drag it to the row area.

- Click the **Amount button** and drag it to the data area. Click the **Amount button** a second time and drag it to the data area. (You need the amount field twice, once to show the dollar amount and once to show the percent.)

- Click **OK** to close the dialog box, then click the **Finish button** to create the pivot table and associated pivot chart. Save the workbook.

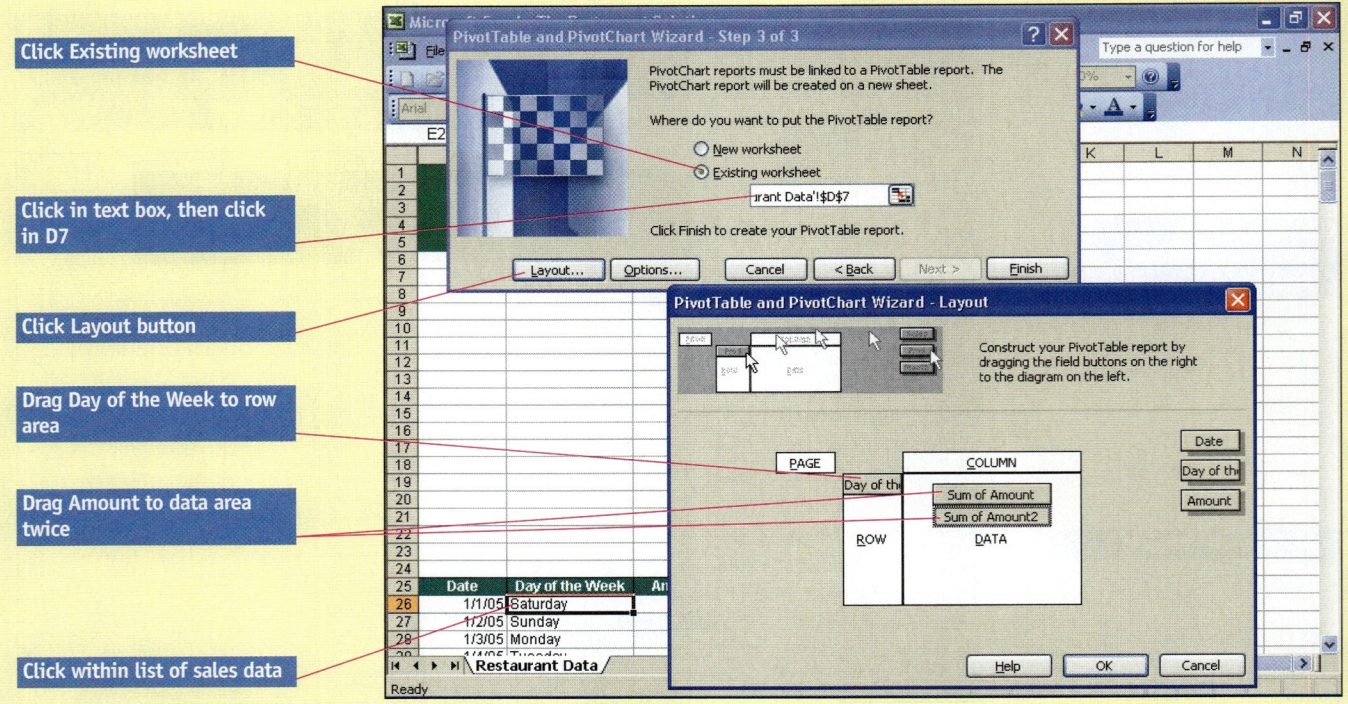

(b) Create the Pivot table (step 2)

FIGURE 8.8 Hands-on Exercise 4 (*continued*)

THE LAYOUT BUTTON

The Layout button is the easiest way to create or modify a pivot table. Right click any cell in an existing pivot table, click the PivotTable Wizard command, then click the Layout button to display the Layout screen. You can add a new field to the row, column, or data area by dragging the field from the field list to the appropriate area. You can delete a field by dragging the field away from the table. You can also change any calculation in the data area by double clicking the field to display a dialog box where you change the function, e.g., from Sum to Average.

Step 3: **Customize the Pivot Table**

- Click the **Restaurant Data tab**, then scroll to the top of the worksheet. You should see the pivot table in Figure 8.8c. Close the Pivot Table field list as we do not need it at this time. Click and drag the Pivot Table toolbar out of the way.

- Click in **cell F8**, the cell containing the total sales for Sunday. Click the **Field Settings button** on the Pivot Table toolbar to display the associated dialog box.

- Click in the **Name box**. Type **Sum of Daily Sales** to replace the original Sum of Amount label. Click the **Number button** to display the Format Cells dialog box. Select the **Currency category** and choose **zero decimal places**. Click **OK** to apply the formatting. Click **OK** a second time to close the dialog box.

- Click in **cell F9**, then click the **Field Settings button** on the Pivot Table toolbar. Click in the **Name box** and enter **Percentage of Weekly Sales**. Click the **Number button** to display the Format Cells dialog box. Select the **Percentage category** and choose **two decimal places**. Click **OK**.

- Click the **Options button** in the PivotTable Field dialog box. Click the **down arrow** in the Show data as list box, click **% of column**, and click **OK**. You should see 9.77% corresponding to the percent of weekly sales for Sunday.

- Use the **Page Setup command** to create a custom footer and to center the worksheet horizontally. Click and drag to select **cells D1:I23**.

- Pull down the **File menu**, click the **Print command**, click the option button to print **Selection**, then click **OK**. (Do not print the individual transactions, as they run for several pages.)

- Save the workbook.

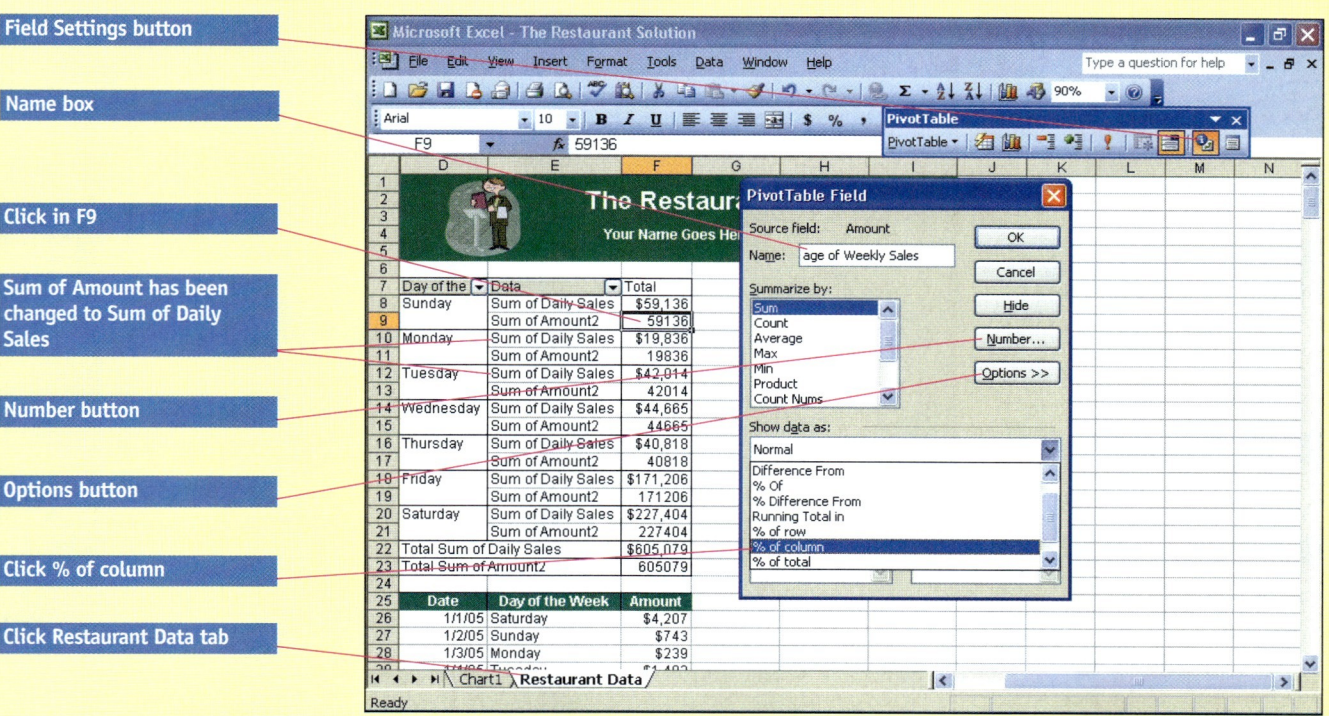

(c) Customize the Pivot Table (step 3)

FIGURE 8.8 Hands-on Exercise 4 (*continued*)

Step 4: **Modify the Pivot Chart**

- Click the **Chart1 worksheet tab** to view the pivot chart in Figure 8.8d. Click the **down arrow** on the Data button, then clear the check box next to the Sum of Daily Sales field as shown in Figure 8.8d. Click **OK**.
- The pivot changes to show just the percent of the weekly total for each day of the week. The scale on the Y axis changes automatically as well.
- Pull down the **Chart menu**, click **Chart Options**, then click the **Legend tab**. Clear the box to Show Legend, then click **OK** to accept this setting and close the Chart Options dialog box.
- Click the **Restaurant Data worksheet tab**. The pivot table has changed to show only a single data field (the percent of weekly sales); that is, anything you do to the pivot chart is automatically reflected in the pivot table and vice versa.
- Click in **cell E9** of the pivot table (the cell containing the percentage of sales for Sunday). Click the **Sort Descending button** on the Standard toolbar to display the weekly sales in descending order. The sales for Saturday now appear in the first row of the pivot table.
- Click the **Chart1 worksheet tab** to return to the pivot chart. The columns representing the days of the week are displayed in descending order to emphasize the relative importance of each day.
- Click in the title (which currently displays "Total") and type **Restaurant Sales by Day of Week**. Click outside the title, then click to select the title. Click the **down arrow** in the Font size box and change to **18 point text**. Click the **Bold button**. Set the fill color to **Teal** and the font color to **White**.
- Save the workbook.

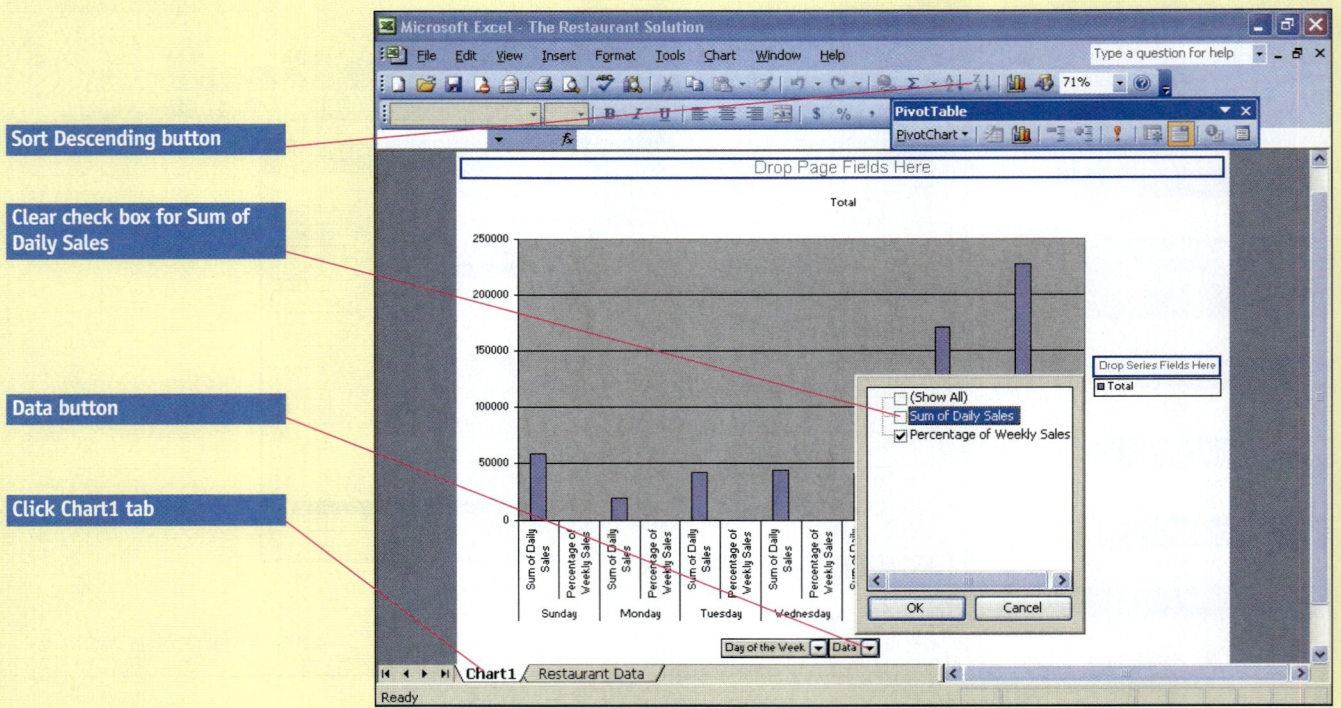

(d) Modify the Pivot Chart (step 4)

FIGURE 8.8 Hands-on Exercise 4 (*continued*)

Step 5: **Complete the Pareto Chart**

- Right click any column within the chart, click the **Format Data series command** to display the associated dialog box, then click the **Options tab**. Use the spin arrow to change the **gap width to zero**, which eliminates the space between the columns.

- Click the **Patterns tab**, then click the **Teal green color** to change the color of the columns. Click **OK** to accept the changes and close the Format Series dialog box.

- Right click anywhere within the gray area of the chart background and click the command to **Format Plot area**. Change the color to **light yellow** and click **OK**.

- Pull down the **View menu**, click **Toolbars**, then click **Drawing** to display the Drawing toolbar as shown in Figure 8.8e.

- Click the **AutoShapes button**, click **Block Arrows**, and select an arrow style.

- Click in the chart (the mouse pointer changes to a thin crosshair), then click and drag to create an arrow. Release the mouse.

- Enter the desired text, **Friday and Saturday account for 65% of weekly sales**, then change the formatting as you see fit. (We used 14-point Italic Teal.)

- Copy the clip art image of the waiter from the Restaurant Data worksheet to the chart. Save the workbook.

- Use the **Page Setup command** to change to landscape printing, and then print the completed chart for your instructor. Close the Drawing toolbar.

- Save the workbook.

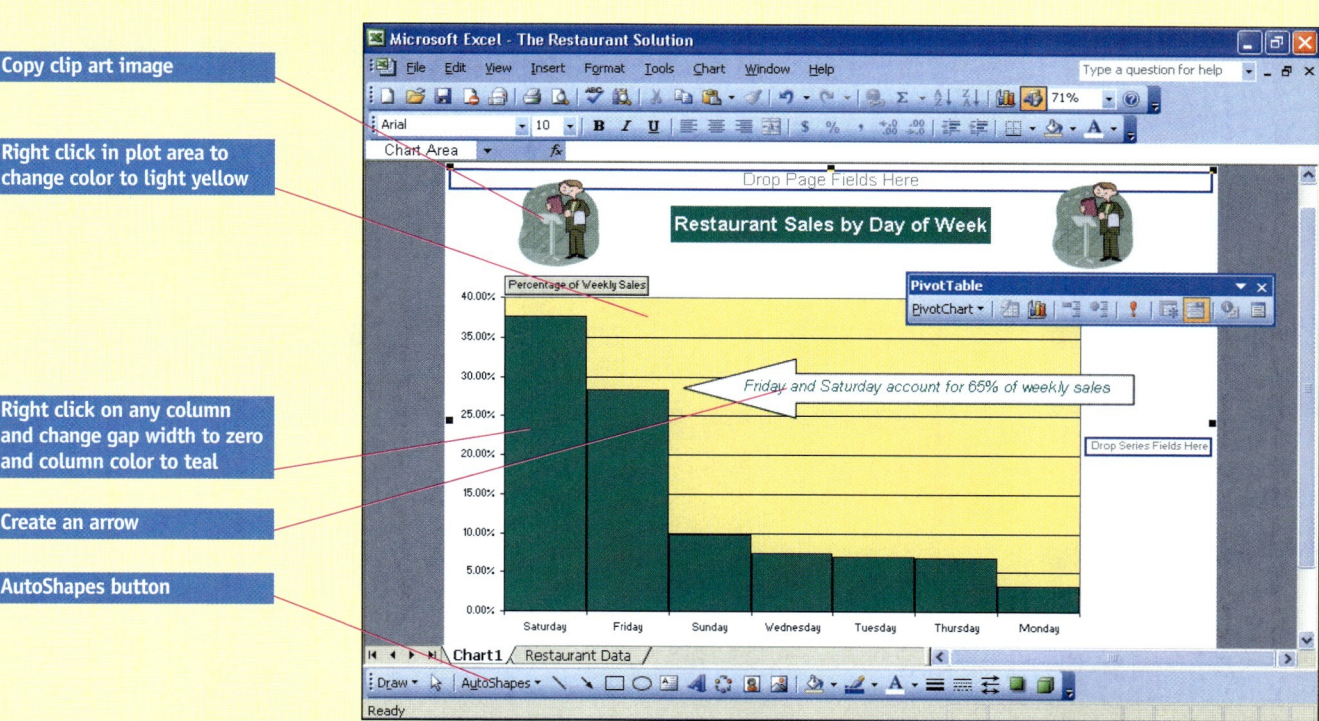

(e) Complete the Pareto Chart (step 5)

FIGURE 8.8   Hands-on Exercise 4 (*continued*)

Step 6: **Shade the Alternate Rows**

- Click the **Restaurant Data tab**. Click and drag to select **rows 18:23**, **right click** the selection, and then click the **Delete command**. (These rows were part of the original pivot table and are no longer relevant.)

- Click and drag to select **cells D20:F384** (the cells containing the restaurant data). Pull down the **Format menu** and click the **Conditional Formatting command** to display the associated dialog box.

- Click the **down arrow** in the Condition 1 list box and choose **Formula Is**. Click in the text box and enter the formula **=MOD(ROW(),2)=1**.

- Click the **Format button** to display the Format Cells dialog box. Click the **Patterns tab**, click **Teal** as the desired fill color, and then click **OK**. You see black letters on a teal (dark) background. The alternate rows will be shaded, but the text will not be easy to read.

- Click the **Format button** a second time to again display the Format Cells dialog box, but this time click the **Font tab**. Click the **down arrow** on the Font color list box and click **White**. Click **OK**. You should see white text on a dark background as shown in Figure 8.8f. Click **OK** to close the Conditional Formatting dialog box.

- Complete the formatting. We widened the columns, added vertical lines between the columns, and centered the entries. Save the workbook.

- Pull down the **File menu**, click the **Print command**, click the option button for **Page(s)** in the Print Range area, and **enter 1** as both the **From** and **To page**; that is, you are printing page one only.

- Exit Excel. Congratulations on a job well done.

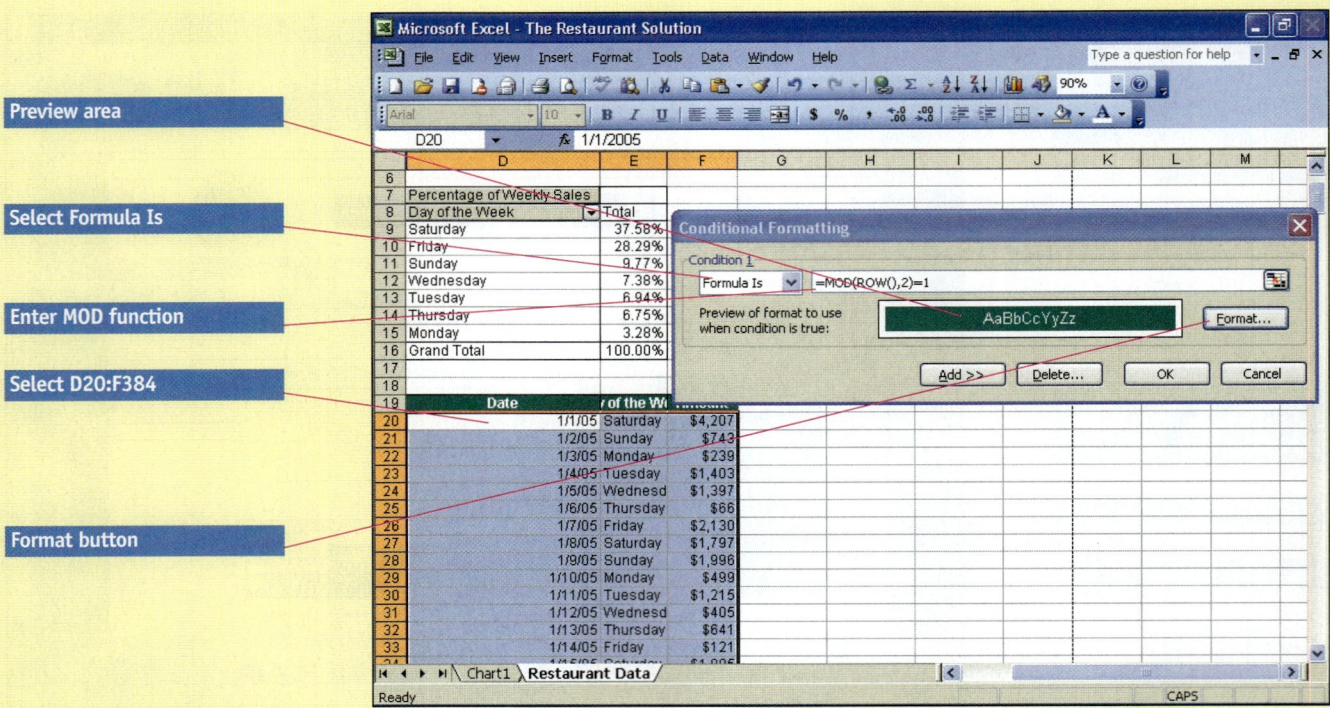

(f) Shade the Alternate Rows (step 6)

FIGURE 8.8   Hands-on Exercise 4 (*continued*)

SUMMARY

Excel is a powerful tool for data analysis. This chapter was built around four independent examples, each of which used a variety of techniques to analyze the data within a list of several hundred records. The techniques included sorting, calculating, filtering, summarizing (subtotals and pivot tables), formatting, and charting.

Several functions were used in the various analyses. These included statistical functions (QUARTILE, RANK, and COUNTIF), logical functions (AND and OR), lookup functions (HLOOKUP and VLOOKUP), date functions (WEEKDAY), and text functions (CONCATENATE and TRIM).

A pivot table provides the ultimate flexibility in data analysis. It divides the records in a list into categories, and then computes summary statistics for those categories. The Group and Show Detail command can create additional fields within the pivot table that were not present in the original data; for example, it creates a quarter field from specific dates. A pivot table does not however, automatically reflect changes in the underlying data, and thus you must execute the Refresh command to update the table whenever the underlying data changes.

A pivot chart is the graphical equivalent of a pivot table, which at first glance resembles any other chart. A pivot chart, however, contains the same shaded buttons as the corresponding pivot table, enabling you to change the chart by dragging the buttons to different areas. A Pareto chart can be easily created from a pivot chart and displays the relative importance of the differences between groups of data. The Pareto chart is associated with the "Pareto Principle" or 80/20 rule, which states that the bulk of activity in any system stems from a small percentage of the transactions.

Formatting is an important consideration and indeed is not typically thought of as an analysis technique. The results of an analysis must be apparent to the end user, however, and this is best accomplished through appropriate formatting. In addition, conditional formatting can present data in different colors, fonts, or styles according to the value of the data; for example, you can shade data depending on whether the value is greater than, equal to, or less than zero. The MOD and ROW functions were also used with conditional formatting in an innovative example to shade the alternate rows in a worksheet.

Regardless of the analysis, it is also important to realize that the data in an Excel workbook may originate from a variety of sources and further that it is essential to go back and forth between different formats and/or different platforms. Incoming data may come from an Excel workbook, a text or CSV (Comma Separated Values) file, an XML document, the Web (via a Web query), and/or an Access database.

KEY WORDS AND CONCEPTS

80/20 rule 425	Group and Show Detail command 416	QUARTILE function 408
Access database 399		RAND function 424
AND function 399	Hide command 420	RANK function 408
AutoFilter command 399	HLOOKUP function 408	Refresh command 416
Calculating 398	IF function 403	RIGHT function 410
Charting 398	Insert Name command 413	Row field 416
Column field 416	LEFT function 410	ROW function 408
CONCATENATE function 410	LEN function 410	Sort command 408
Conditional Formatting 398	LOWER function 410	Sorting 398
COUNT function 405	MOD function 408	Subtotals command 408
COUNTA function 405	Modulo arithmetic 408	Summarizing 398
COUNTIF function 399	Name box 413	TRIM function 410
CSV file 399	OR function 399	Unhide command 401
Custom filter 399	Page field 416	UPPER function 410
Data analysis 398	Pareto chart 425	VLOOKUP function 408
Filtering 398	Pareto Principle 425	Web query 399
Formatting 398	Pivot Chart 416	WEEKDAY function 425
Goal Seek command 399	Pivot Table 398	XML document 399

MULTIPLE CHOICE

1. The data in an Excel workbook can be imported from:
   (a) A text file
   (b) An XML document
   (c) An Access database
   (d) All of the above

2. What value will be returned by the function =IF(A=B, IF(C>D, 10, 20), 30), if A, B, C, and D are all equal to 100?
   (a) 10
   (b) 20
   (c) 30
   (d) Impossible to determine

3. What value will be returned by the function =IF(AND(W<X, Y<Z), 50, 60) if W, X, Y, and Z are equal to 10, 20, 30, and 40, respectively?
   (a) 50
   (b) 60
   (c) True
   (d) False

4. The function =QUARTILE(A1:A100,0) will return:
   (a) The maximum value in the range A1:A100
   (b) The minimum value in the range A1:A100
   (c) The numerical value of the first quartile
   (d) The function is in error; that is, you cannot have the 0th quartile

5. Which of the following is true regarding the lookup functions?
   (a) The HLOOKUP function requires that comparison values (breakpoints) be located in a row *above* the values you want displayed in the cell
   (b) The VLOOKUP function requires that comparison values (breakpoints) be located in a column to the *left* of the values you want displayed in the cell
   (c) Both (a) and (b)
   (d) Neither (a) nor (b)

6. Which column contains the value that will be returned by the function =VLOOKUP(A4,$A$21:$D$25,3)?
   (a) Column A
   (b) Column B
   (c) Column C
   (d) Column D

7. Cells A1 and A2 contain the values 10 and 20, respectively. What value will be returned by the function =AND(A1=10, A2 =21)?
   (a) 10
   (b) 20
   (c) True
   (d) False

8. Cells A1 and A2 contain the values 10 and 20, respectively. What value will be returned by the function =OR(A1=10, A2 =21)?
   (a) 10
   (b) 20
   (c) True
   (d) False

9. Which of the following is equivalent to the expression =D1 & D2?
   (a) JOIN(D1, D2)
   (b) STRING(D1, D2)
   (c) TEXT(D1, D2)
   (d) CONCATENATE(D1, D2)

10. The rule postulated by Vilfredo Pareto is also known as the:
    (a) 80/20 rule
    (b) 70/30 rule
    (c) 60/40 rule
    (d) 50/50 rule

... continued

multiple choice

11. What value is returned by the formula =MOD(10,2)?

(a) 0
(b) 10
(c) 2
(d) Impossible to determine

12. What value(s) is (are) returned by the function =MOD(ROW(),2)?

(a) True or False
(b) Zero or one
(c) Any integer value
(d) Impossible to determine

13. The WEEKDAY function:

(a) Returns a numeric value, as opposed to the actual day
(b) Returns the day of the week as an abbreviation, such as M or T
(c) Returns the actual day of the week, such as Monday or Tuesday
(d) Either (a), (b), or (c) according to the return type specified in the function

14. Which of the following is *not* an input parameter to the Goal Seek command?

(a) The desired value of the end result
(b) The cell containing the end result
(c) The value of the input cell that is required to reach the end result
(d) The cell whose value will change to reach the end result

15. Which of the following is true about pivot charts?

(a) A pivot chart is created automatically for every pivot table
(b) A pivot chart can be created after the corresponding pivot table
(c) Both (a) and (b)
(d) Neither (a) nor (b)

16. Which of the following is not found in a pivot table?

(a) A row field
(b) A column field
(c) A page field
(d) A pivot field

17. Which of the following is a true statement about pivot tables?

(a) Any changes to a pivot table are automatically reflected in the associated pivot chart
(b) Any changes in the underlying list are automatically reflected in the associated pivot table
(c) Both (a) and (b)
(d) Neither (a) nor (b)

18. You want to use the Subtotals command to show total expenses for each department with the departments appearing in alphabetical order. What should you do before executing the Subtotals command?

(a) Sort the list by expenses in ascending order
(b) Sort the list by expenses in descending order
(c) Sort the list by department in ascending order
(d) Sort the list by department in descending order

ANSWERS

1. d	**7.** d	**13.** a
2. b	**8.** c	**14.** c
3. a	**9.** d	**15.** b
4. b	**10.** a	**16.** d
5. c	**11.** a	**17.** a
6. c	**12.** b	**18.** c

PRACTICE WITH EXCEL

1. **Countries of the World:** How much do you know about the world we live in? There are nearly 200 countries, but how many of the 20 largest (or smallest) can you identify? Is your criterion the area of a country or its population? Which countries are the most densely populated? This is your chance to find out.

    a. Open the *Chapter 8 Practice 1—Countries of the World* workbook in Figure 8.9, which presently contains only the Original Data worksheet. Enter your name as indicated.

    b. Click in cell E9. Enter the formula to compute the population density, =INT(D9/C9). Copy this formula to the remaining rows in the worksheet.

    c. Pull down the File menu, click the Page Setup command to display the Page Setup dialog box, then click the Sheet tab. Click the Rows to Repeat at Top list box, then click and drag to select rows 1 through 8. Click the Page tab, click the Fit to button, and enter 1 page for the width. Create a custom footer with the date, your name, and the name of the worksheet tab. Center the worksheet horizontally. Print the worksheet, which should run four pages.

    d. Copy this worksheet three additional times to create the Area, Population, and Density worksheets as shown in Figure 8.9. Rename each worksheet after it has been created.

    e. Click in the newly created Area worksheet. Click in cell B1 and change the title to "The 20 Largest Countries by Area". Click anywhere within the list in column C (the column that contains the area for each country). Click the Sort Descending button to show the countries in descending sequence of area; that is, the largest country Russia is shown first.

    f. Pull down the Data menu, click Filter, then click AutoFilter. Click the down arrow that appears in the Area column, click (Top 10 . . .) to display the associated dialog box, use the spin arrow to select 20 items, then click OK. You see the 20 largest countries by area (Chad is number 20). Print this worksheet for your instructor.

    g. Repeat steps (e) and (f) to create the Population and Density worksheets and print these worksheets as well. Add a cover sheet and then submit the completed assignment to your instructor. Do you have a better appreciation for the world in which all of us live?

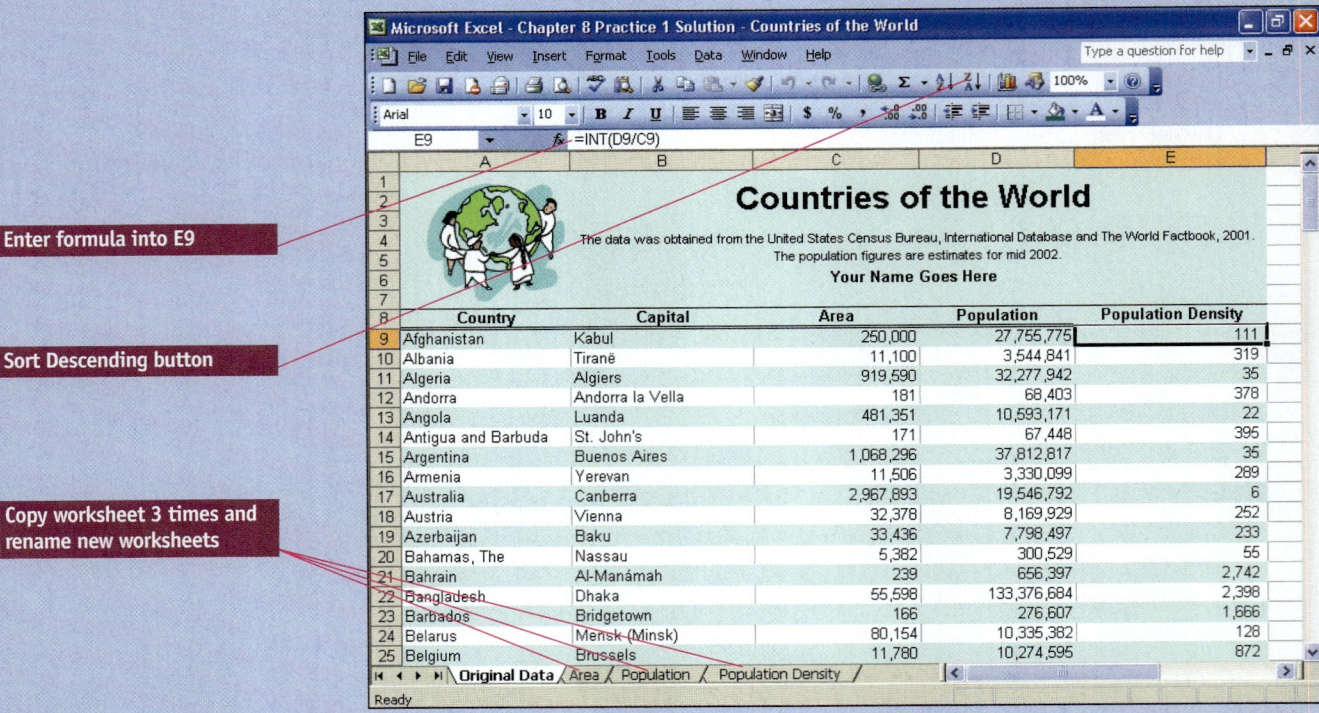

FIGURE 8.9 Countries of the World (exercise 1)

practice exercises

2. **The New SAT:** The worksheet in Figure 8.10 parallels the Admissions Office example from the first hands-on exercise, and thus you can use the original formulas as an aid in completing this assignment. There is, however, one significant difference in that this year's applicants have taken the new SAT, which has a maximum score of 2400, as opposed to the 1600 in the earlier version. The present workbook also has different clip art and background shading to further distinguish it from the original. Proceed as follows:

   a. Open the *Chapter 8 Practice 2—The New SAT* workbook in the Exploring Excel folder. Click in cell F14 and enter the formula to determine early admission. Enter a similar formula into cell G14 to determine if the applicant should be rejected immediately.

   b. Copy the formulas in cells F14 and G14 to the remaining rows in the worksheet.

   c. Click in Cell H14 and enter the formula =D14+E14*600 to compute the applicant's score. This formula yields a maximum score of 4800 (2400 on the SAT and 2400 for the GPA component, given a GPA of 4.0).

   d. Enter a nested IF function into cell I14 to determine the decision for this applicant. Use conditional formatting to display the different decisions in different colors as shown in the figure. Copy the formula in cell I14 to the remaining rows in the worksheet.

   e. Use the Insert Name command to define the range I14:I543 as Final_Decision, then enter the appropriate COUNTIF functions in cells G8:G11. Check that your results match those in the figure.

   f. Complete the worksheet by entering the formulas for the total applicants, total admissions, and acceptance rate in cells I8, I9, and I10. Enter your name in cell I11.

   g. Use the Page Setup command to create an appropriate footer, which includes your name, and then print the *first page* of the worksheet. (Do *not* print the complete worksheet because it runs several pages.)

   h. Use the AutoFilter command to display only the applicants who were granted early admission. Print this page for your instructor as well. Add a cover sheet to complete the assignment.

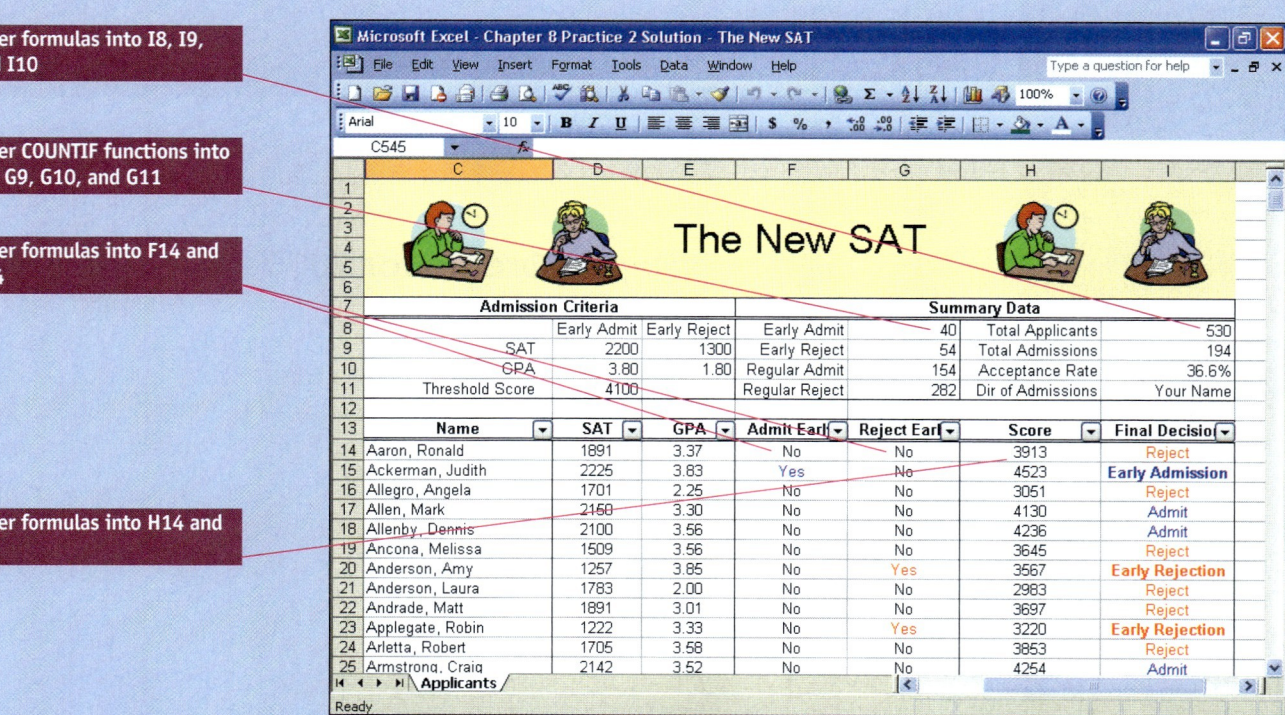

FIGURE 8.10   The New SAT (exercise 2)

practice exercises

3. **Car Trouble:** The worksheet in Figure 8.11 analyzes the repair orders for an automobile dealership to determine the type of complaint that occurred most often. The data were created in an Access database, but are to be brought into an Excel workbook for data analysis. Proceed as follows:

   a. Start Excel and close any open workbooks. Pull down the File menu, click the Open command, change the file type to Access databases, and double click the *Chapter 8 Practice 3—Car Trouble Access database* in the Exploring Excel folder. Click the Open button when asked whether you trust the source of this file. You should see the list of repair orders in a new Excel workbook. Change the name of the worksheet tab to Repair Orders. Save the workbook as Chapter 8 Practice 3 Solution—Car Trouble.

   b. Insert six blank rows at the top of the worksheet, then create a heading with associated clip art. Format the titles in row 7. You don't have to match our formatting exactly, but you are to create an attractive worksheet.

   c. Create a simple pivot table and chart with "Complaint" as the row field and Count of Customer in the data area. Click in the cell containing the summary statistic (cell G9 in our figure) and change the entry to Count of Customer.

   d. The initial pivot table will contain the number of complaints; for example, 35 for the cooling system, as opposed to the percentage as shown in our figure. Accordingly, right click any value in the Total column, click Field Settings to display the Pivot Table dialog box, and click the Options button. Click the down arrow in the Show data as list box, click % of column, and click OK. Click the Sort Descending button to display the percentages in decreasing order.

   e. Modify the default pivot chart to improve its appearance by following the steps in the third hands-on exercise, for instance, by changing the gap width between the columns to zero. Add a title and/or a block arrow to emphasize the category with the greatest percent of defects. Rename the worksheet tab Pareto chart.

   f. Add the finishing touches to the Repair Orders worksheet; for example, borders and conditional formatting to highlight the alternate rows. Print the completed workbook for your instructor. Use the Page Setup command as necessary to modify the printing parameters.

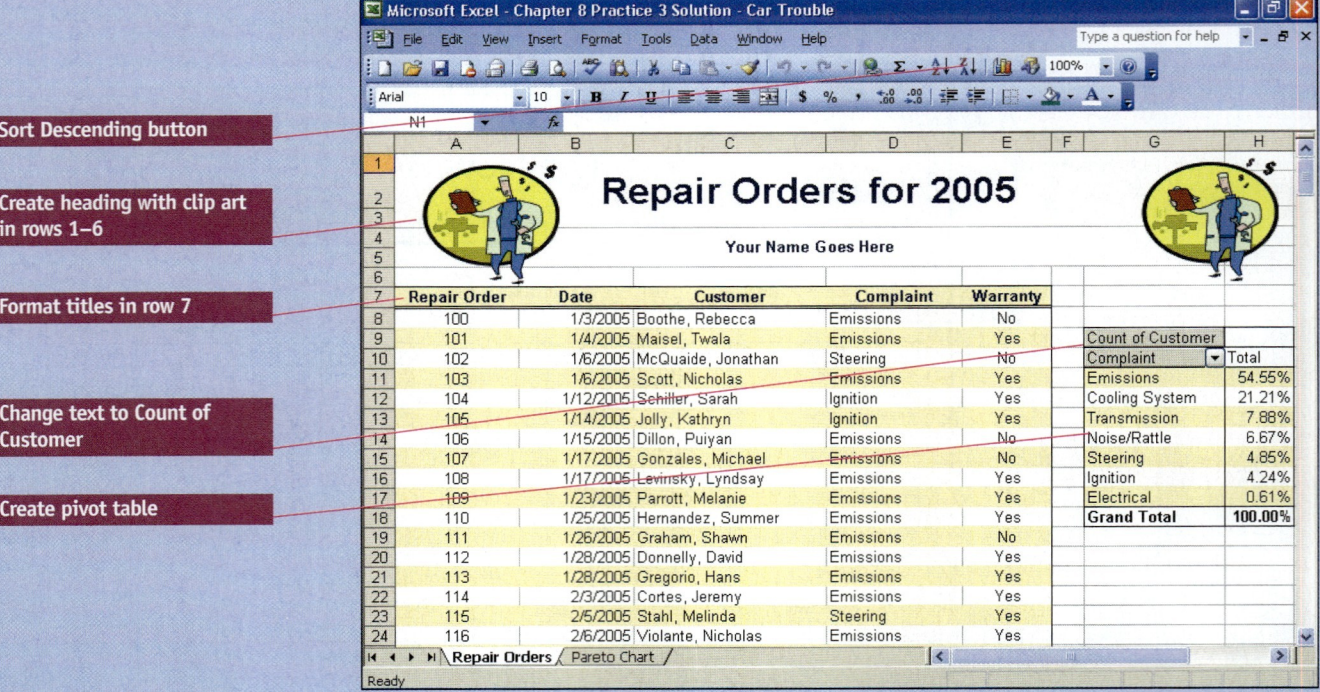

FIGURE 8.11 Car Trouble (exercise 3)

practice exercises

4. **Women's Wear:** The workbook in Figure 8.12 parallels the Men's Store example from the fourth hands-on exercise. The sales data is contained in a text file and imported into an Excel workbook, after which the various pivot tables and pivot charts are created.

   a. Start Excel and close any open workbooks. Pull down the File menu, click the Open command, change the file type to Text files, and then double click the *Chapter 8 Practice 4—Women's Wear* text file to import the data into the workbook. Pull down the File menu and click the Save As command. Change the file type to Microsoft Office Excel workbook. Change the file name to *Chapter 8 Practice 4—Women's Wear Solution*.

   b. The workbook currently has one worksheet. Double click the worksheet tab and change the name to Sales Data. Move to cell A1, then use the Replace command to change all occurrences of the salesperson Lugo to your last name. Excel indicates that it has made 163 replacements.

   c. Create a basic pivot table (and chart) with Category, Salesperson, and Sale Item in the row, column, and page fields, respectively. The data area should contain the order amount in currency format with zero decimal places. The corresponding pivot chart should be a 3-D stacked column chart with the data table below the chart. (Use the default formatting.)

   d. Click the tab for the pivot table. Double click the cell that contains your sales total ($126,461) to create a new worksheet with your sales data. Change the name of this worksheet to your last name. Shade the alternate rows.

   e. Create a second pivot table that adds the quarter as a second row field; that is, the table displays the sales data by quarter and sales category within each quarter. This requires you to use the Group and Show Detail command to group the individual sales dates into sales quarters. Format the pivot table.

   f. Create a Documentation worksheet. You do not have to match our formatting exactly, but your documentation should be essentially the same as ours. Rename and/or rearrange the worksheets to match Figure 8.12.

   g. Use the Page Setup command to create a custom footer for each worksheet that includes the date, the name of the worksheet, and the page within the printed report. Print the entire workbook except for the Sales Data worksheet.

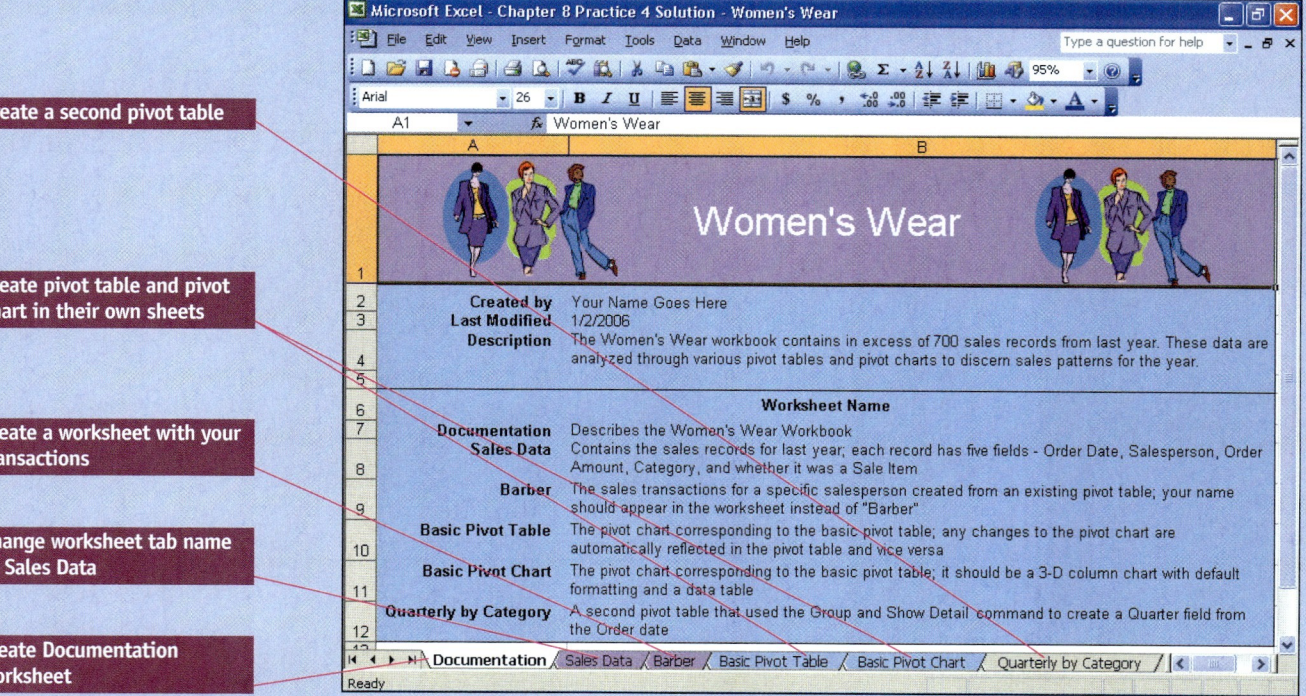

FIGURE 8.12 Women's Wear (exercise 4)

practice exercises

5. **Practice with Pivot Tables:** This exercise provides additional practice with pivot tables by examining the sales records for a computer store. The pivot chart in Figure 8.13 is based on the associated pivot table, which in turn is derived from the Source Data worksheet. The records represent all of the sales information from last year, but there is simply too much data to discern any sales trends. Pivot tables can help. Open the *Chapter 8 Practice 5—Practice with Pivot Tables* workbook and proceed as follows:

   a. Pull down the Edit menu, click the Replace command, enter "Milgrom" as the Find What string, and your last name as the Replace with string. Click the Replace All button, and then click OK when you see the dialog box indicating 110 replacements. Close the Find and Replace Dialog box.

   b. Click in cell A2 (or anywhere within the list). Pull down the Data menu, click the PivotTable and PivotChart Report command, and then create the underlying pivot table (and chart) in its own worksheet. Drag Salesperson to the row area, Category to the Column area, and Order Amount to the data area. Click anywhere in the Grand Total column, then click the Sort Descending button, so that the salesperson with the highest sales total appears first.

   c. Right click any numeric entry within the body of the pivot table, click Field Settings to display the PivotTable Field dialog box, then click the Number command button to display the Format Cells dialog box. Change the formatting to Currency with no decimals. Click OK. Click OK a second time to close the PivotTable dialog box.

   d. Click the worksheet tab for the pivot chart. Pull down the Chart menu, click the Chart Type command, and choose the Stacked Column with 3-D visual effect as the chart type. Check the box for default formatting. Click OK. Use the Chart Options command to display a data table below the chart. Use the Drawing toolbar to create a block arrow indicating that Davis is the leading salesperson.

   e. Change the names of the worksheet tabs to match those in Figure 8.13. Print the pivot chart only if you are *not* continuing with the next exercise. (You do not have to print the pivot table since the data table is displayed below the chart.) Use the Page Setup command to create an appropriate custom footer. Do *not* print the Source Data worksheet, since it runs many pages due to the quantity of data.

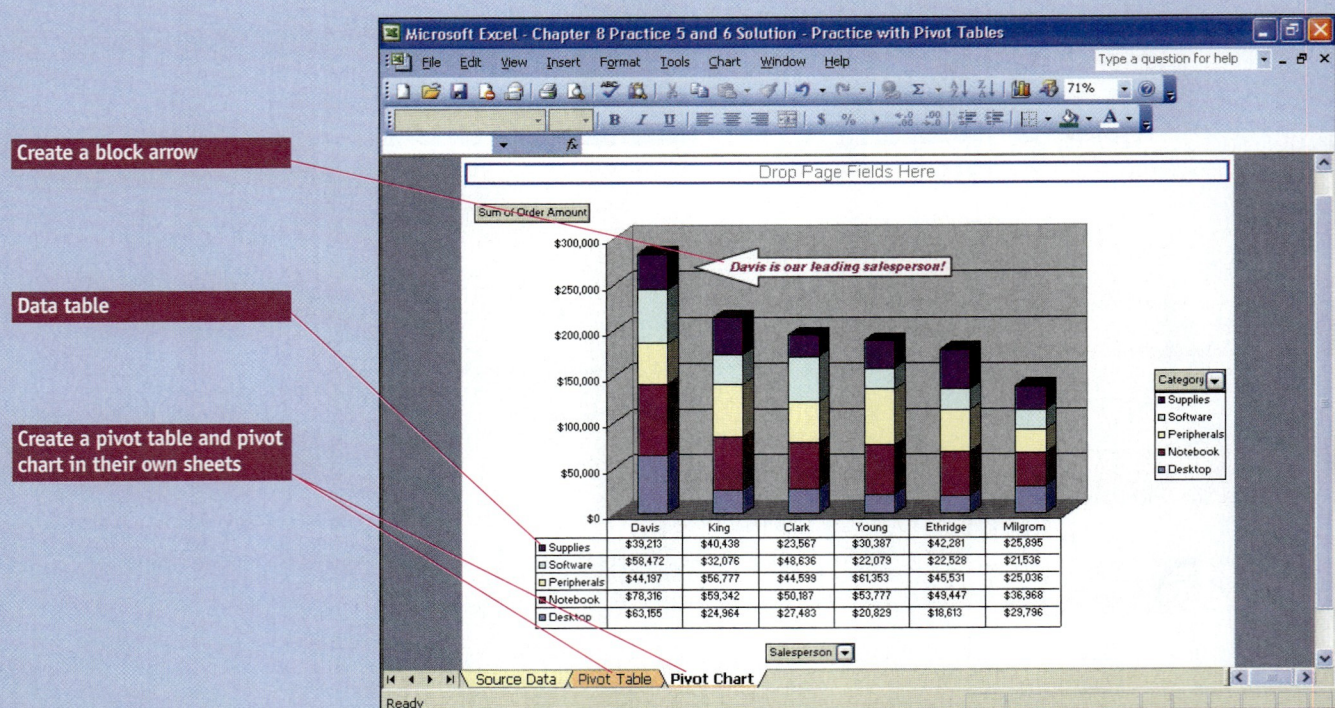

FIGURE 8.13 Practice with Pivot Tables (exercise 5)

practice exercises

6. **Practice with Pivot Tables Continued:** Figure 8.14 extends the analysis from the previous exercise to include the sales quarter, which in turn reveals a disturbing trend in that sales peaked in the first quarter and declined thereafter. Open the completed workbook from the previous exercise and proceed as follows:

   a. Create a new pivot table with two row fields (Order Date and Category) and one column field (Salesperson). Use the Order Amount field in the data area. (Answer Yes when asked if you want the pivot table to be based on an existing report.) Go to the worksheet that contains the newly created pivot table and right click any date in the Order Date area. Click the Group and Show Details command, and click Group to display the Grouping dialog box. Click Quarters in the By list box, then click Months to deselect this grouping. Click OK.

   b. Format the Sales Amount field to currency with no decimal places. Complete the pivot table by choosing an appropriate design. (We used the format from Report 6, but then we had to recreate the pivot table by moving Salesperson back to the column area.)

   c. Double click the cell containing your grand total (cell G35 in Figure 8.14) to create a new worksheet that contains all of your individual transactions. Shade the alternate rows in this worksheet.

   d. Create a new pivot table on its own worksheet (Percentage Analysis in Figure 8.14) that has Salesperson as the row field and Sum of Order Amount in data area. (There are no column or page fields.) Right click any Order Amount in the resulting pivot table, and then click Field Settings to display the PivotTable Field dialog box. Click the Options button, click the down arrow in the Show Data as list box, and then choose % of column. Click OK. Create a second pivot table on the same worksheet that displays the percentage of total sales represented by each category. Create a third pivot table that displays the percentage of total sales represented by each quarter.

   e. Change the names of the worksheet tabs to match those in Figure 8.14. Print the workbook except for the Source Data worksheet. Use the Page Setup command to create an appropriate custom footer for each worksheet (you can group the worksheets to save time).

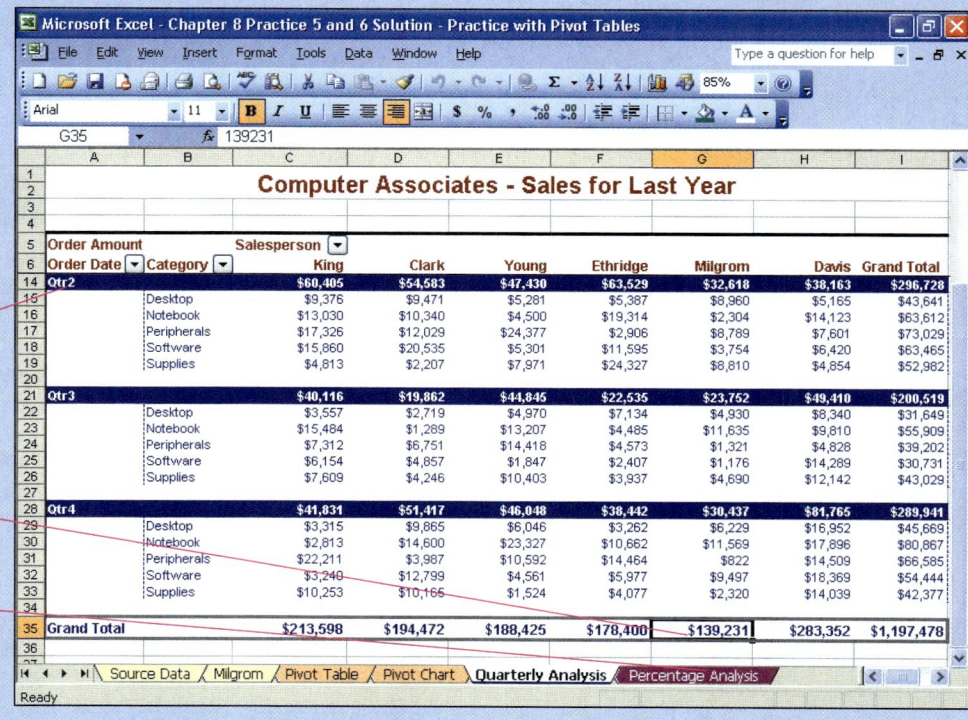

FIGURE 8.14 Practice with Pivot Tables Continued (exercise 6)

practice exercises

7. **Multiple Consolidation Ranges:** The data for a pivot table can come from an Excel list, from a text (CSV, or Comma Separated Value) file, or from an Access database. It can also come from multiple worksheets and/or workbooks as shown in Figure 8.15. In this example, the branch managers from four regional offices have each prepared a worksheet containing summary data for their office, showing the sales of each product in each quarter. Your task is to combine the individual worksheets into a single pivot table. Proceed as follows.

   a. Open the *Chapter 8 Practice 7—Multiple Consolidation Ranges* workbook. Click anywhere in any of the four existing worksheets. Pull down the Data menu and click the Pivot Table and PivotChart Report command. Click the option buttons to select Multiple Consolidation Ranges and to create a Pivot Table. Click Next.

   b. Click the option button that says I will create the page fields in step 2a. Click Next. Specify the range in step 2b of the PivotTable Wizard by clicking the pointing button on the right side of the text box. Click the Sheet tab for Daytona, select cells A2 through E8, click the pointing button to return to the dialog box, then click the Add command button. You should see Daytona!A$2:$E$8 in the All ranges list box. Repeat this step for the other three cities.

   c. Remain in step 2b of the PivotTable Wizard. Click the option button for 1 page field. Select (click) the Daytona range within the All ranges list box, then click in the Field one list box and type Daytona. Do not press the Enter key. Select (click) the Miami range within the All ranges list box, then click in the Field one list box and type Miami. Do not press Enter. Repeat this step for Orlando and Tampa. Click Next.

   d. Select the option to create the pivot table on a new worksheet. Click Finish.

   e. You have a pivot table, but it does not yet match Figure 8.15. Click in cell B3 (the entry in the cell is Column), then click the formula bar and type Quarter (replacing the previous entry). Change the entry in cell A4 from Row to Category in similar fashion. Change the entry in cell A1 from Page1 to City. Now pivot the table to match our figure.

   f. Use the Format Report button on the Pivot Table toolbar to format the pivot table in attractive fashion, change the number format to currency, and then print the pivot table for your instructor.

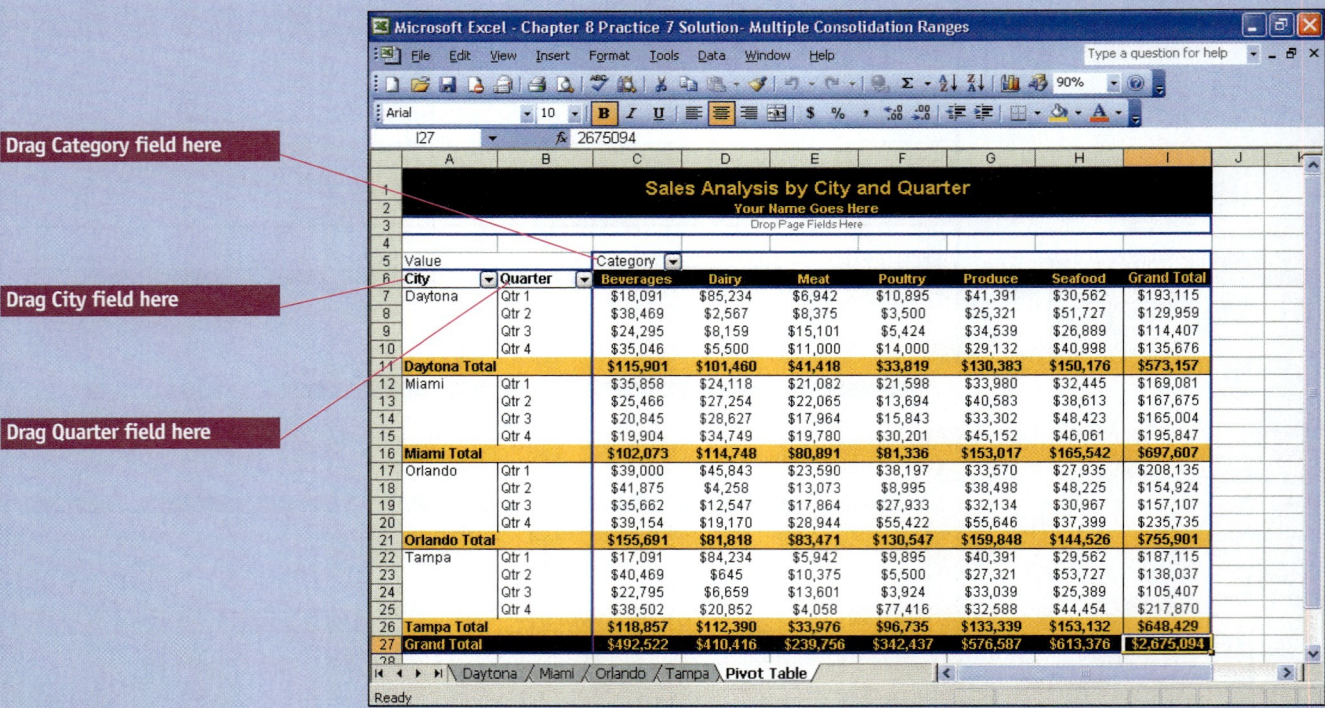

FIGURE 8.15 Multiple Consolidation Ranges (exercise 7)

practice exercises

8. **String (Text) Processing:** Excel contains a variety of text functions, the power of which can be seen in conjunction with the list of names in column A of Figure 8.16. There are two problems with the list as shown; the names are in uppercase, but more importantly, it is not possible to put the list in alphabetical order (by last name) since the last name is embedded within the field. Your task is to convert the list to the format in column G, using a combination of the functions described at the bottom of the worksheet. Proceed as follows:

   a. Open the partially completed, *Chapter 8 Practice 8—String Processing* workbook. The names in your worksheet appear in a *different order* than those in Figure 8.16; your worksheet is in sequence by first name. In addition, "Bob Grauer" does not appear in your worksheet. Click in cell A16 and add your name in uppercase letters.

   b. Click in cell B7 and enter the function =FIND(" ",A7). You should see a 6, which is the position of the space within Brian Street's name.

   c. Click in cell C7 and enter the function =LEFT(A7,B7-1) to isolate the first name; that is, you are taking the leftmost portion of the original name.

   d. Click in cell D7 and enter the function =RIGHT(A7,LEN(A7)-B7) to isolate the last name; that is, you are taking the rightmost portion of the original name.

   e. Convert the first name to a combination of upper and lowercase. Enter =UPPER(LEFT(C7,1))&LOWER(RIGHT(C7,(LEN(C7)-1))) into cell E7.

   f. Copy the formula from cell E7 to cell F7.

   g. Click in cell G7 and enter the function =F7 & ", " & E7 to concatenate the first and last name. You should see "Street, Brian" as shown in Figure 8.16.

   h. Copy the formulas in cells B7 through G7 to the remaining rows in the worksheet. Click anywhere in column G and click the Sort Ascending button to put the names in alphabetical order.

   i. Find your name within the list and change the font to a different color and/or use bold italics for emphasis.

   j. Use conditional formatting for rows 7 through 16 to shade the alternate rows. Print the completed worksheet twice to show both displayed values and cell formulas. (Use the Page Setup command to change to landscape printing.)

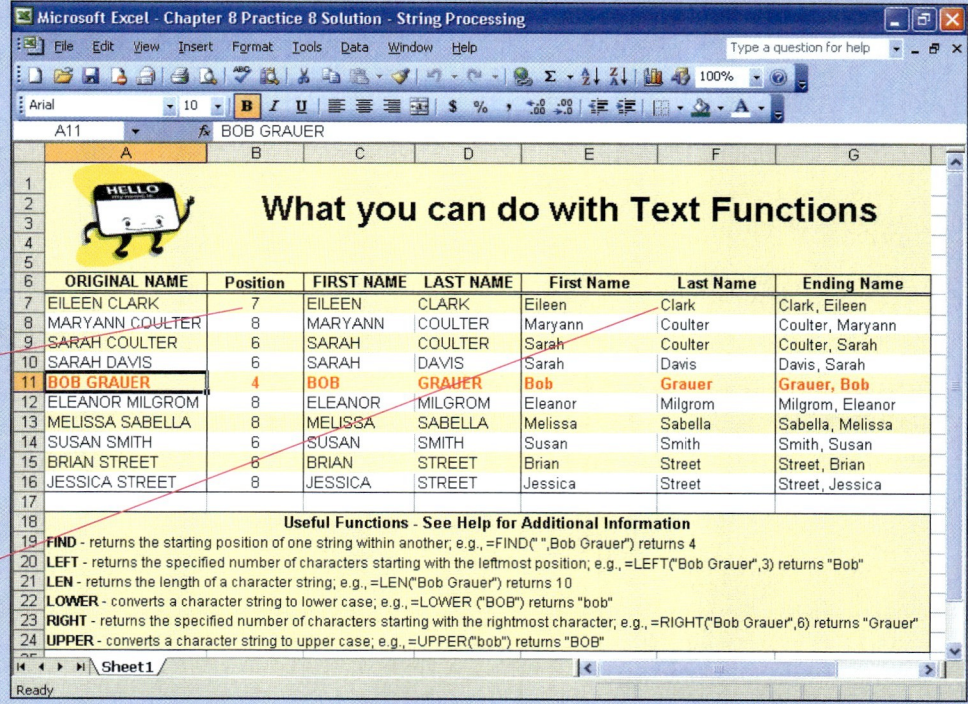

FIGURE 8.16 String Processing (exercise 8)

practice exercises

9. **Generating Test Data:** The names of the students in Figure 8.17 are the same as those in the worksheet in the second hands-on exercise; the students' majors and GPAs are different, however, and consequently the quartile, rank, and honors distinctions are also different since these values depend on the GPA. (The shading has also been changed to avoid confusion with the earlier worksheet.)

   a. Open the partially completed *Chapter 8 Practice 9—Generating Test Data* workbook in the Exploring Excel folder. The worksheet contains the formulas to compute each student's quartile, rank in class, and honors distinction, but it does not contain the student's GPA. Hence you will see the #NUM! and #N/A error messages scattered throughout the worksheet. The error messages disappear when the GPA is entered.

   b. Click in cell E22 (the GPA for the first student), type =RAND(), and press Enter. You will see a random number somewhere between zero and one.

   c. Change the formula in cell E22 to =2.00 + 2*RAND(). This time you see a GPA between 2.00 and 4.00. Now change the formula in cell E22 to =ROUND(($H$5+$H$8*RAND()),2) to round the GPA to two places. Press the F9 (recalculate) key and the GPA changes; each time you press the F9 key the formulas in the worksheet are recalculated.

   d. The determination of the student's major is slightly more complicated. We (arbitrarily) determined the distribution of majors that appear toward the top of the worksheet; 25% of the students are Business majors, 15% are Communication majors, and so on. We then entered the formulas in cells C4 through C9 to compute the cumulative probability (not including the current major), which goes from zero to .95. This enables us to use the VLOOKUP function to take a random number (from zero to one), determine where it falls within the column of cumulative probabilities, and then extract the major. Accordingly, click in cell D22 and enter the formula =VLOOKUP(RAND(),$C$4:$E$9,3).

   e. Copy the formulas in cells D22 and E22 to the next row, which changes Altman's GPA and major; remember, every time a change is made, the entire worksheet is recalculated. (You can go from automatic to manual recalculation using the Options command in the Tools menu.)

   f. Copy the formulas in cells D22 and E22 to the remaining rows in the worksheet, and then print the *first page* of the completed worksheet for your instructor.

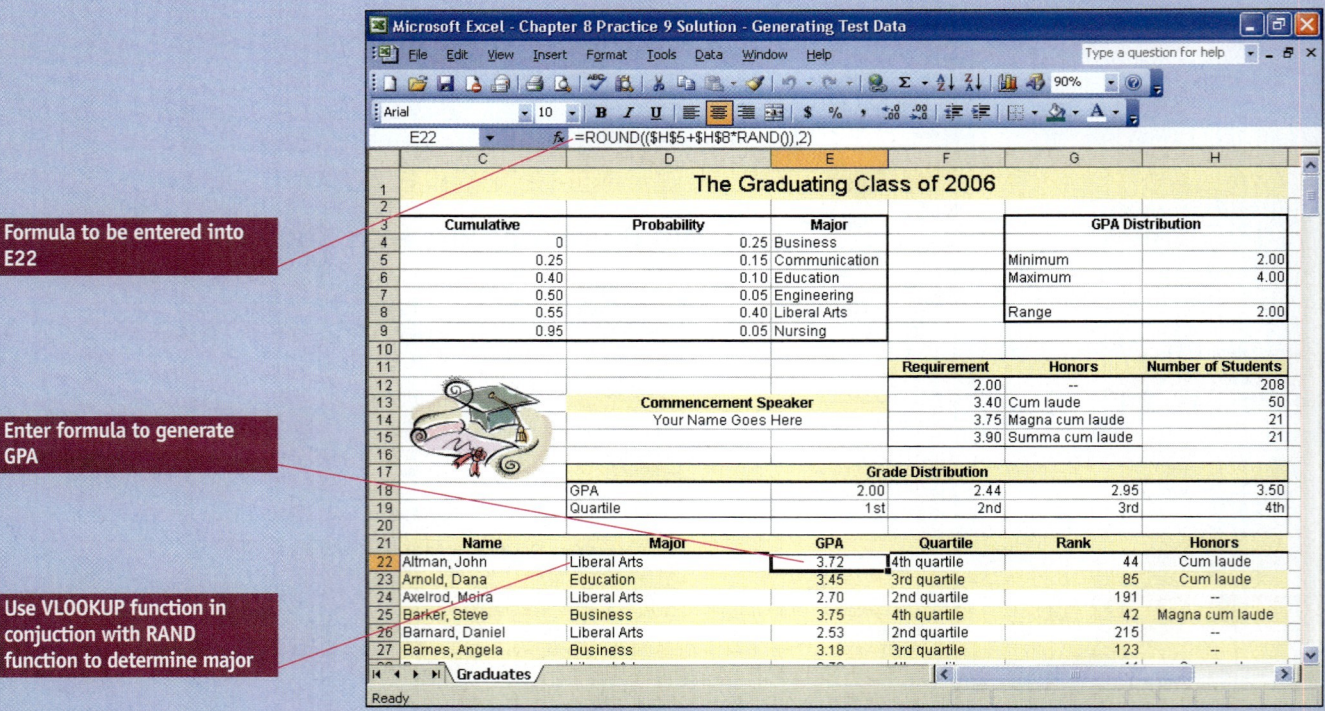

FIGURE 8.17 Generating Test Data (exercise 9)

practice exercises

10. **Data from the Web:** The worksheet in Figure 8.18 displays data from the National Football League toward the end of the 2004 season. The data was obtained directly from the NFL's Web site (www.nfl.com) and can be updated each week during the season by clicking the Refresh Data button on the External Data toolbar.

   a. Start a new workbook, pull down the Data menu, click the Import External Data command, and then click New Web query to display the New Web Query dialog box. Enter the complete address of the site containing the data: http://www.nfl.com/stats/playersort/NFL/QB-PASSING/2004/regular. (You will have to adjust the address for future seasons.)

   b. Click the Go button to display the site that you selected. The site must contain one or more yellow arrows to indicate that data from the site can be imported via a Web query. Click the arrow next to the table you want to import; for example, the statistics for quarterbacks as in our example. The arrow changes to a green check to indicate the data has been selected.

   c. Click the Import button, indicate that the data is to go into cell A5 of the current worksheet, and click OK. The data should appear in your worksheet as shown in Figure 8.18. You can now apply any or all of the techniques you learned in this chapter.

   d. Insert the title and other identifying information as shown in Figure 8.18.

   e. Hide any columns you are not interested in (e.g., columns M and N). Click anywhere in the list, pull down the Data menu, click Filter, then click AutoFilter. Click in the Attempts column and display the top 10 (the quarterbacks with the most attempts). If necessary, sort the data in descending sequence by rating (column O). Print the worksheet for your instructor. Be sure that it fits on one page.

   f. Create a chart of your own choosing that will be meaningful to you. We decided on a side-by-side column chart that displays the touchdowns and interceptions for each quarterback. Press and hold the Ctrl key as you select the Player, Touchdown, and Interception columns. Click the Chart Wizard tool on the Standard toolbar, and let the wizard lead you through the steps to create the chart. Display a data table under the chart. Add an appropriate title, then print the chart for your instructor.

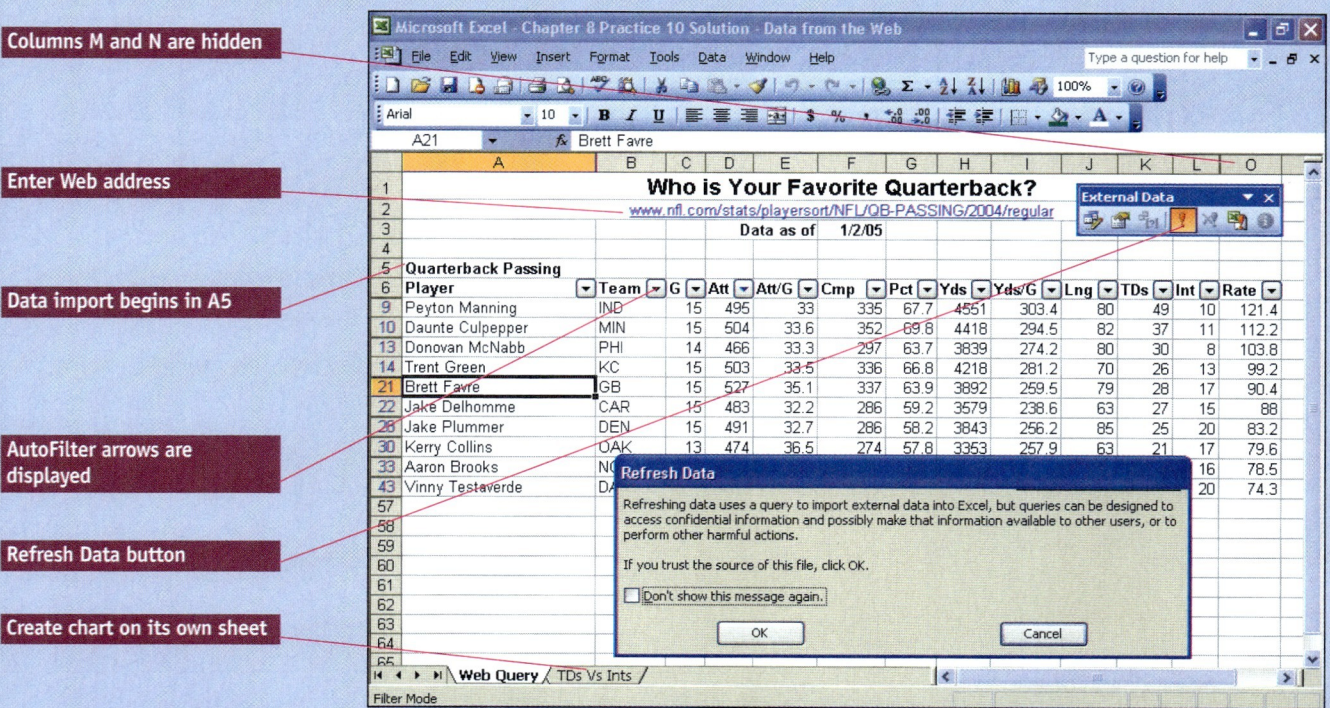

FIGURE 8.18 Data from the Web (exercise 10)

practice exercises

11. **Excel Jeopardy:** How well do you know the functions in Microsoft Excel? The presentation in Figure 8.19 contains a Jeopardy game with 25 answers and questions that review material on Excel functions, most of which were used somewhere in this chapter. We could not resist, however, including a few unexpected (but hopefully intuitive) functions such as the function for Roman numerals in the Math Whiz category. All you have to do is open the presentation and play the game.

   a. Open the *Chapter 8 Practice 11—Office Jeopardy (Excel Functions)* presentation in the Exploring Excel folder. Pull down the Slide Show menu and click the View Show command (or click the F5 key) to view the slide show, which begins with the title slide. Click the mouse to move to slide two (the board). The names of the categories will appear one after another, after which you can select any question in any category. Each dollar amount is a hyperlink to another slide in the presentation.

   b. Select (click) a question; for example, the $400 question in the Math Whiz category, to display the clue, =MOD(22,7). Click the mouse to display the answer "What is 1?" (that appears in the form of a question), then click the answer to return to slide two (the board). Before you click, be sure you see the tiny hand indicating that you are clicking the hyperlink, as opposed to clicking the background of the slide.

   c. You should be back on slide two, the Jeopardy board. Look closely and you will see that the color of the text (i.e., the 400) has changed, indicating that the hyperlink has been followed. Select a different question, view the answer, and return to the game board so that you can be sure of the navigation.

   d. Select a classmate and play the game. There is no "buzzer" so you have to determine an equitable way to gain control of the board and keep score. We leave the details to you and/or we invite you to create additional games of your own design.

   e. Print the presentation in a variety of ways. Select the first two slides, pull down the File menu, click the Print command, choose the option button for Selection, and select Slides in the Print What list box. Click OK to print. Pull down the Print menu a second time and print the entire presentation in Outline view. Study the outline and be sure that you can answer all of the questions.

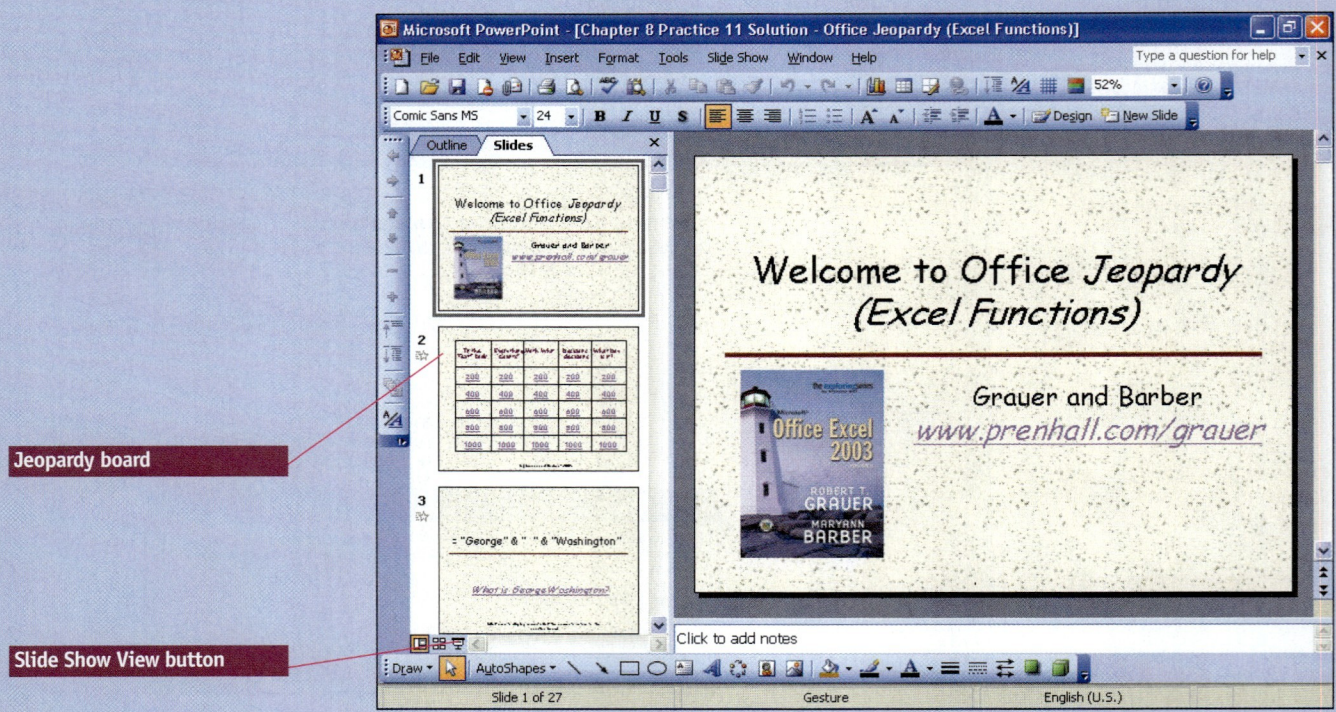

FIGURE 8.19 Excel Jeopardy (exercise 11)

MINI CASES

Medical Specialties

Your proficiency with Excel in general and data analysis in particular has landed you an internship with a new HMO in South Florida. The partners in the HMO are in the process of recruiting physicians to participate in their plan. The practice has just gotten started and fewer than 100 physicians have signed on with the plan. The real recruiting will start next month.

Before proceeding further, however, the partners want to analyze the physicians already in the plan to be sure that they recruit the right specialties in the right geographic areas. Accordingly, the founder of the practice has provided you with the *Chapter 8 Mini Case—Medical Specialties* workbook in the Exploring Excel folder that contains the existing data. There are seven fields for each physician in the workbook: the physician's first name and last name, the city in which he or she practices, the physician's specialty, gender, and date of board certification, and an indication of whether the physician is accepting new patients.

The multiple fields provide the potential for detailed analysis; for example, identifying the female physicians in a designated specialty in a particular city or who were board certified after a specific date. Your immediate task, however, is to examine the list of physicians in order to determine which specialties and/or which cities are underrepresented. This is best accomplished by creating a simple pivot table (on its own worksheet) with the specialty in the row area and the city in the column area. The data area should contain a count of the number of physicians for each combination of city and specialty. The founder of the practice is visually oriented and has requested a chart, as opposed to a table of numerical data.

Print the completed workbook for your instructor. The workbook should contain three worksheets: the complete list of participating physicians, the pivot table, and the corresponding pivot chart (print this worksheet in landscape orientation). Be sure that all of the fields for each physician fit on one page; this worksheet will still require a second page and thus the first several rows with the column headings and descriptive information should appear on both pages.

The Corporate Takeover

The organization you work for has grown quickly through acquisition of local offices throughout the country. Recently, however, management has become concerned about the large payroll (there are more than 300 employees today versus 150 a year ago). They are also concerned about the disparity in salaries from one location to the next, and the potential disparity between men and women in the same position in the same city.

You have just started an internship with the company, and your proficiency in Excel is well known. Your first task is to analyze the employee data within the *Chapter 8 Mini Case—Corporate Takeover* workbook. There are no specific requirements other than to display the average salary and number of employees for each combination of location and title. Any additional pivot tables are up to you. Print the pivot table(s) you create. Management has requested, however, a separate listing of the Los Angeles employees, and another listing of the managers in the company. Use the Page Setup command to create an appropriate footer for every worksheet. This is an excellent opportunity to show what you can do.

Chapter Recap—Drowning In Data

It's a lucky person who is able to combine a hobby with work. You love gardening and have been working part time at a local nursery for the last year, during which time your pay has steadily increased. The owner of the nursery knows of your expertise in Excel and has asked you to analyze the sales data for the last year. She wants to know the most (least) effective salesperson in terms of total sales. She also wants to know which sales category provides the most (least) revenue. The owner also wants to evaluate the data by sales quarter; that is, did business get better or worse during the year?

mini cases

Your predecessor has entered the more than 800 sales receipts from last year into the Excel workbook, but was unable to go further. She did, however, capture all of the necessary data as each record contains four fields: the date of the order, the salesperson who took the order, the amount of the order, and the sales category.

Your assignment is to reread the chapter, paying special attention to the section on pivot tables and pivot charts. You will then open the *Chapter 8 Ending Case Study—Drowning in Data* workbook and use the Replace command to change all occurrences of the salesperson "Street" to your last name. Next, you will create at least two pivot tables that will summarize the data according to the needs of the owner. The owner is very visual, and thus you should create a pivot chart that corresponds to one of the pivot tables. And finally, create one last worksheet that contains all of your sales data.

The pivot tables can appear on individual worksheets, and/or multiple tables can appear on a single worksheet. You should, however, rename each worksheet tab so that it is descriptive of the pivot table(s) it contains. Add a Documentation worksheet that describes the purpose of each worksheet in the workbook. Print the completed workbook *except for the Source Data worksheet*, which runs more than 15 pages because of the quantity of data. Use the Page Setup command to create a custom footer for every worksheet that contains today's date, the name of the worksheet tab, and the page number of the printed report. Each worksheet should fit on one page.

CHAPTER 9

Automating Repetitive Tasks: Macros and Visual Basic for Applications

OBJECTIVES

After reading this chapter you will:

1. Define a macro; describe the relationship between Excel macros and VBA procedures.
2. Record a macro; use the Visual Basic Editor to modify a macro.
3. Use the VBA MsgBox and InputBox statements to enhance a macro.
4. Execute a macro via a keyboard shortcut or button.
5. Describe the Personal Macro workbook.
6. Use the Step Into command to debug a macro.
7. Use the VBA If and Do statements to implement decision making.

hands-on exercises

1. INTRODUCTION TO MACROS
   Input: None
   Output: My Macros

2. THE PERSONAL MACRO WORKBOOK
   Input: None
   Output: Personal Macro workbook

3. DATA MANAGEMENT MACROS
   Input: Employee List Solution (from Chapter 7)
   Output: Employee List Solution (additional changes)

4. ADDITIONAL MACROS
   Input: Employee List Solution (from exercise 3)
   Output: Employee List Solution (additional changes)

5. LOOPS AND DECISION MAKING
   Input: Loops and Decision Making
   Output: Loops and Decision Making Solution

CASE STUDY
UNIVERSAL HEALTH SERVICES

Sarah Davis is excited about her new job with Universal Health Services but unprepared for the volume of subscriber phone calls that she must deal with on a daily basis. Today is typical. Sarah sits down at her desk at 8:15am, 15 minutes early, and already her phone is ringing off the hook. This particular caller is seeking a physician who specializes in internal medicine who is located in Miami. The caller is adamant that the physician be a woman and further that the physician was board certified after January 1, 1985. And, of course, the physician has to be accepting new patients.

The query is not difficult to answer, but it does take time, and therein lies the problem. Universal Health Services is a large health care provider with thousands of subscribers and hundreds of physicians. The list of physicians is maintained within an Excel workbook that Sarah uses to locate physicians for subscribers. The workbook was developed by Sarah's predecessor, and it takes full advantage of database functions, filters, and the associated criteria range, but it does not use macros. Surely there must be a better way, and Sarah intends to find it.

Your assignment is to read the chapter, open the *Chapter 9 Case Study—Universal Health Services* workbook, and create two macros that will enable Sarah to search the physicians' database to service requests from subscribers. The first macro should enable Sarah to enter the desired city, specialty, gender, date of certification, and whether the physician is accepting new patients, and then display the names of qualified physicians (if any) or alternatively, a message that no physicians meet the specified criteria. The second macro should clear the criteria range and display the entire list. Both macros should be completely general and use the range names that have already been defined in the workbook.

Print the workbook for your instructor after the selection macro has been run to identify the physician(s) specified in the opening paragraph. In addition, print the module containing the two macros you created.

INTRODUCTION TO MACROS

Have you ever pulled down the same menus and clicked the same sequence of commands over and over? Easy as the commands may be to execute, it is still burdensome to have to continually repeat the same mouse clicks or keystrokes. If you can think of any task that you do repeatedly, whether in one workbook or in a series of workbooks, you are a perfect candidate to use macros.

A ***macro*** is a set of instructions that tells Excel which commands to execute. It is, in essence, a program, and its instructions are written in Visual Basic, a programming language. Fortunately, however, you don't have to be a programmer to write macros. Instead, you use the macro recorder within Excel to record your commands, and let Excel write the macros for you.

The ***macro recorder*** stores Excel commands, in the form of ***Visual Basic*** instructions, within a workbook. (***Visual Basic for Applications***, or ***VBA***, is a subset of Visual Basic that is built into Microsoft Office.) To use the recorder, you pull down the Tools menu and click the Record New Macro command. From that point on (until you stop recording), every command you execute will be stored by the recorder. It doesn't matter whether you execute commands from pull-down menus via the mouse, or whether you use the toolbar or ***keyboard shortcuts***. The macro recorder captures every action you take and stores the equivalent Visual Basic statements as a macro within the workbook.

Figure 9.1 illustrates a simple macro to enter your name and class in cells A1 and A2 of the active worksheet. The macro is displayed in the ***Visual Basic Editor (VBE)***, which is used to create, edit, execute, and debug Excel macros. The Visual Basic Editor is a separate application (as can be determined from its button on the taskbar in Figure 9.1), and it is accessible from any application in Microsoft Office.

The left side of the VBE window in Figure 9.1 contains the ***Project Explorer***, which is similar in concept and appearance to the Windows Explorer, except that it displays only open workbooks and/or other Visual Basic projects. The Visual Basic statements for the selected module (Module1 in Figure 9.1) appear in the ***Code window*** in the right pane. As you shall see, a Visual Basic module consists of one or more procedures, each of which corresponds to an Excel macro. Thus, in this example, Module1 contains the NameAndCourse procedure corresponding to the Excel macro of the same name. Module1 itself is stored in the My Macros.XLS workbook.

As indicated, a macro consists of Visual Basic statements that were created through the macro recorder. We don't expect you to be able to write the Visual Basic procedure yourself, and you don't have to. You just invoke the recorder and let it capture the Excel commands for you. We do think it is important, however, to understand the macro, and so we proceed to explain its statements. As you read our discussion, do not be concerned with the precise syntax of every statement, but try to get an overall appreciation for what the statements do.

A macro always begins and ends with the Sub and End Sub statements, respectively. The ***Sub statement*** contains the name of the macro—for example, NameAndCourse in Figure 9.1. (Spaces are not allowed in a macro name.) The ***End Sub statement*** is physically the last statement and indicates the end of the macro. Sub and End Sub are Visual Basic keywords and appear in blue.

The next several statements begin with an apostrophe, appear in green, and are known as ***comments***. They provide information about the macro, but do not affect its execution. In other words, the results of a macro are the same, whether or not the comments are included. Comments are inserted automatically by the recorder to document the macro name, its author, and ***shortcut key*** (if any). You can add comments (a comment line must begin with an apostrophe), or delete or modify existing comments, as you see fit. Comments may also be added at the end of a statement by typing an apostrophe, then adding the explanatory text; that is, anything after the apostrophe is considered a comment.

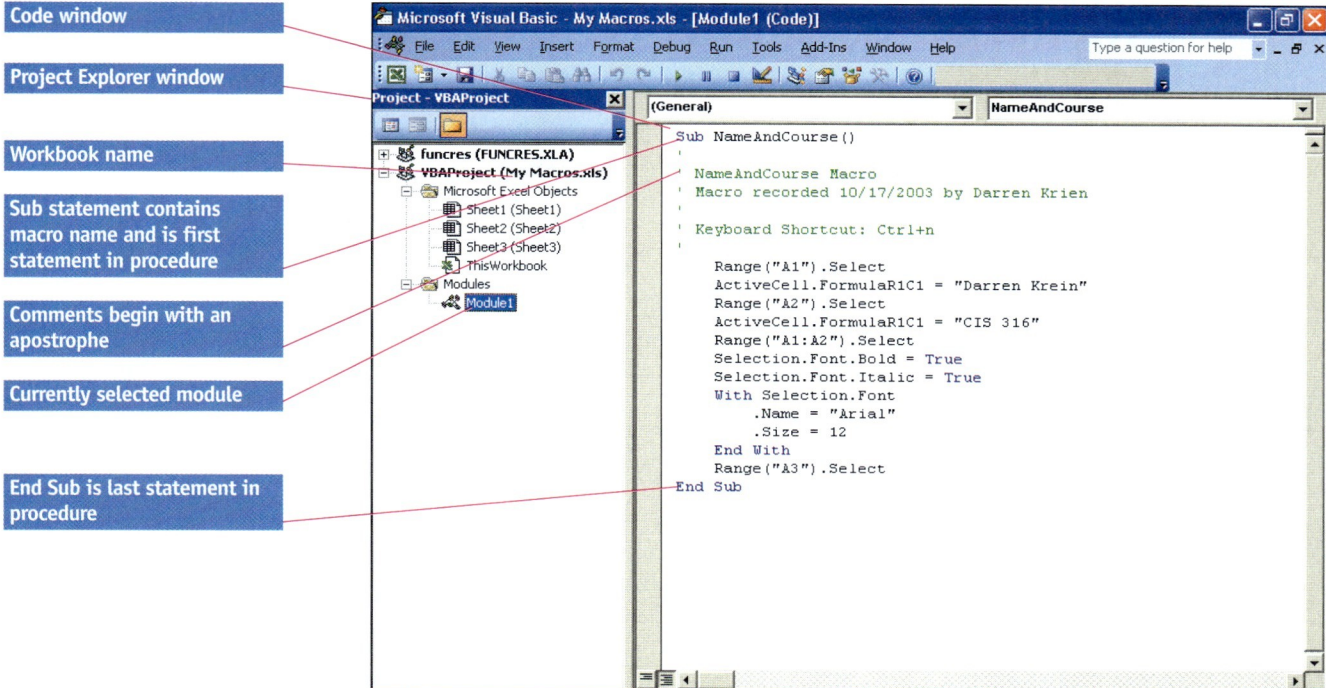

FIGURE 9.1 A Simple Macro

Every other statement is a Visual Basic instruction that was created as a result of an action taken in Excel. For example, the statements

        Range ("A1").Select
and   ActiveCell.FormulaR1C1 = "Darren Krein"

select cell A1 as the active cell, then enter the text "Darren Krein" into the active cell. These statements are equivalent to clicking in cell A1 of a worksheet, typing the indicated entry into the active cell, then pressing the Enter key (or an arrow key) to complete the entry. In similar fashion, the statements

        Range ("A2").Select
and   ActiveCell.FormulaR1C1 = "CIS 316"

select cell A2 as the active cell, then enter the text entry "CIS 316" into that cell. The concept of select-then-do applies equally well to statements within a macro. Thus, the statements

    Range ("A1:A2").Select
    Selection.Font.Bold = True
    Selection.Font.Italic = True

select cells A1 through A2, then change the font for the selected cells to bold italic. The ***With statement*** enables you to perform multiple actions on the same object. All commands between the With and corresponding ***End With statement*** are executed collectively; for example, the statements

    With Selection.Font
        .Name = "Arial"
        .Size = 12
    End With

change the formatting of the selected cells (A1:A2) to 12 point Arial. The last statement in the macro, Range ("A3").Select, selects cell A3, thus deselecting all other cells, a practice we use throughout the chapter.

hands-on exercise 1

Introduction to Macros

Objective To record, run, view, and edit a simple macro; to establish a keyboard shortcut to run a macro. Use Figure 9.2 as a guide in doing the exercise.

Step 1: **Create a Macro**

- Start Excel. Open a new workbook if one is not already open. Save the workbook as **My Macros** in the **Exploring Excel folder**.

- Pull down the **Tools menu**, click (or point to) the **Macro command**, then click **Record New Macro** to display the Record Macro dialog box in Figure 9.2a. (If you don't see the Macro command, click the double arrow at the bottom of the menu to see more commands.)

- Enter **NameAndCourse** as the name of the macro. (Spaces are not allowed in the macro name.)

- The description is entered automatically and contains today's date and the name of the person in whose name this copy of Excel is registered. If necessary, change the description to include your name.

- Click in the **Shortcut Key** check box and enter a **lowercase n**. Ctrl+n should appear as the shortcut as shown in Figure 9.2a. (If you see Ctrl+Shift+N it means you typed an uppercase N rather than a lowercase letter. Correct the entry to a lowercase n.)

- Check that the option to Store macro in **This Workbook** is selected. Click **OK** to record the macro, which displays the Stop Recording toolbar.

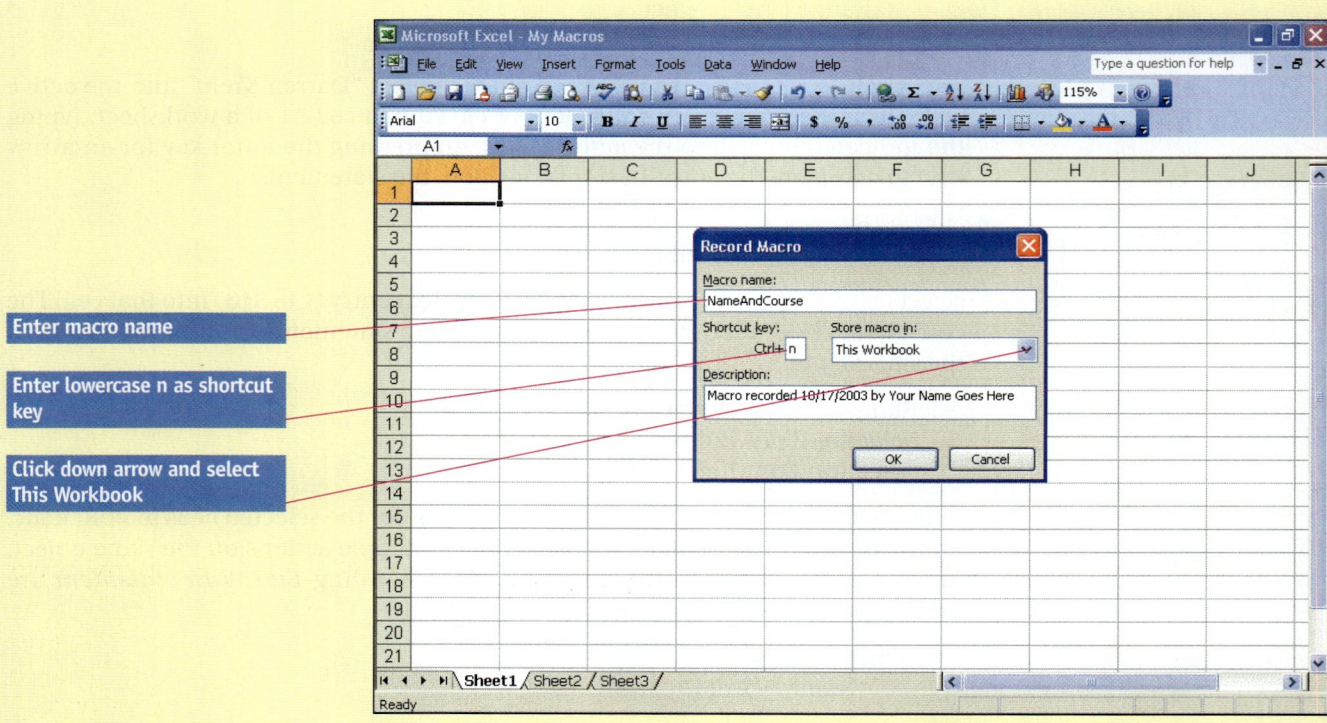

(a) Create a Macro (step 1)

FIGURE 9.2 Hands-on Exercise 1

452   CHAPTER 9: AUTOMATING REPETITIVE TASKS

Step 2: **Record the Macro**

- Look carefully at the Relative References button on the Stop Recording button to be sure it is flush with the other buttons; that is, the button should *not* be pushed in. (See boxed tip on "Is the Button In or Out?")

- You should be in Sheet1, ready to record the macro, as shown in Figure 9.2b. The status bar indicates that you are in the Recording mode:
    - Click in **cell A1** even if it is already selected. Enter your name.
    - Click in **cell A2**. Enter the course you are taking.
    - Click and drag to select **cells A1 through A2**.
    - Click the **Bold button**. Click the **Italic button**.
    - Click the arrow on the **Font Size list box**. Click **12** to change the point size.
    - Click in **cell A3** to deselect all other cells prior to ending the macro.

- Click the **Stop Recording button**. (If you do not see the Stop Recording toolbar, pull down the **Tools button**, click **Macro**, then click the **Stop Recording command**.)

- Save the workbook.

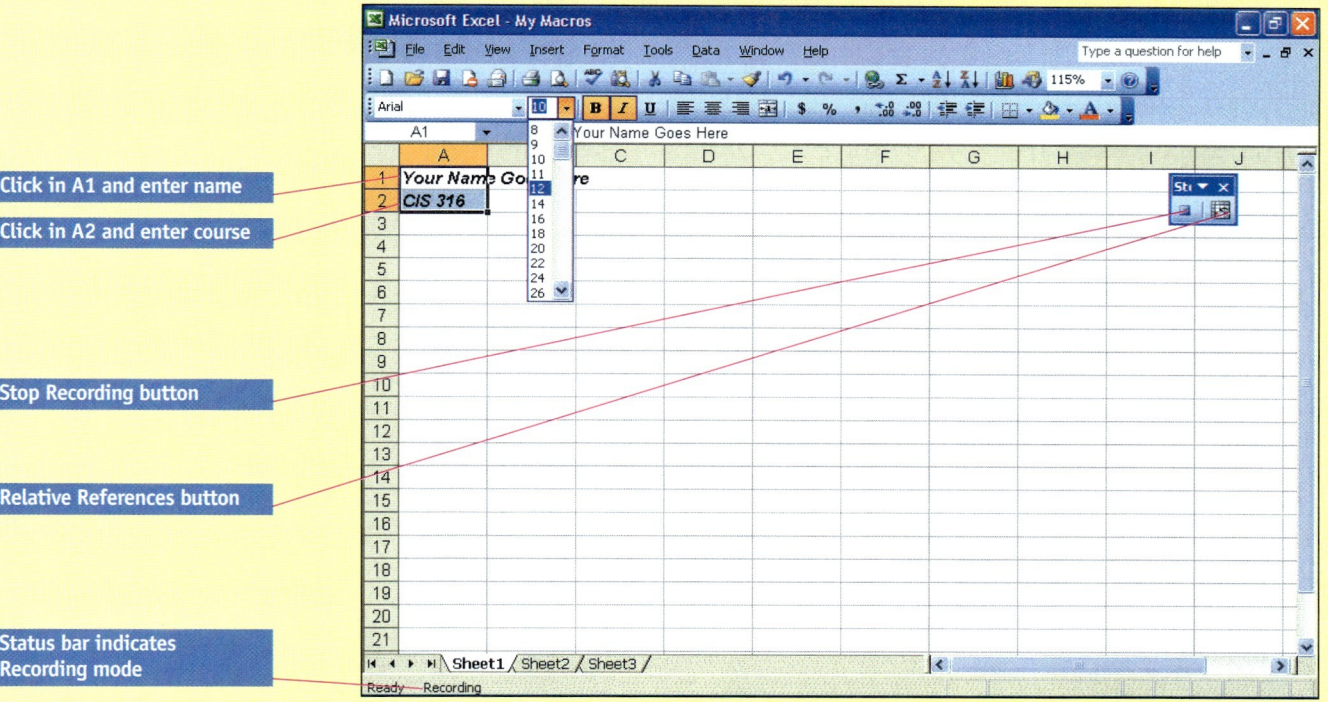

(b) Record the Macro (step 2)

FIGURE 9.2 Hands-on Exercise 1 (*continued*)

IS THE BUTTON IN OR OUT?

The distinction between relative and absolute references within a macro is critical and is described in detail at the end of this exercise. The Relative References button on the Stop Recording toolbar toggles between the two—absolute references when the button is out, relative references when the button is in. The ScreenTip, however, displays Relative References regardless of whether the button is in or out. We wish that Microsoft had made it easier to tell which type of reference you are recording, but they didn't.

Step 3: **Test the Macro**

- To run (test) the macro, you have to remove the contents and formatting from cells A1 and A2. Click and drag to select **cells A1 through A2**.

- Pull down the **Edit menu**. Click **Clear**. Click **All** from the cascaded menu to erase both the contents and formatting from the selected cells. Cells A1 through A2 are empty as shown in Figure 9.2c.

- Pull down the **Tools menu**. Click **Macro**, then click the **Macros . . . command** to display the dialog box in Figure 9.2c.

- Click **NameAndCourse**, which is the macro you just recorded. Click **Run**. Your name and class are entered in cells A1 and A2, then formatted according to the instructions in the macro.

- Clear the contents and formatting in cells A1 and A2. Press **Ctrl+n** (the keyboard shortcut) to rerun the NameAndCourse macro. Your name and class should reappear in cells A1 and A2.

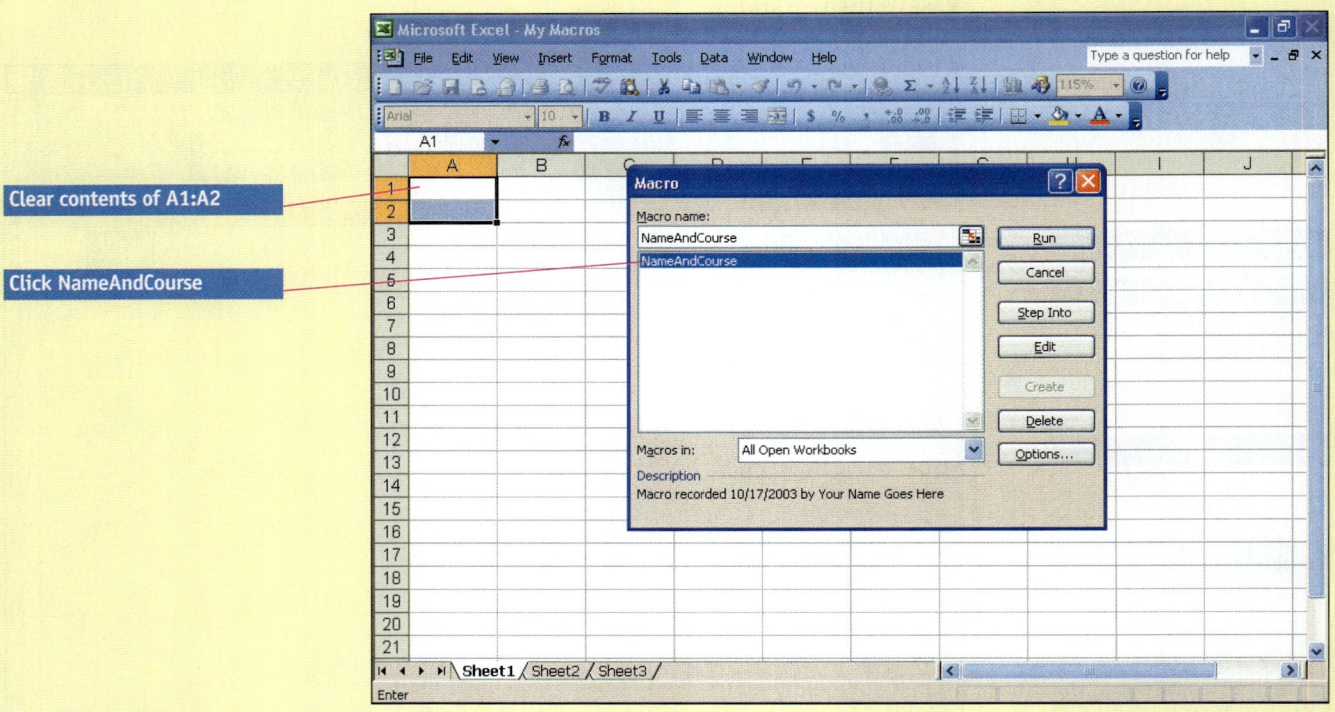

(c) Test the Macro (step 3)

FIGURE 9.2 Hands-on Exercise 1 (*continued*)

THE EDIT CLEAR COMMAND

The Edit Clear command erases the contents of a cell, its formatting, and/or its comments. Select the cell or cells to erase, pull down the Edit menu, click the Clear command, then click All, Formats, Contents, or Comments from the cascaded menu. Pressing the Del key is equivalent to executing the Edit Clear Contents command as it clears the contents of a cell, but retains the formatting and comments.

Step 4: **Start the Visual Basic Editor**

- Pull down the **Tools menu**, click the **Macro command**, then click **Visual Basic Editor** (or press **Alt+F11**) to open the Visual Basic Editor. Maximize the VBE window.
- If necessary, pull down the **View menu**. Click **Project Explorer** to open the Project Explorer window in the left pane. There is currently one open VBA project, My Macros.xls, which is the name of the open workbook in Excel.
- If necessary, click the **plus sign** next to the Modules folder to expand that folder, click (select) **Module1**, pull down the **View menu**, and click **Code** to open the Code window in the right pane. Click the **Maximize button** in the Code window.
- Your screen should match the one in Figure 9.2d. The first statement below the comments should be *Range("A1").Select*, which indicates that the macro was correctly recorded with absolute references.
- If you see a very different statement, *ActiveCell.FormulaR1C1*, it means that you incorrectly recorded the macro with relative references. Right click **Module1** in the Project Explorer window, select the **Remove Module1 command** (respond **No** when asked if you want to export it), then return to step 1 and rerecord the macro.

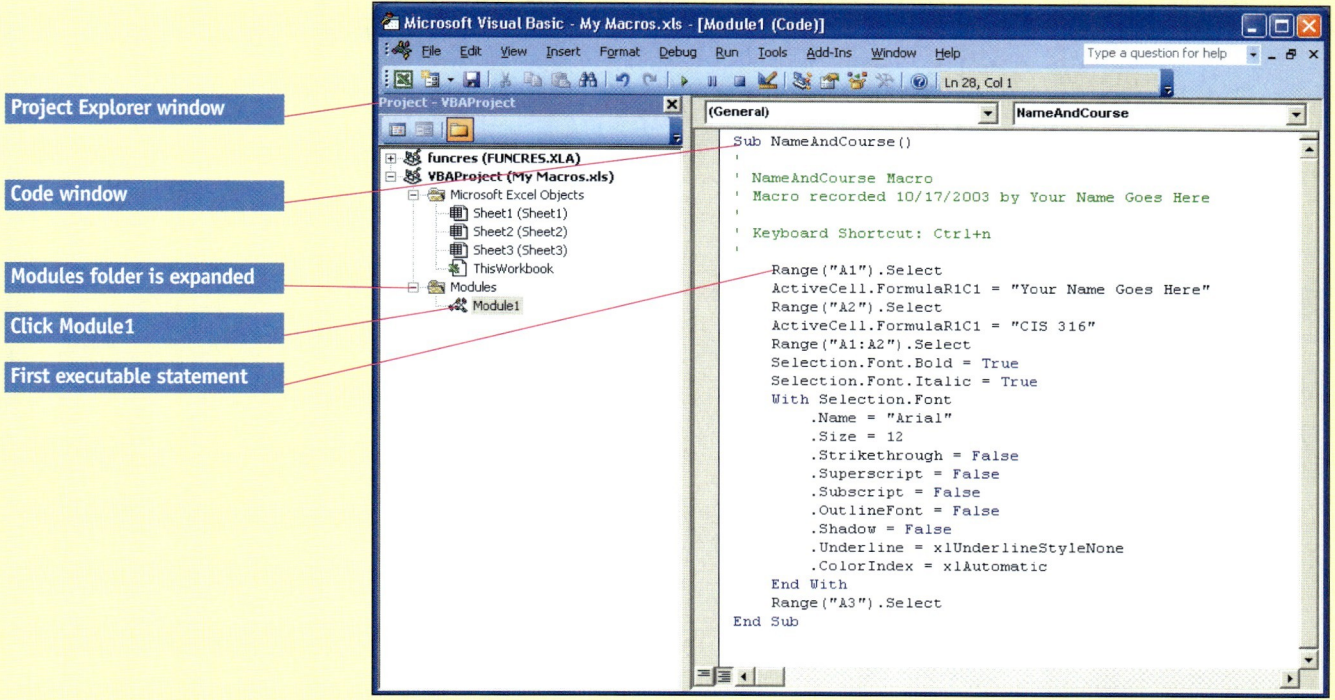

(d) Start the Visual Basic Editor (step 4)

FIGURE 9.2 Hands-on Exercise 1 (*continued*)

THE END RESULT

Excel provides multiple ways to accomplish the same task; for example, you can click the Bold button on the Formatting toolbar, or you can use the Ctrl+B shortcut. The macro recorder records only the end result, with no indication of which technique was used. Thus, you will see Selection.Font.Bold = True (or False) regardless of whether you used the toolbar or the mouse.

Step 5: **Edit the Macro**

- Edit the NameAndCourse macro by changing the font name and size to **"Times New Roman"** and **24**, respectively, as shown in Figure 9.2e.
- Click and drag to select the next seven statements as shown in Figure 9.2e.
- Press the **Del key** to delete these statements from the macro. (These statements contain default values and are unnecessary.) Delete any blank lines as well.
- Press **Alt+F11** to toggle back to the Excel workbook (or click the **Excel button** on the Windows taskbar).
- Clear the entries and formatting in cells A1 and A2 as you did earlier, then rerun the NameAndCourse macro.
- Your name and class should once again be entered in cells A1 and A2 but in a different and larger font. (If the macro does not execute correctly, press **Alt+F11** to toggle back to the Visual Basic Editor to correct your macro.)
- Save the workbook.

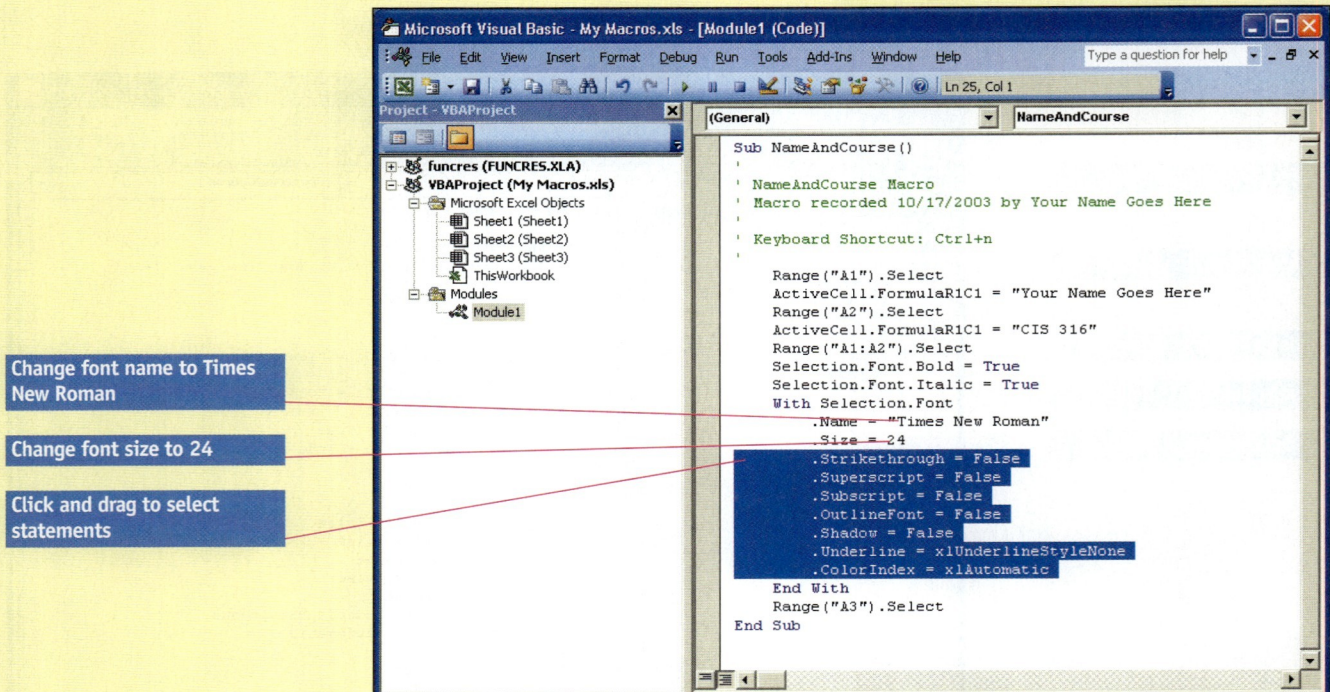

(e) Edit the Macro (step 5)

FIGURE 9.2 Hands-on Exercise 1 (*continued*)

SIMPLIFY THE MACRO

The macro recorder usually sets all possible options for an Excel command or dialog box even if you do not change those options. We suggest, therefore, that you make a macro easier to read by deleting the unnecessary statements. Take a minute, however, to review the statements prior to removing them, so that you can see the additional options. (You can click the Undo button to restore the deleted statements if you make a mistake.)

Step 6: **Create the Erase Macro**

- Pull down the **Tools menu**. Click the **Macro command**, then click **Record New Macro** from the cascaded menu. You will see the Record Macro dialog box.

- Enter **EraseNameAndCourse** as the name of the macro. Do not leave any spaces in the macro name. If necessary, change the description to include your name.

- Click in the **Shortcut Key** check box and enter a **lowercase e**. (Ctrl+e should appear as the shortcut.) Check that the option to Store macro in **This Workbook** is selected.

- Click **OK** to begin recording the macro, which displays the Stop Recording toolbar. Be sure you are recording absolute references (i.e., the Relative References button should be flush on the toolbar).
  - Click and drag to select **cells A1 through A2** as shown in Figure 9.2f, even if they are already selected.
  - Pull down the **Edit menu**. Click **Clear**. Click **All** from the cascaded menu. Cells A1 through A2 should now be empty.
  - Click in **cell A3** to deselect all other cells prior to ending the macro.

- Click the **Stop Recording button** to end the macro.

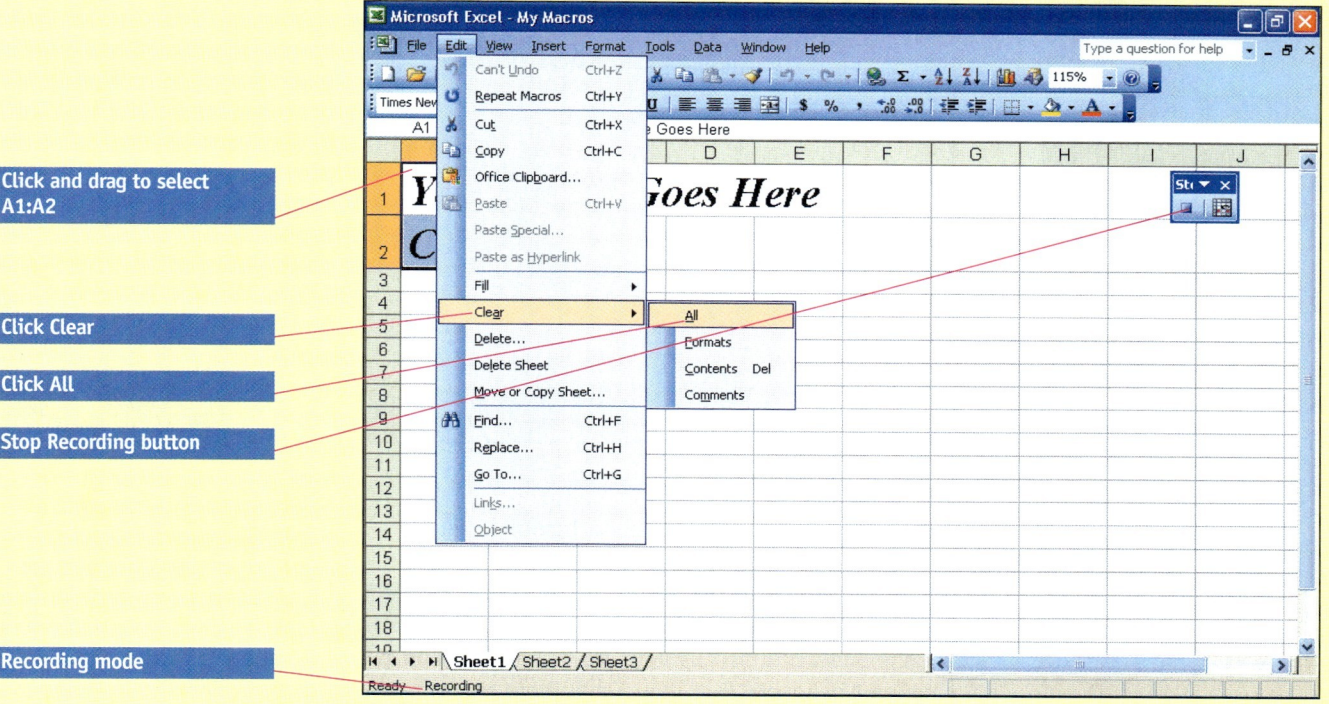

(f) Create the Erase Macro (step 6)

FIGURE 9.2 Hands-on Exercise 1 (*continued*)

TO SELECT OR NOT SELECT

If you start recording, then select a cell(s) within the macro, the selection becomes part of the macro, and the macro will always operate on the same cell. If, however, you select the cell(s) prior to recording, the macro is more general and operates on the selected cells, which may differ every time the macro is executed. Both techniques are valid, and the decision depends on what you want the macro to do.

Step 7: **Shortcut Keys**

- Press **Ctrl+n** to execute the NameAndCourse macro. (You need to reenter your name and course to test the newly created EraseNameAndCourse macro.)
- Your name and course should again appear in cells A1 and A2 as shown in Figure 9.2g.
- Press **Ctrl+e** to execute the EraseNameAndCourse macro. Cells A1 and A2 should again be empty.
- You can press **Ctrl+n** and **Ctrl+e** repeatedly, to enter and then erase your name and course. End this step after having erased the data.
- Save the workbook.

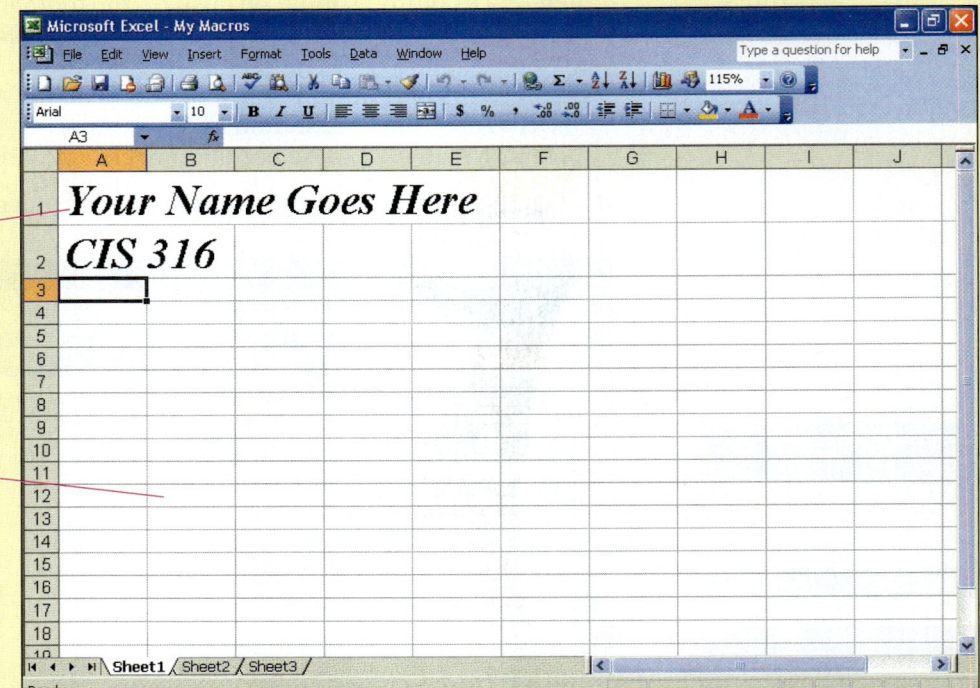

Press Ctrl+n to run the NameAndCourse macro

Press Ctrl+e to run the macro to erase your name and course

(g) Shortcut Keys (step 7)

FIGURE 9.2 Hands-on Exercise 1 (*continued*)

TROUBLESHOOTING

If the macro shortcut keys do not work, it is probably because they were not defined properly. Pull down the Tools menu, click Macro to display a cascaded menu, click the Macros . . . command, then select the desired macro in the Macro Name list box. Click the Options button, then check the entry in the Shortcut Key text box. A lowercase letter creates a shortcut with just the Ctrl key, whereas an uppercase letter uses Ctrl+Shift with the shortcut. Thus, "n" and "N" will establish shortcuts of Ctrl+n and Ctrl+Shift+N, respectively.

Step 8: **Step through the Macro**

- Press **Alt+F11** to switch back to the VBE window. Click the **Close button** to close the **Project window** within the Visual Basic Editor. The Code window expands to take the entire Visual Basic Editor window.

- Point to an empty area on the Windows taskbar, then click the **right mouse button** to display a shortcut menu. Click **Tile Windows Vertically**.

- Your desktop should be similar to Figure 9.2h. It doesn't matter if the workbook is in the left or right window.

- Click in the **Visual Basic Editor window**, then click anywhere within the NameAndCourse macro. Pull down the **Debug menu** and click the **Step Into command** (or press the **F8 key**). The Sub statement is highlighted.

- Press the **F8 key** to move to the first executable statement (the comments are skipped). The statement is highlighted, but it has not yet been executed.

- Press the **F8 key** again to execute this statement (which selects cell A1 and moves to the next statement). Continue to press the **F8 key** to execute the statements one at a time. You see the effect of each statement in the Excel window.

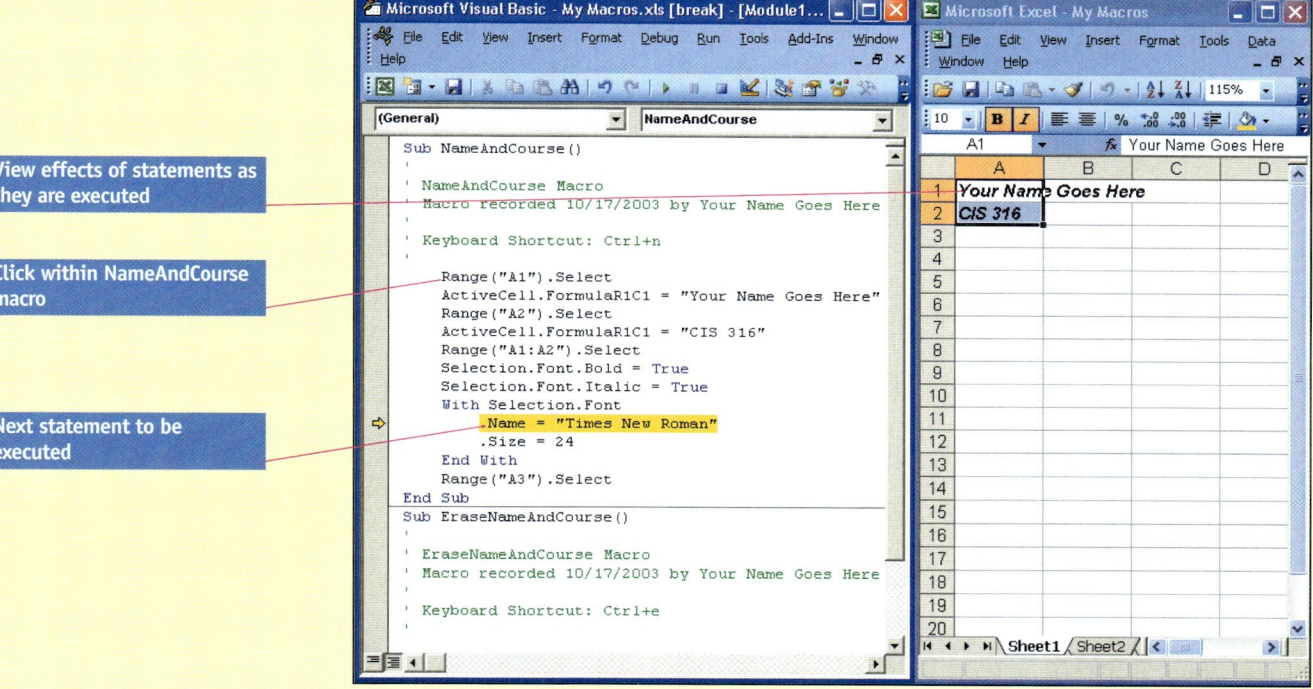

(h) Step through the Macro (step 8)

FIGURE 9.2 Hands-on Exercise 1 (*continued*)

THE STEP INTO COMMAND

The Step Into command is useful to slow down the execution of a macro in the event the macro does not perform as intended. In essence, you execute the macro one statement at a time, while viewing the results of each statement in the associated worksheet. If a statement does not do what you want it to do, just change the statement in the Visual Basic window, then continue to press the F8 key to step through the procedure.

Step 9: **Print the Module**

- Click in the **Visual Basic window**. Pull down the **File menu**. Click **Print** to display the Print - VBAProject dialog box in Figure 9.2i.

- Click the option button to print the current module. Click **OK**. Submit the listing of the current module, which contains the procedures for both macros, to your instructor as proof you did this exercise.

- Close the My Macros workbook. Click **Yes** if asked to save the workbook. The macros are stored within the workbook.

- Exit Excel if you do not wish to continue with the next hands-on exercise at this time.

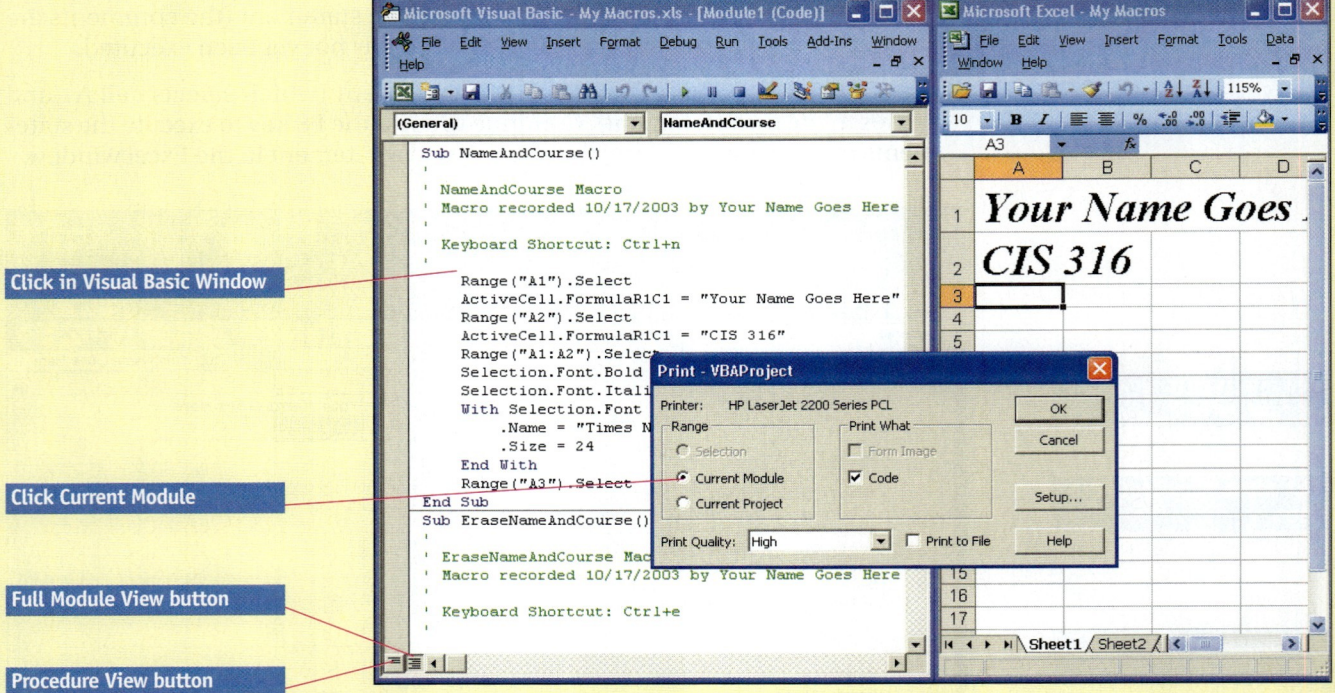

(i) Print the Module (step 9)

FIGURE 9.2 Hands-on Exercise 1 (*continued*)

PROCEDURE VIEW VERSUS FULL MODULE VIEW

The procedures within a module can be displayed individually, or alternatively, multiple procedures can be viewed simultaneously. To go from one view to the other, click the Procedure View button at the bottom of the window to display just the procedure you are working on, or click the Full Module View button to display multiple procedures. You can press Ctrl+PgDn and Ctrl+PgUp to move between procedures in either view. Use the vertical scroll bar to move up and down within the VBA window.

RELATIVE VERSUS ABSOLUTE REFERENCES

One of the most important options to specify when recording a macro is whether the references are to be relative or absolute. A reference is a cell address. An ***absolute reference*** is a constant address that always refers to the same cell. A ***relative reference*** is variable in that the reference will change from one execution of the macro to the next, depending on the location of the active cell when the macro is executed.

To appreciate the difference, consider Figure 9.3, which displays two versions of the NameAndCourse macro from the previous exercise, one with absolute and one with relative references. Figure 9.3a uses absolute references to place your name, course, and date in cells A1, A2, and A3. The data will always be entered in these cells regardless of which cell is selected when you execute the macro.

Figure 9.3b enters the same data, but with relative references, so that the cells in which the data are entered depend on which cell is selected when the macro is executed. If cell A1 is selected, your name, course, and date will be entered in cells A1, A2, and A3. If, however, cell E4 is the active cell when you execute the macro, then your name, course, and date will be entered in cells E4, E5, and E6.

A relative reference is specified by an ***offset*** that indicates the number of rows and columns from the active cell. An offset of (1,0) indicates a cell one row below the active cell. An offset of (0,1) indicates a cell one column to the right of the active cell. In similar fashion, an offset of (1,1) indicates a cell one row below and one column to the right of the active cell. Negative offsets are used for cells above or to the left of the current selection.

Absolute References to cells A1, A2, and A3

```
Range("A1").Select
ActiveCell.FormulaR1C1 = "Darren Krein"
Range("A2").Select
ActiveCell.FormulaR1C1 = "CIS 316"
Range("A3").Select
ActiveCell.FormulaR1C1 = "=TODAY()"
Range("A1:A3").Select
Selection.Font.Italic = True
With Selection.Font
    .Name = "Arial"
    .Size = 12
End With
Range("A4").Select
```

(a) Absolute References

Relative references to cell one row below the active cell

Indicates a column of 3 cells is to be selected

```
ActiveCell.FormulaR1C1 = "Darren Krein"
ActiveCell.Offset(1, 0).Range("A1").Select
ActiveCell.FormulaR1C1 = "CIS 316"
ActiveCell.Offset(1, 0).Range("A1").Select
ActiveCell.FormulaR1C1 = "=TODAY()"
ActiveCell.Offset(-2, 0).Range("A1:A3").Select
Selection.Font.Italic = True
With Selection.Font
    .Name = "Arial"
    .Size = 12
End With
ActiveCell.Offset(3, 0).Range("A1").Select
```

(b) Relative References

FIGURE 9.3 Absolute versus Relative References

Relative references may appear confusing at first, but they extend the power of a macro by making it more general. You will appreciate this capability as you learn more about macros. Let us begin by recognizing that the statement

ActiveCell.Offset (1,0).Range ("A1").Select

means select the cell one row below the active cell. It has nothing to do with cell A1, and you might wonder why the entry Range ("A1") is included. The answer is that the offset specifies the location of the new range (one row below the current cell), and the A1 indicates that the size of that range is a single cell (A1). In similar fashion, the statement

ActiveCell.Offset (–2,0).Range ("A1:A3").Select

selects a range, starting two rows above the current cell, that is one column by three rows in size. Again, it has nothing to do with cells A1 through A3. The offset specifies the location of a new range (two rows above the current cell) and the shape of that range (a column of three cells). If you are in cell D11 when the statement is executed, the selected range will be cells D9 through D11. The selection starts with the cell (cell D9) two rows above the active cell, then it continues from that point to select a range consisting of one column by three rows (cells D9:D11).

RELATIVE VERSUS ABSOLUTE REFERENCES

Relative references appear confusing at first, but they extend the power of a macro by making it more general. Macro statements that have been recorded with relative references include an offset to indicate the number of rows and columns the selection is to be from the active cell. An offset of (–1,0) indicates a cell one row above the active cell, whereas an offset of (0,–1) indicates a cell one column to the left of the active cell. Positive offsets are used for cells below or to the right of the current selection.

THE PERSONAL MACRO WORKBOOK

The hands-on exercise at the beginning of the chapter created the NameAndCourse macro in the My Macros workbook, where it is available to that workbook or to any other workbook that is in memory when the My Macros workbook is open. What if, however, you want the macro to be available at all times, not just when the My Macros workbook is open? This is easily accomplished by storing the macro in the Personal Macro workbook when it is first recorded.

The ***Personal Macro workbook*** opens automatically whenever Excel is loaded. This is because the Personal Macro workbook is stored in the XLStart folder, a folder that Excel checks each time it is loaded into memory. Once open, the macros in the Personal workbook are available to any other open workbook. The following hands-on exercise creates the NameAndCourse macro with relative references, then stores that macro in the Personal Macro workbook.

The exercise also expands the macro to enter the date of execution, and further generalizes the macro to accept the name of the course as input. The latter is accomplished through the Visual Basic ***InputBox function*** that prompts the user for a specific response, then stores that response within the macro. In other words, the Excel macro is enhanced through the inclusion of a VBA statement that adds functionality to the original macro. You start with the macro recorder to translate Excel commands into a VBA procedure, then you modify the procedure by adding the necessary VBA statements. (The InputBox function must be entered manually into the procedure since there is no corresponding Excel command, and hence the macro recorder would not work.)

hands-on exercise
2 The Personal Macro Workbook

Objective To create and store a macro in the Personal Macro workbook; to assign a toolbar button to a macro; to use the Visual Basic InputBox function. Use Figure 9.4 as a guide in the exercise.

Step 1: **The Personal Macro Workbook**

- Start Excel. Be sure to close the My Macros workbook from the previous exercise to avoid any conflict with an existing macro.

- Open a new workbook if one is not already open. Pull down the **Tools menu**, click (or point to) the **Macro command**, then click **Record New Macro** to display the Record Macro dialog box.

- Enter **NameAndCourse** as the name of the macro. Do not leave any spaces in the macro name. Click in the **Shortcut Key** check box and enter a **lowercase n**. Ctrl+n should appear as the shortcut.

- Click the **drop-down arrow** in the Store macro in list box and select the Personal Macro workbook as shown in Figure 9.4a. (If you are working on a network, as opposed to a standalone machine, you may not be able to access the **Personal Macro workbook**, in which case you can save the macro in **This Workbook**.)

- Click **OK** to begin recording the macro, which in turn displays the Stop Recording toolbar.

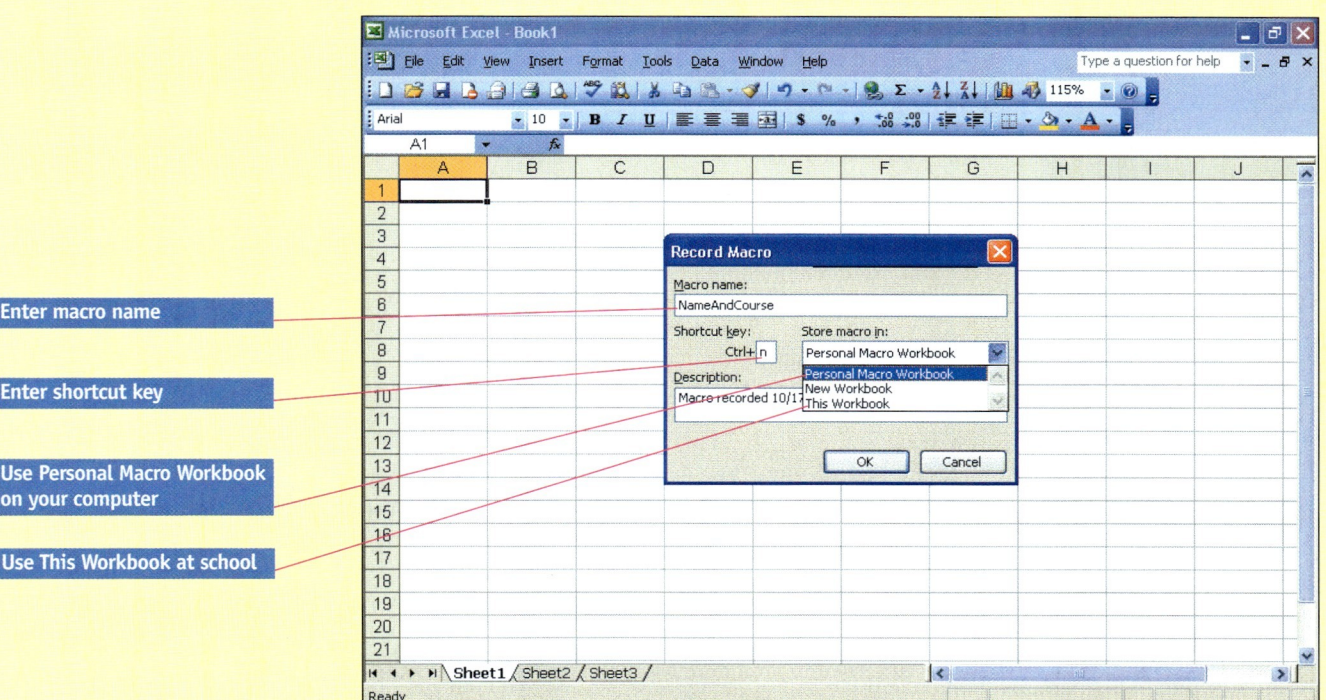

(a) The Personal Macro Workbook (step 1)

FIGURE 9.4 Hands-on Exercise 2

Step 2: **Record with Relative References**

- Click the **Relative References button** on the Stop Recording toolbar so that the button is pushed in as shown in Figure 9.4b.
- The Relative References button functions as a toggle switch—click it, and the button is pushed in to record relative references. Click it again, and you record absolute references. Be sure to record relative references.
- Enter your name in the active cell. Do *not* select the cell.
- Press the **down arrow key** to move to the cell immediately underneath the current cell. Enter the course you are taking.
- Press the **down arrow key** to move to the next cell. Enter **=TODAY()**.
- Click and drag to select the three cells containing the data values you just entered (cells A1 through A3 in Figure 9.4b).
  - Click the **Bold button**. Click the **Italic button**.
  - Click the arrow on the **Font Size list box**. Click **12** to change the point size.
  - Click in **cell A4** to deselect all other cells prior to ending the macro.
- Click the **Stop Recording button** to end the macro.

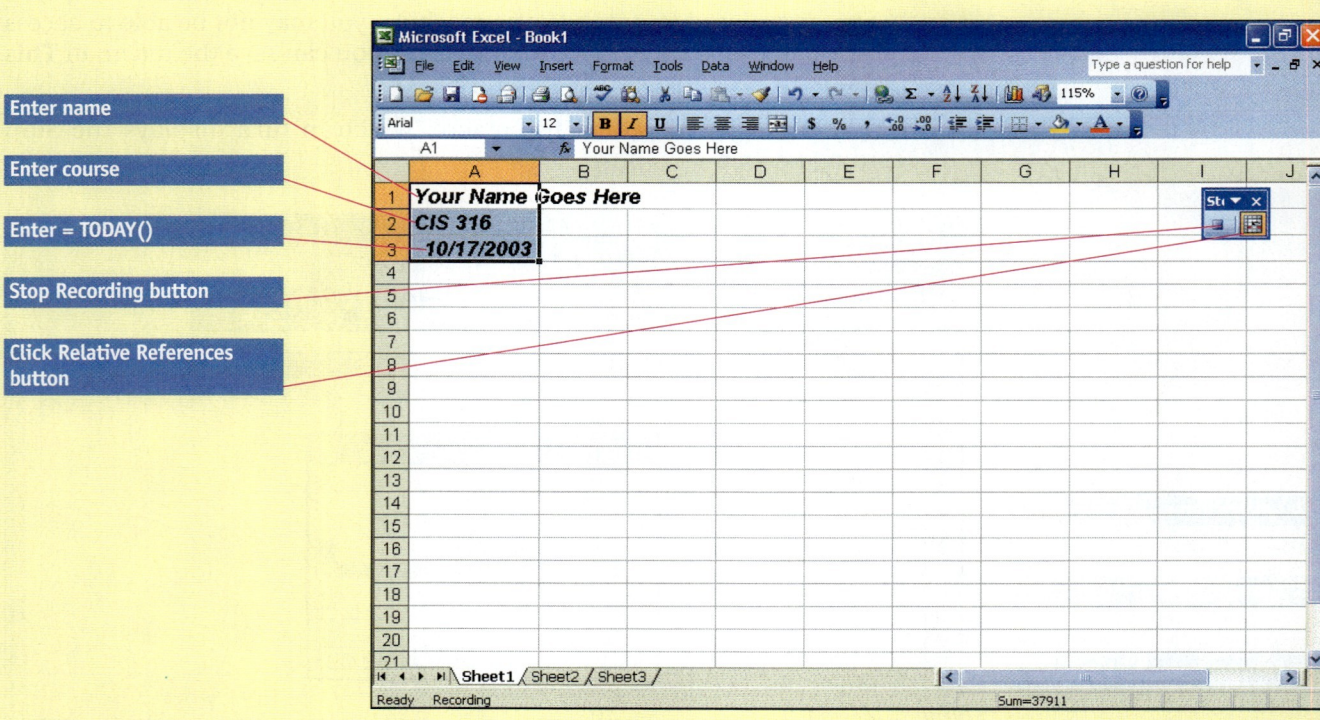

(b) Record with Relative References (step 2)

FIGURE 9.4 Hands-on Exercise 2 (*continued*)

PLAN AHEAD

The macro recorder records everything you do, including entries that are made by mistake or commands that are executed incorrectly. Plan the macro in advance, before you begin recording. Write down what you intend to do, then try out the commands with the recorder off. Be sure you go all the way through the intended sequence of operations prior to turning the macro recorder on.

Step 3: **The Visual Basic Editor**

- Pull down the **Tools menu**, click the **Macro command**, then click **Visual Basic Editor** (or press **Alt+F11**) to open the Visual Basic Editor in Figure 9.4c.

- If necessary, pull down the **View menu**. Click **Project Explorer** to open the Project Explorer window in the left pane.

- There are currently two open VBA projects (Book1, the name of the open workbook, and PERSONAL.XLS, the Personal Macro workbook).

- Click the **plus sign** to expand the Personal Workbook folder, then click the **plus sign** to expand the **Modules** folder within this project.

- Click (select) **Module1**, pull down the **View menu**, and click **Code** to open the Code window in the right pane. Maximize the Code window.

- Close any other open windows within the Visual Basic Editor. The first executable statement should begin with *ActiveCell.FormulaR1C1*.

- If you see a very different statement, *Range("A1").Select*, it means that you incorrectly recorded the macro with absolute references. Right click Module1 in the Project window, select the **Remove Module command** (respond **No** when asked if you want to export it), then return to step 1 and rerecord the macro.

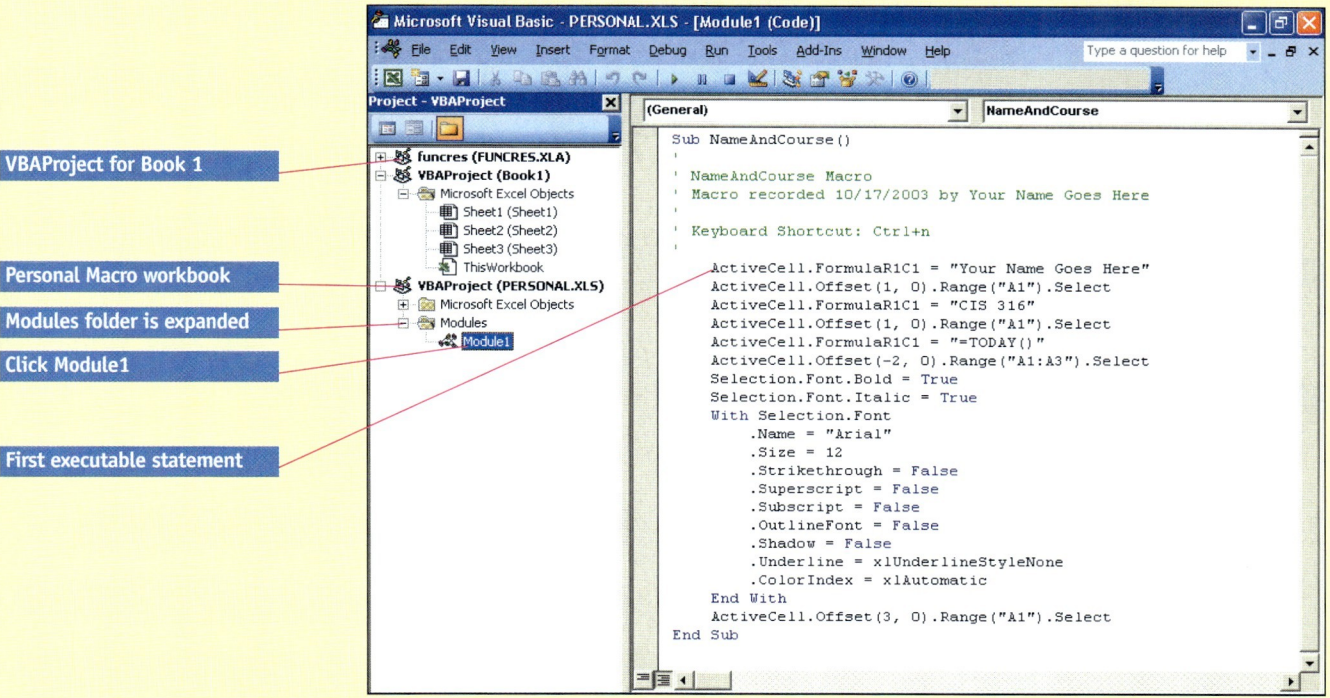

(c) The Visual Basic Editor (step 3)

FIGURE 9.4 Hands-on Exercise 2 (*continued*)

WHAT DOES RANGE ("A1:A3") REALLY MEAN?

The statement ActiveCell.Offset (–2,0).Range ("A1:A3").Select has nothing to do with cells A1 through A3, so why is the entry Range ("A1:A3") included? The effect of the statement is to select three cells (one cell under the other) starting with the cell two rows above the current cell. The offset (–2,0) specifies the starting point of the selected range (two rows above the current cell). The range ("A1:A3") indicates the size and shape of the selected range (a vertical column of three cells).

Step 4: **Edit the Macro**

- Click and drag to select the name of the course, which is found in the third executable statement of the macro. Be sure to include the quotation marks (e.g., "CIS316" in our example) in your selection.

- Enter **InputBox("Enter the Course You Are Taking")** to replace the selected text. Note that as you enter the Visual Basic keyword, *InputBox*, a prompt (containing the correct syntax for this statement) is displayed on the screen as shown in Figure 9.4d.

- Just ignore the prompt and keep typing to complete the entry. Press the **Home key** when you complete the entry to scroll back to the beginning of the line.

- Click immediately after the number **12**, then click and drag to select the next seven statements. Press the **Del key** to delete the highlighted statements from the macro.

- Delete the **Selection.Font.Bold=True** statement. Click the **Save button** to save the modified macro.

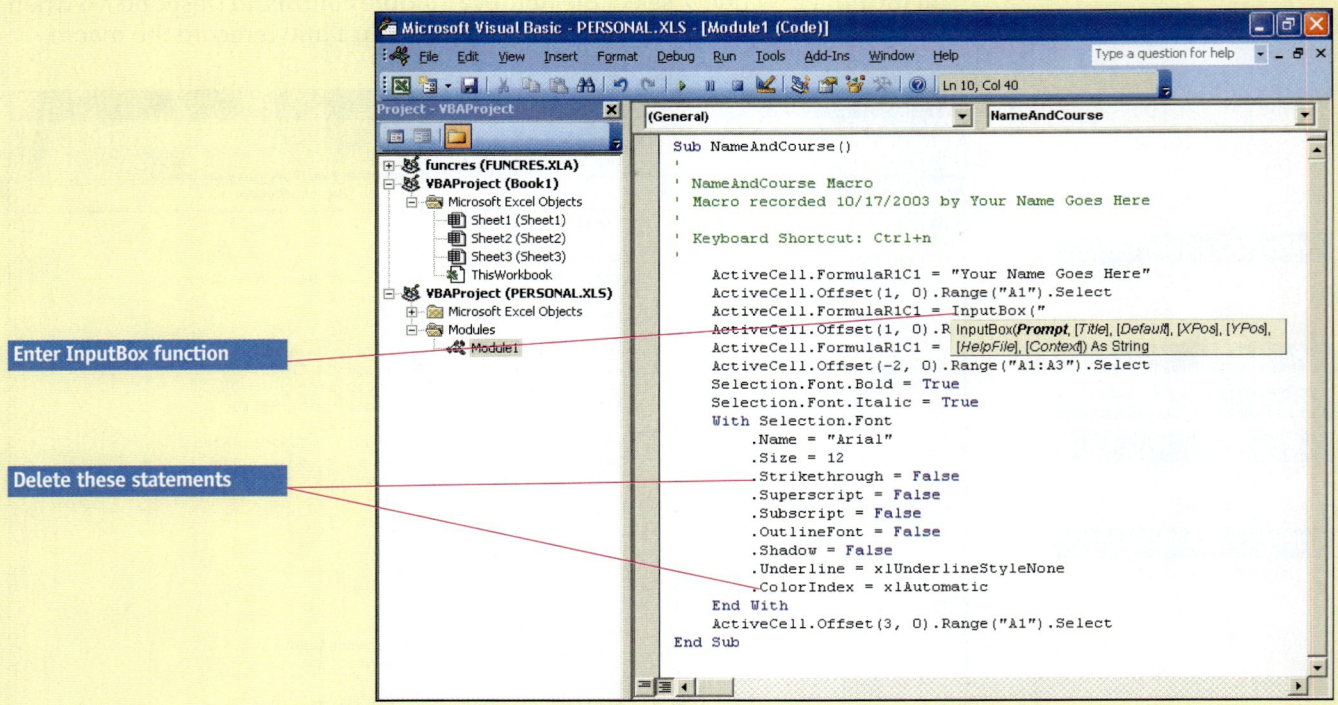

(d) Edit the Macro (step 4)

FIGURE 9.4 Hands-on Exercise 2 (*continued*)

THE INPUTBOX FUNCTION

The InputBox function adds flexibility to a macro by obtaining input from the user when the macro is executed. It is used in this example to generalize the NameAndCourse macro by asking the user for the name of the course, as opposed to storing the name within the macro. The InputBox function, coupled with storing the macro in the Personal Macro workbook, enables the user to personalize any workbook by executing the associated macro.

Step 5: **Test the Revised Macro**

- Press **Alt+F11** to view the Excel workbook. Click in any cell—for example, **cell C5** as shown in Figure 9.4e.

- Pull down the **Tools menu**. Click **Macro**, click the **Macros . . . command**, select **PERSONAL.XLS!NameAndCourse**, then click the **Run command button** to run the macro. (Alternatively you can use the **Ctrl+n** shortcut.)

- The macro enters your name in cell C5 (the active cell), selects the cell one row below, then displays the input dialog box shown in Figure 9.4e.

- Enter any appropriate course and press the **Enter key**. You should see the course you entered followed by the date. All three entries will be formatted according to the commands you specified in the macro.

- Click in a different cell, then press **Ctrl+n** to rerun the macro. The macro will enter your name, the course you specify, and the date in the selected location because it was recorded with relative references.

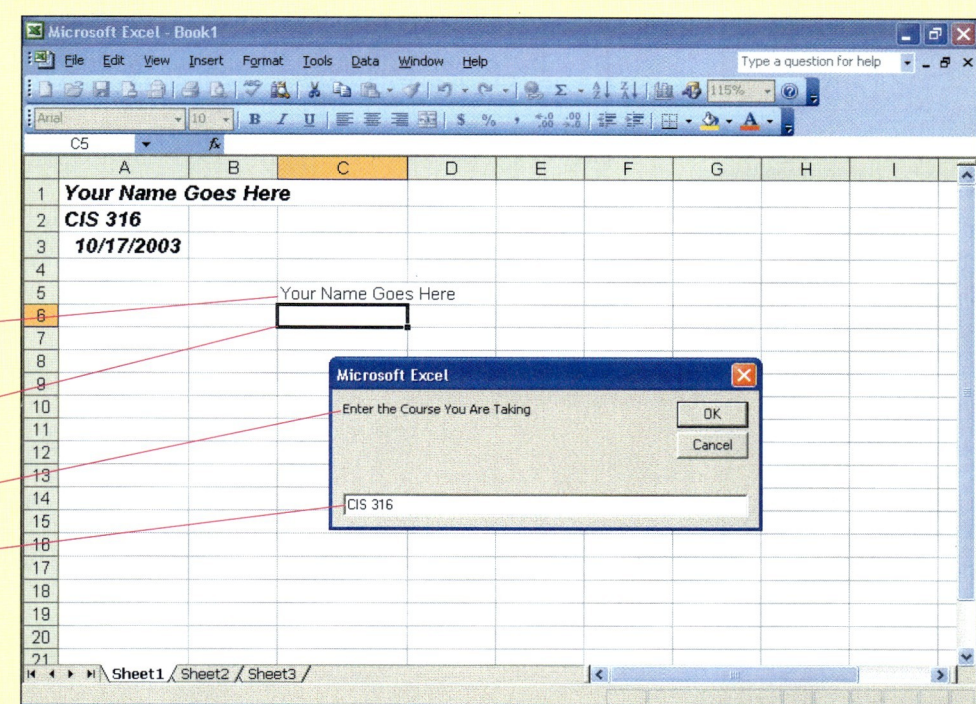

(e) Test the Revised Macro (step 5)

FIGURE 9.4 Hands-on Exercise 2 (*continued*)

RED, GREEN, AND BLUE

Visual Basic automatically assigns different colors to different types of statements (or a portion of those statements). Any statement containing a syntax error appears in red. Comments appear in green. Keywords—such as Sub and End Sub, With and End With, and True and False—appear in blue. The different colors are intended to make the code easier to read. Indentation and/or blank lines can also improve readability.

Step 6: **Add a Custom Button**

- Point to any toolbar, then click the **right mouse button** to display a shortcut menu. Click **Customize** to display the Customize dialog box in Figure 9.4f.
- Click the **Commands tab**. Click the **down arrow** to scroll through the Categories list box until you can select the **Macros category**.
- Click and drag the **Custom (Happy Face) button** to an available space at the right of the Standard toolbar. Release the mouse. (You must drag the button *within* the toolbar.)
- Click the **Modify Selection button** within the Customize dialog box to display the cascaded menu in Figure 9.4f.
- Click and drag to select the name of the button (&Custom Button) and replace it with **NameAndCourse**, to create a ScreenTip for that button. Do not press the Enter key.
- Click the **Assign Macro command** at the bottom of the menu to display the Assign Macro dialog box. Select **PERSONAL.XLS!NameAndCourse** and click **OK**.
- Click **Close** to exit the Custom dialog box.

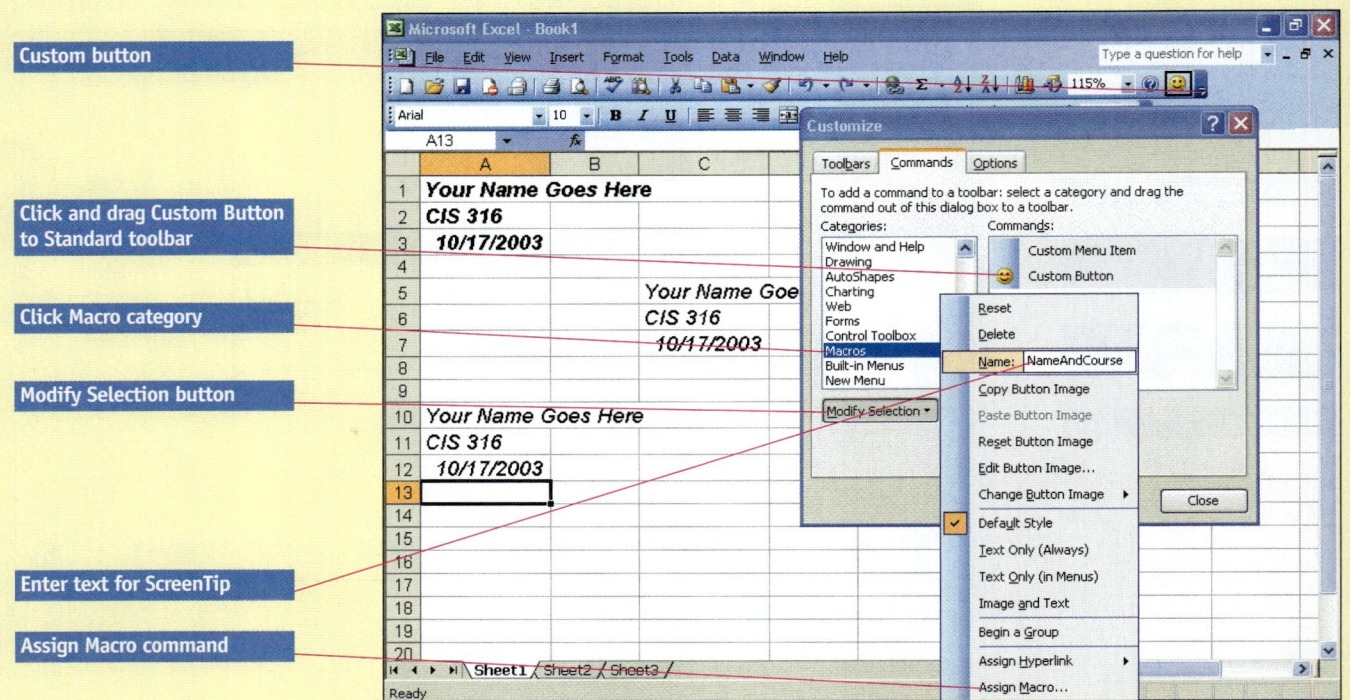

(f) Add a Custom Button (step 6)

FIGURE 9.4 Hands-on Exercise 2 (*continued*)

CUSTOMIZE THE TOOLBAR OR A MENU

You can customize any toolbar or menu to display additional buttons or commands as appropriate. Pull down the View menu, click Toolbars, click Customize to display the Customize dialog box, then click the Commands tab. Choose the category containing the button or command you want, then click and drag that object to an existing toolbar or menu.

Step 7: **Test the Custom Button**

- Click the **New button** on the Standard toolbar to open a new workbook (Book2 in Figure 9.4g; the book number is not important). Click **cell B2** as the active cell from which to execute the macro.

- Point to the **Happy Face button** to display the ScreenTip you just created. The ScreenTip will be useful in future sessions should you forget the function of this button.

- Click the **Happy Face button** to execute the NameAndCourse macro. Enter the name of a course you are taking. The macro inserts your name, course, and today's date in cells B2 through B4.

- Pull down the **File menu** and click the **Exit command** to exit the program.

- Click **No** when prompted to save the changes to Book1 and/or Book2, the workbooks you created in this exercise. Click **Yes** if asked to save the changes to the Personal Workbook.

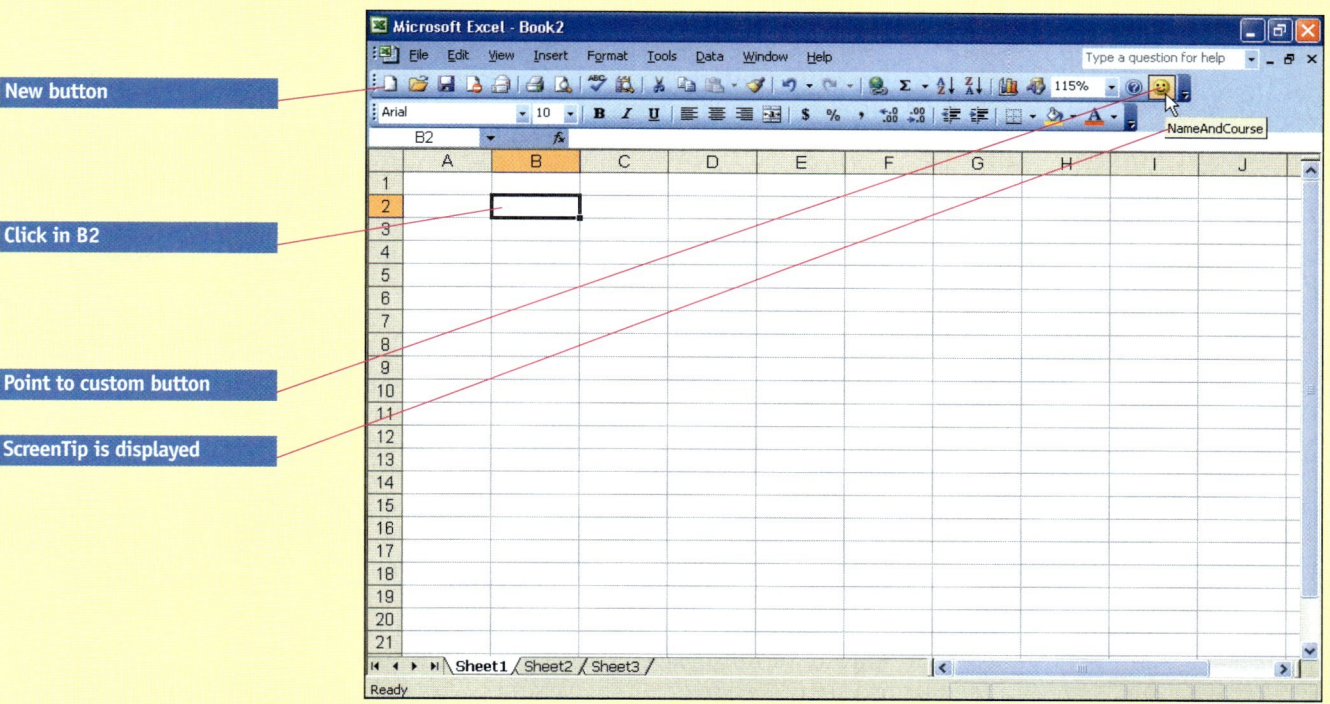

(g) Test the Custom Button (step 7)

FIGURE 9.4   Hands-on Exercise 2 (*continued*)

CHANGE THE CUSTOM BUTTON ICON

The Happy Face icon is automatically associated with the Custom Macro button. You can, however, change the image after the button has been added to a toolbar. Right click the button and click Customize to display the Customize dialog box, which must remain open to change the image. Right click the button a second time to display a different shortcut menu with commands pertaining to the specific button. Click the command to Change Button Image, select a new image, then close the Customize dialog box.

DATA MANAGEMENT MACROS

Thus far we have covered the basics of macros in the context of entering your name, course, and today's date into a worksheet. As you might expect, macros are capable of much more and can be used to automate any repetitive task. The next several pages illustrate the use of macros in conjunction with the list (data) management examples that were presented in an earlier chapter.

Data and information are not synonymous. Data is typically a fact (or facts) about a specific record (or set of records), such as an employee's name or title, or a list of all employees and their titles. Information is something more and refers to data that has been summarized, or otherwise rearranged, into a form perceived as useful by the recipient. A list of all the employees is considered raw data, whereas a subset of that list—such as the employees who worked in Chicago—could be thought of as information derived from that list. Information is also obtained by summarizing the data. Individual salaries are important to the employees who receive those salaries, whereas a manager is more interested in knowing the total of all salaries in order to make decisions. Macros can help in the conversion of data to information.

The worksheet in Figure 9.5a displays the employee list and associated summary statistics from the example in the previous chapter. The list is an area in a worksheet that contains rows of similar data. The first row in the list contains the column labels or field names. Each additional row contains a record. Every record contains the same fields in the same order. The list in Figure 9.5a has 14 records. Each record has six fields: name, location, title, service, hire date, and salary.

A criteria range has been established in cells A17 through F18 for use with the database functions in cells F22 through F26. Criteria values have not been entered in Figure 9.5a, and so the database functions reflect the values of the entire list (all 14 employees).

The worksheet in Figure 9.5b displays selected employees, those who work in Chicago. Look carefully at the worksheet and you will see that only rows 3, 9, 10, and 12 are visible. The other rows within the list have been hidden by the Advanced Filter command, which displays only those employees who satisfy the specified criteria. The summary statistics reflect only the Chicago employees; for example, the DCOUNT function in cell F26 shows four employees (as opposed to the 14 employees in Figure 9.5a).

The previous chapter described how to execute the list management commands to filter the list. The process is not difficult, but it does require multiple commands and keystrokes. Our purpose here is to review those commands and then automate the process through creation of a series of data management macros that will enable you to obtain the desired information with a single click. We begin by reviewing the commands that would be necessary to modify the worksheet in Figure 9.5b to show managers rather than the Chicago employees.

The first step is to clear the existing criterion (Chicago) in cell B18, then enter the new criterion (Manager) in cell C18. You would then execute the Advanced Filter command, which requires the specification of the list (cells A1 through F15), the location of the criteria range (cells A17 through F18), and the option to filter the list in place.

And what if you wanted to see the Chicago employees after you executed the commands to display the managers? You would have to repeat all of the previous commands to change the criterion back to what it was, then filter the list accordingly. Suffice it to say that the entire process can be simplified through creation of the appropriate macros.

The following exercise develops the macro to select the Chicago employees from the worksheet in Figure 9.5a. A subsequent exercise develops two additional macros, one to select the managers and another to select the managers who work in Chicago.

All of the macros use the concept of a ***named range*** to establish a mnemonic name (e.g., database) for a cell range (e.g., A1:F15). The advantage of using a named range in a macro over the associated cell reference is twofold. First, the macro is easier to read. Second, and perhaps more important, a named range adjusts automatically for insertions and/or deletions within the worksheet, whereas a cell reference remains constant. Thus, the use of a named range makes the macro immune to changes in the worksheet in that the macro references a flexible "database," as opposed to a fixed cell range. You can add or delete employee records within the list, and the macro will still work.

Field names are in first row of list → row 1

	A	B	C	D	E	F
1	**Name**	**Location**	**Title**	**Service**	**Hire Date**	**Salary**
2	Adams	Atlanta	Trainee	4.6	11/24/98	$29,500
3	Adamson	Chicago	Manager	4.3	3/16/99	$52,000
4	Brown	Atlanta	Trainee	4.6	11/24/98	$28,500
5	Charles	Boston	Account Rep	4.3	3/16/99	$40,000
6	Coulter	Atlanta	Manager	4.6	11/24/98	$100,000
7	Elofson	Miami	Account Rep	1.7	10/31/01	$47,500
8	Gillenson	Miami	Account Rep	0.7	10/31/02	$55,000
9	James	Chicago	Account Rep	4.7	10/31/98	$42,500
10	Johnson	Chicago	Account Rep	3.7	10/31/99	$47,500
11	Manin	Boston	Account Rep	4.3	3/16/99	$49,500
12	Marder	Chicago	Account Rep	2.7	10/31/00	$38,500
13	Milgrom	Boston	Manager	4.3	3/16/99	$57,500
14	Rubin	Boston	Account Rep	4.3	3/16/99	$45,000
15	Smith	Atlanta	Account Rep	4.6	11/24/98	$65,000
16						
17	**Name**	**Location**	**Title**	**Service**	**Hire Date**	**Salary**
18						
19						
20						
21	**Summary Statistics**					
22	Average Salary					$49,857
23	Maximum Salary					$100,000
24	Minimum Salary					$28,500
25	Total Salary					$698,000
26	Number of Employees					14

Criteria range (A17:F18) → row 17

Database functions (F22:F26) → rows 22–26

(a) All Employees

Filtered list (Chicago employees)

	A	B	C	D	E	F
1	**Name**	**Location**	**Title**	**Service**	**Hire Date**	**Salary**
3	Adamson	Chicago	Manager	4.3	3/16/99	$52,000
9	James	Chicago	Account Rep	4.7	10/31/98	$42,500
10	Johnson	Chicago	Account Rep	3.7	10/31/99	$47,500
12	Marder	Chicago	Account Rep	2.7	10/31/00	$38,500
16						
17	**Name**	**Location**	**Title**	**Service**	**Hire Date**	**Salary**
18		Chicago				
19						
20						
21	**Summary Statistics**					
22	Average Salary					$45,125
23	Maximum Salary					$52,000
24	Minimum Salary					$38,500
25	Total Salary					$180,500
26	Number of Employees					4

Criterion is Chicago

Database functions reflect data for Chicago employees only

(b) Chicago Employees

FIGURE 9.5 Data Management Macros

hands-on exercise 3
Data Management Macros

Objective To create a data management macro in conjunction with an employee list; to create a custom button to execute a macro. Use Figure 9.6 as a guide in completing the exercise.

Step 1: **Data Management Functions**

- Start Excel. Open the **Employee List Solution workbook** that was created in the previous chapter on data management.
- Click anywhere within the employee list. Pull down the **Data Menu**, click **Subtotals**, and click the **Remove All button**.
- Click any cell between A2 and A15, then click the **Sort Ascending button** on the Standard toolbar. The employees should be listed in alphabetical order as shown in Figure 9.6a.
- Clear all entries in the range **A18 through F18**.
- Click in **cell F22**, which contains the DAVERAGE function, to compute the average salary of all employees who satisfy the specified criteria. No criteria have been entered, however, so the displayed value of $49,857 represents the average salary of all 14 employees.
- Click **cell B18**. Enter **Chicago**. Press **Enter**. The average salary changes to $45,125 to indicate the average salary of the four Chicago employees.
- Click **cell C18**. Enter **Manager**. Press **Enter**. The average salary changes to $52,000 to indicate the average salary of the one Chicago manager.
- Save the workbook.

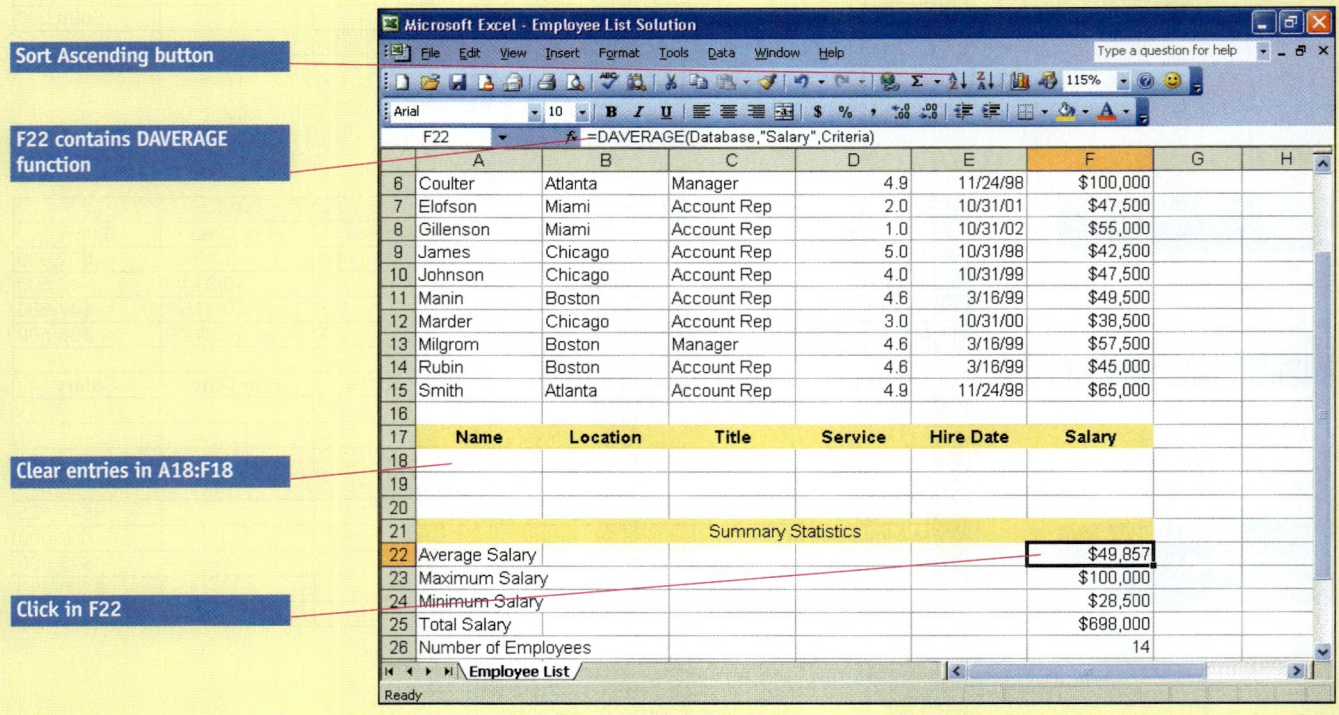

(a) Data Management Functions (step 1)

FIGURE 9.6 Hands-on Exercise 3

472 CHAPTER 9: AUTOMATING REPETITIVE TASKS

Step 2: **The Create Name Command**

- Click and drag to select **cells A17 through F18** as shown in Figure 9.6b. Pull down the **Insert menu**, click **Name**, then click **Create** to display the Create Names dialog box.

- The box to **Create Names in Top Row is already checked. Click OK**. This command assigns the text in each cell in row 17 to the corresponding cell in row 18; for example, cells B18 and C18 will be assigned the names Location and Title, respectively.

- Click and drag to select only **cells A18 through F18**. (You need to assign a name to these seven cells collectively, as you will have to clear the criteria values in row 18 later in the chapter.)

- Pull down the **Insert menu**. Click **Name**. Click **Define**. Enter **CriteriaValues** in the Define Name dialog box. Click **OK**.

- Save the workbook.

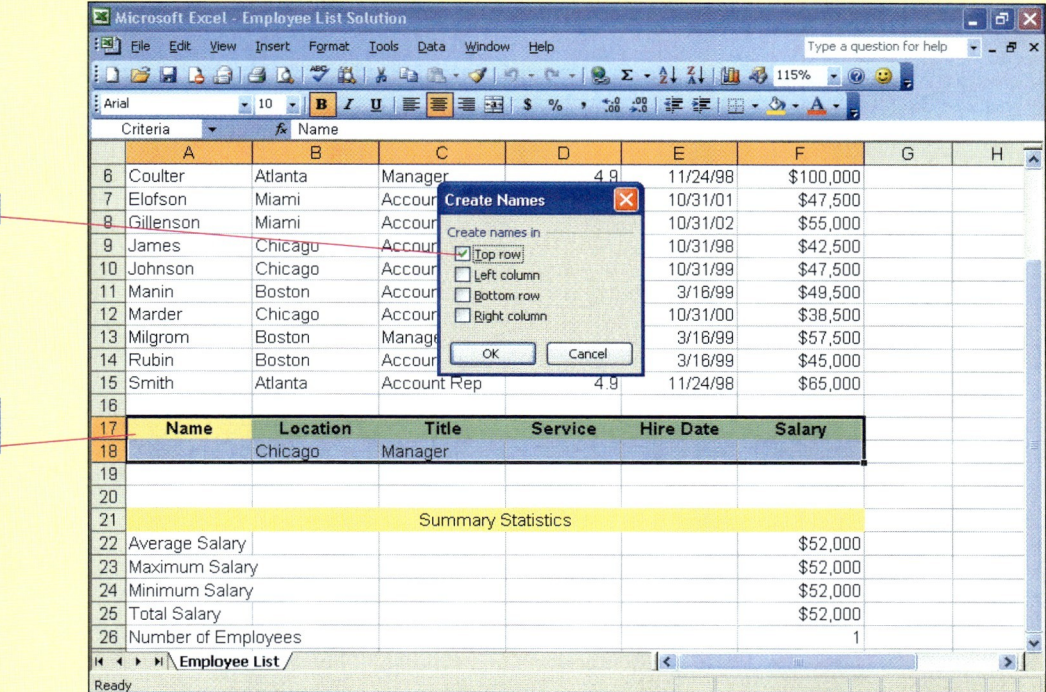

(b) The Create Name Command (step 2)

FIGURE 9.6 Hands-on Exercise 3 (*continued*)

CREATE SEVERAL NAMES AT ONCE

The Insert menu contains two different commands to create named ranges. The Insert Name Define command affects only one cell or range at a time, then has you enter the name into a dialog box. The Insert Name Create command requires you to select adjacent rows or columns, then assigns multiple names from the adjacent row or column in one command. The latter command is very useful in assigning range names within a criteria range.

Step 3: **The Go To Command**

- Pull down the **Edit menu**. Click **Go To** to produce the Go To dialog box in Figure 9.6c. If you do not see the command, click the double arrow to display more commands.

- You should see the names you defined (CriteriaValues, Hire_Date, Location, Name, Salary, Service, and Title) as well as the two names defined previously by the authors (Criteria and Database).

- Click **Database**. Click **OK**. Cells A1 through F15 should be selected, corresponding to cells assigned to the name *Database*.

- Press the **F5 key** (a shortcut for the Edit Go To command), which again produces the Go To dialog box. Click **Criteria**. Click **OK**. Cells A17 through F18 should be selected.

- Click the **drop-down arrow** next to the Name box. Click **Location**. Cell B18 should be selected.

- You are now ready to record the macro.

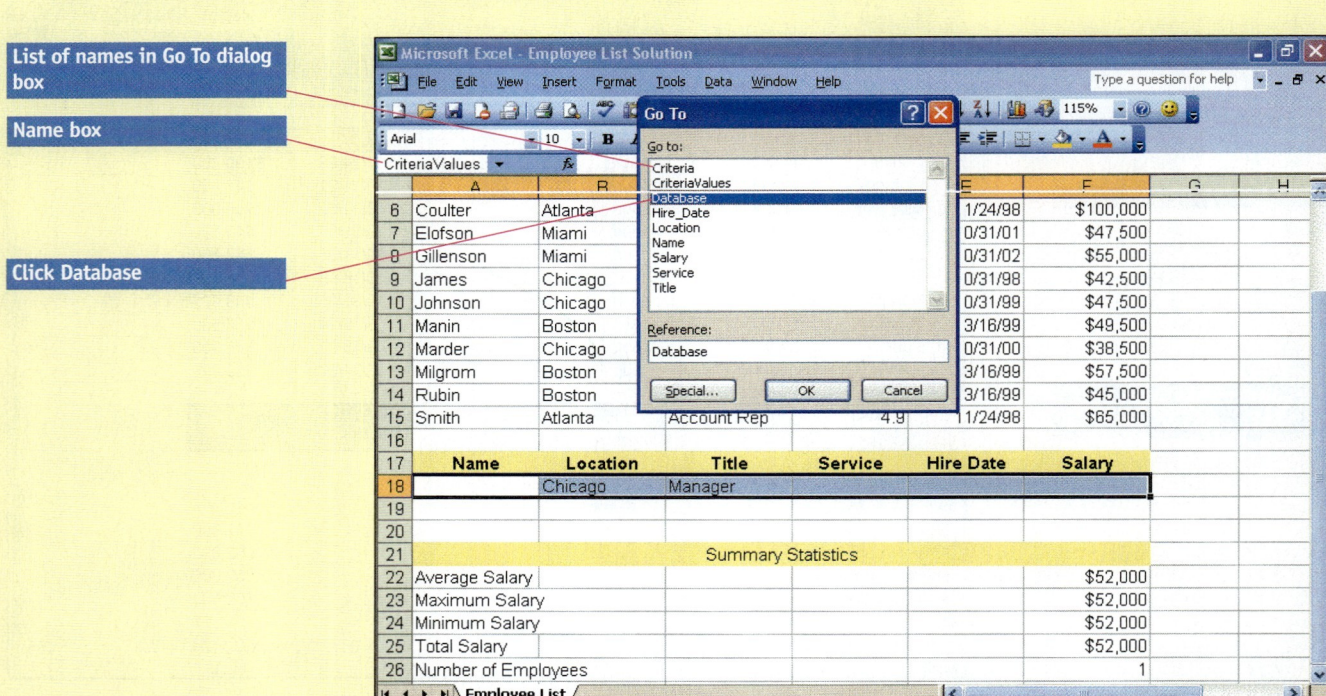

(c) The Go To Command (step 3)

FIGURE 9.6 Hands-on Exercise 3 (*continued*)

THE NAME BOX

Use the Name box (at the left of the Formula bar) to define a range name by selecting the cell(s) in the worksheet to which the name is to apply, clicking the Name box, then entering the name. For example, to assign the name CriteriaValues to cells A18:F18, select the range, click in the Name box, type CriteriaValues, and press Enter. The Name box can also be used to select a previously defined range by clicking the drop-down arrow next to the box and choosing the desired name from the drop-down list.

Step 4: **Record the Macro (Edit Clear command)**

- Pull down the **Tools menu**, click the **Macro command**, then click **Record New Macro** to display the Record Macro dialog box.

- Enter **Chicago** in the Macro Name text box. Verify that the macro will be stored in **This Workbook** and then make sure that the shortcut key text box is empty.

- Click **OK** to begin recording the macro. If necessary, click the **Relative References button** on the Stop Recording toolbar to record Absolute references (the button should be out).

- Pull down the **Edit menu**, click **Go To**, select **CriteriaValues** from the Go To dialog box, and click **OK**. Cells A18 through F18 should be selected as shown in Figure 9.6d. (Alternatively, you can also use the **F5 key** or the **Name box** to select CriteriaValues.)

- Pull down the **Edit menu**. Click **Clear**, then click **All** from the cascaded menu as shown in Figure 9.6d. Cells A18 through F18 (the criteria range) should be empty, and a new criterion can be entered through the macro.

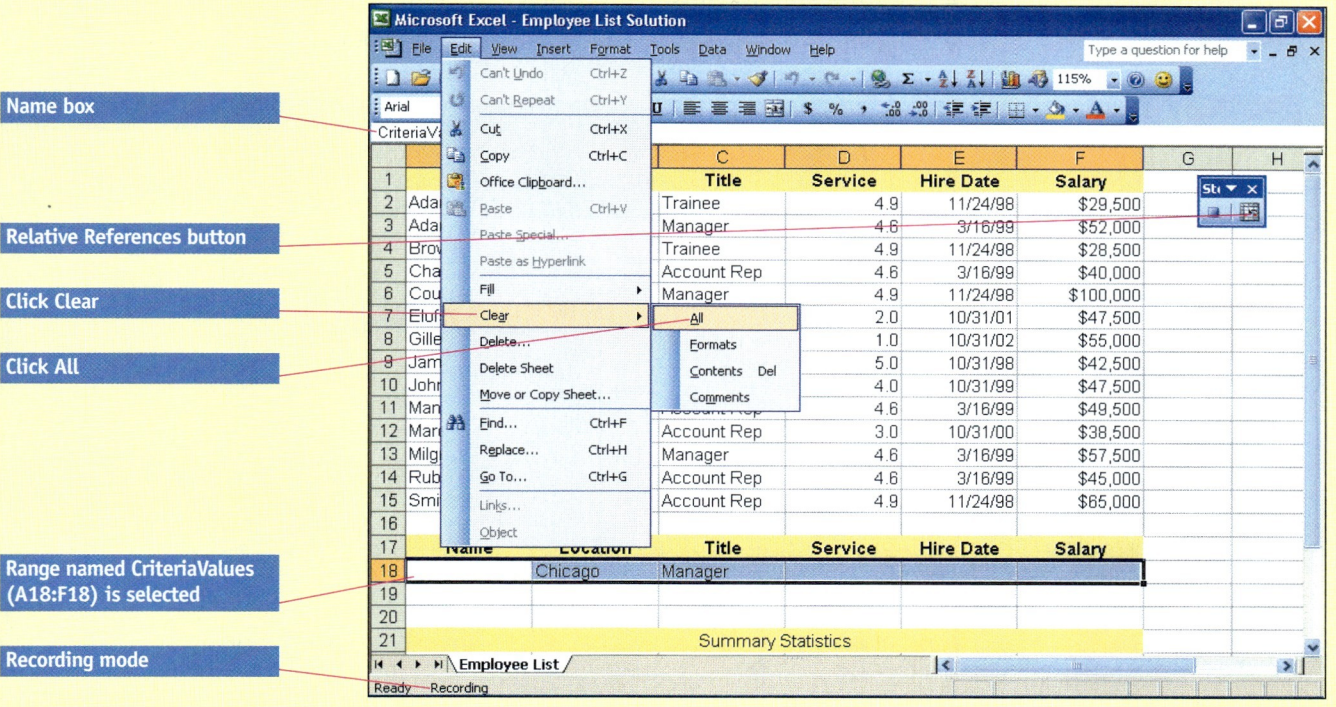

(d) Record the Macro (Edit Clear command) (step 4)

FIGURE 9.6 Hands-on Exercise 3 (*continued*)

GOOD MACROS ARE FLEXIBLE MACROS

The macro to select Chicago employees has to be completely general and work under all circumstances, regardless of what may appear initially in the criteria row. Thus, you have to clear the entire criteria range prior to entering "Chicago" in the Location column. Note, too, the use of range names (e.g., CriteriaValues), as opposed to specific cells (e.g., A18:F18 in this example) to accommodate potential additions or deletions to the employee list. (A macro does not update cell references within its statements to accommodate insertions and/or deletions of rows and columns in the associated worksheet. It is good practice, therefore, to always use range names, as opposed to cell references, within a macro.)

Step 5: **Record the Macro (Advanced Filter command)**

- Pull down the **Edit menu**, click **Go To**, select **Location** from the Go to dialog box, and click **OK**.

- Cell B18 should be selected. Enter **Chicago** to establish the criterion for both the database functions and the Advanced Filter command.

- Click in **cell B2** to position the active cell within the employee list. Pull down the **Data menu**. Click **Filter**, then click **Advanced Filter** from the cascaded menu to display the dialog box in Figure 9.6e.

- Enter **Database** as the List Range. Press the **tab key**. Enter **Criteria** as the Criteria Range.

- Check that the option to **Filter the list, in-place** is checked.

- Click **OK**. You should see only those employees who satisfy the current criteria (i.e., Adamson, James, Johnson, and Marder, who are the employees who work in Chicago).

- Click the **Stop Recording button** to stop recording.

- Click the **Save button** to save the workbook with the macro.

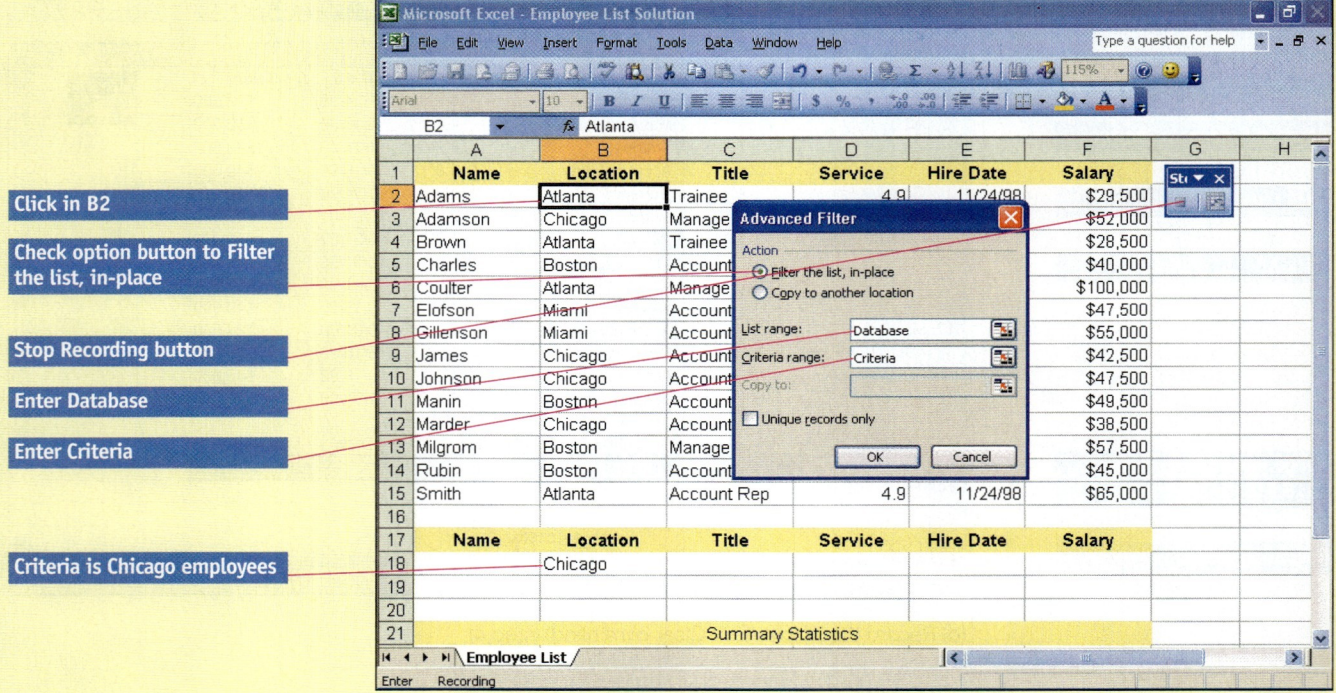

(e) Record the Macro (Advanced Filter command) (step 5)

FIGURE 9.6 Hands-on Exercise 3 (*continued*)

THE FILTER VERSUS THE DATABASE FUNCTIONS

Change the criteria—for example, from Chicago to Chicago Managers—and the values displayed by the database functions (DAVERAGE, DSUM, and so on) change automatically. The filtered records do not change, however, until you reexecute the command to filter the records in place. The advantage of a macro becomes immediately apparent, because the macro is built to change the criteria and filter the records with a single click of the mouse.

Step 6: View the Macro

- Press **Alt+F11** to open the Visual Basic editor as shown in Figure 9.6f. If necessary, pull down the **View menu**. Click **Project Explorer** to open the Project window in the left pane.

- If necessary, expand the **Modules folder**, under the VBA project for Employee List Solution. Click (select) **Module1**, pull down the **View menu**, and click **Code** to display the code for the Chicago macro in the right pane. Maximize the Code window.

- Close any other open windows within the Visual Basic Editor. Your screen should match the one in Figure 9.6f. If necessary, correct your macro so that it matches ours.

- If the correction is minor, it is easiest to edit the macro directly; otherwise delete the macro, then return to step 4 and rerecord the macro from the beginning. (To delete a macro, pull down the Tools menu, click **Macro**, click **Macros . . .**, select the macro you wish to delete, then click the **Delete button**.)

- Click the **View Microsoft Excel button** at the left of the toolbar or press **Alt+F11** to return to the Employee worksheet.

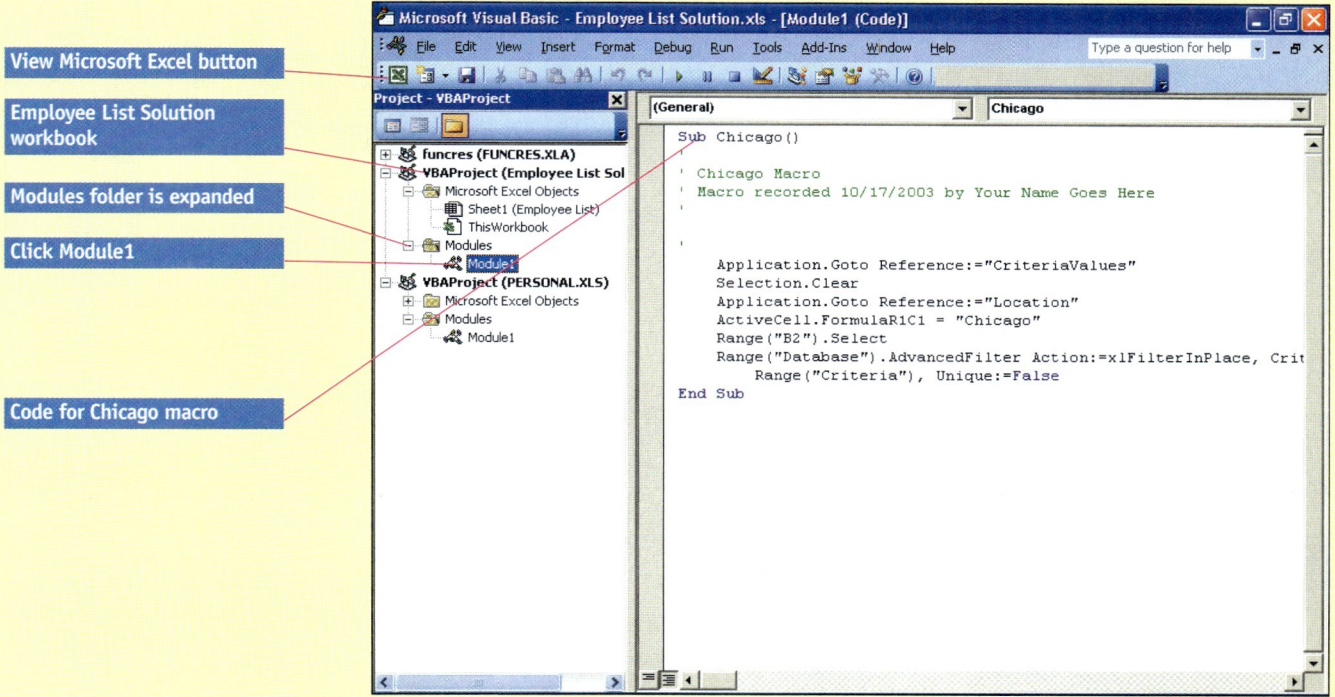

(f) View the Macro (step 6)

FIGURE 9.6 Hands-on Exercise 3 (*continued*)

THE VISUAL BASIC TOOLBAR

The Visual Basic Toolbar consists of seven buttons associated with macros and Visual Basic. You will find a button to run an existing macro, to record (or stop recording) a new macro, and to open (toggle to) the Visual Basic Editor. The toolbar can be displayed (or hidden) by right clicking any visible toolbar, then checking (or clearing) Visual Basic from the list of toolbars.

Step 7: **Assign the Macro**

- Pull down the **View menu**, click **Toolbars**, then click **Forms** to display the Forms toolbar as shown in Figure 9.6g.

- Click the **Button tool** (the mouse pointer changes to a tiny crosshair). Click and drag in the worksheet as shown in Figure 9.6g to draw a command button on the worksheet.

- Be sure to draw the button *below* the employee list, or the button may be hidden when a subsequent Data Filter command is executed.

- Release the mouse, and the Assign Macro dialog box will appear. Choose **Chicago** (the macro you just created) from the list of macro names. Click **OK**.

- The button should still be selected. Click and drag to select the name of the button, **Button 1**.

- Type **Chicago** as the new name. Do *not* press the Enter key. Click outside the button to deselect it.

- Save the workbook.

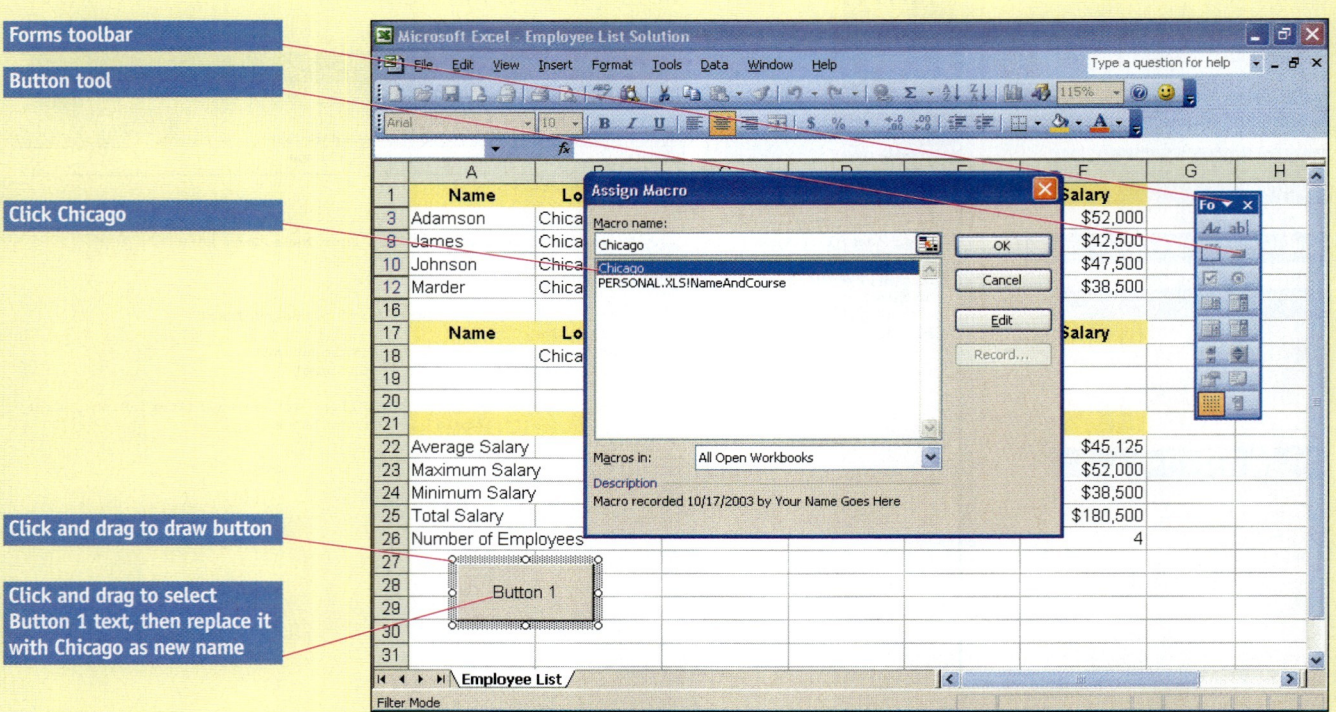

(g) Assign the Macro (step 7)

FIGURE 9.6 Hands-on Exercise 3 (*continued*)

SELECTING A BUTTON

You cannot select a Macro button by clicking it, because that executes the associated macro. Thus, to select a macro button, you must press and hold the Ctrl key as you click the mouse. (You can also select a button by clicking the right mouse button to produce a shortcut menu.) Once the button has been selected, you can edit its name, and/or move or size the button just as you can any other Windows object.

Step 8: **Test the Macro**

- Pull down the **Data menu**, click **Filter**, then click **Show All**.
- Click **cell B12**. Enter **Miami** to change the location for Marder. Press **Enter**. The number of employees in the summary statistics area changes, as do the results of the other summary statistics.
- Click the **Chicago button** as shown in Figure 9.6h to execute the macro. Marder is *not* listed this time because she is no longer in Chicago.
- Pull down the **Data menu**. Click **Filter**. Click **Show All** to display the entire employee list.
- Click **cell B12**. Enter **Chicago** to change the location for this employee back to Chicago. Press **Enter**. Click the **Chicago button** to execute the macro a second time. Marder is once again displayed with the Chicago employees.
- Pull down the **Data menu**. Click **Filter**. Click **Show All**.
- You do not have to print the workbook at this time, since we will print the entire workbook at the end of the next exercise.
- Save the workbook. Exit Excel if you do not want to continue with the next exercise at this time.

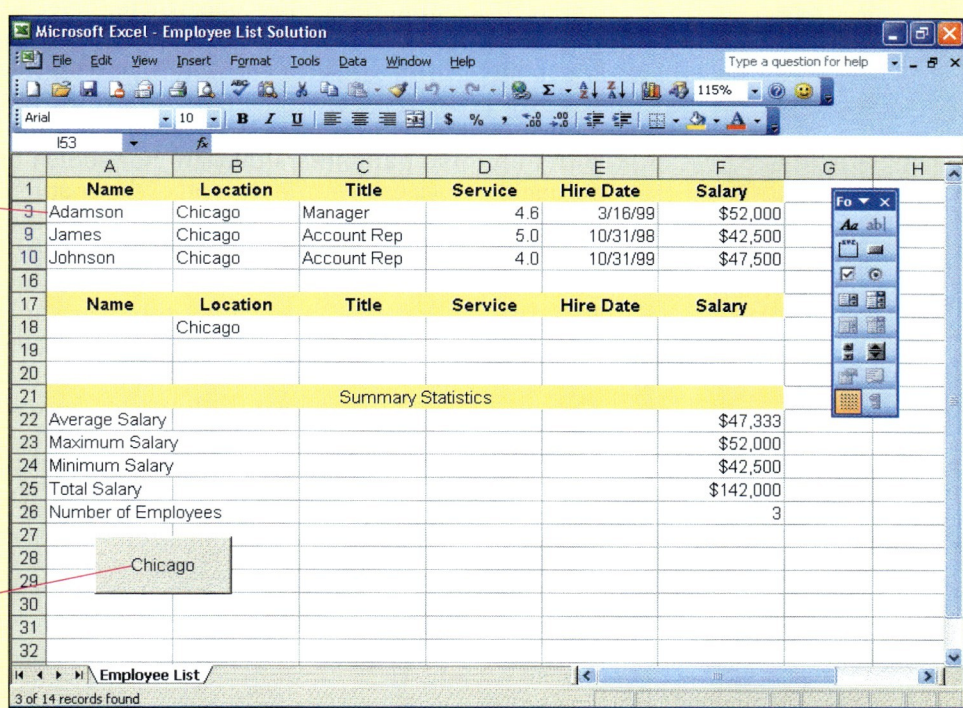

(h) Test the Macro (step 8)

FIGURE 9.6 Hands-on Exercise 3 (*continued*)

EXECUTING A MACRO

There are several different ways to execute a macro. The most basic way is to pull down the Tools menu, click Macro, click Macros . . . to display the Macros dialog box, then double click the desired macro to run it. You can assign a macro to a button within a worksheet or to a custom button on a toolbar, then click the button to run the macro. The fastest way is to use a keyboard shortcut, provided that a shortcut has been defined.

VISUAL BASIC FOR APPLICATIONS

Excel macros were originally nothing more than recorded keystrokes. Earlier versions of Excel had you turn on the macro recorder to capture the associated keystrokes, then "play back" those keystrokes when you ran the macro. Starting with Office 95, however, the recorded keystrokes were translated into Visual Basic commands, which made the macros potentially much more powerful because you could execute Visual Basic programs (known as procedures) from within Excel. (In actuality, Microsoft Office uses a subset of Visual Basic known as *Visual Basic for Applications (VBA)*, and we will use this terminology from now on.)

You can think of the macro recorder as a shortcut to generate the VBA code. Once you have that code, however, you can modify the various statements using techniques common to any programming language. You can move and/or copy statements within a procedure, search for one character string and replace it with another, and so on. And finally, you can insert additional VBA statements that are beyond the scope of ordinary Excel commands. You can, for example, display information to the user in the form of a message box any time during the execution of the macro. You can also accept information from the user into a dialog box for subsequent use in the macro.

Figure 9.7 illustrates the way that these tasks are accomplished in VBA. Figure 9.7a contains the VBA code, whereas Figures 9.7b and 9.7c show the resulting dialog boxes, as they would appear during execution of the associated VBA procedure. The **MsgBox statement** displays information to the user. The text of the message is entered in quotation marks, and the text appears within a dialog box as shown. The user clicks the OK command button to continue. (The MsgBox has other optional parameters that are not shown at this time, but are illustrated through various exercises at the end of the chapter.)

The InputBox function accepts input from the user for subsequent use in the procedure. Note the subtle change in terminology, in that we refer to the InputBox function, but the MsgBox statement. That is because a function returns a value, in this case the name of the location that was supplied by the user. That value is stored in the active cell within the worksheet, where it will be used later in the procedure. There is also a difference in syntax in that the MsgBox statement does not contain parentheses, whereas the InputBox function requires parentheses.

```
MsgBox "The MsgBox statement displays information"
ActiveCell.FormulaR1C1 = InputBox("Enter employee location")
```

(a) Visual Basic Statements

(b) Message Box   (c) Input Box

FIGURE 9.7 VBA Statements

hands-on exercise
4 Creating Additional Macros

Objective To duplicate an existing macro, then modify the copied macro to create an entirely new macro. Use Figure 9.8 as a guide.

Step 1: **Enable Macros**

- Start Excel. Open the **Employee List Solution workbook** from the previous exercise. You should see the warning in Figure 9.8a.

- Click the **More Info button** to display the Help window to learn more about macro virus prevention. (Pull down the **Tools menu**, click **Options**, click the **Security tab**, and click the **Macro Security button** if you do not see the warning message.)

- Click the **Close button** when you are finished reading the information.

- Click the **Enable Macros button** to open the Employee List Solution workbook.

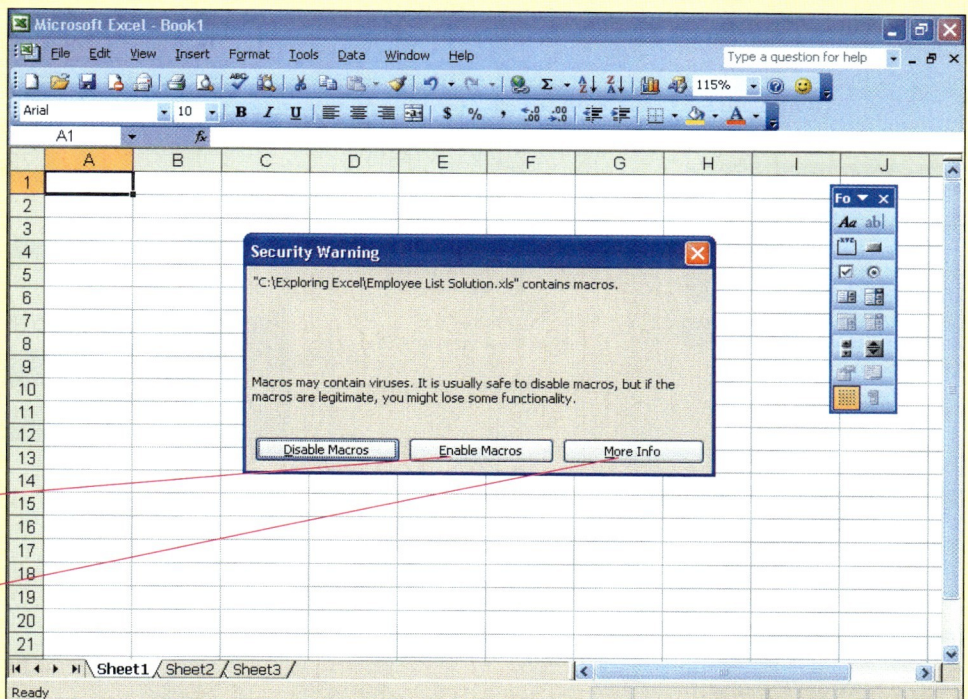

(a) Enable Macros (step 1)

FIGURE 9.8 Hands-on Exercise 4

MACRO SECURITY

A computer virus could take the form of an Excel macro in which case Excel will warn you that a workbook contains a macro, provided the security option is set appropriately. Pull down the Tools menu, click the Options command, click the Security tab, and then set the Macro Security to either High or Medium. High security disables all macros except those from a trusted source. Medium security gives you the option to enable macros. Click the button only if you are sure the macro is from a trusted source.

Step 2: **Copy the Chicago Macro**

- Pull down the **Tools menu**, click the **Macro command**, then click **Visual Basic Editor** (or press **Alt+F11**) to open the Visual Basic Editor.
- Click the **plus sign** on the Modules folder for the Employee List Solution project, select **Module1**, pull down the **View menu**, and click **Code**.
- Click and drag to select the entire Chicago macro as shown in Figure 9.8b.
- Pull down the **Edit menu** and click **Copy**, or press **Ctrl+C**, or click the **Copy button** on the Standard toolbar.
- Click below the End Sub statement to deselect the macro and simultaneously establish the position of the insertion point.
- Pull down the **Edit menu** and click **Paste**, or press **Ctrl+V**, or click the **Paste button** on the Standard toolbar.
- The Chicago macro has been copied and now appears twice in Module1. (If necessary, click the **Full Module View button** to see both procedures.)
- Save the module.

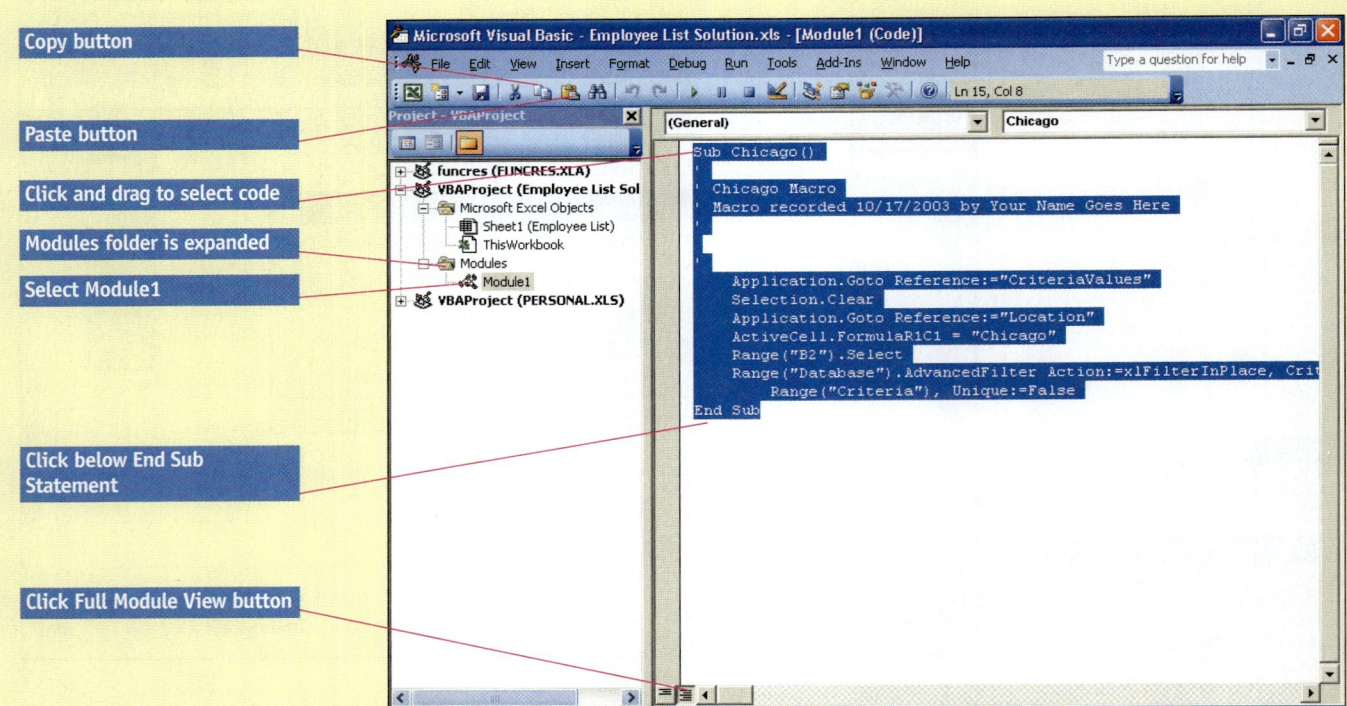

(b) Copy the Chicago Macro (step 2)

FIGURE 9.8   Hands-on Exercise 4 (*continued*)

THE SHIFT KEY

You can select text for editing (or replacement) with the mouse, or alternatively, you can select by using the cursor keys on the keyboard. Set the insertion point where you want the selection to begin, then press and hold the Shift key as you use the cursor keys to move the insertion point to the end of the selection. The selected statements are affected by the next command(s).

Step 3: **Create the Manager Macro**

- Click in front of the second (i.e., the copied) Chicago macro to set the insertion point. Pull down the **Edit menu**. Click **Replace** to display the Replace dialog box as shown in Figure 9.8c.

- Enter **Chicago** in the Find What text box. Press the **tab key**. Enter **Manager** in the Replace With text box. Select the option button to search in the *Current Procedure*. Click the **Find Next command button**.

- Excel searches for the first occurrence of Chicago, which should be in the Sub statement of the copied macro. (If this is not the case, click the **Find Next command button** until your screen matches Figure 9.8c.)

- Click the **Replace command button**. Excel substitutes Manager for Chicago, then looks for the next occurrence of Chicago. Click **Replace**. Click **Replace** a third time to make another substitution. Click **OK** in response to the message that the specified region has been searched. Close the Replace dialog box.

- Click and drag to select **Location** within the Application.Goto.Reference statement in the Manager macro. Enter **Title**. (The criteria within the macro have been changed to employees whose title is Manager.)

- Save the module.

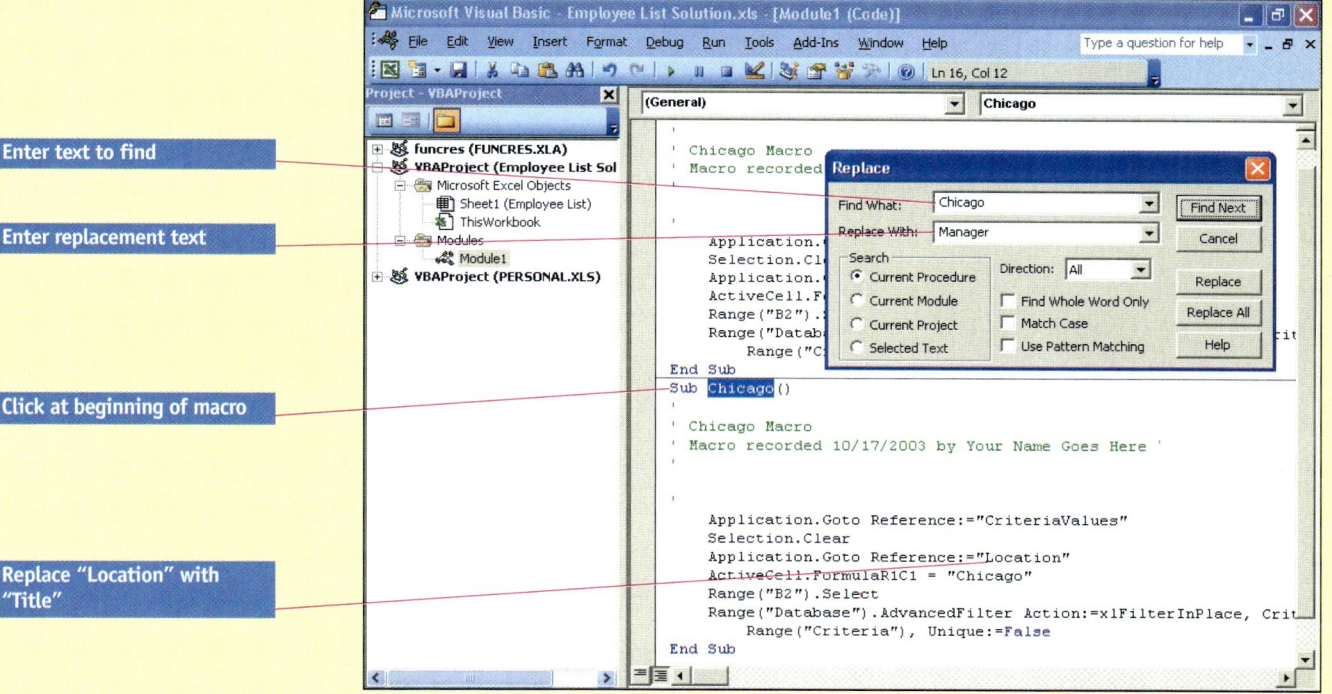

(c) Create the Manager Macro (step 3)

FIGURE 9.8 Hands-on Exercise 4 (*continued*)

THE FIND AND REPLACE COMMANDS

Anyone familiar with a word processor takes the Find and Replace commands for granted, but did you know the same capabilities exist in Excel as well as in the Visual Basic Editor? Pull down the Edit menu and choose either command. You have the same options as in the parallel command in Word, such as a case-sensitive (or insensitive) search or a limitation to a whole-word search.

Step 4: **Run the Manager Macro**

- Click the **Excel button** on the Windows taskbar or press **Alt+F11** to return to the Employee List Solution worksheet.

- Pull down the **Tools menu**. Click **Macro**, then click the **Macros . . . command** to display the Macro dialog box as shown in Figure 9.8d.

- You should see two macros: Chicago, which was created in the previous exercise, and Manager, which you just created. (If the Manager macro does not appear, return to the Visual Basic Editor and correct the appropriate Sub statement to include Manager() as the name of the macro.)

- Select the **Manager macro**, then click **Run** to run the macro, after which you should see three employees (Adamson, Coulter, and Milgrom). If the macro does not execute correctly, return to the Visual Basic Editor to make the necessary corrections, then rerun the macro.

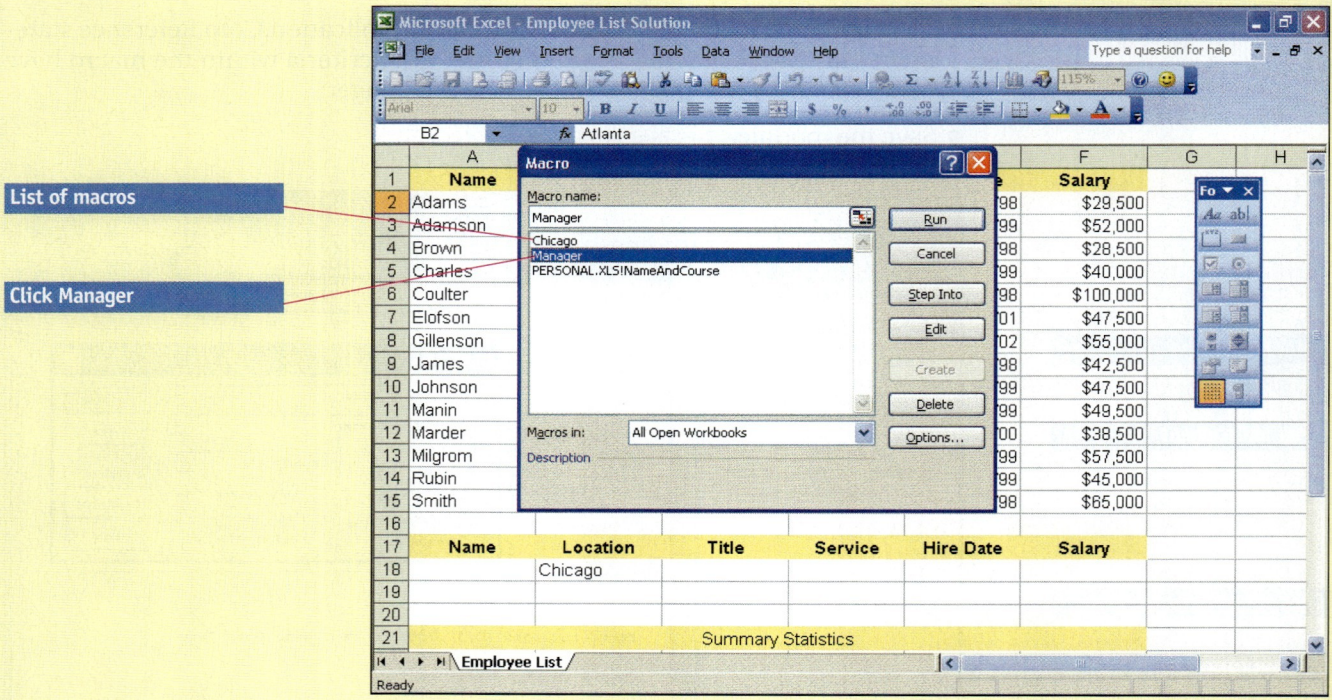

(d) Run the Manager Macro (step 4)

FIGURE 9.8 Hands-on Exercise 4 (*continued*)

THE STEP INTO COMMAND

The Step Into command helps to debug a macro, as it executes the statements one at a time. Pull down the Tools menu, click Macro, click Macros, select the macro to debug, then click the Step Into command button. Move and/or size the Visual Basic Editor window so that you can see both the worksheet and the macro. Pull down the Debug menu and click the Step Into command (or press the F8 function key) to execute the first statement in the macro and view its results. Continue to press the F8 function key to execute the statements one at a time until the macro has completed execution.

Step 5: **Assign a Button**

- Click the **Button tool** on the Forms toolbar (the mouse pointer changes to a tiny crosshair), then click and drag in the worksheet to draw a button on the worksheet. Release the mouse.

- Choose **Manager** (the macro you just created) from the list of macro names as shown in Figure 9.8e. Click **OK** to close the Assign Macro dialog box.

- The button should still be selected. Click and drag to select the name of the button, **Button 2**, then type **Manager** as the new name. Do *not* press the Enter key. Click outside the button to deselect it.

- There should be two buttons on your worksheet, one each for the Chicago and Manager macros.

- Click the **Chicago button** to execute the Chicago macro. You should see four employees with an average salary of $45,125.

- Click the **Manager button** to execute the Manager macro. You should see three employees with an average salary of $69,833.

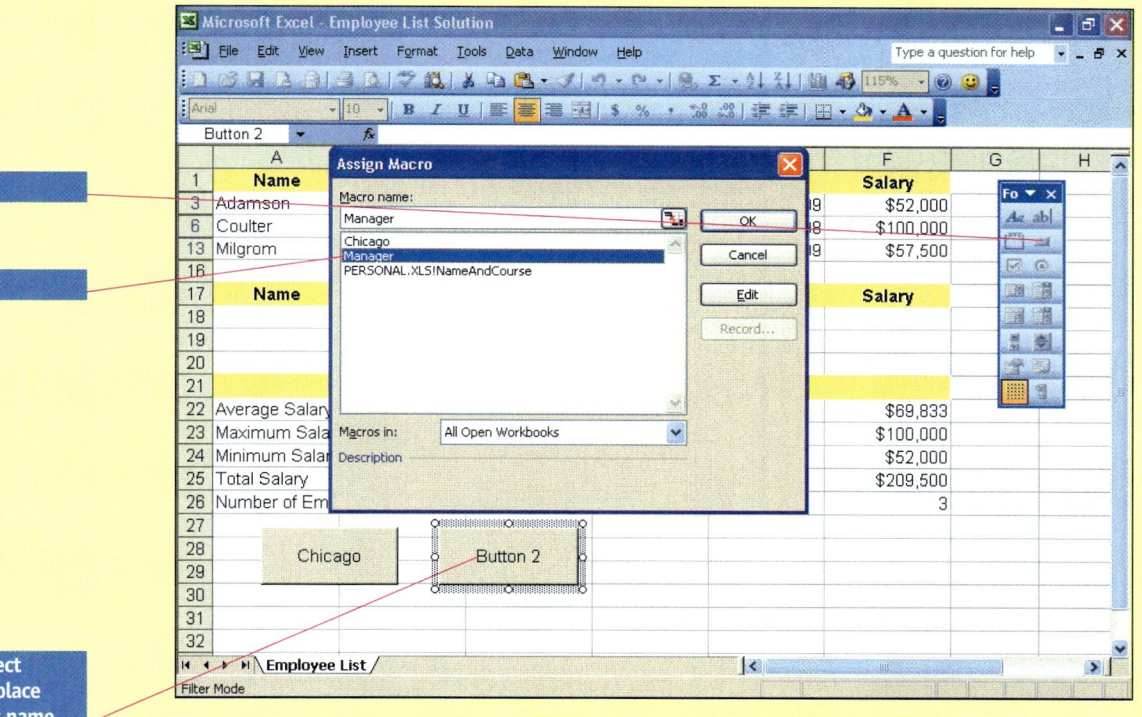

(e) Assign a Button (step 5)

FIGURE 9.8 Hands-on Exercise 4 (*continued*)

CREATE UNIFORM BUTTONS

One way to create buttons of a uniform size is to create the first button, then copy that button to create the others. To copy a button, press the Ctrl key as you select (click) the button, then click the Copy button on the Standard toolbar. Click in the worksheet where you want the new button to appear, then click the Paste button. Click and drag over the name of the button and enter a new name. Right click the border of the new button, then click Assign Macro from the shortcut menu. Select the name of the new macro, then click OK.

Step 6: **Create the ChicagoManager Macro**

- Return to the Visual Basic Editor. Press **Ctrl+Home** to move to the beginning of Module1. Click and drag to select the entire Chicago macro. Be sure to include the End Sub statement in your selection.
- Click the **Copy button** on the Standard toolbar to copy the Chicago macro to the clipboard. Press **Ctrl+End** to move to the end of the module sheet. Click the **Paste button** on the Standard toolbar to complete the copy operation.
- Change **Chicago** to **ChicagoManager** in both the comment statement and the Sub statement as shown in Figure 9.8f.
- Click and drag to select the two statements in the **Manager macro** as shown in Figure 9.8f. Click the **Copy button**.
- Scroll, if necessary, until you can click in the **ChicagoManager macro** at the end of the line, ActiveCell.FormulaR1C1 = "Chicago". Press **Enter** to begin a new line. Click the **Paste button** to complete the copy operation.
- Delete any unnecessary blank lines or spaces that may remain.
- Save the module.

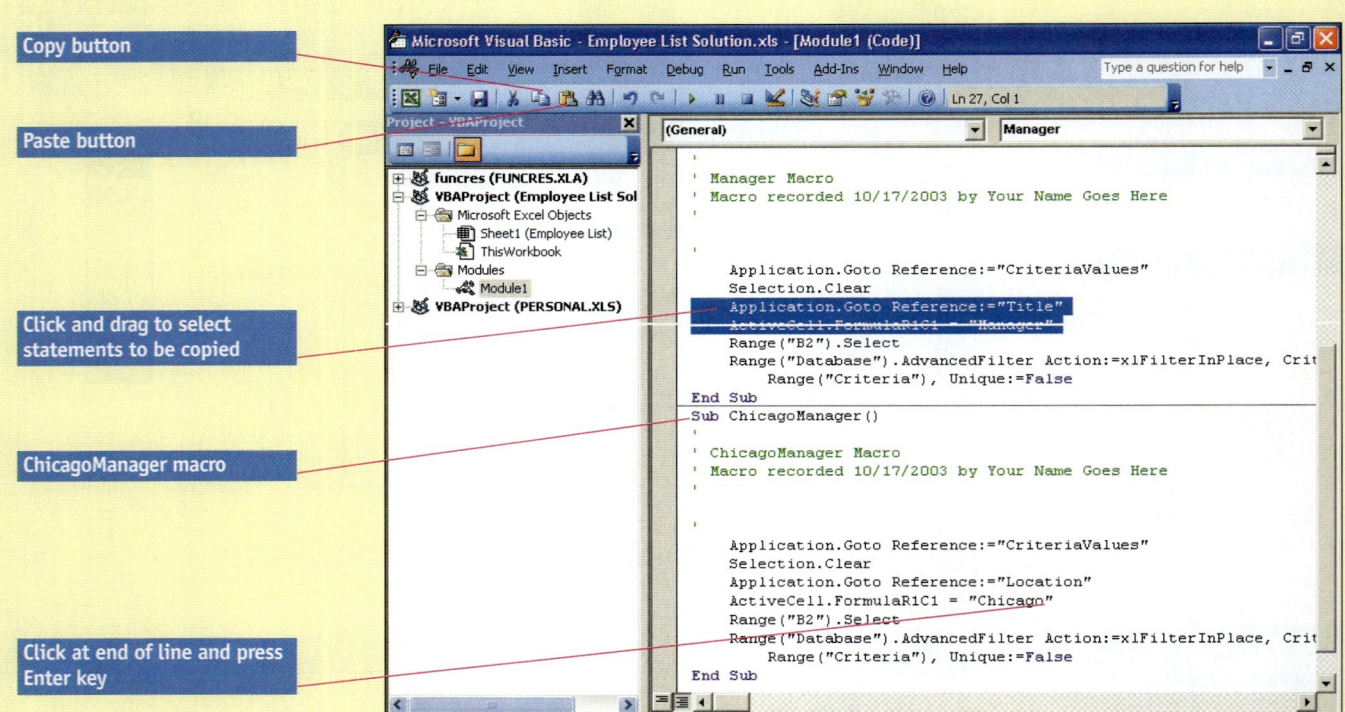

(f) Create the ChicagoManager Macro (step 6)

FIGURE 9.8 Hands-on Exercise 4 (*continued*)

ADD A SHORTCUT

You can add and/or modify the shortcut key associated with a macro at any time. Pull down the Tools menu, click the Macro command, then click Macros to display the Macro dialog box. Select the desired macro and click the Options button to display the Macro Options dialog box, where you assign a shortcut. Type a lowercase letter to create a shortcut with just the Ctrl key, such as Ctrl+m. Enter an uppercase letter to create a shortcut using the Ctrl and Shift keys, such as Ctrl+Shift+M.

Step 7: **The MsgBox Statement**

- Check that the statements in your ChicagoManager macro match those in Figure 9.8g. (The MsgBox statement has not yet been added.)

- Click immediately before the End Sub statement. Press **Enter** to begin a new line, press the **up arrow** to move up one line, then press **Tab** to indent. (Indentation is not a VBA requirement; it is done to enhance the readability of the code.)

- Type the word **MsgBox**, then press the **Space bar**. VBA responds with a Quick Info box that displays the complete syntax of the statement. You can ignore this information at the present time, since we are not entering any additional parameters.

- Enter the rest of the MsgBox statement exactly as it appears in Figure 9.8g. Be sure to include a blank space and the **underscore** at the end of the first line, which indicates that the statement is continued to the next line.

- Save the module, then return to the Excel workbook.

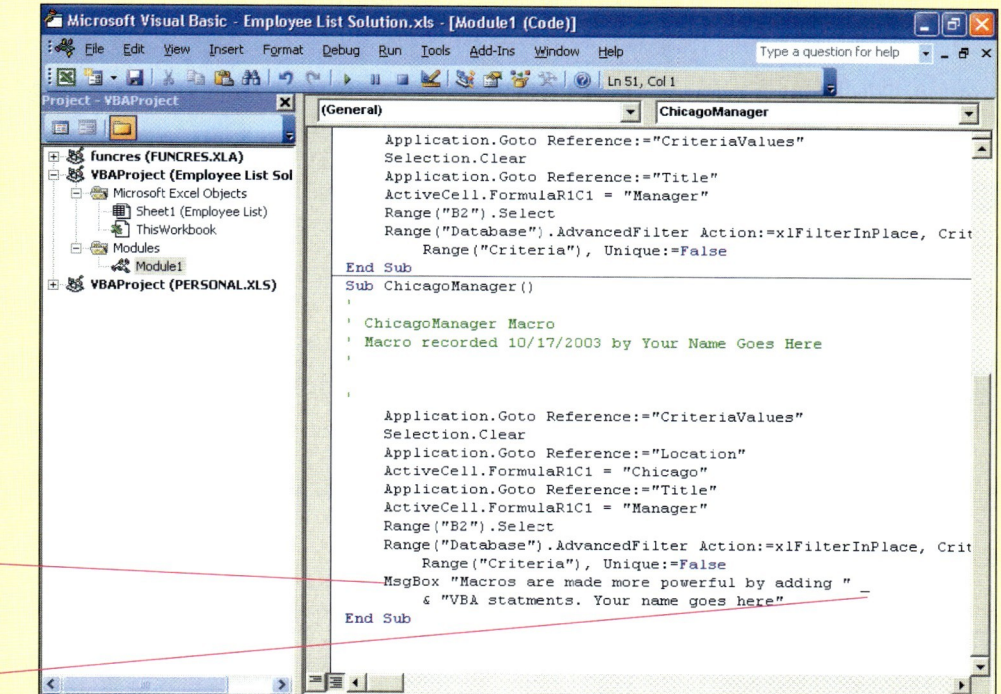

(g) The MsgBox Statement (step 7)

FIGURE 9.8 Hands-on Exercise 4 (*continued*)

THE UNDERSCORE AND AMPERSAND

A VBA statement is continued from one line to the next by typing a blank space followed by an underscore at the end of the line to be continued. You may not, however, break a line in the middle of a literal. Hence, the first line ends with a closing quotation mark, followed by a space and the underscore. The next line starts with an ampersand to indicate continuation of the previous literal, followed by the remainder of the literal in quotation marks.

MICROSOFT OFFICE EXCEL 2003 REVISED

Step 8: Test the ChicagoManager Macro

- You can assign a macro to a command button by copying an existing command button, then changing the name of the button and the associated macro. Right click either of the existing command buttons, click the **Copy command** from the shortcut menu, then click the **Paste button** on the Standard toolbar.

- Click and drag the copied button to the right of the two existing buttons. Click and drag the text of the copied button (which should still be selected) to select the text, then type **Chicago Manager** as the name of the button.

- Click anywhere in the worksheet to deselect the button, then **Right click** the new button, click the **Assign Macro command**, choose the newly created ChicagoManager macro, and click **OK**.

- Click anywhere in the workbook to deselect the button. Save the workbook.

- Click the **Chicago Manager button** to execute the macro. You should see the matching employees as shown in Figure 9.8h, followed by the message box.

- Click **OK**. Return to the VBA editor to correct the macro if it does not execute as intended.

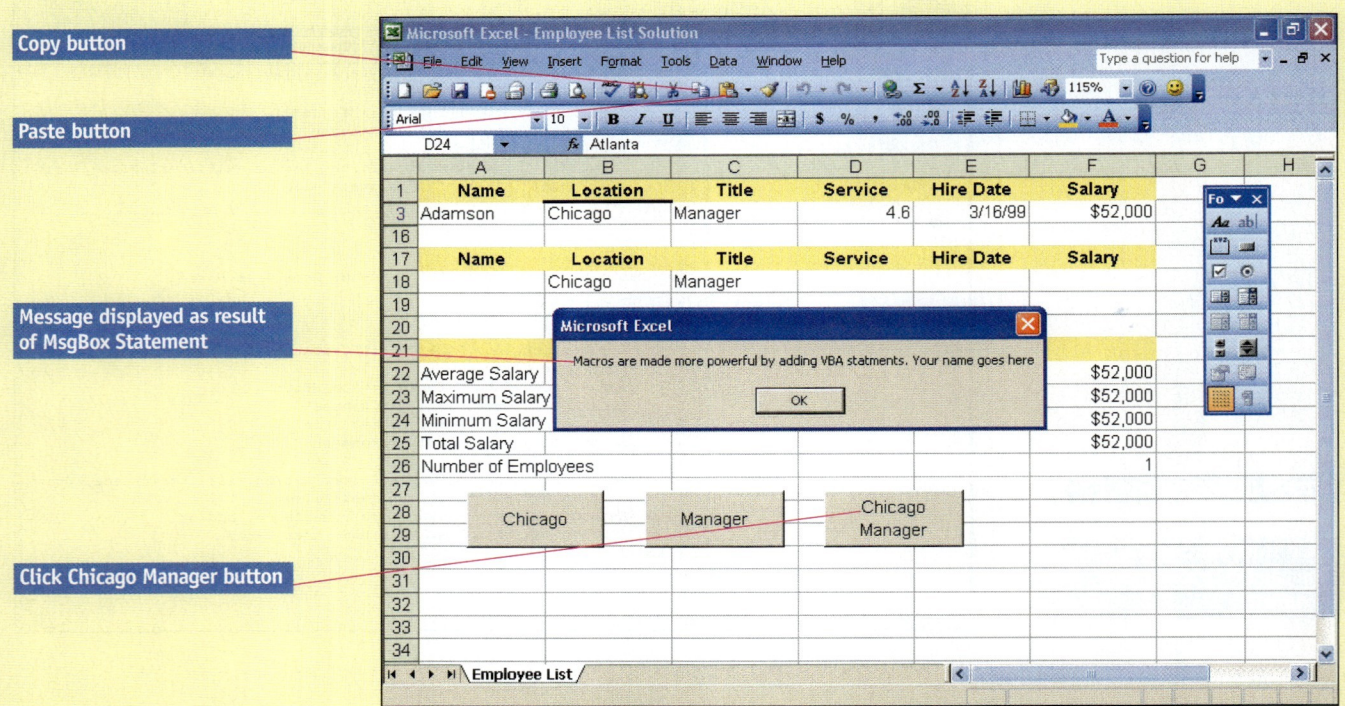

(h) Test the ChicagoManager Macro (step 8)

FIGURE 9.8 Hands-on Exercise 4 (*continued*)

CUSTOMIZE THE MESSAGE BOX

You can add a personal touch to the output of the MsgBox statement by including optional parameters to change the text of the title bar and/or include an icon within the message box. The statement, MsgBox "Hello World", vbinformation, "Your Name on Title Bar" uses both parameters. Be sure to use quotation marks for both the first and last parameter.

488 CHAPTER 9: AUTOMATING REPETITIVE TASKS

Step 9: **Create the AnyCityAnyTitle Macro**

- Press **Alt+F11** to return to the Visual Basic editor. Click and drag to select the entire ChicagoManager macro. Click the **Copy button**, click the blank line below the End Sub statement, then click the **Paste button** to duplicate the module.

- Click and drag the name of the copied macro. Type **AnyCityAnyTitle()** to change the name of the macro. Do not leave any spaces in the macro name. Delete or modify the comments as you see fit.

- Click and drag to select **"Chicago"** as shown in Figure 9.8i. You must include the quotation marks in your selection.

- Type **InputBox("Enter the location")** to replace the specific location with the InputBox function. Be sure to use left and right parentheses and to enclose the literal in quotation marks.

- Click and drag to select **"Manager"**. Type **InputBox("Enter the title")** to replace the specific title with the InputBox function.

- Save the module and return to the Excel workbook.

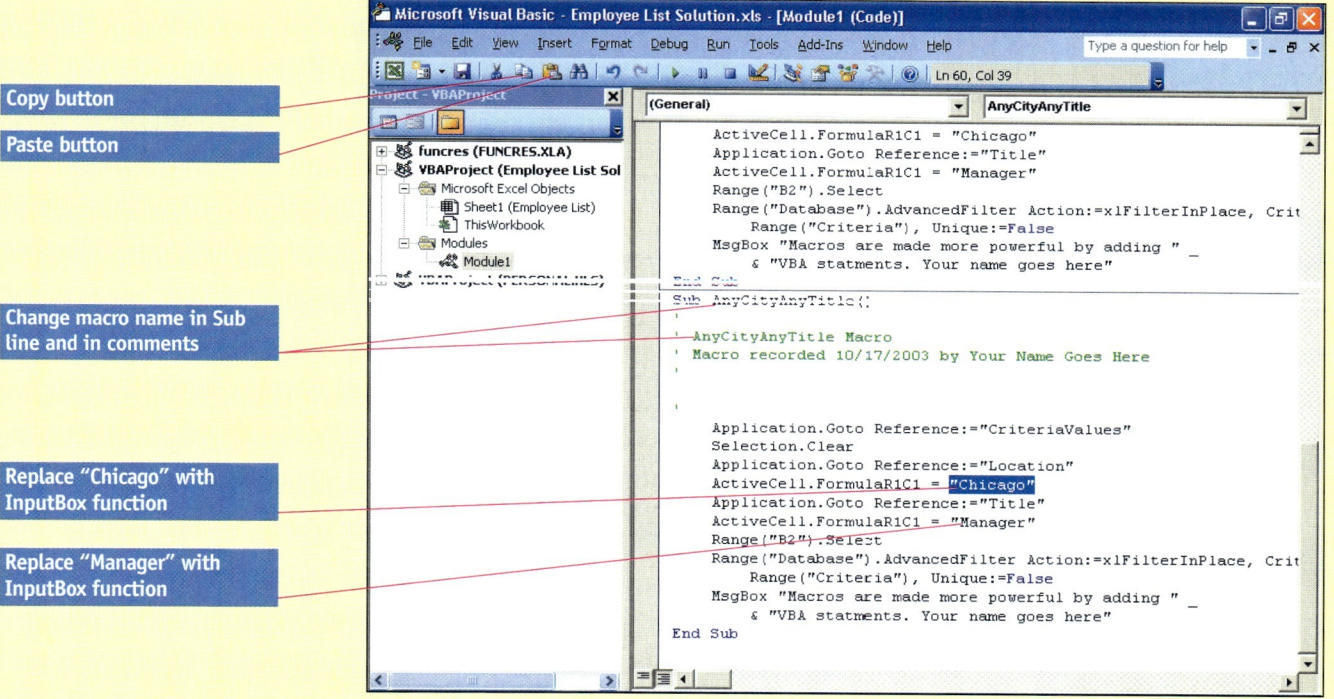

(i) Create the AnyCityAnyTitle Macro (step 9)

FIGURE 9.8 Hands-on Exercise 4 (*continued*)

USE WHAT YOU KNOW

Use the techniques acquired from other applications such as Microsoft Word to facilitate editing within the VBA window. Press the Ins key to toggle between the insert and overtype modes as you modify the statements within a procedure. You can also cut, copy, and paste statements (or parts of statements) within a procedure and from one procedure to another. The Find and Replace commands are also useful.

Step 10: **Test the AnyCityAnyTitle Macro**

- Copy any of the existing command buttons to create a new button for the **AnyCityAnyTitle** macro as shown in Figure 9.8j. Be sure to assign the correct macro to this button.

- Click the **Any City Any Title command button** to run the macro. You will be prompted for the location. Type **Atlanta** and click **OK**. (A second input box will appear in which you will enter the title.)

- At this time Atlanta has been entered into the criteria area, and the summary statistics reflect the Atlanta employees. The filtered list will not change, however, until you have entered the title and completed the Advanced Filter command.

- Enter **Trainee** as the employee title as shown in Figure 9.8j. Click **OK**. The workbook changes to reflect the Atlanta trainees. Click **OK** in response to the message box.

- Return to the VBA editor if the macro does not execute as intended. Save the workbook.

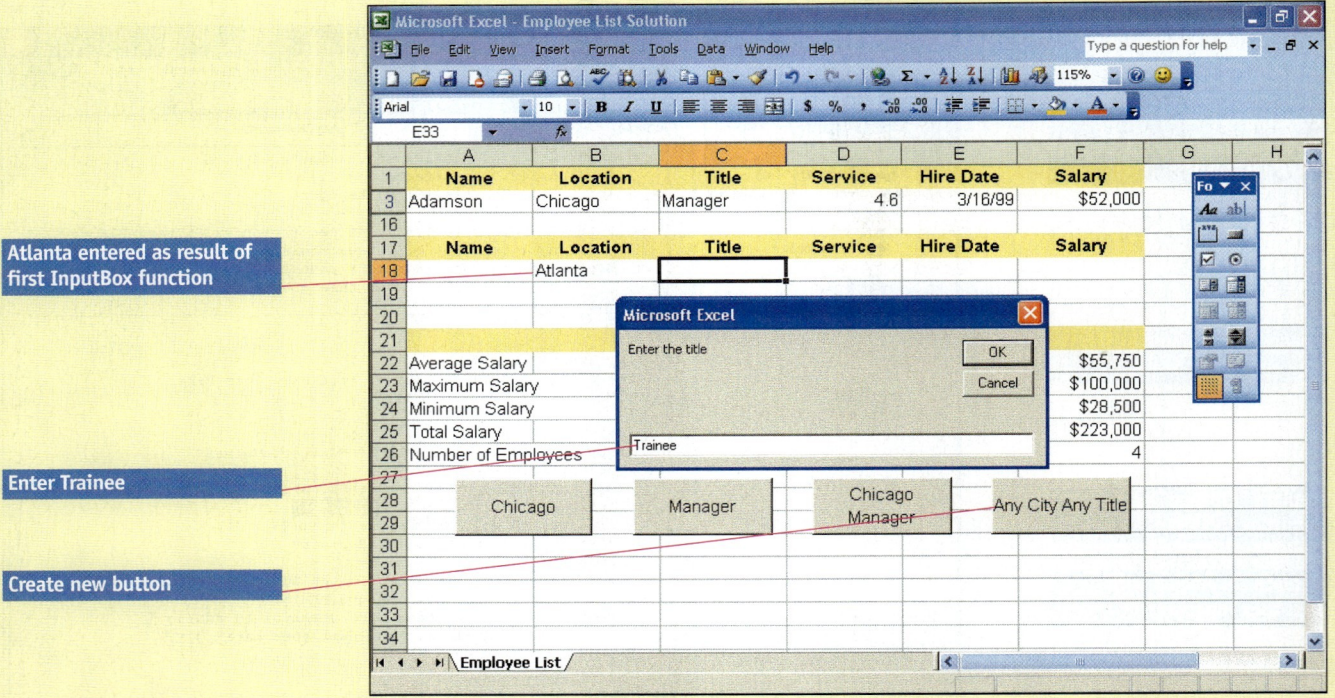

(j) Test the AnyCityAnyTitle Macro (step 10)

FIGURE 9.8 Hands-on Exercise 4 (*continued*)

ONE MACRO DOES IT ALL

The AnyCityAnyTitle macro is the equivalent of the more specific macros that were created earlier; that is, you would enter "Chicago" and "Manager" to replace the Chicago Manager macro. You can also enter "Chicago" as the city and leave the title field blank to select all Chicago employees, or alternatively, leave the city blank and enter "Manager" as the title to select all managers. And finally, you could omit both city and title to select all employees.

Step 11: **Change the Button Properties**

- Press and hold the **Shift** and **Ctrl keys**, then click each of the command buttons to select all four buttons as shown in Figure 9.8k.

- Pull down the **Format menu** and click the **Control command** to display the Format Control dialog box. Click the **Properties tab**, then check the box to **Print object** so that the command buttons will appear on the printed worksheet.

- Click the **Move but don't size with cells option button**. Click **OK** to exit the dialog box and return to the worksheet. Click anywhere in the worksheet to deselect the buttons.

- Click the **Print button** on the Standard toolbar to print the worksheet. Return to the Visual Basic Editor. Pull down the **File menu**, click the **Print command**, select **Current Module**, then click **OK**.

- Save the workbook a final time. Close the workbook. Exit Excel if you don't want to continue with the next exercise at this time.

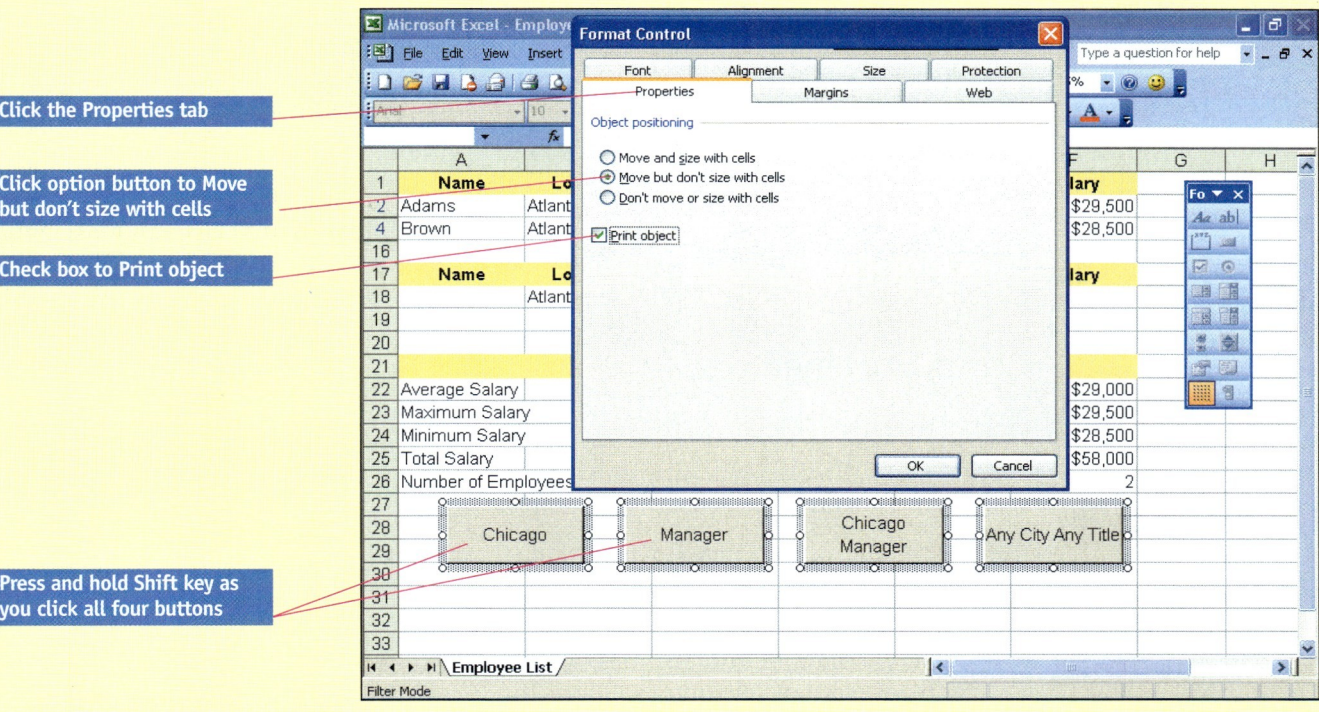

(k) Change the Button Properties (step 11)

FIGURE 9.8 Hands-on Exercise 4 (*continued*)

THE SIZE PROPERTY

Use the Size property to obtain a consistent look for your command buttons. Press and hold the Shift and Ctrl keys as you select the individual buttons. Pull down the Format menu and click the Control command to display the Format Control dialog box. Click the Size tab, enter the width and height for the selected buttons, then click OK. The buttons will be a uniform size, but they may overlap. Click anywhere in the worksheet to deselect the buttons, then right click and drag to reposition a button.

LOOPS AND DECISION MAKING

Excel macros can be made significantly more powerful by incorporating additional Visual Basic statements that enable true programming. These include the If statement for decision making, and the Do statement to implement a *loop* (one or more commands that are executed repeatedly until a condition is met).

Consider, for example, the worksheet and associated macro in Figure 9.9. The worksheet is similar to those used in the preceding exercises, except that the font color of the data for managers is red. Think for a minute how you would do this manually. You would look at the first employee in the list, examine the employee's title to determine if that employee is a manager, and if so, change the font color for that employee. You would then repeat these steps for all of the other employees on the list. It sounds tedious, but that is exactly what you would do if asked to change the font color for the managers.

Now ask yourself whether you could implement the entire process with the macro recorder. You could use the recorder to capture the commands to select a specific row within the list and change the font color. You could not, however, use the recorder to determine whether or not to select a particular row (i.e., whether the employee is a manager) because you have to make that decision by comparing the cell contents to a specific criterion. Nor is there a way to tell the recorder to repeat the process for every employee. In other words, you need to go beyond merely capturing Excel commands. You need to include additional Visual Basic statements within the macro.

The HighlightManager macro in Figure 9.9 uses the If statement to implement a decision (to determine whether the selected employee is a manager) and the Do statement to implement a loop (to repeat the commands until all employees in the list have been processed). To understand how the macro works, you need to know the basic syntax of each statement.

If Statement

The ***If statement*** conditionally executes a statement (or group of statements), depending on the value of an expression (condition). The If statement determines whether an expression is true, and if so, executes the commands between the If and the ***End If statement***. For example:

```
If ActiveCell.Offset(0, 2) = "Manager" Then
    Selection.Font.ColorIndex = 3
End If
```

This If statement determines whether the cell two columns to the right of the active cell (the offset indicates a relative reference) contains the text *Manager*, and if so, changes the font color of the (previously) selected text. The number three corresponds to the color red. No action is taken if the condition is false. Either way, execution continues with the command below the End If.

IF-THEN-ELSE

The If statement includes an optional Else clause whose statements are executed if the condition is false. Consider:

If condition **Then** statements [**Else** statements] **End If**

The condition is evaluated as either true or false. If the condition is true, the statements following Then are executed; otherwise the statements following Else are executed. Either way, execution continues with the statement following End If. Use the Help command for additional information and examples.

Do Statement

The **Do statement** repeats a block of statements until a condition becomes true. For example:

```
Do Until ActiveCell = ""
    ActiveCell.Range("A1:F1").Select
    If ActiveCell.Offset(0, 2) = "Manager" Then
        Selection.Font.ColorIndex = 3
    End If
    ActiveCell.Offset(1, 0).Select
Loop
```

The statements within the loop are executed repeatedly until the active cell is empty (i.e., ActiveCell = ""). The first statement in the loop selects the cells in columns A through F of the current row. Relative references are used, and you may want to refer to the earlier discussion that indicated that A1:F1 specifies the shape of a range rather than a specific cell address.

The If statement determines whether the current employee is a manager and, if so, changes the font color for the selected cells. (The offset (0, 2) refers to the entry two columns to the right of the active cell.) The last statement selects the cell one row below the active cell to process the next employee. (Omission of this statement would process the same row indefinitely, creating what is known as an infinite loop.)

The macro in Figure 9.9 is a nontrivial example that illustrates the potential of Visual Basic to enhance a macro. Try to gain a conceptual understanding of how the macro works, but do not be concerned if you are confused initially. Do the hands-on exercise, and you'll be pleased at how much clearer it will be when you have created the macro yourself. The addition of loops and decision-making statements in a VBA procedure enables true programming within an Excel macro.

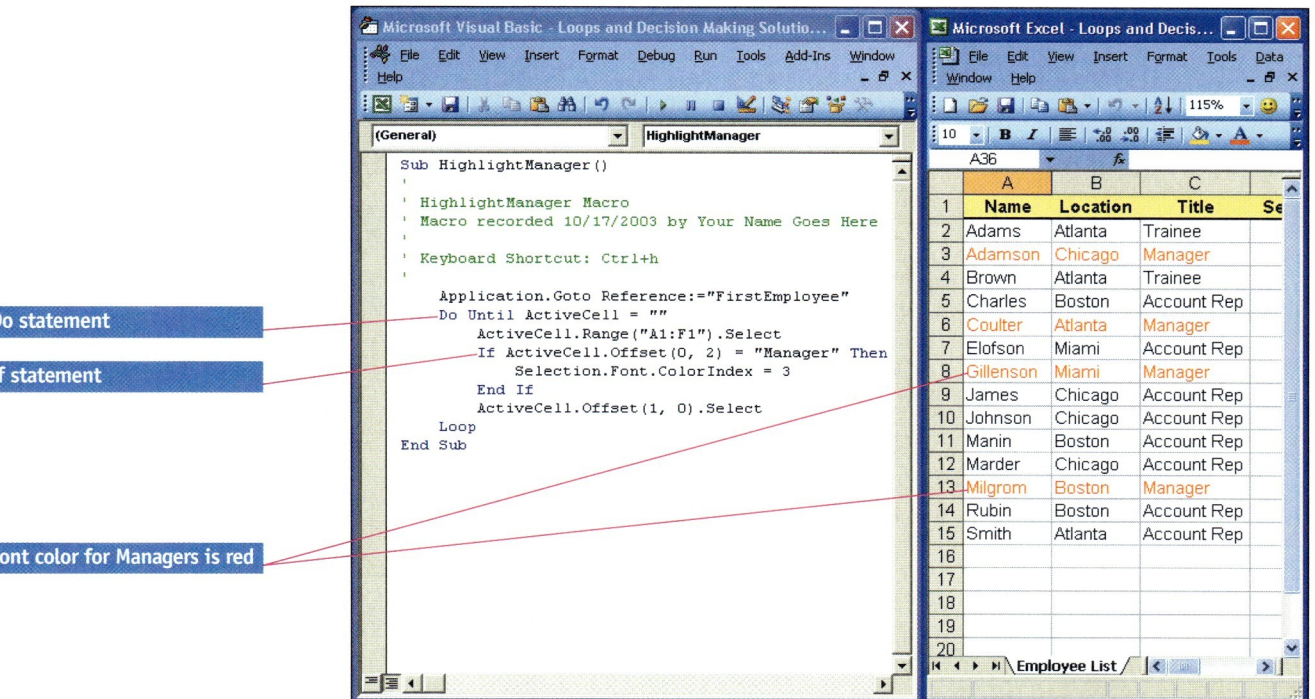

FIGURE 9.9 Loops and Decision Making

hands-on exercise 5

Loops and Decision Making

Objective To implement loops and decision making in a macro through relative references and the Visual Basic Do Until and If statements. Use Figure 9.10 as a guide in doing the exercise.

Step 1: **The ClearColor Macro**

- Open the **Loops and Decision Making workbook** in the **Exploring Excel folder**. Click the button to **Enable Macros** when prompted by the security warning. Close the Forms toolbar.

- Save the workbook as **Loops and Decision Making Solution workbook**. The data for the employees in rows 3, 6, 8, and 13 appears in red to indicate these employees are managers.

- Pull down the **Tools menu**. Click the **Macro command** and click **Macros** to display the dialog box in Figure 9.10a. (Do not be concerned if you do not see the NameAndCourse macro.)

- Select **ClearColor**, then click **Run** to execute this macro and clear the red color from the managerial employees.

- Use the **Font Color button** on the Standard toolbar to change the color of any entry within the list, then rerun the ClearColor macro. It is important to know that the ClearColor macro works, as you will use it throughout the exercise.

- Save the workbook.

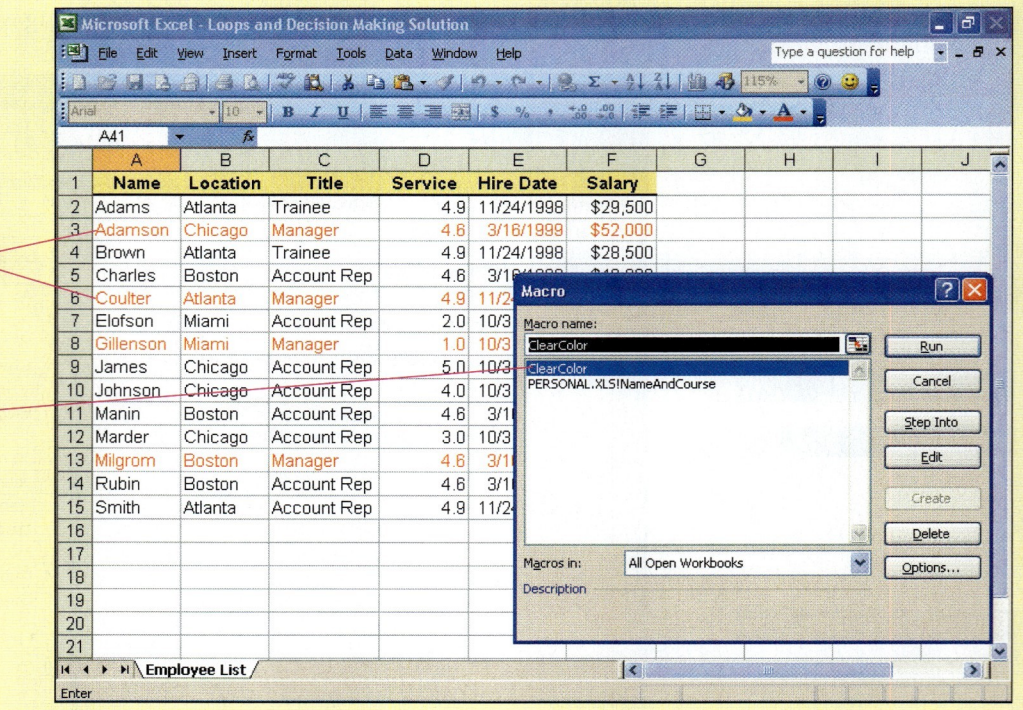

(a) The ClearColor Macro (step 1)

FIGURE 9.10 Hands-on Exercise 5

Step 2: **Record the HighlightManager Macro**

- You must choose the active cell before recording the macro. Click **cell A3**, the cell containing the name of the first manager.

- Pull down the **Tools menu**, click (or point to) the **Macro command**, then click **Record New Macro** (or click the **Record macro button** on the Visual Basic toolbar) to display the Record Macro dialog box.

- Enter **HighlightManager** as the name of the macro. Do not leave any spaces in the macro name. Click in the **Shortcut Key** check box and enter a **lowercase h**. Check that **This Workbook** is selected. Click **OK**.

- The Stop Recording toolbar appears, and the status bar indicates that you are recording the macro as shown in Figure 9.10b. Click the **Relative References button** so that the button is pushed in.

- Click and drag to select **cells A3 through F3** as shown in Figure 9.10b. Click the arrow in the **Font color list box**. Click **Red**. Click the **Stop Recording button**.

- Click anywhere in the worksheet to deselect cells A3 through F3 so you can see the effect of the macro; cells A3 through F3 should be displayed in red.

- Save the workbook.

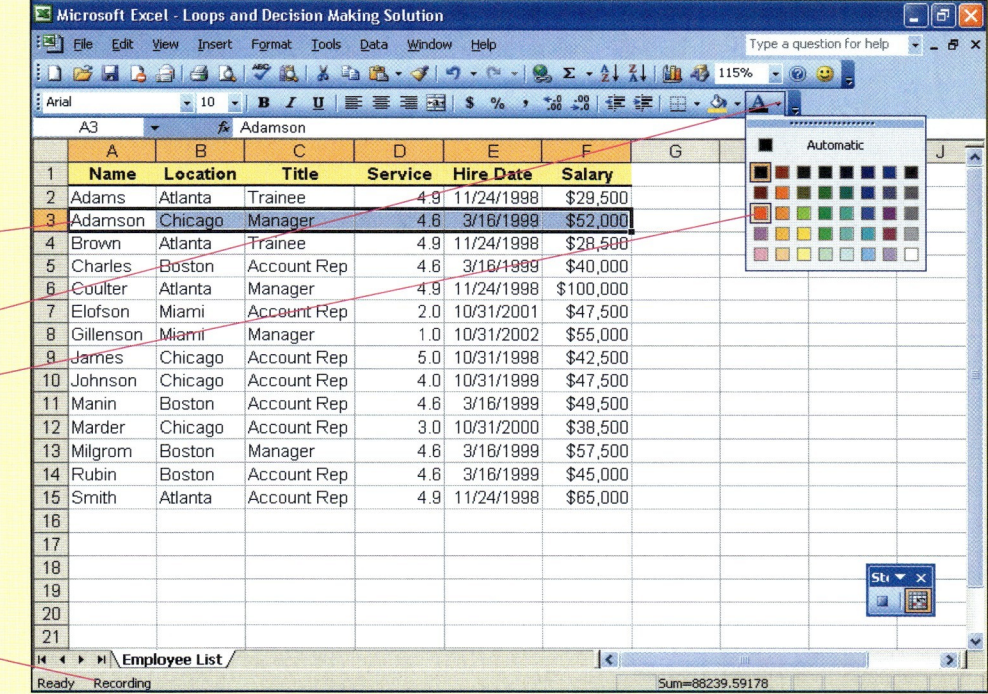

(b) Record the HighlightManager Macro (step 2)

FIGURE 9.10 Hands-on Exercise 5 (*continued*)

A SENSE OF FAMILIARITY

Visual Basic has the basic capabilities found in any other programming language. If you have programmed before, whether in Pascal, C, or even COBOL, you will find all of the familiar logic structures. These include the Do While and Do Until statements, the If-Then-Else statement for decision making, nested If statements, a Case statement, and/or calls to subprograms.

Step 3: **View the Macro**

- Press **Alt+F11** to open the Visual Basic Editor. If necessary, double click the **Modules folder** for the Loops and Decision Making Solution Project within the Project Explorer window to display the two modules within the workbook.

- Select (click) **Module2**. Pull down the **View menu** and click **Code** (or press the **F7 key**) to display the Visual Basic code for the HighlightManager macro you just created as shown in Figure 9.10c.

- Be sure that your code is identical to ours (except for the comments). If you see the absolute reference, Range("A3:F3"), rather than the relative reference in our figure, you need to correct your macro to match ours.

- Click the **close button** (the X on the Project Explorer title bar) to close the Project Explorer window. (You can reopen the Project Explorer at any time by pulling down the View menu.) The Code window expands to occupy the entire Visual Basic Editor window.

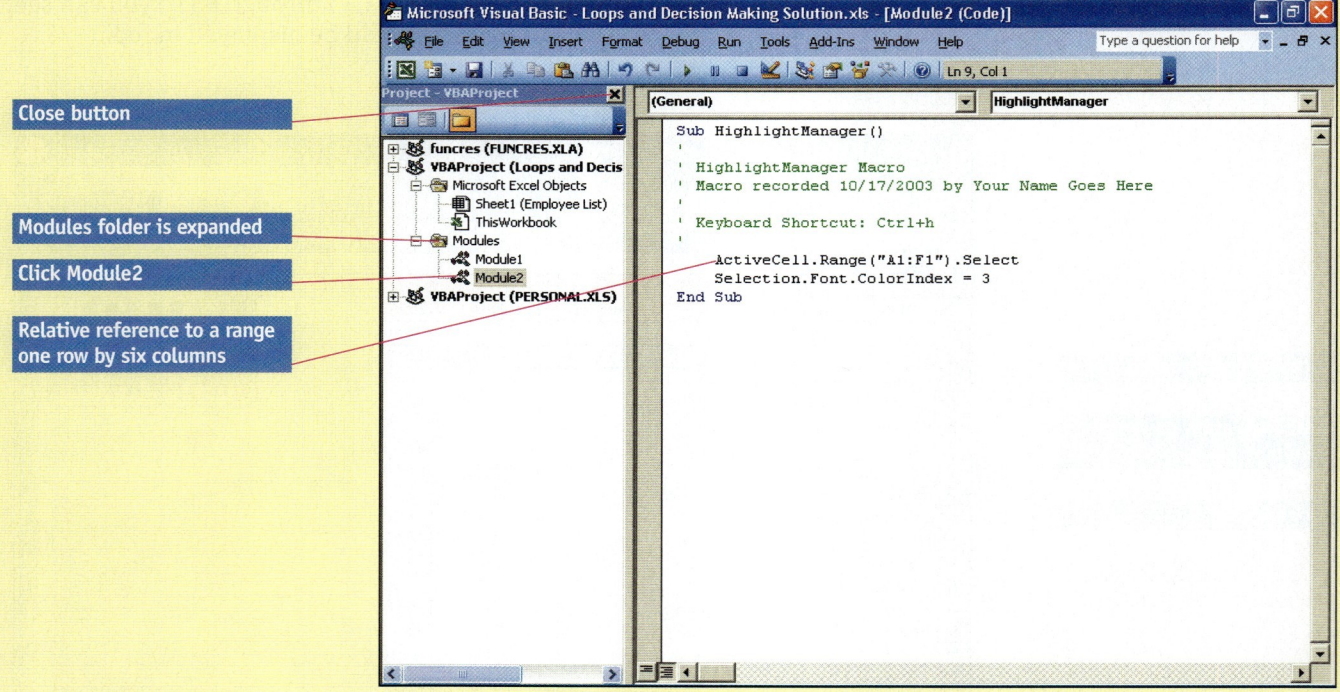

(c) View the Macro (step 3)

FIGURE 9.10 Hands-on Exercise 5 (*continued*)

WHY SO MANY MODULES?

Multiple macros that are recorded within the same Excel session are all stored in the same module. If you close the workbook, then subsequently reopen it, Excel will store subsequent macros in a new module. It really doesn't matter where (in which module) the macros are stored. You can, however, cut and paste macros from one module to another if you prefer to have all of the macros in a single module. Delete the additional (now superfluous) modules after you have copied the procedures.

Step 4: **Test the Macro**

- Point to an empty area on the Windows taskbar, then click the **right mouse button** to display a shortcut menu. Click **Tile Windows Vertically** to tile the open windows (Excel and the Visual Basic Editor).

- Your desktop should be similar to Figure 9.10d except that the additional employees will not yet appear in red. It doesn't matter if the workbook is in the same window as ours. (If additional windows are open on the desktop, minimize each window, then repeat the previous step to tile the open windows.)

- Click the **Excel window**. Click **cell A6** (the cell containing the name of the next manager). Press **Ctrl+h** to execute the HighlightManager macro. The font in cells A6 to F6 changes to red.

- Click **cell A7**. Press **Ctrl+h** to execute the HighlightManager macro. The font for this employee is also in red, although the employee is not a manager.

- Save the workbook.

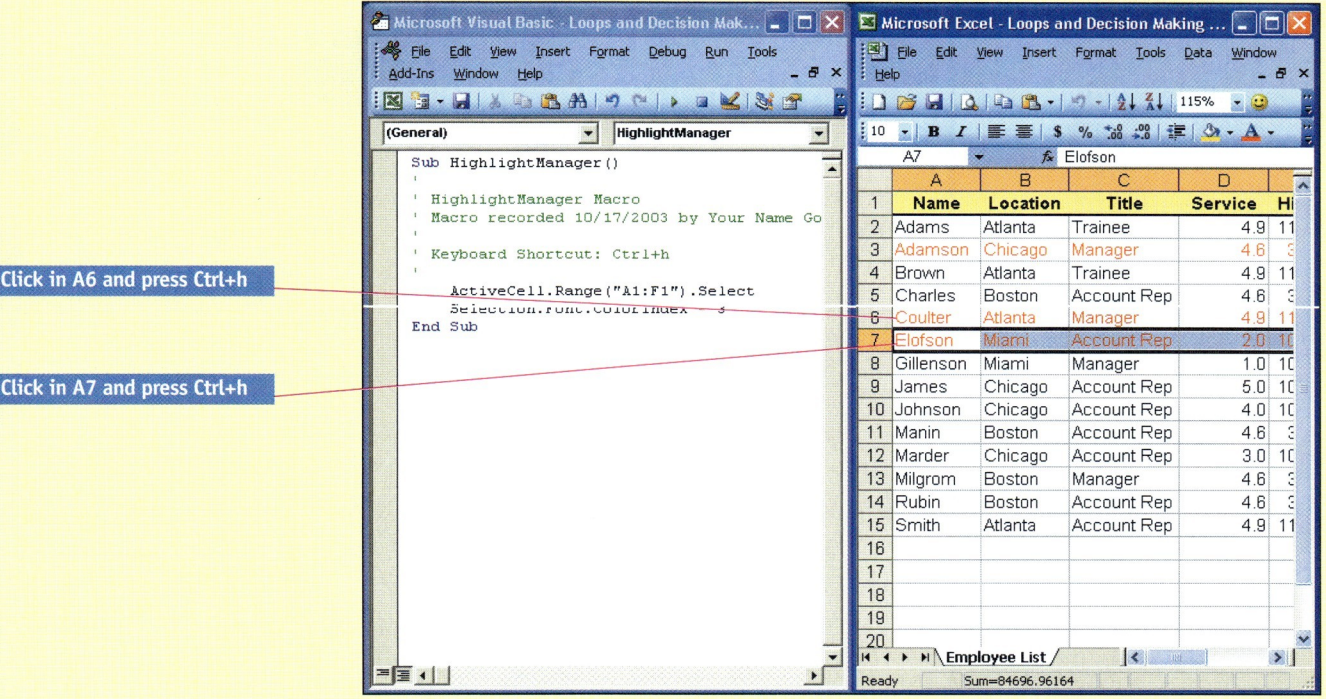

(d) Test the Macro (step 4)

FIGURE 9.10 Hands-on Exercise 5 (*continued*)

THE FIRST BUG

A bug is a mistake in a computer program; hence debugging refers to the process of correcting program errors. According to legend, the first bug was an unlucky moth crushed to death on one of the relays of the electromechanical Mark II computer, bringing the machine's operation to a halt. The cause of the failure was discovered by Grace Hopper, who promptly taped the moth to her logbook, noting, *"First actual case of bug being found."*

Step 5: **Add the If Statement**

- Press **Ctrl+c** to execute the ClearColor macro. The data for all employees is again displayed in black.

- Click in the window containing the **HighlightManager macro**. Add the **If** and **End If** statements exactly as they are shown in Figure 9.10e. Use the **Tab key** (or press the **space bar**) to indent the Selection statement within the If and End If statements.

- Click in the window containing the worksheet, then click **cell A3**. Press **Ctrl+h** to execute the modified HighlightManager macro. The text in cells A3 through F3 is red since this employee is a manager.

- Click **cell A4**. Press **Ctrl+h**. The row is selected, but the color of the font remains unchanged. The If statement prevents these cells from being highlighted because the employee is not a manager. Press **Ctrl+c** to remove all highlighting.

- Save the workbook.

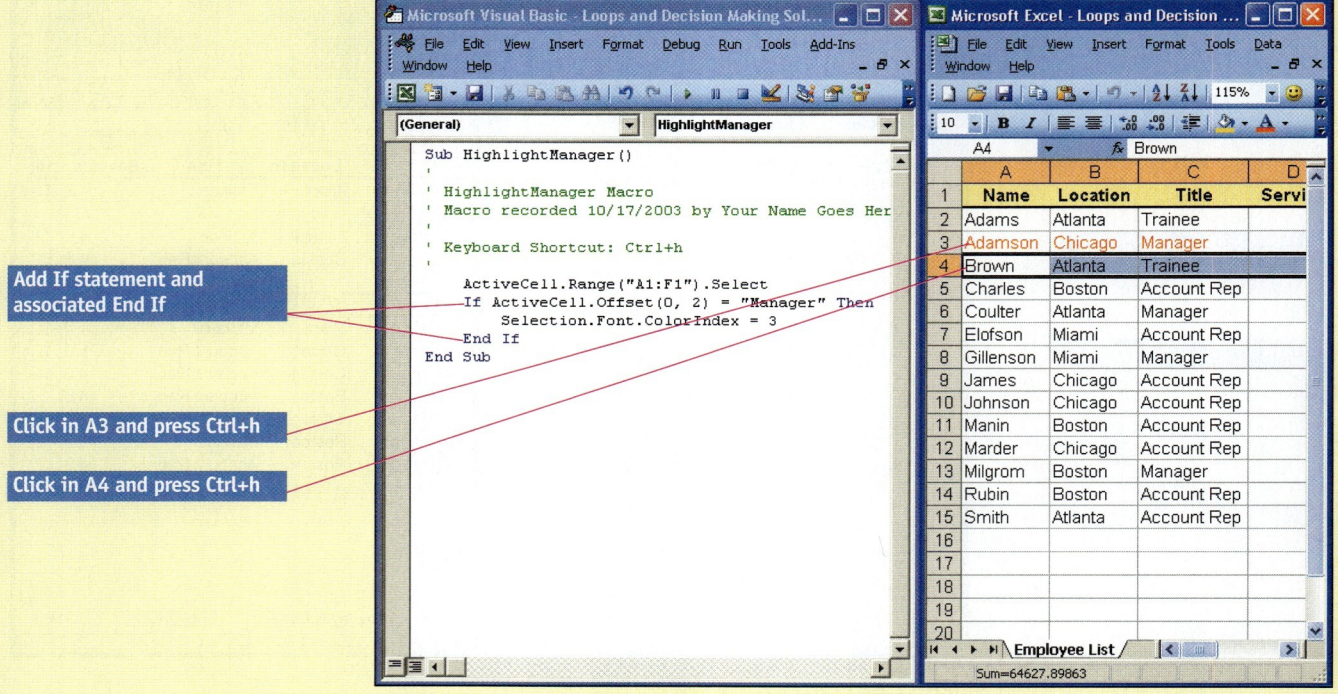

(e) Add the If Statement (step 5)

FIGURE 9.10   Hands-on Exercise 5 (*continued*)

INDENT

Indentation does not affect the execution of a macro. It, does, however, make the macro easier to read, and we suggest you follow common conventions in developing your macros. Indent the conditional statements associated with an If statement by a consistent amount. Place the End If statement on a line by itself, directly under the associated If.

Step 6: **An Endless Loop**

- Click in the window containing the **HighlightManager macro**. Add the **Do Until** and **Loop** statements exactly as they appear in Figure 9.10f. Indent the other statements as shown in the figure.

- Click **cell A3** of the worksheet. Press **Ctrl+h** to execute the macro. Cells A3 through F3 will be displayed in red, but the macro continues to execute indefinitely as it applies color to the same record over and over.

- Press **Ctrl+Break** to cease execution of the macro. You will see the dialog box in Figure 9.10f, indicating that code execution has been interrupted. Click the **End button**.

- Click within the macro code, pull down the **Debug menu**, and click the **Step Into command** (or press the **F8 key**) to enter the macro. The first statement is highlighted in yellow.

- Press the **F8 key** repeatedly to execute the next several steps over and over again. You will see that the macro is stuck in a loop as the If statement is executed indefinitely.

- Click the **Reset button** in the Visual Basic window to end the debugging.

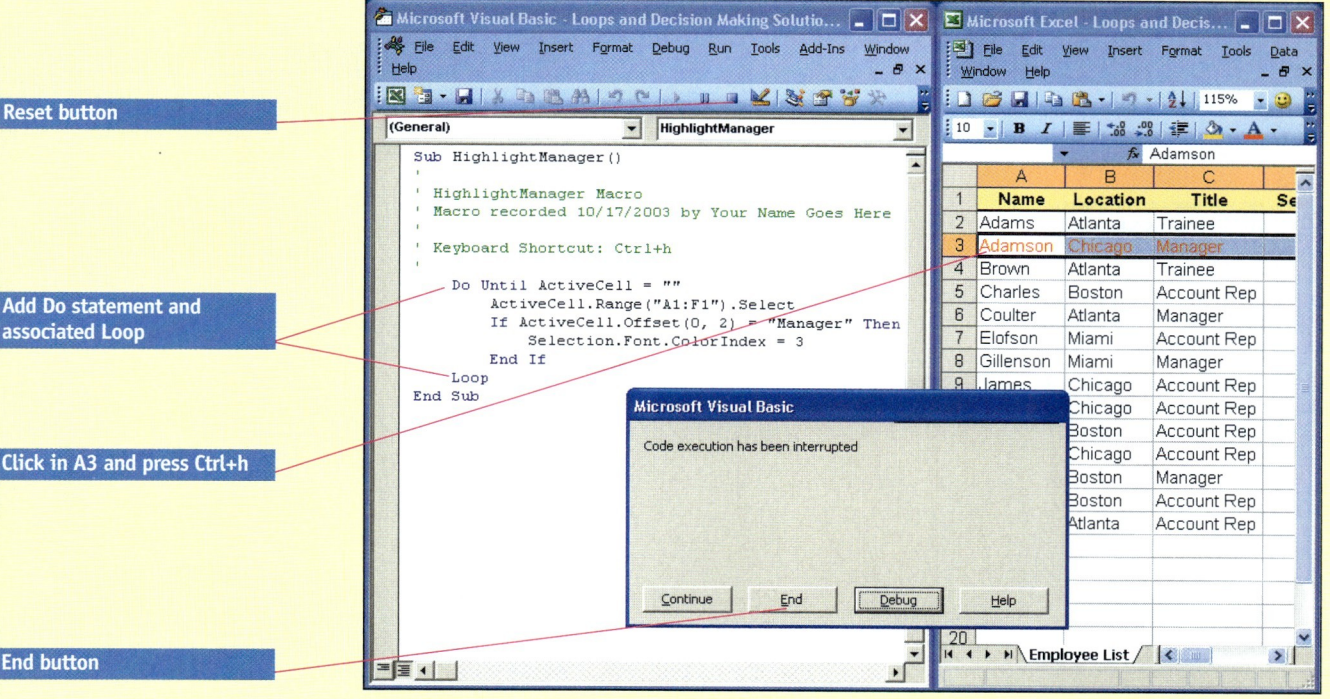

(f) An Endless Loop (step 6)

FIGURE 9.10   Hands-on Exercise 5 (*continued*)

AN ENDLESS LOOP

The glossary in the Programmer's Guide for a popular database contains the following definitions "Endless loop"—See loop, endless and "Loop, endless"—See endless loop.

We don't know whether these entries were deliberate or not, but the point is made either way. Endless loops are a common and frustrating bug. Press Ctrl+Break to halt execution, then click the Debug command button to step through the macro and locate the source of the error.

Step 7: The Completed Macro

- Click in **cell A2** of the worksheet. Click in the **Name Box**. Enter **FirstEmployee** to name this cell. Press **Enter**.

- Click in the window containing the macro. Click after the last comment line and press **Enter** to insert a blank line.

- Add the statement to select the cell named FirstEmployee as shown in Figure 9.10g. This ensures that the macro always begins in row two by selecting the cell named FirstEmployee.

- Click immediately after the End If statement. Press **Enter**. Add the statement containing the offset (1,0) as shown in Figure 9.10g, which selects the cell one row below the current row.

- Click anywhere in the worksheet. Press **Ctrl+c** to clear the color. Press **Ctrl+h** to execute the HighlightManager macro.

- The macro begins by selecting cell A2, then proceeds to highlight all managers in red. Save the workbook a final time.

- Print the workbook and its macro for your instructor. Exit Excel. Congratulations on a job well done.

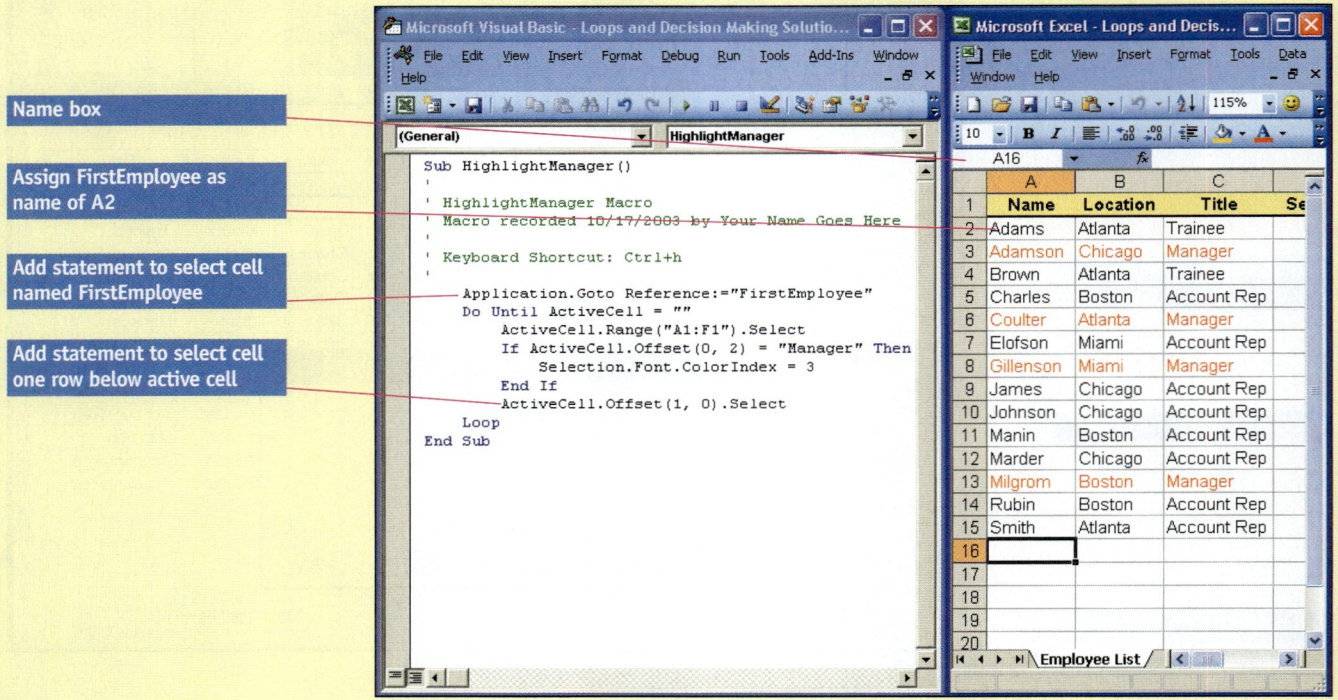

(g) The Completed Macro (step 7)

FIGURE 9.10 Hands-on Exercise 5 (*continued*)

HELP FOR VISUAL BASIC

Click within any Visual Basic keyword, then press the F1 key for context-sensitive help. You will see a help screen containing a description of the statement, its syntax, key elements, and several examples. You can print the help screen by clicking the Printer icon. (If you do not see the help screens, ask your instructor to install Visual Basic Help.)

SUMMARY

A macro is a set of instructions that automates a repetitive task. It is, in essence, a program, and its instructions are written in Visual Basic, a programming language. The macro recorder in Excel records your commands and writes the macro for you. Once a macro has been created, it can be modified in the Visual Basic Editor by manually inserting, deleting, or changing its statements.

Macros are stored in one of two places, either in the current workbook or in a Personal Macro workbook. Macros that are specific to a particular workbook should be stored in that workbook. Generic macros that can be used with any workbook should be stored in the Personal Macro workbook.

A computer virus may be contained in an Excel macro. Thus, Excel will warn you if a workbook you are about to open contains a macro, provided the security option is set appropriately. High security disables all macros except from a previously designated trusted source. Medium security gives you the option to enable macros.

A macro is run (executed) by pulling down the Tools menu and selecting the Run Macro command. A macro can also be executed through a keyboard shortcut, by placing a command button on the worksheet, or by customizing a toolbar to include an additional button to run the macro.

A comment is a nonexecutable statement that begins with an apostrophe. Comments are inserted automatically at the beginning of a macro by the macro recorder to remind you of what the macro does. Comments may be added, deleted, or modified, just as any other statement. A VBA statement is continued from one line to the next by typing a blank space followed by an underscore at the end of the line to be continued. An ampersand concatenates (joins together) two adjacent text strings if a literal has to be continued to a second line.

A macro begins and ends with the Sub and End Sub statements, respectively. The Sub statement contains the name of the macro or VBA procedure. The With statement enables you to perform multiple actions on the same object. All commands between the With and corresponding End With statements are executed collectively.

A macro contains either absolute or relative references. An absolute reference is constant; that is, Excel keeps track of the exact cell address and selects that specific cell. A relative reference depends on the previously selected cell, and is entered as an offset, or number of rows and columns from the current cell. The Relative Reference button on the Stop Recording toolbar toggles between the two.

A good macro is completely general and immune to changes in the underlying workbook. VBA does not, however, update cell references to accommodate insertions or deletions of rows and columns in the associated worksheet. It is good practice, therefore, to always use range names, as opposed to absolute cell references, within a macro.

An Excel macro can be made more powerful through inclusion of Visual Basic statements that enable true programming. These include the MsgBox statement to display information, the InputBox function to obtain user input, the If statement to implement decision making, and the Do statement to implement a loop. The macro recorder creates the initial macro by translating Excel commands to Visual Basic statements. The additional VBA statements are added to the resulting code using the Visual Basic Editor.

A bug is a mistake in a computer program, and debugging is the process of finding and correcting program errors. The Step Into command is useful in debugging as it executes a macro (VBA procedure) one statement at a time to see the effects of each statement.

KEY TERMS

Absolute reference 461	Insert Name command 473	Relative reference 461
Code window 450	Keyboard shortcut 450	Shortcut key 450
Comment 450	Loop 492	Step Into command 459
Debugging .497	Macro 450	Sub statement 450
Do statement 493	Macro recorder 450	Visual Basic 450
End If statement 492	MsgBox statement 480	Visual Basic Editor (VBE) 450
End Sub statement 450	Named range 471	Visual Basic for
End With statement 451	Offset 461	Applications (VBA) 450
If statement 492	Personal Macro workbook 462	With statement 451
InputBox function 462	Project Explorer 450	

MULTIPLE CHOICE

1. Which of the following best describes recording and executing a macro?
   (a) A macro is recorded once and executed once
   (b) A macro is recorded once and executed many times
   (c) A macro is recorded many times and executed once
   (d) A macro is recorded many times and executed many times

2. Which of the following can be used to execute a macro?
   (a) A keyboard shortcut
   (b) A customized toolbar button
   (c) A button on the worksheet
   (d) All of the above

3. A macro can be stored:
   (a) In any Excel workbook
   (b) In the Personal Macro workbook
   (c) Both (a) and (b)
   (d) Neither (a) nor (b)

4. Which of the following is true regarding comments in Visual Basic?
   (a) A comment is executable; that is, its inclusion or omission affects the outcome of a macro
   (b) A comment begins with an apostrophe
   (c) Both (a) and (b)
   (d) Neither (a) nor (b)

5. Which statement must contain the name of the macro?
   (a) The Sub statement at the beginning of the macro
   (b) The first comment statement
   (c) Both (a) and (b)
   (d) Neither (a) nor (b)

6. Which of the following indicates an absolute reference within a macro?
   (a) ActiveCell.Offset(1,1).Range("A1")
   (b) $A$1
   (c) Range("A1")
   (d) All of the above

7. Selection.Offset (1,0).Range ("A1").Select will select the cell that is:
   (a) In the same column as the active cell but one row below
   (b) In the same row as the active cell but one column to the right
   (c) In the same column as the active cell but one row above
   (d) In the same row as the active cell but one column to the left

8. Selection.Offset (1,1).Range ("A1").Select will select the cell that is:
   (a) One cell below and one cell to the left of the active cell
   (b) One cell below and one cell to the right of the active cell
   (c) One cell above and one cell to the right of the active cell
   (d) One cell above and one cell to the left of the active cell

9. Selection.Offset (1,1).Range ("A1:A2").Select will select:
   (a) Cell A1
   (b) Cell A2
   (c) Both (a) and (b)
   (d) Neither (a) nor (b)

10. Which commands are used to duplicate an existing macro so that it can become the basis of a new macro?
    (a) Copy command
    (b) Paste command
    (c) Both (a) and (b)
    (d) Neither (a) nor (b)

11. Which of the following is used to protect a macro from the subsequent insertion or deletion of rows or columns in the associated worksheet?
    (a) Range names
    (b) Absolute references
    (c) Both (a) and (b)
    (d) Neither (a) nor (b)

... continued

multiple choice

12. Which of the following is true regarding a customized button that has been inserted as an object onto a worksheet and assigned to an Excel macro?

    (a) Point to the customized button, then click the left mouse button to execute the associated macro
    (b) Point to the customized button, then click the right mouse button to select the macro button and simultaneously display a shortcut menu
    (c) Point to the customized button, then press and hold the Ctrl key as you click the left mouse to select the button
    (d) All of the above

13. The InputBox function:

    (a) Displays a message (prompt) requesting input from the user
    (b) Stores the user's response in a designated cell
    (c) Both (a) and (b)
    (d) Neither (a) nor (b)

14. You want to create a macro to enter your name into a specific cell. The best way to do this is to:

    (a) Select the cell for your name, turn on the macro recorder with absolute references, then type your name
    (b) Turn on the macro recorder with absolute references, select the cell for your name, then type your name
    (c) Either (a) or (b)
    (d) Neither (a) nor (b)

15. Which of the following is true about indented text in a VBA procedure?

    (a) The indented text is always executed first
    (b) The indented text is always executed last
    (c) The indented text is rendered a comment and is never executed
    (d) None of the above

16. You want to create a macro to enter your name in the active cell (which will vary whenever the macro is used) and the course you are taking in the cell immediately below. The best way to do this is to:

    (a) Select the cell for your name, turn on the macro recorder with absolute references, type your name, press the down arrow, and type the course
    (b) Turn on the macro recorder with absolute references, select the cell for your name, type your name, press the down arrow, and type the course
    (c) Select the cell for your name, turn on the macro recorder with relative references, type your name, press the down arrow, and type the course
    (d) Turn on the macro recorder with relative references, select the cell for your name, type your name, press the down arrow, and type the course

17. A VBA statement contains the reference, ActiveCell.Offset(1,0).Range("A1:A3"). Which cells are selected if cell B3 is the active cell when the command is executed?

    (a) The range B1:B3
    (b) The range B4:B6
    (c) The range A1:A3
    (d) The range A2:A4

18. You have created a named range called AllEmployees, which is assigned to cells A2:H100 in the worksheet. Which of the following actions will change the cells that are included in the named range?

    (a) Inserting or deleting an employee in the middle of the list
    (b) Inserting or deleting a field in the middle of the list
    (c) Both (a) and (b)
    (d) Neither (a) nor (b)

ANSWERS

1. b
2. d
3. c
4. b
5. a
6. c
7. a
8. b
9. d
10. c
11. a
12. d
13. c
14. b
15. d
16. c
17. b
18. c

PRACTICE WITH EXCEL

1. **Data Management Macros:** Figure 9.11 displays an alternate version of the Employee List Solution workbook that was used in the third and fourth hands-on exercises. The existing macros have been deleted and replaced by the five macros represented by the command buttons in the figure. Your assignment is to create the indicated macros and assign the macros to the command buttons. The purpose of each macro should be apparent from the name of the command button.

   a. You can "cut and paste" macros from the Employee List Solution workbook as it existed at the end of the fourth hands-on exercise, or you can create the macros from scratch using the *Chapter 9 Practice 1* workbook (which contains the equivalent workbook used in Hands-on Exercise 3). Choose whichever technique you think is easier. You will need to use the Insert Name Create command to assign names to various cells in the worksheet for use in your macros.

   b. The AllEmployees macro should clear the criteria row, then display all employees within the list (the summary statistics will reflect all employees as well). The other four macros prompt the user for the specific criteria. Note that the user can include relational operators for service or salary, such as >60000 to display employees with salaries greater than $60,000. All of the macros should include a MsgBox statement that displays the indicated message in Figure 9.11.

   c. Run the AnySalary macro, then print the workbook as it appears in Figure 9.11. Print the worksheet with row and column headings and be sure that it fits on a single sheet of paper. Be sure to change the properties of the command buttons so that the buttons appear on the printed worksheet.

   d. Run the AllEmployees macro and then print the worksheet after the macro is complete. Print the worksheet a second time to show the cell formulas.

   e. Change to the Visual Basic Editor, pull down the File menu, click the Print command, then print the current project to print all of the modules (macros) within your workbook.

   f. Add a cover sheet and submit the entire assignment to your instructor.

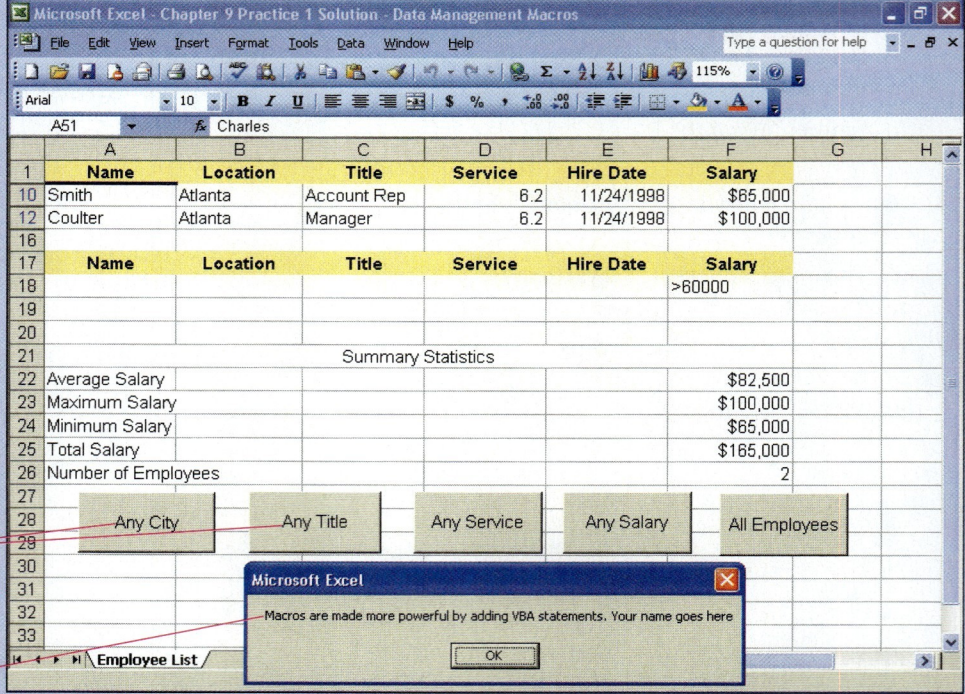

FIGURE 9.11 Data Management Macros (exercise 1)

practice exercises

2. **Employee Selection:** Figure 9.12 extends the previous problem to include one additional macro that prompts the user for city, title, service, and salary. The user enters all four parameters, then the macro displays the selected records within the list together with the summary statistics. It is quite possible, however, that no employee will meet all the criteria, in which case the macro should display a message to that effect as shown.

   a. Your assignment is to complete the previous problem, then add the additional macro to prompt for the multiple criteria. The macro will always ask the user for all four parameters, but you need not enter every parameter. If, for example, you do not specify a city, the macro will return matching employees regardless of the city.

   b. You can include relational operators in the service and/or salary fields as shown in Figure 9.12. The figure is searching for Chicago Account reps with less than eight years of service, earning more than $60,000.

   c. The DAVERAGE function displays a division by zero error message if there is no record that meets the specified criteria. You can hide the error message, however, by using conditional formatting to display the message in white, which renders it invisible. Click in the cell containing the DAVERAGE function. Pull down the Format menu, click Conditional formatting, and then click the drop-down arrow in the left list box to select Formula Is. Click in the box to the right and type =ISERROR(F22), where F22 is the cell containing the function that caused the error. Now click the Format button, click Font, and change the color to white. The message is in the cell, but you cannot see it.

   d. You need to include an If statement in your macro that tests whether the number of qualified employees is equal to zero, and if so, it should display the associated message box. It's easy to do. Use the Insert Name command within the Excel workbook to assign the name "QualifiedEmployees" to cell F26. Then insert a statement in the macro to go to this cell, which makes it the active cell. The If statement can then compare the value of the active cell to zero, and if it is zero, use the MsgBox statement to display the indicated message.

   e. Print the worksheet in Figure 9.12 for your instructor. (The dialog box will not appear on your printout.) Print the module containing the macro.

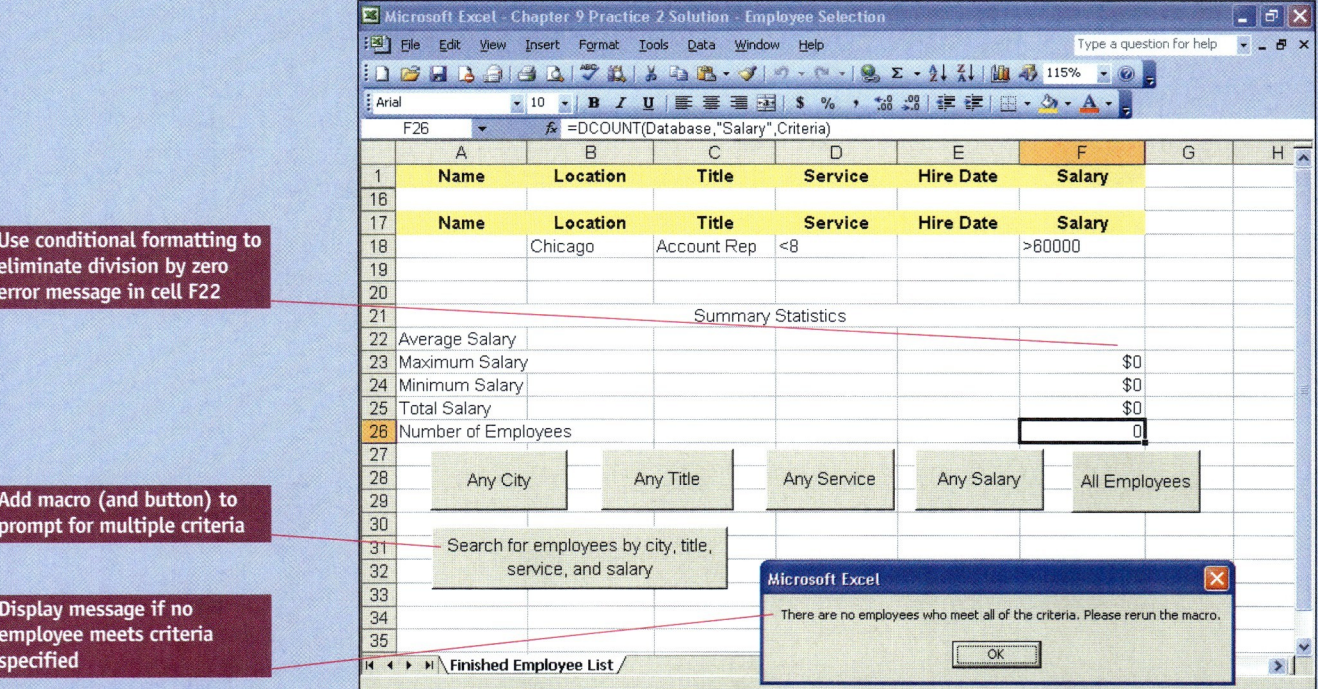

FIGURE 9.12 Employee Selection (exercise 2)

practice exercises

3. **Highlighting Employees:** Figure 9.13 extends the Loops and Decision Making workbook from the fifth hands-on exercise to include command buttons and an additional macro. The new macro highlights the Atlanta and Chicago employees in red and blue, respectively.

   a. Open the Loops and Decision Making Solution workbook from the fifth hands-on exercise. Start the Visual Basic Editor, then copy the existing HighlightManager macro so that you can use it as the basis of the new macro, which will highlight the employees in two locations. Change the name of the copied macro. Then change the offset in the If statement to (0, 1) to reference the location column within the list, and further to compare that value to "Atlanta", as opposed to "Manager".

   b. Switch to the Excel workbook, pull down the Tools menu, select the Macro command, click Macros, select the new macro, click Options, then assign a keyboard shortcut. (We used Ctrl+A.) Press Ctrl+c to execute the ClearColor macro, then press Ctrl+A to test the newly created macro. The Atlanta employees should be highlighted in red.

   c. Return to the VBA editor and insert the ElseIf clause immediately above the existing End If clause. The ElseIf should compare the value of the cell with the appropriate offset to "Chicago", and if that condition is true, highlight the selection in blue (color 5). Test the modified macro.

   d. Add command buttons to the worksheet as shown in Figure 9.13, then test the buttons to be sure that they work properly. You will discover that the macros require one subtle adjustment; that is, if you run the ChicagoandAtlanta macro, followed immediately by the Manager macro (or vice versa), employees from both macros will be highlighted. In other words, you need to clear any existing highlighting prior to running either of the other two. *You can make this happen automatically by including ClearColor (the name of the macro you want to run) as the first statement in the other two macros.*

   e. Print the completed worksheet for your instructor. Be sure to change the properties of the command buttons so that they print with the worksheet.

   f. Print the module containing the code for all three macros. Add a cover sheet to complete the assignment.

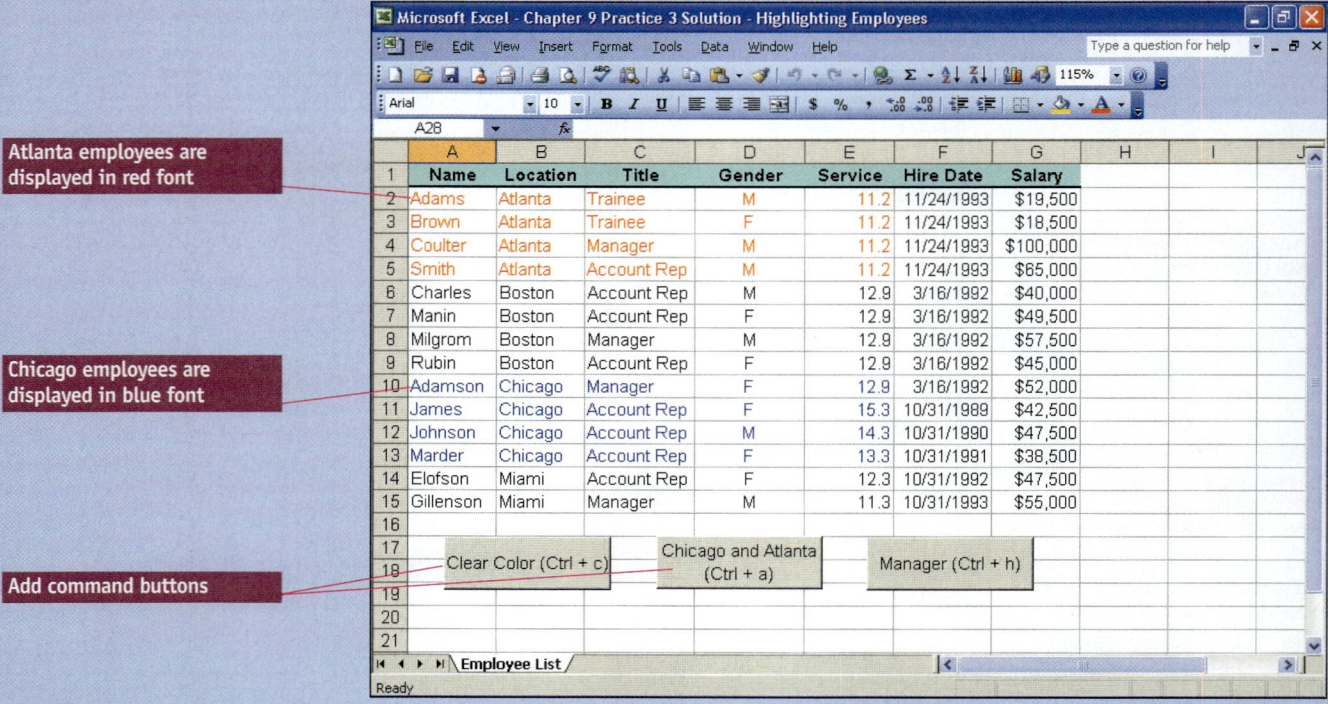

FIGURE 9.13 Highlighting Employees (exercise 3)

practice exercises

4. **Student List:** The worksheet in Figure 9.14 is shown after execution of the macro, Any YearAnyMajor, which prompts the user for these values, then displays the selected students and summary statistics. All of the macros in the worksheet are flexible and use range names, as opposed to specific cell references. We have created three range names for you: Criteria (A19:G20), CriteriaValues (A20:G20), and StudentList (A1:G17), but you will have to create the remaining names as necessary. Proceed as follows:

   a. Open the *Chapter 9 Practice 4* workbook. Click and drag to select cells A19 through G20, then use the Insert Name Create command (using the entries in the top row) to create the additional range names.

   b. Create the macro to show all students. This requires you to clear the range name CriteriaValues, then use the Advanced Filter command (with the range names StudentList and Criteria) to display all of the students.

   c. Display the Forms toolbar. Click the Button tool, draw a button on the worksheet, and assign the AllStudents macro that you just created to the button. Right click the button, click Format Control, click the Properties tab, then check the box to print the object.

   d. Use the macro recorder to create a macro for a specific major, and then edit the macro to substitute the InputBox function for the name of the major. The macro should begin by clearing the criteria area and end by displaying the message box in Figure 9.14.

   e. Return to the Excel workbook. Right click the All Students command button, click the Copy button, click the Paste button, and drag the duplicate button to the right. Right click the new button and assign the AnyMajor macro to the new button. Change the text of the button as well. Test both buttons to be sure that the associated macros work correctly.

   f. The easiest way to create the remaining macros is to duplicate the AnyMajor macro and then make changes in the VBA editor. Copy an existing macro button, and then assign each new macro to a new button.

   g. Execute the macro to display students in any year and any major (use any values you like). Print the completed worksheet and the module(s) containing the macros for your instructor.

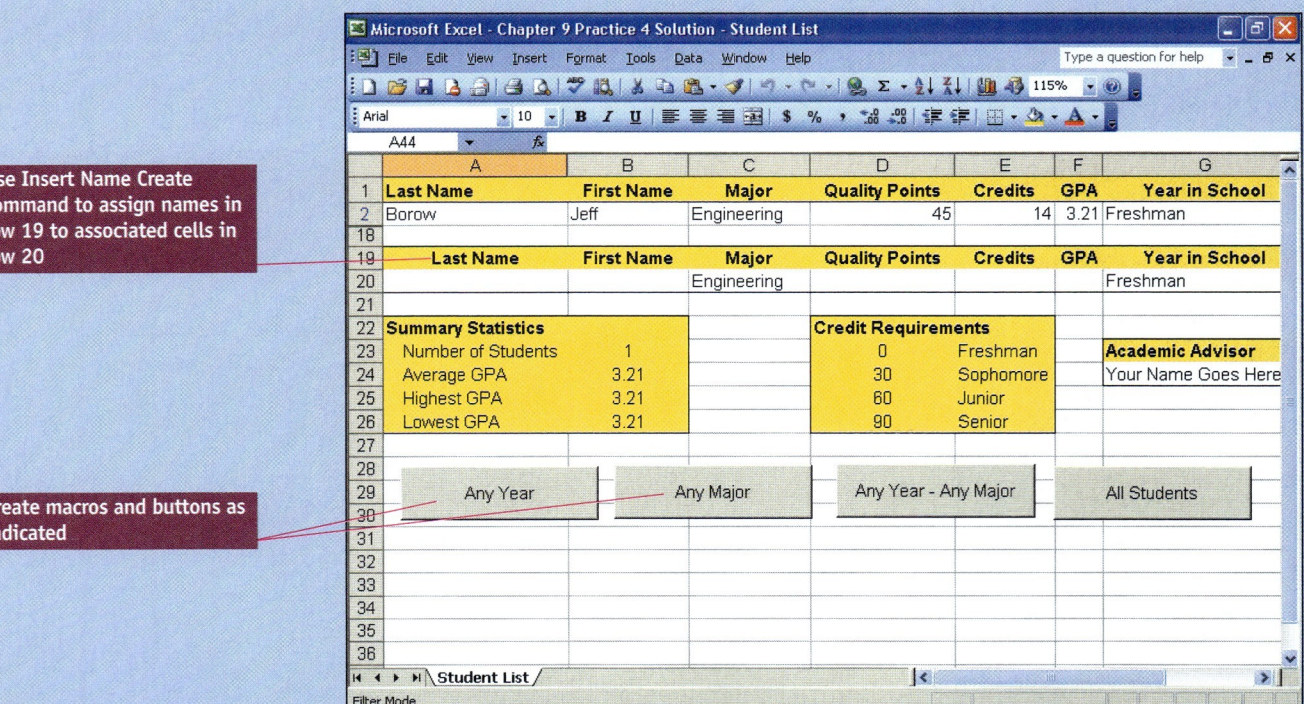

FIGURE 9.14 Student List (exercise 4)

practice exercises

5. **Election Macros:** The workbook in Figure 9.15 displays the returns from the 2004 presidential election. The data, formulas for the difference in popular vote and associated percentage, and formatting have been entered for you. Your task is to create the indicated macros to display the data in different sequences. Open the partially completed *Chapter 9 Practice 5* workbook and proceed as follows:

   a. All macros should use range names, as opposed to specific cell references, so that they are immune to subsequent insertions or deletions of rows or columns in a worksheet. Assign the range names "State", "Difference", and "Percentage", to cells A8, F8, and G8, respectively. Assign "AllResults" to the cell range A8:H59.

   b. Start the macro recorder. Specify Alphabetical as the macro name. Click the down arrow in the Name box and select "State" (to go to cell A8), then click the Ascending Sort button. Click the Stop Recording button.

   c. Press Alt+F11 to display the Visual Basic editor to view the macro you just created. Substitute "AllResults" for A8:H59 and "State" for A8.

   d. Display the Forms toolbar. Click the button tool, draw a button on the worksheet, assign the Alphabetical macro to the button, then enter "Alphabetical" as the button text. Right click the button, click Format Control, click the Properties tab, then check the box to print the object.

   e. Click and drag to select the complete Alphabetical macro (including the Sub and End Sub statements). Press Ctrl+C, click beneath the macro, and then press Ctrl+V to duplicate the macro. Change the name of the duplicate macro to SmallestPercentage. Change *all* occurrences of "State" to "Percentage", effectively changing the sort from column A to column H.

   f. Return to Excel. Right click the Alphabetical command button, click Copy from the menu, click in the worksheet, and click the Paste button, and then drag the duplicate button to the right. Right click the new button and assign the SmallestPercentage macro to the new button. Change the text of the button as well. Test the button to be sure that it works. Create the remaining macros and associated command buttons.

   g. Print the completed worksheet in at least two different sequences. Print the VBA module that contains all five procedures.

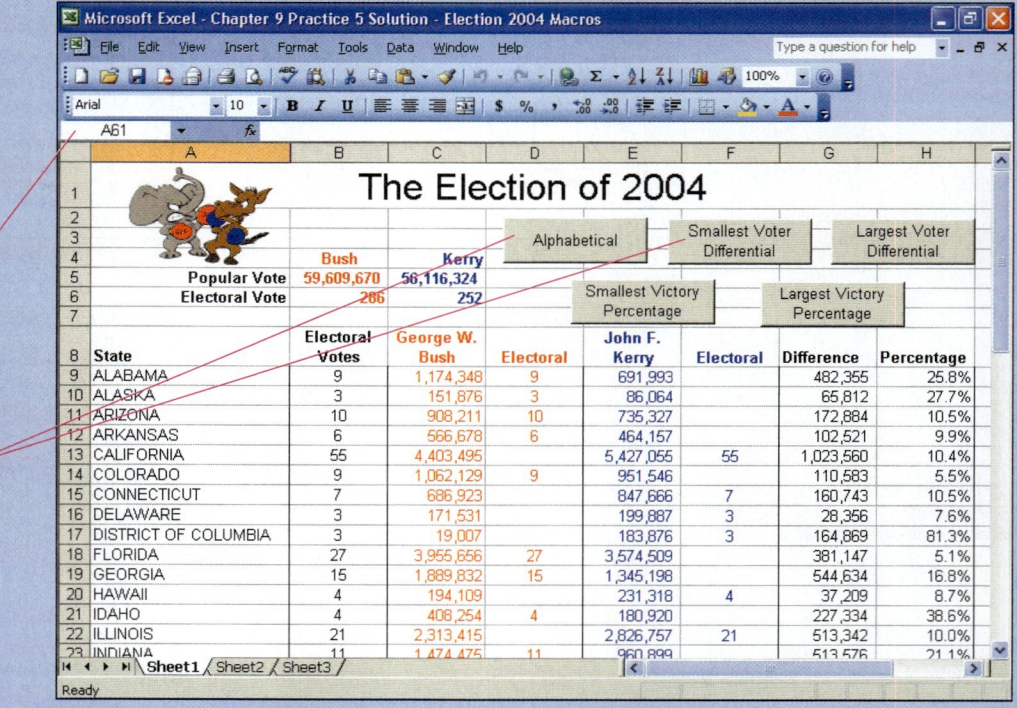

FIGURE 9.15 Election Macros (exercise 5)

practice exercises

6. **Stock Portfolio:** Figure 9.16 displays a worksheet that uses macros in conjunction with Web queries to update a stock portfolio. You have seen this worksheet before, most recently in Chapter 5 when we studied worksheet references within a workbook. Now we complete the example through the introduction of macros.

   a. Open the partially completed *Chapter 9 Practice 6* workbook and click the worksheet tab that contains your portfolio. The macros are already in the worksheet, and all you have to do is click the appropriate command buttons. The macro to enter your investments will prompt you for three investments for which you need to enter the company symbol, number of shares, and purchase price. This macro will also copy the stock symbols you have entered to the end of the stock symbol table in the Stock Prices worksheet.

   b. Click the command button to Update Your Portfolio, which in turn will execute the Web query to retrieve the current price of your investments and automatically calculate the value of your portfolio. The worksheet is password protected to prevent you from accidentally changing any of the formulas that have been entered. (The password is "password", in lowercase letters so you can remove the protection if you like using the Tools menu.)

   c. After you have updated your portfolio, click the button to View Summary to take you to the summary worksheet. The macros for that worksheet have not been created, however, so it is up to you to create the macros and assign them to the indicated command buttons as shown in Figure 9.16. The UpdatePrices macro refreshes the Web query in the Stock Prices worksheet. (It is the same as the UpdateYourPortfolio macro except that it returns to the Summary worksheet.) The BestInvestors and WorstInvestors list the portfolios in descending and ascending order according to the percentage gain or loss.

   d. Print the Summary worksheet for your instructor as well as the worksheet that contains your portfolio. Print the module(s) containing all of the macros within the worksheet. Add a short note explaining the purpose of the various modules that were originally in the workbook.

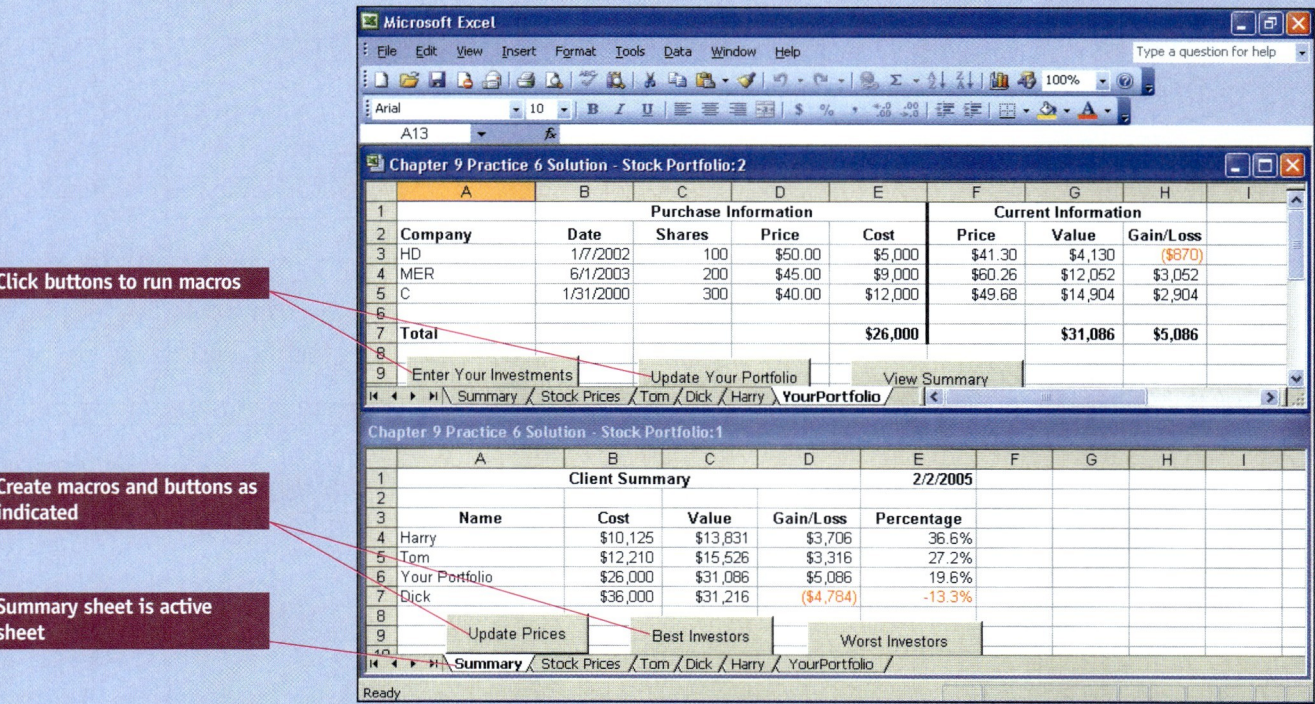

FIGURE 9.16 Stock Portfolio (exercise 6)

MICROSOFT OFFICE EXCEL 2003 REVISED

practice exercises

7. **The Automated Job Search:** The workbook in Figure 9.17 is similar to an earlier workbook in Chapter 7 except that two macros have been added to automate the job search. The ShowAllApplicants macro is already in the workbook; your job is to create the Search macro, which enables you to enter the desired qualifications.

   a. Open the *Chapter 9 Practice 7—Automated Job Search* workbook. Click and drag to select cells A8:H9. Pull down the Insert menu, click Name, then click the Create Command to display the associated dialog box. The box to create the names in the top row is already checked. Click OK.

   b. The easiest way to develop the Search macro is to create a macro with a single criterion, and build on that macro. Pull down the Tools menu, click macro, click Record New Macro, and enter Search as the macro name. Click OK to start recording.

   c. Click the down arrow in the Name box, select CriteriaValues, and then press the Del key to clear the criteria values. There are now 174 "qualified" applicants; that is, every applicant is included in the count because the criteria range is empty. Click the down arrow in the Name box and select Bilingual, so that you are positioned within the criteria range. Type Yes. Click the down arrow in the Name box and select Database. Pull down the Data menu, click Filter, and then click Advanced Filter. Click the option button to filter the list in place, enter Database and Criteria as the list range and criteria range, then click OK. Press Ctrl+Home to move to cell A1. Click the Stop Recording button. You should see 13 qualified applicants.

   d. Open the VBA editor, and locate the macro you just created. Replace the statement that assigns Yes to the cell range Bilingual with an InputBox statement to prompt the user for an entry. Return to Excel; click the button to Show All Applicants, then run the Bilingual macro to test it. Enter No when prompted. You should see 161 applicants.

   e. Expand the Search macro to prompt for the other criteria one at a time, then assign the macro to a command button. (Your macro should contain an If statement to test the value in E5 and then display a message if there are no qualified applicants.) Use the completed macro to search for bilingual applicants for the Director position who require a salary less than $75,000. Print this worksheet. Print the module containing the Search macro.

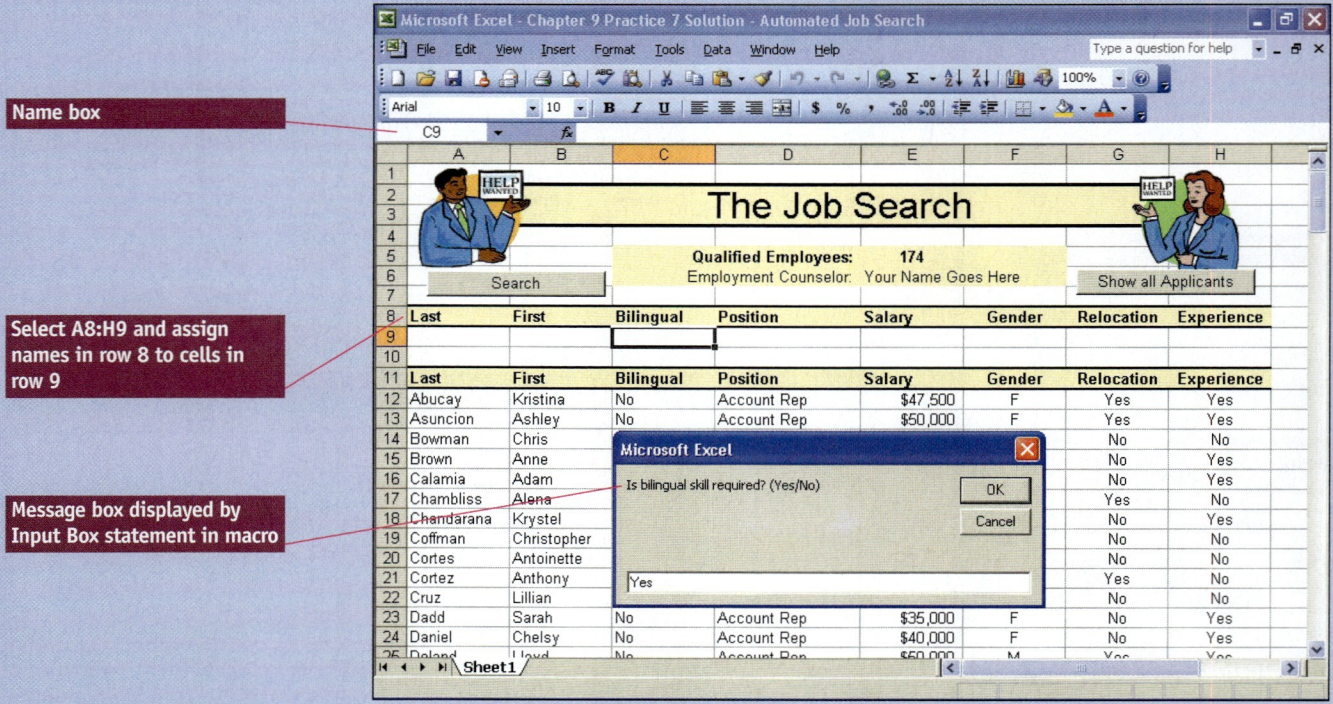

FIGURE 9.17 The Automated Job Search (exercise 7)

practice exercises

8. **Sales Analysis:** The workbook in Figure 9.18 displays selected sales records from a database that contains approximately 750 records from last year. The ShowAllRecords macro is already in the workbook; your job is to create the SelectRecords macro, which prompts you for the sales criteria, then it filters the list to display the selected records.

   a. Open the *Chapter 9 Practice 8—Sales* workbook; a set of criteria have been previously entered, and the appropriate records are displayed.

   b. Pull down the Tools menu, click macro, click Record New Macro, and enter SelectRecords as the macro name. Click OK to start recording. Click the down arrow in the Name box, select CriteriaValues (the range names have been defined for you), and then press the Del key to clear the criteria values. (The summary statistics indicate 757 records, but the list still shows the records for Milgrom.) Click the down arrow in the Name box, select Salesperson, type Davis, and press Enter. (The summary statistics now reflect Davis, but the displayed records continue to show Milgrom.)

   c. Click the down arrow in the Name box and select Database. Pull down the Data menu, click Filter, then click Advanced Filter. Click the option button to filter the list in place, enter Database and Criteria as the list range and criteria range, then click OK. Press Ctrl+Home to move to cell A1. Click the Stop Recording button. The filtered list shows only Davis' records.

   d. Open the VBA editor and locate the macro you just created. Replace the statement that assigns Davis to the cell range Salesperson with an InputBox statement to prompt the user for an entry. Return to Excel; click the button to Show All Records, then run the SelectRecords macro to test it. Enter King as the sales person. You should see 118 records.

   e. Expand the SelectRecords macro to prompt for the other criteria one at a time, then assign the macro to a command button. Your macro should contain an If statement to test the value in C8 (which has the range name Number_Of_Transactions) and then display a message if there are no records that meet the search criteria. Use the completed macro to display the records in Figure 9.18. Print this worksheet. Print the module containing the SelectRecords macro as well.

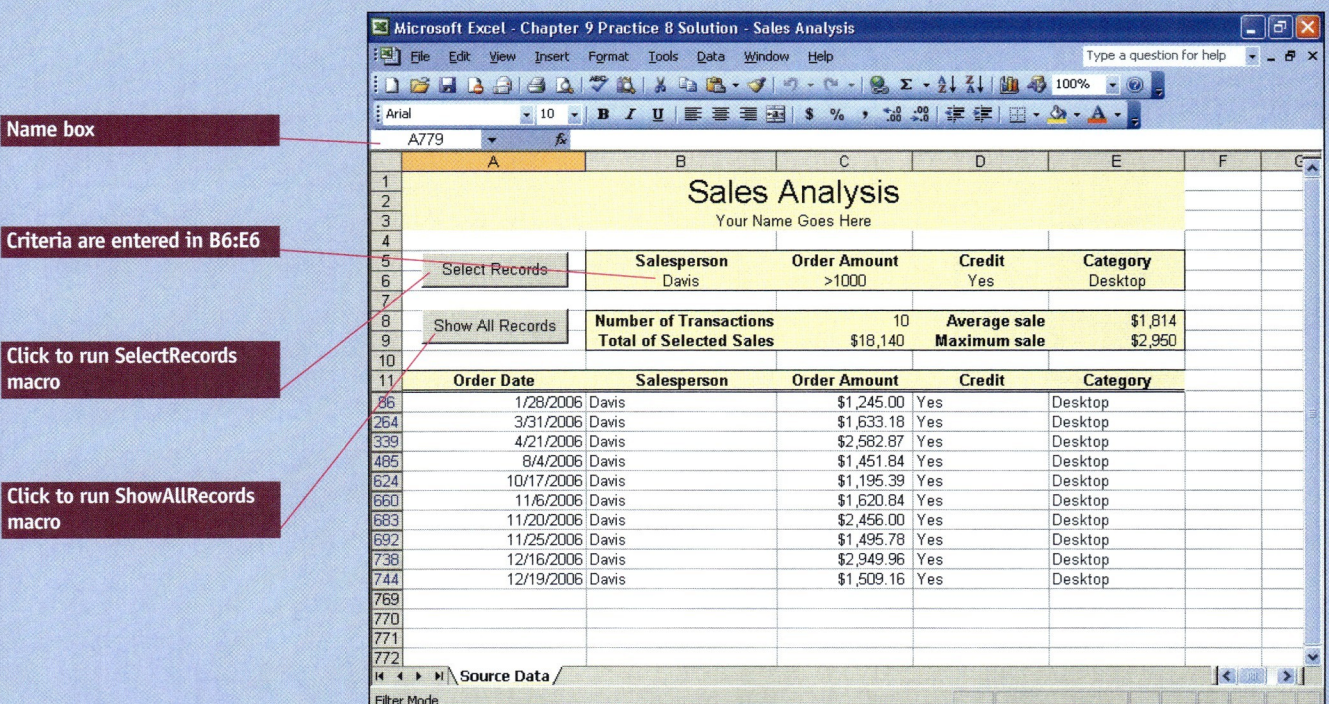

FIGURE 9.18 Sales Analysis (exercise 8)

MICROSOFT OFFICE EXCEL 2003 REVISED 511

practice exercises

9. **Consumer Loans:** Figure 9.19 displays a worksheet containing hypothetical data for a series of consumer loans. The associated workbook also contains four macros: to select loans by type, date, and amount; to clear the associated criteria range and display all loans; to highlight the mortgages in red within the complete list of loans and show the summary statistics for mortgages only; and finally, to remove the highlighting and reset the summary statistics to include all records. We have already created the ShowAllLoans and ClearColor macros for you. Your assignment is to create the remaining two macros. Proceed as follows:

   a. Open the *Chapter 9 Practice 9* workbook in the Exploring Excel folder. Use the concepts from the third and fourth hands-on exercises to create the macro to display loans by type, date, and amount. The user is to be prompted for each parameter. The macro should be written to use the range names that have been defined within the workbook rather than specific cell references. End the macro by selecting cell A1 and displaying the message in Figure 9.19. Assign the macro to a command button.

   b. Use the concepts from the fifth hands-on exercise to create the macro to highlight the mortgages within the complete list of loans, and further to set the criteria range so that the summary statistics for only the mortgages are displayed. (*Hint:* The first statement of this macro should be ShowAllLoans, which will execute the existing macro of that name.) Assign the macro to a command button.

   c. Click the button to run the HighlightMortgages macro. You should see all of the mortgage loans in red. Now click the button to run the LoansByTypeDateandAmount macro. Do not enter a loan type in response to the first prompt (to display loans of all types). Specify a start date after 9/20/2002 and a loan amount less than $100,000. You should see the loans in Figure 9.19.

   d. Print the completed worksheet for your instructor. Use the Page Setup command to be sure the entire worksheet fits on one page. Print the worksheet a second time to show the cell formulas.

   e. Print the VBA module that contains all four procedures. Add a cover sheet to complete the assignment.

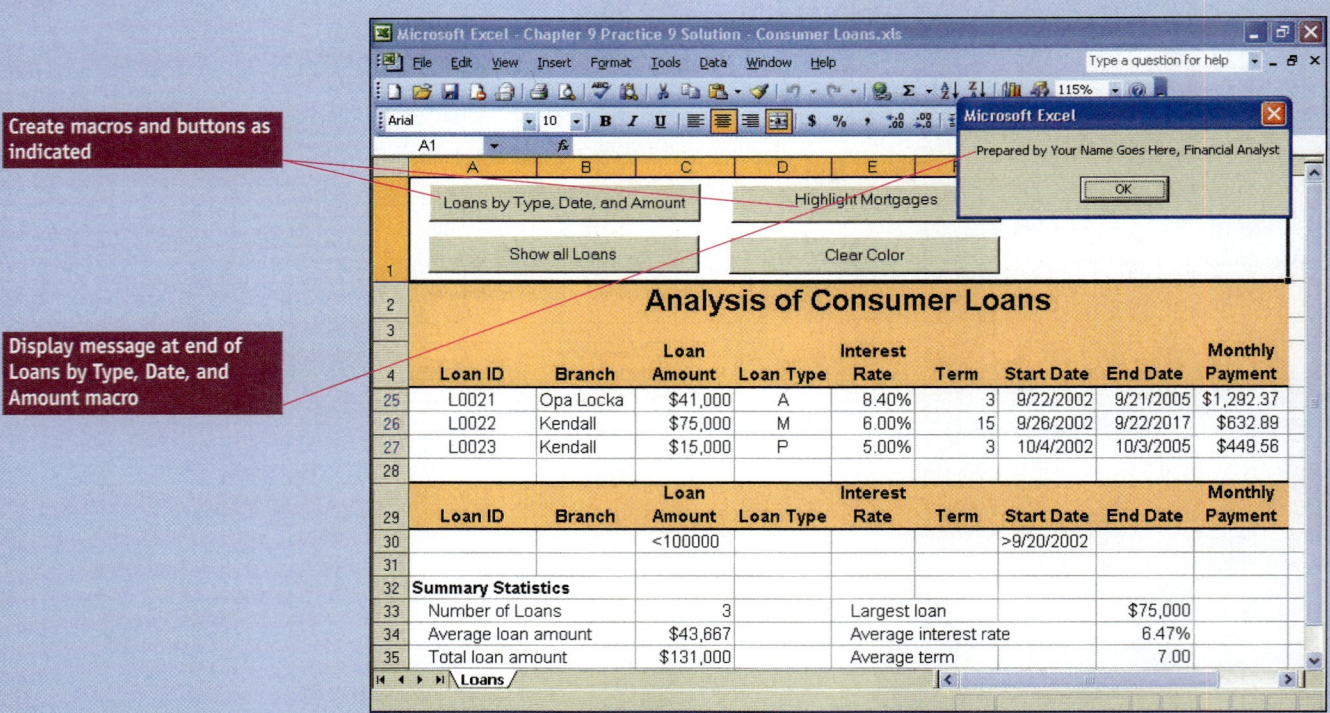

FIGURE 9.19 Consumer Loans (exercise 9)

practice exercises

10. **Create a Custom Function:** The workbook in Figure 9.20 is a variation of an earlier exercise (*Chapter 8 Practice 8*) in which we demonstrated the power of string processing functions. In essence we used a combination of the Find, Left, Right, and Concatenate functions to convert incoming names in the form "Bob Grauer" to "Grauer, Bob". This exercise simplifies the conversion through VBA by creating a custom function; i.e., all the user has to do is click in a cell and enter the custom function =ConvertName("John Doe") to display "Doe, John" in the associated cell. Proceed as follows:

   a. Open the partially completed *Chapter 9 Practice 10—Create a Custom Function* workbook. The names in your worksheet appear in a *different order* than in Figure 9.20; that is, your worksheet is in sequence by first name. In addition, "Bob Grauer" does not appear in your worksheet. Click in cell A12 and add your name in the form "First Name Last Name".

   b. Copy the formulas in cells B11:E11 to cells B12:E12. Use the information displayed at the bottom of the worksheet to see how the functions work. Change the font color in row 12 to red. Boldface the row.

   c. Open the Visual Basic editor. Pull down the Insert menu, click Module to insert a new module, then enter the VBA code in Figure 9.20 to create a new function called CustomName. The function has one argument (the incoming name). The VBA statements in the function correspond to the Excel string processing functions in the worksheet. (The VBA InStr and Len functions correspond to the Excel Find and Length functions, respectively.) Save the workbook.

   d. Return to Excel. Click in cell F7 and enter the formula =ConvertName(A7), then copy this formula to the remaining rows in the worksheet. (You can also pull down the Insert menu, click Function, choose User Defined as the category, and insert the function from the dialog box.) Select a single cell in column F, then click the Sort Ascending button to arrange the names alphabetically.

   e. Print the completed worksheet to show both displayed values and cell formulas. Print the VBA module. Submit all three pages to your instructor.

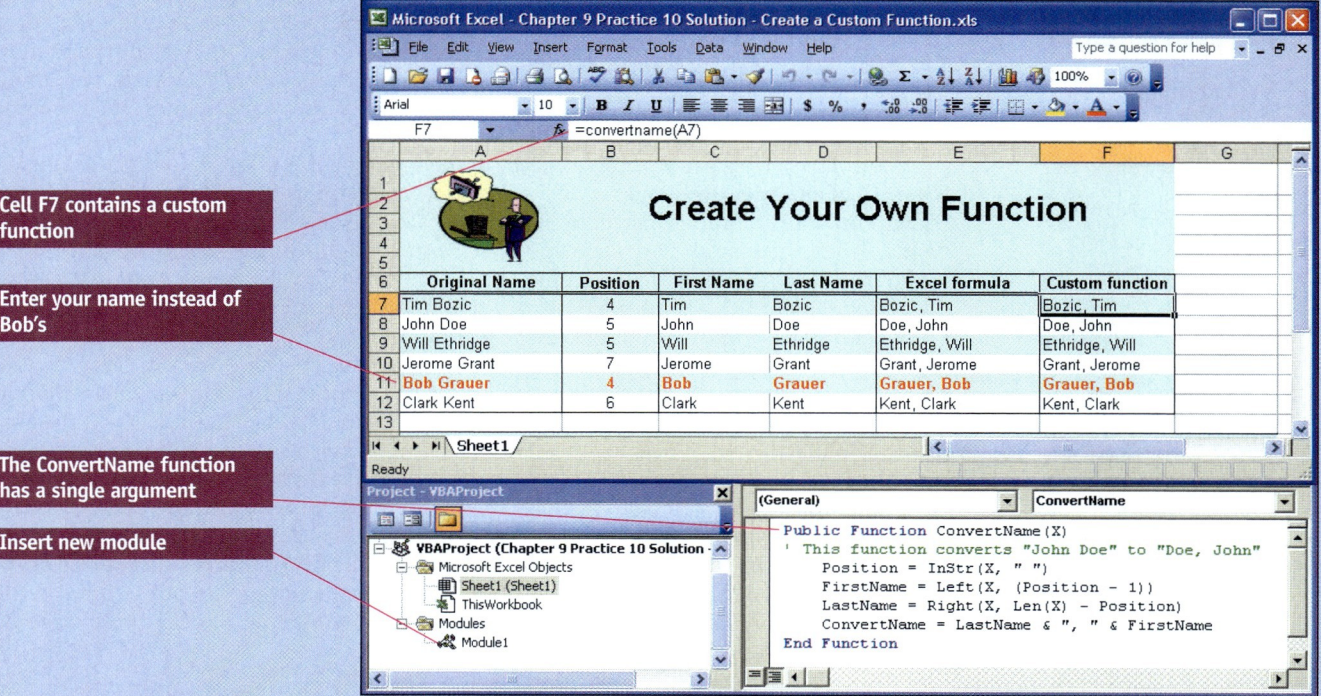

FIGURE 9.20 Create a Custom Function (exercise 10)

MINI CASES

Microsoft Word

Do you use Microsoft Word on a regular basis? Are there certain tasks that you do repeatedly, whether in the same document or in a series of different documents? If so, you would do well to explore the macro capabilities within Microsoft Word. How are these capabilities similar to Excel's? How do they differ?

Starting Up

Your instructor is very impressed with the various Excel workbooks and associated macros that you have created. He would like you to take the automation process one step further and simplify the way in which Excel is started and the workbook is loaded. The problem is open ended, and there are many different approaches. You might, for example, create a shortcut on the desktop to open the workbook. You might also explore the use of the Startup folder in Microsoft Excel.

Extending Excel Macros through VBA

You do not have to know VBA to create Excel macros, but knowledge of VBA will help you to create better macros. VBA is accessible from all major applications in Microsoft Office, so that anything you learn in one application is also applicable to other applications. The VBA syntax is identical. Locate the VBA primer that appears at the end of this text, study the basic statements it contains, and complete the associated hands-on exercises. Write a short note to your instructor that describes similarities and differences from one Office application to the next.

Chapter Recap—The Sleepy Showroom

Simon Key opened the Sleepy Showroom 30 years ago with a limited selection of twin and full-sized mattresses from one vendor. Today he offers a complete product line (twin, full, queen, and king-sized mattresses) in a variety of styles and prices from four different vendors. Simon prides himself on his huge selection; for example, he offers 20 different mattresses from just the Heavenly Sleep Company. The business is very profitable, yet Simon believes he has too many vendors and too many choices from each vendor. He has come to you for advice.

Simon has given you complete access to the financial information for his business in the form of an Excel workbook, which contains detailed information for every item in the showroom. The workbook also contains a criteria range and two database functions that display the units sold and corresponding profit for indicated criteria. The Sleep Wonderfully product line, for example, accounted for only 38% of the units sold, yet it generated 69% of the total profit. You can change the criteria to see similar statistics for other vendors and/or other parameters (e.g., mattress size).

Your assignment is to review the chapter, open the *Chapter 9 Ending Case Study— The Sleepy Showroom* workbook, and create a series of four macros that will enable Simon to change the criteria to see the results for any vendor and/or any size mattress. The first macro should prompt Simon for the vendor and mattress, enter these values within the criteria range, and then filter the list to display only those items that match the indicated criteria. The second macro should clear the criteria range and display the entire list. The third and fourth macros should display the top ten items according to the percent of the total profit and the number of units sold, respectively. All of your macros should use range names, as opposed to specific cell references. (The range names are already defined in the workbook.) Simon has promised you the king-sized bed of your choice and a sizeable bonus if you can improve his bottom line.

CHAPTER 10

A Professional Application: An Enhanced Amortization Schedule

OBJECTIVES

After reading this chapter you will:

1. Explain the importance of data validation in a spreadsheet.
2. Describe the YEAR, MONTH, DAY, and DATE FUNCTIONS.
3. Describe the PMT, IPMT, and PPMT functions.
4. Describe the logical functions AND and OR.
5. Describe the Excel object model.
6. Use the macro recorder to "jump-start" a VBA procedure.
7. Distinguish between event and general procedures.
8. Develop a custom toolbar and attach it to a workbook.
9. Set the print area in a worksheet.
10. Create a user form.
11. Explain how pseudocode is used to develop procedures.

hands-on exercises

1. AMORTIZATION WORKBOOK
   Input: Amortization Schedule
   Output: Amortization Schedule Solution

2. EXPLORING VBA SYNTAX
   Input: Amortization Schedule Solution (from exercise 1)
   Output: Amortization Schedule Solution (additional modifications)

3. EVENT PROCEDURES
   Input: Amortization Schedule Solution (from exercise 2)
   Output: Amortization Schedule Solution (additional modifications)

4. OPTIONAL PAYMENTS
   Input: Amortization Schedule Solution (from exercise 3)
   Output: Amortization Schedule Solution (additional modifications)

CASE STUDY
RETIREMENT PLANNING

Bruce Boundy, your mentor at a financial services firm, has given you a sophisticated worksheet that is used with prospective clients to encourage periodic saving through retirement plans such as a 401K or Roth IRA. The worksheet uses the FV (Future Value) function to forecast the amount of money an individual will have at retirement based on a series of uniform payments during his or her working life. Bruce has asked you to explore the workbook to learn its features and to see the effects of compound interest over time.

The worksheet has an input area in which the user enters four values: the date the plan began (i.e., when contributions started or will start); the number of years the individual plans to contribute (from inception of the plan until retirement); the annual contribution; and the expected rate of return. After all four values have been entered, the summary area displays the projected amount at retirement, the total the individual contributed, and the total that was generated through these savings. The workbook also contains a custom toolbar whereby the user can enter the desired amount at retirement, then vary either the annual contribution or the number of years contributing to reach that goal (if, indeed, the goal is feasible). ■

Your assignment is to read the chapter, noting the various ways in which VBA can be used to enhance an Excel workbook. You will then open the *Chapter 10 Case Study—Retirement Planning* workbook, enter a specific set of parameters for a hypothetical retirement plan of your own, then print the completed worksheet. Explore the workbook to see what other subtle features are built in; for example, the IF function is used throughout the worksheet to print only as many rows as there are years in the forecast, while conditional formatting is used to shade only those rows that do appear. Print the cell formulas, the macros in Module 1, and the Open and Close event procedures in preparation for a class discussion that reviews the entire workbook.

APPLICATION DEVELOPMENT

Any application originates with the client or end user. He or she has a need and is willing to pay a developer to fulfill that need. The developer in turn goes through an iterative process that presents the client with multiple versions of the application, until the finished application is delivered. The key to a successful application is a systematic approach that includes continual testing and interaction between the client and the developer. We suggest these basic steps, which provide a broad outline of the chapter:

1. Determine what the application is to accomplish
2. Design the user interface (the worksheet)
3. Develop the spreadsheet
4. Test and debug the spreadsheet
5. Add automation (macros and VBA procedures) as necessary
6. Test and debug the completed application

The first (and perhaps most important) step is to determine precisely what the application is to accomplish. The client has an idea of his or her requirements, and the developer can make suggestions as to the additional functionality that can be included. The example in this chapter is that of a payment *(amortization)* schedule for a loan, based on parameters supplied by the end user. The client has further specified that he wants to see the scheduled date of each payment, how much of each payment goes toward interest, and how much goes toward principal. He also wants the ability to include optional (extra) payments of principal that will shorten the time required to pay off the loan.

Data validation is an implied requirement of any application, something the developer should bring to the attention of the client if the client does not request it independently. Every input parameter should be checked so that the end results will make sense. The end user should be prevented, for example, from entering a term (more than 30 years) that exceeds the maximum number of possible payments. The user might also be cautioned against (but not prevented from) entering an inappropriate (exorbitant) interest rate. A good worksheet will anticipate errors the user may make during data entry and prevent those errors from occurring.

The application should be flexible, visually appealing, easy to use, and bulletproof. A flexible worksheet enables the user to enter parameters in a clearly defined input area, then bases all of its formulas on those parameters, so that any change in the input automatically changes the body of the worksheet. A worksheet should also be visually appealing and include any logo or other formatting requirements of the client.

The completed application should be easy to use and enable the end user to accomplish tasks that he or she would not otherwise be able to do. The specifications may call for macros or VBA procedures to automate command sequences that are executed from custom toolbars or menus. A bulletproof application will work correctly with any set of input parameters and will prevent the display of zero values when they are not appropriate. The application should also insulate itself from the nontechnical user by protecting the formulas in the worksheet so that they cannot be accidentally (or otherwise) altered or deleted.

Continual testing and debugging are essential. The developer has to ensure that the formulas within the worksheet are correct, and further that any and all VBA procedures are also correct. This is an iterative process that occurs throughout the development cycle. All of these requirements should be clearly specified in advance, after which both client and developer should sign a written statement of the intended specifications and schedule. The end result is a polished application that is suitable for general distribution.

The Enhanced Amortization Schedule

The worksheet in Figure 10.1 is similar to (but different from) the amortization schedule that was developed in Chapter 6. We changed the formatting and clip art, but more significantly, we added functionality using Excel macros and VBA. Hence we will refer to this workbook as the *Enhanced Amortization Schedule* workbook to distinguish it from its predecessor.

The worksheet in Figure 10.1a displays the worksheet as data is being entered. One significant item is what you do *not* see—the payments in the body of the worksheet will not appear until all of the loan parameters have been entered, and further the worksheet will display and print only as many rows (payments) as are necessary. A 30-year loan, for example, requires 360 payments, whereas a 15-year loan takes only 180. Data validation is also built into the worksheet. For example, the worksheet will reject any loans greater than 30 years or any loans with artificially high interest rates.

Figure 10.1b displays the worksheet after the last required parameter has been entered. Only the first several payments are visible, but the information in these rows is indicative of the underlying function. The date of each payment, for example, occurs on the 16th of each month, which is consistent with the specified date of the first payment within the input area. This calculation is accomplished through various date functions and is discussed later in the chapter.

The worksheet also divides the monthly payment of $665.30 into two components, interest and principal. The outstanding balance on the loan is reduced each month by the amount of the payment that went toward principal. Thus, the amount of the next payment that goes toward interest decreases (if only by pennies initially), while the amount that goes toward principal increases.

The summary information in the upper-right portion of the worksheet indicates a total of 360 scheduled payments, which is what you would expect for a 30-year loan. The worksheet also displays the normal payoff date of 2/16/2033, which occurs after the 360th payment has been made. Note, too, that the total interest on the loan is more than $139,000, which is more than the amount of the actual loan.

The client also requested the ability to include additional payments toward principal, which is reflected in Figure 10.1c. Here we see that a constant (optional) payment of $100 a month will reduce the total interest over the life of the loan to just over $89,000 (a savings of more than $50,000). The loan is paid off after 247 payments on September 16, 2023, almost 10 years earlier than the original loan. The borrower has paid $24,700 (247 payments of $100 each) in early payments, but this is not truly "additional" money. It is principal that would have been paid eventually during the original 30-year schedule. The borrower has simply elected to make these payments earlier than necessary in order to reduce the total interest.

Figure 10.1d displays some of the underlying formulas and may appear unduly complicated. We prefer to say, however, that these formulas add functionality, as opposed to complexity. Consider, for example, the ***AND function***, =AND(C4>0, C5>0,C6>0,C7>0), that appears in cell D6. The AND function returns one of two values, true or false. It is considered true if all of its arguments are true, and false otherwise. In this example the AND function is checking the values in cells C4 through C7, and it requires that each of these entries be greater than zero if the function is to be true. In other words, we can check the value in cell D6 (which has been assigned the name DataEntered) to determine if all of the required parameters have been supplied, and if so, we can display these values in the body of the worksheet.

Cell A14 contains the formula =IF(DataEntered, 1,0). Recall that the IF function has three arguments—a condition that is evaluated as true or false, the value if the condition is true, and the value if the condition is false. Thus, the number of the first payment will be 1 if all parameters have been entered, and zero otherwise. (The Options command has been set to hide zero values in the spreadsheet.) All of the other formulas in the worksheet are based on the value in cell A14, which in turn allows us to display only as many rows (payments) as are necessary.

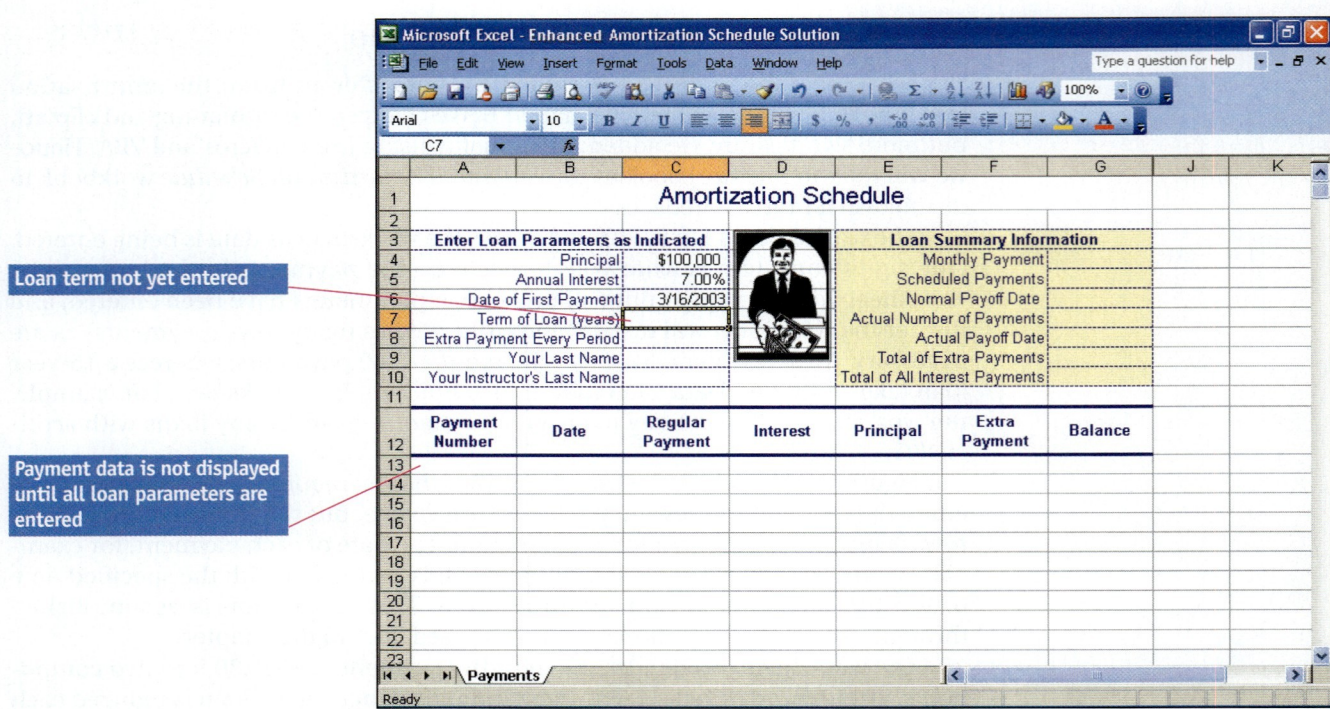

(a) Data Entry

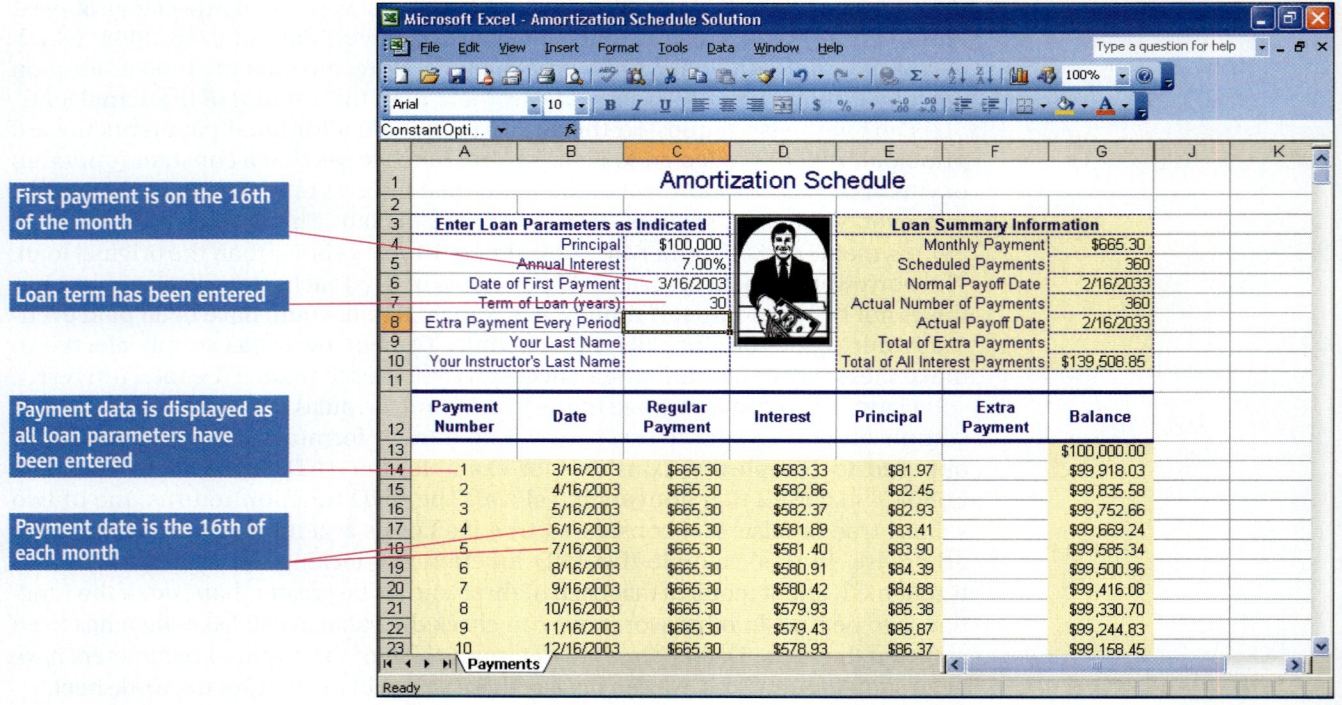

(b) 30-year Mortgage

FIGURE 10.1 The Enhanced Amortization Schedule Workbook

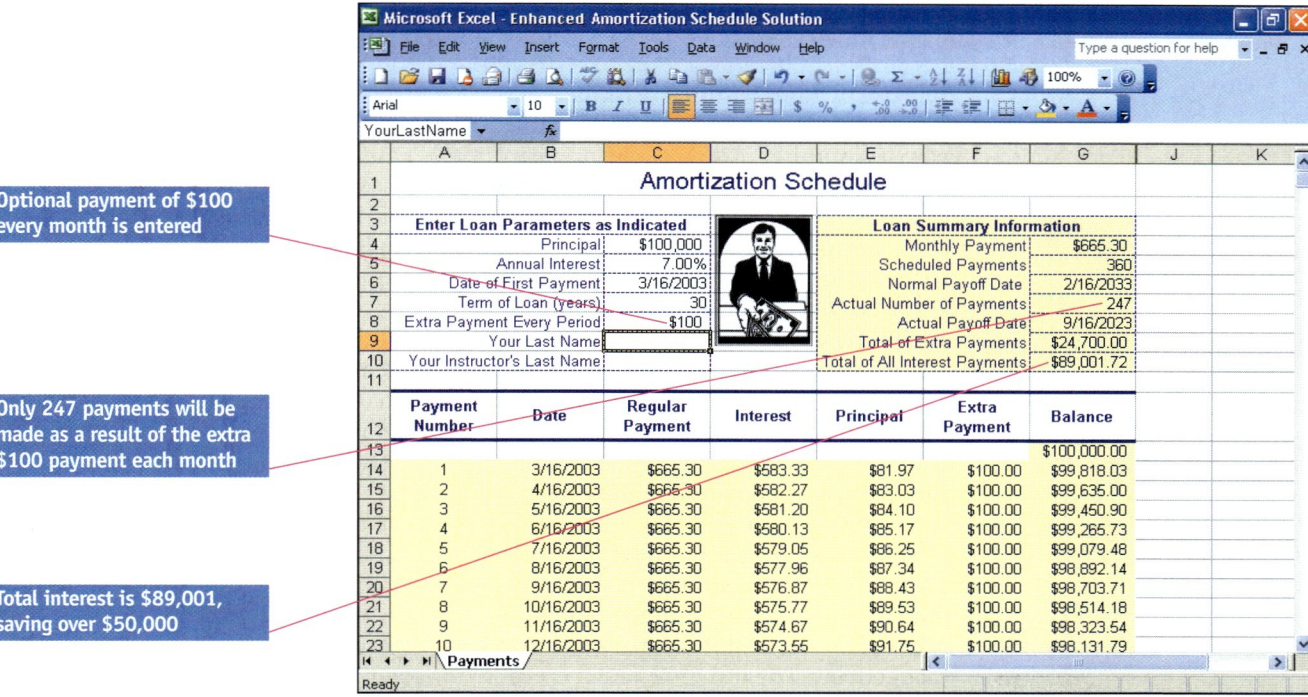

(c) Optional Extra Payment

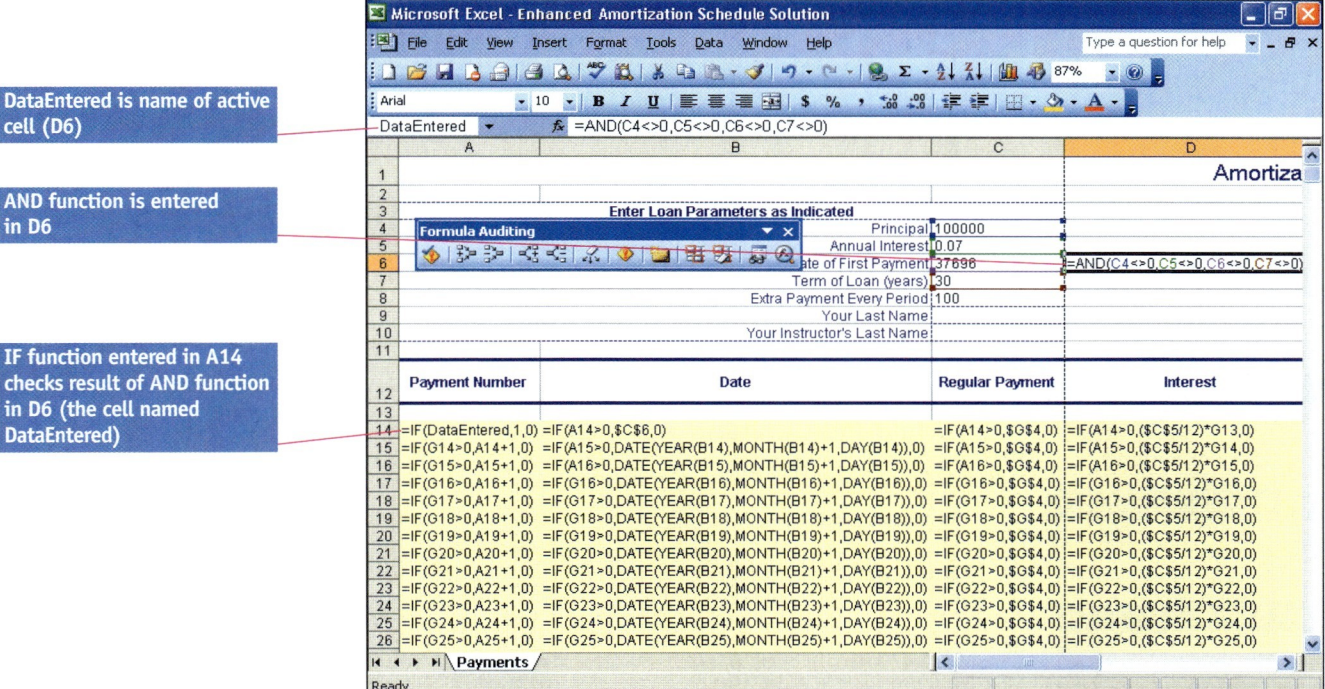

(d) Partial Cell Formulas

FIGURE 10.1 The Enhanced Amortization Schedule Workbook (*continued*)

DATE FUNCTIONS

The use of dates within a worksheet has been discussed at various points in the text. Recall that Excel stores a date as an integer (serial number) equivalent to the elapsed number of days since January 1, 1900. Thus, January 1, 1900, is stored as the number 1; January 2, 1900, as the number 2; and so on. The fact that dates are stored as integer numbers enables you to perform date arithmetic as illustrated in the age calculation in Figure 10.2. To determine an individual's age, we take the (integer) value of today's date, subtract the birth date, and then divide the result by 365. (The **TODAY function** always returns today's date and is updated automatically each time you open the workbook.)

It's easy enough to determine tomorrow's date because all you have to do is add one to the integer value of today's date. What if, however, you want to determine next month's date? Do you add 30 or 31? And what if today's date is February 15? Do you add 28 or 29 to display March 15? Fortunately, Excel includes additional date functions that accomplish these tasks very easily.

The **DATE function** has three arguments: year, month, and day. The cell formula in cell B5, for example, is =DATE(1982,3,16), and it displays the date as March 16, 1982, through the appropriate formatting command. (We could have entered the date directly, but we wanted to illustrate the Date function.) Excel also has the **DAY, MONTH**, and **YEAR functions** that return the numeric day, month, and year, respectively. The function =MONTH(B3), for example, returns the numeric month of the date in cell B3. In similar fashion, =MONTH(B3)+1 adds one to the numeric month. Excel is smart enough to know that if today's date is sometime in December, next month will occur in January.

Look now at the cell formulas for cells B11 and B13 that display next month's date and next year's date, respectively. These formulas may have seemed complex initially, but on closer inspection are easy to understand. The various date functions are used in the following exercise to determine the payment schedule.

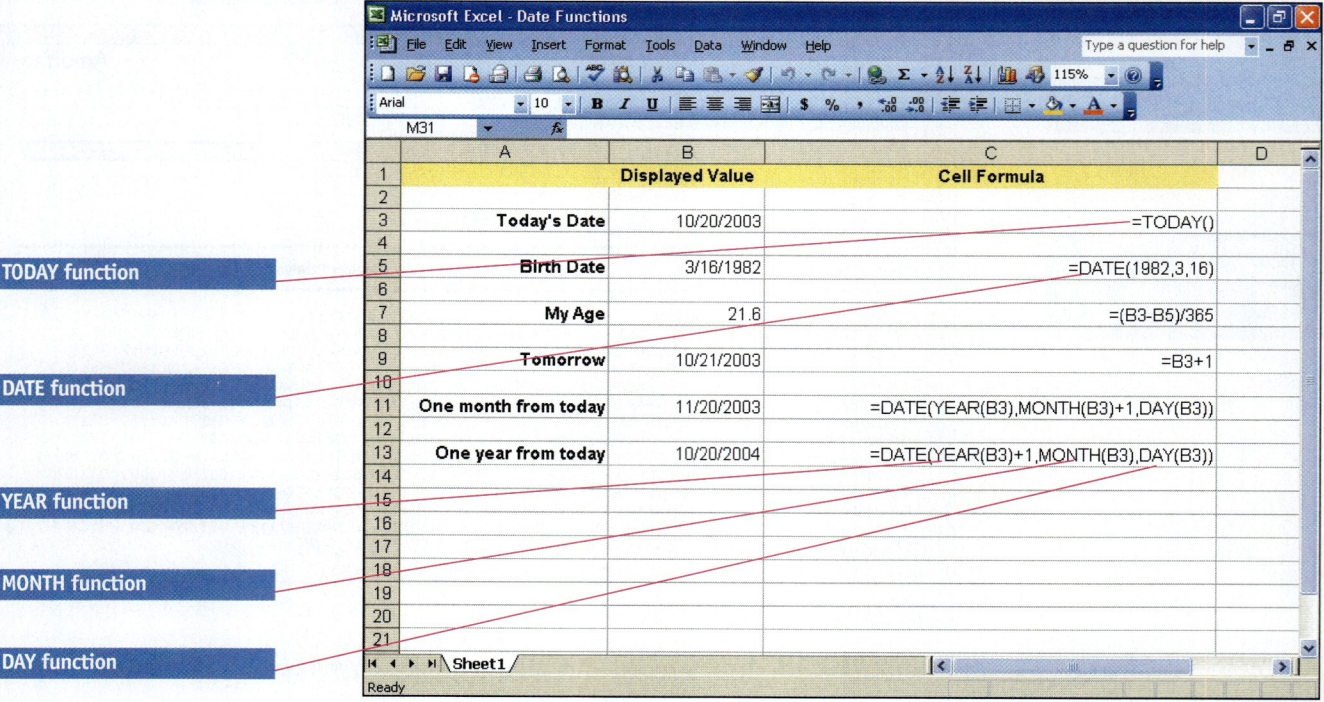

FIGURE 10.2 Date Functions

hands-on exercise

1 The Enhanced Amortization Schedule Workbook

Objective Explore the enhanced amortization schedule workbook with respect to data validation, cell protection, optional extra payments, and a variable print area. Use Figure 10.3 as a guide in the exercise.

Step 1: **Data Entry and Validation**

- Start Excel. Open the **Enhanced Amortization Schedule workbook** in the **Exploring Excel folder**. Click the button to **Enable macros**. (This exercise, however, accomplishes all of its tasks without the use of macros.)

- Save the workbook as **Enhanced Amortization Schedule Solution** so that you can return to the original workbook if necessary. Click in **cell C4**. Enter **$100,000** and press **Enter**.

- Enter **.09** as the interest rate, which in turn displays the message box in Figure 10.3a. Click **No**, then enter **.07** as the interest rate. This time the value is accepted, and you see 7.00% in cell B5.

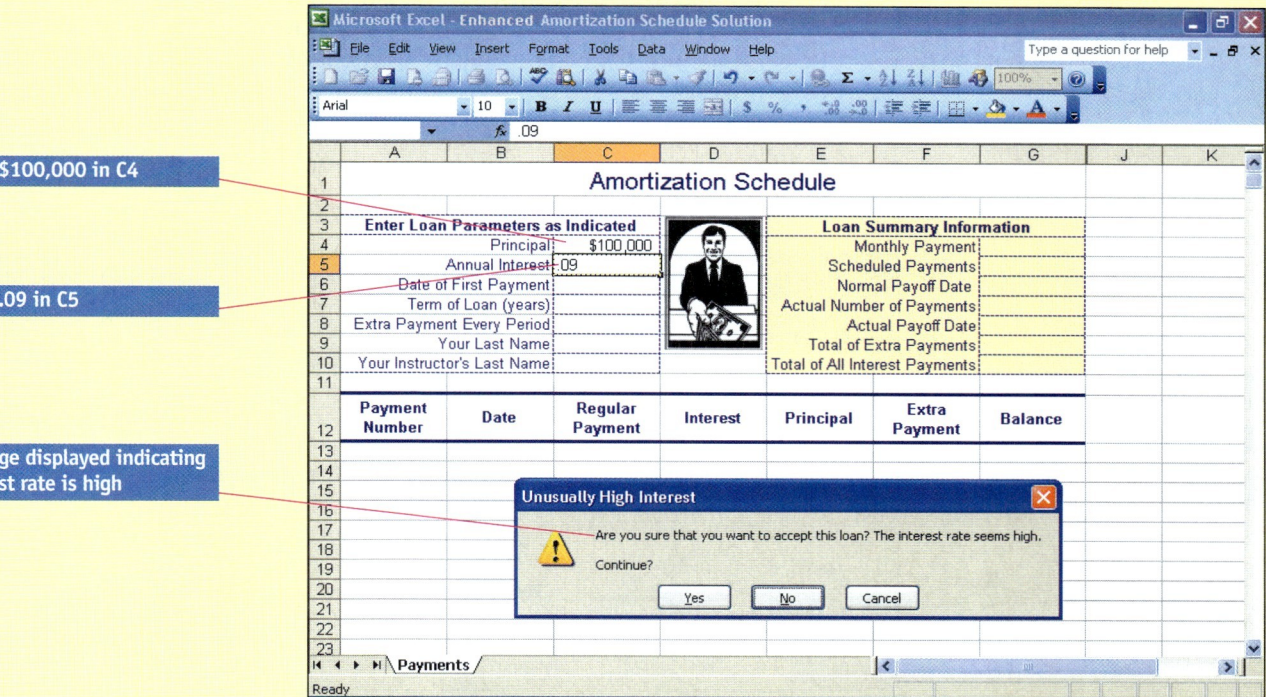

(a) Data Entry and Validation (step 1)

FIGURE 10.3 Hands-on Exercise 1

DATA VALIDATION

The Data Validation command enables you to restrict the values that can be entered into a specific cell. Click in the cell where you want to impose validation, then pull down the Data menu, and click the Validation command to display the Data Validation dialog box. (The command is disabled if the worksheet is protected.)

Step 2: **A Protected Worksheet**

- Complete the entries in **cells C6 and C7** as shown in Figure 10.3b. Enter the date of the first payment so as to reflect the 15th of next month. (Your dates will differ from ours.) The monthly payments and summary information appear as soon as you complete the last required entry (the term of the loan).

- Click in **cell A1** and attempt to enter a new title for the worksheet. You will see a message box indicating that the cell is protected and that you cannot change its value. Click **OK** after you have read the message.

- Pull down the **Tools menu**, click the **Protection command**, and click the **Unprotect Sheet command** to unprotect the worksheet. (You are not prompted for a password because we protected the worksheet without a password.) The worksheet is now unprotected, and you have full access to all of its cells.

- Click the clip art to select the image and display the sizing handles. Click and drag any of the four corners to increase (decrease) the size of the clip art.

- The Picture toolbar should be displayed automatically. If not, right click the clip art and click the command to **Show Picture toolbar** as shown in Figure 10.3b. Experiment with the different tools:
  - Click the **Crop tool**, then click and drag the bottom border of the figure up to delete (crop) this part of the figure. Click the **Undo button**.
  - Click the **Rotate tool** to rotate the figure 90 degrees to the left. Click the **Undo button** to reverse the command.
  - Click the **Increase (Decrease) Brightness tool** to see the effect (if any).

- Click off the figure to deselect it and continue working. The Picture toolbar closes automatically. Save the workbook.

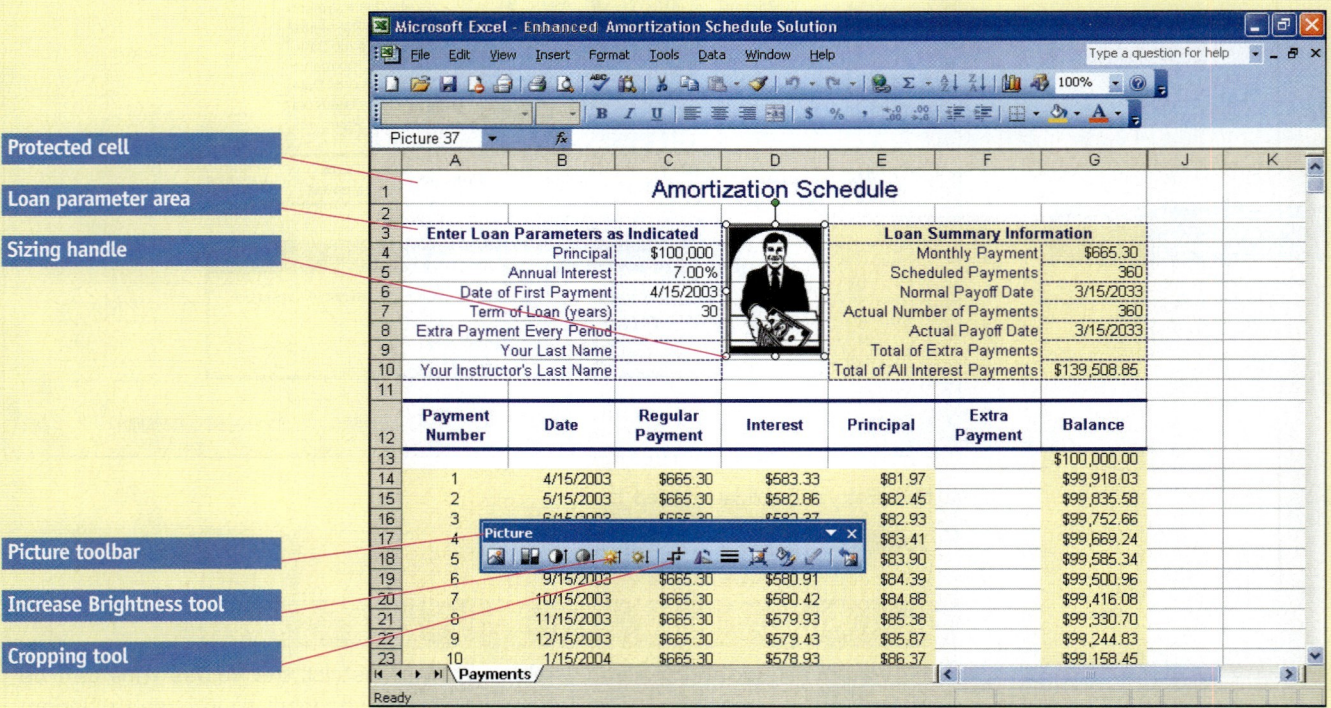

(b) A Protected Worksheet (step 2)

FIGURE 10.3 Hands-on Exercise 1 (*continued*)

Step 3: **The Logical AND Function**

- Click and drag the clip art image to the right as shown in Figure 10.3c. The displayed value in cell D6 is "TRUE", and the monthly payments and summary information are displayed in G4:G10.
- Click in **cell C7** and delete the term of the loan. The value in cell D6 changes to "FALSE", and the payments and summary information are no longer visible.
- Click the **Undo button** to restore the 30 in cell C7. The loan parameters are now complete, and the value of cell D6 returns to "TRUE".
- Click in **cell D6** and note the following:
  - The formula bar contains a logical AND function with four arguments, all of which have to be true for the function to be true. In other words, data has to be entered in cells C4, C5, C6, and C7 for the value in cell D6 to be true.
  - The Name box displays "DataEntered" to indicate that cell D6 is associated with this range name, which can be used in any worksheet formula.
- Click in **cell A14**, the cell containing the formula for the first payment. The IF function checks the value of the range name "DataEntered", and if that value is true, enters the number 1 for the payment number. If the value is false, however, zero is entered for the payment number. (Zero values are not displayed.)
- Click and drag the clip art image back to its original place in the worksheet.

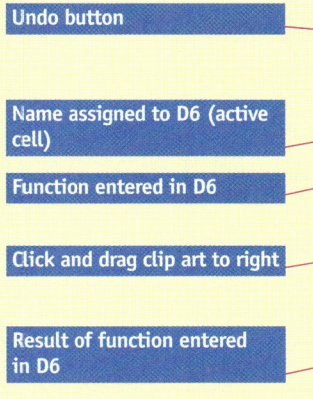
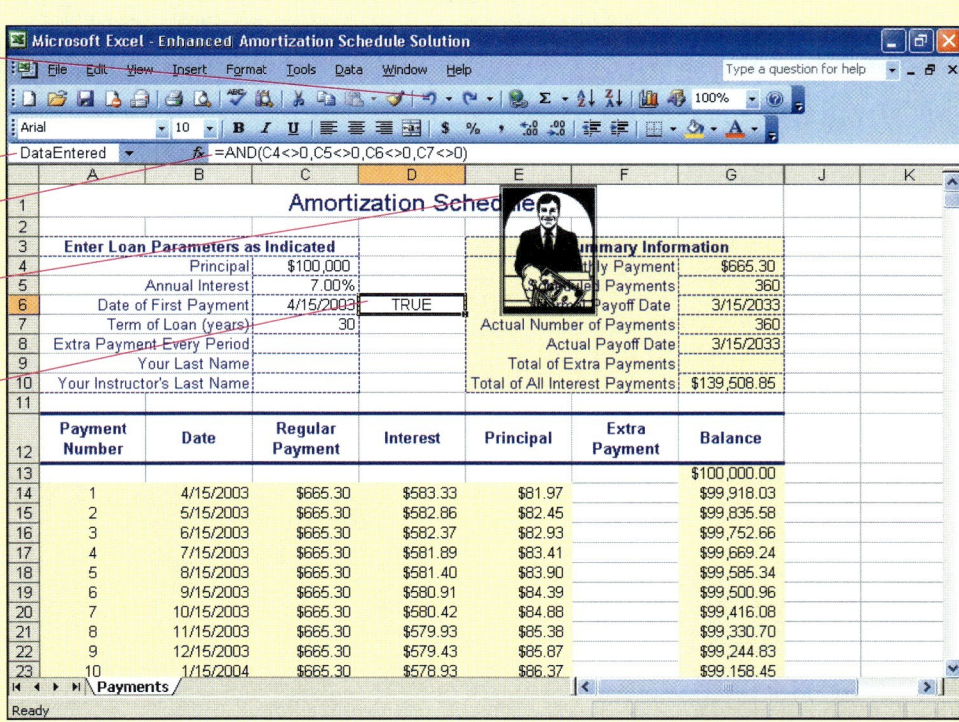

(c) The Logical AND Function (step 3)

FIGURE 10.3 Hands-on Exercise 1 (*continued*)

SUPPRESS ZERO VALUES

Many spreadsheets are visually enhanced by suppressing the display of zero values. The amortization worksheet, for example, contains formulas to compute 360 monthly loan payments, but it displays the entries for only those cells with nonzero values. Pull down the Tools menu, click the Options command, click the View tab, and clear the box for Zero values. Click OK.

Step 4: **Check the Calculations**

- The formulas in columns D and E to compute the portion of each payment towards interest and principal, respectively, are not trivial. It is important, therefore, to verify the results through alternate calculations.

- Click and drag to select **columns G and J**. (Columns H and I are not visible because they are currently hidden.) Pull down the **Format menu**, click the **Column command**, then click **Unhide** to display columns H and I, as shown in Figure 10.3d.

- Click in **cell H14** to examine the amount of the first payment that goes toward interest. The displayed value of $583.33 is obtained through the IPMT function and matches the amount in cell D14.

- Click in **cell I14** to examine the amount of the first payment that goes toward principal. The displayed value of $81.97 is obtained through the PPMT function and matches the amount in cell E14.

- Click and drag the column headings to select **columns H and I**. Pull down the **Format menu**, click the **Column command**, then click **Hide** to suppress these columns. Save the workbook.

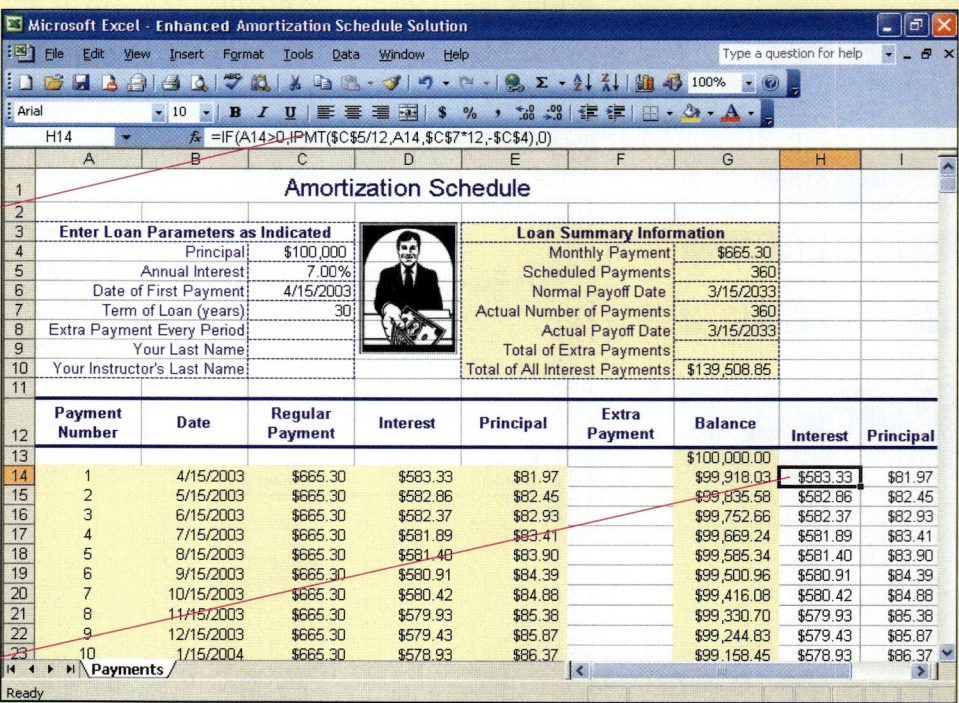

(d) Check the Calculations (step 4)

FIGURE 10.3 Hands-on Exercise 1 (*continued*)

THE IPMT AND PPMT FUNCTIONS

The IPMT and PPMT functions compute the portion of a monthly payment that goes toward interest and principal, respectively. These functions refer to the original principal and cannot accommodate extra payments toward principal. Hence, they could not be used in the body of the worksheet, but serve only to validate that the formulas in columns D and E are correct. These formulas are for the developer to check his or her work, not the user.

Step 5: **What If?**

- Examine the information in the summary area of the worksheet. The total interest for the 30-year loan is found in cell G10 and is equal to $139,508.

- Change the term of the loan to **15 years**, and the interest decreases to $61,789, a savings of almost $80,000. Note, too, that the payoff date is now 15 years (less one month, but 180 payments) from the initial payment.

- Change the starting date to the first of next month as shown in Figure 10.3e. The payoff date changes, as do the dates for the individual payments.

- Click in **cell C8** and enter **$100** as an optional extra payment you hope to make each month toward principal. The payoff date, actual number of payments, and total interest decrease further.

- Enter **your last name** and **your instructor's last name** in **cells C9 and C10**.

- Pull down the **Tools menu**, click the **Protection command**, and click the **Protect Sheet command** to protect the worksheet. Leave the password blank. Click **OK**.

- Save the workbook.

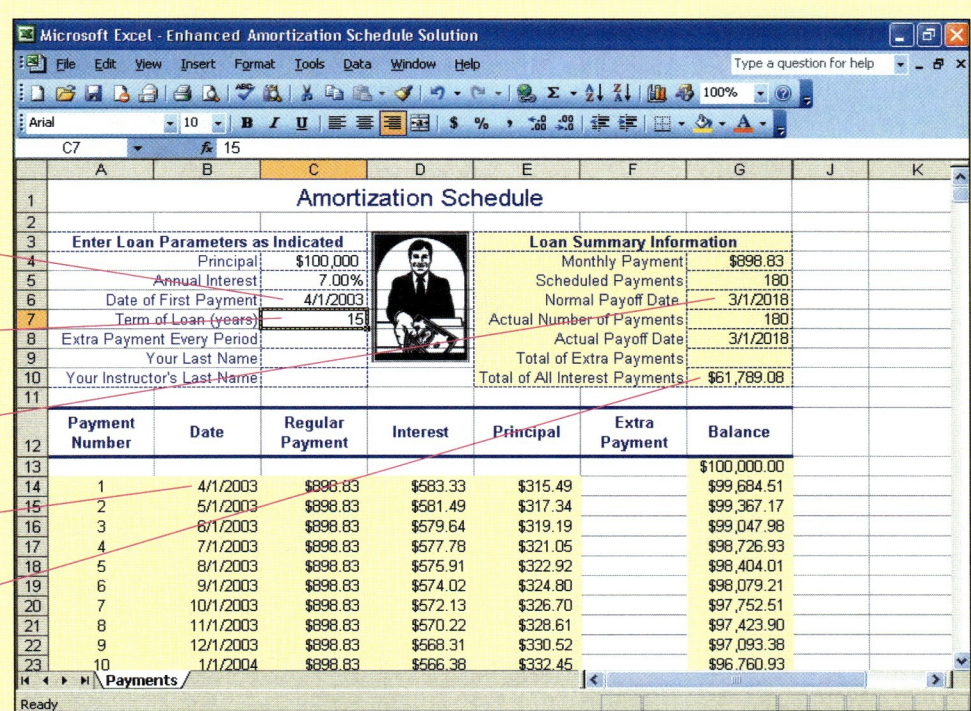

(e) What If? (step 5)

FIGURE 10.3 Hands-on Exercise 1 (*continued*)

PROTECTING A WORKSHEET

Protecting a worksheet is a two-step process. First, you unlock all of the cells that are subject to change, then you protect the worksheet. Select the cell(s) you want to unlock, pull down the Format menu, click the Cells command, then select the Protection tab in the Format Cells dialog box. Clear the Locked check box. To protect the worksheet, pull down the Tools menu, click Protection, then click the Protect Sheet command to display the Protect Sheet dialog box, where you can enter a password. *Be careful, because once you password-protect a worksheet, you cannot unprotect it without the password.*

Step 6: **The Print Preview Command**

- Click the **Print Preview button** to see how your worksheet will appear when it is printed, as shown in Figure 10.3f. Click the **Zoom button**, if necessary, so that you see the worksheet more easily.

- Look at the status bar and note that the entire worksheet requires three pages. Click the **Next button** on the Print Preview toolbar to view page two of the printout, which repeats the column headings, then begins with payment number 46. (You may see a different payment number, depending on your printer.)

- Click the **Next button** to move to page 3, which again repeats the payment headings and starts with payment 103 and continues to the last payment.

- Click the **Print button** to print the worksheet for your instructor. Click **OK** when you see the Print dialog box.

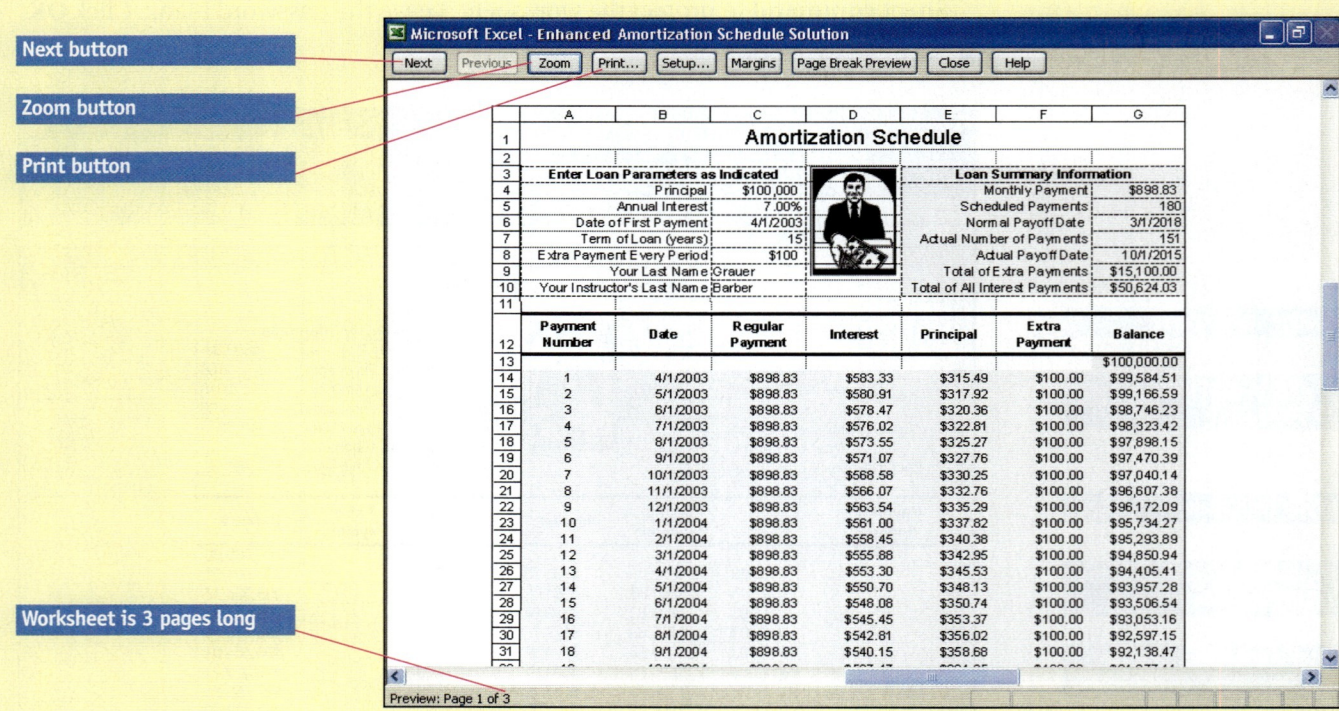

(f) The Print Preview Command (step 6)

FIGURE 10.3 Hands-on Exercise 1 (*continued*)

THE MULTIPLE-PAGE PRINTOUT—REPEATING ROWS AND COLUMNS

It is very helpful to repeat one or more rows and/or columns of a worksheet if the worksheet extends to several printed pages. Pull down the File menu and click the Page Setup command to display the Page Setup dialog box. Click the Sheet tab. Click in the Rows to repeat at top text box, then click and drag in the worksheet to select the row(s) you want to repeat. Click in the Columns to repeat at left text box, click and drag in the worksheet to select the columns, then click OK to accept the settings and close the dialog box. Use the Print Preview command to see the effect of these changes.

Step 7: **Print the Cell Formulas**

- We want you to print the cell formulas so that you will be able to study the worksheet in detail. We are going to change the term of the loan, however, so that the worksheet will take fewer pages.

- Click in **cell C7** and change the term of the loan to **1 year**. The displayed values will change, but the formulas remain constant. Press **Ctrl+~** (the ~ character appears immediately below the Esc key) to display cell formulas.

- Unprotect the worksheet. Click and drag the column borders to see the entire formula within a cell as shown in Figure 10.3g.

- Click the **Print Preview button**. The worksheet should require three pages. All of the rows fit on one page, but the wider columns spill over to pages two and three. Click **Print**. Click **OK**.

- Close the workbook. Click **No** if asked whether to save the changes. Exit Excel if you do not want to continue with the next exercise at this time.

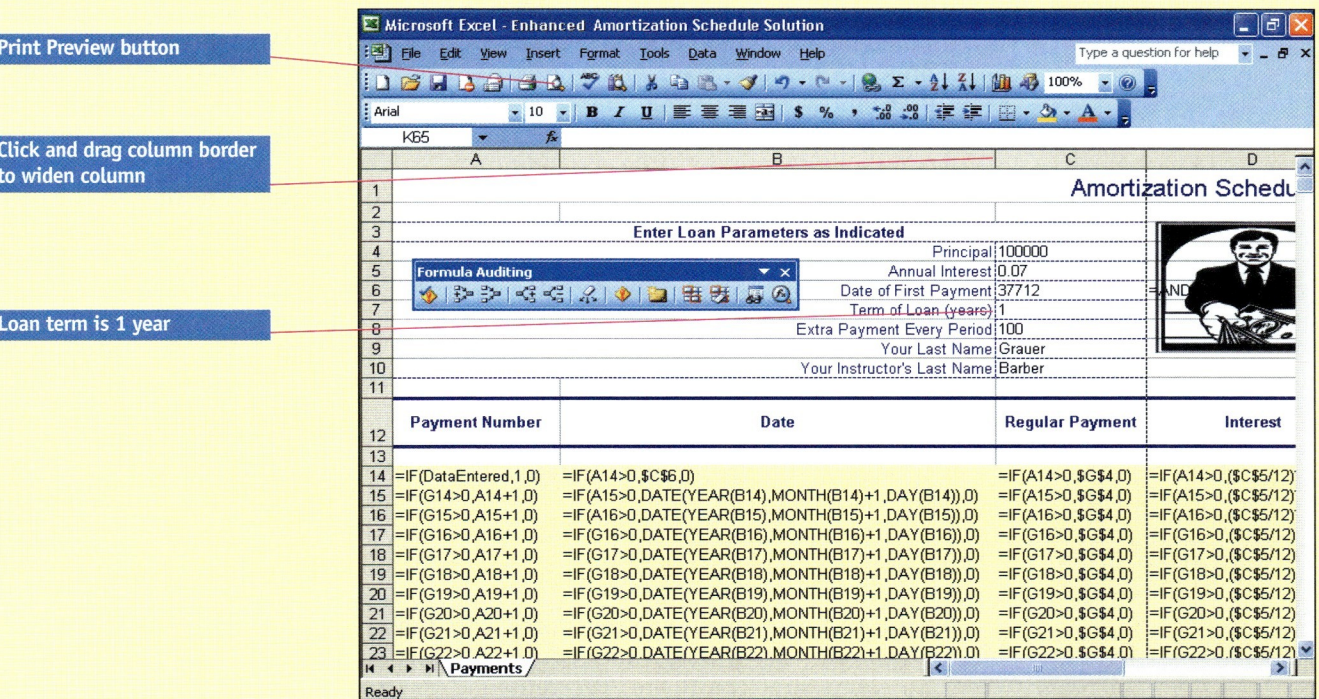

(g) Print the Cell Formulas (step 7)

FIGURE 10.3 Hands-on Exercise 1 (*continued*)

CHANGING THE PRINT AREA

It's easy to set a print area manually. You select the range that is to print, pull down the File menu, click Print Area, and then click Set Print Area. (You can clear the print area by choosing the Clear Print Area command.) The problem with this technique is that the desired print area changes according to the number of required payments, each of which adds a row to the worksheet. We have, however, found a way to set the print area dynamically, according to the number of rows in a worksheet. If this does not happen in your worksheet, press Ctrl+r to execute a macro to reset the dynamic print area. See exercises 3 and 4 at the end of the chapter.

EXPLORING VBA SYNTAX

You could study VBA for weeks on end prior to coding a simple procedure. We prefer to plunge right in, use the **macro recorder** to capture Excel commands, and then learn about VBA through inference and observation. Nevertheless, you need a grasp of basic terminology as presented in this section.

VBA accomplishes its tasks by manipulating **objects**. The objects within Excel include workbooks, worksheets, ranges, charts, pivot tables, and individual cells. The **object model** describes the hierarchical way in which different objects are related to one another. The workbook object, for example, contains the worksheet object, which in turn contains the range object, and so on.

A **collection** is a group of similar objects within the object model. The worksheet collection is a group of individual worksheets. A specific object within a collection is referenced by the collection name followed by the object name enclosed in quotation marks within parentheses. Worksheets("Documentation"), for example, refers to the worksheet named "Documentation" within the Worksheets collection. In similar fashion, Range("Principal") refers to the range object named "Principal" within the Range collection. A reference to an object may be qualified (joined together with periods) over several objects. Thus, Worksheets("Payments"). Range("Principal") refers to the range named "Principal" in the worksheet named "Payments". If you omit the worksheet reference, the current worksheet is assumed. (VBA recognizes "Sheets" as a synonym for "Worksheets", and you may see either reference in a VBA statement.)

A **method** is an action performed by an object. You specify the object, and then you indicate the method. The statements Range("Principal").Select and Range("Principal").Clear apply the Select and Clear methods, respectively, to the indicated range object. A **property** is an attribute of an object, such as whether it is visible. You specify the object, the property, and the value of the property; for example, Sheets("Payments").Visible = True or Sheets("Payments").Visible = False.

That's all there is. The object model defines the relationships of the objects to one another and defines the methods and properties associated with each object. The object model also provides a link between the user interface and VBA, enabling VBA to manipulate Excel objects such as workbooks, worksheets, and specific cell ranges.

Three Simple Procedures

Figure 10.4 displays three procedures from the Amortization Schedule workbook to illustrate VBA syntax. A procedure is created in one of two ways—by entering statements directly into the VBA editor and/or by using the macro recorder to capture Excel commands and convert them to their VBA equivalents. You can also combine the two techniques by starting with the recorder to capture basic statements, then view the resulting syntax and embellish those statements with additional VBA statements.

The procedure in Figure 10.4a is used by the developer to verify his or her calculations. The procedure displays two hidden columns that contain the **IPMT** and **PPMT functions**, to compute the amount of each payment for interest and principal, respectively. (See step 4 in the previous hands-on exercise.) The procedure was created entirely through the macro recorder. The resulting VBA statements are easily understood within the context of our basic definitions. The Unprotect method is applied to the active worksheet object so that its contents may be modified. The named range called ValidationColumns is selected, and its hidden property is set to False. The Protect method is then applied to the worksheet so that it cannot be modified further. You might not be able to write the procedure from scratch, but you can understand its statements once they have been created for you. All of a sudden, VBA does not seem so intimidating.

VBA statements were generated by macro recorder

```
Sub DisplayValidationColumns()
    ActiveSheet.Unprotect
    Application.Goto Reference:="ValidationColumns"
    Selection.EntireColumn.Hidden = False
    ActiveSheet.Protect
End Sub
```

(a) Display Validation Columns (Macro Recorder)

If statement tests to see if data has been entered in cell named DataEntered

Else clause

MsgBox statement

```
Sub DisplayValidationColumns()
    ActiveSheet.Unprotect
    If Range("DataEntered").Value = True Then
        Application.Goto Reference:="ValidationColumns"
        Selection.EntireColumn.Hidden = False
        MsgBox "This macro displays additional columns for validation " _
            & "of the spreadsheet formulas using the IPMT and PPMT " _
            & "functions, respectively. The values should match the " _
            & "corresponding columns in the body of the spreadsheet " _
            & "provided that no extra payments are made.", _
                vbInformation, ApplicationTitle
    Else
        MsgBox "Validation meaningless - Loan parameters not entered", _
                vbInformation, ApplicationTitle
    End If
    ActiveSheet.Protect
End Sub
```

(b) Display Validation Columns (Additional VBA Statements)

User is prompted for a Yes or No response, and response is tested against vbYes

```
Public Sub EnableSinglePayments()
    If MsgBox("This procedure unprotects the extra payments " _
        & "columns enabling you to enter individual payments. " _
        & "Do you want to unprotect the spreadsheet?", _
        vbYesNo + vbQuestion, ApplicationTitle) = vbYes _
    Then
        ActiveSheet.Unprotect
    Else
        ActiveSheet.Protect
    End If
End Sub
```

(c) Enable Single Payments

FIGURE 10.4 VBA Procedures

The real power of VBA, however, lies in the ability to add VBA statements that do not have an Excel equivalent to procedures that were created by the macro recorder. The procedure in Figure 10.4b expands the procedure to display the hidden columns by first testing to see that data has been entered in the main body of the worksheet, because it does not make sense to display the validation columns if the data is incomplete. Thus, we took the procedure in Figure 10.4a and added the If . . . Else . . . End If construct to see if data has been entered.

Figure 10.4c displays a procedure that expands the functionality of the worksheet by enabling the user to enter individual payments within the optional payments column. The new procedure uses the *MsgBox function*, as opposed to a simple *MsgBox statement*. The MsgBox function displays a prompt to the user, then returns a value such as which button was clicked.

hands-on exercise 2

Exploring VBA Syntax

Objective To use the Excel macro recorder to jump-start the creation of VBA procedures; to add VBA statements to create more powerful procedures. Use Figure 10.5 as a guide in the exercise.

Step 1: **Open the VBA Editor**

- Start Excel. Open the **Enhanced Amortization Schedule Solution** from the previous exercise. Click the button to **Enable macros**.

- Pull down the **Tools menu**, click the **Macro command**, then click the **Visual Basic Editor command** (or use the **Alt+F11** keyboard shortcut) to open the editor. You should see a window similar to Figure 10.5a.

- If necessary, pull down the **View menu** and click **Project Explorer** to display the Project Explorer pane at the left of the window.

- Click the **plus sign** next to the Modules folder to list the existing modules, then double click **Module1** to display its contents in the code window.

- Click and drag to select the public constant, **Your Name Goes Here**. (Do not select the quotation marks.)

- Type your name, and it will replace the selected text. Click the **Save button** to save the changes to Module1.

- Click the **View Microsoft Excel button** to return to the workbook.

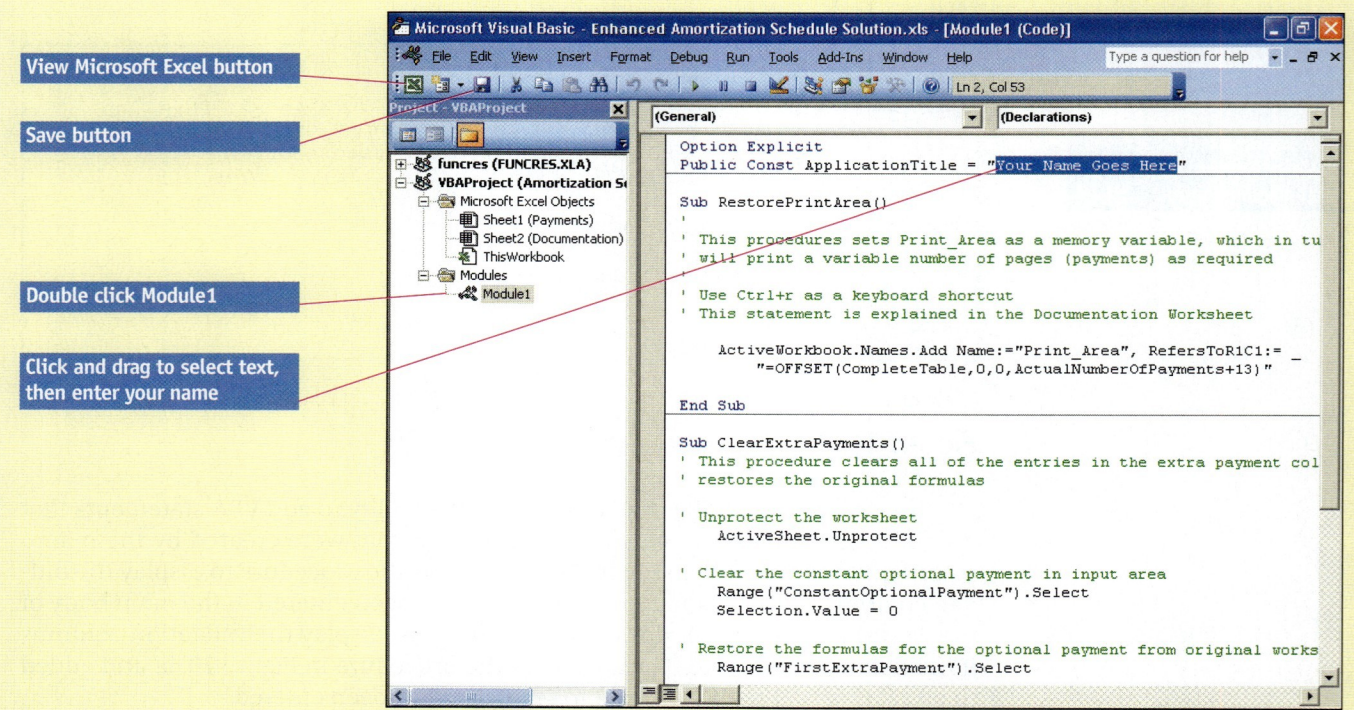

(a) Open the VBA Editor (step 1)

FIGURE 10.5 Hands-on Exercise 2

530 CHAPTER 10: A PROFESSIONAL APPLICATION

Step 2: **Record the Display Validation Columns Macro**

- Pull down the **Tools menu** and click the **Macro command**, then click **Record New Macro** to display the Record Macro dialog box. Enter **DisplayValidationColumns** (spaces are not allowed) as the name of the macro.

- Click in the **Shortcut Key** text box and enter a **lowercase d**. Ctrl+d should appear as the shortcut. Be sure that the macro is stored in This Workbook. Click **OK** to begin recording and display the Stop Recording toolbar in Figure 10.5b.

- Pull down the **Tools menu**, click **Protection**, and click the **Unprotect Sheet command**. (A password is not required.)

- Click the **down arrow** in the Name box and click **ValidationColumns** to select columns H and I. You see only a thick vertical line between columns G and J because the columns are still hidden.

- Pull down the **Format menu**, click the **Column command**, and click **Unhide**. You should see the validation columns. Pull down the **Tools menu**, click **Protection**, and click the **Protect Sheet command**. Click **OK**. (A password is not required.)

- Click the **Stop Recording button**. (If you do not see the Stop Recording toolbar, pull down the **Tools menu**, click **Macro**, and then click **Stop Recording**.)

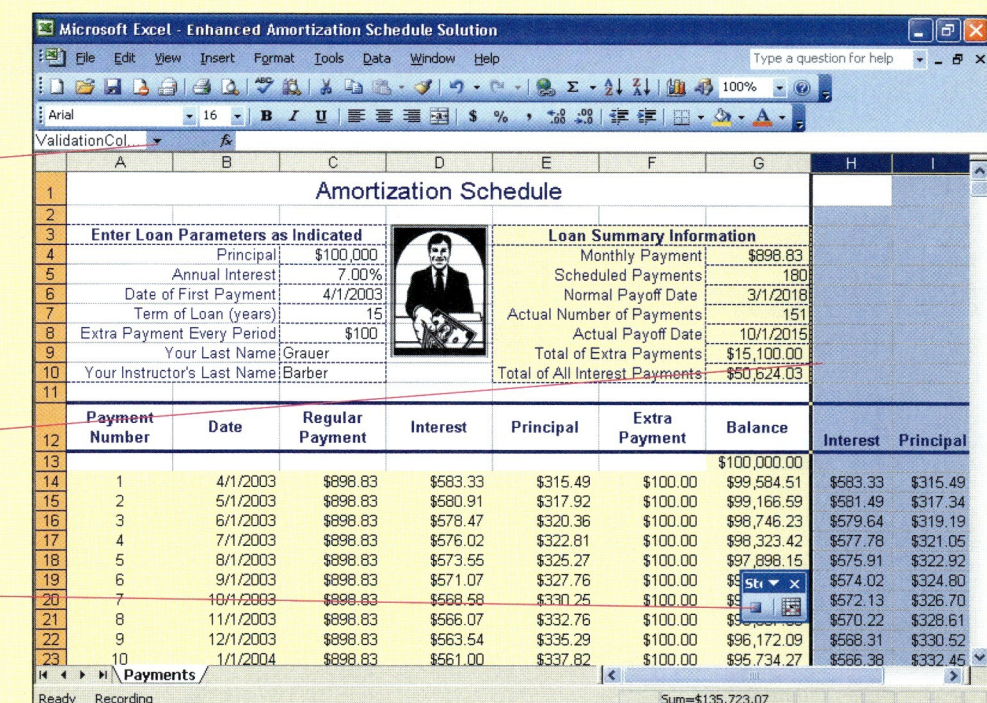

(b) Record the Display Validation Columns Macro (step 2)

FIGURE 10.5 Hands-on Exercise 2 (*continued*)

INSULATE YOUR MACROS AND PROCEDURES

Excel formulas adjust automatically for the insertion or deletion of rows and columns. This is not true of macros and VBA procedures; that is, if you record a macro to go to a specific column, such as column H, then you subsequently add or remove a column, the macro will no longer work. You can prevent this from happening by defining range names within the worksheet, and referring to those range names within a macro.

Step 3: **Create the Hide Validation Columns Macro**

- Press **Alt+F11** to open the VBA editor. Double click **Module2**.
- You should see the DisplayValidationColumns procedure in Figure 10.5c. Modify your procedure to match our code. (The second procedure is not yet there.)
- Return to Excel. Pull down the **Tools menu**, click the **Macro command**, then click **Record New Macro** to display the Record Macro dialog box.
- Enter **HideValidationColumns** as the name of the macro. Click in the **Shortcut Key** text box and enter a **lowercase h**. Click **OK** to begin recording.
- Pull down the **Tools menu**, click **Protection**, and click **Unprotect Sheet**. Click the **down arrow** in the Name box and click **ValidationColumns** to select columns H and I. Do this even if the columns are still selected.
- Pull down the **Format menu**, click the **Column command**, and click the **Hide command**. The validation columns should no longer be visible.
- Pull down the **Tools menu**, click **Protection**, click **Protect Sheet**, then click **OK**. Click the **Stop Recording button** to complete the macro. Save the workbook.
- Now test the two macros by using the keyboard shortcuts. Press **Ctrl+d** to display the columns. Press **Ctrl+h** to hide the columns.

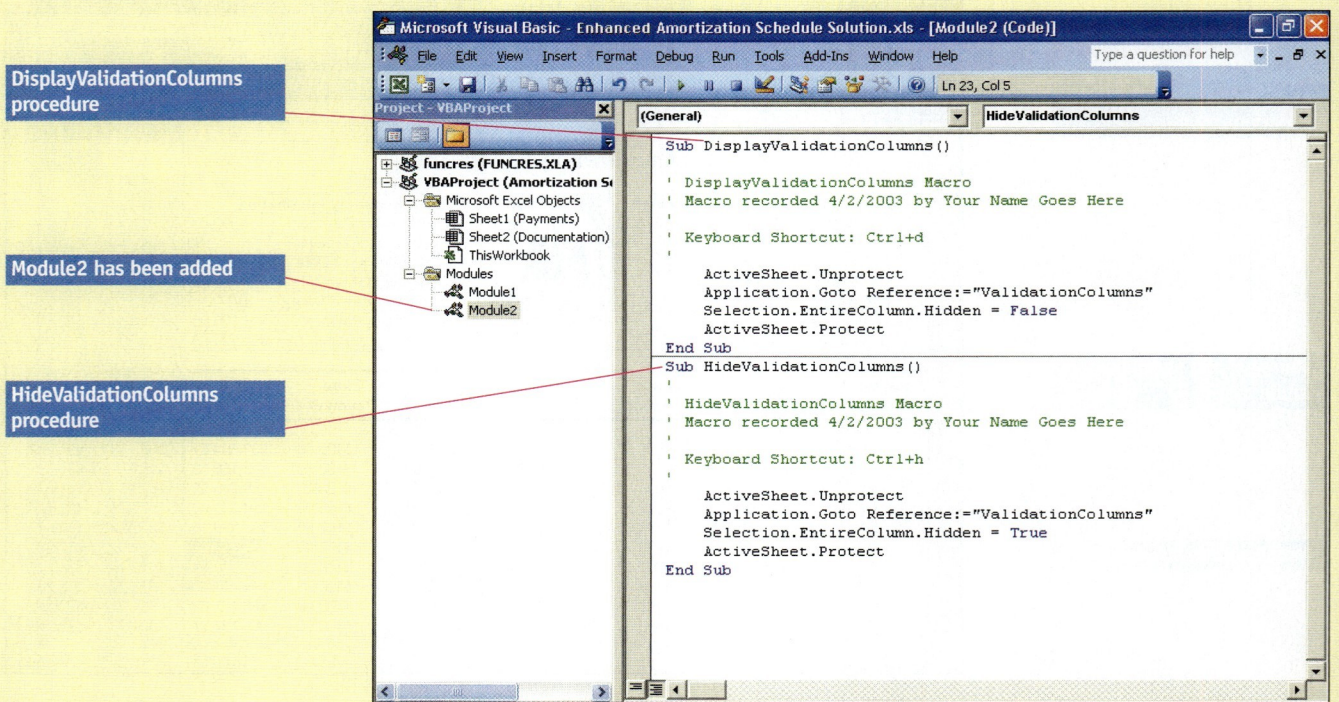

(c) Create the Hide Validation Columns Macro (step 3)

FIGURE 10.5 Hands-on Exercise 2 (*continued*)

WHICH MODULE IS IT IN?

All macros that are recorded within the same Excel session will be stored in the same module. If you close the workbook, however, then subsequently reopen it, Excel will store subsequent macros in a new module. It really doesn't matter where (in which module) the macros are stored. You can, however, move a macro from one module to another for organizational purposes.

Step 4: **Complete the Display Validation Columns Procedure**

- Press **Alt+F11** to return to the VBA editor as shown in Figure 10.5d.

- Think for a minute about what you are doing. You know that the basic macro works, but you want to enhance the macro to include error checking and meaningful messages to the user.

- Click at the end of the first statement, ActiveSheet.Unprotect, in the first procedure, and press the **Enter key**. Add the first line of the **If statement**, indent the next two existing lines, then click after the keyword False and press **Enter** twice.

- Enter the first **MsgBox statement**, continuing from one line to the next as shown in Figure 10.5d. Type **Else**, press **Enter**, then complete the second **MsgBox statement**. Complete the If statement by adding the **End If** delimiter.

- Check that your code matches Figure 10.5d. Click the **Save button**.

- Return to the Excel worksheet to test the procedure. Delete one input parameter, then press **Ctrl+d** to (attempt) to display the validation columns.

- You should see the message box indicating that the validation is meaningless because the loan parameters are not entered. If the procedure does not work as intended, press **Alt+F11** to return to the VBA editor and make corrections.

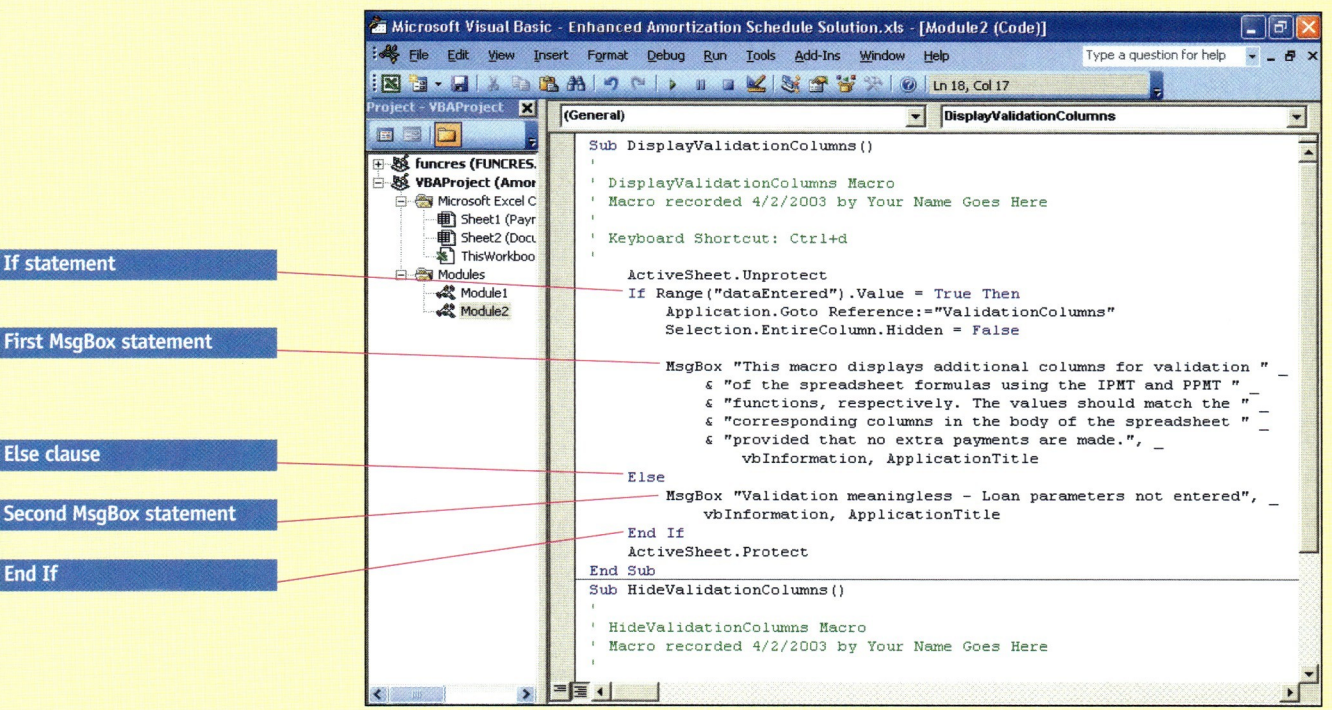

(d) Complete the Display Validation Columns Procedure (step 4)

FIGURE 10.5 Hands-on Exercise 2 (*continued*)

THE UNDERSCORE AND THE AMPERSAND

A VBA Statement is continued from one line to the next by typing an underscore at the end of the line to be continued. You may not, however, break a line in the middle of a literal. Hence, several lines within the MsgBox statement end with a closing quotation mark, followed by a space and the underscore. Each continued line starts with an ampersand to indicate continuation (concatenation) of the previous literal, followed by the remainder of the literal in quotation marks.

Step 5: **Create the Enable Single Payments Procedure**

- The procedure we are about to create enables the user to enter single payments within the extra payments columns. Return to the VBA editor. Press **Ctrl+End** to move to the end of the current module.

- Pull down the **Insert menu** and click the **Procedure command** to display the Add Procedure dialog box. Enter **EnableSinglePayments** (spaces are not allowed) as the procedure name. Select option buttons for **Sub** and **Public**. Click **OK**.

- The Sub and End Sub statements are created automatically. Click the **Procedure View button** to view only this procedure. Complete the procedure as shown in Figure 10.5e. You are using the **MsgBox function**, which means that:
  - The parameters of the MsgBox function are enclosed in parentheses. (Parentheses are not used when MsgBox is used as a statement.)
  - The MsgBox function returns a value, in this case an indication of which button the user clicked, Yes or No.
  - The value returned by the MsgBox function is compared to the VBA intrinsic constant vbYes.

- Click the **Save button**. Click the **Excel button** to test the procedure.

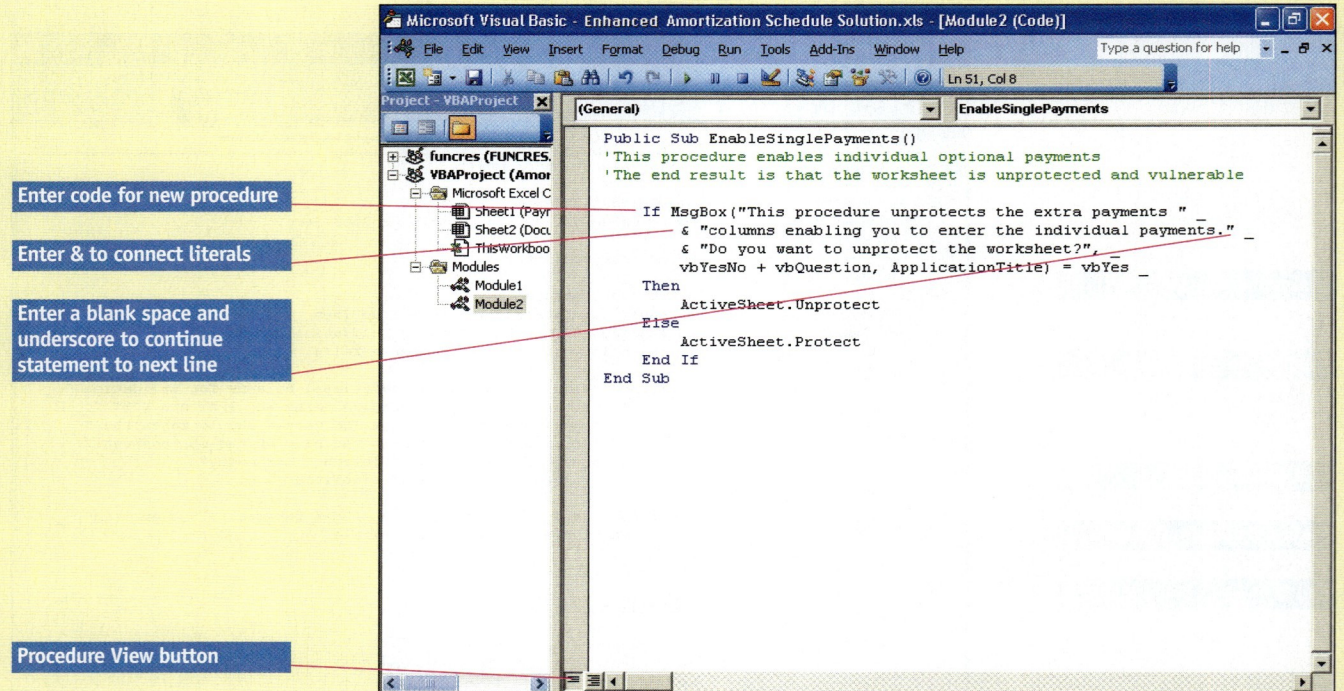

(e) Create the Enable Single Payments Procedure (step 5)

FIGURE 10.5 Hands-on Exercise 2 (*continued*)

USE WHAT YOU KNOW

Use the techniques acquired from other Office applications to facilitate editing within the VBA window. Press the Ins key to toggle between the insert and overtype modes as you modify the statements within a VBA procedure. You can also cut, copy, and paste statements (or parts of statements) within a procedure and from one procedure to another. You can access these commands via buttons on the Standard toolbar, as commands in the Edit menu, or by using the appropriate keyboard shortcuts.

Step 6: **Test the Procedure**

- You should be back in Excel. Delete the entry in **cell C8**. Pull down the **Tools menu**, click **Macro**, then click **Macros** to display the Macro dialog box.

- Double click the **EnableSinglePayments macro** that was just created. You should see the message box in Figure 10.5f. Click **No**.

- Click anywhere in **column F**, the column that contains the optional extra payments, and try to enter a value. You should see a message indicating that the cell is protected and that you cannot alter its contents. Click **OK** when you have read this message.

- Rerun the **EnableSinglePayments macro**, but this time click **Yes**, indicating that you want to enter extra payments. This will unprotect the worksheet.

- Return to any cell in column F and enter **$1000** as an optional payment for that month. This time Excel accepts the payment. Click the **Undo button** to cancel the extra payment.

- If the procedure does not function as intended, return to the Visual Basic editor and correct it. Save the workbook.

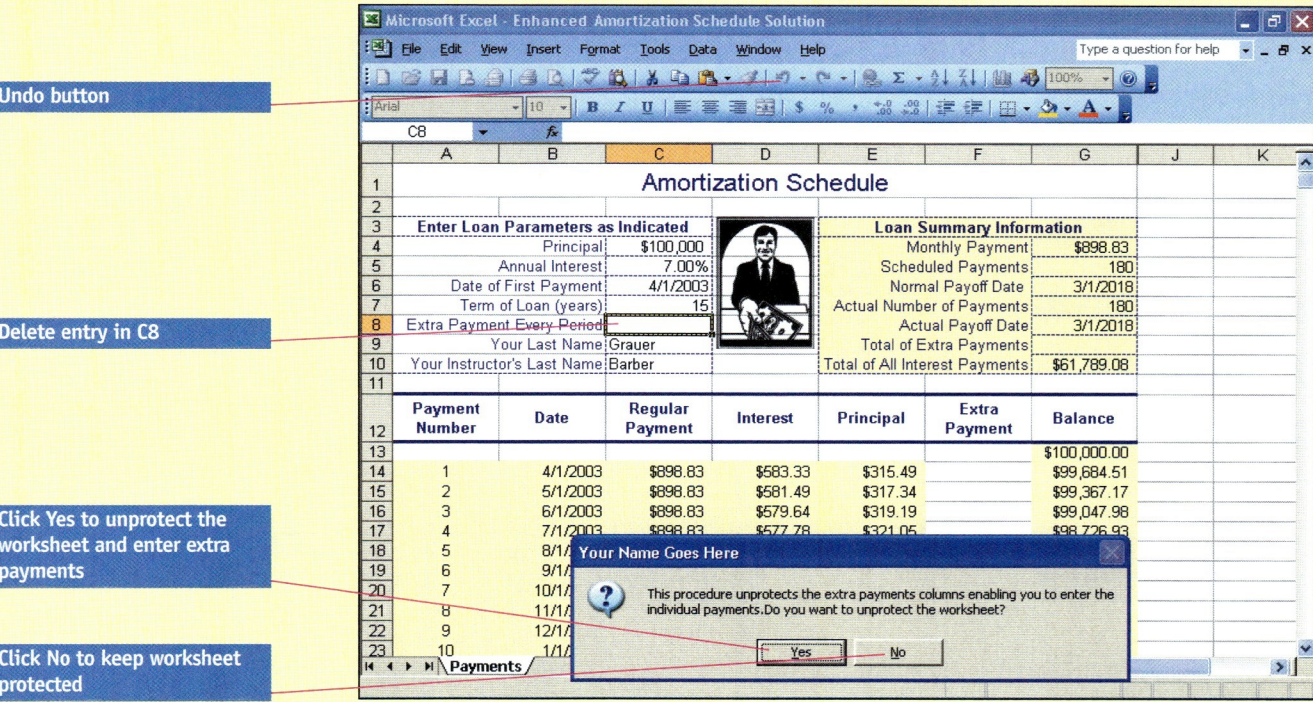

(f) Test the Procedure (step 6)

FIGURE 10.5   Hands-on Exercise 2 (*continued*)

ADD A MACRO SHORTCUT

You can add and/or modify the shortcut key associated with a macro at any time. Pull down the Tools menu, click the Macro command, then click Macros to display the Macro dialog box. Select the desired macro and click the Options button to display the Macro Options dialog box, where you assign a shortcut. Type a lowercase letter to create a shortcut with just the Ctrl key such as Ctrl+e. Enter an uppercase letter to create a shortcut using the Ctrl and Shift keys such as Ctrl+Shift+E.

Step 7: **Create a Custom Toolbar**

- Pull down the **View menu**, click the **Toolbars command**, then click **Customize** to display the Customize dialog box. Click the **Toolbars tab**, then click the **New button** to create a new toolbar.

- Type **Amortization Schedule** as the toolbar name and click **OK**. You will see a floating toolbar as shown in Figure 10.5g. Click the **Commands tab** within the Custom dialog box, then scroll until you can select the **Macros category**.

- Click and drag the **Custom button** (with the smiley face image) to the newly created toolbar. Release the mouse. The smiley face appears on the toolbar. Click (select) the **smiley face button**, then click the **Modify Selection button** in the Customize dialog box.

- Click the **Name command** within the menu options, select the existing text, and type **Display Validation Columns** as the name of the button.

- Click the **Change Button Image command**. Choose an icon. We selected the **eye**.

- Click the **Modify Selection button**, click **Assign macro** and choose the **DisplayValidationColumns macro**. Click **OK**. Close the dialog box. Save the workbook.

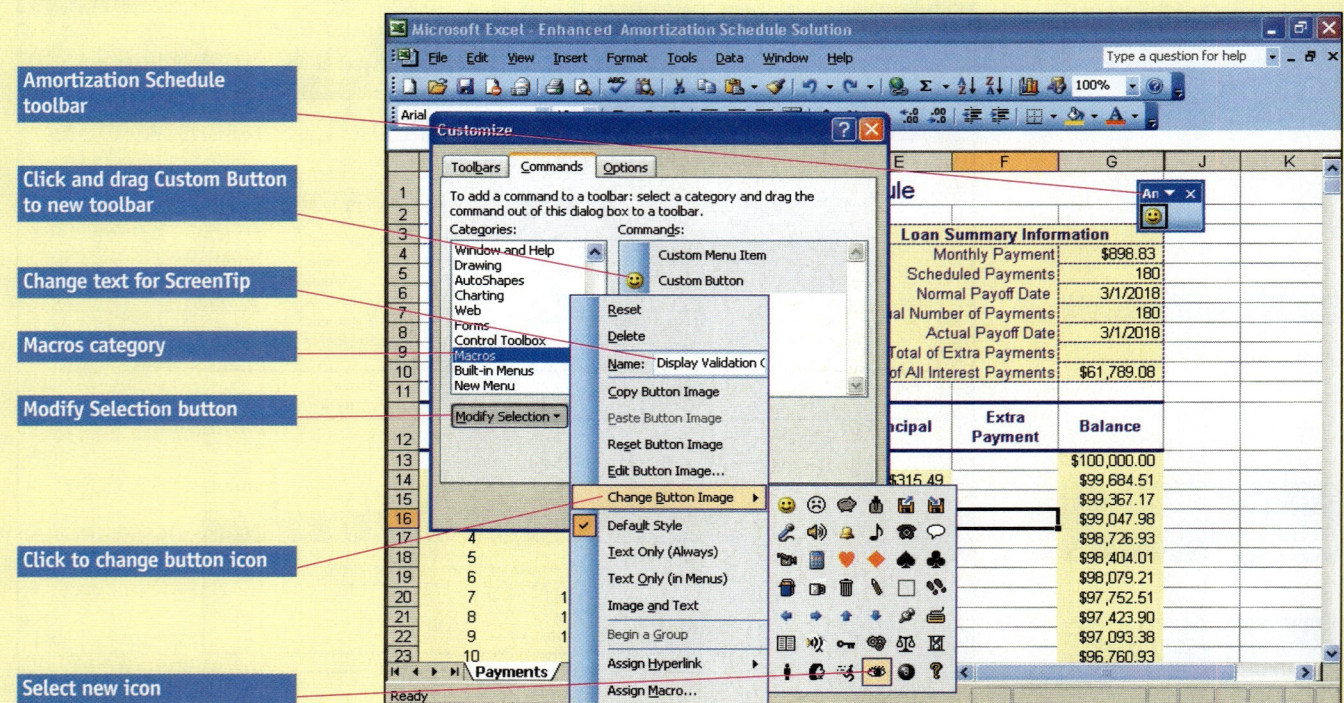

(g) Create a Custom Toolbar (step 7)

FIGURE 10.5 Hands-on Exercise 2 (*continued*)

MOVING AND/OR REMOVING A BUTTON

You can change the position of any button on a custom toolbar and/or remove the button altogether. Pull down the View menu, click Toolbars, then click the Customize command to display the Customize dialog box. To change the position of a button, select the button, then drag it to its new position. To remove the button, just drag the button off the toolbar. The same techniques apply to any standard toolbar within Microsoft Office.

Step 8: **Test the Toolbar Button**

- Point to the newly created toolbar button. You should see the name (ScreenTip) you entered, just as you would with any other toolbar button.

- Click the button to display the validation columns. Click **OK** after you have read the message.

- If necessary, pull down the **View menu**, click **Toolbars**, and click the **Customize command** to correct any element (the description, image, or macro) that did not work correctly.

- Add buttons for the **HideValidationColumns** and **EnableSinglePayments** macros. We used the runner and piggy bank icons, respectively.

- Test these buttons as shown in Figure 10.5h after they have been created. Make corrections as necessary.

- Save the workbook.

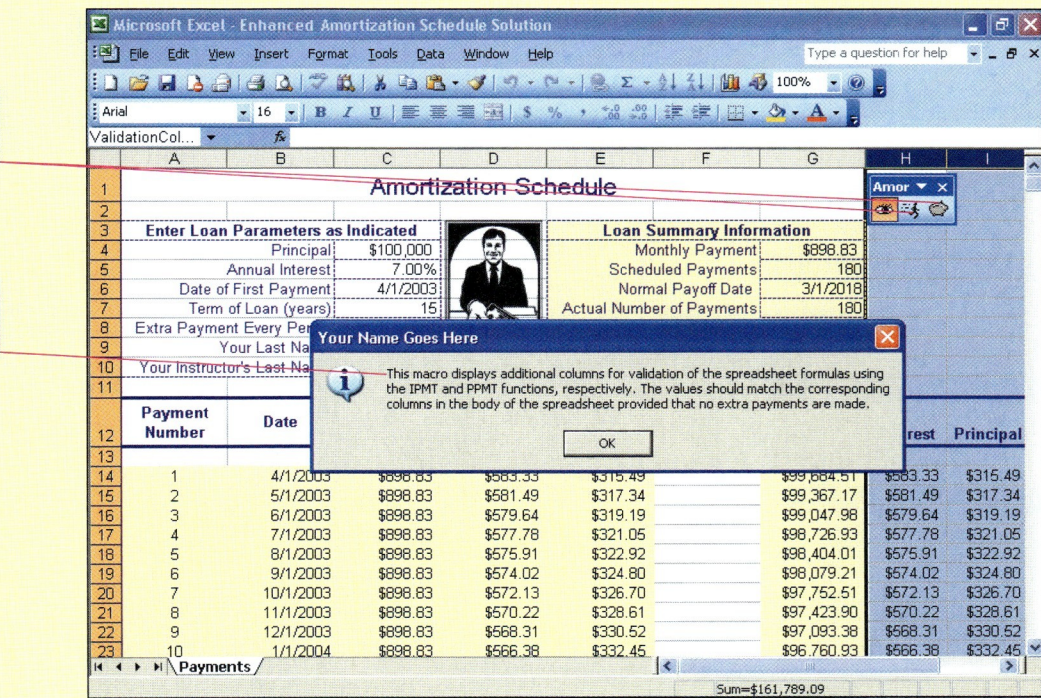

(h) Test the Toolbar Button (step 8)

FIGURE 10.5 Hands-on Exercise 2 (*continued*)

MODIFY THE BUTTON'S IMAGE

Excel provides only a limited number of images from which to choose, so it is convenient to be able to modify the images that are provided. Pull down the View menu, click Toolbars, click Customize to display the Customize dialog box, and click the Commands tab. Select the toolbar button, click Modify Selection, then click the Edit Button Image command to display the Button editor. Each button consists of 256 squares in a 16 by 16 grid. You can change the color of any square by selecting a new color, then clicking the appropriate square within the grid. You can also erase any square by double clicking the square. Click OK.

Step 9: **Attach the Toolbar**

- *This step is very important.* You must attach the custom toolbar to your workbook, so that it (the toolbar) will travel with the workbook if you copy the file and try to use it on a different computer.

- Pull down the **View menu**, click **Toolbars**, and click the **Customize command** to display the Customize dialog box. Click the **Toolbars tab**, then click the **Attach button** to display the Attach Toolbars dialog box in Figure 10.5i.

- Select the Amortization Schedule toolbar in the left pane, then click the **Copy button** to copy the custom toolbar to this workbook. (The custom toolbar resides in a special Excel folder that is stored on your computer and not in the workbook. Only after you attach the toolbar will it travel with the workbook.) Click **OK**. Click **Close**.

- Close the Amortization Schedule toolbar. Save the workbook. Exit Excel if you do not want to continue with the next exercise at this time.

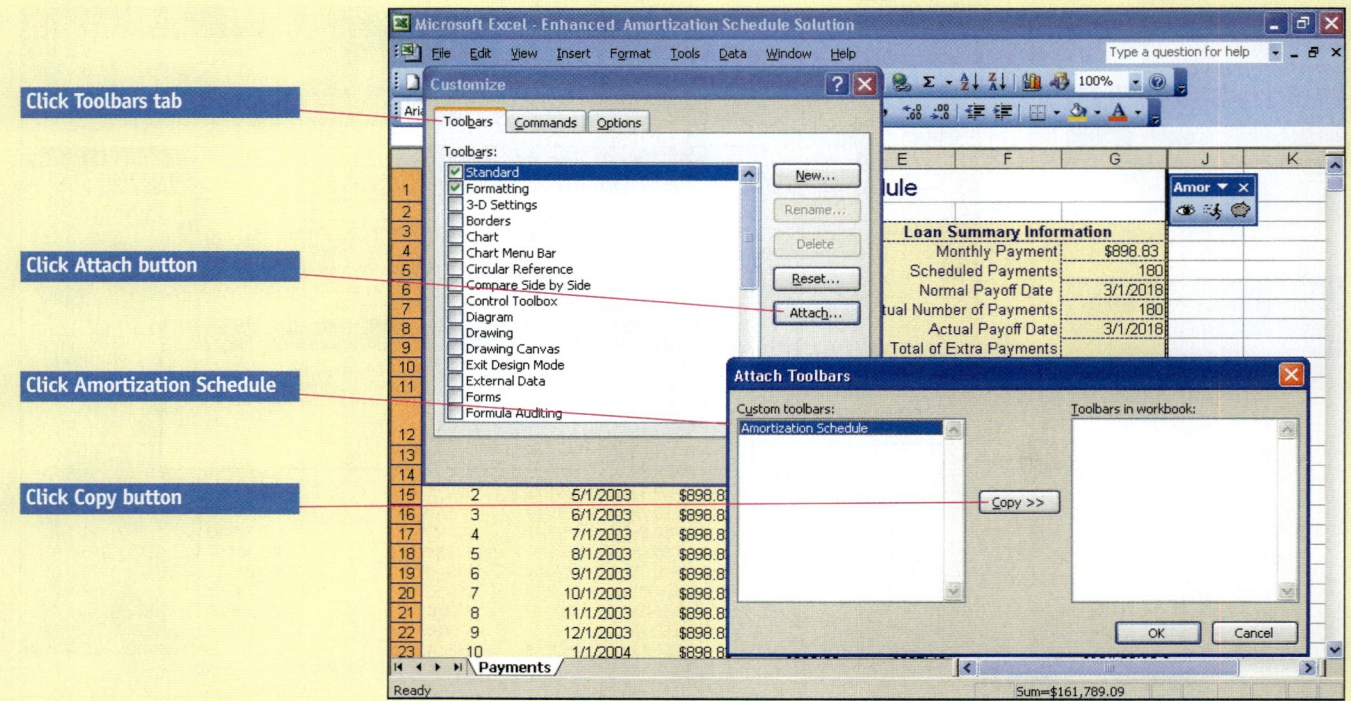

(i) Attach the Toolbar (step 9)

FIGURE 10.5 Hands-on Exercise 2 (*continued*)

ATTACHING TOOLBARS

The copy of the toolbar that is stored in a workbook reflects its contents at the time you attach the toolbar. Thus, if you subsequently modify a toolbar after attaching it, the changes are not automatically stored within the workbook. Pull down the View menu, click Toolbars, click Customize, click the Toolbars tab, then click the Attach button. Select the old toolbar in the Toolbars in workbook area at the right of the Attach Toolbar dialog box. Click the Delete button to delete the old toolbar. Select the new toolbar at the left of the dialog box, then click the Copy command to attach the new version. Click OK and save the workbook.

EVENT PROCEDURES

VBA has two types of procedures. There are **general procedures** such as those in the preceding exercise that are executed explicitly by the user whenever the user chooses. VBA also recognizes **event procedures** that are executed automatically when a specified event occurs. An **event** is defined as any action that is recognized by an application. Opening, closing, or printing a workbook is an event, as is clicking a button on a **custom toolbar**. (The Excel object model describes the specific events that are recognized by VBA.)

You can enhance an Excel application by deciding which events are significant, and what is to happen when those events occur. Then you develop the appropriate event procedures to execute automatically in conjunction with those events. This is in contrast to a traditional program that is executed sequentially, beginning with the first line of code and continuing in order through the remainder of the program. It is the program, not the user, that determines the order in which the statements are executed. VBA, on the other hand, is event-driven, meaning that the order in which the procedures are executed depends on the events that occur. It is the user, rather than the program, that determines which events occur, and consequently which procedures are executed.

The **Open workbook event procedure** is common to many applications. It accomplishes a variety of tasks such as the display of a custom toolbar or splash screen, checking for special conditions to alert the user, and/or performing other tasks for the developer. The **Before Close event procedure** is also common and typically hides the custom toolbar and displays a closing message to the user, such as a reminder to back up the system. It may also check for special conditions and/or perform one or more tasks for the developer.

Figures 10.6a and 10.6b display the results of these two event procedures for the Amortization Schedule workbook. The Open workbook event procedure in Figure 10.6a displays the custom toolbar and a splash screen. A **splash screen** is a simple form that appears for a brief period of time to identify an application, and then it disappears from view. (The form itself is created in the VBA editor as described in the next section.) The Open workbook event procedure may also include additional code to accomplish other tasks, but you may not be aware of the additional actions by merely looking at the worksheet.

Figure 10.6b displays the results of the Before Close event procedure. The custom toolbar has been hidden from view and a message is displayed to the user. The message box is different from the splash screen and requires the user to click OK to close the dialog box. Again, there may be additional code within the Before Close event procedure, the effects of which are not visible from this figure.

Remember too that an event procedure is executed regardless of how the event is triggered. Think about the various ways in which you close a workbook. You may pull down the File menu and click the Close command, or you can click the Close button in the application window, or you can use the Ctrl+F4 keyboard shortcut. All of these commands close the active workbook and in turn will trigger the Before Close event procedure.

SIGN YOUR DOCUMENTS

Excel displays a security warning prior to opening any Excel workbook that contains a VBA procedure. You can, however, display a different dialog box that identifies the publisher of the workbook and that the workbook is to be trusted as a safe source. This is accomplished by applying a digital signature, an electronic, encryption-based stamp of authentication, which confirms the origin of a document, and further that the document has not been altered since it was last saved by the signer. (See step 9 in Hands-on Exercise 3.)

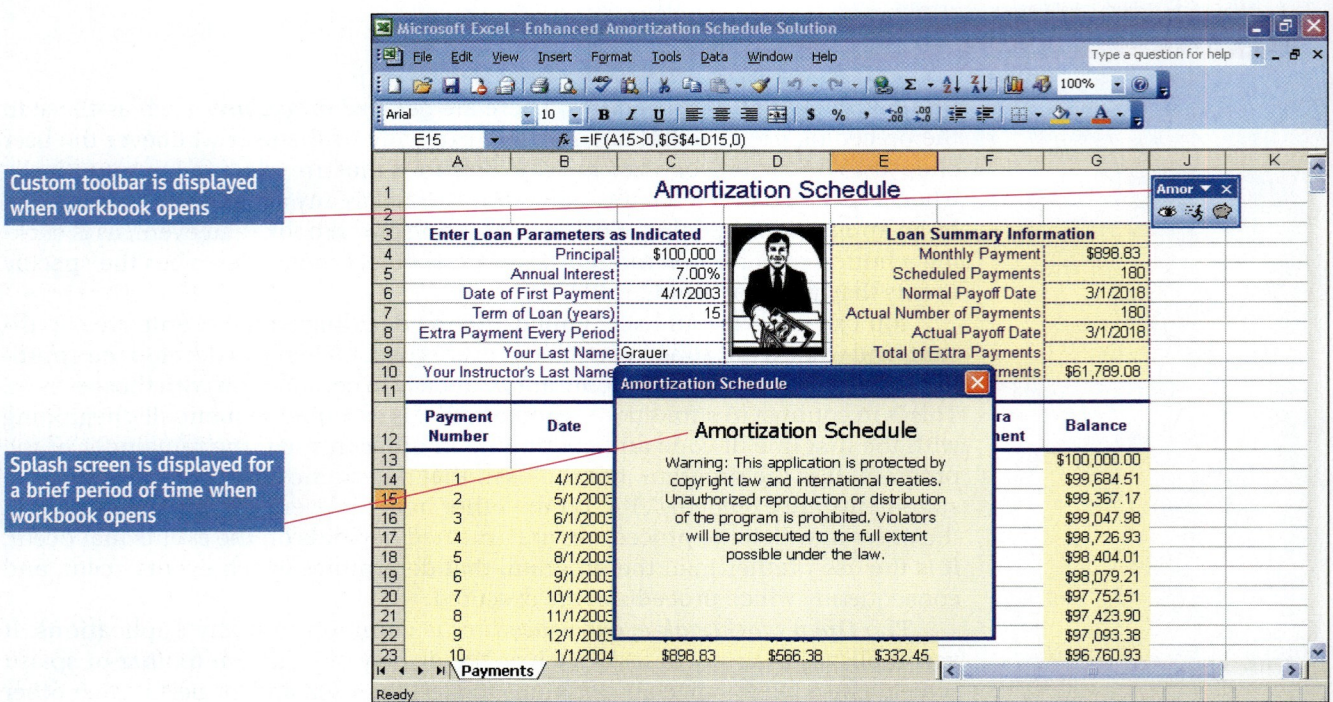

(a) The Open Workbook Event Procedure

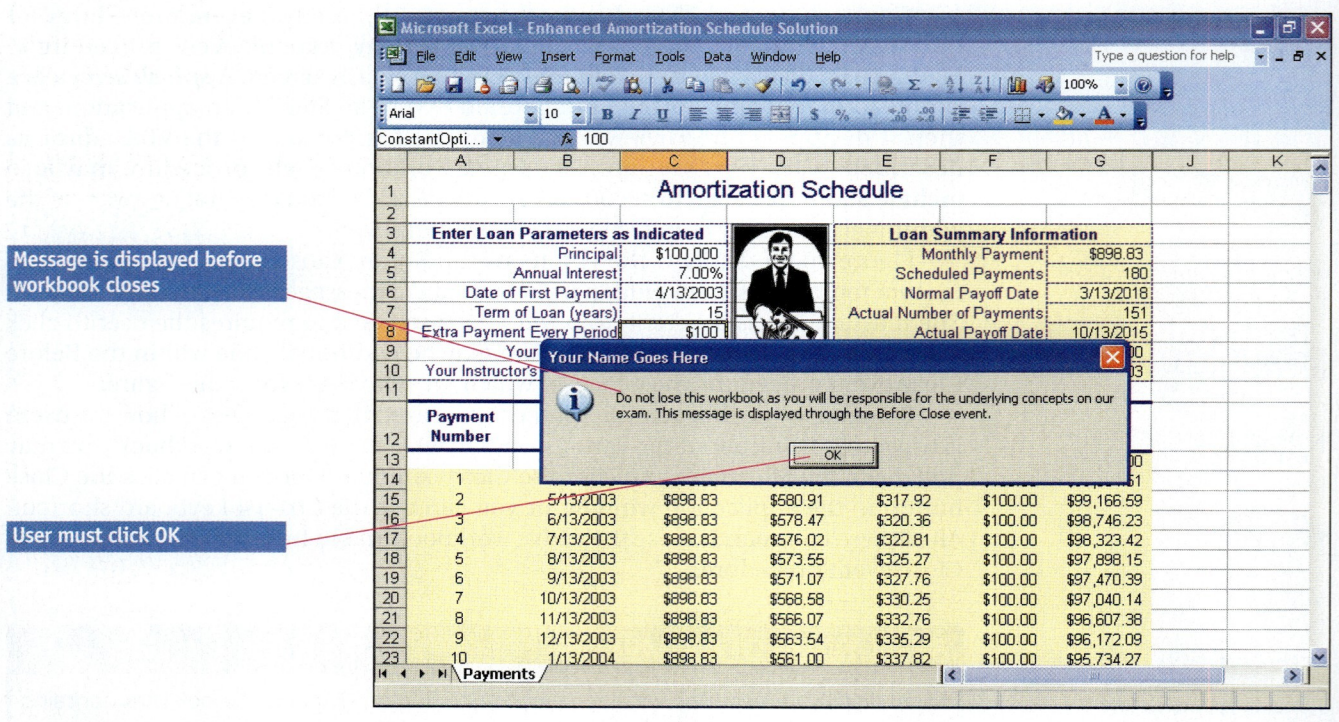

(b) The Before Close Event Procedure

FIGURE 10.6 Event Procedures

USER FORMS

A *user form* is typically created to facilitate data entry and is most commonly associated with Microsoft Access. A user form can also be created in Excel to enter data into a worksheet and/or to display a splash screen, which in turn requires several steps. First, you create the user form. Next, you develop the procedure(s) to load (display) the form. And finally, you create the procedure to unload (hide) the form.

Figure 10.7 depicts the creation of a splash screen for the Enhanced Amortization Schedule workbook. The Project Explorer window in the upper-left pane contains a Forms folder, which contains a single object, UserForm1. The form itself appears in Design view in the upper-right pane. You start with a blank form, then use the controls on the Toolbox to create the form. Click the appropriate tool (e.g., the "A" or label tool), then click and drag on the form to create the corresponding control. Once the label has been created, you click within the control and enter the desired text.

Every object (control) on a form as well as the form itself has a distinct set of properties (attributes) that are displayed and modified in the ***Properties window*** in the lower-left portion of the screen. You select the object on the form, and then you change the desired property, such as the font style, color, or size.

Once the form has been created, you have to develop the procedure to display the form, and another procedure to hide the form after it has been on the screen for the specified amount of time. The form is displayed by a single line of code, UserForm1.Show, which appears in the Open workbook event procedure. (The event procedure is not visible in Figure 10.7.)

The ***UserForm Activate event procedure*** in the lower-right portion of Figure 10.7 executes automatically when the form is opened. The ***OnTime method*** sets the amount of time the form is visible by adding five seconds to the Now function that contains the current time. The OnTime method then calls a third procedure, CloseScreen, which contains a single statement to unload (hide) the form. It's easier than it sounds as you will see in our next hands-on exercise.

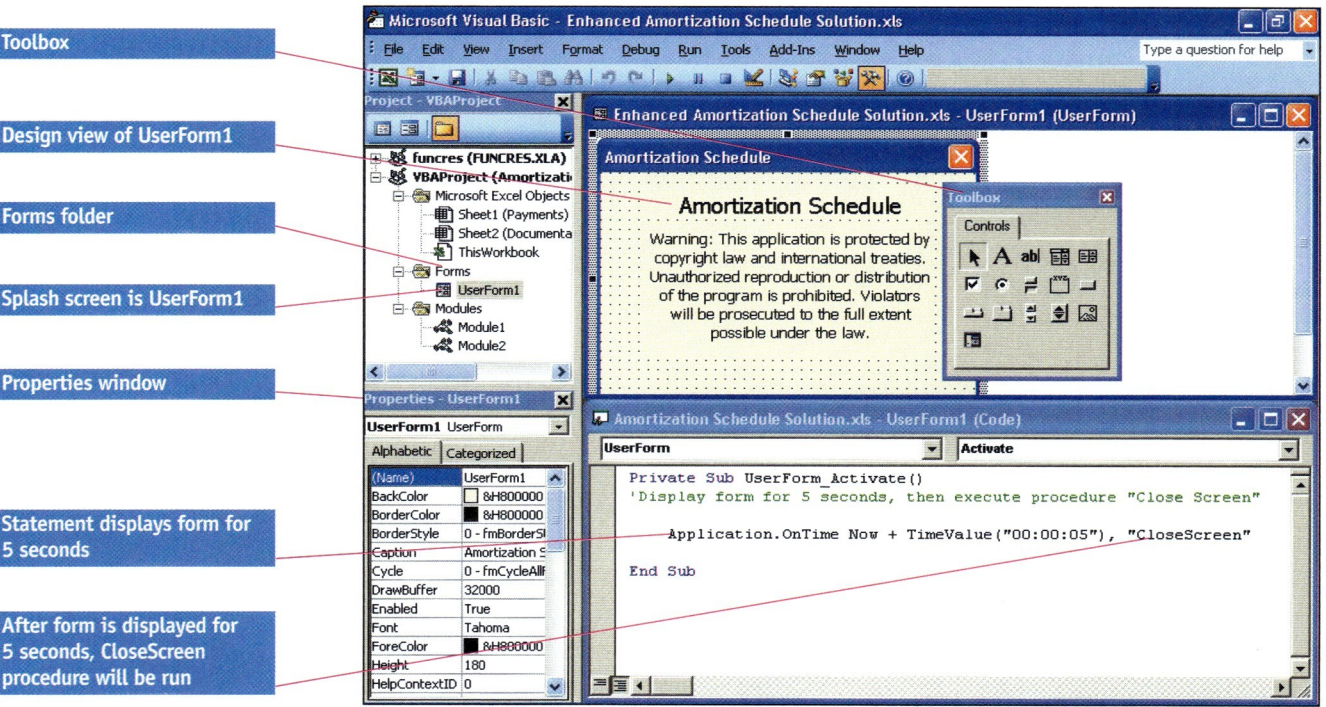

FIGURE 10.7 Creating a User Form

hands-on exercise

3 Event Procedures

Objective To create an Open workbook event procedure that displays a splash screen and custom toolbar; to create a Before Close event procedure to close the custom toolbar and display a message to the user. Use Figure 10.8 as a guide.

Step 1: **Start the Macro Recorder**

- Start Excel. Open the **Enhanced Amortization Schedule Solution** workbook from the previous exercise. Click the button to **Enable macros**.
- Pull down the **Tools menu**, click the **Macro command**, then click **Record New Macro** to display the Record Macro dialog box. You can accept the default name (such as Macro1), since we are using the recorder just to obtain the correct VBA syntax. Click **OK** to begin recording the macro.
- Pull down the **View menu**, click the **Toolbars command**, then click the **Amortization Schedule toolbar** as shown in Figure 10.8a.
- Click the **Stop Recording button**. (If you do not see the button, pull down the **Tools menu**, click the **Macro command**, and then click **Stop Recording**.)

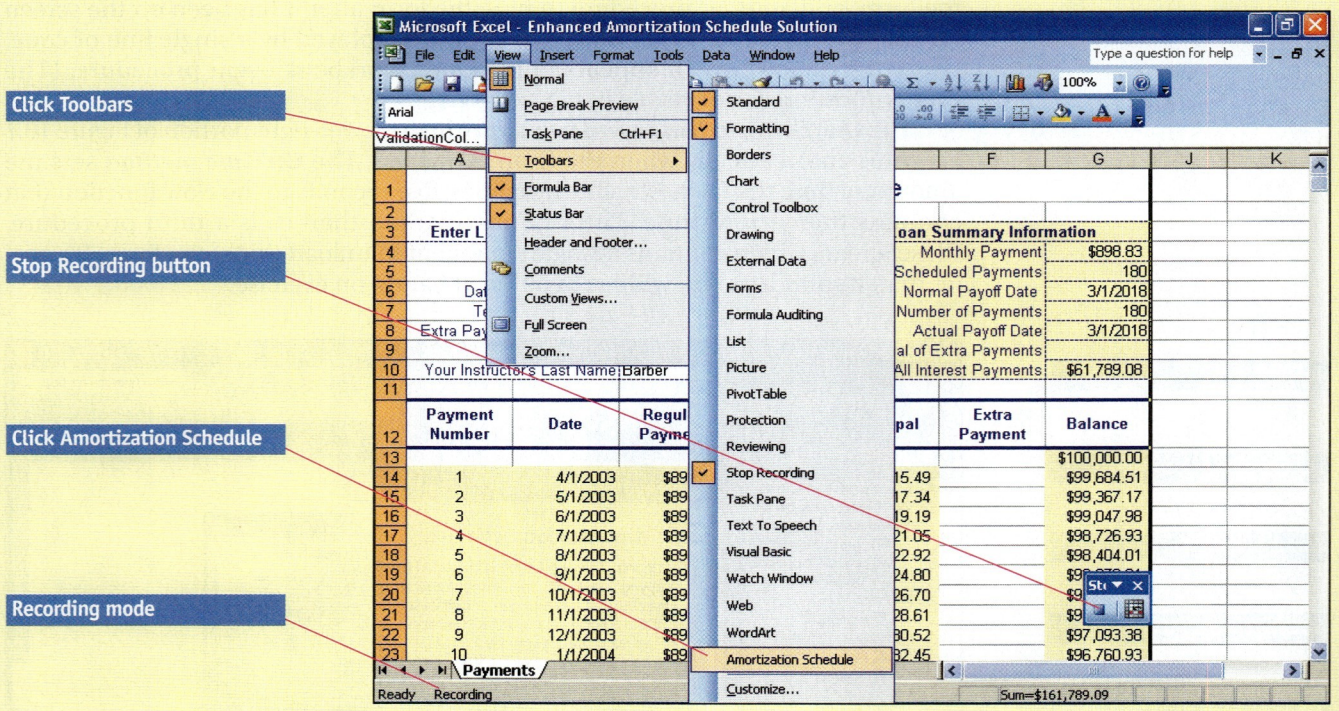

(a) Start the Macro Recorder (step 1)

FIGURE 10.8 Hands-on Exercise 3

WRITE VBA THE EASY WAY

The statement, Application.CommandBars("Amortization Schedule").Visible = True, displays the Amortization Schedule toolbar. It's easy to understand the statement, but it is not so easy to write it. The good news is you do not have to. Start the macro recorder and create a macro to display the toolbar. Stop the recorder, open the VBA editor, then use the generated code as the basis of a more sophisticated VBA procedure.

Step 2: **Create the Open Workbook Event Procedure**

- Press **Alt+F11** to open the VBA editor. Open the **Modules folder**, then select the newest module that contains the macro you just recorded.

- You should see a procedure called Macro1 that contains a single statement to display the Amortization Schedule toolbar. Select that statement, then click the **Copy button** on the Standard toolbar.

- Double click **ThisWorkbook** within the Project Explorer to display the code for the event procedures within the workbook. (There are none so far.)

- Click the **down arrow** in the Object list box (the leftmost list box) to select **Workbook**. The **Open workbook event procedure** is created automatically. The insertion point appears below the procedure header.

- Press the **Tab key** or **space bar** to indent the code, then click the **Paste button** (or use the **Ctrl+V** keyboard shortcut) to paste the VBA statement to display the Amortization schedule toolbar.

- Add the additional statements and comments as shown in Figure 10.8b. Click the **Save button** to save the event procedures within the workbook.

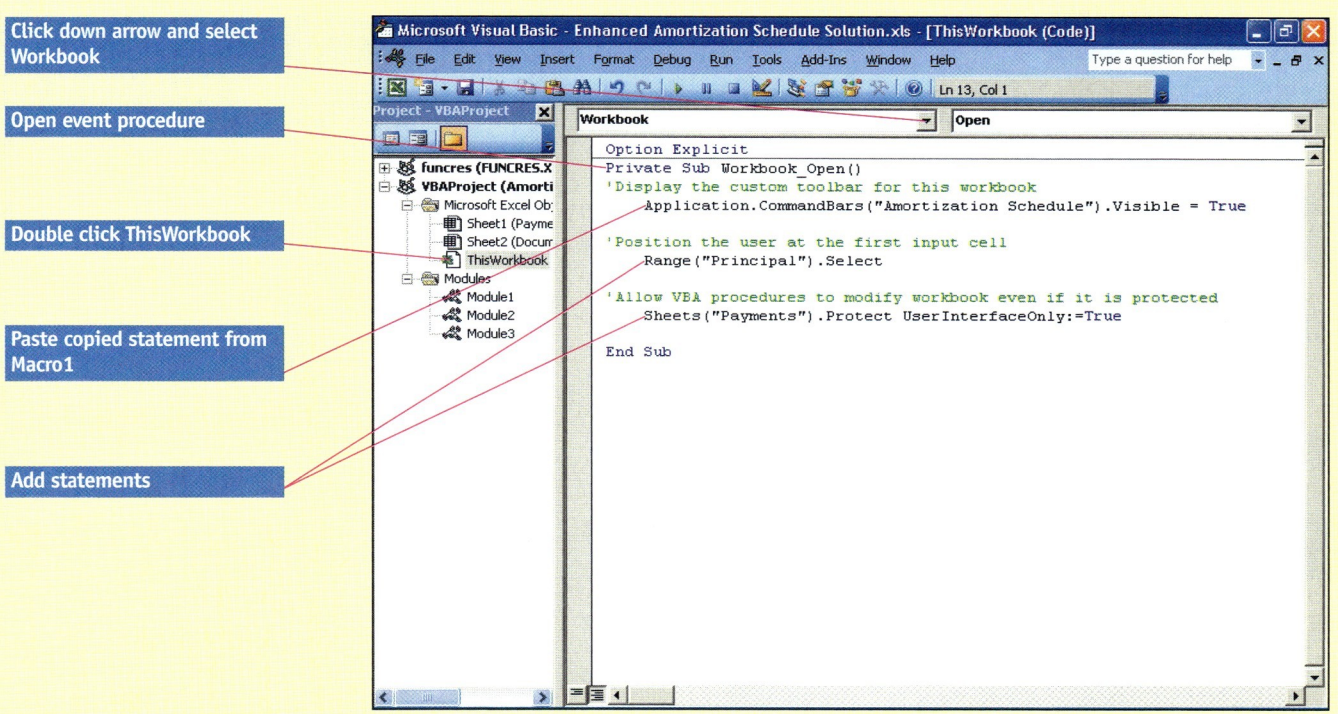

(b) Create the Open Workbook Event Procedure (step 2)

FIGURE 10.8 Hands-on Exercise 3 (*continued*)

PROTECT USER INTERFACE ONLY

A worksheet is protected to prevent the end user from accidentally (or otherwise) altering or deleting the formulas in the worksheet. The developer, however, should be able to modify the worksheet without having to protect and unprotect the worksheet within individual procedures. This is accomplished by setting the UserInterfaceOnly property. All VBA procedures will be able to modify the worksheet. The user, however, will be prevented from doing so when protection is in effect.

Step 3: Create the Before Close Event Procedure

- Click the **down arrow** in the Procedure list box (at the top of the right side of the Code window), then scroll until you can select the **Before Close event**. The Before Close event procedure is created automatically as shown in Figure 10.8c.

- Enter the statement and associated comment to hide the Amortization Schedule toolbar. You can type the statement directly, or you can copy the existing statement from the Open workbook event procedure and change the **Visible property** to **False**.

- Create the **MsgBox statement** that will be displayed prior to the workbook closing. The VBA syntax requires the underscore character when the MsgBox statement is continued from one line to the next. The ampersand is used to concatenate (join together) the various literals within the statement.

- Click the **Save button**. (You can remove the module that contains the Macro1 "dummy" procedure. Right click the module, click **Remove Module3**, then click **No** when asked to export the module. This macro was created only to obtain the basic VBA syntax for the event procedures and has no further purpose.)

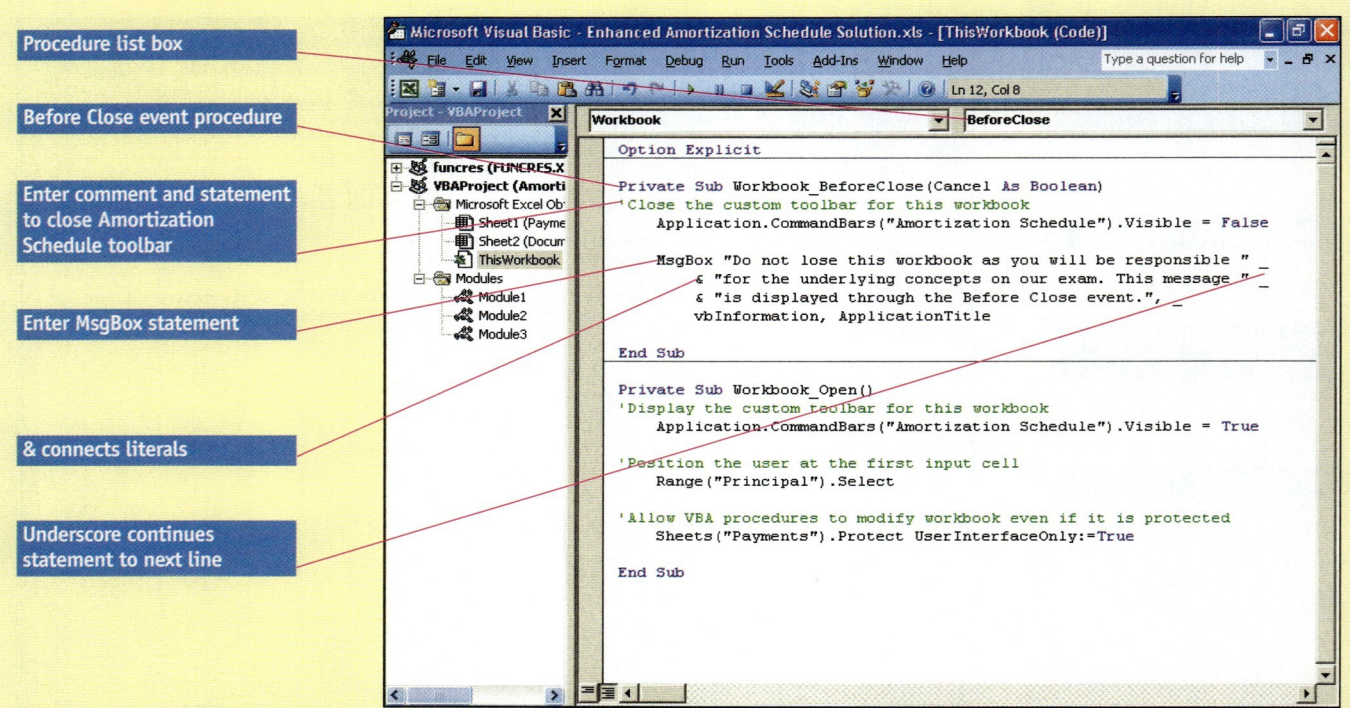

(c) Create the Before Close Event Procedure (step 3)

FIGURE 10.8 Hands-on Exercise 3 (*continued*)

EVENT PROCEDURES VERSUS GENERAL PROCEDURES

Event procedures such as opening and closing a workbook execute only when the designated event occurs. General procedures can be executed at any time. The macro recorder cannot be used with event procedures. Thus, we create a "dummy" macro to obtain the VBA statement to display a toolbar, we copy that statement to the event procedure, and then we delete the "dummy" procedure since it is no longer necessary.

Step 4: **Test the Procedures**

- Return to the Excel worksheet. The Amortization Schedule toolbar should still be visible on your screen (but not in our figure). If you do not see the toolbar, pull down the **View menu**, click **Toolbars** to display the list of available toolbars, then click the **Amortization Schedule toolbar**.

- Pull down the **File menu** and click the **Close command** to close the workbook but leave the Excel application open.

- The Amortization Schedule toolbar disappears, after which you should see the message box in Figure 10.8d, which is displayed by the Before Close event procedure that you just created.

- Read the statement carefully, and make a note of any potential corrections. Click **OK** after you have read the message. Click **Yes** if you are prompted to save the changes to the workbook.

- Excel should still be open. Pull down the **File menu**, click the **Open command**, then double click the **Amortization Schedule Solution** workbook.

- Click the button to **Enable macros**. The workbook opens and you should see the Amortization Schedule toolbar. Make corrections as necessary to the event procedures. Save the workbook.

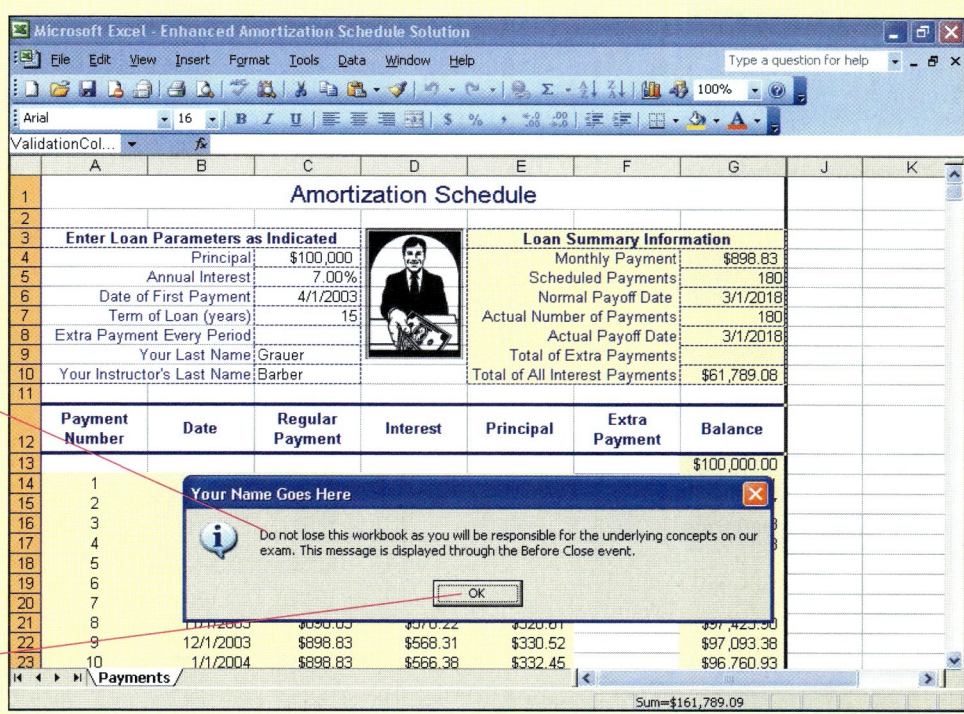

(d) Test the Procedures (step 4)

FIGURE 10.8   Hands-on Exercise 3 (*continued*)

THE WEEKDAY FUNCTION TEST FOR SPECIAL CONDITIONS

Use the WEEKDAY function within the Open and Before Close event procedures to test for special conditions. You can, for example, use the Open event to test for Monday, the first day of the business week, then display a message to check for new interest rates. In similar fashion, you can use the Before Close event to display a message on Friday, reminding the user to perform a weekly backup. See exercise 5 at the end of the chapter.

Step 5: **Create the User Form**

- Press **Alt+F11** to return to the Visual Basic Editor. Pull down the **Insert menu** and click **UserForm** to create a new user form as shown in Figure 10.8e. The form is stored within the Forms folder that appears automatically within the Project Explorer.

- The toolbox should appear automatically. If not, you can click the **Toolbox button** on the Standard toolbar to toggle the toolbox on and off. Do not be concerned if the size and/or position of the window for the form is different from ours.

- Click the **Label tool** (the large letter "A"), then click and drag in the form to create the first label, containing the title of the form. Click and drag within the newly created label to select the default text, **Label1**, then type **Amortization Schedule** to replace the existing text.

- Click the **Label tool** a second time. Click and drag in the form to create the second label, then enter the text shown in the figure.

- Click the **Save button** to save the form.

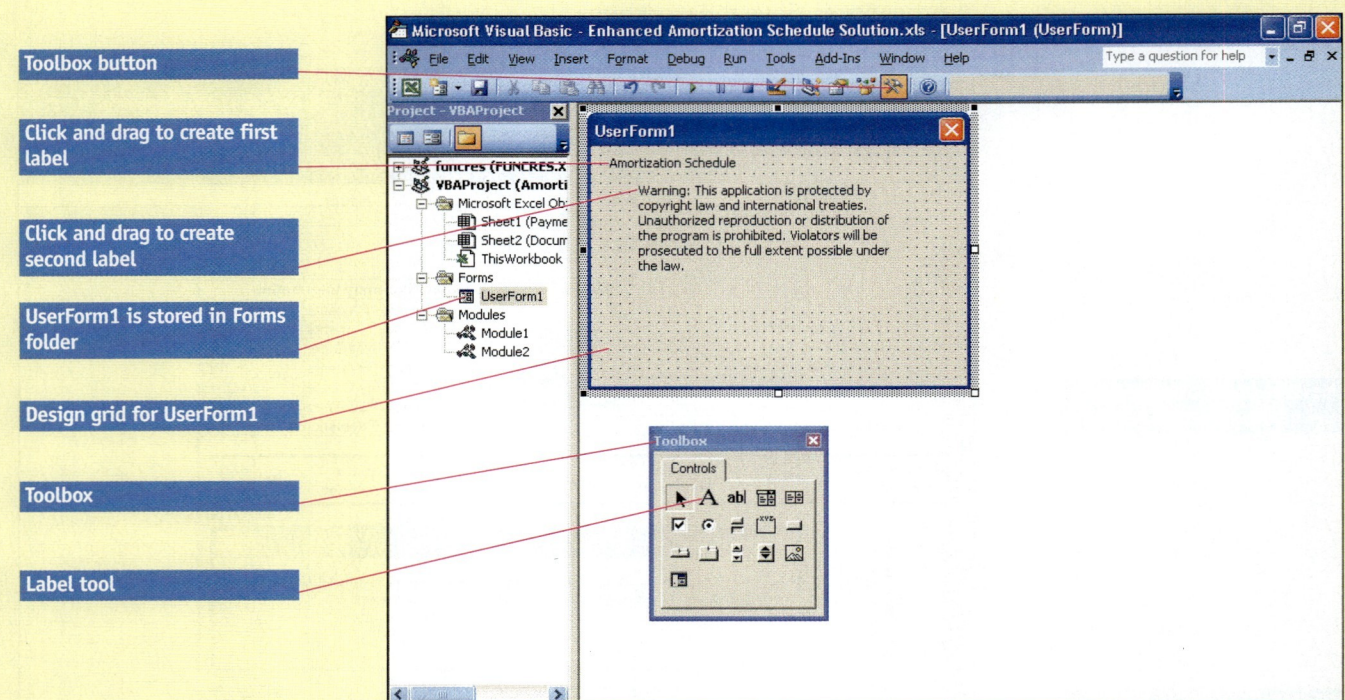

(e) Create the User Form (step 5)

FIGURE 10.8   Hands-on Exercise 3 (*continued*)

MANAGE THE OPEN WINDOWS

Multiple windows are open simultaneously within the VBA editor. Every module and form has its own window. The Project Explorer and Properties sheet are also open in separate windows. It may be helpful, therefore, to close the windows that you do not need. You can also move and size windows within the VBA editor. And finally, you can use the Window menu to tile or cascade the open windows.

Step 6: **Modify the Form Properties**

- Pull down the **View menu** and click the **Properties Window command** (or press the **F4 keyboard shortcut**) to open the Properties window in Figure 10.8f. Click the **Alphabetic tab** so that the properties are displayed alphabetically.

- Click the **second label** (the copyright notice), and you see its properties as shown in Figure 10.8f. Change the **Name property** to **CopyrightNotice**.

- Click in the **Back Color text box** to display a down arrow, then click the **down arrow** to display the available colors. Click the **System tab**, then choose the ToolTip color.

- Change the name and back color of the other label in similar fashion. Change the back color and caption property (to **Amortization Schedule**) of the form itself. Experiment further with the available properties (we changed the font size and alignment). Set a time limit. Five minutes is enough. Close the Properties window.

- Check that the user form is still selected in the Project Explorer. Click the background area on the form. Click the **View Code** and **View Object buttons** to switch between the code and the form, respectively. It doesn't matter if you see both windows simultaneously, or if one window overlays the other. The Code window contains only a Sub and End Sub. Save the form.

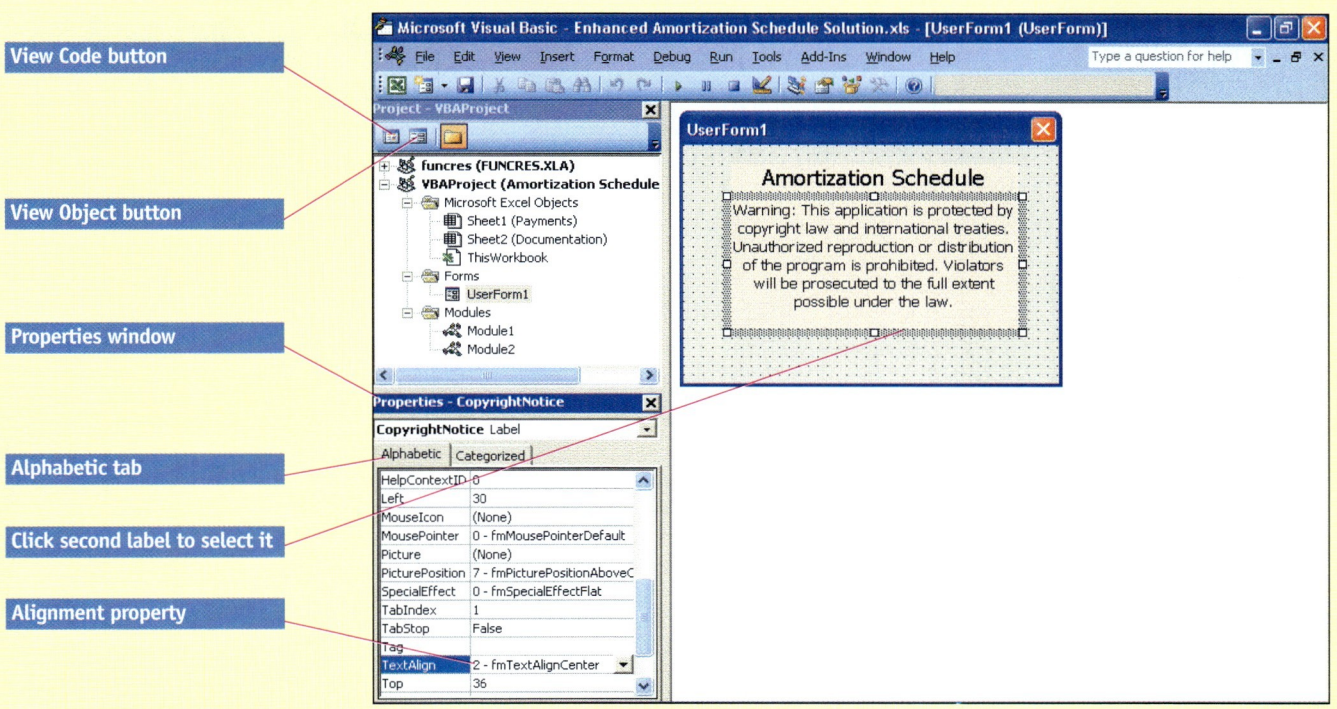

(f) Modify the Form Properties (step 6)

FIGURE 10.8 Hands-on Exercise 3 (*continued*)

THE SPLASH SCREEN

There are four distinct steps to creating a splash screen. First, you create the screen as a user form. Next, you create the Activate event procedure to display the form for a specified time. You then modify the Open workbook event procedure to load the user form when the workbook opens. And finally, you have to create a public procedure to unload the form after it has been displayed for the specified amount of time.

Step 7: **Create the Code for the User Form**

- Display the Code window for the user form. Click the **down arrow** in the Procedure list box (near the top of the VBA window) and select the **Activate event**. Delete the UserForm_Click procedure that is created by default.

- Enter the code for the **ActivateForm** event procedure as shown in Figure 10.8g. This procedure will display the form for five seconds once the form is activated, then it calls a second procedure to unload the form.

- It is still necessary to load the form initially within the Open workbook event procedure. Double click **ThisWorkbook** within the Project Explorer to return to the events associated with the workbook.

- Locate the **Open workbook procedure**. Add the statement **UserForm1.Show** on a separate line, after the statement to display the Amortization Schedule toolbar.

- You're almost finished but not quite. You still have to create the procedure to unload the form after the five seconds are up.

- Double click **Module1** within the Project Explorer window and create the **CloseScreen procedure**, which consists of three statements: **Public Sub CloseScreen()**, **Unload UserForm1**, and **End Sub**. Save the project.

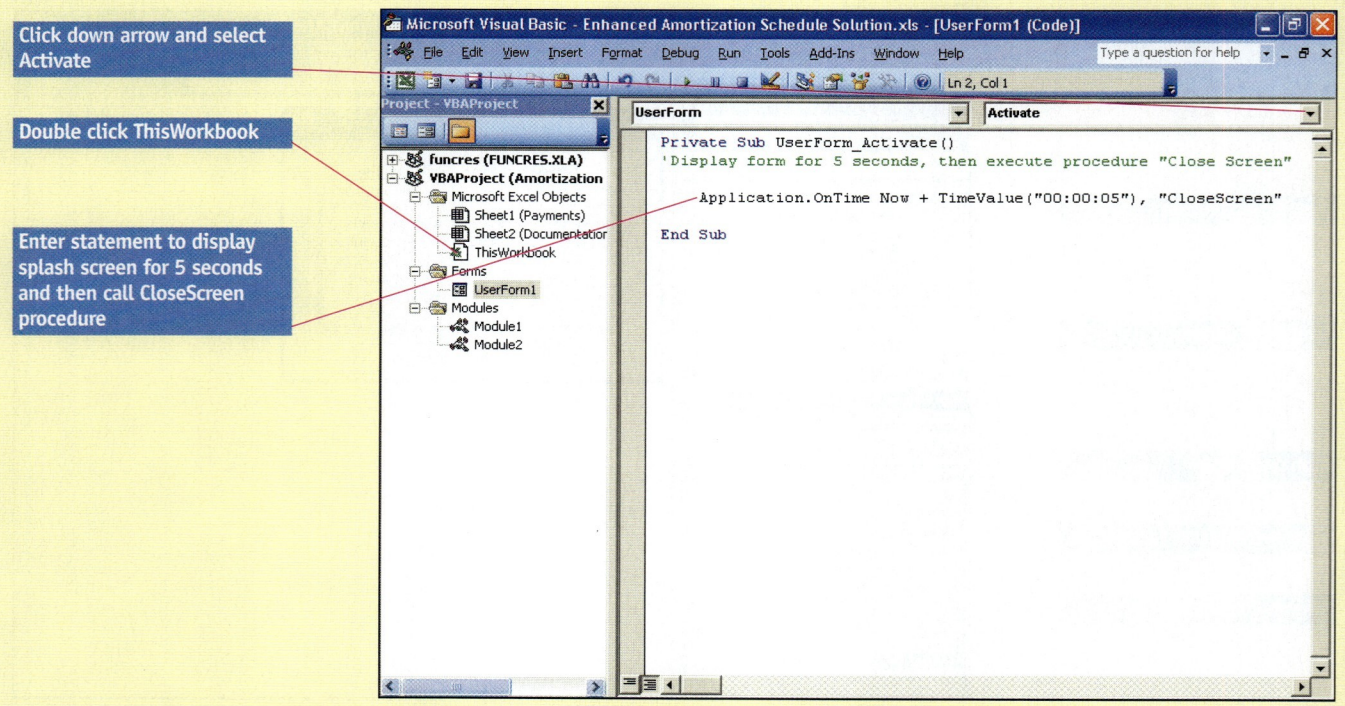

(g) Create the Code for the User Form (step 7)

FIGURE 10.8 Hands-on Exercise 3 (*continued*)

PUBLIC VERSUS PRIVATE PROCEDURES

The Amortization Schedule workbook is a VBA project. Each module in the project contains one or more procedures. Each procedure is either public or private. The scope of a procedure determines how the procedure can be accessed. A public procedure can be called from any module within the VBA project. A private procedure, however, can be accessed only from within the module in which it is stored.

Step 8: **Test the Splash Screen**

- Return to the Excel window. Close the workbook, but remain in Excel. Click **Yes** if asked whether to save the changes.

- Reopen the **Amortization Schedule Solution workbook** that appears at the top of the list of recently opened workbooks. Click the button to **Enable macros** when you see the security warning.

- The workbook opens and the Amortization Schedule toolbar is displayed, followed by the splash screen as shown in Figure 10.8h. The splash screen should remain for approximately five seconds, then it closes automatically.

- Enter any set of loan parameters, then test each of the toolbar buttons to be sure that they work properly. If the buttons do not function as intended, it could be because you forgot to attach the custom toolbar at the end of the previous exercise. Return to that exercise and repeat the steps correctly.

- Save the workbook. Exit Excel if you do not want to apply a digital signature to the workbook.

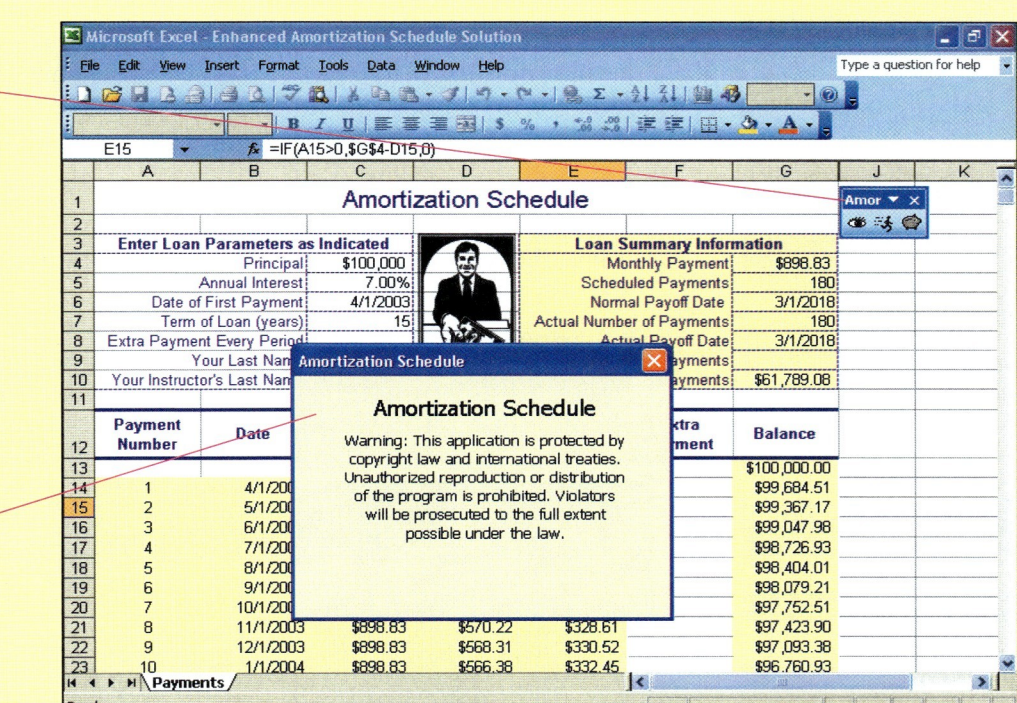

(h) Test the Splash Screen (step 8)

FIGURE 10.8 Hands-on Exercise 3 (*continued*)

SCREEN CAPTURE

The ability to capture a screen, then print the captured screen as part of a document, is very useful. The process is quite simple. Press the PrintScreen key any time you want to capture a screen to copy the screen to the Windows clipboard, an area of memory that is accessible to any Windows application. Next, start (or switch to) a Word document, and then execute the Paste command in the Edit menu to paste the contents of the clipboard into the current document. The screen is now part of the Word document, where it can be moved and sized like any other Windows object. See exercise 10 at the end of the chapter.

MICROSOFT OFFICE EXCEL 2003 REVISED

Step 9: **Authenticate the Workbook**

- You cannot digitally sign a workbook unless you have a digital signature. Click the **Start button**, click **All Programs**, click **Microsoft Office**, click **Microsoft Office Tools**, and then click **Digital Certificate for VBA Projects**.

- Type **Your Name** in the Create Digital Certificate dialog box. Click **OK** to create your signature and close the dialog box.

- The Amortization Schedule Solution workbook should still be open. Press **Alt+F11** to switch to the VBA editor. Pull down the **Tools menu** and click the **Digital Signature command** to display the associated dialog box.

- Click the **Choose button** to display the Select Certificate dialog box, click the signature you just created, click **OK** to close the Select Certificate dialog box, then click **OK** a second time to close the Digital Signature dialog box. Close the VBA editor.

- Save the workbook. Close the workbook, but leave Excel open. Pull down the **File menu** and click the **Enhanced Amortization Schedule Solution workbook** that appears at the bottom of the File menu.

- You should see the Security Warning in Figure 10.8i. Your name should appear as the publisher of the workbook. Look closely, however, and note the message that indicates your credentials cannot be trusted. This is because your certificate has not been authenticated by a formal certification agency.

- Click the button to **Enable Macros** to return to the Excel workbook. You will see the splash screen, amortization toolbar, and so on.

- Close the workbook. Exit Excel if you do not want to continue with the next exercise at this time.

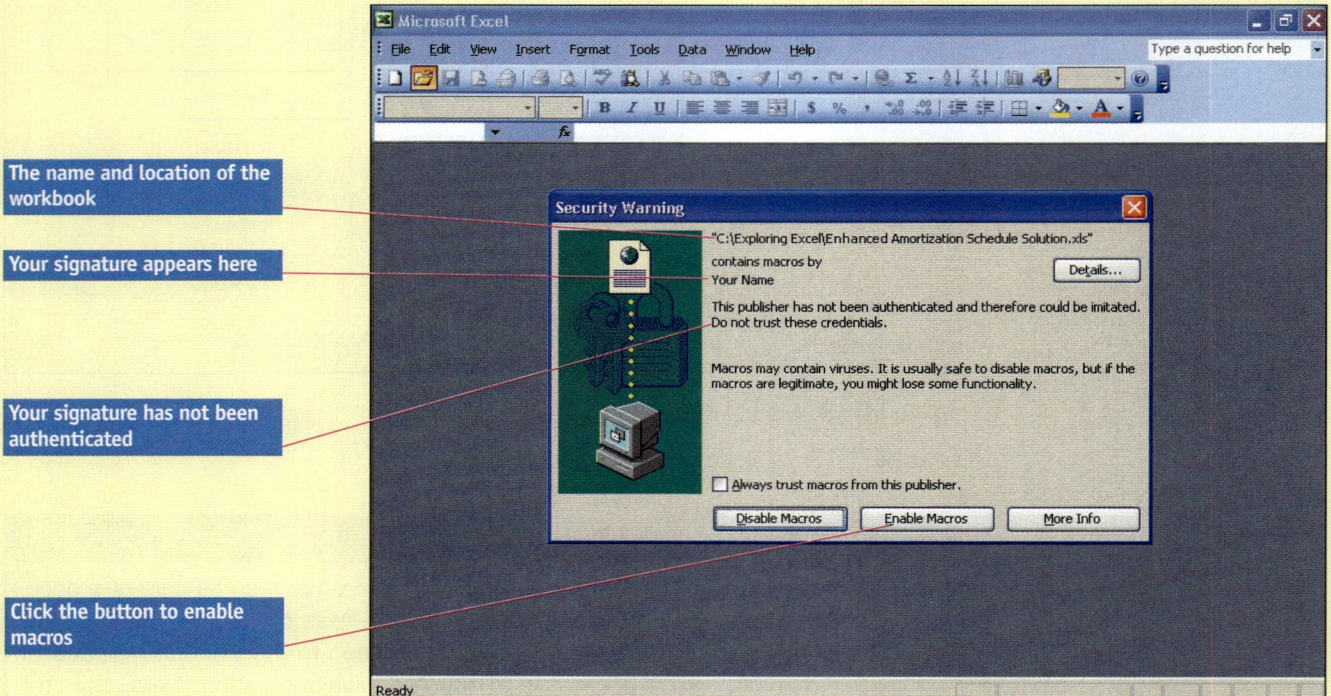

(i) Authenticate the Workbook (step 9)

FIGURE 10.8 Hands-on Exercise 3 (*continued*)

MORE COMPLEX PROCEDURES

A good application lets a user accomplish tasks that he or she could not (easily) do through ordinary Excel commands. The original amortization worksheet gave the user the capability to apply an optional extra payment *every month*. What if, however, the user wanted to see the effect of an *annual* optional payment (that is, an extra payment once a year)? This is best accomplished through a VBA procedure that prompts the user for the amount of the annual payment and the date it is to begin, after which the procedure applies that payment annually until the loan is paid off. Such a procedure entails more complex logic than what we have shown so far.

The difficulty (if any) is not the VBA per se, but rather the underlying logic. Think carefully about the implication of the preceding sentence. VBA is a powerful tool, and because it is powerful, developers use it to implement sophisticated procedures that entail nontrivial logic.

Pseudocode or "neat notes to oneself" is the most common way of expressing logic. Pseudocode does not have any precise syntax and is intended only to convey the logic within a program. One develops pseudocode by thinking in very general terms about the steps required to solve the problem. Our problem, simply stated, is to write a VBA procedure that will apply an annual extra payment to the existing payments table until the loan is paid off. This requires that we

1. Ask the user for the amount of the extra payment.

2. Ask the user when the extra payments are to begin.

3. Determine where in the table the payments are to begin.

4. Apply the extra payments annually until the loan is paid off.

This version of the pseudocode is almost trivial, but it does get you started thinking about the problem. You prompt the user for the amount and date of the periodic payment, go to the first date in the table where the payments are to begin, and then apply the periodic payment annually until the loan is paid off. The logic is accurate and complete, but it is not sufficiently detailed to provide a real help in writing the procedure.

It is necessary, therefore, to further develop the steps that determine when the payments are to begin, and how to apply the payments within the table. The expanded pseudocode is shown in Figure 10.9a and includes decision making and loops. To determine the first extra payment, you go to the first date within the payments table, then look at each successive date within the table until you reach a date greater than or equal to the date the payments are to begin. You then move the active cell to the payments column within this row.

Once you have the position of the first extra payment, you create a second loop in which you apply a payment once a year until the loan is paid off. This is accomplished through a **switch**, a programming term for a variable that assumes one of two values. We set the switch (PayoffMade in this example) to "No" outside of the loop, then we go through the loop until the loan has been paid off. The first statement in the loop applies the extra payment to the active cell, after which the If statement compares the balance at the end of that year to zero. If the loan has been paid off, the switch is set to "Yes" and the loop is terminated. If the loan has not been paid, we move one year down in the table and return to the top of the loop.

Only when you are comfortable with this logic should you begin to write the VBA procedure, starting with the macro recorder to provide basic syntax. We used the macro recorder to capture the statement to select a specific cell (FirstTableDate in this example). We also used it to get the syntax for the relative references to various cells within the table. Once we had these basic statements, we added the additional VBA control structures to complete the procedure. The indentation within the procedure and the blank lines between statements are there only to enhance the readability.

User supplies amount and start date for extra payments

```
Input amount of extra payment and date payments are to begin

Set active date to first table date
Do Until active cell >= Date that payments are to begin
      Check next date
Loop
Move active cell to the extra payment column in this row

PayoffMade = "No"
Do Until PayoffMade = "Yes"
      Apply extra payment here
      If Ending Balance at end of year <=0
            PayoffMade = "Yes"
      Else
            Drop active cell 12 rows (1 year)
      End if
Loop

Display summary area
```

Determines where in table payments begin

Applies extra payments until loan is paid off

(a) Pseudocode

User supplies amount and start date for extra payment

Determines where in table payments begin

Applies extra payments until loan is paid off

```
Sub PeriodicExtraPayments()
    Dim DateExtraPaymentsBegin As Date
    Dim AmountofExtraPayment As Currency
    Dim PayoffMade As String
    AmountofExtraPayment = InputBox("Enter amount of extra payment")
    DateExtraPaymentsBegin = InputBox("Enter date when payments begin")

    Application.Goto Reference:="FirstTableDate"

    Do Until ActiveCell >= DateExtraPaymentsBegin
        ActiveCell.Offset(1, 0).Range("A1").Select
    Loop

    ActiveCell.Offset(0, 4).Range("A1").Select

    PayoffMade = "No"
    Do Until PayoffMade = "Yes"
        ActiveCell = AmountofExtraPayment
        If ActiveCell.Offset(11, 1) <= 0 Then 'Check one year later
            PayoffMade = "Yes"
        Else
            ActiveCell.Offset(12, 0).Select    'New Payment necessary
        End If
    Loop

    Range("TotalOfExtraPayments").Select

End Sub
```

(b) The VBA Procedure

FIGURE 10.9 Periodic Extra Payments

hands-on exercise
4 Periodic Optional Payments

Objective Develop a procedure to apply periodic extra payments to a loan until the loan is paid off. Use Figure 10.10 as a guide in the exercise.

Step 1: **Start the Macro Recorder**

- Open the **Enhanced Amortization Schedule Solution** and click the button to **Enable macros**. Pull down the **Tools menu** to start recording a new macro. Enter **PeriodicExtraPayment** as the name of the macro. Click **OK** to begin recording.

- The Relative Reference button on the Stop Recording toolbar should be out, so that you are recording absolute references. Click the **down arrow** in the Name box at the upper left of the window, then select **FirstTableDate**, which positions you in cell B14.

- Click the **Relative Reference button** to record relative references from now on. Click in **cell B15** as shown in Figure 10.10a to move down one row.

- Click the **Stop Recording button**. Save the workbook.

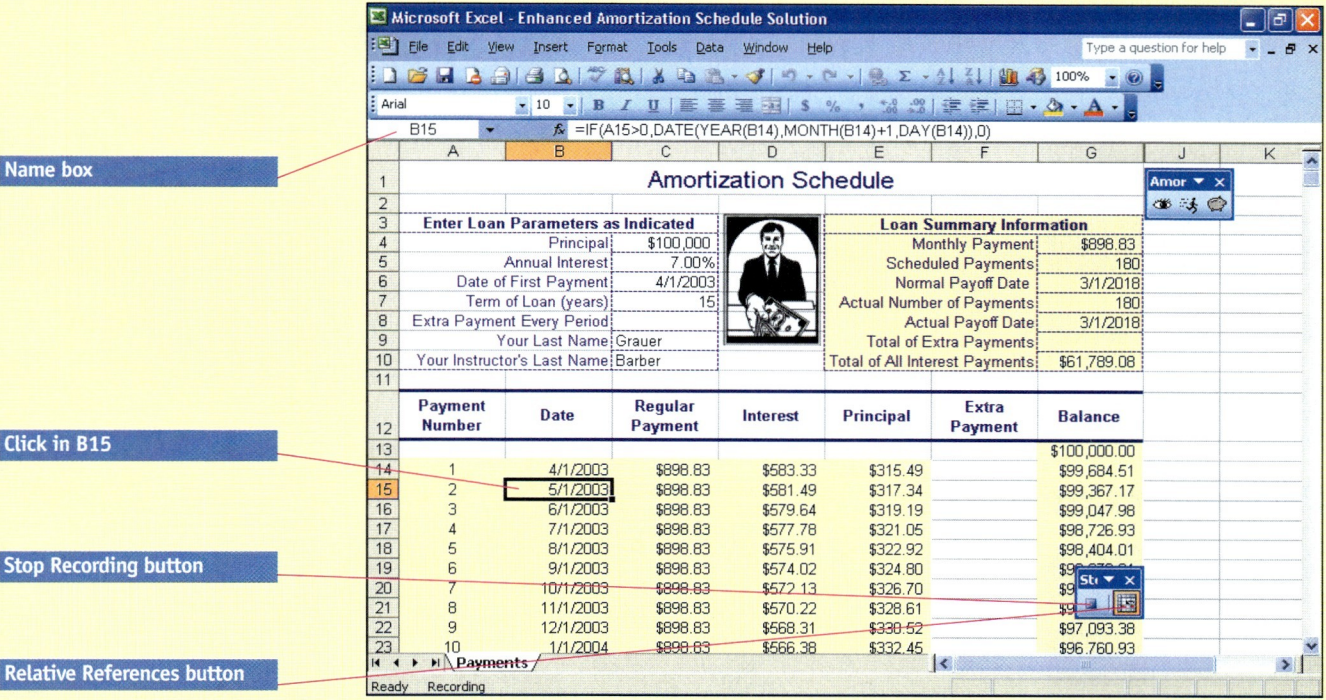

(a) Start the Macro Recorder (step 1)

FIGURE 10.10 Hands-on Exercise 4

IS THE BUTTON IN OR OUT?

The Relative Reference button on the Stop Recording toolbar toggles between relative (the button is in) and absolute (the button is out) references. The ScreenTip, however, displays "Relative References" regardless of whether the button is in or out. We wish that Microsoft had made it easier to tell which type of reference you are recording, but it didn't.

Step 2: **View and Add Code**

- Press **Alt+F11** to open the VBA editor. Open the **Modules folder**. Double click the module that contains the current macro (Module3 in our figure).

- You should see two statements within the procedure. The first statement, **Application.Goto Reference: ="FirstTableDate"** goes to the first date within the table (cell B14).

- The second statement, **ActiveCell.Offset(1,0).Range("A1").Select** moves the active cell down one row, but remains in column B. (The Range property can be deleted—see the boxed tip below.)

- Add the remaining statements as shown in Figure 10.10b.
    - The **Dim statement** defines a variable
    - The **InputBox function** prompts the user for the value of this variable.
    - The **Do** and **Loop statements** go down the column of dates until the starting date is reached.
    - The **Offset property** selects the cell four columns to the right of the active cell (the Extra Payment column).

- Save the procedure.

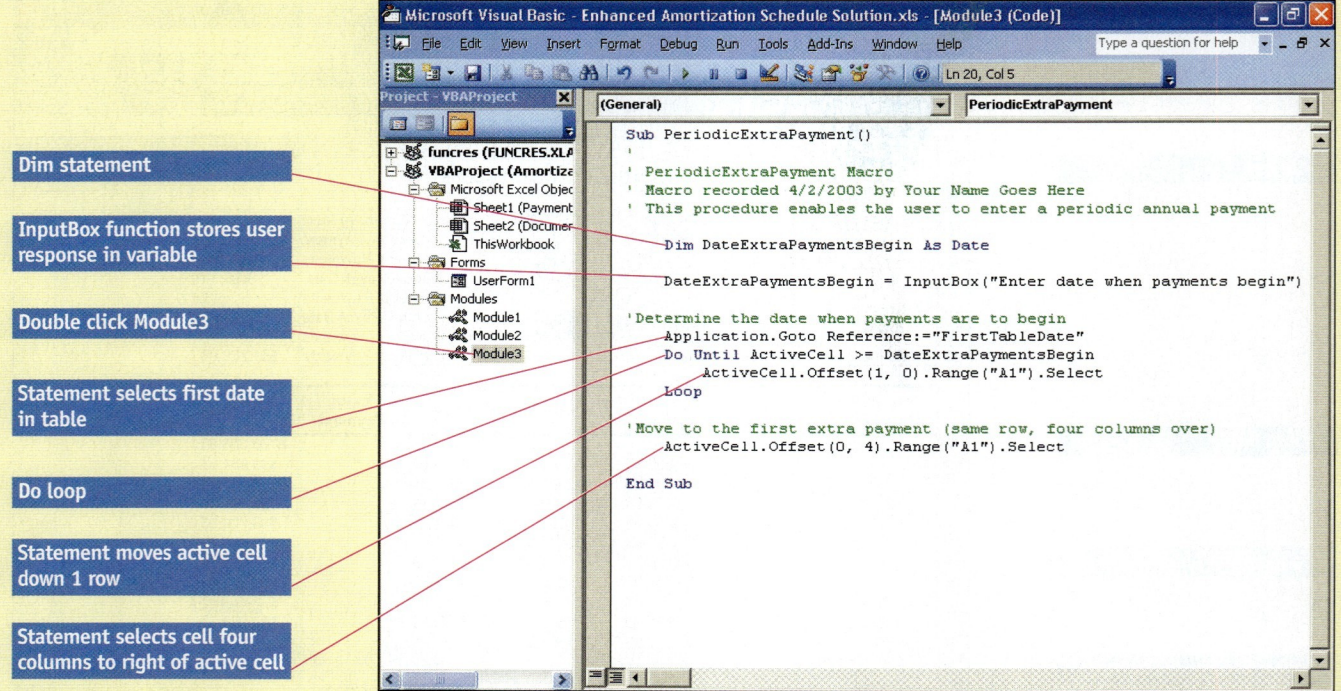

(b) View and Add Code (step 2)

FIGURE 10.10 Hands-on Exercise 4 (*continued*)

WHAT DOES RANGE("A1") REALLY MEAN?

The statement ActiveCell.Offset(1,0).Range("A1").Select has nothing to do with cell A1, so why is the entry (Range"A1") included? The Range property describes the number and shape of the selected cells—Range("A1") refers to a single cell. The default, however, is to select a single cell; therefore the Range property can be deleted, which results in the simpler statement ActiveCell.Offset(1,0).Select. If, however, you were selecting multiple cells, the Range property would be necessary.

Step 3: **Step through the Procedure**

- Point to a blank area at the right of the Windows taskbar, and then click the **right mouse button**. Click the command to **Show the Desktop**.
- Click the **VBA** and **Excel buttons** on the taskbar. **Right click** a blank area of the taskbar a second time, then click the command to **Tile Windows Vertically**.
- Your desktop should be similar to Figure 10.10c. It does not matter if the Excel window is on the left or right. Click in the Excel zoom box and lower the zoom percentage to **75%** to view more entries within the payments table.
- Click in the window containing the VBA editor. Close the Project Explorer. Click after the Sub statement within the PeriodicExtraPayment procedure.
- Press the **F8 key** or click the **Step Into button** on the Debug toolbar. The procedure header is highlighted. Press the **F8 key** a second time.
- The InputBox statement is highlighted, indicating that it will be executed next. Press the **F8 key** again to display the input box in the figure. Type any date that occurs two or three months after the first payment, then press **Enter.**
- Press the **F8 key** continually until you reach the date at which payments are to begin. At that point, the cell four columns to the right is selected.
- Press the **F8 key** one last time to move below the End Sub statement.

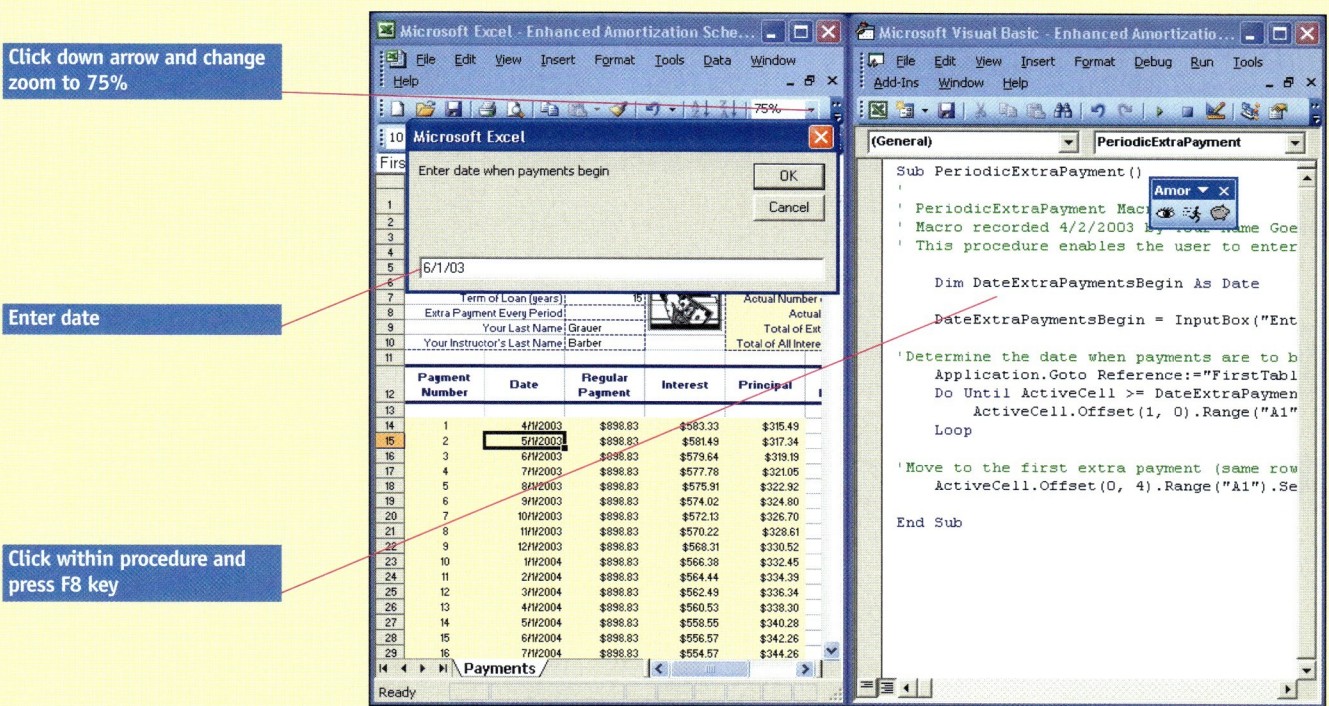

(c) Step through the Procedure (step 3)

FIGURE 10.10 Hands-on Exercise 4 (*continued*)

DIVIDE AND CONQUER

The logic to apply periodic payments is nontrivial and consists of three basic building blocks—obtain input from the user, determine the cell for the first extra payment, and apply periodic payments until the loan is paid off. The best way to develop the procedure is to code and test each block in sequence. Once you are sure of one step, move on to the next.

Step 4: **Add Additional Code**

- Maximize the VBA window. Add the additional statements to complete the procedure as shown in Figure 10.10d. Note the following:
  - The additional Dim statements define the amount of the extra payment and the switch to control the loop to apply the payments.
  - The additional InputBox function obtains the amount of the extra payment.
  - The additional loop applies the first extra payment, then continues to apply an annual payment until the loan is paid off.
  - The last statement selects a cell in the summary portion of the worksheet so that the user sees the relevant information about the loan in a single place.
- Add indentation, blank lines, and comments as you see fit to enhance the readability of the code. (These elements will make the procedure easier to follow and are not required by VBA.)
- Save the procedure.

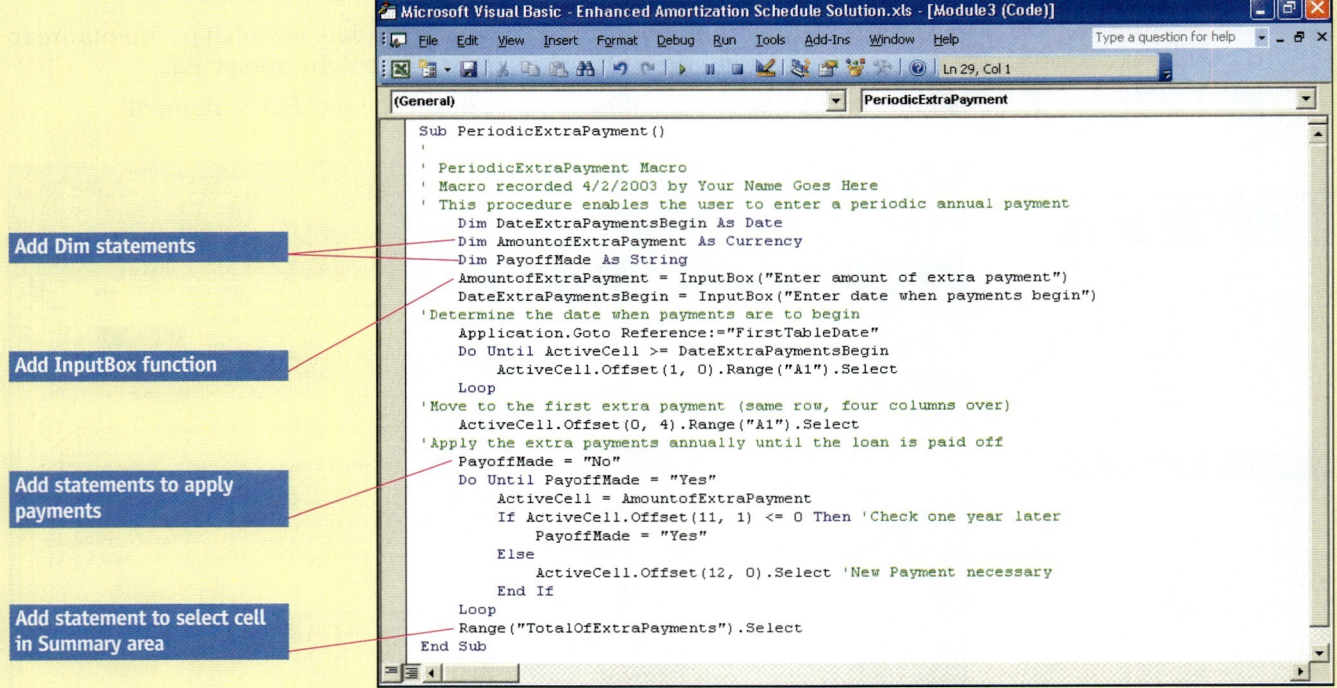

(d) Add Additional Code (step 4)

FIGURE 10.10 Hands-on Exercise 4 (*continued*)

SETTING A SWITCH

The use of a switch to control an action within a procedure is a common programming technique. The PayoffMade switch in this example is initially set to "no", prior to applying the first optional payment. The procedure then steps through the table to apply additional payments, testing after each optional payment to see if the loan is paid off, and if so, resetting the switch to "yes". At that point the loop is terminated and control passes to the next sequential statement.

Step 5: Test the Procedure

- Return to Excel. Maximize the Excel window. Check that your loan parameters match those in Figure 10.10e. (Your dates will be different.)

- Pull down the **Tools menu**, click **Macro**, click **Macros . . .**, then run the **PeriodicExtraPayment** procedure that you completed in the previous step. Enter **$1,500** and a date two months after the first payment as the amount of the extra payment and the date the payments are to begin.

- The macro executes, and if all goes well, you will see the summary information in our figure. The actual number of payments has been reduced to 145 (from 180). The total of the extra payments was $18,000.

- If you did not get these results, check that your loan parameters match ours and try again. If you still do not get these results, return to the previous step and check your code. If you cannot find an obvious error, tile the Excel and VBA windows as described in step 3 and step through the procedure.

- Pull down the **Tools menu**, click **Macro**, then click **Macros . . .** and run the **ClearExtraPayments** macro that we provided with the workbook. The extra payments disappear, and the loan requires the full 180 payments.

- Delete the term of the loan so that the loan parameters are incomplete. The individual payments disappear from the body of the worksheet. Rerun the **PeriodicExtraPayment** procedure.

- You are prompted for the amount of the extra payment and the starting date. This time the procedure is stuck in a loop because it cannot find the starting date. Press **Ctrl+Break** to stop the execution of the macro.

- Click the **Debug button** in the dialog box that appears. This takes you to the Visual Basic editor, where you can correct the code.

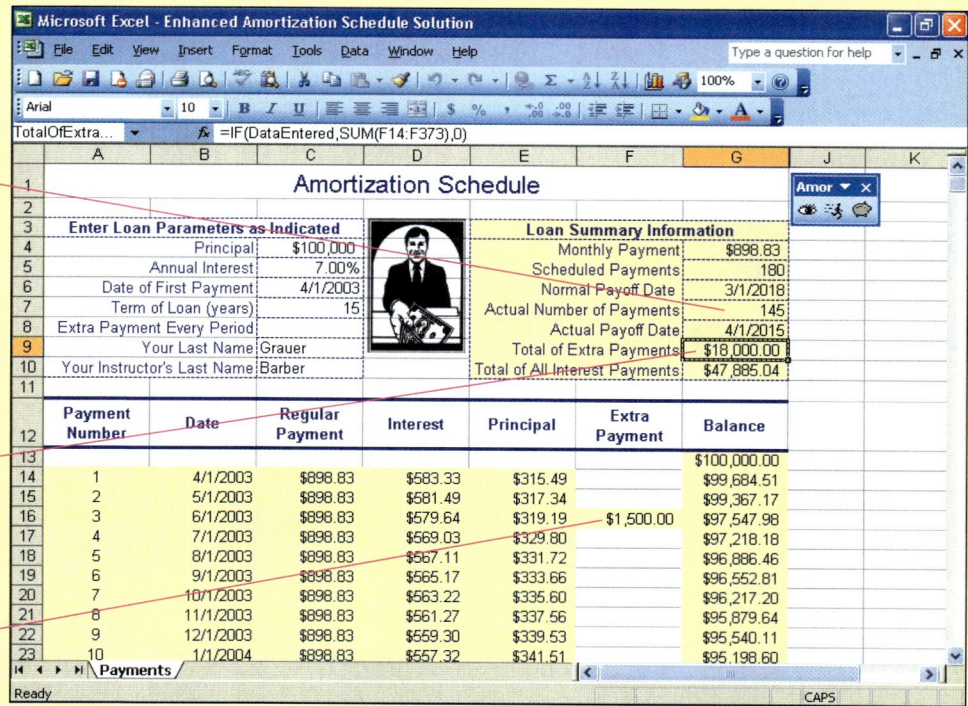

(e) Test the Procedure (step 5)

FIGURE 10.10 Hands-on Exercise 4 (*continued*)

Step 6: Revise the Procedure

- You are back in the Visual Basic editor within the PeriodicExtraPayment procedure. One line within the procedure is highlighted, indicating where the procedure stopped executing.

- Click the **Reset button** (the tiny square) on the Standard toolbar. The highlighting disappears. You can now add the additional VBA statements to complete the procedure.

- The procedure executes correctly as long as the loan parameters were entered. It does not work, however, if the information is missing. Hence you need to test for the parameters within an If statement.

- Modify the procedure as shown in Figure 10.10f to include the **If statement**, the associated **Else clause**, and the concluding **End If**.
    - The If statement toward the top of the procedure tests to see if the loan parameters are present in the worksheet.
    - The Else clause displays an error message if the loan parameters are missing.

- Save the revised procedure.

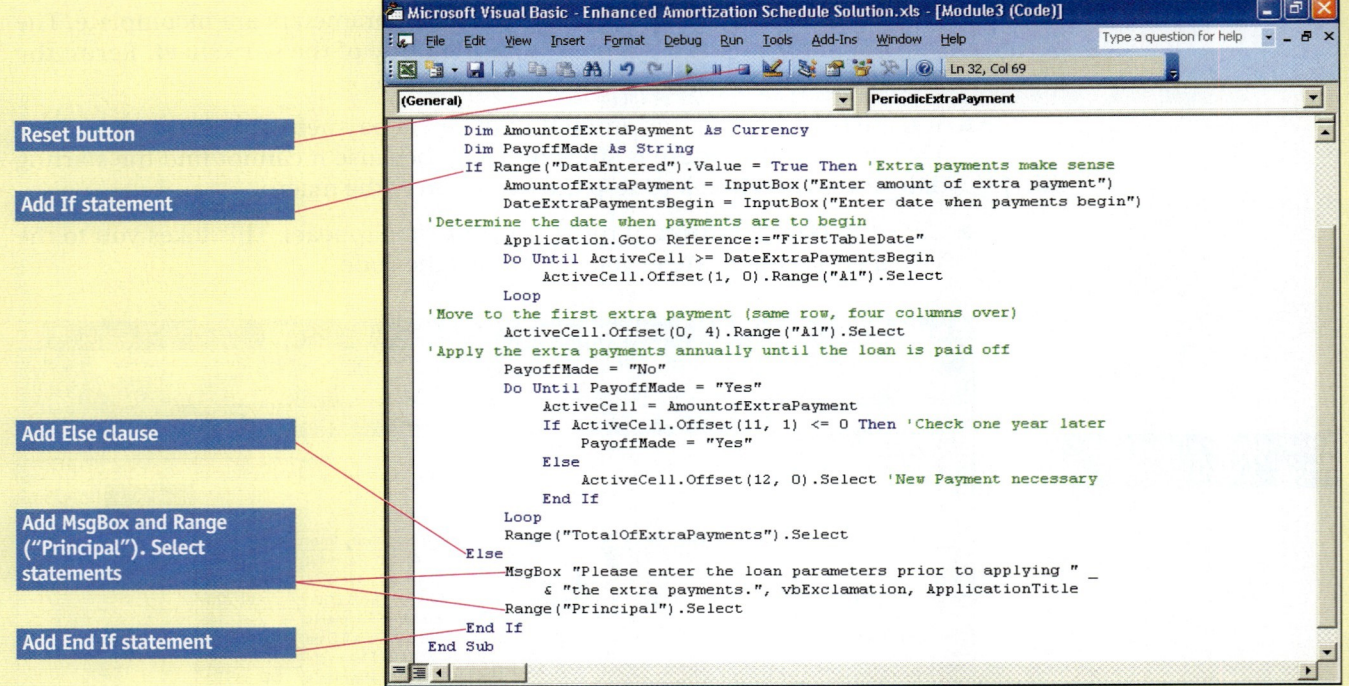

(f) Revise the Procedure (step 6)

FIGURE 10.10 Hands-on Exercise 4 (*continued*)

TEST UNDER ALL CONDITIONS

The most important characteristic of an application is that it works, and further that it works under all circumstances. It must be "bulletproof," and thus it should be tested under any and all conditions that might occur. The user should not try to apply periodic extra payments if loan parameters have not been entered, but what if that happens? The developer should have anticipated the possibility and built in the additional code to prevent the application from crashing.

558   CHAPTER 10: A PROFESSIONAL APPLICATION

Step 7: **Retest the Procedure**

- Click the **Excel button** on the Windows taskbar to return to Excel. Check that the loan information is still incomplete, then pull down the **Tools menu** and retest the **PeriodicExtraPayment procedure**.

- You should see the message box in Figure 10.10g that indicates the missing data. Click **OK** to close the dialog box.

- Pull down the **View menu**, click the **Toolbars command**, click **Customize**, and then modify the custom toolbar from the earlier exercise to include buttons for the additional procedures you developed. Use the **smiley face** and **sad face** for the **PeriodicExtraPayment** and **ClearExtraPayments procedures**, respectively.

- You must also attach the modified toolbar to your workbook. Pull down the **View menu**, click **Toolbars**, and click the **Customize command** to display the Customize dialog box. Click the **Toolbars tab**, then click the **Attach button** to display the Attach Toolbars dialog box.

- Select the Amortization Schedule toolbar in the right pane and click the **Delete button** to remove the old version. Select the **Amortization Schedule toolbar** in the left pane and click the **Copy button**. Click **OK**. Click **Close**.

- Save the workbook. The application is complete, but we provide additional practice through end-of-chapter exercises. Exit Excel.

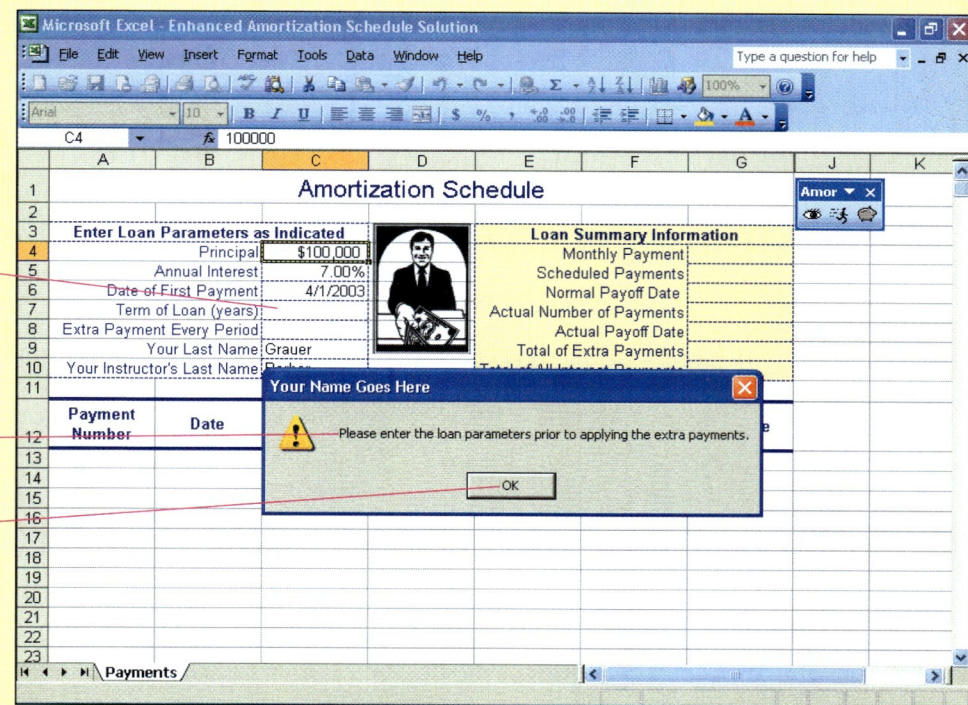

(g) Retest the Procedure (step 7)

FIGURE 10.10 Hands-on Exercise 4 (*continued*)

PRINT THE VBA CODE

It is good practice to obtain hard copy of the modules you have created for future study. Press Alt+F11 to return to the VBA editor. Select Module1. Pull down the File menu and click the Print command to display the Print dialog box. Select the option to print the current module, then click OK. Print any other modules in similar fashion.

SUMMARY

This chapter focused on the development of the Enhanced Amortization Schedule workbook, a professional application that is suitable for distribution to individuals who need not be proficient in Excel. The workbook is visually appealing. It includes data validation to ensure sensible results and automation to facilitate ease of use. The workbook also enables the end user to do things that he or she could not do without benefit of VBA.

Excel contains various date functions to facilitate date arithmetic and/or to isolate the individual components of a date. The TODAY function returns the current date. The DATE function creates a date from three individual arguments (year, month, and day). The DAY, MONTH, and YEAR functions each have a single argument (a numeric date) and return the numeric day, month, and year, respectively.

VBA accomplishes its tasks by manipulating objects. Each object (such as a workbook, worksheet, a single cell, or chart) has a well-defined set of characteristics called properties, and each object can perform a set of actions called methods. The object model describes the hierarchical way the different objects are related to one another. Each application in Microsoft Office has its own object model. A collection is a group of similar objects within the object model.

An event is any action that is recognized by an application. An event procedure is a procedure that is activated in response to a specific event. To use VBA effectively, you decide which events are significant, and what is to happen when those events occur. Then you develop the appropriate event procedures. Event procedures are distinguished from general procedures that can be executed any time at the discretion of the user.

A custom toolbar can be created as a convenient way to run the procedures for any application. The toolbar must be attached to the workbook to distribute the toolbar with the workbook. The custom toolbar can be displayed and hidden automatically through the Open workbook and Before Close event procedures.

A user form is a convenient way to enter data within an application. A splash screen is a simple form that consists entirely of text. There are two essential tasks to display a splash screen. First, you have to create the form and then you develop the procedure(s) to display (and hide) the form.

Pseudocode or "neat notes to oneself" is the most common way of expressing logic. Pseudocode does not have any precise syntax and is intended only to convey the logic within a procedure.

A digital signature is an electronic, encryption-based stamp of authentication, which confirms the origin of a document, and further that the document has not been altered since it was last saved by the signer. You can create your own signature using a tool within Microsoft Office. Any certificate that you create yourself is unauthenticated, however, and generates a warning in the Security Warning box if the security level is set to High or Medium. You can also obtain an authenticated digital certificate from an internal security administrator and/or a variety of commercial sources.

KEY TERMS

Amortization 516	IPMT function 528	Properties window 541
AND function 517	Macro recorder 528	Property 528
Before Close	Method 528	Pseudocode 551
event procedure 539	MONTH function 520	Splash screen 539
Collection 528	MsgBox function 529	Switch 551
Custom toolbar 539	MsgBox statement 529	TODAY function 520
Data validation 516	Object 528	User form 541
DATE function 520	Object model 528	UserForm Activate
DAY function 520	OnTime method 541	event procedure 541
Digital signature 539	Open workbook event	WEEKDAY function 545
Event 539	procedure 539	YEAR function 520
Event procedure 539	PPMT function 528	Zero suppression 523
General procedure 539	Print area 527	

MULTIPLE CHOICE

1. Which of the following will display the date November 16, 2002?
   (a) =DATE(11,16,2002)
   (b) =DATE(2002, 11, 16)
   (c) =DATE(2002, 16, 11)
   (d) =11/16/2002

2. Given that cell A4 contains the date 1/21/2002, what date will be displayed as a result of the function =DATE(YEAR(A4)+1,MONTH(A4)+2,DAY(A4)+3)?
   (a) 2/23/2005
   (b) 1/24/2005
   (c) 3/24/2003
   (d) 2/22/2003

3. What values will be returned by the logical functions =AND(10>5, 6<3) and =OR (10>5, 6<3)?
   (a) Both functions will return True
   (b) Both functions will return False
   (c) True and False, respectively
   (d) False and True, respectively

4. Which of the following is true about the PPMT function?
   (a) It determines the periodic payment for a loan
   (b) It determines the amount of a periodic payment that goes toward principal
   (c) It will adjust automatically if an additional payment toward principal was made during the preceding period
   (d) All of the above

5. What is a program switch?
   (a) A setting to start or stop the macro recorder
   (b) A variable that assumes one of two values, typically "yes" or "no"
   (c) An indication of whether the macro recorder is relative or absolute
   (d) All of the above

6. A single workbook, worksheet, chart, or range is called a(n):
   (a) Object
   (b) Property
   (c) Method
   (d) Collection

7. Which of the following is true, given the VBA statements Selection.Copy and Selection.Value=0?
   (a) Selection is a VBA object
   (b) Copy is a method of the Selection object
   (c) Value is a property of the Selection object
   (d) All of the above

8. Given the statement If MsgBox("Are you George?", vbyesno) = vbNo Then . .
   (a) MsgBox is used as a function rather than a statement
   (b) The question mark icon will be displayed within the message box
   (c) The Then portion of the If statement will address anyone named George
   (d) All of the above

9. Which of the following is typically *not* done in conjunction with adding a button to a custom toolbar?
   (a) An image is selected for the button
   (b) A description is written for the button
   (c) A macro is assigned to the button
   (d) A sound is assigned to the button

10. Which of the following is true regarding a VBA procedure that attempts to modify one or more cells in a protected worksheet?
    (a) The procedure *must* include an Unprotect worksheet statement at the beginning of the procedure
    (b) The procedure *must* include an Unprotect worksheet statement at the beginning and a Protect worksheet statement at the end
    (c) The procedure need not include Protect or Unprotect statements provided the Open workbook event procedure enables changes to the user interface
    (d) The procedure need not include Protect or Unprotect statements provided the Close workbook event procedure enables changes to the user interface

. . . continued

multiple choice

11. Which of the following is *not* necessary to create a splash screen?
    (a) Create a user form as the basis of the splash screen, then modify the Open workbook event procedure to show the user form
    (b) Create the Activate Form event procedure to set the timer
    (c) Create an Open Form event procedure
    (d) Create a public procedure to unload the form

12. Which of the following is least appropriate in the Open workbook event procedure?
    (a) A statement to display a custom toolbar
    (b) A message to the user to back up the system at the end of the session
    (c) A statement to display a splash screen
    (d) A statement to protect the user interface only

13. Which of the following will trigger the Before Close event procedure?
    (a) Pulling down the File menu and clicking the Close command
    (b) Pulling down the File menu and clicking the Exit command
    (c) Clicking either Close button at the upper right of the Excel window
    (d) All of the above

14. Which of the following best describes how to protect a worksheet but still enable the user to change the value of selected cells within the worksheet?
    (a) Unprotect the cells that are to change, then protect the entire sheet
    (b) Unlock the cells that are to change, then protect the entire worksheet
    (c) Protect the entire worksheet, then unlock the cells that are to change
    (d) Protect the entire worksheet, then unprotect the cells that are to change

15. Which of the following is a true statement about pseudocode?
    (a) It is defined as neat notes to oneself
    (b) It is required by the VBA editor for all procedures that include loops and decision making
    (c) It has a precise set of syntactical rules
    (d) It is displayed automatically within the VBA editor as the associated procedure is executing

16. A group of similar objects within the object model is called a(n):
    (a) Module
    (b) Procedure
    (c) Attribute
    (d) Collection

17. An action performed by an object is called a:
    (a) Command
    (b) Property
    (c) Method
    (d) Procedure

18. Worksheets("Forecast").Range("NextYear") refers to:
    (a) The range "NextYear" in the current worksheet
    (b) The range "NextYear" in the current worksheet in the current workbook
    (c) The range "NextYear" in the worksheet named "Forecast" in the current workbook
    (d) The range "NextYear" in the workbook named "Forecast"

ANSWERS

1. b
2. c
3. d
4. b
5. b
6. a
7. d
8. a
9. d
10. c
11. c
12. b
13. d
14. b
15. a
16. d
17. c
18. c

PRACTICE WITH EXCEL AND VBA

1. **Practice with Dates:** Open the partially completed version of the workbook in Figure 10.11 in *Chapter 10 Practice 1* in the Exploring Excel folder. (Click the button to Enable Macros.) The workbook will open, and you will see the message box that is displayed in the figure indicating that the dates in the workbook are reset automatically. Click OK after you have read the message.

    a. The invoice dates in your worksheet will differ from those in our figure, but the values in the Days Elapsed column should be identical to ours after you complete the worksheet. Enter the appropriate formula into cell B4 and change the formatting as necessary. Copy the formula in cell B4 to the remaining rows in the column.

    b. Enter the appropriate formulas for the first invoice to compute current amount due, as well as the amounts that are 30, 60, and 90 days late. Two of these formulas are simple If statements (the current amount due, and the amount over 90 days). The other two formulas require nested If statements (an IF function within an IF function). We suggest you do the 60-day formula first, since that is the easier one. Then once you have that formula, you will be able to extend it to the 30-day formula.

    c. Copy the formulas for the first invoice to the remaining rows in the column. Add the formulas to compute the totals in each category, then compare your values to ours. The dollar amounts in each column should match Figure 10.11 even though the individual invoice dates are different.

    d. Open the Visual Basic editor and look at the Open workbook event procedure. What is the significance of the "UpdateDates" statement that is found in this event procedure?

    e. Add your name and birth date in the indicated cells, then add the formula to compute your age as shown in the worksheet. Format the worksheet appropriately, then print it two ways, once to show the displayed values, and once to show the cell formulas.

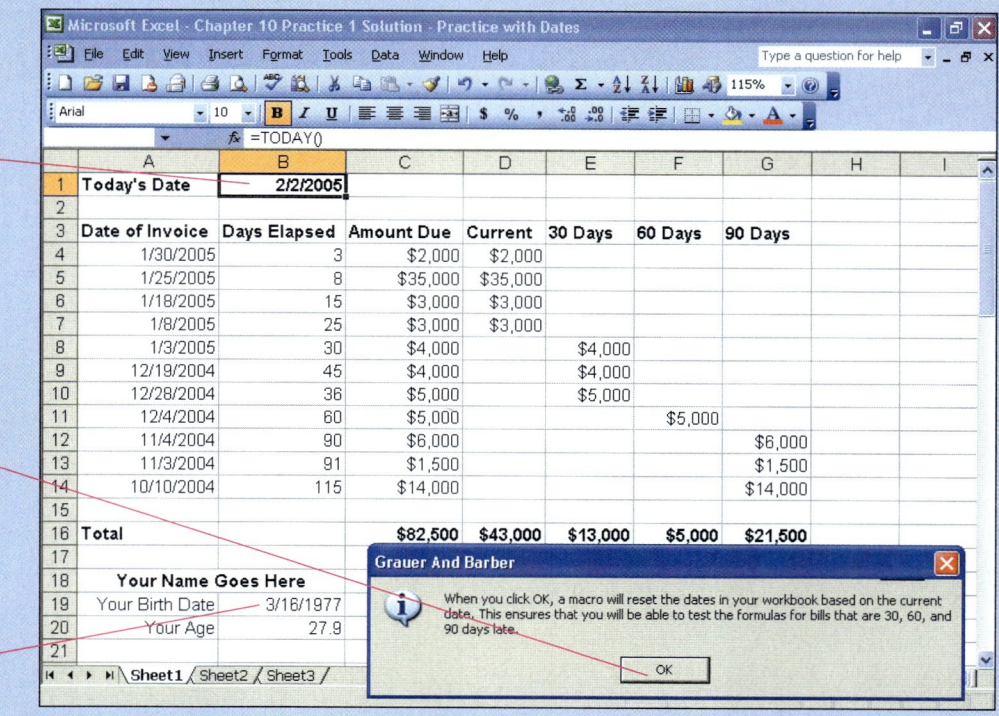

FIGURE 10.11 Practice with Dates (exercise 1)

practice exercises

2. **Change the Magnification:** The screen in Figure 10.12 displays a pair of procedures that increase and decrease the magnification percentage within the Excel window. These procedures do not do anything that the user could not accomplish manually. They are, however, more convenient ways to change the magnification incrementally and are truly useful in that regard. They also serve to illustrate how simple Excel macros are enhanced through the inclusion of VBA statements.

   a. Open the Enhanced Amortization Schedule Solution workbook and start the macro recorder. Click in the Zoom box and change the magnification to 110. Stop the recorder. Press Alt+F11 to open the Visual Basic Editor.

   b. Locate the module that contains the macro you just created, which contains the single statement ActiveWindow.Zoom =110. That changes the zoom property of the active window to 110. The single statement, plus a little imagination, is all you need to create the procedures in Figure 10.12.

   c. Add a Dim statement to define the variable intMagnification as an integer. The second statement sets this variable 10% higher than the current magnification. It does not change the magnification, however, because you have to check that you do not exceed the maximum magnification (400%) that is permitted—hence the If statement prior to changing the actual magnification, which is controlled by the Zoom property of the ActiveWindow object.

   d. Use the completed procedure to increase the magnification as the basis for the procedure to decrease the magnification. (You can enter the entire procedure manually, or you can copy the existing procedure, then make the necessary modifications.)

   e. Add two additional buttons (an up and a down arrow, respectively) to the custom toolbar to execute these procedures. Be sure to attach the modified toolbar to the completed workbook. Save the workbook.

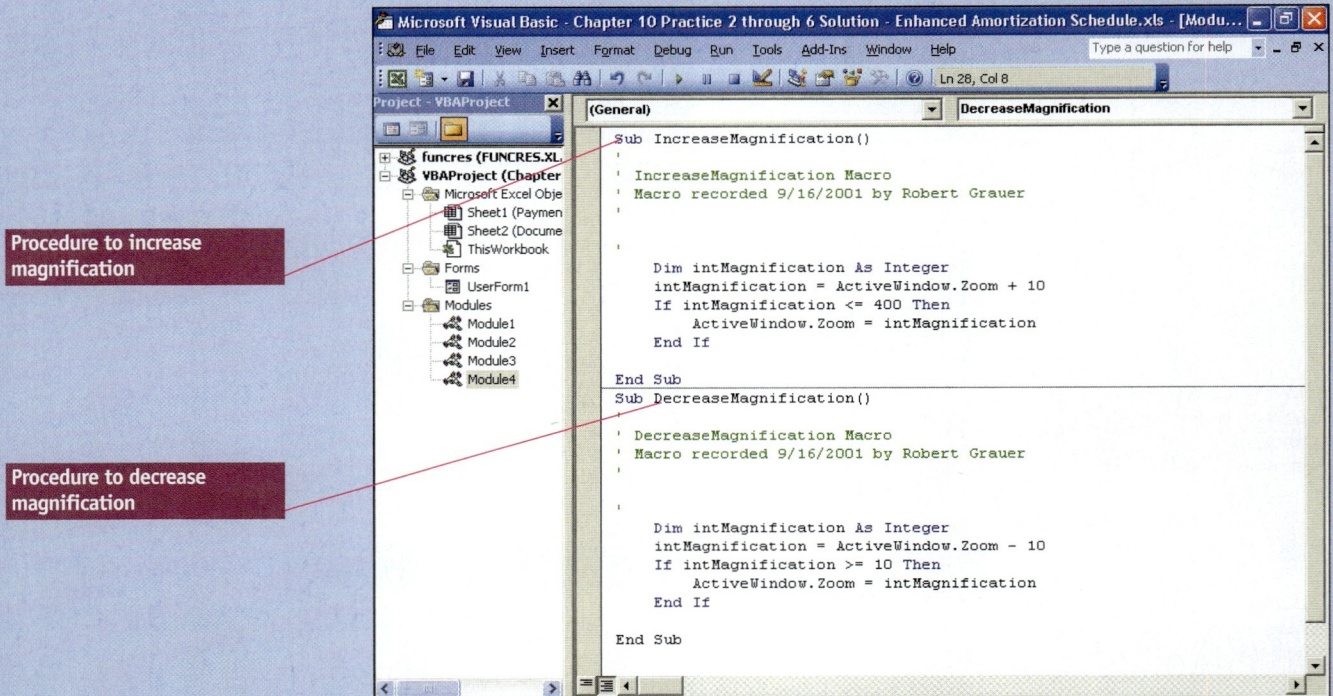

FIGURE 10.12 Change the Magnification (exercise 2)

practice exercises

3. **Toggle the Documentation Worksheet:** Figure 10.13 displays the Documentation worksheet that is included in the Enhanced Amortization Schedule Solution workbook. This worksheet explains how the OFFSET function is used in conjunction with a memory variable to set a variable print area to print only as many rows as there are payments. This is not an easy concept, and so we include the complete explanation within the workbook so that you can apply this technique to other workbooks that you might create.

   The purpose of this exercise, however, is to create a VBA procedure that will toggle the Documentation worksheet on and off. Thus, if the worksheet is hidden, the procedure will display it; if the worksheet is visible, the procedure will hide it. The logic is simple, but you need to obtain the VBA statement to display or hide the worksheet. Proceed as follows:

   a. Open the Enhanced Amortization Schedule Solution workbook that you have been working on throughout the chapter. Start the macro recorder. Pull down the Format menu, click Sheet, click the Unhide command, select the worksheet, then click OK. (The Documentation worksheet is hidden initially, and so the Unhide command is active. If the worksheet is already visible, however, click the Hide command instead of Unhide.) Stop the recorder.

   b. Start the Visual Basic editor to view the code in the macro you just created. You will see a single VBA statement that sets the Visible property for the Documentation worksheet to True. Use this statement as the basis of the procedure that will toggle the worksheet on or off. You have to add an If/Else statement that hides a visible worksheet and displays a hidden worksheet.

   c. Assign a button (use the book image) to add the procedure to the custom toolbar. Test the button to be sure that it works properly.

   d. Add your name to cell A2 in the documentation worksheet, then print the documentation worksheet for your instructor.

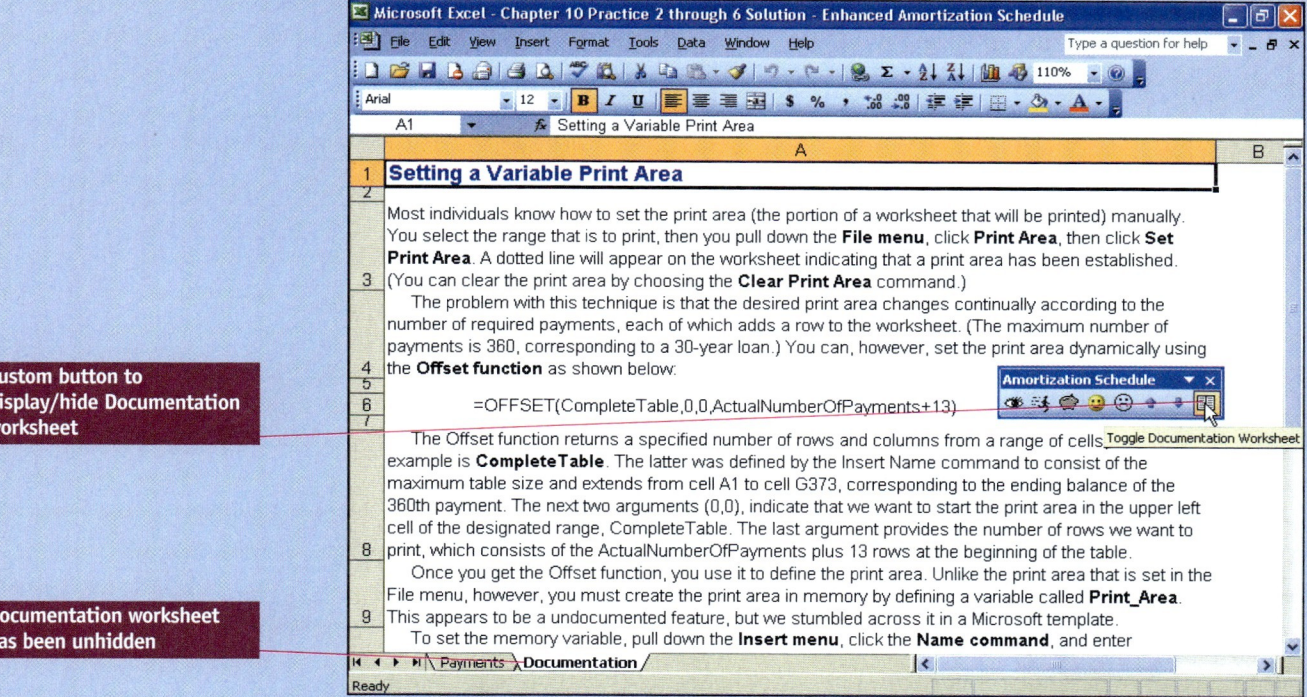

FIGURE 10.13 Toggle the Documentation Worksheet (exercise 3)

practice exercises

4. **Print the Summary Area:** Figure 10.14 displays two VBA procedures, one to print the summary area of the worksheet and a second to reset the print area. The PrintSummaryOnly procedure has not yet been created and is the subject of this exercise. The RestorePrintArea procedure was included in the original workbook; it incorporates the information that was contained in the Documentation worksheet from the previous exercise.

   a. Open the Enhanced Amortization Schedule Solution workbook. Enter the parameters for any loan, but specify the term as two years. Click the Print Preview button and notice that the printout fits on one page. Change the term of the loan to 10 years, click Print Preview a second time, and the printout requires three pages.

   b. Pull down the File menu, click Print Area, then click the Clear Print Area command. Click the Print Preview button. The printout requires seven pages even though many of the pages are blank. This is because the previous step had you clear the print area which had been set to print only as many rows as contained nonzero values. Close the Print Preview window, and press Ctrl+r, which is the keyboard shortcut for the RestorePrintArea procedure in the workbook. The printout once again takes three pages.

   c. You will set the print area to print just the summary portion of the worksheet. Start the macro recorder. Name the macro PrintSummaryOnly. Click the down arrow in the Name box, select the SummaryArea range name, then pull down the File menu, click Print Area, then click the command to Set the print area. Click the Print button. Stop the macro recorder.

   d. Open the VBA editor to examine the statements you just created. They are similar to, but different from, the code in Figure 10.14. Look closely at the recorded statements, however, and see how they can be simplified to create the code in Figure 10.14. The last statement runs the RestorePrintArea procedure, so that the print area will be automatically reset.

   e. Add a button (use the calculator button) to the custom toolbar to run the Print Summary Area procedure. Add a second button (the pencil) to restore the print area. Attach the toolbar to the workbook.

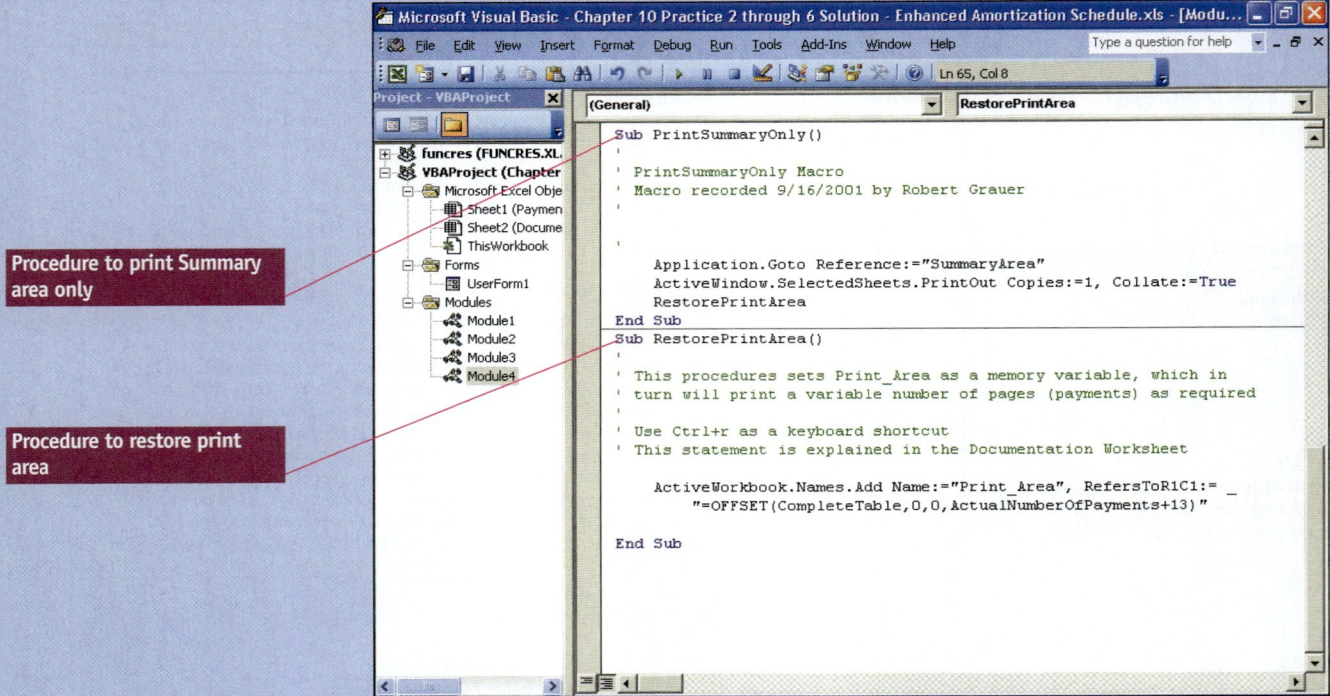

FIGURE 10.14 Print the Summary Area (exercise 4)

practice exercises

5. **Nested Ifs and Other Logic:** A nested If statement (or "an If within an If") is a common logic structure in every programming language. It tests an initial condition, then it tests a second condition if the first condition is true. Open the Enhanced Amortization Schedule Solution workbook and expand the Before Close event procedure as shown in Figure 10.15. The original procedure has been modified to accomplish several additional tasks.

   a. The procedure checks to see whether your name or your instructor's last name has been omitted from the worksheet, and if so, it gives the user the option to cancel the Close command. First, the procedure sets the active cell to the range name "YourLastName". It then checks that cell and the cell one row below for null values. If either cell is blank, the second If statement is executed.

   b. The MsgBox function within the nested If displays a message to the user and displays Yes and No buttons within the resulting message box. The user's response is compared to the VBA intrinsic constant, vbNo. If the user clicked the No button, then the comparison is true, the close operation is canceled, and the switch to close the workbook is set to No.

   c. The second nested If statement tests to see if the workbook is to be closed, and if so, it hides the custom toolbar, and also displays a message to the user. The custom toolbar is then deleted from the collection of custom toolbars (but not from this workbook). This ensures that the toolbar will work correctly if the workbook is subsequently opened in a different folder.

   d. A second If statement tests for the day of the week (Friday in this example) and displays an appropriate message.

   e. There is a lot of logic here, and hence you might want to close the workbook two or three times (with different responses) to better appreciate the underlying logic. Print this procedure for your professor.

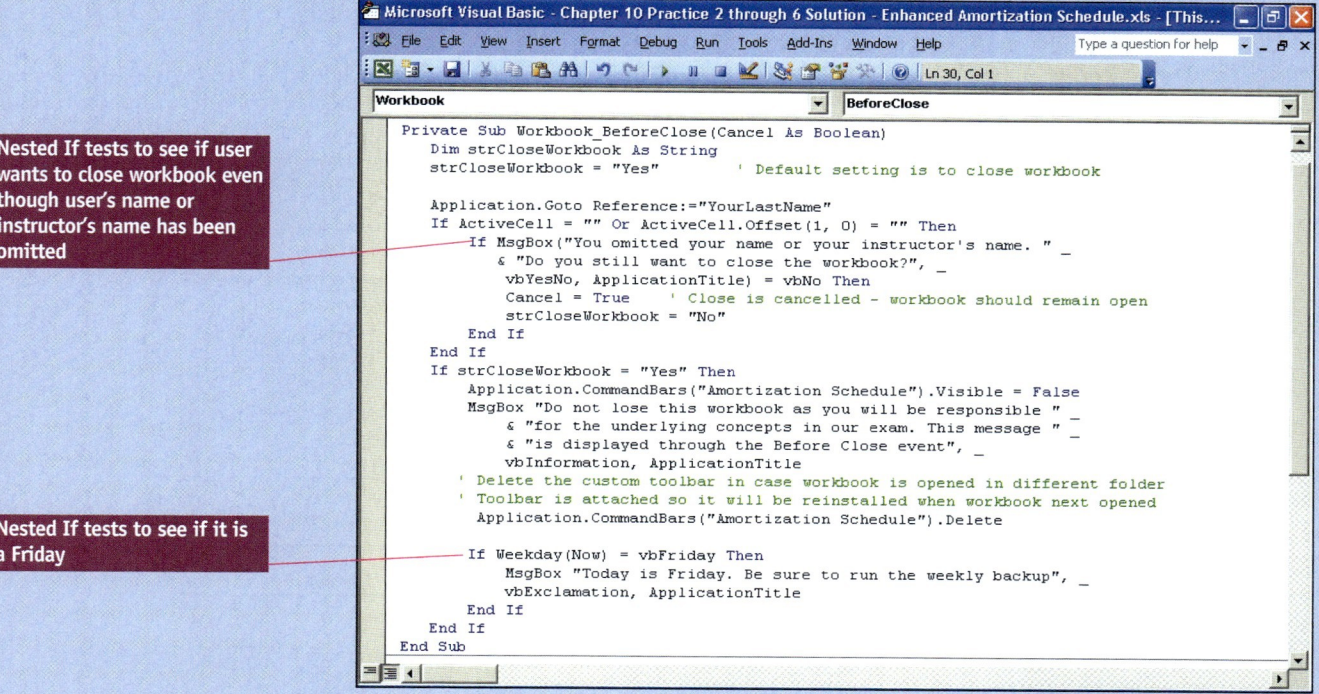

FIGURE 10.15 Nested Ifs and Other Logic (exercise 5)

practice exercises

6. **Custom Menus and Toolbars:** Figure 10.16 displays the completed Enhanced Amortization Schedule Solution workbook immediately prior to closing the workbook. The custom toolbar (and corresponding menu) contains a total of 10 buttons that were created during the various hands-on exercises and end-of-chapter problems. Compare your toolbar to ours to be sure that you have completed the entire application.

   a. The eye and runner correspond to the procedures to display and hide the validation columns, respectively, and were developed in the second hands-on exercise.

   b. The piggy bank icon runs the procedure to enable individual optional payments of principal and was created in the second hands-on exercise.

   c. The smiley and sad faces contain the procedures to apply an optional payment and clear the optional payments column, respectively. The procedures were developed in the fourth hands-on exercise.

   d. The up and down arrows increase and decrease the magnification within the Excel window. These procedures were developed in problem 2 at the end of the chapter.

   e. The book toggles the documentation worksheet on or off and was developed in problem 3 at the end of the chapter.

   f. The calculator and pencil print the summary area and restore the print area, respectively. These procedures were created in problem 4 at the end of the chapter.

   g. You can also create a custom menu with the same commands. Pull down the View menu, click Tools, click Customize to display the Customize dialog box, then click the Commands tab and scroll until you can select New Menu. Click and drag the New Menu command to the right of the menu bar, then release the mouse to create a menu called "New Menu". Select the new menu on the menu bar, click the Modify Selection button in the Customize dialog box, then change the name of the menu to Amortization.

   h. You are now ready to add commands to the menu. Select the Macros category in the Category area, then drag a Custom button to the Amortization menu. Pull down the menu, select the Custom Button command and assign a macro. Repeat this process to add additional commands.

   i. Complete the Amortization menu. Press the Print Screen key to capture this screen, start Word, then paste the screen into a Word document to submit to your instructor.

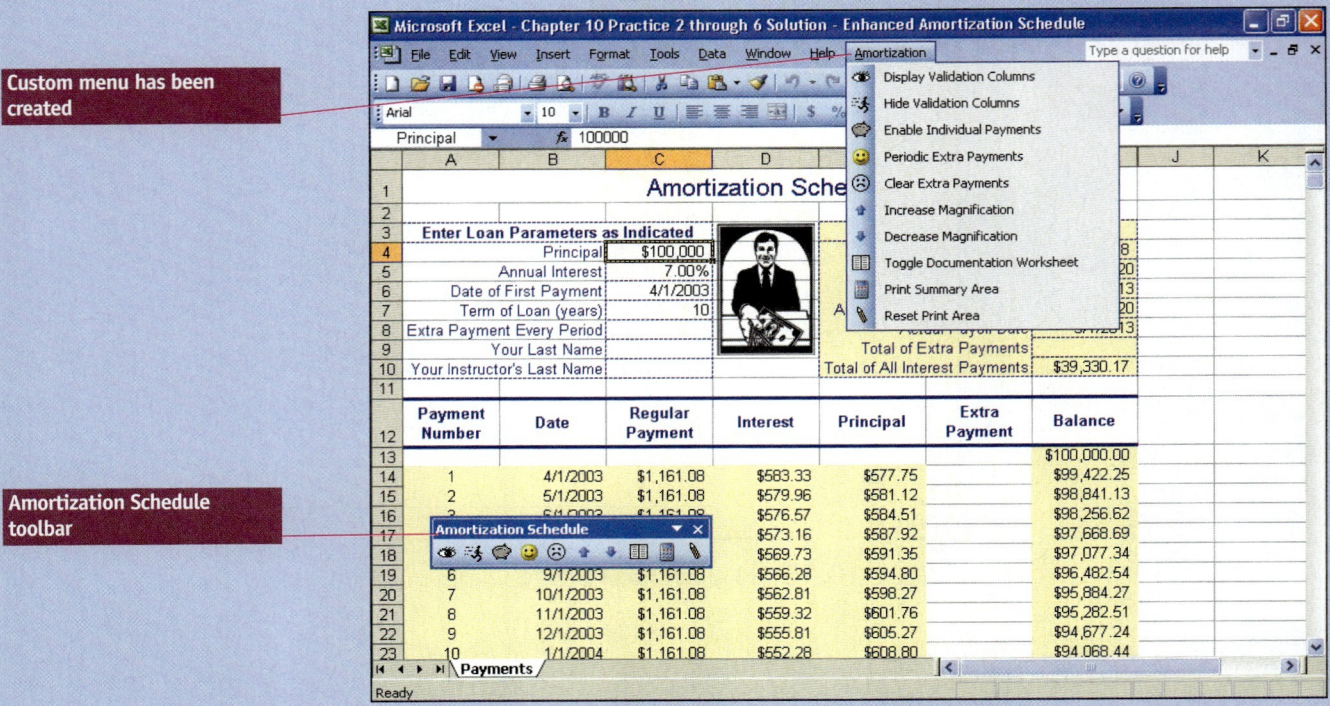

FIGURE 10.16 Custom Menus and Toolbars (exercise 6)

practice exercises

7. **The Get Out of Debt Worksheet:** The Get Out of Debt workbook in Figure 10.17 is similar to the Enhanced Amortization Schedule Solution application that was developed in the chapter. The new workbook is designed to let you practice all of the skills in the chapter within the context of a different application. It is also intended as a gentle reminder to think twice about using your credit card, because once you acquire this type of debt, it is very difficult to get out from under.

   a. Open the partially completed version of this workbook in *Chapter 10 Practice 7* and complete the basic worksheet. Unprotect the worksheet (a password is not required) so that you can make the necessary modifications.

   b. Implement a validation requirement in cell C7, the cell that contains the projected monthly payment, to ensure that the payment is greater than the interest due in the first month. Use the Insert Name command to assign the range name FirstMonthInterest to cell D13, then use this name as needed throughout the worksheet.

   c. Enter the appropriate If functions in cells E8 and G8 to display the indicated error message and remaining balance (if, in fact, there is a remaining balance after 30 years). These functions check the value in the cell G372, which has been assigned the range name, BalanceAfter30Years. Display these values in red, bold, and italics. Test the functions by entering appropriate values in the spreadsheet; for example, if you make the minimum monthly payment (the amount the credit card company requires), you will still owe $4,800 after 30 years, after paying out more than $25,000 in interest. Press the Print Screen key to capture this screen, start Word, then paste the screen into a Word document to submit to your instructor.

   d. Click the Retry button and drop your monthly payment by $1.00. Not only are you still in debt, but the debt has almost quadrupled to more than $18,000. This is *not* a spreadsheet error, but rather an indication of the power of compound interest. It is wonderful when it works for you, as in a retirement account, but a disaster when it works against you with debt.

   e. Change the monthly payment to $100. You are finally out of debt, but it took more than seven years. Add your name and your instructor's name in the appropriate cells, then print this worksheet for your instructor.

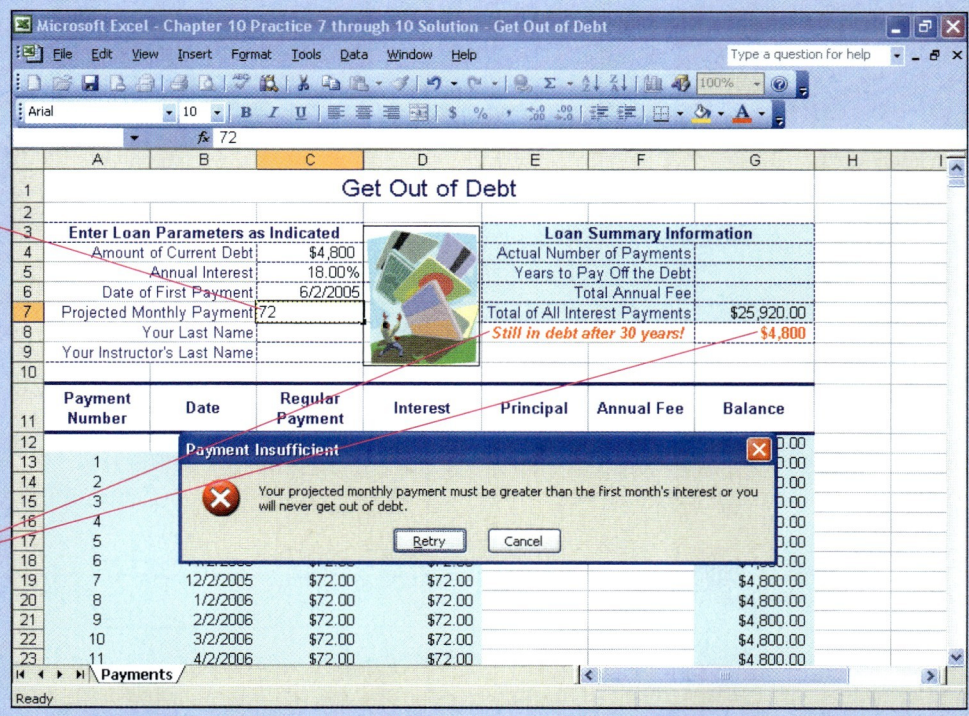

FIGURE 10.17 The Get Out of Debt Worksheet (exercise 7)

practice exercises

8. **Expand the Application:** Create a custom toolbar (and/or a custom menu) to execute the procedures that are already in the workbook to print the summary area and to reset the print area. Use the same icons (the calculator and the pencil) that were used in the Enhanced Amortization Schedule Solution workbook. Include additional procedures as described below:

   a. Create a general procedure that imposes an annual fee once a year within the body of the worksheet. The procedure should prompt the user for the amount of the fee and the first date that it takes effect. The logic parallels that of the periodic extra payments module in the other workbook. Add a button for this procedure to the custom toolbar using the sad face image.

   b. Use the procedure you just created to enter an annual fee of $50 that takes effect the first month. Compare the results of this calculation with those of the previous exercise; that is, an annual fee of $50 extends the time required to pay off your loan by another seven months. Click the toolbar button to print the summary area for these parameters.

   c. Create a second general procedure to clear the annual fee. Add this procedure to the custom toolbar using the smiley face button.

   d. Create an Open workbook event procedure to display the custom toolbar and to enable VBA procedures to modify a protected worksheet. This logic parallels that in the Amortization workbook. You do not need a splash screen at this time.

   e. Create a Before Close event procedure to hide the custom toolbar and display a meaningful message (choose your own text) as shown in Figure 10.18. The procedure should also check for the presence of your name and your instructor's name prior to closing. You can copy the code from the Enhanced Amortization Schedule Solution workbook as appropriate.

   f. Add your name and your instructor's name to the worksheet in the indicated cells. Print the summary portion of this worksheet for your instructor.

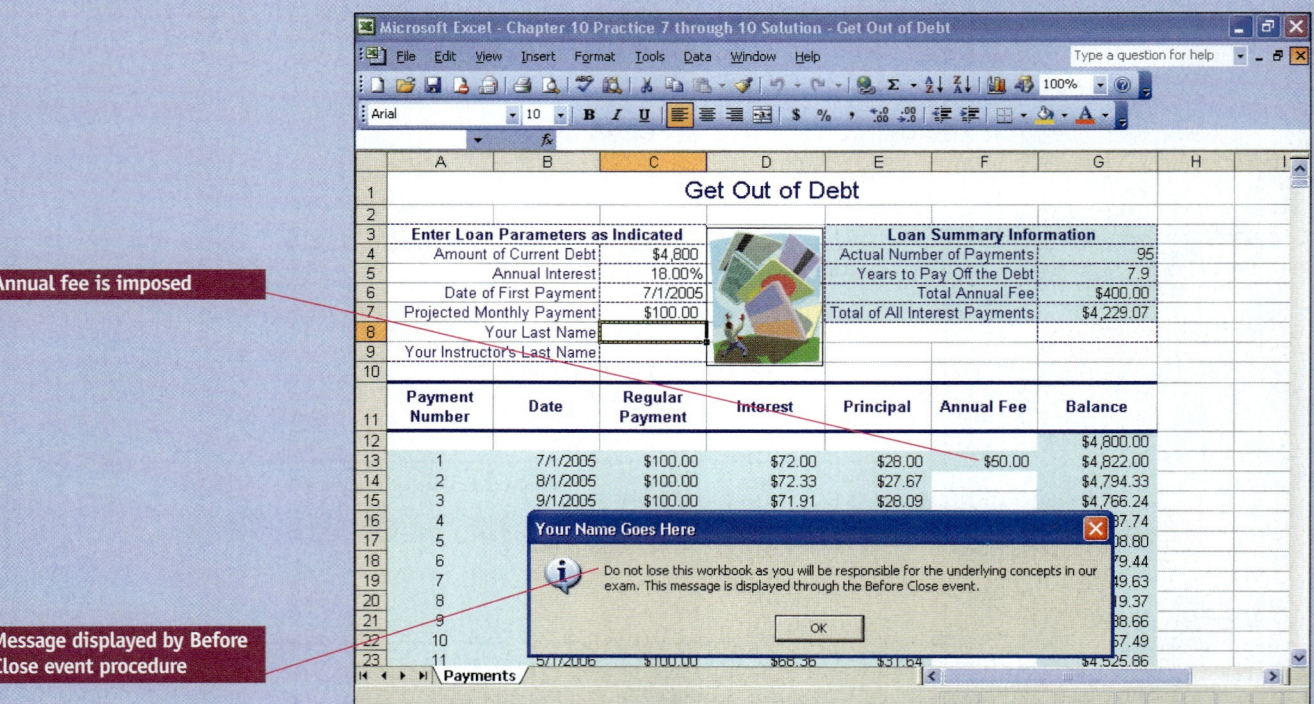

FIGURE 10.18 Expand the Application (exercise 8)

practice exercises

9. **The Get Out of Debt Procedure:** The procedure in Figure 10.19 uses the PMT function to calculate the required monthly payment to pay off the debt within a specified amount of time. The procedure uses existing values within the worksheet for the principal and annual interest rate. It displays an Input Box that prompts the user for the desired number of monthly payments, and then places the result of the calculation (vbPayment) into cell C7 (that has been associated with the range name ProjectedMonthlyPayment).

   a. Open the Get Out of Debt workbook and create the procedure in Figure 10.19. Our procedure includes the statement ClearAnnualFee, which runs the procedure we created in the previous exercise to erase any annual fee that may have been entered into the worksheet. Explain why this is necessary for the Get Out of Debt procedure to work correctly.

   b. Add the completed procedure to the custom toolbar using the image of a heart for the button image.

   c. Test the procedure using the existing loan parameters of $4,800 at 18% interest. Specify that you want to pay off the loan in 36 months. If you do the work correctly, the projected monthly payment should be $173.53. Be sure that your name and your instructor's name have both been entered into the worksheet, then print the payment schedule for your instructor.

   d. Look closely at your worksheet. The value in cell G4 (the cell that contains the actual number of payments) is also 36, which corresponds to the number of months you specified. This is significant because the computation associated with cell G4 is independent of the Get Out of Debt procedure, and thus serves to validate the calculations in the worksheet.

   e. What is the value in cell G48 of the worksheet? How does this serve to further validate the worksheet?

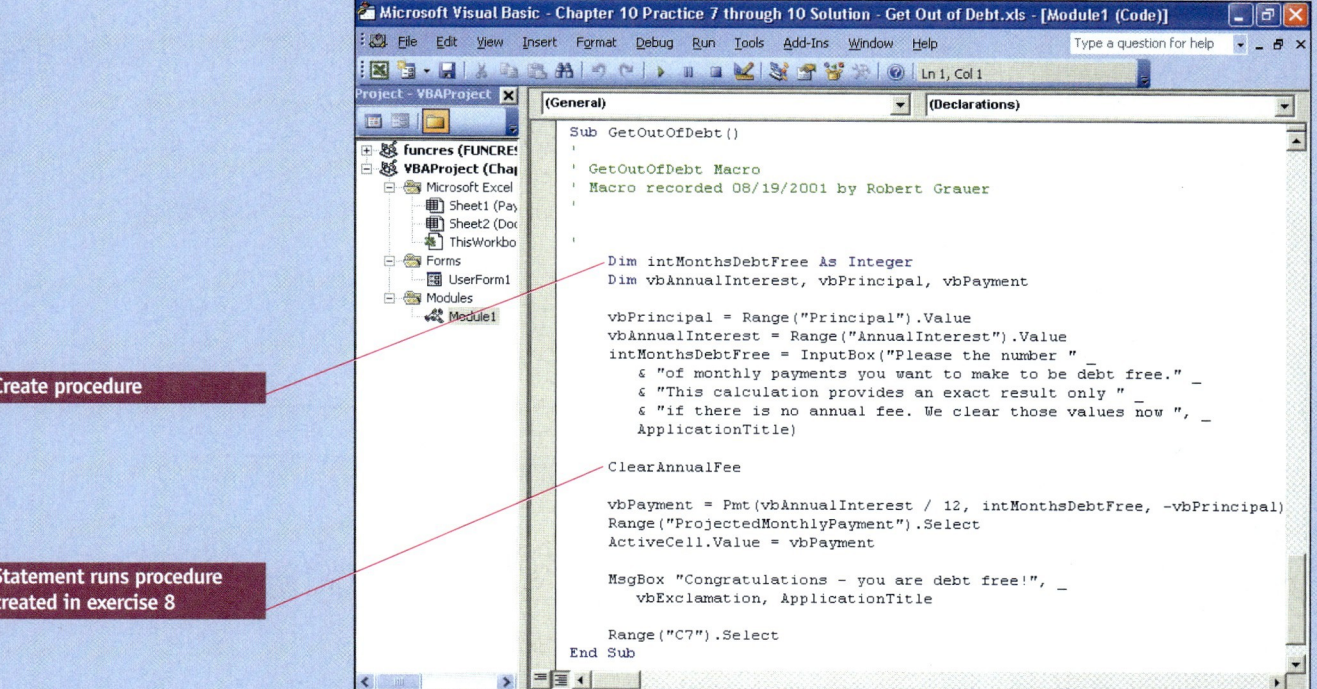

FIGURE 10.19 The Get Out of Debt Procedure (exercise 9)

practice exercises

10. **The Completed Application:** Complete the Get Out of Debt application by adding all of the functionality implied by Figure 10.20. This step is actually quite easy in that you can copy code from the Amortization Schedule Solution workbook as necessary.
    a. Add the procedures and corresponding buttons to toggle the documentation worksheet on and off, and to increase or decrease the magnification in the Excel window.
    b. Add a splash screen that is displayed for 5 seconds when the workbook is opened initially. Press the PrintScreen key to capture the splash screen when it appears, then paste the screen into a Word document. Print the Word document for your instructor to show that you created the splash screen successfully.
    c. Print the procedures within the workbook for your instructor. You can print the VBA procedures from within the VBA editor, but the procedures are printed without any formatting. You get a better result by printing from within Microsoft Word. Open the VBA editor, select the procedures you want to print, then click the Copy button (or use the Ctrl+C keyboard shortcut) to copy these procedures to the Windows clipboard.
    d. Start Microsoft Word and open a new document. Click the Paste button (or use the Ctrl+V keyboard shortcut) to paste the contents of the clipboard (the VBA procedures) into the Word document.
    e. Return to the VBA editor to copy the contents of the other modules to the Word document in similar fashion.
    f. Format the procedures in the Word document as you see fit. We suggest you use a monospaced font such as Courier New so that the indentation and alignment are easier to see. We also suggest that you boldface the Sub and End Sub statements of each procedure, and that you insert a horizontal border to separate the procedures from one another.
    g. Add a title page, then submit the completed assignment to your instructor.

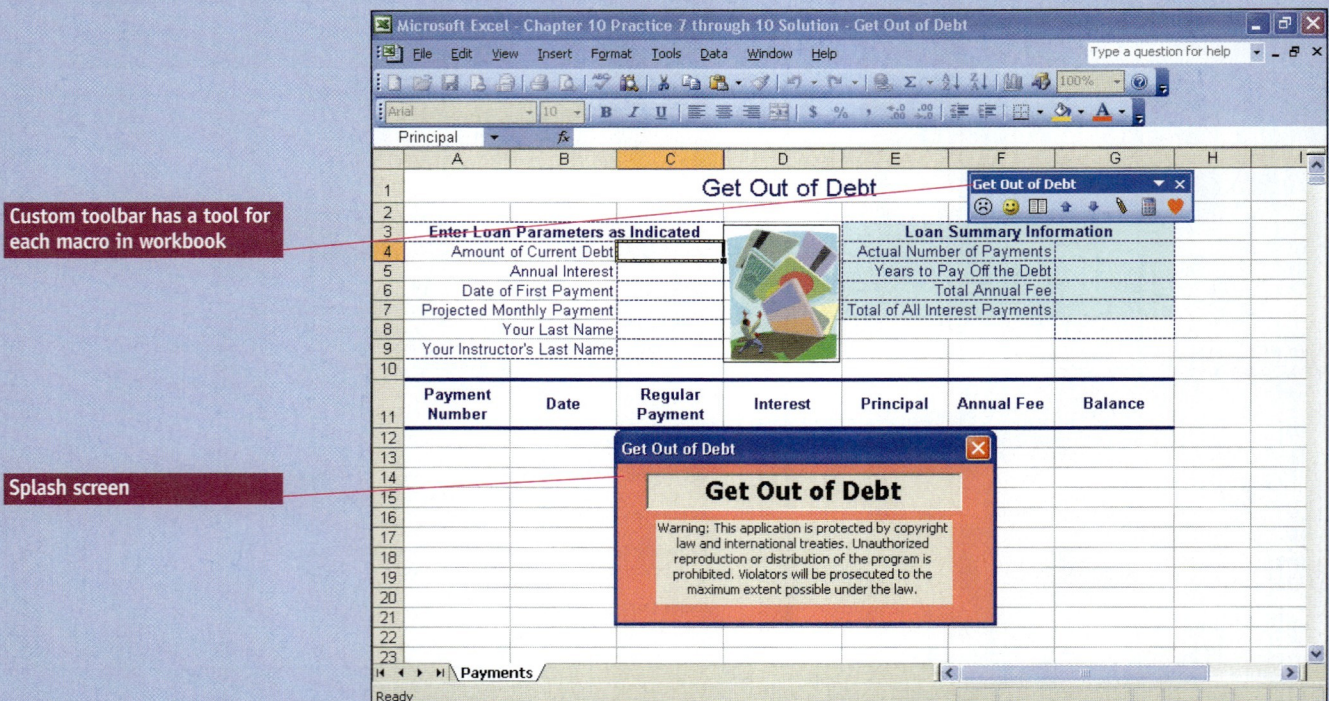

FIGURE 10.20 The Completed Application (exercise 10)

practice exercises

11. **The Mind Reader:** The puzzle in Figure 10.21 was created for the Web by Andy Naughton (www.cyberglass.co.uk) and converted to an Excel workbook by the authors. We thank Andy for permission to use his very clever puzzle. Open the *Chapter 10 Practice 11* workbook, enable the macros, and follow the directions. Choose any two-digit number; add the digits, then subtract the sum from the original number. If you choose 75, for example, the sum is 12, and you wind up with 63 (75 – 12). Look for the number in the table, notice the symbol next to the number, then click the Show Me button. The puzzle will read your mind and display the symbol that is next to your number.

    Click the button to play again. Choose a different number, do the math, and more than likely you will get a different symbol. But no matter how many times you play the game, the puzzle will always be able to guess the symbol. Are you intrigued? We were. Now let's see if we can determine how the puzzle works.

    a. Open the VBA editor and look at Module 1. There are four procedures. Run each procedure to determine what each procedure does. (You may want to tile the Excel and VBA windows to step through each procedure to see the effect of each statement.)

    b. You now know the function of each procedure, but that does not explain how the puzzle works. Return to the Excel window and click the button to Play Again to reset the puzzle. Pull down the Format menu, click the Sheet command, click Unhide, and then unhide the Symbols worksheet. Look at the formula in cell C2. What is the purpose of the RAND function? Press the F9 (Calculate) key. How does the worksheet change?

    c. Click in cell C3 of the Symbols worksheet and examine the formula. How does that formula relate to the value in cell C2 and the table of symbols in column A? Press the F9 key. What happens to the worksheet?

    d. Click the tab for the ReadYourMind worksheet. It would be very helpful to see the cell formulas in this worksheet except that we have protected the worksheet to hide the formulas. We'll give you one more hint. Pull down the Tools menu, click the Protection command, and click the Unprotect Sheet command. A password is not required. Now look at the formulas in the table of symbols to see if you can find the pattern.

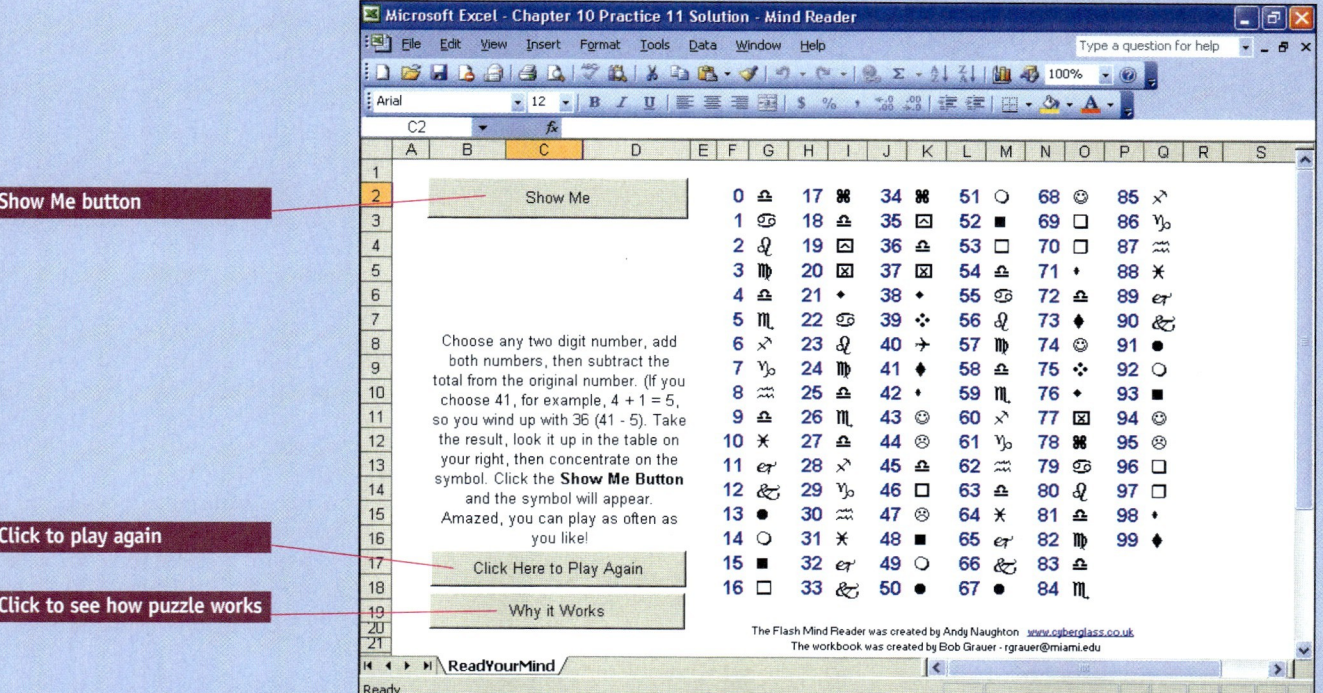

FIGURE 10.21 The Mind Reader (exercise 11)

MINI CASES

The Robot and the Wall

This problem is an exercise in logic and has nothing to do with VBA per se. A robot is sitting on a chair facing a wall a short distance away. Your assignment is to provide the necessary instructions to the robot to stand up, walk to the wall, then turn around, walk back, and sit down in the chair. The robot understands a set of very basic commands—Stand, Sit, Turn (90 degrees to the right), and Step.

The robot can also raise its arms and sense the wall with its fingertips. It cannot, however, sense the chair on its return trip, since the chair is below arm level. Accordingly, the robot must count the number of steps to the wall or chair by using another set of commands—Add (increment a counter by 1), Subtract (decrement the counter by 1), Initialize Counter to zero, Arms Up, and Arms Down. The wall is an integer number of steps away.

Open the partially completed PowerPoint presentation, *Chapter 10 Mini Case—The Robot and the Wall*, which describes this assignment. Enter the completed pseudocode on a new slide, and then present your solution to the class. Ask for a volunteer to play the part of the robot.

VBA Review

After reading this chapter, you should be familiar with the syntax of Visual Basic. You should also be comfortable with the definition of key terms such as object model, collection, method, and property. We have, therefore created a Word document to review this material. Open the *Chapter 10 Mini Case—VBA Review* document in the Exploring Excel folder, fill in the blanks, add a cover page, and submit the completed document to your instructor.

Chapter Recap—Refinance Now

You purchased your first home three years ago. It's in a great neighborhood, your neighbors are friendly, you have a large yard for your dog, and you are truly at home. You took out a 30-year mortgage for $100,000 at 7.5%, which resulted in a monthly payment of just under $700. You have paid approximately $25,000 to the bank (principal and interest) during the three years you have lived in the house, but are shocked to learn that you still owe approximately $97,000 on the mortgage. In other words, you have paid approximately $22,000 in interest and only $3,000 in principal.

The good news is that interest rates are at or near their lowest level in 40 years. You have been approached by multiple mortgage brokers about the benefits of refinancing, yet you still have doubts about whether you should refinance. You know that your monthly payment will go down, but you will incur additional closing costs of 4% to obtain the new loan on the remaining principal of $97,000; thus, you plan to roll the closing costs into the new mortgage to avoid an out-of-pocket expense. You can obtain either a 15- or 30-year mortgage, and you want to explore the advantages of each. Is it possible that the lower interest rates on a new 15-year loan could keep your payments at the same level as your existing 30-year mortgage?

Your assignment is to create a simple workbook that will compare your existing mortgage to a new 15-year mortgage at 5%. It should show the monthly payment, the savings per month, and the total interest over the life of each loan. It should also determine the number of months to break even on the new 30-year mortgage. This is a simple workbook that does not require macros or VBA.

You are then to review the chapter and create the loan amortization workbook that is described within the chapter. The end result is a sophisticated workbook that includes macros and a custom toolbar that allows you to make extra payments. Use the completed workbook to enter one additional payment a year; that is, how long will it take you to pay off a 30-year mortgage if you make 13 payments a year (one every month as scheduled, plus an extra payment once a year)?

CHAPTER 11

Extending VBA: Processing Worksheets and Workbooks

OBJECTIVES

After reading this chapter you will:

1. Use the Dir function to open all workbooks in a specific folder.
2. Explain how the Len function indicates an "empty" folder.
3. Use the On Error and Exit Sub statements for error trapping.
4. Use the Forms toolbar to add a command button to a worksheet.
5. Use the For/Next statement to process all worksheets in a workbook.
6. Change the color of a worksheet tab based on a value in the worksheet.
7. Explain how to "divide and conquer" to create an application.
8. Call one VBA procedure from another procedure.

hands-on exercises

1. CREATE SUMMARY WORKBOOK
   Input: Expense Statement; Expense Summary
   Output: Expense Statement (modified to include your name); Expense Summary Solution

2. ERROR TRAPPING
   Input: Expense Summary Solution
   Output: Expense Summary Solution (additional modifications)

3. CREATE SUMMARY WORKSHEET
   Input: Expense Summary Solution (from exercise 2)
   Output: Expense Summary Solution (additional modifications)

4. BETTER SUMMARY WORKBOOK
   Input: Better Summary
   Output: Better Summary Solution

CASE STUDY
BON VOYAGE TRAVEL

You love your new job at the Bon Voyage Travel agency. It's challenging, exciting, and the travel benefits are phenomenal. You are busy all day long, fielding calls from clients, booking hotels, flights, cruises, and so on. Each booking requires you to create an individual invoice for that client, which is based on an Excel workbook.

The only drawback comes at the end of the day because you cannot leave until you have consolidated the data from each individual workbook into a summary workbook, retaining each client's data on a separate worksheet in the summary workbook. You also have to evaluate each invoice to see if it qualifies for "premium status," which is determined by the amount of the invoice. It's time consuming, tedious, and rather boring. Were it not for this daily "nuisance," your job would be much easier and you would be much happier. There must be a better way. ■

Your assignment is to read the chapter to see how macros and VBA can automate the consolidation process. We have, in fact, done much of the work for you. Open the *Chapter 11 Case Study Invoice* workbook in the Bon Voyage Travel folder, which is found in the Exploring Excel folder. Complete the invoice by entering the details for a dream vacation. The worksheet is protected and you can enter data only in the shaded cells. Save the workbook. Now you are ready to create the daily summary.

Open the *Chapter 11 Case Study—Bon Voyage Summary* workbook in the Exploring Excel folder. Click the button to enable macros, and then click "Yes" when asked whether to create the summary workbook. Enter the folder that contains the invoices, "C:\Exploring Excel\Bon Voyage Travel", then sit back as the individual invoices are brought into the summary workbook. Now enter $7,500 as the amount to qualify as a premium client, and then watch as the summary worksheet is built. Your name should appear first under invoice number 10000. Print the summary worksheet. Click the macro button to find a client worksheet, enter your name, and then print your worksheet after it is selected. And if you are really ambitious, create the macro to print the selected worksheets (i.e., premium, regular, or every worksheet according to the user's response).

THE EXPENSE SUMMARY APPLICATION

A good application enables an end user to accomplish tasks that he or she could not (easily) do through ordinary Excel commands. Consider, for example, the Expense Summary workbook that appears in Figure 11.1. Each employee submits an expense statement at the beginning of each month with his or her expenses for the previous month. The expense statements are submitted as separate Excel workbooks such as the one in Figure 11.1a. Your task is to consolidate the individual workbooks to create a summary workbook, as shown in Figure 11.1b.

Each individual workbook contains a single worksheet listing the expenses for that employee. The summary workbook, on the other hand, contains multiple worksheets with one worksheet for each employee. The summary workbook also contains a summary worksheet that lists the expenses for all employees, as well as an indication of whether the expenses are approved or require further review.

You could build the summary workbook manually using specific Excel commands to open each employee workbook, and copy the associated worksheet to the summary workbook. You then have to review the employee expenses on each worksheet and copy the relevant information to the summary worksheet. This is tedious, to say the least, and it is also prone to error. And what if there were 100 employees, as opposed to five? Clearly, you need to automate the process.

You should not, however, attempt to write a single VBA procedure to build the summary workbook because it is too complicated. It is better to divide the overall task into a series of smaller, more manageable tasks, each of which requires its own procedure. The procedures are developed and tested individually, then executed collectively to create the summary workbook. This is the methodology that we follow throughout the chapter. The end result will be an "empty" workbook that contains multiple procedures to obtain the individual employee data and produce the summary information. You will be able to click a single command button and build the entire workbook.

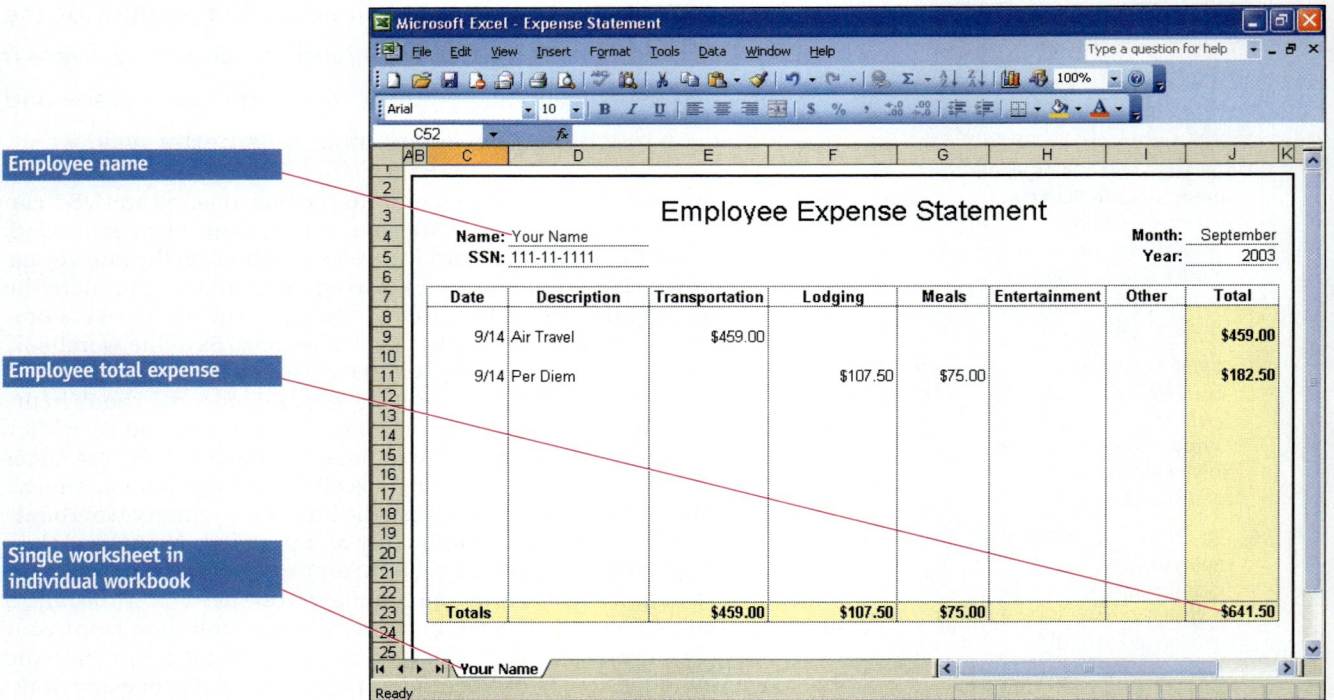

(a) Individual Expense Statement

FIGURE 11.1 The Expense Summary Application

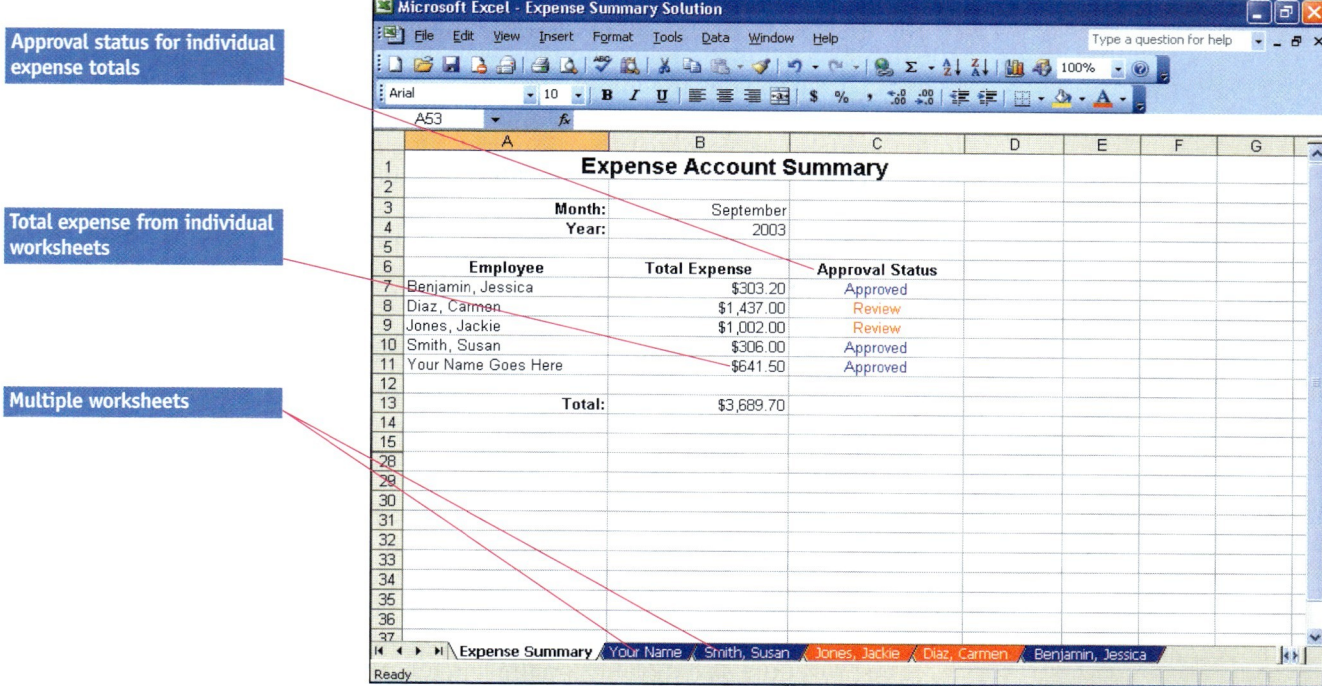

(b) Summary Workbook

FIGURE 11.1   The Expense Summary Application (*continued*)

A QUICK REVIEW

The VBA procedures to create the summary workbook use many VBA statements that do not have equivalent Excel commands. These statements are presented collectively in the VBA primer at the end of this text, and it is important that you are comfortable with their use and syntax. A quick summary is shown below.

The ***MsgBox statement*** displays information to the user. It has one required argument, which is the message (or prompt) that is displayed to the user. The other two arguments, the icon that is to be displayed in the message box, and the text of the title bar, are optional. The ***InputBox function*** displays a prompt for information, and then it stores that information for later use.

Every variable must be declared (defined) before it can be used. This is accomplished through the ***Dim*** (short for Dimension) ***statement*** that appears at the beginning of a procedure. The Dim statement indicates the name of the variable and its type (for example, whether it will hold a character string or an integer number), which in turn reserves the appropriate amount of memory for that variable.

The ability to make decisions within a procedure and then branch to alternative sets of statements is implemented through the ***If. . .Then. . .Else statement***. The Else clause is optional, but may be repeated multiple times within an If statement.

The ***For. . .Next statement*** (or For. . .Next loop as it is also called) executes all statements between the words For and Next a specified number of times, using a counter to keep track of the number of times the loop is executed. The ***Do Until*** and/or the ***Do While statements*** are used when the number of iterations is not known in advance.

Remember, too, that a VBA procedure is created in one of two ways—by entering statements directly into the VBA editor and/or by using the macro recorder to capture Excel commands and convert them to their VBA equivalents. You can also combine the two techniques by starting with the macro recorder to capture basic statements, view the resulting syntax, and then embellish the original statements.

The Dir Function

The first task in creating the summary workbook is to open the individual workbooks in order to copy the information for each employee to the summary workbook. This requires a procedure to process all of the workbooks in a specified folder, which is accomplished through the Visual Basic Dir function. The **Dir function** returns the name of the first file that matches a specified character string. For example, *Dir(C:\Expense Statements*.xls)* returns the name of the first Excel workbook in the Expense Statements folder on drive C. The file name of the workbook that was found can be stored in a variable for subsequent processing by the following statement:

> strWorkbookName = Dir("C:\Expense Statements*.xls")

The next workbook in the folder is obtained by calling the Dir function without any arguments as shown below:

> strWorkbookName = Dir

The two Dir statements are used in conjunction with one another to process all of the workbooks in a folder, as shown in Figure 11.2. The initial Dir statement is executed once to be sure that the specified folder exists, and further, to obtain the name of the first workbook in that folder. The second Dir statement is placed in a loop to access every other workbook in that folder.

The procedure also depends on the Len function to determine when all of the workbooks have been processed. The **Len function** returns the number of characters in the specified variable. (A length of zero indicates an empty character string, which implies that no more workbooks were found.) The Len function appears in an If statement immediately following the initial Dir statement to ensure that the folder contains at least one workbook. The function is also used to terminate the Do While loop after the last employee workbook has been processed; i.e., the loop ends when the length of the file name is zero to indicate there are no more workbooks in the folder.

The procedure in Figure 11.2 contains statements that were inserted by the macro recorder as well as VBA statements that were entered directly. The recorder was used to capture the keystrokes to open a specified workbook, to select a worksheet in the workbook, to copy the selected sheet to the Expense Summary workbook, and finally to close the workbook. The remaining statements were entered explicitly by the developer.

```
Public Sub OpenAllWorkbooks()
    Dim strWorkbookName

    strWorkbookName = Dir("C:\Exploring Excel\Expense Statements\*.xls")
    If Len(strWorkbookName) > 0 Then
        Do While Len(strWorkbookName) > 0
            Workbooks.Open Filename:= _
                "C:\Exploring Excel\Expense Statements\" & strWorkbookName
            Sheets(1).Select
            Sheets(1).Copy After:=Workbooks("Expense Summary Solution.xls").Sheets(1)
            Workbooks(strWorkbookName).Close
            strWorkbookName = Dir
        Loop
    Else
        MsgBox "Error - The folder C:\Exploring Excel\Expense Statements " _
            & "does not exist and/or there are no workbooks in the folder. " _
            & "Please check the folder name and then rerun the macro.", _
            vbCritical, ApplicationTitle
    End If
End Sub
```

Labels: Initial Dir function; Len function; Dir Statement within loop

FIGURE 11.2 The Open All Workbooks Procedure

hands-on exercise

1 Create the Summary Workbook

Objective Run a VBA procedure to combine worksheets from multiple workbooks into a single workbook. Use Figure 11.3 as a guide in the exercise.

Step 1: **Open the Expense Statement Workbook**

- Open the **Expense Statement workbook** in the Exploring Excel Folder. Click the button to **Enable Macros** to display the worksheet in Figure 11.3a.

- Enter your name into **cell D4** in the indicated format. Type your **last name, a comma and a space**, then **your first name**.

- Press the **Tab key** to move to **cell J4**, where you will enter the **previous month** (the month for which you are submitting expenses). You can type the month yourself, or you can select the month by clicking the **down arrow** in the list box.

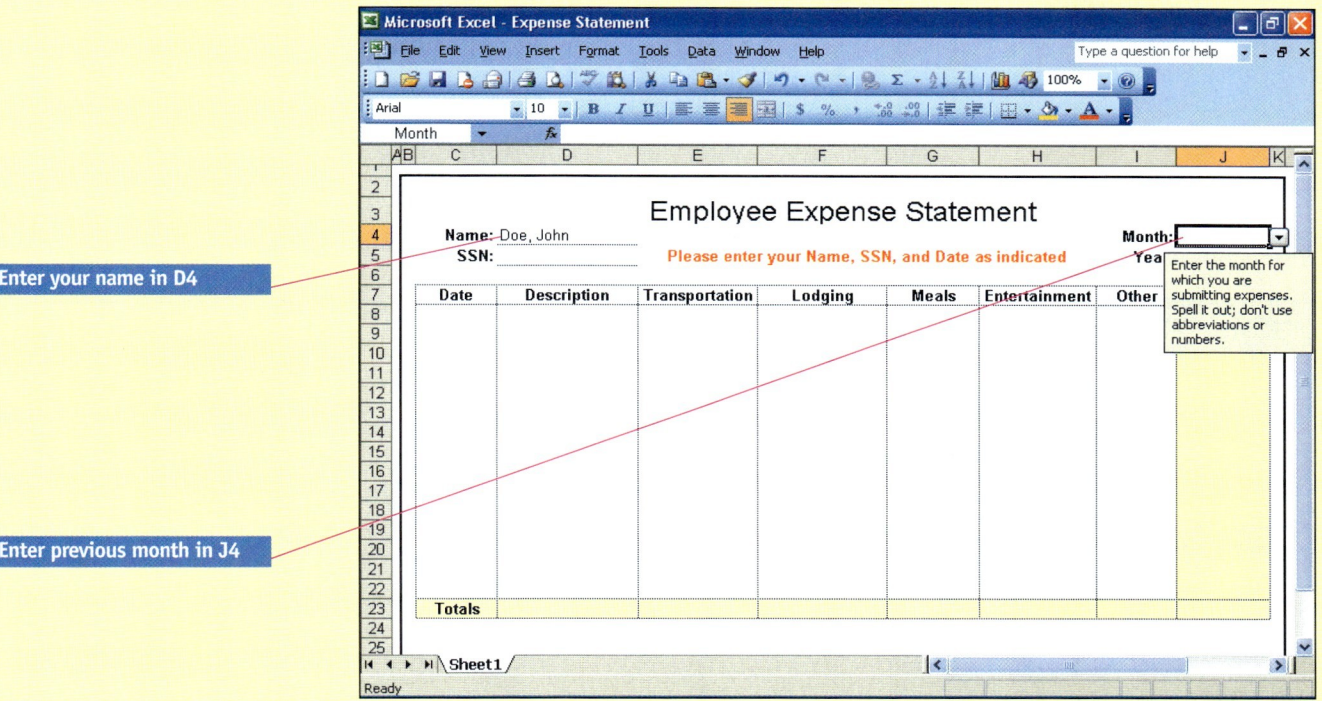

(a) Open the Expense Statement Workbook (step 1)

FIGURE 11.3 Hands-on Exercise 1

DATA VALIDATION

The Expense Statement worksheet uses the Data Validation command to ensure that the user enters a valid month. Pull down the Tools menu, click Protection, then click the Unprotect Sheet command. Scroll down in the worksheet until you can click and drag to select rows 27 to 40, pull down the Format menu, click Row, then click Unhide. Now click in cell J4, pull down the Data menu, and click the Validation command to see how the input for this cell is restricted to the list in cells C28 to C39. Click the Undo command twice to reverse the last commands and hide these rows. Reprotect the worksheet.

Step 2: **Understanding the Workbook**

- Click in **cell D5** and enter a *hypothetical* Social Security number such as **111-11-1111**. The text in cell E5 is no longer visible. Delete the Social Security number, and the text reappears.

- Click in **cell E5** as shown in Figure 11.3b. The formula in this cell uses the OR function within an IF function to determine if any of four cells is blank, and if so, it displays the text requesting you to enter the appropriate information.

- Click in **cell D5** and reenter **111-11-1111**.

- The year is entered automatically into the worksheet. Click in **cell J5** to see how this is accomplished. (The worksheet assumes that you are always entering expenses for the previous month.)

- The Expense Statement workbook contains a single worksheet that is named Sheet1. Close the workbook. Click **Yes** when prompted to save the changes.

- Reopen the **Expense Statement workbook**, enable macros, and notice that the worksheet tab has been renamed to match your name as it was entered into cell D4. Press **Alt+F11** to open the Visual Basic Editor, then look at the Before Close event procedure to see how we changed the worksheet tab.

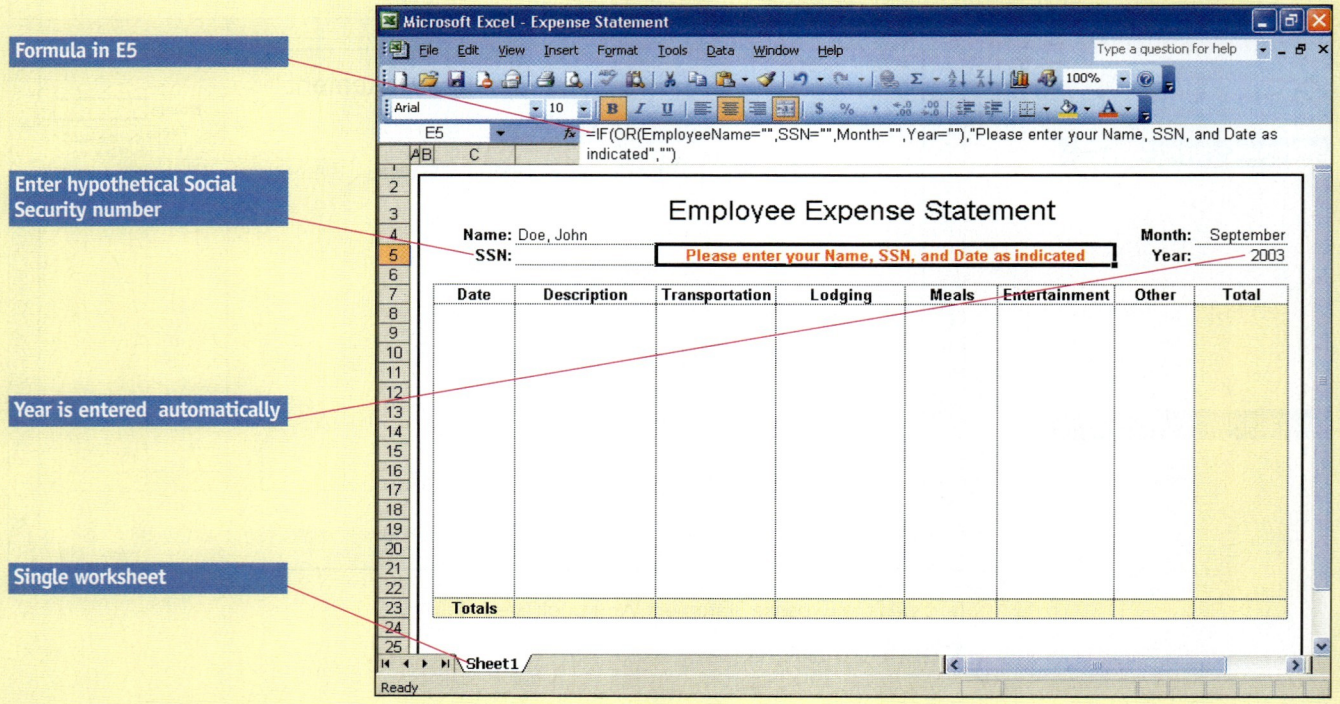

(b) Understanding the Workbook (step 2)

FIGURE 11.3 Hands-on Exercise 1 (*continued*)

EVENT-DRIVEN PROGRAMMING

The Open Workbook and Before Close event procedures may contain VBA code to accomplish certain "housekeeping" at the beginning and end of an application, respectively. The Before Close event procedure in this application confirms that the employee name has been entered, and if so, it changes the worksheet tab to reflect the employee name. This becomes important in subsequent steps, when the individual worksheets are combined into a summary workbook.

Step 3: **The Expense Statements Folder**

- Return to the Excel workbook. Click in **cell C9**. Enter an appropriate date—that is, a date in which the month matches the value in cell J4. You can enter the date with or without the year—for example, as 9/14 or as 9/14/03. (The year will not be displayed.)

- Enter the indicated description and expense for this date as shown in Figure 11.3c. Use the **Tab key** to move from one column to the next within the row. The total is computed automatically.

- Enter the second set of expenses into row 11. You can choose any date (within the month), but use the Description and the dollar amounts that are shown in the figure.

- Pull down the **File menu** and click the **Save As command** to display the Save As dialog box in Figure 11.3c. Double click the **Expense Statements folder** that exists within the Exploring Excel folder.

- Click in the **File name** text box and save the workbook in Expense Statements folder as **Your Last Name - Expense Statement**.

- Pull down the **File menu** and click the **Close command** (or click the **Close button** in the document window) to close your workbook. Click **Yes** if prompted to save the changes.

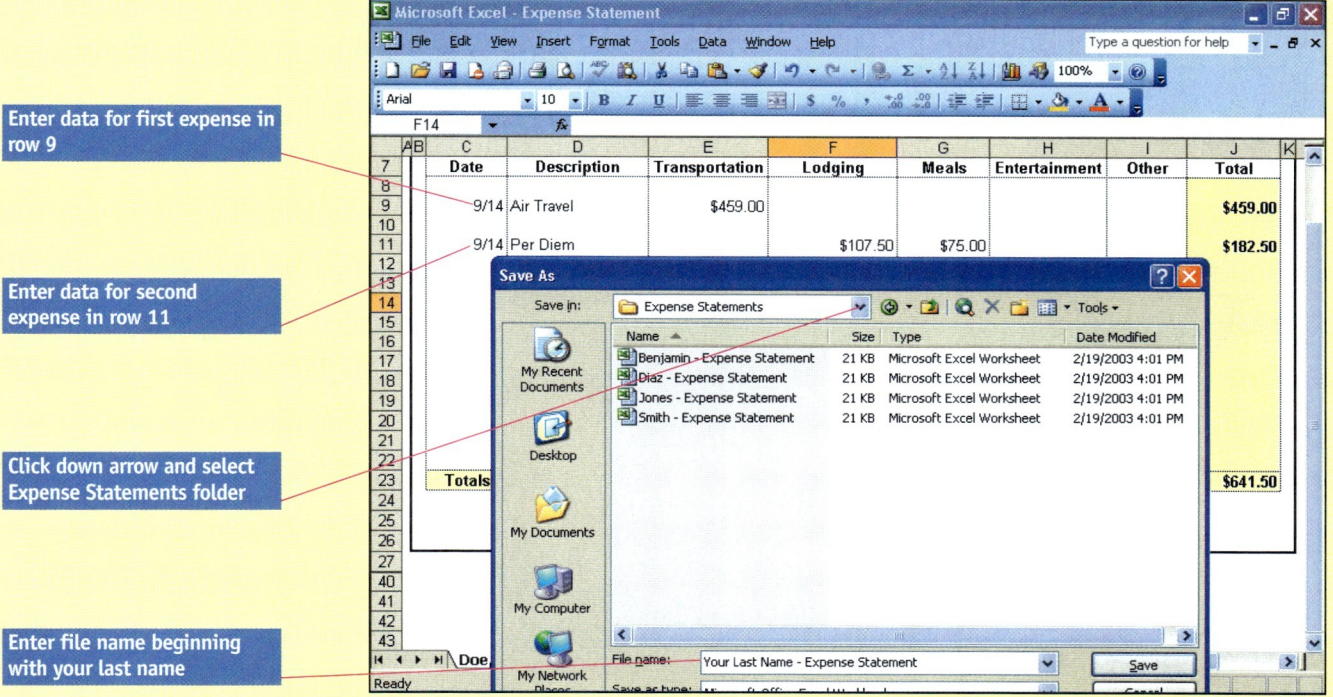

(c) The Expense Statements Folder (step 3)

FIGURE 11.3 Hands-on Exercise 1 (*continued*)

THE EXPENSE STATEMENTS FOLDER

The Expense Statements folder has been created for you. It contains four existing workbooks, each of which represents the expenses of a different employee. You have just added your workbook to this folder. The next step in this exercise will copy the expense worksheet from each of these workbooks into a summary workbook.

Step 4: **Run the Open All Workbooks Procedure**

- Open the **Expense Summary workbook** in the Exploring Excel folder. Click the button to **Enable macros**. Save the workbook as **Expense Summary Solution** so that you can return to the original workbook if necessary.

- The workbook consists of a single worksheet. The month and year are entered automatically and should reflect last month (the month for which the expenses are being submitted).

- Pull down the **Tools menu**, click **Macro**, then click **Macros...** to display the Macro dialog box as shown in Figure 11.3d. Select the **OpenAllWorkbooks macro**, then click the **Run button** to execute the VBA procedure.

- The procedure opens the first employee workbook in the Expense Statements folder, then it displays a message asking whether you want to save the changes to this workbook. Click **No**. (If this does not occur, skip the remainder of this step, and go to step 5.)

- The procedure continues to open each employee workbook in the folder, prompting you to save each workbook. Click **No** and continue in this fashion until all five workbooks have been opened.

- Save the Expense Summary Solution workbook.

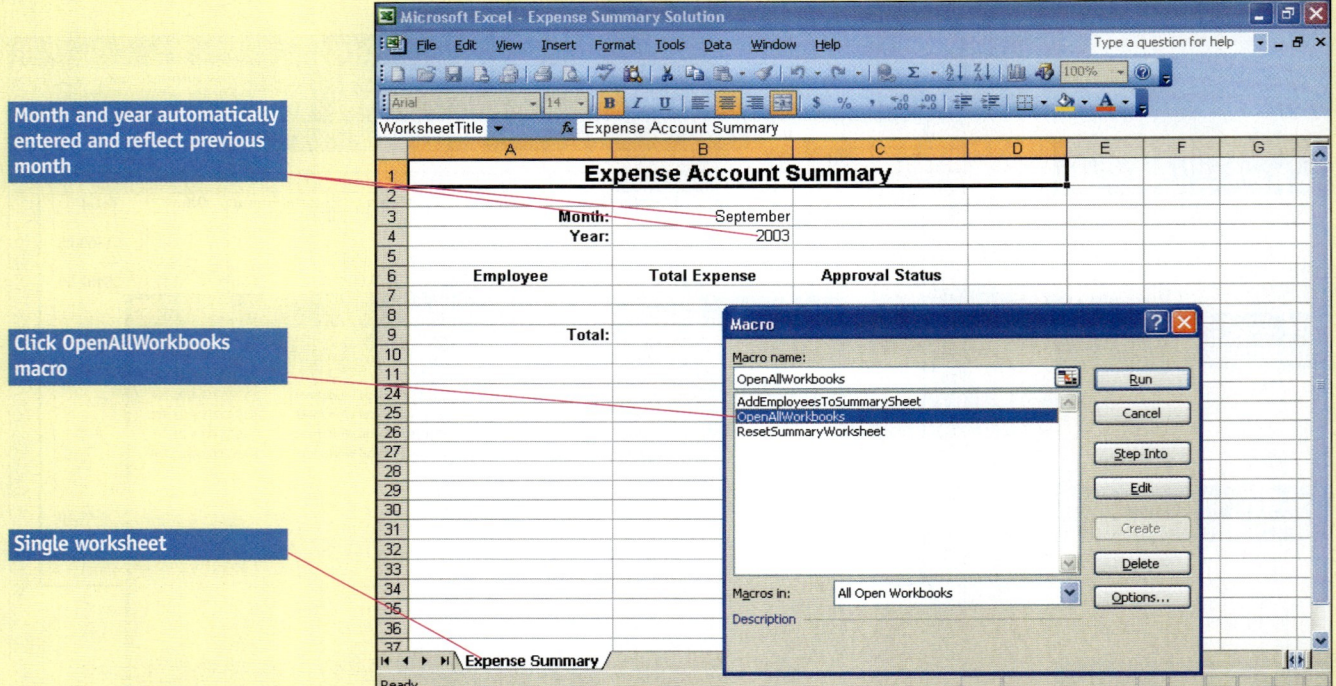

(d) Run the Open All Workbooks Procedure (step 4)

FIGURE 11.3 Hands-on Exercise 1 (*continued*)

SAVING THE INDIVIDUAL WORKBOOKS

Our application takes "poetic license" in that the individual employee workbooks are modified each time they are opened through date functions. This was done to keep the workbooks current; that is, the employee workbooks will reference the same month for which you are submitting your expense report. The contents (dates) in the workbooks change, however, and thus Excel prompts you to save the changes.

Step 5: **Debugging**

- Your actions in this step depend on the success of the previous step:
  - ❏ If the procedure executed successfully, press **Alt+F11** to open the editor.
  - ❏ If the procedure did not execute correctly, Click **OK** in response to the error message in Figure 11.3e, then press **Alt+F11** to open the VBA editor.

- Double click **Module1** within Project Explorer to display the procedures within this module. Locate the OpenAllWorkbooks procedure that was shown earlier in Figure 11.2. Note the following:
  - ❏ The Dir function obtains the names of the Excel workbooks in the **Expense Statements folder**, which is located in the Exploring Excel folder on drive C.
  - ❏ If your procedure did not execute correctly, it is most likely because the folder does not exist on your system and/or it is on a different drive. Make the necessary changes, either by changing the folder name and/or location using Windows Explorer or by modifying the procedure. Return to the previous step and reexecute the procedure.

- Close the VBA window to return to Excel.

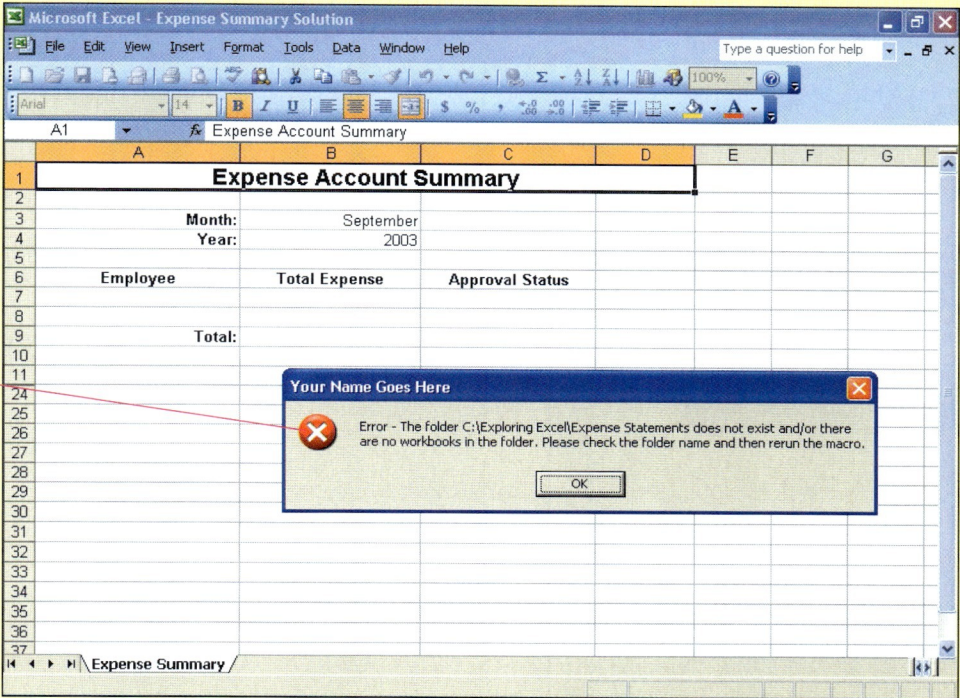

Error message indicates that designated folder was not found

(e) Debugging (step 5)

FIGURE 11.3 Hands-on Exercise 1 (*continued*)

ANTICIPATE USER ERRORS

The developer will understand why a procedure fails to execute properly and/or the meaning of the associated error message. The end user will not, however, and thus a good application anticipates mistakes that a user may make and displays meaningful messages to correct the problem. The OpenAllWorkbooks procedure checks the value returned by the initial Dir function, then displays the appropriate message if the function does not locate an Excel workbook.

Step 6: **The Expense Summary Workbook**

- You should see the Expense Summary Solution workbook as shown in Figure 11.3f. There are a total of six worksheets:
  - The Expense Summary worksheet that existed at the start of the exercise. This worksheet does not yet contain any employee information.
  - A worksheet with your name that contains the expenses you entered earlier.
  - Four additional worksheets that contain the expenses of other employees.

- Select the worksheet containing your expenses. Recall that you entered the month manually into cell J4, and further that you were instructed to enter the previous month. (Expenses are submitted in the current month for the previous month.)

- Select any other employee worksheet. The month and year in this worksheet should match the values in your worksheet. This was accomplished through the use of Date functions and a VLOOKUP function to provide consistency among the worksheets. (See boxed tip.)

- Save the Expense Summary Solution workbook. Exit Excel if you do not want to continue with the next exercise at this time.

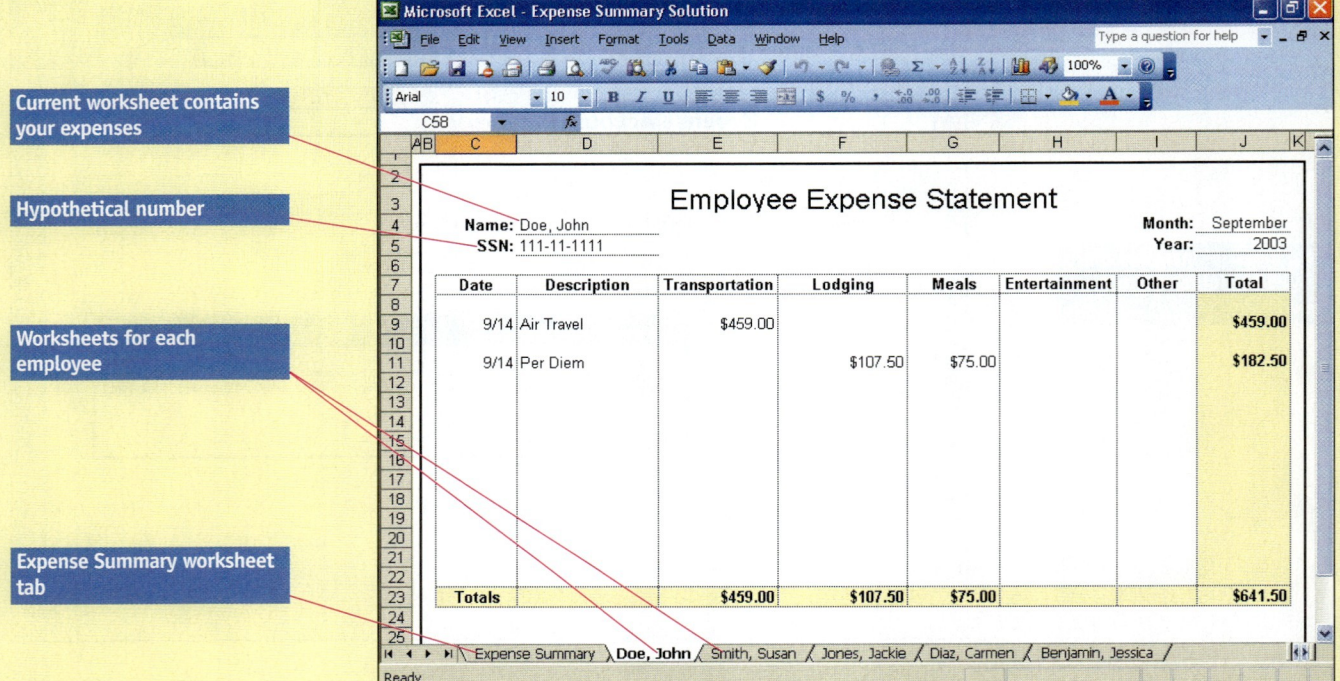

Current worksheet contains your expenses

Hypothetical number

Worksheets for each employee

Expense Summary worksheet tab

(f) The Expense Summary Workbook (step 6)

FIGURE 11.3 Hands-on Exercise 1 (*continued*)

THE VLOOKUP FUNCTION

Cell D28 in each employee worksheet contains the Excel formula =Month(Today())-1 to determine the previous month. This is a numeric value, however, and it is converted to text through a VLOOKUP function. Click in cell J4 of any employee worksheet to display the formula =VLOOKUP(D28,B28:C39,2). The VLOOKUP function takes the numeric month in cell D28 and applies it to a table of the month names in cells B28 through C39. Unprotect the worksheet, then unhide the indicated rows to see these functions.

DISPLAYING A SPECIFIC WORKSHEET

The summary workbook that has been created contains a worksheet for each employee who submitted an expense report. Our next task is to display the expenses for a specific employee on demand, perhaps when speaking to that employee to obtain additional documentation for his or her expenses. This could be done within the Excel interface, without benefit of a VBA procedure, simply by clicking the worksheet tab for that employee. It's easy to find the worksheet in a workbook with only a few employees, but much more tedious in a large workbook. Excel does not have a command to sort the worksheets within a workbook. Accordingly, we will develop a procedure to display a specific worksheet.

The user is prompted to enter the name of a specific employee as shown in Figure 11.4a, after which the procedure selects (displays) the associated worksheet. It sounds easy, and it is, provided the user enters the employee name *exactly* as it appears on a worksheet tab within the summary workbook. If the user makes a mistake, even one as insignificant as omitting the comma or space, an error results and the worksheet will not be displayed. You may know that "Smith John" and "Smith, John" are one and the same, but VBA does not. If it cannot find the worksheet, it will display a rather intimidating error message, "Run Time Error 9—Subscript Out of Range", and the user is left to decipher the meaning of this message.

Error Trapping

The preceding error is a **run-time error** that occurs during the execution of a procedure. (A **syntax error** occurs prior to execution and must be corrected to execute the procedure.) A run-time error terminates a procedure immediately, then it displays an explanation in a message box. The developer may know the meaning of the message, but the typical user does not. Thus, a good application will anticipate (trap) errors that are likely to occur and take appropriate action when they do occur. This is accomplished through the **On Error statement** that transfers control to a special error-handling section at the end of the procedure. The latter contains additional processing statements and/or simply displays a more meaningful error message.

Consider now the procedure in Figure 11.4b. The Dim statement at the beginning of the procedure defines the variable strEmployeeName. The user is asked to enter the employee's name, and the result is stored in strEmployeeName. The next statement selects the appropriate worksheet, which in turn displays the worksheet in the Excel window. Syntactically, the statement is specifying a **worksheet object** and applying the Select method to the object. The generic format for that statement is Sheets("SheetName").Select. Instead of the worksheet name, however, we use the variable strEmployeeName, which contains the name of the desired worksheet. (Quotation marks are not used, or else VBA would attempt to display a worksheet called "strEmployeeName".)

The **Exit Sub statement** follows, and it terminates the procedure. The Exit Statement is essential because, without it, the procedure would continue to execute and process the statements in the error-handling routine.

Now consider what happens in the event of an error. The On Error statement takes effect any time a run-time error occurs. The procedure ceases its normal processing and jumps to the section called ErrorHandler. (ErrorHandler is a user-defined name, as opposed to a VBA reserved word.) The ErrorHandler section (note the colon to indicate that ErrorHandler is a label and not an executable statement) appears at the end of the procedure. It consists of a single MsgBox statement to display a more helpful error message. Additional statements could be added to this section to take further action. The End Sub statement is reached, and the procedure terminates. The procedure in Figure 11.4b is a simple, but solid, example of **error trapping**.

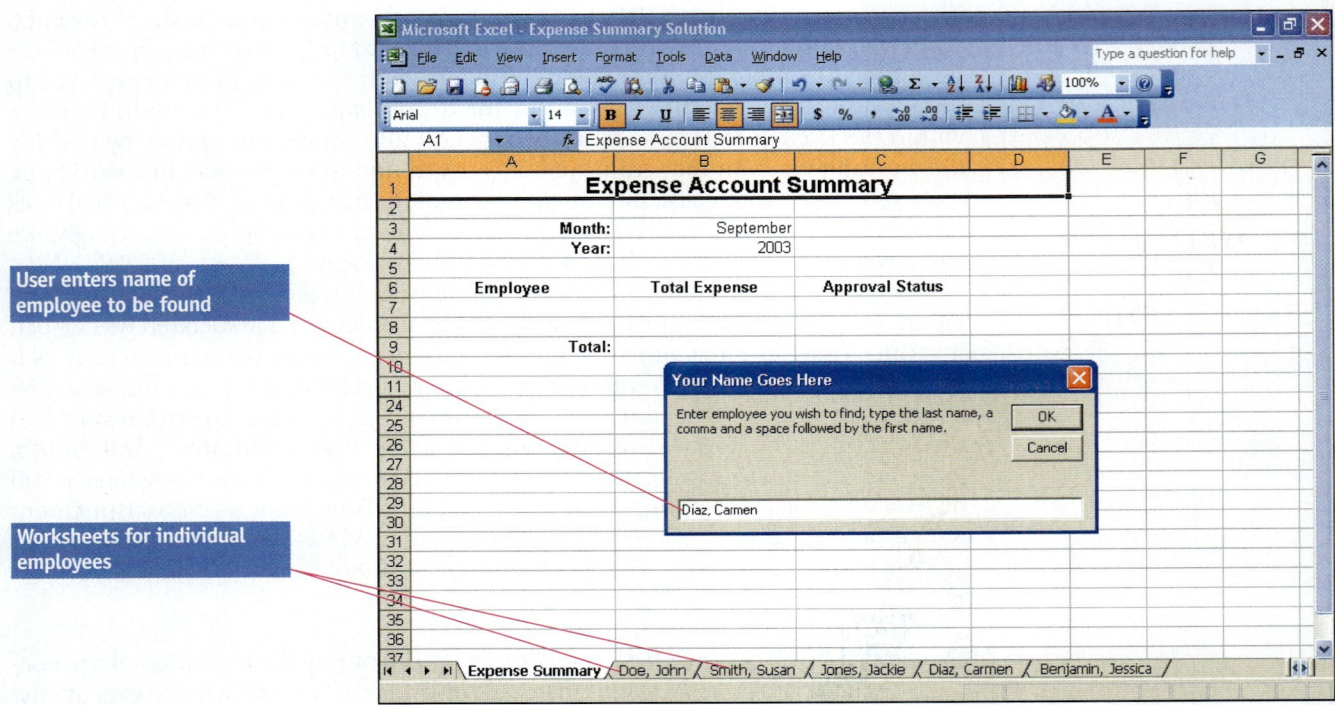

(a) Excel Workbook

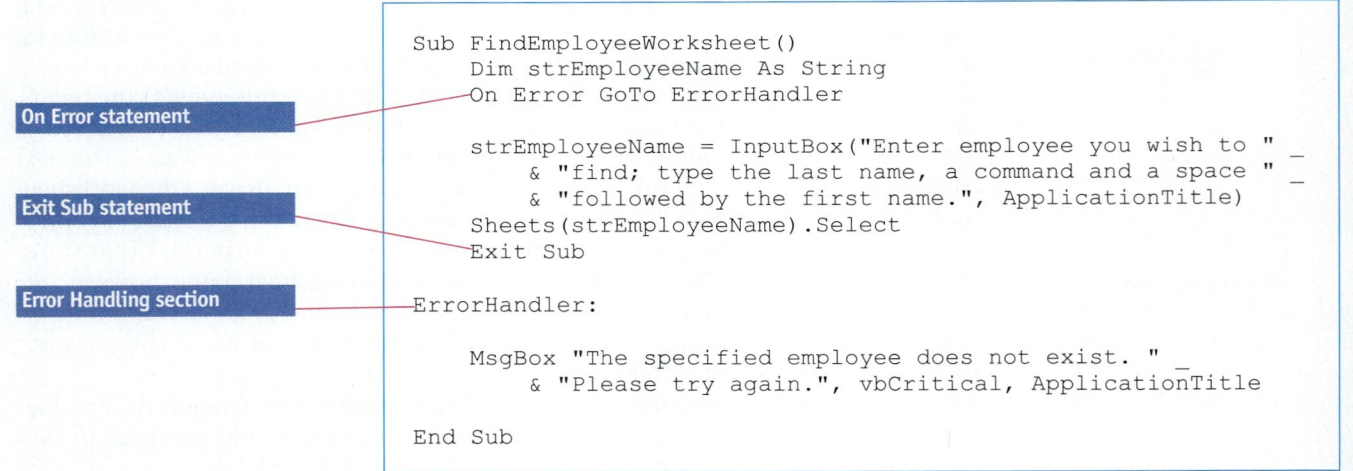

(b) VBA Procedure

FIGURE 11.4 Finding an Employee Worksheet

hands-on exercise

2 Error Trapping

Objective Develop a VBA procedure to display a specific worksheet within a workbook; include the appropriate error-trapping statements.

Step 1: Start the Macro Recorder

- Open the **Expense Summary Solution workbook** from the last exercise. Click the button to **Enable Macros**. Click the **Expense Summary worksheet tab**.

- Pull down the **Tools menu**, click the **Macro command**, then click **Record New Macro** to display the Record Macro dialog box in Figure 11.5a.

- Enter **FindEmployeeWorksheet** as the name of the procedure. Click the **Shortcut Key** check box and enter a **lowercase f. Ctrl+f** should appear as the keyboard shortcut. Click **OK** to begin recording.

- Click the worksheet tab for **Susan Smith**. Click the **Stop Recording button**. (If you do not see the Stop Recording toolbar, pull down the **Tools menu**, click **Macro**, and click the **Stop Recording command**.)

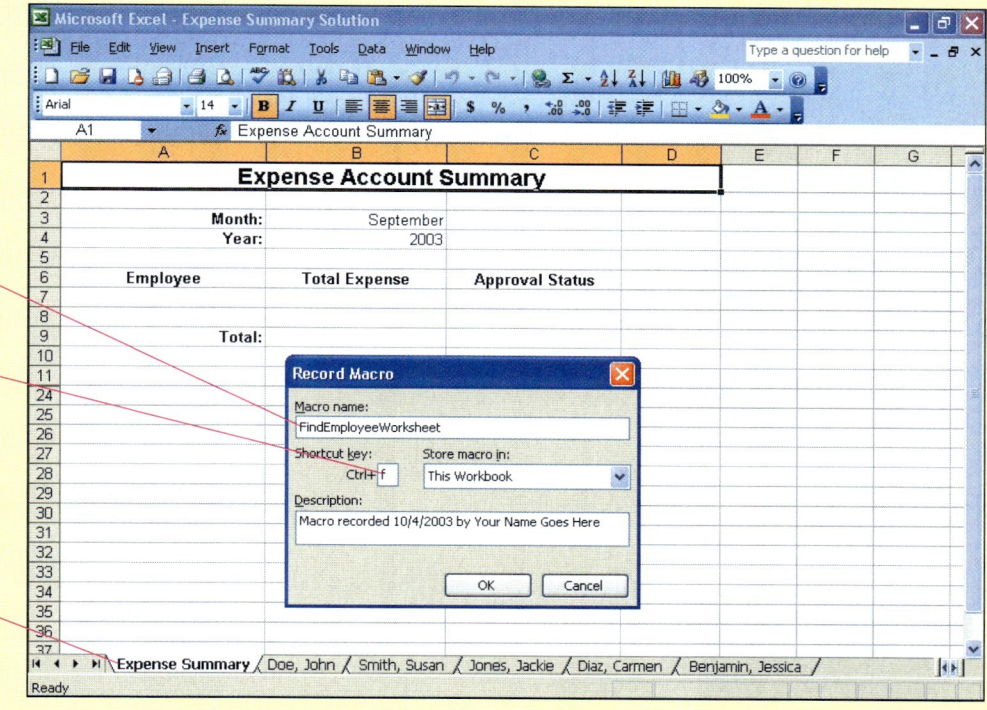

(a) Start the Macro Recorder (step 1)

FIGURE 11.5 Hands-on Exercise 2

KEYBOARD SHORTCUTS

You can add and/or modify the shortcut key associated with a macro at any time. Pull down the Tools menu, click the Macro command, then click Macros. . . to display the Macro dialog box. Select the desired macro and click the Options button to display the Macro Options dialog box, where you assign a shortcut.

Step 2: **Modify the Procedure**

- Press **Alt+F11** to display the VBA editor. Open Project Explorer if it is not visible. You will see that Module2 has been added to the Modules folder. Double click **Module2** to display its contents.

- The procedure at this point consists of a single executable statement, Sheets("Smith, Susan").Select. The other statements include the procedure header and End Sub statement and various comments. Enter the additional code as shown in Figure 11.5b:
  - Add the **Comment statements** as indicated.
  - The **Dim statement** defines the variable strEmployeeName that will contain the name of the employee whose worksheet you want to display.
  - The **InputBox function** prompts the user for the employee name, then stores the result in the strEmployeeName variable.

- Click and drag to select **"Smith, Susan"** (include the quotation marks) as shown in Figure 11.5b. Type **strEmployeeName**. The statement now reads **Sheets(strEmployeeName).Select**.

- Save the procedure.

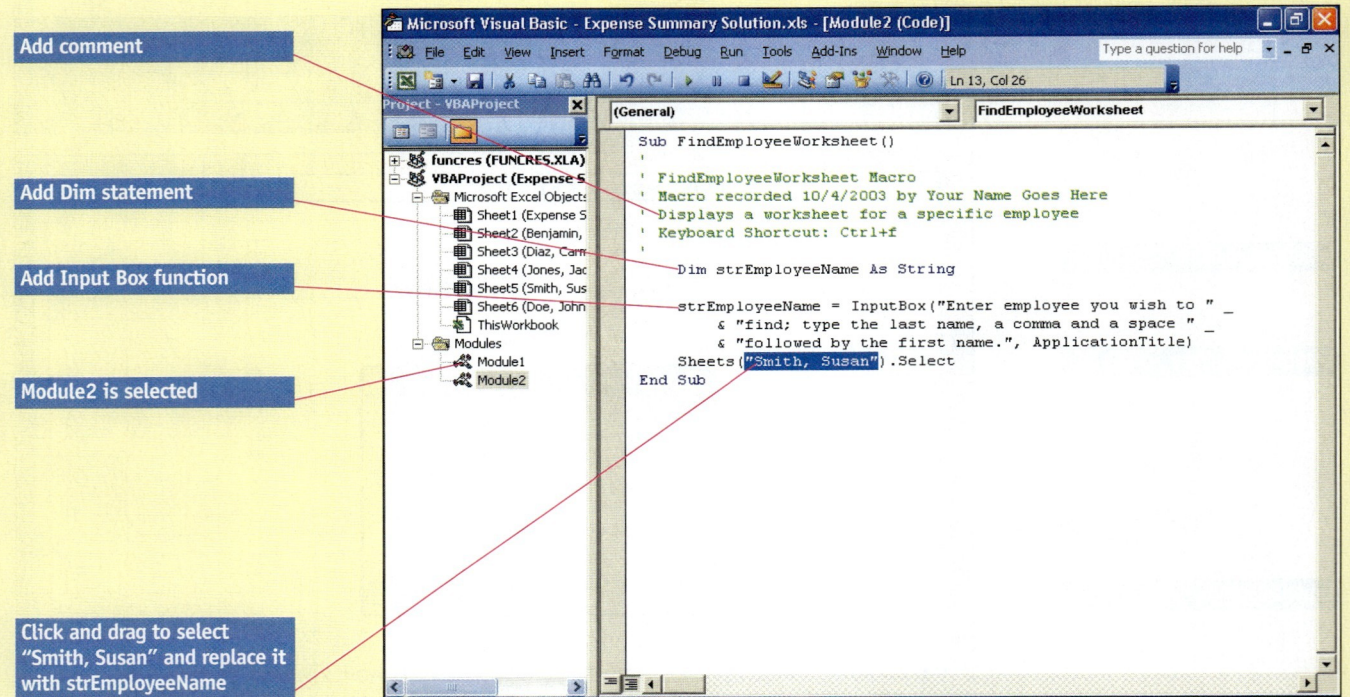

(b) Modify the Procedure (step 2)

FIGURE 11.5 Hands-on Exercise 2 (*continued*)

UNDERSTANDING THE VBA SYNTAX

The syntax of any VBA statement is easy to follow if you go back to the basics. VBA accomplishes its tasks by manipulating objects such as workbooks and worksheets. A collection is a group of similar objects. A method is an action that is performed on an object. Given this information, it is easy to understand the statement, *Sheets("Susan Smith").Select*. VBA is applying the Select method to a specific worksheet within the worksheets collection.

Step 3: **Test the Procedure**

- Return to the Excel window and select the **Expense Summary worksheet**. **Press Ctrl+f** to test the procedure you just created. You should see the message box in Figure 11.5c that asks you to enter an employee name.

- Enter the name that appears on any worksheet tab, but be sure to enter the name correctly. Click **OK** and you should see the worksheet for that employee.

- Press **Ctrl+f** to rerun the procedure, but this time, misspell the name of the employee you wish to find. You will see an error message, "Run-time error 9: Subscript out of range".

- Click the **Debug button**. You are back in the VBA editor, and the statement that caused the problem—Sheets(strEmployeeName).Select—is highlighted.

- Click the **Reset (square) button** on the Standard toolbar to reset the procedure to modify its code, as described in the next step.

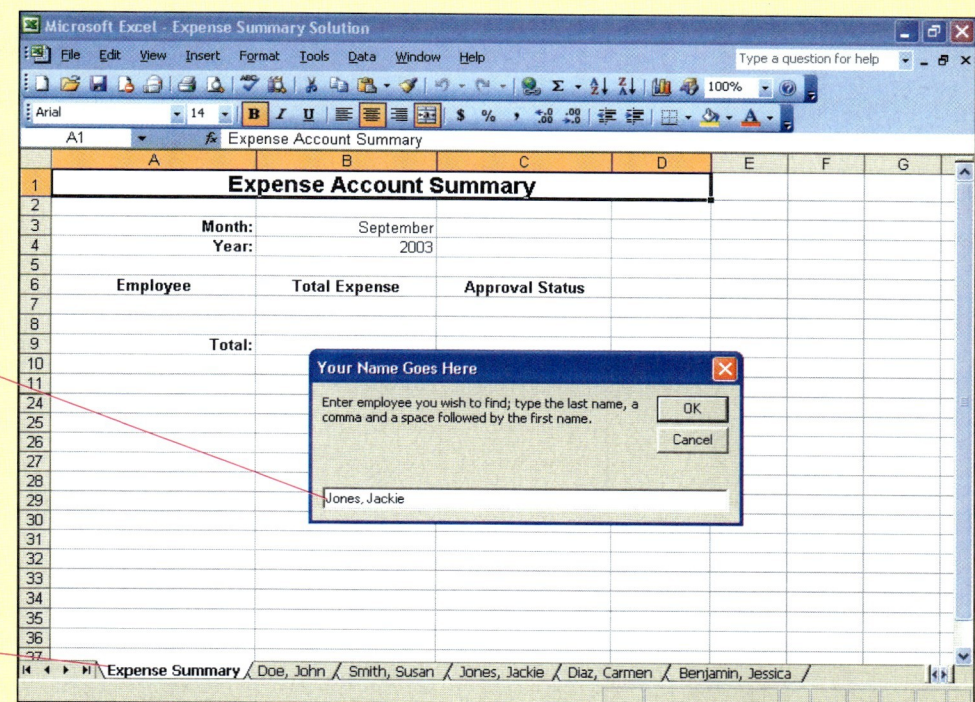

(c) Test the Procedure (step 3)

FIGURE 11.5 Hands-on Exercise 2 (*continued*)

RUN-TIME ERRORS

A run-time (execution) error results when VBA is unable to perform a specific task. VBA displays an explanation for the error, which typically does not make sense to the end user. The error in this example occurs because VBA was unable to reference a specific worksheet because it (the worksheet) does not exist. The internal subscript used by VBA to reference the worksheet within the workbook is out of range and hence the error message. A good application will anticipate (trap) the errors a user is apt to make and provide more meaningful explanations than the standard error messages.

Step 4: **Add the Error Handling**

- You can insulate a procedure against runtime errors by including the appropriate code. Add the additional statements as shown in Figure 11.5d:
  - The **On Error statement** suppresses the normal error message and transfers control to the user-defined location ErrorHandler, which appears elsewhere in the procedure. This statement is executed automatically whenever an error occurs during the procedure.
  - The **Exit Sub statement** exits the procedure immediately, effectively bypassing the statements within the ErrorHandler routine.
  - The **MsgBox statement** within the ErrorHandler routine displays a meaningful message to the user that describes the nature of the error.
- Save the procedure. Return to the Excel window, then press **Ctrl+f** to rerun the procedure to locate a specific employee. **Misspell the employee's name** to test the modified procedure. You should see the message box indicating that the employee worksheet cannot be found. Click **OK**.

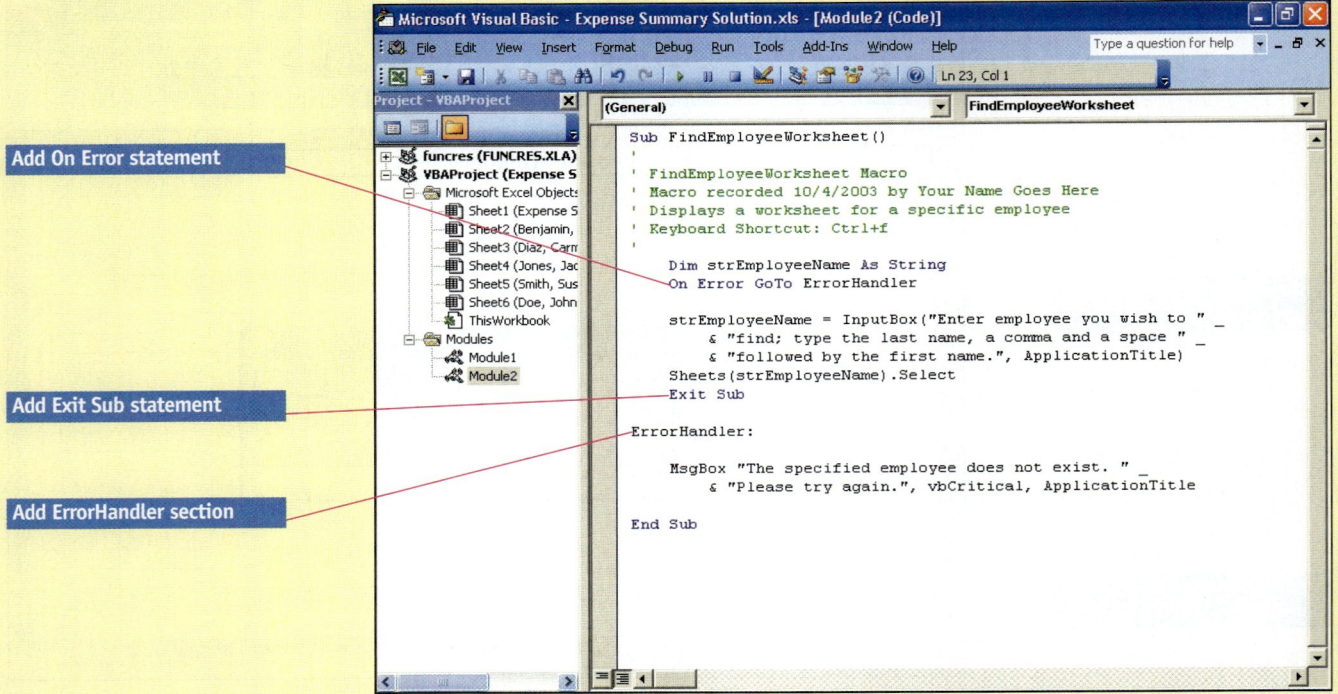

(d) Add the Error Handling (step 4)

FIGURE 11.5 Hands-on Exercise 2 (*continued*)

TOGGLE COMMENTS ON AND OFF

A comment is used primarily to explain the logic within a VBA procedure, but it can also render a statement nonexecutable (as opposed to deleting it altogether). Click at the beginning of the On Error statement within the procedure, type an apostrophe, and then press the down arrow. The statement turns green, indicating that it has been converted to a comment, and thus will not affect the outcome of the procedure. Now reexecute the procedure, misspell the employee name, and you once again see the VBA error message. Remove the apostrophe, try the procedure again, and you see the meaningful error message.

Step 5: **Create a Command Button**

- Select the **Expense Summary worksheet**. Pull down the **View menu**, click **Toolbars**, then click **Forms** to display the Forms toolbar. Click the **Button tool** (the mouse pointer changes to a tiny crosshair).

- Click and drag in the worksheet to draw a command button. Release the mouse. The Assign Macro dialog box will appear as shown in Figure 11.5e. Select **FindEmployeeWorksheet** (the procedure you just created). Click **OK**.

- The button should still be selected. Click and drag to select the name of the button, **Button 1**. Type **Find Employee Worksheet** as the new name. Do not press the Enter key.

- Click outside of the button to deselect it. Right click the button you just created to display a context-sensitive menu, click the **Format Control** to display the associated dialog box, then click the **Properties tab**. Click the Option button that says **Don't move or size with cells**. Click **OK**.

- Add a second command button to run the **OpenAllWorkbooks procedure**.

- Close the Forms toolbar. Save the workbook.

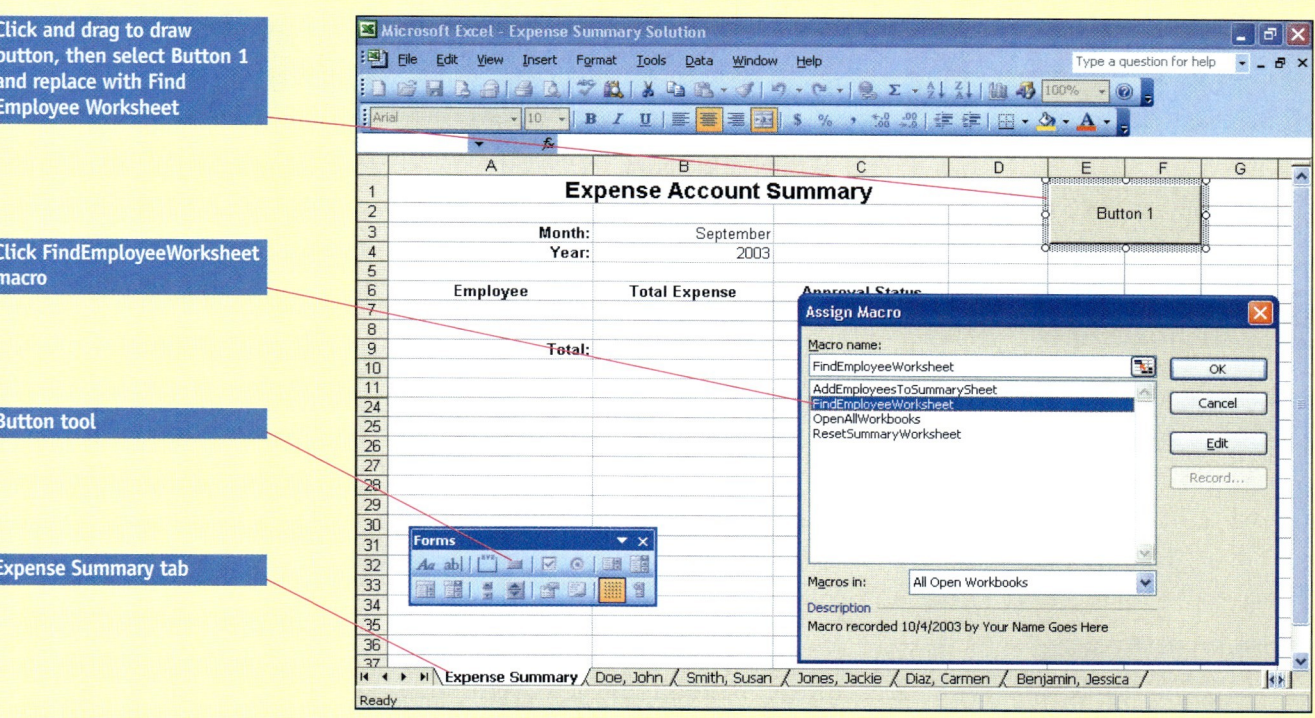

(e) Create a Command Button (step 5)

FIGURE 11.5 Hands-on Exercise 2 (*continued*)

COMMAND BUTTON PROPERTIES

A command button is not physically in a cell, but it will (by default) move and/or resize itself in conjunction with the cells on which it is placed. This is a potential problem if you insert and/or delete rows or columns within a worksheet. Hence we find it convenient to fix the button properties so that the button is unaffected by subsequent changes in the worksheet. Note, too, that you cannot select a command button by clicking it, because that would execute the associated VBA procedure. You can, however, right click the button to display a context-sensitive menu, which in turn selects the button.

Step 6: **Test the Command Buttons**

- You should see two command buttons as shown in Figure 11.5f. Select (click) the worksheet tab for the first employee.
- Press and hold the **Shift key** as you click the name of the last worksheet to select all of the employee worksheets.
- Point to any tab and click the **right mouse button**, then click the **Delete command**. Click the **Delete button** to confirm that you want to delete the employee worksheets.
- Click the command button to **Open All Workbooks**, which in turn runs the procedure from the first exercise. Click **No** when prompted to save the contents of each workbook.
- Select the **Expense Summary** worksheet. Click the button to **Find Employee Worksheet**. Misspell the employee name to test the error handing. Click **OK** when you see the message box in Figure 11.5f.
- Save the workbook. Exit Excel if you do not want to continue with the next exercise at this time.

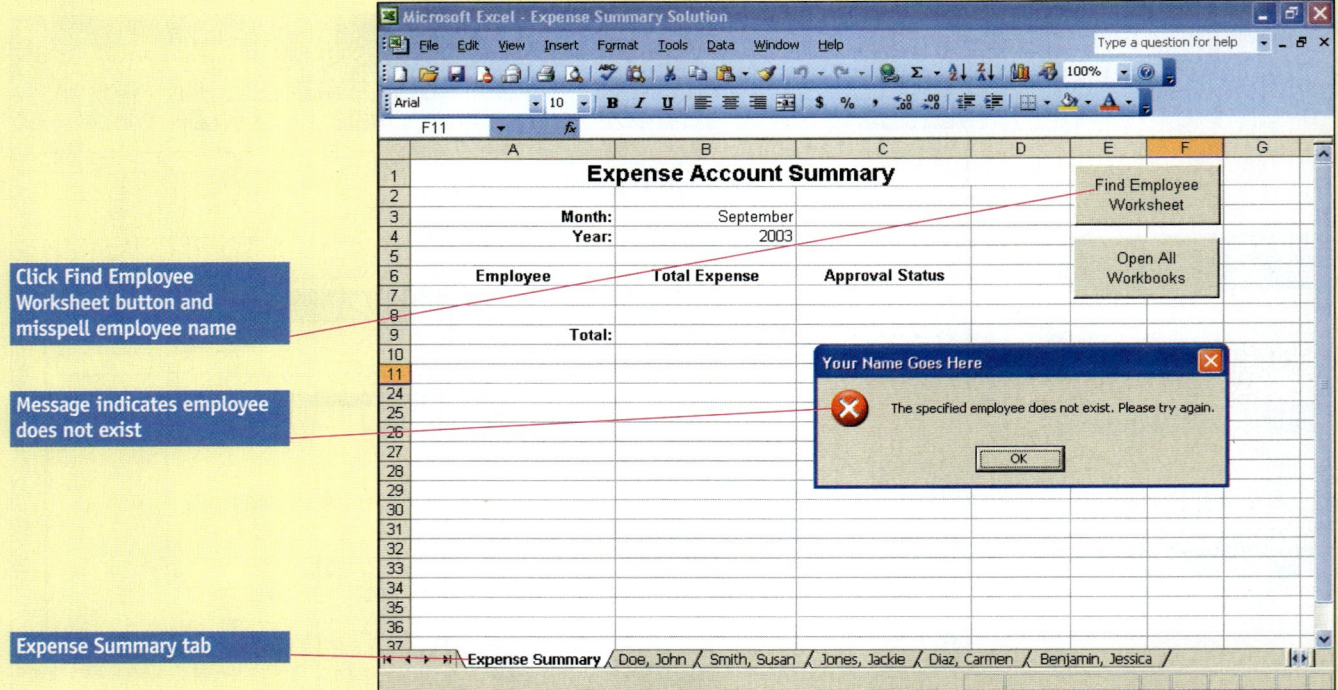

(f) Test the Command Buttons (step 6)

FIGURE 11.5 Hands-on Exercise 2 (*continued*)

DUPLICATE WORKSHEETS

Excel will not allow you to create multiple worksheets with the same name within a workbook. It is important, therefore, to delete the employee worksheets before running the procedure to add the employee information to the summary workbook. If you inadvertently run the procedure twice in a row, Excel will insert the second worksheet, but will append a subscript to its name within the worksheet tab, such as Your Name(2). Select the first sheet to be deleted, then press and hold the Ctrl key to select the remaining worksheets, click the right mouse button, then click the Delete command to remove the duplicate sheets.

PROCESSING WORKSHEETS IN A WORKBOOK

The Expense Summary workbook contains a single summary worksheet as well as a detailed worksheet for each employee who submitted an expense workbook. Our next task is to process all of the worksheets within the summary workbook. We will develop two separate procedures:

- A procedure to examine the individual worksheets in order to approve the indicated expenses or send the expense worksheet for further review. (The approval criterion is simple. The individual preparing the summary worksheet is asked to enter the threshold amount for the total expense for one employee, below which the expenses are approved automatically.)

- A second procedure to copy the total expense from each employee worksheet, as well as an indication of whether that amount was approved, to a row on the summary worksheet.

Figure 11.6a displays the detailed worksheet for one employee in conjunction with the first procedure. The individual preparing the summary workbook is prompted initially for the threshold amount ($1,000 in this example—the Input Box is not visible in this figure), that value is compared to the employee's total expense in cell J23 ($641.50 on this worksheet), and the approval status is entered into cell D25. Conditional formatting is used in the cell to display "Approved" or "Review" in blue or red, respectively. The procedure also modifies the worksheet tab so that you can see at a glance the status of individual employees. (The ability to change the color of a worksheet tab was introduced in Office XP.)

Figure 11.6b contains the associated VBA procedure, which includes a For . . . Next statement to process all of the worksheets within the workbook. (Technically speaking, it is processing each worksheet object within the worksheets collection.) The logic is not difficult, but it helps to examine the logic in pseudocode prior to looking at the actual VBA statements. Consider this:

```
Input threshold amount for automatic approval
For each worksheet in the workbook
    If this is an employee worksheet
        Unprotect this worksheet
        If the expenses are less than or equal to threshold amount
            Approve these expenses and set worksheet tab to blue
        Else
            Review these expenses and set worksheet tab to red
        End if
        Protect this worksheet
    End If
Next worksheet
```

Loop to process every worksheet

Determines whether expenses are approved

The For. . .Next loop automatically processes all of the worksheets within the workbook. Realize, however, that the first worksheet is a summary (rather than an employee) worksheet and thus the If statement to process only employee worksheets is required. The second If statement compares the total expense on the employee worksheet to the threshold amount and takes the appropriate action.

Figure 11.6b displays the associated VBA procedure. The Dim statement defines the variable mysheet as a worksheet object, which controls the For. . .Next statement that drives the procedure. The loop looks at every worksheet within the workbook, checks to see that each worksheet is an employee worksheet, and if so, compares the total expense on that worksheet to the threshold amount. (WorksheetTitle, TotalExpense, and ApprovedRejected are range names on the Excel worksheet.) The ColorIndex property is set to 5 (blue) or 3 (red), respectively, to indicate whether the expenses are approved or subject to further review.

Employee's total expense is compared to threshold amount

Approval status is entered

Tab color reflects approval status

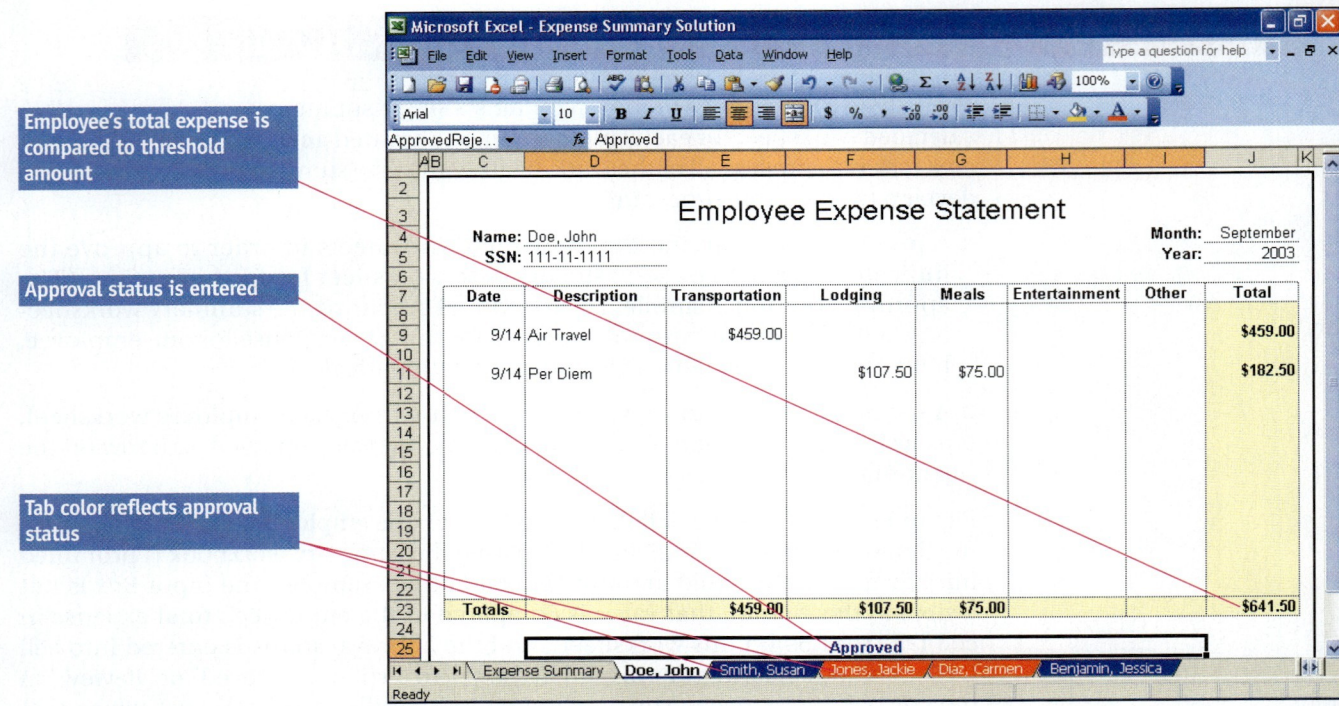

(a) Employee Worksheet

User is prompted for threshold amount

Worksheet tab color is set to blue

Worksheet tab color is set to red

Summary worksheet is selected when loop is exited

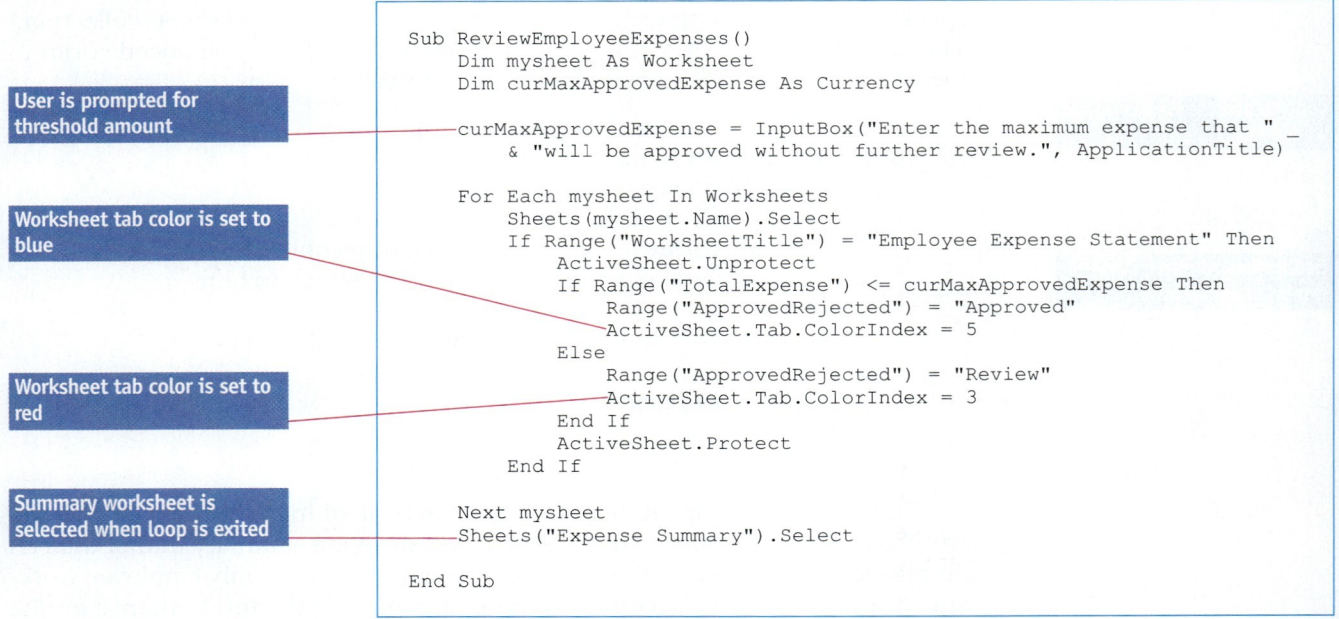

(b) VBA Procedure

FIGURE 11.6 Review Employee Expenses

Adding Employees to the Summary Worksheet

Our next task is to copy the information from the individual employee worksheets (within the summary workbook) to a summary worksheet as shown in Figure 11.7. The summary worksheet contains a single line for each employee with his or her name, the total expense for that employee, and an indication of the approval status. (**Conditional Formatting** is used to display the status in red or blue for "review" or "approved", respectively.) Row 7, for example, contains the data for Jessica Benjamin, and it reflects the data in the associated worksheet. The color of the worksheet tab also indicates the approval status.

Each of the entries in this row contains a formula that references the appropriate cell from Jessica's worksheet. Cell B7 displays Jessica's total expenses ($303.20) according to the formula ='Benjamin,Jessica'!TotalExpense. The name of the worksheet is enclosed in apostrophes and corresponds to a worksheet tab at the bottom of the window. The exclamation point indicates a worksheet reference. TotalExpense is a range name on that worksheet.

Figure 11.7b displays the procedure to process all of the employee worksheets in the summary workbook and build the appropriate formulas on the summary worksheet. The procedure is easier to understand if we look first at the underlying logic as expressed in pseudocode. Consider the following:

> Select the cell for the first employee on the summary worksheet [*Sets insertion point on Summary worksheet*]
>
> For each worksheet in the workbook
>   If this is an employee worksheet [*Tests for employee worksheet*]
>   Store the name of this worksheet for use in a cell formula
>   Select the active cell in the summary worksheet
>   Enter the formula to reference cell D4 in the employee worksheet
>   Move one column to the right (on the summary worksheet)
>   Enter the formula for the total expenses in the employee worksheet
>   Move one column to the right (on the summary worksheet)
>   Enter the formula for the approval status in the employee worksheet
>   Move down one row and two columns to the left (for the next employee) [*Adjusts insertion point for next employee*]
>   Insert a blank row to update the Sum function for the new employee
>   End If
> Next worksheet
>
> Delete extra blank row after all employees have been processed
> Sort the employees in alphabetical order [*Sorts Summary worksheet after all employees were added*]

The procedure begins by selecting the cell that will contain the first employee on the summary worksheet, then it enters a loop to process all of the worksheets in the workbook. The first statement within the loop is an If statement to check that the worksheet is an employee worksheet; we do not want to copy information from the summary worksheet itself. We then build three formulas on the current row of the summary worksheet. The offset property is used to create a relative reference to various cells on this row; for example, Offset (0,1) refers to the cell on the same row, but one column to the right.

Each formula begins with a reference to the current worksheet name, which is then concatenated (joined) to the other parts of the formula. The ampersand indicates concatenation in the formula and joins one character string to another. After the third formula has been created, we drop down one row and move two columns to the left for the next employee. A blank row is inserted to accommodate this employee, and the loop continues.

After all of the employee data has been copied to the summary worksheet, we exit the loop and delete a superfluous blank line after the last employee. The employees are then displayed in alphabetical order by last name. The summary worksheet is complete.

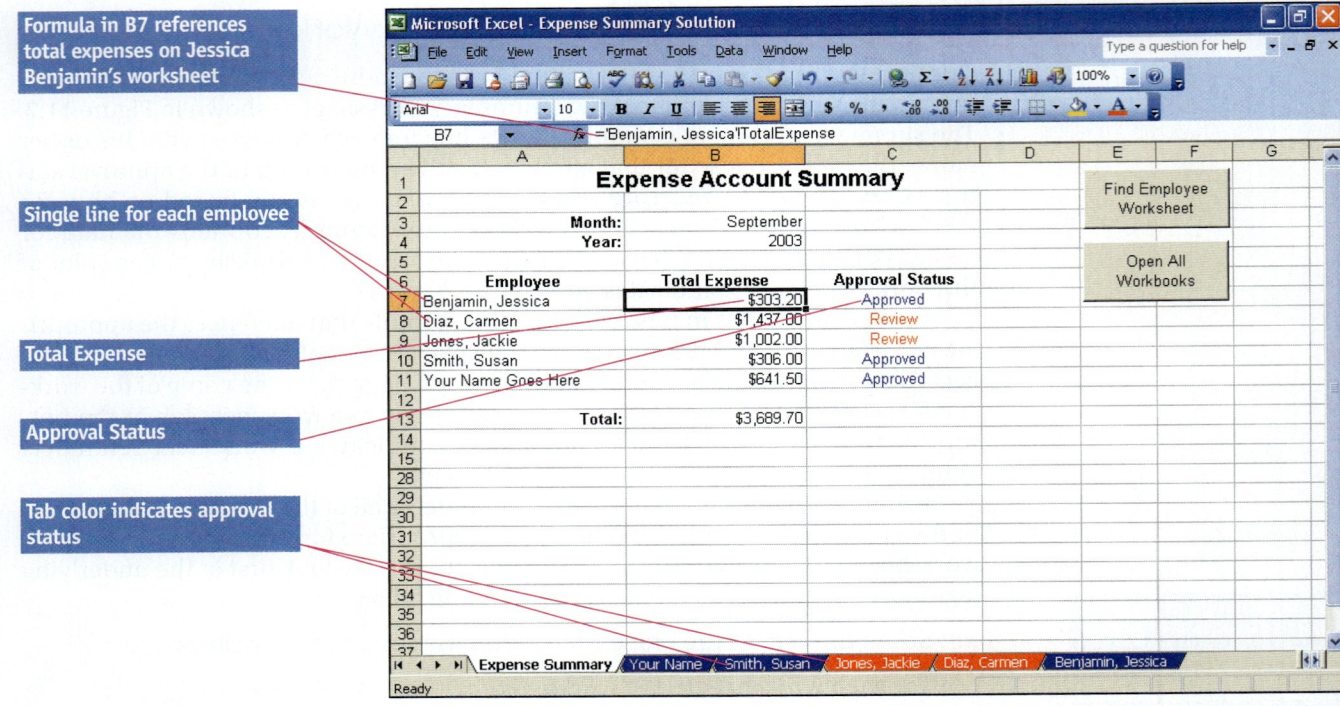

(a) The Summary Worksheet

(b) VBA Procedure

FIGURE 11.7 Create the Summary Worksheet

hands-on exercise 3
Create the Summary Worksheet

Objective Create two procedures to process the worksheets in a workbook. Use Figure 11.8 as a guide in the exercise.

Step 1: **Start the Macro Recorder**

- Open the **Expense Summary Solution workbook** from the previous exercise. Enable the macros. Click the worksheet tab that contains your expenses.
- Click the **down arrow** in the Name box to see the range names that have been previously defined in this worksheet. Note the following:
  - The range name WorksheetTitle refers to cell C3, which contains the title of this worksheet, "Employee Expense Statement".
  - The range name ApprovedRejected refers to cell D25. This cell is presently blank, but it will contain an indication of whether the expenses are approved.
  - The range name TotalExpense refers to cell J23, which contains the total expenses for this employee.
- Pull down the **Tools menu**, click the **Macro command**, then click **Record New Macro** to display the Record Macro dialog box in Figure 11.8a.
- Enter **ReviewEmployeeExpenses** as the name of the procedure, enter the description shown, and then click **OK** to begin recording.
- Pull down the **Tools menu**, click **Protection**, then click **Unprotect Sheet**.
- If you are using Excel 2002 or a later release, right click the worksheet tab to display a context-sensitive menu, click **Tab Color** to display the Format Tab Color dialog box, click a **Blue square** from the palette, then click **OK**.
- Click the **Expense Summary worksheet tab**. Click the **Stop Recording button**.

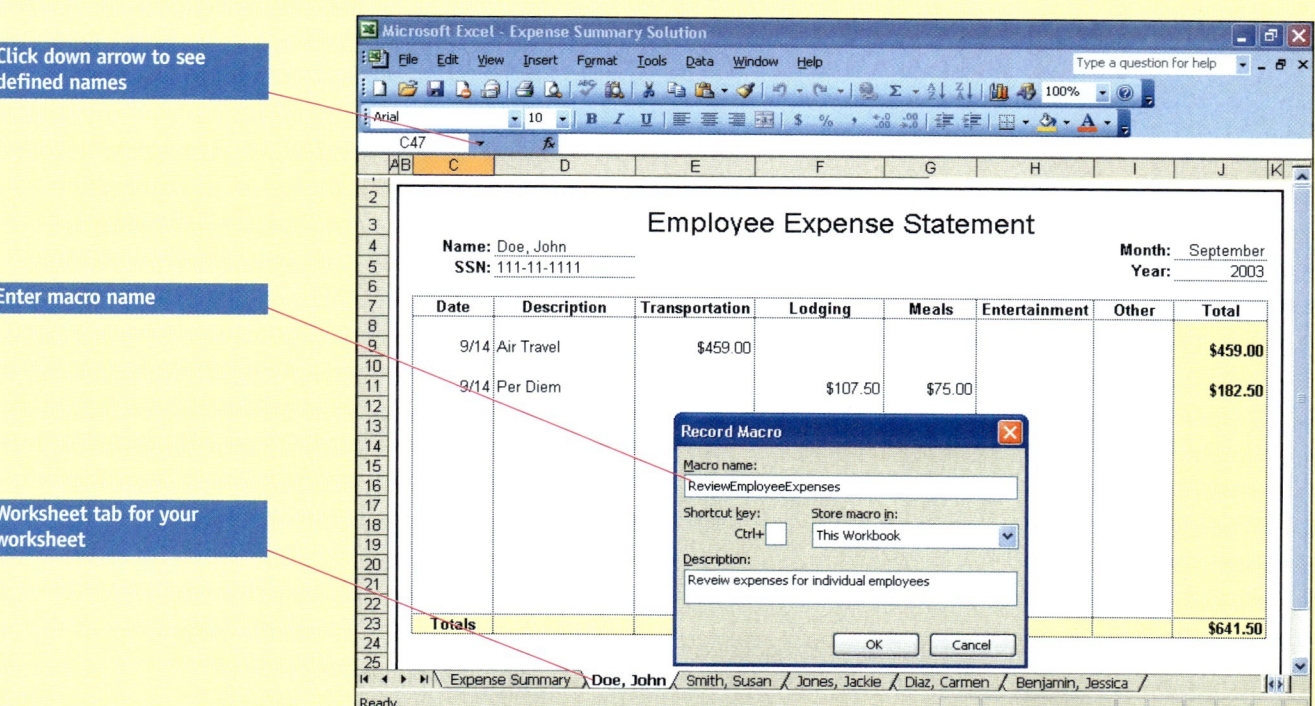

(a) Start the Macro Recorder (step 1)

FIGURE 11.8 Hands-on Exercise 3

Step 2: **Loops and Decision Making**

- Press **Alt+F11** to display the VBA editor. If necessary, pull down the **View menu** and click **Project Explorer** (or use the **Ctrl+r** keyboard shortcut) to display the Project Explorer window.
- Open the modules folder, then double click the last module that appears to display the procedures in that module. Locate the **ReviewEmployeeExpenses procedure** that you just created.
- Close Project Explorer. Your procedure contains only a few of the statements in Figure 11.8b. Proceed as follows:
  - Add the **Dim statement** at the beginning of the procedure to define the variable **mysheet**. Add the **For** and **Next statements** as shown in the figure.
  - Change Sheets("Your Name").Select, to **Sheets(mysheet.Name).Select**.
  - Add the **If** and **End If** statements to test for an employee worksheet.
  - Change the statement for tab color to **ActiveSheet.Tab.ColorIndex = 5**. (This statement will not appear in Office 2000.)
  - Add the statement to protect the worksheet. Check that your procedure matches Figure 11.8b. Save the procedure.
- Click in the procedure, then click the **RunSub button** to run the procedure, then click the **Excel button** to see the results. All of the worksheet tabs (except the summary tab) should be blue. Save the workbook.

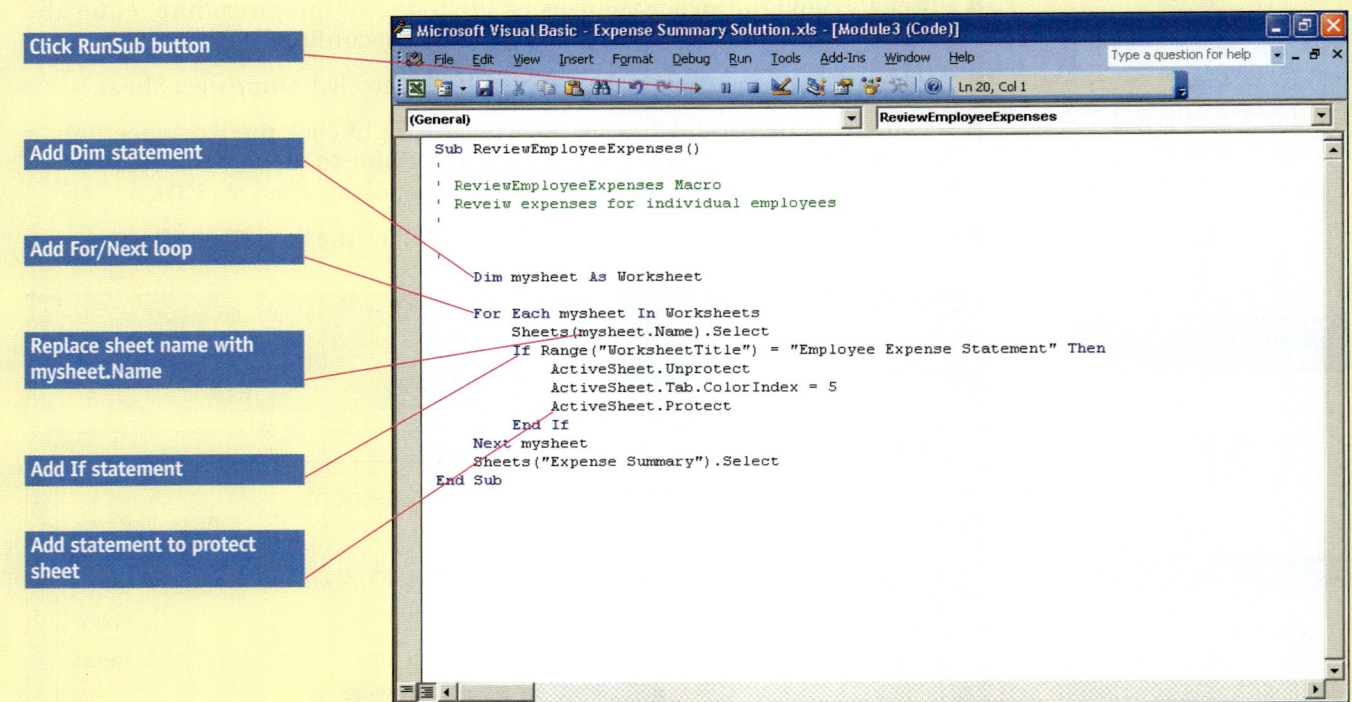

(b) Loops and Decision Making (step 2)

FIGURE 11.8 Hands-on Exercise 3 (*continued*)

CHANGE THE COLOR OF A WORKSHEET TAB

The ability to change the color of a worksheet tab was introduced in Excel 2002. The tab color can be changed in two ways—in VBA by setting the Tab.ColorIndex property and/or from the Excel interface. (Right click the tab, click the Tab Color command to display the associated dialog box, select a color, and click OK.) The feature does not exist in Excel 2000.

Step 3: **Complete the Procedure**

- Return to the VBA editor to complete the procedure as shown in Figure 11.8c. Add a second **Dim statement** to define the **curMaxApprovedExpense** variable. Add **the Input Box function** to prompt the user for the value of this variable.

- Add the second (nested) **If statement** to compare the value in the range named "TotalExpenses" to the maximum approved expense, then take the appropriate action. Enter **"Approved"** in the range named "ApprovedRejected" if the expenses are less than or equal to the maximum amount.

- Add the **Else clause**, which enters "Review" in the range named "ApprovedRejected" and changes the tab color to red if the expenses are greater than the threshold amount. (A color index of 3 changes the worksheet tab to red.)

- Add the **End If** delimiter to complete the statement. Save the procedure. Run the procedure. Enter **$1,000** when prompted for the maximum expense.

- Click the **View Microsoft Excel button** to view the workbook, which should contain a combination of red and blue worksheet tabs. Click any blue tab (e.g., Susan Smith) and you should see an approved message at the bottom of the worksheet. Click any red tab (e.g., Jackie Jones) and you should see the review message.

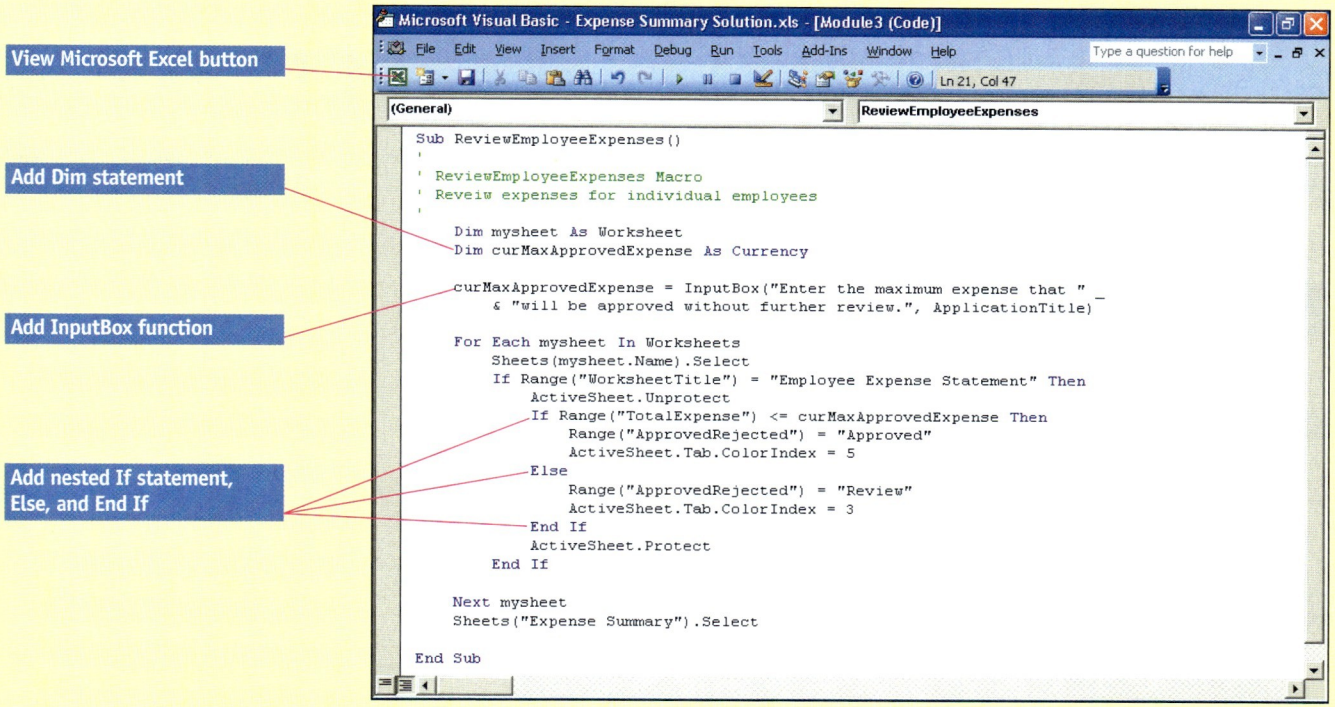

(c) Complete the Procedure (step 3)

FIGURE 11.8 Hands-on Exercise 3 (*continued*)

NESTED IF STATEMENTS

A nested If statement (or an If within an If) is easy to understand if you indent properly and follow basic syntax. Recall that an ordinary If statement tests a condition, then follows one of two paths, depending on whether the condition is true or false. The If statement must end with the End If delimiter, but the Else clause is optional. A nested If simply adds another If statement to either path. Each If (within the nested If) has its own End If delimiter. Indentation is used to make the statement easier to read.

Step 4: **Step through a Procedure**

- Return to the VBA editor. Pull down the **View menu** to display the Project Explorer window, then double click **Module1** to open its code window. Locate the **AddEmployeesToSummarySheet** procedure. Close Project Explorer.

- Point to a blank area at the right of the Windows taskbar and then click the **right mouse button**. Click the command to **Show the Desktop**.

- Click the **VBA** and **Excel buttons** on the taskbar to reopen these windows. Right click a blank area of the taskbar a second time, then click the command to **Tile Windows Vertically**.

- Your desktop should be similar to Figure 11.8d. Click in the Excel window, then click on the **Expense Summary tab** to select that worksheet. Click in the window containing the VBA editor. Click after the **Sub statement**.

- Press the **F8 key**. The procedure header is highlighted. Press the **F8 key** a second time. The Sheets("Expense Summary").Range("FirstEmployee").Select statement is highlighted.

- Continue to press the **F8 key** to view the progress of the procedure as it is executed one statement at a time. Each employee worksheet is selected in succession, and the appropriate information is moved to the summary worksheet.

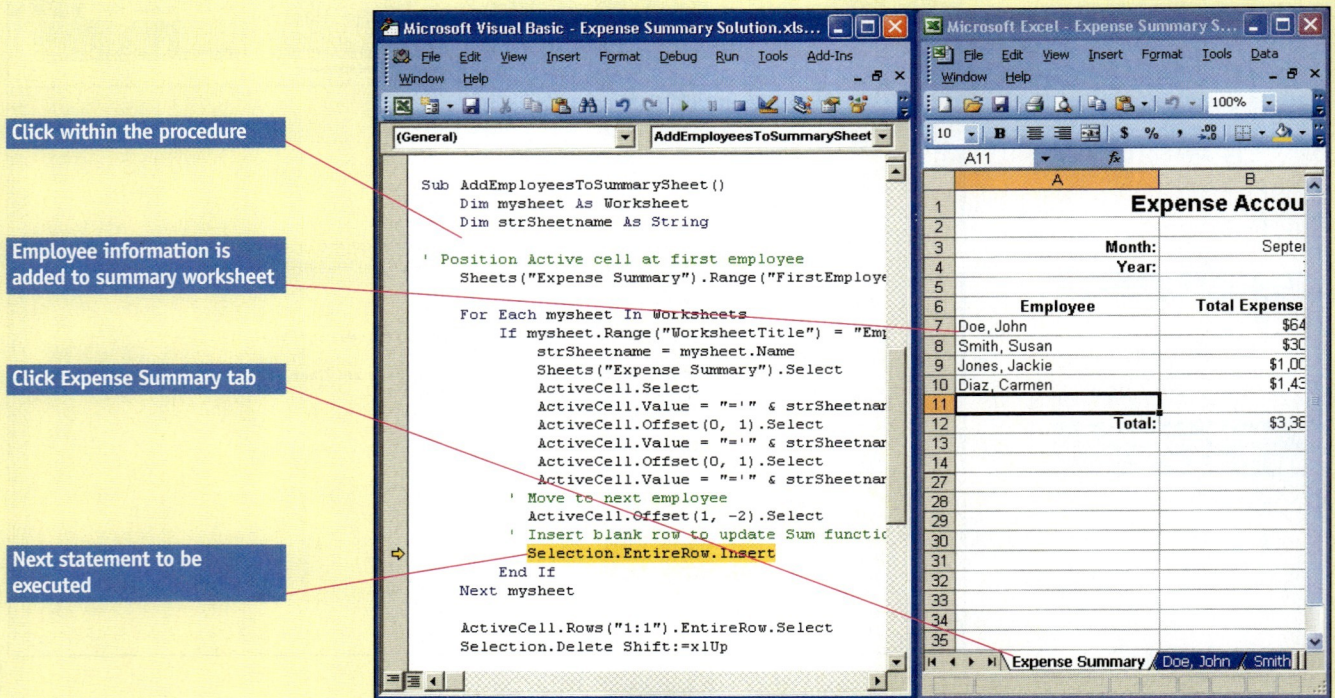

(d) Step through a Procedure (step 4)

FIGURE 11.8   Hands-on Exercise 3 (*continued*)

RELATIVE REFERENCES—THE OFFSET PROPERTY

The Offset property returns a range of cells that is offset (displaced) from the active cell by a designated number of rows and columns; for example, ActiveCell.Offset(0,1).Range("A1").Select selects the cell in the same row and one column to the right of the active cell. The Range object may be omitted if you are selecting only a single cell.

Step 5: **Check Your Progress**

- Maximize the Excel window to check your progress as shown in Figure 11.8e. The total expense for each employee as well as the approval status has been copied to the summary worksheet. The color of the worksheet tabs corresponds to the approval status for each employee.

- Click in any cell in the body of the worksheet—for example, **cell B8**, which contains the total expenses for Susan Smith on our worksheet. Look at the formula bar to see the contents of this cell, ='Smith, Susan'!TotalExpense.

- The employees are not yet in alphabetical order. We could sort the employees at this point, without modifying the existing procedure. We want the procedure to include this function, however, and so we will use the macro recorder to obtain these commands.

- Pull down the **Tools menu**, click the **Macro command**, then click **Record New Macro** to display the Record Macro dialog box. Enter **Dummy** as the name of the procedure. The keyboard shortcut and description are optional. Click **OK**.

- Click the **down arrow** in the Name box and select **FirstEmployee**. Click the **Sort Ascending button**. Click the **Stop Recording button**.

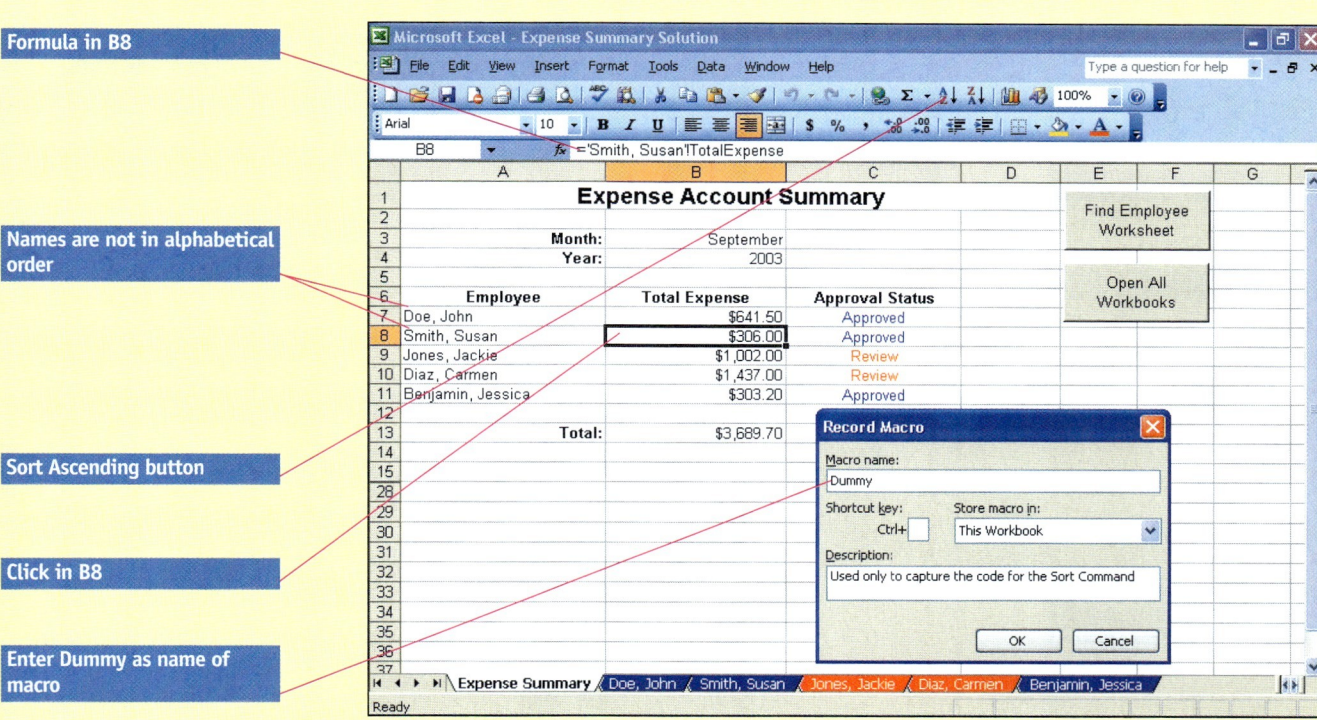

(e) Check Your Progress (step 5)

FIGURE 11.8 Hands-on Exercise 3 (continued)

WORKSHEET REFERENCES—THE EXCLAMATION MARK

An Excel formula may reference cells in other worksheets, in which case you need to include the name of the worksheet with the cell address; for example, =Sheet4!A1, references cell A1 in the worksheet called Sheet4. The name of the worksheet is always followed by an exclamation point. The cell reference, A1, may be replaced by a named range such as TotalExpense. The name of the worksheet is enclosed in apostrophes if it (the worksheet name) contains a space, as in 'Smith, Susan'!TotalExpense.

Step 6: **Complete the Procedure**

- Press **Alt+F11** to return to the VBA editor. Maximize the window. Open Project Explorer and double click the module that contains the newly recorded Dummy procedure.

- Click and drag to select the four lines of code in that procedure. You will see a statement to select the cell called "FirstEmployee", followed by a Sort statement that is continued over several lines. Select all four lines.

- Click the **Copy button** on the Standard toolbar or use the **Ctrl+C** keyboard shortcut to copy these statements to the clipboard.

- Switch to the **AddEmployeesToSummarySheet** procedure on Module1 that you were working on earlier. Click to the left of the **End Sub** statement and press the **Enter key** to insert a blank line, then click the **up arrow key** to move to the blank line.

- Click the **Paste button** or use the **Ctrl+V** keyboard shortcut. Close Project Explorer. The statements from the Dummy procedure should appear as shown in Figure 11.8f.

- Save the procedure.

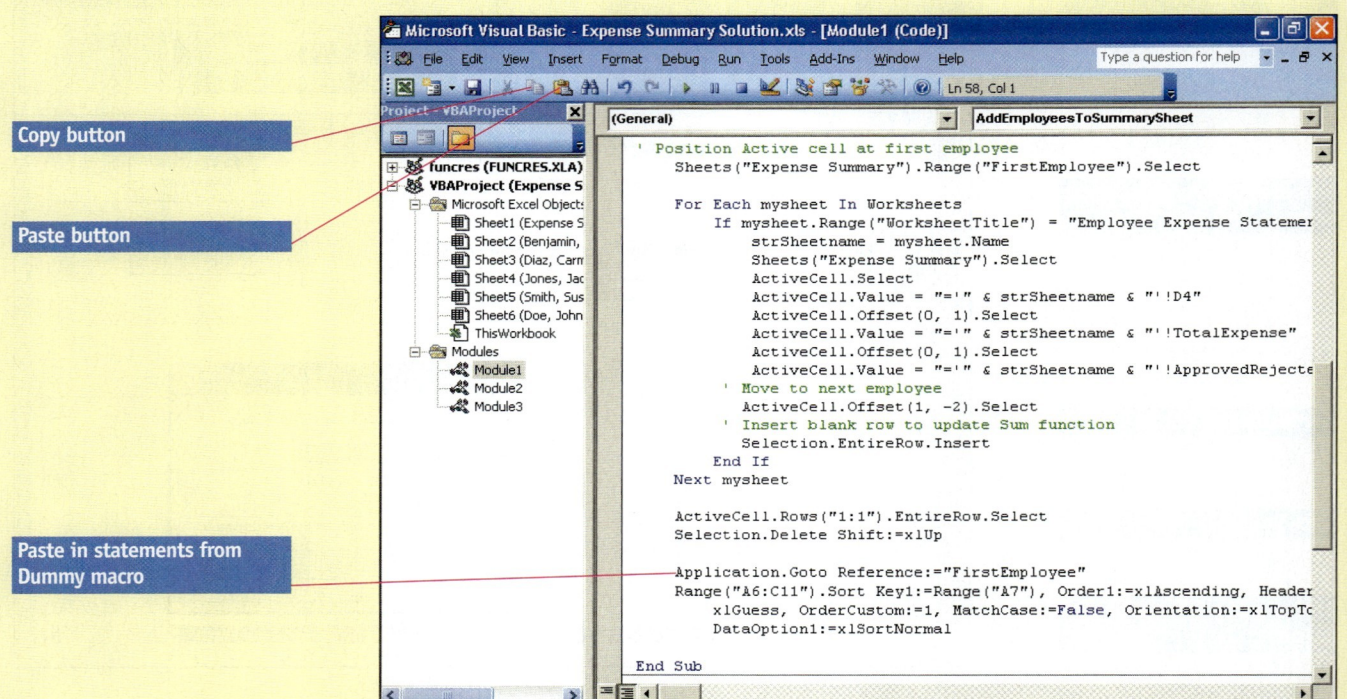

(f) Complete the Procedure (step 6)

FIGURE 11.8 Hands-on Exercise 3 (*continued*)

BE FLEXIBLE AND USE WHAT YOU KNOW

There is no single way to create a VBA procedure. You can use the Excel macro recorder to "jump-start" the process to obtain the syntax for lesser-known VBA statements. You can also create a procedure by entering code directly into the VBA editor. Once you have the procedure, you can return to the macro recorder to capture additional statements you may not have thought of initially. Be flexible and use the editing techniques that you learned in other applications.

Step 7: **Test the Completed Procedure**

- Click the **Excel button** to return to the Excel worksheet, where you can test the completed procedure. First, however, you need to delete and/or clear the rows containing the employee information. Thus:
    - Click and drag to select **rows 8 through 11** (do not select row 7) as shown in Figure 11.8g. Right click the selected rows to display the context-sensitive menu, then click the **Delete command** to remove these rows.
    - Click and drag to select the entries in **row 7**. Press the **Del key** to erase the contents of these cells—the cells, however, remain in the workbook.
    - Click in **cell A7**. Be sure that the Name box contains the reference FirstEmployee (since this reference is used in a VBA procedure).
    - Click in **cell B9**. Be sure that this cell contains the formula =Sum(B7:B8).

- Pull down the **Tools menu** and rerun the **AddEmployeesToSummarySheet** procedure. The employee data is added to the worksheet, but this time the employees should be in alphabetical order.

- Save the workbook.

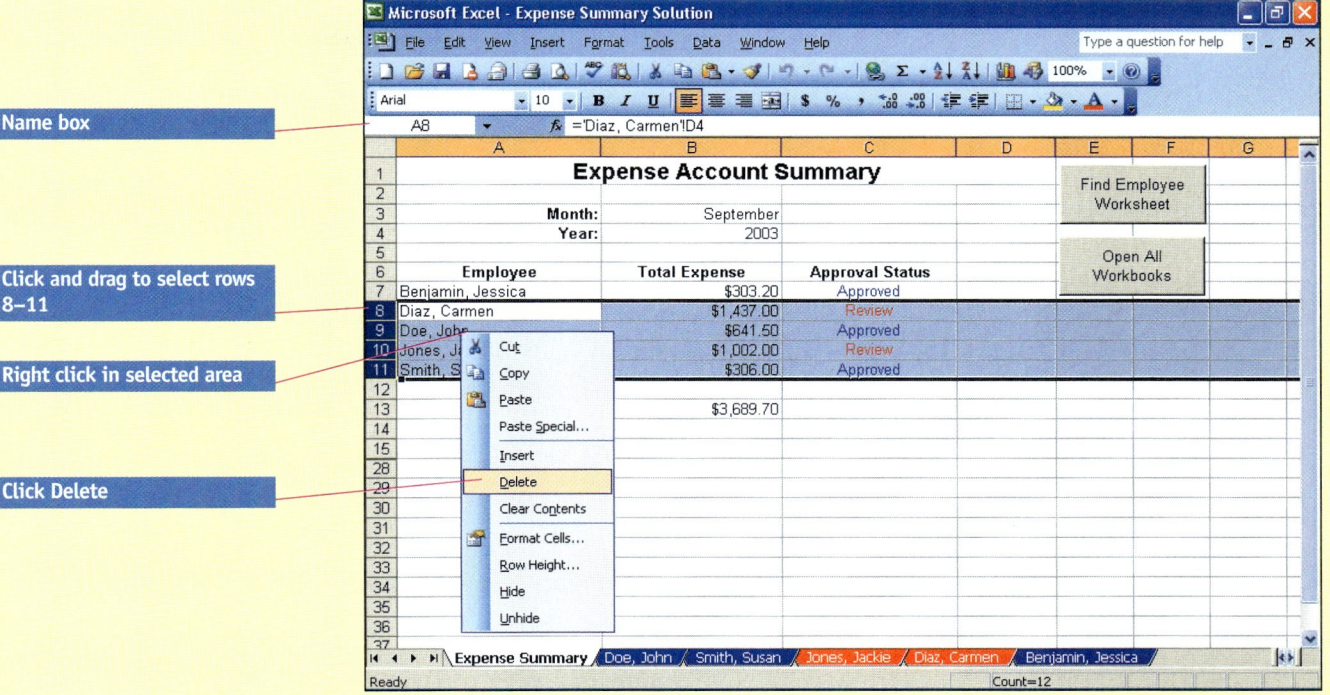

(g) Test the Completed Procedure (step 7)

FIGURE 11.8 Hands-on Exercise 3 (*continued*)

KEYBOARD SHORTCUTS

We have created a procedure to reset (clear) the Summary worksheet and have assigned the keyboard shortcut Ctrl+r to that procedure. You can test this procedure in conjunction with the procedure to add the employee data to the summary worksheet. Thus, press Ctrl+a to add the employee data, then press Ctrl+r to clear the summary data. You can execute the latter procedure several times in succession. The first procedure should be executed only once; that is, if you add the employee data twice in a row, you will wind up with duplicate rows for each employee.

Step 8: **Print the Cell Formulas**

- Press **Ctrl+~** to display the cell formulas as shown in Figure 11.8h. (Press **Ctrl+~** a second time to return to the displayed values.)

- Click and drag to select the row headers for **rows 15 through 28** (rows 16 through 27 are currently hidden). Right click the selected rows, then click the **Unhide command** to display these cells.

- Click in **cell B3**, the cell containing the month for which the expenses were submitted. Note how the VLOOKUP function uses the data in rows 16 to 27 to display the current month.

- Click and drag to adjust the column widths. Pull down the **File menu**, select the **Page Setup command** and switch to **Landscape printing**. Select the **scaling option** to force the output onto one page. Print the formulas for the summary worksheet.

- Close the workbook. Do not save the workbook when the cell formulas are displayed. Exit Excel if you do not want to continue with the next hands-on exercise at this time.

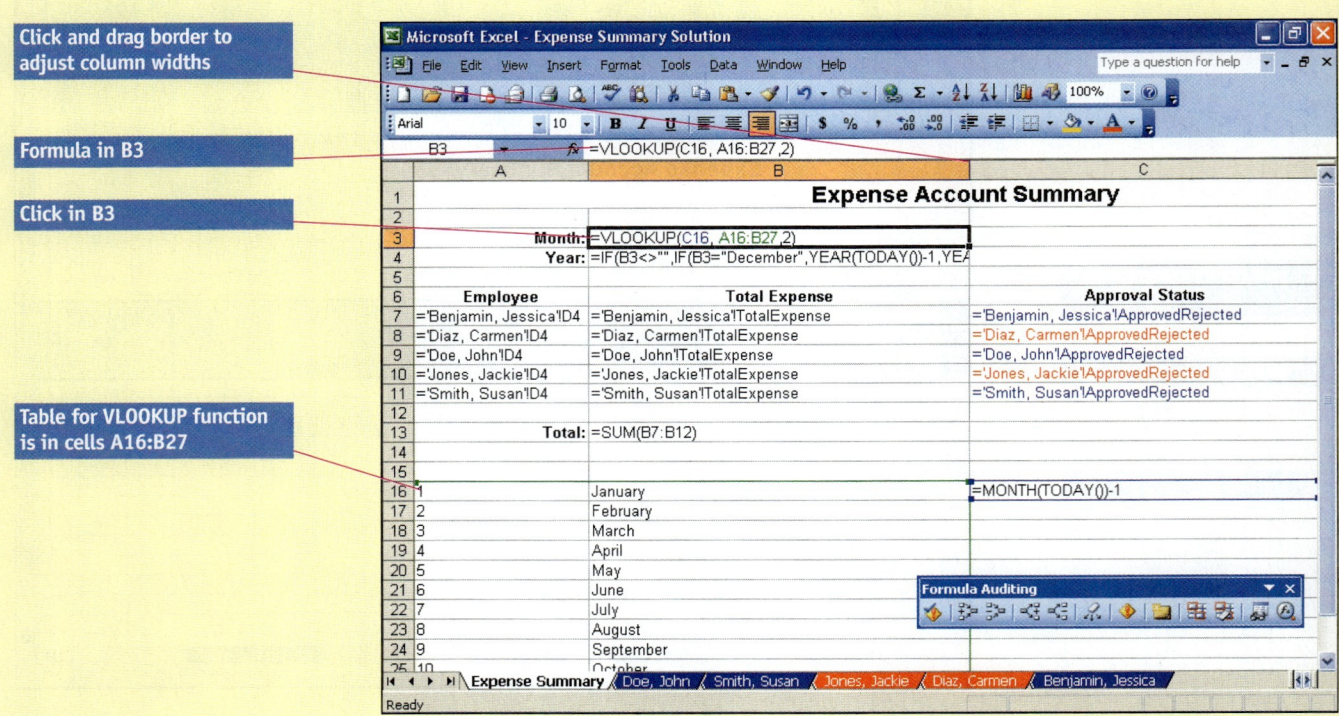

(h) Print the Cell Formulas (step 8)

FIGURE 11.8 Hands-on Exercise 3 (*continued*)

PRINT THE CELL FORMULAS—THE PAGE SETUP COMMAND

A worksheet should always be printed twice—once to show the displayed values and once to show the underlying cell formulas. Use the keyboard shortcut, Ctrl+~ to toggle between the two. Pull down the File menu and click the Page Setup command to change settings as necessary, when printing the cell formulas. You may want to change the orientation, column width, and/or margins.

A BETTER SUMMARY WORKBOOK

The summary workbook is finished, but you had to complete three hands-on exercises to accomplish that task. First, you had to open each individual workbook to copy the information for that employee to a new worksheet in the summary workbook. Next, you had to review the expenses on each worksheet within the summary workbook, and finally, you had to add the individual employee data to the summary worksheet. It would be much easier if you could execute a single procedure and with one click of the mouse, create the entire workbook. This is accomplished by creating a simple procedure that calls the three procedures (you ran individually) as shown below:

```
Public Sub CreateSummaryWorkbook()
    OpenAllWorkbooks
    ReviewEmployeeExpenses
    AddEmployeesToSummarySheet
End Sub
```

Three procedures are executed in succession

The CreateSummaryWorkbook procedure calls three procedures in succession, resulting in the completed summary workbook. The subordinate procedures may reside in the same module or in different modules provided that they have been defined as public procedures. The *scope* of a procedure refers to its availability or use by another procedure. **Public procedures** are available to any procedure in any module. **Private procedures** are available only to other procedures in the same module.

What if, however, the OpenAllWorkbooks procedure was unable to locate the folder containing the individual employee workbooks? It would be pointless to run the subsequent procedures because the summary worksheet would not contain any employee data. Accordingly, we modified the CreateSummaryWorkbook procedure to include an If statement to check that the number of worksheets in the summary workbook is greater than one (i.e., that the summary workbook contains the individual employee worksheets), and if so, it executes the next two procedures. (There is no need to include an error message since the OpenAllWorkbooks procedure contains its own error message if it is unsuccessful.) The modified procedure becomes:

```
Public Sub CreateSummaryWorkbook()
    OpenAllWorkbooks
    If Worksheets.Count > 1
        ReviewEmployeeExpenses
        AddEmployeesToSummarySheet
    End If
End Sub
```

These procedures are executed provided there is at least one employee worksheet

The workbook in Figure 11.9a displays the "empty" summary workbook prior to adding the employee information. The user clicks the Create Summary Workbook command button to execute the associated procedure, which runs the three individual procedures, one after the other.

Look closely at the input box in Figure 11.9a, which is displayed by a modified OpenAllWorkbooks procedure in Figure 11.9b. The user is prompted to enter the path of the folder that contains the employee workbooks. This is a more general approach than was used in the first hands-on exercise in which the name of the folder was coded directly into the macro. The user's response (the name of the folder) is stored in the variable strPathName, which becomes an argument in the subsequent Dir statements. The end result is a flexible procedure that lets the user specify where the individual expense statements are stored.

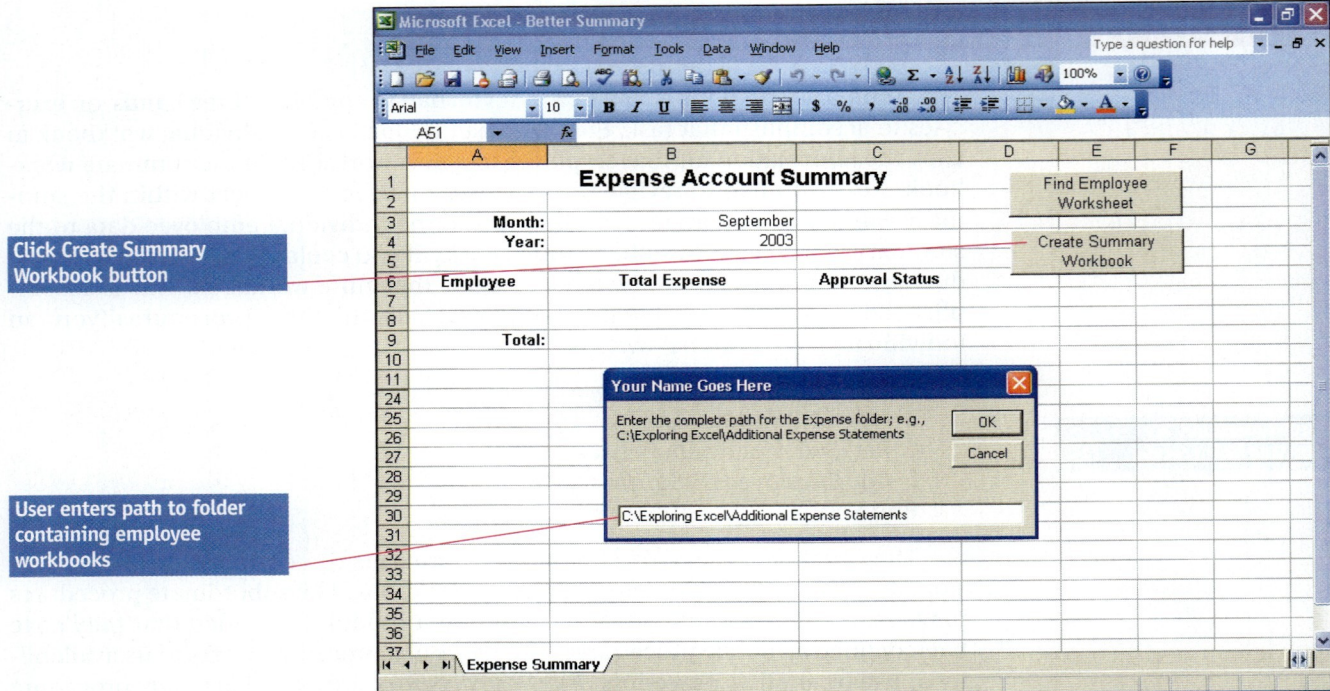

(a) Variable Input Folder

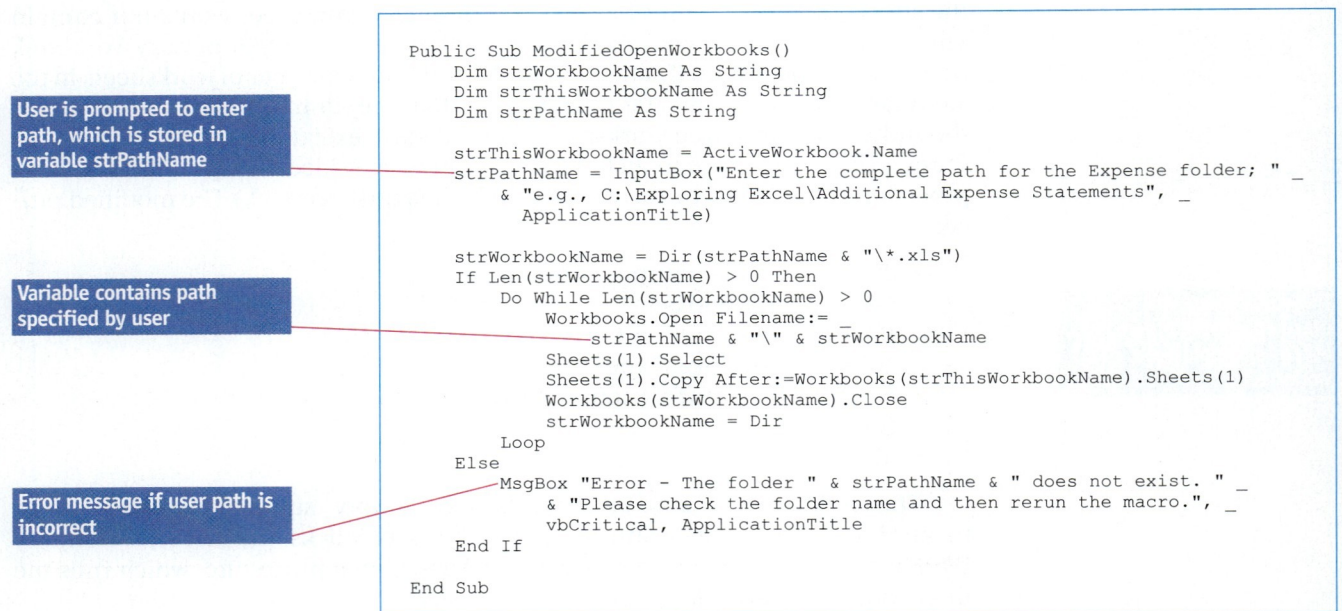

(b) The VBA Procedure

FIGURE 11.9   An Improved Summary Worksheet

hands-on exercise
4 A Better Summary Workbook

Objective Use a modified version of the Expense Summary workbook with additional flexibility and automation. Use Figure 11.10 as a guide in the exercise.

Step 1: **Open the Better Workbook**

- Open the **Better Summary workbook** in the Exploring Excel folder. Click the button to **Enable Macros** in response to the security warning.
- You will see the message box in Figure 11.10a. Click **No**. You will see a second message indicating that you can run the procedure at a later time. Click **OK**.
- Save the workbook as **Better Summary Solution** so that you can return to the original workbook if necessary.
- The Better Summary workbook contains a single (empty) summary worksheet and parallels the Expense Summary workbook you were using earlier. The command buttons correspond to the command buttons that you added in a previous hands-on exercise.
- The previous month (the month for which expenses are submitted) is determined automatically using Date functions. The year is also entered automatically.

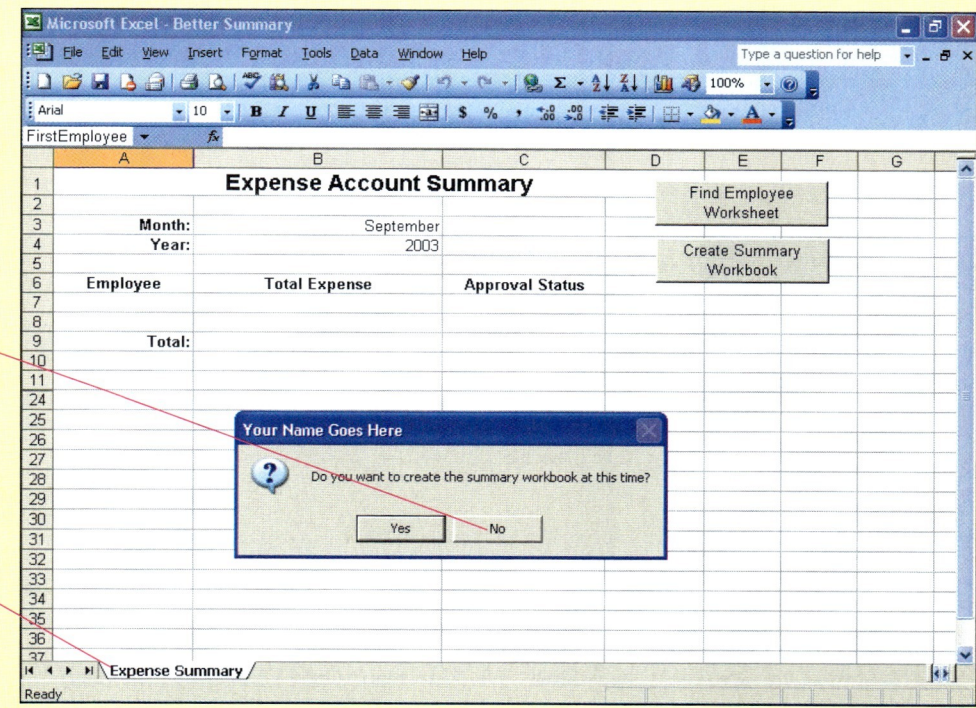

(a) Open the Better Workbook (step 1)

FIGURE 11.10 Hands-on Exercise 4

A BETTER SUMMARY WORKBOOK

The workbook in this exercise improves on its predecessor in two important ways. It is more general because it enables the user to enter the folder containing the employee workbooks, verifies that the folder exists, and displays an error message if it doesn't. It is also easier to use because the summary workbook is created with a single mouse click, as opposed to executing multiple procedures.

Step 2: Event Procedures

- Press **Alt+F11** to open the VBA Editor. Maximize this window. If necessary, pull down the **View menu** to display the Project Explorer window.
- Double click **ThisWorkbook** within the list of Excel objects to display the event procedures for this workbook as shown in Figure 11.10b. (The BeforeClose event procedure has not yet been created.) Close Project Explorer.
- Look at the Open Workbook event procedure. The MsgBox function asks the user whether to create the summary workbook, and if so, runs a general procedure called CreateSummaryWorkbook. (We examine this procedure in step 3.)
- If necessary, click the **down arrow** on the Object list box and select **Workbook**. Click the **down arrow** on the Procedure list box and select the **BeforeClose** event to create this event procedure.
- Enter the statements in the BeforeClose event procedure as shown in Figure 11.10b. Save the workbook. Click the **Close button** to close the window containing the event procedures.

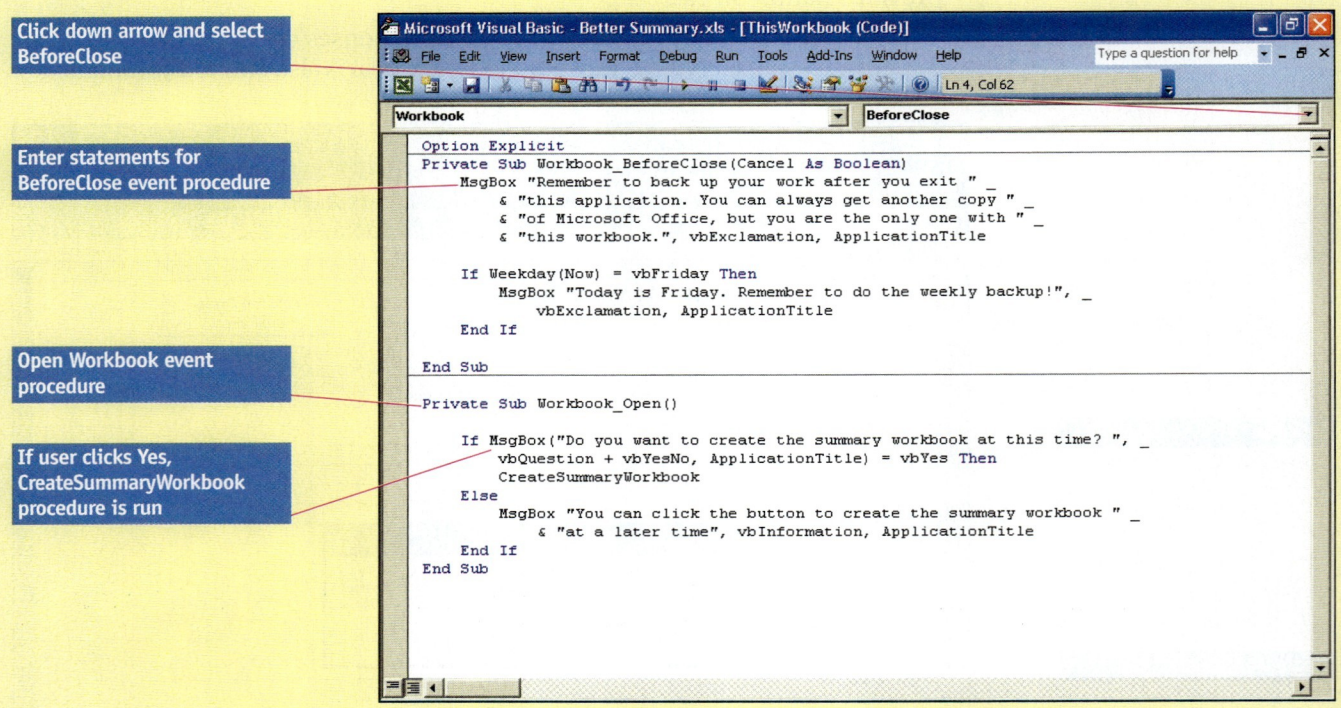

(b) Event Procedures (step 2)

FIGURE 11.10 Hands-on Exercise 4 (*continued*)

DAYS OF THE WEEK—INTRINSIC CONSTANTS

You can test for a specific day of the week using a combination of the Weekday and Now functions in conjunction with VBA intrinsic (predefined) constants. The Now function returns today's date. Thus, the expression Weekday(Now) returns today's day, which is then compared to a specific day of the week such as vbFriday. In other words, the condition in the If statement will be considered true if today is Friday. Use the Help function in VBA to search for other sets of intrinsic constants.

Step 3: **Test the CreateSummaryWorkbook Procedure**

- Open Project Explorer. Double click **Module1** to display the code for this module. Maximize the code window. Close Project Explorer.

- Click within the **CreateSummaryWorkbook procedure**, then click the **Procedure View button** at the bottom of the window to display one procedure at a time. (Use the **PgUp** and **PgDn keys** to move between procedures.)

- Right click an empty area of the taskbar, then click the **Show the Desktop command**. Click the Excel and VBA buttons to reopen these windows.

- Right click the taskbar a second time and click the **Tile Windows Vertically command** to display the windows as shown in Figure 11.10c. Close Project Explorer.

- Click the **Run button** on the VBA standard toolbar. Enter an **invalid folder** when prompted for the name of the folder that contains the expense statements. Click **OK**. You will see the error message in Figure 11.10c. Click **OK**.

- Rerun the **CreateSummaryWorkbook** procedure, but this time, enter the correct folder, **C:\Exploring Excel\Additional Expense Statements**. Click **No** when prompted to save each employee workbook.

- You will be asked for the maximum expense. Enter **$1,000**. Click **OK**. The summary workbook is created for you.

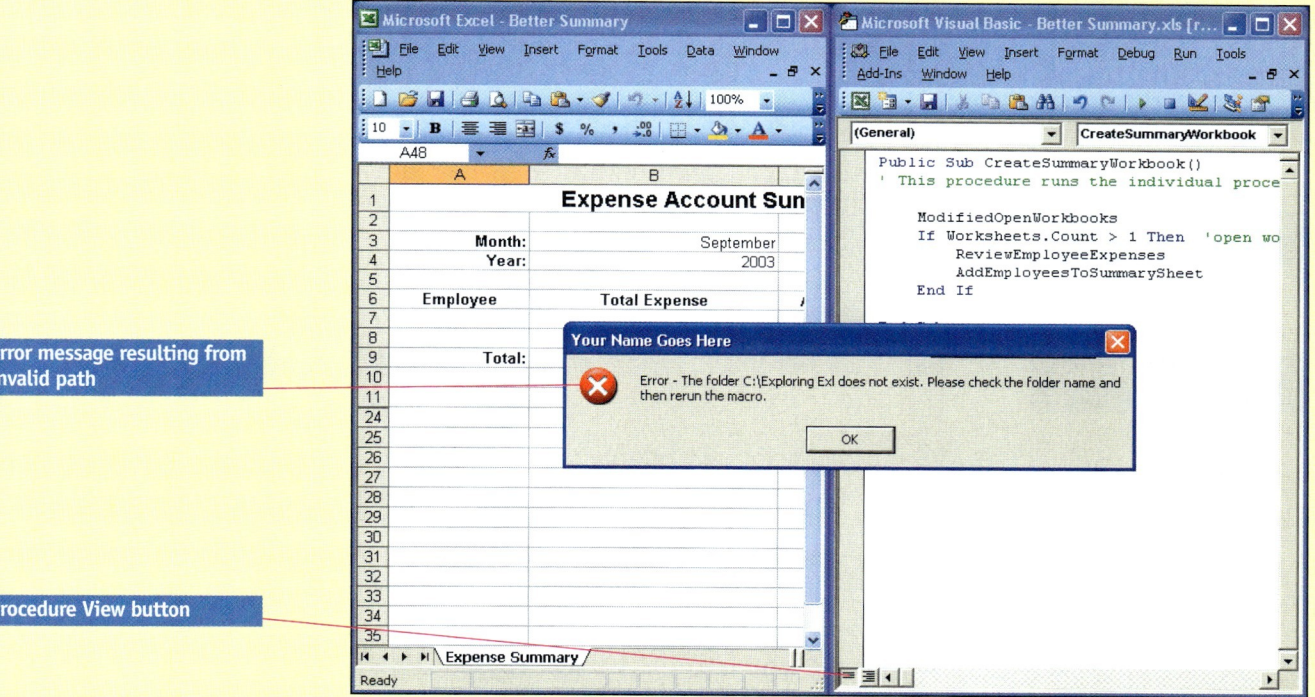

(c) Test the CreateSummaryWorkbook Procedure (step 3)

FIGURE 11.10 Hands-on Exercise 4 (*continued*)

OBJECTS, COLLECTIONS, AND PROPERTIES

A collection is a set of similar objects. For example, the worksheets collection is the set of worksheets in a workbook. Collections, like objects, have properties that can be tested. The statement If Worksheets.Count > 1 in our procedure is testing the Count property of the Worksheets collection to ensure that there are multiple worksheets within the workbook before executing the next two commands.

Step 4: **Find an Employee's Worksheet**

- Maximize the Excel window. You should see the summary worksheet with the employees listed in alphabetical order as shown in Figure 11.10d. (The input box is not yet visible.)

- The names in the worksheet are different from those in the earlier exercise because we used a different folder to obtain the employee workbooks.

- Save the workbook. Print the summary worksheet for your instructor as proof you completed the exercise.

- Click the button to **Find Employee Worksheet**. Disregard the message in the box and enter only the employee's last name; for example, enter **Beesaw**, then click **OK**. You will see an error message indicating that the specified employee does not exist.

- Click **OK** in response to the error message. Click the **Find Employee Worksheet button** a second time, and enter the name correctly as shown in Figure 11.10d. Click **OK**.

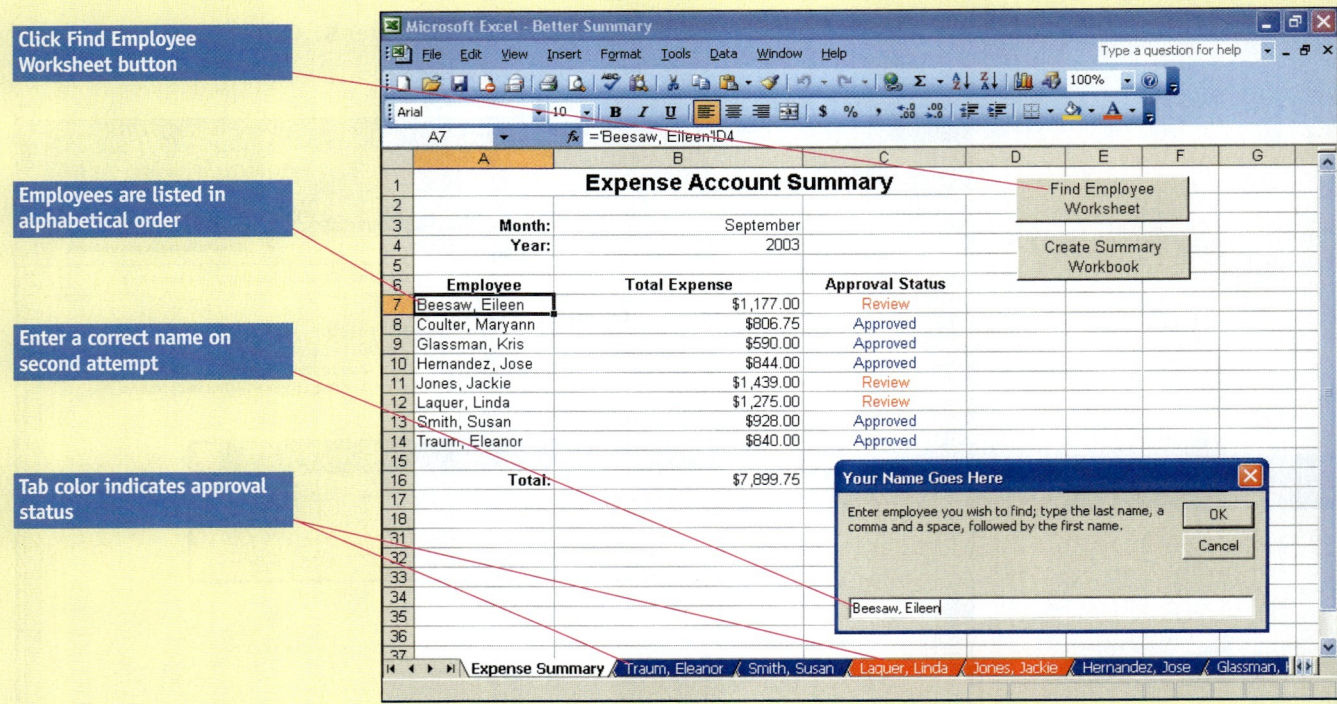

(d) Find an Employee's Worksheet (step 4)

FIGURE 11.10 Hands-on Exercise 4 (*continued*)

ENTER THE EMPLOYEE'S LAST NAME

The existing procedure requires you to enter the employee's complete name in a precise syntax. What if, however, you know only the last name? You can develop an alternate procedure to prompt the user for the employee's last name, then search through the workbook to see if any worksheet tab contains that name. The resulting procedure will be driven by a For. . .Next statement to process all of the worksheets within the workbook. It also requires elementary string processing to search for the last name within the combination of first and last name that appears on the worksheet tab. See exercise 3 at the end of the chapter.

Step 5: **Exit the Application**

- You should see the worksheet for Eileen Beesaw as shown in Figure 11.10e. Note the indication to review Eileen's expenses at the bottom of the worksheet is consistent with the red color of the worksheet tab.

- Take a minute to review all that was accomplished in this exercise.
  - ❏ You opened the Better Summary workbook and were asked if you wanted to create the summary workbook. If you answered yes, you were asked to enter the name of the folder that contained the employee workbooks.
  - ❏ Each employee workbook was opened automatically, the worksheets were copied to the summary workbook, the expenses on the individual worksheets were evaluated, and the associated information was copied to the summary worksheet.
  - ❏ You were able to display an employee worksheet that needed review.
  - ❏ The BeforeClose event procedure reminds the user to back up the workbook.

- Press **Alt+F11** to switch to the VBA editor. Print the event procedures as well as the procedures in Module1 for your instructor. Close the VBA window.

- Exit Excel. Congratulations on a job well done.

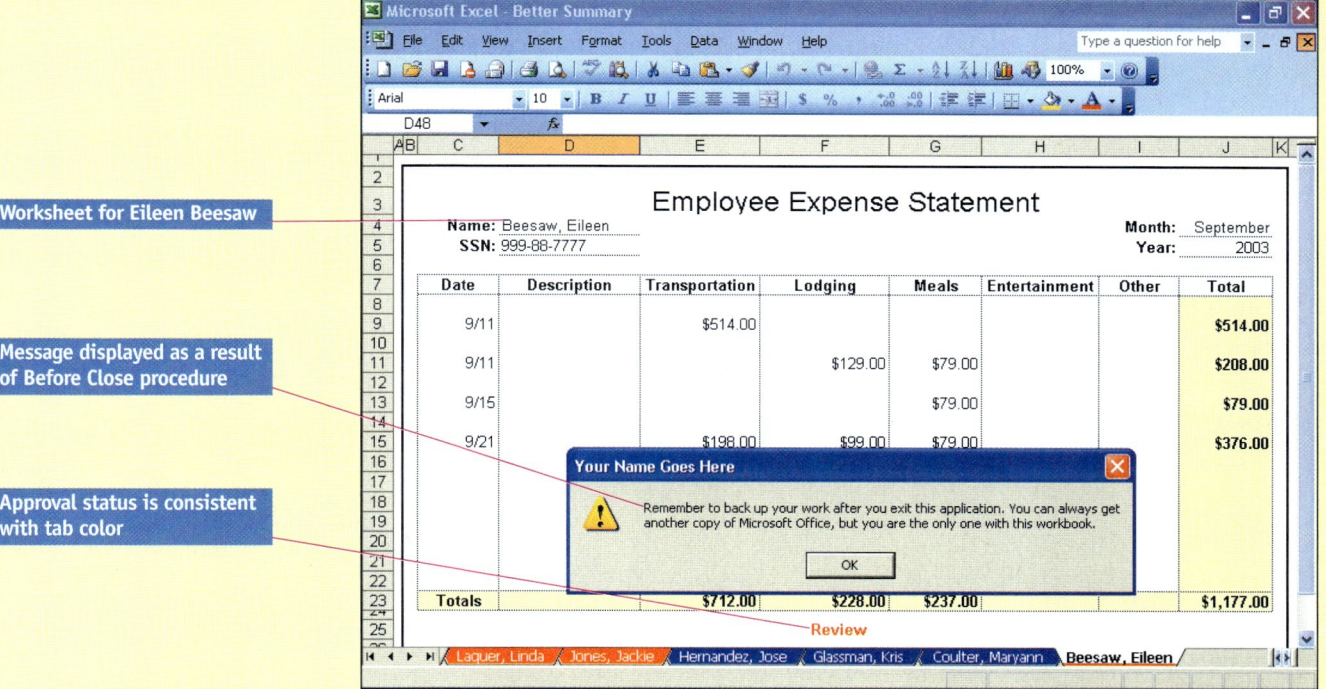

(e) Exit the Application (step 5)

FIGURE 11.10   Hands-on Exercise 4 (continued)

PRINT THE PROCEDURES FROM MICROSOFT WORD

The Print command within the VBA editor will print all of the procedures in the current module or in the entire project. The command is limited, however, in that it prints the procedures without formatting of any kind, and thus we find it helpful to print the final version of our procedures using Microsoft Word. The end result is a more polished document from which to study. See exercise 6 at the end of the chapter.

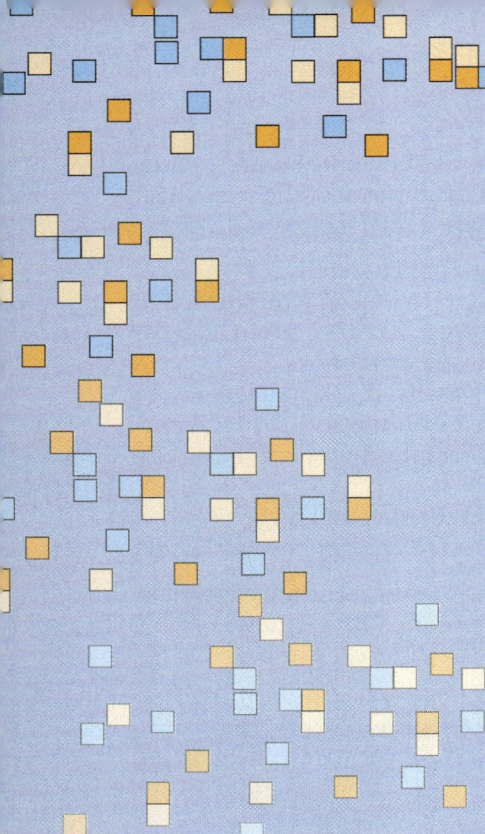

SUMMARY

The chapter developed an Excel application to process employee expenses that exist initially in individual workbooks. The overall objective is to automate the process of consolidating data from different sources. A "divide and conquer" approach is used to divide a complex task into smaller, more manageable tasks. The end result is an "empty" summary workbook that contains multiple VBA procedures to accomplish the objective. These procedures include several VBA statements that do not have equivalent Excel menu commands such as MsgBox, InputBox, If. . .Else, For. . .Next, Do Until, and Do While. (The VBA primer at the end of the text contains detailed information on these statements.)

The reader is presented with an expense statement workbook at the beginning of the chapter and asked to enter a set of hypothetical expenses to gain familiarity with the application. The completed workbook is then saved in an Expense Statement folder that contains additional workbooks from other employees, which in turn will be incorporated into the summary workbook.

The Visual Basic Dir function is used to process all of the workbooks in the Expense Statement folder. The first time this function is called, it returns the name of the first file in the folder, then each subsequent time the function is called, it returns the next file (if any) in the same folder. Eventually no additional files are found and the function returns a null value. The Dir function is incorporated into a loop that opens each individual workbook, then copies the information from that workbook onto a worksheet in the summary workbook.

Two additional procedures are developed to process the employee worksheets once they have been added to the summary workbook. The first procedure evaluates the expenses on each worksheet to indicate immediate approval or further review. Conditional formatting is used to display the approved or rejected expenses in blue or red, respectively. The color of the worksheet tab is also changed to reflect the approval status. A second procedure then copies information from the individual worksheets to a summary worksheet.

Both procedures use the For. . .Next statement to process all of the worksheets within the worksheets collection (i.e., with a specified workbook). The three procedures to create the summary workbook may be executed individually (as was done in the first three hands-on exercises). The procedures may also be executed collectively from a single procedure as illustrated in the fourth hands-on exercise.

The scope of a procedure or variable refers to its availability or use by another procedure. Public procedures are available to any procedure in any module. Private procedures are available only to other procedures in the same module.

A procedure was also developed to display a specific worksheet. The user is prompted for the employee's first and last name, after which the worksheet is displayed, provided the information was entered correctly. The procedure also introduces error processing in the event that the worksheet cannot be found. This is accomplished through the On Error statement that transfers control to a special error-handling section at the end of the procedure.

KEY TERMS

Conditional Formatting 595	Exit Sub statement 585	On Error statement 585
Debugging 583	For. . .Next statement 577	Private procedure 605
Dim statement 577	If. . .Then. . .Else statement 577	Public procedure 605
Dir function 578	InputBox function 577	Run-time error 585
Do Until statement 577	Intrinsic constant 608	Scope 605
Do While statement 577	Len function 578	Syntax error 585
Error Trapping 585	MsgBox statement 577	Worksheet object 585

MULTIPLE CHOICE

1. The statement strWorkbookName = Dir("C:\My Assignments*.xls") will:
   (a) Open the My Assignments workbook on drive C
   (b) Return the names of all workbooks in the My Assignments folder
   (c) Return the name of the first workbook in the My Assignments folder
   (d) Display the message "File Does Not Exist" if there are no workbooks in the My Assignments folder

2. What happens if the Dir function cannot find the specified file?
   (a) The function returns an empty (zero length) character string
   (b) The associated procedure displays an error message
   (c) The associated procedure ceases execution
   (d) All of the above

3. The statement strWorkbookName = Dir(strFolderName & "*.xls") will:
   (a) Open the workbook called strFolderName
   (b) Return the name of the first workbook in the folder called strFolderName
   (c) Return the name of the first workbook in the folder where the folder name is stored in the variable strFolderName
   (d) Display the message "File Does Not Exist" if there are no workbooks in the strFolderName folder

4. Which of the following is a true statement?
   (a) A run-time error occurs because the user violated a syntactical requirement of VBA
   (b) The statement that produced a run-time error is indicated in red within the VBA procedure
   (c) A run-time error is accompanied by a standard VBA error message unless the procedure includes an error-handling procedure
   (d) All of the above

5. How do you implement an error-handling procedure?
   (a) Include an On Error statement that transfers control elsewhere in the procedure if a run-time error occurs
   (b) Develop an error-handling section that is referenced by the On Error statement
   (c) Include an Exit Sub statement to bypass the error-handling code if the error does not occur
   (d) All of the above

6. Which of the following statements is true regarding VBA syntax?
   (a) An underscore at the end of a line indicates continuation
   (b) An ampersand indicates concatenation of a character string
   (c) An apostrophe at the beginning of a line indicates a comment
   (d) All of the above

7. Where does the macro recorder store the macros (procedures) it creates?
   (a) In a hidden worksheet called Module1
   (b) In a hidden worksheet, but not necessarily Module1
   (c) In Module1 of the current project
   (d) In a module of the current project, but not necessarily Module1

8. The statement ActiveCell.Offset(1, -2).Select moves to the cell that is:
   (a) One row down and two columns to the left of the current cell
   (b) One row down and two columns to the right of the current cell
   (c) One row up and two columns to the left of the current cell
   (d) One row up and two columns to the right of the current cell

9. The Excel formula ='Smith'!TotalExpense is
   (a) Syntactically incorrect because a worksheet tab must include the employee's first and last name
   (b) Syntactically incorrect because a cell formula must contain a relative or absolute cell reference
   (c) Referencing the range name TotalExpense on the current worksheet
   (d) Referencing the range name TotalExpense on the worksheet called Smith

10. What value will be returned by the function Len(strName), given that the variable strName was previously initialized to "Your Name"?
    (a) Seven
    (b) Nine
    (c) Eleven
    (d) Impossible to determine

... continued

multiple choice

11. Which of the following statements is true, given the VBA statement ActiveWorkbook.Sheets("Jessica Benjamin").Tab.ColorIndex = 3?
    (a) ActiveWorkbook is used as a qualifier to indicate the specific workbook that contains the indicated worksheets collection
    (b) "JessicaBenjamin" is a worksheet within the worksheets collection of the active workbook
    (c) ColorIndex is a property of the Tab object
    (d) All of the above

12. Which of the following is a true statement?
    (a) Every If statement must include an Else clause
    (b) Every If statement must include an End If delimiter
    (c) An If statement must be precisely indented if it is to compile correctly
    (d) All of the above

13. Given that the variable strName contains the value "George", what will be displayed by the statement, msgbox "Hello", & strName & ". How are you?"?
    (a) HelloGeorge. How are you?
    (b) HelloGeorge.How are you?
    (c) Hello George.How are you?
    (d) Hello George. How are you?

14. The statement If Worksheets.Count > 1 is:
    (a) Applying the Count method to a worksheet object
    (b) Testing the Count property of a worksheet object
    (c) Applying the Count method to the worksheets collection
    (d) Testing the Count property of the worksheets collection

15. Given the partial statement MsgBox("Do you want to continue?", vbYesNo), which of the following is true?
    (a) The user will see the indicated prompt and Yes and No command buttons
    (b) A question mark icon will appear in the resulting message box
    (c) "Your Name Goes Here" will appear on the title bar of the message box
    (d) All of the above

16. Which statement will prompt the user to enter his or her name and store the result in a variable called strUserName?
    (a) InputBox.strUserName
    (b) strUserName = MsgBox("Please enter your name.")
    (c) strUserName = InputBox("Please enter your name.")
    (d) InputBox("Please enter strUserName.")

17. Given the statement Sheets("Sheet1").Select
    (a) Sheets is the collection, Select is the method
    (b) Sheets is the object, Select is the method
    (c) Sheets is the collection, Select is the property
    (d) Sheets is the object, Select is the property

18. If the variable strName is set to "George", the expression "Good morning, strName" will return:
    (a) Good morning, George
    (b) Good morning, strName
    (c) Good morning George
    (d) Good morning strName

ANSWERS

1. c	7. d	13. a
2. a	8. a	14. d
3. c	9. d	15. a
4. c	10. b	16. c
5. d	11. d	17. a
6. d	12. b	18. b

PRACTICE WITH EXCEL AND VBA

1. **Finding the Month and Day:** The workbook in Figure 11.11 illustrates table lookup functions in conjunction with date functions. Proceed as follows:
   a. Create a new workbook. Enter the title of the worksheet into cell A1, then merge cells A1 through D1 to center the title at the top of the worksheet. Enter the indicated labels into cells A3, A4, and C4. Enter the tables for the day of the week and month of the year into cells A9 through B15 and C9 through D20, respectively. Widen columns as necessary.
   b. Enter any date into cell B3. Use the Weekday and Month functions in cells B8 and D8, respectively, to obtain the numerical value for the day of the week and month of the year, respectively. Cell B8, for example, will contain the function =Weekday(B3).
   c. Enter a VLOOKUP function into cell B4 to display the day of the week based on the numeric value in cell B8 and the associated table. Enter a second VLOOKUP function into cell D4 to display the month of the year based on the numeric value in cell D8 and the associated table.
   d. Modify the formulas in cells B4 and D4 to include an IF statement that displays a blank value if cell B3 is empty. Modify the formulas in cells B8 and D8 to include similar If statements. Delete the date in cell B3 to test the revised formulas.
   e. Create an Open Workbook event procedure to prompt the user for his or her birth date to enter the response into cell B3.
   f. Turn on the macro recorder to create a "dummy" macro to hide rows 8 through 20 in the worksheet. Modify the Open Workbook event procedure to prompt the user as shown in Figure 11.11. Use the VBA statements that were captured in part e to hide the indicated rows.
   g. Print the cell formulas for the completed worksheet. Print the Open Workbook event procedure. Capture the screen in Figure 11.11 and use that as a cover sheet when you submit the completed assignment.

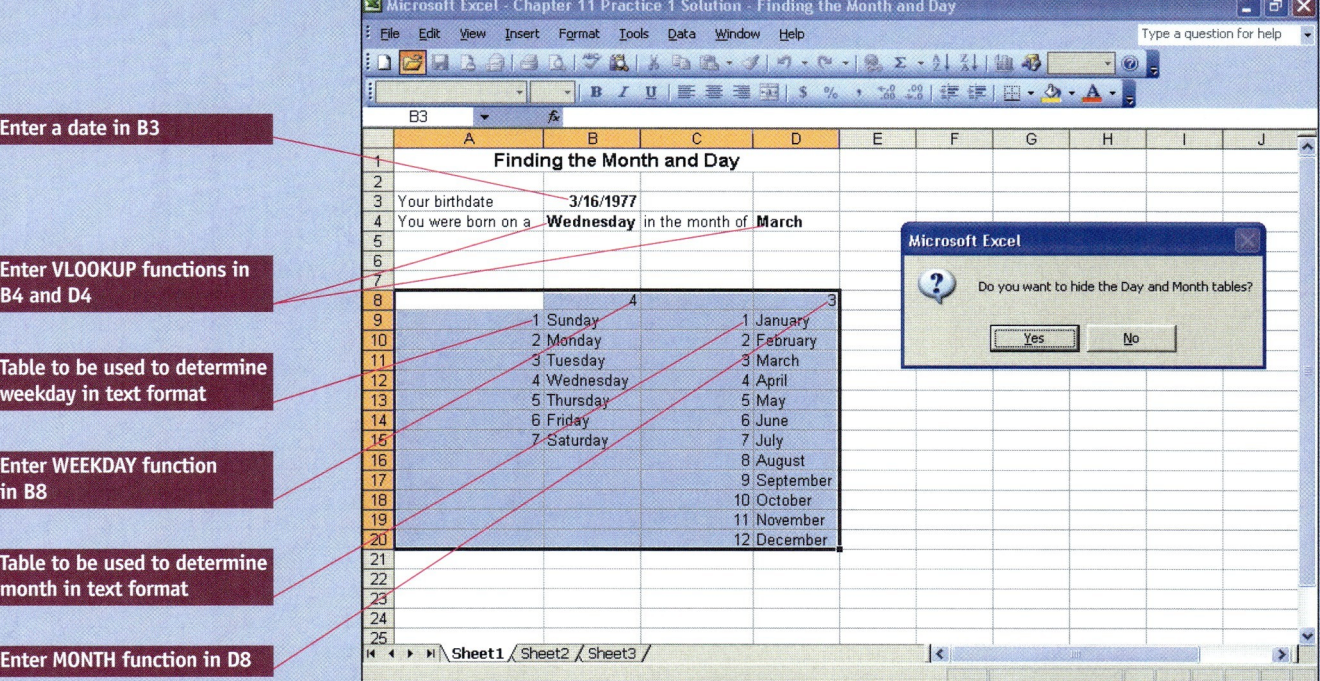

FIGURE 11.11 Finding the Month and Day (exercise 1)

practice exercises

2. **A Puzzle for You:** The workbook in Figure 11.12 contains a traditional puzzle that you may have seen before. Even so, you may not be able to solve every entry. We don't want you to be unduly frustrated, and so we have included the answers in the workbook, but you have to find the hidden password to see the solution. The intent of the exercise, however, is not to solve the puzzle per se, but to use your knowledge of Excel and VBA to display the password. Proceed as follows:

   a. Open the *Chapter 11 Practice 2* workbook in the Exploring Excel folder. Click the button to Enable Macros to see the worksheet in Figure 11.12. Try to solve as many of the entries as possible, without resorting to the answers. There are 26 questions. A good score is 20 or better.

   b. You can begin your quest for the solution without knowing the password. Use the appropriate Excel command to display the gridlines and the row and column headings.

   c. Look for a hidden worksheet. Does this worksheet contain any hints to help you find the password?

   d. Locate the VBA procedure that will display the cell formulas, provided you make the necessary change. Once you run the modified procedure, the password will become obvious to you.

   e. Use the password to unhide the columns containing the solution to complete the workbook.

   f. Print the workbook two ways, once to show the displayed values and once to show the cell formulas. (You will not be able to print the cell formulas until you complete part d correctly.) Print all of the VBA procedures within the workbook.

   g. Add a cover sheet, then submit the completed assignment to your instructor. Include a brief discussion of how you found the hidden password. Can you create an Excel workbook with another puzzle that contains the solution and a hidden password?

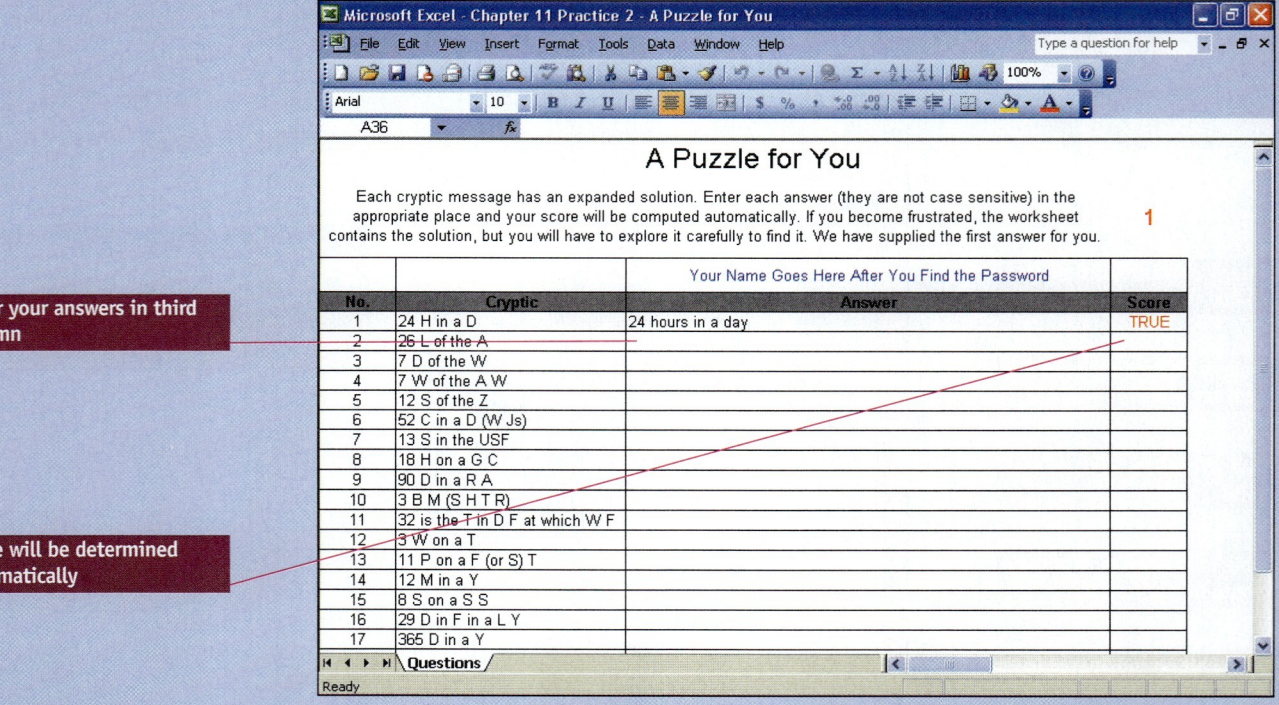

FIGURE 11.12   A Puzzle for You (exercise 2)

practice exercises

3. **Search for an Employee's Last Name:** Figure 11.13 displays a procedure to search for an employee's last name, and then to display the associated worksheet. It achieves the same result as the procedure in the second hands-on exercise, but it allows the user to enter only the last name, as opposed to the combination of last name and first name. It also introduces additional programming techniques. Open the *Chapter 11 Practice 3* workbook and click "Yes" when asked whether to create the summary workbook. (Use the expense statements in the Additional Expense Statements folder and specify $1,000 as the amount required for review.) You now have the same workbook as at the end of the fourth hands-on exercise. You will improve this workbook by adding additional procedures, beginning with the procedure in Figure 11.13, which can be added to any existing module.

   a. Use the VBA Help function to determine the meaning of the Visual Basic Like function. What is the statement Like strEmployeeName & "*" searching for?

   b. The variable strFoundWorksheet is an example of a programming switch. It is set to "No" prior to looking at the first worksheet, then set to "Yes" if the last name entered by the user matches the last name in any worksheet tab within the workbook. What action will the procedure take if the designated name cannot be found?

   c. What happens if the procedure locates a worksheet that contains the designated last name? Is it possible to locate more than one worksheet for the same last name?

   d. What is the significance of the intrinsic constant vbQuestion? How is it used in this procedure?

   e. Test the completed procedure to be sure that it works correctly. Print the completed procedure for your instructor.

   f. Modify the error-handling section in the FindEmployeeWorksheet procedure to execute this procedure if the combination of the employee's first and last name is not found. Is this a meaningful enhancement to the earlier procedure?

   g. Submit your answers to the various questions in this exercise to your instructor. Be sure to include the printed procedure with your submission. Add a cover sheet to complete the assignment.

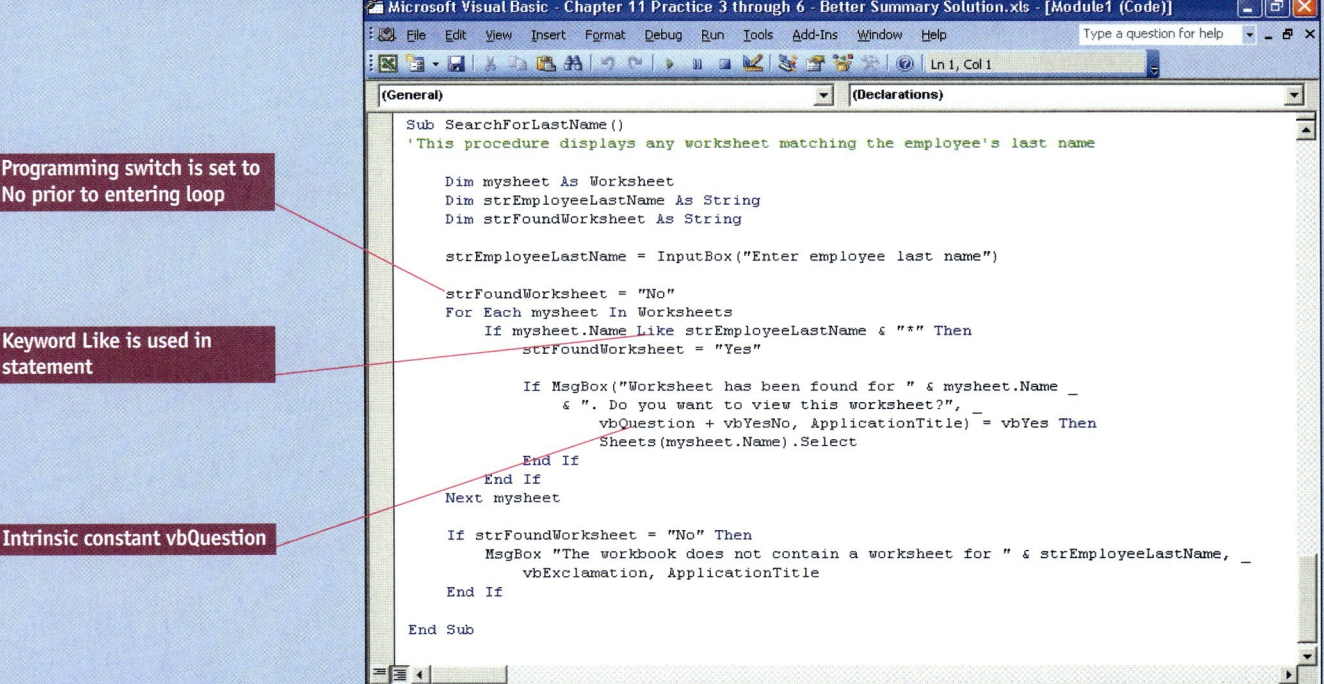

FIGURE 11.13 Search for an Employee's Last Name (exercise 3)

practice exercises

4. **Print Selected Worksheets:** The completed summary workbook has evaluated the expenses for each employee and colored the corresponding worksheet tabs to blue or red, respectively, indicating expenses that are approved or expenses subject to further review. Either (or both) sets of worksheets may be printed at different times by manually selecting the worksheets. It's better to do it automatically.

   The SelectSheetsForPrinting procedure in Figure 11.14 prompts the user to determine which set of worksheets to print, then it calls one of three other procedures to comply with the request. Your assignment is to complete the four required procedures using Figure 11.14 as a guide.

   a. Use the macro recorder to capture the Excel key strokes to print the selected worksheet. Once you have the Print statement, use it as the basis for three separate procedures—to print the approved expense worksheets, to print the worksheets for further review, and to print every employee worksheet. Look closely at Figure 11.14 to see the beginning of the PrintApprovedExpenses procedure.

   b. Create the SelectSheetsForPrinting procedure as shown in Figure 11.14. The Msgbox statement within this procedure inserts line feeds within the message box to force a break from one line to the next. (You can see this message box by looking at Figure 11.15 in the next exercise.) The procedure also uses a Case statement to test the user's response to ensure that it is valid. Note, too, the use of the Visual Basic UCase function to make the user's response case insensitive.

   c. Return to Excel and execute the SelectSheetsForPrinting procedure. Capture the screen that displays the input box asking for the user's response and use that image as the cover sheet for this assignment.

   d. Print all four procedures for your instructor as proof you completed this exercise. Include a short note describing how to call one procedure from another. Add a cover sheet with your name and date.

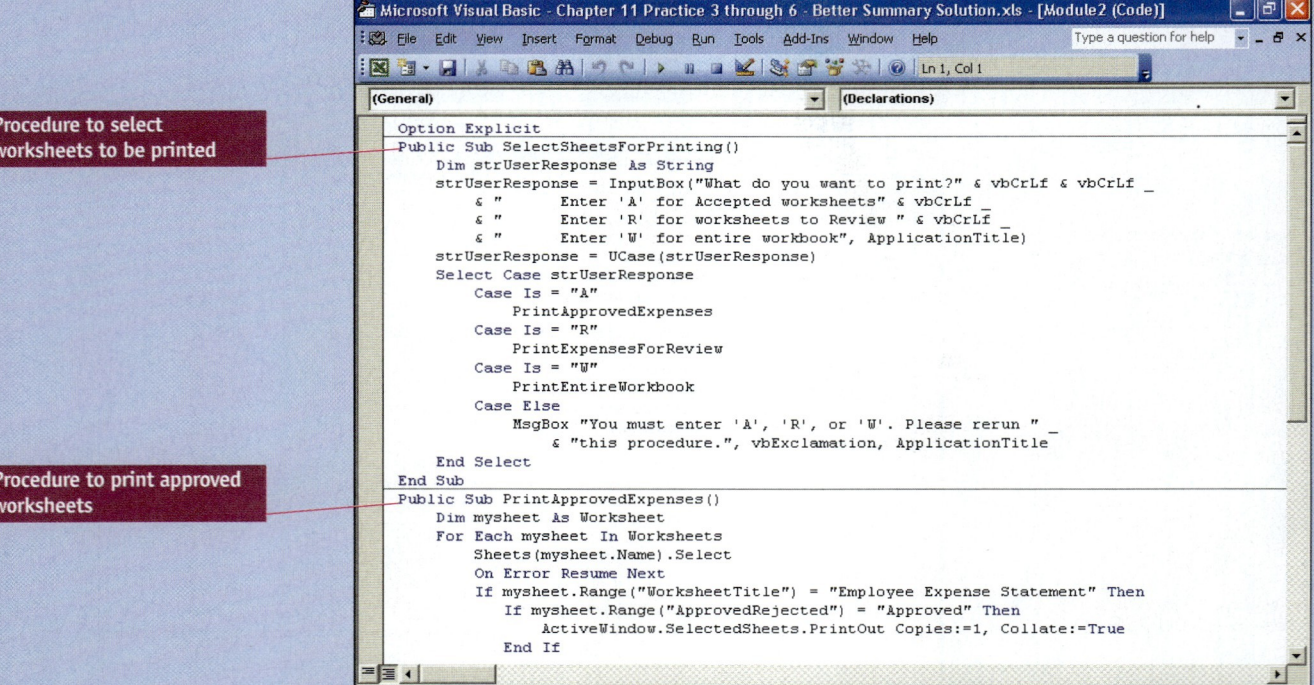

FIGURE 11.14 Print Selected Worksheets (exercise 4)

practice exercises

5. **Add Command Buttons:** The workbook in Figure 11.15 contains a total of five command buttons that collectively execute all of the procedures associated with the Better Summary workbook that has been developed throughout the chapter.

   a. Complete the fourth hands-on exercise in the chapter, which creates the basic version of the Better Summary Solution workbook. There are two command buttons on the summary worksheet at this point.

   b. Complete practice exercise 3 to develop the procedure to search for an employee using only the last name. Add the command button corresponding to this procedure to the worksheet.

   c. Add the fourth command button to change the approval criterion, which runs the ReviewEmployeeExpenses procedure from the third hands-on exercise. Click the button and change the approval criterion to $500 (rather than $1,000 used earlier).

   d. Complete the previous problem to print selected worksheets, then add the fifth command button to run this procedure. Enter "A" to print just the approved worksheet(s).

   e. You can improve the appearance of the worksheet by creating command buttons of uniform size. Choose any command button and size it appropriately. Now right click that button, click the Format Control command, and click the Size tab to see the size of your button. Click the Properties tab and check the box to Print Object. Change the properties of the other command buttons in similar fashion.

   f. Print the summary worksheet (with the command buttons) for your instructor as proof you did this exercise. Use landscape printing if necessary to print the worksheet on a single page.

   g. Create a custom menu that contains five commands that are equivalent to the command buttons in the worksheet. Which technique do you prefer—command buttons on the worksheet or a custom menu? Summarize your thoughts in a short note to your instructor.

   h. Capture the screen in Figure 11.15 (or a different screen that displays the custom menu) to use as a cover sheet for your completed assignment.

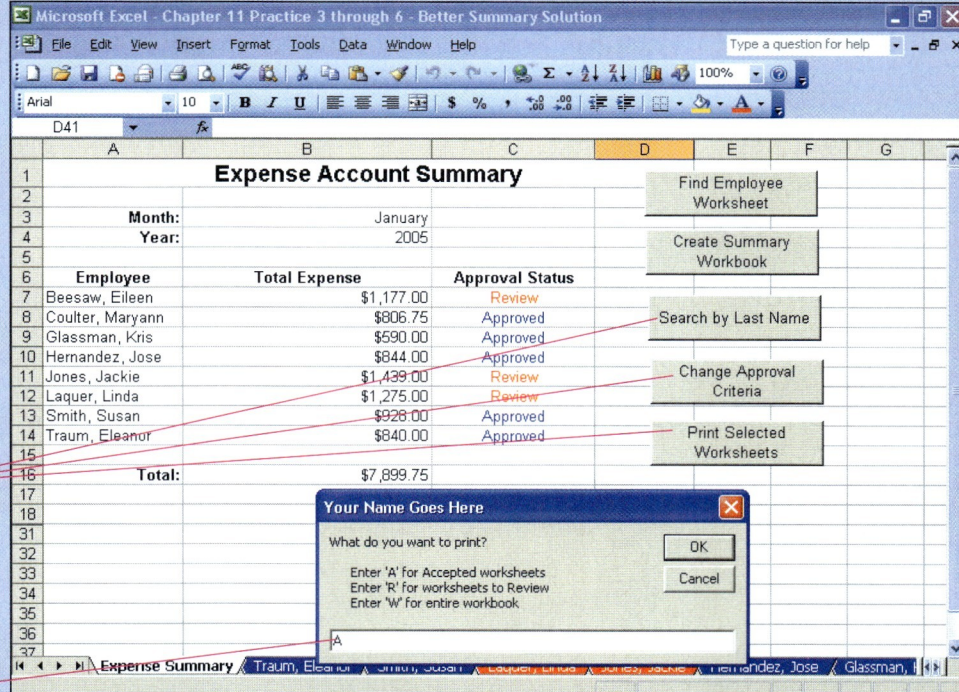

FIGURE 11.15 Add Command Buttons (exercise 5)

practice exercises

6. **Print the VBA Procedures in Microsoft Word:** You can print VBA procedures from within the VBA editor, but the procedures are printed without any formatting. You get a better result by printing from within Microsoft Word as shown in Figure 11.16. Complete the previous exercise to create all of the VBA procedures, and then print the procedures as described below.

   a. Open the VBA editor, select ThisWorkbook within Project Explorer, and click and drag to select all of the statements in both event procedures. Click the Copy button (or use the Ctrl+C keyboard shortcut) to copy these procedures to the Windows clipboard.

   b. Start Microsoft Word and open a new document. Click the Paste button (or use the Ctrl+V keyboard shortcut) to paste the contents of the clipboard (the VBA procedures) into the Word document.

   c. Use the Windows taskbar to return to the VBA editor to copy the contents of the other modules to the Word document in similar fashion. Be sure to copy all of the procedures in all of the modules.

   d. Format the procedures in the Word document as you see fit. We suggest you use a monospaced font such as Courier New so that the indentation and alignment are easier to see. We also suggest that you boldface the Sub and End Sub statements of each procedure, and that you insert a horizontal border to separate the procedures from one another.

   e. Experiment with styles and a table of contents. Format each procedure in a heading style, then use the Reference command in the Insert menu to create the table of contents automatically.

   f. Add a title page, then submit the completed assignment to your instructor. Do you think the additional formatting is worth the trouble? What happens if a procedure changes in the Excel workbook?

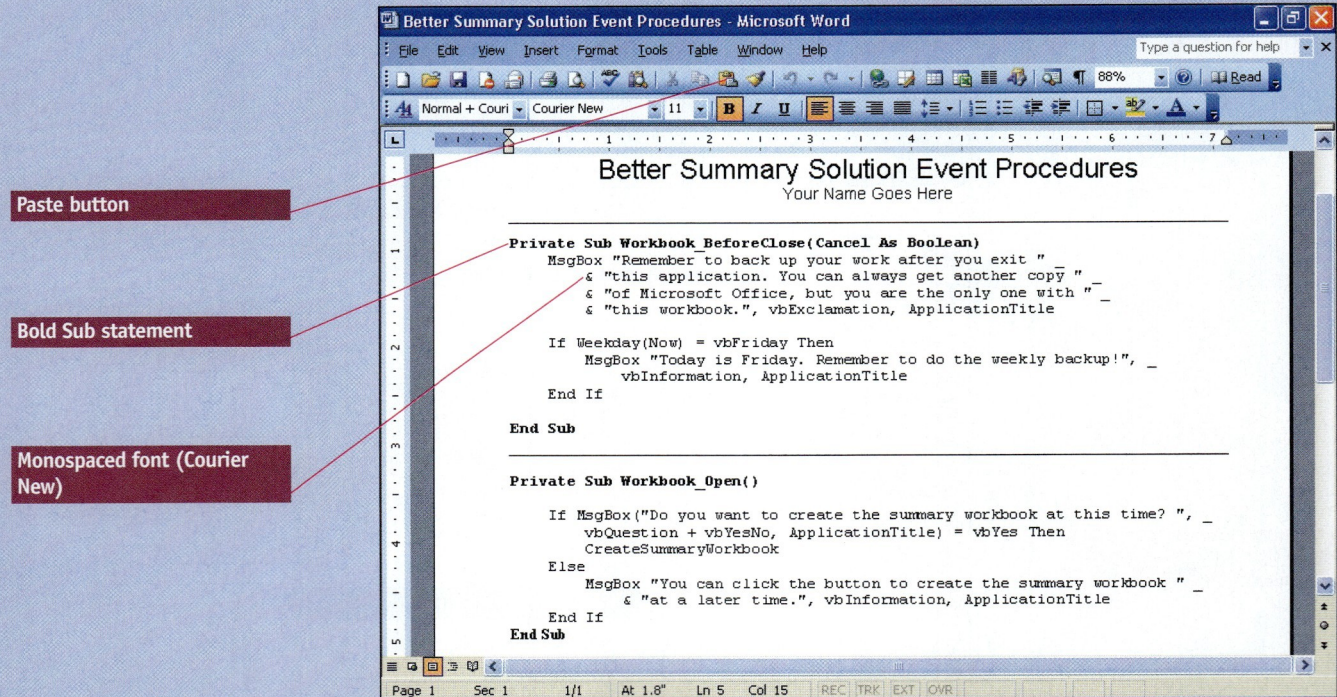

FIGURE 11.16 Print the VBA Procedures in Microsoft Word (exercise 6)

practice exercises

7. **Random Numbers as Test Data:** Open the partially completed version of the workbook in Figure 11.17, which can be found in the *Chapter 11 Practice 7* workbook in the Exploring Excel folder. You will not be able to duplicate the figure exactly, however, because the random number function is used to generate test data for the workbook. Proceed as follows:

   a. Click in cell C4 and note that the formula contains the expression 70+20*Rand( ). The random number function returns a value between 0 and 1, so that the expression returns a value between 70 and 90. (The Round function is used in the actual cell formula to eliminate the decimal portion.)

   b. Pull down the Tools menu, click the Options command, click the Calculation tab, then click the Calculate Now button. The test grade changes. Press the F9 (shortcut) key. The value changes again. Click in Cell G1, enter your name, and press the Enter key. The random numbers change again because the spreadsheet is automatically recalculated each time you change the contents of a cell.

   c. Copy the formulas in cells C4 to G4 to rows 5 through 21 to generate the grades for the remaining students. Press the F9 key once or twice to see how the grades change.

   d. The worksheet you just created will be used in a subsequent problem, where it will be combined with other grade books. Pull down the File menu and click the Save As command to display the Save As dialog box in Figure 11.17. Change the folder to VBA Grade Books (within the Exploring Excel folder). This folder was created automatically when you installed the practice files. Change the file name to Section R. Click the Save button.

   e. The last step is to convert the formulas (containing the random numbers) in the workbook to fixed values so that they remain constant. Click and drag to select cells C4 through G21. Click the Copy button. Pull down the Edit menu, click the Paste Special command to display the Paste Special dialog box, click the option button for Values, then click OK.

   f. Press the F9 key to recalculate the spreadsheet. The displayed values do not change because the formulas have been converted to a constant value.

   g. Save the spreadsheet a final time.

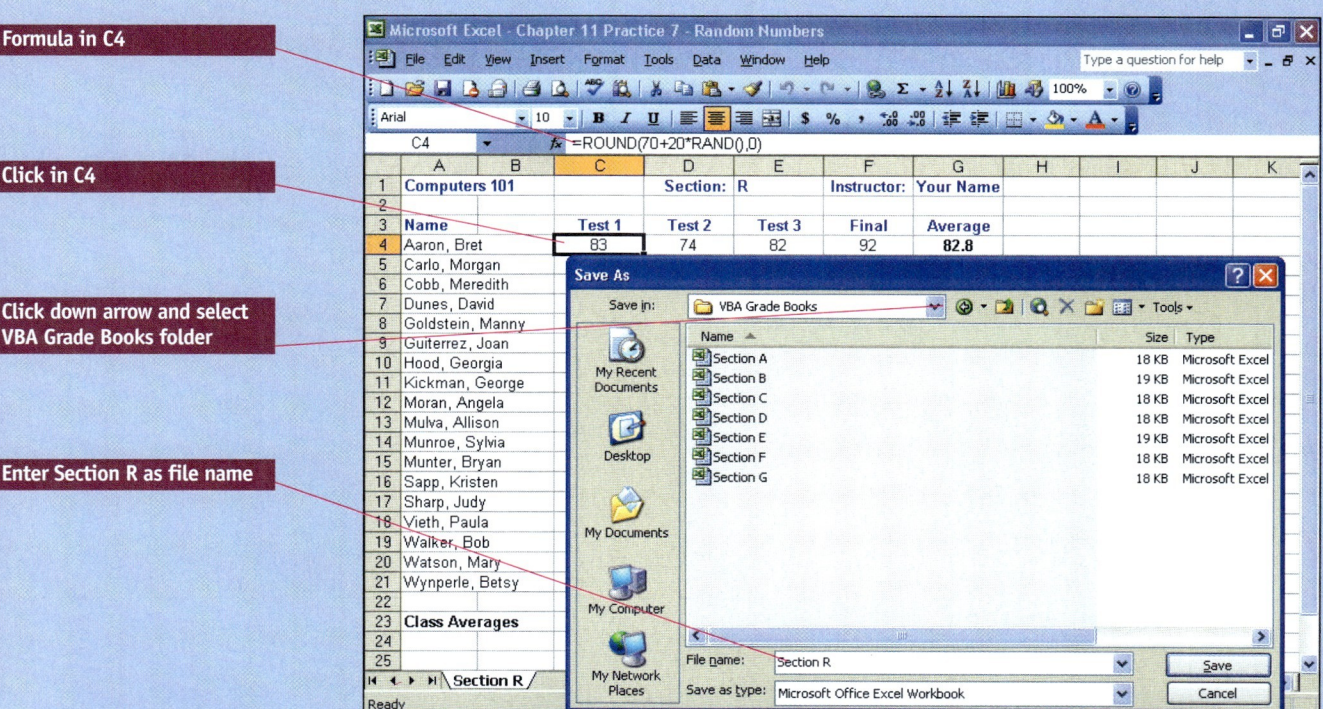

FIGURE 11.17 Random Numbers as Test Data (exercise 7)

MICROSOFT OFFICE EXCEL 2003 REVISED

practice exercises

8. **The Composite Grade Book:** The workbook in Figure 11.18 is similar in concept to the expense summary workbook that was developed in the chapter. We started with an empty summary workbook and developed the necessary procedures to create the composite grade book by inserting data from individual workbooks. Proceed as follows:

   a. Open the partially completed workbook in *Chapter 11 Practice 8* to display a partially completed workbook. Click Yes when asked whether to create the Summary Grade Book.

   b. You will be prompted for the path to the individual grade books. Type C:\Exploring Excel\VBA Grade Books (assuming that you used the default location when you installed the practice files).

   c. Sit back and relax. The individual grade books will be brought into the summary workbook, after which the summary worksheet will be created. You will not be prompted to save the changes to the individual workbooks because there are no calculations associated with opening and closing these workbooks.

   d. The appearance of Section R in the workbook and on the summary worksheet depends on whether you did the previous exercise, and further, whether you saved this workbook in the VBA Grade Books folder as instructed.

   e. Print the All Sections worksheet two ways—once to show the displayed values, and once to show the cell contents.

   f. Open the VBA editor and print the event procedures that exist within this workbook. What differences (if any) are there in the procedures in this workbook compared to those in the Better Summary that you developed earlier? What differences (if any) are there in the procedures in Module1 compared to the comparable procedures in the Better Summary workbook?

   g. Add a cover sheet and submit the assignment to your instructor.

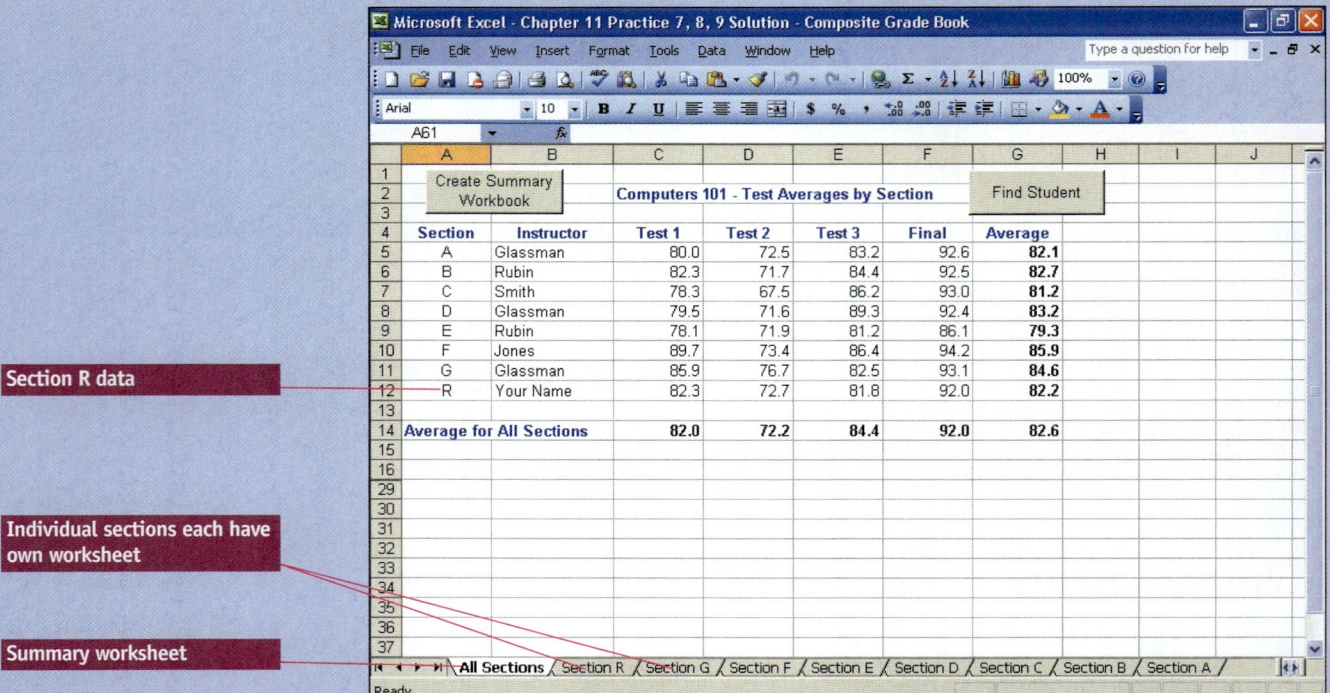

FIGURE 11.18 The Composite Grade Book (exercise 8)

practice exercises

9. **Locate a Student:** This exercise continues the development of the Composite Grade Book by developing a procedure to locate a specific student. It is similar to the Expense Summary workbook from the chapter, except that you are searching for student names within a worksheet, as opposed to an employee name on a worksheet tab.

   a. Open the *Chapter 11 Practice 8* workbook from the previous exercise. What happens if you click the Find Student command button? Is this a reasonable action for the original workbook?

   b. You will replace the original procedure with the VBA code in Figure 11.19, but first we want you to see how the procedure was created. Start the macro recorder. Pull down the Edit menu, click the Find command, then search for a student, "Smith, Doe". Click the Stop Recording button. Which part of the procedure in Figure 11.19 was adopted from the macro you just recorded?

   c. Replace the existing FindStudent procedure in the *Chapter 11 Practice 8* workbook with the VBA code in Figure 11.19. Test the procedure by looking for two students, one who is somewhere in the workbook, and one who is not in the workbook at all. Does the procedure work correctly in both instances?

   d. Place an apostrophe in front of the On Error statement to convert the statement to a comment. Rerun the procedure, specifying the name of a student who is not in the workbook. Does the procedure run successfully? What is the purpose of the On Error statement?

   e. Summarize your answers in a short note to your instructor. Add a cover sheet to complete the assignment.

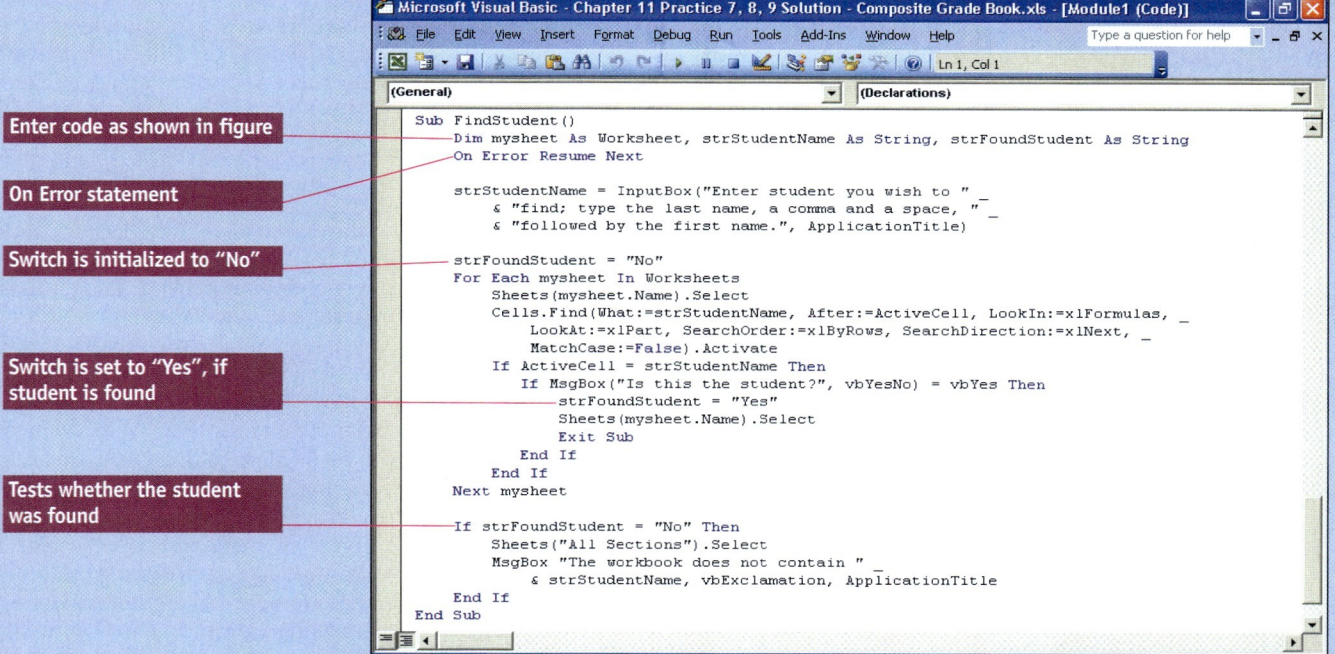

FIGURE 11.19 Locate a Student (exercise 9)

MINI CASES

Your Own Help Manual

Detailed help is available on any VBA topic if only you will take the trouble to look. Start the VBA editor, pull down the Help menu, and select Visual Basic Help (or press the F1 key) to display the Visual Basic Help window. You will see the same type of Help screen that is common to all Office applications. Click the Contents tab, select at least five topics of interest to you, and print the associated Help pages. Add a cover sheet and submit the information to your instructor.

Cleaning Up VBA Code

The macro recorder jump-starts the process of creating a VBA procedure by capturing Excel commands and converting them to their VBA equivalents. The result, however, can be cluttered (inefficient) code that can be simplified by going to the VBA editor and deleting the superfluous entries. For example, turn on the macro recorder, pull down the File menu, click the Page Setup command, and change to Landscape orientation. Turn off the recorder, then look at the resulting procedure.

You may be somewhat surprised at the number of statements because the recorder set every property associated with printing a worksheet. If your intention is just to change the orientation property, you can replace the entire procedure with the single statement, ActiveSheet.PageSetup.Orientation = xlLandscape. Not only is this easier to read, but it runs much more efficiently. You can find similar examples if you use the recorder to change the font or style. A different example is obtained by selecting a cell on a different worksheet.

Turn on the macro recorder, click the tab for Sheet2, select cell A5, then turn off the recorder. The macro recorder produces two statements, Sheets("Sheet2").Select and Range("A5").Select, but you can combine the statements using qualification to Sheets("Sheet2").Range("A5").Select. Study the procedures you created in this chapter and the previous chapter for other examples. Add a cover sheet and submit your assignment to your instructor.

Chapter Recap—End of the Month

It happens at the end of every month—you want to leave the office at a reasonable hour, but are inundated with a set of employee expense statements, each in a separate workbook. You cannot leave until you have extracted the data from each individual workbook into a summary workbook, retaining each employee's data on a separate worksheet in the summary workbook. You then have to evaluate each employee's expenses individually to see whether the total is under the allocated amount.

It's time consuming, tedious, and rather boring. Were it not for this monthly "nuisance," your job would be much easier and you would be much happier. If only there were a way to make it happen with the push of a button or two, then you could be spending that extra time making plans for the weekend. Just when you were feeling down about your work, a colleague suggested that you automate the entire process using Excel macros and VBA.

Your assignment is to review the chapter and complete all four hands-on exercises, which have you create the Better Summary Solution workbook. The completed workbook will contain all of the macros to consolidate the expense statements as applied to a specific set of employee worksheets. Prove to yourself how easy the automation procedure is by using the completed workbook to process a different set of expense statements.

Open the *Better Summary Solution* workbook. Pull down the Tools menu, click Macro, run the macro to Reset the Summary Worksheet, then manually delete all of the existing employee worksheets from the Better Summary Solution workbook. Now click the button to Create Summary workbook and enter "*C:\Exploring Excel\Chapter 11 Case Study*" as the name of the folder containing the new set of employee expense statements. You will be prompted to save each workbook in this folder, after which you will be prompted for the maximum allowable expense. Enter $1,000, and then sit back as the new summary workbook is created for you. Print the new summary worksheet for your instructor.

APPENDIX A

Toolbars for Microsoft® Office Excel 2003

TOOLBARS

- 3-D Settings
- Borders
- Chart
- Circular Reference
- Compare Side by Side
- Control Toolbox
- Diagram
- Drawing
- Drawing Canvas
- Exit Design Mode
- External Data
- Formatting
- Forms
- Formula Auditing
- Full Screen
- List and XML
- Organization Chart
- Picture
- Pivot Table
- Protection
- Reviewing
- Shadow Settings
- Standard
- Stop Recording
- Text to Speech
- Visual Basic
- Watch Window
- Web
- WordArt

OVERVIEW

Microsoft Excel has 29 predefined toolbars that provide access to commonly used commands. The toolbars are displayed in Figure A.1 and are listed here for convenience. They are: the Standard, Formatting, 3-D Settings, Borders, Chart, Circular Reference, Compare Side by Side, Control Toolbox, Diagram, Drawing, Drawing Canvas, Exit Design Mode, External Data, Forms, Formula Auditing, Full Screen, List, Organization Chart, Picture, Pivot Table, Protection, Reviewing, Shadow Settings, Stop Recording, Text to Speech, Visual Basic, Watch Window, Web, and WordArt. The Standard and Formatting toolbars are displayed by default and appear on the same row immediately below the menu bar. The other predefined toolbars are displayed (hidden) at the discretion of the user, and in some cases, are displayed automatically when their corresponding features are in use (e.g., the Chart toolbar and the Pivot Table toolbar).

The buttons on the toolbars are intended to be indicative of their function. Clicking the Printer button (the sixth button from the left on the Standard toolbar), for example, executes the Print command. If you are unsure of the purpose of any toolbar button, point to it, and a ScreenTip will appear that displays its name.

You can display multiple toolbars at one time, move them to new locations on the screen, customize their appearance, or suppress their display.

- To separate the Standard and Formatting toolbars and simultaneously display all of the buttons for each toolbar, pull down the Tools menu, click the Customize command, click the Options tab, then check the box to show the toolbars on two rows. Alternatively, the toolbars appear on the same row, so that only a limited number of buttons are visible on each toolbar; hence you may need to click the double arrow at the end of the toolbar to view additional buttons. Additional buttons will be added to either toolbar as you use the associated feature, and conversely, buttons will be removed from the toolbar if the feature is not used.

- To display or hide a toolbar, pull down the View menu and click the Toolbars command. Select (deselect) the toolbar that you want to display (hide). The selected toolbar will be displayed in the same position as when last displayed. You may also point to any toolbar and click with the right mouse button to bring up a shortcut menu, after which you can select the toolbar to be displayed (hidden). If the toolbar to be displayed is not listed, click the Customize command, click the Toolbars tab, check the box for the toolbar to be displayed, and then click the Close button.

625

- To change the size of the buttons, suppress the display of the ScreenTips, or display the associated shortcut key (if available), pull down the View menu, click Toolbars, and click Customize to display the Customize dialog box. If necessary, click the Options tab, then select (deselect) the appropriate check box. Alternatively, you can right click on any toolbar, click the Customize command from the context-sensitive menu, then select (deselect) the appropriate check box from within the Options tab in the Customize dialog box.

- Toolbars are either docked (along the edge of the window) or floating (in their own window). A toolbar moved to the edge of the window will dock along that edge. A toolbar moved anywhere else in the window will float in its own window. Docked toolbars are one tool wide (high), whereas floating toolbars can be resized by clicking and dragging a border or corner as you would with any window.
  - To move a docked toolbar, click anywhere in the background area and drag the toolbar to its new location. You can also click and drag the move handle (the single vertical line) at the left of the toolbar.
  - To move a floating toolbar, drag its title bar to its new location.

- To customize one or more toolbars, display the toolbar on the screen. Then pull down the View menu, click Toolbars, and click Customize to display the Customize dialog box. Alternatively, you can click on any toolbar with the right mouse button and select Customize from the shortcut menu.
  - To move a button, drag the button to its new location on that toolbar or any other displayed toolbar.
  - To copy a button, press the Ctrl key as you drag the button to its new location on that toolbar or any other displayed toolbar.
  - To delete a button, drag the button off the toolbar and release the mouse button.
  - To add a button, click the Commands tab in the Customize dialog box, select the category (from the Categories list box) that contains the button you want to add, then drag the button to the desired location on the toolbar.
  - To restore a predefined toolbar to its default appearance, pull down the View menu, click Toolbars, click Customize, click the Toolbars tab, select (highlight) the desired toolbar, and click the Reset command button.

- Buttons can also be moved, copied, or deleted without displaying the Customize dialog box.
  - To move a button, press the Alt key as you drag the button to the new location.
  - To copy a button, press the Alt and Ctrl keys as you drag the button to the new location.
  - To delete a button, press the Alt key as you drag the button off the toolbar.

- To create your own toolbar, pull down the View menu, click Toolbars, click Customize, click the Toolbars tab, then click the New command button. Alternatively, you can click on any toolbar with the right mouse button, select Customize from the shortcut menu, click the Toolbars tab, and then click the New command button.
  - Enter a name for the toolbar in the dialog box that follows. The name can be any length and can contain spaces.
  - The new toolbar will appear on the screen. Initially it will be big enough to hold only one button. Add, move, and delete buttons following the same procedures as outlined above. The toolbar will automatically size itself as new buttons are added and deleted.
  - To delete a custom toolbar, pull down the View menu, click Toolbars, click Customize, and click the Toolbars tab. *Verify that the custom toolbar to be deleted is the only one selected (highlighted)*. Click the Delete command button. Click Yes to confirm the deletion. (Note that a predefined toolbar cannot be deleted.)

MICROSOFT OFFICE EXCEL 2003 TOOLBARS

Standard

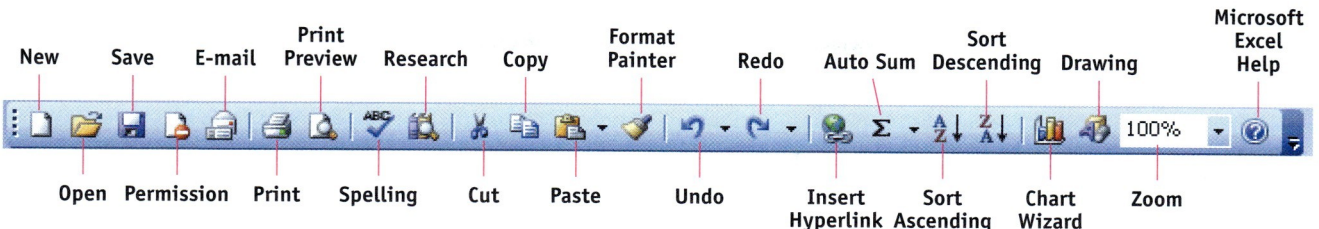

Formatting

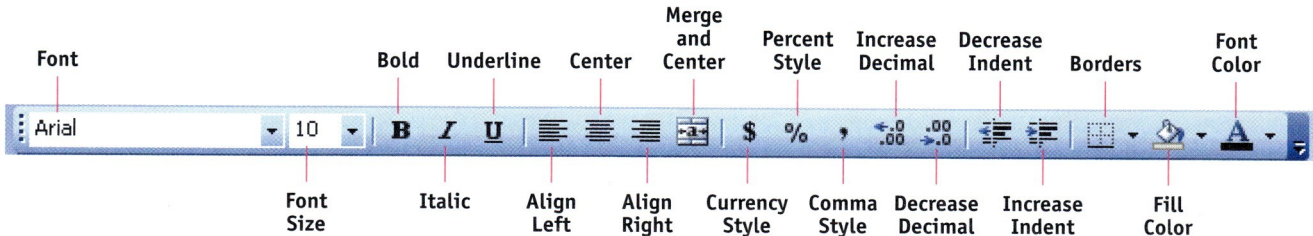

3-D Settings

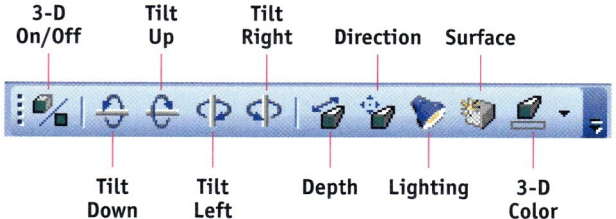

Borders

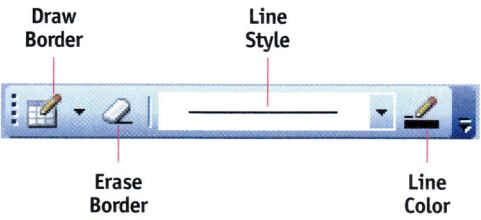

FIGURE A.1 Toolbars

Chart

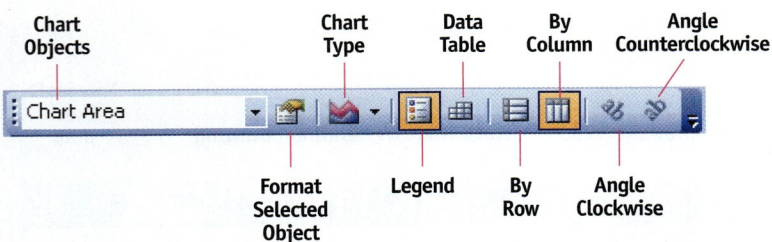

Circular Reference

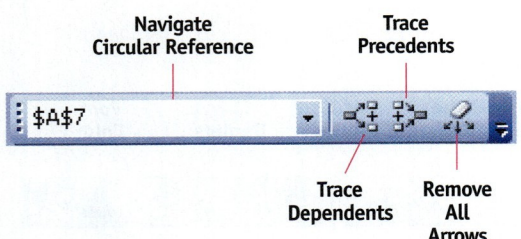

Compare Side by Side

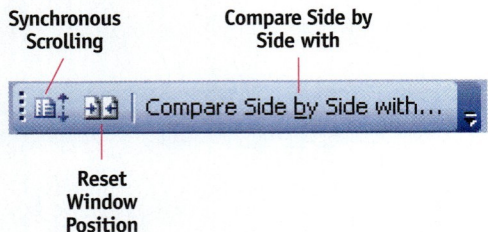

Control Toolbox

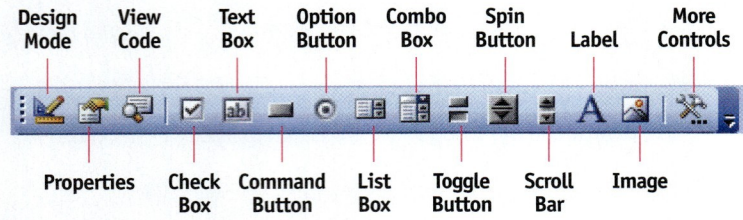

FIGURE A.1 Toolbars (*continued*)

Diagram

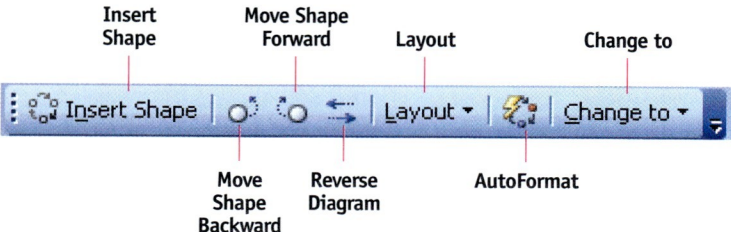

Drawing

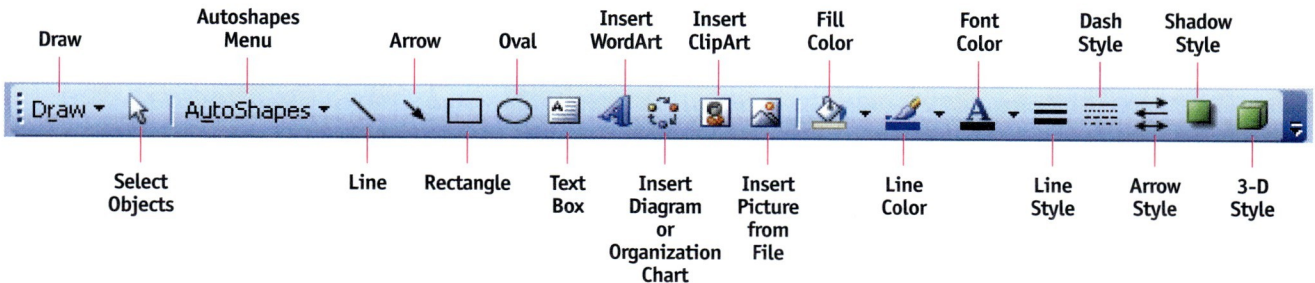

Drawing Canvas

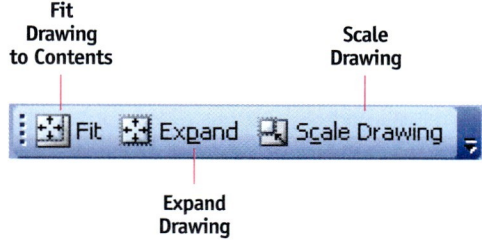

Exit Design Mode

Design Mode

FIGURE A.1 Toolbars (*continued*)

External Data

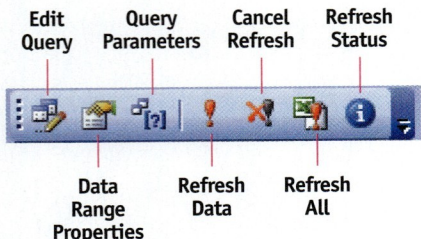

Forms

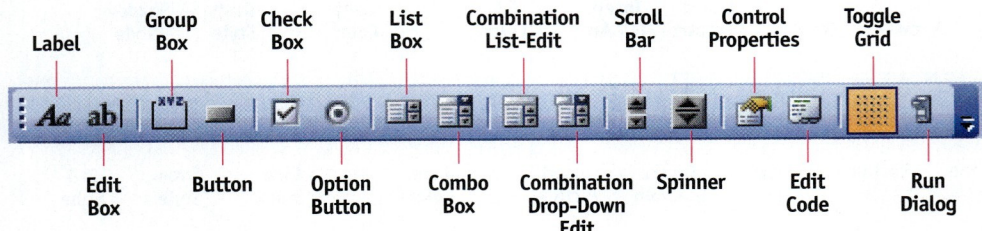

Formula Auditing

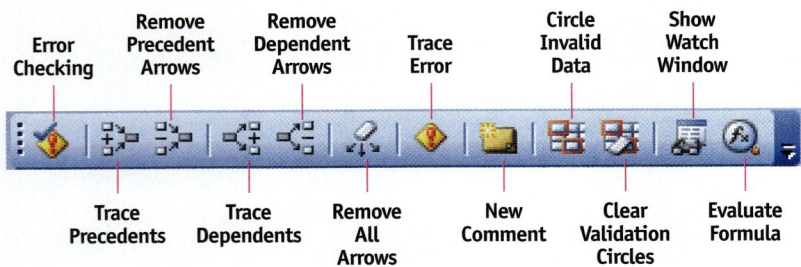

Full Screen

FIGURE A.1 Toolbars (*continued*)

List

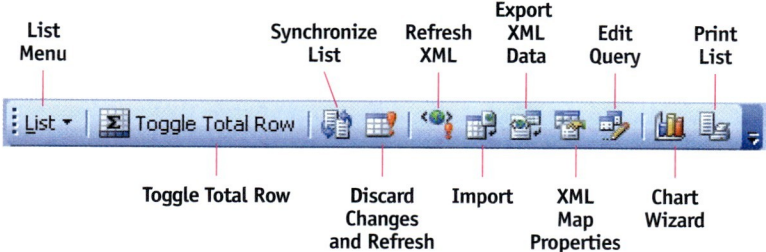

Organization Chart

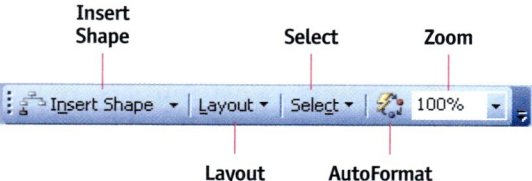

Picture

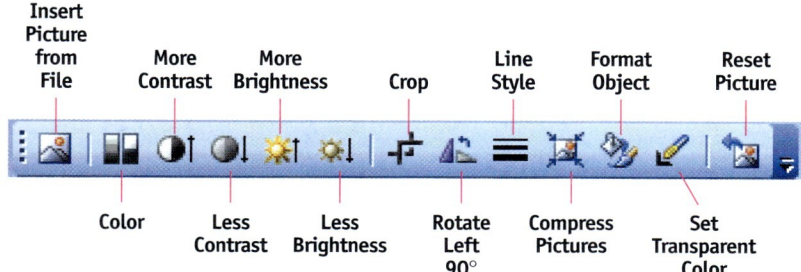

Pivot Table

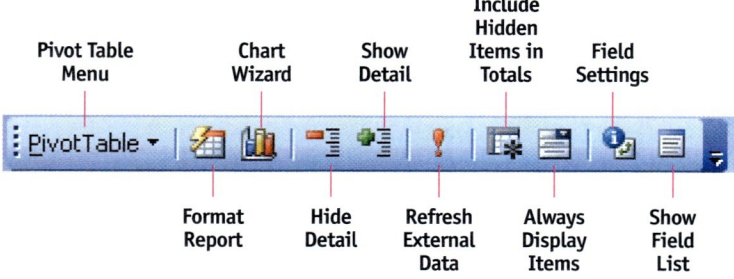

FIGURE A.1 Toolbars (*continued*)

Protection

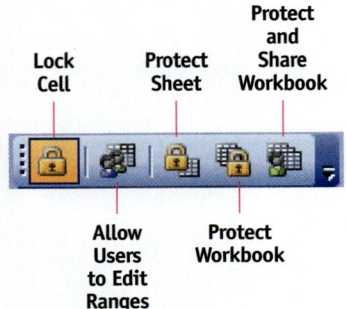

Reviewing

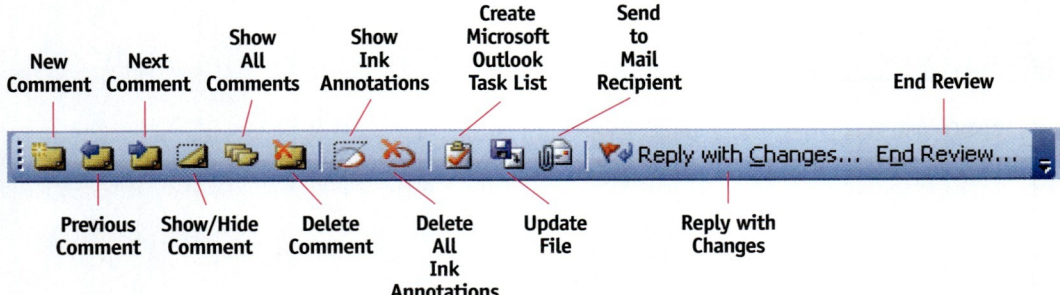

Shadow Settings

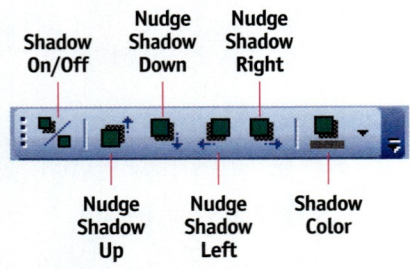

FIGURE A.1 Toolbars (continued)

Stop Recording

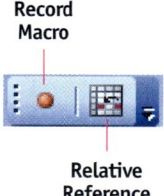

Text to Speech

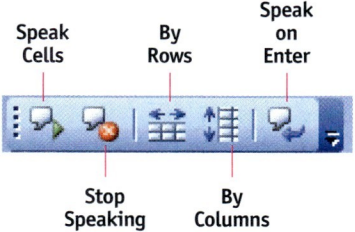

Visual Basic

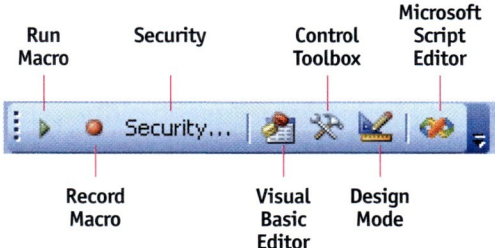

Watch Window

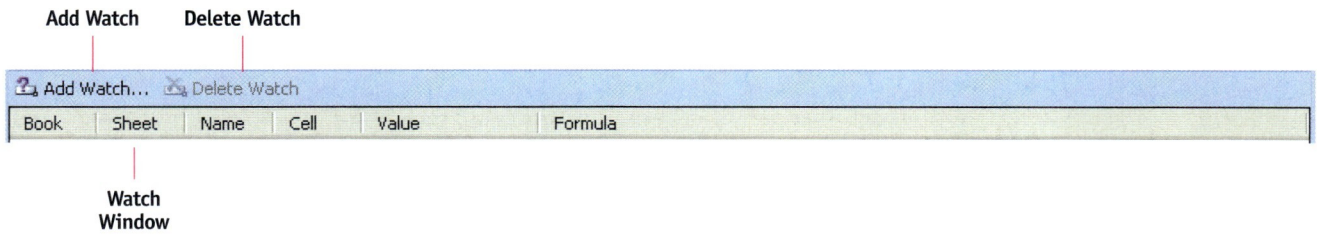

FIGURE A.1 Toolbars (*continued*)

Web

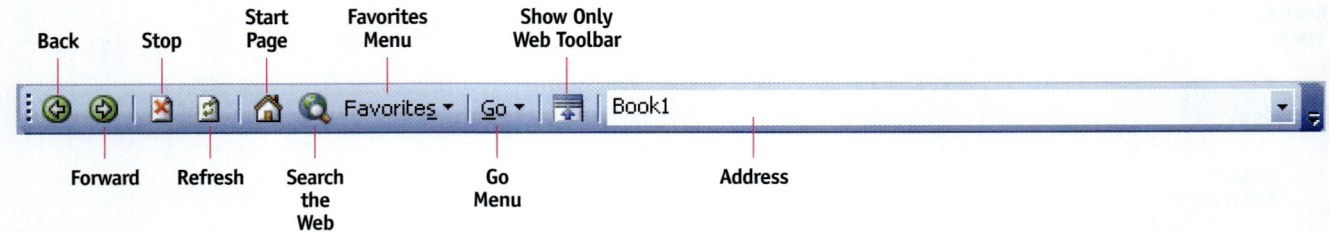

WordArt

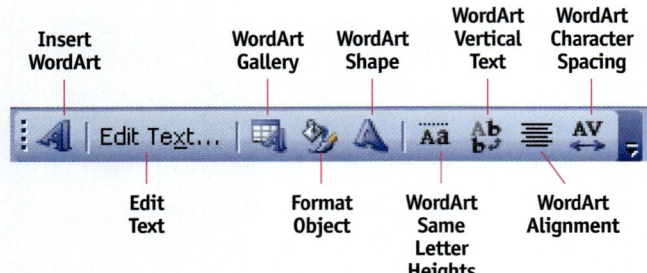

FIGURE A.1   Toolbars (*continued*)

APPENDIX B

Solver: A Tool for Optimization

CASE STUDY
MAXIMIZE PROFIT

Assume that you are the production manager for a company that manufactures computers. Your company divides its product line into two basic categories—desktop computers and laptops. Each product is sold under two labels, a discount line and a premium line. As production manager you are to determine how many computers of each type, and of each product line, to make each week.

Your decision is subject to various constraints that must be satisfied during the production process. Each computer requires a specified number of hours for assembly. Discount and premium-brand desktops require two and three hours, respectively. Discount and premium-brand laptops use three and five hours, respectively. The factory is working at full capacity, and you have only 4,500 hours of labor to allocate among the various products.

Your production decision is also constrained by demand. The marketing department has determined that you cannot sell more than 800 desktop units, nor more than 900 laptops, per week. The total demand for the discount and premium lines is 700 and 1,000 computers, respectively, per week.

Your goal (objective) is to maximize the total profit, which is based on a different profit margin for each type of computer. A desktop and a laptop computer from the discount line have unit profits of $600 and $800, respectively. The premium desktop and laptop computers have unit profits of $1,000 and $1,300, respectively. How many computers of each type do you manufacture each week to maximize the total profit?

This is a complex problem, but one that can be easily solved provided you can design a spreadsheet that is equivalent to Figure B.1. The top half of the spreadsheet contains the information about the individual products. There are three numbers associated with each product—the quantity that will be produced, the number of hours required, and the unit profit. The bottom half of the spreadsheet contains the information about the available resources, such as the total number of labor hours that are available. The spreadsheet also contains various formulas that relate the resources to the quantities that are produced. Cell E8, for example, will contain a formula that computes the total number of hours used, based on the quantity of each computer and the associated hourly requirements.

The problem is to determine the values of cells B2 through B5, which represent the quantity of each computer to produce. You might be able to solve the problem manually through trial and error, by substituting different values and seeing the impact on profit. That is exactly what Solver will do for you, only it will do it much more quickly. (Solver uses various optimization techniques that are beyond the scope of this discussion.)

Once Solver arrives at a solution, assuming that it can find one, it creates a report such as the one shown in Figure B.2. The solution shows the value of the target cell (the profit in this example), based on the values of the adjustable cells (the quantity of each type of computer). The solution that will maximize profit is to manufacture 700 discount laptops and 800 premium desktops for a profit of $1,270,000.

The report in Figure B.2 also examines each constraint and determines whether it is binding or not binding. A *binding constraint* is one in which the resource is fully utilized (i.e., the slack is zero). The number of available hours, for example, is a binding constraint because every available hour is used, and hence the value of the target cell (profit) is limited by the amount of this resource (the number of hours). Or stated another way, any increase in the number of available hours (above 4,500) will also increase the profit.

A *nonbinding constraint* is just the opposite. It has a nonzero slack (i.e., the resource is not fully utilized), and hence it does not limit the value of the target cell. The laptop demand, for example, is not binding because a total of only 700 laptops were produced, yet the allowable demand was 900 (the value in cell E13). In other words, there is a slack value of 200 for this constraint, and increasing the allowable demand will have no effect on the profit. (The demand could actually be decreased by up to 200 units with no effect on profit.)

	A	B	C	D	E
1		Quantity	Hours	Unit Profit	
2	**Discount desktop**		2	$600	
3	**Discount laptop**		3	$800	
4	**Premium desktop**		3	$1,000	
5	**Premium laptop**		5	$1,300	
6					
7		Constraints			
8	Total number of hours used				
9	Labor hours available				4,500
10	Number of desktops produced				
11	Total demand for desktop computers				800
12	Number of laptops produced				
13	Total demand for laptop computers				900
14	Number of discount computers produced				
15	Total demand for discount computers				700
16	Number of premium computers produced				
17	Total demand for premium computers				1,000
18	Hourly cost of labor				$20
19	**Profit**				

FIGURE B.1 The Initial Worksheet

- Problem is to determine values of cells B2:B5, given the constraints
- E8 will contain formula to compute total hours used
- Formula to calculate total profit will be entered in E19

Target Cell (Max)

Cell	Name	Original Value	Final Value
$E$19	Profit	$0	$1,270,000

Adjustable Cells

Cell	Name	Original Value	Final Value
$B$2	Discount desktop Quantity	0	0
$B$3	Discount laptop Quantity	0	700
$B$4	Premium desktop Quantity	0	800
$B$5	Premium laptop Quantity	0	0

Constraints

Cell	Name	Cell Value	Formula	Status	Slack
$E$8	Total number of hours used	4500	$E$8<=$E$9	Binding	0
$E$10	Number of desktops produced	800	$E$10<=$E$11	Binding	0
$E$12	Number of laptops produced	700	$E$12<=$E$13	Not Binding	200
$E$14	Number of discount computers produced	700	$E$14<=$E$15	Binding	0
$E$16	Number of premium computers produced	800	$E$16<=$E$17	Not Binding	200
$B$2	Discount desktop Quantity	0	$B$2>=0	Binding	0
$B$3	Discount laptop Quantity	700	$B$3>=0	Not Binding	700
$B$4	Premium desktop Quantity	800	$B$4>=0	Not Binding	800
$B$5	Premium laptop Quantity	0	$B$5>=0	Binding	0

FIGURE B.2 The Solution

- Value of target cell (E19)
- Quantities to be produced (B2:B5)
- Constraints
- Status indicates whether constraint is binding or not binding

SOLVER

The information required by Solver is entered through the **Solver Parameters dialog box** as shown in Figure B.3. The dialog box is divided into three sections: the target cell, the adjustable cells, and the constraints. The dialog box in Figure B.3 corresponds to the spreadsheet shown earlier in Figure B.1.

The *target cell* identifies the goal (or objective function)—that is, the cell whose value you want to maximize, minimize, or set to a specific value. Our problem seeks to maximize profit, the formula for which is found in cell E19 (the target cell) of the underlying spreadsheet.

The *adjustable cells* (or decision variables) are the cells whose values are adjusted until the constraints are satisfied and the target cell reaches its optimum value. The changing cells in this example contain the quantity of each computer to be produced and are found in cells B2 through B5.

The *constraints* specify the restrictions. Each constraint consists of a cell or cell range on the left, a relational operator, and a numeric value or cell reference on the right. (The constraints can be entered in any order, but they always appear in alphabetical order.) The first constraint references a cell range, cells B2 through B5, and indicates that each of these cells must be greater than or equal to zero. The remaining constraints reference a single cell rather than a cell range.

The functions of the various command buttons are apparent from their names. The Add, Change, and Delete buttons are used to add, change, or delete a constraint. The Options button enables you to set various parameters that determine how Solver attempts to find a solution. The Reset All button clears all settings and resets all options to their defaults. The Solve button begins the search for a solution.

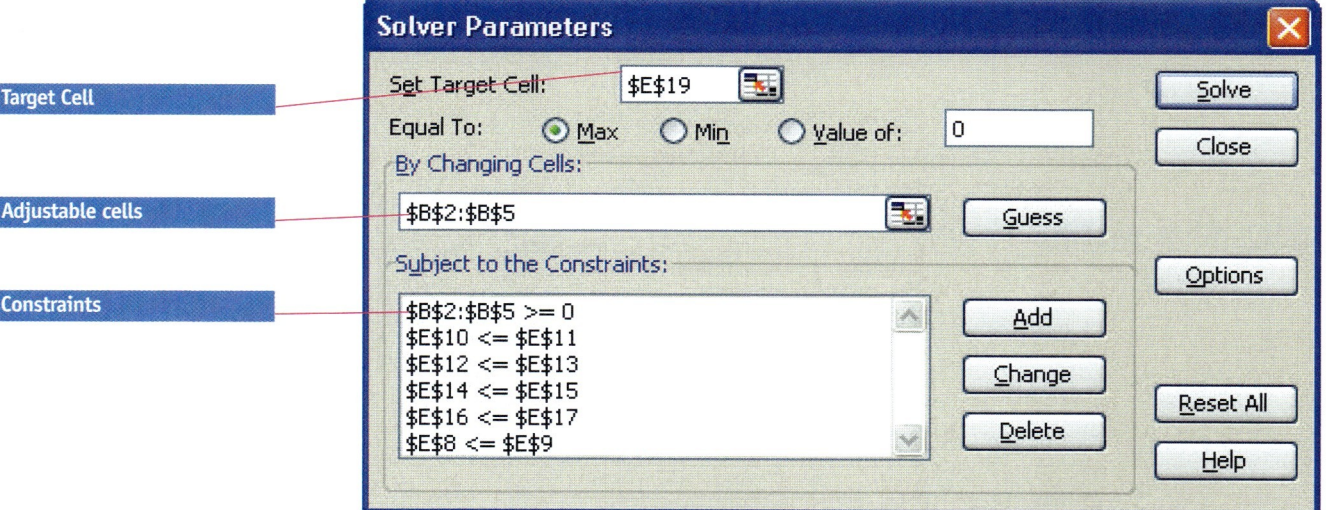

FIGURE B.3 Solver Parameters Dialog Box

THE GREATER-THAN-ZERO CONSTRAINT

One constraint that is often overlooked is the requirement that the value of each adjustable cell be greater than or equal to zero. Physically, it makes no sense to produce a negative number of computers in any category. Mathematically, however, a negative value in an adjustable cell may produce a higher value for the target cell. Hence the nonnegativity (greater than or equal to zero) constraint should always be included for the adjustable cells.

hands-on exercise

1 Maximize Profit

Objective To use Solver to maximize profit; to create a report containing binding and nonbinding constraints. Use Figure B.4 as a guide in the exercise.

Step 1: **Enter the Cell Formulas**

- Start Excel. Open the **Optimization workbook** in the Exploring Excel folder. Save the workbook as **Optimization Solution** so that you can return to the original workbook if necessary.

- If necessary, click the tab for the **Production Mix worksheet**, then click **cell E8** as shown in Figure B.4a.

- Enter the formula shown in Figure B.4a to compute the total number of hours used in production.

- Enter the remaining cell formulas as shown below:
    - Cell E10 (Number of desktops produced) **=B2+B4**
    - Cell E12 (Number of laptops produced) **=B3+B5**
    - Cell E14 (Number of discount computers produced) **=B2+B3**
    - Cell E16 (Number of premium computers produced) **=B4+B5**
    - Cell E19 (Profit) **=B2*D2+B3*D3+B4*D4+B5*D5–E18*E8**

- Save the workbook.

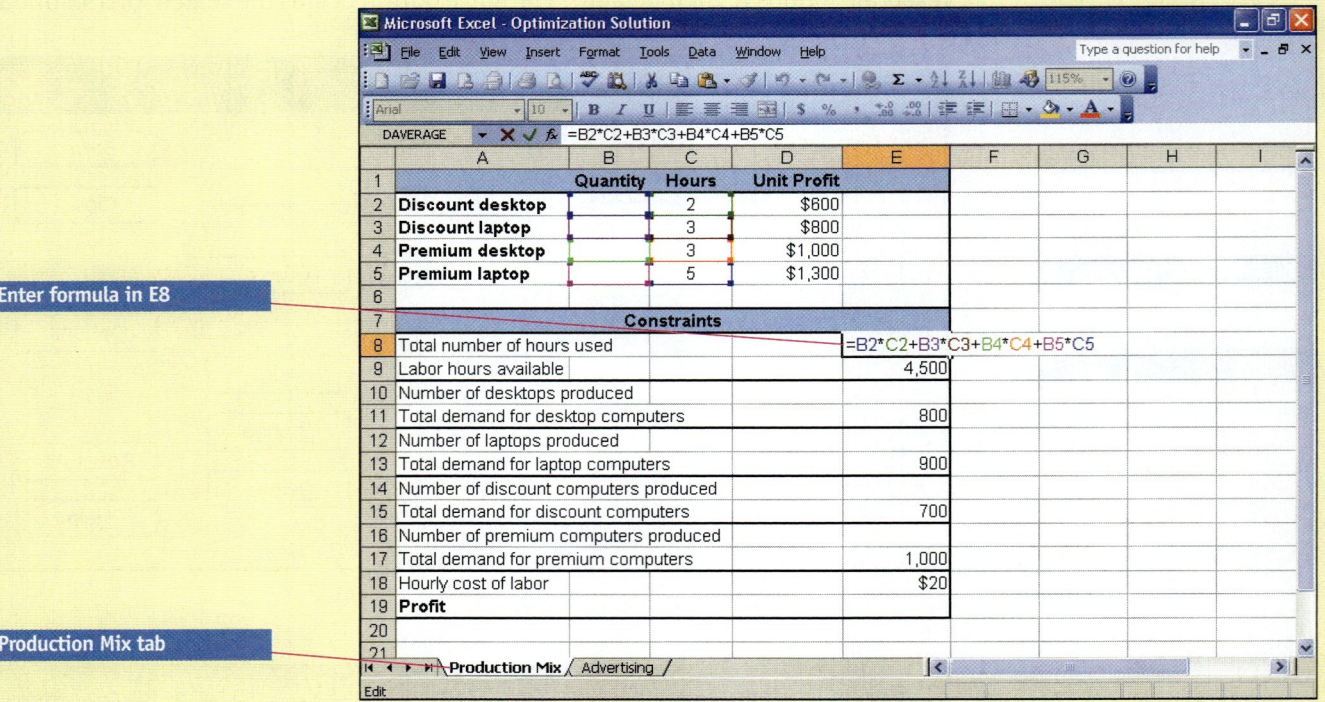

(a) Enter the Cell Formulas (step 1)

FIGURE B.4 Hands-on Exercise 1

Step 2: **Set the Target and Adjustable Cells**

- Check that the formula in cell E19 is entered correctly as shown in Figure B.4b. Pull down the **Tools menu**. Click **Solver** to display the Solver Parameters dialog box shown in Figure B.4b.

- If necessary, click in the text box for **Set Target Cell**. Click in **cell E19** to set the target cell. The Max option button is selected by default.

- Click in the **By Changing Cells** text box. Click and drag **cells B2 through B5** in the worksheet to select these cells.

- Click the **Add command button** to add the first constraint as described in step 3.

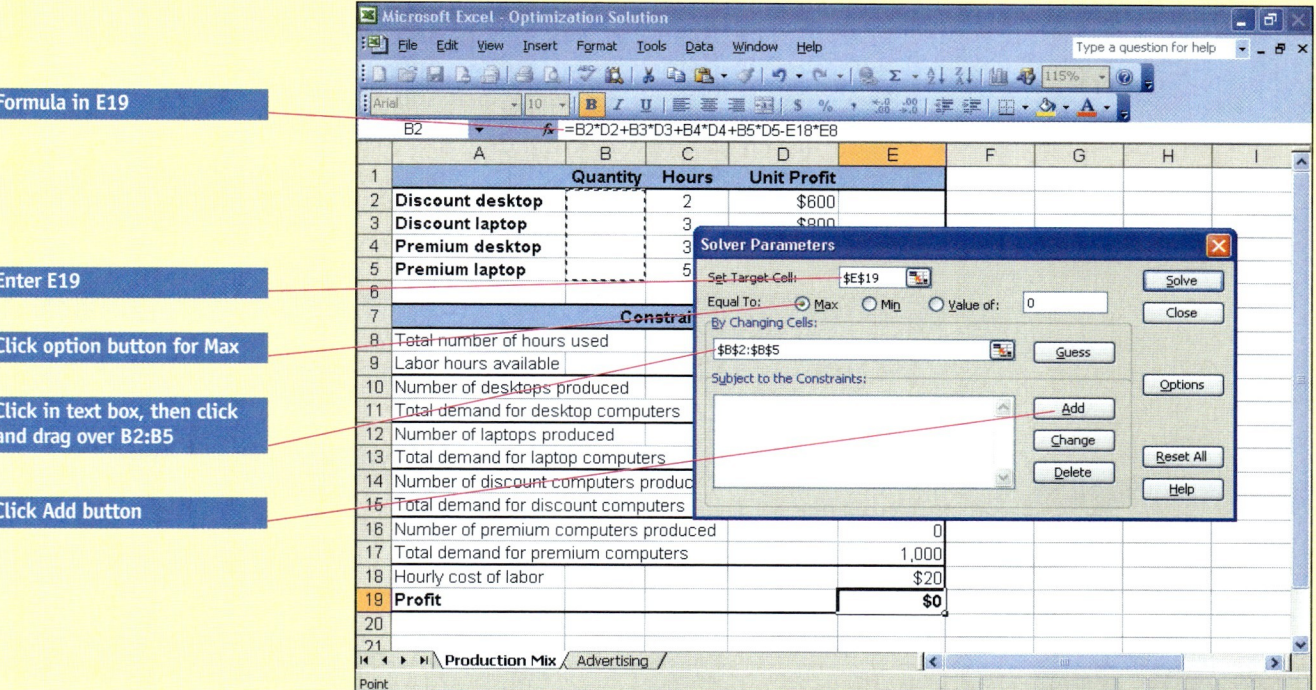

(b) Set the Target and Adjustable Cells (step 2)

FIGURE B.4 Hands-on Exercise 1 (*continued*)

MISSING SOLVER

Solver is an optional component of Microsoft Excel, and hence it may not be installed on your system. If you are working on a computer at school, your instructor should be able to notify the network administrator to correct the problem. If you are working on your own machine, pull down the Tools menu, click the Add-Ins command, check the box for Solver, then click OK to close the Add-Ins dialog box. Click Yes when asked to install Solver. You will need the Microsoft Office CD.

Step 3: Enter the Constraints

- You should see the Add Constraint dialog box in Figure B.4c with the insertion point (a flashing vertical line) in the Cell Reference text box.
  - Click in **cell E8** (the cell containing the formula to compute the total number of hours used). The <= constraint is selected by default.
  - Click in the **Constraint** text box, which will contain the value of the constraint, then click **cell E9** in the worksheet to enter the cell reference.
  - Click **Add** to complete this constraint and add another.

- You will see a new (empty) Add Constraint dialog box, which enables you to enter additional constraints. Use pointing to enter each of the constraints shown below. (Solver automatically enters each reference as an absolute reference.)
  - Enter the constraint **E10<=E11**. Click **Add**.
  - Enter the constraint **E12<=E13**. Click **Add**.
  - Enter the constraint **E14<=E15**. Click **Add**.
  - Enter the constraint **E16<=E17**. Click **Add**.

- Add the last constraint. Click and drag to select **cells B2 through B5**. Click the drop-down arrow for the relational operators and click the **>=** operator. Type **0** in the text box to indicate that the production quantities for all computers must be greater than or equal to zero. Click **OK**.

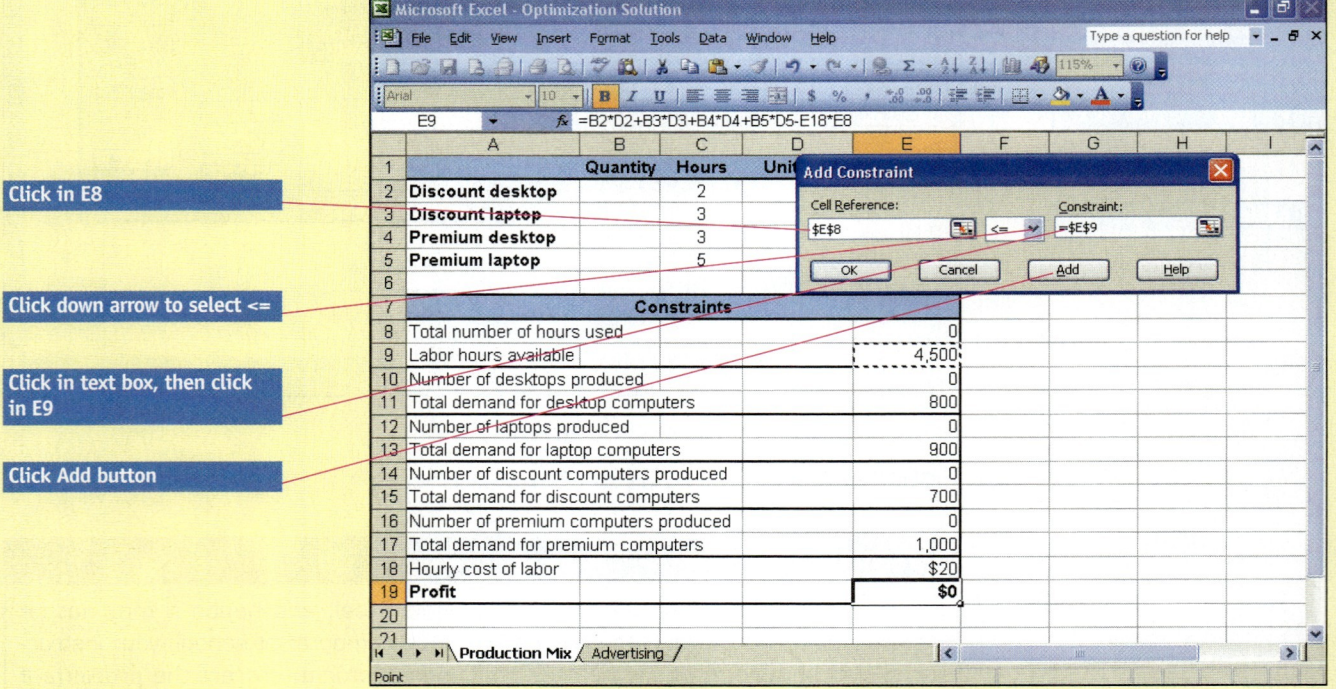

(c) Enter the Constraints (step 3)

FIGURE B.4 Hands-on Exercise 1 (*continued*)

ADD VERSUS OK

Click the Add button to complete the current constraint and display an empty dialog box to enter another constraint. Click OK only when you have completed the last constraint and want to return to the Solver Parameters dialog box to solve the problem.

Step 4: **Solve the Problem**

- Check that the contents of the Solver Parameters dialog box match those of Figure B.4d. (The constraints appear in alphabetical order rather than the order in which they were entered.)
  - To change the Target cell, click the **Set Target Cell** text box, then click the appropriate target cell in the worksheet.
  - To change (edit) a constraint, select the constraint, then click the **Change button**.
  - To delete a constraint, select the constraint and click the **Delete button**.
- Click the **Solve button** to solve the problem.
- You should see the Solver Results dialog box, indicating that Solver has found a solution. The maximum profit is $1,270,000. The option button to Keep Solver Solution is selected by default.
- Click **Answer** in the Reports list box, then click **OK** to generate the report. You will see the report being generated, after which the Solver Results dialog box closes automatically.
- Save the workbook.

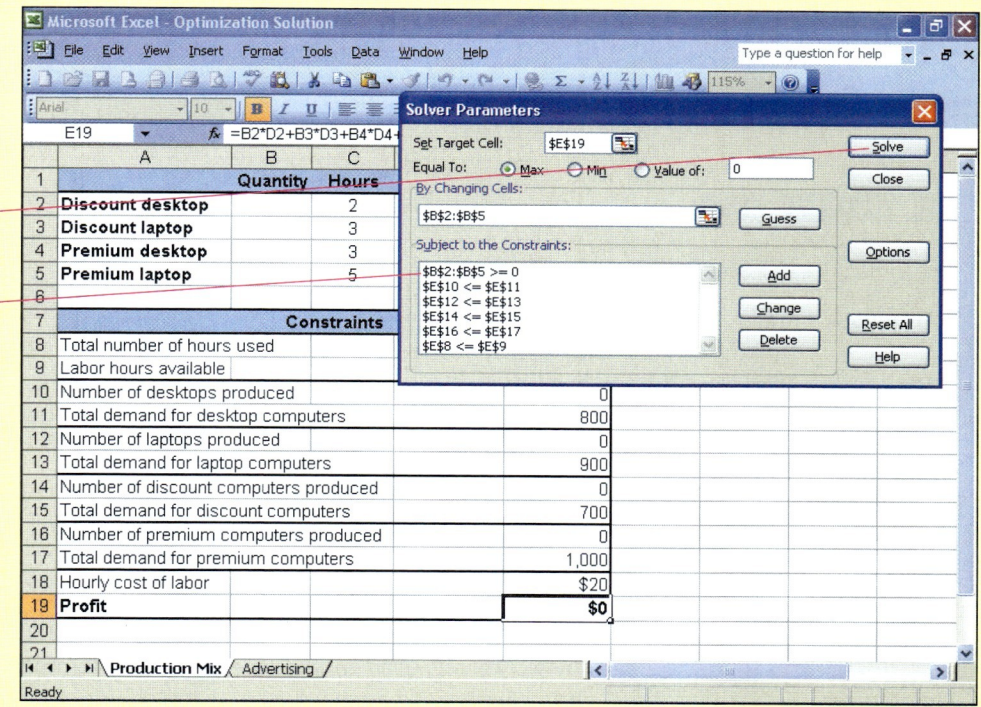

(d) Solve the Problem (step 4)

FIGURE B.4 Hands-on Exercise 1 (*continued*)

Step 5: **View the Report**

- Click the **Answer Report 1 worksheet tab** to view the report as shown in Figure B.4e. Click in **cell A4**, the cell immediately under the entry showing the date and time the report was created. (The gridlines and row and column headings are suppressed by default for this worksheet.)

- Enter your name in boldface as shown in the figure, then press **Enter** to complete the entry. Print the answer sheet and submit it to your instructor as proof you did the exercise.

- Save the workbook. Exit Excel if you do not wish to continue with the next exercise at this time.

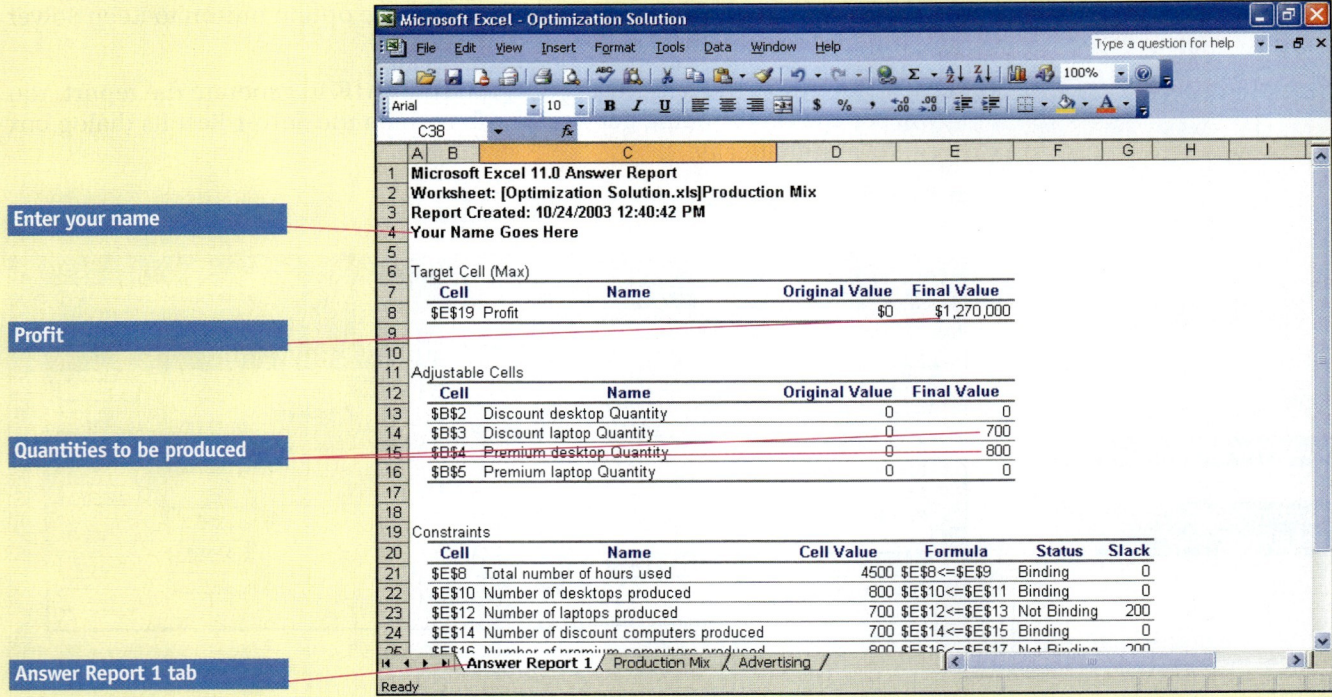

(e) View the Report (step 5)

FIGURE B.4 Hands-on Exercise 1 (*continued*)

VIEW OPTIONS

Any worksheet used to create a spreadsheet model will display gridlines and row and column headers by default. Worksheets containing reports, however, especially reports generated by Excel, often suppress these elements to make the reports easier and more appealing to read. To suppress (display) these elements, pull down the Tools menu, click Options, click the View tab, then clear (check) the appropriate check boxes under Window options.

EXAMPLE 2—MINIMIZE COST

The example just concluded introduced you to the basics of Solver. We continue now with a second hands-on exercise, to provide additional practice, and to discuss various subtleties that can occur. This time we present a minimization problem in which we seek to minimize cost subject to a series of constraints. The problem will focus on the advertising campaign that will be conducted to sell the computers you have produced.

The director of marketing has allocated a total of $125,000 in his weekly advertising budget. He wants to establish a presence in both magazines and radio, and requires a minimum of four magazine ads and ten radio ads each week. Each magazine ad costs $10,000 and is seen by one million readers. Each radio commercial costs $5,000 and is heard by 250,000 listeners. How many ads of each type should be placed to reach at least 10 million customers at minimum cost?

All of the necessary information is contained within the previous paragraph. You must, however, display that information in a worksheet before you can ask Solver to find a solution. Accordingly, reread the previous paragraph, then try to set up a worksheet from which you can call Solver. (Our worksheet appears in step 1 of the following hands-on exercise. Try, however, to set up your own worksheet before you look at ours.)

FINER POINTS OF SOLVER

Figure B.5 displays the **Solver Options dialog box** that enables you to specify how Solver will approach the solution. The Max Time and Iterations entries determine how long Solver will work on finding the solution. If either limit is reached before a solution is found, Solver will ask whether you want to continue. The default settings of 100 seconds and 100 *iterations* are sufficient for simpler problems, but may fall short for complex problems with multiple constraints.

The Precision setting determines how close the computed values in the constraint cells come to the specified value of the resource. The smaller the precision, the longer Solver will take in arriving at a solution. The default setting of .0000001 is adequate for most problems and should not be decreased. The remaining options are beyond the scope of our discussion.

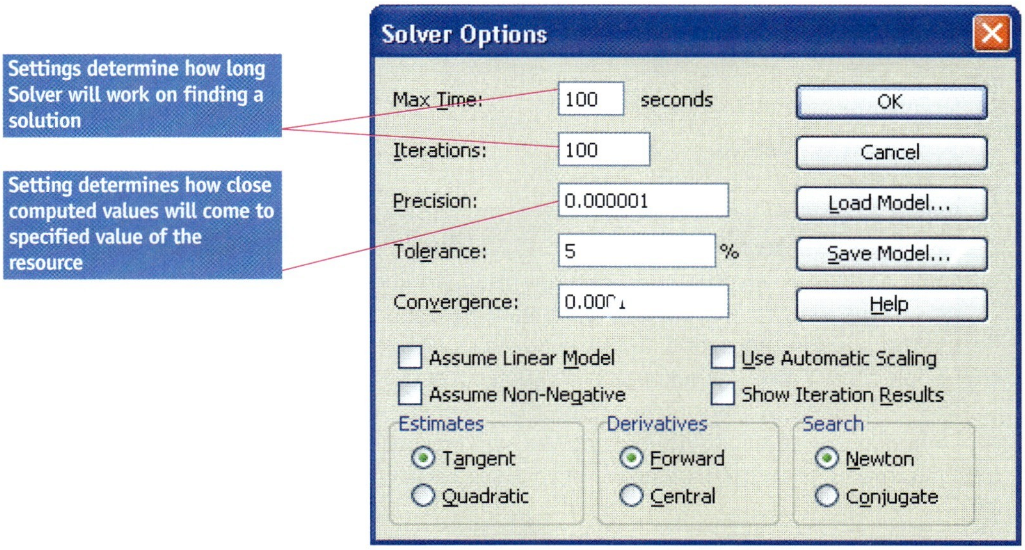

FIGURE B.5 Options Dialog Box

hands-on exercise 2

Minimize Cost

Objective To use Solver to minimize cost; to impose an integer constraint and examine its effect on the optimal solution; to relax a constraint in order to find a feasible solution. Use Figure B.6 as a guide in the exercise.

Step 1: **Enter the Cell Formulas**

- Open the **Optimization Solution workbook** from the previous exercise.
- Click the tab for the **Advertising worksheet**, then click in **cell E6**. Enter the formula **=B2*C2+B3*C3** as shown in Figure B.6a.
- Click in **cell E10**. Enter the formula **=B2*D2+B3*D3** to compute the size of the audience. Save the workbook.

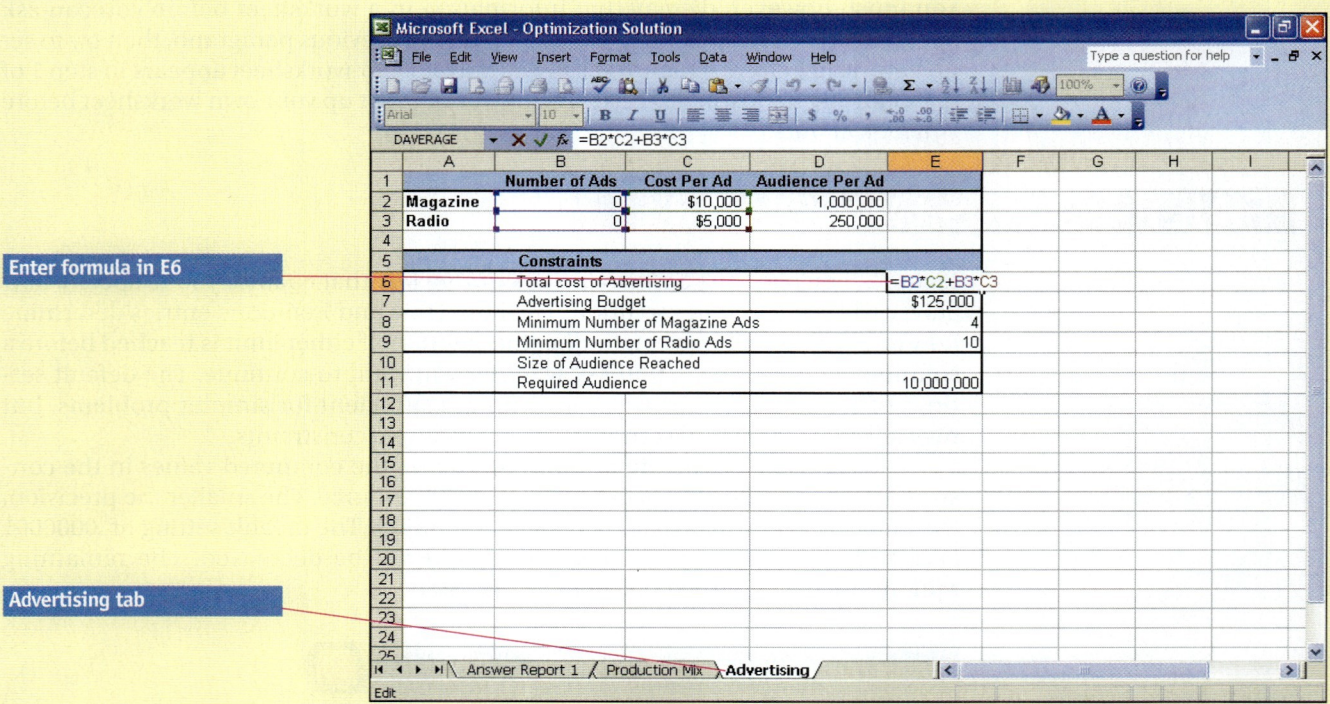

(a) Enter the Cell Formulas (step 1)

FIGURE B.6 Hands-on Exercise 2

USE THE TASK PANE

The easiest way to reopen a recently used workbook is to use the task pane. Pull down the View menu and toggle the Task Pane command on so that the task pane is displayed in the right side of the application window. Click the name of the workbook in the Open a workbook area to reopen the workbook. You can also open a recently used workbook from the list that appears at the bottom of the File menu. Another way is to click the Windows Start button, click the My Recent Documents command, then click the name of the workbook when it appears in the submenu.

Step 2: **Set the Target and Adjustable Cells**

- Pull down the **Tools menu**. Click **Solver** to display the Solver Parameters dialog box shown in Figure B.6b.

- Set the target cell to **cell E6**. Click the **Min (Minimize) option button**. Click in the **By Changing Cells** text box.

- Click and drag **cells B2 and B3** in the worksheet to select these cells as shown in Figure B.6b.

- Click the **Add command button** to add the first constraint as described in step 3.

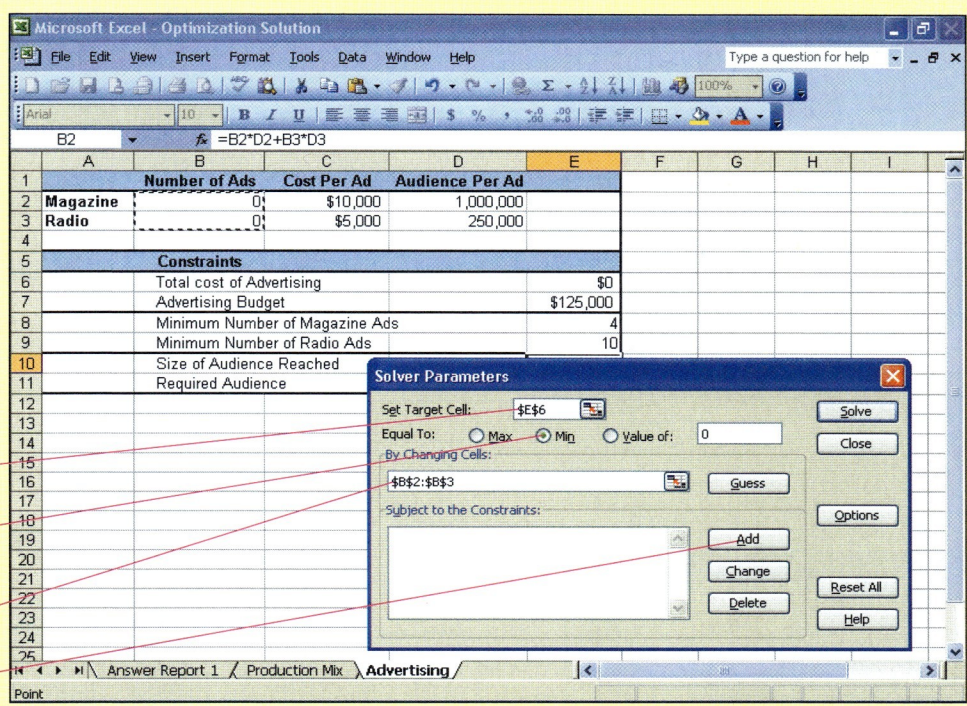

(b) Set the Target and Adjustable Cells (step 2)

FIGURE B.6 Hands-on Exercise 2 (*continued*)

REVIEW THE TERMINOLOGY

Solver is an optimization technique that allows you to maximize or minimize the value of an objective function, such as profit or cost, respectively. The formula to compute the objective function is stored in the target cell within the worksheet. Other cells in the worksheet contain the variables or adjustable cells. Another set of cells contains the value of the available resources or constraints. This type of optimization problem is referred to as linear programming.

Step 3: **Enter the Constraints**

- You should see the Add Constraint dialog box in Figure B.6c with the insertion point (a flashing vertical line) in the Cell Reference text box.
  - Click in **cell E6** (the cell containing the total cost of advertising).
  - The <= constraint is selected by default.
  - Click in the text box to contain the value of the constraint, then click **cell E7** to enter the cell reference in the Add Constraint dialog box. Click **Add**.

- You will see a new (empty) Add Constraint dialog box, which enables you to enter additional constraints. Use pointing to enter each of the constraints shown below. (Solver converts each reference to an absolute reference.)
  - Enter the constraint E10>=E11. Click **Add**.
  - Enter the constraint B2>=E8. Click **Add**.
  - Enter the constraint B3>=E9. Click **OK** since this is the last constraint.

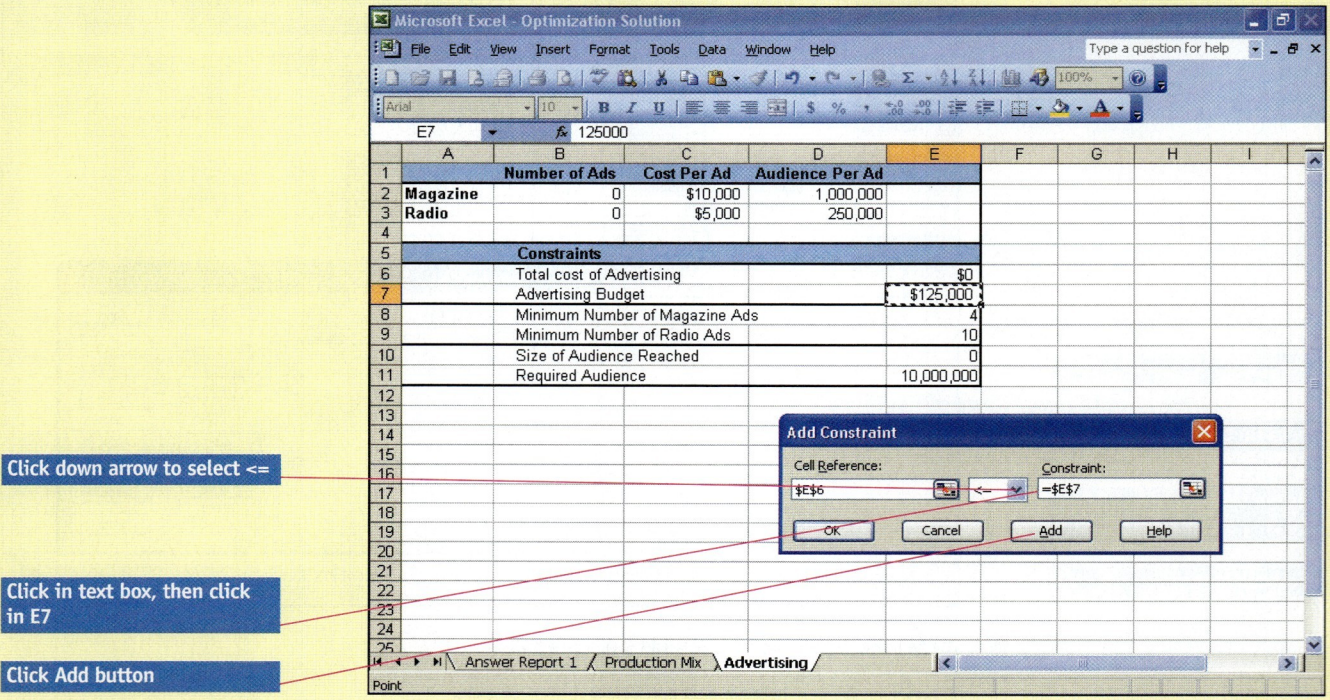

(c) Enter the Constraints (step 3)

FIGURE B.6 Hands-on Exercise 2 (*continued*)

SHOW ITERATION RESULTS

Solver uses an iterative (repetitive) approach in which each iteration (trial solution) is one step closer to the optimal solution. It may be interesting, therefore, to examine the intermediate solutions, especially if you have a knowledge of optimization techniques, such as linear programming. Click the Options command button in the Solver Parameters dialog box, check the Show Iterations Results box, click OK to close the Solver Options dialog box, then click the Solve command button in the usual fashion. A Show Trial Solutions dialog box will appear as each intermediate solution is displayed in the worksheet. Click Continue to move from one iteration to the next until the optimal solution is reached.

Step 4: **Solve the Problem**

- Check that the contents of the Solver Parameters dialog box match those in Figure B.6d. (The constraints appear in alphabetical order rather than the order in which they were entered.)

- Click the **Solve button** to solve the problem. The Solver Results dialog box appears and indicates that Solver has arrived at a solution.

- The option button to Keep Solver Solution is selected by default. Click **OK** to close the Solver Results dialog box and display the solution.

- Save the workbook.

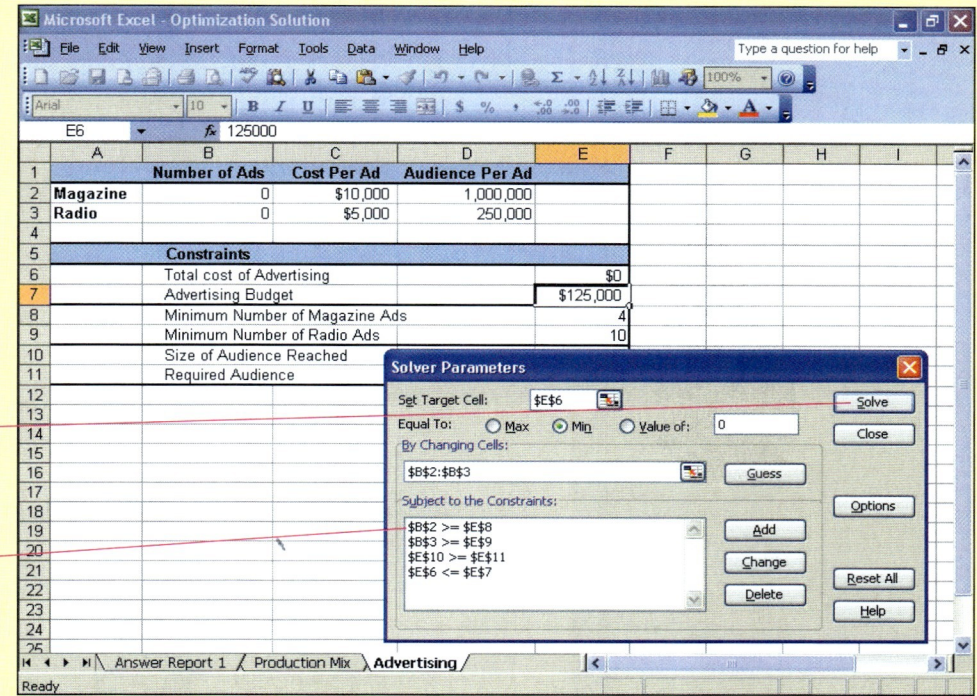

(d) Solve the Problem (step 4)

FIGURE B.6 Hands-on Exercise 2 (*continued*)

USE POINTING TO ENTER CELL FORMULAS

A cell reference can be typed directly into a formula, or it can be entered more easily through pointing. To use pointing, select (click) the cell to contain the formula, type an equal sign to begin entering the formula, then click (or move to) the cell containing the value to be used. Type any arithmetic operator to place the cell reference into the formula, then continue pointing to additional cells. Press the Enter key (instead of typing an arithmetic operator) to complete the formula.

Step 5: **Impose an Integer Constraint**

- The number of magazine ads in the solution is 7.5 as shown in Figure B.6e. This is a noninteger number, which is reasonable in the context of Solver but not in the "real world" as one cannot place half an ad.

- Pull down the **Tools menu**. Click **Solver** to once again display the Solver Parameters dialog box. Click the **Add button** to display the Add Constraint dialog box in Figure B.6e.

- The insertion point is already positioned in the Cell Reference text box. Click and drag to select **cells B2 through B3**. Click the **drop-down arrow** in the Constraint list box and click **int** (for integer).

- Click **OK** to accept the constraint and close the Add Constraint dialog box.

- The Solver Parameters dialog box appears on your monitor with the integer constraint added. Click **Solve** to solve the problem.

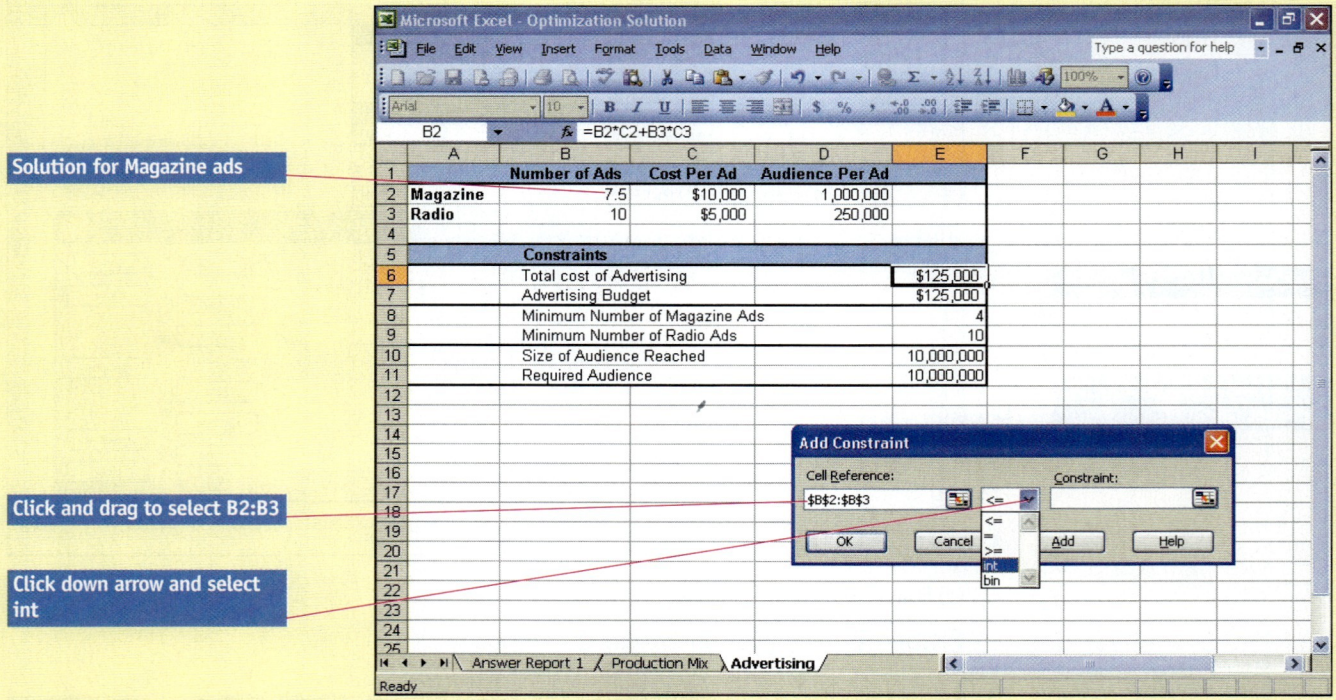

(e) Impose an Integer Constraint (step 5)

FIGURE B.6   Hands-on Exercise 2 (*continued*)

DO YOU REALLY NEED AN INTEGER SOLUTION?

It seems like such a small change, but specifying an integer constraint can significantly increase the amount of time required for Solver to reach a solution. The examples in this chapter are relatively simple and did not take an inordinate amount of time to solve. Imposing an integer constraint on a more complex problem, however, may challenge your patience as Solver struggles to reach a solution.

Step 6: **The Infeasible Solution**

- You should see the dialog box in Figure B.6f, indicating that Solver could *not* find a solution that satisfied the existing constraints. This is because the imposition of the integer constraint would raise the number of magazine ads from 7.5 to 8, which would increase the total cost of advertising to $130,000, exceeding the budget of $125,000.

- The desired audience can still be reached but only by relaxing one of the binding constraints. You can, for example, retain the requisite number of magazine and radio ads by increasing the budget. Alternatively, the budget can be held at $125,000, while still reaching the audience by decreasing the required number of radio ads.

- Click **Cancel** to exit the dialog box and return to the worksheet.

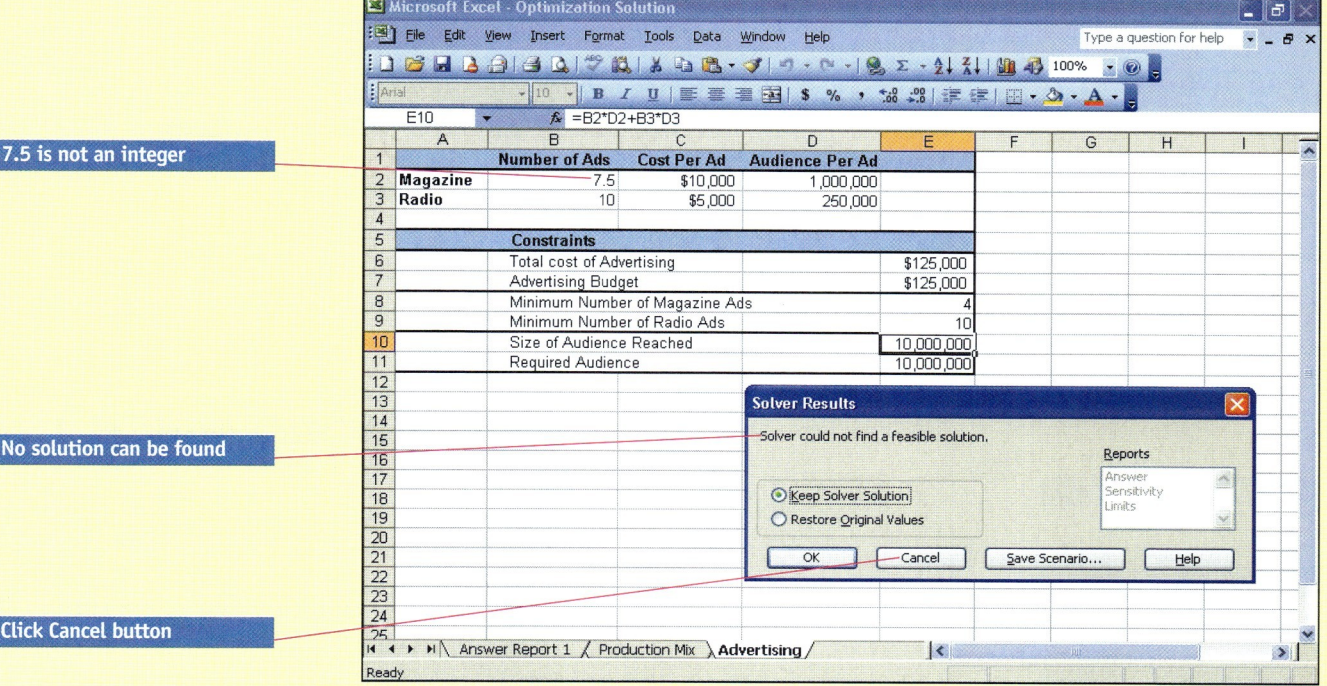

(f) The Infeasible Solution (step 6)

FIGURE B.6 Hands-on Exercise 2 (*continued*)

UNABLE TO FIND A SOLUTION

Solver is a powerful tool, but it cannot do the impossible. Some problems simply do not have a solution because the constraints may conflict with one another, and/or because the constraints exceed the available resources. Should this occur, and it will, check your constraints to make sure they were entered correctly. If Solver is still unable to reach a solution, it will be necessary to relax one or more of the constraints.

Step 7: **Relax a Constraint**

- Click in **cell E9** (the cell containing the minimum number of radio ads). Enter **9** and press **Enter**.

- Pull down the **Tools menu**. Click **Solver** to display the Solver Parameters dialog box. Click **Solve**. This time Solver finds a solution as shown in Figure B.6g.

- Click **Answer** in the Reports list box, then click **OK** to generate the report. You will see the report being generated, after which the Solver Results dialog box closes automatically.

- Click the **Answer Report 2 worksheet tab** to view the report. Add your name to the report, boldface your name, print the answer report, and submit it to your instructor.

- Save the workbook.

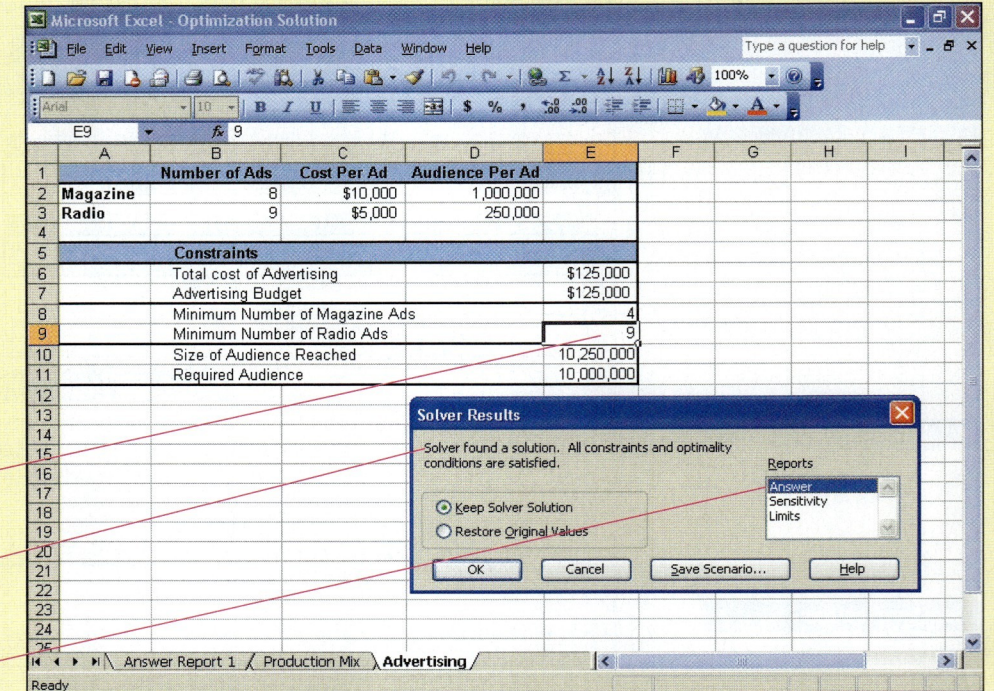

(g) Relax a Constraint (step 7)

FIGURE B.6 Hands-on Exercise 2 (*continued*)

SENSITIVITY, BINDING, AND NONBINDING CONSTRAINTS

A sensitivity report shows the effect of increasing resources associated with the binding and nonbinding constraints within the optimization problem. A binding constraint has a limiting effect on the objective value; that is, relaxing a binding constraint by increasing the associated resource will improve the value of the objective function. Conversely, a nonbinding constraint does not have a limiting effect, and increasing its resource has no effect on the value of the objective function.

Step 8: **Add the Documentation Worksheet**

- This step creates a documentation worksheet similar to the one in Chapter 6. Pull down the **Insert menu** and click the **Worksheet command**.

- Double click the **tab** of the newly inserted worksheet. Enter **Documentation** as the new name and press **Enter**. If necessary, click and drag the worksheet tab to move it to the beginning of the workbook.

- Enter the descriptive entries in **cells A3, A4, and A6** as shown in Figure B.6h. Use boldface as shown. Increase the width of column A.

- Enter your name in **cell B3**. Enter **=Today( )** in **cell B4**. Press **Enter**. Click the **Left Align button** to align the date as shown in the figure.

- Increase the width of column B, then click in **cell B6** and enter the indicated text. Do not press the Enter key until you have completed the entry.

- Click in **cell B6**, then pull down the **Format menu** and click the **Cells command** to display the Format Cells dialog box. Click the **Alignment tab**, click the box to **Wrap Text**, then click **OK**.

- Point to **cell A6**, then click the **right mouse button** to display a shortcut menu. Click **Format Cells** to display the Format Cells dialog box. If necessary, click the **Alignment tab**, click the **drop-down arrow** in the Vertical list box, and select **Top**. Click **OK**.

- Click in **cell A1**. Enter **Solver—An Optimization Technique**. Change the font size to **18**. Click and drag to select **cells A1** and **B1**. Click the **Merge and Center button** to center the title across cells A1 and B1.

- Complete the entries in the remainder of the worksheet. Check the worksheet for spelling. Save the workbook. Print the documentation worksheet.

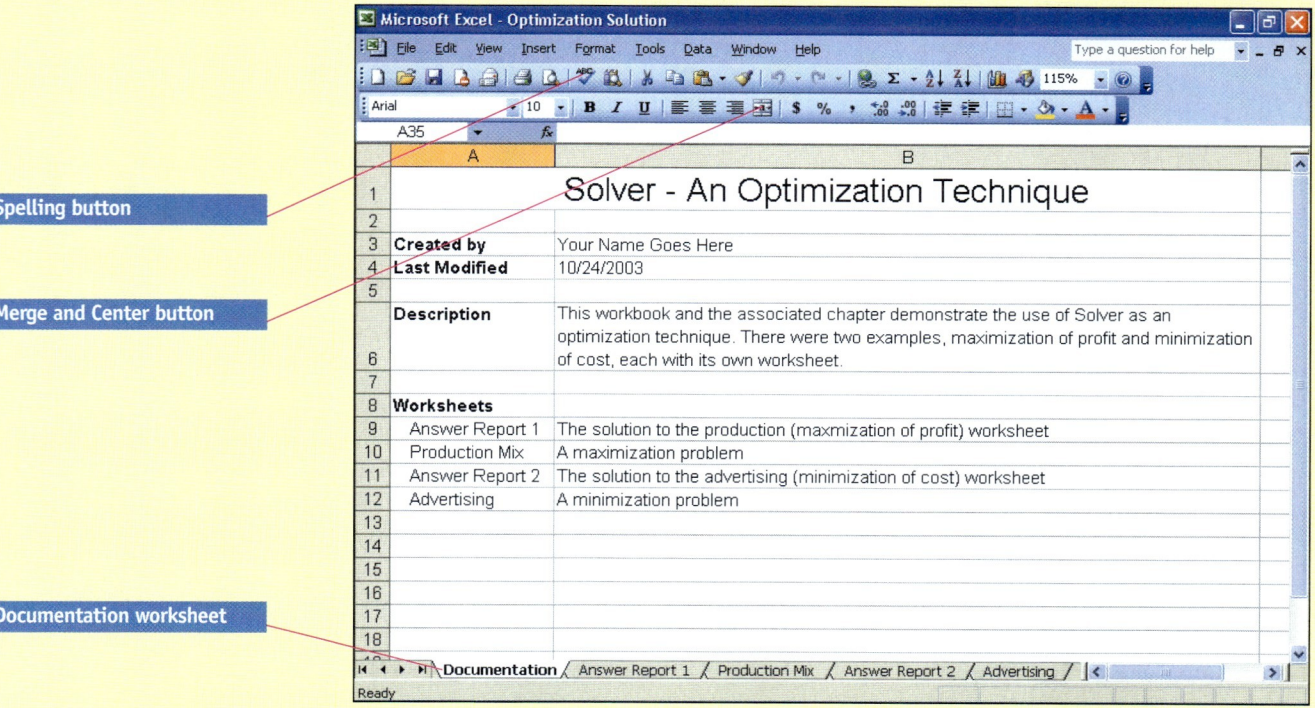

(h) Add the Documentation Worksheet (step 8)

FIGURE B.6 Hands-on Exercise 2 (*continued*)

SUMMARY

Solver is an optimization and resource allocation tool that helps you achieve a desired goal, such as maximizing profit or minimizing cost. The information required by Solver is entered through the Solver Parameters dialog box, which is divided into three sections: the target cell, the adjustable cells, and the constraints.

The target cell identifies the goal (or objective function), which is the cell whose value you want to maximize, minimize, or set to a specific value. The adjustable cells are the cells whose values are changed until the constraints are satisfied and the target cell reaches its optimum value. The constraints specify the restrictions. Each constraint consists of a comparison containing a cell or cell range on the left, a relational operator, and a numeric value or cell reference on the right.

The Solver Options dialog box lets you specify how Solver will attempt to find a solution. The Max Time and Iterations entries determine how long Solver will work on finding a solution. If either limit is reached before a solution is found, Solver will ask whether you want to continue. The default settings of 100 seconds and 100 iterations are sufficient for simpler problems, but may not be enough for complex problems with multiple constraints.

KEY TERMS

Adjustable cells 637
Binding constraint 635
Constraint 637
Iteration 643
Nonbinding constraint 635
Solver 637
Solver Options
   dialog box 643
Solver Parameters
   dialog box..................637
Target cell 637

APPENDIX C

Using XML with Microsoft® Excel 2003

OBJECTIVES

After reading this chapter you will be able to:

1. Define XML; describe how XML differs from HTML.
2. Describe the XML syntax; create an XML document using the Notepad accessory.
3. Explain how Internet Explorer is XML-enabled and how Notepad is not.
4. Import and refresh XML data into an Excel worksheet.

hands-on exercises

1. INTRODUCTION TO XML
   Input: None
   Output: Apartment (XML)

2. EXCEL AND XML
   Input: SalesData (XML)
   Output: SalesData (modified XML), SalesData workbook

OVERVIEW

Today's corporate enterprise runs a variety of applications on different hardware and different operating systems. Individuals within the organization are accessing the same data from different cities or countries, using notebooks, desktops, cell phones, mainframes, and a variety of other hardware. The applications vary greatly, but the one thing in common is the data that moves through the organization. Thus, the various applications and system components have to understand one another so that data can be captured once, and then reused as often as necessary. The solution is to adopt a common standard that describes data in such a way that it can be used by any application.

XML (eXtensible Markup Language) is an industry standard for structuring data across applications, operating systems, and hardware devices. It enables data to be sent and retrieved between disparate and otherwise incompatible systems; in theory, you can start a transaction on a PC at your office, check on the status of that transaction on your way home using a cell phone or PDA, then check further on your PC when you arrive home. XML is but the latest step in the evolution of markup languages. It follows the *Standard Generalized Markup Language (SGML)*, which you may not recognize, and *Hypertext Markup Language (HTML)*, which you should recognize because it made the World Wide Web possible. Despite its success, however, HTML has significant limitations and hence the development of XML. Our intent is not to make you an XML expert, but to provide an overview of its capability and implementation within Microsoft Excel 2003. ■

Your assignment is to read the material, paying special attention to the development and characteristics of XML and its use within the organization. You will complete two hands-on exercises that describe how to create a simple XML document, and how Microsoft Excel 2003 supports XML technology.

INTRODUCTION TO XML

XML (eXtensible Markup Language) describes the structure of data, but not its appearance or formatting. Its elements are created by the user for each individual application, as opposed to a central authority. But what does this really mean? What is a markup language and what makes it extensible? Why is it so flexible? The text below provides insight into the significance of XML:

2 bedrooms/2 bathrooms – $600 per month – (305) 111-2222

You should recognize the sentence immediately as an advertisement for an apartment that might have been taken from the classified section of a newspaper. It makes sense to you, but not to a computer that cannot discern the individual entries within the text; that is, the computer has no way of interpreting the sentence without additional information. Now look at the same text as it would appear in XML:

<Apartment>

    <Description> 2 bedrooms/2 bathrooms </Description>

    <Rent> $600 per month </Rent>

    <Telephone> (305) 111-2222 </Telephone>

</Apartment>

The data has been "marked up" with various ***tags*** (enclosed in angled brackets) to give it structure. Each piece of data is enclosed in a beginning and ending tag, where the name of the tag was defined by the user. Various tags are nested within one another; for example, the Description, Rent, and Telephone tags are nested within the Apartment tag. The tags seem rather obvious, but no one said that XML was complicated. XML is simply data about data; its tags are defined by the user according to the application, and they can be read by any XML-compliant application and processed accordingly.

Look further and you will see that the XML document does not contain any information about how to display the data; XML describes the data itself rather than the formatting of the data. XML is very different therefore from HTML, which specifies how to display the data, but not the meaning of the data. The distinction is apparent if we examine the apartment listing as it would appear in HTML:

<B><I> 2 bedrooms/2 bathrooms – $600 per month – (305) 111-2222 </I></B>

HTML uses a finite set of predefined tags, such as <B> or <I>, for bold and italics, respectively. XML, however, is much more general because it has an infinite number of tags that are defined as necessary in different applications. In other words, XML is ***extensible***, meaning that it can be expanded as necessary to include additional data. Consider:

<Apartment>

    <Description> 2 bedrooms/2 bathrooms </Description>

    <Availability> Immediate occupancy </Availability>

    <Amenities> Swimming pool; close to campus </Amenities>

    <Telephone> (305)111-2222 </Telephone>

    <Rent> $600 per month </Rent>

    <Security> 1 month </Security>

</Apartment>

The original document has been expanded to include information on availability, amenities, and security deposit for our apartment listing. The syntax is straightforward, but it behooves us to make the following observations:

1. An XML document is divided into *elements*. Each element contains a start tag, an ending tag, and the associated data. The start tag contains the name of the element. The ending tag contains the element's name preceded by a slash.

2. XML tags are case sensitive; for example, <Security> 1 month </security> is *incorrect* because the start and ending tags are not the same case.

3. XML elements can be nested to any depth, but each inner element (or child) must be entirely contained within the outer element (or parent); for example, the Description and Availability elements are nested within the Apartment element.

Figure C.1 displays an XML document that was created in the ***Notepad accessory***, a simple text editor that is provided with Windows. The ***XML declaration*** in line one specifies the XML version and ***character encoding*** used in the document. Our document uses the Unicode Transformation Format that corresponds to the standard ASCII character scheme, wherein each character is represented by 8 bits. The question mark and angled brackets are part of the declaration. (A declaration is not required, but it is good practice to include it.) The document also contains a comment in line two to identify the author. The indentation throughout the document makes it easier to read and is not required.

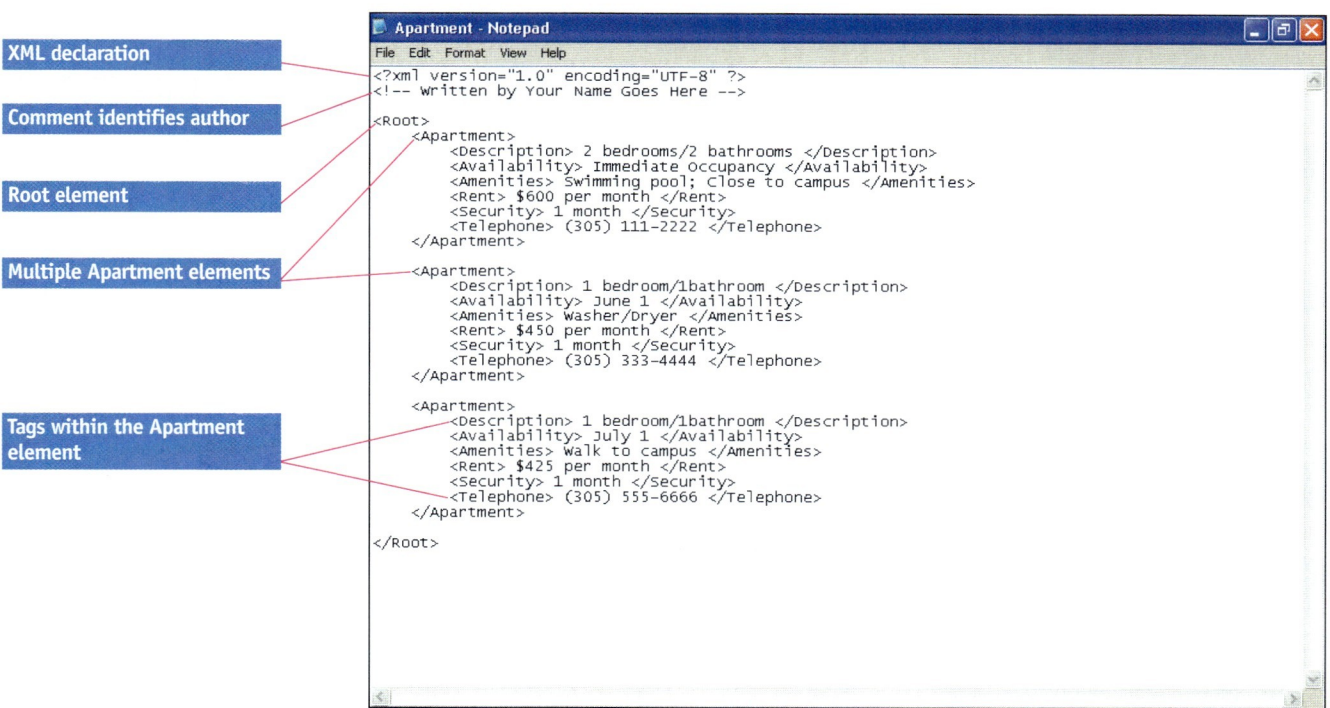

FIGURE C.1 Introduction to XML

Figure C.1 includes a ***root element*** to permit multiple occurrences of the apartment element within the same XML document; that is, each apartment element is nested within the root element. The root element may also be given a different name—for example, "Listing" or "ClassifiedListing"—that is more descriptive of the data in the document. The completed document is in essence a "data file" with multiple apartment records that can be used by any XML-compliant application. We continue with a hands-on exercise in which you create the document in Figure C.1.

hands-on exercise 1
Introduction to XML

Objective Use the Notepad accessory to create and edit a simple XML document; use Internet Explorer to view the XML document. Use Figure C.2 as a guide.

Step 1: **Create the XML Document**

- Click the **Start button**, click **All Programs**, click **Accessories**, and then open and maximize the **Notepad accessory**. Enter the text of the document exactly as it appears in Figure C.2a. Note the following:
  - We omitted the starting bracket in front of the Telephone tag deliberately to show you what happens when you make a syntax error.
  - The indentation (four spaces in our example) is not required, but is included to make the document easier to read.

- Pull down the **File menu**. Click the **Save command** to display the Save As dialog box. Click the **Create New Folder button** to create the **Exploring XML folder**.

- Enter **Apartment.xml** as the file name, select **Text Documents** as the file type, and **UTF-8** as the encoding type. Click the **Save button**. Close Notepad.

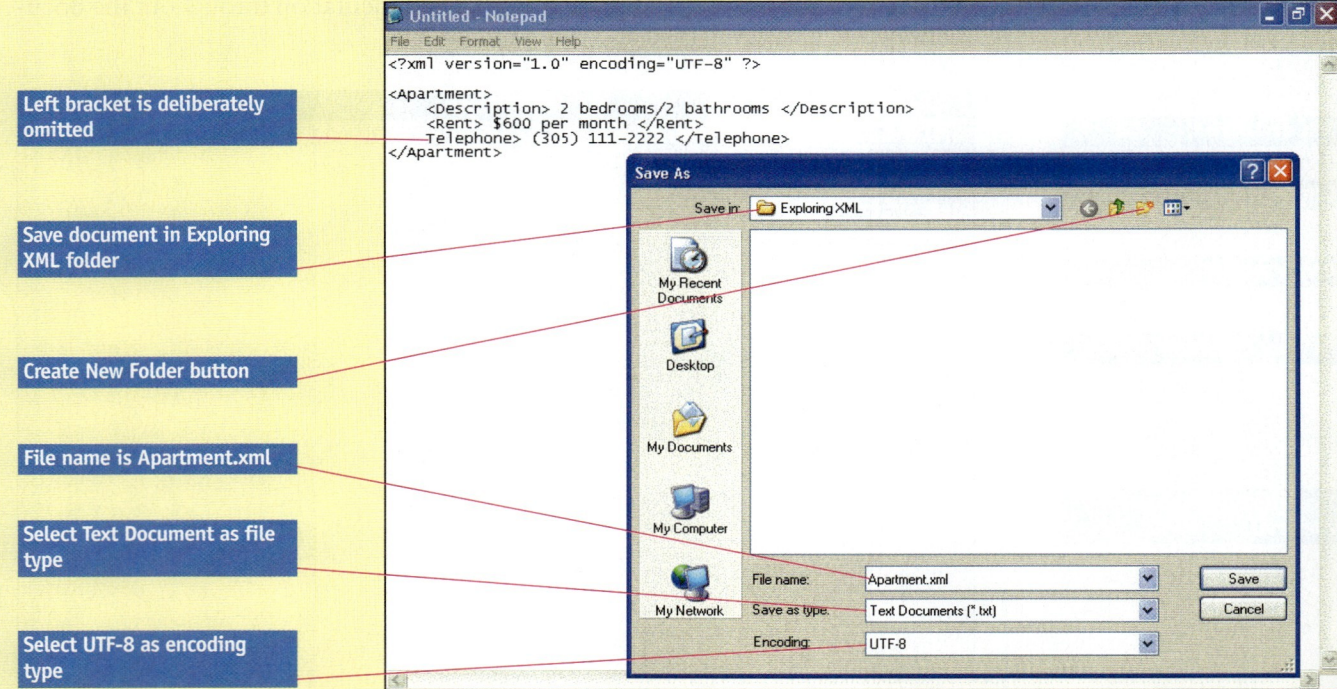

(a) Create the XML Document (step 1)

FIGURE C.2 Hands-on Exercise 1

CHARACTER ENCODING

Every character (e.g., the letters of the alphabet, punctuation symbols, numbers, and so on) is stored internally (in memory or in auxiliary storage) as a numeric value. The character encoding determines which number represents which character; for example, UTF-8 stands for Unicode Transformation Format and corresponds to the standard ASCII character scheme wherein each character is represented by one byte (8 bits). Other encoding schemes are also possible.

Step 2: **Check for Errors**

- Start Internet Explorer. Pull down the **File menu**, click the **Open command**, then click the **Browse button** in the Open dialog box. Change to the **Exploring XML folder**.
- Click the **drop-down arrow** in the Files of type list box and select **All files**, and then (try to) open the **Apartment.xml document** that you just created. The document will not open because of the omitted bracket in front of the Telephone tag (and/or because you made additional errors).
- You should see an error message similar to the one in Figure C.2b. Click the tool to **Edit with XML editor** on the Standard toolbar in Internet Explorer.
- The document opens in Notepad. Click in front of the Telephone tag and insert the left bracket (and/or correct any additional errors you may have made).
- Pull down the **File menu** and click the **Save command**. Click in the **Internet Explorer window**, and then click the **Refresh button** on the Standard toolbar.
- The XML document will open, provided you have corrected all of the errors.

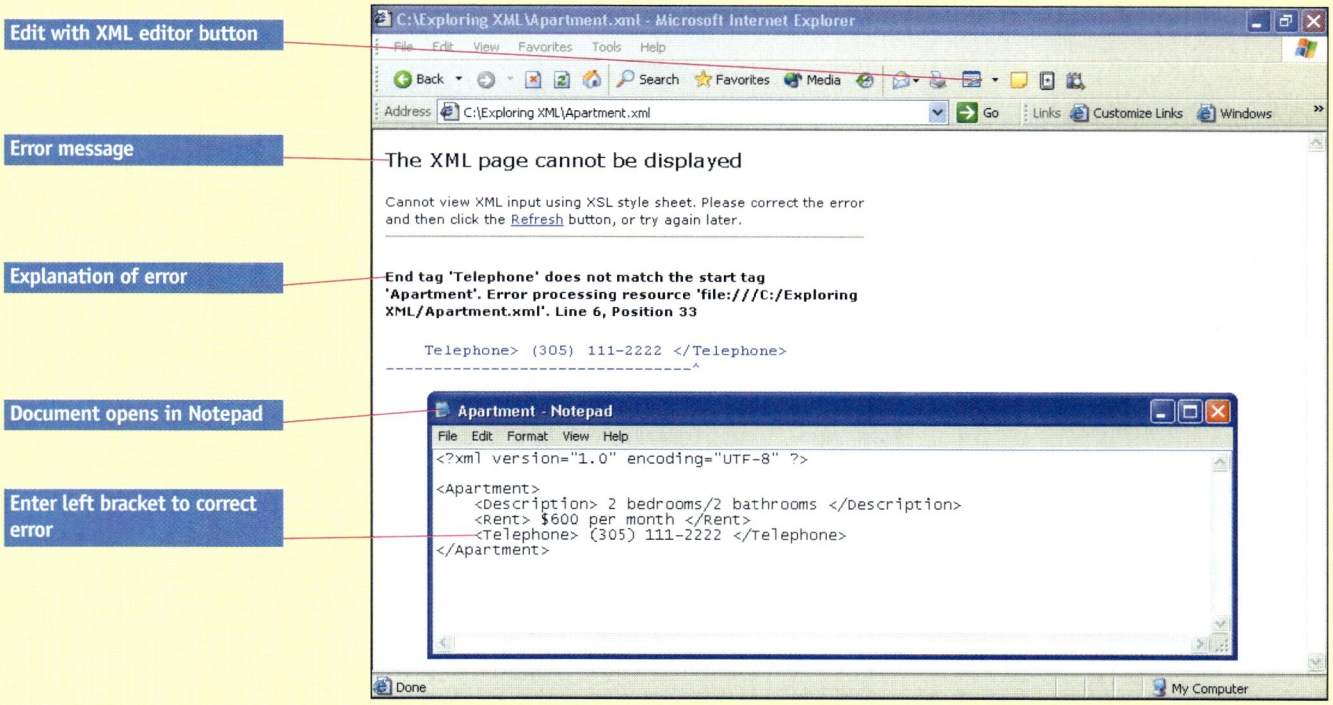

(b) Check for Errors (step 2)

FIGURE C.2   Hands-on Exercise 1 (*continued*)

NOTEPAD VERSUS INTERNET EXPLORER

The creation of an XML document is an iterative process that requires the user to switch back and forth between the Notepad accessory and Internet Explorer. You create the document in Notepad, view it in Internet Explorer, and return to Notepad to make the necessary changes. You must remember to save the document in Notepad and to click the Refresh button in Internet Explorer to see the latest version. The document is displayed differently in each application. Notepad is a simple text editor and does not handle the XML tags differently from other text. Internet Explorer is XML-aware and displays the tags and associated data with different formatting.

Step 3: Expand the Document

- You should see the corrected XML document as shown in the Internet Explorer window of Figure C.2c. There are two ways to return to the Notepad accessory:
  - We recommend that you click the **Notepad button** on the Windows taskbar since the Apartment document is still open.
  - Alternatively, you can click the **Edit with XML editor button** on the Internet Explorer toolbar, but this opens a second copy of Notepad if the document is already open. Multiple copies are confusing, but will not cause a problem, provided you remember to save all of your editing changes.
- Add the comment as shown in the second line. The syntax is very precise; that is, the comment begins and ends with <!-- and -->, respectively.
- Add the **Availability**, **Amenities**, and **Security elements** to complete the description of the apartment listing. Save the document.
- Click in the **Internet Explorer window**. Click the **Refresh button** on the Internet Explorer toolbar to view the expanded document.
- Correct any errors by returning to Notepad. Save the document after each editing change. Be sure to click the **Refresh button** to see the results of those changes in Internet Explorer.

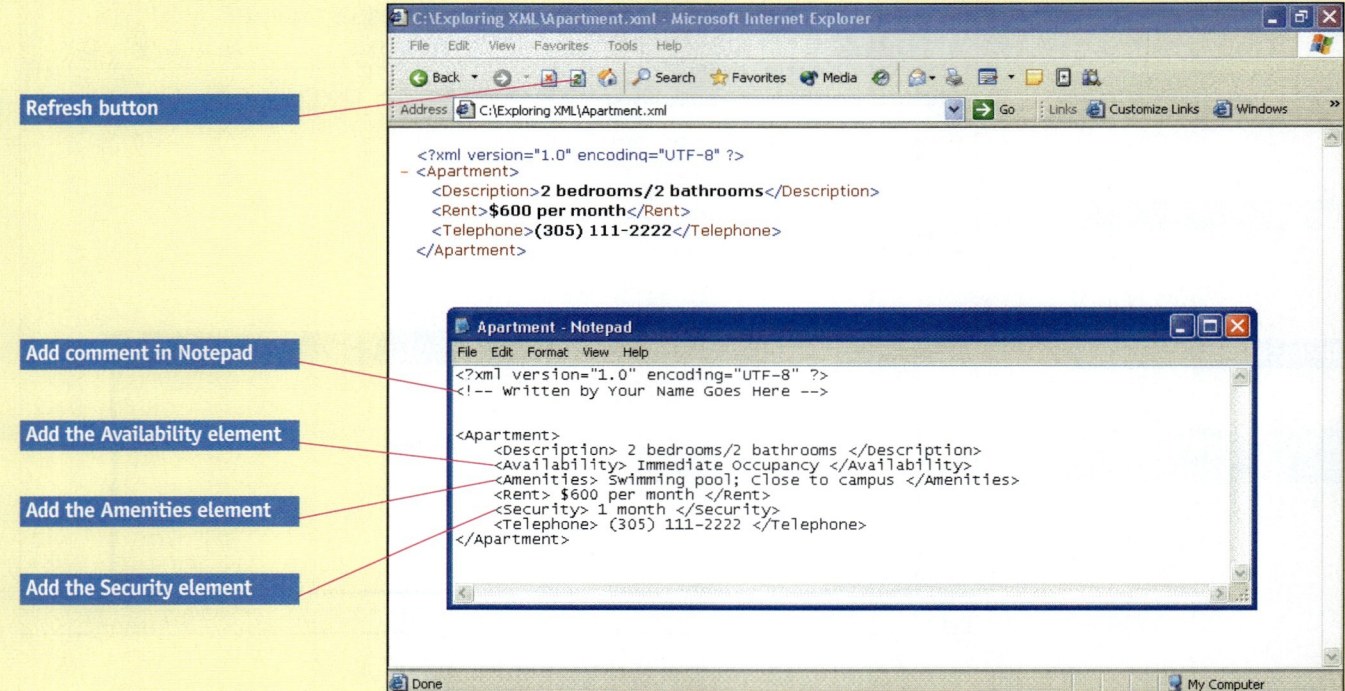

(c) Expand the Document (step 3)

FIGURE C.2 Hands-on Exercise 1 (*continued*)

A QUICK REVIEW OF XML SYNTAX

Each element in an XML document contains a start tag, an ending tag, and the associated data. The start tag contains the name of the element. The ending tag contains the element's name preceded by a slash. The element name can contain letters, numbers, and other characters, but it cannot start with a number or punctuation character, nor can it start with the letters xml. Element names may not contain spaces (an underscore or initial caps are used instead) and are case sensitive.

Step 4: **Add the Root Element**

- Continue the development of the XML document by adding the Root element as shown in the Notepad window in Figure C.2d.
  - Click at the end of the second line, which contains the comment. Press **Enter** to start a new line.
  - Type **<Root>** to create the root element.
  - Press **Ctrl+End** to move to the end of the document. Press **Enter**.
  - Type **</Root>** to complete the root element. Press **Enter**.
  - Add indentation (four spaces per line) or not as you see fit. The indentation in our document is not required.

- Add a second Apartment element as shown in Figure C.2d that contains only the Description element. Save the document.

- Click in the **Internet Explorer window**. Click the **Refresh button** on the Internet Explorer toolbar to view the expanded document.

- Correct any errors by returning to Notepad. Save the document after each editing change. Be sure to click the **Refresh button** to see the results of those changes in Internet Explorer.

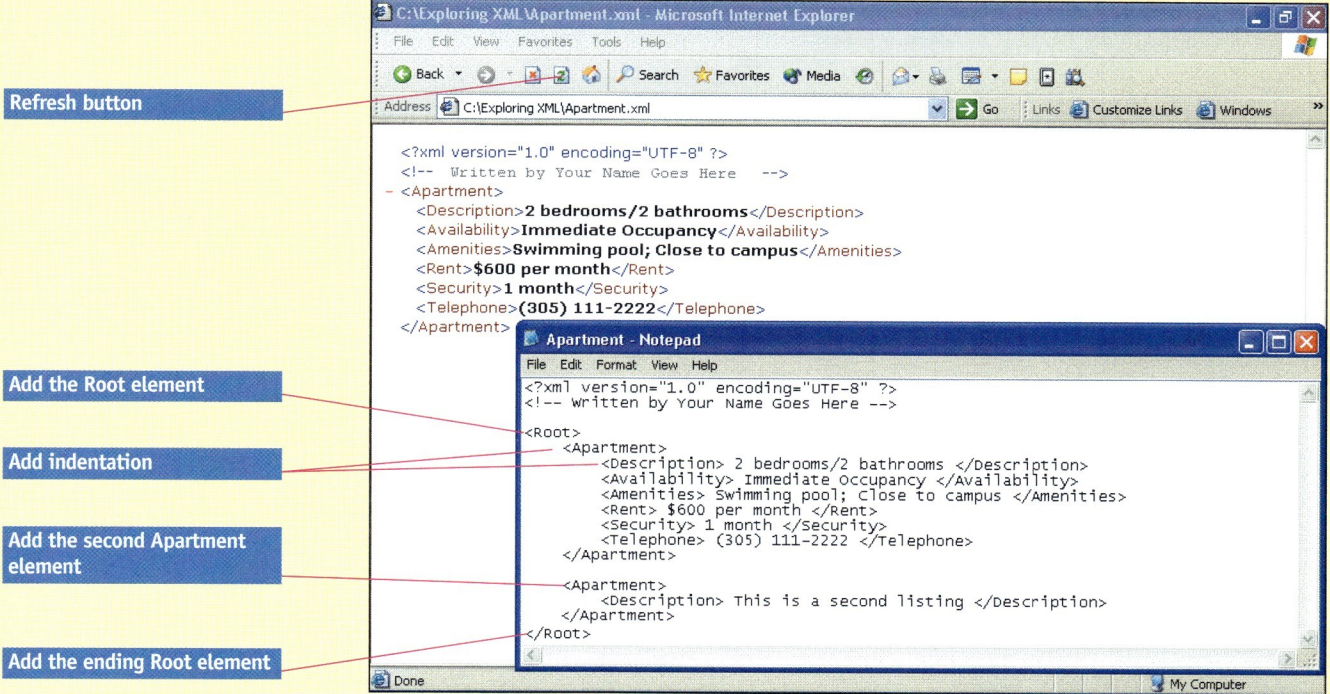

(d) Add the Root Element (step 4)

FIGURE C.2   Hands-on Exercise 1 (*continued*)

USE WHAT YOU KNOW

Notepad is a Windows accessory that follows common conventions and keyboard shortcuts; for example, Ctrl+X, Ctrl+C, and Ctrl+V are keyboard shortcuts to cut, copy, and paste, respectively. Other shortcuts are also available, such as Ctrl+S and Ctrl+P to save and print the document, respectively. (You can also use the Alt key plus an underlined letter to pull down a menu, such as Alt+F to pull down the file menu, and then type the letter S or P to save or print.) And don't forget the Edit menu, which provides access to the Find and Replace commands.

Step 5: **Complete the Document**

- You should be back in Internet Explorer as shown in Figure C.2e. (The third apartment listing for a 1 bedroom/1 bath apartment has not yet been entered.)
- Click the – **sign** that appears next to the second Apartment element. The minus sign changes to a plus sign and the information within the Apartment element is no longer visible.
- Click the – **sign** next to the Root element, which collapses the Root element. Click the + **sign** (that now appears) next to the Root element to expand the element.
- Use Notepad to add a third apartment listing (**1 bedroom/1 bathroom**) as shown in Figure C.2e. Check the document for accuracy, save it, and then print the completed document from Notepad for your instructor.
- Close Notepad. Click **Yes** if you are prompted to save the changes.
- Click in the **Internet Explorer window**, click the **Refresh button**, and then print the XML document from Internet Explorer. How does this document differ from the one printed in Notepad?
- Close Internet Explorer.

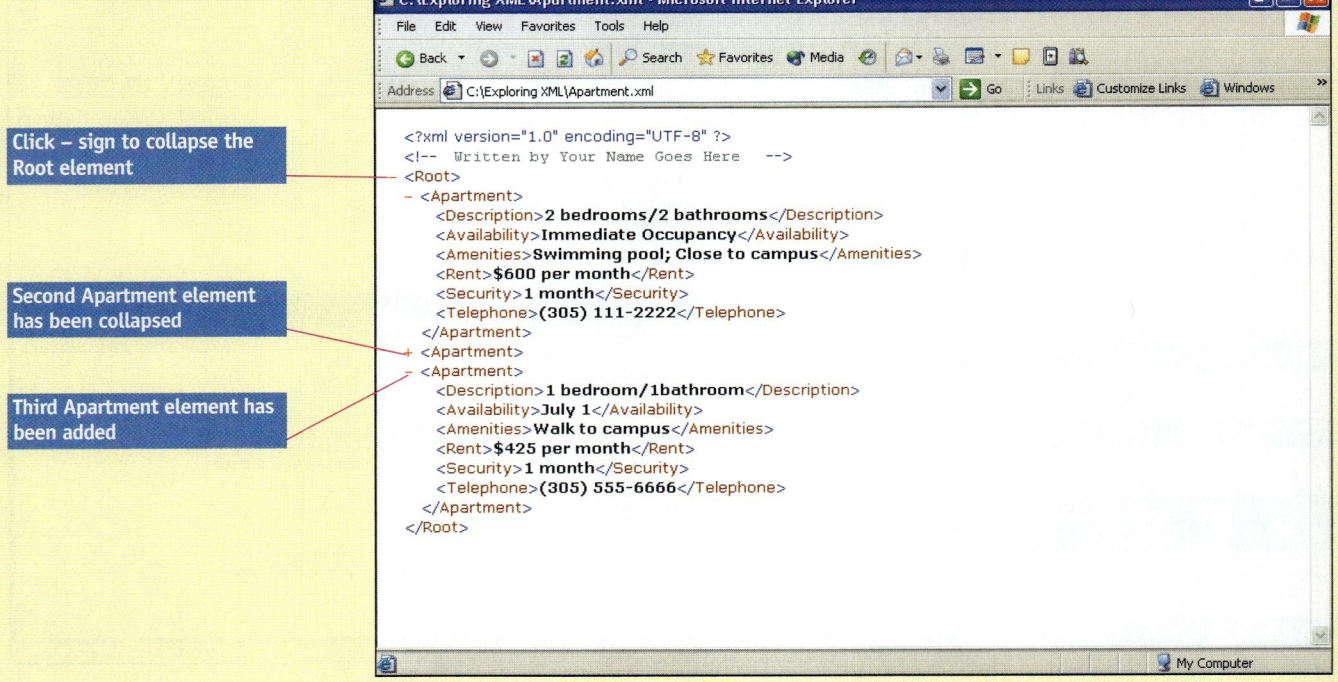

(e) Complete the Document (step 5)

FIGURE C.2 Hands-on Exercise 1 (*continued*)

EXPAND AND COLLAPSE THE DATA

The plus and minus signs that appear next to the elements within an XML document follow the same conventions as the plus and minus signs next to the folders in Windows Explorer. Click a plus sign and the data expands. Click a minus sign and the data collapses. Internet Explorer is XML-aware and prints the document to show only the expanded elements. Notepad, however, is unaware of the XML tags and prints the entire document.

MICROSOFT EXCEL AND XML

Microsoft Excel is designed to analyze and manipulate data, but the source of that data is irrelevant. It may originate within a worksheet, it may be imported from an Access table or query, it may come from a text file, or as you might expect in a chapter on XML, from an XML document as shown in Figure C.3. In this example, the workbook is linked dynamically to an XML document, which originated from a corporate mainframe that updates the sales performance of its account representatives on a daily basis. The mainframe generates the raw data; Excel is used to analyze the data to see how well the organization is meeting its sales goals.

Microsoft Excel provides full XML support that enables the exchange of information between an XML source document and an Excel workbook. You attach the XML definition (schema) to the workbook and then you map the XML elements in the schema to the cells in the workbook. The data is brought into the worksheet as a *list* (a contiguous set of rows and columns), as indicated by the blue line around the data. The drop-down arrows that appear in each field heading indicate that the AutoFilter command (which enables you to display selected records) is on.

The *XML source pane* in Figure C.3 contains six fields for each employee, which are mapped to the associated worksheet. The worksheet also contains an additional field, PercentOfGoal in column G, which is calculated by dividing the YearToDate sales by the SalesGoal. *Conditional formatting* is used to display values of 100% or more in blue; that is, the worksheet highlights those employees who have reached their goals. The worksheet also calculates the company totals for the SalesGoal, YearToDate, and PercentOfGoal fields in cells E17, F17, and G17, respectively.

Think again about the relationship between XML and Excel. The mainframe generates the XML data, which is then linked to an Excel workbook for analysis. The underlying XML data changes continually (e.g., the sales data may be updated daily on the mainframe), but the data in the workbook will remain current by executing the *refresh command* every time the workbook is opened.

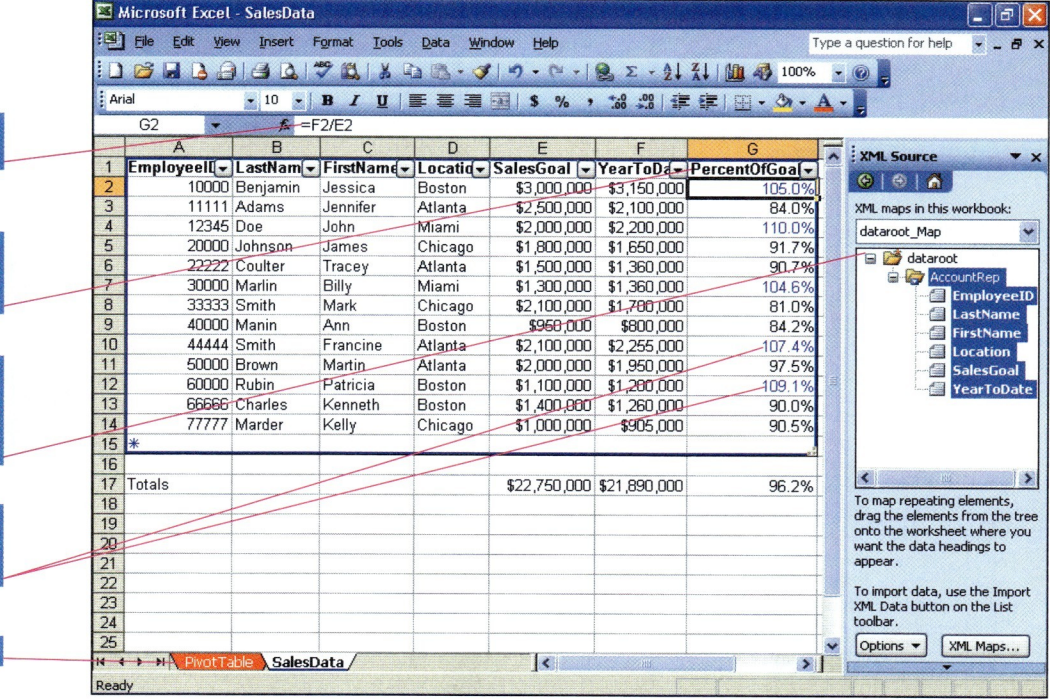

FIGURE C.3 Excel and XML

MICROSOFT OFFICE EXCEL 2003 REVISED 661

hands-on exercise 2

Excel and XML

Objective Import and refresh XML data into a workbook; create a pivot table. Use Figure C.4 as a guide. (You will need to download the practice files.)

Step 1: **Import the XML Data**

- Start Excel. Pull down the **Data menu**, click the **XML command**, and click the **Import command** to display the Import XML dialog box.

- Change to the **Exploring XML folder** (in the **Exploring Excel folder**), select the **SalesData document**, and click the **Import button**. (Click **OK** if you see a message saying that the XML source does not refer to a schema.)

- You should see the Import Data dialog box. The option button to put the data as an XML list in an existing worksheet is already selected, with cell A1 specified by default. Click **OK**. The XML data is imported into the workbook.
  - ❏ The first row in the list contains the field names, which identify the data in that column.
  - ❏ The down arrow next to each field name implies that the AutoFilter command (in the Data menu) is on.

- Open the **XML Source task pane** as shown in Figure C.4a. Click the **Options button** within the task pane to see the available options for an XML list. Press **Esc** to suppress the option list.

- **Right click** the tab for Sheet2 to display a context-sensitive menu and click the **Delete command**. Delete Sheet3 in similar fashion.

- Save the workbook as **SalesData** in the **Exploring XML folder**. Close the task pane so that you have more room in which to work.

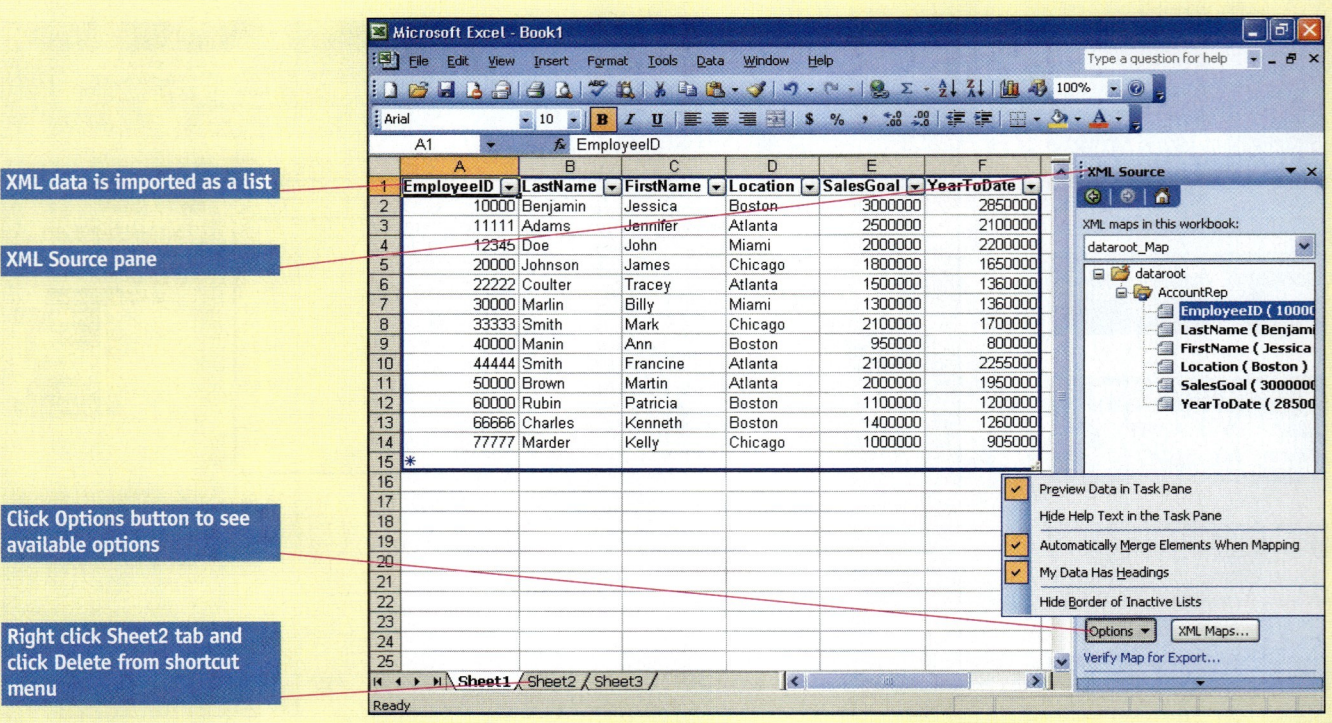

(a) Import the XML Data (step 1)

FIGURE C.4 Hands-on Exercise 2

Step 2: **Analyze the Data**

- Click in **cell G1** and type **PercentOfGoal** as the column heading. Click in **cell G2**. Type an **equal sign**, click in **cell F2**, type a **/**, then click in **cell E2** and press **Enter**. You will see .95. Widen column G as necessary.

- Change the formatting in **cell G2** to **Percent with one decimal**. Copy the formula in **cell G2** to **cells G3:G14** to display the percent of goal for each employee. Format cells **E2:F17** as **Currency** with **zero decimal places**.

- Click in **cell A16** and enter **Totals**. Click in **cell E16** and enter the formula **=SUM(E2:E15)**. Copy this formula to **cell F16**. Copy the formula from **cell G14** to **cell G16** to compute the percent of goal for the company as a whole.

- Click and drag to select **cells G2:G17**. Pull down the **Format menu** and click **Conditional Formatting** to display the dialog box in Figure C.4b. Click the arrow in the list box and select **greater than or equal to**. Enter **100%**.

- Click the **Format button**, click the **Font tab** in the Format Cells dialog box, then change the color to **blue**. Click **OK** to close the Conditional Formatting dialog box, then click **OK** to close the Format Cells dialog box.

- The sales percentages for employees who have made goal are shown in blue.

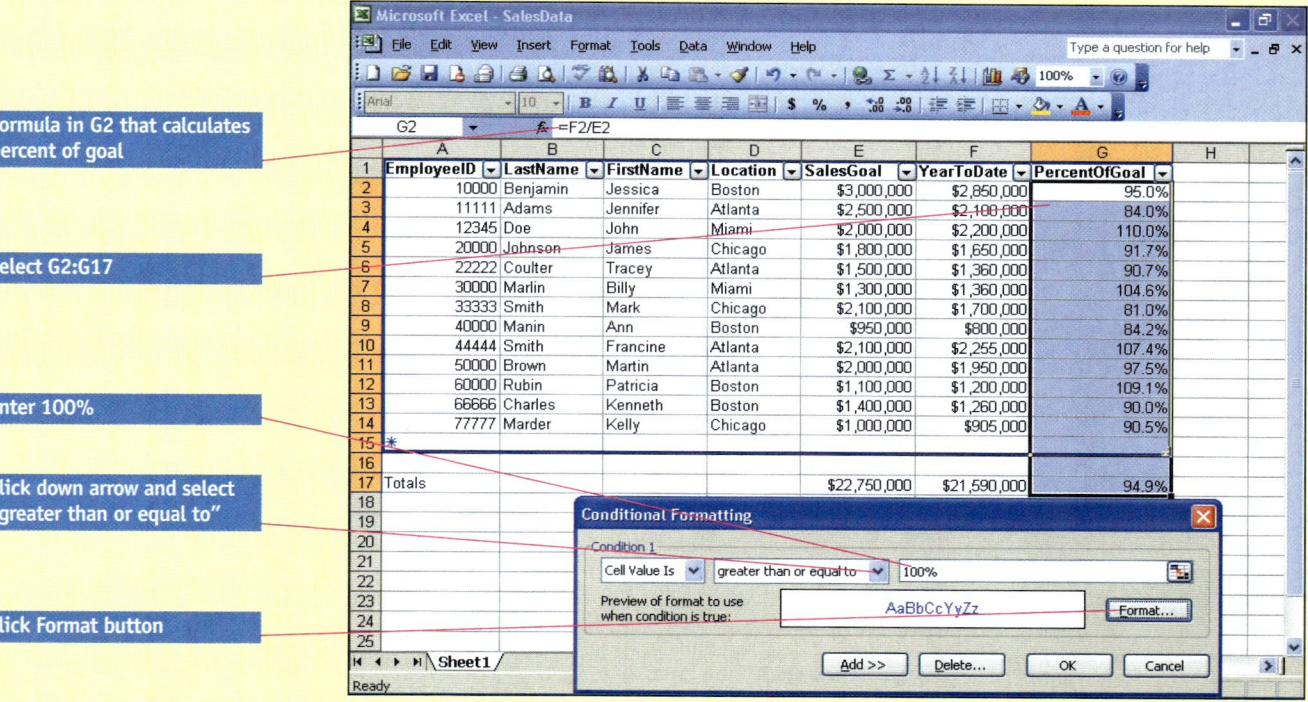

(b) Analyze the Data (step 2)

FIGURE C.4   Hands-on Exercise 2 (*continued*)

USE POINTING TO ENTER FORMULAS

A cell reference can be typed directly into a formula, or it can be entered more easily through pointing. Select the cell to contain the formula, type an equal sign to begin the formula, click (or move to) the cell containing the reference, then press the F4 key as necessary to change from relative to absolute or mixed references. Type any arithmetic operator to place the cell reference in the formula, then continue pointing to additional cells. Press Enter to complete the formula.

Step 3: **Create the Pivot Table**

- Click anywhere in the employee list. Pull down the **Data menu** and then click **PivotTable and PivotChart Report** to start the Pivot Table Wizard.
- Select the options indicating the data comes from a **Microsoft Office Excel list or database** and that you want to create just a **PivotTable**. Click **Next**.
- Cells A1 through G14 have been selected automatically. Click **Next**.
- The option button to put the pivot table report into a new worksheet is selected. Click **Finish**. A new worksheet has been added to the workbook as shown in Figure C.4c.
- Click the **Location field button** and drag it to the row area. Click the **SalesGoal field button** and drag it to the data area. Click the **YearToDate field button** and drag it to the data area.
- Click the **PercentOfGoal field button** and drag it to the data area; release the mouse when you see the message on the status bar indicating that you are dropping the field in the data area. Save the workbook.

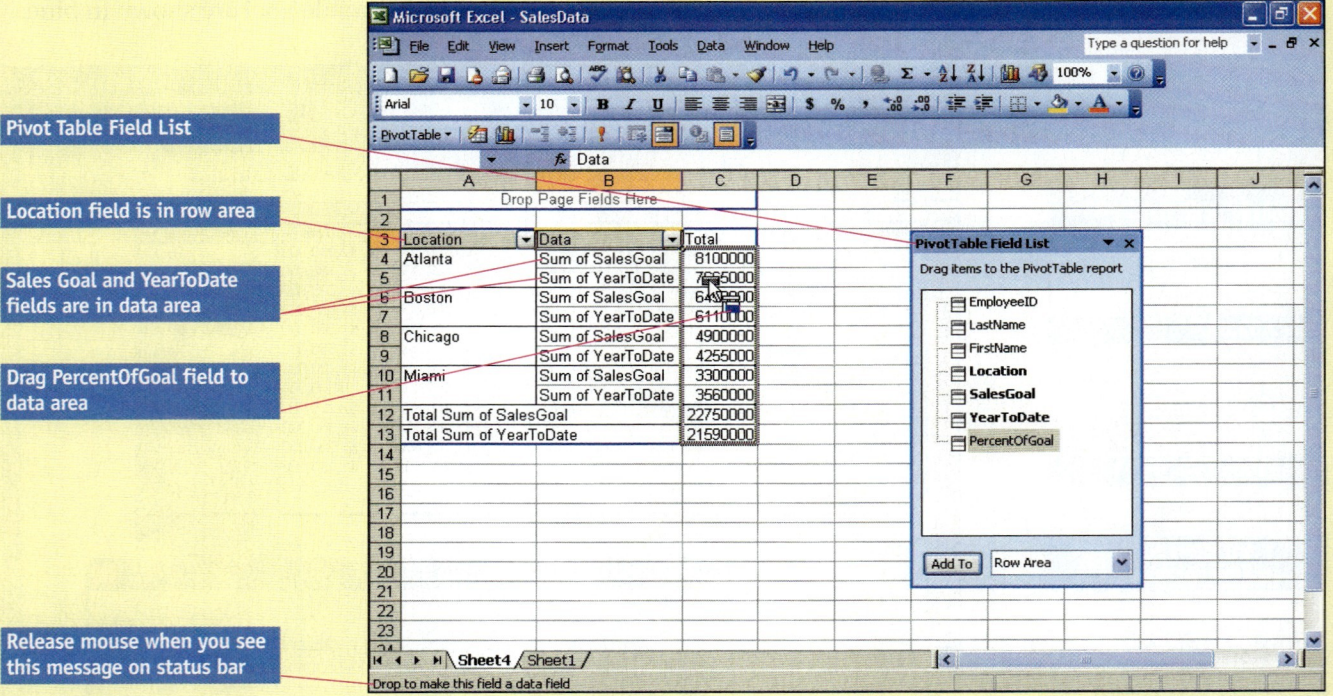

(c) Create the Pivot Table (step 3)

FIGURE C.4 Hands-on Exercise 2 (*continued*)

MODIFY THE PIVOT TABLE

Don't be discouraged if you fail to create the pivot table correctly on your first attempt. Right click any cell in the pivot table to display a context-sensitive menu, click the PivotTable Wizard command, then click the Layout button to display an alternate screen that makes it easy to change the fields and associated calculations within the table. You can add a new field to the row, column, or data area by dragging the field from the field list at the left to the appropriate area in the table. Conversely, you can delete a field simply by dragging the field away from the table.

Step 4: **Complete the Pivot Table**

- Close the pivot table field list. Right click in **cell C6** to display a context-sensitive menu, and then click the **Field Settings command** to display the PivotTable Field dialog box in Figure C.4d.

- Select the **Average function**. Click the **Number command button**, change to **Percentage format**, and specify **one decimal place**. Click **OK** to close the Format Cells dialog box.

- Click **OK** a second time to close the PivotTable Field dialog box. You should see the average percent of goal for each location (e.g., 94.9% for Atlanta).

- Change the formatting for the **SalesGoal** and **YearToDate** fields to **Currency** with **no decimals** in similar fashion.

- Double click the worksheet tab to select the sheet name (Sheet4 in our worksheet), type **PivotTable** as the new name, and press **Enter**. **Right click** the worksheet tab, click the **Tab color command**, choose a color, and click **OK**.

- Change the name of Sheet1 to **SalesData**. Change the color of the tab to **blue**.

- Save the workbook.

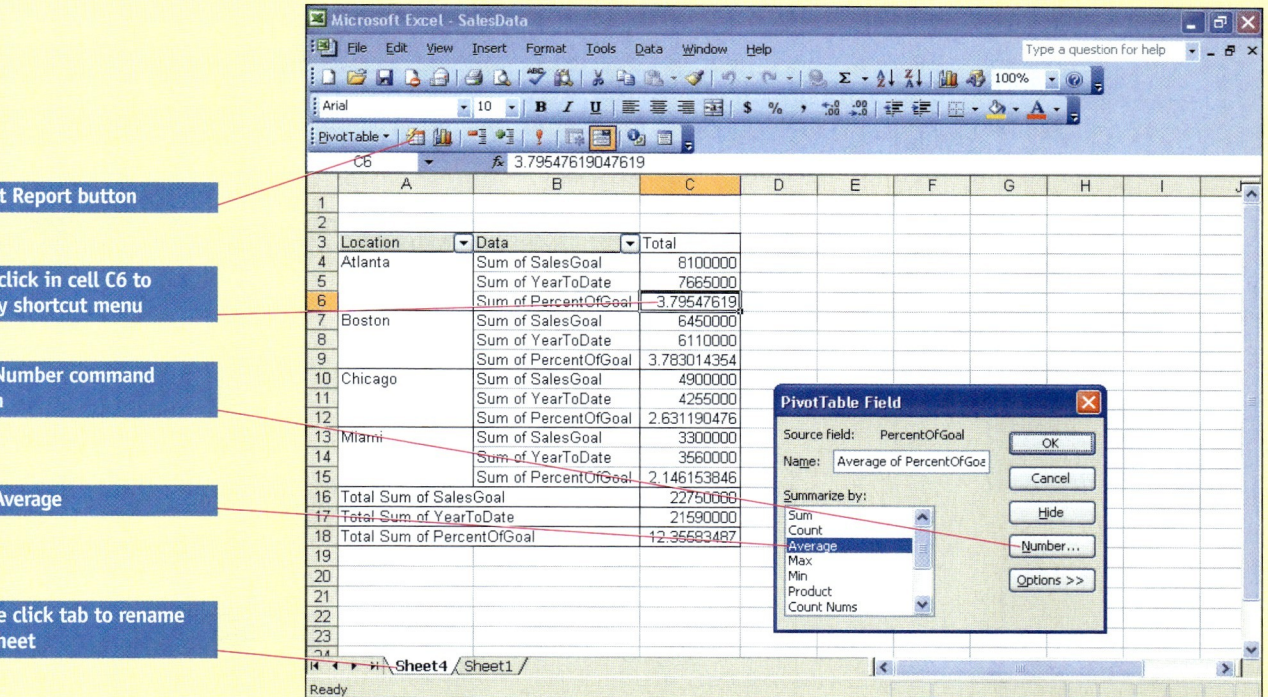

(d) Complete the Pivot Table (step 4)

FIGURE C.4 Hands-on Exercise 2 (continued)

THE FORMAT REPORT BUTTON

Why settle for a traditional report in black and white or shades of gray when you can choose from preformatted reports in a variety of styles and colors? Click the Format Report button on the Pivot Table toolbar to display the AutoFormat dialog box, where you select the style of your report. (To return to the default formatting, scroll to the end of the AutoFormat dialog box and select PivotTable Classic.)

Step 5: **Edit the XML Data**

- Start **Windows Explorer**, change to the **Exploring XML folder**, then double click the **SalesData.xml file** to open the document in Internet Explorer. Click the tool to **Edit with XML editor** on the Standard toolbar in Internet Explorer.

- The SalesData XML document should open in Notepad as shown in Figure C.4e. (If this does not occur, click the **Start button**, click **All Programs**, click the **Accessories group**, and open **Notepad**. Pull down the **File menu** and open the **SalesData.xml document**.)

- Click and drag to select the **YearToDate** sales for Jessica Benjamin, then type **3150000** to replace the existing value. Pull down the **File menu** and click the **Save command**.

- Click in the **Internet Explorer window**, and then click the **Refresh button**. You should see the updated value for the year-to-date sales. Print the updated XML document for your instructor.

- Close Internet Explorer. Close Notepad.

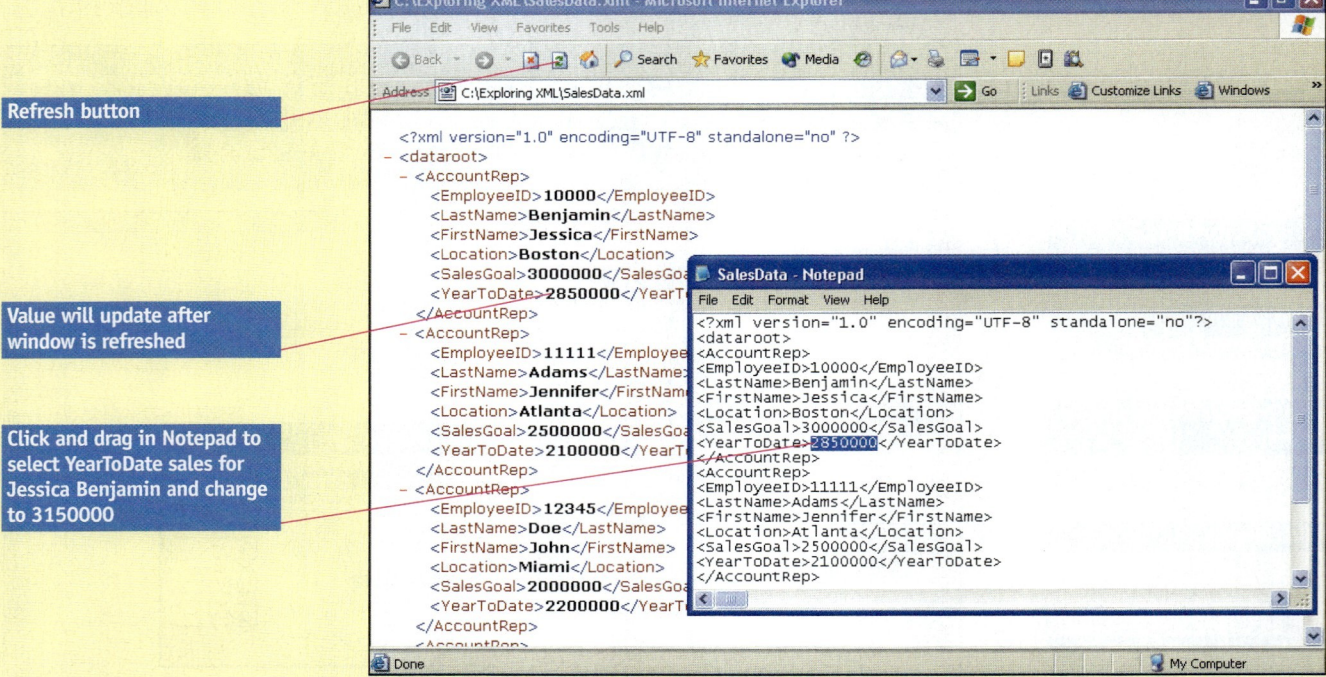

(e) Edit the XML Data (step 5)

FIGURE C.4 Hands-on Exercise 2 (*continued*)

INTERNET EXPLORER VERSUS NOTEPAD

Internet Explorer is an XML-aware application that automatically indents XML elements to show their relationships to one another, and that further displays the XML tags in different colors for ease of reading. Internet Explorer cannot, however, edit an XML document. Notepad, on the other hand, is a simple text editor that does not treat XML tags differently from other text. You can, however, indent the various tags by pressing the space bar as necessary. The indentation (if any) has no effect on the resulting code.

Step 6: **Refresh the Data**

- You should be back in Excel. **Right click** any cell in the employee list to display the context-sensitive menu in Figure C.4f, click the **XML command**, and then click **Refresh XML data**.

- The data for Jessica Benjamin is updated to reflect year-to-date sales of $3,150,000 and 105% of goal. The company totals have been updated as well to show year-to-date sales of $21,890,000 and 96.2% of goal.

- Click the tab for the **PivotTable**, click anywhere in the pivot table, then click the **Refresh Data button** on the PivotTable toolbar. (The pivot table has to be manually refreshed whenever the underlying data in the workbook changes.)

- The pivot table is updated to show company year-to-date sales of $21,890,000 and 95.8% of goal. The latter is different from the "same number" on the Employee worksheet, but it is not an error. (See the boxed tip below.)

- Print both worksheets. Use the **Page Setup command** to be sure that each worksheet fits on a single sheet of paper. Save the workbook. Exit Excel.

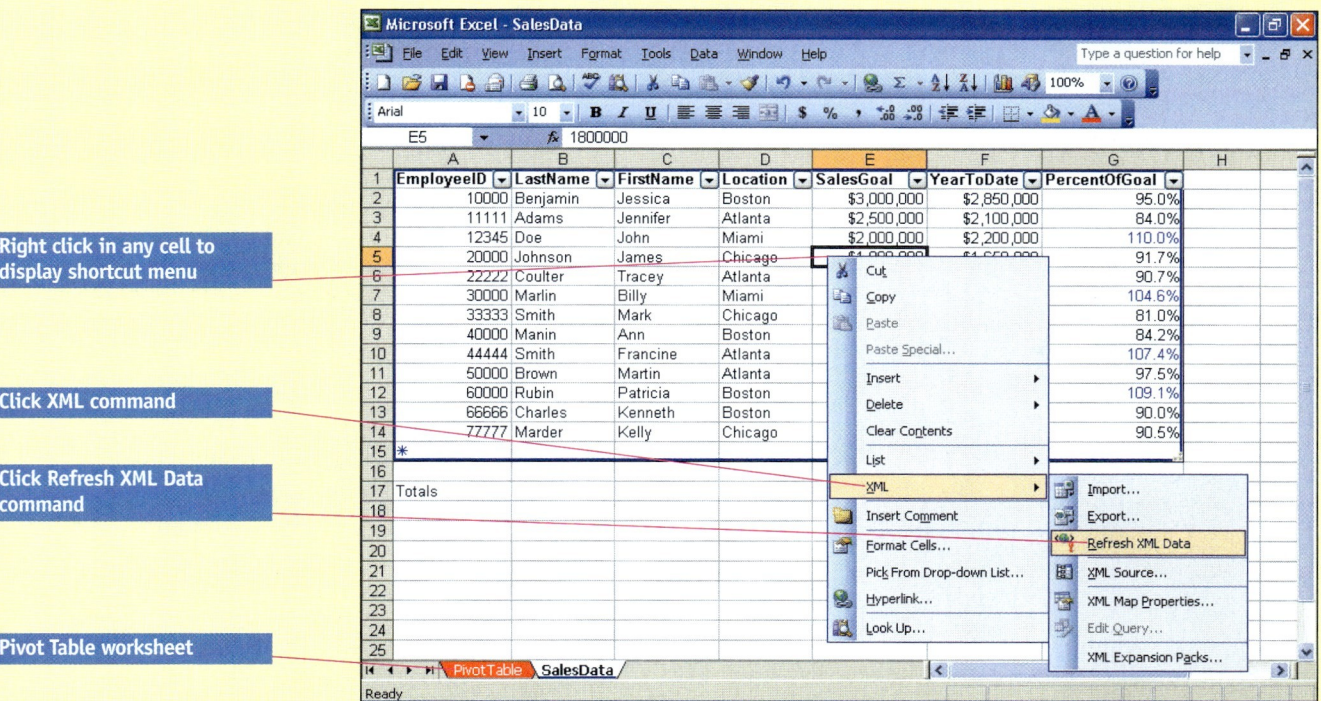

(f) Refresh the Data (step 6)

FIGURE C.4 Hands-on Exercise 2 (*continued*)

TWO DIFFERENT AVERAGES

The percent of goal for the company is computed differently in the two worksheets. The SalesData worksheet sums the SalesGoal and YearToDate fields for all 13 employees, and then it divides one number by the other; that is, the value in cell G16 is computed by the formula =F16/E16 and is displayed as 96.2%. The pivot table, however, takes the average percent of goal of all the employees; thus, it effectively adds the values in column G, then it divides by the number of employees. Both averages are "correct," but in this example, the average in the SalesData worksheet is the more meaningful result.

SUMMARY

XML (eXtensible Markup Language) is an industry standard for structuring data across applications, operating systems, and hardware devices. The XML syntax, known officially as the XML recommendation, was developed by the World Wide Web Consortium (commonly known as W3C), a public organization with the sole purpose of creating standards or recommendations for the Internet. (W3C also published the HTML specification. You can learn more about the organization and its standards by visiting their Web site at www.w3.org.)

XML is the latest step in the evolution of markup languages. It is not intended to replace HTML (Hypertext Markup language), which describes the formatting of a document rather than its structure. HTML uses a finite set of tags, such as <B> or <I>, for bold and italic, respectively. XML is more general because it is extensible (expandable) and thus has an infinite number of tags that are defined as necessary by the developer. XML is "data about data" and it does not contain any information about how to display that data.

An XML document is divided into elements. Each element contains a start tag, an ending tag, and the associated data. The start tag contains the name of the element. The ending tag contains the element's name preceded by a slash. XML tags are case sensitive; that is, the start and ending tags must match. XML elements can be nested to any depth, but each inner element (or child) must be entirely contained within the outer element (or parent). Every XML document has a root element, which is the single element in an XML file that contains all other elements.

The creation of an XML document is an iterative process that requires the user to switch back and forth between an editor (e.g., the Notepad accessory) and Internet Explorer. You create the document in Notepad, view it in Internet Explorer, and return to Notepad to make the necessary changes. It is important to save the document in Notepad after each set of changes, and to click the Refresh button in Internet Explorer to see the latest version. The document is displayed differently in each application. Notepad is a simple text editor and does not handle the XML tags differently from other text. Internet Explorer is XML-aware and displays the tags and associated data with appropriate formatting.

An XML document may contain a reference to a schema and/or a style sheet. The schema (XSD file) contains the rules, such as which fields are required and/or the type of data each field may contain. The style sheet (XSL document) describes the formatting or display of the data. Both documents, the schema and the style sheet, may be viewed and edited with the Notepad accessory.

XML is fully supported throughout Microsoft Office 2003. XML documents may be imported and/or exported into Word, Excel, and Access. Microsoft Office InfoPath 2003 is a new application in the Office suite that simplifies the creation of an XML form.

KEY TERMS

Character encoding 655
Conditional formatting 661
Element 655
Extensible .654
HTML (Hypertext
   Markup Language) 653
List 661

Notepad accessory 655
Pivot table .664
Refresh command 661
Root element 655
SGML (Standard Generalized
   Markup Language) 653
Tag 654

XML-aware 657
XML declaration 655
XML (eXtensible
   Markup Language) 653
XML source pane 661

CHAPTER 1

Getting Started with VBA:
Extending Microsoft Office 2003

OBJECTIVES

After reading this chapter you will:

1. Describe the relationship of VBA to Microsoft Office 2003.
2. Explain how to create, edit, and run a VBA procedure.
3. Use the MsgBox statement and InputBox function.
4. Explain how to debug a procedure by stepping through its statements.
5. Use the If...Then...Else statement to implement a decision.
6. Explain the Case statement.
7. Create a custom toolbar.
8. Describe several statements used to implement a loop.
9. Describe event-driven programming.

hands-on exercises

1. INTRODUCTION TO VBA
   Input: None
   Output: VBA workbook

2. DECISION MAKING
   Input: VBA workbook
   Output: VBA workbook

3. LOOPS AND DEBUGGING
   Input: VBA workbook
   Output: VBA workbook

4. EVENT-DRIVEN PROGRAMMING
   Input: VBA workbook; Financial Consultant workbook
   Output: VBA workbook; Financial Consultant workbook

5. EVENT-DRIVEN PROGRAMMING
   Input: VBA Switchboard and Security database
   Output: VBA Switchboard and Security database

CASE STUDY
ON-THE-JOB TRAINING

Your first job is going exceedingly well. The work is very challenging and your new manager, Phyllis Simon, is impressed with the Excel workbooks that you have developed thus far. Phyllis has asked you to take it to the next level by incorporating VBA procedures into future projects. You have some knowledge of Excel macros and have already used the macro recorder to record basic macros. You are able to make inferences about the resulting code, but you will need additional proficiency in VBA to become a true expert in Excel.

The good news is that you work for a company that believes in continuing education and promotes from within. Phyllis has assigned you to a new interdepartmental team responsible for creating high-level Excel applications that will be enhanced through VBA. Moreover, you have been selected to attend a week-long seminar to learn VBA so that you can become a valued member of the team. The seminar will be held in San Diego, California, where there is a strong temptation to study sand and surf rather than VBA. Thus, Phyllis expects you to complete a series of VBA procedures upon your return—just to be sure that you were not tempted to skip class and dip your toes into the water.

Your assignment is to read this chapter on VBA and focus on the first three hands-on exercises that develop the syntax for basic VBA statements—MsgBox, InputBox, decision making through If/Else and Case statements, and iteration through the For...Next and Do Until statements. You will then open the partially completed *VBA Case Study—On-the-Job Training*, start the VBA editor, and then complete the tasks presented in the procedures in Module1. (The requirements for each procedure appear as comments within the procedure.) Add a command button for each macro to the Excel workbook, and then print the worksheet and a copy of the completed module for your instructor. Last, but not least, create a suitable event procedure for closing the workbook.

INTRODUCTION TO VBA

Visual Basic for Applications (VBA) is a powerful programming language that is accessible from all major applications in Microsoft Office XP. You do not have to know VBA to use Office effectively, but even a basic understanding will help you to create more powerful documents. Indeed, you may already have been exposed to VBA through the creation of simple macros in Word or Excel. A ***macro*** is a set of instructions (i.e., a program) that simplifies the execution of repetitive tasks. It is created through the ***macro recorder*** that captures commands as they are executed, then converts those commands into a VBA program. (The macro recorder is present in Word, Excel, and PowerPoint, but not in Access.) You can create and execute macros without ever looking at the underlying VBA, but you gain an appreciation for the language when you do.

The macro recorder is limited, however, in that it captures only commands, mouse clicks, and/or keystrokes. As you will see, VBA is much more than just recorded keystrokes. It is a language unto itself, and thus, it contains all of the statements you would expect to find in any programming language. This lets you enhance the functionality of any macro by adding extra statements as necessary—for example, an InputBox function to accept data from the user, followed by an If . . . Then . . . Else statement to take different actions based on the information supplied by the user.

This supplement presents the rudiments of VBA and is suitable for use with any Office application. We begin by describing the VBA editor and how to create, edit, and run simple procedures. The examples are completely general and demonstrate the basic capabilities of VBA that are found in any programming language. We illustrate the MsgBox statement to display output to the user and the InputBox function to accept input from the user. We describe the For . . . Next statement to implement a loop and the If . . . Then . . . Else and Case statements for decision making. We also describe several debugging techniques to help you correct the errors that invariably occur. The last two exercises introduce the concept of event-driven programming, in which a procedure is executed in response to an action taken by the user. The material here is application-specific in conjunction with Excel and Access, but it can be easily extended to Word or PowerPoint.

One last point before we begin is that this supplement assumes no previous knowledge on the part of the reader. It is suitable for someone who has never been exposed to a programming language or written an Office macro. If, on the other hand, you have a background in programming or macros, you will readily appreciate the power inherent in VBA. VBA is an incredibly rich language that can be daunting to the novice. Stick with us, however, and we will show you that it is a flexible and powerful tool with consistent rules that can be easily understood and applied. You will be pleased at what you will be able to accomplish.

VBA is a programming language, and like any other programming language its programs (or procedures, as they are called) are made up of individual statements. Each ***statement*** accomplishes a specific task such as displaying a message to the user or accepting input from the user. Statements are grouped into ***procedures***, and procedures, in turn, are grouped into ***modules***. Every VBA procedure is classified as either public or private. A ***private procedure*** is accessible only from within the module in which it is contained. A ***public procedure***, on the other hand, can be accessed from any module.

The statement, however, is the basic unit of the language. Our approach throughout this supplement will be to present individual statements, then to develop simple procedures using those statements in a hands-on exercise. As you read the discussion, you will see that every statement has a precise ***syntax*** that describes how the statement is to be used. The syntax also determines the ***arguments*** (or parameters) associated with that statement, and whether those arguments are required or optional.

THE MSGBOX STATEMENT

The **MsgBox statement** displays information to the user. It is one of the most basic statements in VBA, but we use it to illustrate several concepts in VBA programming. Figure 1a contains a simple procedure called MsgBoxExamples, consisting of four individual MsgBox statements. All procedures begin with a ***procedure header*** and end with the ***End Sub statement***.

The MsgBox statement has one required argument, which is the message (or prompt) that is displayed to the user. All other arguments are optional, but if they are used, they must be entered in a specified sequence. The simplest form of the MsgBox statement is shown in example 1, which specifies a single argument that contains the text (or prompt) to be displayed. The resulting message box is shown in Figure 1b. The message is displayed to the user, who responds accordingly, in this case by clicking the OK button.

Example 2 extends the MsgBox statement to include a second parameter that displays an icon within the resulting dialog box as shown in Figure 1c. The type of icon is determined by a VBA ***intrinsic*** (or predefined) ***constant*** such as vbExclamation, which displays an exclamation point in a yellow triangle. VBA has many such constants that enable you to simplify your code, while at the same time achieving some impressive results.

Example 3 uses a different intrinsic constant, vbInformation, to display a different icon. It also extends the MsgBox statement to include a third parameter that is displayed on the title bar of the resulting dialog box. Look closely, for example, at Figures 1c and 1d, whose title bars contain "Microsoft Excel" and "Grauer/Barber", respectively. The first is the default entry (given that we are executing the procedure from within Microsoft Excel). You can, however, give your procedures a customized look by displaying your own text in the title bar.

Procedure header

```
Public Sub MsgBoxExamples()
'This procedure was written by John Doe on 6/10/2003

    MsgBox "Example 1 - VBA is not difficult"
    MsgBox "Example 2 - VBA is not difficult", vbExclamation
    MsgBox "Example 3 - VBA is not difficult", vbInformation, "Grauer/Barber"
    MsgBox "Example 4 - VBA is not difficult", , "Your name goes here"
End Sub
```

End Sub statement

(a) VBA Code

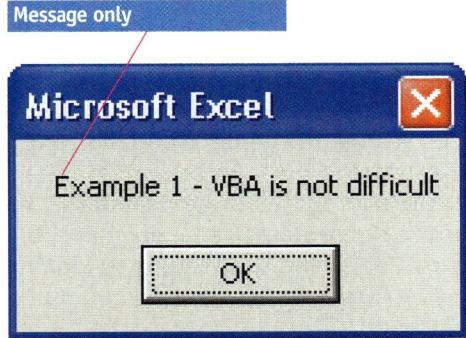

(b) Example 1—One Argument

(c) Example 2—Two Arguments

FIGURE 1 The MsgBox Statement

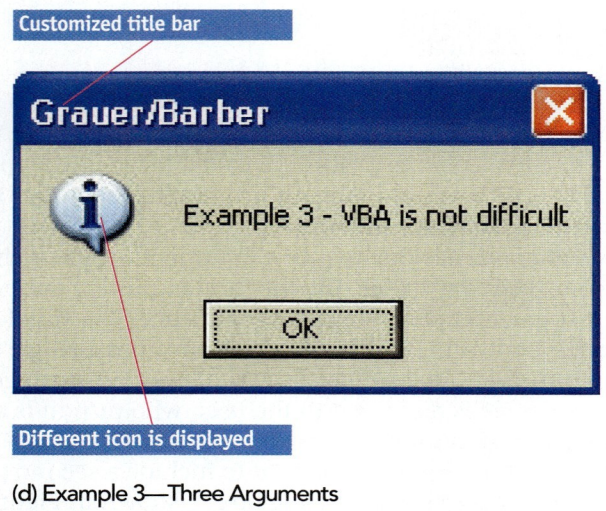
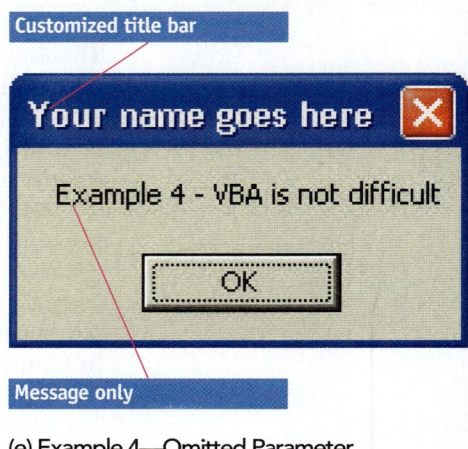

(d) Example 3—Three Arguments (e) Example 4—Omitted Parameter

FIGURE 1 The MsgBox Statement (*continued*)

Example 4 omits the second parameter (the icon), but includes the third parameter (the entry for the title bar). The parameters are positional, however, and thus the MsgBox statement contains two commas after the message to indicate that the second parameter has been omitted.

THE INPUTBOX FUNCTION

The MsgBox statement displays a prompt to the user, but what if you want the user to respond to the prompt by entering a value such as his or her name? This is accomplished using the ***InputBox function***. Note the subtle change in terminology in that we refer to the InputBox *function*, but the MsgBox *statement*. That is because a function returns a value, in this case the user's name, which is subsequently used in the procedure. In other words, the InputBox function asks the user for information, then it stores that information (the value returned by the user) for use in the procedure.

Figure 2 displays a procedure that prompts the user for a first and last name, after which it displays the information using the MsgBox statement. (The Dim statement at the beginning of the procedure is explained shortly.) Let's look at the first InputBox function, and the associated dialog box in Figure 2b. The InputBox function displays a prompt on the screen, the user enters a value ("Bob" in this example), and that value is stored in the variable that appears to the left of the equal sign (strFirstName). The concept of a variable is critical to every programming language. Simply stated, a ***variable*** is a named storage location that contains data that can be modified during program execution.

The MsgBox statement then uses the value of strFirstName to greet the user by name as shown in Figure 2c. This statement also introduces the ampersand to ***concatenate*** (join together) two different character strings, the literal "Good morning", followed by the value within the variable strFirstName.

The second InputBox function prompts the user for his or her last name. In addition, it uses a second argument to customize the contents of the title bar (VBA Primer in this example) as can be seen in Figure 2d. Finally, the MsgBox statement in Figure 2e displays both the first and last name through concatenation of multiple strings. This statement also uses the ***underscore*** to continue a statement from one line to the next.

VBA is not difficult, and you can use the MsgBox statement and InputBox function in conjunction with one another as the basis for several meaningful procedures. You will get a chance to practice in the hands-on exercise that follows shortly.

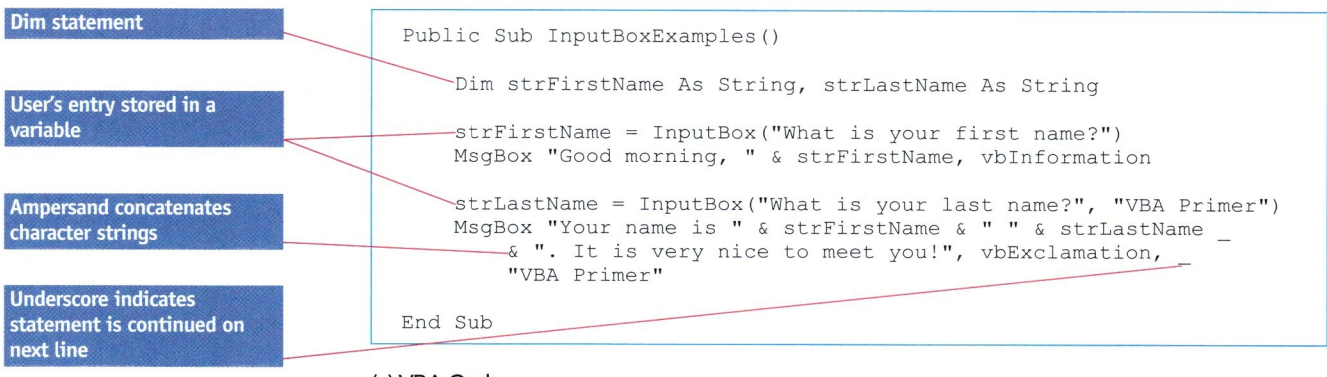

Dim statement

User's entry stored in a variable

Ampersand concatenates character strings

Underscore indicates statement is continued on next line

(a) VBA Code

(b) InputBox

(c) Concatenation

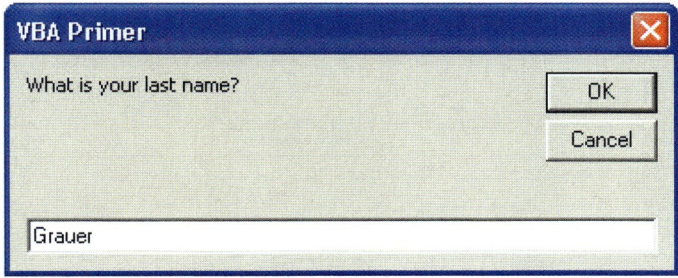

(d) Input Box Includes Argument for Title Bar

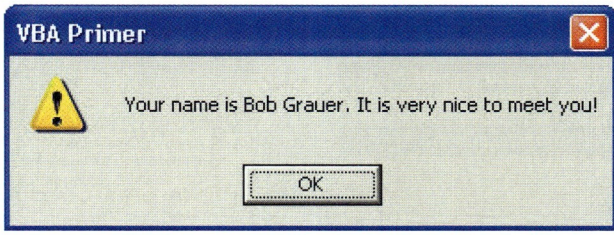

(e) Concatenation and Continuation

FIGURE 2 The InputBox Function

Declaring Variables

Every variable must be declared (defined) before it can be used. This is accomplished through the ***Dim*** (short for Dimension) ***statement*** that appears at the beginning of a procedure. The Dim statement indicates the name of the variable and its type (for example, whether it will hold characters or numbers), which in turn reserves the appropriate amount of memory for that variable.

A variable name must begin with a letter and cannot exceed 255 characters. It can contain letters, numbers, and various special characters such as an underscore, but it cannot contain a space or the special symbols !, @, &, $, or #. Variable names typically begin with a prefix to indicate the type of data that is stored within the variable such as "str" for a character string or "int" for integers. The use of a prefix is optional with respect to the rules of VBA, but it is followed almost universally.

THE VBA EDITOR

All VBA procedures are created using the ***Visual Basic editor*** as shown in Figure 3. You may already be familiar with the editor, perhaps in conjunction with creating and/or editing macros in Word or Excel, or event procedures in Microsoft Access. Let's take a moment, however, to review its essential components.

The left side of the editor displays the ***Project Explorer***, which is similar in concept and appearance to the Windows Explorer, except that it displays the objects associated with the open document. If, for example, you are working in Excel, you will see the various sheets in a workbook, whereas in an Access database you will see forms and reports.

The VBA statements for the selected module (Module1 in Figure 3) appear in the code window in the right pane. The module, in turn, contains declarations and procedures that are separated by horizontal lines. There are two procedures, MsgBoxExamples and InputBoxExamples, each of which was explained previously. A ***comment*** (nonexecutable) statement has been added to each procedure and appears in green. It is the apostrophe at the beginning of the line, rather than the color, that denotes a comment.

The ***Declarations section*** appears at the beginning of the module and contains a single statement, ***Option Explicit***. This option requires every variable in a procedure to be explicitly defined (e.g., in a Dim statement) before it can be used elsewhere in the module. It is an important option and should appear in every module you write.

The remainder of the window should look reasonably familiar in that it is similar to any other Office application. The title bar appears at the top of the window and identifies the application (Microsoft Visual Basic) and the current document (VBA Examples.xls). The right side of the title bar contains the Minimize, Restore, and Close buttons. A menu bar appears under the title bar. Toolbars are displayed under the menu bar. Commands are executed by pulling down the appropriate menu, via buttons on the toolbar, or by keyboard shortcuts.

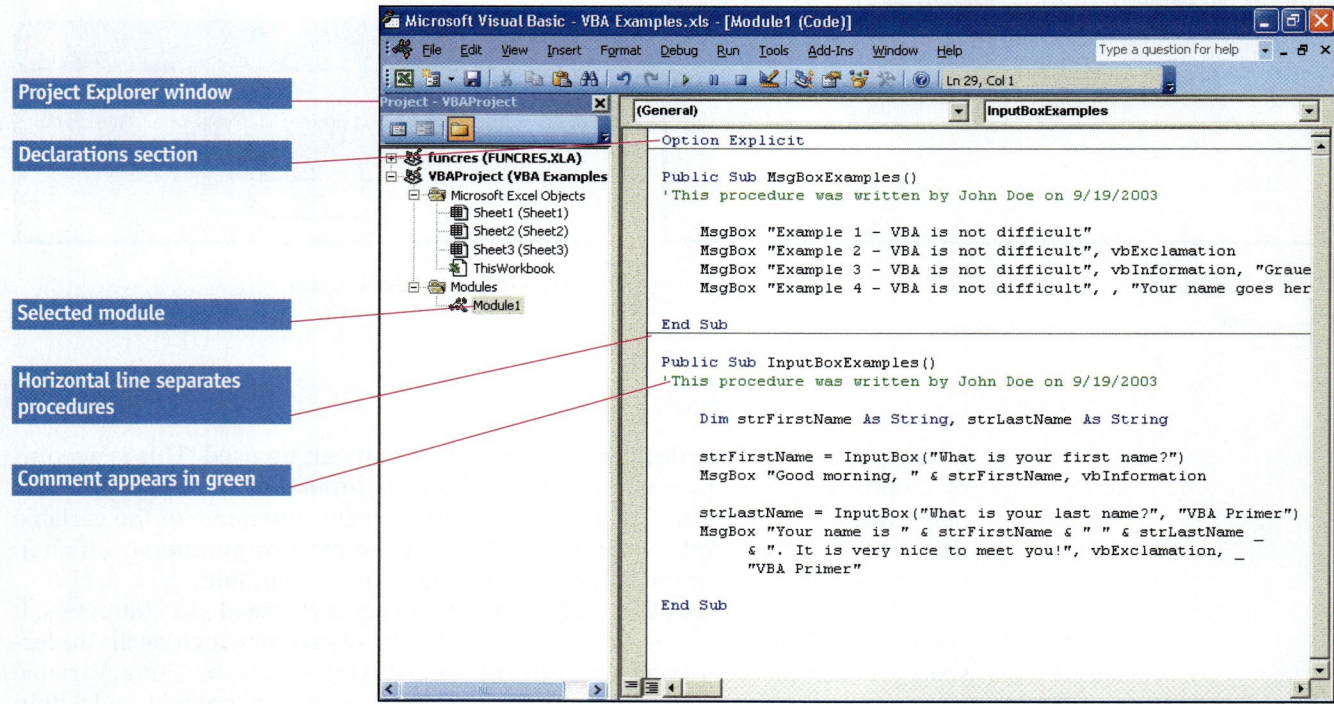

FIGURE 3 The VBA Editor

hands-on exercise 1

Introduction to VBA

Objective To create and test VBA procedures using the MsgBox and InputBox statements. Use Figure 4 as a guide in the exercise. You can do the exercise in any Office application.

Step 1a: Start Microsoft Excel

- We suggest you do the exercise in either Excel or Access (although you could use Word or PowerPoint just as easily). Go to step 1b for Access.

- Start **Microsoft Excel** and open a new workbook. Pull down the **File menu** and click the **Save command** (or click the **Save button** on the Standard toolbar) to display the Save As dialog box. Choose an appropriate drive and folder, then save the workbook as **VBA Examples**.

- Pull down the **Tools menu**, click the **Macro command**, then click the **Visual Basic Editor command** as shown in Figure 4a. Go to step 2.

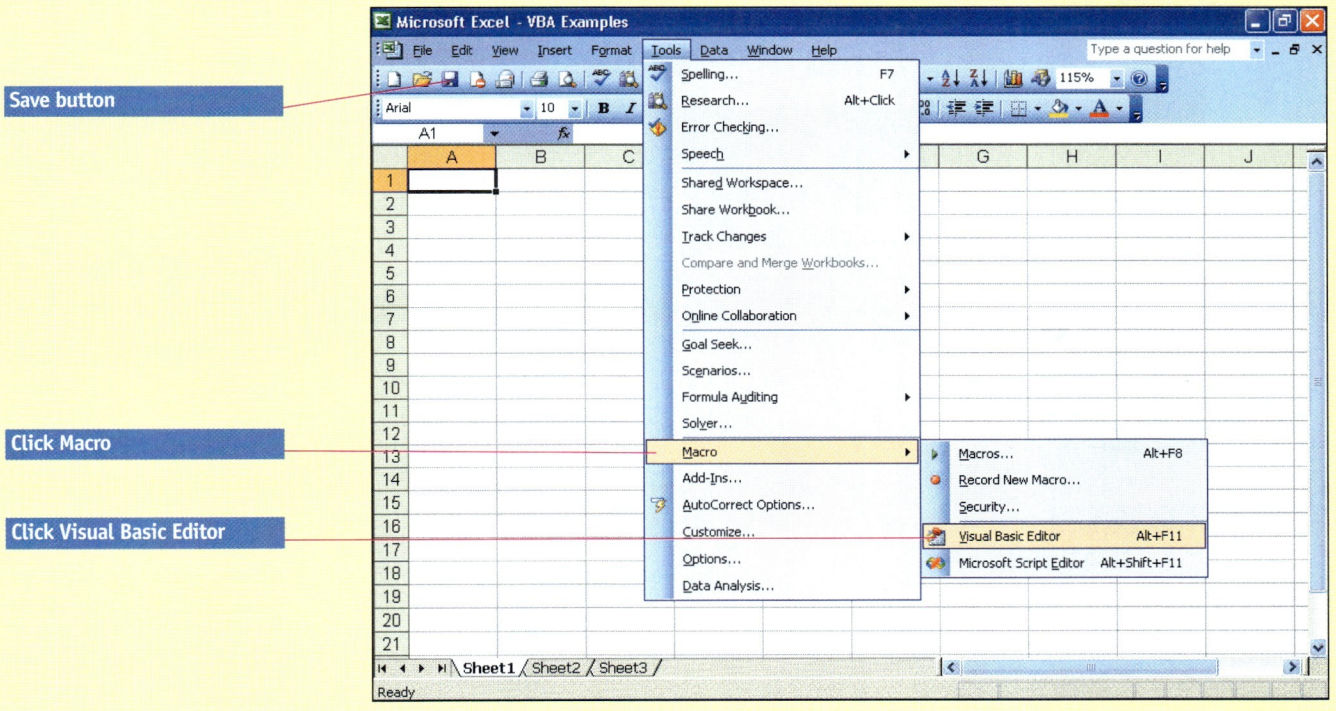

(a) Start Microsoft Excel (step 1a)

FIGURE 4 Hands-on Exercise 1

Step 1b: Start Microsoft Access

- Start **Microsoft Access** and choose the option to create a **Blank Access database**. Save the database as **VBA Examples**.

- Pull down the **Tools menu**, click the **Macro command**, then click the **Visual Basic Editor command**. (You can also use the **Alt+F11** keyboard shortcut to open the VBA editor without going through the Tools menu.)

Step 2: **Insert a Module**

- You should see a window similar to Figure 4b, but Module1 is not yet visible. Close the Properties window if it appears.

- If necessary, pull down the **View menu** and click **Project Explorer** to display the Project Explorer pane at the left of the window. Our figure shows Excel objects, but you will see the "same" window in Microsoft Access.

- Pull down the **Insert menu** and click **Module** to insert Module1 into the current project. The name of the module, Module1 in this example, appears in the Project Explorer pane.

- The Option Explicit statement may be entered automatically, but if not, click in the code window and type the statement **Option Explicit**.

- Pull down the **Insert menu** a second time, but this time select **Procedure** to display the Add Procedure dialog box in Figure 4b. Click in the **Name** text box and enter **MsgBoxExamples** as the name of the procedure. (Spaces are not allowed in a procedure name.)

- Click the option buttons for a **Sub procedure** and for **Public scope**. Click **OK**. The sub procedure should appear within the module and consist of the Sub and End Sub statements.

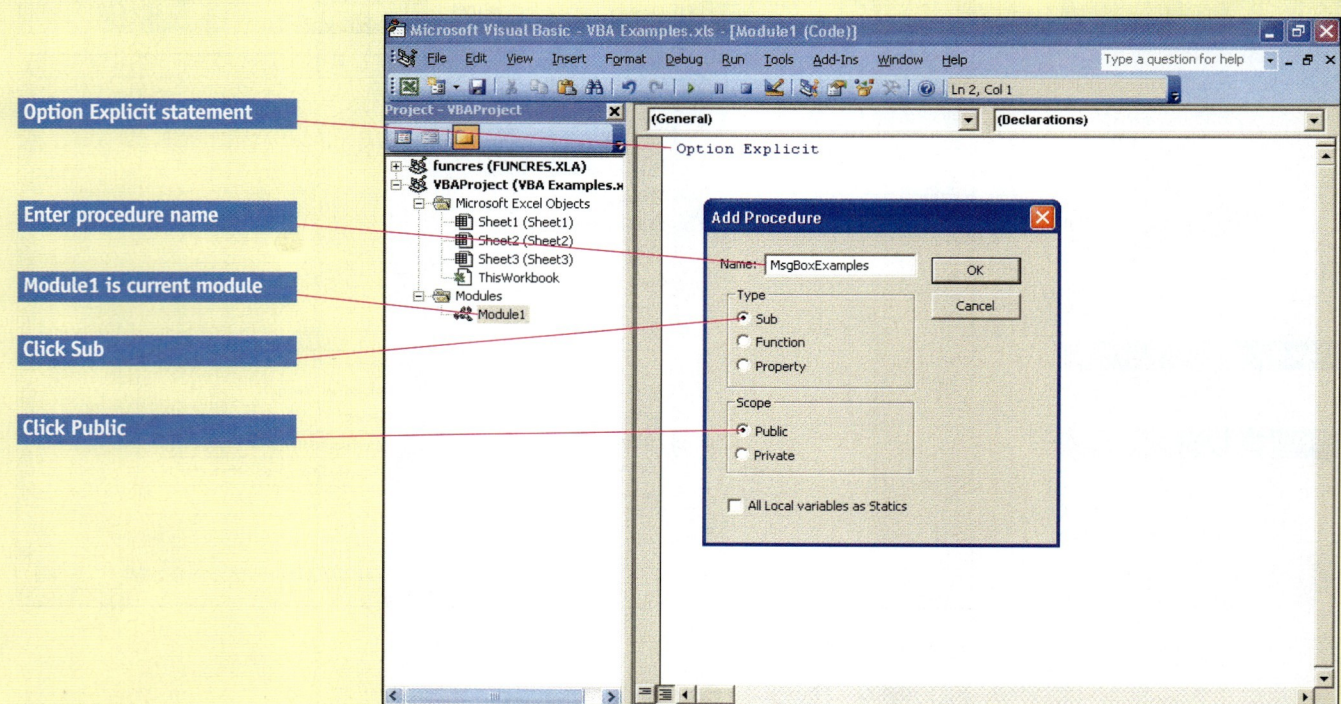

(b) Insert a Module (step 2)

FIGURE 4   Hands-on Exercise 1 (*continued*)

THE OPTION EXPLICIT STATEMENT

The Option Explicit statement is optional, but if it is used it must appear in a module before any procedures. The statement requires that all variables in the module be declared explicitly by the programmer (typically with a Dim, Public, or Private statement), as opposed to VBA making an implicit assumption about the variable. It is good programming practice and it should be used every time.

Step 3: **The MsgBox Statement**

- The insertion point (the flashing cursor) appears below the first statement. Press the **Tab key** to indent the next statement. (Indentation is not a VBA requirement, but is used to increase the readability of the statement.)

- Type the keyword **MsgBox**, then press the **space bar**. VBA responds with Quick Info that displays the syntax of the statement as shown in Figure 4c.

- Type a **quotation mark** to begin the literal, enter the text of your message, **This is my first VBA procedure**, then type the closing **quotation mark**.

- Click the **Run Sub button** on the Standard toolbar (or pull down the **Run menu** and click the **Run Sub command**) to execute the procedure.

- You should see a dialog box, containing the text you entered, within the Excel workbook (or other Office document) on which you are working.

- After you have read the message, click **OK** to return to the VBA editor.

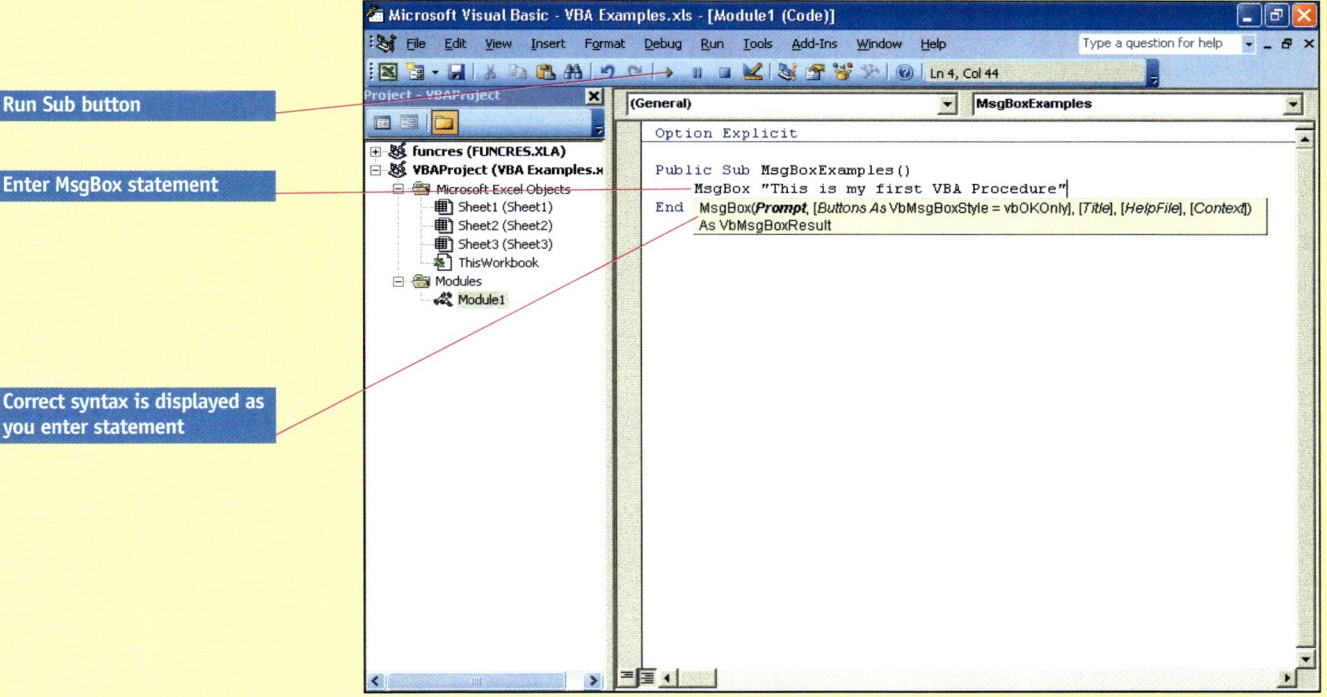

(c) The MsgBox Statement (step 3)

FIGURE 4 Hands-on Exercise 1 (*continued*)

QUICK INFO—HELP WITH VBA SYNTAX

Press the space bar after entering the name of a statement (e.g., MsgBox), and VBA responds with a Quick Info box that displays the syntax of the statement. You see the arguments in the statement and the order in which those arguments appear. Any argument in brackets is optional. If you do not see this information, pull down the Tools menu, click the Options command, then click the Editor tab. Check the box for Auto Quick Info and click OK.

Step 4: **Complete the Procedure**

- You should be back within the MsgBoxExamples procedure. If necessary, click at the end of the MsgBox statement, then press **Enter** to begin a new line. Type **MsgBox** and press the **space bar** to begin entering the statement.

- The syntax of the MsgBox statement will appear on the screen. Type a **quotation mark** to begin the message, type **Add an icon** as the text of this message, then type the closing **quotation mark**. Type a **comma**, then press the **space bar** to enter the next parameter.

- VBA automatically displays a list of appropriate parameters, in this case a series of intrinsic constants that define the icon or command button that is to appear in the statement.

- You can type the first several letters (e.g., **vbi**, for vbInformation), then press the **space bar**, or you can use the **down arrow** to select **vbInformation** and then press the **space bar**. Either way you should complete the second MsgBox statement as shown in Figure 4d. Press **Enter**.

- Enter the third MsgBox statement as shown in Figure 4d. Note the presence of the two consecutive commas to indicate that we omitted the second parameter within the MsgBox statement. Enter your name instead of John Doe where appropriate. Press **Enter**.

- Enter the fourth (and last) MsgBox statement following our figure. Select **vbExclamation** as the second parameter, type a **comma**, then enter the text of the title bar, as you did for the previous statement.

- Click the **Save button** to save the changes to the module.

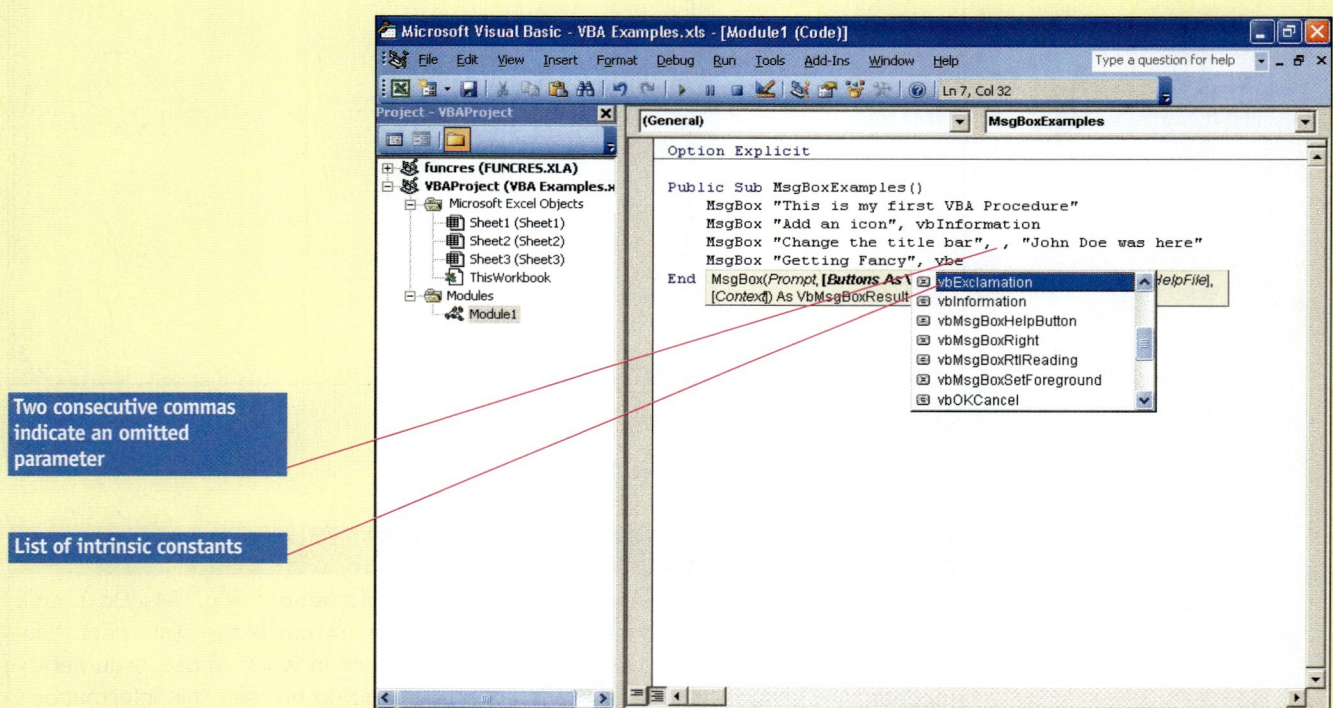

(d) Complete the Procedure (step 4)

FIGURE 4 Hands-on Exercise 1 (*continued*)

Step 5: **Test the Procedure**

- It's convenient if you can see the statements in the VBA procedure at the same time you see the output of those statements. Thus we suggest that you tile the VBA editor and the associated Office application.

- Minimize all applications except the VBA editor and the Office application (e.g., Excel).

- Right click the taskbar and click **Tile Windows Horizontally** to tile the windows as shown in Figure 4e. (It does not matter which window is on top. (If you see more than these two windows, minimize the other open window, then right click the taskbar and retile the windows.)

- Click anywhere in the VBA procedure, then click the **Run Sub button** on the Standard toolbar.

- The four messages will be displayed one after the other. Click **OK** after each message.

- Maximize the VBA window to continue working.

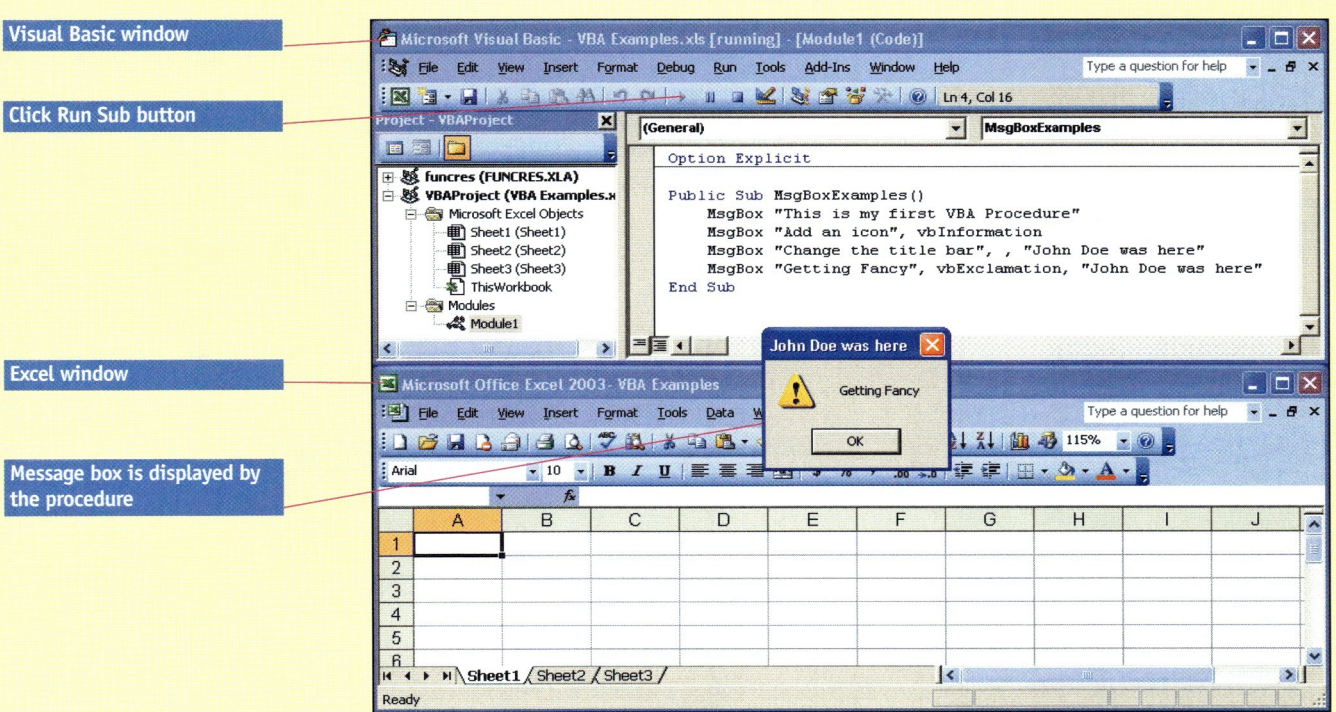

(e) Test the Procedure (step 5)

FIGURE 4 Hands-on Exercise 1 (*continued*)

HIDE THE WINDOWS TASKBAR

You can hide the Windows taskbar to gain additional space on the desktop. Right click any empty area of the taskbar to display a context-sensitive menu, click Properties to display the Taskbar properties dialog box, and if necessary click the Taskbar tab. Check the box to Auto Hide the taskbar, then click OK. The taskbar disappears from the screen but will reappear as you point to the bottom edge of the desktop.

Step 6: **Comments and Corrections**

- All VBA procedures should be documented with the author's name, date, and other comments as necessary to explain the procedure. Click after the procedure header. Press the **Enter key** to leave a blank line.

- Press **Enter** a second time. Type an **apostrophe** to begin the comment, then enter a descriptive statement similar to Figure 4f. Press **Enter** when you have completed the comment. The line turns green to indicate it is a comment.

- The best time to experiment with debugging is when you know your procedure is correct. Go to the last MsgBox statement and delete the quotation mark in front of your name. Move to the end of the line and press **Enter**.

- You should see the error message in Figure 4f. Unfortunately, the message is not as explicit as it could be; VBA cannot tell that you left out a quotation mark, but it does detect an error in syntax.

- Click **OK** in response to the error. Click the **Undo button** twice, to restore the quotation mark, which in turn corrects the statement.

- Click the **Save button** to save the changes to the module.

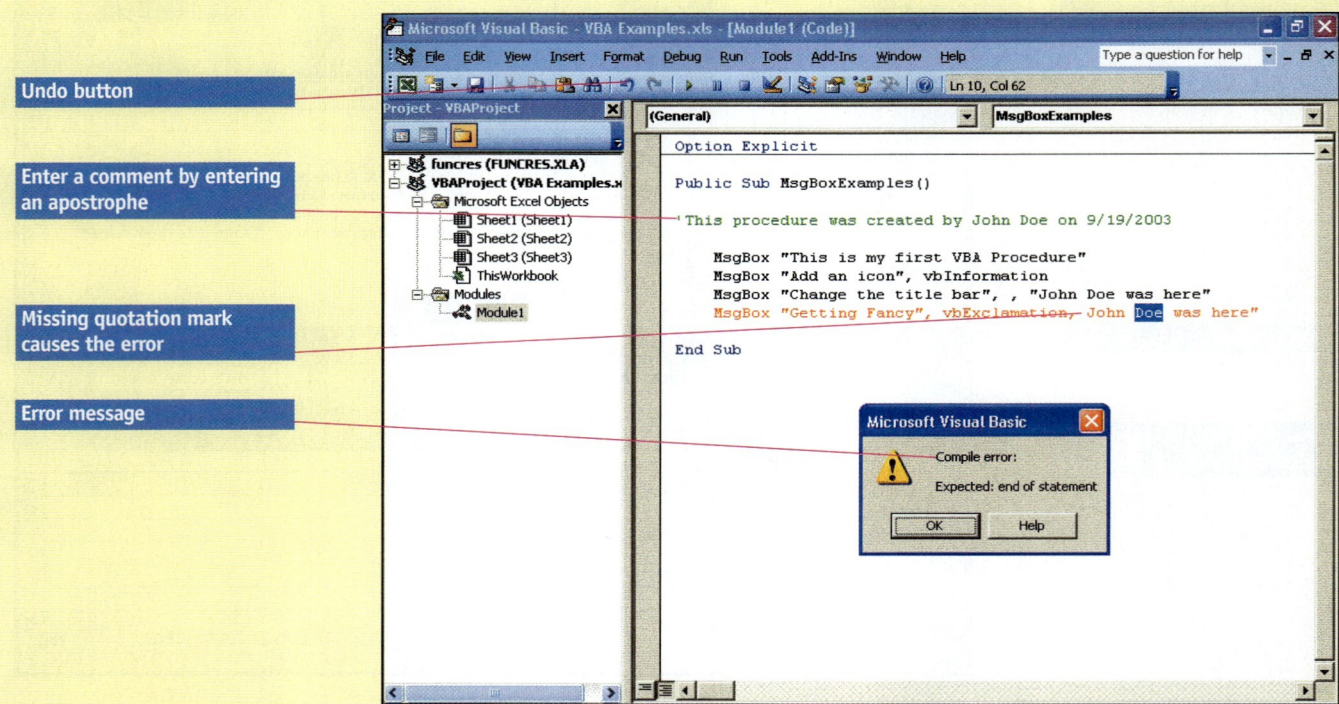

(f) Comments and Corrections (step 6)

FIGURE 4   Hands-on Exercise 1 (*continued*)

RED, GREEN, AND BLUE

Visual Basic for Applications uses different colors for different types of statements (or a portion of those statements). Any statement containing a syntax error appears in red. Comments appear in green. Keywords, such as Sub and End Sub, appear in blue.

Step 7: **Create a Second Procedure**

- Pull down the **Insert menu** and click **Procedure** to display the Add Procedure dialog box. Enter **InputBoxExamples** as the name of the procedure. (Spaces are not allowed in a procedure name.)

- Click the option buttons for a **Sub procedure** and for **Public scope**. Click **OK**. The new sub procedure will appear within the existing module below the existing MsgBoxExamples procedure.

- Enter the statements in the procedure as they appear in Figure 4g. Be sure to type a space between the ampersand and the underscore in the second MsgBox statement. Click the **Save button** to save the procedure before testing it.

- You can display the output of the procedure directly in the VBA window if you minimize the Excel window. Thus, **right click** the Excel button on the taskbar to display a context-sensitive menu, then click the **Minimize command**. There is no visible change on your monitor.

- Click the **Run Sub button** to test the procedure. This time you see the Input box displayed on top of the VBA window because the Excel window has been minimized.

- Enter your first name in response to the initial prompt, then click **OK**. Click **OK** when you see the message box that says "Hello".

- Enter your last name in response to the second prompt and click **OK**. You should see a message box similar to the one in Figure 4g. Click **OK**.

- Return to the VBA procedure to correct any mistakes that might occur. Save the module.

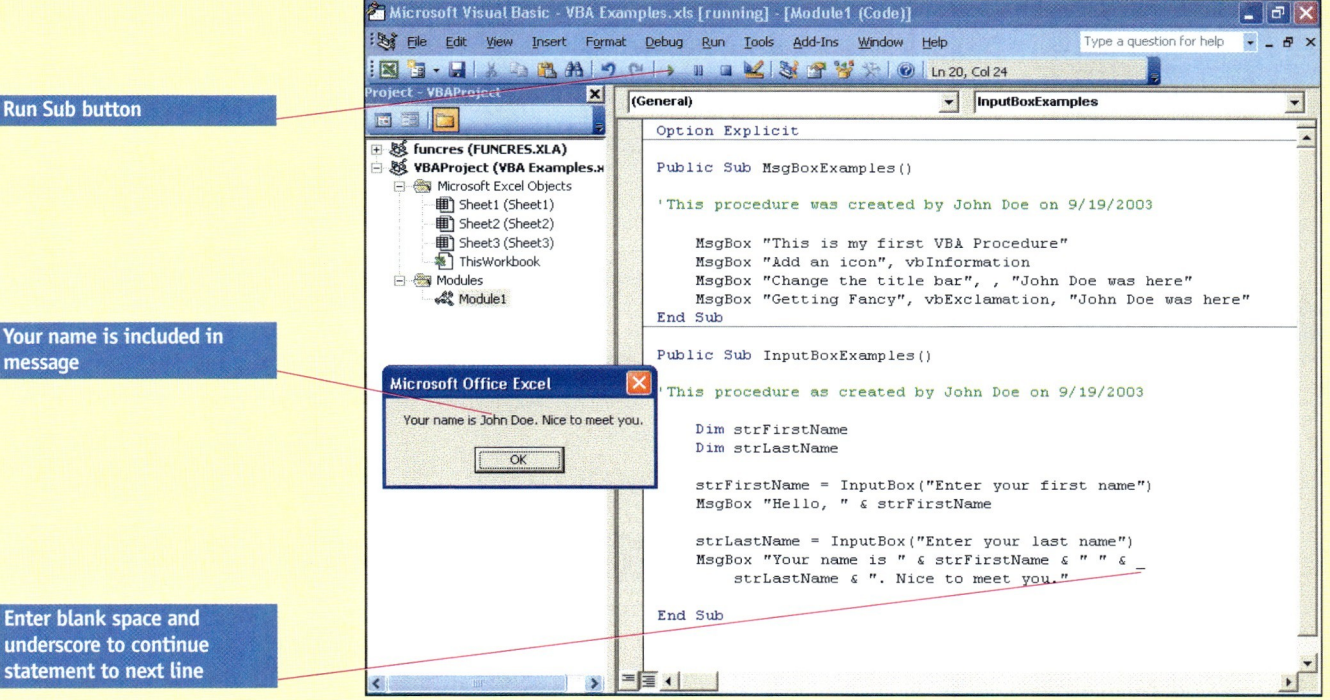

(g) Create a Second Procedure (step 7)

FIGURE 4 Hands-on Exercise 1 (*continued*)

Step 8: **Create a Public Constant**

- Click after the Options Explicit statement and press **Enter** to move to a new line. Type the statement to define the constant, **ApplicationTitle**, as shown in Figure 4h, and press **Enter**.

- Click anywhere in the MsgBoxExamples procedure, then change the third argument in the last MsgBox statement to ApplicationTitle. Make the four modifications in the InputBoxExamples procedure as shown in Figure 4h.

- Click anywhere in the InputBoxExamples procedure, then click the **Run Sub button** to test the procedure. The title bar of each dialog box will contain a descriptive title corresponding to the value of the ApplicationTitle constant.

- Change the value of the ApplicationTitle constant in the General Declarations section, then rerun the InputBoxExamples procedure. The title of every dialog box changes to reflect the new value.

- Save the procedure. Do you see the advantage of defining a title in the General Declarations section?

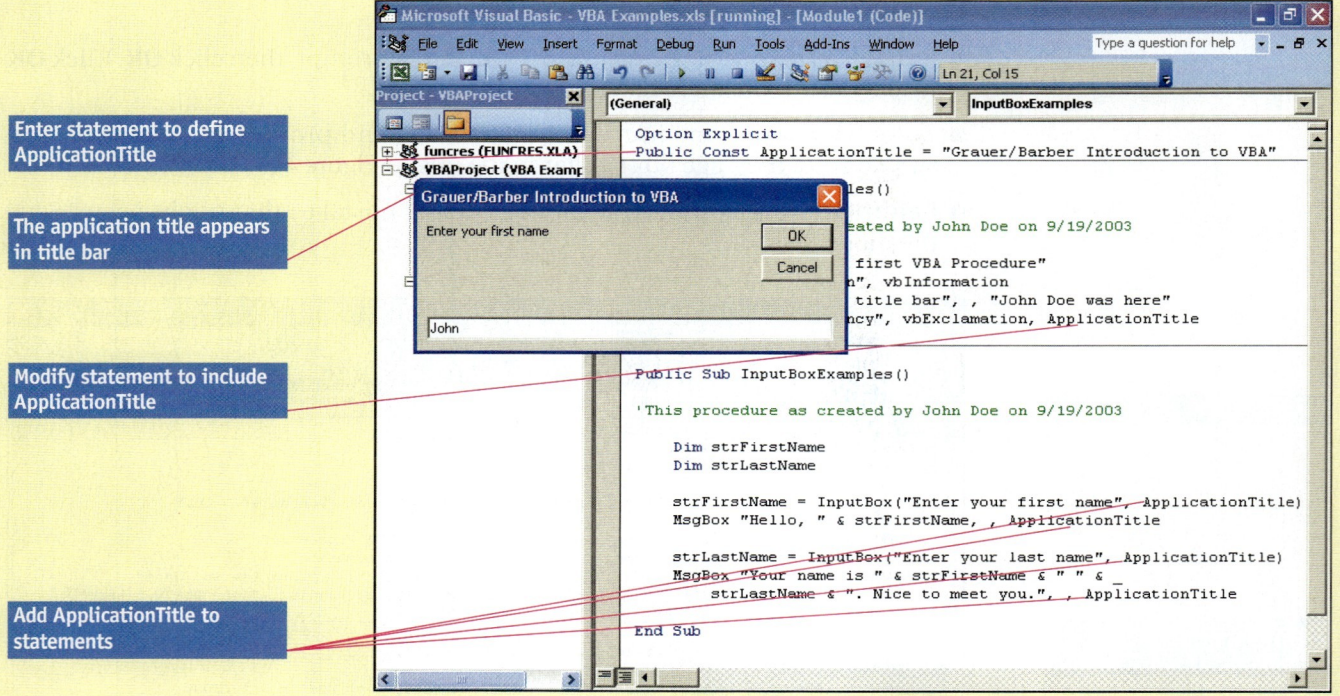

(h) Create a Public Constant (step 8)

FIGURE 4 Hands-on Exercise 1 (*continued*)

CONTINUING A VBA STATEMENT—THE & AND THE UNDERSCORE

A VBA statement can be continued from one line to the next by typing a space at the end of the line to be continued, typing the underscore character, then continuing on the next line. You may not, however, break a line in the middle of a literal (character string). Thus, you need to complete the character string with a closing quotation mark, add an ampersand (as the concatenation operator to display this string with the character string on the next line), then leave a space followed by the underscore to indicate continuation.

Step 9: **Help with VBA**

- You should be in the VBA editor. Pull down the **Help menu** and click the **Microsoft Visual Basic Help command** to open the Help pane.
- Type **Input Box function** in the Search box, then click the arrow to initiate the search. The results should include a hyperlink to InputBox function. Click the **hyperlink** to display the Help screen in Figure 4i.
- Maximize the Help window, then explore the information on the InputBox function to reinforce your knowledge of this statement.
    - Click the **Print button** to print this page for your instructor.
    - Click the link to **Example** within the Help window to see actual code.
    - Click the link to **See Also**, which displays information about the MsgBox statement.
- Close the Help window, but leave the task pane open. Click the **green** (back) **arrow** within the task pane to display the Table of Contents for Visual Basic Help, then explore the table of contents.
    - Click any closed book to open the book and "drill down" within the list of topics. The book remains open until you click the icon a second time to close it.
    - Click any question mark icon to display the associated help topic.
- Close the task pane. Pull down the **File menu** and click the **Close and Return to Microsoft Excel command** (or click the **Close button** on the VBA title bar) to close the VBA window and return to the application. Click **Yes** if asked whether to save the changes to Module1.
- You should be back in the Excel (or Access) application window. Close the application if you do not want to continue with the next exercise at this time.
- Congratulations. You have just completed your first VBA procedure. Remember to use Help any time you have a question.

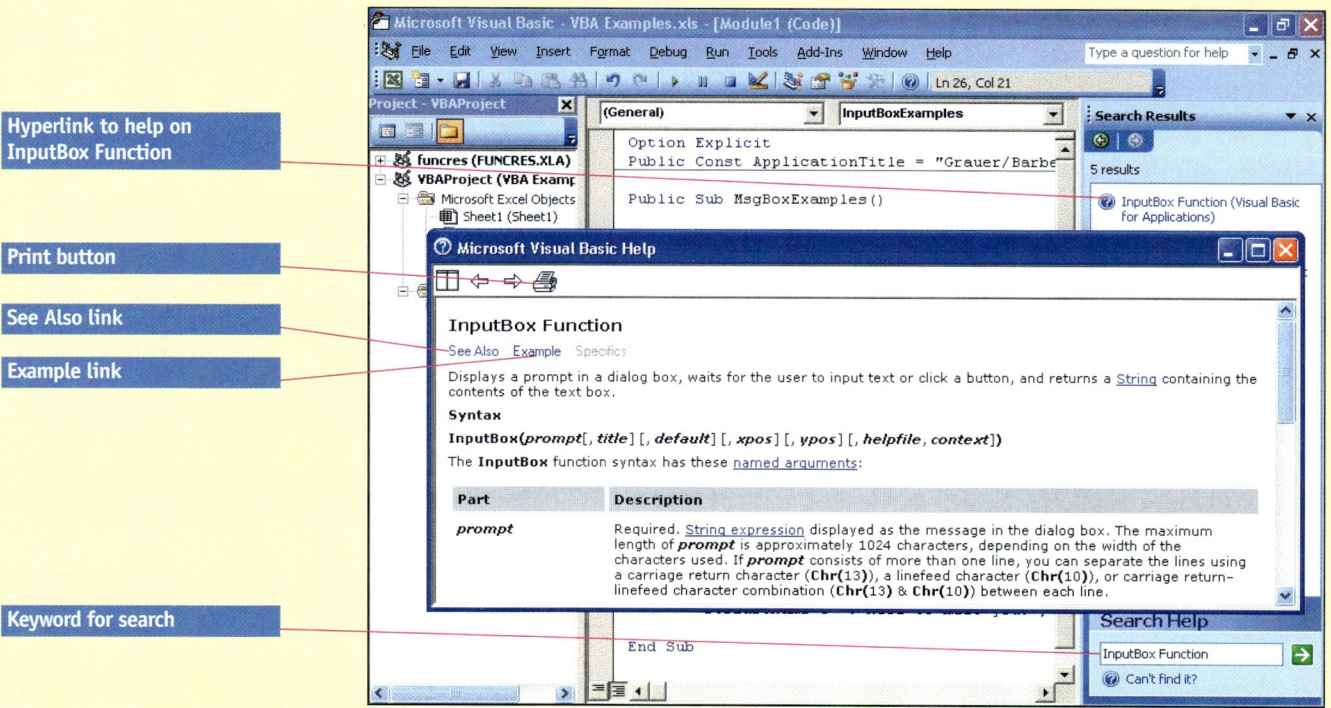

(i) Help with VBA (step 9)

FIGURE 4 Hands-on Exercise 1 (*continued*)

MICROSOFT OFFICE EXCEL 2003 REVISED

IF . . . THEN . . . ELSE STATEMENT

The ability to make decisions within a program, and then execute alternative sets of statements based on the results of those decisions, is crucial to any programming language. This is typically accomplished through an **If statement**, which evaluates a condition as either true or false, then branches accordingly. The If statement is not used in isolation, however, but is incorporated into a procedure to accomplish a specific task as shown in Figure 5a. This procedure contains two separate If statements, and the results are displayed in the message boxes shown in the remainder of the figure.

The InputBox statement associated with Figure 5b prompts the user for the name of his or her instructor, then it stores the answer in the variable strInstructorName. The subsequent If statement then compares the user's answer to the literal "Grauer". If the condition is true (i.e., Grauer was entered into the input box), then the message in Figure 5c is displayed. If, however, the user entered any other value, then the condition is evaluated as false, the MsgBox is not displayed, and processing continues with the next statement in the procedure.

The second If statement includes an optional **Else clause**. Again, the user is asked for a value, and the response is compared to the number 50. If the condition is true (i.e., the value of intUserStates equals 50), the message in Figure 5d is displayed to indicate that the response is correct. If, however, the condition is false (i.e., the user entered a number other than 50), the user sees the message in Figure 5e. Either way, true or false, processing continues with the next statement in the procedure. That's it—it's simple and it's powerful, and we will use the statement in the next hands-on exercise.

You can learn a good deal about VBA by looking at existing code and making inferences. Consider, for example, the difference between literals and numbers. **Literals** (also known as **character strings**) are stored differently from numbers, and this is manifested in the way that comparisons are entered into a VBA statement. Look closely at the condition that references a literal (strInstructorName = "Grauer") compared to the condition that includes a number (intUserStates = 50). The literal ("Grauer") is enclosed in quotation marks, whereas the number (50) is not. (The prefix used in front of each variable, "str" and "int", is a common VBA convention to indicate the variable type—a string and an integer, respectively. Both variables are declared in the Dim statements at the beginning of the procedure.)

Note, too, that indentation and spacing are used throughout a procedure to make it easier to read. This is for the convenience of the programmer and not a requirement for VBA. The If, Else, and End If keywords are aligned under one another, with the subsequent statements indented under the associated keyword. We also indent a continued statement, such as a MsgBox statement, which is typically coded over multiple lines. Blank lines can be added anywhere within a procedure to separate blocks of statements from one another.

THE MSGBOX FUNCTION—YES OR NO

A simple MsgBox statement merely displays information to the user. MsgBox can also be used as a function, however, to accept information from the user such as clicking a Yes or No button, then combined with an If statement to take different actions based on the user's input. In essence, you enclose the arguments of the MsgBox function in parentheses (similar to what is done with the InputBox function), then test for the user response using the intrinsic constants vbYes and vbNo. The statement, If MsgBox("Are you having fun?", vbYesNo)=vbYes asks the user a question, displays Yes and No command buttons, then tests to see if the user clicked the Yes button.

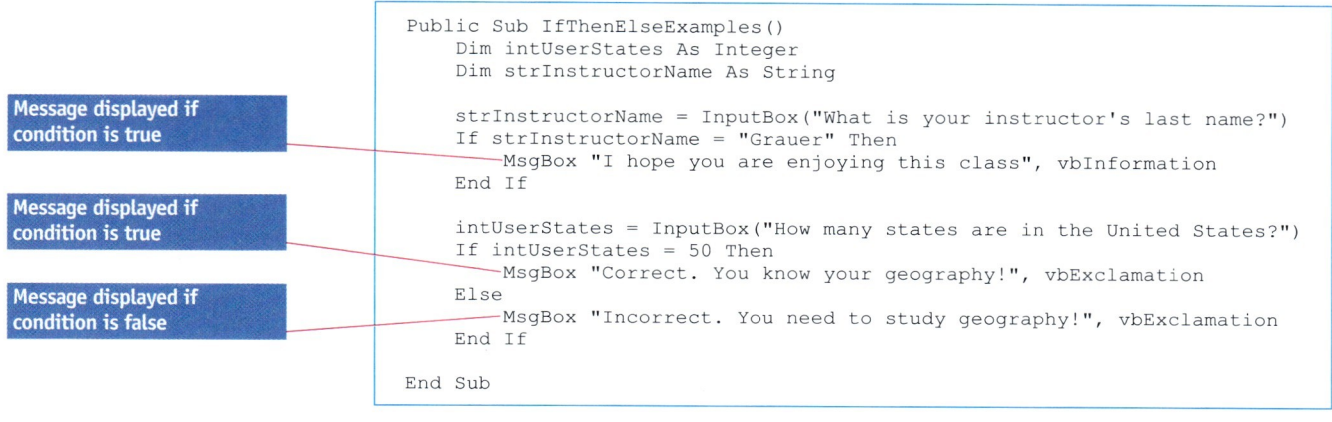

(a) VBA Code

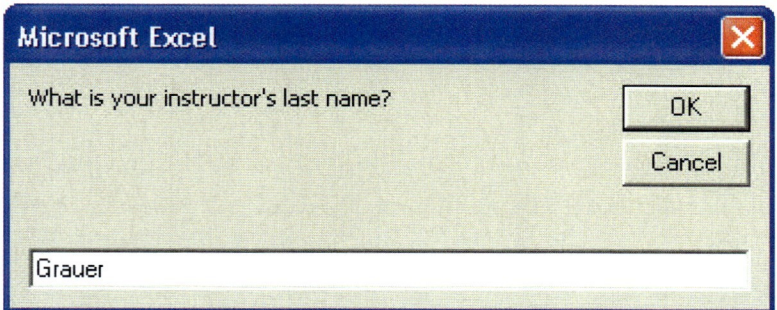

(b) InputBox Prompts for User Response

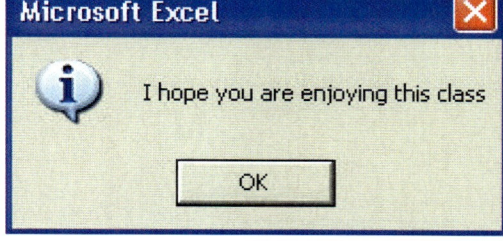

(c) Condition Is True

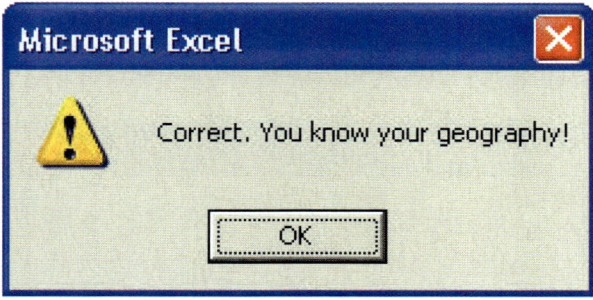

(d) Answer Is Correct (condition is true)

(e) Answer Is Wrong (condition is false)

FIGURE 5   The If Statement

CASE STATEMENT

The If statement is ideal for testing simple conditions and taking one of two actions. Although it can be extended to include additional actions by including one or more ElseIf clauses (If...Then...ElseIf...ElseIf...), this type of construction is often difficult to follow. Hence the **Case statement** is used when multiple branches are possible.

The procedure in Figure 6a accepts a student's GPA, then displays one of several messages, depending on the value of the GPA. The individual cases are evaluated in sequence. (The GPAs must be evaluated in descending order if the statement is to work correctly.) Thus, we check first to see if the GPA is greater than or equal to 3.9, then 3.75, then 3.5, and so on. If none of the cases is true, the statement following the Else clause is executed.

Note, too, the format of the comparison in that numbers (such as 3.9 or 3.75) are not enclosed in quotation marks because the associated variable (sngUserGPA) was declared as numeric. If, however, we had been evaluating a string variable (such as, strUserMajor), quotation marks would have been required around the literal values (e.g., Case Is = "Business", Case Is = "Liberal Arts", and so on.) The distinction between numeric and character (string) variables is important.

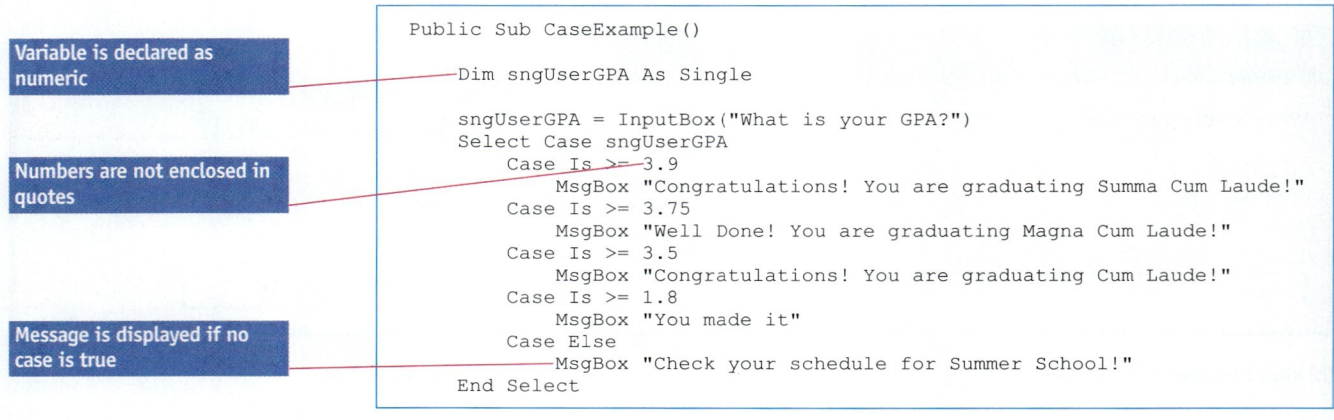

(a) VBA Code

(b) Enter the GPA

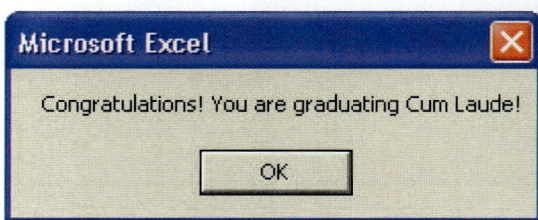

(c) Third Option Is Selected

FIGURE 6 The Case Statement

CUSTOM TOOLBARS

A VBA procedure can be executed in several different ways. It can be run from the Visual Basic editor by pulling down the Run menu and clicking the Run Sub button on the Standard toolbar, or using the F5 function key. It can also be run from within the Office application (Word, Excel, or PowerPoint, but not Access), by pulling down the Tools menu, clicking the Macro command, then choosing the name of the macro that corresponds to the name of the procedure.

Perhaps the best way, however, is to create a ***custom toolbar*** that is displayed within the application as shown in Figure 7. (A custom menu can also be created that contains the same commands as the custom toolbar.) The toolbar has its own name (Bob's Toolbar), yet it functions identically to any other Office toolbar. You have your choice of displaying buttons only, text only, or both buttons and text. Our toolbar provides access to four commands, each corresponding to a procedure that was discussed earlier. Click the Case Example button, for example, and the associated procedure is executed, starting with the InputBox statement asking for the user's GPA.

A custom toolbar is created via the Toolbars command within the View menu. The new toolbar is initially big enough to hold only a single button, but you can add, move, and delete buttons following the same procedure as for any other Office toolbar. You can add any command at all to the toolbar; that is, you can add existing commands from within the Office application, or you can add commands that correspond to VBA procedures that you have created. Remember, too, that you can add more buttons to existing office toolbars.

Once the toolbar has been created, it is displayed or hidden just like any other Office toolbar. It can also be docked along any edge of the application window or left floating as shown in Figure 7. It's fun, it's easy, and as you may have guessed, it's time for the next hands-on exercise.

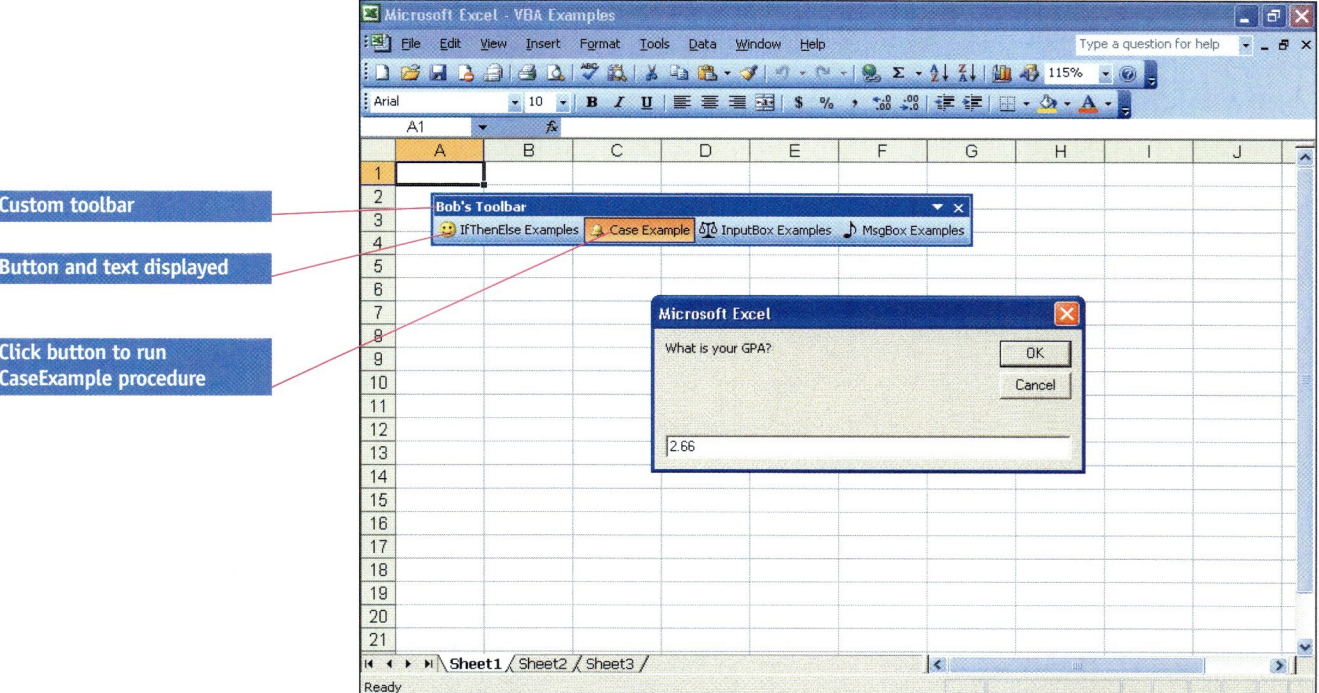

FIGURE 7 Custom Toolbars

hands-on exercise

2 Decision Making

Objective To create procedures with If . . . Then . . . Else and Case statements, then create a custom toolbar to execute those procedures. Use Figure 8 as a guide in the exercise.

Step 1: **Open the Office Document**

- Open the **VBA Examples workbook** or Access database from the previous exercise. The procedure differs slightly, depending on whether you are using Access or Excel.
  - In Access, you simply open the database.
  - In Excel you will be warned that the workbook contains a macro as shown in Figure 8a. Click the button to **Enable Macros**.
- Pull down the **Tools menu**, click the **Macro command**, then click the **Visual Basic Editor command**. You can also use the **Alt+F11** keyboard shortcut to open the VBA editor without going through the Tools menu.

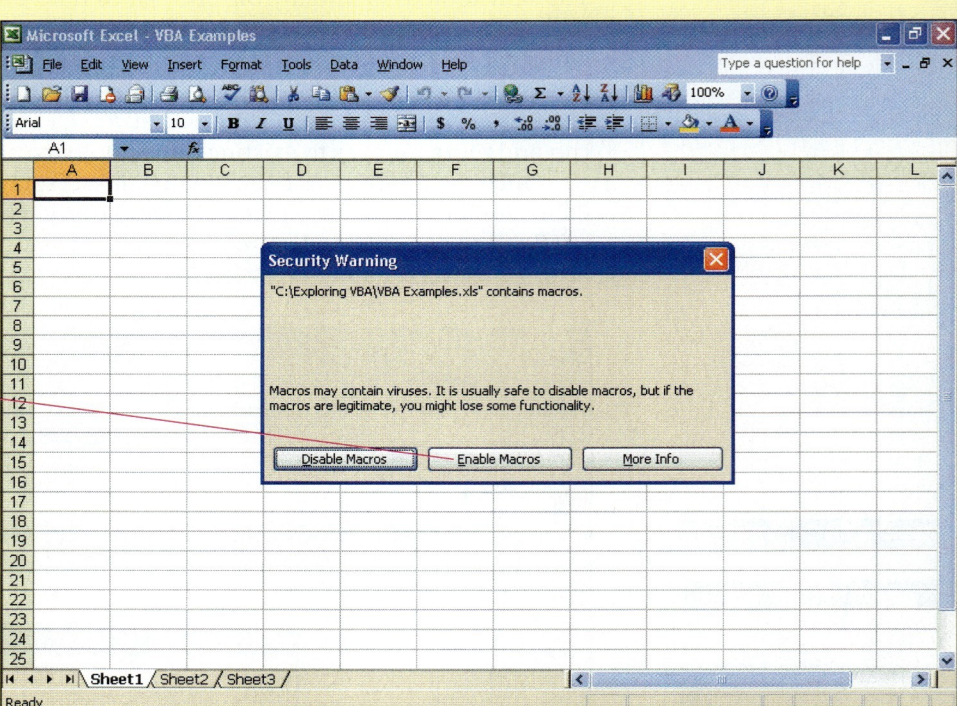

Click Enable Macros

(a) Open the Office Document (step 1)

FIGURE 8 Hands-on Exercise 2

MACRO SECURITY

A computer virus could take the form of an Excel macro; thus, Excel will warn you that a workbook contains a macro, provided the security option is set appropriately. Pull down the Tools menu, click the Options command, click the Security tab, and then set the Macro Security to either High or Medium. High security disables all macros except those from a trusted source. Medium security gives you the option to enable macros. Click the button only if you are sure the macro is from a trusted source.

Step 2: **Insert a New Procedure**

- You should be in the Visual Basic editor as shown in Figure 8b. If necessary, double click **Module1** in the Explorer Window to open this module. Pull down the **Insert menu** and click the **Procedure command** to display the Add Procedure dialog box.

- Click in the **Name** text box and enter **IfThenElseExamples** as the name of the procedure. Click the option buttons for a **Sub procedure** and for **Public scope**. Click **OK** to create the procedure.

- The Sub procedure should appear within the module and consist of the Sub and End Sub statements as shown in Figure 8b.

- Click within the newly created procedure, then click the **Procedure View button** at the bottom of the window. The display changes to show just the current procedure.

- Click the **Save button** to save the module with the new procedure.

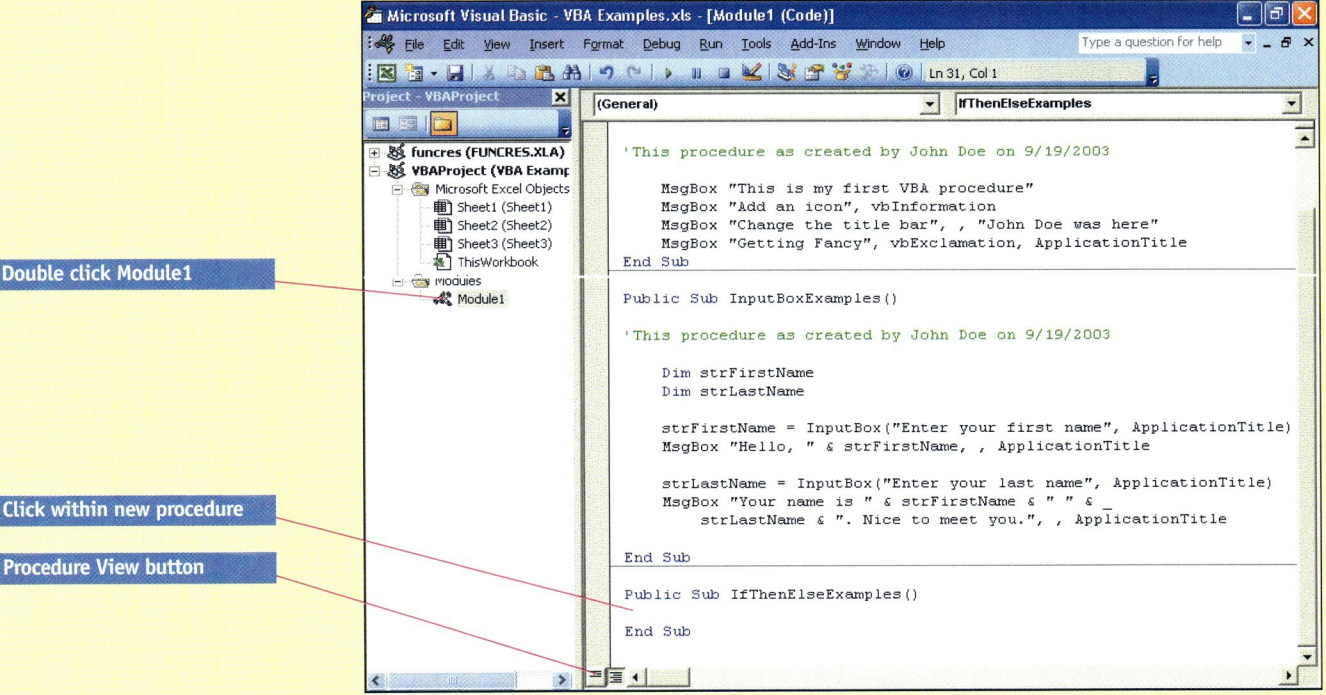

(b) Insert a New Procedure (step 2)

FIGURE 8   Hands-on Exercise 2 (*continued*)

PROCEDURE VIEW VERSUS FULL MODULE VIEW

The procedures within a module can be displayed individually, or alternatively, multiple procedures can be viewed simultaneously. To go from one view to the other, click the Procedure View button at the bottom of the window to display just the procedure you are working on, or click the Full Module View button to display multiple procedures. You can press Ctrl+PgDn and Ctrl+PgUp to move between procedures in either view.

MICROSOFT OFFICE EXCEL 2003 REVISED   689

Step 3: **Create the If...Then...Else Procedure**

- Enter the IfThenElseExamples procedure as it appears in Figure 8c, but use your instructor's name instead of Bob's. Note the following:
  - The Dim statements at the beginning of the procedure are required to define the two variables that are used elsewhere in the procedure.
  - The syntax of the comparison is different for string variables versus numeric variables. String variables require quotation marks around the comparison value (e.g., strInstructorName = "Grauer"). Numeric variables (e.g., intUserStates = 50) do not.
  - Indentation and blank lines are used within a procedure to make the code easier to read, as distinct from a VBA requirement. Press the **Tab key** to indent one level to the right.
  - Comments can be added to a procedure at any time.
- Save the procedure.

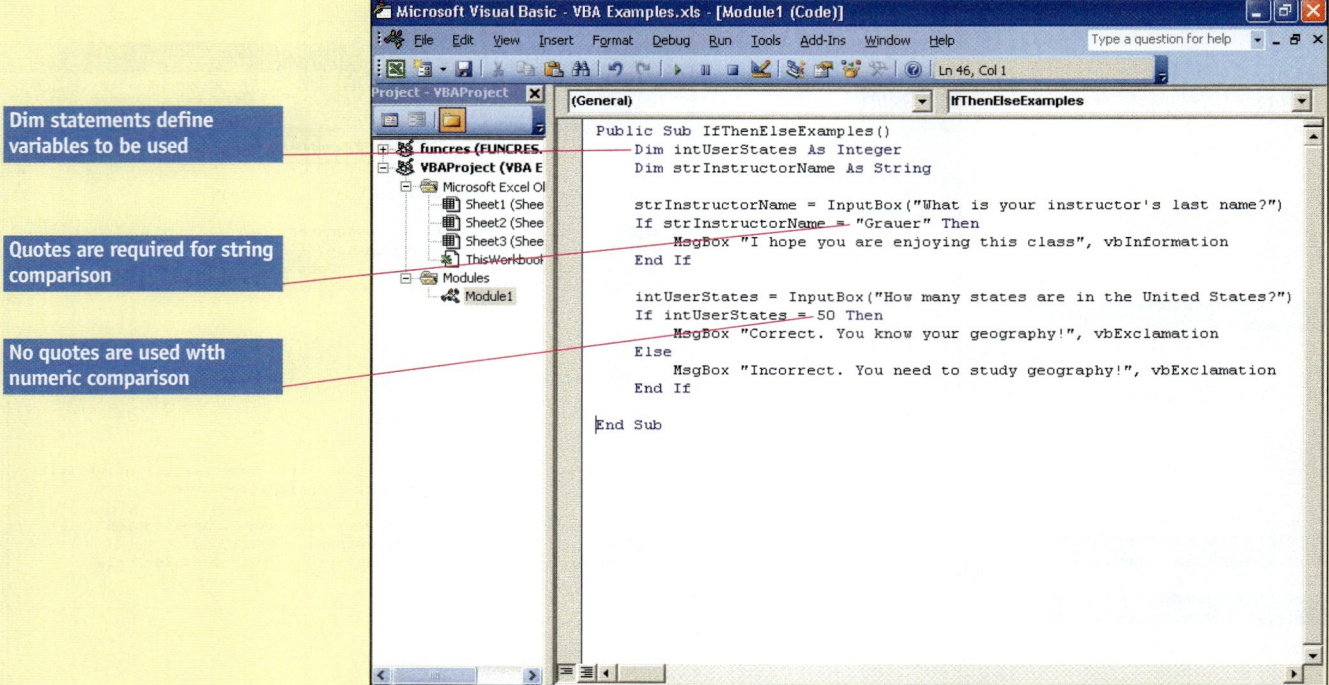

(c) Create the If...Then...Else Procedure (step 3)

FIGURE 8   Hands-on Exercise 2 (continued)

THE COMPLETE WORD TOOL

It's easy to misspell a variable name within a procedure, which is why the Complete Word tool is so useful. Type the first several characters in a variable name (such as "intU" or "strI" in the current procedure), then press Ctrl+Space. VBA will complete the variable name for you, provided that you have already entered a sufficient number of letters for a unique reference. Alternatively, it will display all of the elements that begin with the letters you have entered. Use the down arrow to scroll through the list until you find the item, then press the space bar to complete the entry.

Step 4: Test the Procedure

- The best way to test a procedure is to display its output directly in the VBA window (without having to switch back and forth between that and the application window). Thus, right click the Excel button on the taskbar to display a context-sensitive menu, then click the **Minimize command**.

- There is no visible change on your monitor. Click anywhere within the procedure, then click the **Run Sub button**. You should see the dialog box in Figure 8d.

- Enter your instructor's name, exactly as it was spelled within the VBA procedure. Click **OK**.

- You should see a second message box that hopes you are enjoying the class. This box will be displayed only if you spell the instructor's name correctly. Click **OK**.

- You should see a second input box that asks how many states are in the United States. Enter **50** and click **OK**. You should see a message indicating that you know your geography. Click **OK** to close the dialog box.

- Click the **Run Sub button** a second time, but enter a different set of values in response to the prompts. Misspell your instructor's name, and you will not see the associated message box.

- Enter any number other than 50, and you will be told to study geography.

- Continue to test the procedure until you are satisfied it works under all conditions. We cannot overemphasize the importance of thorough testing!

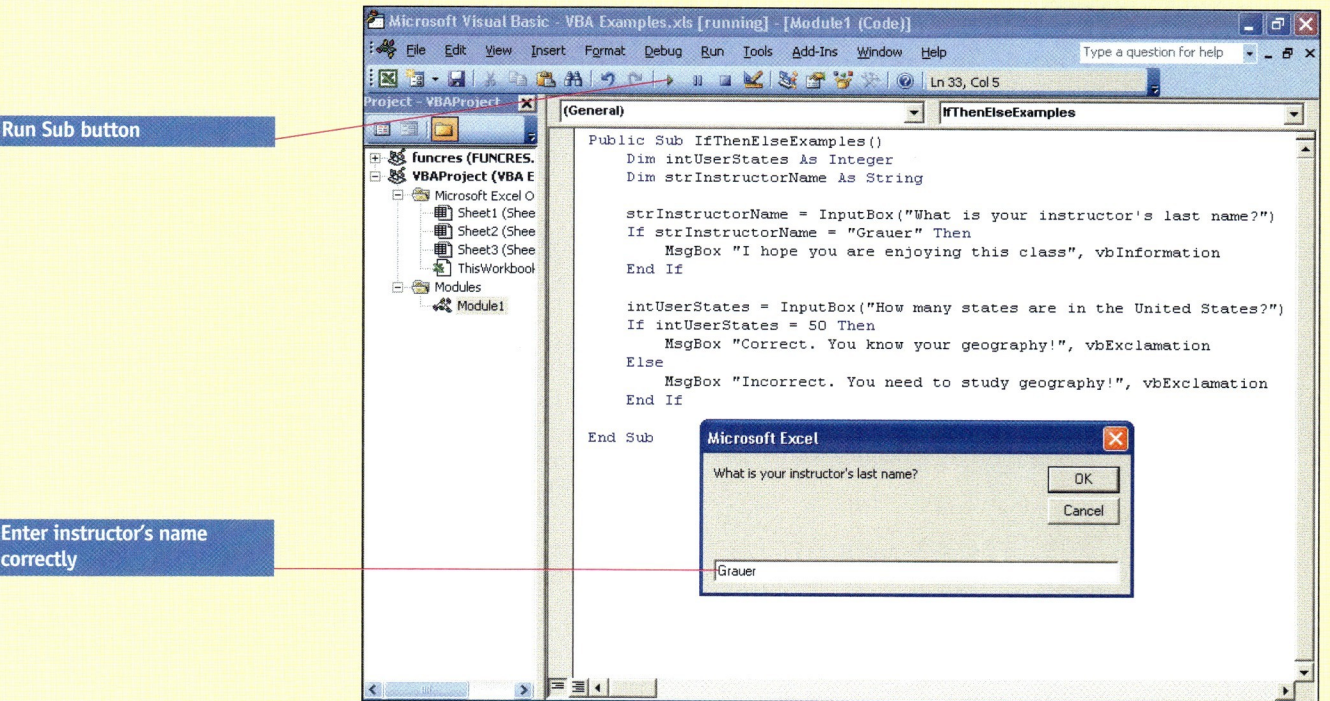

(d) Test the Procedure (step 4)

FIGURE 8 Hands-on Exercise 2 (*continued*)

Step 5: **Create and Test the CaseExample Procedure**

- Pull down the **Insert menu** and create a new procedure called **CaseExample**, then enter the statements exactly as they appear in Figure 8e. Note:
  - The variable sngUserGPA is declared to be a single-precision floating-point number (as distinct from the integer type that was used previously). A floating-point number is required in order to maintain a decimal point.
  - The GPA must be tested in descending order if the statement is to work correctly.
  - You may use any editing technique with which you are comfortable. You could, for example, enter the first case, copy it four times in the procedure, then modify the copied text as necessary.
  - The use of indentation and blank lines is for the convenience of the programmer and not a requirement of VBA.
- Click the **Run Sub button**, then test the procedure. Be sure to test it under all conditions; that is, you need to run it several times and enter a different GPA each time to be sure that all of the cases are working correctly.
- Save the procedure.

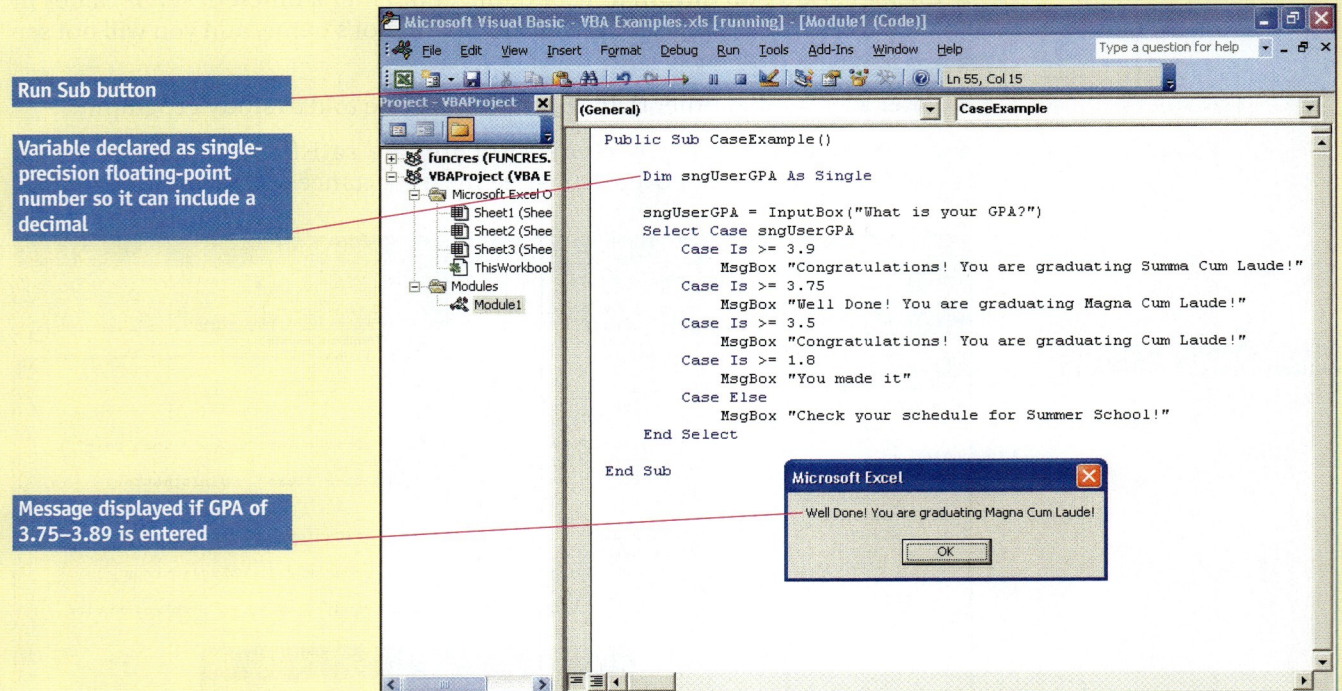

(e) Create and Test the CaseExample Procedure (step 5)

FIGURE 8 Hands-on Exercise 2 (*continued*)

RELATIONAL OPERATORS

The condition portion of an If or Case statement uses one of several relational operators. These include =, <, and > for equal to, less than, or greater than, respectively. You can also use >=, <=, or <> for greater than or equal to, less than or equal to, or not equal. This is basic, but very important, information if you are to code these statements correctly.

Step 6: **Create a Custom Toolbar**

- Click the **View Microsoft Excel** (or **Access**) **button** to display the associated application window. Pull down the **View menu**, click (or point to) the **Toolbars command**, then click **Customize** to display the Customize dialog box in Figure 8f. (Bob's toolbar is not yet visible.) Click the **Toolbars tab**.

- Click the **New button** to display the New Toolbar dialog box. Enter the name of your toolbar—e.g., **Bob's toolbar**—then click **OK** to create the toolbar and close the New Toolbar dialog box.

- Your toolbar should appear on the screen, but it does not yet contain any buttons. If necessary, click and drag the title bar of your toolbar to move the toolbar within the application window.

- Toggle the check box that appears next to your toolbar within the Customize dialog box on and off to display or hide your toolbar. Leave the box checked to display the toolbar and continue with this exercise.

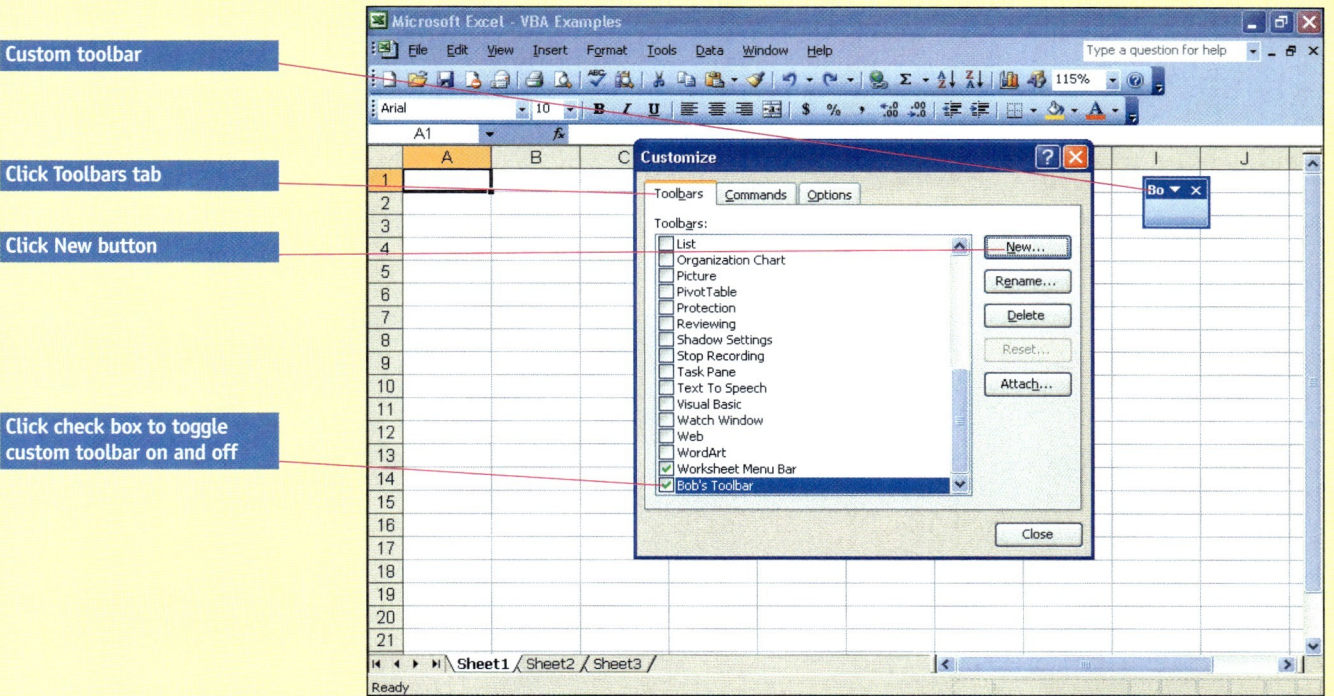

(f) Create a Custom Toolbar (step 6)

FIGURE 8 Hands-on Exercise 2 (*continued*)

FIXED VERSUS FLOATING TOOLBARS

A toolbar may be docked (fixed) along the edge of the application window, or it can be displayed as a floating toolbar anywhere within the window. You can switch back and forth by dragging the move handle of a docked toolbar to move the toolbar away from the edge. Conversely, you can drag the title bar of a floating toolbar to the edge of the window to dock the toolbar. You can also click and drag the border of a floating toolbar to change its size.

Step 7: **Add Buttons to the Toolbar**

- Click the **Commands tab** in the Customize dialog box, click the **down arrow** in the Categories list box, then scroll until you can select the **Macros category**. (If you are using Access and not Excel, you need to select the **File category**, then follow the steps as described in the boxed tip on the next page.)

- Click and drag the **Custom button** to your toolbar and release the mouse. A "happy face" button appears on the toolbar you just created. (You can remove a button from a toolbar by simply dragging the button from the toolbar.)

- Select the newly created button, then click the **Modify Selection command button** (or right click the button to display the context-sensitive menu) in Figure 8g. Change the button's properties as follows:
    - Click the **Assign Macro command** at the bottom of the menu to display the Assign Macro dialog box, then select the **IfThenElseExamples macro** (procedure) to assign it to the button. Click **OK**.
    - Click the **Modify Selection button** a second time.
    - Click in the **Name Textbox** and enter an appropriate name for the button, such as **IfThenElseExamples**.
    - Click the **Modify Selection button** a third time, then click **Text Only (Always)** to display text rather than an image.

- Repeat this procedure to add buttons to the toolbar for the MsgBoxExamples, InputBoxExamples, and CaseExample procedures that you created earlier.

- Close the Customize dialog box when you have completed the toolbar.

- Save the workbook.

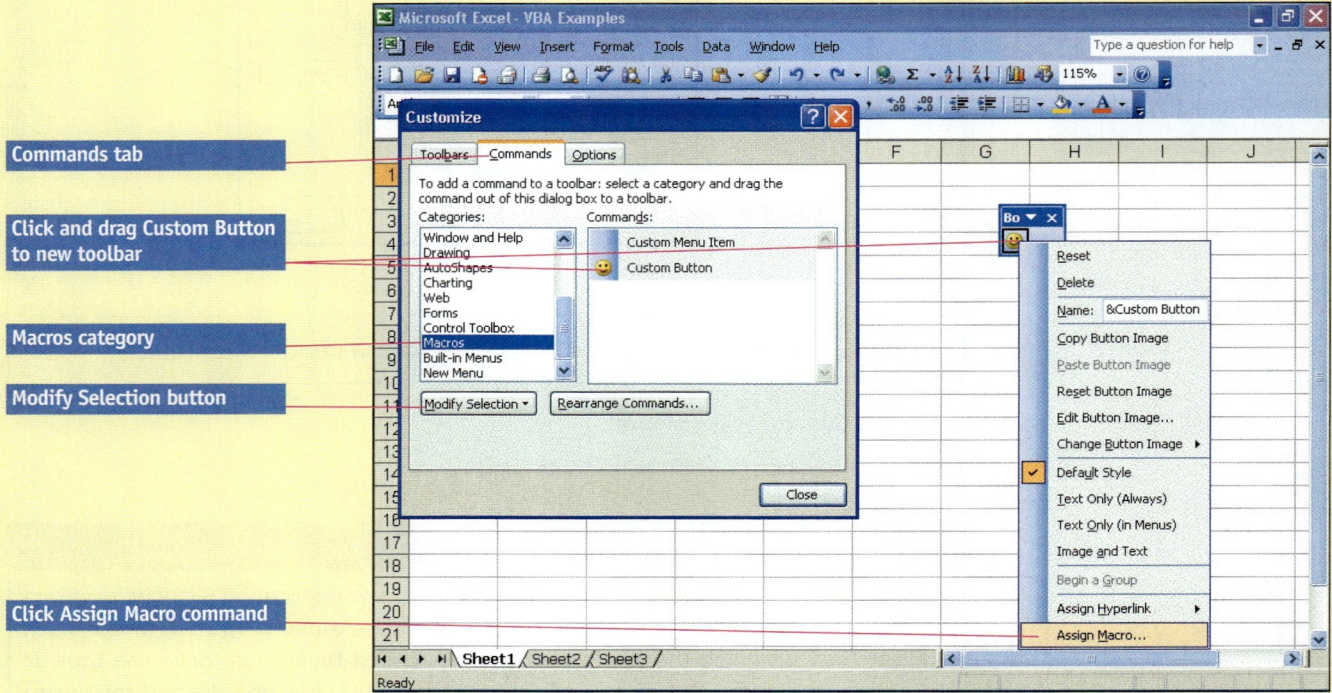

(g) Add Buttons to the Toolbar (step 7)

FIGURE 8   Hands-on Exercise 2 (*continued*)

Step 8: **Test the Custom Toolbar**

- Click any command on your toolbar as shown in Figure 8h. We clicked the **InputBoxExamples button**, which in turn executed the InputBoxExamples procedure that was created in the first exercise.

- Enter the appropriate information in any input boxes that are displayed. Click **OK**. Close your toolbar when you have completed testing it.

- If this is not your own machine, you should delete your toolbar as a courtesy to the next student. Pull down the **View menu**, click the **Toolbars command**, click **Customize** to display the Customize dialog box, then click the **Toolbars tab**. Select (highlight) the toolbar, then click the **Delete button** in the Customize dialog box. Click **OK** to delete the button. Close the dialog box.

- Exit Office if you do not want to continue with the next exercise.

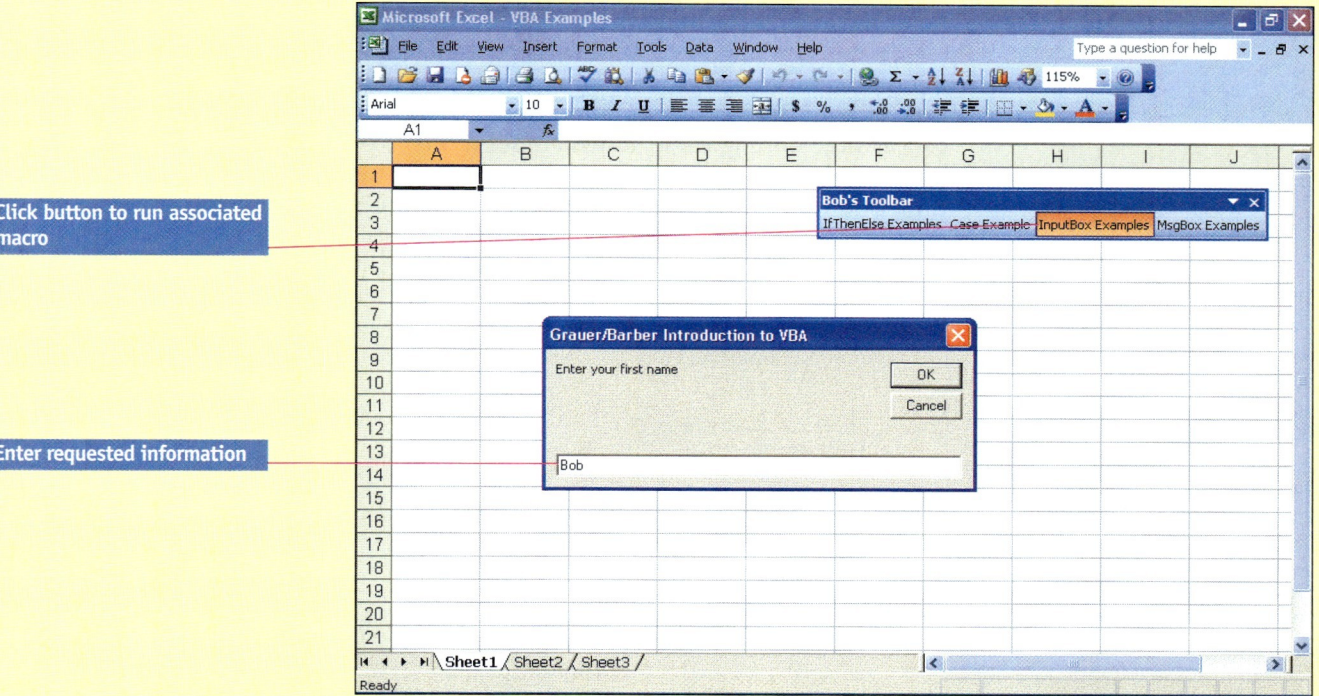

(h) Test the Custom Toolbar (step 8)

FIGURE 8 Hands-on Exercise 2 (*continued*)

ACCESS IS DIFFERENT

The procedure to add buttons to a custom toolbar in Access is different from the procedure in Excel. Pull down the View menu, click the Toolbars command, then click the Customize command. Select the File category within the Customize dialog box, then click and drag the Custom command to the newly created toolbar. Select the command on the toolbar, then click the Modify Selection command button in the dialog box. Click Properties, click the On Action text box, then type the name of the procedure you want to run in the format, =procedurename(). Close the dialog boxes, then press Alt+F11 to return to the VBA editor. Change the keyword "Sub" that identifies the procedure to "Function". Return to the database window, then test the newly created toolbar.

MICROSOFT OFFICE EXCEL 2003 REVISED

FOR . . . NEXT STATEMENT

The **For . . . Next statement** executes all statements between the words For and Next a specified number of times, using a counter to keep track of the number of times the statements are executed. The statement, For intCounter = 1 to N, executes the statements within the loop N times.

The procedure in Figure 9 contains two For . . . Next statements that sum the numbers from 1 to 10, counting by 1 and 2, respectively. The Dim statements at the beginning of the procedure declare two variables, intSumofNumbers to hold the sum and intCounter to hold the value of the counter. The sum is initialized to zero immediately before the first loop. The statements in the loop are then executed 10 times, each time incrementing the sum by the value of the counter. The result (the sum of the numbers from 1 to 10) is displayed after the loop in Figure 9b.

The second For . . . Next statement increments the counter by 2 rather than by 1. (The increment or step is assumed to be 1 unless a different value is specified.) The sum of the numbers is reset to zero prior to entering the second loop, the loop is entered, and the counter is initialized to the starting value of 1. Each subsequent time through the loop, however, the counter is incremented by 2. Each time the value of the counter is compared to the ending value, until it (the counter) exceeds the ending value, at which point the For . . . Next statement is complete. Thus the second loop will be executed for values of 1, 3, 5, 7, and 9. After the fifth time through the loop, the counter is incremented to 11, which is greater than the ending value of 10, and the loop is terminated.

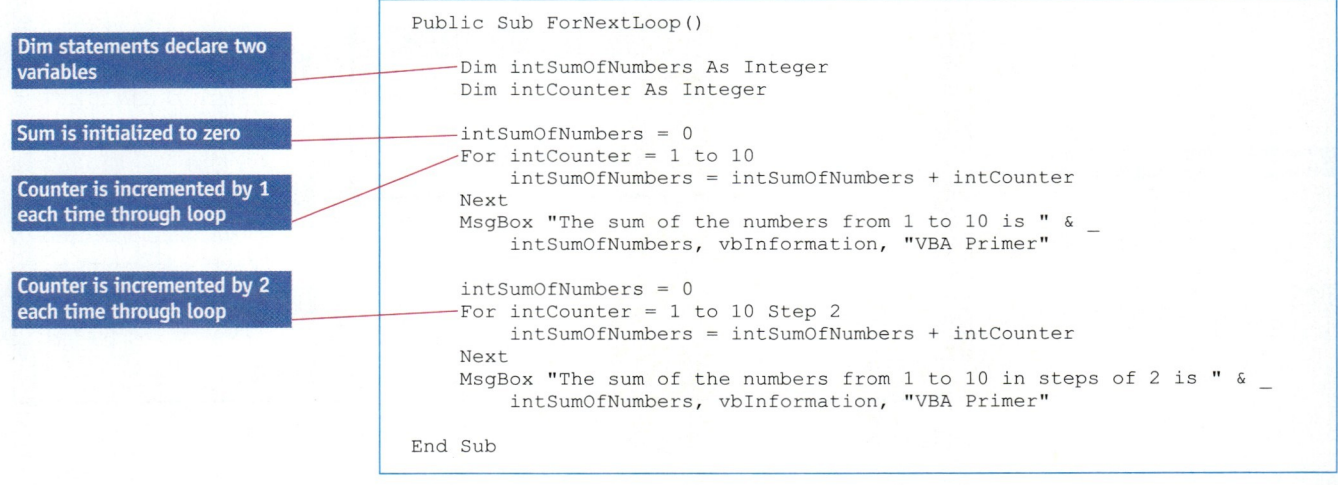

```
Public Sub ForNextLoop()

    Dim intSumOfNumbers As Integer
    Dim intCounter As Integer

    intSumOfNumbers = 0
    For intCounter = 1 to 10
        intSumOfNumbers = intSumOfNumbers + intCounter
    Next
    MsgBox "The sum of the numbers from 1 to 10 is " & _
        intSumOfNumbers, vbInformation, "VBA Primer"

    intSumOfNumbers = 0
    For intCounter = 1 to 10 Step 2
        intSumOfNumbers = intSumOfNumbers + intCounter
    Next
    MsgBox "The sum of the numbers from 1 to 10 in steps of 2 is " & _
        intSumOfNumbers, vbInformation, "VBA Primer"

End Sub
```

(a) VBA Code

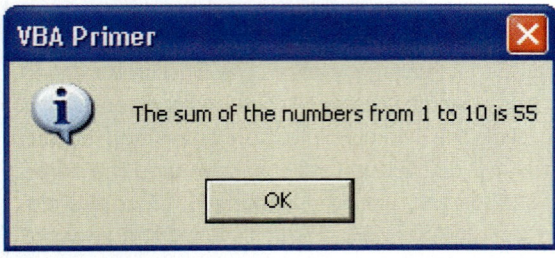

(b) In Increments of 1

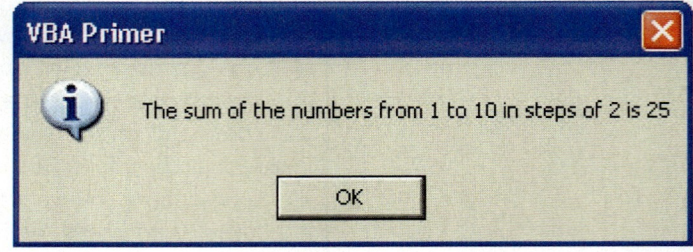

(c) In Increments of 2

FIGURE 9 For . . . Next Loops

DO LOOPS

The For . . . Next statement is ideal when you know in advance how many times you want to go through a loop. There are many instances, however, when the number of times through the loop is indeterminate. You could, for example, give a user multiple chances to enter a password or answer a question. This type of logic is implemented through a Do loop. You can repeat the loop as long as a condition is true (Do While), or until a condition becomes true (Do Until). The choice depends on how you want to state the condition.

Regardless of which keyword you choose, Do While or Do Until, two formats are available. The difference is subtle and depends on whether the keyword (While or Until) appears at the beginning or end of the loop. Our discussion will use the Do Until statement, but the Do While statement works in similar fashion.

Look closely at the procedure in Figure 10a, which contains two different loops. In the first example the Until condition appears at the end of the loop, which means the statements in the loop are executed, and then the condition is tested. This ensures that the statements in the loop will be executed at least once. The second loop, however, places the Until condition at the beginning of the loop, so that it (the condition) is tested prior to the loop being executed. Thus, if the condition is satisfied initially, the second loop will never be executed. In other words, there are two distinct statements **Do . . . Loop Until** and **Do Until . . . Loop**. The first statement executes the loop, then tests the condition. The second statement tests the condition, then enters the loop.

```
Public Sub DoUntilLoop()

    Dim strCorrectAnswer As String, strUserAnswer As String

    strCorrectAnswer = "Earth"

    Do
        strUserAnswer = InputBox("What is the third planet from the sun?")
    Loop Until strUserAnswer = strCorrectAnswer
    MsgBox "You are correct, earthling!", vbExclamation

    strUserAnswer = InputBox("What is the third planet from the sun?")
    Do Until strUserAnswer = strCorrectAnswer
        strUserAnswer = InputBox("Your answer is incorrect. Try again.")
    Loop
    MsgBox "You are correct, earthling!", vbExclamation

End Sub
```

Until appears at end of loop

Until appears at beginning of loop

(a) (VBA Code)

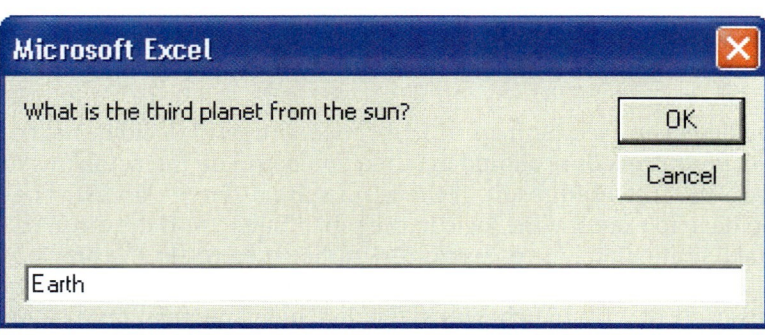

(b) Input the Answer

(c) Correct Response

FIGURE 10 Do Until Loops

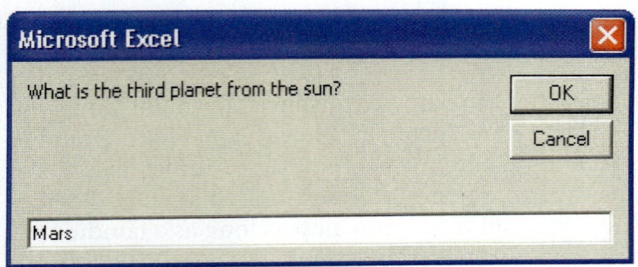
(d) Wrong Answer Initially

(e) Second Chance

FIGURE 10 Do Until Loops (*continued*)

It's tricky, but stay with us. In the first example the user is asked the question within the loop, and the loop is executed repeatedly until the user gives the correct answer. In the second example the user is asked the question outside of the loop, and the loop is bypassed if the user answers it correctly. The latter is the preferred logic because it enables us to phrase the question differently, before and during the loop. Look carefully at the difference between the InputBox statements and see how the question changes within the second loop.

DEBUGGING

As you learn more about VBA and develop more powerful procedures, you are more likely to make mistakes. The process of finding and correcting errors within a procedure is known as ***debugging*** and it is an integral part of programming. Do not be discouraged if you make mistakes. Everyone does. The important thing is how quickly you are able to find and correct the errors that invariably occur. We begin our discussion of debugging by describing two types of errors, ***compilation errors*** and ***execution*** (or ***run-time***) ***errors***.

A compilation error is simply an error in VBA syntax. (Compilation is the process of translating a VBA procedure into machine language, and thus a compilation error occurs when the VBA editor is unable to convert a statement to machine language.) Compilation errors occur for many reasons, such as misspelling a keyword, omitting a comma, and so on. VBA recognizes the error before the procedure is run and displays the invalid statement in red together with an associated error message. The programmer corrects the error and then reruns the procedure.

Execution errors are caused by errors in logic and are more difficult to detect because they occur without any error message. VBA, or for that matter any other programming language, does what you tell it to do, which is not necessarily what you want it to do. If, for example, you were to compute the sales tax of an item by multiplying the price by 60% rather than 6%, VBA will perform the calculation and simply display the wrong answer. It is up to you to realize that the results of the procedure are incorrect, and you will need to examine its statements and correct the mistake.

So how do you detect an execution error? In essence, you must decide what the expected output of your procedure should be, then you compare the actual result of the procedure to the intended result. If the results are different, an error has occurred, and you have to examine the logic in the procedure to find the error. You may see the mistake immediately (e.g., using 60% rather than 6% in the previous example), or you may have to examine the code more closely. And as you might expect, VBA has a variety of tools to help you in the debugging process. These tools are accessed from the ***Debug toolbar*** or the ***Debug menu*** as shown in Figure 11 on the next page.

The procedure in Figure 11 is a simple For . . . Next loop to sum the integers from 1 to 10. The procedure is correct as written, but we have introduced several debugging techniques into the figure. The most basic technique is to step through the statements in the procedure one at a time to see the sequence in which the statements are executed. Click the **Step Into button** on the Debug toolbar to enter (step into) the procedure, then continue to click the button to move through the procedure. Each time you click the button, the statement that is about to be executed is highlighted.

Another useful technique is to display the values of selected variables as they change during execution. This is accomplished through the **Debug.Print statement** that displays the values in the **Immediate window**. The Debug.Print statement is placed within the For . . . Next loop so that you can see how the counter and the associated sum change during execution.

As the figure now stands, we have gone through the loop nine times, and the sum of the numbers from 1 to 9 is 45. The Step Into button is in effect so that the statement to be executed next is highlighted. You can see that we are back at the top of the loop, where the counter has been incremented to 10, and further, that we are about to increment the sum.

The **Locals window** is similar in concept except that it displays only the current values of all the variables within the procedure. Unlike the Immediate window, which requires the insertion of Debug.Print statements into a procedure to have meaning, the Locals window displays its values automatically, without any effort on the part of the programmer, other than opening the window. All three techniques can be used individually, or in conjunction with one another, as the situation demands.

We believe that the best time to practice debugging is when you know there are no errors in your procedure. As you may have guessed, it's time for the next hands-on exercise.

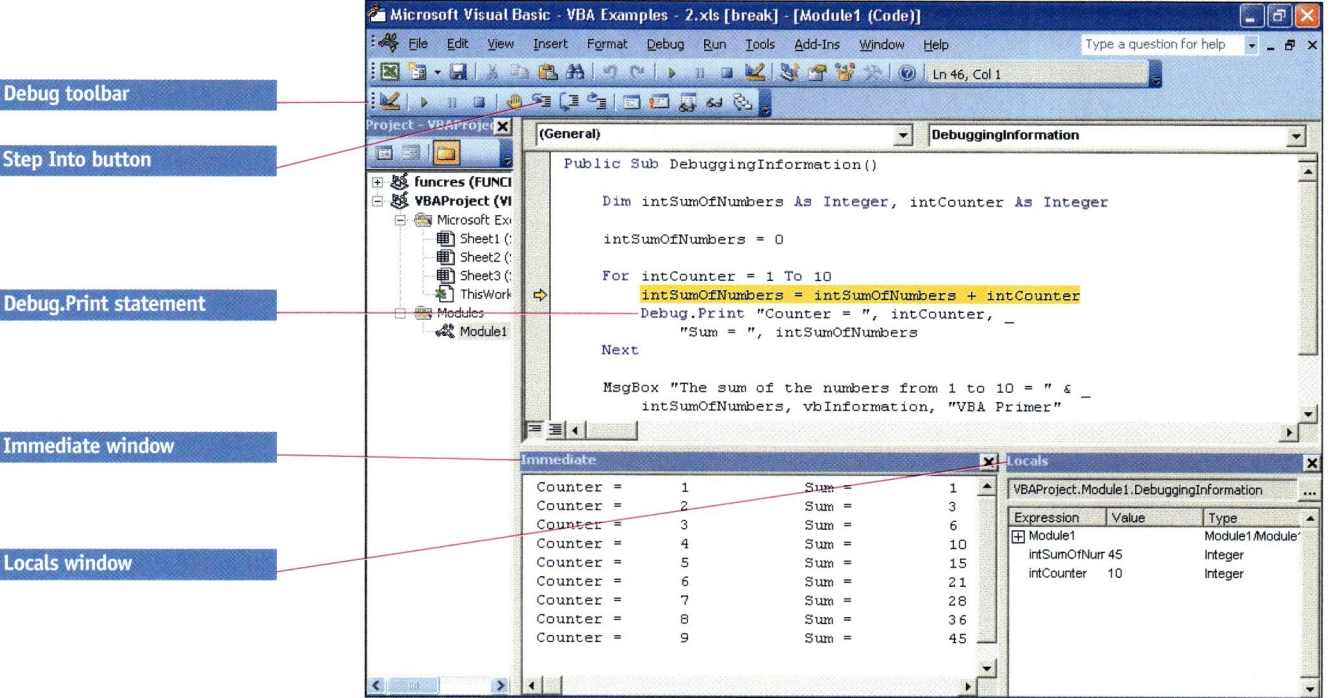

FIGURE 11 Debugging

hands-on exercise 3

Loops and Debugging

Objective To create a loop using the For . . . Next and Do Until statements; to open the Locals and Immediate windows and illustrate different techniques for debugging. Use Figure 12 as a guide in the exercise.

Step 1: **Insert a New Procedure**

- Open the **VBA Examples workbook** or the Access database from the previous exercise. Either way, pull down the **Tools menu**, click the **Macro command**, then click **Visual Basic editor** (or use the **Alt+F11** keyboard shortcut) to start the VBA editor.

- If necessary, double click **Module1** within the Project Explorer window to open this module. Pull down the **Insert menu** and click the **Procedure command** to display the Add Procedure dialog box.

- Click in the **Name** text box and enter **ForNextLoop** as the name of the procedure. Click the option buttons for a **Sub procedure** and for **Public scope**. Click **OK** to create the procedure.

- The Sub procedure should appear within the module and consist of the Sub and End Sub statements as shown in Figure 12a.

- Click the **Procedure View button** at the bottom of the window as shown in Figure 12a. The display changes to show just the current procedure, giving you more room in which to work.

- Save the module.

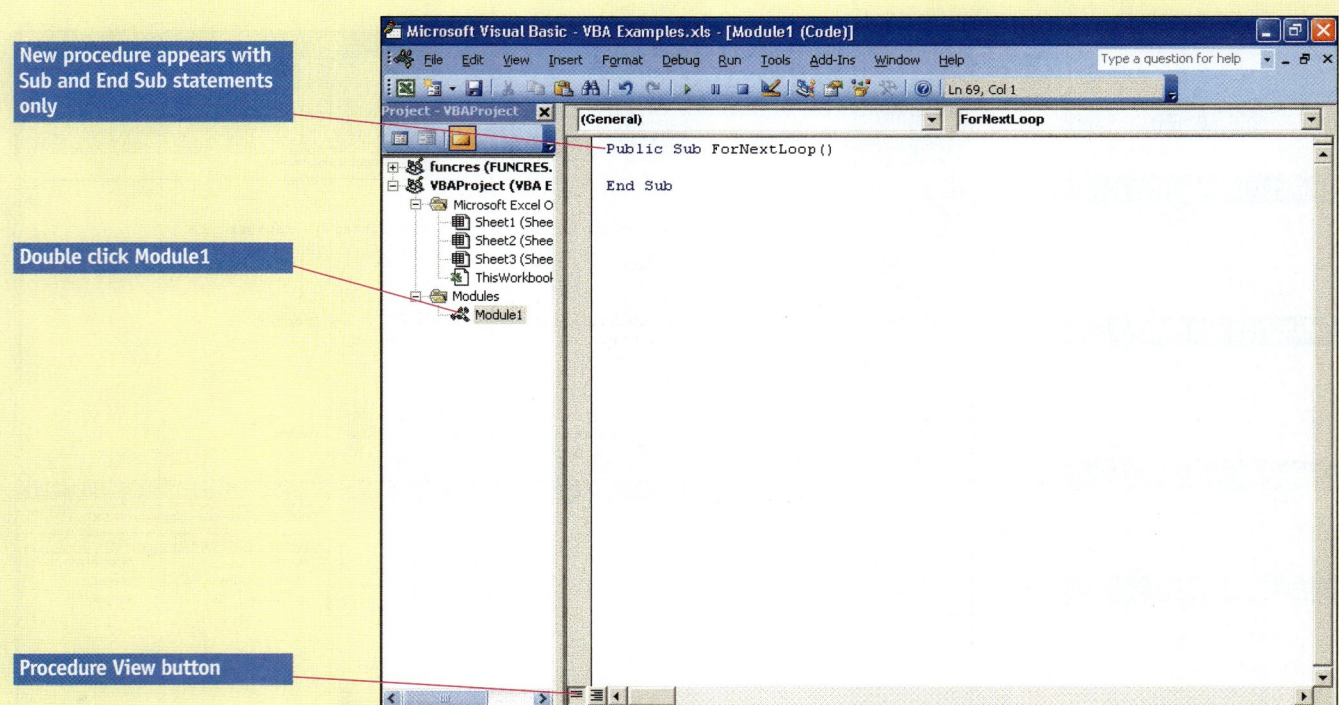

(a) Insert a New Procedure (step 1)

FIGURE 12 Hands-on Exercise 3

Step 2: **Test the For ... Next Procedure**

- Enter the procedure exactly as it appears in Figure 12b. Note the following:
  - A comment is added at the beginning of the procedure to identify the author and the date.
  - Two variables are declared at the beginning of the procedure, one to hold the sum of the numbers and the other to serve as a counter.
  - The sum of the numbers is initialized to zero. The For ... Next loop varies the counter from 1 to 10.
  - The statement within the For ... Next loop increments the sum of the numbers by the current value of the counter. The equal sign is really a replacement operator; that is, replace the variable on the left (the sum of the numbers) by the expression on the right (the sum of the numbers plus the value of the counter.
  - Indentation and spacing within a procedure are for the convenience of the programmer and not a requirement of VBA. We align the For and Next statements at the beginning and end of a loop, then indent all statements within a loop.
  - The MsgBox statement displays the result and is continued over two lines as per the underscore at the end of the first line.
  - The ampersand concatenates (joins together) the text and the number within the message box.
- Click the **Save button** to save the module. Right click the **Excel button** on the Windows taskbar to display a context-sensitive menu, then click the **Minimize command**.
- Click the **Run Sub button** to test the procedure, which should display the MsgBox statement in Figure 12b. Correct any errors that may occur.

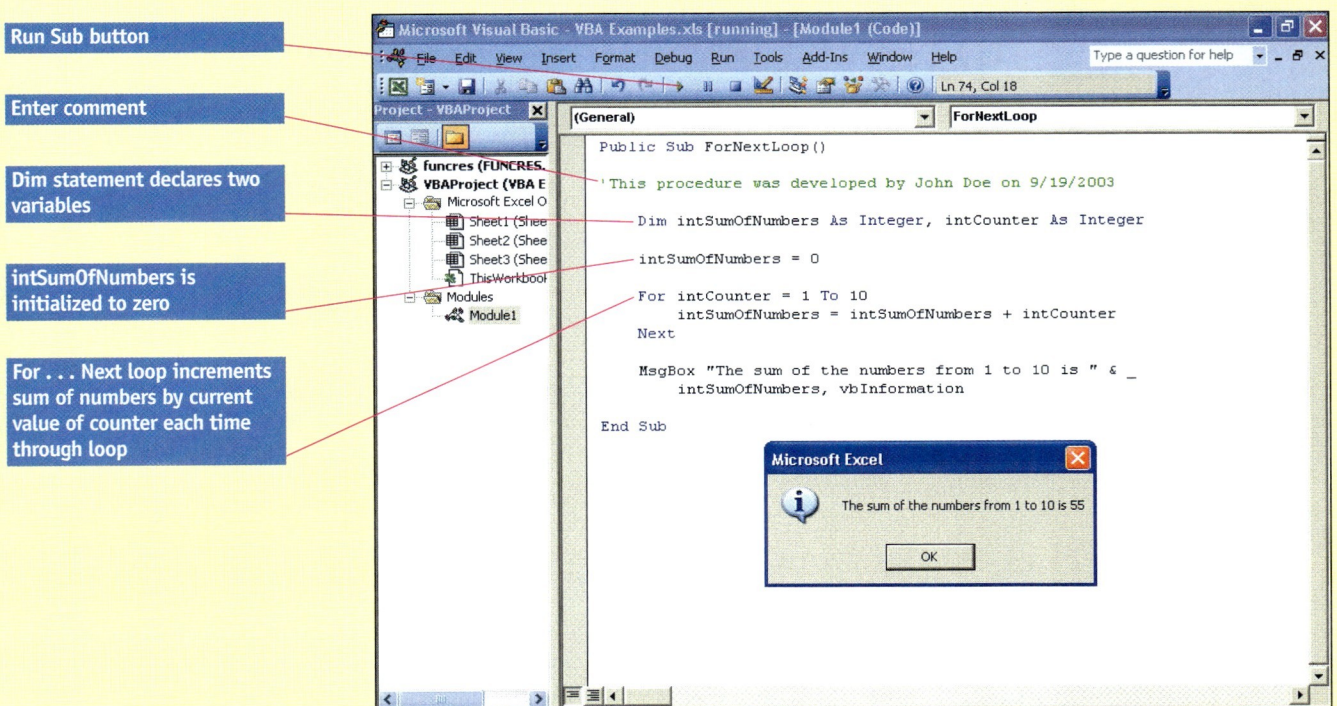

(b) Test the For ... Next Procedure (step 2)

FIGURE 12   Hands-on Exercise 3 (*continued*)

Step 3: **Compilation Errors**

- The best time to practice debugging is when you know that the procedure is working properly. Accordingly, we will make some deliberate errors in our procedure to illustrate different debugging techniques.

- Pull down the **View menu**, click the **Toolbars command**, and (if necessary) toggle the Debug toolbar on, then dock it under the Standard toolbar.

- Click on the statement that initializes intSumOfNumbers to zero and delete the "s" at the end of the variable name. Click the **Run Sub button**.

- You will see the message in Figure 12c. Click **OK** to acknowledge the error, then click the **Undo button** to correct the error.

- The procedure header is highlighted, indicating that execution is temporarily suspended and that additional action is required from you to continue testing. Click the **Run Sub button** to retest the procedure.

- This time the procedure executes correctly and you see the MsgBox statement indicating that the sum of the numbers from 1 to 10 is 55. Click **OK**.

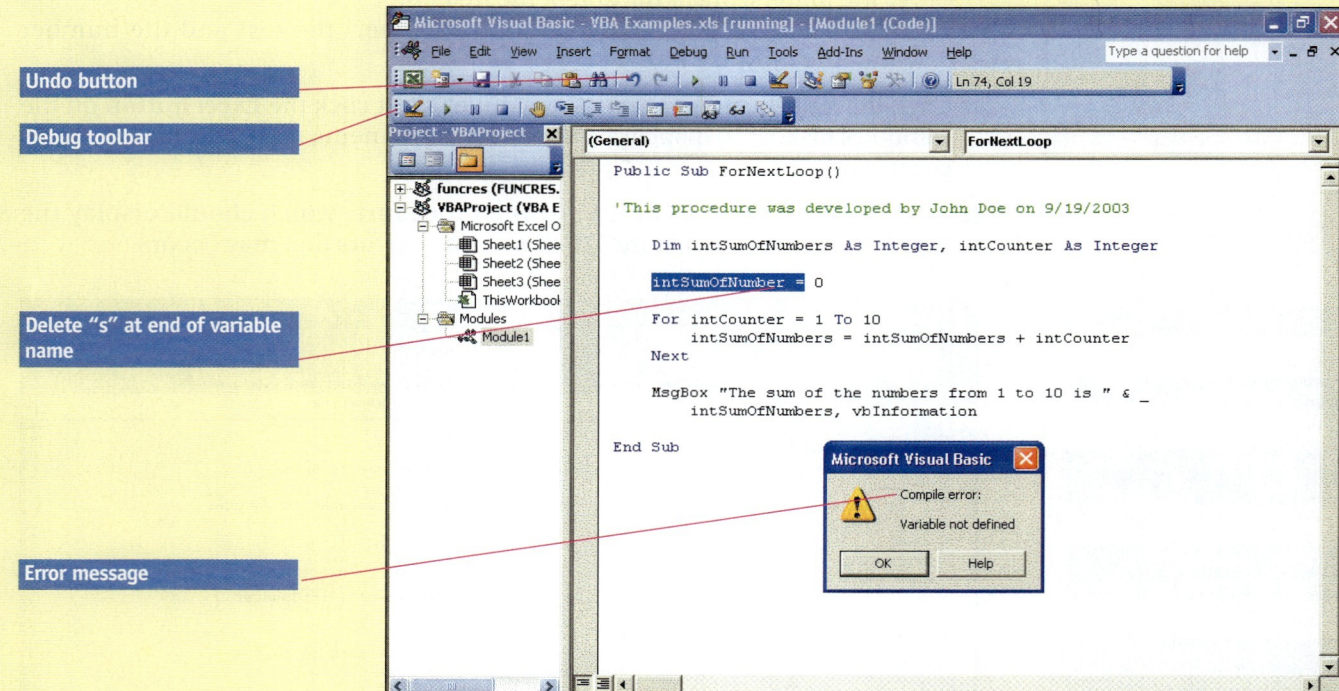

(c) Compilation Error (step 3)

FIGURE 12   Hands-on Exercise 3 (*continued*)

USE HELP AS NECESSARY

Pull down the Help menu at any time (or press the F1 key) to access the VBA Help facility to explore at your leisure. Use the Print command to create hard copy. (You can also copy the help text into a Word document to create your own reference manual.) The answers to virtually all of your questions are readily available if only you take the time to look.

Step 4: **Step through a Procedure**

- Pull down the **View menu** a second time and click the **Locals Window command** (or click the **Locals Window button** on the Debug toolbar).

- If necessary, click and drag the top border of the Locals window to size the window appropriately as shown in Figure 12d.

- Click anywhere within the procedure. Pull down the **Debug menu** and click the **Step Into command** (or click the **Step Into button** on the Debug toolbar). The first statement (the procedure header) is highlighted, indicating that you are about to enter the procedure.

- Click the **Step Into button** (or use the **F8** keyboard shortcut) to step into the procedure and advance to the next executable statement. The statement that initializes intSumOfNumbers to zero is highlighted, indicating that this statement is about to be executed.

- Continue to press the **F8 key** to step through the procedure. Each time you execute a statement, you can see the values of intSumOfNumbers and intCounter change within the Locals window. (You can click the **Step Out button** at any time to end the procedure.)

- Correct errors as they occur. Click the **Reset button** on the Standard or Debug toolbars at any time to begin executing the procedure from the beginning.

- Eventually you exit from the loop, and the sum of the numbers (from 1 to 10) is displayed within a message box.

- Click **OK** to close the message box. Press the **F8 key** a final time, then close the Locals window.

- Do you see how stepping through a procedure helps you to understand how it works?

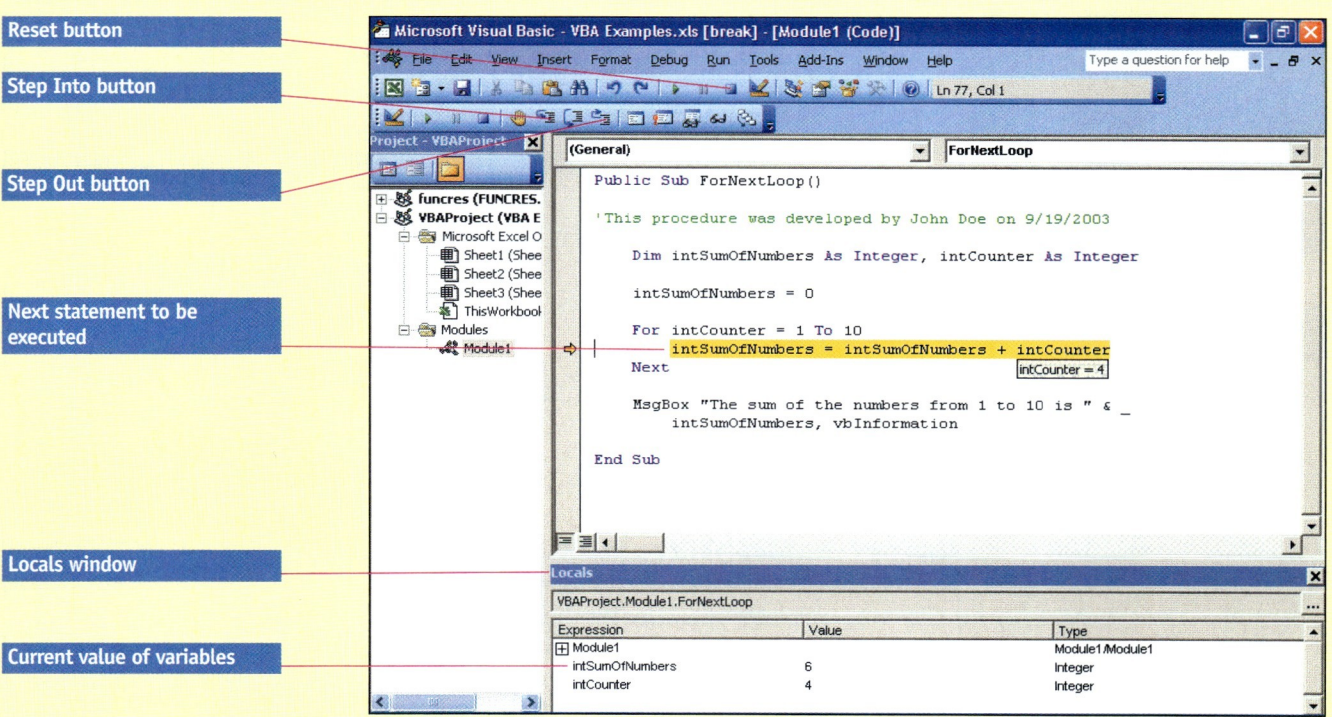

(d) Step through a Procedure (step 4)

FIGURE 12 Hands-on Exercise 3 (*continued*)

Step 5: The Immediate Window

- You should be back in the VBA window. Click immediately to the left of the Next statement and press **Enter** to insert a blank line. Type the **Debug.Print** statement exactly as shown in Figure 12e. (Click **OK** if you see a message indicating that the procedure will be reset.)

- Pull down the **View menu** and click the **Immediate Window command** (or click the **Immediate Window button** on the Debug toolbar). The Immediate window should be empty, but if not, you can click and drag to select the contents, then press the **Del key** to clear the window.

- Click anywhere within the For . . . Next procedure, then click the **Run Sub button** to execute the procedure. You will see the familiar message box indicating that the sum of the numbers is 55. Click **OK**.

- You should see 10 lines within the Immediate window as shown in Figure 12e, corresponding to the values displayed by the Debug.Print statement as it was executed within the loop.

- Close the Immediate window. Do you see how displaying the intermediate results of a procedure helps you to understand how it works?

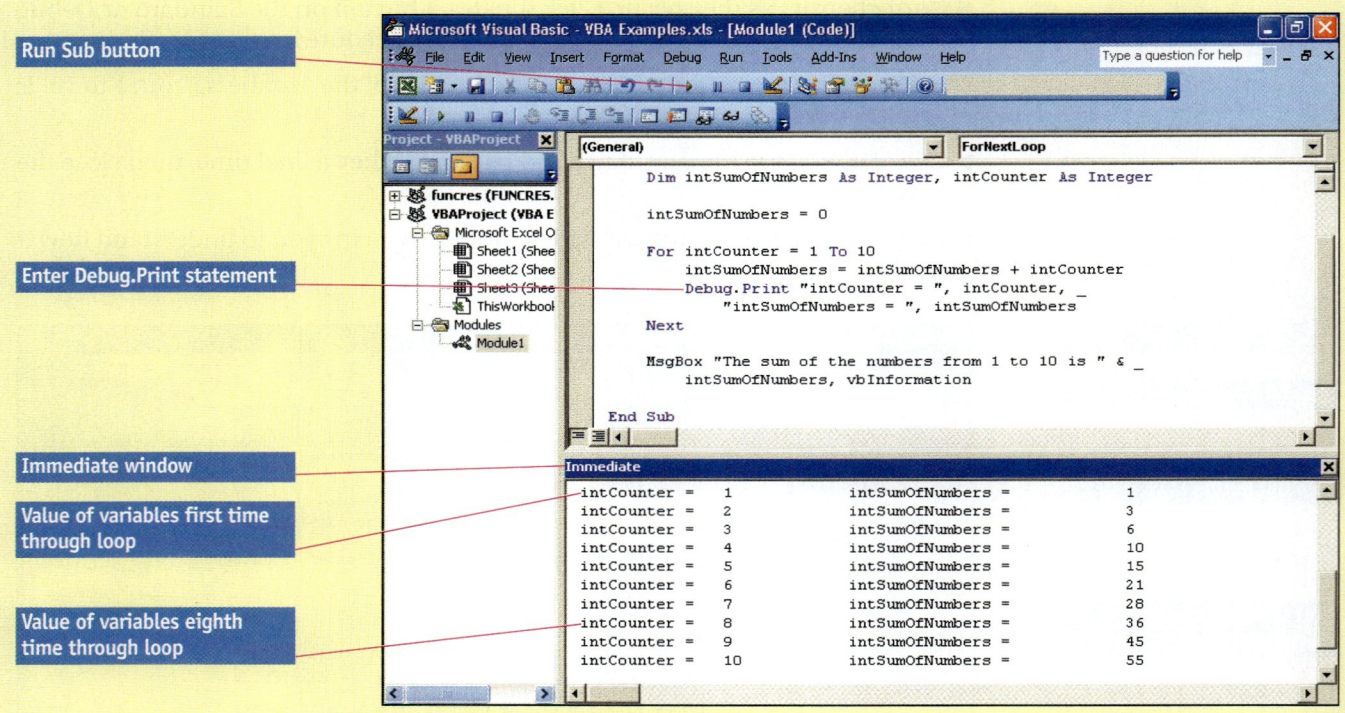

(e) The Immediate Window (step 5)

FIGURE 12 Hands-on Exercise 3 (*continued*)

INSTANT CALCULATOR

Use the Print method (action) in the Immediate window to use VBA as a calculator. Press Ctrl+G at any time to display the Immediate window. Click in the window, then type the statement Debug.Print, followed by your calculation, for example, Debug.Print 2+2, and press Enter. The answer is displayed on the next line in the Immediate window.

Step 6: **A More General Procedure**

- Modify the existing procedure to make it more general—for example, to sum the values from any starting value to any ending value:
  - Click at the end of the existing Dim statement to position the insertion point, press **Enter** to create a new line, then add the second **Dim statement** as shown in Figure 12f.
  - Click before the For statement, press **Enter** to create a blank line, press **Enter** a second time, then enter the two **InputBox statements** to ask the user for the beginning and ending values.
  - Modify the For statement to execute from **intStart** to **intEnd** rather than from 1 to 10.
  - Change the MsgBox statement to reflect the values of intStart and intEnd, and a customized title bar. Note the use of the ampersand and the underscore, to indicate concatenation and continuation, respectively.

- Click the **Save button** to save the module.

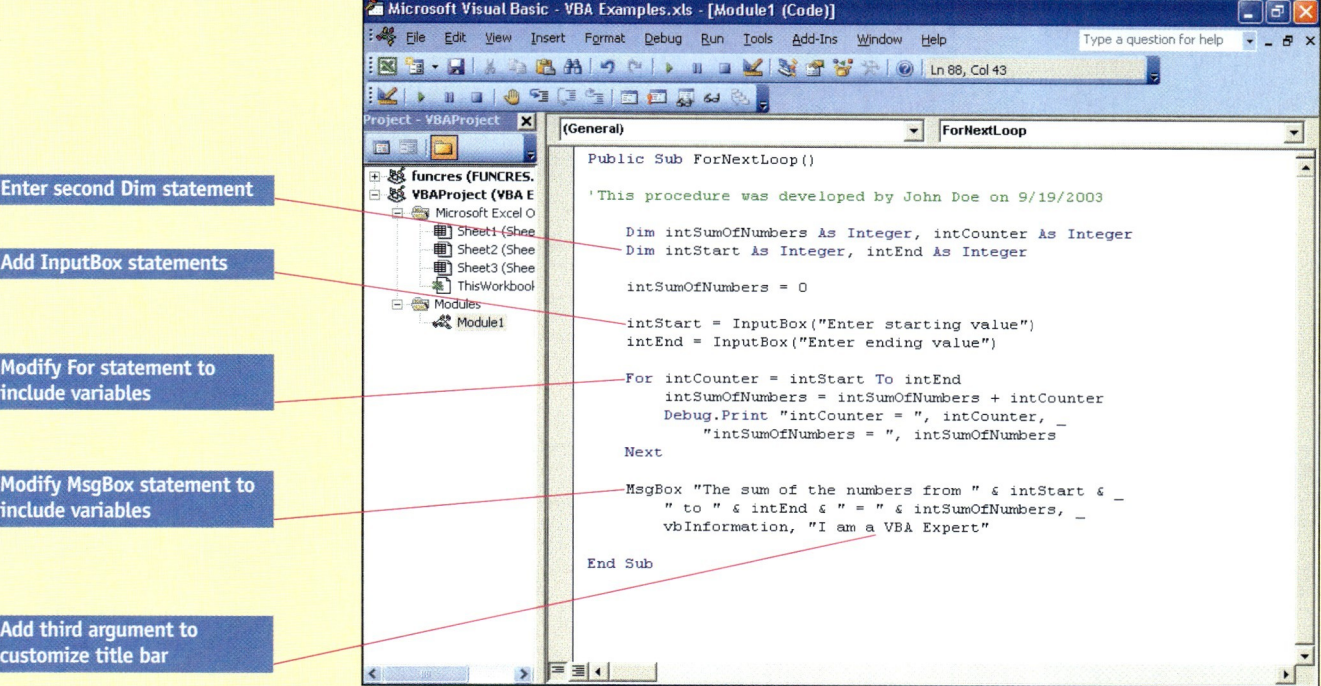

(f) A More General Procedure (step 6)

FIGURE 12 Hands-on Exercise 3 (*continued*)

USE WHAT YOU KNOW

Use the techniques acquired from other applications such as Microsoft Word to facilitate editing within the VBA window. Press the Ins key to toggle between the insert and overtype modes as you modify the statements within a VBA procedure. You can also cut, copy, and paste statements (or parts of statements) within a procedure and from one procedure to another. The Find and Replace commands are also useful.

Step 7: **Test the Procedure**

- Click the **Run Sub button** to test the procedure. You should be prompted for a beginning and an ending value. Enter any numbers you like, such as 10 and 20, respectively, to match the result in Figure 12g.

- The value displayed in the MsgBox statement should reflect the numbers you entered. For example, you will see a sum of 165 if you entered 10 and 20 as the starting and ending values.

- Look carefully at the message box that is displayed in Figure 12g. Its title bar displays the literal "I am a VBA expert", corresponding to the last argument in the MsgBox statement.

- Note, too, the spacing that appears within the message box, which includes spaces before and after each number. Look at your results and, if necessary, modify the MsgBox statement so that you have the same output. Click **OK**.

- Save the procedure.

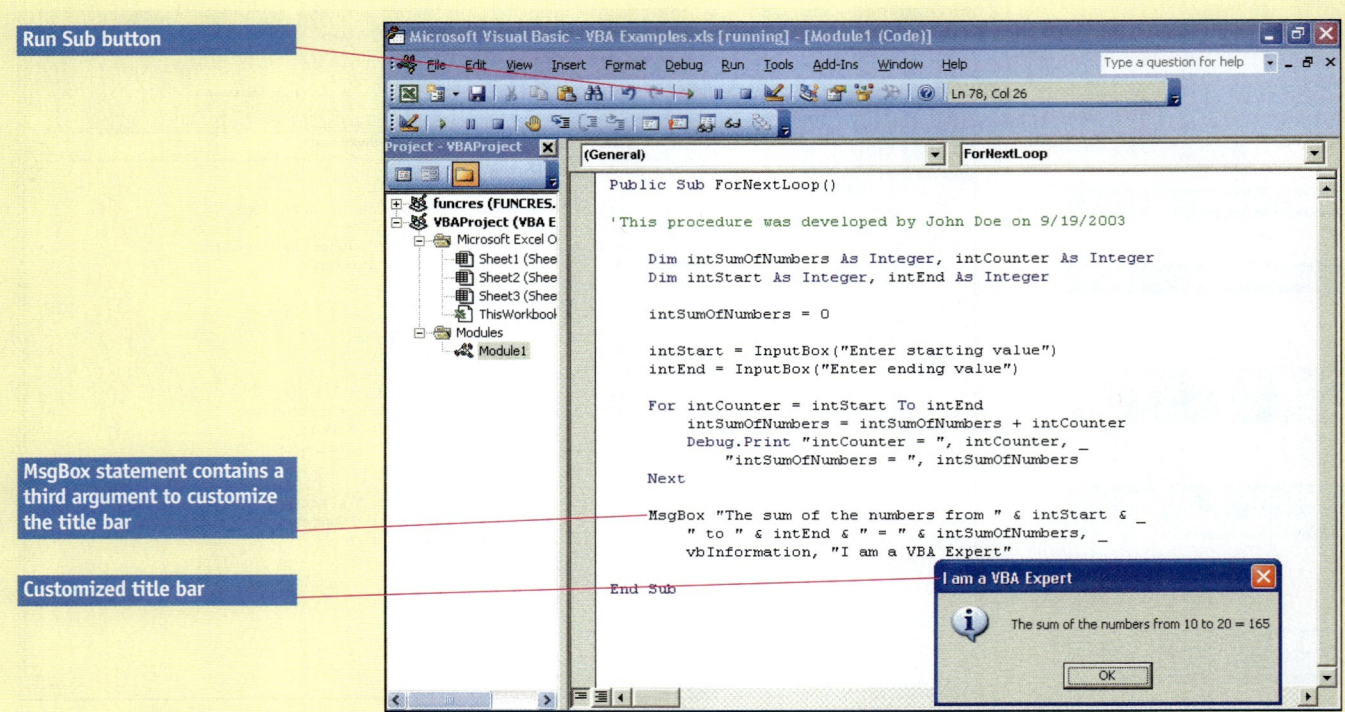

(g) Test the Procedure (step 7)

FIGURE 12 Hands-on Exercise 3 (*continued*)

CHANGE THE INCREMENT

The For . . . Next statement can be made more general by supplying an increment within the For statement. Try For intCount = 1 To 10 Step 2, or more generally, For intCount = intStart to intEnd Step intStepValue. "Step" is a Visual Basic keyword and must be entered that way. intCount, intEnd, and intStepValue are user-defined variables. The variables must be defined at the beginning of a procedure and can be initialized by requesting values from the user through the InputBox statement.

Step 8: **Create a Do Until Loop**

- Pull down the **Insert menu** and click the **Procedure command** to insert a new procedure called **DoUntilLoop**. Enter the procedure as it appears in Figure 12h. Note the following:
  - Two string variables are declared to hold the correct answer and the user's response, respectively.
  - The variable strCorrectAnswer is set to "Earth", which is the correct answer for our question.
  - The initial InputBox function prompts the user to enter his/her response to the question. A second InputBox function appears in the loop that is executed if and only if the user enters the wrong answer.
  - The Until condition appears at the beginning of the loop, so that the loop is entered only if the user answers incorrectly. The loop executes repeatedly until the correct answer is supplied.
  - A message to the user is displayed at the end of the procedure after the correct answer has been entered.

- Click the **Run Sub button** to test the procedure. Enter the correct answer on your first attempt, and you will see that the loop is never entered.

- Rerun the procedure, answer incorrectly, then note that a second input box appears, telling you that your answer was incorrect. Click **OK**.

- Once again you are prompted for the answer. Enter **Earth**. Click **OK**. The procedure ends.

- Save the procedure.

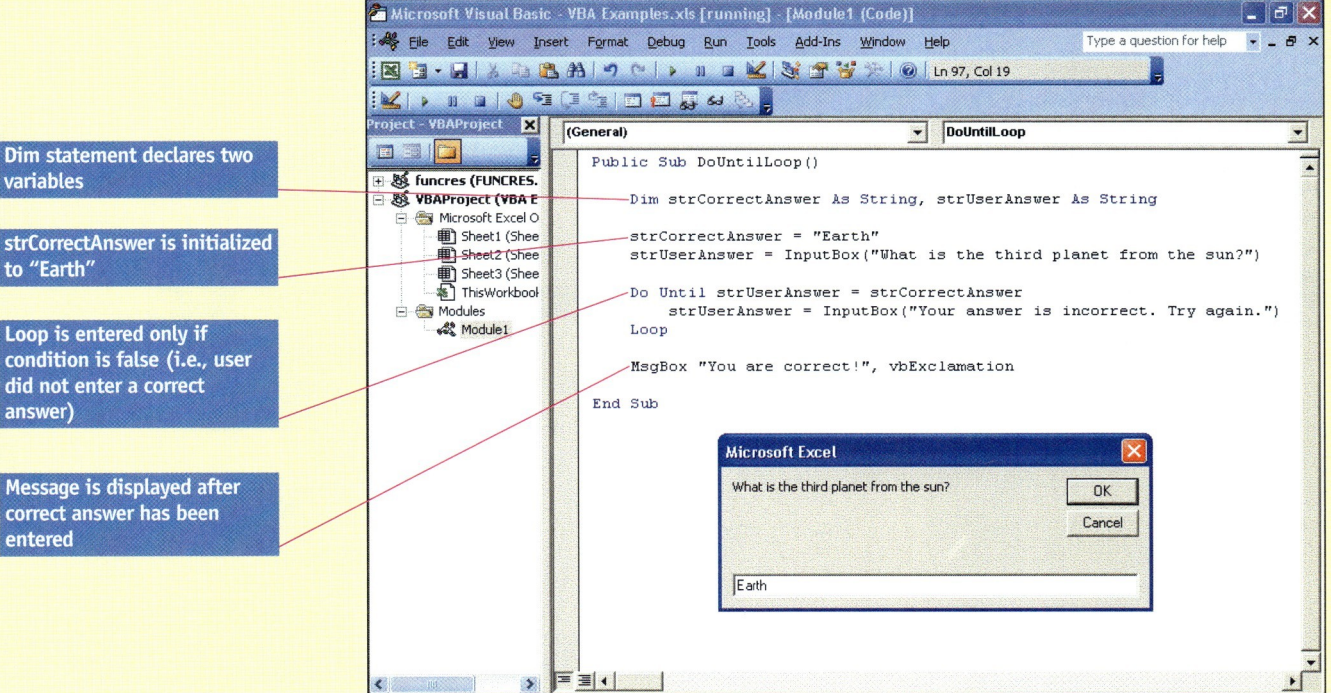

(h) Create a Do Until Loop (step 8)

FIGURE 12   Hands-on Exercise 3 (*continued*)

Step 9: **A More Powerful Procedure**

- Modify the procedure as shown in Figure 12i to include the statements to count and print the number of times the user takes to get the correct answer.
  - The variable intNumberOfAttempts is declared as an integer and is initialized to 1 after the user inputs his/her initial answer.
  - The Do loop is expanded to increment intNumberOfAttempts by 1 each time the loop is executed.
  - The MsgBox statement after the loop is expanded prints the number of attempts the user took to answer the question.
- Save the module, then click the **Run Sub button** to test the module. You should see a dialog box similar to the one in Figure 12i. Click **OK**. Do you see how this procedure improves on its predecessor?
- Pull down the **File menu** and click the **Print command** to display the Print dialog box. Click the option button to print the current module for your instructor. Click **OK**.
- Close the Debug toolbar. Exit Office if you do not want to continue with the next hands-on exercise at this time.

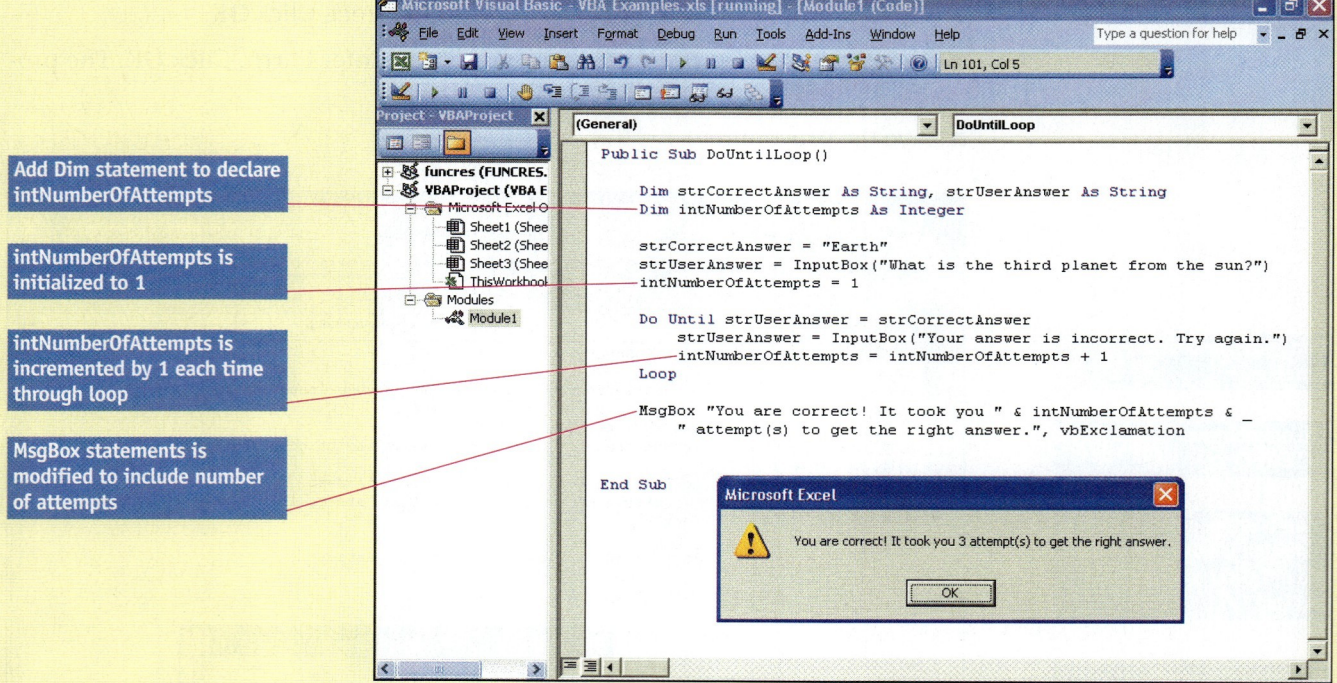

(i) A More Powerful Procedure (step 9)

FIGURE 12   Hands-on Exercise 3 (*continued*)

IT'S NOT EQUAL, BUT REPLACE

All programming languages use statements of the form N = N + 1, in which the equal sign does not mean equal in the literal sense; that is, N cannot equal N + 1. The equal sign is really a replacement operator. Thus, the expression on the right of the equal sign is evaluated, and that result replaces the value of the variable on the left. In other words, the statement N = N + 1 increments the value of N by 1.

PUTTING VBA TO WORK (MICROSOFT EXCEL)

Our approach thus far has focused on VBA as an independent entity that can be run without specific reference to the applications in Microsoft Office. We have covered several individual statements, explained how to use the VBA editor to create and run procedures, and how to debug those procedures, if necessary. We hope you have found the material to be interesting, but you may be asking yourself, "What does this have to do with Microsoft Office?" In other words, how can you use your knowledge of VBA to enhance your ability in Microsoft Excel or Access? The answer is to create ***event procedures*** that run automatically in response to events within an Office application.

VBA is different from traditional programming languages in that it is event-driven. An ***event*** is defined as any action that is recognized by an application such as Excel or Access. Opening or closing an Excel workbook or an Access database is an event. Selecting a worksheet within a workbook is also an event, as is clicking on a command button on an Access form. To use VBA within Microsoft Office, you decide which events are significant, and what is to happen when those events occur. Then you develop the appropriate event procedures.

Consider, for example, Figure 13, which displays the results of two event procedures in conjunction with opening and closing an Excel workbook. (If you are using Microsoft Access instead of Excel, you can skip this discussion and the associated exercise, and move to the parallel material for Access that appears after the next hands-on exercise.) The procedure associated with Figure 13a displays a message that appears automatically after the user executes the command to close the associated workbook. The procedure is almost trivial to write, and consists of a single MsgBox statement. The effect of the procedure is quite significant, however, as it reminds the user to back up his or her work after closing the workbook. Nor does it matter how the user closes the workbook—whether by pulling down the menu or using a keyboard shortcut—because the procedure runs automatically in response to the Close Workbook event, regardless of how that event occurs.

The dialog box in Figure 13b prompts the user for a password and appears automatically when the user opens the workbook. The logic here is more sophisticated in that the underlying procedure contains an InputBox statement to request the password, a Do Until loop that is executed until the user enters the correct password or exceeds the allotted number of attempts, then additional logic to display the worksheet or terminate the application if the user fails to enter the proper password. The procedure is not difficult, however, and it builds on the VBA statements that were covered earlier.

The next hands-on exercise has you create the two event procedures that are associated with Figure 13. As you do the exercise, you will gain additional experience with VBA and an appreciation for the potential event procedures within Microsoft Office.

HIDING AND UNHIDING A WORKSHEET

Look carefully at the workbooks in Figures 13a and 13b. Both figures reference the identical workbook, Financial Consultant, as can be seen from the title bar. Look at the worksheet tabs, however, and note that two worksheets are visible in Figure 13a, whereas the Calculations worksheet is hidden in Figure 13b. This was accomplished in the Open workbook procedure and was implemented to hide the calculations from the user until the correct password was entered.

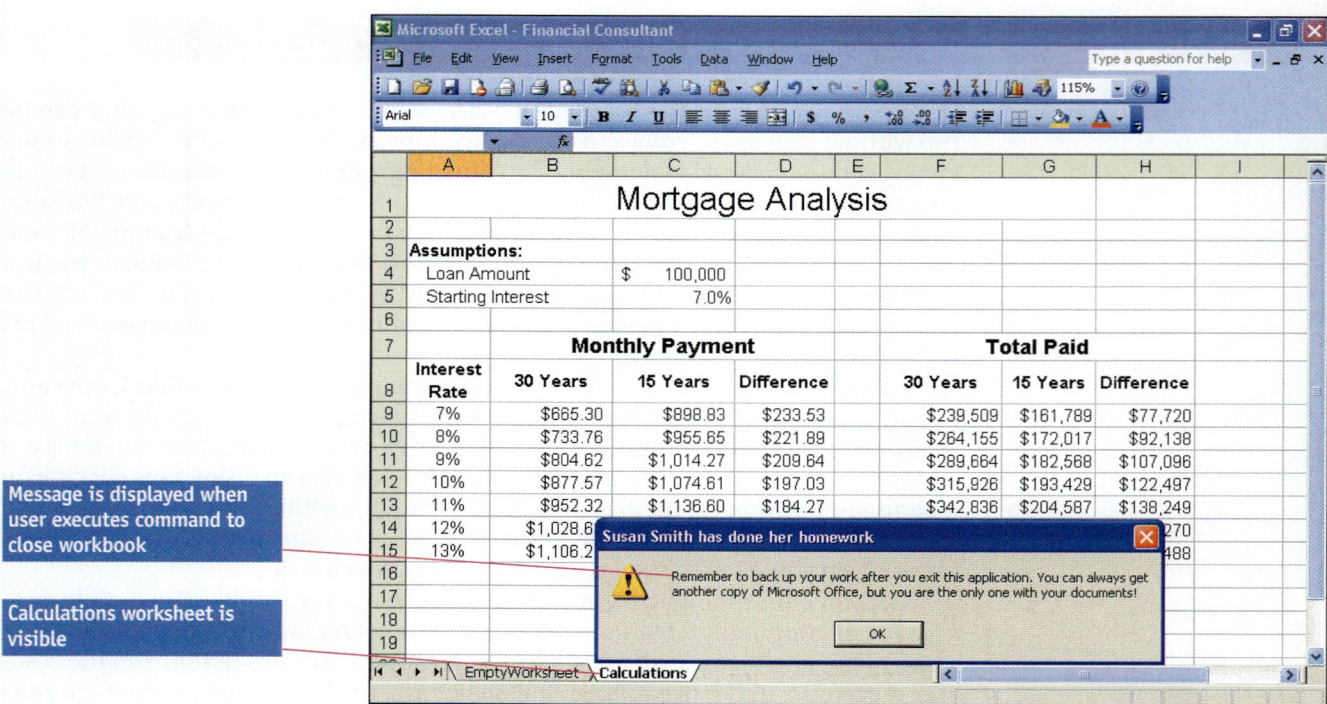

(a) Message to the User (Close Workbook event)

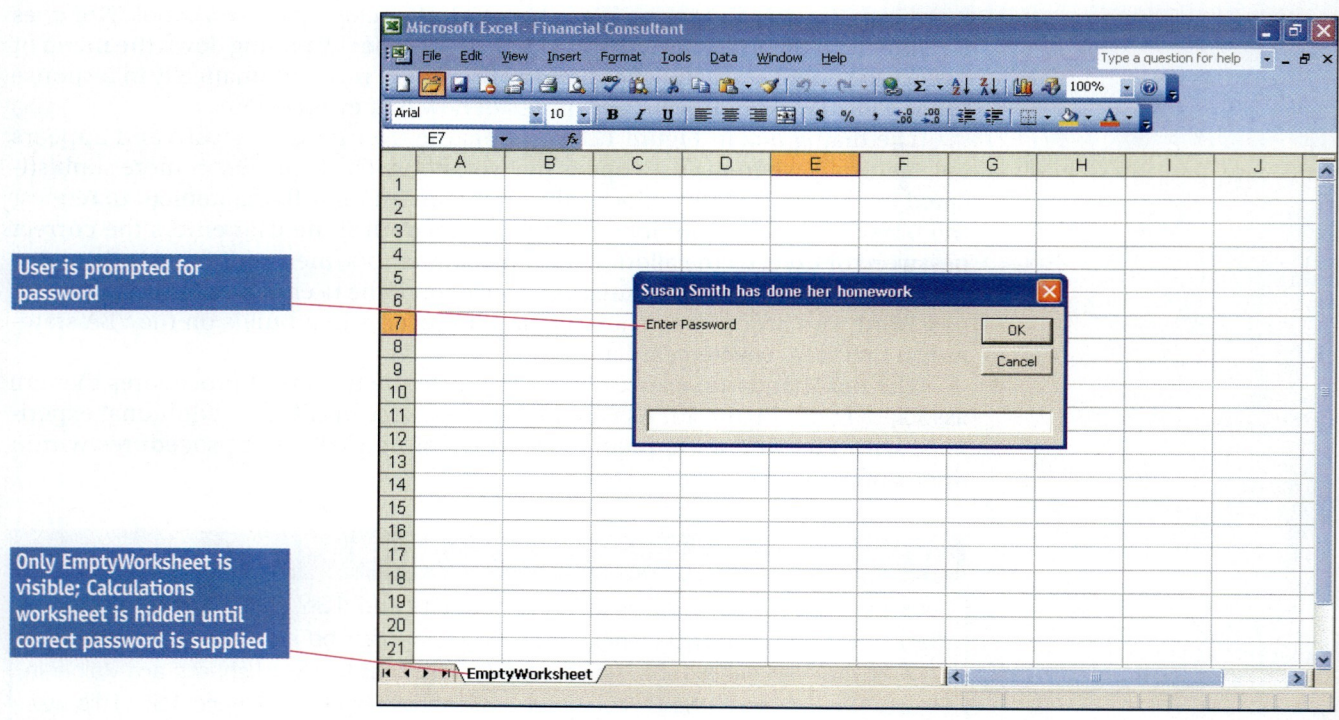

(b) Password Protection (Open Workbook event)

FIGURE 13 Event-Driven Programming

hands-on exercise
4 Event-Driven Programming (Microsoft Excel)

Objective To create an event procedure to implement password protection that is associated with opening an Excel workbook; to create a second event procedure that displays a message to the user upon closing the workbook. Use Figure 14 as a guide in the exercise.

Step 1: **Create the Close Workbook Procedure**

- Open the **VBA Examples workbook** you have used for the previous exercises and enable the macros. If you have been using Access rather than Excel, start Excel, open a new workbook, then save the workbook as **VBA Examples**.

- Pull down the **Tools menu**, click the **Macro command**, then click the **Visual Basic Editor command** (or use the **Alt+F11** keyboard shortcut).

- You should see the Project Explorer pane as shown in Figure 14a, but if not, pull down the **View menu** and click the **Project Explorer**. Double click **ThisWorkbook** to create a module for the workbook as a whole.

- Enter the **Option Explicit statement** if it is not there already, then press **Enter** to create a new line. Type the statement to declare the variable, **ApplicationTitle**, using your name instead of Susan Smith.

- Click the **down arrow** in the Object list box and select **Workbook**, then click the **down arrow** in the Procedure list box and select the **BeforeClose event** to create the associated procedure. (If you choose a different event by mistake, click and drag to select the associated statements, then press the **Del key** to delete the procedure.)

- Enter the comment and MsgBox statement as it appears in Figure 14a.

- Save the procedure.

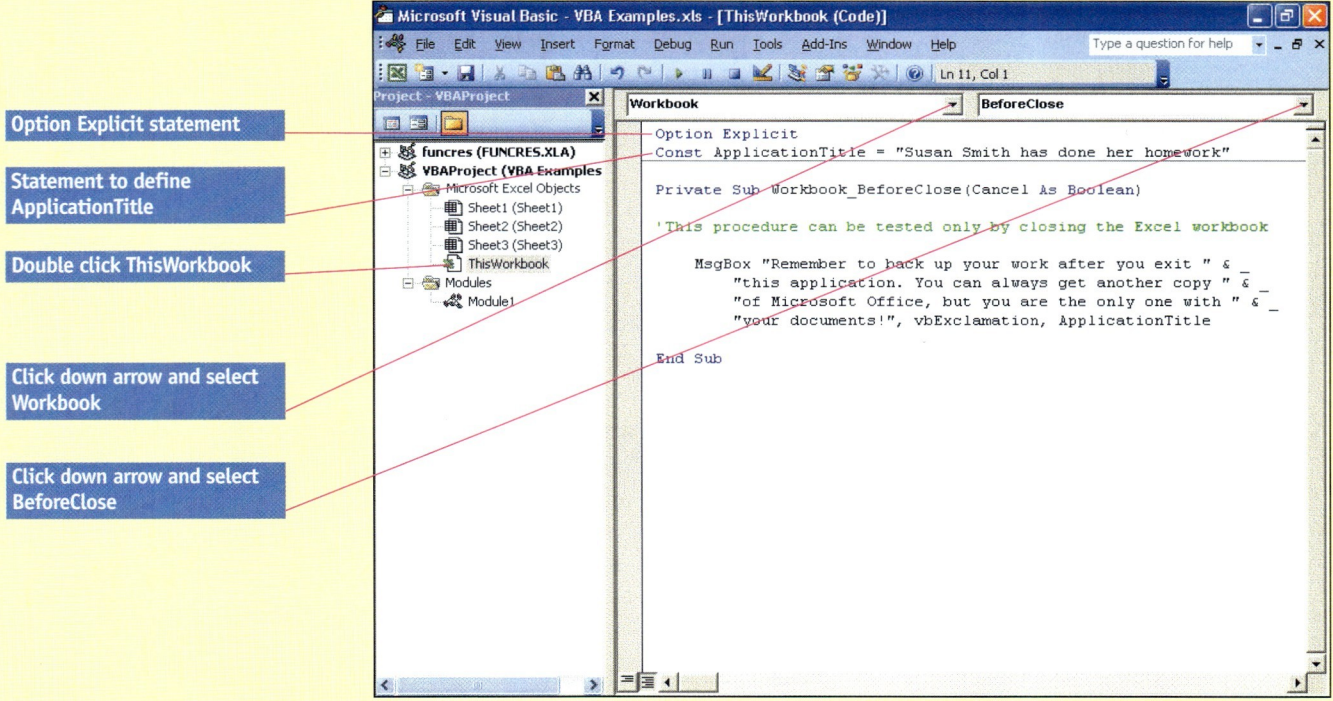

(a) Create the Close Workbook Procedure (step 1)

FIGURE 14 Hands-on Exercise 4

MICROSOFT OFFICE EXCEL 2003 REVISED   711

Step 2: Test the Close Workbook Procedure

- Click the **View Microsoft Excel button** on the Standard toolbar or on the Windows taskbar to view the Excel workbook. The workbook is not empty; that is, it does not contain any cell entries, but it does contain multiple VBA procedures.

- Pull down the **File menu** and click the **Close command**, which runs the procedure you just created and displays the dialog box in Figure 14b. Click **OK** after you have read the message, then click **Yes** if asked to save the workbook.

- Pull down the **File menu** and reopen the **VBA Examples workbook**, enabling the macros. Press **Alt+F11** to return to the VBA window to create an additional procedure.

- Double click **ThisWorkbook** from within the Project Explorer pane to return to the BeforeClose procedure and make the necessary corrections, if any.

- Save the procedure.

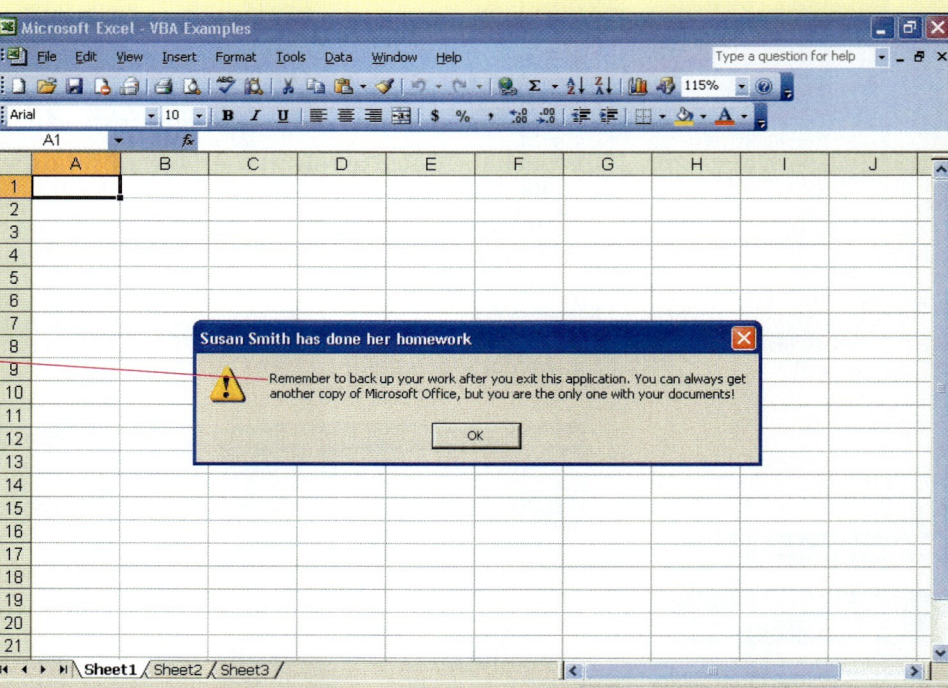

Message is displayed when you execute the Close command

(b) Test the Close Workbook Procedure (step 2)

FIGURE 14 Hands-on Exercise 4 (*continued*)

THE MOST RECENTLY OPENED FILE LIST

One way to open a recently used workbook is to select the workbook directly from the File menu. Pull down the File menu, but instead of clicking the Open command, check to see if the workbook appears on the list of the most recently opened workbooks located at the bottom of the menu. If so, just click the workbook name, rather than having to make the appropriate selections through the Open dialog box.

Step 3: **Start the Open Workbook Event Procedure**

- Click within the Before Close procedure, then click the **Procedure View button** at the bottom of the Code window. Click the **down arrow** in the Procedure list box and select the **Open event** to create an event procedure.

- Enter the VBA statements as shown in Figure 14c. Note the following:
  - Three variables are required for this procedure—the correct password, the password entered by the user, and the number of attempts.
  - The user is prompted for the password, and the number of attempts is set to 1. The user is given two additional attempts, if necessary, to get the password correct. The loop is bypassed, however, if the user supplies the correct password on the first attempt.

- Minimize Excel. Save the procedure, then click the **Run Sub button** to test it. Try different combinations in your testing; that is, enter the correct password on the first, second, and third attempts. The password is case-sensitive.

- Correct errors as they occur. Click the **Reset button** at any time to begin executing the procedure from the beginning. Save the procedure.

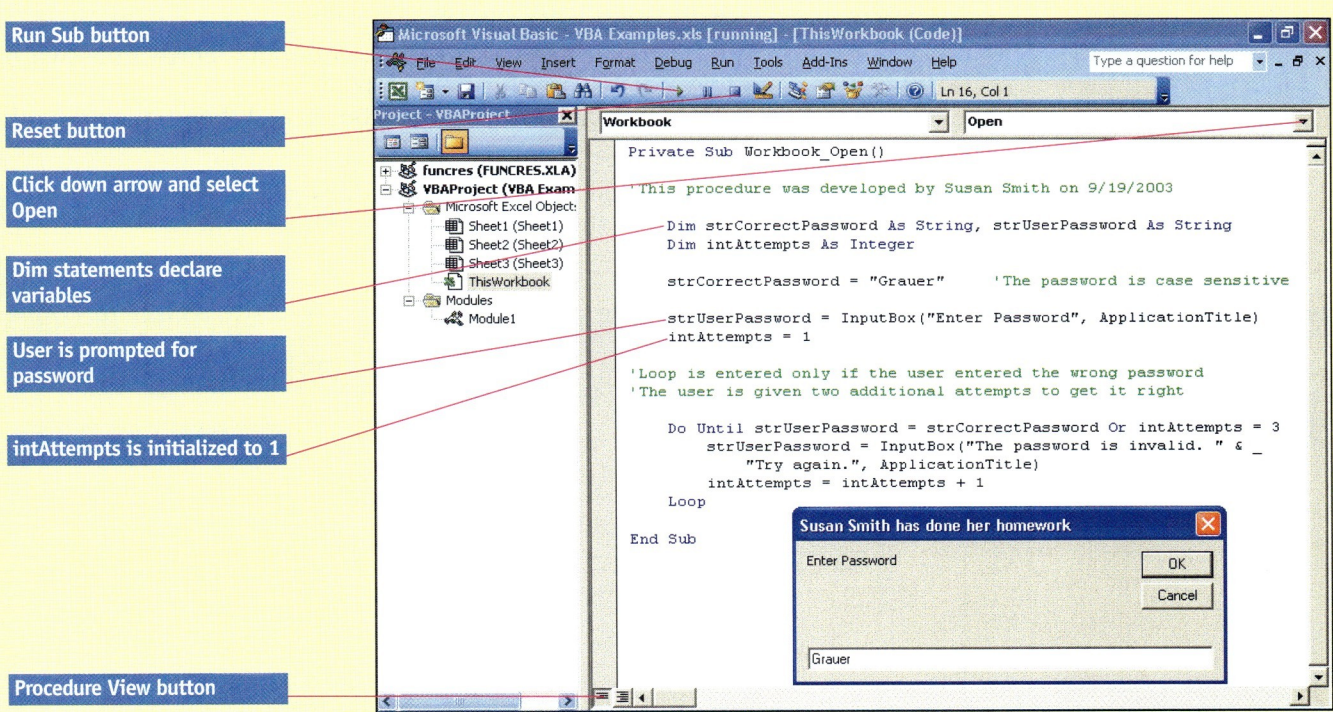

(c) Start the Open Workbook Event Procedure (step 3)

FIGURE 14 Hands-on Exercise 4 (*continued*)

THE OBJECT AND PROCEDURE BOXES

The Object box at the top of the code window displays the selected object such as an Excel workbook, whereas the Procedure box displays the name of the events appropriate to that object. Events that already have procedures appear in bold. Clicking an event that is not bold creates the procedure header and End Sub statements for that event.

Step 4: **Complete the Open Workbook Event Procedure**

- Enter the remaining statements in the procedure as shown in Figure 14d. Note the following:
  - The If statement determines whether the user has entered the correct password and, if so, displays the appropriate message.
  - If, however, the user fails to supply the correct password, a different message is displayed, and the workbook will close due to the **Workbooks.Close statement** within the procedure.
  - As a precaution, put an apostrophe in front of the Workbooks.Close statement so that it is a comment, and thus it is not executed. Once you are sure that you can enter the correct password, you can remove the apostrophe and implement the password protection.
- Save the procedure, then click the **Run Sub button** to test it. Be sure that you can enter the correct password (**Grauer**), and that you realize the password is case-sensitive.
- Delete the apostrophe in front of the Workbooks.Close statement. The text of the statement changes from green to black to indicate that it is an executable statement rather than a comment. Save the procedure.
- Click the **Run Sub button** a second time, then enter an incorrect password three times in a row. You will see the dialog box in Figure 14d, followed by a message reminding you to back up your workbook, and then the workbook will close.
- The first message makes sense, the second does not make sense in this context. Thus, we need to modify the Close Workbook procedure when an incorrect password is entered.

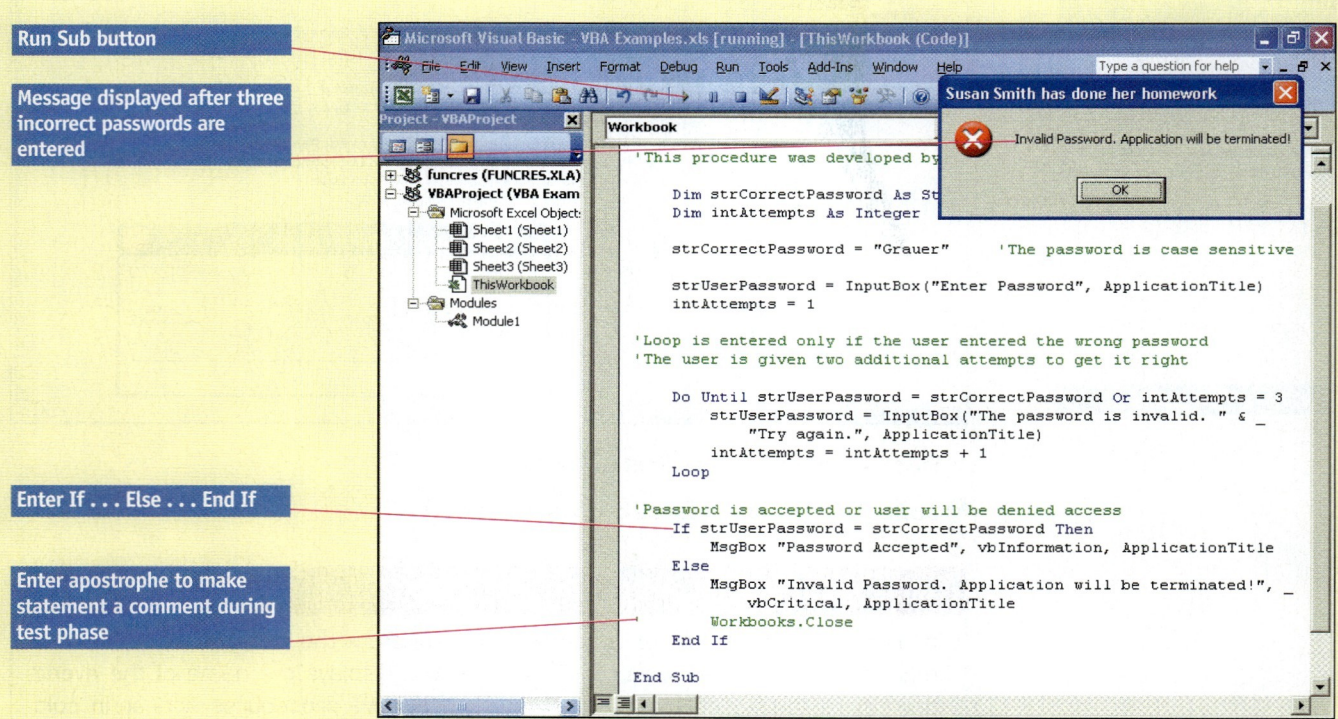

(d) Complete the Open Workbook Event Procedure (step 4)

FIGURE 14 Hands-on Exercise 4 (*continued*)

Step 5: **Modify the Before Close Event Procedure**

- Reopen the **VBA Examples workbook**. Click the button to **Enable Macros**.
- Enter the password, **Grauer** (the password is case-sensitive), press **Enter**, then click **OK** when the password has been accepted.
- Press **Alt+F11** to reopen the VBA editor, and (if necessary) double click **ThisWorkbook** within the list of Microsoft Excel objects.
- Click at the end of the line defining the ApplicationTitle constant, press **Enter**, then enter the statement to define the **binNormalExit** variable as shown in Figure 14e. (The statement appears initially below the line ending the General Declarations section, but moves above the line when you press Enter.)
- Modify the BeforeClose event procedure to include an If statement that tests the value of the binNormalExit variable as shown in Figure 14e. You must, however, set the value of this variable in the Open Workbook event procedure as described in step 6.
- Save the procedure.

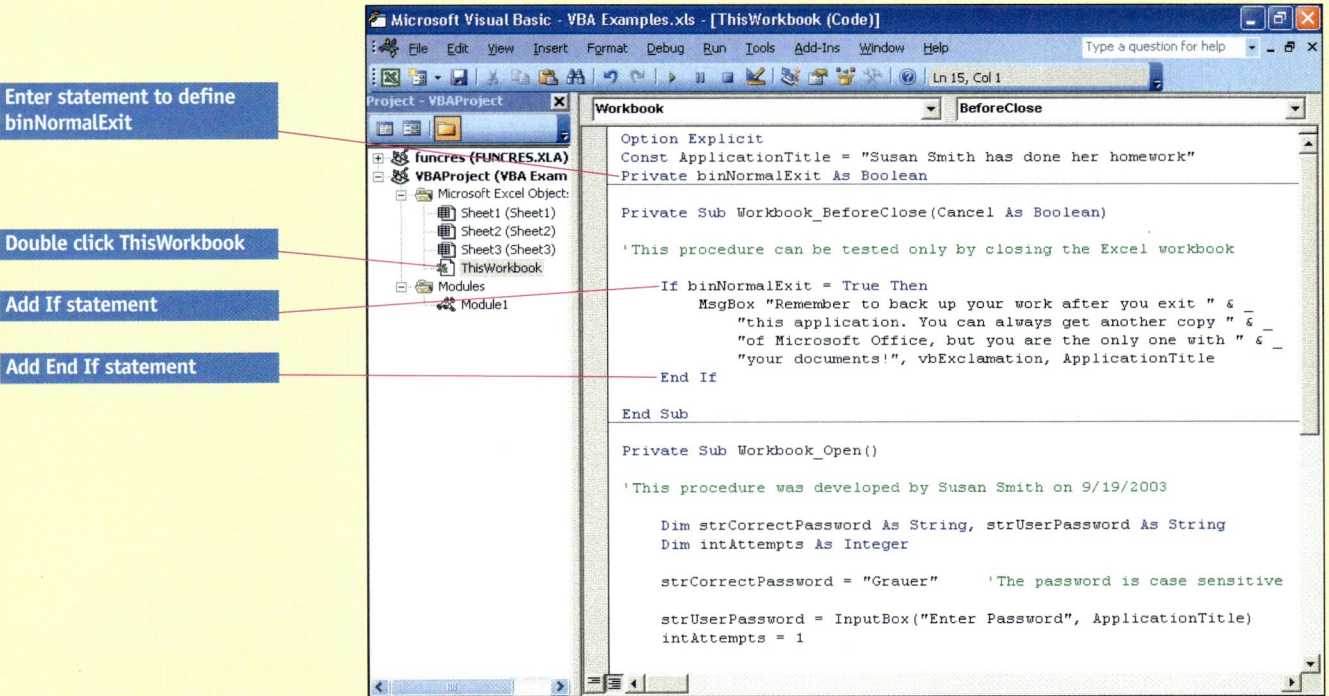

(e) Modify the Before Close Event Procedure (step 5)

FIGURE 14 Hands-on Exercise 4 (*continued*)

SETTING A SWITCH

The use of a switch (binNormalExit, in this example) to control an action within a procedure is a common programming technique. The switch is set to one of two values according to events that occur within the system, then the switch is subsequently tested and the appropriate action is taken. Here, the switch is set when the workbook is opened to indicate either a valid or invalid user. The switch is then tested prior to closing the workbook to determine whether to print the closing message.

Step 6: **Modify the Open Workbook Event Procedure**

- Scroll down to the Open Workbook event procedure, then modify the If statement to set the value of binNormalExit as shown in Figure 14f:
  - Take advantage of the Complete Word tool to enter the variable name. Type the first few letters, "**binN**", then press **Ctrl+Space**, and VBA will complete the variable name.
  - The indentation within the statement is not a requirement of VBA per se, but is used to make the code easier to read. Blank lines are also added for this purpose.
  - Comments appear throughout the procedure to explain its logic.
  - Save the modified procedure.

- Click the **Run Sub button**, then enter an incorrect password three times in a row. Once again, you will see the dialog box indicating an invalid password.

- Click **OK**. This time you will not see the message reminding you to back up your workbook. The workbook closes as before.

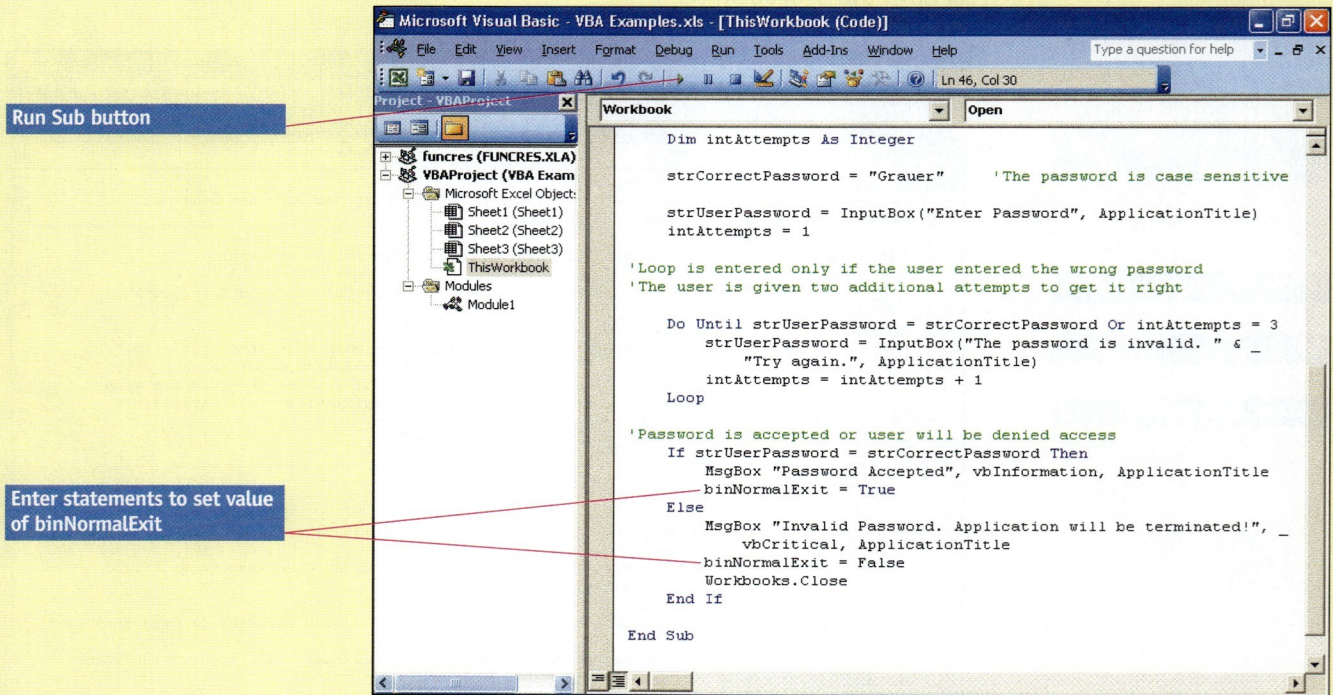

(f) Modify the Open Workbook Event Procedure (step 6)

FIGURE 14 Hands-on Exercise 4 (*continued*)

TEST UNDER ALL CONDITIONS

We cannot overemphasize the importance of thoroughly testing a procedure, and further, testing it under all conditions. VBA statements are powerful, but they are also complex, and a misplaced or omitted character can have dramatic consequences. Test every procedure completely at the time it is created, while the logic of the procedure is fresh in your mind.

Step 7: **Open a Second Workbook**

- Reopen the **VBA Examples workbook**. Click the button to **Enable Macros**.

- Enter the password, **Grauer**, then press **Enter**. Click **OK** when you see the second dialog box telling you that the password has been accepted.

- Pull down the **File menu** and click the **Open command** (or click the **Open button** on the Standard toolbar) and open a second workbook. We opened a workbook called **Financial Consultant**, but it does not matter which workbook you open.

- Pull down the **Window menu**, click the **Arrange command**, click the **Horizontal option button**, and click **OK** to tile the workbooks as shown in Figure 14g. The title bars show the names of the open workbooks.

- Pull down the **Tools menu**, click **Macro**, then click **Visual Basic editor**.

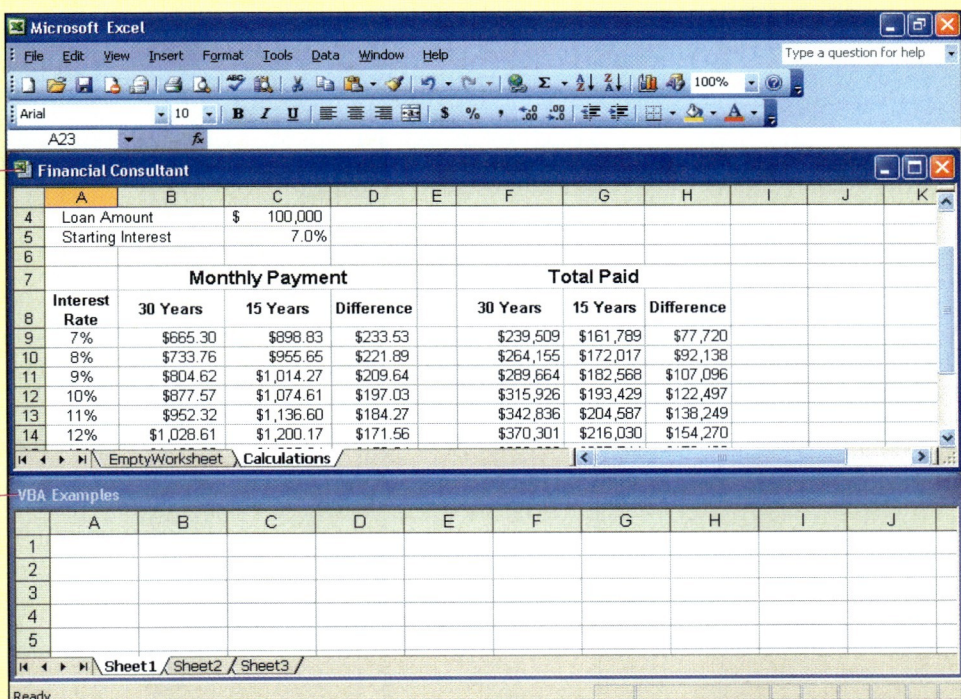

(g) Open a Second Workbook (step 7)

FIGURE 14   Hands-on Exercise 4 (*continued*)

THE COMPARISON IS CASE-SENSITIVE

Any literal comparison (e.g., strInstructorName = "Grauer") is case-sensitive, so that the user has to enter the correct name and case for the condition to be true. A response of "GRAUER" or "grauer", while containing the correct name, will be evaluated as false because the case does not match. You can, however, use the UCase (uppercase) function to convert the user's response to uppercase, and test accordingly. In other words, UCase(strInstructorName) = "GRAUER" will be evaluated as true if the user enters "Grauer" in any combination of upper- or lowercase letters.

Step 8: **Copy the Procedure**

- You should be back in the Visual Basic editor as shown in Figure 14h. Copy the procedures associated with the Open and Close Workbook events from the VBA Examples workbook to the other workbook, Financial Consultant.
  - Double click **ThisWorkbook** within the list of Microsoft Excel objects under the VBA Examples workbook.
  - Click and drag to select the definition of the ApplicationTitle constant in the General Declarations section, the binNormalExit definition, plus the two procedures (to open and close the workbook) in their entirety.
  - Click the **Copy button** on the Standard toolbar.
  - If necessary, expand the Financial Consultant VBA Project, then double click **ThisWorkbook** with the list of Excel objects under the Financial Consultant workbook. Click underneath the **Option Explicit command**.
  - Click the **Paste button** on the Standard toolbar. The VBA code should be copied into this module as shown in Figure 14h.
- Click the **Save button** to save the module.

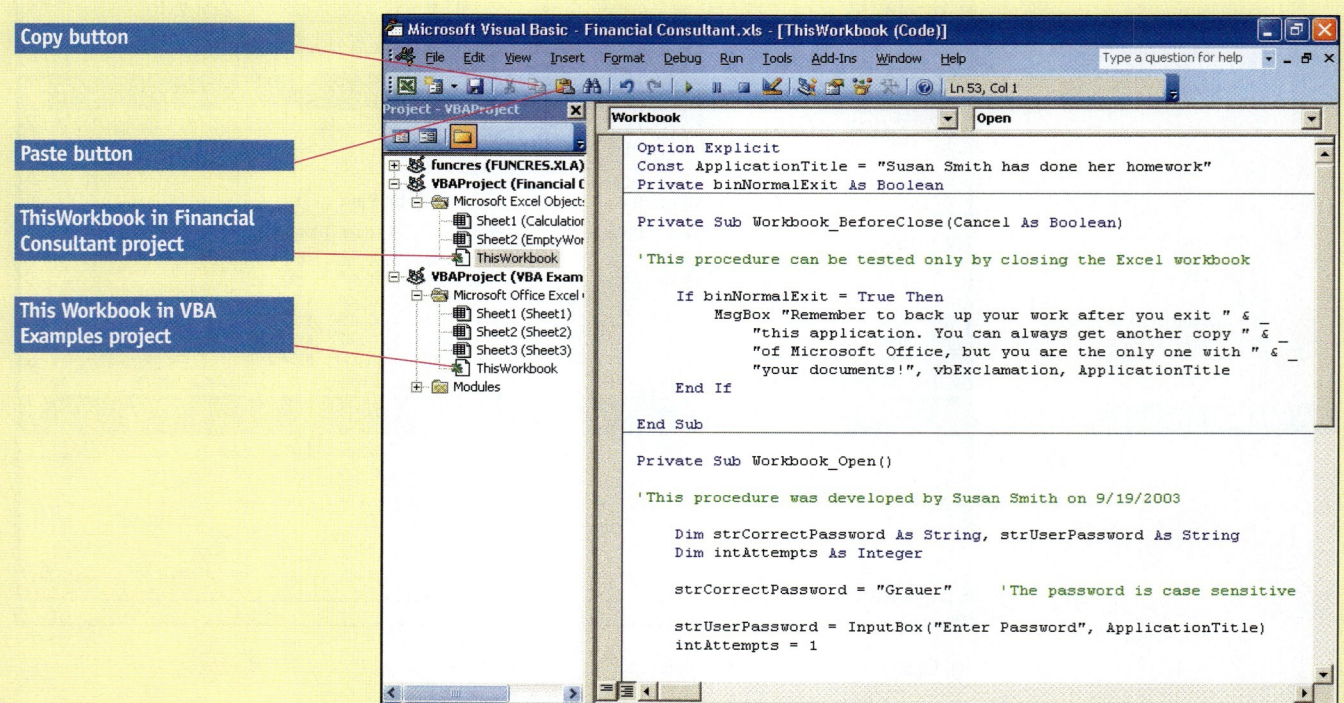

(h) Copy the Procedure (step 8)

FIGURE 14 Hands-on Exercise 4 (*continued*)

THE VISIBLE PROPERTY

The Calculations worksheet sheet should be hidden until the user enters the correct password. This is accomplished by setting the Visible property of the worksheet to false at the beginning of the Open Workbook event procedure, then setting it to true after the correct password has been entered. Click in the Open Workbook event procedure after the last Dim statement, press Enter, then enter the statement Sheet1.Visible = False to hide the Calculations worksheet. Scroll down in the procedure (below the MsgBox statement within the If statement that tests for the correct password), then enter the statement Sheet1.Visible = True followed by the statement Sheet1.Activate to select the worksheet.

Step 9: **Test the Procedure**

- Click the **View Microsoft Excel button** on the Standard toolbar within the VBA window (or click the **Excel button** on the Windows taskbar) to view the Excel workbook. Click in the window containing the Financial Consultant workbook (or whichever workbook you are using), then click the **Maximize button**.

- Pull down the **File menu** and click the **Close command**. (The dialog box in Figure 14i does not appear initially because the value of binNormalExit is not yet set; you have to open the workbook to set the switch.) Click **Yes** if asked whether to save the changes to the workbook.

- Pull down the **File menu** and reopen the workbook. Click the button to **Enable Macros**, then enter **Grauer** when prompted for the password. Click **OK** when the password has been accepted.

- Close this workbook, close the **VBA Examples workbook**, then pull down the **File menu** and click the **Exit command** to quit Excel.

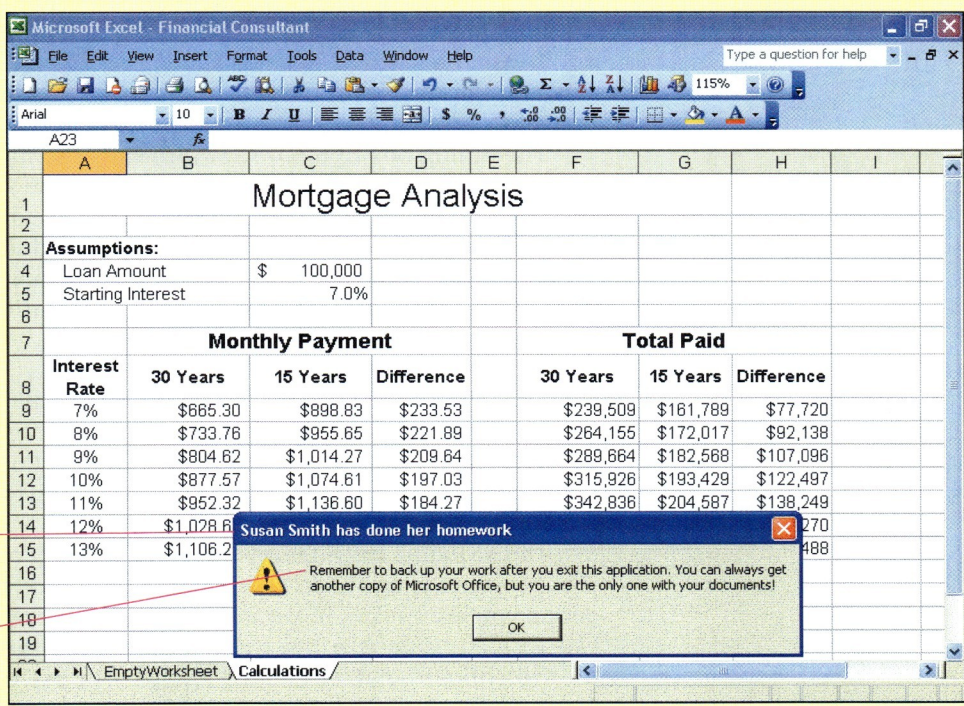

(i) Test the Procedure (step 9)

FIGURE 14 Hands-on Exercise 4 (*continued*)

SCREEN CAPTURE

Prove to your instructor that you have completed the hands-on exercise correctly by capturing a screen, then pasting the screen into a Word document. Do the exercise until you come to the screen that you want to capture, then press the PrintScreen key at the top of the keyboard. Click the Start button, start Word, and open a Word document, then pull down the Edit menu and click the Paste command to bring the captured screen into the Word document. Right click the screen within the Word document, click the Format Picture command, click the Layout tab, and select the Square layout. Click OK to close the dialog box. You can now move and size the screen within the document.

PUTTING VBA TO WORK (MICROSOFT ACCESS)

The same VBA procedure can be run from multiple applications in Microsoft Office, despite the fact that the applications are very different. The real power of VBA, however, is its ability to detect events that are unique to a specific application and to respond accordingly. An event is defined as any action that is recognized by an application. Opening or closing an Excel workbook or an Access database is an event. Selecting a worksheet within a workbook is also an event, as is clicking on a command button on an Access form. To use VBA within Microsoft Office, you decide which events are significant, and what is to happen when those events occur. Then you develop the appropriate ***event procedures*** that execute automatically when the event occurs.

Consider, for example, Figure 15, which displays the results of two event procedures in conjunction with opening and closing an Access database. (These are procedures similar to those we created in the preceding pages in conjunction with opening and closing an Excel workbook.) The procedure associated with Figure 15a displays a message that appears automatically after the user clicks the Switchboard button to exit the database. The procedure is almost trivial to write, and consists of a single MsgBox statement. The effect of the procedure is quite significant, however, as it reminds the user to back up his or her work. Indeed, you can never overemphasize the importance of adequate backup.

The dialog box in Figure 15b prompts the user for a password and appears automatically when the user opens the database. The logic here is more sophisticated in that the underlying procedure contains an InputBox statement to request the password, a Do Until loop that is executed until the user enters the correct password or exceeds the allotted number of attempts, then additional logic to display the switchboard or terminate the application if the user fails to enter the proper password. The procedure is not difficult, however, and it builds on the VBA statements that were covered earlier.

The next hands-on exercise has you create the event procedures that are associated with the database in Figure 15. The exercise references a switchboard, or user interface, that is created as a form within the database. The switchboard displays a menu that enables a nontechnical person to move easily from one object in the database (e.g., a form or report) to another.

The switchboard is created through a utility called the Switchboard Manager that prompts you for each item you want to add to the switchboard, and which action you want taken in conjunction with that menu item. You could do the exercise with any database, but we suggest you use the database we provide to access the switchboard that we created for you. The exercise begins, therefore, by having you download a data disk from our Web site.

EVENT-DRIVEN VERSUS TRADITIONAL PROGRAMMING

A traditional program is executed sequentially, beginning with the first line of code and continuing in order through the remainder of the program. It is the program, not the user, that determines the order in which the statements are executed. VBA, on the other hand, is event-driven, meaning that the order in which the procedures are executed depends on the events that occur. It is the user, rather than the program, that determines which events occur, and consequently which procedures are executed. Each application in Microsoft Office has a different set of objects and associated events that comprise the application's object model.

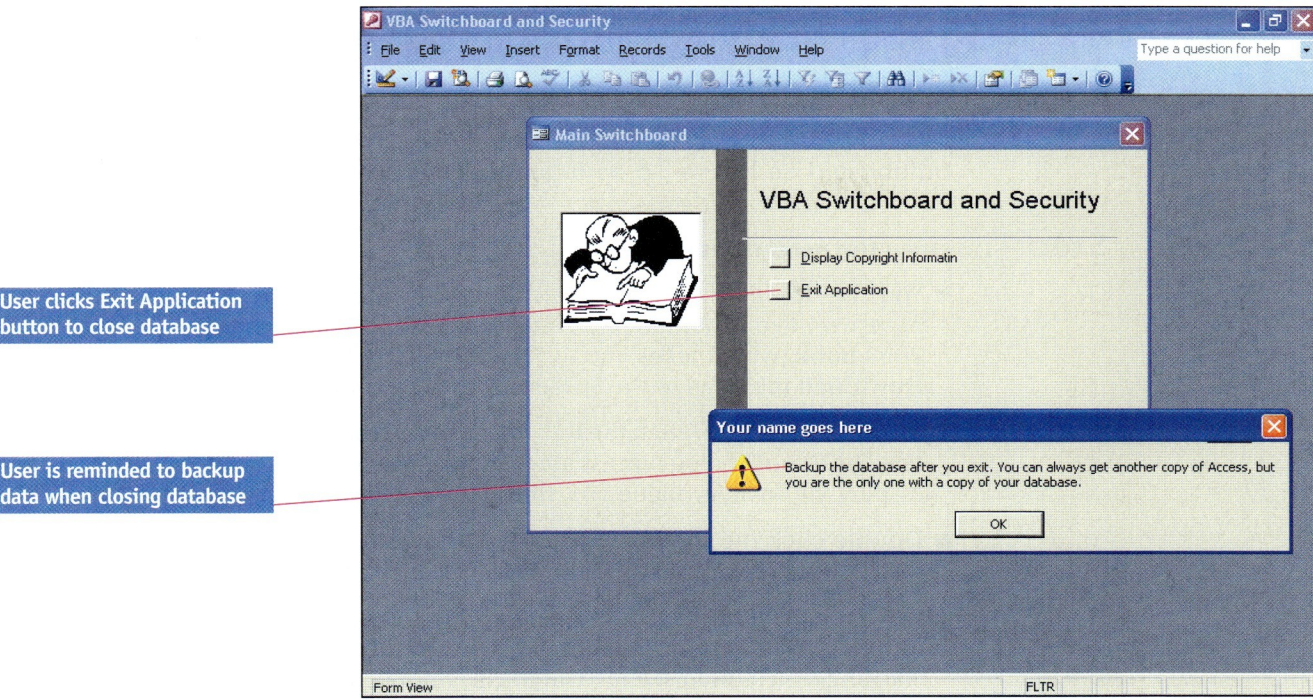

(a) Reminder to the User (Exit Application event)

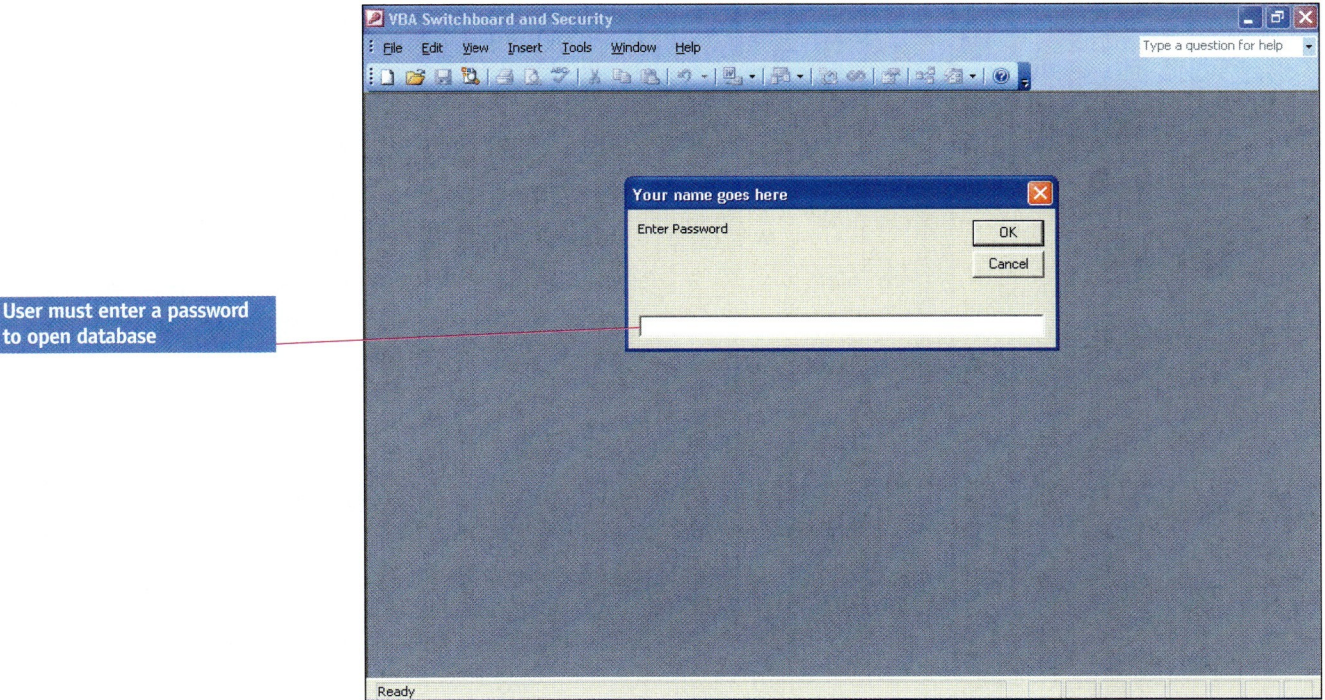

(b) Password Protection (Open Form event)

FIGURE 15   Event-Driven Programming (Microsoft Access)

hands-on exercise

5 Event-Driven Programming (Microsoft Access)

Objective To implement password protection for an Access database; to create a second event procedure that displays a message to the user upon closing the database. Use Figure 16 as a guide in the exercise.

Step 1: **Open the Access Database**

- You can do this exercise with any database, but we suggest you use the database we have provided. Go to **www.prenhall.com/grauer**, click the **Office 2003 book**, which takes you to the Office 2003 home page. Click the **Student Download tab** to go to the Student Download page.

- Scroll until you can click the link for **Getting Started with VBA**. You will see the File Download dialog box asking what you want to do. Click the **Save button** to display the Save As dialog box, then save the file on your desktop.

- Double click the file after it has been downloaded and follow the onscreen instructions to expand the self-extracting file that contains the database.

- Go to the newly created **Exploring VBA folder** and open the **VBA Switchboard and Security database**. Click the **Open button** when you see the security warning. You should see the Database window in Figure 16a.

- Pull down the **Tools menu**, click the **Macro command**, then click the **Visual Basic Editor command**. Maximize the VBA editor window.

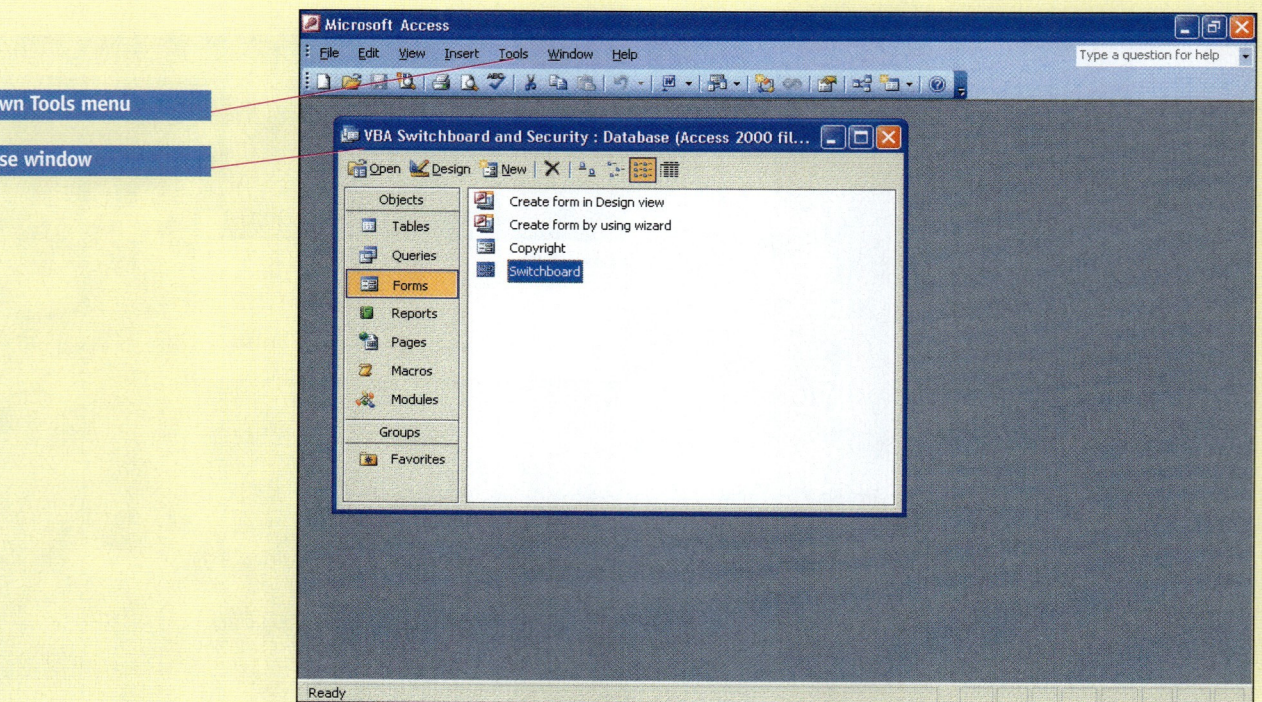

(a) Open the Access Database (step 1)

FIGURE 16 Hands-on Exercise 5

722 GETTING STARTED WITH VBA

Step 2: **Create the ExitDatabase Procedure**

- Pull down the **Insert menu** and click **Module** to insert Module1. Complete the **General Declarations section** by adding the Option Explicit statement (if necessary) and the definition of the ApplicationTitle constant as shown in Figure 16b.

- Pull down the **Insert menu** and click **Procedure** to insert a new procedure called **ExitDatabase**. Click the option buttons for a **Sub procedure** and for **Public scope**. Click **OK**.

- Complete the ExitDatabase procedure by entering the **MsgBox** and **DoCmd.Quit** statements. The DoCmd.Quit statement will close Access, but it is entered initially as a comment by beginning the line with an apostrophe.

- Click anywhere in the procedure, then click the **Run Sub button** to test the procedure. Correct any errors that occur, then when the MsgBox displays correctly, **delete the apostrophe** in front of the DoCmd.Quit statement.

- Save the module. The next time you execute the procedure, you should see the message box you just created, and then Access will be terminated.

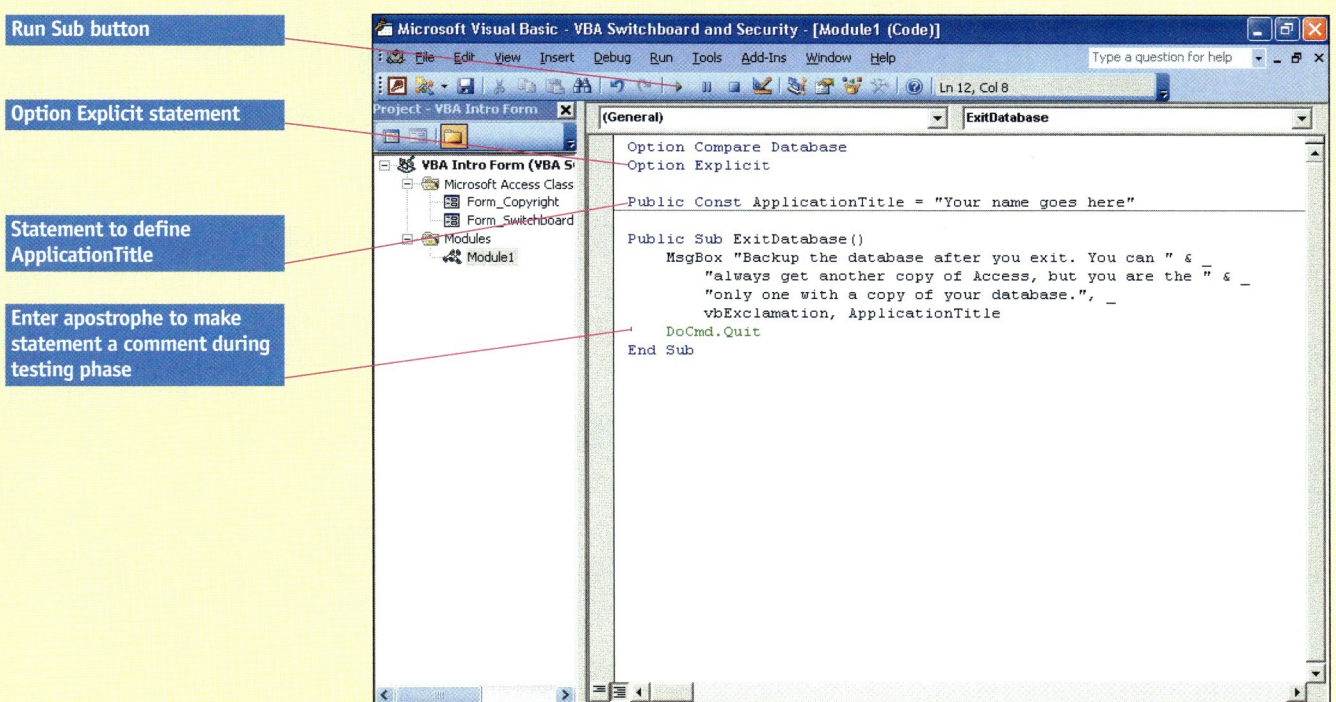

(b) Create the ExitDatabase Procedure (step 2)

FIGURE 16 Hands-on Exercise 5 (*continued*)

CREATE A PUBLIC CONSTANT

Give your application a customized look by adding your name or other identifying message to the title bar of the message and/or input boxes that you use. You can add the information individually to each statement, but it is easier to declare a public constant from within a general module. That way, you can change the value of the constant in one place and have the change reflected automatically throughout your application.

Step 3: **Modify the Switchboard**

- Click the **View Microsoft Access button** on the Standard toolbar within the VBA window to switch to the Database window (or use the **F11** keyboard shortcut).
- Pull down the **Tools menu**, click the **Database Utilities command**, then choose **Switchboard Manager** to display the Switchboard Manager dialog box in Figure 16c.
- Click the **Edit button** to edit the Main Switchboard and display the Edit Switchboard Page dialog box. Select the **&Exit Application command** and click its **Edit button** to display the Edit Switchboard Item dialog box.
- Change the command to **Run Code**. Enter **ExitDatabase** in the Function Name text box. Click **OK**, then close the two other dialog boxes.
- The switchboard has been modified so that clicking the Exit button will run the VBA procedure you just created.

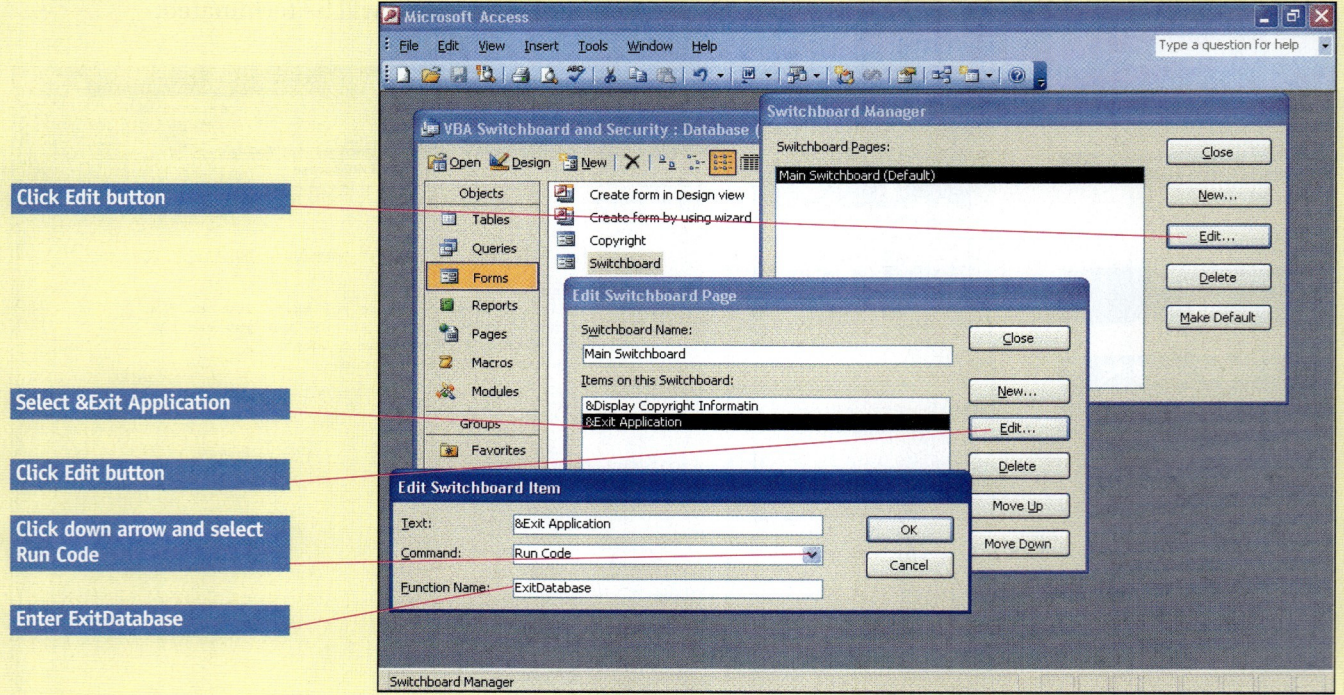

(c) Modify the Switchboard (step 3)

FIGURE 16 Hands-on Exercise 5 (*continued*)

CREATE A KEYBOARD SHORTCUT

The & has special significance when used within the name of an Access object because it creates a keyboard shortcut to that object. Enter "&Exit Application", for example, and the letter E (the letter immediately after the ampersand) will be underlined and appear as "Exit Application" on the switchboard. From there, you can execute the item by clicking its button, or you can use the Alt+E keyboard shortcut (where "E" is the underlined letter in the menu option).

Step 4: **Test the Switchboard**

- If necessary, click the **Forms button** in the Database window. Double click the **Switchboard form** to open the switchboard as shown in Figure 16d. The switchboard contains two commands.

- Click the **Display Copyright Information command** to display a form that we use with all our databases. (You can open this form in Design view and modify the text to include your name, rather than ours. If you do, be sure to save the modified form, then close it.)

- Click the **Exit Application command** (or use the **Alt+E** keyboard shortcut). You should see the dialog box in Figure 16d, corresponding to the MsgBox statement you created earlier. Click **OK** to close the dialog box.

- Access itself will terminate because of the DoCmd.Quit statement within the ExitDatabase procedure. (If this does not happen, return to the VBA editor and remove the apostrophe in front of the DoCmd statement.)

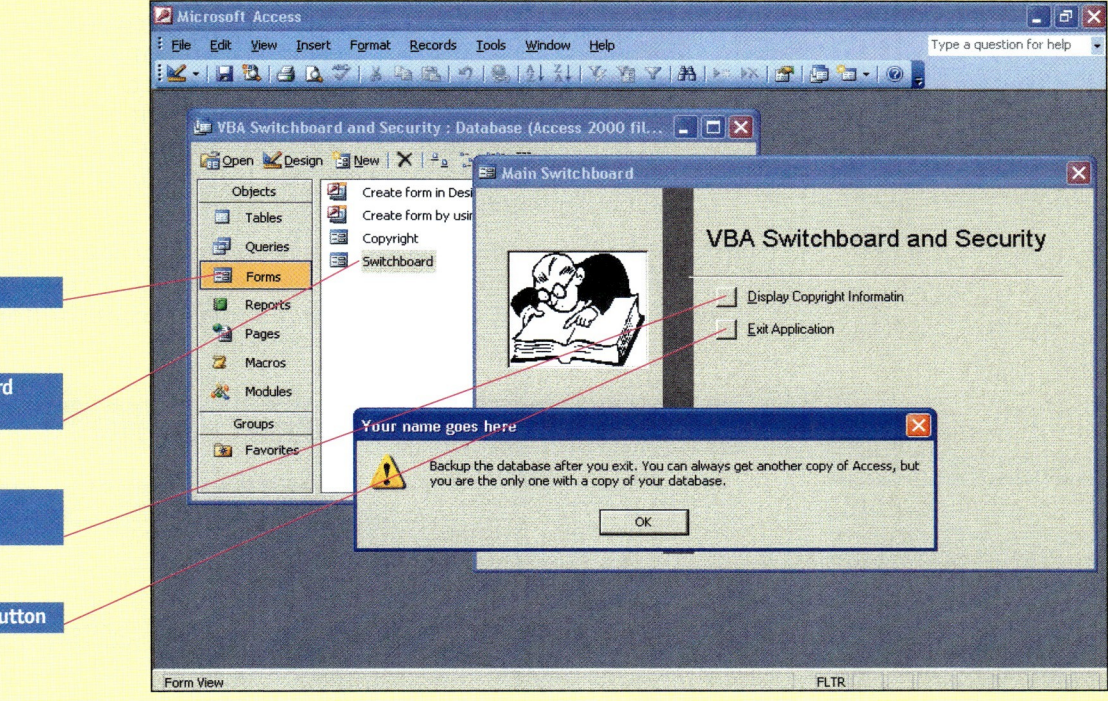

(d) Test the Switchboard (step 4)

FIGURE 16 Hands-on Exercise 5 (*continued*)

BACK UP IMPORTANT FILES

It's not a question of *if* it will happen, but *when*—hard disks die, files are lost, or viruses may infect a system. It has happened to us, and it will happen to you, but you can prepare for the inevitable by creating adequate backup before the problem occurs. The essence of a backup strategy is to decide which files to back up (your data), how often to do the backup (whenever it changes), and where to keep the backup (away from your computer). Do it!

Step 5: **Complete the Open Form Event Procedure**

- Start Access and reopen the **VBA Switchboard and Security database**. Press **Alt+F11** to start the VBA editor.

- Click the **plus sign** next to Microsoft Office Access Class objects, double click the module called **Form_Switchboard**, then look for the partially completed **Form_Open procedure** as shown in Figure 16e.

- The procedure was created automatically by the Switchboard Manager. You must, however, expand this procedure to include password protection. Note the following:
  - Three variables are required—the correct password, the password entered by the user, and the number of attempts.
  - The user is prompted for the password, and the number of attempts is set to 1. The user is given two additional attempts, if necessary, to get the correct password.
  - The If statement at the end of the loop determines whether the user has entered the correct password, and if so, it executes the original commands that are associated with the switchboard. If, however, the user fails to supply the correct password, an invalid password message is displayed and the **DoCmd.Quit** statement terminates the application.
  - We suggest you place an **apostrophe** in front of the statement initially so that it becomes a comment, and thus it is not executed. Once you are sure that you can enter the correct password, you can remove the apostrophe and implement the password protection.

- Save the procedure. You cannot test this procedure from within the VBA window; you must cause the event to happen (i.e., open the form) for the procedure to execute. Click the **View Microsoft Access button** on the Standard toolbar to return to the Database window.

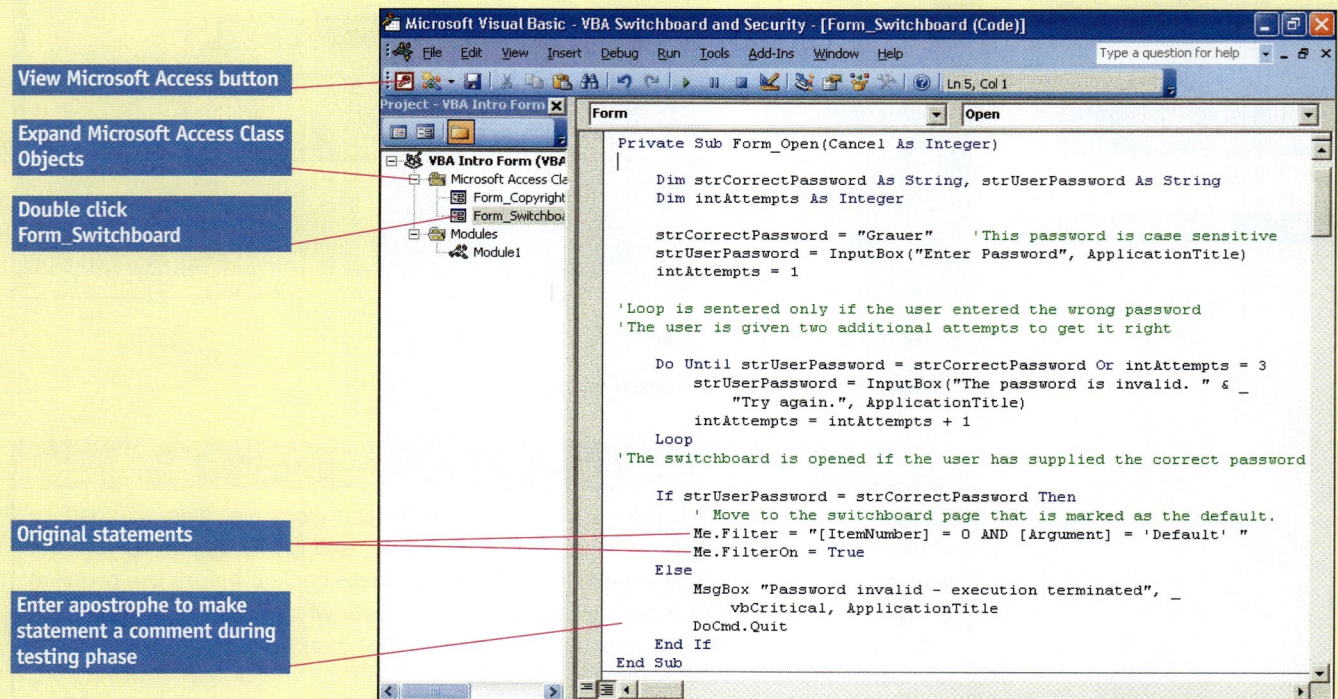

(e) Complete the Open Form Event Procedure (step 5)

FIGURE 16 Hands-on Exercise 5 (*continued*)

Step 6: **Test the Procedure**

- Close all open windows within the Access database except for the Database window. Click the **Forms button**, then double click the **Switchboard form**.

- You should be prompted for the password as shown in Figure 16f. The password (in our procedure) is **Grauer**.

- Test the procedure repeatedly to include all possibilities. Enter the correct password on the first, second, and third attempts to be sure that the procedure works as intended. Each time you enter the correct password, you will have to close the switchboard, then reopen it.

- Test the procedure one final time, by failing to enter the correct password. You will see a message box indicating that the password is invalid and that execution will be terminated. Termination will not take place, however, because the DoCmd.Quit statement is currently entered as a comment.

- Press **Alt+F11** to reopen the VBA editor. Open the **Microsoft Access Class Objects folder** and double click on **Form_Switchboard**. Delete the apostrophe in front of the DoCmd.Quit statement. The text of the statement changes from green to black to indicate that it is an executable statement. Save the procedure.

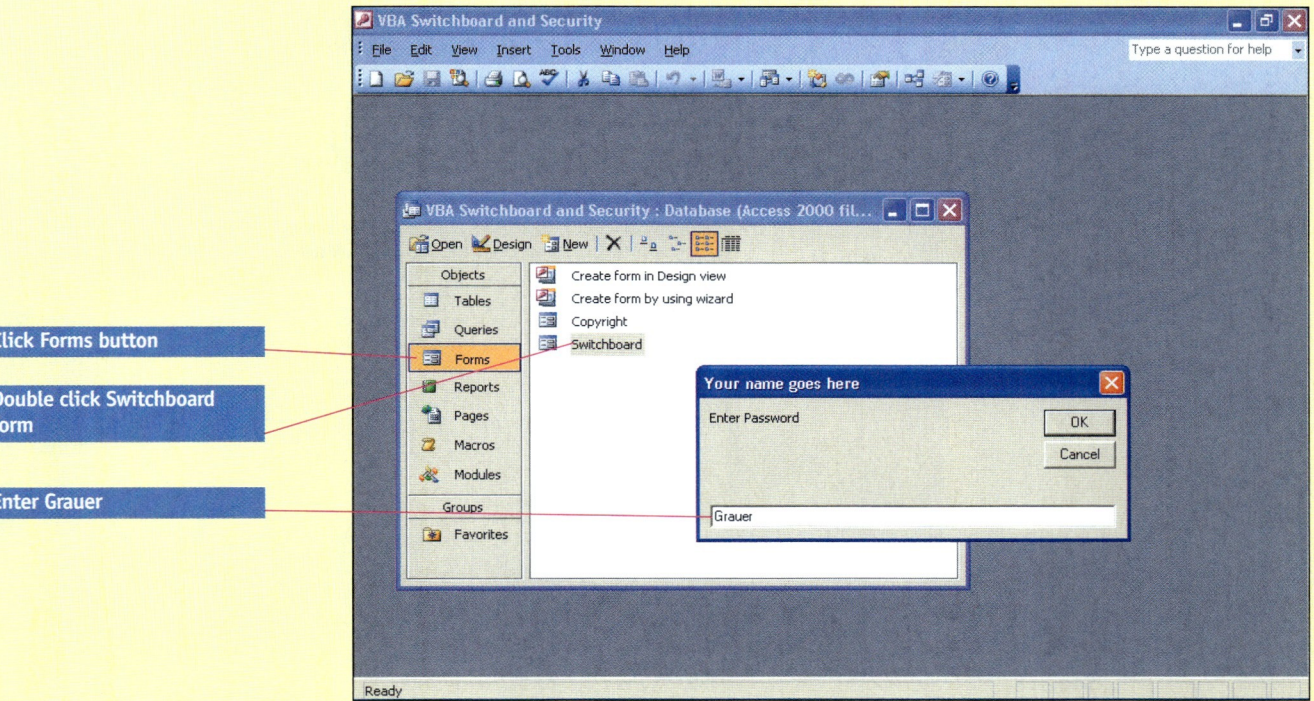

(f) Test the Procedure (step 6)

FIGURE 16 Hands-on Exercise 5 (*continued*)

TOGGLE COMMENTS ON AND OFF

Comments are used primarily to explain the purpose of VBA statements, but they can also be used to "comment out" code as distinct from deleting the statement altogether. Thus, you can add or remove the apostrophe in front of the statement, to toggle the comment on or off.

Step 7: Change the Startup Properties

- Click the **View Microsoft Access button** on the VBA Standard toolbar to return to the Database window.

- Close all open windows except the Database window. Pull down the **Tools menu** and click **Startup** to display the Startup dialog box as shown in Figure 16g.

- Click in the **Application Title** text box and enter the title of the application, **VBA Switchboard and Security** in this example.

- Click the **drop-down arrow** in the Display Form/Page list box and select the **Switchboard form** as the form that will open automatically in conjunction with opening the database.

- Clear the check box to display the Database window. Click **OK** to accept the settings and close the dialog box.

- The next time you open the database, the switchboard should open automatically, which in turn triggers the Open Form event procedure that will prompt the user to enter a password.

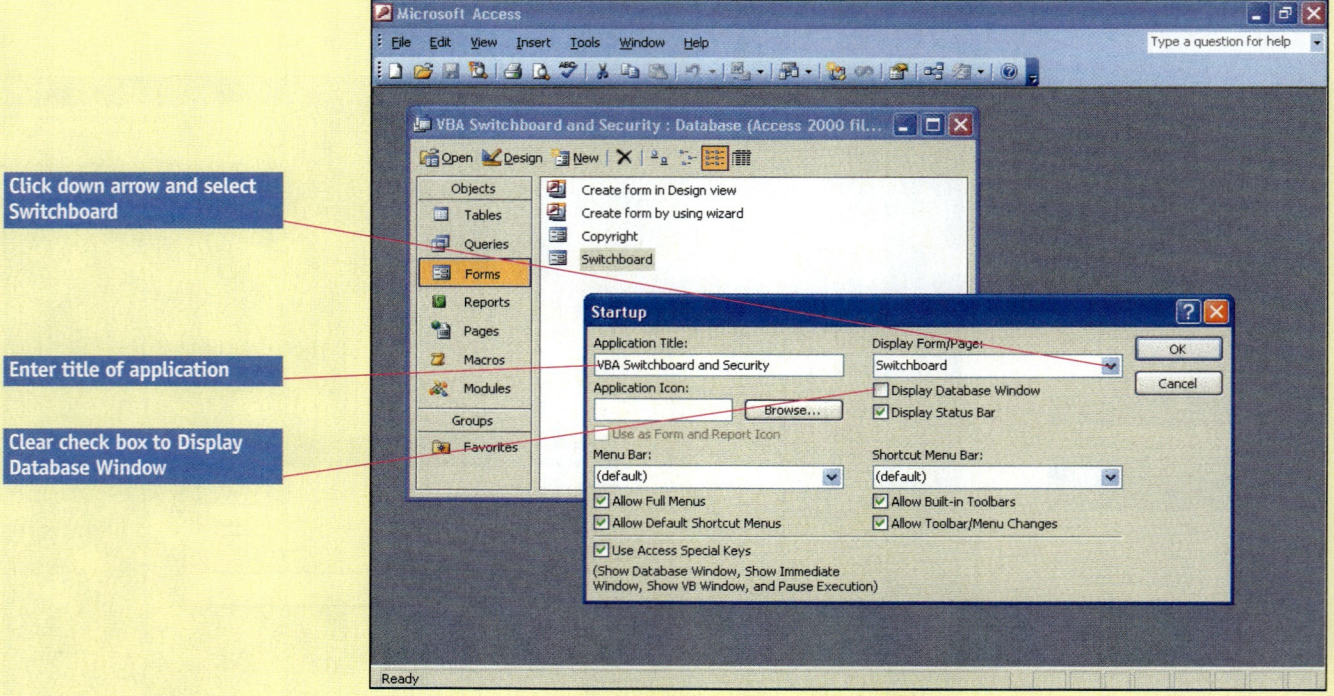

(g) Change the Startup Properties (step 7)

FIGURE 16   Hands-on Exercise 5 (*continued*)

HIDE THE DATABASE WINDOW

Use the Startup property to hide the Database window from the novice user. You avoid confusion and you may prevent the novice from accidentally deleting objects in the database. Of course, anyone with some knowledge of Access can restore the Database window by pulling down the Window menu, clicking the Unhide command, then selecting the Database window from the associated dialog box. Nevertheless, hiding the Database window is a good beginning.

Step 8: **Test the Database**

- Close the database, then reopen the database to test the procedures we have created in this exercise. The sequence of events is as follows:
  - The database is loaded and the switchboard is opened but is not yet visible. The Open Form procedure for the switchboard is executed, and you are prompted for the password as shown in Figure 16h.
  - The password is entered correctly and the switchboard is displayed. The Database window is hidden, however, because the Startup Properties have been modified.

- Click the **Exit Application command** (or use the **Alt+E** keyboard shortcut). You will see the message box reminding you to back up the system, after which the database is closed and Access is terminated.

- Reopen the database. This time, however, you are to enter the wrong password three times in a row. You should see a message indicating that the execution was terminated due to an invalid password.

- Testing is complete and you can go on to add the other objects to your Access database. Congratulations on a job well done.

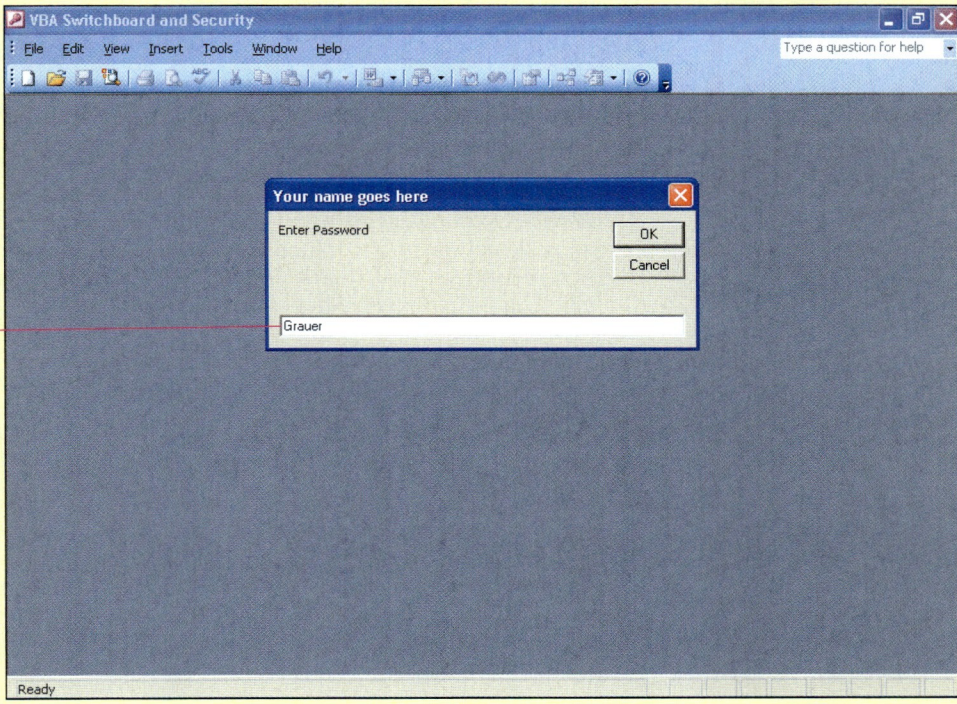

Enter password

(h) Test the Database (step 8)

FIGURE 16 Hands-on Exercise 5 (*continued*)

RESTORING HIDDEN MENUS AND TOOLBARS

You can use the Startup property to hide menus and/or toolbars from the user by clearing the respective check boxes. A word of caution, however—once the menus are hidden, it is difficult to get them back. Start Access, pull down the File menu, and click Open to display the Open dialog box, select the database to open, then press and hold the Shift key when you click the Open button. This powerful technique is not widely known.

SUMMARY

Visual Basic for Applications (VBA) is a powerful programming language that is accessible from all major applications in Microsoft Office XP. A VBA statement accomplishes a specific task such as displaying a message to the user or accepting input from the user. Statements are grouped into procedures, and procedures in turn are grouped into modules. Every procedure is classified as either private or public.

The MsgBox statement displays information to the user. It has one required argument, which is the message (or prompt) that is displayed to the user. The other two arguments—the icon that is to be displayed in the dialog box and the text of the title bar—are optional. The InputBox function displays a prompt to the user requesting information, then it stores that information (the value returned by the user) for use later in the procedure.

Every variable must be declared (defined) before it can be used. This is accomplished through the Dim (short for Dimension) statement that appears at the beginning of a procedure. The Dim statement indicates the name of the variable and its type (for example, whether it will hold a character string or an integer number), which in turn reserves the appropriate amount of memory for that variable.

The ability to make decisions within a procedure, then branch to alternative sets of statements is implemented through the If . . . Then . . . Else or Case statements. The Else clause is optional, but may be repeated multiple times within an If statement. The Case statement is preferable to an If statement with multiple Else clauses.

The For . . . Next statement (or For . . . Next loop as it is also called) executes all statements between the words For and Next a specified number of times, using a counter to keep track of the number of times the loop is executed. The Do . . . Loop Until and/or Do Until . . . Loop statements are used when the number of times through the loop is not known in advance.

VBA is different from traditional programming languages in that it is event-driven. An event is defined as any action that is recognized by an application, such as Excel or Access. Opening or closing an Excel workbook or an Access database is an event. Selecting a worksheet within a workbook is also an event, as is clicking on a command button on an Access form. To use VBA within Microsoft Office, you decide which events are significant, and what is to happen when those events occur. Then you develop the appropriate event procedures.

KEY TERMS

Argument 670	Event 709	Private procedure 670
Case statement 686	Event procedure (Access) 720	Procedure 670
Character string 684	Event procedure (Excel) 709	Procedure header 671
Comment 674	Execution error 698	Project Explorer 674
Compilation error 698	For . . . Next Statement 696	Public procedure 670
Complete Word tool 690	Full Module view 689	Run-time error 698
Concatenate 672	If statement 684	Statement 670
Custom toolbar 687	Immediate window 699	Step Into button 699
Debug menu 698	InputBox function 672	Syntax 670
Debug toolbar 698	Intrinsic constant 671	Underscore 672
Debug.Print statement 699	Literal 684	Variable 672
Debugging 698	Locals window 699	VBA 670
Declarations section 674	Macro 670	Visible property 718
Dim statement 673	Macro recorder 670	Visual Basic editor 674
Do Loops 697	Module 670	Visual Basic
Else clause 684	MsgBox statement 671	for Applications 670
End Sub statement 671	Option Explicit 674	

MULTIPLE CHOICE

1. Which of the following applications in Office XP has access to VBA?
   (a) Word
   (b) Excel
   (c) Access
   (d) All of the above

2. Which of the following is a valid name for a VBA variable?
   (a) Public
   (b) Private
   (c) strUserFirstName
   (d) int Count Of Attempts

3. Which of the following is true about an If statement?
   (a) It evaluates a condition as either true or false, then executes the statement(s) following the keyword "Then" if the condition is true
   (b) It must contain the keyword Else
   (c) It must contain one or more ElseIf statements
   (d) All of the above

4. Which of the following lists the items from smallest to largest?
   (a) Module, procedure, statement
   (b) Statement, module, procedure
   (c) Statement, procedure, module
   (d) Procedure, module, statement

5. Given the statement, MsgBox "Welcome to VBA", "Bob was here", which of the following is true?
   (a) "Welcome to VBA" will be displayed within the resulting message box
   (b) "Welcome to VBA" will appear on the title bar of the displayed dialog box
   (c) The two adjacent commas will cause a compilation error
   (d) An informational icon will be displayed with the message

6. Where are the VBA procedures associated with an Office document stored?
   (a) In the same folder, but in a separate file
   (b) In the Office document itself
   (c) In a special VBA folder on drive C
   (d) In a special VBA folder on the local area network

7. The Debug.Print statement is associated with the:
   (a) Locals window
   (b) Immediate window
   (c) Project Explorer
   (d) Debug toolbar

8. Which of the following is the proper sequence of arguments for the MsgBox statement?
   (a) Text for the title bar, prompt, button
   (b) Prompt, button, text for the title bar
   (c) Prompt, text for the title bar, button
   (d) Button, prompt, text for the title bar

9. Which of the following is a true statement about Do loops?
   (a) Placing the Until clause at the beginning of the loop tests the condition prior to executing any statements in the loop
   (b) Placing the Until clause at the end of the loop executes the statements in the loop, then it tests the condition
   (c) Both (a) and (b)
   (d) Neither (a) nor (b)

10. Given the statement, For intCount = 1 to 10 Step 3, how many times will the statements in the loop be executed (assuming that there are no statements in the loop to terminate the execution)?
    (a) 10
    (b) 4
    (c) 3
    (d) Impossible to determine

... continued

multiple choice

11. Which of the following is a *false* statement?
    (a) A dash at the end of a line indicates continuation
    (b) An ampersand indicates concatenation
    (c) An apostrophe at the beginning of a line signifies a comment
    (d) A pair of quotation marks denotes a character string

12. What is the effect of deleting the apostrophe that appears at the beginning of a VBA statement?
    (a) A compilation error will occur
    (b) The statement is converted to a comment
    (c) The color of the statement will change from black to green
    (d) The statement is made executable

13. Which of the following If statements will display the indicated message if the user enters a response other than "Grauer" (assuming that "Grauer" is the correct password)?
    (a) If strUserResponse <> "Grauer" Then MsgBox "Wrong password"
    (b) If strUserResponse = "Grauer" Then MsgBox "Wrong password"
    (c) If strUserResponse > "Grauer" Then MsgBox "Wrong password"
    (d) If strUserResponse < "Grauer" Then MsgBox "Wrong password"

14. Which of the following will execute the statements in the loop at least once?
    (a) Do . . . Loop Until
    (b) Do Until ….. Loop
    (c) Both (a) and (b)
    (d) Neither (a) nor (b)

15. The copy and paste commands can be used to:
    (a) Copy statements within a procedure
    (b) Copy statements from a procedure in one module to a procedure in another module within the same document
    (c) Copy statements from a module in an Excel workbook to a module in an Access database
    (d) All of the above

16. Which of the following is true about indented text in a VBA procedure?
    (a) The indented text is always executed first
    (b) The indented text is always executed last
    (c) The indented text is rendered a comment and is never executed
    (d) None of the above

17. Which statement will prompt the user to enter his or her name and store the result in a variable called strUser?
    (a) InputBox.strUser
    (b) strUser = MsgBox("Enter your name")
    (c) strUser = InputBox("Enter your name")
    (d) InputBox("Enter strUser")

18. Given that strUser is currently set to "George", the expression "Good morning, strName" will return:
    (a) Good morning, George
    (b) Good morning, strName
    (c) Good morning George
    (d) Good morning strName

ANSWERS

1. d   7. b   13. a
2. c   8. b   14. a
3. a   9. c   15. d
4. c   10. b   16. d
5. a   11. a   17. c
6. b   12. d   18. b

CHAPTER 1

Getting Started with Microsoft® Windows® XP

OBJECTIVES

After reading this chapter you will:

1. Describe the Windows desktop.
2. Use the Help and Support Center to obtain information.
3. Describe the My Computer and My Documents folders.
4. Differentiate between a program file and a data file.
5. Download a file from the Exploring Office Web site.
6. Copy and/or move a file from one folder to another.
7. Delete a file, and then recover it from the Recycle Bin.
8. Create and arrange shortcuts on the desktop.
9. Use the Search Companion.
10. Use the My Pictures and My Music folders.
11. Use Windows Messenger for instant messaging.

hands-on exercises

1. WELCOME TO WINDOWS XP
   Input: None
   Output: None

2. DOWNLOAD PRACTICE FILES
   Input: Data files from the Web
   Output: Welcome to Windows XP (a Word document)

3. WINDOWS EXPLORER
   Input: Data files from exercise 2
   Output: Screen Capture within a Word document

4. INCREASING PRODUCTIVITY
   Input: Data files from exercise 3
   Output: None

5. FUN WITH WINDOWS XP
   Input: None
   Output: None

CASE STUDY
UNFORESEEN CIRCUMSTANCES

Steve and his wife Shelly have poured their life savings into the dream of owning their own business, a "nanny" service agency. They have spent the last two years building their business and have created a sophisticated database with numerous entries for both families and nannies. The database is the key to their operation. Now that it is up and running, Steve and Shelly are finally at a point where they could hire someone to manage the operation on a part-time basis so that they could take some time off together.

Unfortunately, their process for selecting a person they could trust with their business was not as thorough as it should have been. Nancy, their new employee, assured them that all was well, and the couple left for an extended weekend. The place was in shambles on their return. Nancy could not handle the responsibility, and when Steve gave her two weeks' notice, neither he nor his wife thought that the unimaginable would happen. On her last day in the office Nancy "lost" all of the names in the database—the data was completely gone!

Nancy claimed that a "virus" knocked out the database, but after spending nearly $1,500 with a computer consultant, Steve was told that it had been cleverly deleted from the hard drive and could not be recovered. Of course, the consultant asked Steve and Shelly about their backup strategy, which they sheepishly admitted did not exist. They had never experienced any problems in the past, and simply assumed that their data was safe. Fortunately, they do have hard copy of the data in the form of various reports that were printed throughout the time they were in business. They have no choice but to manually reenter the data.

Your assignment is to read the chapter, paying special attention to the information on file management. Think about how Steve and Shelly could have avoided the disaster if a backup strategy had been in place, then summarize your thoughts in a brief note to your instructor. Describe the elements of a basic backup strategy. Give several other examples of unforeseen circumstances that can cause data to be lost.

WELCOME TO WINDOWS® XP

Windows® XP is the newest and most powerful version of the Windows operating system. It has a slightly different look than earlier versions, but it maintains the conventions of its various predecessors. You have seen the Windows interface many times, but do you really understand it? Can you move and copy files with confidence? Do you know how to back up the Excel spreadsheets, Access databases, and other documents that you work so hard to create? If not, now is the time to learn.

We begin with an introduction to the desktop, the graphical user interface that lets you work in intuitive fashion by pointing at icons and clicking the mouse. We identify the basic components of a window and describe how to execute commands and supply information through different elements in a dialog box. We stress the importance of disk and file management, but begin with basic definitions of a file and a folder. We also introduce Windows Explorer and show you how to move or copy a file from one folder to another. We discuss other basic operations, such as renaming and deleting a file. We also describe how to recover a deleted file (if necessary) from the Recycle Bin.

Windows XP is available in different versions. Windows ***XP Home Edition*** is intended for entertainment and home use. It includes a media player, new support for digital photography, and an instant messenger. Windows ***XP Professional Edition*** has all of the features of the Home Edition plus additional security to encrypt files and protect data. It includes support for high-performance multiprocessor systems. It also lets you connect to your computer from a remote station.

The login screen in Figure 1 is displayed when the computer is turned on initially and/or when you are switching from one user account to another. Several individuals can share the same computer. Each user, however, retains his or her individual desktop settings, individual lists of favorite and recently visited Web sites, as well as other customized Windows settings. Multiple users can be logged on simultaneously, each with his or her programs in memory, through a feature known as ***fast user switching***.

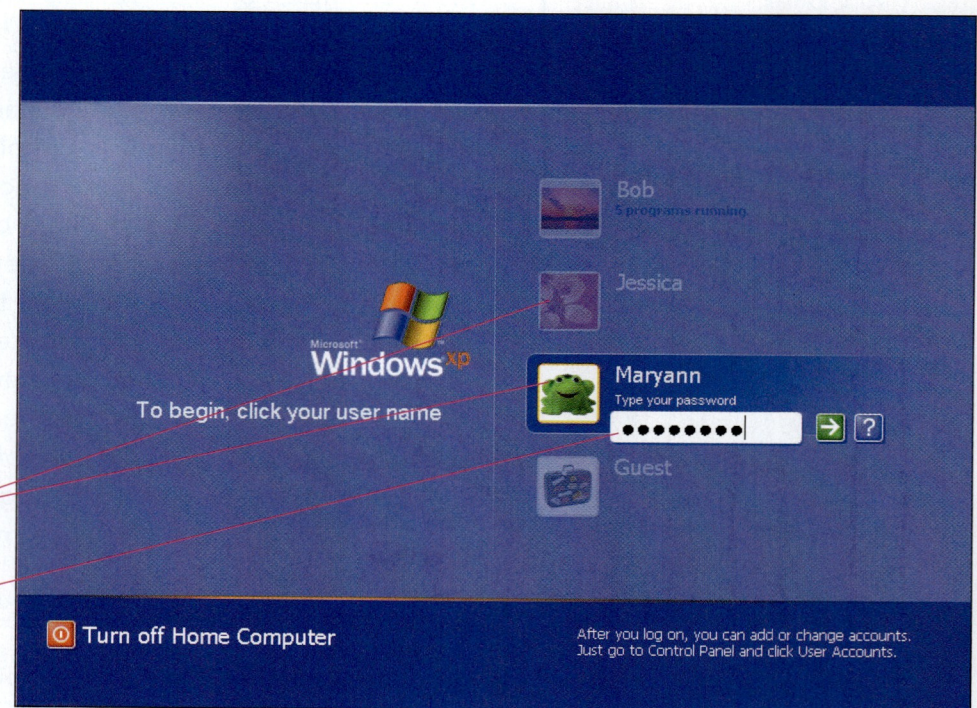

Multiple users can be logged on

Accounts can be password-protected

FIGURE 1   Windows XP Login

734   GETTING STARTED WITH MICROSOFT WINDOWS XP

THE DESKTOP

Windows XP, as well as all previous versions of Windows, creates a working environment for your computer that parallels the working environment at home or in an office. You work at a desk. Windows operations take place on the ***desktop***. There are physical objects on a desk such as folders, a dictionary, a calculator, or a phone. The computer equivalents of those objects appear as icons (pictorial symbols) on the desktop. Each object on a real desk has attributes (properties) such as size, weight, and color. In similar fashion, Windows assigns properties to every object on its desktop. And just as you can move the objects on a real desk, you can rearrange the objects on the Windows desktop.

Windows XP has a new interface, but you can retain the look and feel of earlier versions as shown in Figure 2. The desktop in Figure 2a uses the default ***Windows XP theme*** (the wallpaper has been suppressed), whereas Figure 2b displays the "same" desktop using the ***Windows Classic theme***. The icons on either desktop are used to access specific programs or other functions.

The ***Start button***, as its name suggests, is where you begin; it works identically on both desktops. Click the Start button to see a menu of programs and other functions. The Windows XP ***Start menu*** in Figure 2a is divided into two columns. The column on the left displays the most recently used programs for easy access, whereas the column on the right contains a standard set of entries. It also shows the name of the individual who is logged into the computer. The ***Classic Start menu*** in Figure 2b contains only a single column. (Note the indication of the Windows XP Professional operating system that appears at the left of the menu.)

Do not be concerned if your desktop is different from ours. Your real desk is arranged differently from those of your friends, just as your Windows desktop will also be different. Moreover, you are likely to work on different systems—at school, at work, or at home; what is important is that you recognize the common functionality that is present on all desktops.

Look now at Figure 2c, which displays an entirely different desktop, one with four open windows that is similar to a desk in the middle of a working day. Each window in Figure 2c displays a program or a folder that is currently in use. The ability to run several programs at the same time is known as ***multitasking***, and it is a major benefit of the Windows environment. Multitasking enables you to run a word processor in one window, create a spreadsheet in a second window, surf the Internet in a third window, play a game in a fourth window, and so on. You can work in a program as long as you want, then change to a different program by clicking its window.

The ***taskbar*** at the bottom of the desktop contains a button for each open window, and it enables you to switch back and forth between the open windows by clicking the appropriate button. A ***notification area*** appears at the right end of the taskbar. It displays the time and other shortcuts. It may also provide information on the status of such ongoing activities as a printer or Internet connection.

The desktop in Figure 2d is identical to the desktop in Figure 2c except that it is displayed in the Windows Classic theme. The open windows are the same, as are the contents of the taskbar and notification area. The choice between the XP theme or Windows Classic (or other) theme is one of personal preference.

Moving and Sizing a Window

A window can be sized or moved on the desktop through appropriate actions with the mouse. To ***size a window***, point to any border (the mouse pointer changes to a double arrow), then drag the border in the direction you want to go—inward to shrink the window or outward to enlarge it. You can also drag a corner (instead of a border) to change both dimensions at the same time. To ***move a window*** while retaining its current size, click and drag the title bar to a new position on the desktop.

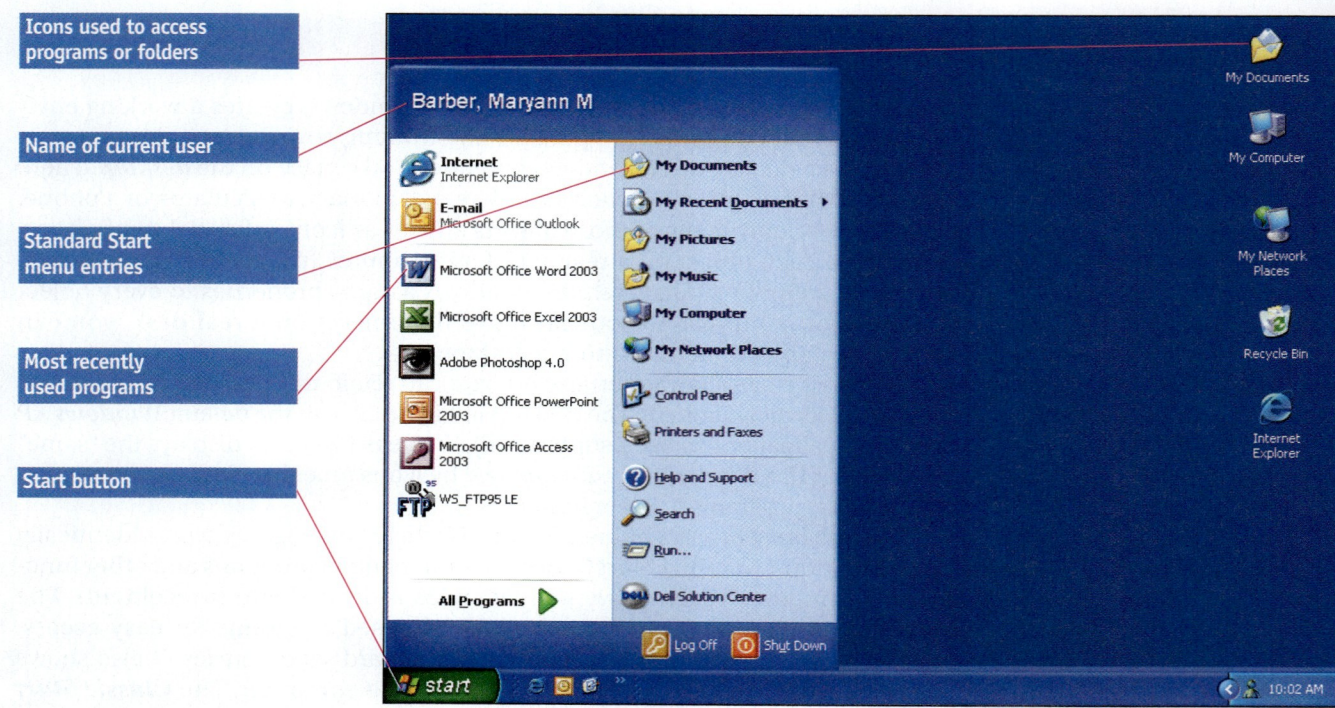

(a) Windows XP Theme and Start Menu

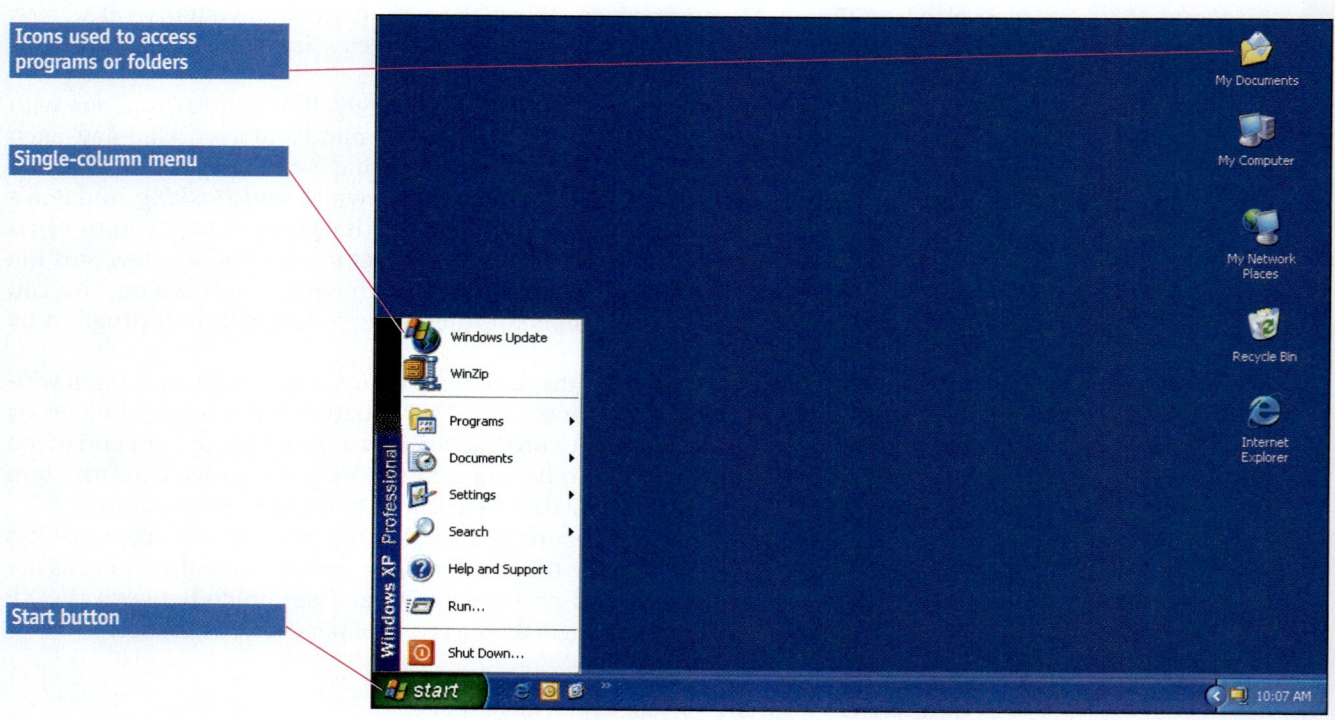

(b) Windows Classic Theme and Start Menu

FIGURE 2   The Desktop and Start Menu

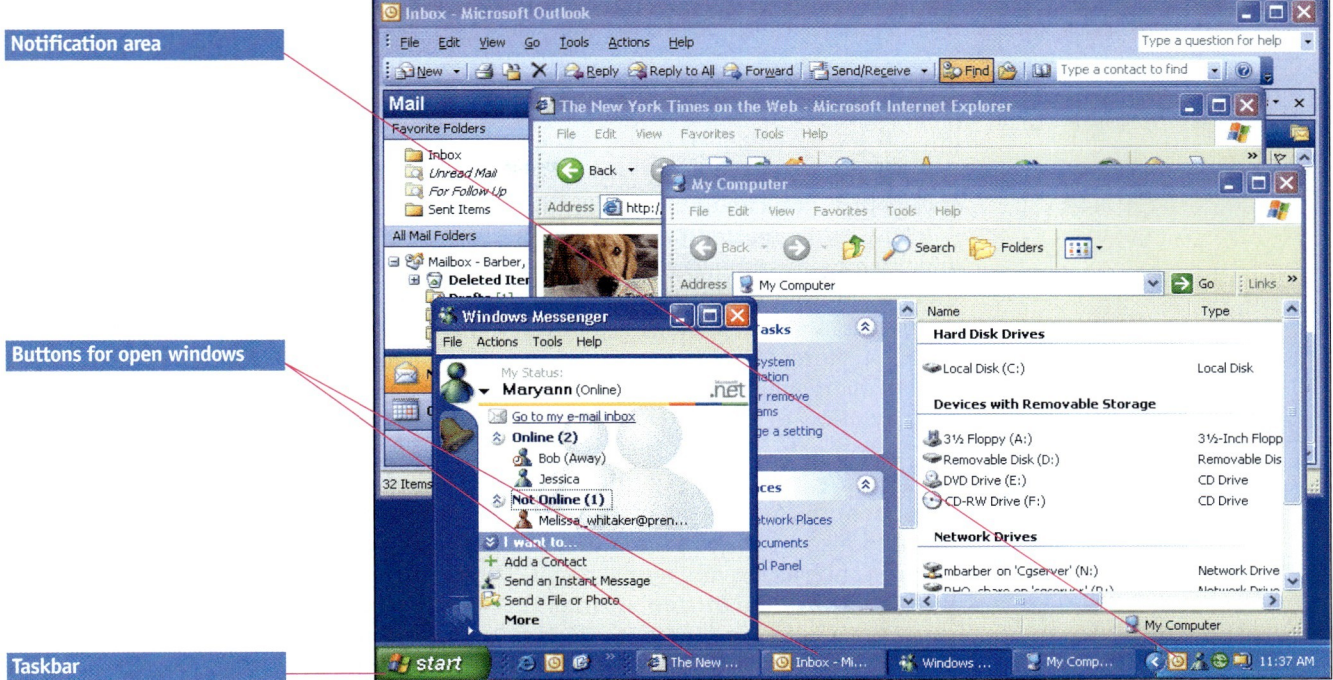

(c) Windows XP Theme

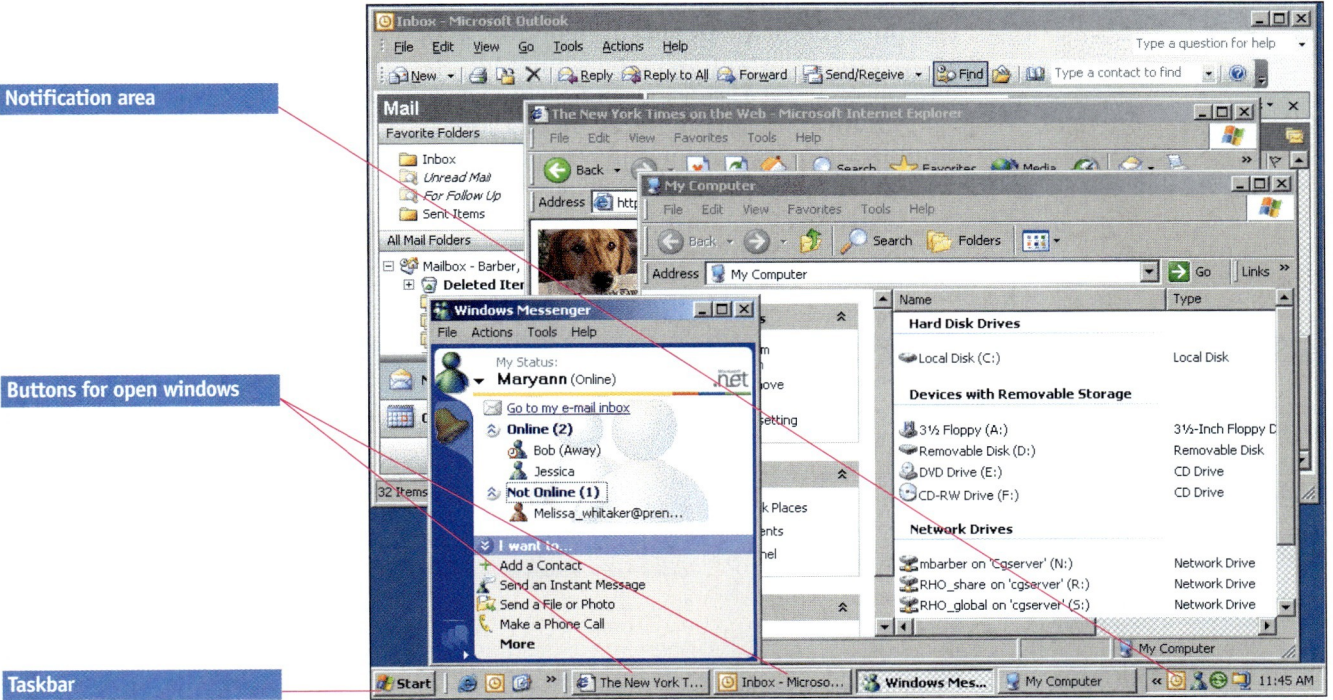

(d) Windows Classic Theme

FIGURE 2   The Desktop and Start Menu (*continued*)

ANATOMY OF A WINDOW

All Windows applications share a common user interface and possess a consistent command structure. This means that every Windows application works essentially the same way, which provides a sense of familiarity from one application to the next. In other words, once you learn the basic concepts and techniques in one application, you can apply that knowledge to every other application.

The *My Computer folder* in Figure 3 is used to illustrate basic technology. This folder is present on every system, and its contents depend on the hardware of the specific computer. Our system, for example, has one local disk, a floppy drive, a removable disk (an Iomega Zip® drive), a DVD drive, and a CD-RW (recordable) drive. Our intent at this time, however, is to focus on the elements that are common to every window. A *task pane* (also called a task panel) is displayed at the left of the window to provide easy access to various commands that you might want to access from this folder.

The *title bar* appears at the top of every window and displays the name of the folder or application. The icon at the extreme left of the title bar identifies the window and also provides access to a control menu with operations relevant to the window, such as moving it or sizing it. Three buttons appear at the right of the title bar. The *Minimize button* shrinks the window to a button on the taskbar, but leaves the window in memory. The *Maximize button* enlarges the window so that it takes up the entire desktop. The *Restore button* (not shown in Figure 3) appears instead of the Maximize button after a window has been maximized, and restores the window to its previous size. The *Close button* closes the window and removes it from memory and the desktop.

The *menu bar* appears immediately below the title bar and provides access to pull-down menus. One or more *toolbars* appear below the menu bar and let you execute a command by clicking a button, as opposed to pulling down a menu. The *status bar* at the bottom of the window displays information about the window as a whole or about a selected object within a window.

A vertical (or horizontal) *scroll bar* appears at the right (or bottom) border of a window when its contents are not completely visible and provides access to the unseen areas. The vertical scroll bar at the right of the task panel in Figure 3 implies that there are additional tasks available that are not currently visible. A horizontal scroll bar does not appear since all of the objects in the My Computer folder are visible at one time.

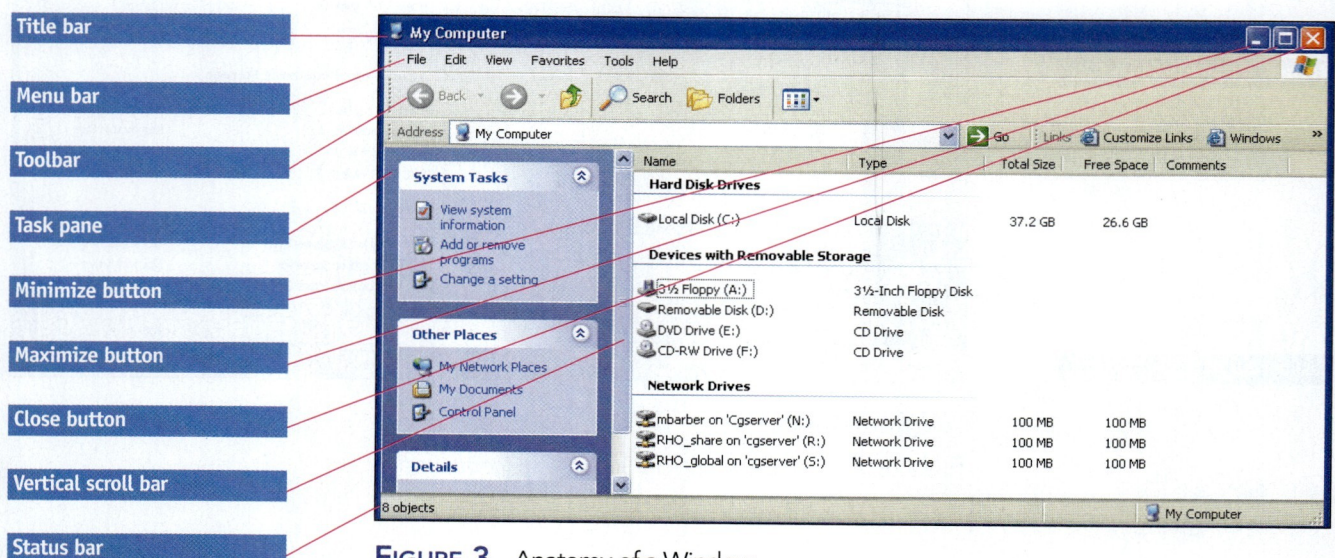

FIGURE 3   Anatomy of a Window

Pull-down Menus

The menu bar provides access to ***pull-down menus*** that enable you to execute commands within an application (program). A pull-down menu is accessed by clicking the menu name or by pressing the Alt key plus the underlined letter in the menu name; for example, press Alt+V to pull down the View menu. (You may have to press the Alt key to see the underlines.) Figure 4 displays three pull-down menus that are associated with the My Computer folder.

Commands within a menu are executed by clicking the command or by typing the underlined letter. Alternatively, you can bypass the menu entirely if you know the equivalent shortcuts shown to the right of the command in the menu (e.g., Ctrl+X, Ctrl+C, or Ctrl+V to cut, copy, or paste as shown within the Edit menu). A dimmed command (e.g., the Paste command in the Edit menu) means the command is not currently executable, and that some additional action has to be taken for the command to become available.

An ellipsis (. . .) following a command indicates that additional information is required to execute the command; for example, selection of the Format command in the File menu requires the user to specify additional information about the formatting process. This information is entered into a dialog box (discussed in the next section), which appears immediately after the command has been selected.

A check next to a command indicates a toggle switch, whereby the command is either on or off. There is a check next to the Status Bar command in the View menu of Figure 4, which means the command is in effect (and thus the status bar will be displayed). Click the Status Bar command and the check disappears, which suppresses the display of the status bar. Click the command a second time and the check reappears, as does the status bar in the associated window.

A bullet next to an item, such as Icons in the View menu, indicates a selection from a set of mutually exclusive choices. Click a different option within the group—such as Thumbnails—and the bullet will move from the previous selection (Icons) to the new selection (Thumbnails).

An arrowhead after a command (e.g., the Arrange Icons by command in the View menu) indicates that a submenu (also known as a cascaded menu) will be displayed with additional menu options.

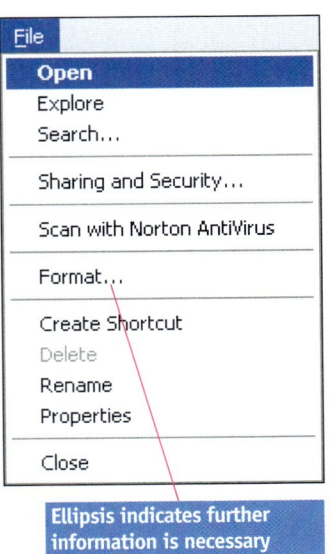
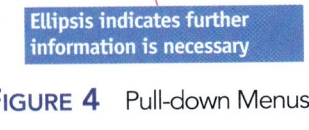
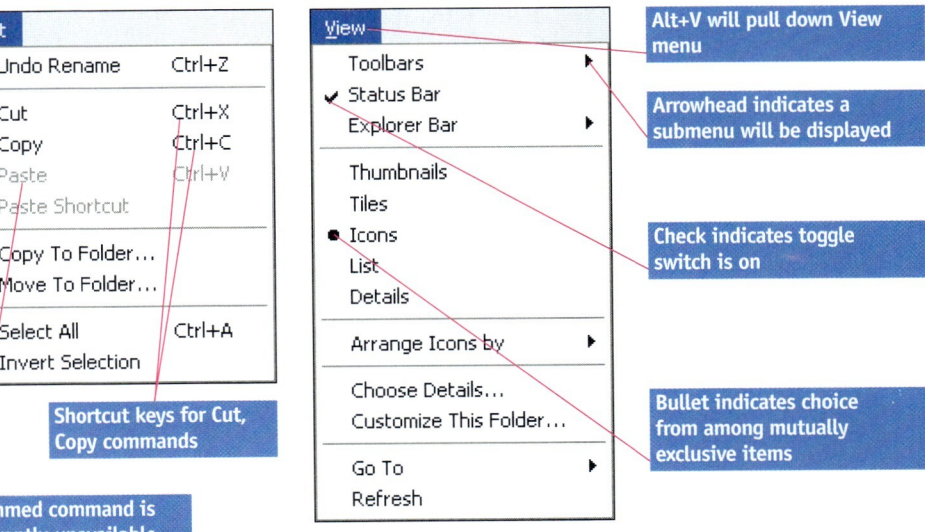

FIGURE 4 Pull-down Menus

Dialog Boxes

A ***dialog box*** appears when additional information is necessary to execute a command. Click the Print command in Internet Explorer, for example, and you are presented with the Print dialog box in Figure 5, requesting information about precisely what to print and how. The information is entered into the dialog box in different ways, depending on the type of information that is required. The tabs at the top of the dialog box provide access to different sets of options. The General tab is selected in Figure 5.

Option (radio) buttons indicate mutually exclusive choices, one of which *must* be chosen, such as the page range. In this example you can print all pages, the selection (if it is available), the current page (if there are multiple pages), or a specific set of pages (such as pages 1–4), but you can choose *one and only one* option. Any time you select (click) an option, the previous option is automatically deselected.

A ***text box*** enters specific information such as the pages that will be printed in conjunction with selecting the radio button for pages. A ***spin button*** is another way to enter specific information such as the number of copies. Click the up or down arrow to increase or decrease the number of pages, respectively. You can also enter the information explicitly by typing it into a spin box, just as you would a text box.

Check boxes are used instead of option buttons if the choices are not mutually exclusive or if an option is not required. The Collate check box is checked, whereas the Print to file box is not checked. Individual options are selected and cleared by clicking the appropriate check box, which toggles the box on and off. A ***list box*** (not shown in Figure 5) displays some or all of the available choices, any one of which is selected by clicking the desired item.

The ***Help button*** (a question mark at the right end of the title bar) provides help for any item in the dialog box. Click the button, then click the item in the dialog box for which you want additional information. The Close button (the X at the extreme right of the title bar) closes the dialog box without executing the command.

All dialog boxes also contain one or more ***command buttons***, the function of which is generally apparent from the button's name. The Print button in Figure 5, for example, initiates the printing process. The Cancel button does just the opposite and ignores (cancels) any changes made to the settings, then closes the dialog box without further action.

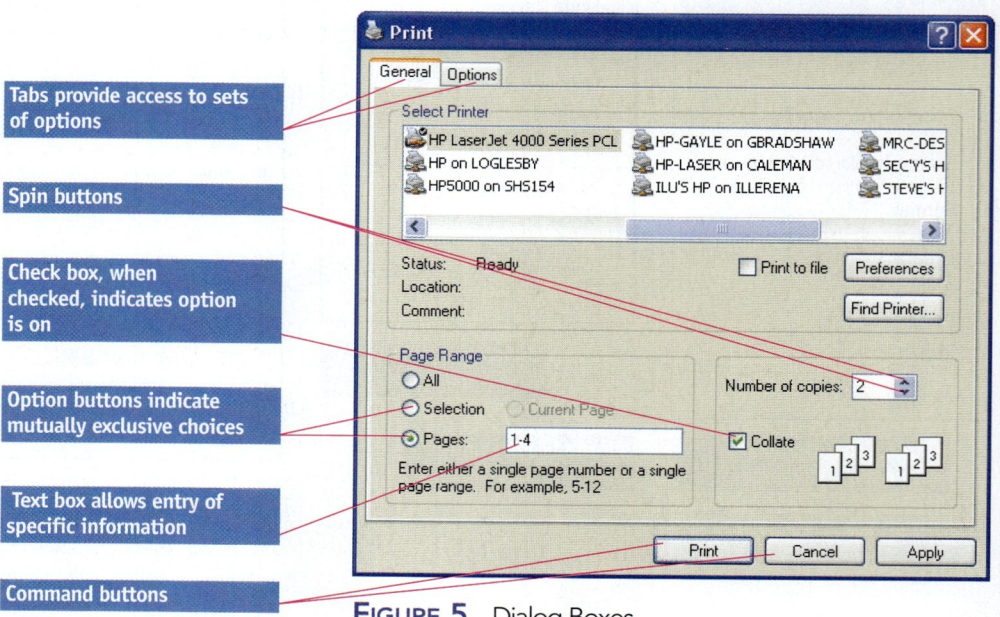

FIGURE 5 Dialog Boxes

HELP AND SUPPORT CENTER

The *Help and Support Center* combines such traditional features as a search function and an index of help topics. It also lets you request remote help from other Windows XP users, and/or you can access the Microsoft Knowledge base on the Microsoft Web site. Click the Index button, type the keyword you are searching for, then double click the subtopic to display the associated information in the right pane. The mouse is essential to Windows, and you are undoubtedly familiar with its basic operations such as pointing, clicking, and double clicking. Look closely, however, at the list of subtopics in Figure 6 and you might be surprised at the amount of available information. Suffice it to say, therefore, that you will find the answer to almost every conceivable question if only you will take the trouble to look.

The toolbar at the top of the window contains several buttons that are also found in *Internet Explorer 6.0*, the Web browser that is built into Windows XP. The Back and Forward buttons enable you to navigate through the various pages that were viewed in the current session. The Favorites button displays a list of previously saved (favorite) help topics from previous sessions. The History button shows all pages that were visited in this session.

The Support button provides access to remote sources for assistance. Click the Support button, then click the link to ask a friend to help, which in turn displays a Remote Assistance screen. You will be asked to sign in to the Messenger service (Windows Messenger is discussed in more detail in a later section). Your friend has to be running Windows XP for this feature to work, but once you are connected, he or she will be able to view your computer screen. You can then chat in real time about the problem and proposed solution. And, if you give permission, your friend can use his or her mouse and keyboard to work on your computer. Be careful! It is one thing to let your friend see your screen. It is quite a leap of faith, however, to give him or her control of your machine.

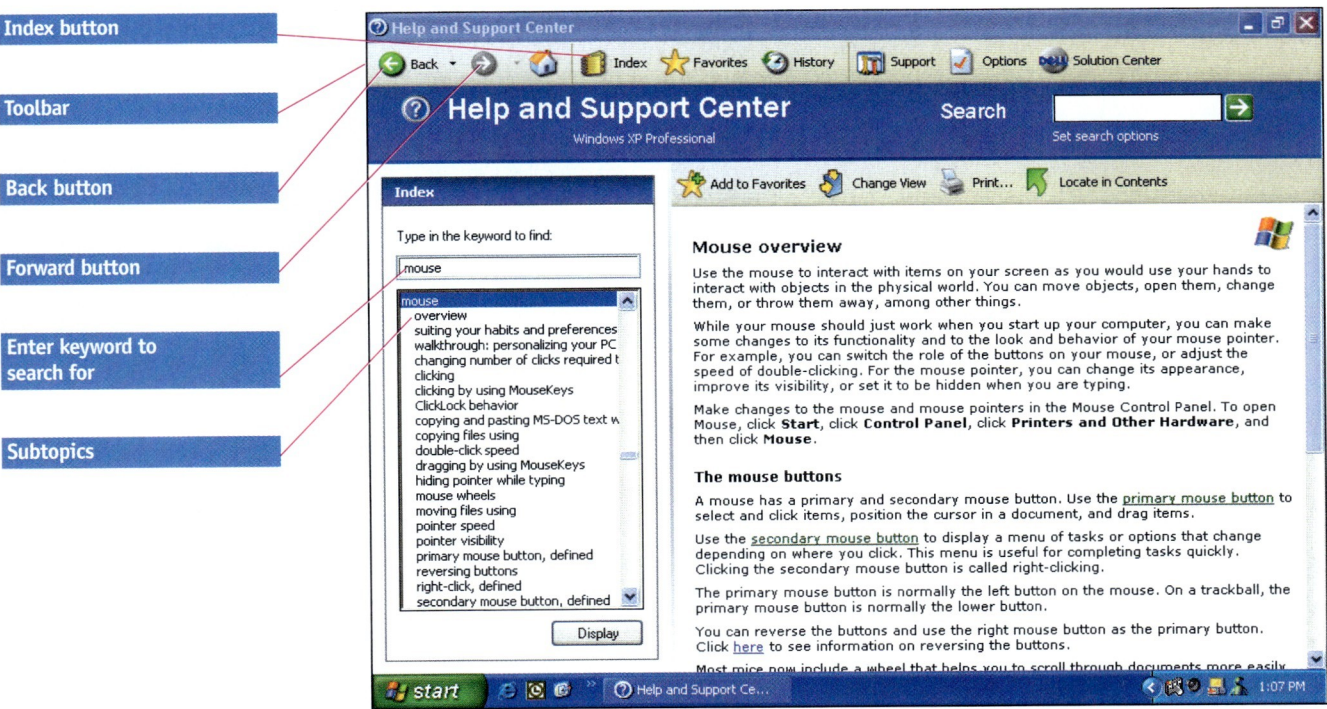

FIGURE 6 Help and Support Center

hands-on exercise
1 Welcome to Windows XP

Objective To log on to Windows XP and customize the desktop; to open the My Computer folder; to move and size a window; to format a floppy disk and access the Help and Support Center. Use Figure 7 as a guide.

Step 1: **Log On to Windows XP**

- Turn on the computer and all of the peripheral devices. The floppy drive should be empty prior to starting your machine.
- Windows XP will load automatically, and you should see a login screen similar to Figure 7a. (It does not matter which version of Windows XP you are using.) The number and names of the potential users and their associated icons will be different on your system.
- Click the icon for the user account you want to access. You may be prompted for a password, depending on the security options in effect.

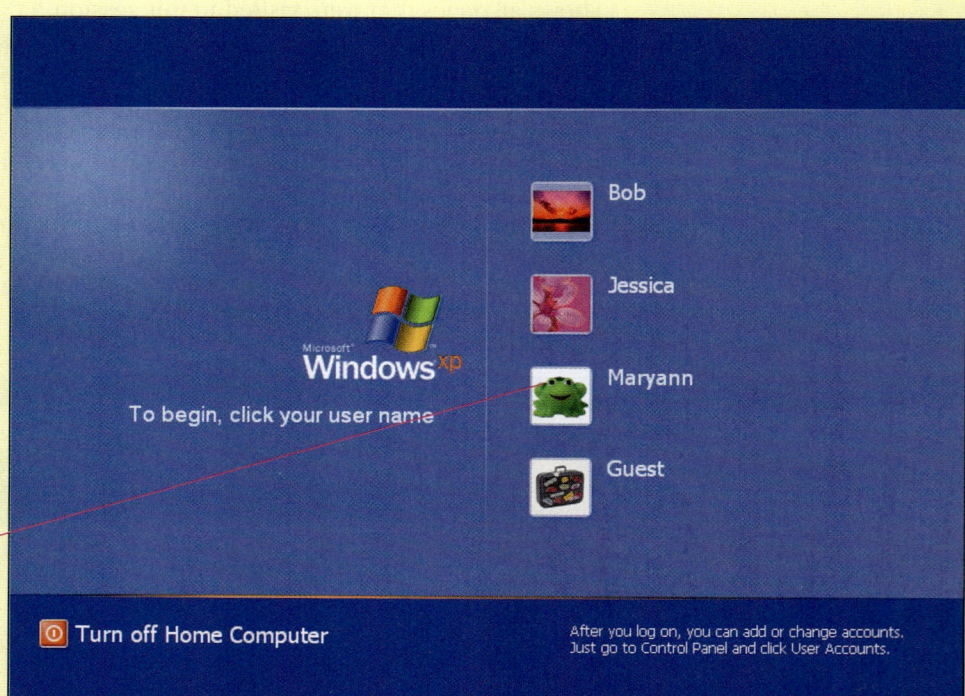

Click icon for user account to be accessed

(a) Log On to Windows XP (step 1)

FIGURE 7 Hands-on Exercise 1

USER ACCOUNTS

The available user names are created automatically during the installation of Windows XP, but you can add or delete users at any time. Click the Start button, click Control Panel, switch to the Category view, and select User Accounts. Choose the desired task, such as creating a new account or changing an existing account, then supply the necessary information. Do not expect, however, to be able to modify user accounts in a school setting.

742 GETTING STARTED WITH MICROSOFT WINDOWS XP

Step 2: **Choose the Theme and Start Menu**

- Check with your instructor to see if you are able to modify the desktop and other settings at your school or university. If your network administrator has disabled these commands, skip this step and go to step 3.

- Point to a blank area on the desktop, click the **right mouse button** to display a context-sensitive menu, then click the **Properties command** to open the Display Properties dialog box. Click the **Themes tab** and select the **Windows XP theme** if it is not already selected. Click **OK**.

- We prefer to work without any wallpaper (background picture) on the desktop. **Right click** the desktop, click **Properties**, then click the **Desktop tab** in the Display Properties dialog box. Click **None** as shown in Figure 7b, then click **OK**. The background disappears.

- The Start menu is modified independently of the theme. **Right click** a blank area of the taskbar, click the **Properties command** to display the Taskbar and Start Menu Properties dialog box, then click the **Start Menu tab**.

- Click the **Start Menu option button**. Click **OK**.

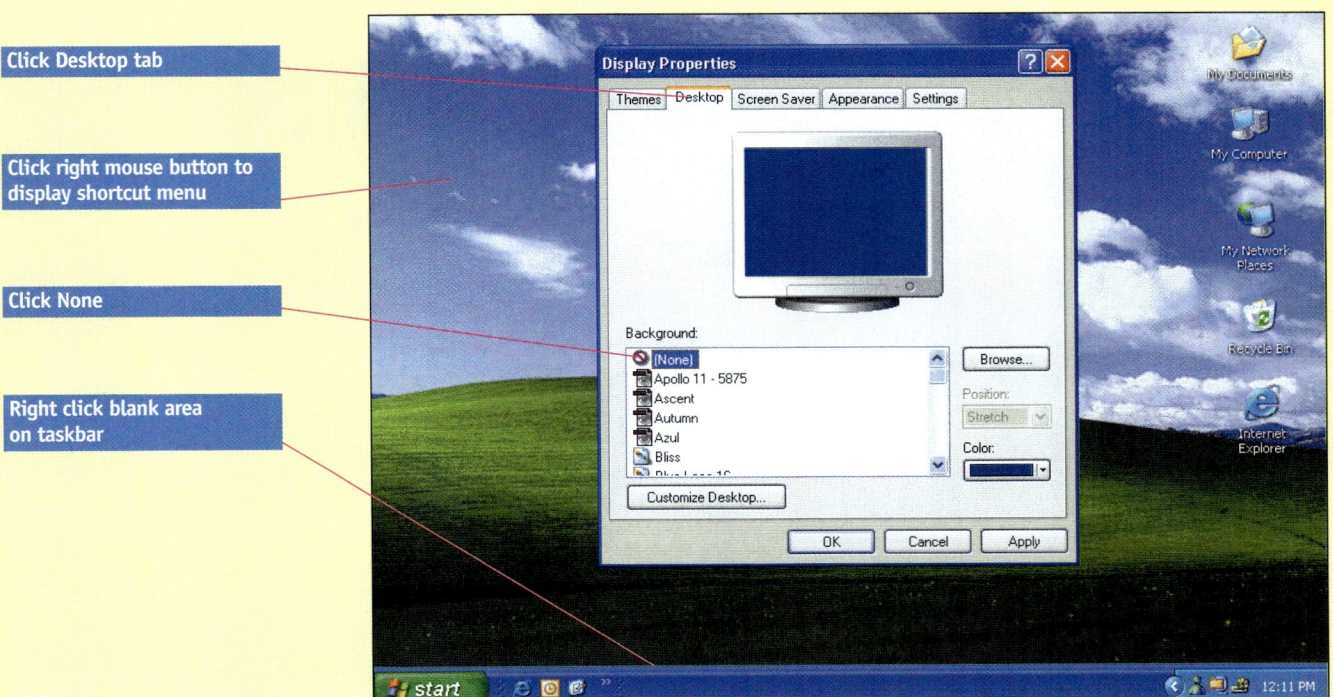

(b) Choose the Theme and Start Menu (step 2)

FIGURE 7 Hands-on Exercise 1 (*continued*)

> ### IMPLEMENT A SCREEN SAVER
> A screen saver is a delightful way to personalize your computer and a good way to practice with basic commands in Windows XP. Right click a blank area of the desktop, click the Properties command to open the Display Properties dialog box, then click the Screen Saver tab. Click the down arrow in the Screen Saver list box, choose the desired screen saver, then set the option to wait an appropriate amount of time before the screen saver appears. Click OK to accept the settings and close the dialog box.

Step 3: **Open the My Computer Folder**

- Click the **Start button** to display a two-column Start menu that is characteristic of Windows XP. Click **My Computer** to open the My Computer folder. The contents of your window and/or its size and position on the desktop will be different from ours.

- Pull down the **View menu** as shown in Figure 7c to make or verify the following selections. (You have to pull down the View menu each time you make an additional change.)
  - The **Status Bar command** should be checked. The Status Bar command functions as a toggle switch. Click the command and the status bar is displayed; click the command a second time and the status bar disappears.
  - Click the **Tiles command** to change to this view. Selecting the Tiles view automatically deselects the previous view.

- Pull down the **View menu**, then click (or point to) the **Toolbars command** to display a cascaded menu. If necessary, check the commands for the **Standard Buttons** and **Address Bar**, and clear the other commands.

- Click the **Folders button** on the Standard Buttons toolbar to toggle the task panel on or off. End with the task panel displayed as shown in Figure 7c.

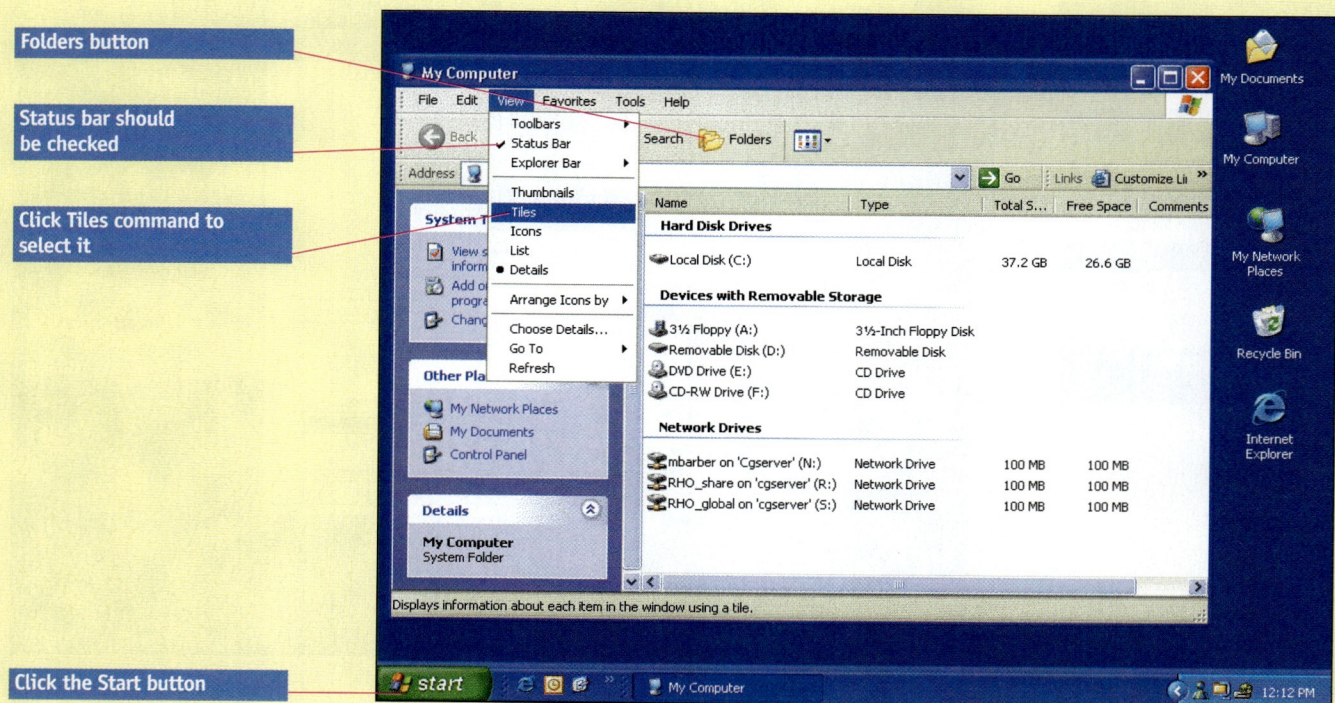

(c) Open the My Computer Folder (step 3)

FIGURE 7   Hands-on Exercise 1 (*continued*)

DESIGNATING THE DEVICES ON A SYSTEM

The first (usually only) floppy drive is always designated as drive A. (A second floppy drive, if it were present, would be drive B.) The first hard (local) disk on a system is always drive C, whether or not there are one or two floppy drives. Additional local drives, if any, such as a zip (removable storage) drive, a network drive, a CD and/or a DVD, are labeled from D on.

Step 4: **Move and Size a Window**

- Move and size the My Computer window on your desktop to match the display in Figure 7d.
  - To change the width or height of the window, click and drag a border (the mouse pointer changes to a double arrow) in the direction you want to go; drag the border inward to shrink the window or outward to enlarge it.
  - To change the width and height at the same time, click and drag a corner rather than a border.
  - To change the position of the window, click and drag the title bar.

- Click the **Minimize button** to shrink the My Computer window to a button on the taskbar. My Computer is still active in memory although its window is no longer visible. Click the **My Computer button** on the taskbar to reopen the window.

- Click the **Maximize button** so that the My Computer window expands to fill the entire screen. Click the **Restore button** (which replaces the Maximize button and is not shown in Figure 7d) to return the window to its previous size.

- Practice these operations until you can move and size a window with confidence.

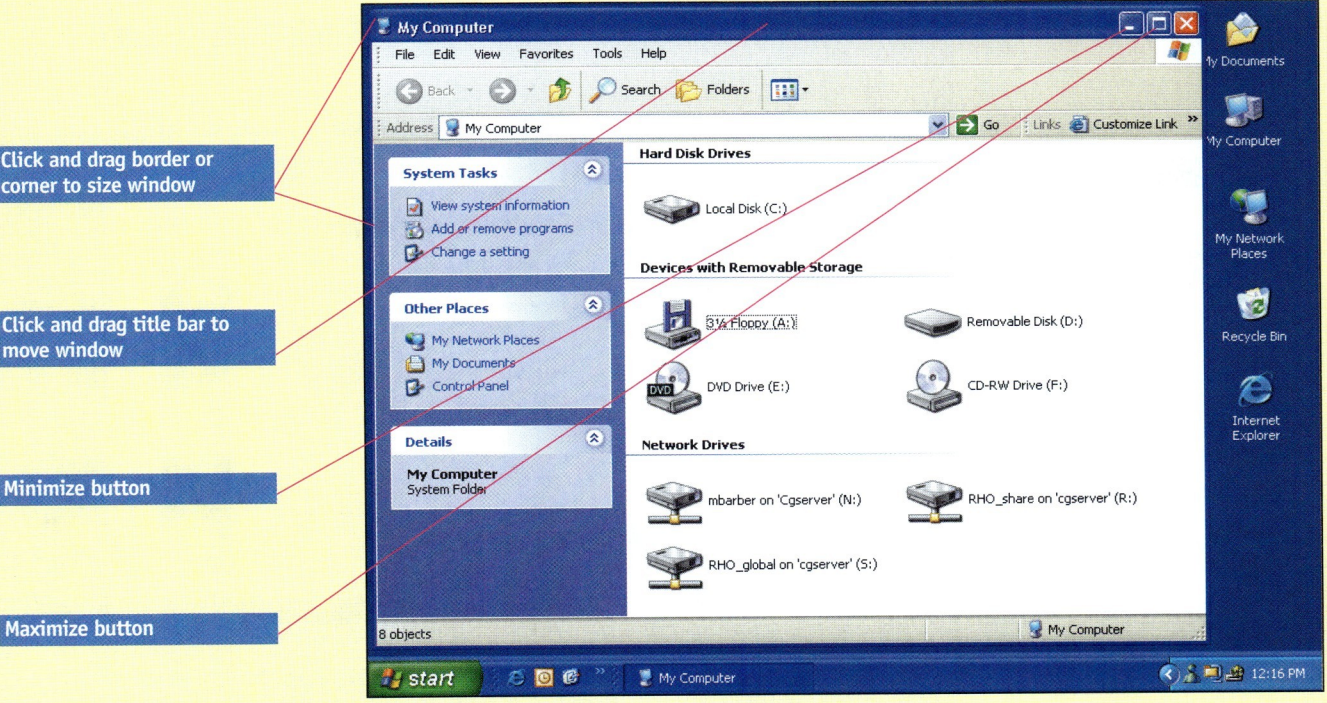

(d) Move and Size a Window (step 4)

FIGURE 7 Hands-on Exercise 1 (*continued*)

MINIMIZING VERSUS CLOSING AN APPLICATION

Minimizing a folder or an application leaves the object open in memory and available at the click of the appropriate button on the taskbar. Closing it, however, removes the object from memory, which also causes it to disappear from the taskbar. The advantage of minimizing an application or folder is that you can return to it immediately with the click of the mouse. The disadvantage is that too many open applications will eventually degrade the performance of a system.

Step 5: **Capture a Screen**

- Prove to your instructor that you have sized the window correctly by capturing the desktop that currently appears on your monitor. Press the **Print Screen key** to copy the current screen display to the **clipboard**, an area of memory that is available to every application.

- Nothing appears to have happened, but the screen has in fact been copied to the clipboard and can be pasted into a Word document. Click the **Start button**, click the **All Programs command**, then start **Microsoft Word** and begin a new document.

- Enter the title of your document (I Did My Homework) followed by your name as shown in Figure 7e. Press the **Enter key** two or three times to leave blank lines after your name.

- Pull down the **Edit menu** and click the **Paste command** (or click the **Paste button** on the Standard toolbar) to copy the contents of the clipboard into the Word document.

- Print this document for your instructor. There is no need to save this document. Exit Word.

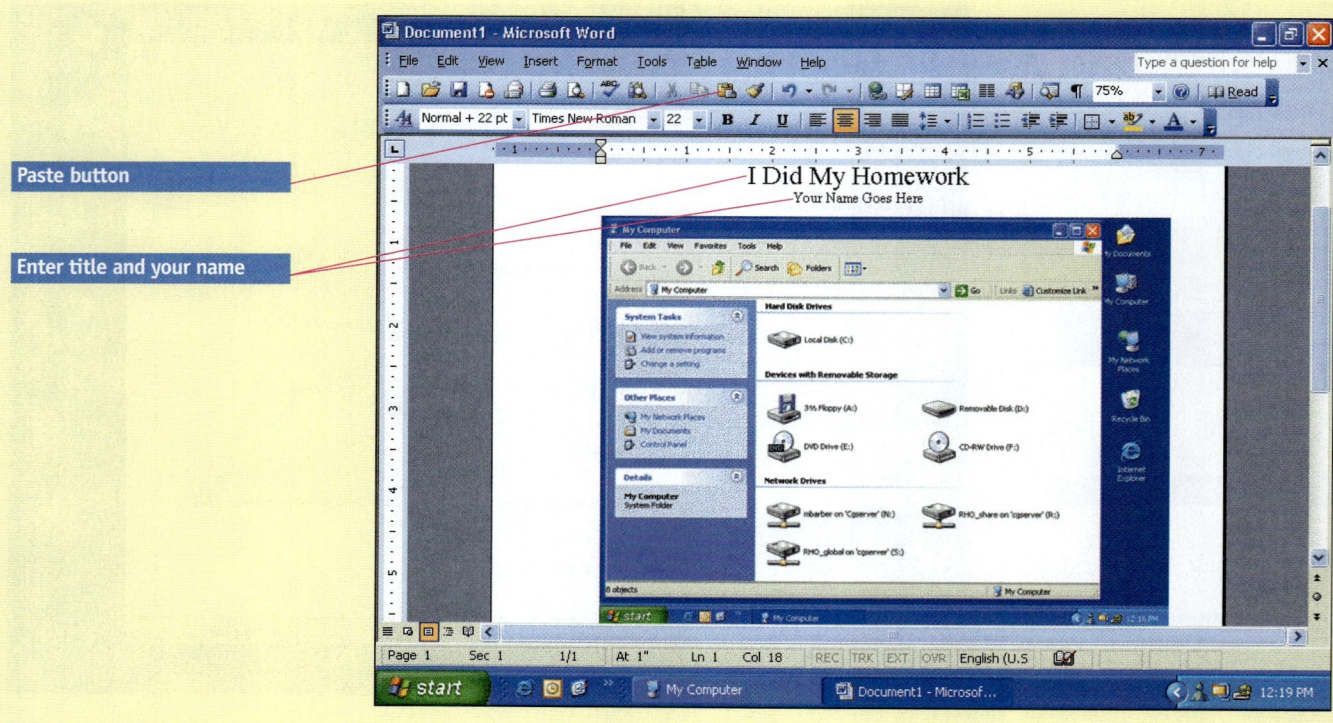

(e) Capture a Screen (step 5)

FIGURE 7   Hands-on Exercise 1 (*continued*)

THE FORMAT PICTURE COMMAND

Use the Format Picture command to facilitate moving and/or sizing an object within a Word document. Right click the picture to display a context-sensitive menu, then click the Format Picture command to display the associated dialog box. Click the Layout tab, choose any layout other than Inline with text, and click OK. You can now click and drag the picture to position it elsewhere within the document.

Step 6: **Format a Floppy Disk**

- Place a floppy disk into drive A. Select (click) **drive A** in the My Computer window, then pull down the **File menu** and click the **Format command** to display the Format dialog box in Figure 7f.
  - Set the **Capacity** to match the floppy disk you purchased (1.44MB for a high-density disk and 720KB for a double-density disk. The easiest way to determine the type of disk is to look for the label HD or DD, respectively.).
  - Click the **Volume label text box** if it's empty, or click and drag over the existing label if there is an entry. Enter a new label (containing up to 11 characters), such as **Bob's Disk**.
  - You can check the **Quick Format box** if the disk has been previously formatted, as a convenient way to erase the contents of the disk.
- Click the **Start button,** then click **OK**—after you have read the warning message—to begin the formatting operation. The formatting process erases anything that is on the disk, so be sure that you do not need anything on the disk.
- Click **OK** after the formatting is complete. Close the dialog box, then save the formatted disk for the next exercise. Close the My Computer window.

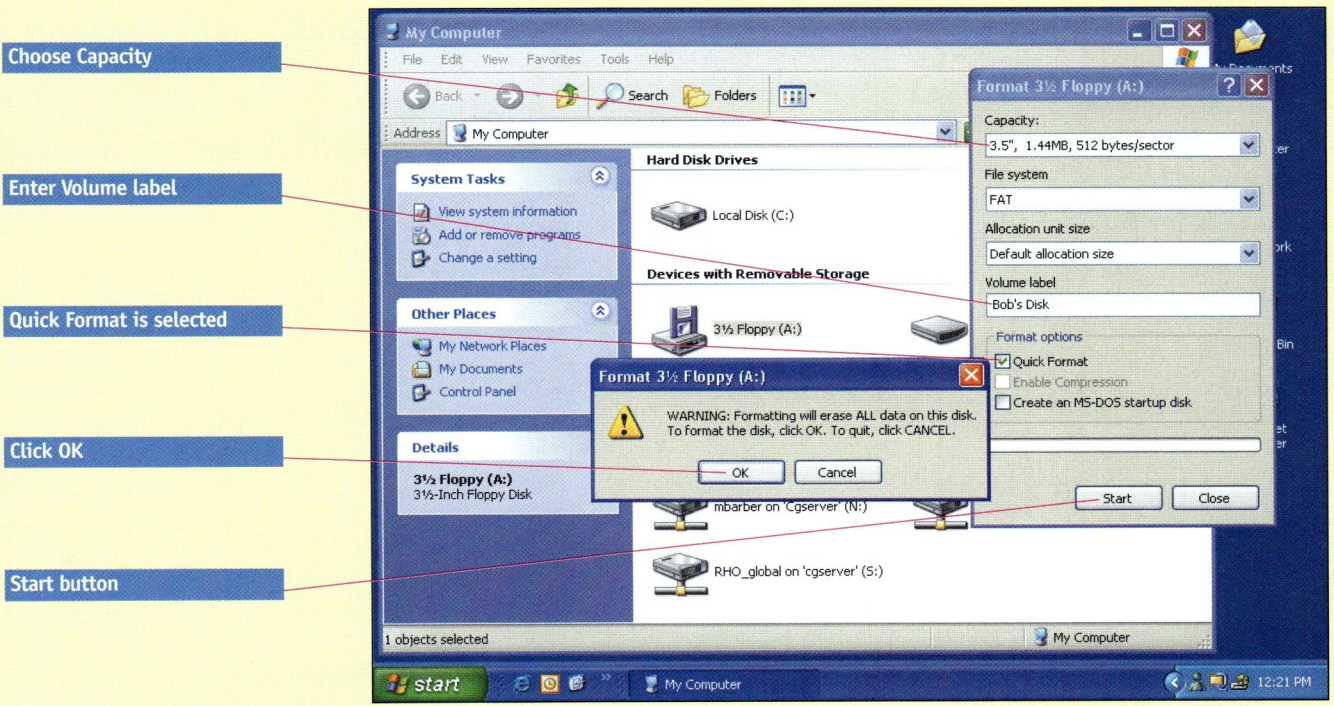

(f) Format a Floppy Disk (step 6)

FIGURE 7 Hands-on Exercise 1 (*continued*)

THE DEMISE OF THE FLOPPY DISK

You may be surprised to discover that your system no longer has a floppy disk drive, but it is only the latest victim in the march of technology. Long-playing records have come and gone. So too have 8-track tapes and the laser disk. The 3½-inch floppy disk has had a long and successful run, but it, too, is slated for obsolescence with Dell's recent announcement that it will no longer include a floppy drive as a standard component in desktop systems. Still, the floppy disk will "live forever" in the Save button that has the floppy disk as its icon.

Step 7: **The Help and Support Center**

- Click the **Start button**, then click the **Help and Support command** to open the Help and Support Center. Click the **Index button** to open the index pane. The insertion point moves automatically to the text box where you enter the search topic.

- Type **help**, which automatically moves you to the available topics within the index. Double click **central location for Help** to display the information in the right pane as shown in Figure 7g.

- Toggle the display of the subtopics on and off by clicking the plus and minus sign, respectively. Click the **plus sign** next to Remote Assistance, for example, and the topic opens. Click the **minus sign** next to Tours and articles, and the topic closes.

- Right click anywhere within the right pane to display the context-sensitive menu shown in Figure 7g. Click the **Print command** to print this information for your instructor.

- Close the Help and Support window.

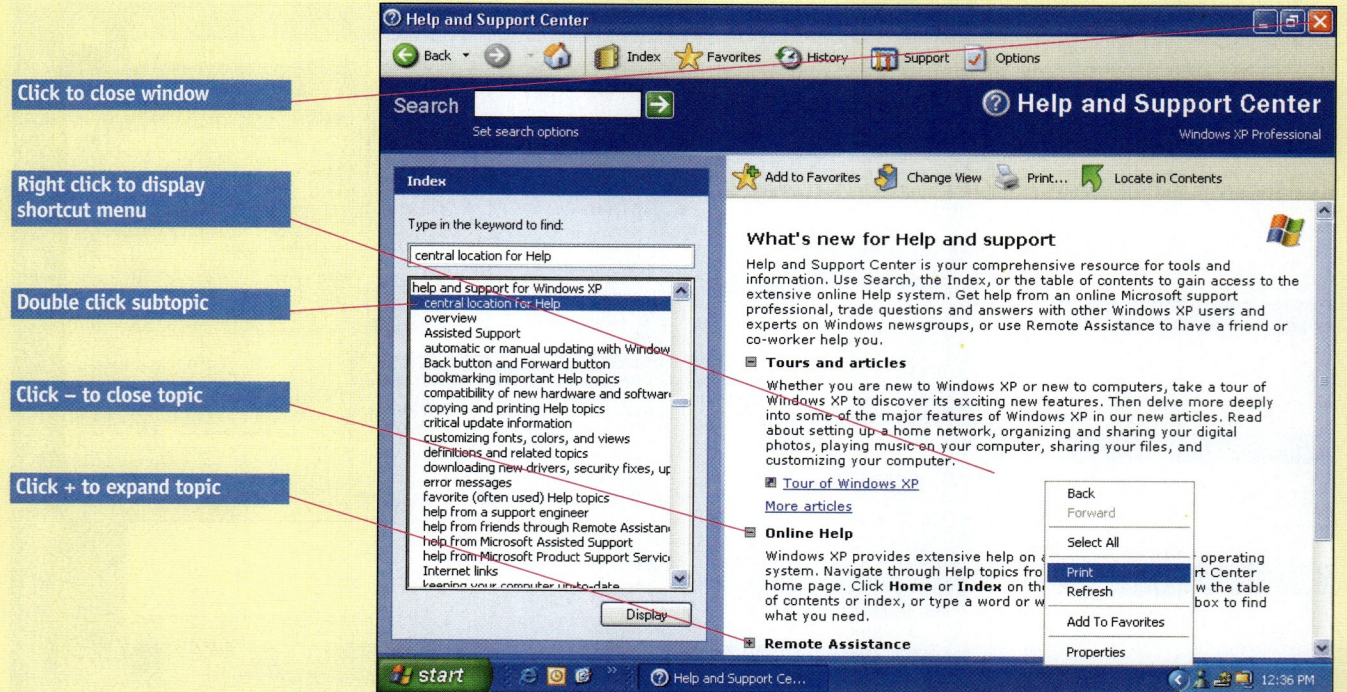

(g) The Help and Support Center (step 7)

FIGURE 7   Hands-on Exercise 1 (*continued*)

THE FAVORITES BUTTON

Do you find yourself continually searching for the same information? If so, you can make life a little easier by adding the page to a list of favorite help topics. Start the Help and Support Center, use the Index button to display the desired information in the right pane, and then click the Add to Favorites button to add the topic to your list of favorites. You can return to the topic at any time by clicking the Favorites button at the top of the Help and Support window, then double clicking the bookmark.

Step 8: **Log (or Turn) Off the Computer**

- It is very important that you log off properly, as opposed to just turning off the power. This enables Windows to close all of its system files and to save any changes that were made during the session.

- Click the **Start button** to display the Start menu in Figure 7h, then click the **Log Off button** at the bottom of the menu. You will see a dialog box asking whether you want to log off or switch users.
  - ❑ Switching users leaves your session active. All of your applications remain open, but control of the computer is given to another user. You can subsequently log back on (after the new user logs off) and take up exactly where you left off.
  - ❑ Logging off ends your session, but leaves the computer running at full power. This is the typical option you would select in a laboratory setting at school.

- To turn the computer off, you have to log off as just described, then select the **Turn Computer Off command** from the login screen. Welcome to Windows XP!

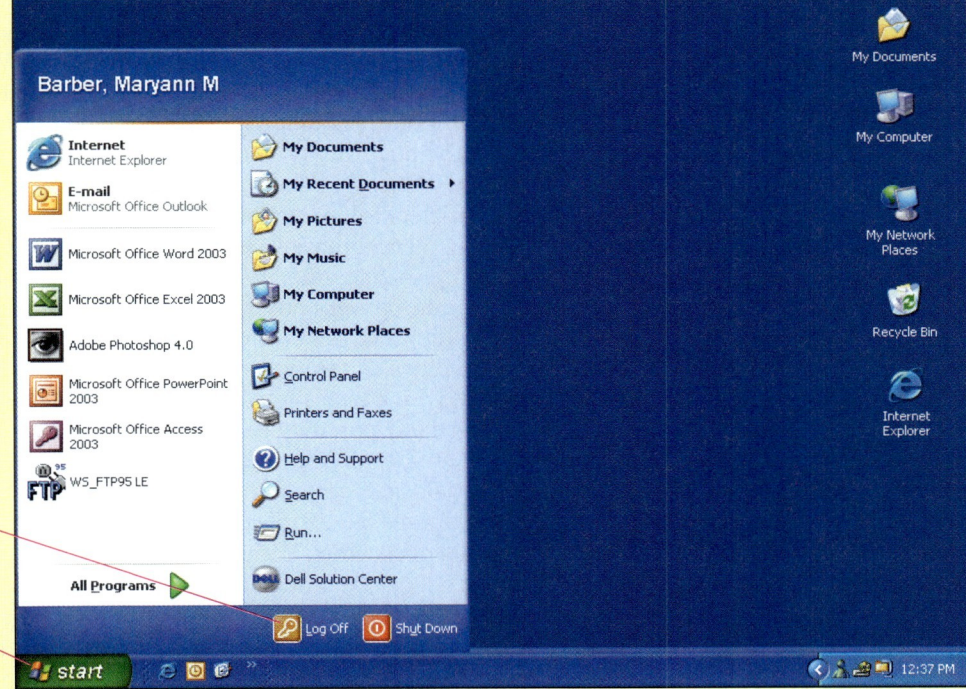

(h) Log (or Turn) Off Computer (step 8)

FIGURE 7   Hands-on Exercise 1 (*continued*)

THE TASK MANAGER

The Start button is the normal way to exit Windows. Occasionally, however, an application may "hang"—in which case you want to close the problem application but continue with your session. Press Ctrl+Alt+Del to display the Windows Task Manager dialog box, then click the Applications tab. Select the problem application (it will most likely say "not responding"), and click the End Task button. This capability is often disabled in a school setting.

FILES AND FOLDERS

A ***file*** is a set of instructions or data that has been given a name and stored on disk. There are two basic types of files, ***program files*** and ***data files***. Microsoft Word and Microsoft Excel are examples of program files. The documents and workbooks that are created by these programs are data files. A program file is executable because it contains instructions that tell the computer what to do. A data file is not executable and can be used only in conjunction with a specific program. In other words, you execute program files to create and/or edit the associated data files.

Every file has a ***filename*** that identifies it to the operating system. The filename can contain up to 255 characters and may include spaces and other punctuation. (Filenames cannot contain the following characters: \, /, :, *, ?, ", <, >, and |.) We find it easier, however, to restrict the characters in a filename to letters, numbers, and spaces, as opposed to having to remember the special characters that are not permitted.

Files are kept in ***folders*** to better organize the thousands of files on a typical system. A Windows folder is similar to an ordinary manila folder that holds one or more documents. To continue the analogy, an office worker stores his or her documents in manila folders within a filing cabinet. Windows stores its files in electronic folders that are located on a disk, CD-ROM, or other device.

Many folders are created automatically by Windows XP, such as the My Computer or My Documents folders that are present on every system. Other folders are created whenever new software is installed. Additional folders are created by the user to hold the documents he or she creates. You might, for example, create a folder for your word processing documents and a second folder for your spreadsheets. You could also create a folder to hold all of your work for a specific class, which in turn might contain a combination of word processing documents and spreadsheets. The choice is entirely up to you, and you can use any system that makes sense to you. A folder can contain program files, data files, or even other folders.

Figure 8 displays the contents of a hypothetical folder with nine documents. Figure 8a displays the folder in ***Tiles view***. Figure 8b displays the same folder in ***Details view***, which also shows the date the file was created or last modified. Both views display a file icon next to each file to indicate the ***file type*** or application that was used to create the file. *Introduction to E-mail*, for example, is a PowerPoint presentation. *Basic Financial Functions* is an Excel workbook.

The two figures have more similarities than differences, such as the name of the folder (*Homework*), which appears in the title bar next to the icon of an open folder. The Minimize, Restore, and Close buttons are found at the right of the title bar. A menu bar with six pull-down menus appears below the title bar. The Standard Buttons toolbar is below the menu, and the Address bar (indicating the drive and folder) appears below the toolbar. Both folders also contain a task pane that provides easy access to common tasks for the folder or selected object.

Look closely and you will see that the task panes are significantly different. This is because there are no documents selected in Figure 8a, whereas the *Milestones in Communications* document is selected (highlighted) in Figure 8b. Thus, the File and Folder Tasks area in Figure 8a pertains to folders in general, whereas the available tasks in Figure 8b are pertinent to the selected document. The Details areas in the two task panes are also consistent with the selected objects and display information about the Homework folder and selected document, respectively. A status bar appears at the bottom of both windows and displays the contents of the selected object.

The last difference between the task panes reflects the user's preference to open or close the Other Places area. Click the upward chevron in Figure 8a to suppress the display and gain space in the task pane, or click the downward chevron in Figure 8b to display the specific links to other places. The task pane is new to Windows XP and did not appear in previous versions of Windows.

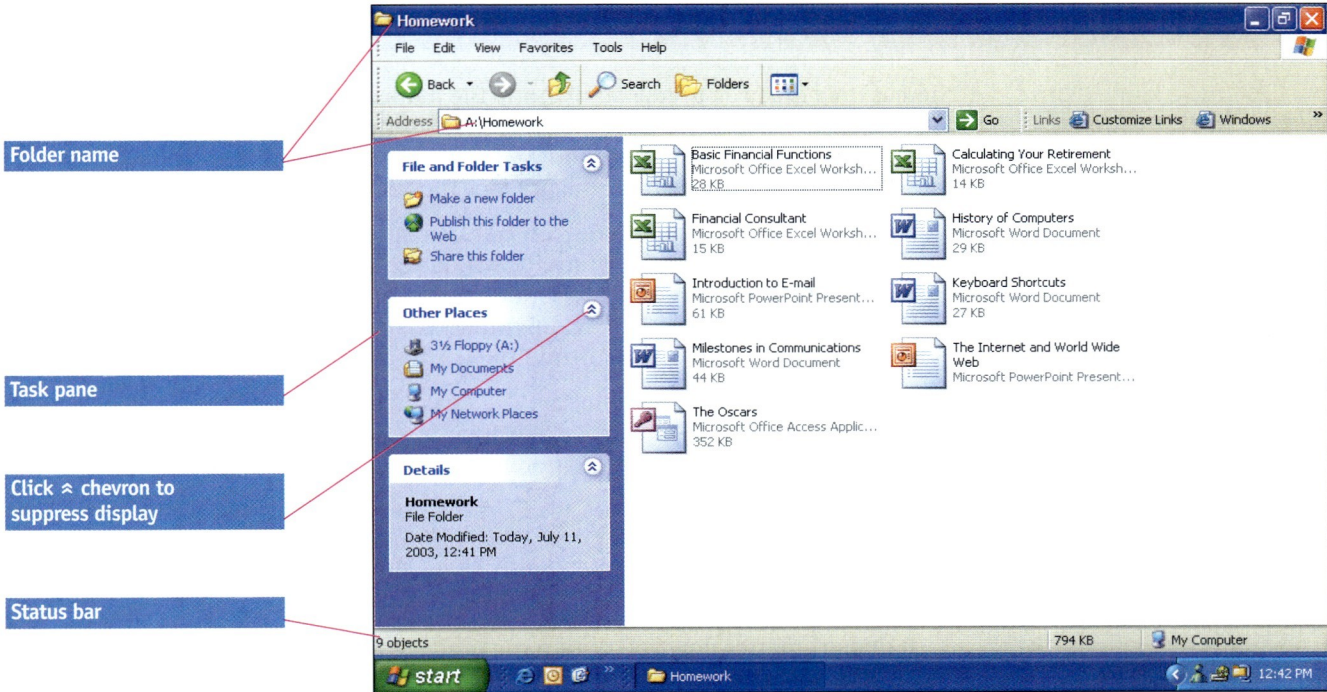

(a) Tiles View

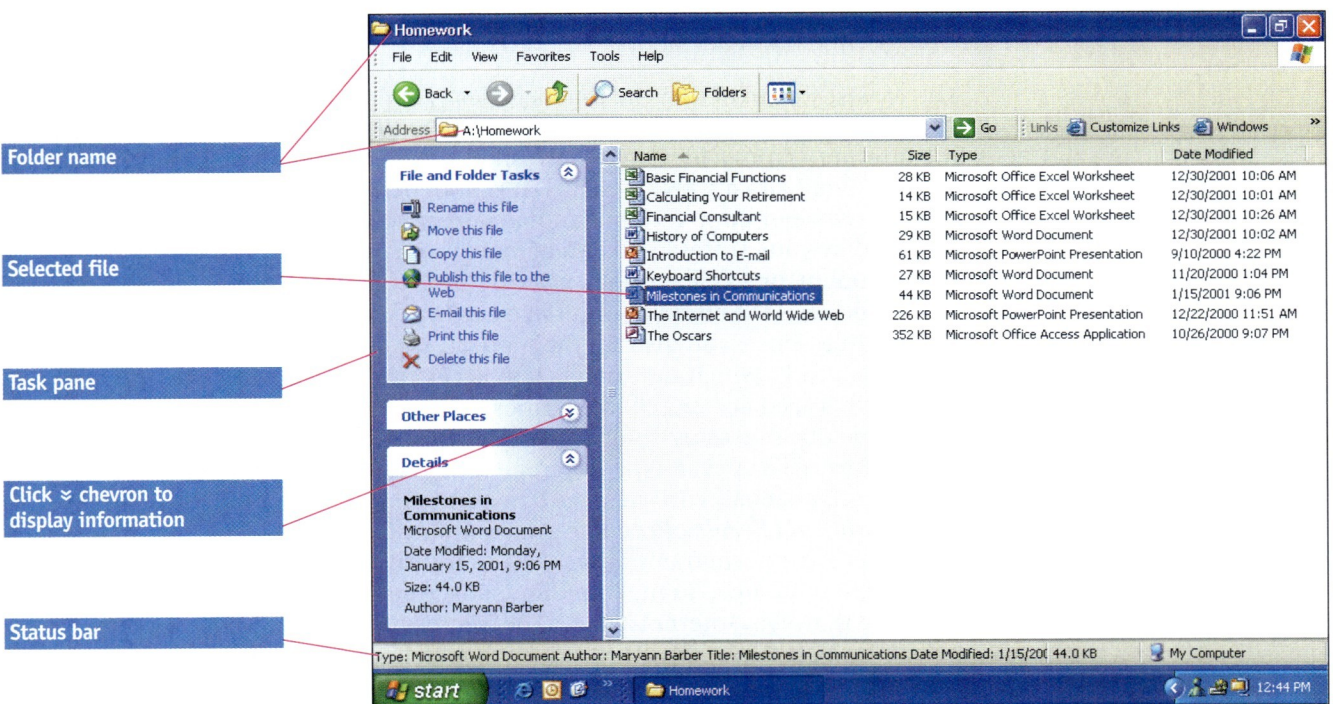

(b) Details View

FIGURE 8 Files and Folders

THE EXPLORING OFFICE PRACTICE FILES

There is only one way to master disk and file management and that is to practice at the computer. To do so requires that you have a series of files with which to work. We have created these files for you, and we use the files in the next two hands-on exercises. Your instructor will make the practice files available to you in different ways:

- The files can be downloaded from our Web site at www.prenhall.com/grauer. Software and other files that are downloaded from the Internet are typically compressed (made smaller) to reduce the amount of time it takes to transmit the file. In essence, you will download a single *compressed file* and then uncompress the file into multiple files onto a local drive as described in the next hands-on exercise.

- The files may be on a network drive at your school or university, in which case you can copy the files from the network drive to a floppy disk.

- There may be an actual "data disk" in the computer lab. Go to the lab with a floppy disk, then use the Copy Disk command (on the File menu of My Computer when drive A is selected) to duplicate the data disk and create a copy for yourself.

It doesn't matter how you obtain the practice files, only that you are able to do so. Indeed, you may want to try different techniques to gain additional practice with Windows XP. Note, too, that Windows XP provides a *firewall* to protect your computer from unauthorized access while it is connected to the Internet. (See exercise 2 at the end of the chapter.)

CONNECTING TO THE INTERNET

The easiest way to obtain the practice files is to download the files from the Web, which requires an Internet connection. There are two basic ways to connect to the Internet—from a local area network (LAN) or by dialing in. It's much easier if you connect from a LAN (typically at school or work) since the installation and setup have been done for you, and all you have to do is follow the instructions provided by your professor. If you connect from home, you will need a modem, a cable modem, or a DSL modem, and an Internet Service Provider (or ISP).

A *modem* is the hardware interface between your computer and the telephone system. In essence, you instruct the modem, via the appropriate software, to connect to your ISP, which in turn lets you access the Internet. A cable modem provides high-speed access (20 to 30 times that of an ordinary modem) through the same type of cable as used for cable TV. A DSL modem also provides high-speed access through a special type of phone line that lets you connect to the Internet while simultaneously carrying on a conversation.

An *Internet Service Provider* is a company or organization that maintains a computer with permanent access to the Internet. America Online (AOL) is the largest ISP with more than 30 million subscribers, and it provides a proprietary interface as well as Internet access. The Microsoft Network (MSN) is a direct competitor to AOL. Alternatively, you can choose from a host of other vendors who provide Internet access without the proprietary interface of AOL or MSN.

Regardless of which vendor you choose as an ISP, be sure you understand the fee structure. The monthly fee may entitle you to a set number of hours per month (after which you pay an additional fee), or it may give you unlimited access. The terms vary widely, and you should shop around for the best possible deal. Price is not the only consideration, however. Reliability of service is also important. Be sure that the equipment of your provider is adequate so that you can obtain access whenever you want.

hands-on exercise

2 Download the Practice Files

Objective To download a file from the Web and practice basic file commands. The exercise requires a formatted floppy disk and access to the Internet. Use Figure 9 as a guide.

Step 1: **Start Internet Explorer**

- Click the **Start button**, click the **All Programs command**, and then click **Internet Explorer** to start the program. If necessary, click the **Maximize button** so that Internet Explorer takes the entire desktop.

- Click anywhere within the **Address bar**, which automatically selects the current address (so that whatever you type replaces the current address). Enter **www.prenhall.com/grauer** (the http:// is assumed). Press **Enter**.

- You should see the Exploring Office Series home page as shown in Figure 9a. Click the book for **Office 2003**, which takes you to the Office 2003 home page.

- Click the **Student Downloads tab** (at the top of the window) to go to the Student Download page.

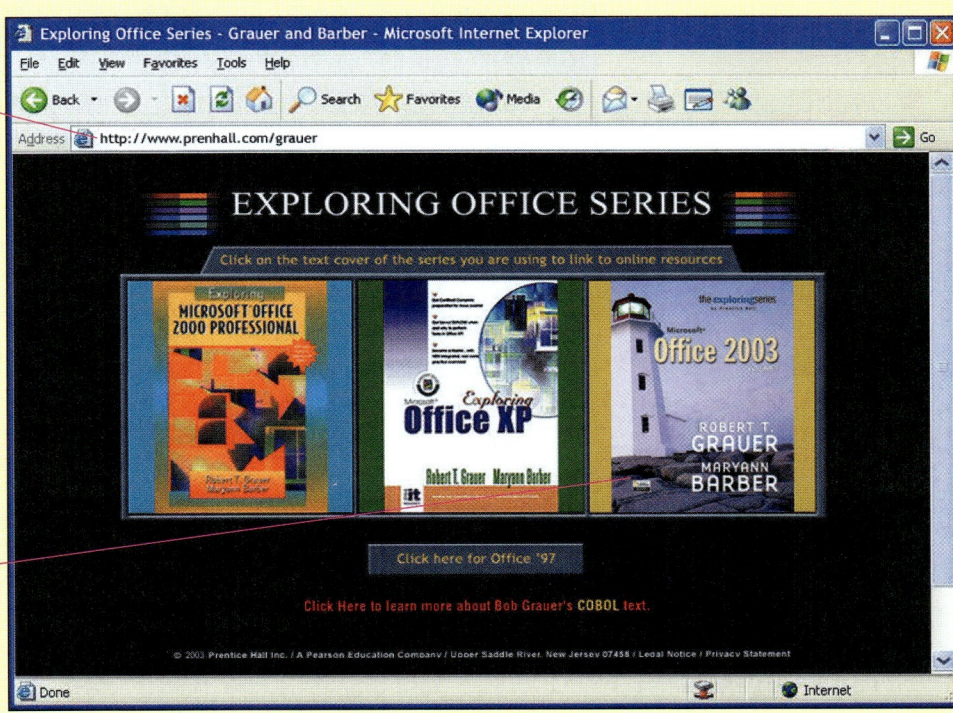

(a) Start Internet Explorer (step 1)

FIGURE 9 Hands-on Exercise 2

A NEW INTERNET EXPLORER

The installation of Windows XP automatically installs a new version of Internet Explorer. Pull down the Help menu and click the About Internet Explorer command to display the current release (version 6.0). Click OK to close the About Internet Explorer window.

Step 2: **Download the Practice Files**

- You should see the Student Download page in Figure 9b. Place the formatted floppy disk from the first exercise in drive A. Be sure there are no files on this disk.

- Scroll down the page until you see the link to the student data disk for **Windows XP**. Click the link to download the practice files.

- You will see the File Download dialog box, asking what you want to do. Click the **Save button** to display the Save As dialog box. Click the **drop-down arrow** on the Save in list box, and select (click) **drive A**.

- Click **Save** to download the file. The File Download window may reappear and show you the status of the downloading operation as it takes place.

- If necessary, click **Close** when you see the dialog box indicating that the download is complete. Minimize Internet Explorer.

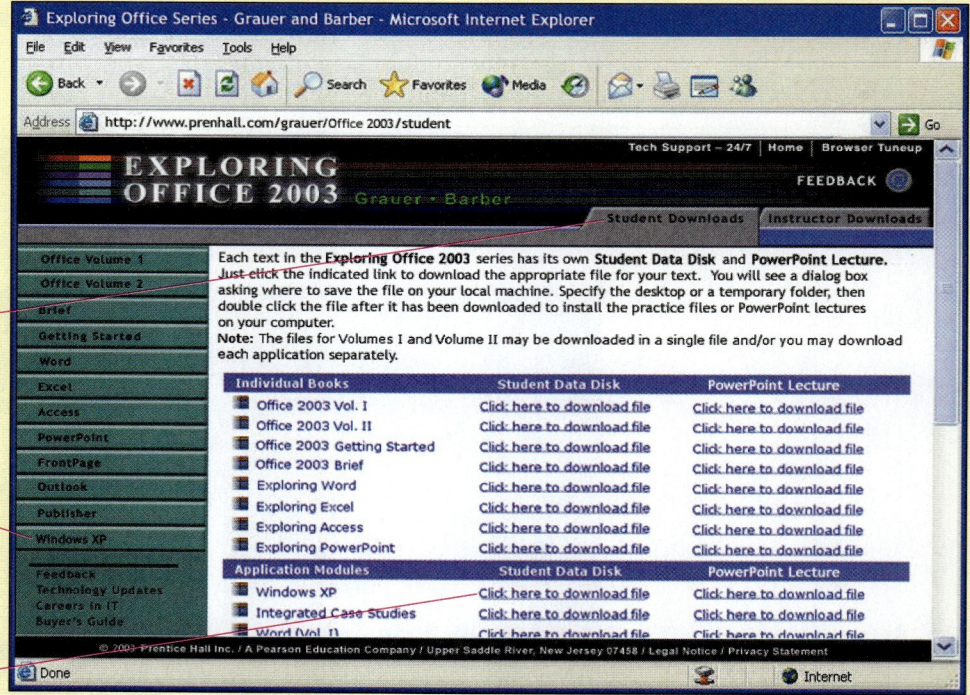

(b) Download the Practice Files (step 2)

FIGURE 9   Hands-on Exercise 2 (*continued*)

EXPLORE OUR WEB SITE

The Exploring Office Series Web site offers an online study guide (multiple-choice, true/false, and matching questions) for each individual textbook to help you review the material in each chapter. You can take practice quizzes by yourself and/or e-mail the results to your instructor. These online study guides are available via the tabs in the left navigation bar. You can return to the Student Download page at any time by clicking the tab toward the top of the window and/or you can click the link to Home to return to the home page for the Office 2003 Series. And finally, you can click the Feedback button at the top of the screen to send a message directly to Bob Grauer.

Step 3: **Install the Practice Files**

- Click the **Start button**, then click the **My Computer command** on the menu to open the My Computer folder. If necessary, click the Maximize button so that the My Computer window takes up the entire desktop. Change to the **Details view**.

- Click the icon for **drive A** to select it. The description of drive A appears at the left of the window. Double click the icon for **drive A** to open this drive. The contents of the My Computer window are replaced by the contents of drive A as shown in Figure 9c.

- Double click the **XPData file** to install the practice files, which displays the dialog box in Figure 9c. When you have finished reading, click **OK** to continue the installation and display the WinZip Self-Extractor dialog box.

- Check that the Unzip To Folder text box specifies **A:** to extract the files to the floppy disk. Click the **Unzip button** to extract (uncompress) the practice files and copy them onto the designated drive.

- Click **OK** after you see the message indicating that the files have been unzipped successfully. Close the WinZip dialog box.

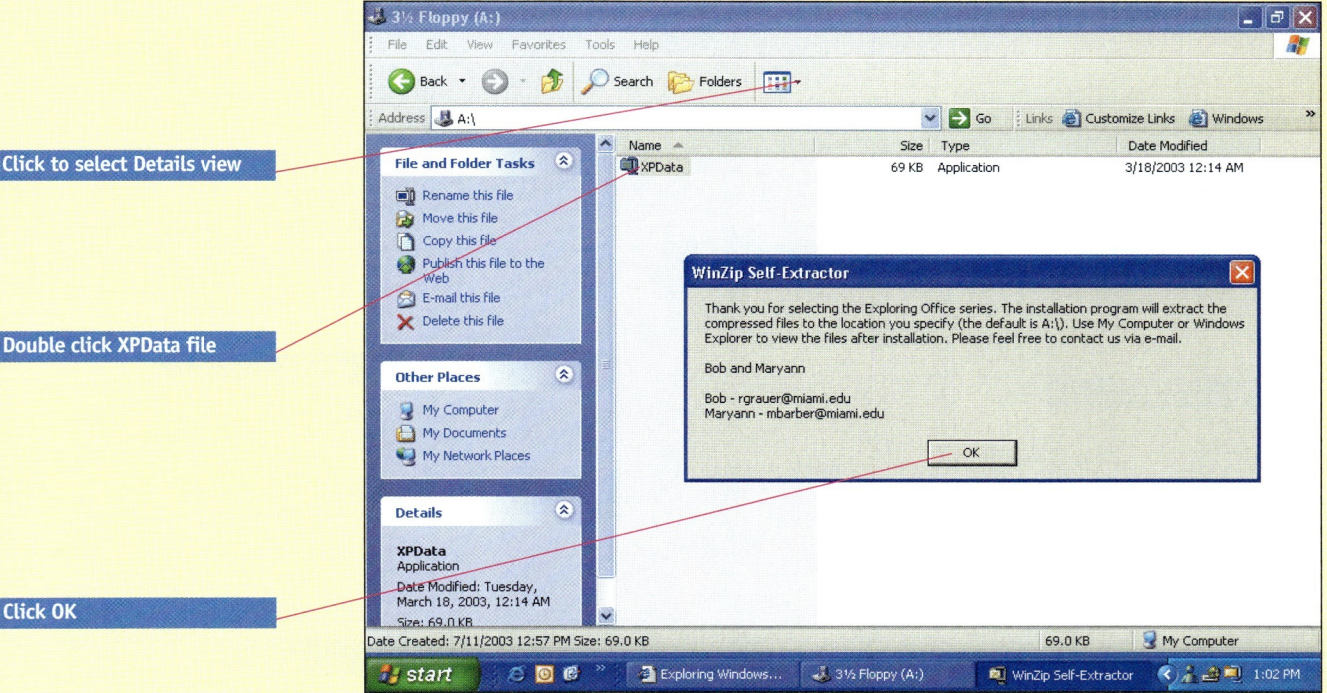

(c) Install the Practice Files (step 3)

FIGURE 9 Hands-on Exercise 2 (*continued*)

DOWNLOADING A FILE

Software and other files are typically compressed (made smaller) to reduce the amount of storage space the files require on disk and/or the time it takes to download the files. In essence, you download a compressed file (which may contain multiple individual files), then you uncompress (expand) the file on your local drive to access the individual files. After the file has been expanded, it is no longer needed and can be deleted.

Step 4: **Delete the Compressed File**

- The practice files have been extracted to drive A and should appear in the Drive A window. If you do not see the files, pull down the **View menu** and click the **Refresh command**.

- If necessary, pull down the **View menu** and click **Details** to change to the Details view in Figure 9e. You should see a total of eight files in the drive A window. Seven of these are the practice files on the data disk. The eighth file is the original file that you downloaded earlier. This file is no longer necessary, since it has been already been expanded.

- Select (click) the **XPData file**. Click the **Delete this file command** in the task pane (or simply press the **Del key**). Pause for a moment to be sure you want to delete this file, then click **Yes** when asked to confirm the deletion as shown in Figure 9d.

- The XPData file is permanently deleted from drive A. (Items deleted from a floppy disk or network drive are not sent to the Recycle bin, and cannot be recovered.)

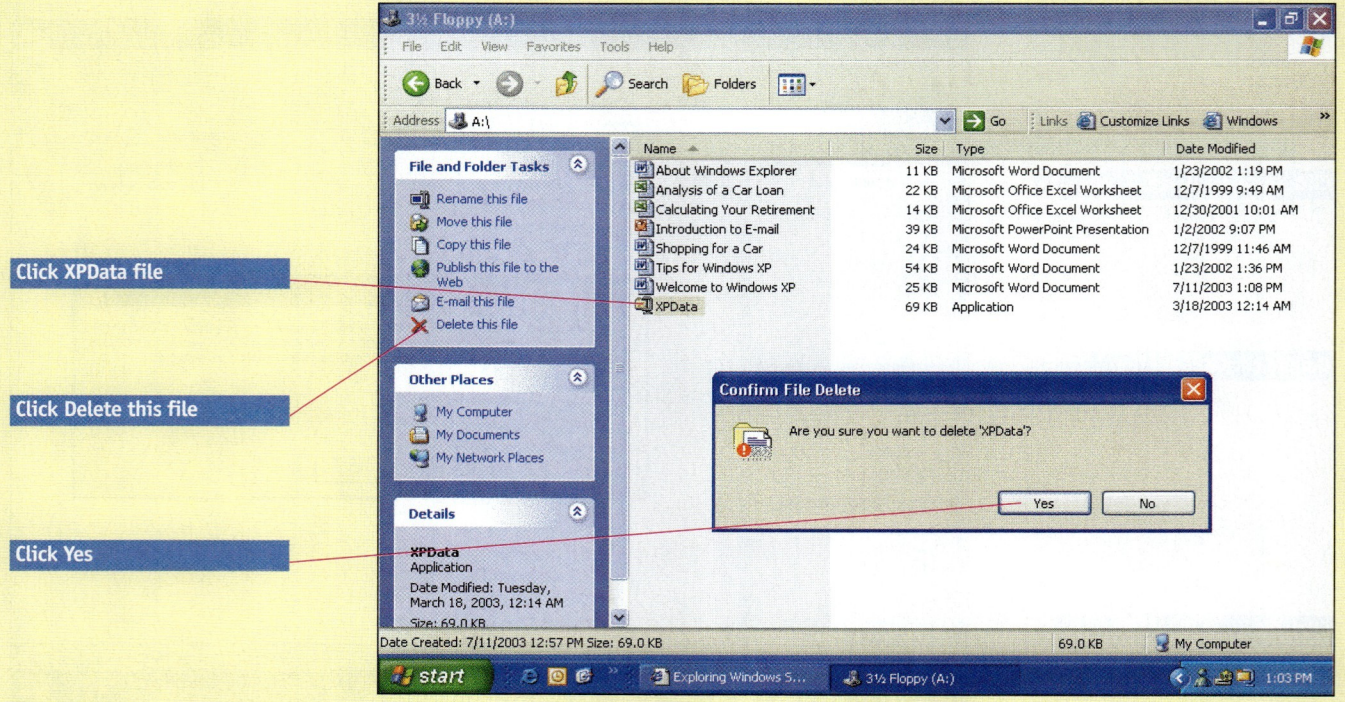

(d) Delete the Compressed File (step 4)

FIGURE 9 Hands-on Exercise 2 (*continued*)

SORT BY NAME, DATE, FILE TYPE, OR SIZE

The files in a folder can be displayed in ascending or descending sequence, by name, date modified, file type, or size, by clicking the appropriate column heading. Click Size, for example, to display files in the order of their size. Click the column heading a second time to reverse the sequence; that is, to switch from ascending to descending, and vice versa. Click a different column heading to display the files in a different sequence.

Step 5: **Modify a Document**

- Double click the **Welcome to Windows XP** document from within My Computer to open the document as shown in Figure 9e. (The document will open in the WordPad accessory if Microsoft Word is not installed on your machine.)

- Maximize the window for Microsoft Word. Read the document, and then press **Ctrl+End** to move to the end of the document. Do not be concerned if your screen does not match ours exactly.

- Add the sentence shown in Figure 9e, press the **Enter key** twice, then type your name. Click the **Save button** on the Standard toolbar to save the document.

- Pull down the **File menu**, click the **Print command**, and click **OK** (or click the **Print button** on the Standard toolbar) to print the document and prove to your instructor that you did the exercise.

- Pull down the **File menu** and click **Exit** to close Microsoft Word. You should be back in the My Computer folder.

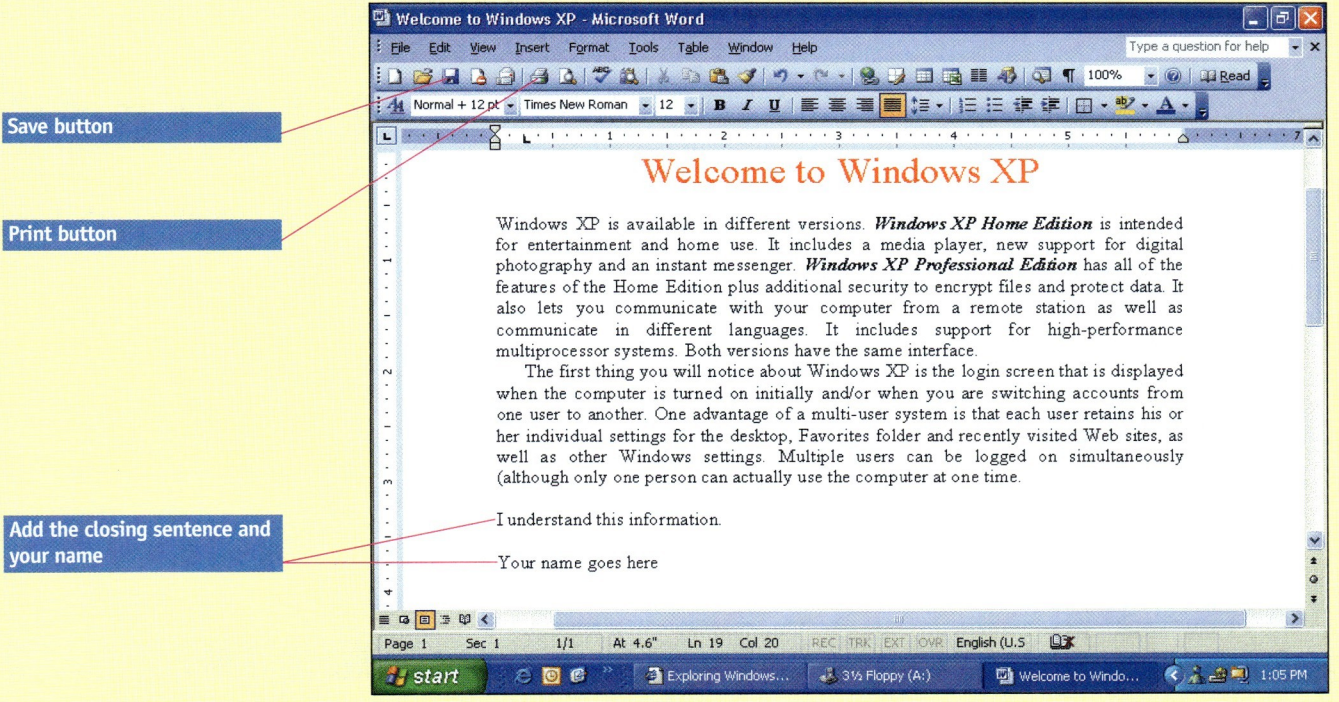

(e) Modify a Document (step 5)

FIGURE 9   Hands-on Exercise 2 (*continued*)

THE DOCUMENT, NOT THE APPLICATION

The Windows operating system is document oriented, which means that you are able to think in terms of the document rather than the application that created it. You can still open a document in traditional fashion, by starting the application that created the document, then using the File Open command in that program to retrieve the document. It's often easier, however, to open the document from within a folder by double clicking its icon. Windows will start the associated application and then open the document for you.

Step 6: **Create a New Folder**

- Look closely at the date and time that are displayed next to the Welcome to Windows XP document in Figure 9f. It should show today's date and the current time (give or take a minute) because that is when the document was last modified. Your date will be different from ours.

- Look closely and see that Figure 9f also contains an eighth document, called "Backup of Welcome to Windows XP." This is a backup copy of the original document that will be created automatically by Microsoft Word if the appropriate options are in effect. (See the boxed tip below.)

- Click **a blank area** in the right pane to deselect the Welcome to Windows XP document. The commands in the File and Folder Tasks area change to basic folder operations.

- Click the command to **Make a New folder**, which creates a new folder with the default name "New Folder". Enter **New Car** as the new name. You will move files into this folder in step 7.

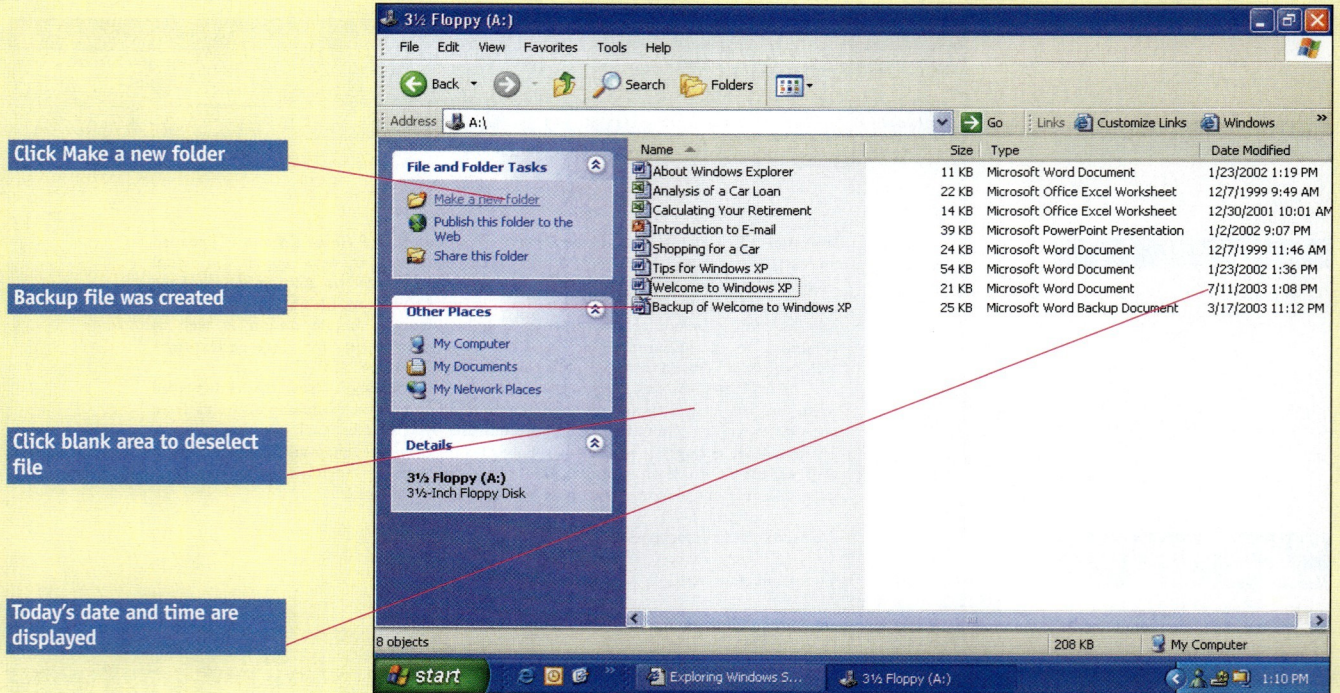

(f) Create a New Folder (step 6)

FIGURE 9 Hands-on Exercise 2 (*continued*)

USE WORD TO CREATE A BACKUP COPY

Microsoft Word enables you to automatically keep the previous version of a document as a backup copy. The next time you are in Microsoft Word, pull down the Tools menu, click the Options command, click the Save tab, then check the box to Always create backup copy. Every time you save a file from this point on, the previously saved version is renamed "Backup of document," and the document in memory is saved as the current version. The disk will contain the two most recent versions of the document, enabling you to retrieve the previous version if necessary.

Step 7: **Move the Files**

- There are different ways to move a file from one folder to another. The most basic technique is to
  - Select (click) the **Analysis of a Car Loan** workbook to highlight the file, then click the **Move this file command** in the task pane.
  - You will see the Move Items dialog box in Figure 9g. Click the plus sign (if it appears) next to the 3½ floppy disk to expand the disk and view its folders. Click the **New Car folder**, then click the **Move button**.
  - The selected file is moved to the New Car folder and the dialog box closes. The Analysis of a Car Loan document no longer appears in the right pane of Figure 9g because it has been moved to a new folder.

- If the source and destination folders are both on the same drive, as in this example, you can simply click and drag the file to its new destination. Thus, click and drag the **Shopping for a Car** Word document to the New Car folder. Release the mouse when the file is directly over the folder to complete the move.

- Double click the **New Car folder** to view the contents of this folder, which should contain both documents. The Address bar now says A:\New Car.

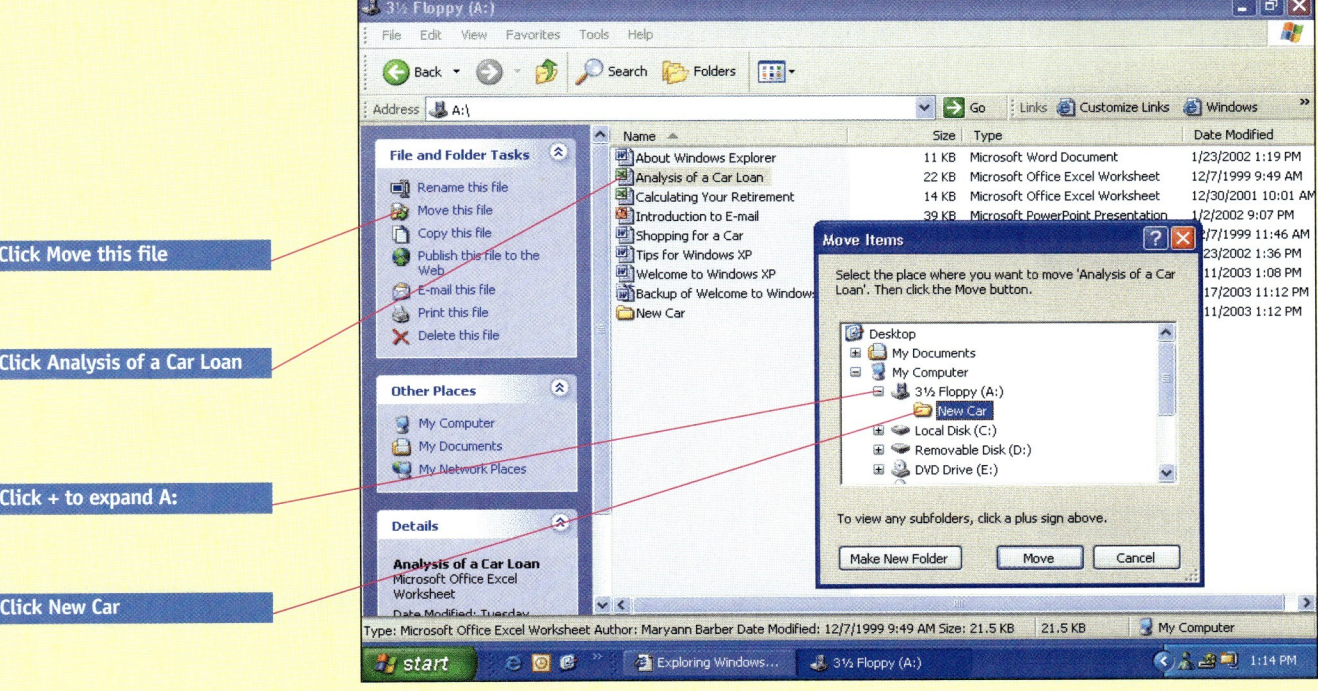

(g) Move the Files (step 7)

FIGURE 9 Hands-on Exercise 2 (*continued*)

THE PLUS AND MINUS SIGNS

Any drive, be it local or on the network, may be expanded or collapsed to display or hide its folders. A minus sign indicates that the drive has been expanded and that its folders are visible. A plus sign indicates the reverse; that is, the device is collapsed and its folders are not visible. Click either sign to toggle to the other. Clicking a plus sign, for example, expands the drive, then displays a minus sign next to the drive to indicate that the folders are visible. Clicking a minus sign has the reverse effect.

Step 8: **A Look Ahead**

- Click the **Folders button** to display a hierarchical view of the devices on your computer as shown in Figure 9h. This is the same screen that is displayed through Windows Explorer, a program that we will study after the exercise.

- The Folders button functions as a toggle switch; click the button a second time and the task pane (also called task panel) returns. Click the **Folders button** to return to the hierarchical view.

- The New Car folder is selected (highlighted) in the left pane because this is the folder you were working in at the previous step. The contents of this folder are displayed in the right pane.

- Click the icon for the **3½ floppy drive** to display the contents of drive A. The right pane displays the files on drive A as well as the New Car folder.

- Close the My Computer folder. Close Internet Explorer. Log off if you do not want to continue with the next exercise at this time.

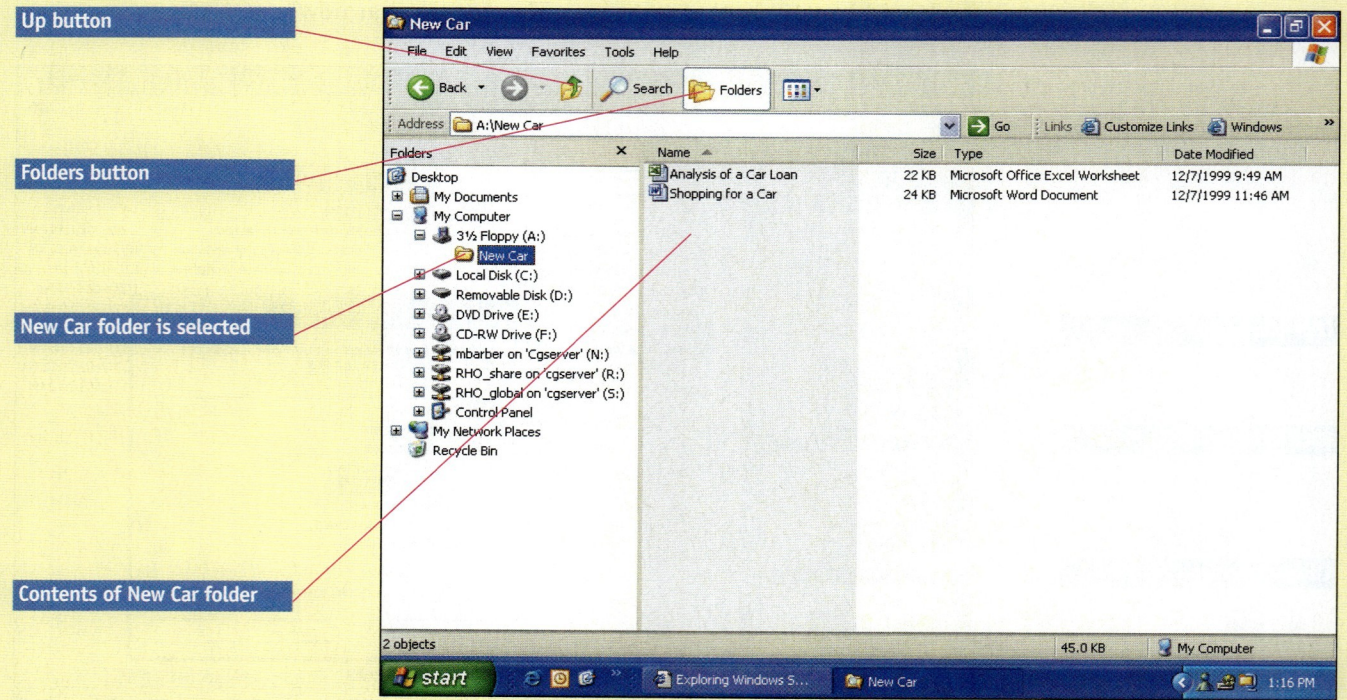

(h) A Look Ahead (step 8)

FIGURE 9 Hands-on Exercise 2 (*continued*)

NAVIGATING THE HIERARCHY

Click the Up button on the Standard Buttons toolbar to move up one level in the hierarchy in the left pane and display the associated contents in the right pane. Click the Up button when you are viewing the New Car folder, for example, and you are returned to drive A. Click the Up button a second time and you will see the contents of My Computer. Note, too, how the contents of the Address bar change each time you view a different folder in the right pane.

WINDOWS EXPLORER

Windows Explorer is a program that displays a hierarchical (tree) structure of the devices on your system. Consider, for example, Figure 10a, which displays the contents of a hypothetical Homework folder as it exists on our computer. The hierarchy is displayed in the left pane, and the contents of the selected object (the Homework folder) are shown in the right pane. The advantage of viewing the folder in this way (as opposed to displaying the task pane) is that you see the location of the folder on the system; that is; the Homework folder is physically stored on drive A.

Let's explore the hierarchy in the left pane. There is a minus sign next to the icon for drive A to indicate that this drive has been expanded and thus you can see its folders. Drive C, however, has a plus sign to indicate that the drive is collapsed and that its contents are not visible. Look closely and you see that both drive A and drive C are indented under My Computer, which in turn is indented under the desktop. In other words, the desktop is at the top of the hierarchy and it contains the My Computer folder, which in turn contains drive A and drive C. The desktop also contains a My Documents folder, but the plus sign next to the My Documents folder indicates the folder is collapsed. My Computer, on the other hand, has a minus sign and you can see its contents, which consist of the drives on your system as well as other special folders (Control Panel and Shared Documents).

Look carefully at the icon next to the Homework folder in the left pane of the figure. The icon is an open folder, and it indicates that the (Homework) folder is the active folder. The folder's name is also shaded, and it appears in the title bar. Only one folder can be active at one time, and its contents are displayed in the right pane. The Milestones in Communications document is highlighted (selected) in the right pane, which means that subsequent commands will affect this document, as opposed to the entire folder. If you wanted to work with a different document in the Homework folder, you would select that document. To see the contents of a different folder, such as Financial Documents, you would select (click) the icon for that folder in the left pane (which automatically closes the Homework folder). The contents of the Financial Documents folder would then appear in the right pane.

You can create folders at any time just like the Homework and Financial Documents folders that we created on drive A. You can also create folders within folders; for example, a correspondence folder may contain two folders of its own, one for business correspondence and one for personal letters.

Personal Folders

Windows automatically creates a set of personal folders for every user. These include the ***My Documents folder*** and the ***My Pictures folder*** and ***My Music folder*** within the My Documents folder. The My Documents folder is collapsed in Figure 10a, but it is expanded in Figure 10b, and thus its contents are visible. The My Music folder is active, and its contents are visible in the right pane.

Every user has a unique set of personal folders, and thus Windows has to differentiate between the multiple "My Documents" folders that may exist. It does so by creating additional folders to hold the documents and settings for each user. Look closely at the Address bar in Figure 10b. Each back slash indicates a new folder, and you can read the complete path from right to left. Thus, the My Music folder that we are viewing is contained in My Documents folder within Maryann's folder, which in turn is stored in a Documents and Settings folder on drive C.

Fortunately, however, Windows does the housekeeping for you. All you have to do is locate the desired folder—for example, My Music or My Pictures—in the left pane, and Windows does the rest. ***Personal folders*** are just what the name implies—"personal," meaning that only one person has access to their content. Windows also provides a ***Shared Documents folder*** for files that Maryann may want to share with others.

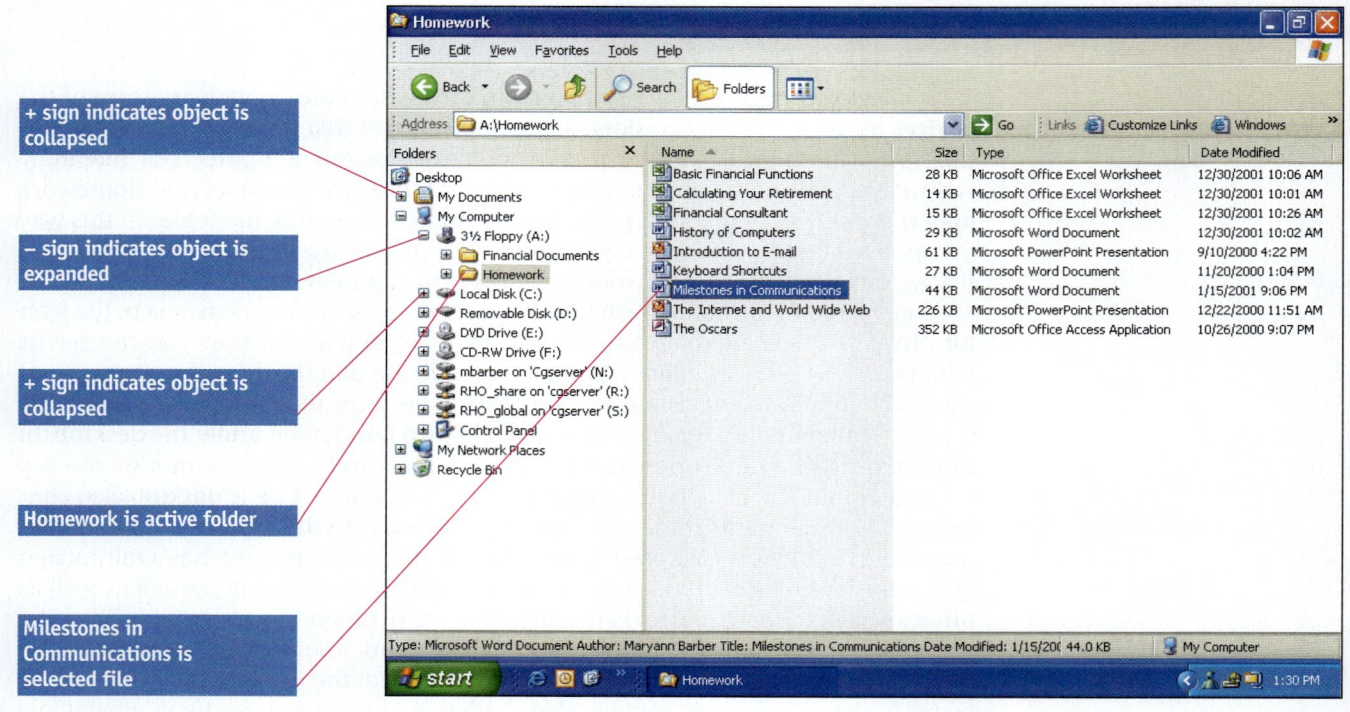

(a) Homework Folder

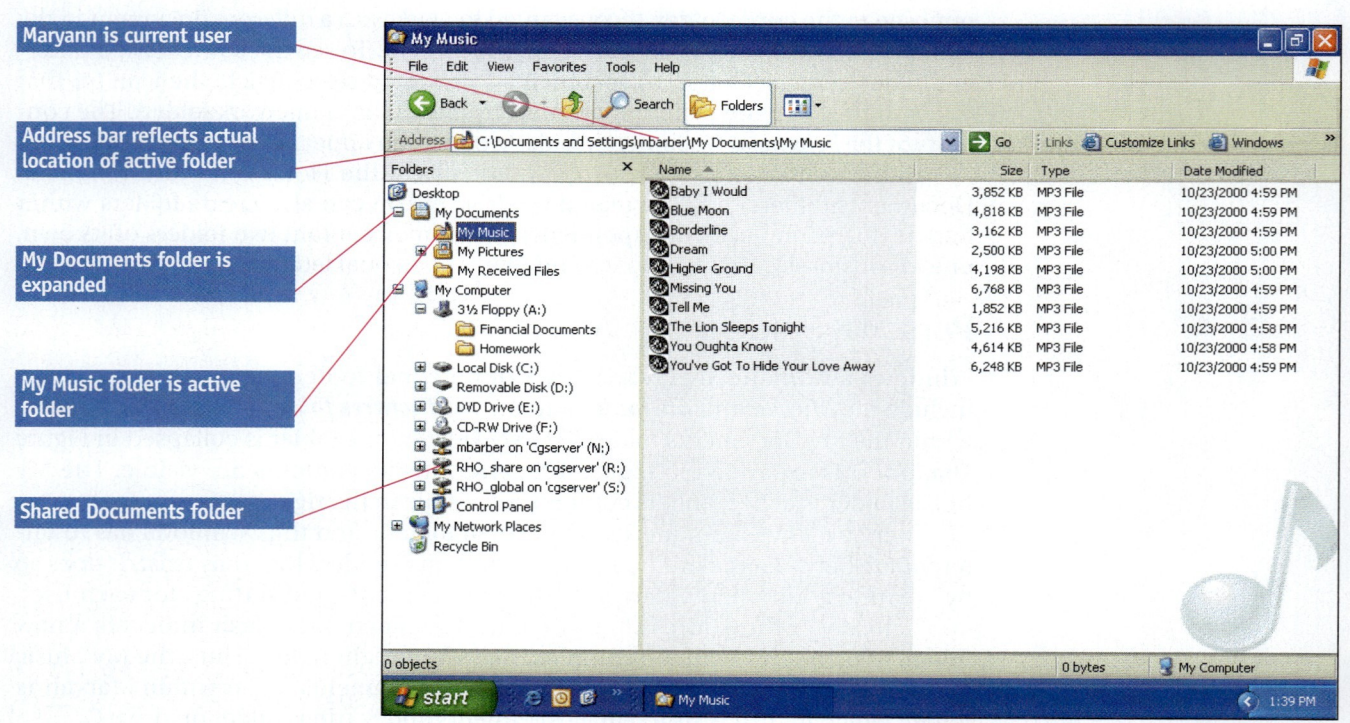

(b) My Music Folder

FIGURE 10   Windows Explorer

Moving and Copying a File

The essence of file management is to **move** and ***copy a file*** or folder from one location to another. This can be done in different ways. The easiest is to click and drag the file icon from the source drive or folder to the destination drive or folder, within Windows Explorer. There is one subtlety, however, in that the result of dragging a file (i.e., whether the file is moved or copied) depends on whether the source and destination are on the same or different drives. Dragging a file from one folder to another folder on the same drive moves the file. Dragging a file to a folder on a different drive copies the file. The same rules apply to dragging a folder, where the folder and every file in it are moved or copied, as per the rules for an individual file.

This process is not as arbitrary as it may seem. Windows assumes that if you drag an object (a file or folder) to a different drive (e.g., from drive C to drive A), you want the object to appear in both places. Hence, the default action when you click and drag an object to a different drive is to copy the object. You can, however, override the default and move the object by pressing and holding the Shift key as you drag.

Windows also assumes that you do not want two copies of an object on the same drive, as that would result in wasted disk space. Thus, the default action when you click and drag an object to a different folder on the same drive is to move the object. You can override the default and copy the object by pressing and holding the Ctrl key as you drag. It's not as complicated as it sounds, and you get a chance to practice in the hands-on exercise, which follows shortly.

Deleting a File

The ***Delete command*** deletes (erases) a file from a disk. The command can be executed in different ways, most easily by selecting a file, then pressing the Del key. It's also comforting to know that you can usually recover a deleted file, because the file is not (initially) removed from the disk, but moved instead to the Recycle Bin, from where it can be restored to its original location. Unfortunately, files deleted from a floppy disk are not put into the Recycle Bin and hence cannot be recovered.

The ***Recycle Bin*** is a special folder that contains all files that were previously deleted from any hard disk on your system. Think of the Recycle Bin as similar to the wastebasket in your room. You throw out (delete) a report by tossing it into a wastebasket. The report is gone (deleted) from your desk, but you can still get it back by taking it out of the wastebasket as long as the basket wasn't emptied. The Recycle Bin works the same way. Files are not deleted from the hard disk per se, but moved instead to the Recycle Bin from where they can be restored to their original location. (The protection afforded by the Recycle Bin does not extend to files deleted from a floppy disk.)

Backup

It's not a question of *if* it will happen, but *when*—hard disks die, files are lost, or viruses may infect a system. It has happened to us and it will happen to you, but you can prepare for the inevitable by creating adequate backup *before* the problem occurs. The essence of a ***backup strategy*** is to decide which files to back up, how often to do the backup, and where to keep the backup.

Our strategy is very simple—back up what you can't afford to lose, do so on a daily basis, and store the backup away from your computer. You need not copy every file, every day. Instead, copy just the files that changed during the current session. Realize, too, that it is much more important to back up your data files than your program files. You can always reinstall the application from the original disks or CD, or if necessary, go to the vendor for another copy of an application. You, however, are the only one who has a copy of the term paper that is due tomorrow. Once you decide on a strategy, follow it, and follow it faithfully!

hands-on exercise

3 | Windows Explorer

Objective Use Windows Explorer to move, copy, and delete a file; recover a deleted file from the Recycle Bin. Use Figure 11 as a guide.

Step 1: Create a New Folder

- Place the floppy disk from the previous exercise into drive A. Click the **Start Button**, click the **All Programs command**, click **Accessories**, then click **Windows Explorer**. Click the **Maximize button**.

- Expand or collapse the various devices on your system so that My Computer is expanded, but all of the devices are collapsed.

- Click (select) **drive A** in the left pane to display the contents of the floppy disk. You should see the New Car folder that was created in the previous exercise.

- Point to a blank area anywhere in the **right pane**, click the **right mouse button**, click the **New command**, then click **Folder** as the type of object to create.

- The icon for a new folder will appear with the name of the folder (New Folder) highlighted. Type **Windows Information** to change the name. Press **Enter**.

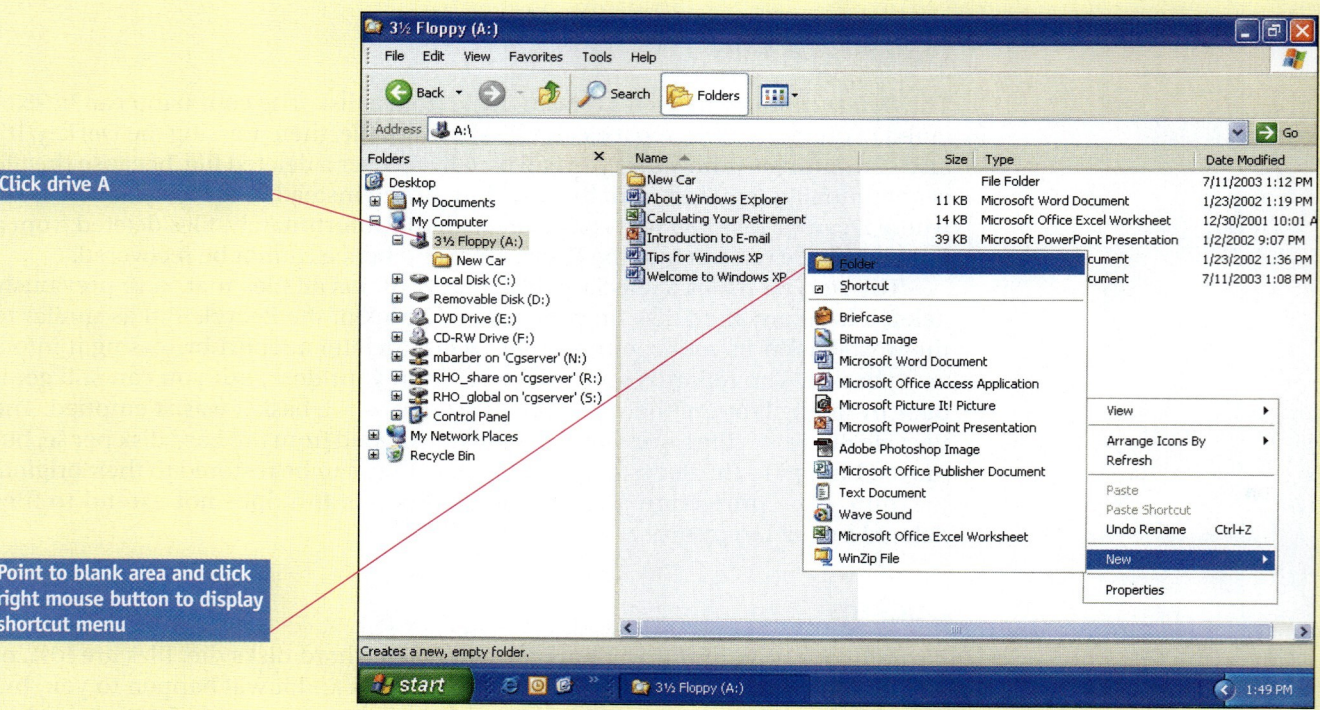

Click drive A

Point to blank area and click right mouse button to display shortcut menu

(a) Create a New Folder (step 1)

FIGURE 11 Hands-on Exercise 3 (*continued*)

THE RENAME COMMAND

Right click the file or a folder whose name you want to change to display a context-sensitive menu, and then click the Rename command. The name of the folder will be highlighted with the insertion point at the end of the name. Enter (or edit) the new (existing) name and press Enter.

764 GETTING STARTED WITH MICROSOFT WINDOWS XP

Step 2: **Move the Files**

- If necessary, change to the **Details view** and click the **plus sign** next to drive A to expand the drive as shown in Figure 11b. Note the following:
  - The left pane shows that drive A is selected. The right pane displays the contents of drive A (the selected object in the left pane). The folders are shown first and appear in alphabetical order. If not, press the **F5 (Refresh) key** to refresh the screen.
  - There is a minus sign next to the icon for drive A in the left pane, indicating that it has been expanded and that its folders are visible. Thus, the folder names also appear under drive A in the left pane.
- Click and drag the **About Windows Explorer** document in the right pane to the **Windows Information folder** in the left pane, to move the file into that folder.
- Click and drag the **Tips for Windows XP** and the **Welcome to Windows XP** documents to move these documents to the **Windows Information folder**.
- Click the **Windows Information folder** in the left pane to select the folder and display its contents in the right pane. You should see the three files that were just moved.
- Click the **Up button** to return to drive A.

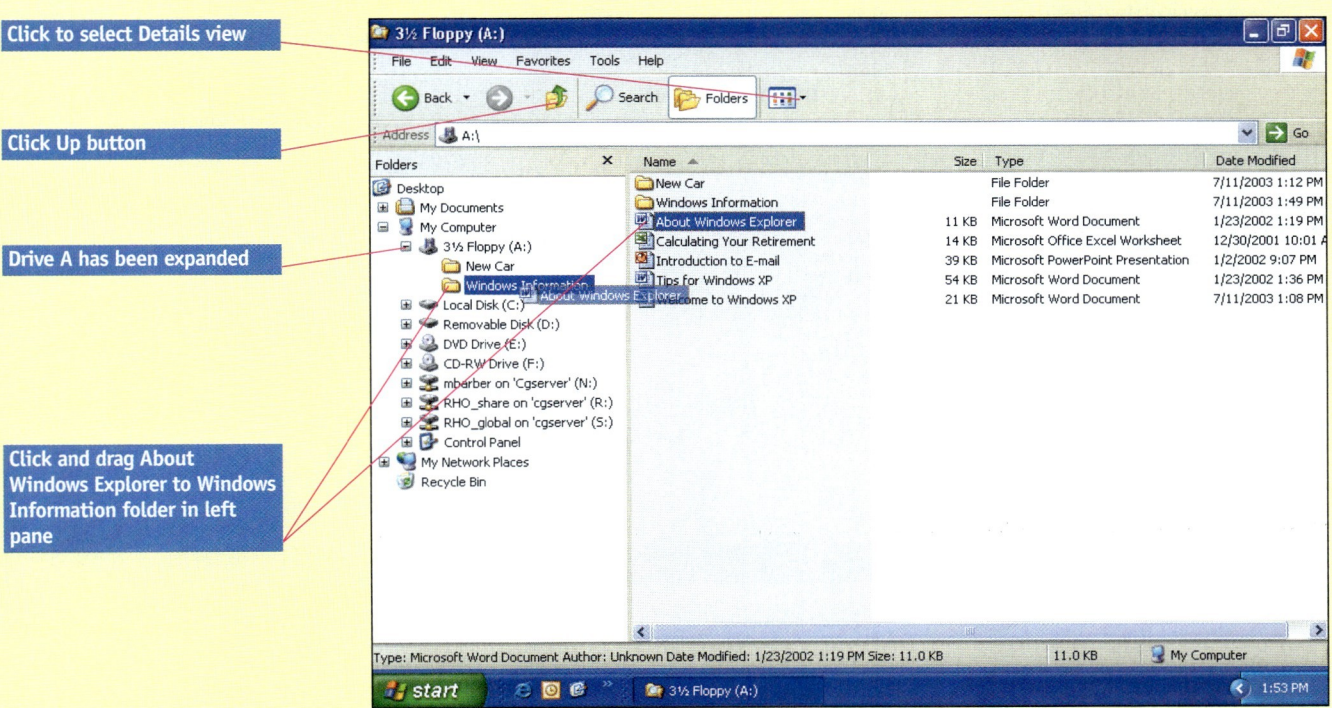

(b) Move the Files (step 2)

FIGURE 11   Hands-on Exercise 3 (*continued*)

SELECT MULTIPLE FILES

Selecting (clicking) one file automatically deselects the previously selected file. You can, however, select multiple files by clicking the first file, then pressing and holding the Ctrl key as you click each additional file. Use the Shift key to select multiple files that are adjacent to one another by clicking the icon of the first file, then pressing and holding the Shift key as you click the icon of the last file.

Step 3: **Copy a Folder**

- Point to the **Windows Information folder** in the right pane, then **right click and drag** this folder to the **My Documents folder** (on drive C) in the left pane. Release the mouse to display a context-sensitive menu.

- Click the **Copy Here command** as shown in Figure 11c.
  - You may see a Copy files message box as the individual files within the Windows Information folder are copied to the My Documents folder.
  - If you see the Confirm Folder Replace dialog box, it means that you (or another student) already copied these files to the My Documents folder. Click the **Yes to All button** so that your files replace the previous versions in the My Documents folder.

- Click the **My Documents folder** in the left pane. Pull down the **View menu** and click the **Refresh command** (or press the **F5 key**) so that the hierarchy shows the newly copied folder. (Please remember to delete the Windows Information folder from drive C at the end of the exercise.)

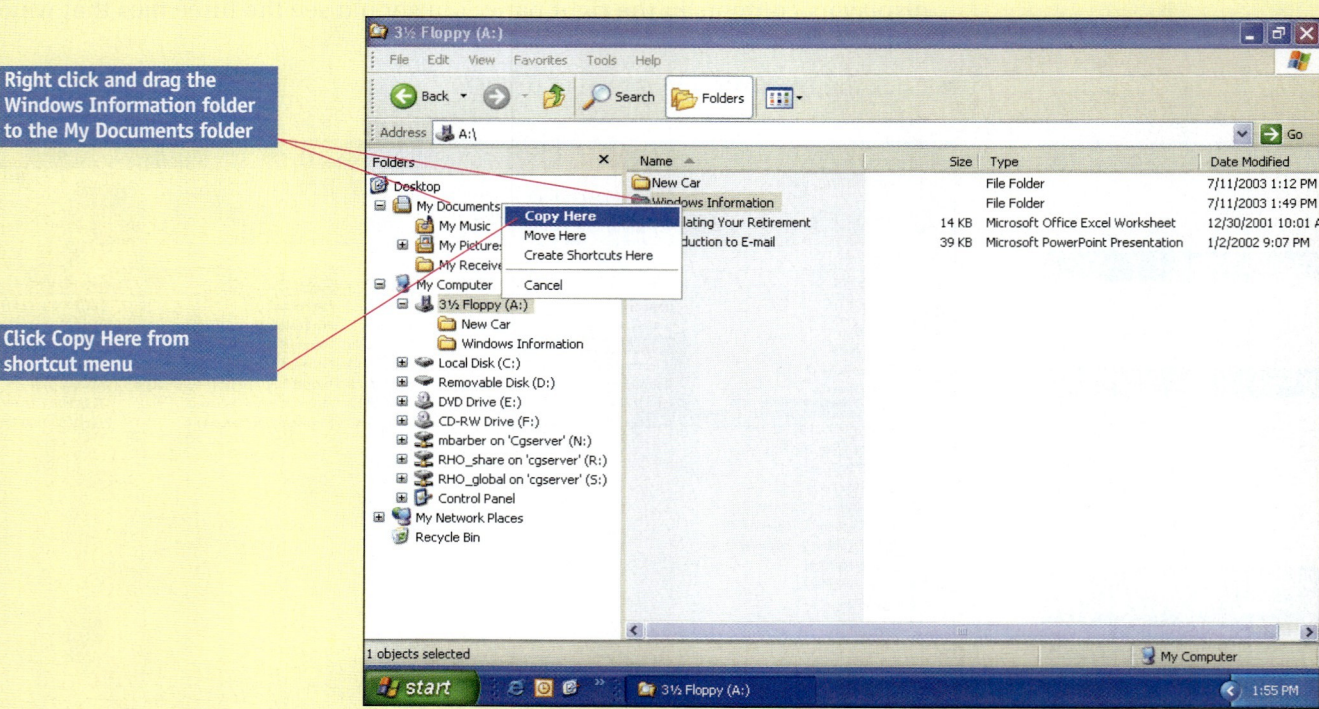

(c) Copy a Folder (step 3)

FIGURE 11 Hands-on Exercise 3 (*continued*)

RIGHT CLICK AND DRAG

The result of dragging a file with the left mouse button depends on whether the source and destination folders are on the same or different drives. Dragging a file to a folder on a different drive copies the file, whereas dragging the file to a folder on the same drive moves the file. If you find this hard to remember, and most people do, click and drag with the right mouse button to display a context-sensitive menu asking whether you want to copy or move the file. This simple tip can save you from making a careless (and potentially serious) error. Use it!

Step 4: **Modify a Document**

- Click the **Windows Information folder** within the My Documents folder to make it the active folder and to display its contents in the right pane. Change to the **Details view**.

- Double click the **About Windows Explorer** document to start Word and open the document. Do not be concerned if the size and/or position of the Microsoft Word window are different from ours. Read the document.

- If necessary, click inside the document window, then press **Ctrl+End** to move to the end of the document. Add the text shown in Figure 11d.

- Pull down the **File menu** and click **Save** to save the modified file (or click the **Save button** on the Standard toolbar). Pull down the **File menu** and click **Exit** to exit from Microsoft Word.

- Pull down the **View menu** and click the **Refresh command** (or press the **F5 key**) to update the contents of the right pane. The date and time associated with the About Windows Explorer document (on drive C) have been changed to indicate that the file has been modified.

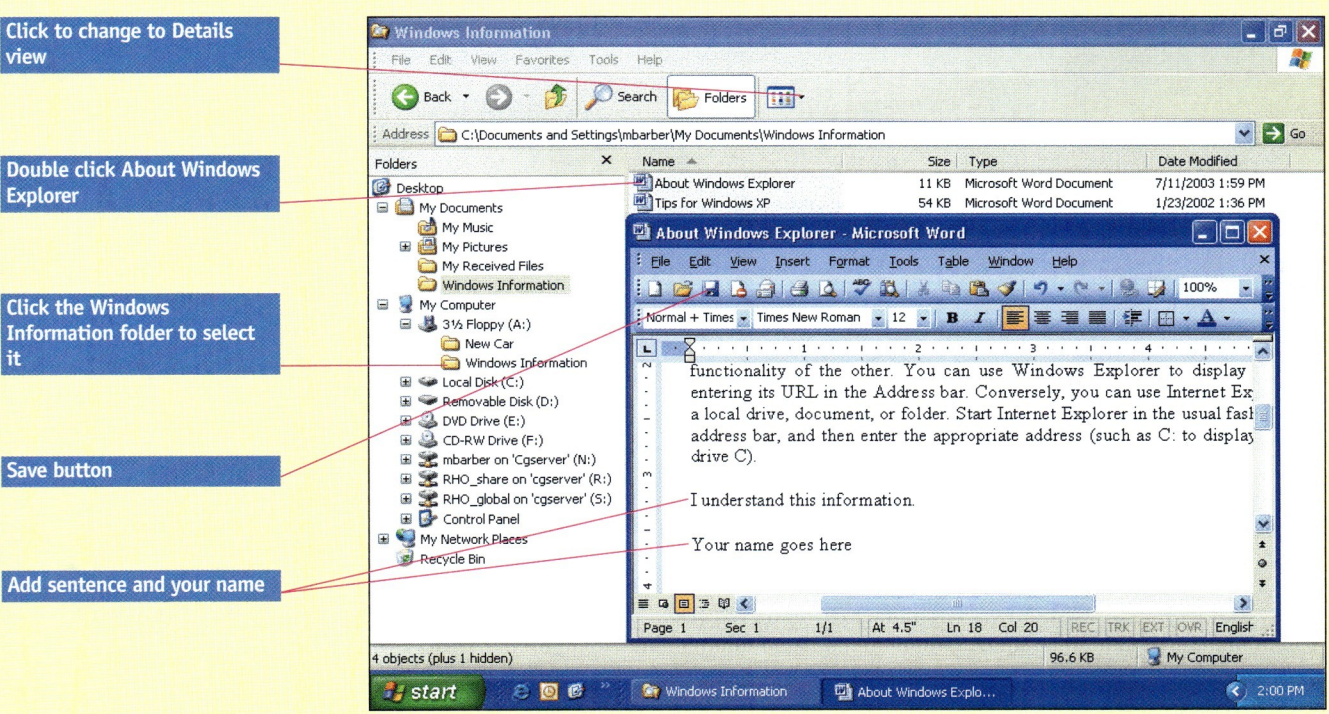

(d) Modify a Document (step 4)

FIGURE 11 Hands-on Exercise 3 (*continued*)

KEYBOARD SHORTCUTS

Most people begin with the mouse, but add keyboard shortcuts as they become more proficient. Ctrl+B, Ctrl+I, and Ctrl+U are shortcuts to boldface, italicize, and underline, respectively. Ctrl+X (the X is supposed to remind you of a pair of scissors), Ctrl+C, and Ctrl+V correspond to Cut, Copy, and Paste, respectively. Ctrl+Home and Ctrl+End move to the beginning or end of a document. These shortcuts are not unique to Microsoft Word, but are recognized in virtually every Windows application.

Step 5: **Copy (Back up) a File**

- Verify that the **Windows Information folder** (on drive C) is the active folder, as denoted by the open folder icon. Click and drag the icon for the **About Windows Explorer** document from the right pane to the **Windows Information folder** on **drive A** in the left pane.

- You will see the message in Figure 11e, indicating that the folder (on drive A) already contains a file called About Windows Explorer and asking whether you want to replace the existing file.

- Click **Yes** because you want to replace the previous version of the file on drive A with the updated version from the My Documents folder.

- You have just backed up a file by copying the About Windows Explorer document from a folder on drive C to the disk in drive A. In other words, you can use the floppy disk to restore the file to drive C should anything happen to it.

- Keep the floppy disk in a safe place, away from the computer.

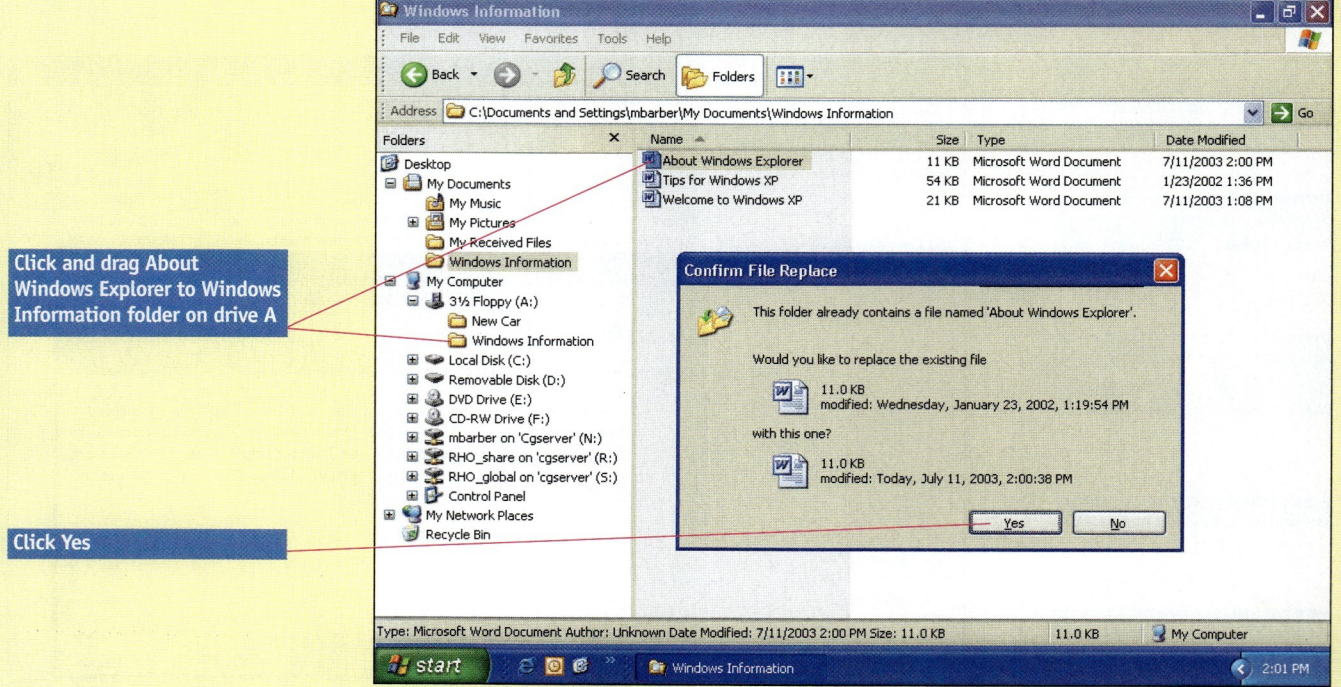

(e) Copy (Back up) a File (step 5)

FIGURE 11 Hands-on Exercise 3 (*continued*)

THE MY DOCUMENTS FOLDER

The My Documents folder is created by default with the installation of Windows XP. There is no requirement that you store your documents in this folder, but it is convenient, especially for beginners who may lack the confidence to create their own folders. The My Documents folder is also helpful in a laboratory environment where the network administrator may prevent you from modifying the desktop and/or from creating your own folders on drive C, in which case you will have to use the My Documents folder.

Step 6: **Delete a Folder**

- Select (click) **Windows Information folder** within the My Documents folder in the left pane. Pull down the **File menu** and click **Delete** (or press the **Del key**).

- You will see the dialog box in Figure 11f, asking whether you are sure you want to delete the folder and send its contents to the Recycle Bin, which enables you to restore the folder at a later date.

- Click **Yes** to delete the folder. The folder disappears from drive C. Note that you have deleted the folder and its contents.

- Now pretend that you do not want to delete the folder. Pull down the **Edit menu**. Click **Undo Delete**.

- The deletion is cancelled and the Windows Information folder reappears in the left pane. If you do not see the folder, pull down the **View menu** and click the **Refresh command** (or press the **F5 key**).

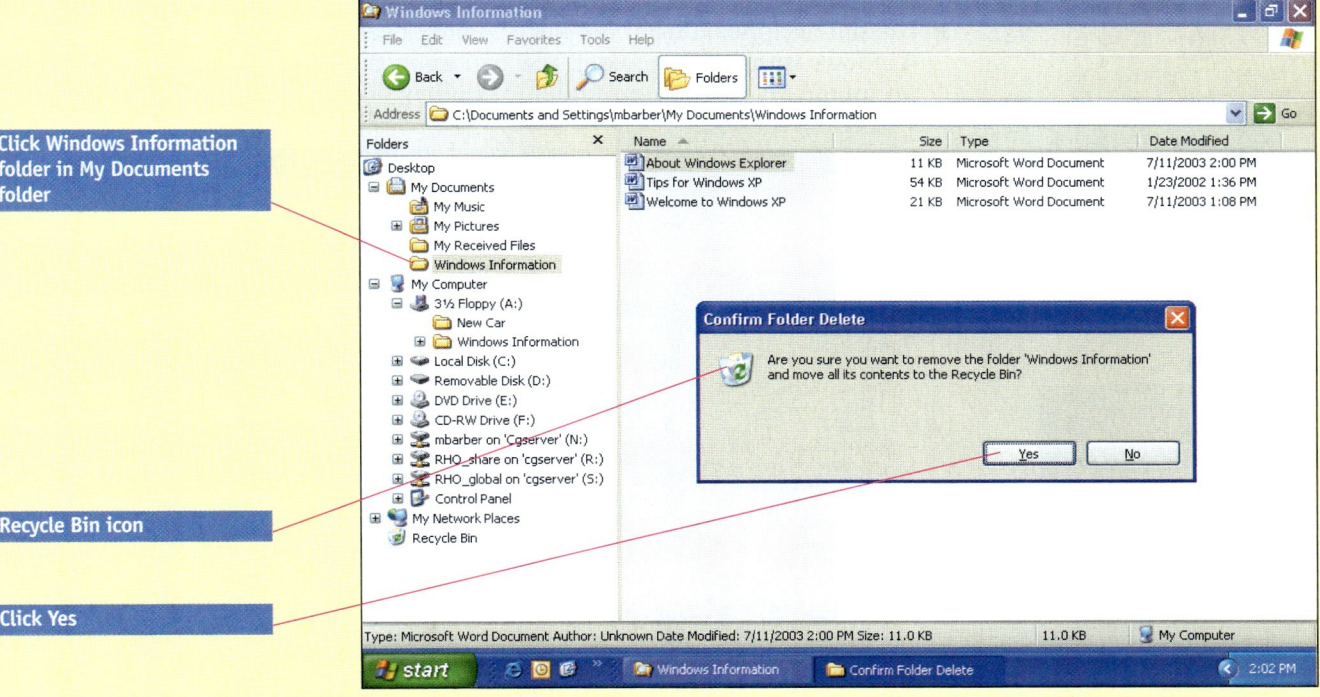

(f) Delete a Folder (step 6)

FIGURE 11 Hands-on Exercise 3 (*continued*)

CUSTOMIZE WINDOWS EXPLORER

Increase or decrease the size of the left pane within Windows Explorer by dragging the vertical line separating the left and right panes in the appropriate direction. You can also drag the right border of the various column headings (Name, Size, Type, and Modified) in the right pane to increase or decrease the width of the column and see more or less information in that column. And best of all, you can click any column heading to display the contents of the selected folder in sequence by that column. Click the heading a second time and the sequence changes from ascending to descending and vice versa.

Step 7: **The Recycle Bin**

- If necessary, select the **Windows Information folder** within the My Documents folder in the left pane. Select (click) the **About Windows Explorer** file in the right pane. Press the **Del key**, then click **Yes** when asked to delete the file.

- Click the **down arrow** in the vertical scroll bar in the left pane until you can click the icon for the **Recycle Bin**.

- The Recycle Bin contains all files that have been previously deleted from the local (hard) disks, and hence you will see a different number of files than those displayed in Figure 11g.

- Change to the **Details view**. Pull down the **View menu**, click (or point to) **Arrange Icons by**, then click **Date Deleted** to display the files in this sequence. Execute this command a second time (if necessary) so that the most recently deleted file appears at the top of the window.

- Right click the **About Windows Explorer** file to display the context-sensitive menu in Figure 11g, then click the **Restore command**.

- The file disappears from the Recycle bin because it has been returned to the Windows Information folder. You can open the Windows Information folder within the My Documents folder to confirm that the file has been restored.

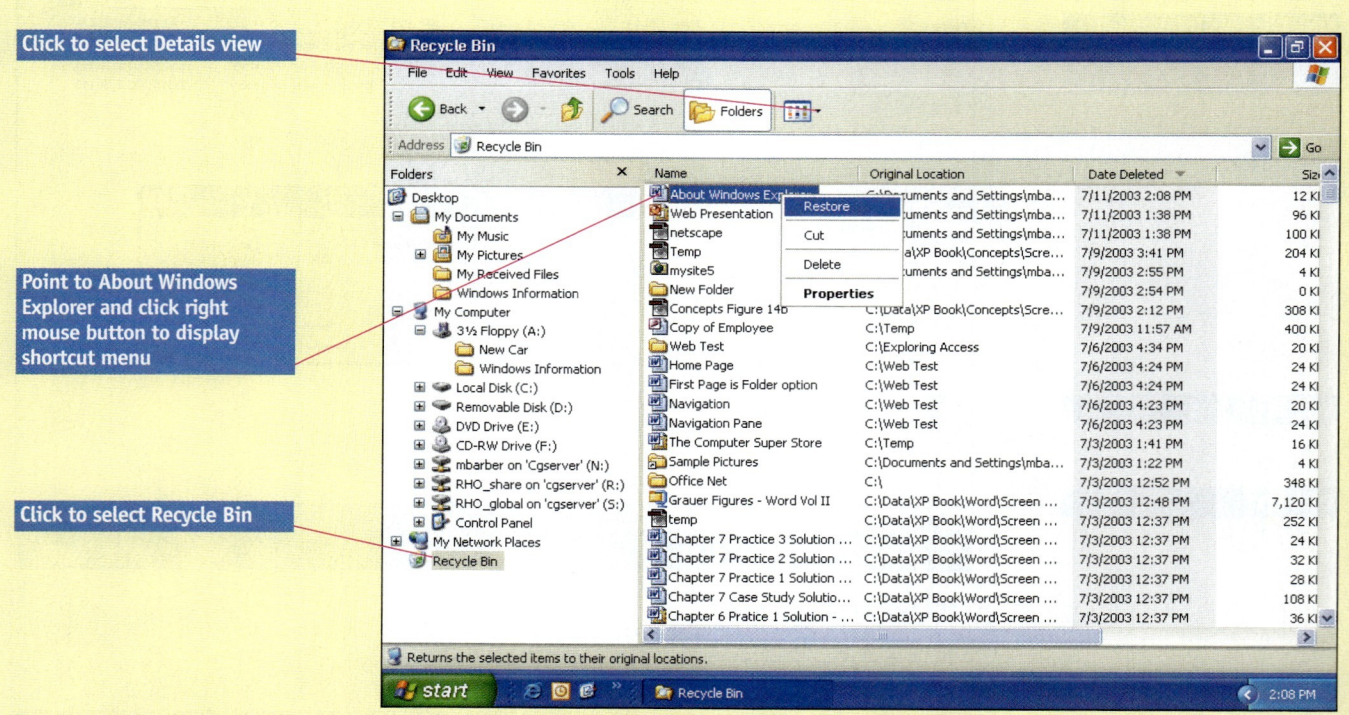

(g) The Recycle Bin (step 7)

FIGURE 11 Hands-on Exercise 3 (*continued*)

TWO WAYS TO RECOVER A FILE

The Undo command is present in Windows Explorer. Thus, you do not need to resort to the Recycle Bin to recover a deleted file provided you execute the Undo command immediately (within a few commands) after the Delete command was issued. Some operations cannot be undone (in which case the Undo command will be dimmed), but Undo is always worth a try.

Step 8: **The Group By Command**

- Select (click) the **Windows Information folder** on drive A. You should see the contents of this folder (three Word documents) in the right pane.

- Pull down the **View menu**, (click or) point to the **Arrange Icons by command**, then click the **Show in Groups command** from the cascaded menu.

- You see the same three files as previously, but they are displayed in groups according to the first letter in the filename. Click the **Date Modified** column, and the files are grouped according to the date they were last modified.

- The Show in Groups command functions as a toggle switch. Execute the command and the files are displayed in groups; execute the command a second time and the groups disappear.

- Select (click) the icon for **drive A** in the left pane to display the contents of drive A. You should see two folders and two files. Pull down the **View menu**, (click or) point to the **Arrange Icons by command**, and then click the **Show in Groups command** from the cascaded menu.

- Change to the **Details view**. Click the **Type column** to group the objects by folder and file type.

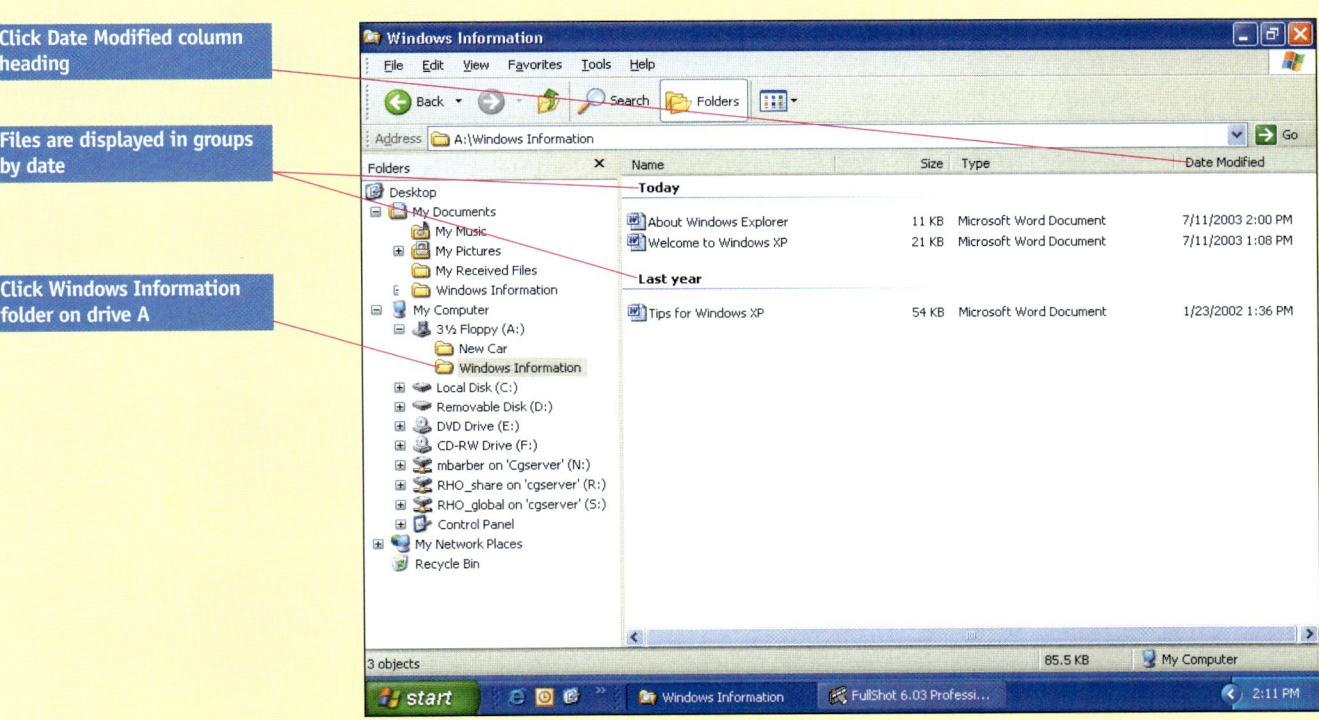

(h) The Group By Command (step 8)

FIGURE 11   Hands-on Exercise 3 (*continued*)

KEEP THE VIEW

Once you set the desired view in a folder, you may want to display every other folder according to those parameters. Pull down the Tools menu, click the Folder Options command, and click the View tab. Click the button to Apply to All folders, then click Yes when prompted to confirm. Click OK to close the Folder Options dialog box. The next time you open another folder, it will appear in the same view as the current folder.

Step 9: **Complete the Exercise**

- Prove to your instructor that you have completed the exercise correctly by capturing the screen on your monitor. Press the **Print Screen key**. Nothing appears to have happened, but the screen has been copied to the clipboard.

- Click the **Start button**, click the **All Programs command**, then start Microsoft Word and begin a new document. Enter the title of your document, followed by your name as shown in Figure 11i. Press the **Enter key** two or three times.

- Pull down the **Edit menu** and click the **Paste command** (or click the **Paste button** on the Standard toolbar) to copy the contents of the clipboard into the Word document.

- Print this document for your instructor. There is no need to save this document. Exit Word.

- Delete the **Windows Information folder** from the My Documents folder as a courtesy to the next student. Close Windows Explorer.

- Log off if you do not want to continue the next exercise at this time. (Click the **Start button**, click **Log Off**, then click **Log Off** a second time to end your session.)

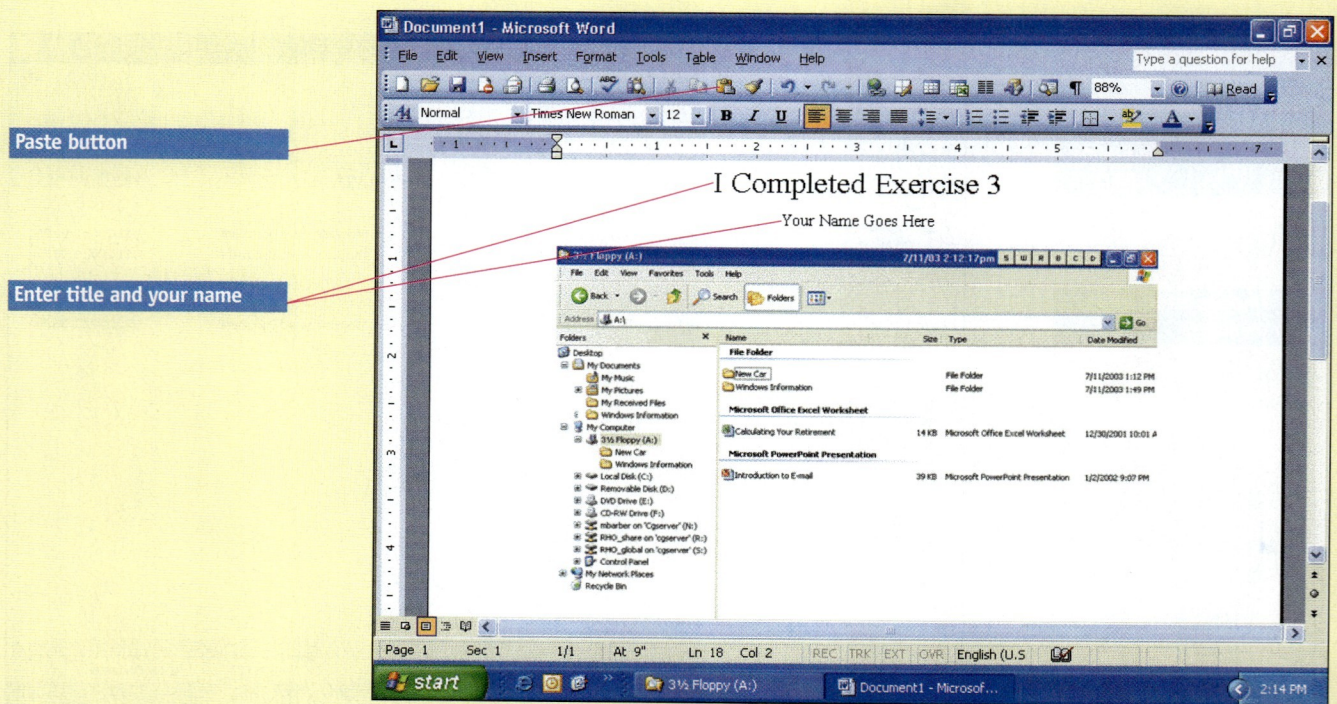

(i) Complete the Exercise (step 9)

FIGURE 11 Hands-on Exercise 3 (*continued*)

SWITCHING USERS VERSUS LOGGING OFF

Windows XP gives you the choice of switching users or logging off. Switching users leaves all of your applications open, but it relinquishes control of the computer to another user. This lets you subsequently log back on (after the new user logs off) and take up exactly where you were. Logging off, on the other hand, closes all of your applications and ends the session, but it leaves the computer running at full power and available for someone else to log on.

772 GETTING STARTED WITH MICROSOFT WINDOWS XP

INCREASING PRODUCTIVITY

You have learned the basic concepts of disk and file management, but there is so much more. Windows XP has something for everyone. It is easy and intuitive for the novice, but it also contains sophisticated tools for the more knowledgeable user. This section describes three powerful features to increase your productivity. Some or all of these features may be disabled in a school environment, but the information will stand you in good stead on your own computer.

The Control Panel

The ***Control Panel*** affects every aspect of your system. It determines the appearance of your desktop, and it controls the performance of your hardware. You can, for example, change the way your mouse behaves by switching the function of the left and right mouse buttons and/or by replacing the standard mouse pointers with animated icons that move across the screen. You will not have access to the Control Panel in a lab environment, but you will need it at home whenever you install new hardware or software. You should be careful about making changes, and you should understand the nature of the new settings before you accept any of the changes.

The Control Panel in Windows XP organizes its tools by category as shown in Figure 12. Point to any category and you see a Screen Tip that describes the specific tasks within that category. The Appearance and Themes category, for example, lets you select a screen saver or customize the Start menu and taskbar. You can also switch to the Classic view that displays every tool in a single screen, which is consistent with all previous versions of Windows.

The task pane provides access to the ***Windows Update*** function, which connects you to a Web site where you can download new device drivers and other updates to Windows XP. You can also configure your system to install these updates automatically as they become available. Some updates, especially those having to do with Internet security, are absolutely critical.

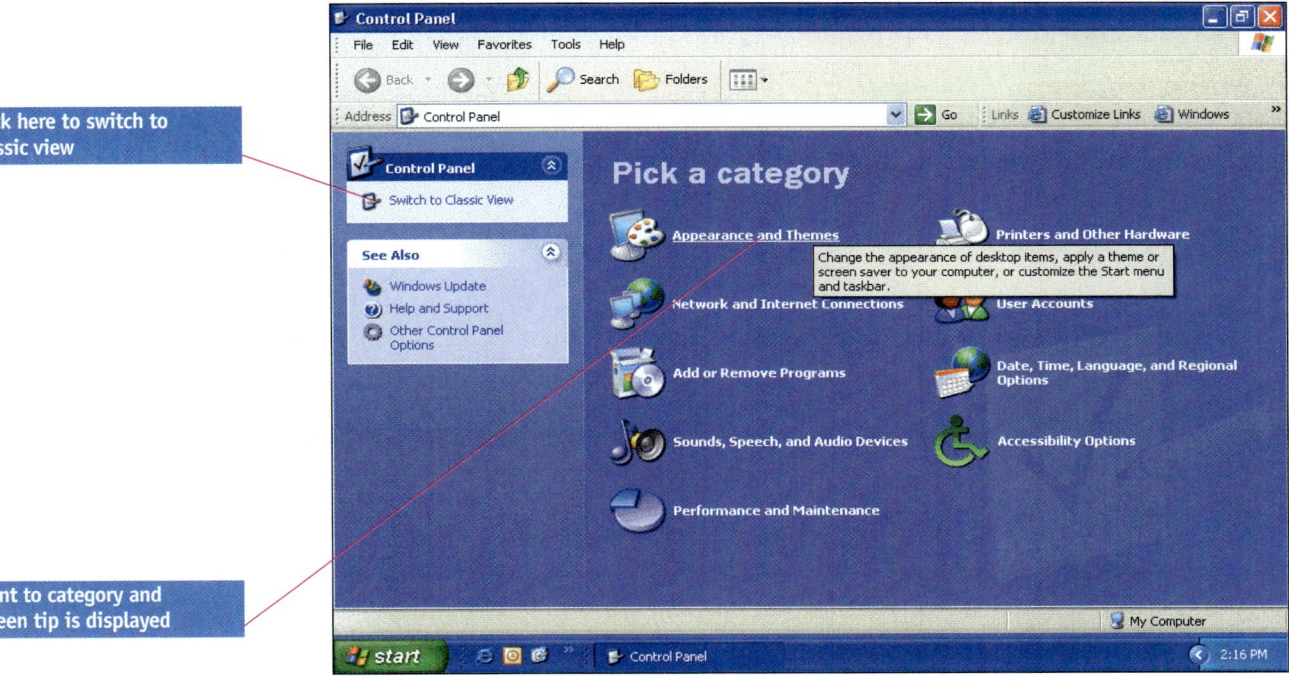

FIGURE 12   The Control Panel

Shortcuts

A ***shortcut*** is a link to any object on your computer, such as a program, file, folder, disk drive, or Web page. Shortcuts can appear anywhere, but are most often placed on the desktop or on the Start menu. The desktop in Figure 13 contains a variety of shortcuts, each of which contains a jump arrow to indicate a shortcut icon. Double click the shortcut to Election of Officers, for example, and you start Word and open this document. In similar fashion, you can double click the shortcut for a Web page (Exploring Windows Series), folder, or disk drive (drive A) to open the object and display its contents.

Creating a shortcut is a two-step process. First, you use Windows Explorer to locate the object such as a file, folder, or disk drive. Then you select the object, use the right mouse button to drag the object to the desktop, and then click the Create Shortcut command from the context-sensitive menu. A shortcut icon will appear on the desktop with the phrase "shortcut to" as part of the name. You can create as many shortcuts as you like, and you can place them anywhere on the desktop or in individual folders. You can also right click a shortcut icon after it has been created to change its name. Deleting the icon deletes the shortcut and not the object.

Windows XP also provides a set of predefined shortcuts through a series of desktop icons that are shown at the left border of the desktop in Figure 13. Double click the My Computer icon, for example, and you open the My Computer folder. These desktop icons were displayed by default in earlier versions of Windows, but not in Windows XP. They were added through the Control Panel as you will see in our next exercise.

Additional shortcuts are found in the **Quick Launch toolbar** that appears to the right of the Start button. Click any icon and you open the indicated program. And finally, Windows XP will automatically add to the Start menu shortcuts to your most frequently used programs. Desktop shortcuts are a powerful technique that will increase your productivity by taking you directly to a specified document or other object.

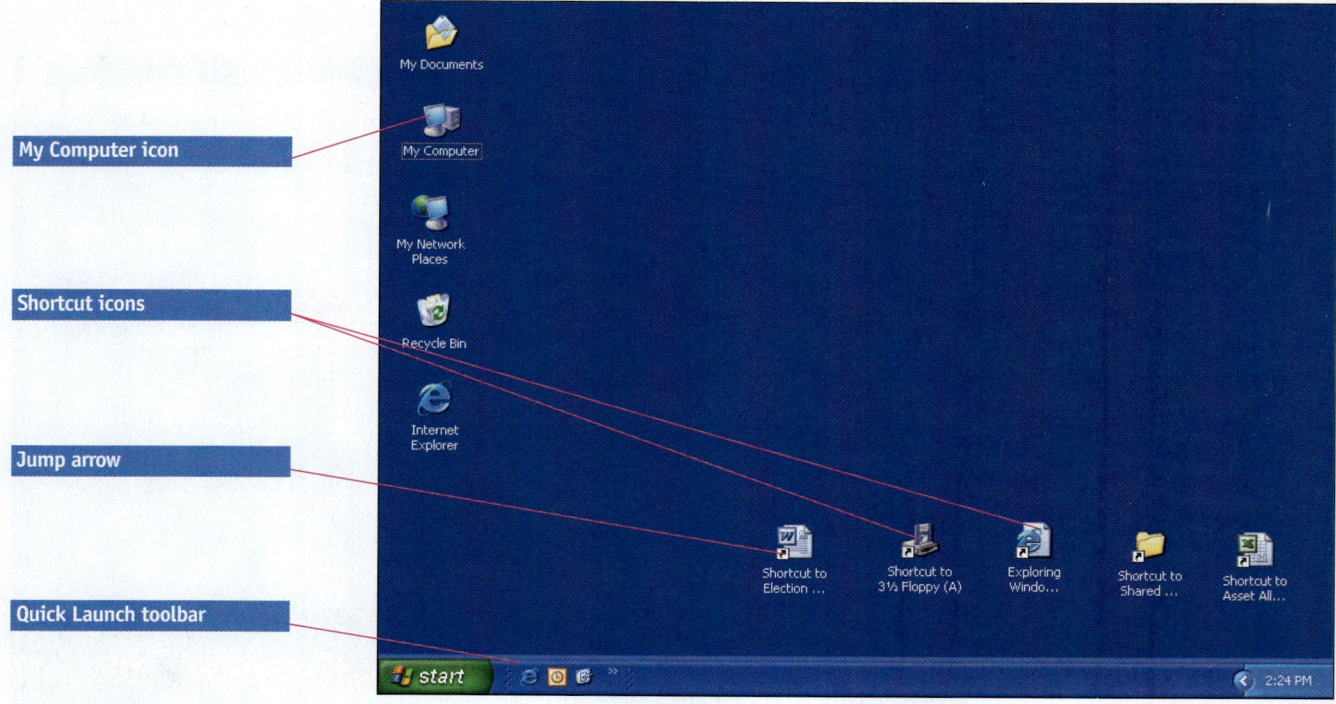

FIGURE 13 Desktop with Shortcuts

774 GETTING STARTED WITH MICROSOFT WINDOWS XP

The Search Companion

Sooner or later you will create a file, and then forget where (in which folder) you saved it. Or you may create a document and forget its name, but remember a key word or phrase in the document. Or you may want to locate all files of a certain file type—for example, all of the sound files on your system. The **Search Companion** can help you to solve each of these problems and is illustrated in Figure 14.

The Search Companion is accessed from within any folder by clicking the Search button on the Standard Buttons toolbar to open the search pane at the left of the folder. You are presented with an initial search menu (not shown in Figure 14) that asks what you want to search for. You can search your local machine for media files (pictures, music, or video), documents (such as spreadsheets or Word documents), or any file or folder. You can also search the Help and Support Center or the Internet.

Once you choose the type of information, you are presented with a secondary search pane as shown in Figure 14. You can search according to a variety of criteria, each of which will help to narrow the search. In this example we are looking for any document on drive C that has "Windows" as part of its filename and further, contains the name "Maryann" somewhere within the document. The search is case sensitive. This example illustrates two important capabilities, namely that you can search on the document name (or part of its name) and/or its content.

Additional criteria can be entered by expanding the chevrons for date and size. You can, for example, restrict your search to all documents that were modified within the last week, the past month, or the last year. You can also restrict your search to documents of a certain size. Click the Search button after all of the criteria have been specified to initiate the search. The results of the search (the documents that satisfy the search criteria) are displayed in the right pane. You can refine the search if it is unsuccessful and/or you can open any document in which you are interested. The Search Companion also has an indexing service to make subsequent searches faster.

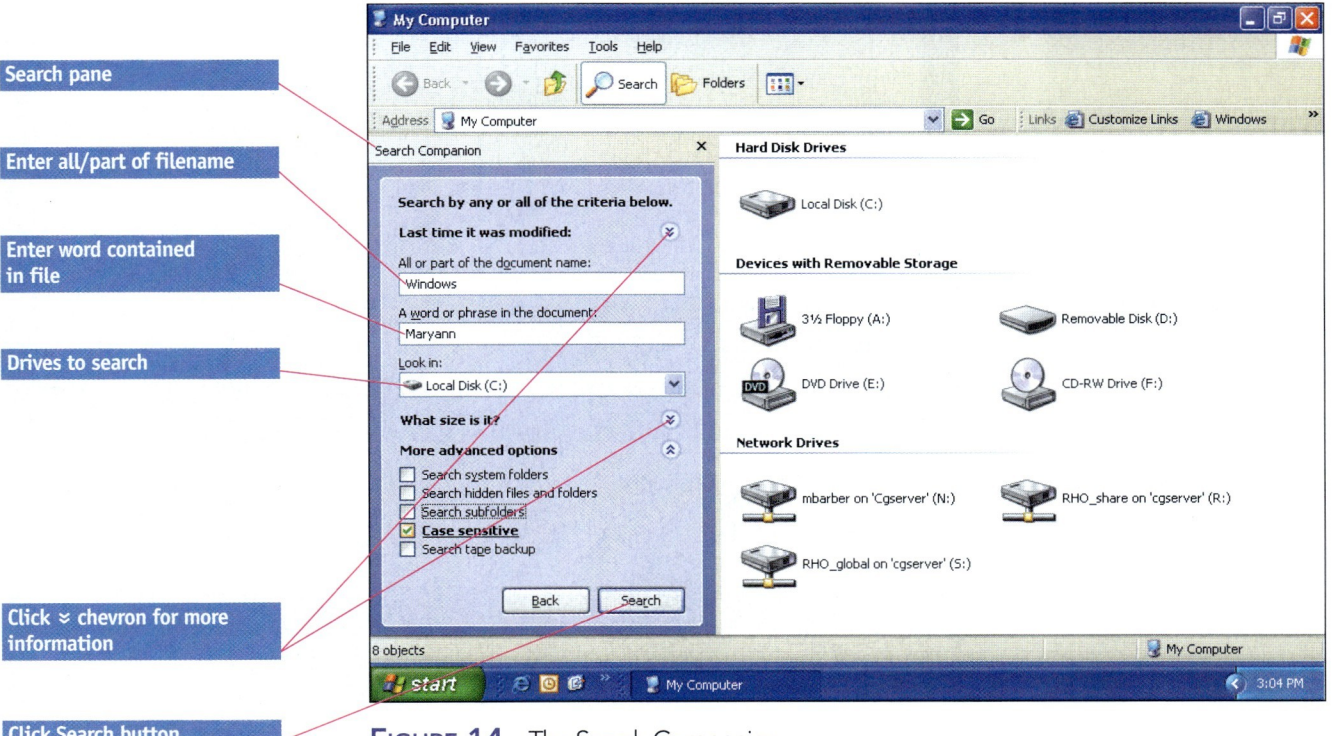

FIGURE 14   The Search Companion

hands-on exercise 4

Increasing Productivity

Objective To create and use shortcuts; to locate documents using the Search Companion; to customize your system using the Control Panel; to obtain a passport account. The exercise requires an Internet connection. Use Figure 15 as a guide.

Step 1: **Display the Desktop Icons**

- Log on to Windows XP. Point to a blank area on the desktop, click the **right mouse button** to display a context-sensitive menu, then click the **Properties command** to open the Display Properties dialog box in Figure 15a.

- Click the **Desktop tab** and then click the **Customize Desktop button** to display the Desktop Items dialog box.

- Check the boxes to display all four desktop icons. Click **OK** to accept these settings and close the dialog box, then click **OK** a second time to close the Display Properties dialog box.

- The desktop icons should appear on the left side of your desktop. Double click any icon to execute the indicated program or open the associated folder.

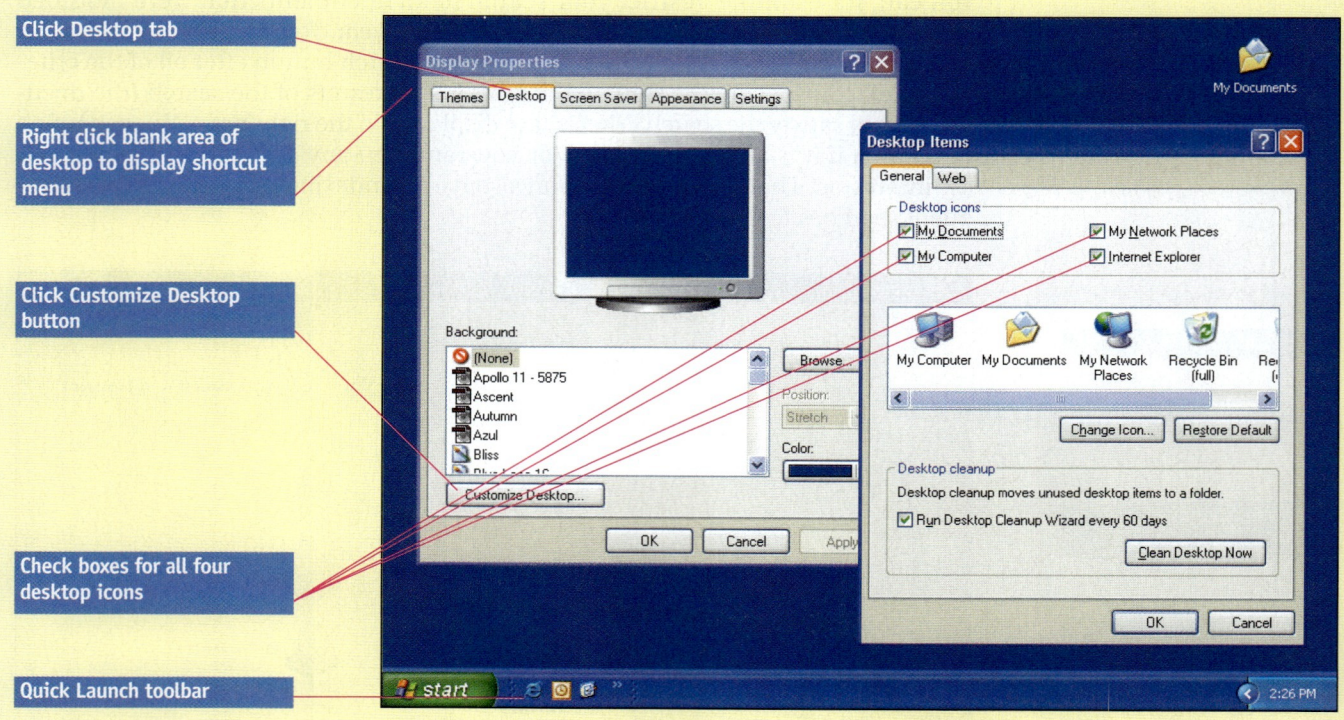

(a) Display the Desktop Icons (step 1)

FIGURE 15 Hands-on Exercise 4

THE QUICK LAUNCH TOOLBAR

The Quick Launch toolbar is a customizable toolbar that executes a program or displays the desktop with a single click. Right click a blank area of the taskbar, point to (or click) the Toolbars command, then check the Quick Launch toolbar to toggle its display on or off.

776 GETTING STARTED WITH MICROSOFT WINDOWS XP

Step 2: **Create a Web Shortcut**

- Start Internet Explorer. You can double click the newly created icon at the left of the desktop, or you can single click its icon in the Quick Launch toolbar. Click the **Restore button** so that Internet Explorer is not maximized, that is, so that you can see a portion of the desktop.

- Click in the Address bar and enter the address **www.microsoft.com/ windowsxp** to display the home page of Windows XP. Now that you see the page, you can create a shortcut to that page.

- Click the **Internet Explorer icon** in the Address bar to select the entire address, point to the Internet Explorer icon, then click and drag the icon to the desktop (you will see a jump arrow as you drag the text). Release the mouse to create the shortcut in Figure 15b.

- Prove to yourself that the shortcut works. Close Internet Explorer, and then double click the shortcut you created. Internet Explorer will open, and you should see the desired Web page. Close (or minimize) Internet Explorer since you do not need it for the remainder of the exercise.

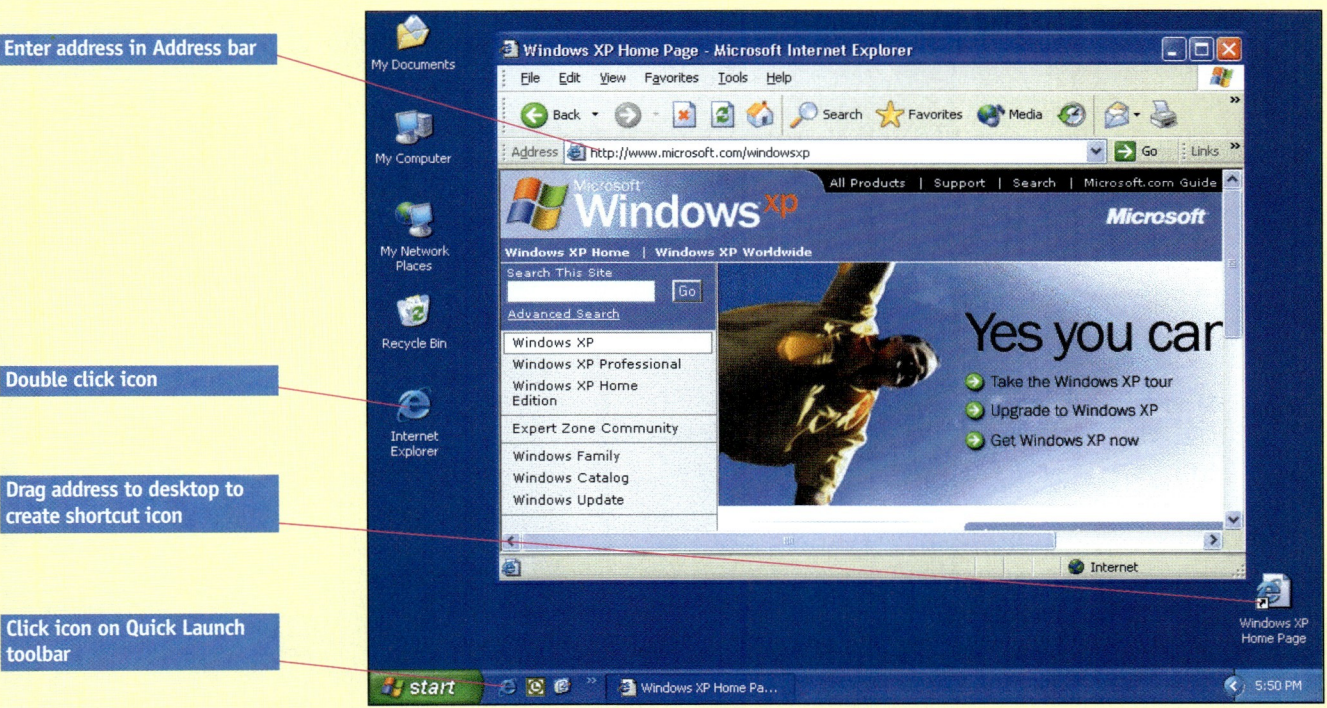

(b) Create a Web Shortcut (step 2)

FIGURE 15 Hands-on Exercise 4 (*continued*)

WORKING WITH SHORTCUTS

You can work with a shortcut icon just as you can with any other icon. To move a shortcut, drag its icon to a different location on the desktop. To rename a shortcut, right click its icon, click the Rename command, type the new name, then press the enter key. To delete a shortcut, right click its icon, click the Delete command, and click Yes in response to the confirming prompt. Deleting a shortcut deletes just the shortcut and not the object to which the shortcut refers.

Step 3: **Create Additional Shortcuts**

- Double click the **My Computer icon** to open this folder. Place the floppy disk from hands-on exercise 3 into the floppy drive. Double click the icon for **drive A** to display the contents of the floppy disk as shown in Figure 15c.

- The contents of the Address bar have changed to A:\ to indicate the contents of the floppy disk. You should see two folders and two files.

- Move and size the window so that you see a portion of the desktop. Right click and drag the icon for the **Windows Information folder** to the desktop, then release the mouse. Click the **Create Shortcuts Here command** to create the shortcut.

- Look for the jump arrow to be sure you have created a shortcut (as opposed to moving or copying the folder). If you made a mistake, right click a blank area of the desktop, then click the **Undo command** to reverse the unintended move or copy operation.

- Right click and drag the icon for the **PowerPoint presentation** to the desktop, release the mouse, and then click the **Create Shortcuts Here command**.

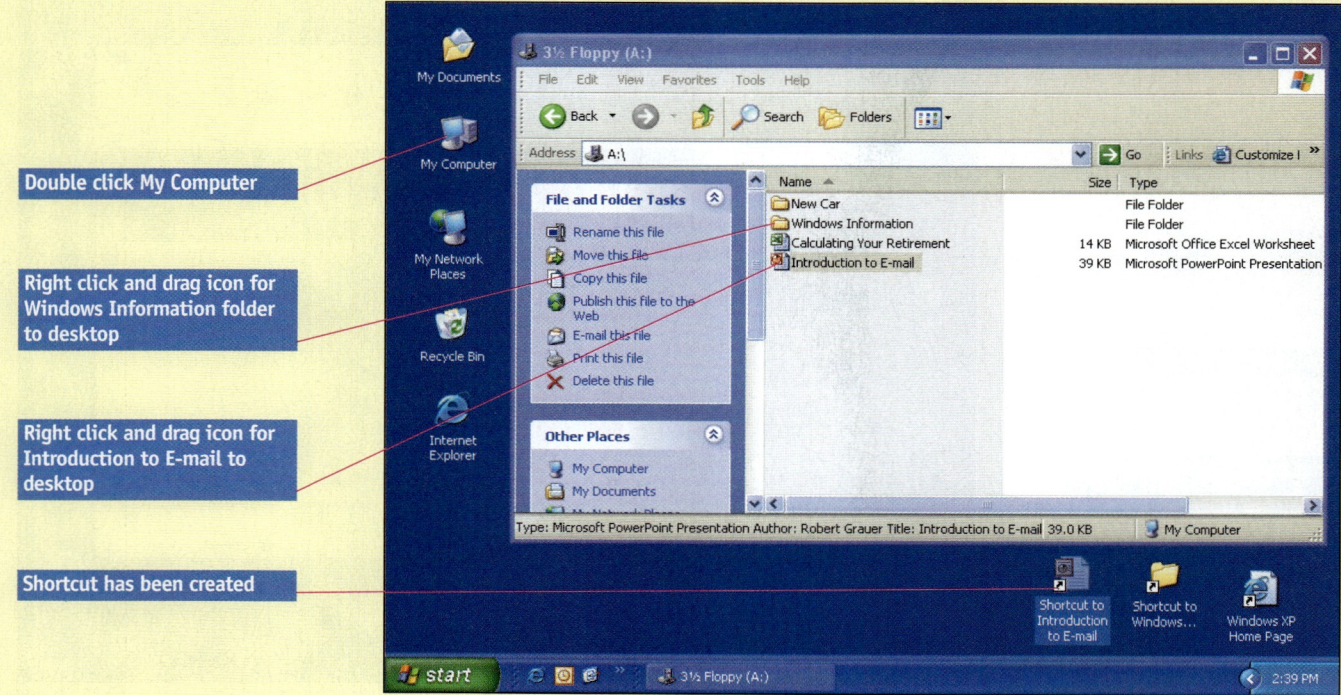

(c) Create Additional Shortcuts (step 3)

FIGURE 15 Hands-on Exercise 4 (*continued*)

THE ARRANGE ICONS COMMAND

The most basic way to arrange the icons on your desktop is to click and drag an icon from one place to another. It may be convenient, however, to have Windows arrange the icons for you. Right click a blank area of the desktop, click (or point to) the Arrange Icons by command, then click Auto Arrange. All existing shortcuts, as well as any new shortcuts, will be automatically aligned along the left edge of the desktop. Execute the Auto Arrange command a second time to cancel the command, and enable yourself to manually arrange the icons.

Step 4: **Search for a Document**

- Maximize the My Computer window. Click the **Search button** on the Standard Buttons toolbar to display the Search pane. The button functions as a toggle switch. Click the button and the Search pane appears. Click the button a second time and the task pane replaces the Search Companion.

- The initial screen (not shown in Figure 15d) in the Search Companion asks what you are searching for. Click **Documents (word processing, spreadsheet, etc.)**.

- You may be prompted to enter when the document was last modified. Click the option button that says **Don't Remember**, then click **Use advanced search options**. You should see the screen in Figure 15d.

- Enter the indicated search criteria. You do not know the document name and thus you leave this text box blank. The other criteria indicate that you are looking for any document that contains "interest rate" that is located on drive A, or in any subfolder on drive A.

- Click the **Search button** to initiate the search. You will see a Search dialog box to indicate the progress of the search, after which you will see the relevant documents.

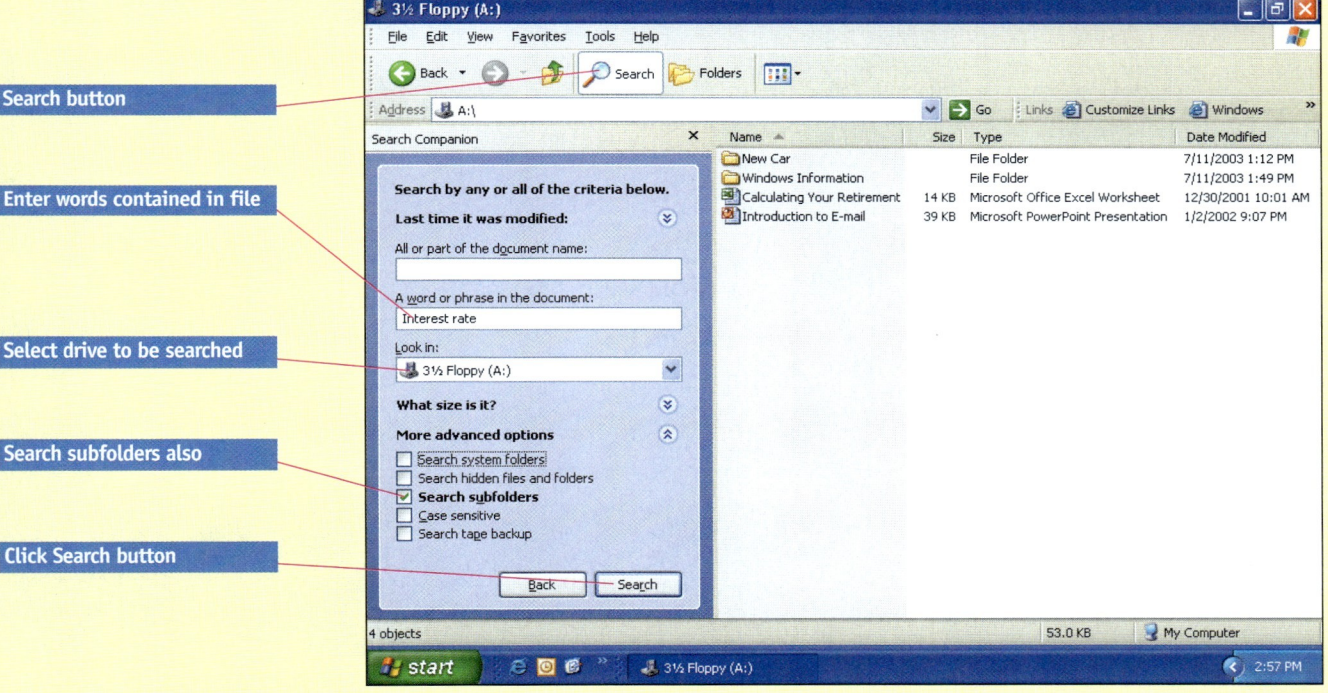

(d) Search for a Document (step 4)

FIGURE 15 Hands-on Exercise 4 (*continued*)

YOU DON'T NEED THE COMPLETE FILENAME

You can enter only a portion of the filename, and the Search Companion will still find the file(s). If, for example, you're searching for the file "Marketing Homework," you can enter the first several letters such as "Marketing" and Windows will return all files whose name begins with the letters you've entered—for example, "Marketing Homework" and "Marketing Term Paper."

Step 5: **Search Results**

- The search should return two files that satisfy the search criteria as shown in Figure 15e. Click the **Views button** and select **Tiles view** if you want to match our figure. If you do not see the same files, it is for one of two reasons:
  ❑ You did not specify the correct search criteria. Click the **Back button** and reenter the search parameters as described in step 4. Repeat the search.
  ❑ Your floppy disk is different from ours. Be sure to use the floppy disk as it existed at the end of the previous hands-on exercise.
- Click the **Restore button** so that you again see a portion of the desktop. Right click and drag the **Calculating Your Retirement** workbook to the desktop to create a shortcut on the desktop.
- Close the Search Results window, close the My Documents window, then double click the newly created shortcut to open the workbook.
- Retirement is a long way off, but you may want to experiment with our worksheet. It is never too early to start saving.
- Exit Excel when you are finished.

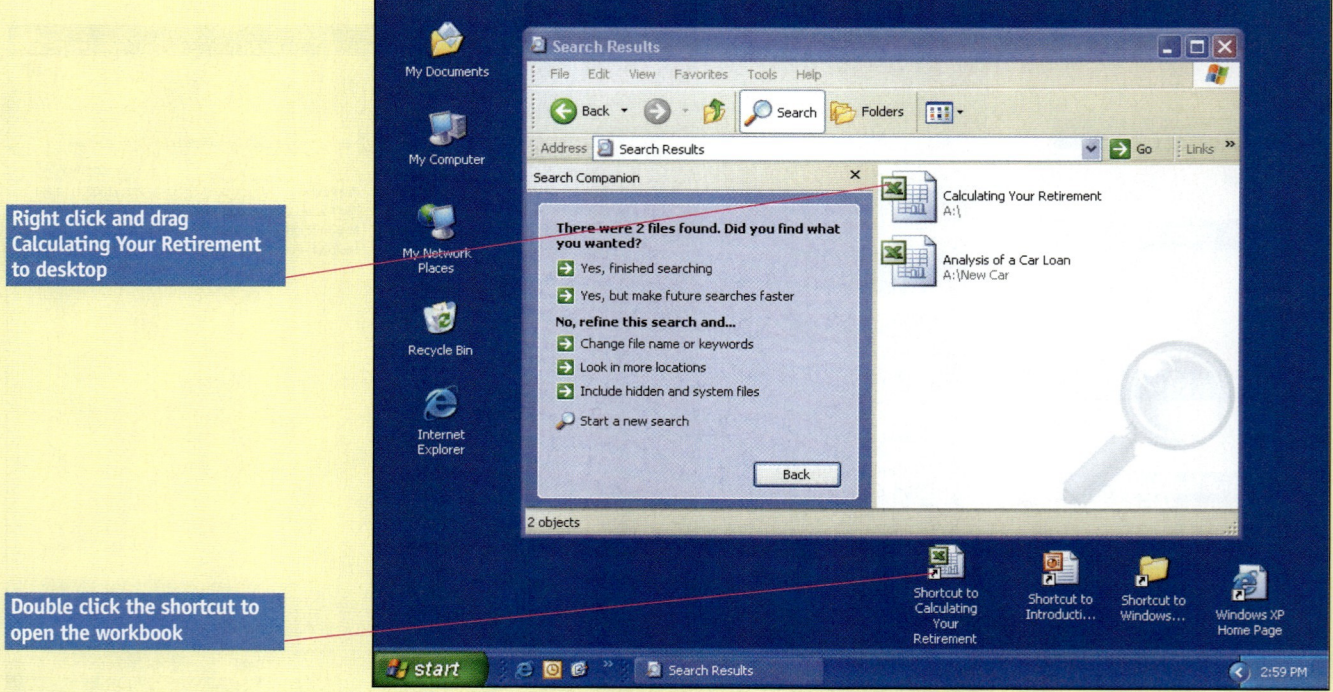

(e) Search Results (step 5)

FIGURE 15 Hands-on Exercise 4 (*continued*)

SHORTCUT WIZARD

Shortcuts can be created in many ways, including the use of a wizard. Right click a blank area of the desktop, click (or point) to the New command, then choose Shortcut to start the wizard. Enter the Web address in the indicated text box (or click the Browse button to locate a local file). Click Next, then enter the name for the shortcut as it is to appear on the desktop. Click the Finish button to exit the wizard. The new shortcut should appear on the desktop.

Step 6: **Open the Control Panel Folder**

- Click the **Start button**, then click **Control Panel** to open the Control Panel folder. Click the command to **Switch to Classic View** that appears in the task pane to display the individual icons as shown in Figure 15f. Maximize the window.

- Double click the **Taskbar and Start Menu icon** to display the associated dialog box. Click the **Taskbar tab**, then check the box to **Auto-hide the taskbar.** Your other settings should match those in Figure 15f. Click **OK** to accept the settings and close the dialog box.

- The taskbar (temporarily) disappears from your desktop. Now point to the bottom edge of the desktop, and the taskbar reappears. The advantage of hiding the taskbar in this way is that you have the maximum amount of room in which to work; that is, you see the taskbar only when you want to.

- Double click the **Fonts folder** to open this folder and display the fonts that are installed on your computer. Change to the **Details view**.

- Double click the icon of any font other than the standard fonts (Arial, Times New Roman, and Courier New) to open a new window that displays the font. Click the **Print button**. Close the Font window.

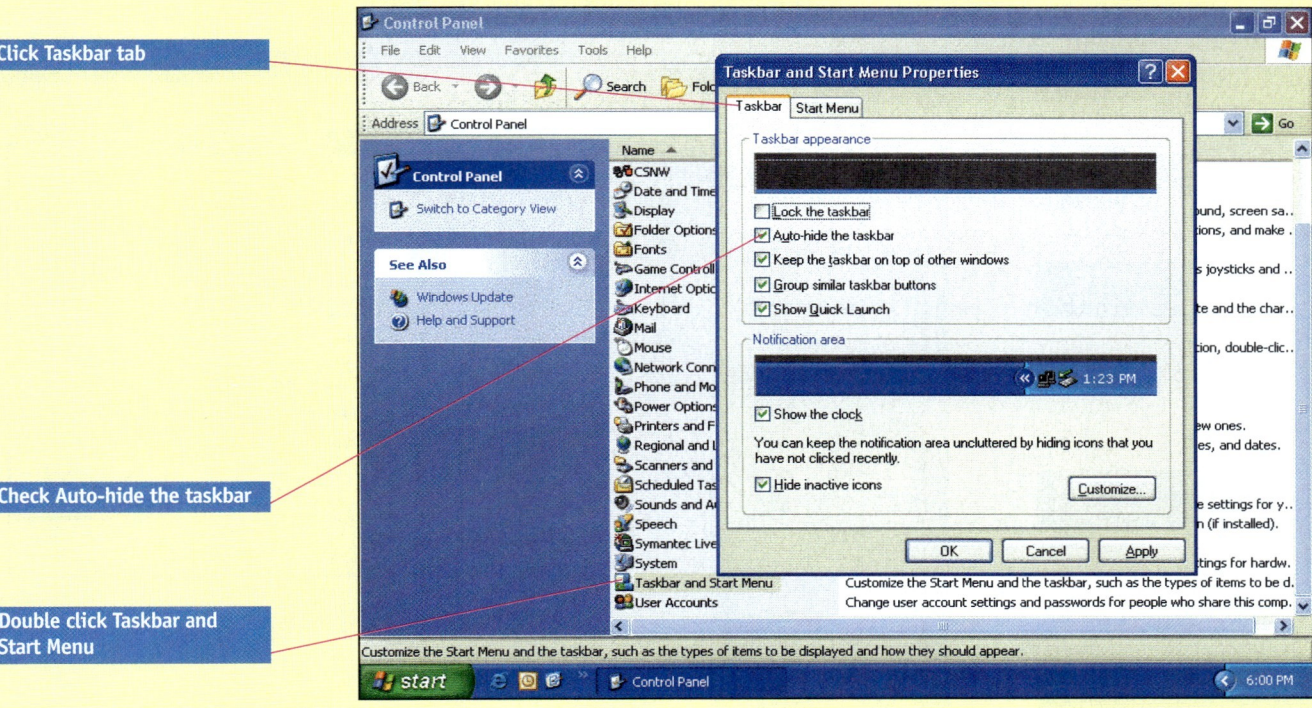

(f) Open the Control Panel Folder (step 6)

FIGURE 15   Hands-on Exercise 4 (*continued*)

MODIFY THE START MENU

Click and drag a shortcut icon to the Start button to place the shortcut on the Start menu. It does not appear that anything has happened, but the shortcut will appear at the top of the Start menu. Click the Start button to display the Start menu, then press the Esc key to exit the menu without executing a command. You can delete any item from the menu by right clicking the item and clicking the Unpin from the Start menu command.

Step 7: **Obtain a .NET Passport**

- Click the **Back button** to return to the Control Panel, then double click the **User Accounts icon** in the Control Panel folder. Maximize the User Accounts window so that it takes the entire desktop.

- Click the icon corresponding to the account that is currently logged to display a screen similar to Figure 15g. Click the command to **Set up my account to use a .NET passport**. You will see the first step in the Passport Wizard.

- Click the link to **View the privacy statement**. This starts Internet Explorer and goes to the .NET Passport site on the Web. Print the privacy agreement. It runs nine pages, but it contains a lot of useful information.

- Close Internet Explorer after you have printed the agreement. You are back in the Passport Wizard. Click **Next** to continue.

- Follow the instructions on the next several screens. You will be asked to enter your e-mail address and to supply a password. Click **Finish** when you have reached the last screen.

- You will receive an e-mail message after you have registered successfully. You will need your passport in our next exercise when we explore Windows Messenger and the associated instant messaging service.

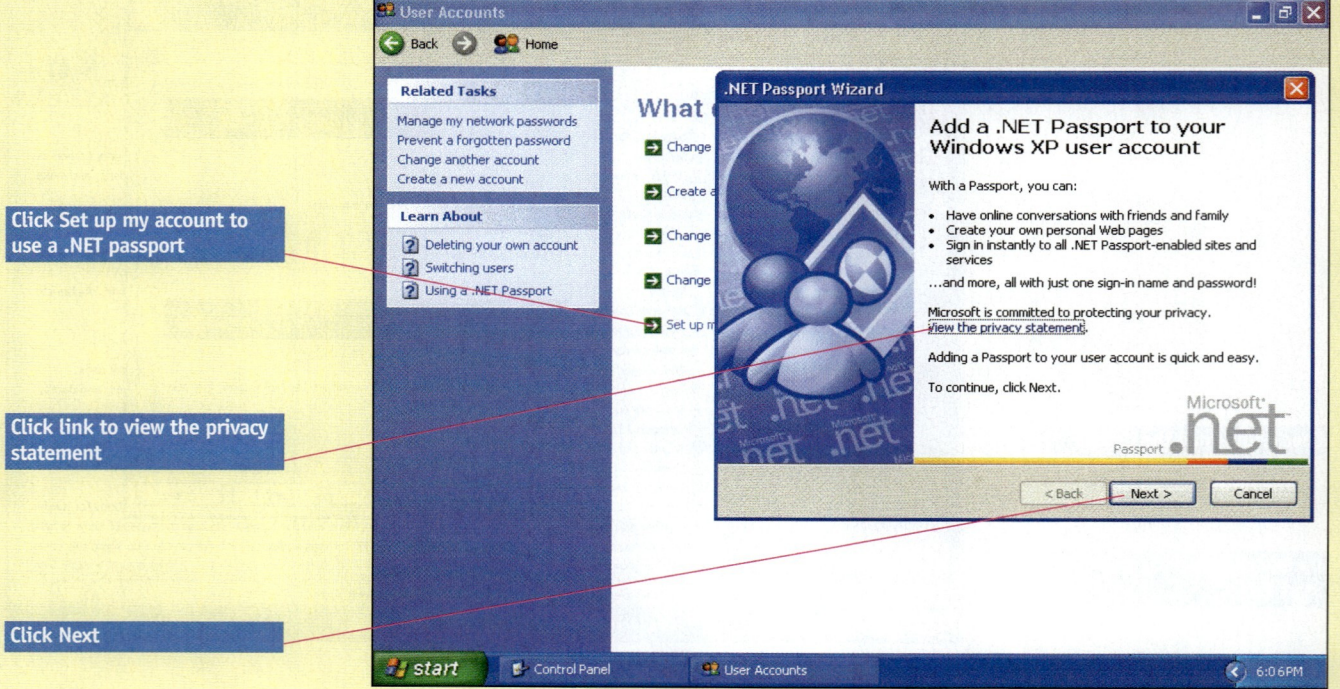

(g) Obtain a .NET Passport (step 7)

FIGURE 15 Hands-on Exercise 4 (*continued*)

UPDATING YOUR PASSPORT

You can modify the information in your passport profile at any time. Open the Control Panel, click User Accounts, select your account, then click the command to Change Your .NET passport. You can change your password, change the question that will remind you about your password should you forget it, and/or change the information that you authorize the passport service to share with others.

Step 8: **Windows Update**

- Close the User Accounts window to return to the Control Panel folder. Click the link to **Windows Update** to display a screen similar to Figure 15h.

- Click the command to **Scan for updates**. (This command is not visible in our figure.) This command will take several seconds as Windows determines which (if any) updates it recommends. Our system indicates that there are no critical updates but that additional updates are available.

- Click the link(s) to review the available updates. You do not have to install the vast majority of available updates. It is essential, however, that you install any updates deemed critical. One critical update appeared shortly after the release of Windows XP and closed a hole in the operating system that enabled hackers to break into some XP machines.

- Click the link to **View installation history** to see which updates were previously installed. Print this page for your instructor.

- Close the Update window. Log off the computer if you do not want to continue with the next exercise at this time.

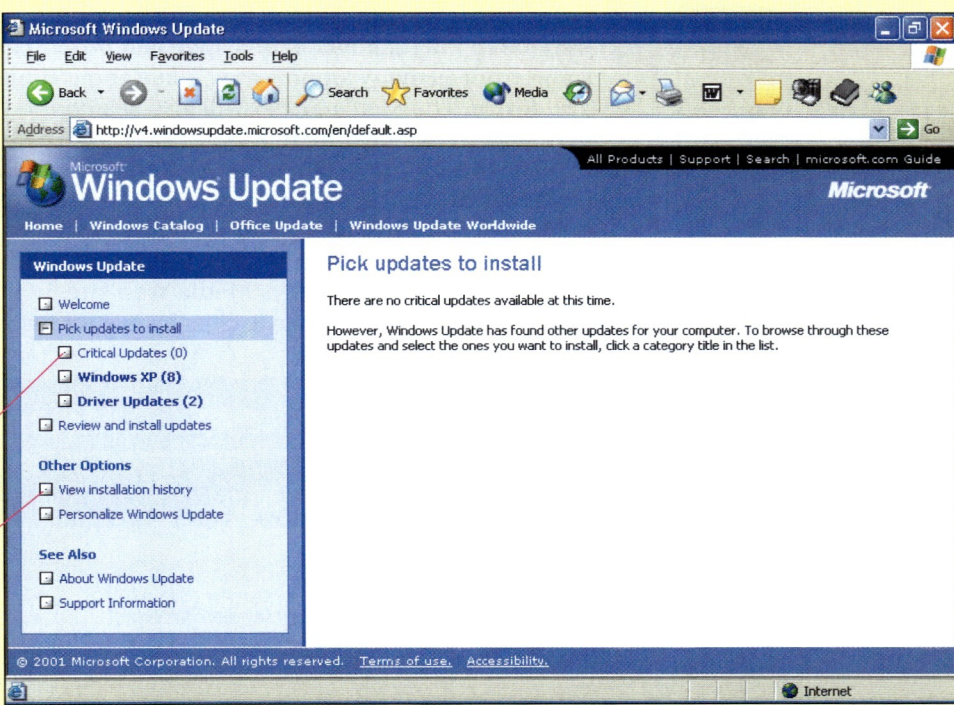

(h) Windows Update (step 8)

FIGURE 15   Hands-on Exercise 4 (*continued*)

THE SHOW DESKTOP BUTTON

The Show Desktop button or command minimizes every open window and returns you immediately to the desktop. You can get to this command in different ways, most easily by clicking the Show Desktop icon on the Quick Launch toolbar. The button functions as a toggle switch. Click it once and all windows are minimized. Click it a second time and the open windows are restored to their position on the desktop.

FUN WITH WINDOWS XP

The "XP" in Windows XP is for the experience that Microsoft promises individuals who adopt its operating system. Windows XP makes it easy to enjoy music and video, work with **digital photographs**, and chat with your friends. This section describes these capabilities and then moves to a hands-on exercise in which you practice at the computer. All of the features are available on your own machine, but some may be disabled in a laboratory setting. It's not that your professor does not want you to have fun, but listening to music or engaging in instant messaging with your friends is not practical in a school environment. Nevertheless, the hands-on exercise that follows enables you to practice your skills in disk and file management as you work with multiple files and folders.

Windows Media Player

The **Windows Media Player** combines the functions of a radio, a CD, or DVD player, and an information database into a single program. It lets you listen to radio stations anywhere in the world, play a CD, or watch a DVD movie (provided you have the necessary hardware). You can copy selections from a CD to your computer, organize your music by artist and album, and then create a customized **playlist** to play the music in a specified order. The playlist may include as many songs from as many albums as you like and is limited only by the size of your storage device. The Media Player will also search the Web for audio or video files and play clips from a favorite movie.

The buttons at the left of the Media Player enable you to switch from one function to the next. The Radio Tuner button is active in Figure 16, and the BBC station is selected. Think of that—you are able to listen to radio stations from around the world with the click of a button. The Media Guide button connects you to the home page of the Windows Media Web site, where you can search the Web for media files and/or play movie clips from your favorite movies.

FIGURE 16 Windows Media Player

Digital Photography

Windows XP helps you to organize your pictures and share them with others. The best place to store photographs is in the My Pictures folder or in a subfolder within this folder as shown in Figure 17. The complete path to the folder appears in the Address bar and is best read from right to left. Thus, you are looking at pictures in the Romance Folder, which is in the My Pictures folder, which in turn is stored in a My Documents folder. Remember that each user has his or her unique My Documents folder, so the path must be further qualified. Hence, you are looking at the My Documents folder, within a folder for Jessica (one of several users), within the Documents and Settings folder on drive C. The latter folder maintains the settings for all of the users that are registered on this system.

The pictures in Figure 17 are shown in the ***Thumbnails view***, which displays a miniature image of each picture in the right pane. (Other views are also available and are accessed from the View menu or Views button.) The Picture Tasks area in the upper right lists the functions that are unique to photographs. You can view the pictures as a slide show, which is the equivalent of a PowerPoint presentation without having to create the presentation. You can print any picture, use it as the background on your desktop, or copy multiple pictures to a CD, provided you have the necessary hardware. You can also order prints online. You choose the company; select print sizes and quantities, supply the billing and shipping information, and your photographs are sent to you.

One photo is selected (BenWendy) in Figure 17, and the associated details are shown in the Details area of the task pane. The picture is stored as a JPG file, a common format for photographs. It was created on January 21, 2002.

The File and Folder Tasks area is collapsed in our figure, but you can expand the area to gain access to the normal file operations (move, copy, and delete). You can also e-mail the photograph from this panel. Remember, too, that you can click the Folders button on the Standard Buttons toolbar to switch to the hierarchical view of your system, which is better suited to disk and file management.

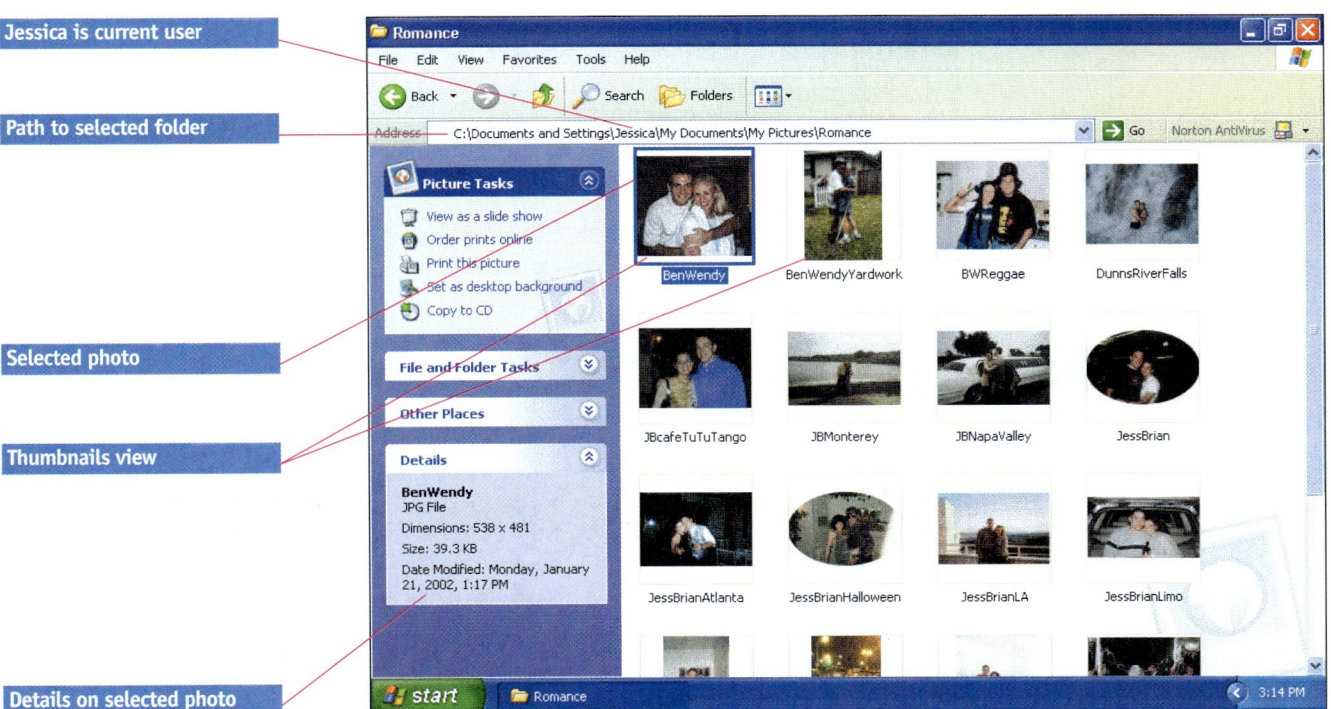

FIGURE 17 Working with Pictures

Windows Messenger

Windows Messenger is an instant messaging system in which you chat with friends and colleagues over the Internet. (It is based on the same technology as the "buddies list" that was made popular by America Online.) You need an Internet connection, a list of contacts, and a ***Microsoft passport*** that is based on your e-mail address. The passport is a free Microsoft service that enables you to access any passport-enabled Internet site with a single user name and associated password. (Step 7 in the previous hands-on exercise described how to obtain a passport.)

You can initiate a conversation at any time by monitoring the contacts list to see who is online and starting a chat session. Up to four people can participate in the same conversation. It is easy, fun, and addictive. You know the instant someone signs on, and you can begin chatting immediately. The bad news, however, is that it is all too easy to chat incessantly when you have real work to do. Hence you may want to change your status to indicate that you are busy and unable to participate in a conversation.

Figure 18 displays a conversation between Maryann and Bob. The session began when Maryann viewed her contact list, noticed that Bob was online, and started a conversation. Each person enters his or her message at the bottom of the conversation window, and then clicks the Send button. Additional messages can be sent without waiting for a response. Emoticons can be added to any message for effect. Note, too, the references to the file transfer that appear within the conversation, which are the result of Maryann clicking the command to send a file or photo, then attaching the desired file.

Windows Messenger is more than just a vehicle for chatting. If you have speakers and a microphone, you can place phone calls from your computer without paying a long distance charge. The most intriguing feature, however, is the ability to ask for remote assistance, whereby you can invite one of your contacts to view your desktop as you are working in order to ask for help. It is as if your friend were in the room looking over your shoulder. He or she will see everything that you do and can respond immediately with suggestions.

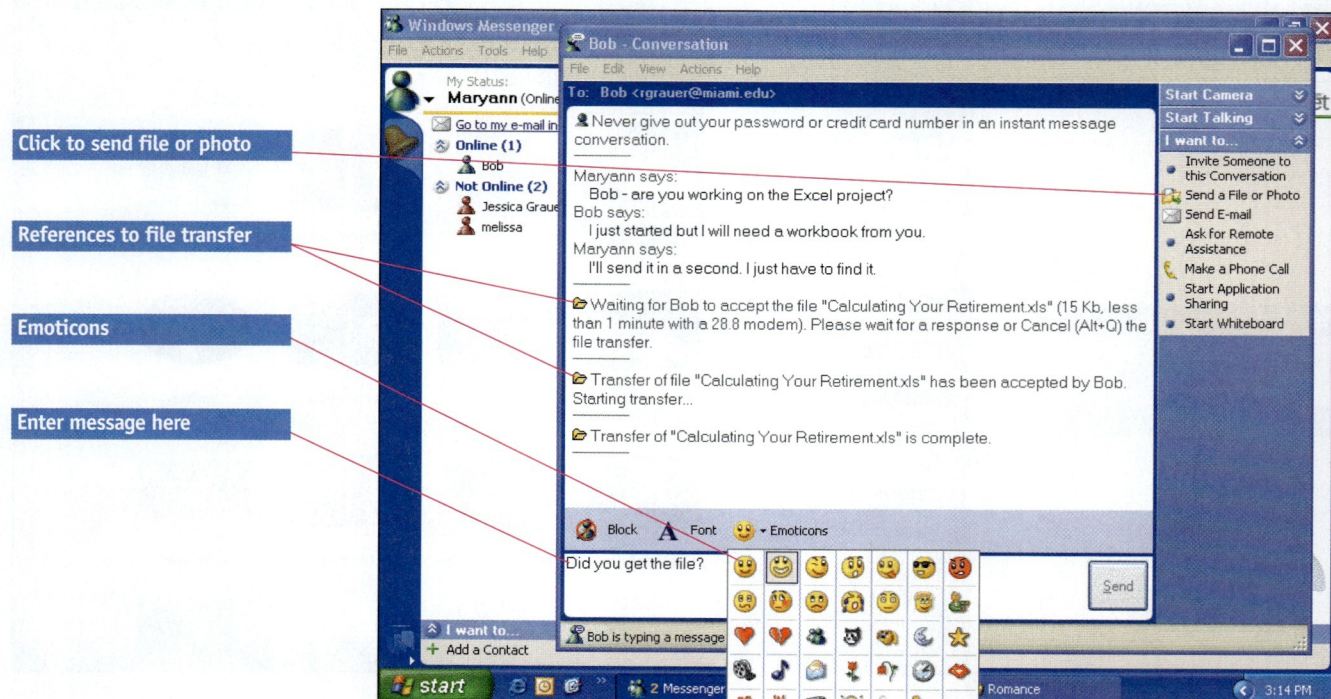

FIGURE 18 Windows Messenger

hands-on exercise
5 Fun with Windows XP

Objective To use Windows Media Player, work with photographs, and experiment with Windows Messenger. Check with your professor regarding the availability of the resources required for this exercise. Use Figure 19.

Step 1: **Open the Shared Music Folder**

- Start Windows Explorer. Click the **Folders button** to display the tree structure. You need to locate some music to demonstrate the Media Player.

- The typical XP installation includes some files within the Shared Documents folder. Expand the My Computer folder to show the **Shared Documents folder**, expand the **Shared Music folder**, and then open the **Sample Music folder** as shown in Figure 19a.

- Point to any file (it does not matter if you have a different selection of music) to display the ScreenTip describing the music. Double click the file to start the Media Player and play the selected music.

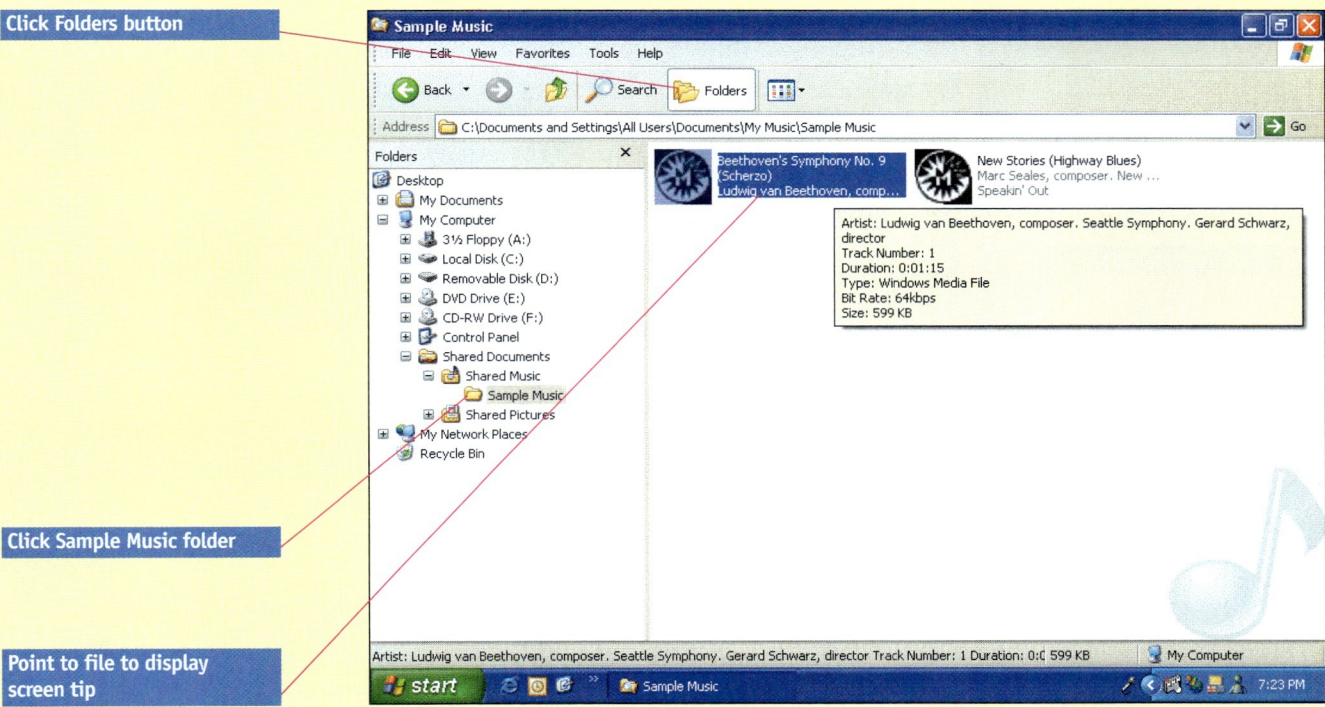

(a) Open the Shared Music Folder (step 1)

FIGURE 19 Hands-on Exercise 5

SHARED FOLDERS VERSUS PERSONAL FOLDERS

Windows XP automatically creates a unique My Documents folder for every user, which in turn contains a unique My Pictures folder and My Music folder within the My Documents folder. These folders are private and cannot be accessed by other users. Windows also provides a Shared Documents folder that is accessible to every user on a system.

Step 2: **Listen to the Music**

- You should hear the music when the Windows Media Player opens in its own window as shown in Figure 19b. The controls at the bottom of the window are similar to those on any CD player.
    - You can click the **Pause button**, then click the **Play button** to restart the music at that point.
    - You can click the **Stop button** to stop playing altogether.
    - You can also drag the slider to begin playing at a different place.

- You can also adjust the volume as shown in Figure 19b. Double click the **Volume Control icon** in the notification area at the right of the taskbar to display the Volume Control dialog box. Close this window.

- Click the **Radio Tuner button** at the side of the Media Player window. The system pauses as it tunes into the available radio stations.

- Select a radio station (e.g., **BBC World**) when you see the list of available stations, then click the **Play button** after you choose a station.

- You will see a message at the bottom of the window indicating that your computer is connecting to the media, after which you will hear the radio station.

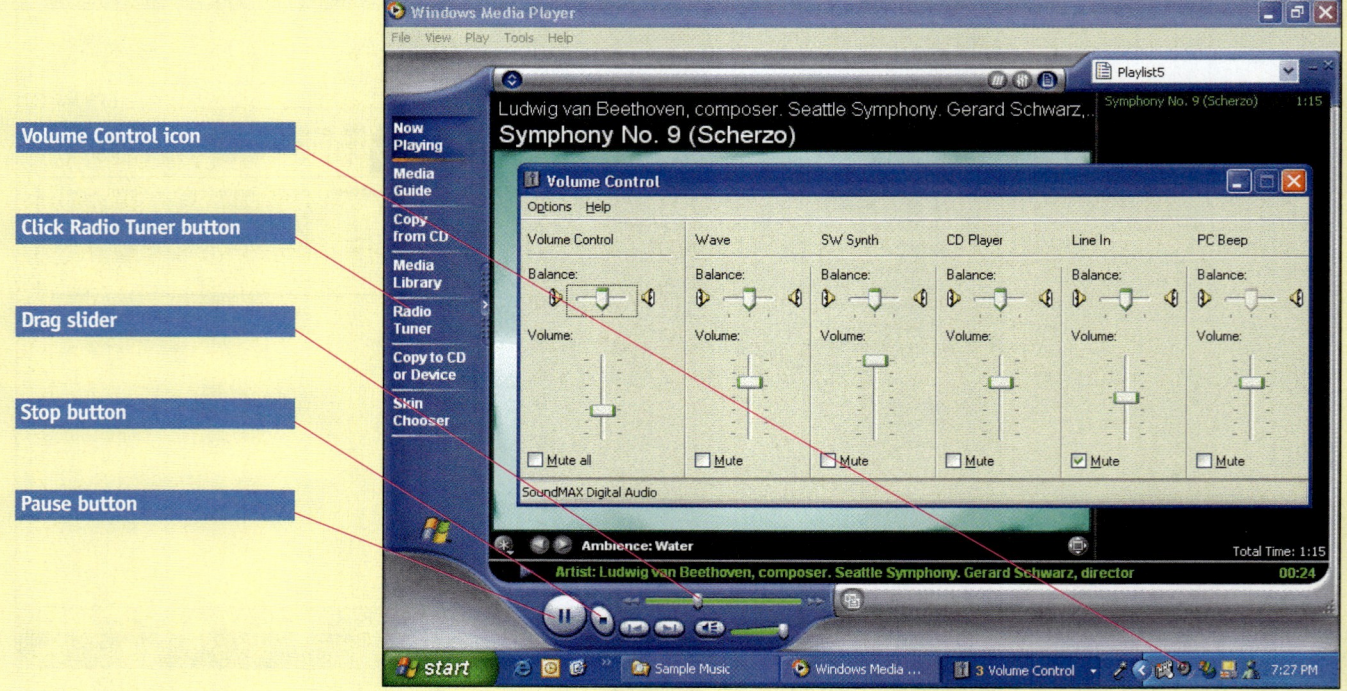

(b) Listen to the Music (step 2)

FIGURE 19   Hands-on Exercise 5 (*continued*)

OTHER MEDIA PLAYERS

If you double click a music (MP3) file, and a program other than Windows Media starts to play, it is because your system has another media player as its default program. You can still use the Windows Media Player, but you will have to start the program explicitly from the Start menu. Once the Media Player is open, pull down the File menu and click the Open command, then select the music file you want to play.

Step 3:   **Create a Playlist**

- Click the **Media Library button** at the side of the Media player to display the media files that are currently on your computer.
  - The left pane displays a tree structure of your media library. Thus, you click the plus or minus sign to collapse or expand the indicated folder.
  - The right pane displays the contents of the selected object (the My Music playlist) in Figure 19c.

- Do not be concerned if your media library is different from ours. Click the **New playlist button**, enter **My Music** as the name of the new list, and click **OK**.

- Click the newly created playlist in the left pane to display its contents in the left pane. The playlist is currently empty.

- Start **Windows Explorer**. Open the **My Music Folder** within the My Documents folder. If necessary, click the **Restore button** to move and size Windows Explorer so that you can copy documents to the Media library.

- Click and drag one or more selections from the My Music folder to the right pane of the Media library to create the playlist. Close Windows Explorer.

- Click the **down arrow** in the list box at the upper right of the Media Gallery and select the My Music playlist to play the songs you have selected.

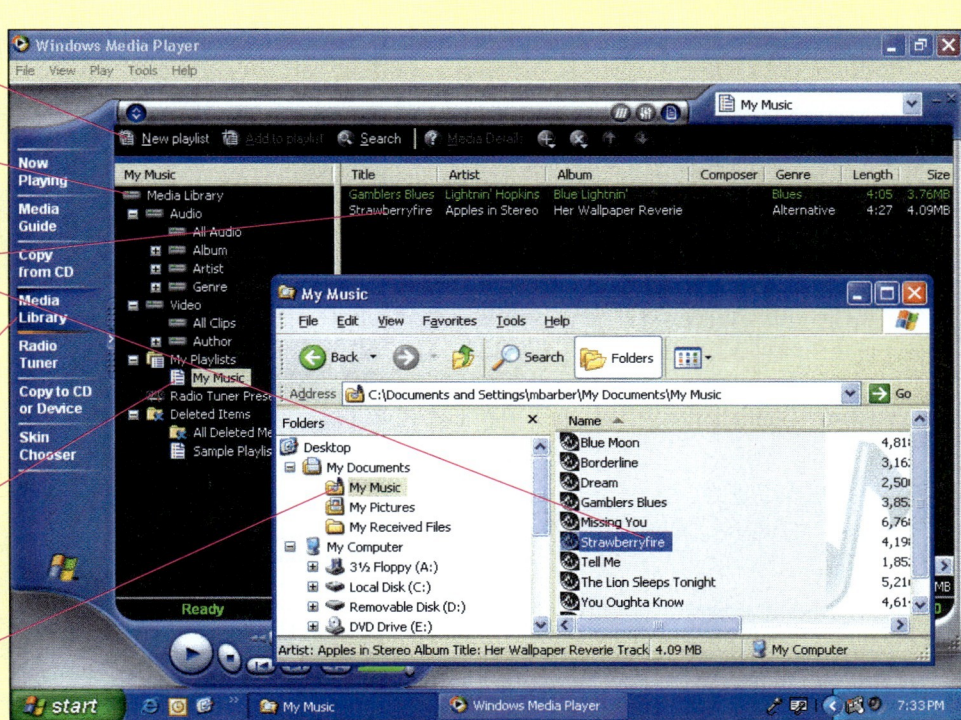

(c) Create a Playlist (step 3)

FIGURE 19 Hands-on Exercise 5 (*continued*)

THE MEDIA GUIDE

Click the Media Guide button at the left of the Media Player to display the home page of the Windows Media Site. You can also get there by starting Internet Explorer and entering windowsmedia.com in the Address bar. Either way, you will be connected to the Internet and can search the Web for media files and/or play clips from your favorite movie.

Step 4: **Create a Pictures Folder**

- You can use your own pictures, or if you don't have any, you can use the sample pictures provided with Windows XP. Start (or maximize) Windows Explorer. Open the **My Pictures folder** within the **My Documents folder**.

- Do not be concerned if the content of your folder is different from ours. Our folder already contains various subfolders with different types of pictures in each folder.

- Click the **Views button** and change to the **Thumbnails view**. This view is especially useful when viewing folders that contain photographs because (up to four) images are displayed on the folder icon.

- Right click anywhere in the right pane to display a context-sensitive menu as shown in Figure 19d. Click **New**, and then click **Folder** as the type of object to create.

- The icon for a new folder will appear with the name of the folder (New Folder) highlighted. Enter a more appropriate name (we chose **Romance** because our pictures are those of a happy couple), and press **Enter**.

- Copy your pictures from another folder, a CD, or floppy disk to the newly created folder.

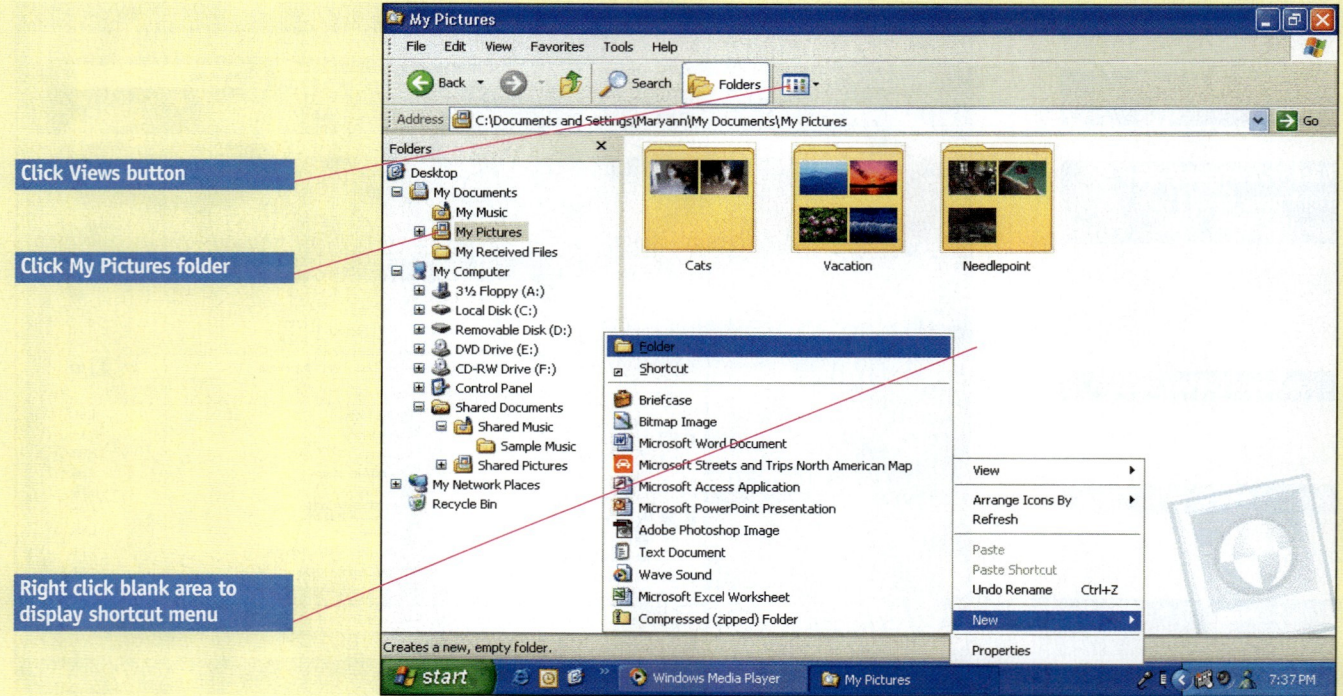

(d) Create a Pictures Folder (step 4)

FIGURE 19 Hands-on Exercise 5 (*continued*)

DESIGN GALLERY LIVE

The Microsoft Design Gallery is an excellent source of photographs and other media. Start Internet Explorer and go to the Design Gallery at dgl.microsoft.com. Enter the desired topic in the Search for text box, indicate that you want to search everywhere, and specify that the results should be photos. Download one or more of the photos that are returned by the search and use those pictures to complete this exercise.

Step 5: **Display Your Pictures**

- Double click the newly created folder to display its contents. Click the **Folders button** to display the Windows Explorer task pane, as opposed to the hierarchy structure. Click the **Views button** and change to the **Filmstrip view** as shown in Figure 19e.

- Click the **Next Image** or (**Previous Image**) **button** to move from one picture to the next within the folder. If necessary, click the buttons to rotate pictures clockwise or counterclockwise so that the pictures are displayed properly within the window.

- Click the command to **View as a slide show**, then display your pictures one at a time on your monitor. This is a very easy way to enjoy your photographs. Press the **Esc key** to stop.

- Choose any picture, then click the command to **Print this picture** that appears in the left pane. Submit this picture to your instructor.

- Choose a different picture and then click the command to **Set as desktop background**. Minimize Windows Explorer.

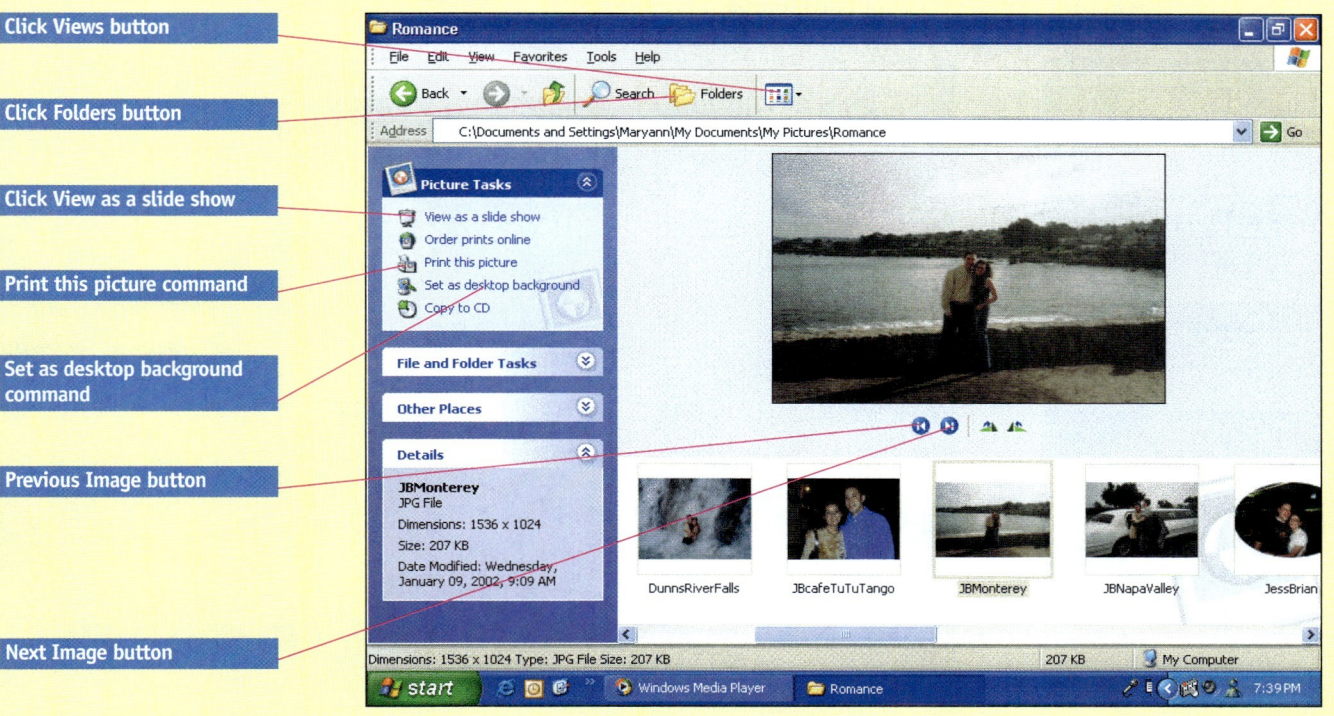

(e) Display Your Pictures (step 5)

FIGURE 19 Hands-on Exercise 5 (*continued*)

CHANGE THE VIEW

Click the down arrow next to the Views button on the Standard toolbar to change the way files are displayed within a folder. The Details view provides the most information and includes the filename, file type, file size, and the date that the file was created or last modified. (Additional attributes are also possible.) Other views are more visual. The Thumbnails view displays a miniature image of the file and is best used with clip art, photographs, or presentations. The Filmstrip view is used with photographs only.

Step 6: **Customize the Desktop**

- Your desktop should once again be visible, depending on which (if any) applications are open. If you do not see the desktop, right click a blank area of the taskbar, then click the **Show Desktop command**.

- You should see the picture you selected earlier as the background for your desktop. The picture is attractive (you chose it), but it may be distracting.

- To remove the picture, **right click** the background of the desktop and click the **Properties command** to display the Display Properties dialog box in Figure 19f.

- Click the **Desktop tab**, then click **None** in the Background list box. Click **OK** to accept this setting and close the dialog box. The picture disappears.

- Regardless of whether you keep the background, you can use your pictures as a screen saver. Redisplay the Display Properties dialog box. Click the **Screen Saver tab** in the Display Properties box, then choose **My Picture Slideshow** from the screen saver list box.

- Wait a few seconds and the picture within the dialog box will change, just as it will on your desktop. Click **OK** to accept the screen saver and close the Display Properties dialog box.

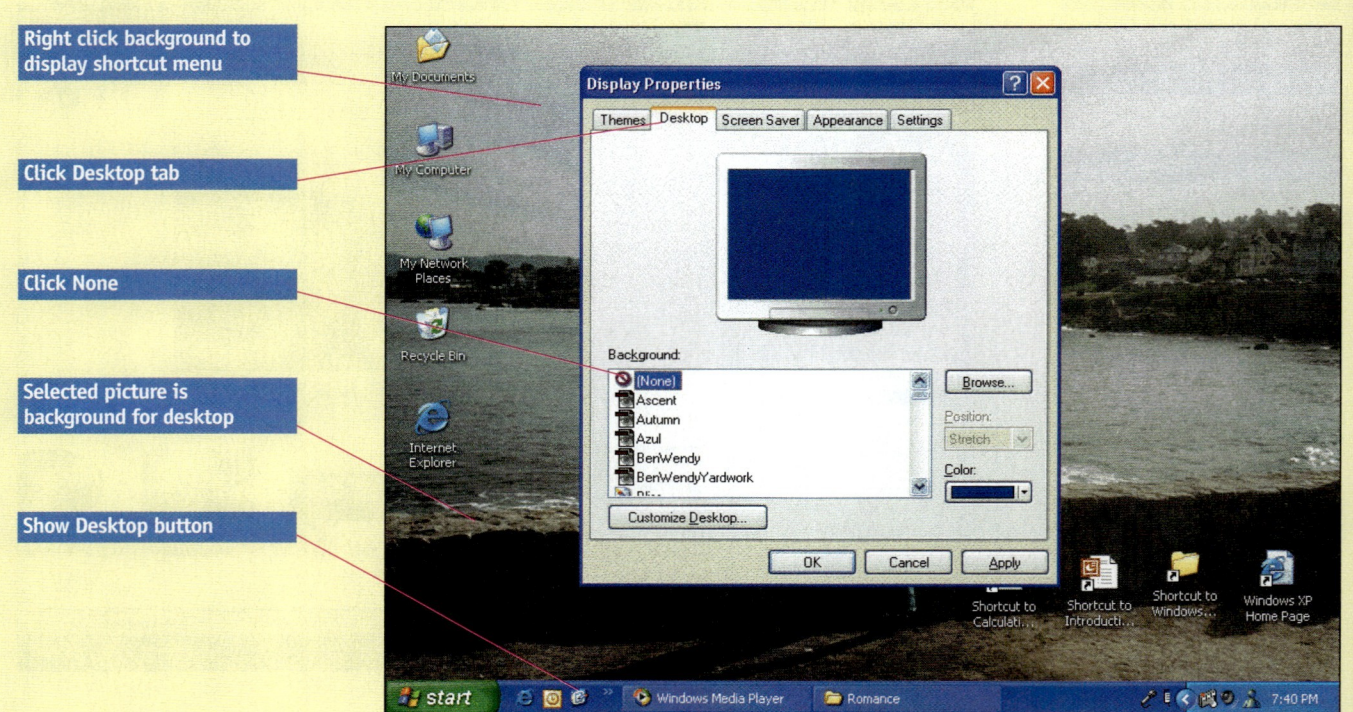

Right click background to display shortcut menu

Click Desktop tab

Click None

Selected picture is background for desktop

Show Desktop button

(f) Customize the Desktop (step 6)

FIGURE 19 Hands-on Exercise 5 (*continued*)

CHANGE THE RESOLUTION

The resolution of a monitor refers to the number of pixels (picture elements or dots) that are displayed at one time. The higher the resolution, the more pixels are displayed, and hence you see more of a document at one time. You can change the resolution at any time. Right click the desktop, click the Properties command to show the Display Properties dialog box, then click the Settings tab. Drag the slider bar to the new resolution, then click OK.

Step 7: **Start Windows Messenger**

- You need a passport to use Windows Messenger. Double click the **Windows Messenger icon** in the notification area of the taskbar to sign in.

- Maximize the Messenger window. You will see a list of your existing contacts with an indication of whether they are online.

- Add one or more contacts. Pull down the **Tools menu**, click the command to **Add a Contact**, then follow the onscreen instructions. (The contact does not have to have Windows XP to use instant messaging.)

- Double click any contact that is online to initiate a conversation and open a conversation window as shown in Figure 19g.

- Type a message at the bottom of the conversation window, then click the **Send button** to send the message. The text of your message will appear immediately on your contact's screen. Your friend's messages will appear on your screen.

- Continue the conversation by entering additional text. You can press the **Enter key** (instead of clicking the **Send button**) to send the message. You can also use **Shift + enter** to create a line break in your text.

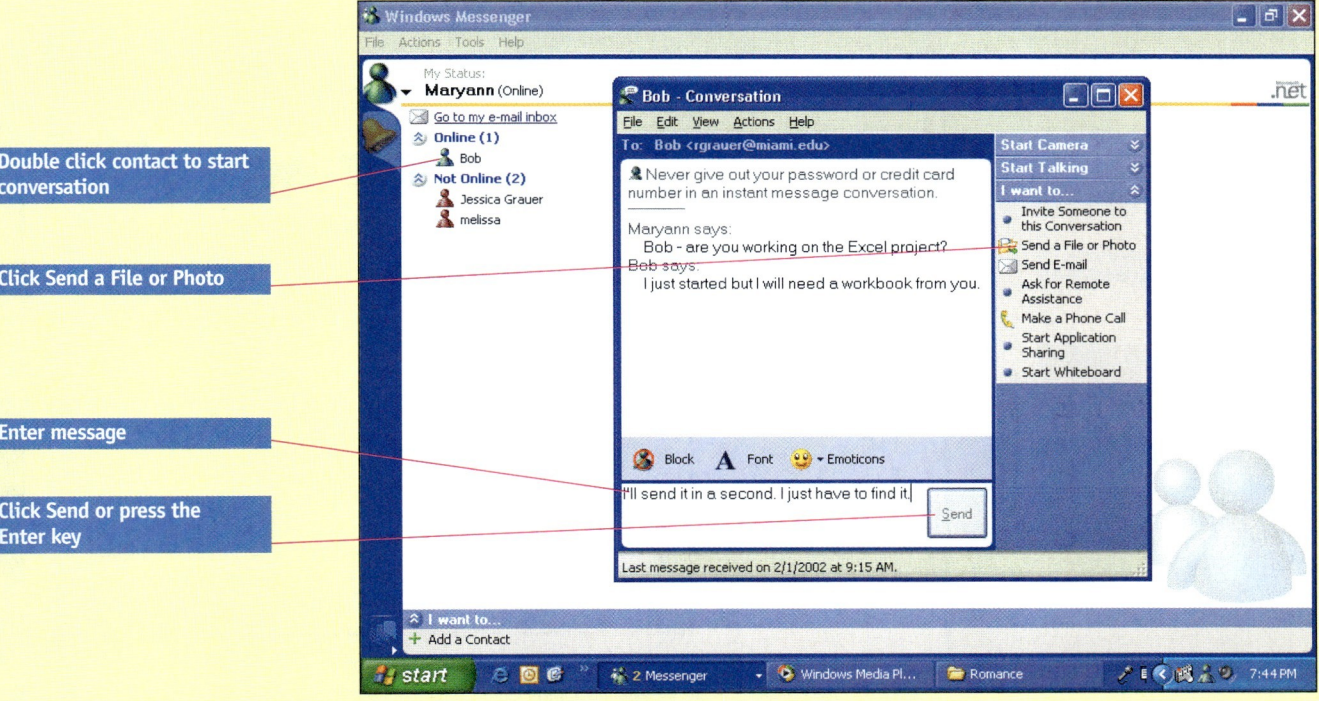

(g) Start Windows Messenger (step 7)

FIGURE 19   Hands-on Exercise 5 (*continued*)

CHANGE YOUR STATUS

Anyone on your contact list knows immediately when you log on; thus, the larger your contact list, the more likely you are to be engaged in idle chitchat when you have real work to do. You can avoid unwanted conversations without being rude by changing your status. Click the down arrow next to your name in the Messenger window and choose a different icon. You can appear offline or simply indicate that you are busy. Either way you will be more likely to get your work done.

Step 8: **Attach a File**

- Click the command to **Send a File or Photo**, which displays the Send a File dialog box in Figure 19h. It does not matter which file you choose, since the purpose of this step is to demonstrate the file transfer capability.

- A series of three file transfer messages will appear on your screen. Windows Messenger waits for your friend to accept the file transfer, then it indicates the transfer has begun, and finally, that the transfer was successful.

- Click the command to **Invite someone to this conversation** if you have another contact online. You will see a second dialog box in which you select the contact.

- There are now three people in the conversation. (Up to four people can participate in one conversation.) Your friends' responses will appear on your screen as soon as they are entered.

- Send your goodbye to end the conversation, then close the conversation window to end the chat session. You are still online and can participate in future conversations.

- Close Windows Messenger. You will be notified if anyone wants to contact you.

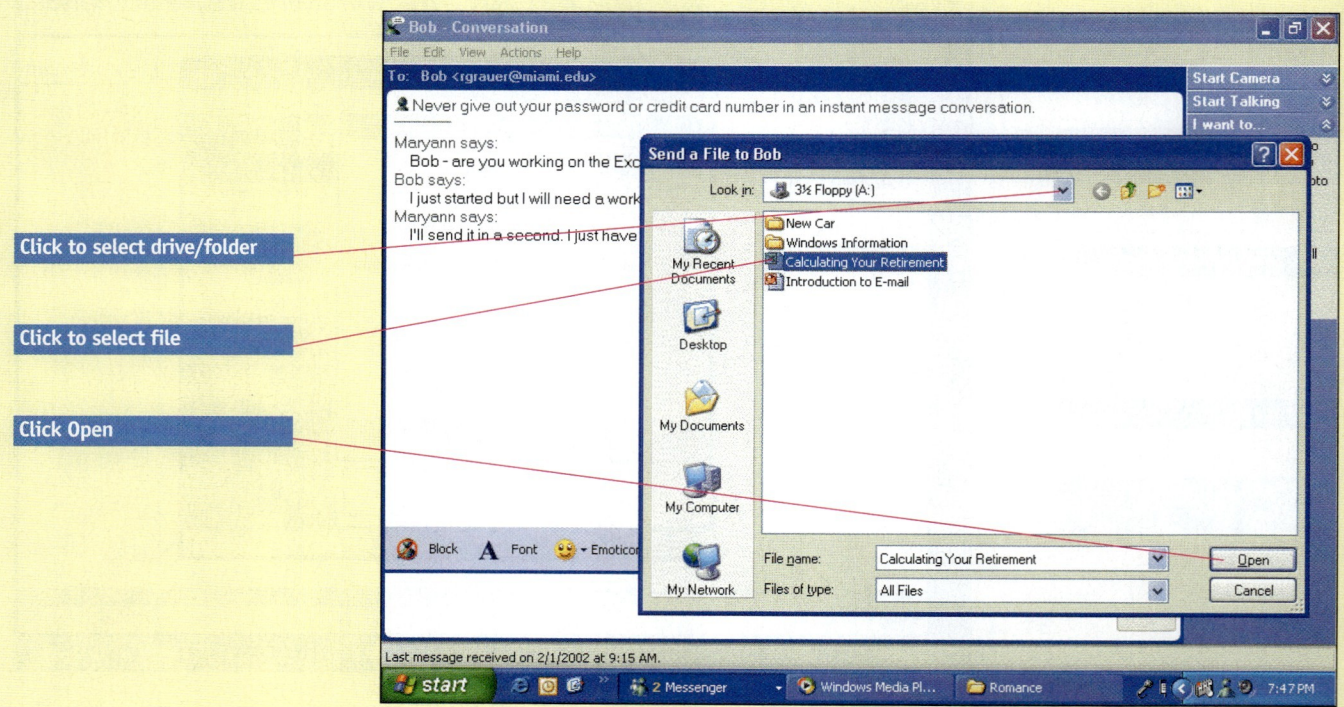

(h) Attach a File (step 8)

FIGURE 19 Hands-on Exercise 5 (*continued*)

E-MAIL VERSUS INSTANT MESSAGING

E-mail and instant messaging are both Internet communication services, but there are significant differences. E-mail does not require both participants to be online at the same time. E-mail messages are also permanent and do not disappear when you exit your e-mail program. Instant messaging, however, requires both participants to be online. Its conversations are not permanent and disappear when you end the session.

Step 9: **Ask for Assistance**

- Your contacts do not require Windows XP to converse with you using Windows Messenger. Windows XP is required, however, to use the remote assistance feature.

- Click the **Start button**, then click the **Help and Support command** to display the home page of the Help and Support Center. Click the **Support button**, then click the command to **Ask a friend to help**.

- A Remote Assistance screen will open in the right pane. Click the command to **Invite someone to help**, which will display your contact list as shown in Figure 19i. You can choose any contact who is online, or you can enter the e-mail address of someone else.

- You will see a dialog box indicating that an invitation has been sent. Once your friend accepts the invitation, he or she will be able to see your screen. A chat window will open up in which you can discuss the problem you are having. Close the session when you are finished.

- Pull down the **File menu** and click the command to **Sign out**. The Windows Messenger icon in the notification will indicate that you have signed out.

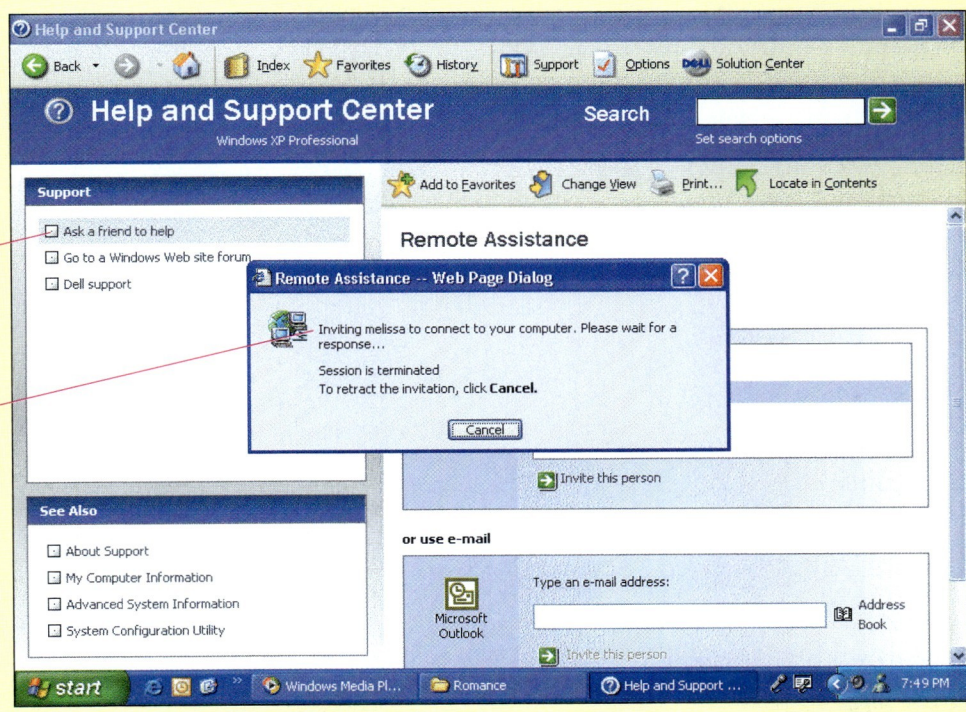

(i) Ask for Assistance (step 9)

FIGURE 19 Hands-on Exercise 5 (*continued*)

SUPPORT ONLINE

Microsoft provides extensive online support in a variety of formats. Start at the Windows XP home page (www.microsoft.com/windowsxp), then click the Support button to see what is available. You will be able to search the Microsoft Knowledge Base for detailed information on virtually any subject. You can also post questions and participate in threaded discussions in various newsgroups. Support is available for every Microsoft product.

SUMMARY

Windows XP is the newest and most powerful version of the Windows operating system. It has a slightly different look than earlier versions, but it maintains the conventions of its predecessors. All Windows operations take place on the desktop. Every window contains the same basic elements, which include a title bar, a Minimize button, a Maximize or Restore button, and a Close button. All windows may be moved and sized. The taskbar contains a button for each open program and enables you to switch back and forth between those programs by clicking the appropriate button. You can obtain information about every aspect of Windows through the Help and Support Center.

A file is a set of data or set of instructions that has been given a name and stored on disk. There are two basic types of files, program files and data files. A program file is an executable file, whereas a data file can be used only in conjunction with a specific program. Every file has a filename and a file type.

Files are stored in folders to better organize the hundreds (or thousands) of files on a disk. A folder may contain program files, data files, and/or other folders. Windows automatically creates a set of personal folders for every user. These include the My Documents folder and the My Pictures folder and My Music folder within the My Documents folder. Windows also provides a Shared Documents folder that can be accessed by every user. The My Computer folder is accessible by all users and displays the devices on a system.

Windows Explorer facilitates every aspect of disk and file management. It presents a hierarchical view of your system that displays all devices and, optionally, the folders on each device. Any device may be expanded or collapsed to display or hide its folders.

Windows XP contains several tools to help you enjoy your system. The Windows Media Player combines the functions of a radio, CD player, DVD player, and an information database into a single program. Windows Messenger is an instant messaging system in which you chat with friends and colleagues over the Internet.

The Control Panel affects every aspect of your system. It determines the appearance of your desktop and it controls the performance of your hardware. A shortcut is a link to any object on your computer, such as a program, file, folder, disk drive, or Web page. The Search Companion enables you to search for a file according to several different criteria.

KEY TERMS

Backup strategy 763
Check box 740
Classic Start menu 735
Close button .738
Command button 740
Compressed file 752
Control Panel 773
Copy a file 763
Data file 750
Delete command 763
Desktop 735
Details view .750
Dialog box 740
Digital photographs 784
Fast user switching 734
File 750
File type 750
File name 750
Filmstrip view 791
Firewall 752
Folder 750
Help and Support Center 741
Help button .740
Internet Explorer 6.0 741
Internet Service Provider 752

List box 740
Maximize button 738
Menu bar 738
Microsoft passport 786
Minimize button 738
Modem 752
Move a file 763
Move a window 735
Multitasking .735
My Computer folder 738
My Documents folder 761
My Music folder 761
My Pictures folder 761
Notification area 735
Option button 740
Personal folders 761
Playlist 784
Program file .750
Pull-down menu 739
Quick Launch toolbar 774
Radio button 740
Recycle Bin 763
Rename command 764
Restore button 738
Scroll bar 738

Search Companion 775
Shared Documents folder 761
Shortcut 774
Size a window 735
Spin button .740
Start button .735
Start menu 735
Status bar 738
Task pane 738
Taskbar 735
Text box 740
Thumbnails view 785
Tiles view 750
Title bar 738
Toolbar 738
Windows Classic theme 735
Windows Explorer 761
Windows Media Player 784
Windows Messenger 786
Windows Update 773
Windows® XP 734
Windows XP theme 735
XP Home Edition 734
XP Professional Edition 734

MULTIPLE CHOICE

1. Which of the following is true regarding a dialog box?
   - (a) Option buttons indicate mutually exclusive choices
   - (b) Check boxes imply that multiple options may be selected
   - (c) Both (a) and (b)
   - (d) Neither (a) nor (b)

2. Which of the following is the first step in sizing a window?
   - (a) Point to the title bar
   - (b) Pull down the View menu to display the toolbar
   - (c) Point to any corner or border
   - (d) Pull down the View menu and change to large icons

3. Which of the following is the first step in moving a window?
   - (a) Point to the title bar
   - (b) Pull down the View menu to display the toolbar
   - (c) Point to any corner or border
   - (d) Pull down the View menu and change to large icons

4. Which button appears immediately after a window has been maximized?
   - (a) The Close button
   - (b) The Minimize button
   - (c) The Maximize button
   - (d) The Restore button

5. What happens to a window that has been minimized?
   - (a) The window is still visible but it no longer has a Minimize button
   - (b) The window shrinks to a button on the taskbar
   - (c) The window is closed and the application is removed from memory
   - (d) The window is still open but the application has been removed from memory

6. What is the significance of a faded (dimmed) command in a pull-down menu?
   - (a) The command is not currently accessible
   - (b) A dialog box appears if the command is selected
   - (c) A Help window appears if the command is selected
   - (d) There are no equivalent keystrokes for the particular command

7. The Recycle Bin enables you to restore a file that was deleted from
   - (a) Drive A
   - (b) Drive C
   - (c) Both (a) and (b)
   - (d) Neither (a) nor (b)

8. Which of the following was suggested as essential to a backup strategy?
   - (a) Back up all program files at the end of every session
   - (b) Store backup files at another location
   - (c) Both (a) and (b)
   - (d) Neither (a) nor (b)

9. A shortcut may be created for
   - (a) An application or a document
   - (b) A folder or a drive
   - (c) Both (a) and (b)
   - (d) Neither (a) nor (b)

10. What happens if you click the Folders button (on the Standard Buttons toolbar in the My Computer folder) twice in a row?
    - (a) The left pane displays a task pane with commands for the selected object
    - (b) The left pane displays a hierarchical view of the devices on your system
    - (c) The left pane displays either a task pane or the hierarchical view depending on what was displayed prior to clicking the button initially
    - (d) The left pane displays both the task pane and a hierarchical view

... continued

multiple choice

11. The Search Companion can
    (a) Locate all files containing a specified phrase
    (b) Restrict its search to a specified set of folders
    (c) Both (a) and (b)
    (d) Neither (a) nor (b)

12. Which views display miniature images of photographs within a folder?
    (a) Tiles view and Icons view
    (b) Thumbnails view and Filmstrip view
    (c) Details view and List view
    (d) All views display a miniature image

13. Which of the following statements is true?
    (a) A plus sign next to a folder indicates that its contents are hidden
    (b) A minus sign next to a folder indicates that its contents are hidden
    (c) A plus sign appears next to any folder that has been expanded
    (d) A minus sign appears next to any folder that has been collapsed

14. Ben and Jessica are both registered users on a Windows XP computer. Which of the following is a *false statement* regarding their personal folders?
    (a) Ben and Jessica each have a My Documents folder
    (b) Ben and Jessica each have a My Pictures folder that is stored within their respective My Documents folders
    (c) Ben can access files in Jessica's My Documents folder
    (d) Jessica cannot access files in Ben's My Documents folder

15. When is a file permanently deleted?
    (a) When you delete the file from Windows Explorer
    (b) When you empty the Recycle Bin
    (c) When you turn the computer off
    (d) All of the above

16. What happens if you (left) click and drag a file to another folder on the same drive?
    (a) The file is copied
    (b) The file is moved
    (c) The file is deleted
    (d) A shortcut menu is displayed

17. How do you shut down the computer?
    (a) Click the Start button, then click the Turn Off Computer command
    (b) Right click the Start button, then click the Turn Off Computer command
    (c) Click the End button, then click the Turn Off Computer command
    (d) Right click the End button, then click the Turn Off Computer command

18. Which of the following can be accomplished with Windows Messenger?
    (a) You can chat with up to three other people in the conversation window
    (b) You can place telephone calls (if you have a microphone and speaker) without paying long-distance charges
    (c) You can ask for remote assistance, which enables your contact to view your screen as you are working
    (d) All of the above

ANSWERS

1. c
2. c
3. a
4. d
5. b
6. a
7. b
8. b
9. c
10. c
11. c
12. b
13. a
14. c
15. b
16. b
17. a
18. d

PRACTICE WITH WINDOWS XP

1. **Two Different Views:** The document in Figure 20 is an effective way to show your instructor that you understand the My Computer folder, the various views available, the task pane, and the hierarchy structure. It also demonstrates that you can capture a screen for inclusion in a Word document. Proceed as follows:
    a. Open the My Computer folder, click the Views button, and switch to the Tiles view. Click the Folders button to display the task pane. Size the window as necessary so that you will be able to fit two folders onto a one-page document as shown in Figure 20.
    b. Press and hold the Alt key as you press the Print Screen key to copy the My Computer window to the Windows clipboard. (The Print Screen key captures the entire screen. Using the Alt key, however, copies just the current window.) Click the Start menu, click Programs, and then click Microsoft Word to start the program. Maximize the window.
    c. Enter the title of the document, press Enter, and type your name. Press the Enter key twice in a row to leave a blank line.
    d. Pull down the Edit menu. Click the Paste command to copy the contents of the clipboard to the document. Press the Enter key to add a figure caption, then press the Enter key two additional times.
    e. Click the taskbar to return to the My Computer folder. Change to the Details view. Click the Folders button to display the hierarchy structure, as opposed to the task pane. Expand My Computer in the left pane, but collapse all of the individual devices. Press Alt+Print Screen to capture the My Computer folder in this configuration.
    f. Click the taskbar to return to your Word document. Press Ctrl+V to paste the contents of the clipboard into your document. Enter an appropriate caption below the figure. Save the completed document and print it for your instructor.

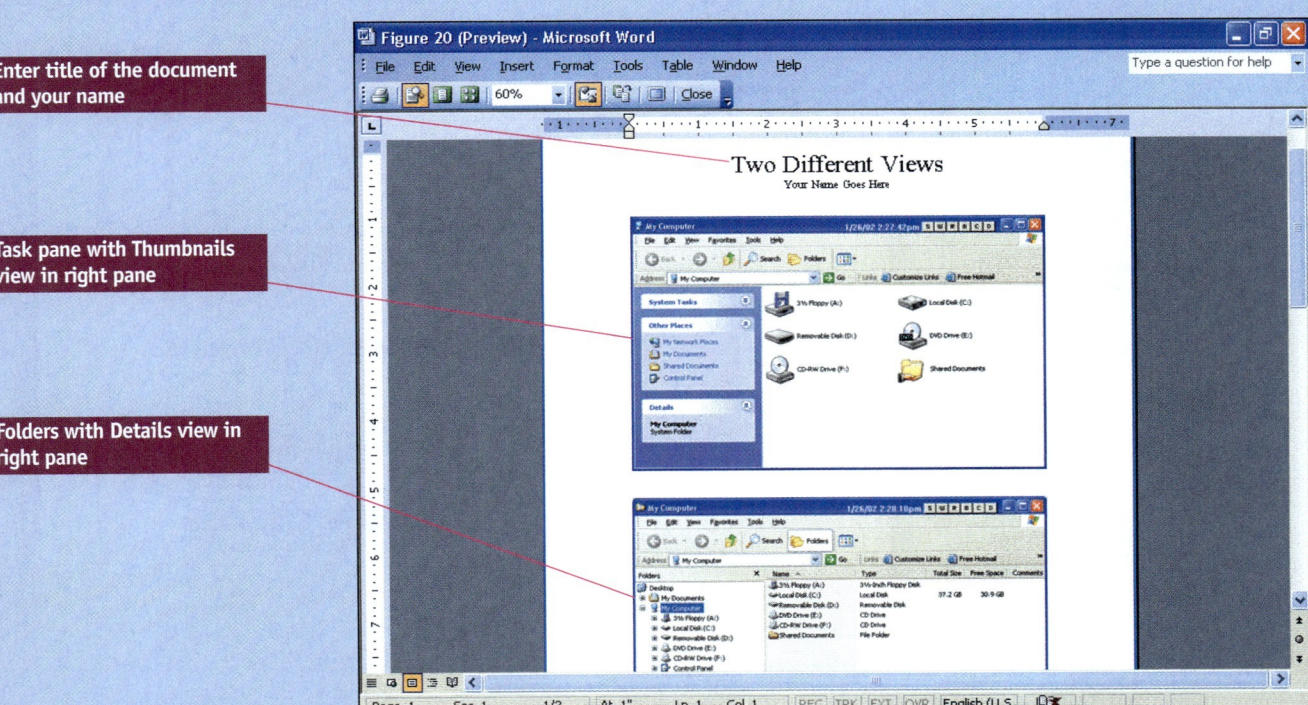

FIGURE 20 Two Different Views (exercise 1)

MICROSOFT OFFICE EXCEL 2003 REVISED

practice exercises

2. **Network Connections:** The document in Figure 21 displays the network connections on our system as well as the status of one of those connections. Your assignment is to create the equivalent document for your computer. Proceed as follows:

   a. Open the Control Panel, switch to the Classic view, then double click the Network Connections icon to display the Network Connections folder. (You can also get to this folder from My Computer, by clicking the link to My Network Places, and then clicking Network Connections from within the Network Tasks area.)

   b. Maximize the Network Connections folder so that it takes the entire desktop. Change to the Tiles view. Click the Folders button to display the task pane. Select (click) a connection, then click the link to View status of the connection, to display the associated dialog box.

   c. Press the Print Screen key to print this screen. Start Microsoft Word and open a new document. Press the Enter key several times, then click the Paste button to copy the contents of the clipboard into your document.

   d. Press Ctrl+Home to return to the beginning of the Word document, where you can enter the title of the document and your name. Compose a paragraph similar to the one in our figure that describes the network connections on your computer. Print this document for your instructor.

   e. Experiment with the first two network tasks that are displayed in the task pane. How difficult is it to set up a new connection? How do you set a firewall to protect your system from unauthorized access when connected to the Internet? How do you establish a home or small office network?

   f. Use the Help and Support Center to obtain additional information. Print one or two Help screens for your instructor.

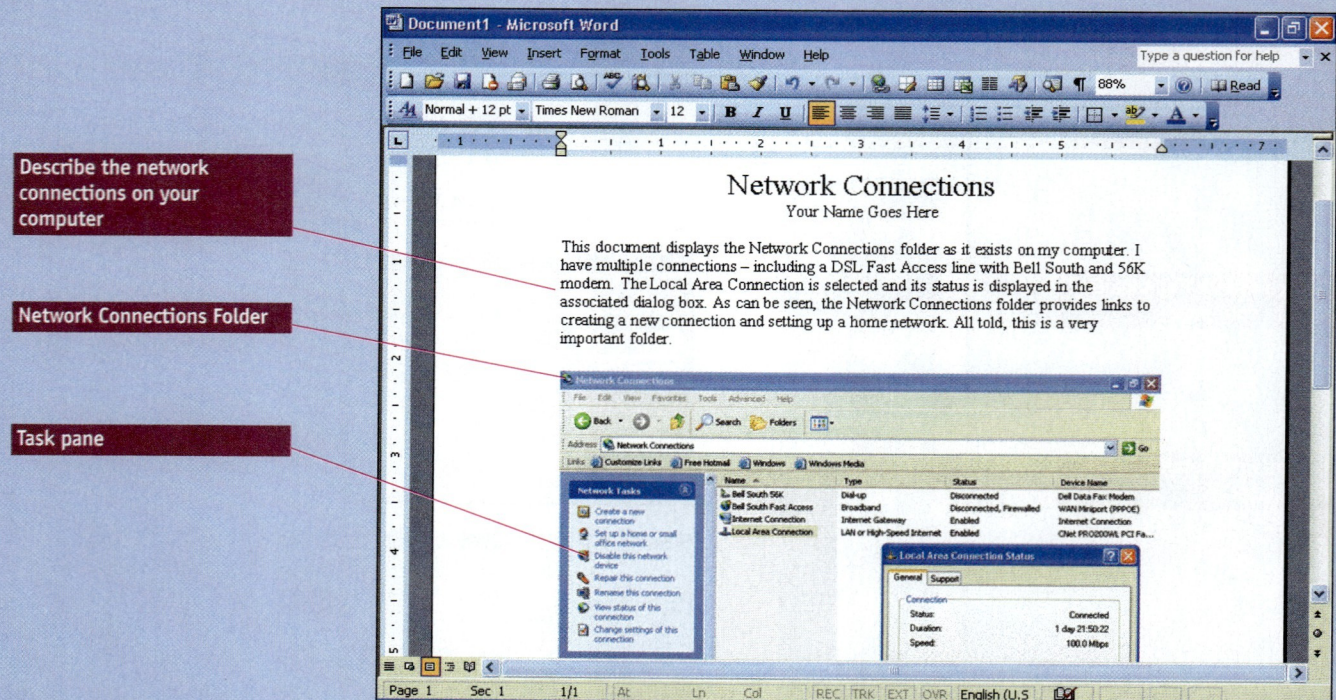

FIGURE 21 Network Connections (exercise 2)

800 GETTING STARTED WITH MICROSOFT WINDOWS XP

practice exercises

3. **Create Your Own Folders:** Folders are the key to the Windows storage system. Folders can be created at any time and in any way that makes sense to you. The My Courses folder in Figure 22, for example, contains five folders, one folder for each class you are taking. In similar fashion, the Correspondence folder in this figure contains two additional folders according to the type of correspondence. Proceed as follows:

   a. Place the floppy disk from hands-on exercise 3 into drive A. Start Windows Explorer. Click the Folders button to display the hierarchy structure in the left pane. Change to the Details view.

   b. Create a Correspondence folder on drive A. Create a Business folder and a Personal folder within the Correspondence folder.

   c. Create a My Courses folder on drive A. Create a separate folder for each course you are taking within the My Courses folder. The names of your folders will be different from ours.

   d. Pull down the View menu, click the Arrange Icons by command, and click the command to Show in Groups. Click the Date Modified column header to group the files and folders by date. The dates you see will be different from the dates in our figure.

   e. The Show in Groups command functions as a toggle switch. Execute the command, and the files are displayed in groups; execute the command a second time, and the groups disappear. (You can change the grouping by clicking the desired column heading.)

   f. Use the technique described in problems 1 and 2 to capture the screen in Figure 22 and incorporate it into a document. Add a short paragraph that describes the folders you have created, then submit the document to your instructor.

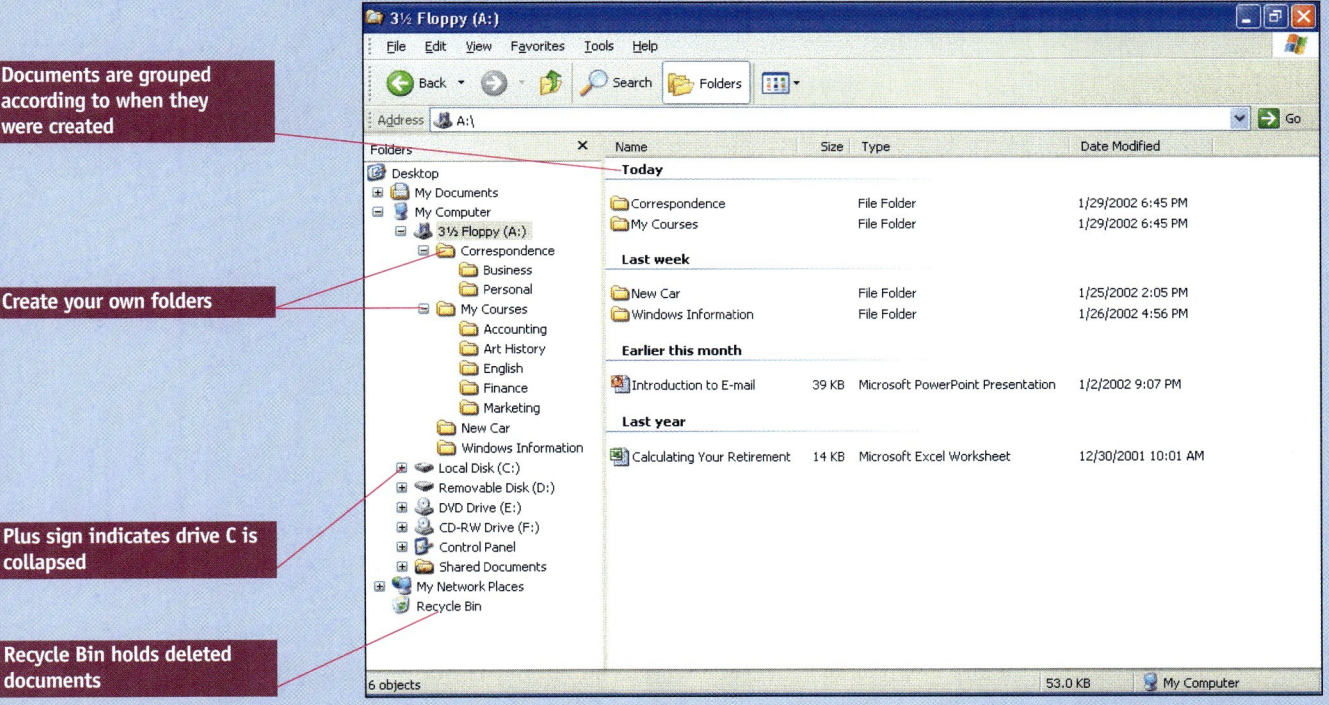

FIGURE 22   Create Your Own Folders (exercise 3)

practice exercises

4. **What's New in Windows XP:** Anyone, whether an experienced user or a computer novice, can benefit from a quick overview of new features in Windows XP. Click the Start button, click Help and Support, and then click the link to What's New in Windows XP. Click the second link in the task pane (taking a tour or tutorial), select the Windows XP tour, and choose the desired format. We chose the animated tour with animation, music, and voice narration.

   a. Relax and enjoy the show as shown in Figure 23. The task bar at the bottom of the figure contains three buttons to restart the show, exit, or toggle the music on and off. Exit the tutorial when you are finished. You are back in the Help and Support window, where you can take a tour of the Windows Media Player. Try it. Click the Close button at the upper right of any screen or press Escape to exit the tour. Write a short note to your instructor with comments about either tour.

   b. Return to the Help and Support Center and find the topic, "What's New in Home Networking." Print two or three subtopics that describe how to create a home network. Does the task seem less intimidating after you have read the information?

   c. Locate one or more topics on new features in digital media such as burning a CD or Windows Movie Maker. Print this information for your instructor.

   d. Return once again to the Help and Support Center to explore some of the other resources that describe new features in Windows XP. Locate the link to Windows News Groups, and then visit one of these newsgroups online. Locate a topic of interest and print several messages within a threaded discussion. Do you think newsgroups will be useful to you in the future?

   e. You can also download a PowerPoint presentation by the authors that describes new features in Windows XP. Go to www.prenhall.com/grauer, click the text for Office XP, then click the link to What's New in Windows XP, from where you can download the presentation.

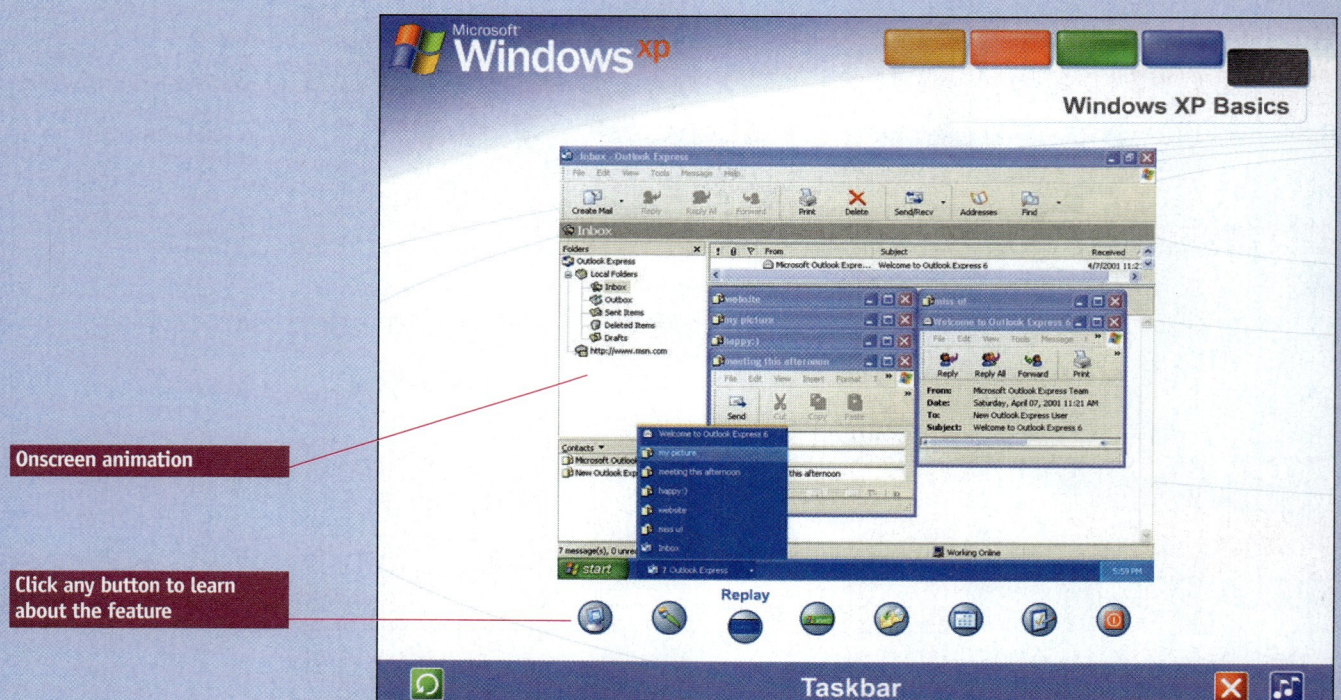

FIGURE 23   What's New in Windows XP (exercise 4)

practice exercises

5. **Keyboard Shortcuts:** Almost every command in Windows can be executed in different ways, using either the mouse or the keyboard. Most people start with the mouse and add keyboard shortcuts as they become more proficient. There is no right or wrong technique, just different techniques, and the one you choose depends entirely on personal preference. If, for example, your hands are already on the keyboard, it is faster to use the keyboard equivalent if you know it.

   There is absolutely no need to memorize these shortcuts, nor should you even try. A few, however, have special appeal and everyone has favorites. You are probably familiar with general Windows shortcuts such as Ctrl+X, Ctrl+C, and Ctrl+V to cut, copy, and paste, respectively. (The X is supposed to remind you of a pair of scissors.) Ctrl+Z is less well known and corresponds to the Undo command. You can find additional shortcuts through the Help command.

   a. Use the Help and Support Center to display the information in Figure 24, which shows the available shortcuts within a dialog box. Two of these, Tab and Shift+Tab, move forward and backward, respectively, from one option to the next within the dialog box. The next time you are in a physician's office or a dentist's office, watch the assistant as he or she labors over the keyboard to enter information. That person will typically type information into a text box, then switch to the mouse to select the next entry, return to the keyboard, and so on. Tell that person about Tab and Shift+Tab; he or she will be forever grateful.

   b. The Help and Support Center organizes the shortcuts by category. Select the Natural keyboard category (not visible in Figure 24), then note what you can do with the ⊞ key. Press the ⊞ key at any time, and you display the Start menu. Press ⊞+M and you minimize all open windows. There are several other, equally good shortcuts in this category.

   c. Select your five favorite shortcuts in any category, and submit them to your instructor. Compare your selections to those of your classmates. Do you prefer the mouse or your newly discovered shortcuts?

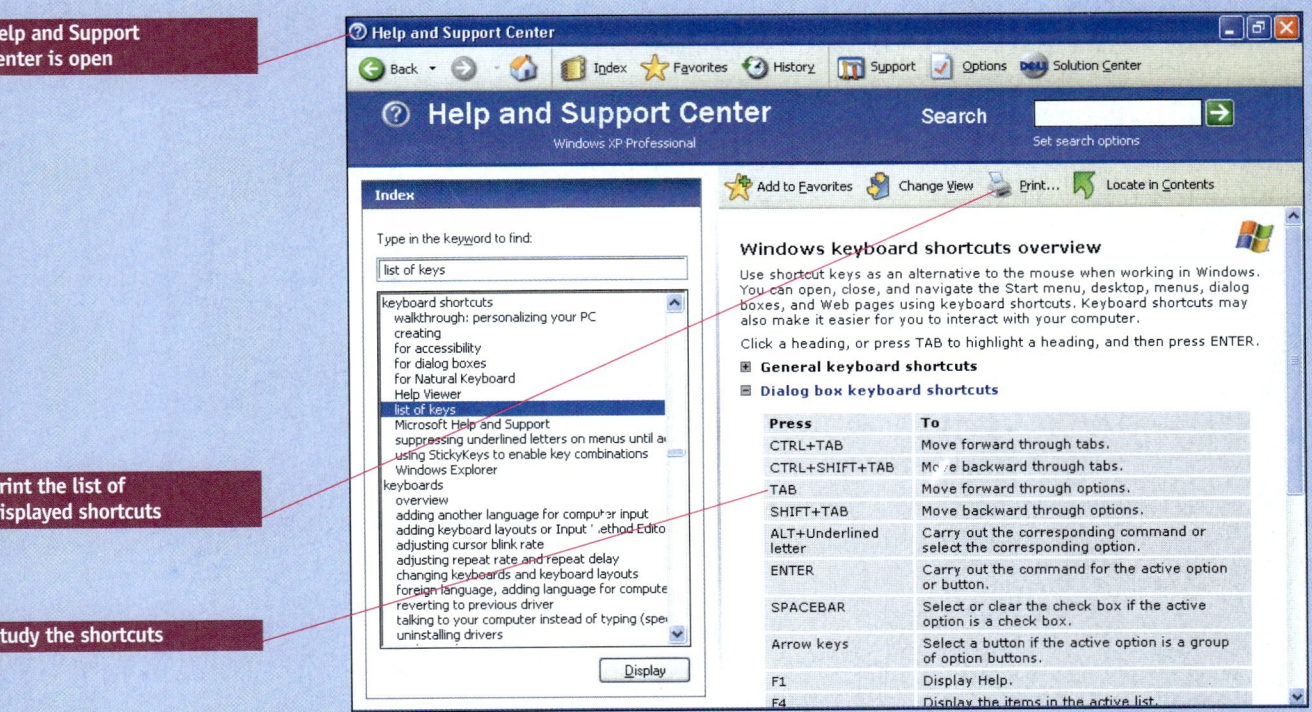

FIGURE 24 Keyboard Shortcuts (exercise 5)

MINI CASES

Planning for Disaster

Do you have a backup strategy? Do you even know what a backup strategy is? You had better learn, because sooner or later you will wish you had one. You will erase a file, be unable to read from a floppy disk, or worse yet, suffer a hardware failure in which you are unable to access the hard drive. The problem always seems to occur the night before an assignment is due. The ultimate disaster is the disappearance of your computer, by theft or natural disaster. Describe, in 250 words or less, the backup strategy you plan to implement in conjunction with your work in this class.

Tips for Windows XP

Print the *Tips for Windows XP* document that was downloaded as one of the practice files in the hands-on exercises. This document contains many of the boxed tips that appeared throughout the chapter. Read the document as a review and select five of your favorite tips. Create a new document for your instructor consisting of the five tips you selected. Add a cover page titled, "My Favorite Tips." Include your name, your professor's name, and a reference to the Grauer/Barber text from where the tips were taken.

File Compression

You've learned your lesson and have come to appreciate the importance of backing up all of your data files. The problem is that you work with large documents that exceed the 1.44MB capacity of a floppy disk. Accordingly, you might want to consider the acquisition of a file compression program to facilitate copying large documents to a floppy disk in order to transport your documents to and from school, home, or work. You can download an evaluation copy of the popular WinZip program at www.winzip.com. Investigate the subject of file compression and submit a summary of your findings to your instructor.

The Threat of Virus Infection

A computer virus is an actively infectious program that attaches itself to other programs and alters the way a computer works. Some viruses do nothing more than display an annoying message at an inopportune time. Most, however, are more harmful, and in the worst case, erase all files on the disk. Use your favorite search engine to research the subject of computer viruses to answer the following questions. When is a computer subject to infection by a virus? What precautions does your school or university take against the threat of virus infection in its computer lab? What precautions, if any, do you take at home? Can you feel confident that your machine will not be infected if you faithfully use a state-of-the-art anti-virus program that was purchased in June 2002?

Your First Consultant's Job

Go to a real installation such as a doctor's or attorney's office, the company where you work, or the computer lab at school. Determine the backup procedures that are in effect, then write a one-page report indicating whether the policy is adequate and, if necessary, offering suggestions for improvement. Your report should be addressed to the individual in charge of the business, and it should cover all aspects of the backup strategy; that is, which files are backed up and how often, and what software is used for the backup operation. Use appropriate emphasis (for example, bold italics) to identify any potential problems. This is a professional document (it is your first consultant's job), and its appearance should be perfect in every way.

Index

#DIV/0 error, 364
(displayed as cell value), 94
#REF error message, 194
3-D reference, 240
80/20 rule, 425

A

Absolute reference, 33, 68, 180
   in a macro, 461–462
   shortcut for, 72
Accept or reject changes, 298
Access database, 399, 418
Accounting format, 43
Active cell, 7
Adjustable cells, 637
Advanced Filter command, 353, 361
Age (calculation of), 219
Alignment, 44
Amortization schedule, 309–318, 516
   with VBA, 517–559
Ampersand, 487, 533, 682
Analysis ToolPak, 360, 392
AND function, 309, 399, 401, 517, 523
Argument, 170, 670
Arrange command, 232, 244
Arrange Icons command, 778
Arrange Windows command, 190
Ascending sequence, 339
Ask a Question list box, 6, 36
Assumptions (isolation of), 31, 56, 180, 276, 288
Attach a file, 794
AutoComplete, 25
AutoCorrect command, 345
AutoFill capability, 201, 257
AutoFilter command, 200, 210, 352, 359, 399
AutoFit column width, 248
AutoFormat command, 131, 241, 247
AutoSum, 127, 246
AVERAGE function, 193

B

Back up, 725, 763
Bar chart, 119
Before Close event procedure, 539, 711–712
Binding constraint, 635
Bold button, 47

Border tab, 46, 50
Breakpoint, 196

C

Calculating, 398
Calendar (creation of), 58
Capital gain, 96
Car loan, 168–169
Case statement, 686, 692
Category label, 116
Cell, 4
Cell formula, 5
   displaying, 27
   printing, 52, 178, 254, 527
Cell reference, 4
Changing cells, 279
Character encoding, 655, 656
Character string, 684
Chart, 116
Chart sheet, 122
Chart toolbar, 126
Chart type, 124, 132
Chart Wizard, 124–125, 128–129, 140
Charting, 398
Check box, 740
Checkbook (creation of), 59
Circle invalid data, 292, 323
Circular reference, 298, 331
Classic Start menu, 735
Clipboard, 33, 40
Close button, 738
Close command, 9
Code window, 450
Collapse Dialog button, 205
Collection, 528, 609
Column (hiding), 363
Column chart, 119
Column field (in pivot table), 416
Column width, 38, 94
   pound signs in, 184
Combination chart, 161, 164
Command button, 740
   assigning to a macro, 478, 485
   properties of, 491, 591
Comment, 23, 70, 77, 299, 450, 590, 674, 680
   toggle on or off, 727
Common user interface, 148
Compare and merge workbooks, 330
Compilation error, 698, 702
Complete Word tool, 690
Compressed file, 752
Computer (purchase of), 107

CONCATENATE function, 410
Concatenate, 672, 682
Conditional formatting, 83, 96, 278, 285, 304, 398, 595, 661
   locate cells with, 404
   shade alternate rows, 408–409, 412, 432
Consolidating data, 230–233
Constant, 5
Constraint, 637
Context-sensitive menu, 245
Continuation (of VBA statement), 487, 682
Control panel, 773, 781
Copy a file, 763
Copy command, 32
   shortcut for, 185
COUNT function, 193, 405
COUNTA function, 193, 405, 408
COUNTIF function, 399, 405
Create List command, 344
Create Name command, 473
Credit card (amortization of), 328–329
Criteria range, 353–354, 366
Crop tool, 522
CSV format, 9, 399
   exporting of, 349
Currency (conversion of), 106
Currency format, 43
Custom filter, 399
Custom format, 43, 278
Custom function (creation of),
Custom menu, 568
Custom series, 257
Custom sort sequence, 339
Custom toolbar, 536–538, 687, 693–695
Custom view, 254, 286
Cut command
   shortcut for, 185

D

Data, 350
Data analysis, 398
Data file, 750
Data form, 338
Data management macros, 470–491
Data point, 116
Data series, 116
   formatting of, 135, 158, 377
   multiple data series, 136–145
Data table (versus mixed references), 333

Data validation, 516, 521, 579
Data Validation command, 292–293, 300, 313
Database, 336
Database functions, 355, 363–366
Date (entering of), 348
Date arithmetic, 89, 358, 427
Date format, 43
DATE function, 311, 520
DAVERAGE function, 355, 364
DAY function, 311, 520
DCOUNT function, 355, 365
Debug menu, 698
Debug toolbar, 698
Debug.Print statement, 699
Debugging, 497, 583, 698
Declarations section, 674
Decrease Brightness tool, 522
Decrease decimal, 75
Default location, 85
Define Name command, 279
Delete command, 19, 337, 763
  worksheet, 30
Delimited format, 341
Dependent cells, 292, 296
Dependent workbook, 255
Depreciation, 113
Descending sequence, 339
Desktop, 735
  customization of, 792
Destination range, 32
Details view, 750
Dialog box (shortcuts for), 28, 740
Digital photography, 785
Digital signature, 539, 550
Dim statement, 577, 673
Dir function, 578
Division by zero, 364
DMAX function, 355, 365
DMIN function, 355, 365
Do Loops, 697, 707–708
Do statement, 493
Do Until statement, 577
Do While statement, 577
Docked toolbar, 134
Documentation worksheet, 249, 424
Drawing toolbar, 126
DSUM function, 355, 365

E

Edit, 5
Edit Clear command, 347, 454
Edit Delete command, 347
Element, 655
Else clause, 684, 690
Embedded chart, 122, 130
End If statement, 492
End Sub statement, 450, 671

End With statement, 451
Error checking, 364
Error Trapping, 585, 590
Evaluate formula tool, 308, 332
Event, 539, 709
Event procedure, 539, 544, 709
Execution error, 698
Exit command, 9
Exit Sub statement, 585
Exploded pie chart, 117
Exporting data, 349
Extensible, 654
Extensible Markup Language (*See* XML)
External Data toolbar, 89
External reference, 255, 259

F

Fast user switching, 734
Favorites button, 748
Field, 336
Field name, 336
File, 336, 750
  selection of, 765
File management (in Excel), 10
File menu, 9
File name, 9, 750
File type, 9, 750
Fill handle, 70, 73, 83, 201, 282
Filmstrip view, 791
Filtered list, 352
Filtering 398
Find and Replace command, 52, 183, 483
Firewall, 752
Fixed toolbar, 693
Fixed width format, 341
Floating toolbar, 134, 693
Floppy disk
  demise of, 747
  formatting of, 747
Folder, 750
  copying of, 766
  creation of, 37, 758, 764
  deletion of, 769
Fonts folder, 781
For Next Statement, 577, 696, 701, 705–706
Form command, 338
Format Cells command, 43
Format Painter, 82
Format Style command, 75
Formatting 398
Formatting toolbar, 7–8, 42–46, 57
  clearing of, 49
FormOpen event procedure, 726
Formula, 5
  versus function, 74

Formula Auditing toolbar, 27, 292, 294
Formula bar, 7
Fraction format, 43
Freeze Panes command, 197–198
Full module view, 689
Function, 5, 170
  creation of, 513
  versus formula, 74, 194
FV function, 170, 176

G

Garbage in, Garbage out (GIGO), 337
General format, 43
General procedure, 539, 544
Go To command, 203, 356
Goal Seek command, 172, 175, 399, 407
Group and Show Detail command, 416, 422
Group By command, 771
Grouping worksheets, 241, 246

H

Help and Support Center, 741, 748, 795, 803
Help, 683
Help button, 740
Hide command, 401, 420
Hiding rows and columns, 197, 199, 209
HLOOKUP function, 196, 215, 411
Home mortgage, 179–180
Hopper, Grace, 497
Horizontal scroll bar, 142, 233
HTML, 78, 342, 379, 653
Hyperlink, 78, 84, 103
HyperText Markup Language (*See* HTML)

I

IF function, 195, 204, 403
If statement (in VBA), 492, 498, 577, 684, 690
Immediate window, 699, 704
Import data, 365, 418
  from Microsoft Access, 438
Import External Data command, 89, 92
Increase Brightness tool, 522
Increase decimal, 75
Indent text, 278, 284
INDEX function, 311, 317
Information, 350
Initial conditions, 276
InputBox function, 462, 466, 577, 672, 681
Insert Columns command, 299, 337

Insert command, 19
  cells, 26
  column, 26
  comment, 23, 70, 77
  function, 171, 174
  hyperlink, 84
  row, 24
  worksheet, 30
Insert Name command, 287, 356, 362, 437, 473
Insert Rows command, 337
Internal rate of return (*See* IRR function)
Internet, 78
Internet Explorer, 741
Internet Service Provider, 752
Intrinsic constant, 608, 671
Invalid data (circling of), 292, 323
IPMT function, 186, 315, 524, 528
IRA (Individual Retirement Account), 181
IRR function, 301, 304
ISERROR function, 306, 364
Italic button, 47
Iteration, 643

K

Key, 336
Keyboard shortcuts, 185, 450, 767, 803
  dialog box, 28

L

Landscape orientation, 21
LEFT function, 202, 410
LEN function, 410
  in VBA, 578
Linking, 145, 255, 258
List, 336–337, 661
List box, 740
Literal, 684
Locals window, 699
Log off, 749, 772
Log on, 742
Loop, 492
LOWER function, 410

M

Macro, 450, 670
  execution of, 479
Macro recorder, 450, 528, 670
Macro security, 481, 688
MATCH function, 311, 317
MAX function, 193
Maximize button, 738
Media Guide, 789

Menu (changing of), 14
Menu bar, 738
Merge and Center command, 187
Merge cells, 44, 47
Method, 528
Microsoft Access
  importing from, 365, 418, 438
Microsoft passport, 782, 786
MIN function, 193
Minimize button, 738, 745
Mixed references, 33, 108, 181, 189
  versus Data Table, 333
  shortcut for, 72
MOD function, 408
Modem, 752
Module, 670
Module view, 460
Modulo arithmetic, 408, 412
MONTH function, 311, 520
Move a file, 759, 763, 765
Move a window, 735, 745
Move operation, 34–35
MsgBox function, 529, 684
MsgBox statement, 480, 488, 529, 577, 671, 677–679
Multiple data series, 136–145
Multitasking, 87, 145, 735
My Computer folder, 738, 744
My Documents folder, 761, 768
My Music folder, 761
My Pictures folder, 761, 790

N

Name box, 7, 287, 362, 413, 429, 474
Named range, 471
  use in a macro, 475
Nested IF, 208, 212, 222, 403
  in VBA procedure, 567, 599
Network Connections folder, 800
New Window command, 232
Nonbinding constraint, 635
Noncontiguous range, 177
Notepad accessory, 655
  versus Internet Explorer, 657, 666
Notification area, 735
Now() function, 91
Number format, 43

O

Object, 145, 528
Object Linking and Embedding (OLE), 145–152, 160, 267
Object model, 528
Office Assistant, 18
Office clipboard, 33, 40
Offset, 461
Offset property, 600

On Error statement, 585
OnTime method, 541
Open command, 9, 22
Open workbook event procedure, 539
Option button, 740
Option Explicit, 674, 676
Options command, 316
OR function, 399, 517, 580
Outline symbols, 357

P

Page Break Preview command, 159, 197, 199, 208, 406
Page field (in pivot table), 373, 416
Page Setup command, 21, 28, 253
  repeating rows and columns, 526
Pareto chart, 425
Pareto Principle, 425
Paste command
  shortcut for, 185
Paste Options button, 39
Patterns tab, 46
Percentage format, 43, 48
Personal folders, 761
Personal Macro workbook, 462–463
Pi (function), 61, 65
Picture toolbar, 522
Pie chart, 117
Pivot chart, 369, 372–377, 386, 395, 416
  modification of, 420, 430
Pivot Table Wizard, 369
Pivot Table, 398, 664
  customization of, 375, 429
  formatting of, 374
  grouping data, 422
  layout button, 428
  multiple consolidation ranges, 272, 419, 442
  refreshing of, 380, 416, 423
Places bar, 9
Play list, 784, 789
PMT function, 170, 174, 312
Pointing, 70, 80, 81
Portrait orientation, 21
PowerPoint (with Excel chart), 165
PPMT function, 186, 315, 524, 528
Practice files (downloading of), 12, 753–755
Precedent cells, 292, 297
Print area, 210, 527, 565
Print command, 9
Print Preview command, 29, 253, 526
Private procedure, 548, 605, 670
Procedure header, 671
Procedure view, 460, 689
Procedure, 559
  printing from Microsoft Word, 611
  stepping through, 600

Procedure, 670
Program file, 750
Project Explorer, 450, 674
Properties window, 541
Property, 528
Protect Worksheet command, 525
Protected workbook, 306
Protected worksheet, 301
Pseudocode, 551
Public constant, 682, 723
Public procedure, 548, 605, 670
Pull-down menu, 739

Q

QUARTILE function, 408, 411
Quick Launch toolbar, 774, 776

R

Radio button, 740
RAND function, 424, 444
Range, 32
RANK function, 207, 408, 411
Record, 336
Record New Macro command, 452
Recycle Bin, 763, 770
Redo command, 17–18
Refresh command
   Web query, 89
   Pivot table, 369, 416, 423, 661
Relational operator, 195, 692
Relative reference button, 453, 553
Relative reference, 33, 68, 180
   in a macro, 461–462, 464
   shortcut for, 72
Rename command, 764
Repeat columns, 526
Repeat rows, 526
Research task pane, 95
Resolution (changing of), 792
Restore button, 738
Result cells, 279
Reviewing toolbar, 291, 294
Right click, 766
RIGHT function, 202, 410
Right mouse button, 143, 234
Root element, 655, 659
Rotate text, 278, 284
Rotate tool, 522
Roth IRA, 190, 218, 323
ROUND function, 206, 222
Round trip HTML, 78, 86
Row field (in pivot table), 416
ROW function, 408
Row height, 38
Rows to repeat (in Page Setup command), 406

Rule of 72, 227
Run-time error, 585, 589, 698

S

Save As command, 9
Save As Web Page command, 78, 85
Save command, 9
Scenario, 279, 288
Scenario list box, 289
Scenario Manager, 279
Scenario summary, 279, 290, 325, 327
Schema, 342
Scientific format, 43
Scope, 605
Screen capture, 549
Screen capture, 719
Screen capture, 746
Screen saver, 743
Screen Tip, 7
Scroll bar, 738
Scrolling, 197
Search Companion, 775, 779–780
Select-then-do, 43
SGML, 653
Shading (alternate rows), 408–409, 412, 432
Shared Documents folder, 761, 787
Shared workbook, 291
Shortcut key (with macros), 450, 452, 458, 486
Shortcut Wizard, 780
Shortcut, 774, 777–778
Show Desktop button, 783, 792
Side-by-side column charts, 137
Single File Web Page, 378
Single File Web Page, 78
Size a window, 735, 745
Sizing handles, 122
Social Security number (formatting of), 202
Solver Options dialog box, 643
Solver Parameters dialog box, 637
Solver, 635–651
   installation of, 639
Sort ascending button, 346
Sort command, 339–340, 346, 408
Sort command, 51, 76, 192
Sort descending button, 346
Sorting 398
Source range, 32
Source workbook, 255
Special format, 43
Spell check, 182, 252, 345
Spin button, 740
Splash screen, 539, 547–549
Split cells, 44

Spreadsheet, 2
Stacked column charts, 137–138
Standard Generalized Markup Language (See SGML)
Standard toolbar, 7–8
Start button, 735
Start menu, 735
   modification of, 781
Statement, 670
Statistical functions, 193
Status bar, 7, 738
Step Into command, 459, 484, 699, 703
Stop Recording button, 453
Style, 278, 303
Sub statement, 450
Subtotals command, 357, 367–368, 390, 408, 415
SUM function, 194
Summarizing, 398
Switch, 551, 556, 715
Switchboard (modification of), 724
Switching users, 772
Syntax error, 585, 670

T

Tab color property, 598
Tag, 654
Target cell, 637
Task Manager, 749
Task pane, 6, 22, 738
Taskbar, 145, 147, 735
Template, 63, 88, 168, 301
Templates folder, 301
Test data (creation of), 424, 444
Text box, 740
   creation of, 134
Text format, 43
Text Import Wizard, 341, 343, 418
Three-dimensional column chart, 122
Three-dimensional pie chart, 117
Thumbnails view, 785
Tiles view, 750
Time format, 43, 91, 112
Title bar, 738
TODAY function, 90, 358, 520
Toolbar, 7–8, 625–626
   attachment of, 538,
   custom, 468, 536, 568
   listing of, 627–634
   separation of, 13
Top Ten Auto filter, 359, 384
Tracers, 292
Track Changes command, 291
Trend line, 307
TRIM function, 410

U

Ucase function, 717
Underscore (as continuation), 487, 533, 672, 682
Undo command, 17–18
Unfreeze Panes command, 197
Unhide command, 197, 209, 401, 420
Unlock cells, 301
Unprotect a worksheet, 63, 597
Up button, 765
UPPER function, 410
User accounts, 11, 742
User form, 541, 546–547
UserForm Activate procedure, 541

V

Variable, 672
VBA, 450, 670
VBA syntax, 677
View menu, 771
Visible property, 718
Visual Basic, 450
Visual Basic Editor, 450, 455, 465, 674
Visual Basic for Applications (*See* VBA)
Visual Basic toolbar, 477
VLOOKUP function, 196, 205, 408, 584
    with WEEKDAY function 425–426

W

Watch window, 331
Web page (creation of), 80–88, 103
Web Page Preview command, 78
Web query, 399
    creation of, 445
Web query, 89–90, 92–97, 106
    creation of, 93, 445
    data range properties, 97
Weekday function (in VBA), 608
WEEKDAY function, 425–426, 545
Wild card, 355
Windows Classic theme, 735
Windows clipboard (*See* Clipboard)
Windows Explorer, 761, 764–772
    customization of, 769
Windows Media Player, 784
Windows Messenger, 786, 793–794
Windows taskbar
    hiding of, 679
Windows Update, 773, 783
Windows XP (log on), 11
Windows XP theme, 735
Windows XP, 734
    log off, 749
    log on, 742
    new features, 802
With statement, 451
Work group, 291
Workbook, 6
    authentication of, 550
    properties of, 250
    protection of, 307
    reference, 255, 270
WorkbookOpen event procedure, 713–714, 716
Worksheet
    copying, 141, 236–238
    hiding, 139, 420, 709
    inserting, 242
    moving, 141, 238
    protecting, 525
    renaming, 139
    selecting, 247
    summing, 243
    unhiding, 139, 420
Worksheet object, 585
Worksheet reference, 162, 239–240, 601
Worksheet tab (color of), 16, 598
Workspace, 260
Wrap text command, 251

X

X axis, 119
XML, 342, 379, 393, 653
    importing of, 662
    syntax of, 658
XML declaration, 655
XML document, 399
XML source pane, 661, 662
XML-aware, 657
XP Home Edition, 734
XP Professional Edition, 734

Y

Y axis, 119
YEAR function, 311, 520

Z

Zero suppression, 523
Zodiac (signs of), 228
Zoom percentage, 41, 236